>The
>Downloader's
>Music
>Source Book

>
>
>
>>>CARLTON BOOKS
>

⏮ COMPILED BY DAVE McALEER ⏭

This is a Carlton book

First published in Great Britain by
Carlton Books Limited 2005
20 Mortimer Street
London W1T 3JW

Text copyright © Dave McAleer 2005
Design copyright © Carlton Books Ltd 2005

ISBN 1 84442 501 0

Typeset by E-Type, Liverpool
Printed and bound in Singapore

>CONTENTS

>

>

>

INTRODUCTION

Downloading recordings via the internet is the most revolutionary thing to happen to music since Thomas Edison perfected a method of putting it onto a cylinder disc over 125 years ago.

The internet is the record shop of the future, and the sale of downloaded tracks will soon surpass those of physical records all over the world. It has already happened in the world's biggest record market, the USA, where downloads outsell CD singles by about 20-1, a ratio that is increasing all the time. The media may now be full of stories of doom and gloom regarding singles sales, but it won't be long before they are reporting regular million-plus sales of downloaded tracks. The fact that, figuratively speaking, there will be a record dealer in everyone's house must mean that future download sales will break sales records previously set by vinyl, cassette and CD singles.

The purpose of *The Downloader's Music Source Book* is to act as a reminder to you of all those fantastic hits of the last 40 years that you may have temporarily forgotten about but would like to add to the growing collection of downloads on your digital music player or PC. It is not intended to be a chart book, but it does include all the biggest hits both in the USA and the UK over the last 40 years. If you recall the title of a favourite song from the past but not the act's name, then check out the title index, or if you simply want a reminder of what hits were recorded by any of your favourite acts, just check out the artist listing. Or just flick through and let the songs jump off the page. It's as simple as downloading a track!

For those of you who may still be download virgins and are worried about doing it for the first time, have no fear. Simply open up your favourite search engine – Google or Yahoo, for instance – and type in the name of any of the scores of sites where music can be downloaded, such as iTunes, MSN, MusicMatch, MusicNow, MyCoke, or Napster. Once you get to the site, the actual downloading is made very simple. On your first visit you may need to fill in your personal details before you can order tracks, but on subsequent visits you will be able to quickly get down to the business of downloading music. You will be amazed at how many tracks are available to you and how easy it is to purchase them. All you need to do is key in the track you require and the artist who performs it. This book gives you the exact titles and correct act names, which will make the task of ordering a track to download even easier.

Among the 23000+ tracks included here you will be able to find forgotten favourites, lost hits and hopefully tons of other tracks that you would like to add to your collection. Also, we strongly suggest that you experiment and try tracks and acts that you might otherwise have overlooked. Most sites either allow you to 'stream' (that is, just listen to but not download) a track for around 1p or 1c, or to listen to a part of it for free, therefore giving you a chance to hear any track before you decide whether to purchase it or not. This way you can experiment in musical areas that you might otherwise have not ventured into, without hurting your pocket too much. For instance, UK record buyers might like to check out US hits they missed, and vice versa. As you have probably noticed, your *Downloader's Music Source Book* can also be used as a pop quiz book for the whole family (as the music covers such a wide span of time), and some less scrupulous readers may wish to refer to it when they attend such quizzes!

The title listing section includes hit songs and artists of the last 40 years in alphabetical order by title, along with the year that they were successful, while the artist listing shows every major hit of the period listed in alphabetical order by artist, and again includes the year. Please note that a track where two or more acts shared the billing is listed under each artist involved (unless it was their sole entry in this book, in which case it can be found under the first named act only).

I'd like to thank the record collectors whose plight in trying to find certain tracks alerted me to the need for a book such as this. I hope that it not only helps you get more enjoyment from music collecting by making the search for tracks far simpler, but also inspires you to expand your musical horizons.

Dave McAleer

MP3 WEBSITES

www.apple.com

Offers more than one million tracks from all four majors and more than 600 leading independent labels. Free 30-second previews of all songs. You can download complete albums or single tracks and burn CDs.

www.artistdirect.com

Users can download selected free tracks from high-profile artists courtesy of the record label.

www.bignoisemusic.com

Oxfam's download service has 300,000 tracks and counting, plus regularly updated exclusives. 10% of their revenue goes to fight poverty. Not Mac-compatible yet, though.

www.buymusic.com

Everything from Top 100 to Oldies, Soul to Metal. Over 500,000 tracks. Search by genre, artist or song.

www.connect.com

Music from all major labels and many indies.

www.entertainment.msn.co.uk/music

Big on-line music store offering DVDs and concert tickets as well as downloads.

www.emusic.com

Subscription-based service that allows the first 50 MP3 downloads for free. Catalogue of over 400,000 tracks.

www.epitonic.com

Free, legal downloads (as long as they're not for commercial use). The music is by independent or underground artists, mainly US based. This site has a strong editorial identity, and is well worth a visit if you are interested in expanding your musical horizons.

www.listen.com

Listen.com has been building a huge digital music subscription service since 1998. It offers over 800,000 tracks, from well-established artists as well as newcomers.

www.MyCokeMusic.com

Easy to use and good for first-timers. But this site is not Mac-compatible.

www.mp3.com

One of the largest archives of MP3s on the web. Browse by genre or search by album, artist or song.

www.musicmatch.com

Winner of *PC Magazine*'s Editor's Choice award for Best Music Player five times in a row, this site has a jukebox, radio and music store for downloads of over 800,000 songs from 60,000 albums.

www.musicnow.com

This subscription-based service is easy to navigate with an option to browse by genre. It also offers 40 ad-free radio stations.

www.napster.com

This site is back – all legal with over 700,000 tracks, 65,000 albums and 45,000 artists. Adds new releases from major and independent labels every Tuesday.

www.real.com/rhapsody

Videos, free games and over 60 ad-free radio stations. Burn your own CDs from a catalogue of over 600,000 songs.

www.vitaminic.com

Offers unlimited access to a wide range of music for an annual or six-monthly subscription fee. Unsigned artists can promote their work on this site too.

www.wippit.com

Cheap and cheerful. Lets you pay per download. Steadily growing catalogue from more than 200 labels, including EMI and BMG.

www.dominorecordco.com

Indie home to the likes of Franz Ferdinand, Stephen Malkmus and Four Tet. Offers regularly updated archive of free downloads.

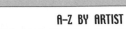

ARTIST	SONG TITLE	DATE
A+	Enjoy Yourself	1999
A	Good Time	2003
	Nothing	2002
	Starbucks	2002
A1	Be The First To Believe	1999
	Caught In The Middle	2002
	Everytime/Ready Or Not	1999
	Like A Rose	2000
	Make It Good	2002
	No More	2001
	Same Old Brand New You	2000
	Summertime Of Our Lives	1999
	Take On Me	2000
A HOUSE	Here Come The Good Times	1994
A TEENS	Halfway Around The World	2001
	Mamma Mia	1999
	Super Trouper	1999
	Upside Down	2001
A.T.F.C. presents ONEPHATDEEVA		
	In And Out Of My Life	1999
A.T.F.C. featuring LISA MILLETT		
	Sleep Talk	2002
A.T.F.C. presents ONEPHATDEEVA featuring		
LISA MILLETT	Bad Habit	2000
A.T.G.O.C.	Repeated Love	1998
AALIYAH	Are You That Somebody?	1998

ARTIST	SONG TITLE	DATE
	At Your Best (You Are Love)	1994
	Back and Forth	1994
	Come Over	2003
	Don't Know What To Tell Ya	2003
	Down With The Clique	1995
	4 Page Letter	1997
	Got To Give It Up	1996
	I Care 4 You	2002
	I Don't Wanna	2000
	If Your Girl Only Knew/One In A Million	1997
	Journey To The Past	1998
	More Than A Woman	2002
	The One I Gave My Heart To/Hot Like Fire	1997
	Rock The Boat	2001
	The Thing I Like	1995
	Try Again	2000
AALIYAH featuring TIMBALAND		
	We Need A Resolution	2001
ABBA	Angel Eyes/Voulez Vous	1979
	Chiquitita	1979
	Dancing Queen	1976
	The Day Before You Came	1982
	Does Your Mother Know	1979
	Fernando	1976
	Gimme! Gimme! Gimme! (A Man After Midnight)	1979

ARTIST	SONG TITLE	DATE
	Head Over Heels	1982
	Honey, Honey	1974
	I Do, I Do, I Do, I Do, I Do	1976
	I Have A Dream	1979
	Knowing Me, Knowing You	1977
	Lay All Your Love On Me	1981
	Mamma Mia	1976
	Money, Money, Money	1976
	The Name Of The Game	1977
	One Of Us	1981
	Ring Ring	1974
	S.O.S.	1975
	Summer Night City	1978
	Super Trouper	1980
	Take A Chance On Me	1978
	Thank You For The Music	1983
	Under Attack	1982
	Waterloo	1974
	When All Is Said And Done	1982
	The Winner Takes It All	1980
RUSS ABBOT	All Night Holiday	1985
	Atmosphere	1984
GREGORY ABBOTT	Shake You Down	1986
ABC	All Of My Heart	1982
	Be Near Me	1985

ARTIST	SONG TITLE	DATE
	(How To Be A) Millionaire	1986
	The Look Of Love	1982
	The Night You Murdered Love	1987
	One Better World	1989
	Poison Arrow	1983
	S.O.S.	1984
	Tears Are Not Enough	1981
	That Was Then But This Is Now	1983
	When Smokey Sings	1987
PAULA ABDUL	Blowing Kisses In The Wind	1991
	Cold Hearted	1989
	Forever Your Girl	1989
	(It's Just) The Way You Love Me	1988
	Knocked Out	1990
	My Love Is For Real	1995
	Opposites Attract	1990
	The Promise Of A New Day	1991
	Rush Rush	1991
	Straight Up	1988
	Vibeology	1992
	Will You Marry Me?	1992
ABIGAIL	Smells Like Teen Spirit	1994
COLONEL ABRAMS	I'm Not Gonna Let You (Get The Best Of Me)	1986
	Trapped	1985

ARTIST	SONG TITLE	DATE
ABS	Stop Sign	2003
	What You Got	2002
ABS featuring NODESHA		
	Miss Perfect	2003
ABSOLUTE featuring SUZANNE PALMER		
	I Believe	1997
ABSOLUTELY FABULOUS		
	Absolutely Fabulous	1994
AC/DC	Are You Ready?	1991
	Back In Black	1980
	Big Gun	1993
	For Those About To Rock (We Salute You)	1982
	Guns For Hire	1983
	Hard As A Rock	1995
	Heatseeker	1988
	Highway To Hell (Live)	1992
	Let's Get It Up	1982
	Moneytalks	1990
	Nervous Shakedown	1984
	Rock 'n' Roll Ain't Noise Pollution	1980
	Rock 'n' Roll Damnation	1978
	Shake Your Foundations	1986
	That's The Way I Wanna Rock 'n' Roll	1988
	Thunderstruck	1990
	Touch Too Much	1980
	Who Made Who	1986

ARTIST	SONG TITLE	DATE
	Whole Lotta Rosie	1980
	You Shook Me All Night Long	1980
ACE	How Long	1975
ACE OF BASE	All That She Wants	1993
	Always Have, Always Will	1998
	Beautiful Life	1995
	Cruel Summer	1998
	Don't Turn Around	1994
	Everytime It Rains	1999
	Happy Nation	1994
	Life Is A Flower	1998
	Living In Danger	1994
	Lucky Love	1996
	The Sign	1994
	Wheel Of Fortune	1993
ACEN	Trip II The Moon	1992
BARBARA ACKLIN	Love Makes A Woman	1968
ACT ONE	Tom The Peeper	1974
AD LIBS	The Boy From New York City	1965
ADAM & THE ANTS	Ant Rap	1981
	Antmusic	1980
	Cartrouble	1981
	Deutscher Girls	1982
	Dog Eat Dog	1980
	Kings Of The Wild Frontier	1980
	Prince Charming	1981

ARTIST	SONG TITLE	DATE
	Stand And Deliver	1981
	Young Parisians	1980
ADAM ANT	Apollo 9	1984
	Desperate But Not Serious	1982
	Friend Or Foe	1982
	Goody Two Shoes	1982
	Puss 'N Boots	1983
	Room At The Top	1990
	Wonderful	1995
ADAM featuring AMY		
	Zombie	1995
ARTHUR ADAMS	You Got The Floor	1981
BRYAN ADAMS	All I Want Is You	1992
	Back To You	1997
	Can't Stop This Thing We Started	1991
	Cloud Number 9	1999
	Cuts Like A Knife	1983
	Do I Have To Say The Words?	1992
	18 Til I Die	1997
	(Everything I Do) I Do It For You	1991
	Have You Ever Really Loved A Woman?	1995
	Hearts On Fire	1987
	Heat Of The Night	1987
	Heaven	1985
	Here I Am	2002
	I'm Ready	1998

ARTIST	SONG TITLE	DATE
	Let's Make A Night To Remember	1996
	On A Day Like Today	1998
	One Night Love Affair	1985
	The Only Thing That Looks Good On Me Is You	1996
	Open Road	2004
	Please Forgive Me	1993
	Run To You	1984
	Somebody	1985
	Star	1996
	Straight From The Heart	1983
	Summer Of '69	1985
	There Will Never Be Another Tonight	1991
	This Time	1983
	Thought I'd Died And Gone To Heaven	1992
	Victim Of Love	1987
BRYAN ADAMS & TINA TURNER		
	It's Only Love	1985
BRYAN ADAMS featuring MELANIE C		
	When You're Gone	1998
BRYAN ADAMS/ROD STEWART/STING		
	All For Love	1993
(BARBRA STREISAND & BRYAN ADAMS)		
	I Finally Found Someone	1996
(CHICANE featuring BRYAN ADAMS)		
	Don't Give Up	2000

ARTIST	SONG TITLE	DATE
JOHNNY ADAMS	Reconsider Me	1969
OLETA ADAMS	Don't Let The Sun Go Down On Me	1991
	Get Here	1990
	Never Knew Love	1995
	Rhythm Of Life	1995
RYAN ADAMS	Answering Bell	2002
	Nuclear	2002
	So Alive	2004
	Wonderwall	2004
ADAMSKI	Killer	1990
	N-R-G	1990
	The Space Jungle	1990
CANNONBALL ADDERLEY		
	Mercy, Mercy, Mercy	1967
ADDRISI BROTHERS	Slow Dancin' Don't Turn Me On	1977
	We've Got To Get It On Again	1972
ADEVA	Don't Let It Show On Your Face	1992
	I Thank You	1989
	Respect	1989
	Warning	1989
	(FRANKIE KNUCKLES featuring ADEVA)	
	Too Many Fish	1995
	Whadda U Want (From Me)	1995
	(MONIE LOVE vs ADEVA)	
	Ring My Bell	1991

ARTIST	SONG TITLE	DATE
	(PAUL SIMPSON featuring ADEVA)	
	Musical Freedom (Moving On Up)	1989
ADVENTURES OF STEVIE V		
	Body Language	1990
	Dirty Cash (Money Talks)	1990
ADVENTURES	Broken Land	1988
ADVERTS	Gary Gilmour's Eyes	1977
	No Time To Be 21	1978
AEROSMITH	Amazing	1993
	Angel	1988
	Back In The Saddle	1977
	Come Together	1978
	Crazy/Blind Man	1994
	Cryin'	1993
	Dream On	1976
	Dude (Looks Like A Lady)	1987
	Eat The Rich	1993
	Falling In Love (Is Hard On The Knees)	1997
	Hole In My Soul	1997
	I Don't Want To Miss A Thing	1998
	Jaded	2001
	Janie's Got A Gun	1989
	Last Child	1976
	Livin' On The Edge	1993
	Love In An Elevator	1989
	The Other Side	1990

ARTIST	SONG TITLE	DATE
	Pink	1998
	Rag Doll	1988
	Shut Up And Dance	1994
	Sweet Emotion	1975
	Walk This Way	1976
	What It Takes	1990
AFI	Girl's Not Grey	2003
AFRO MEDUSA	Pasilda	2000
AFROMAN	Because I Got High	2001
	Crazy Rap	2002
AFTER 7	Can't Stop	1990
	Heat Of The Moment	1989
	Nights Like This	1991
	Ready Or Not	1990
	'Til You Do Me Right	1995
AFTER THE FIRE	Der Kommissar	1983
	One Rule For You	1979
AFTERNOON DELIGHTS		
	General Hospi-Tale	1981
AFTERSHOCK	Slave To The Vibe	1993
AGE OF LOVE	The Age Of Love	1998
AGENT SUMO	Why?	2002
AGNELLI & NELSON	El Nino	1998
	Embrace	2000
	Everyday	1999
	Hudson Street	2000

ARTIST	SONG TITLE	DATE
CHRISTINA AGUILERA		
	Beautiful	2003
	The Christmas Song (Chestnuts Roasting On An Open Fire)	1999
	Come On Over Baby (All I Want Is You)	2000
	Fighter	2003
	Genie In A Bottle	1999
	I Turn To You	2000
	The Voice Within	2003
	What A Girl Wants	1999
CHRISTINA AGUILERA featuring LIL' KIM		
	Can't Hold Us Down	2003
CHRISTINA AGUILERA featuring REDMAN		
	Dirrty	2002
CHRISTINA AGUILERA, LIL' KIM, MYA & PINK		
	Lady Marmalade	2001
	(RICKY MARTIN & CHRISTINA AGUILERA) Nobody Wants To Be Lonely	2001
A-HA	The Blood That Moves The Body	1988
	Cry Wolf	1986
	Crying In The Rain	1990
	Dark Is The Night	1993
	Hunting High And Low	1986
	I've Been Losing You	1986
	The Living Daylights	1987
	Manhattan Skyline	1987

ARTIST	SONG TITLE	DATE
	Shapes That Go Together	1994
	Stay On These Roads	1988
	Summer Moved On	2000
	The Sun Always Shines On TV	1985
	Take On Me	1985
	Touchy!	1988
	Train Of Thought	1986
	You Are The One	1988
AHMAD!	Back In The Day	1994
CLAY AIKEN	Invisible	2003
AIR SUPPLY	All Out Of Love	1980
	Even The Nights Are Better	1982
	Every Woman In The World	1980
	Here I Am (Just When You Thought I Was Over You)	1981
	Just As I Am	1985
	Lost In Love	1980
	Making Love Out Of Nothing At All	1983
	The One That You Love	1981
	Sweet Dreams	1981
	Two Less Lonely People In The World	1982
	Young Love	1982
AIR	All I Need	1998
	Kelly Watch The Stars	1998
	Playground Love	2000
	Radio No. 1	2001

ARTIST	SONG TITLE	DATE
	Sexy Boy	1998
AIRHEAD	Counting Sheep	1991
AIRHEADZ	Stanley (Here I Am)	2001
AIRSCAPE	L'Esperanza	1999
	Pacific Melody	1997
JEWEL AKENS	The Birds And The Bees	1965
AKON featuring STYLES P.		
	Locked Up	2004
ALABAMA	The Closer You Get	1983
	Feels So Right	1981
	Love In The First Degree	1981
	Take Me Down	1982
ALABAMA featuring *NSYNC		
	God Must Have Spent A Little More Time On You	1999
ALABAMA 3	Ain't Goin' To Goa	1998
ALARM	Absolute Reality	1985
	A New South Wales/The Rock	1989
	Rain In The Summertime	1987
	68 Guns	1983
	Spirit Of '76	1986
	Strength	1985
	Where Were You Hiding When The Storm Broke?	1984
MORRIS ALBERT	Feelings	1975
ALCATRAZ	Give Me Luv	1996

ARTIST	SONG TITLE	DATE
ALCAZAR	Crying At The Discoteque	2001
	Sexual Guarantee	2002
	This Is The World We Live In	2004
ALDA	Girls Night Out	1998
	Real Good Time	1998
ALENA	Turn It Around	1999
ALESSI	Oh, Lori	1977
ALEXIA	Gimme Love	1998
	The Music I Like	1998
	Uh La La La	1998
JOHN ALFORD	Blue Moon/Only You	1996
	If/Keep On Running	1996
	Smoke Gets In Your Eyes	1996
ALI AND FRAZIER	Uptown Top Ranking	1993
TATYANA ALI	Daydreamin'	1998
	Everytime	1999
TATYANA ALI featuring WILL SMITH		
	Boy You Knock Me Out	1999
ALIAS	More Than Words Can Say	1990
	Waiting For Love	1991
ALICE DEEJAY	Back In My Life	1999
	Celebrate Our Love	2001
	The Lonely One	2000
	Will I Ever	2000
	(DJ JURGEN presents ALICE DEEJAY)	
	Better Off Alone	1999

ARTIST	SONG TITLE	DATE
ALICE IN CHAINS	Angry Chair	1993
	Down In A Hole	1993
	Grind	1995
	Heaven Beside You	1996
	Them Bones	1993
	Would?	1993
ALIEN ANT FARM	Movies	2002
	Smooth Criminal	2001
ALISHA'S ATTIC	Air We Breathe	1997
	Alisha Rules The World	1996
	Barbarella	1999
	I Am, I Feel	1996
	The Incidentals	1998
	Indestructible	1997
	Push It All Aside	2001
	Wish I Were You	1999
ALIVE & KICKING	Tighter, Tighter	1970
ALIZEE	Moi... Lolita	2002
ALL ABOUT EVE	December	1989
	Every Angel	1988
	Farewell Mr. Sorrow	1991
	Martha's Harbour	1988
	Phased (EP)	1992
	Road To Your Soul	1989
	Scarlet	1990
	What Kind Of Fool	1988

ARTIST	SONG TITLE	DATE
	Wild Hearted Woman	1988
ALL SAINTS	All Hooked Up	2001
	Black Coffee	2000
	Bootie Call	1998
	I Know Where It's At	1998
	Never Ever	1998
	Pure Shores	2000
	Under The Bridge/Lady Marmalade	1998
	War Of Nerves	1998
ALL SEEING I	Beat Goes On	1998
	1st Man In Space	1999
ALL SEEING I featuring TONY CHRISTIE		
	Walk Like A Panther '98	1999
ALL STAR TRIBUTE What's Going On		2001
ALL-AMERICAN REJECTS		
	Swing, Swing	2003
ALL-4-ONE	I Can Love You Like That	1995
	I Swear	1994
	So Much In Love	1994
	Someday	1996
DAVIE ALLAN & THE ARROWS		
	Blue's Theme	1967
GARY ALLAN	Man To Man	2003
	Tough Little Boys	2003
DEBORAH ALLEN	Baby I Lied	1983
DONNA ALLEN	Joy And Pain	1989

ARTIST	SONG TITLE	DATE
	Real	1995
	Serious	1987
	(EAST 57TH STREET featuring DONNA ALLEN)	
	Saturday	1997
ALLMAN BROTHERS BAND		
	Crazy Love	1979
	Ramblin' Man	1973
	Straight From The Heart	1981
GREGG ALLMAN	Midnight Rider	1973
ALLSTARS	Back When/Going All The Way	2002
	Best Friends	2001
	The Land Of Make Believe	2002
	Things That Go Bump In The Night/Is	
	There Something I Should Know	2001
ALLURE	All Cried Out	1998
ALLURE featuring NAS		
	Head Over Heels	1997
ALMIGHTY	Addiction	1993
	All Sussed Out	1996
	Devil's Toy	1991
	Do You Understand	1996
	Free 'n' Easy	1991
	Jonestown Mind	1995
	Over The Edge	1993
	Wrench	1994
MARC ALMOND	Adored And Explored	1995

ARTIST	SONG TITLE	DATE
	Bitter Sweet	1988
	The Days Of Pearly Spencer	1992
	Jacky	1991
	A Lover Spurned	1990
	My Hand Over My Heart	1992
	Stories Of Johnny	1985
	Tears Run Rings	1988
MARC ALMOND featuring GENE PITNEY		
	Something's Gotten Hold Of My Heart	1989
(BRONSKI BEAT & MARC ALMOND)		
	I Feel Love (Medley)	1985
(SOFT CELL/MARC ALMOND)		
	Tainted Love	1991
ALOOF	One Night Stand	1996
HERB ALPERT	A Banda	1967
	Casino Royale	1967
	Diamonds	1987
	Flamingo	1966
	The Happening	1967
	Keep Your Eye On Me	1987
	The Lonely Bull (El Solo Torro)	1963
	Making Love In The Rain	1987
	Mame	1966
	Rise	1979
	Rotation	1979
	Route 101	1982

ARTIST	SONG TITLE	DATE
	Spanish Flea	1965
	A Taste Of Honey	1965
	This Guy's In Love With You	1968
	Tijuana Taxi	1965
	Wade In The Water	1967
	What Now My Love	1966
	Without Her	1969
	The Work Song	1966
	Zorba The Greek	1965
ALPHAVILLE	Big In Japan	1984
ALSOU	Before You Love Me	2001
ALTERED IMAGES	Bring Me Closer	1983
	Don't Talk To Me About Love	1983
	Happy Birthday	1981
	I Could Be Happy	1981
	Pinky Blue	1982
	See Those Eyes	1982
ALTERN 8	Activ 8 (Come With Me)	1991
	Evapor 8	1992
	Hypnotic St-8	1992
	Infiltrate 202	1991
ALTHIA AND DONNA		
	Uptown Top Ranking	1977
SHOLA AMA	Imagine	2000
	Much Love	1998
	Someday I'll Find You/I've Been To A	

ARTIST	SONG TITLE	DATE
	Marvellous Party	1998
	Still Believe	1999
	Who's Loving My Baby	1997
	You Might Need Somebody	1997
	You're The One I Love	1997
	(GLAMMA KID featuring SHOLA AMA)	
	Taboo	1999
	(PIRATES featuring ENYA, SHOLA AMA, NAILA BOSS & ISHANI)	
	You Should Really Know	2004
EDDIE AMADOR	House Music	1998
	Rise	2000
RUBY AMANFU	Sugah	2003
AMAZING RHYTHM ACES		
	Third Rate Romance	1975
AMAZULU	Don't You Just Know It	1985
	Excitable	1985
	Montego Bay	1986
	Mony Mony	1987
	Too Good To Be Forgotten	1986
AMBASSADORS OF FUNK/MC MARIO		
	Supermarioland	1992
AMBER	Sexual	2000
	This Is Your Night	1996
AMBOY DUKES	Journey To The Center Of The Mind	1968
AMBROSIA	Biggest Part Of Me	1980

ARTIST	SONG TITLE	DATE
	Holdin' On To Yesterday	1975
	How Much I Feel	1978
	Magical Mystery Tour	1977
	You're The Only Woman (You & I)	1980
AMEN CORNER	Bend Me, Shape Me	1968
	Gin House Blues	1967
	Hello Susie	1969
	High In The Sky	1968
	(If Paradise Is) Half As Nice	1969
	The World Of Broken Hearts	1967
AMEN! UK	Passion	1997
	People Of Love	1997
AMERICA	The Border	1983
	Daisy Jane	1975
	Don't Cross The River	1973
	A Horse With No Name	1972
	I Need You	1972
	Lonely People	1974
	Sister Golden Hair	1975
	Tin Man	1974
	Today's The Day	1976
	Ventura Highway	1972
	You Can Do Magic	1982
AMERICAN BREED	Bend Me, Shape Me	1967
	Green Light	1968
	Step Out Of Your Mind	1967

ARTIST	SONG TITLE	DATE
AMERICAN HI-FI	Flavor Of The Weak	2001
AMERIE featuring LUDACRIS		
	Why Don't We Fall In Love	2002
	(LL COOL J featuring AMERIE)	
	Paradise	2002
ED AMES	My Cup Runneth Over	1967
	Who Will Answer?	1967
AMILLIONSONS	Misti Blu	2002
AMIRA	My Desire	2001
CHERIE AMORE	I Don't Want Nobody (Tellin' Me What	
	To Do)	2000
VANESSA AMOROSI	Absolutely Everybody	2000
AMOS	Let Love Shine	1995
	(JEREMY HEALY & AMOS)	
	Argentina	1997
	Stamp!	1996
TORI AMOS	Caught A Lite Sneeze	1996
	Cornflake Girl	1994
	Crucify	1992
	Hey Jupiter/Professional Widow	1996
	Past The Mission	1994
	Pretty Good Year	1994
	Professional Widow (It's Got To Be Big)	1997
	Silent All These Years	1992
	Spark	1998
	Talula	1996

ARTIST	SONG TITLE	DATE
	Winter	1992
	(BT featuring TORI AMOS)	
	Blue Skies	1996
AMOURE	Is That Your Final Answer?	2000
ANASTACIA	Cowboys & Kisses	2001
	I'm Outta Love	2000
	Left Outside Alone	2004
	Made For Lovin' You	2001
	Not That Kind	2001
	One Day In Your Life	2002
	Paid My Dues	2001
	Sick And Tired	2004
	Why'd You Lie To Me	2002
	You'll Never Be Alone	2002
AND WHY NOT?	The Face	1990
	Something You Got	1990
ANGRY ANDERSON	Suddenly	1988
CARLEEN ANDERSON		
	Let It Last	1995
	Mama Said	1994
	Maybe I'm Amazed	1998
	Nervous Breakdown	1994
	True Spirit	1994
LAURIE ANDERSON	O Superman	1981
LYNN ANDERSON	Rose Garden	1970

ARTIST	SONG TITLE	DATE
SUNSHINE ANDERSON		
	Heard It All Before	2001
PETER ANDRE	All About Us	1997
	Flava	1996
	I Feel You	1996
	Insania	2004
	Kiss The Girl	1998
	Lonely	1997
	Natural	1997
	Only One	1996
	The Right Way	2004
PETER ANDRE featuring BUBBLER RANX		
	Mysterious Girl	1996
PETER ANDRE featuring WARREN G		
	All Night All Right	1998
CHRIS ANDREWS	Stop That Girl	1966
	To Whom It Concerns	1965
	Whatcha Gonna Do Now?	1966
	Yesterday Man	1965
JESSICA ANDREWS	Who I Am	2001
MICHAEL ANDREWS featuring GARY JULES		
	Mad World	2003
ANDROIDS	Do It With Madonna	2003
ANEKA	Japanese Boy	1981
ANGEL CITY	Do You Know (I Go Crazy)	2004
	Touch Me	2004

ARTIST	SONG TITLE	DATE
ANGEL CITY featuring LARA MCALLEN		
	Love Me Right (Oh Sheila)	2003
ANGELETTES	Don't Let Him Touch You	1972
ANGELIC	Can't Keep Me Silent	2001
	It's My Turn	2000
	Stay With Me	2001
ANGELIC UPSTARTS	I'm An Upstart	1979
	Teenage Warning	1979
ANGELICA	Angel Baby	1991
ANIMAL NIGHTLIFE	Love Is Just The Great Pretender	1985
	Mr. Solitaire	1984
ANIMAL	Wipe Out	1994
ANIMALS	Baby Let Me Take You Home	1964
	Bring It On Home To Me	1965
	Don't Bring Me Down	1966
	Don't Let Me Be Misunderstood	1965
	The House Of The Rising Sun	1964
	I'm Crying	1964
	Inside Looking Out	1966
	It's My Life	1965
	We Gotta Get Out Of This Place	1965
	(ERIC BURDON & THE ANIMALS)	
	Good Times	1967
	Help Me Girl	1966
	Monterey	1967
	San Franciscan Nights	1967

ARTIST	SONG TITLE	DATE
	See See Rider	1966
	Sky Pilot (Part I)	1968
	When I Was Young	1967
ANIMOTION	Let Him Go	1985
	Obsession	1985
	Room To Move	1989
PAUL ANKA	Anytime (I'll Be There)	1976
	Diana	1957
	Goodnight My Love	1969
	This Is Love	1978
	Times Of Your Life	1975
PAUL ANKA/ODIA COATES		
	I Believe There's Nothing Stronger Than	
	Our Love	1975
	I Don't Like To Sleep Alone	1975
	One Man Woman/One Woman Man	1974
	(You're) Having My Baby	1974
ANA ANN	Ride	2002
ANNIE	Chewing Gum	2004
ANOTHER BAD CREATION		
	Iesha	1991
	Playground	1991
ANOTHER LEVEL	Be Alone No More	1998
	Bomb Diggy	1999
	Freak Me	1998

ARTIST	SONG TITLE	DATE
	From The Heart	1999
	Guess I Was A Fool	1998
ANOTHER LEVEL featuring TQ		
	Summertime	1999
ANOTHER LEVEL/GHOSTFACE KILLAH		
	I Want You For Myself	1999
MARC ANTHONY	I Need To Know	1999
	You Sang To Me	2000
	(LITTLE LOUIE & MARC ANTHONY)	
	Ride On The Rhythm	1998
MIKI ANTHONY	If It Wasn't For The Reason That I	
	Love You	1973
RICHARD ANTHONY		
	If I Loved You	1964
	Walking Alone	1963
ANTHRAX	Got The Time	1991
	I Am The Law	1987
	I'm The Man	1987
	In My World	1990
	Make Me Laugh	1988
	Only	1993
ANTHRAX featuring CHUCK D		
	Bring The Noise	1991
ANTICAPPELLA	Express Your Freedom	1995
	2/231	1991

ARTIST	SONG TITLE	DATE
ANTICAPPELLA featuring MC FIXX IT		
	Move Your Body	1994
APACHE INDIAN	Arranged Marriage	1993
	Chok There	1993
	Nuff Vibes (EP)	1993
APACHE INDIAN featuring FRANKIE PAUL		
	Raggamuffin Girl	1995
APACHE INDIAN WITH TIM DOG		
	Make Way For The Indian	1995
APHEX TWINS	Come To Daddy	1997
	On	1993
	Windowlicker	1999
APHRODITE'S CHILD		
	Rain And Tears	1968
APOLLO 100	Joy	1972
APOLLO 440	Ain't Talkin' 'Bout Dub	1997
	Astral America	1994
	Charlie's Angels 2000	2000
	(Don't Fear) The Reaper	1995
	Krupa	1996
	Liquid Cool	1994
	Lost In Space	1998
	Raw Power	1997
	Stop The Rock	1999
	(JEAN MICHEL JARRE & APOLLO 440)	
	Rendez-Vous '98	1998

ARTIST	SONG TITLE	DATE
FIONA APPLE	Criminal	1997
	Fast As You Can	2000
KIM APPLEBY	Don't Worry	1990
	G.L.A.D.	1991
	Mama	1991
APPLEJACKS	Like Dreamers Do	1964
	Tell Me When	1964
	Three Little Words	1964
APPLETON	Don't Worry	2003
	Everything Eventually	2003
	Fantasy	2002
CRABBY APPLETON	Go Back	1970
APRIL WINE	Just Between You And Me	1981
	Roller	1979
	You Could Have Been A Lady	1972
AQUA	Around The World	2000
	Barbie Girl	1997
	Cartoon Heroes	2000
	Doctor Jones	1998
	Good Morning Sunshine	1998
	Lollipop (Candyman)	1997
	My Oh My	1998
	Turn Back Time	1998
AQUAGEN	Hard To Say I'm Sorry	2003
	(WARP BROTHERS vs AQUAGEN)	
	Phatt Bass	2000

ARTIST	SONG TITLE	DATE
AQUALUNG	Brighter Than Sunshine	2003
	Strange And Beautiful (I'll Put A Spell On You)	2002
ARBORS	The Letter	1969
ARCADIA	Election Day	1985
	The Promise	1986
TASMIN ARCHER	Arienne	1993
	In Your Care	1993
	Lords Of The New Church	1993
	Shipbuilding	1994
	Sleeping Satellite	1993
ARCHIES	Bang-Shang-A-Lang	1968
	Jingle Jangle	1969
	Sugar Sugar	1969
	Who's Your Baby?	1970
ARCHITECHS	Show Me The Money	2001
ARCHITECHS featuring NANA		
	Body Groove	2000
JANN ARDEN	Insensitive	1996
TINA ARENA	Chains	1996
	Heaven Help My Heart	1995
	Show Me Heaven	1995
	Sorrento Moon (I Remember)	1996
	Whistle Down The Wind	1998
ARGENT	God Gave Rock 'n' Roll To You	1973
	Hold Your Head Up	1972

ARTIST	SONG TITLE	DATE
	Tragedy	1972
ARIEL	A9	2000
ARKARNA	House On Fire	1997
JOAN ARMATRADING		
	Drop The Pilot	1983
	Love And Affection	1976
	Me Myself I	1980
ARMIN	Communication	2000
LOUIS ARMSTRONG	Hello, Dolly!	1964
	We Have All The Time In The World	1994
	What A Wonderful World/Cabaret	1968
ARMY OF LOVERS	Crucified	1992
ARNEE & THE TERMINATERS		
	I'll Be Back	1991
DAVID ARNOLD/BJORK		
	Play Dead	1993
	(DAVID MCALMONT/DAVID ARNOLD)	
	Diamonds Are Forever	1997
	(PROPELLERHEADS/DAVID ARNOLD)	
	On Her Majesty's Secret Service	1997
EDDY ARNOLD	I Want To Go With You	1966
	The Last Word In Lonesome Is Me	1966
	Make The World Go Away	1965
P.P. ARNOLD	Angel Of The Morning	1968
	The First Cut Is The Deepest	1967

ARTIST	SONG TITLE	DATE
(BEATMASTERS WITH P.P. ARNOLD)		
	Burn It Up	1988
ARRESTED DEVELOPMENT		
	Ease My Mind	1994
	Mr. Wendal/Revolution	1993
	People Everyday	1992
	Tennessee	1992
STEVE ARRINGTON	Dancin' In The Key Of Life	1985
	Feel So Real	1985
ARRIVAL	Friends	1970
	I Will Survive	1970
ARROW	Hot Hot Hot	1994
	Long Time	1985
ARROWS	My Last Night With You	1975
	A Touch Too Much	1974
ARSENAL F.C.	Good Old Arsenal	1971
	Hot Stuff	1998
	Shouting For The Gunners	1993
ART COMPANY	Susanna	1984
ART OF NOISE	Close (To The Edit)	1984
	Paranoimia	1986
ART OF NOISE featuring DUANE EDDY		
	Peter Gunn	1986
ART OF NOISE featuring TOM JONES		
	Kiss	1988

ARTIST	SONG TITLE	DATE
ARTFUL DODGER & ROBBIE CRAIG featuring		
CRAIG DAVID	Woman Trouble	2000
ARTFUL DODGER & ROMINA JOHNSON		
	Movin Too Fast	2000
ARTFUL DODGER featuring CRAIG DAVID		
	Re-Rewind The Crowd Say Bo Selecta	1999
ARTFUL DODGER featuring LIFFORD		
	Please Don't Turn Me On	2000
ARTFUL DODGER featuring MELANIE BLATT		
	Twentyfourseven	2001
ARTFUL DODGER featuring MICHELLE ESCOFFERY		
	Think About Me	2001
(DREEM TEEM vs ARTFUL DODGER MZ MAY & MC ALISTAIR)		
	It Ain't Enough	2001
ARTIFICIAL FUNK featuring NELLIE ETTISON		
	Together	2003
ARTISTS AGAINST AIDS WORLDWIDE		
	What's Going On?	2001
ARTISTS UNITED AGAINST APARTHEID		
	Sun City	1985
ASH	Angel Interceptor	1995
	Burn Baby Burn	2001
	Candy	2001
	Envy	2002

ARTIST	SONG TITLE	DATE
	Girl From Mars	1995
	Goldfinger	1996
	Jesus Says	1998
	A Life Less Ordinary	1997
	Oh Yeah	1996
	Orpheus	2004
	Shining Light	2001
	Sometimes	2001
	Starcrossed	2004
	There's A Star	2002
	Wild Surf	1998
ASHA	J.J. Tribute	1995
ASHANTI	Baby	2002
	Foolish	2002
	Happy	2002
	Rain On Me	2003
	Rock Wit U (Awww Baby)	2003
(FAT JOE featuring ASHANTI)		
	What's Luv?	2002
(IRV GOTTI presents JA RULE, ASHANTI, CHARLI BALTIMORE)		
	Down 4 U	2002
(JA RULE featuring ASHANTI)		
	Always On Time	2001
	Mesmerize	2003

ARTIST	SONG TITLE	DATE
(JA RULE featuring R. KELLY & ASHANTI)		
	Wonderful	2004
RICHARD ASHCROFT		
	Buy It In Bottles	2003
	C'mon People (We're Making It Now)	2000
	Check The Meaning	2002
	Money To Burn	2000
	Science Of Silence	2003
	A Song For The Lovers	2000
JOHN ASHER	Let's Twist Again	1975
ASHFORD & SIMPSON		
	Found A Cure	1979
	Solid	1984
ASHTON GARDNER & DYKE		
	Resurrection Shuffle	1971
ASIA	Don't Cry	1983
	Heat Of The Moment	1982
	Only Time Will Tell	1982
	The Smile Has Left Your Eyes	1983
ASIAN DUB FOUNDATION		
	Buzzin'	1998
ASSEMBLED MULTITUDE		
	Overture From Tommy	1970
ASSEMBLY	Never Never	1983
ASSOCIATES	Club Country	1982

ARTIST	SONG TITLE	DATE
	Love Hangover/18 Carat Love Affair	1982
	Party Fears Two	1982
ASSOCIATION	Along Comes Mary	1966
	Cherish	1966
	Everything That Touches You	1968
	Never My Love	1967
	Pandora's Golden Heebie Jeebies	1966
	Time For Livin'	1968
	Windy	1967
RICK ASTLEY	Cry For Help	1991
	Giving Up On Love	1989
	Hold Me In Your Arms	1989
	Hopelessly	1993
	It Would Take A Strong Man	1988
	Never Gonna Give You Up	1987
	She Wants To Dance With Me	1989
	Take Me To Your Heart	1988
	Together Forever	1988
	When I Fall In Love/My Arms Keep Missing You	1987
	Whenever You Need Somebody	1987
ASWAD	Beauty's Only Skin Deep	1989
	Don't Turn Around	1988
	Give A Little Love	1988
	Next To You	1990
	On And On	1989

ARTIST	SONG TITLE	DATE
	Shine	1994
	Warriors	1994
	You're No Good	1995
	(YAZZ & ASWAD)	
	How Long	1993
ATB	Don't Stop	1999
	Killer	2000
	Let U Go	2001
	9pm (Till I Come)	1999
ATB featuring YORK		
	The Fields Of Love	2001
ATC	Around The World (La La La La La)	2001
ATHLETE	El Salvador	2003
	You Got The Style	2002
ATL	Calling All Girls	2004
	Make It Up With Love	2004
ATLANTA RHYTHM SECTION		
	Alien	1981
	Do It Or Die	1979
	Doraville	1974
	I'm Not Gonna Let It Bother Me Tonight	1978
	Imaginary Lover	1978
	So Into You	1977
	Spooky	1979

ARTIST	SONG TITLE	DATE
ATLANTIC OCEAN	Body In Motion	1994
	Waterfall	1996
ATLANTIC STARR	Always	1987
	Circles	1982
	Everybody's Got Summer	1994
	Masterpiece	1992
	Secret Lovers	1985
ATOMIC KITTEN	Eternal Flame	2001
	Follow Me	2000
	I Want Your Love	2000
	If You Come To Me	2003
	It's Ok!	2002
	The Last Goodbye/Be With You	2002
	Love Doesn't Have To Hurt	2003
	Right Now	1999
	See Ya	2000
	The Tide Is High (Get The Feeling)	2002
	Whole Again	2001
ATOMIC KITTEN featuring KOOL & THE GANG		
	Ladies Night	2003
ATOMIC ROOSTER	Devil's Answer	1971
	Tomorrow Night	1971
AUDIO BULLYS	The Things/Turned Away	2003
	We Don't Care	2003
AUDIOSLAVE	Cochise	2003
	Like A Stone	2003

ARTIST	SONG TITLE	DATE
AUDIOWEB	Bankrobber	1997
	Policeman Skank... (The Story Of My Life)	1998
AUF DER MAUR	Followed The Waves	2004
	Real A Lie	2004
AURORA	The Day It Rained Forever	2002
	Dreaming	2002
	Hear You Calling	2000
AURORA featuring NAIMEE COLEMAN		
	Ordinary World	2000
AURRA	You And Me Tonight	1986
PATTI AUSTIN (with JAMES INGRAM)		
	Baby Come To Me	1982
AUTOGRAPH	Turn Up The Radio	1984
PETER AUTRY	Walking In The Air	1987
AUTUMN	My Little Girl	1971
AVALANCHES	Frontier Psychiatrist	2001
	Since I Left You	2001
AVANT	Don't Take Your Love Away	2004
	Makin' Good Love	2002
	Separated	2000
AVANT featuring KETARA WYATT		
	My First Love	2000
	(KEKE WYATT featuring AVANT) Nothing In This World	2002

ARTIST	SONG TITLE	DATE
AVANT-GARDE	Naturally Stoned	1968
AVERAGE WHITE BAND		
	Cut The Cake	1975
	If I Ever Lose This Heaven	1975
	Let's Go Round Again (Pt 1)	1980
	Pick Up The Pieces	1974
	Queen Of My Soul	1976
	School Boy Crush	1975
AWESOME 3 featuring JULIE MCDERMOTT		
	Don't Go (96 Remix)	1996
AYLA	Ayla	1999
AZ	Sugar Hill	1995
AZ YET	Last Night	1996
AZ YET featuring PETER CETERA		
	Hard To Say I'm Sorry	1997
STEVE AZAR	I Don't Have To Be Me ('Til Monday)	2002
CHARLES AZNAVOUR		
	The Old-Fashioned Way (Les Plaisirs Demodes)	1973
	She	1974
AZTEC CAMERA	All I Need Is Everything/Jump	1984
	Good Morning Britain	1990
	How Men Are	1988
	Oblivious	1983
	Somewhere In My Heart	1988
	Working In A Goldmine	1988

ARTIST	SONG TITLE	DATE
AZYMUTH	Jazz Carnival	1980
B B & Q BAND	Genie	1985
	(I'm A) Dreamer	1986
B REAL/BUSTA RHYMES/COOLIO/LL COOL J/ METHOD MAN	Hit 'Em High (The Monstars' Anthem)	1997
B*WITCHED	Blame It On The Weatherman	1999
	C'est La Vie	1999
	Jesse Hold On	1999
	Jump Down	2000
	Rollercoaster	1998
	To You I Belong	1998
B*WITCHED featuring LADYSMITH BLACK MAMBAZO		
	I Shall Be There	1999
DEREK B	Bad Young Brother	1988
	Goodgroove	1988
HOWIE B	Angels Go Bald: Too	1997
JON B	Are U Still Down	1998
	Don't Talk	2001
	Pretty Girl	1995
	They Don't Know	1998
JON B featuring BABYFACE		
	Someone To Love	1995
LISA B	Fascinated	1993
	You And Me	1994
STEVIE B	Because I Love You (The Postman Song)	1990
	Dream About You/Funky Melody	1995

ARTIST	SONG TITLE	DATE
	I Wanna Be The One	1989
	I'll Be By Your Side	1991
	In My Eyes	1989
	Love And Emotion	1990
	Love Me For Life	1990
B-ROCK & THE BIZZ		
	My Baby Daddy	1997
MARK B & BLADE	Ya Don't See The Signs	2001
ERIC B. & RAKIM	Follow The Leader	1988
	I Know You Got Soul	1988
	Paid In Full	1987
	(JODY WATLEY WITH ERIC B. & RAKIM)	
	Friends	1989
B.G. featuring BABY, TURK, MANNIE FRESH, JUVENILE		
	Bling Bling	1999
B.M.R. featuring FELICIA		
	Check It Out (Everybody)	1999
B.V.S.M.P.	I Need You	1988
B15 featuring CHRISSY D & LADY G		
	Girls Like Us	2000
B2K	Girlfriend	2003
	Gots Ta Be	2002
	Uh Huh	2002
B2K featuring FABOLOUS		
	Badaboom	2004

ARTIST	SONG TITLE	DATE
B2K featuring P. DIDDY		
	Bump, Bump, Bump	2003
BABE INSTINCT	Disco Babes From Outer Space	1999
BABY BUMPS	Burning	1998
	I Got This Feeling	2000
BABY D	(Everybody's Got To Learn Sometime)	
	I Need Your Loving	1995
	Let Me Be Your Fantasy	1994
	So Pure	1996
	Take Me To Heaven	1996
BABYBIRD	Back Together	1999
	Bad Old Man	1998
	Candy Girl	1997
	Cornershop	1997
	The F-Word	2000
	Goodnight	1996
	If You'll Be Mine	1998
	You're Gorgeous	1996
BABYFACE	And Our Feelings	1994
	Everytime I Close My Eyes	1997
	It's No Crime	1989
	My Kinda Girl	1990
	Never Keeping Secrets	1993
	Tender Lover	1989
	There She Goes	2001
	This Is For The Lover In You	1996

ARTIST	SONG TITLE	DATE
	When Can I See You	1994
	Whip Appeal	1990
BABYFACE featuring TONI BRAXTON		
	Give U My Heart	1992
BABYFACE featuring STEVIE WONDER		
	How Come, How Long	1997
(JAY-Z featuring BABYFACE & FOXY BROWN)		
	Sunshine	1997
(JON B featuring BABYFACE)		
	Someone To Love	1995
BABYLON ZOO	Animal Army	1996
	The Boy With The X-Ray Eyes	1996
	Spaceman	1996
BABYS	Back On My Feet Again	1980
	Every Time I Think Of You	1979
	Isn't It Time	1977
BACCARA	Sorry I'm A Lady	1978
	Yes Sir, I Can Boogie	1977
BURT BACHARACH	Trains And Boats And Planes	1965
BACHELORS	Can I Trust You	1966
	Chapel In The Moonlight	1965
	Charmaine	1963
	Diane	1964
	Faraway Places	1963
	Hello, Dolly!	1966
	I Believe	1964

ARTIST	SONG TITLE	DATE
	I Wouldn't Trade You For The World	1964
	In The Chapel In The Moonlight	1965
	Love Me With All Of Your Heart	1966
	Marie	1965
	Marta	1967
	No Arms Can Ever Hold You	1964
	Oh How I Miss You	1967
	Ramona	1964
	The Sound Of Silence	1966
	True Love For Evermore	1965
	Walk With Faith In Your Heart	1966
	Whispering	1963
BACHMAN-TURNER OVERDRIVE		
	Hey You	1975
	Let It Ride	1974
	Roll On Down The Highway	1975
	Take It Like A Man	1976
	Takin' Care Of Business	1974
	You Ain't Seen Nothin' Yet	1974
TAL BACHMAN	She's So High	1999
BACKSTREET BOYS	All I Have To Give	1999
	Anywhere For You	1997
	As Long As You Love Me	1997
	The Call	2001
	Drowning	2001
	Everybody (Backstreet's Back)	1998

ARTIST	SONG TITLE	DATE
	Get Down (You're The One For Me)	1996
	I Want It That Way	1999
	I'll Never Break Your Heart	1998
	Larger Than Life	1999
	More Than That	2001
	The One	2000
	Quit Playing Games (With My Heart)	1997
	Shape Of My Heart	2000
	Show Me The Meaning Of Being Lonely	2000
	We've Got It Goin' On	1996
BACKYARD DOG	Baddest Ruffest	2001
BAD BOYS INC	Don't Talk About Love	1993
	Love Here I Come	1994
	More To This World	1994
	Take Me Away (I'll Follow You)	1994
	Walking On Air	1993
	Whenever You Need Someone	1993
BAD COMPANY	Can't Get Enough	1974
	Feel Like Makin' Love	1975
	Good Lovin' Gone Bad	1975
	How About That	1992
	If You Needed Somebody	1990
	Mo' Fire	2003
	Movin' On	1975
	Rock 'n' Roll Fantasy	1979
	Walk Through Fire	1991

ARTIST	SONG TITLE	DATE
	Young Blood	1976
BAD ENGLISH	Possession	1990
	Price Of Love	1989
	When I See You Smile	1989
BAD MANNERS	Buona Sera	1981
	Can Can	1981
	Just A Feeling	1981
	Lip Up Fatty	1980
	Lorraine	1981
	My Girl Lollipop (My Boy Lollipop)	1982
	Ne-Ne Na-Na Na-Na Nu-Nu	1980
	Special Brew	1980
	Walkin' In The Sunshine	1981
BADDIEL & SKINNER & LIGHTNING SEEDS		
	Three Lions	1996
BADFINGER	Baby Blue	1972
	Come And Get It	1970
	Day After Day	1971
	No Matter What	1970
BADLY DRAWN BOY		
	All Possibilities	2003
	Born Again	2003
	Disillusion	2000
	Once Around The Block	2000
	Pissing In The Wind	2001
	Silent Sigh	2002

ARTIST	SONG TITLE	DATE
	Something To Talk About	2002
	Year Of The Rat	2004
	You Were Right	2002
ERYKAH BADU	Bag Lady	2000
	Next Lifetime	1997
	On & On	1997
ERYKAH BADU featuring COMMON		
	Love Of My Life (An Ode To Hip Hop)	2002
(BUSTA RHYMES featuring ERYKAH BADU)		
	One	1998
(MACY GRAY featuring ERYKAH BADU)		
	Sweet Baby	2001
(ROOTS featuring ERYKAH BADU)		
	You Got Me	1999
JOAN BAEZ	Diamonds And Rust	1975
	Farewell Angelina	1965
	It's All Over Now, Baby Blue	1965
	The Night They Drove Old Dixie Down	1971
	There But For Fortune	1965
	We Shall Overcome	1965
BAHA MEN	Move It Like This	2002
	Who Let The Dogs Out	2000
	You All Dat	2001
PHILIP BAILEY	Walking On The Chinese Wall	1985
PHILIP BAILEY & PHIL COLLINS		
	Easy Lover	1984

ARTIST	SONG TITLE	DATE
MERRIL BAINBRIDGE		
	Mouth	1996
DAN BAIRD	I Love You Period	1992
ADRIAN BAKER	Sherry	1975
ANITA BAKER	Body & Soul	1994
	Caught Up In The Rapture	1986
	Giving You The Best That I Got	1988
	Just Because	1989
	Sweet Love	1986
ARTHUR BAKER/BACKBEAT DISCIPLES featuring		
AL GREEN	The Message Is Love	1989
GEORGE BAKER SELECTION		
	Little Green Bag	1970
	Paloma Blanca	1975
HYLDA BAKER & ARTHUR MULLARD		
	You're The One That I Want	1978
BALANCE	Breaking Away	1981
LONG JOHN BALDRY		
	It's Too Late Now	1969
	Let The Heartaches Begin	1967
	Mexico	1968
	When The Sun Comes Shining Thru	1968
BALEARIC BILL	Destination Sunshine	1999
MARTY BALIN	Atlanta Lady (Something About Your Love)	1981
DAVID BALL	Riding With Private Malone	2001
	Thinkin' Problem	1994

ARTIST	SONG TITLE	DATE
KENNY BALL	Acapulco 1922	1963
	Casablanca	1963
	Hello, Dolly!	1964
	Rondo	1963
	Sukiyaki	1963
MICHAEL BALL	From Here To Eternity	1994
	Love Changes Everything	1989
	One Step Out Of Time	1992
	(Something Inside) So Strong	1996
BALLOON FARM	A Question Of Temperature	1968
STEVE BALSAMO	Sugar For The Soul	2002
BALTIMORA	Tarzan Boy	1993
CHARLI BALTIMORE		
	Money	1998
	(IRV GOTTI presents JA RULE, ASHANTI, CHARLI BALTIMORE)	
	Down 4 U	2002
	(JA RULE featuring CHARLI 'CHUCK' BALTIMORE)	
	Down Ass Chick	2002
AFRIKA BAMBAATAA		
	Got To Get Up	1998
AFRIKA BAMBAATAA & THE SOUL SONIC FORCE		
	Renegades Of Funk	1984
AFRIKA BAMBAATAA AND FAMILY featuring UB40		
	Reckless	1988

ARTIST	SONG TITLE	DATE
	(LEFTFIELD/BAMBAATAA)	
	Afrika Shox	1999
BAMBOO	Bamboogie	1998
	The Strutt	1998
BANANARAMA	Cruel Summer	1984
	Do Not Disturb	1985
	I Can't Help It	1988
	I Heard A Rumour	1987
	I Want You Back	1988
	Long Train Running	1991
	Love In The First Degree/Mr. Sleaze	1987
	Love Truth And Honesty	1988
	More, More, More	1993
	Movin' On	1992
	Na Na Hey Hey Kiss Him Goodbye	1983
	Nathan Jones	1988
	Only Your Love	1990
	Preacher Man	1991
	Robert De Niro's Waiting	1984
	Rough Justice	1984
	Shy Boy	1982
	Trick Of The Night	1987
	Venus	1986
BANANARAMA WITH FUN BOY THREE		
	Really Saying Something	1982

ARTIST	SONG TITLE	DATE
BANANARAMA/LANANEENEENOONOO		
	Help	1989
	(FUN BOY THREE & BANANARAMA)	
	It Ain't What You Do It's The Way That	
	You Do It	1982
BAND	Don't Do It	1972
	Rag Mama Rag	1970
	Up On Cripple Creek	1969
	The Weight	1968
BAND AID	Do They Know It's Christmas?	1984
BAND AID II	Do They Know It's Christmas?	1989
BAND AKA	Joy	1983
BAND OF GOLD	Love Songs Are Back Again (Medley)	1984
BANDERAS	This Is Your Life	1991
BANDITS	Take It And Run	2003
	2 Step Rock	2003
HONEY BANE	Turn Me On Turn Me Off	1981
BANGLES	Be With You	1989
	Eternal Flame	1989
	Hazy Shade Of Winter	1987
	If She Knew What She Wants	1986
	In Your Room	1988
	Manic Monday	1986
	Something That You Said	2003
	Walk Like An Egyptian	1986
	Walking Down Your Street	1987

ARTIST	SONG TITLE	DATE
LLOYD BANK$	On Fire	2004
DARRELL BANKS	Open The Door To Your Heart	1966
BANNED	Little Girl	1977
PATO BANTON	Baby Come Back	1994
PATO BANTON & THE REGGAE REVOLUTION		
	Groovin'	1996
PATO BANTON WITH RANKING ROGER		
	Bubbling Hot	1995
PATO BANTON WITH STING		
	Spirits In A Material World	1996
BAR-KAYS	Shake Your Rump To The Funk	1976
	Soul Finger	1967
KEITH BARBOUR	Echo Park	1969
BARDEUX	When We Kiss	1988
BARDO	One Step Further	1982
BOBBY BARE	Miller's Cave	1964
BAREFOOT MAN	Big Panty Woman	1998
BARENAKED LADIES		
	It's All Been Done	1999
	One Week	1998
	Pinch Me	2000
GARY BARLOW	For All That You Want	1999
	Forever Love	1996
	Love Won't Wait	1997
	Open Road	1997
	So Help Me Girl	1997

ARTIST	SONG TITLE	DATE
	Stronger	1999
BARNDANCE BOYS	Yippie-I-Oh	2003
JIMMY BARNES & INXS		
	Good Times	1991
RICHARD BARNES	Go North	1970
	Take To The Mountains	1970
BARRACUDAS	Summer Fun	1980
J.J. BARRIE	No Charge	1976
BARRON KNIGHTS	Call Up The Groups	1964
	Live In Trouble	1977
	Merry Gentle Pops	1965
	Never Mind The Presents	1980
	An Olympic Record	1968
	Pop Go The Workers	1965
	A Taste Of Aggro	1978
	Under New Management	1966
JOHN BARRY	From Russia With Love	1963
JOHN BARRY ORCHESTRA		
	Theme From 'The Persuaders'	1971
LEN BARRY	1-2-3	1965
	Like A Baby	1966
	Somewhere	1966
MICHAEL BARRYMORE		
	Too Much For One Heart	1995
BARTHEZZ	Infected	2002
	On The Move	2001

ARTIST	SONG TITLE	DATE
CHRIS BARTLEY	The Sweetest Thing This Side Of Heaven	1967
ROB BASE & D.J. E-Z ROCK		
	Get On The Dance Floor	1989
	It Takes Two	1988
BASEMENT JAXX	Bingo Bango	2000
	Fly Life	1997
	Get Me Off	2002
	Jump N' Shout	1999
	Jus I Kiss	2001
	Red Alert	1999
	Rendez-Vu	1999
	Romeo	2001
	Where's Your Head At?	2001
BASEMENT JAXX featuring DIZZEE RASCAL		
	Lucky Star	2003
BASEMENT JAXX featuring JC CHASEZ		
	Plug It In	2004
BASEMENT JAXX featuring LISA KEKAULA		
	Good Luck	2004
BASIA	Cruising For Bruising	1990
	Time And Tide	1988
TONI BASIL	Mickey	1982
BASS BUMPERS	The Music's Got Me	1994
FONTELLA BASS	Recovery	1966
	Rescue Me	1965

ARTIST	SONG TITLE	DATE
FONTELLA BASS & BOBBY MCCLURE		
	Don't Mess Up A Good Thing	1965
NORMAN BASS	How U Like Bass	2001
BASS-O-MATIC	Fascinating Rhythm	1990
SHIRLEY BASSEY	Big Spender	1967
	For All We Know	1971
	Goldfinger	1965
	Gone	1964
	I (Who Have Nothing)	1963
	My Special Dream	1964
	Never, Never, Never (Grande, Grande, Grande)	1973
	No Regrets	1965
	Something	1970
SHIRLEY BASSEY/BRYN TERFEL		
	World In Union	1999
(PROPELLERHEADS featuring SHIRLEY BASSEY)		
	History Repeating	1997
BASSHEADS	Back To The Old School	1992
	Is There Anybody Out There?	1991
	Who Can Make Me Feel Good?	1992
MIKE BATT	Summertime City	1975
BAUHAUS	She's In Parties	1983
	Ziggy Stardust	1982
BAY CITY ROLLERS		
	All Of Me Loves All Of You	1974

ARTIST	SONG TITLE	DATE
	Bye Bye Baby	1975
	Give A Little Love	1975
	I Only Wanna Be With You	1976
	It's A Game	1977
	Keep On Dancing	1971
	Love Me Like I Love You	1976
	Money Honey	1976
	Remember (Sha-La-La)	1974
	Saturday Night	1975
	Shang-A-Lang	1974
	Summerlove Sensation	1974
	The Way I Feel Tonight	1977
	You Made Me Believe In Music	1977
DUKE BAYSEE	Sugar Sugar	1994
BAZ	Believers	2001
TONY CAMILLO'S BAZUKA		
	Dynomite	1975
BBC CONCERT ORCHESTRA/BBC SYMPHONY CHORUS		
	Ode To Joy (From Beethoven's Symphony No. 9)	1996
BBE	Deeper Love (Symphonic Paradise)	1998
	Desire	1998
	Flash	1997
	Seven Days And One Week	1996
BBG featuring DINA TAYLOR		
	Snappiness	1990

ARTIST	SONG TITLE	DATE
BBMAK	Back Here	2001
	Out Of My Heart	2002
	Still On Your Side	2001
BE BOP DELUXE	Hot Valves (EP)	1976
	Ships In The Night	1976
BEACH BOYS	Barbara Ann	1966
	The Beach Boys Medley	1981
	Bluebirds Over The Mountain	1968
	Break Away	1969
	California Girls	1965
	California Saga	1973
	Come Go With Me	1981
	Cottonfields	1970
	Dance, Dance, Dance	1964
	Darlin'	1967
	Do It Again	1968
	Do You Wanna Dance?	1965
	Don't Worry Baby	1964
	Friends	1968
	Fun, Fun, Fun	1964
	Getcha Back	1985
	God Only Knows	1966
	Good Timin'	1979
	Good Vibrations	1966
	Help Me, Rhonda	1965
	Heroes And Villains	1967

ARTIST	SONG TITLE	DATE
	I Can Hear Music	1969
	I Get Around	1964
	It's O.K.	1976
	Kokomo	1988
	Lady Lynda	1979
	The Little Girl I Once Knew	1965
	Rock And Roll Music	1976
	Sloop John B	1966
	Surfin' U.S.A.	1974
	Then I Kissed Her	1967
	When I Grow Up (To Be A Man)	1964
	Wild Honey	1967
	Wouldn't It Be Nice	1966
(FAT BOYS & THE BEACH BOYS)		
	Wipeout	1987
(STATUS QUO WITH THE BEACH BOYS)		
	Fun, Fun, Fun	1996
BEASTIE BOYS	Alive	1999
	Body Movin'	1998
	Ch-Check It Out	2004
	Get It Together/Sabotage	1994
	Girls/She's Crafty	1987
	Hey Ladies	1989
	Intergalactic	1998
	No Sleep Till Brooklyn	1987
	Remote Control/3 MCS & 1DJ	1999

ARTIST	SONG TITLE	DATE
	She's On It	1987
	Sure Shot	1994
	Triple Trouble	2004
	(You Gotta) Fight For Your Right (To Party)	1986
BEAT	Best Friend/Stand Down Margaret (Dub)	1980
	Can't Get Used To Losing You	1983
	Doors Of Your Heart	1981
	Drowning/All Out To Get You	1981
	Hands Off She's Mine	1980
	Mirror In The Bathroom	1980
	Tears Of A Clown/Ranking Full Stop	1979
	Too Nice To Talk To	1980
	(SPECIAL AKA/MADNESS/SELECTER/BEAT)	
	The 2 Tone EP	1993
BEATCHUGGERS featuring ERIC CLAPTON		
	Forever Man (How Many Times)	2000
BEATLES	Ain't She Sweet	1964
	All You Need Is Love	1967
	And I Love Her	1964
	Baby It's You	1995
	Baby You're A Rich Man	1967
	Back In The U.S.S.R.	1976
	The Ballad Of John And Yoko	1969
	The Beatles Movie Medley	1982
	Can't Buy Me Love	1964
	Come Together/Something	1969

ARTIST	SONG TITLE	DATE
	Day Tripper/We Can Work It Out	1965
	Do You Want To Know A Secret	1964
	Eight Days A Week	1965
	Free As A Bird	1995
	From Me To You	1963
	Got To Get You Into My Life	1976
	A Hard Day's Night	1964
	Hello, Goodbye	1967
	Help!	1965
	Hey Jude	1968
	I Don't Want To Spoil The Party	1965
	I Feel Fine	1964
	I Saw Her Standing There	1964
	I Want To Hold Your Hand	1964
	I'll Cry Instead	1964
	Lady Madonna	1968
	Let It Be	1970
	The Long And Winding Road/For You Blue	1970
	Love Me Do	1964
	Magical Mystery Tour (Double EP)	1967
	Matchbox	1964
	Nowhere Man	1966
	P.S. I Love You	1964
	Paperback Writer	1966
	Penny Lane/Strawberry Fields Forever	1967
	Please Please Me	1964

ARTIST	SONG TITLE	DATE
	Rain	1966
	Real Love	1996
	Revolution	1968
	She Loves You	1964
	She's A Woman	1964
	Slow Down	1964
	Thank You Girl	1964
	Ticket To Ride	1965
	Twist And Shout	1986
	Yellow Submarine/Eleanor Rigby	1966
	Yesterday	1965
BEATLES WITH BILLY PRESTON		
	Don't Let Me Down	1969
	Get Back	1969
BEATLES WITH TONY SHERIDAN		
	My Bonnie	1964
BEATMASTERS featuring BETTY BOO		
	Hey D.J. I Can't Dance To.../Ska Train	1989
BEATMASTERS featuring MERLIN		
	Who's In The House	1989
BEATMASTERS featuring THE COOKIE CREW		
	Rok Da House	1988
BEATMASTERS WITH P.P. ARNOLD		
	Burn It Up	1988
BEATS INTERNATIONAL		
	Dub Be Good To Me	1990

ARTIST	SONG TITLE	DATE
	Won't Talk About It	1990
BEAU BRUMMELS	Just A Little	1965
	Laugh, Laugh	1965
	You Tell Me Why	1965
BEAUTIFUL SOUTH	Bell Bottomed Tear	1992
	Blackbird On The Wire	1997
	Closer Than Most	2000
	Don't Marry Her	1996
	Dumb	1998
	Everybody's Talkin'	1994
	Good As Gold	1994
	How Long's A Tear Take To Dry?	1999
	I'll Sail This Ship Alone	1989
	Just A Few Things That I Ain't	2003
	A Little Time	1990
	Livin' Thing	2004
	Old Red Eyes Is Back	1992
	One Last Love Song	1994
	Perfect 10	1998
	Pretenders To The Throne	1995
	Prettiest Eyes	1994
	Rotterdam	1996
	Song For Whoever	1989
	We Are Each Other	1992
	You Keep It All In	1989

ARTIST	SONG TITLE	DATE
GILBERT BECAUD	A Little Love And Understanding	1975
BECK	Deadweight	1997
	Devil's Haircut	1996
	Loser	1994
	Mixed Bizness	2000
	The New Pollution	1997
	Sexx Laws	1999
	Sissyneck	1997
	Tropicalia	1998
	Where It's At	1996
JEFF BECK	Hi-Ho Silver Lining	1967
	I've Been Drinking	1973
	Love Is Blue	1968
	Tallyman	1967
	(DONOVAN WITH THE JEFF BECK GROUP)	
	Goo Goo Bababajagal (Love Is Hot)	1969
ROBIN BECK	The First Time	1988
VICTORIA BECKHAM		
	A Mind Of Its Own	2002
	Not Such An Innocent Girl	2001
	This Groove/Let Your Head Go	2004
	(TRUE STEPPERS & DANE BOWERS featuring	
	VICTORIA BECKHAM)	
	Out Of Your Mind	2000
DANIEL BEDINGFIELD		
	Friday	2003

ARTIST	SONG TITLE	DATE
	Gotta Get Thru This	2002
	I Can't Read You	2003
	If You're Not The One	2002
	James Dean (I Wanna Know)	2002
	Never Gonna Leave Your Side	2003
	Nothing Hurts Like Love	2004
NATASHA BEDINGFIELD		
	Single	2004
	These Words	2004
BEDROCK	Heaven Scent	1999
BEDROCK featuring KYO		
	For What You Dream Of	1996
BEDROCKS	Ob-La-Di, Ob-La-Da	1968
BEE GEES	Alive	1972
	Alone	1997
	Boogie Child	1977
	Don't Forget To Remember	1969
	Fanny (Be Tender With My Love)	1975
	First Of May	1969
	For Whom The Bell Tolls	1993
	He's A Liar	1981
	Holiday	1967
	How Can You Mend A Broken Heart	1971
	How Deep Is Your Love	1977
	How To Fall In Love Part 1	1994
	I Could Not Love You More	1997

ARTIST	SONG TITLE	DATE
	I Started A Joke	1968
	I've Gotta Get A Message To You	1968
	Jive Talkin'	1975
	Jumbo/The Singer Sang His Song	1968
	Lonely Days	1970
	Love So Right	1976
	Love You Inside Out	1979
	Massachusetts (The Night The Lights	
	Went Out In)	1967
	My World	1972
	New York Mining Disaster 1941	1967
	Night Fever	1978
	Nights On Broadway	1975
	One	1989
	Paying The Price Of Love	1993
	Run To Me	1972
	Secret Love	1991
	Spirits (Having Flown)	1980
	Stayin' Alive	1977
	Still Waters (Run Deep)	1997
	This Is Where I Came In	2001
	To Love Somebody	1967
	Tomorrow, Tomorrow	1969
	Too Much Heaven	1978
	Tragedy	1979

ARTIST	SONG TITLE	DATE
	The Woman In You	1983
	Words	1968
	World	1967
	You Should Be Dancing	1976
	You Win Again	1987
	(CELINE DION WITH THE BEE GEES)	
	Immortality	1998
BEENIE MAN	King Of The Dancehall	2004
	Street Life	2003
	Who Am I	1998
BEENIE MAN featuring JANET		
	Feel It Boy	2002
BEENIE MAN featuring MS THING		
	Dude	2004
BEENIE MAN featuring MYA		
	Girls Dem Sugar	2001
	(JAMELIA featuring BEENIE MAN)	
	Money	2000
BEES	Wash In The Rain	2004
BEF featuring LALAH HATHAWAY		
	Family Affair	1991
LOU BEGA	Mambo No. 5 (A Little Bit Of...)	1999
BEGGAR & CO	Mule (Chant No. 2)	1981
	(Somebody) Help Me Out	1981
BEGINERZ	Reckless Girl	2002

ARTIST	SONG TITLE	DATE
BEGINNING OF THE END		
	Funky Nassau	1971
BEL AMOUR	Bel Amour	2001
BELL & JAMES	Livin' It Up (Friday Night)	1979
BELL & SPURLING	Goldenballs (Mr Beckham To You)	2002
	Sven Sven Sven	2001
BELL BIV DEVOE	B.B.D. (I Thought It Was Me)	1990
	Do Me	1990
	Gangsta	1992
	Poison	1990
	Something In Your Eyes	1993
ARCHIE BELL & THE DRELLS		
	Here I Go Again	1972
	I Can't Stop Dancing	1968
	The Soul City Walk	1976
	(There's Gonna Be A) Showdown	1973
	Tighten Up	1968
BENNY BELL	Shaving Cream	1975
MADELINE BELL	I'm Gonna Make You Love Me	1968
MAGGIE BELL	Hazell	1978
	(B.A. ROBERTSON & MAGGIE BELL)	
	Hold Me	1981
VINCENT BELL	Airport Love Theme (Gwen And Vern)	1970
WILLIAM BELL	A Tribute To A King	1968
	Tryin' To Love Two	1977

ARTIST	SONG TITLE	DATE
	(JUDY CLAY & WILLIAM BELL)	
	Private Number	1968
BELLAMY BROTHERS		
	If I Said You Had A Beautiful Body	1979
	Let Your Love Flow	1976
BELLE & SEBASTIAN		
	Belle & Sebastian Present 'Books'	2004
	I'm A Cuckoo	2004
	I'm Waking Up To Us	2001
	Jonathan David	2001
	Legal Man	2000
	Step Into My Office Baby	2003
	3..6..9.. Seconds Of Light (EP)	1997
BELLE & THE DEVOTIONS		
	Love Games	1984
BELLE STARS	The Clapping Song	1982
	Iko Iko	1989
	Sign Of The Times	1983
	Sweet Memory	1983
BELLEFIRE	All I Want Is You	2002
	Perfect Bliss	2001
	Say Something Anyway	2004
BELLINI	Samba De Janeiro	1997
BELLS	Stay Awhile	1971
BELLY	Feed The Tree	1993
	Now They'll Sleep	1995

ARTIST	SONG TITLE	DATE
	Seal My Fate	1995
BELOVED	Hello	1990
	Outerspace Girl	1993
	Satellite	1996
	The Sun Rising	1989
	Sweet Harmony	1993
	You Got Me Thinking	1993
	Your Love Takes Me Higher	1990
BENNY BENASSI presents THE BIZ		
	No Matter What You Do	2004
	Satisfaction	2003
PAT BENATAR	All Fired Up	1988
	Fire And Ice	1981
	Heartbreaker	1979
	Hit Me With Your Best Shot	1980
	Invincible (Theme From The Legend Of Billie Jean)	1985
	Little Too Late	1983
	Looking For A Stranger	1983
	Love Is A Battlefield	1983
	Ooh Ooh Song	1985
	Promises In The Dark	1981
	Sex As A Weapon	1985
	Shadows Of The Night	1982
	Treat Me Right	1981
	We Belong	1984

ARTIST	SONG TITLE	DATE
	We Live For Love	1980
ERIC BENET featuring FAITH EVANS		
	Georgy Porgy	1999
ERIC BENET featuring TAMIA		
	Spend My Life With You	1999
BENNET	Mum's Gone To Iceland	1997
CLIFF BENNETT & THE REBEL ROUSERS		
	Got To Get You Into My Life	1966
	One Way Love	1964
TONY BENNETT	The Good Life	1963
	(I Left My Heart) In San Francisco	1965
	If I Ruled The World	1965
	The Very Thought Of You	1965
	Who Can I Turn To	1964
GARY BENSON	Don't Throw It All Away	1975
GEORGE BENSON	Feel Like Makin' Love	1983
	Give Me The Night	1980
	The Greatest Love Of All	1977
	In Your Eyes	1983
	Lady Love Me (One More Time)	1983
	Love Ballad	1979
	Love X Love	1980
	Nature Boy	1977
	Never Give Up On A Good Thing	1982
	On Broadway	1978
	Shiver	1986

ARTIST	SONG TITLE	DATE
	Supership	1975
	This Masquerade	1976
	Turn Your Love Around	1981
	20/20	1985
RHIAN BENSON	Say How I Feel	2004
BENTLEY RHYTHM ACE		
	Bentleys Gonna Sort You Out!	1997
	Theme From Gutbuster	2000
DIERKS BENTLEY	What Was I Thinkin'	2003
BROOK BENTON	Going Going Gone	1964
	Rainy Night In Georgia	1970
BENZ	Miss Parker	1996
	Urban City Girl	1996
BERLIN	No More Words	1984
	Take My Breath Away	1986
	You Don't Know	1987
BERRI	Shine Like A Star	1995
	The Sunshine After The Rain	1995
CHUCK BERRY	Go Go Go	1963
	Memphis Tennessee	1963
	My Ding-A-Ling	1972
	Nadine (Is It You?)	1964
	No Particular Place To Go	1964
	The Promised Land	1965
	Reelin' & Rockin'	1972
	Run Rudolph Run	1963

ARTIST	SONG TITLE	DATE
	You Never Can Tell	1964
DAVE BERRY	Baby It's You	1964
	The Crying Game	1964
	Little Things	1965
	Mama	1966
	Memphis Tennessee	1963
	My Baby Left Me	1964
	This Strange Effect	1965
MIKE BERRY	Don't You Think It's Time	1963
	If I Could Only Make You Care	1980
	My Little Baby	1963
	Sunshine Of Your Smile	1980
NICK BERRY	Every Loser Wins	1986
	Heartbeat	1992
BETA BAND	Assessment	2004
	Broke/Won	2001
BETTER THAN EZRA		
	Good	1995
BEYONCE	Crazy In Love	2003
	Me, Myself And I	2004
	Naughty Girl	2004
	Work It Out	2002
BEYONCE featuring SEAN PAUL		
	Baby Boy	2003
B-52'S	Deadbeat Club	1990
	Good Stuff	1992

ARTIST	SONG TITLE	DATE
	Love Shack	1989
	Roam	1989
	Rock Lobster/Planet Claire	1986
BC-52S	(Meet) The Flintstones	1994
BHANGRA KNIGHTS vs HUSAN		
	Husan	2003
BIDDU ORCHESTRA	Rain Forest	1976
	Summer Of '42	1975
BIFFY CLYRO	Glitter And Trauma	2004
	My Recovery Injection	2004
	Questions & Answers	2003
BIG AUDIO DYNAMITE		
	E=mc2	1986
	Medicine Show	1986
BIG AUDIO DYNAMITE II		
	Rush	1991
BIG BROTHER & THE HOLDING COMPANY		
	Piece Of My Heart	1968
BIG BROVAZ	Ain't What You Do	2003
	Baby Boy	2003
	Favourite Things	2003
	Nu Flow	2002
	OK	2003
	Yours Fatally	2004
BIG COUNTRY	Alone	1993
	Chance	1983

ARTIST	SONG TITLE	DATE
	East Of Eden	1984
	Fields Of Fire (400 Miles)	1983
	In A Big Country	1983
	Just A Shadow	1985
	King Of Emotion	1988
	Look Away	1986
	One Great Thing	1986
	Peace In Our Time	1989
	Republican Party Reptile (EP)	1991
	Ships (Where Were You?)	1993
	The Teacher	1986
	Where The Rose Is Sown	1984
	Wonderland	1984
BIG DADDY	Dancing In The Dark	1985
BIG DISH	Miss America	1991
BIG FUN	Blame It On The Boogie	1989
	Can't Shake The Feeling	1989
	Handful Of Promises	1990
BIG FUN & SONIA	You've Got A Friend	1990
BIG MOUNTAIN	Baby I Love Your Way	1994
BIG PUNISHER featuring JOE		
	Still Not A Player	1998
	(JENNIFER LOPEZ featuring BIG PUN & FAT JOE)	
	Feelin' So Good	2000
BIG ROOM GIRL featuring DARYL PANDY		
	Raise Your Hands	1999

ARTIST	SONG TITLE	DATE
BIG SOUND AUTHORITY		
	This House (Is Where Your Love Stands)	1985
BIG THREE	By The Way	1963
	Some Other Guy	1963
BIG TIME CHARLIE	On The Run	1999
BIG TIME CHARLIE featuring SOOZY Q		
	Mr Devil	2000
BIG TYMERS	Still Fly	2002
BARRY BIGGS	Side Show	1976
	Three Ring Circus	1977
	Work All Day	1976
	You're My Life	1977
IVOR BIGGUN	The Winker's Song (Misprint)	1978
ACKER BILK	Aria	1976
MR ACKER BILK & THE LEON YOUNG STRING CHORALE		
	A Taste Of Honey	1963
BILL & BEN	Flobbadance	2002
BILLIE	Because We Want To	1998
	Girlfriend	1998
	Honey To The Bee	1999
	She Wants You	1998
BILLIE PIPER	Day & Night	2000
	Something Deep Inside	2000
	Walk Of Life	2000

ARTIST	SONG TITLE	DATE
BIMBO JET	El Bimbo	1975
BINARY FINARY	1998	1998
BINGO BOYS	How To Dance	1991
BIRDLAND	Sleep With Me	1990
ZOE BIRKETT	Treat Me Like A Lady	2003
JANE BIRKIN & SERGE GAINSBOURG		
	Je T'aime... Moi Non Plus	1969
BIS	Eurodisco	1998
	The Secret Vampire Soundtrack (EP)	1996
ELVIN BISHOP	Fooled Around And Fell In Love	1976
STEPHEN BISHOP	Everybody Needs Love	1978
	It Might Be You	1983
	On And On	1977
	Save It For A Rainy Day	1976
BIZ MARKIE	Just A Friend	1990
BENNY BENASSI presents THE BIZ		
	No Matter What You Do	2004
	Satisfaction	2003
BIZARRE INC.	I'm Gonna Get You	1992
	Keep The Music Strong	1996
	Playing With Knives	1991
	Such A Feeling	1991
	Surprise	1996
	Took My Love	1993
BIZZ NIZZ	Don't Miss The Partyline	1990

ARTIST	SONG TITLE	DATE
BJORK	Alarm Call	1998
	All Is Full Of Love	1999
	Army Of Me	1995
	Bachelorette	1997
	Big Time Sensuality	1993
	Cocoon	2002
	Hidden Place	2001
	Human Behavior	1993
	Hyperballad	1996
	I Miss You	1997
	Isobel	1995
	It's In Our Hands	2002
	It's Oh So Quiet	1995
	Pagan Poetry	2001
	Possibly Maybe	1996
	Venus As A Boy	1993
	Violently Happy	1994
	Who Is It	2004
BJORK & DAVID ARNOLD		
	Play Dead	1993
BJORN AGAIN	Erasure-Ish (A Little Respect/Stop!)	1992
BLACK & WHITE ARMY		
	Black & White Army	1998
BLACK BOX	Everybody Everybody	1990
	Fantasy	1990
	I Don't Know Anybody Else	1990

ARTIST	SONG TITLE	DATE
	I Got The Vibration/A Positive Vibration	1996
	Not Anyone	1995
	Ride On Time	1989
	Rockin' To The Music	1993
	Strike It Up	1991
	The Total Mix	1990
BLACK BOX RECORDER		
	The Facts Of Life	2000
BLACK CONNECTION		
	Give Me Rhythm	1998
BLACK CROWES	Hard To Handle	1990
	High Head Blues/A Conspiracy	1995
	Remedy	1992
	She Talks To Angels	1991
	Wiser Time	1995
BLACK DUCK	Whiggle In Line	1994
BLACK EYED PEAS	Hey Mama	2004
	Let's Get It Started	2004
	Shut Up	2003
	Where Is The Love?	2003
BLACK EYED PEAS featuring MACY GRAY		
	Request & Line	2001
BLACK GORILLA	Gimme Dat Banana	1977
BLACK GRAPE	Fat Neck	1996
	Get Higher	1997
	In The Name Of The Father	1995

ARTIST	SONG TITLE	DATE
	Kelly's Heroes	1995
	Reverend Black Grape	1995
BLACK GRAPE featuring JOE STRUMMER & KEITH ALLEN		
	England's Irie	1996
BLACK LEGEND	You See The Trouble With Me	2000
(SHORTIE vs BLACK LEGEND)		
	Somebody	2001
BLACK MACHINE	How Gee	1994
BLACK OAK ARKANSAS		
	Jim Dandy	1973
BLACK REBEL MOTORCYCLE CLUB		
	Love Burns	2002
	Spread Your Love	2002
	Stop	2003
BLACK SABBATH	Hard Road	1978
	Neon Knights	1980
	Never Say Die	1978
	Paranoid	1970
	Turn Up The Night	1982
	TV Crimes	1992
BLACK	Paradise	1988
	Sweetest Smile	1987
	Wonderful Life	1987
CILLA BLACK	Alfie	1966
	Anyone Who Had A Heart	1964
	Baby We Can't Go Wrong	1974

ARTIST	SONG TITLE	DATE
	Conversations	1969
	Don't Answer Me	1966
	A Fool Am I	1966
	I Only Live To Love You	1967
	I've Been Wrong Before	1965
	If I Thought You'd Ever Change Your Mind	1969
	It's For You	1964
	Love Of The Loved	1963
	Love's Just A Broken Heart	1966
	Something Tells Me (Something Is Gonna Happen Tonight)	1971
	Step Inside Love	1968
	Surround Yourself With Sorrow	1969
	What Good Am I?	1967
	Where Is Tomorrow?	1968
	You're My World	1964
	You've Lost That Lovin' Feelin'	1965
CLINT BLACK	When I Said I Do	1999
FRANK BLACK	Men In Black	1996
TONY BLACKBURN	So Much Love	1968
BLACKBYRDS	Happy Music	1976
	Walking In Rhythm	1975
BLACKFOOT	Highway Song	1979
	Train, Train	1979
BLACKFOOT SUE	Sing Don't Speak	1972
	Standing In The Road	1972

ARTIST	SONG TITLE	DATE
BLACKGIRL	90s Girl	1994
BLACK LACE	Agadoo	1984
	Do The Conga	1984
	Hokey Cokey	1985
	Superman (Gioca Jouer)	1983
BLACKOUT	Mr DJ	2001
BLACKOUT ALLSTARS		
	I Like It	1996
BLACK SLATE	Amigo	1980
BLACKSTREET	Before I Let You Go	1994
	Booti Call	1994
	Don't Leave Me	1997
	Fix	1997
	(Money Can't) Buy Me Love	1997
	U Blow My Mind	1995
	Wizzy Wow	2003
BLACKSTREET & MYA featuring MASE & BLINKY BLINK		
	Take Me There	1998
BLACKSTREET featuring DR DRE		
	No Diggity	1996
BLACKSTREET featuring TEDDY RILEY		
	Baby Be Mine	1993
BLACKSTREET WITH JANET		
	Girlfriend/Boyfriend	1999
	(FOXY BROWN featuring BLACKSTREET)	
	Get Me Home	1997

ARTIST	SONG TITLE	DATE
	(JANET featuring BLACKSTREET)	
	I Get Lonely	1998
	(JAY-Z featuring BLACKSTREET)	
	The City Is Mine	1998
	(MASE featuring BLACKSTREET)	
	Get Ready	1999
BAND OF THE BLACK WATCH		
	Dance Of The Cuckoos (The Laurel And Hardy Theme)	1975
	Scotch On The Rocks	1975
RICHARD BLACKWOOD		
	Mama — Who Da Man?	2000
	Someone There For Me	2000
RICHARD BLACKWOOD featuring DEETAH		
	1-2-3-4 Get With The Wicked	2000
BLAIR	Have Fun, Go Mad!	1995
PETER BLAKE	Lipsmackin' Rock 'n' Rollin'	1977
BLAMELESS	Breathe (A Little Deeper)	1996
JACK BLANCHARD & MISTY MORGAN		
	Tennessee Birdwalk	1970
BLANCMANGE	Blind Vision	1983
	The Day Before You Came	1984
	Don't Tell Me	1984
	Living On The Ceiling	1982
	That's Love, That It Is	1983
	Waves	1983

ARTIST	SONG TITLE	DATE
	What's Your Problem	1985
BOBBY BLAND	Ain't Nothing You Can Do	1964
BLANK & JONES	Cream	1999
BLAQUE	Bring It All To Me	1999
BLAQUE IVORY	808	1999
BLAST featuring VDC		
	Crayzy Man	1994
	Princes Of The Night	1994
MEL BLATT	Do Me Wrong	2003
	(ARTFUL DODGER featuring MELANIE BLATT)	
	Twentyfourseven	2001
BLAZIN' SQUAD	Crossroads	2002
	Flip Reverse	2003
	Here 4 One	2004
	Love On The Line	2002
	Reminisce/Where The Story Ends	2003
	We Just Be Dreamin'	2003
BLEACHIN'	Peakin'	2000
BLESSID UNION OF SOULS		
	Hey Leonardo (She Likes Me For Me)	1999
	I Believe	1995
	I Wanna Be There	1997
	Let Me Be The One	1995
BLESSING	Highway 5 '92	1992
MARY J. BLIGE	All That I Can Say	1999
	Be Happy	1994

ARTIST	SONG TITLE	DATE
	Everything	1997
	Family Affair	2001
	Give Me You	2000
	I Can Love You	1997
	I'm Goin' Down	1995
	Love Is All We Need	1997
	Mary Jane (All Night Long)	1995
	Missing You	1997
	My Love	1994
	No More Drama	2001
	Not Gon' Cry	1996
	Ooh!	2003
	Real Love	1992
	Reminisce	1993
	Seven Days	1998
	Sweet Thing	1993
	You Don't Have To Worry	1993
	(You Make Me Feel Like) A Natural Woman	1995
	You Remind Me	1992
MARY J. BLIGE featuring COMMON		
	Dance For Me	2002
MARY J. BLIGE featuring EVE		
	Not Today	2003
MARY J. BLIGE featuring JA RULE		
	Rainy Dayz	2002

ARTIST	SONG TITLE	DATE
MARY J. BLIGE featuring METHOD MAN		
	Love At 1st Sight	2003
(GEORGE MICHAEL & MARY J. BLIGE)		
	As	1999
(JAY-Z featuring MARY J. BLIGE)		
	Can't Knock The Hustle	1997
(METHOD MAN/MARY J. BLIGE)		
	I'll Be There For You/You're All I Need	
	To Get By	1995
(WYCLEF JEAN featuring MARY J. BLIGE)		
	911	2000
BLIND MELON	Change	1994
	Galaxie	1995
	No Rain	1993
BLINK-182	All The Small Things	1999
	Down	2004
	Feeling This	2003
	First Date	2001
	I Miss You	2004
	The Rock Show	2001
	What's My Age Again?	1999
BLOC PARTY	Helicopter	2004
	Little Thoughts/Tulips	2004
BLOCKSTER	Grooveline	1999
	You Should Be...	1999

ARTIST	SONG TITLE	DATE
KRISTINE BLOND	Love Shy	1998
	You Make Me Go Oooh	2002
BLONDIE	Atomic	1980
	Call Me	1980
	Denis	1978
	Dreaming	1979
	Good Boys	2003
	Hanging On The Telephone	1978
	Heart Of Glass	1979
	(I'm Always Touched) By Your Presence	
	Dear	1978
	Island Of Lost Souls	1982
	Maria	1999
	Nothing Is Real But The Girl	1999
	One Way Or Another	1979
	Picture This	1978
	Rapture	1981
	Sunday Girl	1979
	The Tide Is High	1980
	Union City Blue	1979
	War Child	1982
BLOOD, SWEAT & TEARS		
	And When I Die	1969
	Go Down Gamblin'	1971
	Hi-De-Ho	1970

ARTIST	SONG TITLE	DATE
	Lucretia Mac Evil	1970
	Spinning Wheel	1969
	You've Made Me So Very Happy	1969
BLOODHOUND GANG		
	The Bad Touch	2000
	The Ballad Of Chasey Lain	2000
BLOODROCK	D.O.A.	1971
BLOODSTONE	Natural High	1973
	Outside Woman	1974
BOBBY BLOOM	Heavy Makes You Happy	1971
	Montego Bay	1970
BLOW MONKEYS	Digging Your Scene	1986
	It Doesn't Have To Be That Way	1987
	Out With Her	1987
	This Is Your Life	1988
BLOW MONKEYS/SYLVIA TELLA		
	Choice?	1989
KURTIS BLOW	Christmas Rappin'	1979
	If I Ruled The World	1986
ANGEL BLU/JAIMESON		
	True	2003
	Take Control	2004
BLUE	Gonna Capture Your Heart	1977
BLUE	All Rise	2001
	Breathe Easy	2004
	Bubblin'	2004

ARTIST	SONG TITLE	DATE
	Fly By II	2002
	Guilty	2003
	If You Come Back	2001
	One Love	2002
	Too Close	2001
	U Make Me Wanna	2003
BLUE featuring ELTON JOHN		
	Sorry Seems To Be The Hardest Word	2002
BLUE featuring STEVIE WONDER & ANGIE STONE		
	Signed, Sealed, Delivered, I'm Yours	2003
BLUE ADONIS featuring LIL' MISS MAX		
	Disco Cop	1998
BLUE BAMBOO	ABC And D	1994
BLUE BOY	Remember Me	1997
	Sandman	1997
BLUE CHEER	Summertime Blues	1968
BLUE HAZE	Smoke Gets In Your Eyes	1972
BLUE MAGIC	Sideshow	1974
	Three Ring Circus	1974
BLUE MERCEDES	I Want To Be Your Property	1987
BLUE MINK	Banner Man	1971
	By The Devil (I Was Tempted)	1973
	Good Morning Freedom	1970
	Melting Pot	1969
	Our World	1970
	Randy	1973

ARTIST	SONG TITLE	DATE
	Stay With Me	1972
BLUE OYSTER CULT		
	Burnin' For You	1981
	(Don't Fear) The Reaper	1976
BLUE PEARL	(Can You) Feel The Passion	1992
	Little Brother	1990
	Naked In The Rain	1990
BLUE RIDGE RANGERS		
	Hearts Of Stone	1973
	Jambalaya (On The Bayou)	1972
BLUE RONDO A LA TURK		
	Me And Mr Sanchez	1981
BARRY BLUE	Dancin' (On A Saturday Night)	1973
	Do You Wanna Dance?	1973
	Hot Shot	1974
	Miss Hit And Run	1974
	School Love	1974
BLUEBELLS	Cath	1984
	I'm Falling	1984
	Young At Heart	1993
BLUES BROTHERS	Everybody Needs Somebody To Love	1990
	Gimme Some Lovin'	1980
	Rubber Biscuit	1979
	Soul Man	1978
	Who's Making Love	1980
BLUES IMAGE	Ride Captain Ride	1970

ARTIST	SONG TITLE	DATE
BLUES MAGOOS	(We Ain't Got) Nothin' Yet	1966
BLUES TRAVELER	Hook	1995
	Run-Around	1995
BLUE SWEDE	Hooked On A Feeling	1974
	Never My Love	1974
BLUETONES	After Hours	2002
	Are You Blue Or Are You Blind?	1995
	Autophilia	2000
	Bluetonic	1995
	Cut Some Rug/Castle Rock	1996
	Fast Boy/Liquid Lips	2003
	If …	1998
	Keep The Home Fires Burning	2000
	Marblehead Johnson	1996
	Never Going Nowhere	2003
	Sleazy Bed Track	1998
	Slight Return	1996
	Solomon Bites The Worm	1998
BLUE ZOO	Cry Boy Cry	1982
COLIN BLUNSTONE	I Don't Believe In Miracles	1972
	Say You Don't Mind	1972
	(DAVE STEWART: GUEST VOCALS COLIN BLUNSTONE)	
	What Becomes Of The Brokenhearted	1981
BLUR	Bang	1991
	Beetlebum	1997

ARTIST	SONG TITLE	DATE
	Charmless Man	1996
	Chemical World	1993
	Coffee + TV	1999
	Country House	1995
	Crazy Beat	2003
	End Of A Century	1994
	For Tomorrow	1993
	Girls And Boys	1994
	Good Song	2003
	Mor	1997
	Music Is My Radar	2000
	No Distance Left To Run	1999
	On Your Own	1997
	Out Of Time	2003
	Parklife	1994
	Popscene	1992
	Song 2	1997
	Stereotypes	1996
	Sunday Sunday	1993
	Tender	1999
	There's No Other Way	1991
	To The End	1994
	The Universal	1995
BM DUBS presents MR RUMBLE featuring BRASSTOOTH & KEE	Whoomp There It Is	2001

ARTIST	SONG TITLE	DATE
BMU	U Will Know	1995
BO SELECTA	Proper Crimbo	2003
BOB & EARL	Harlem Shuffle	1969
BOB & MARCIA	Pied Piper	1971
	Young, Gifted And Black	1970
BOB THE BUILDER	Can We Fix It	2000
	Mambo No. 5	2001
ANDREA BOCELLI	Canto Della Terra	1999
	(SARAH BRIGHTMAN & ANDREA BOCELLI) Time To Say Goodbye (Con Te Partiro)	1997
BODEANS	Closer To Free	1996
BODY COUNT	Born Dead	1994
BODYSNATCHERS	Let's Do Rock Steady	1980
HAMILTON BOHANNON		
	Disco Stomp	1975
	Foot Stompin' Music	1975
	South African Man	1975
CJ BOLLAND	It Ain't Gonna Be Me	1999
	The Prophet	1997
	Sugar Is Sweeter	1996
MICHAEL BOLTON	The Best Of Love/Go The Distance	1997
	Can I Touch You... There?	1995
	Completely	1994
	Drift Away	1992
	Georgia On My Mind	1990
	How Am I Supposed To Live Without You	1989

ARTIST	SONG TITLE	DATE
	How Can We Be Lovers	1990
	Lean On Me	1994
	Love Is A Wonderful Thing	1991
	A Love So Beautiful	1995
	Reach Out I'll Be There	1993
	Said I Love You....But I Lied	1993
	(Sittin' On) The Dock Of The Bay	1988
	Soul Of My Soul	1994
	Soul Provider	1989
	Steel Bars	1992
	That's What Love Is All About	1987
	Time, Love And Tenderness	1991
	To Love Somebody	1992
	When A Man Loves A Woman	1991
	When I'm Back On My Feet Again	1990
MICHAEL BOLTON featuring KENNY G		
	Missing You Now	1992
BOMB THE BASS	Beat Dis	1988
	Megablast/Don't Make Me Wait	1988
	Say A Little Prayer	1988
	Winter In July	1991
BOMB THE BASS featuring JUSTIN WARFIELD		
	Bug Powder Dust	1994
BOMB THE BASS featuring SPIKEY TEE		
	Darkheart	1994

ARTIST	SONG TITLE	DATE
BOMBALURINA	Itsy Bitsy Teeny Weeny Yellow Polka Dot Bikini	1990
	Seven Little Girls Sitting In The Back Seat	1990
BOMBERS	(Everybody) Get Dancin'	1979
BOMFUNK MC'S	Freestyler	2000
	Up Rocking Beats	2000
BON JOVI	All About Lovin' You	2003
	Always	1994
	Bad Medicine	1988
	Bed Of Roses	1993
	Born To Be My Baby	1988
	Dry County	1994
	Everyday	2002
	Hey God	1996
	I Believe	1993
	I'll Be There For You	1989
	I'll Sleep When I'm Dead	1993
	In These Arms	1993
	It's My Life	2000
	Keep The Faith	1992
	Lay Your Hands On Me	1989
	Lie To Me	1995
	Livin' On A Prayer	1986
	Living In Sin	1989
	Misunderstood	2002

ARTIST	SONG TITLE	DATE
	Never Say Goodbye	1987
	One Wild Night	2001
	Please Come Home For Christmas	1994
	Real Life	1999
	Runaway	1984
	Say It Isn't So	2000
	Someday I'll Be Saturday Night	1995
	Something For The Pain	1995
	Thank You For Loving Me	2000
	These Days	1996
	This Ain't A Love Song	1995
	Wanted Dead Or Alive	1987
	You Give Love A Bad Name	1986
JON BON JOVI	Blaze Of Glory	1990
	Janie, Don't Take Your Love To Town	1997
	Midnight In Chelsea	1997
	Miracle	1990
	Queen Of New Orleans	1997
BON	Boys	2001
GARY U.S. BONDS	This Little Girl	1981
	Out Of Work	1982
BONE THUGS-N-HARMONY		
	Days Of Our Livez	1997
	If I Could Teach The World	1997
	Ist Of Tha Month	1996
	Look Into My Eyes	1997

ARTIST	SONG TITLE	DATE
	Tha Crossroad	1996
	Thuggish Ruggish Bone	1994
BONE THUGS-N-HARMONY featuring PHIL COLLINS		
	Home	2003
	(MO THUGS FAMILY featuring BONE THUGS-N-HARMONY)	
	Ghetto Cowboy	1998
BONECRUSHER featuring KILLER MIKE & T.I.		
	Never Scared	2003
ELBOW BONES & THE RACKETEERS		
	A Night In New York	1984
BONEY M	Belfast	1977
	Boney M Megamix	1992
	Daddy Cool	1976
	Gotta Go Home/El Lute	1979
	Hooray Hooray, It's A Holi-Holiday	1979
	I'm Born Again	1979
	Ma Baker	1977
	Mary's Boy Child/Oh My Lord	1978
	Painter Man	1979
	Rasputin	1978
	Rivers Of Babylon/Brown Girl In The Ring	1978
	Sunny	1977
	We Kill The World (Don't Kill The World)	1981

ARTIST	SONG TITLE	DATE
BONEY M vs HORNY UNITED		
	Ma Baker — Somebody Screamed	1999
BONIFACE	Cheeky	2002
GRAHAM BONNET	Night Games	1981
GRAHAM BONNEY	Super Girl	1966
BONO/WYCLEF JEAN		
	New Day	1999
KARLA BONOFF	Personally	1982
BONZO DOG DOO-DAH BAND		
	I'm The Urban Spaceman	1968
BOO RADLEYS	C'mon Kids	1996
	Find The Answer Within	1995
	From The Bench At Belvidere	1995
	It's Lulu	1995
	Ride The Tiger	1997
	Wake Up Boo!	1995
	What's In The Box? (See Whatcha Got)	1996
BETTY BOO	Doin' The Doo	1990
	Let Me Take You There	1992
	24 Hours	1990
	Where Are You Baby?	1990
	(BEATMASTERS featuring BETTY BOO)	
	Hey D.J. I Can't Dance To... /Ska Train	1989
BOOGIE BOX HIGH	Jive Talkin'	1987
BOOGIE PIMPS	Somebody To Love	2004
	Sunny	2004

ARTIST	SONG TITLE	DATE
BOOKER T. & THE MG'S		
	Green Onions	1979
	Groovin'	1967
	Hang 'Em High	1968
	Hip-Hug-Her	1967
	Mrs Robinson	1969
	Soul Clap '69	1969
	Soul Limbo	1968
	Time Is Tight	1969
BOOM!	Falling	2001
TAKA BOOM/EYE TO EYE		
	Just Can't Get Enough (No No No No)	2001
	(JOEY NEGRO featuring TAKA BOOM)	
	Must Be The Music	2000
BOOMKAT	The Wreckoning	2003
BOOMTOWN RATS	Banana Republic	1980
	Diamond Smiles	1979
	The Elephant's Graveyard (Guilty)	1981
	House On Fire	1982
	I Don't Like Mondays	1979
	Like Clockwork	1978
	Looking After Number One	1977
	Mary Of The Fourth Form	1977
	Rat Trap	1978
	She's So Modern	1978
	Someone's Looking At You	1980

ARTIST	SONG TITLE	DATE
DANIEL BOONE	Beautiful Sunday	1972
	Daddy Don't You Walk So Fast	1971
DEBBY BOONE	You Light Up My Life	1977
BOOTH AND THE BAD ANGEL		
	I Believe	1996
KEN BOOTHE	Crying Over You	1974
	Everything I Own	1974
BOSTON	Amanda	1986
	Can'tcha Say (You Believe In Me)/Still In Love	1987
	Don't Look Back	1978
	Long Time	1977
	A Man I'll Never Be	1978
	More Than A Feeling	1976
	Peace Of Mind	1977
	We're Ready	1986
JUDY BOUCHER	Can't Be Without You Tonight	1987
	You Caught My Eye	1987
BOURGEOIS TAGG	I Don't Mind At All	1987
BRENT BOURGEOIS	Dare To Fall In Love	1990
TOBY BOURKE WITH GEORGE MICHAEL		
	Waltz Away Dreaming	1997
BOW WOW WOW	C'30, C'60, C'90 Go	1980
	Go Wild In The Country	1982
	I Want Candy	1982

ARTIST	SONG TITLE	DATE
DANE BOWERS	Another Lover	2001
	Shut Up And Forget About It	2001
(TRUE STEPPERS & DANE BOWERS featuring VICTORIA BECKHAM)		
	Out Of Your Mind	2000
(TRUE STEPPERS featuring DANE BOWERS)		
	Buggin	2000
DAVID BOWIE	Absolute Beginners	1986
	Alabama Song	1980
	Ashes To Ashes	1980
	Baal's Hymn (EP)	1982
	Beauty And The Beast	1978
	Blue Jean	1984
	Boys Keep Swingin'	1979
	Buddha Of Suburbia	1993
	Cat's People (Putting Out Fire)	1982
	China Girl	1983
	D.J.	1979
	Day-In Day-Out	1987
	Dead Man Walking	1997
	Diamond Dogs	1974
	Drive-In Saturday (Seattle-Phoenix)	1973
	Everyone Says 'Hi'	2002
	Fame	1975
	Fame 90 (Gass Mix)	1990

ARTIST	SONG TITLE	DATE
	Fashion	1980
	Golden Years	1975
	Hallo Spaceboy	1996
	The Heart's Filthy Lesson	1995
	Heroes	1977
	The Jean Genie	1972
	John, I'm Only Dancing	1972
	Jump They Say	1993
	Knock On Wood	1974
	The Laughing Gnome	1973
	Let's Dance	1983
	Life On Mars?	1973
	Little Wonder	1997
	Loving The Alien	1985
	Miracle Goodnight	1993
	Modern Love	1983
	Never Let Me Down	1987
	Rebel Rebel	1974
	Rock 'n' roll Suicide	1974
	Scary Monsters (And Super Creeps)	1981
	Seven	2000
	Sorrow	1973
	Sound And Vision	1977
	Space Oddity	1972
	Starman	1972
	Strangers When We Meet/The Man Who	

ARTIST	SONG TITLE	DATE
	Sold The World (Live)	1995
	Survive	2000
	Thursday's Child	1999
	Time Will Crawl	1987
	TVC 15	1976
	Underground	1986
	Up The Hill Backwards	1981
	Wild As The Wind	1981
	Young Americans	1975
DAVID BOWIE & BING CROSBY		
	Peace On Earth/Little Drummer Boy	1982
DAVID BOWIE & MICK JAGGER		
	Dancing In The Street	1985
DAVID BOWIE & PAT METHENY GROUP		
	This Is Not America	1985
DAVID BOWIE featuring AL B. SURE!		
	Black Tie White Noise	1993
(QUEEN & DAVID BOWIE)		
	Under Pressure	1981
BOWLING FOR SOUP		
	Girl All The Bad Guys Want	2002
	1985	2004
GEORGE BOWYER	Guardians Of The Land	1998
BOX TOPS	Choo Choo Train	1968
	Cry Like A Baby	1968
	I Met Her In Church	1968

ARTIST	SONG TITLE	DATE
	The Letter	1967
	Neon Rainbow	1967
	Soul Deep	1969
	Sweet Cream Ladies, Forward March	1968
BOY GEORGE	The Crying Game	1993
	Everything I Own	1987
	Keep Me In Mind	1987
	Live My Life	1987
	Sold	1987
	To Be Reborn	1987
BOY KRAZY	That's What Love Can Do	1993
BOY MEETS GIRL	Oh Girl	1985
	Waiting For A Star To Fall	1988
TOMMY BOYCE & BOBBY HART		
	Alice Long	1968
	I Wonder What She's Doing Tonight	1967
	Out & About	1967
BOYS	Crazy	1990
	Dial My Heart	1989
BOYS CLUB	I Remember Holding You	1988
BOYS DON'T CRY	I Wanna Be A Cowboy	1986
BOYSTOWN GANG	Can't Take My Eyes Off You	1982
BOYZ II MEN	Can't Let Her Go	1998
	End Of The Road	1992
	4 Seasons Of Loneliness	1997
	I Will Get There	1999

ARTIST	SONG TITLE	DATE
	I'll Make Love To You	1994
	In The Still Of The Night (I'll Remember)	1992
	It's So Hard To Say Goodbye To Yesterday	1991
	Let It Snow	1993
	Motownphilly	1991
	On Bended Knee	1994
	A Song For Mama	1997
	Thank You	1995
	Uhh Ahh	1991
	Water Runs Dry	1995
	(MARIAH CAREY & BOYZ II MEN)	
	One Sweet Day	1995
BOYZONE	All That I Need	1998
	Baby Can I Hold You/Shooting Star	1997
	Coming Home Now	1996
	A Different Beat	1996
	Every Day I Love You	1999
	Father And Son	1995
	I Love The Way You Love Me	1998
	Isn't It A Wonder	1997
	Key To My Life	1995
	Love Me For A Reason	1994
	No Matter What	1998
	Picture Of You	1997
	So Good	1995

ARTIST	SONG TITLE	DATE
	When The Going Gets Tough	1999
	Words	1996
	You Needed Me	1999
BILLY BRAGG	Accident Waiting To Happen (EP)	1992
	Between The Wars (EP)	1985
	Levi Stubb's Tears	1986
	Sexuality	1991
BILLY BRAGG AND THE BLOKES		
	Take Down The Union Jack	2002
(WET WET WET/BILLY BRAGG WITH CARA TIVEY)		
	With A Little Help From My Friends/She's Leaving Home	1988
BRAIDS	Bohemian Rhapsody	1996
BRAINBUG	Benedictus/Nightmare	1997
	Nightmare	1997
BRAINCHILD	Symmetry C	1999
BRAM TCHAIKOVSKY		
	Girl Of My Dreams	1979
WILFRED BRAMBELL & HARRY H. CORBETT		
	Steptoe & Son At Buckingham Palace (Parts 1 & 2)	1963
BRAN VAN 3000	Drinking In LA	1999
BRAN VAN 3000 featuring CURTIS MAYFIELD		
	Astounded	2001
BRANCACCIO & AISHER		
	It's Gonna Be … (A Lovely Day)	2002

ARTIST	SONG TITLE	DATE
MICHELLE BRANCH	All You Wanted	2002
	Are You Happy Now?	2003
	Breathe	2003
	Everywhere	2001
	Goodbye To You	2002
(SANTANA featuring MICHELLE BRANCH)		
	The Game Of Love	2002
BRAND NEW	The Quiet Things That No One Ever Knows	2004
	Sic Transit Gloria…Glory Fades	2004
BRAND NEW HEAVIES		
	Apparently Nothing	2000
	Back To Love	1994
	Don't Let It Go To Your Head	1992
	Dream Come True	1992
	Dream On Dreamer	1994
	Midnight At The Oasis	1994
	Saturday Nite	1999
	Shelter	1998
	Sometimes	1997
	Spend Some Time	1994
	Stay This Way	1992
	Ultimate Trunk Funk (EP)	1992
	You Are The Universe	1997
	You've Got A Friend	1997

ARTIST	SONG TITLE	DATE
BRANDY	Afrodisiac	2004
	Almost Doesn't Count	1999
	Baby	1995
	Best Friend	1995
	Brokenhearted	1995
	Full Moon	2002
	Have You Ever?	1998
	I Wanna Be Down	1994
	Sittin' Up In My Room	1995
	What About Us?	2002
BRANDY & MONICA		
	The Boy Is Mine	1998
BRANDY & RAY J	Another Day In Paradise	2001
BRANDY featuring KANYE WEST		
	Talk About Our Love	2004
BRANDY featuring MASE		
	Top Of The World	1998
BRANDY, TAMIA, GLADYS KNIGHT & CHAKA KHAN		
	Missing You	1996
LAURA BRANIGAN	Gloria	1982
	How Am I Supposed To Live Without You	1983
	The Lucky One	1984
	Power Of Love	1987
	Self Control	1984
	Solitaire	1983
	Spanish Eddie	1985

ARTIST	SONG TITLE	DATE
BRASS CONSTRUCTION		
	Ha Cha Cha (Funktion)	1977
	Movin'	1976
	Music Makes You Feel Like Dancing	1980
BRASS RING	The Disadvantages Of You	1967
	The Phoenix Love Theme (Senza Fine)	1966
BRAT PACK	You're The Only Woman	1990
THE BRAT	Chalk Dust — The Umpire Strikes Back	1982
BRAVADO	Harmonica Man	1994
BRAVO ALL STARS	Let The Music Heal Your Soul	1998
LOS BRAVOS	Black Is Black	1966
	I Don't Care	1966
ALAN BRAXE & FRED FALKE		
	Intro	2000
DHAR BRAXTON	Jump Back (Set Me Free)	1986
TONI BRAXTON	Another Sad Love Song	1993
	Breathe Again	1993
	He Wasn't Man Enough	2000
	I Belong To You/How Many Ways	1994
	I Don't Want To/I Love Me Some Him	1997
	Just Be A Man About It	2000
	Love Shoulda Brought You Home	1992
	Unbreak My Heart	1996
	You Mean The World To Me	1994
	You're Makin' Me High/Let It Flow	1996

ARTIST	SONG TITLE	DATE
TONI BRAXTON featuring LOON		
	Hit The Freeway	2003
TONI BRAXTON WITH KENNY G		
	How Could An Angel Break My Heart	1997
(BABYFACE featuring TONI BRAXTON)		
	Give U My Heart	1992
BRAXTONS	The Boss	1997
	Slow Flow	1997
	So Many Ways	1997
BREAD	Aubrey	1973
	Baby I'm-A Want You	1971
	Diary	1972
	Everything I Own	1972
	Guitar Man	1972
	If	1971
	It Don't Matter To Me	1970
	Let Your Love Go	1971
	Lost Without Your Love	1976
	Make It With You	1970
	Mother Freedom	1971
	Sweet Surrender	1972
BREAK MACHINE	Are You Ready	1984
	Break Dance Party	1984
	Street Dance	1984
BREAKBEAT ERA	Breakbeat Era	1998
BREAKFAST CLUB	Right On Track	1987

ARTIST	SONG TITLE	DATE
BREATHE	Does She Love That Man?	1990
	Don't Tell Me Lies	1989
	Hands To Heaven	1988
	How Can I Fall	1988
	Say A Prayer	1990
BRECKER BROTHERS		
	East River	1978
BREED 77	The River	2004
BREEDERS	Cannonball	1993
JO BREEZER	Venus And Mars	2001
BEVERLY BREMMERS		
	Don't Say You Don't Remember	1971
	We're Free	1972
BRENDA & THE TABULATIONS		
	Dry Your Eyes	1967
	Right On The Tip Of My Tongue	1971
BRENDON	Gimme Some	1977
BREWER AND SHIPLEY		
	One Toke Over The Line	1971
BRIAN & MICHAEL (BURKE & JERK)		
	Matchstalk Men And Matchstalk Cats And Dogs (Lowry's Song)	1978
BRICK	Dazz	1976
	Dusic	1977
EDIE BRICKELL	Good Times	1994

ARTIST	SONG TITLE	DATE
EDIE BRICKELL & THE NEW BOHEMIANS		
	What I Am	1989
ALICIA BRIDGES	I Love The Night Life (Disco 'Round)	1978
BRIGHOUSE AND RASTRICK		
	The Floral Dance	1977
BRIGHTER SIDE OF DARKNESS		
	Love Jones	1972
SARAH BRIGHTMAN		
	I Lost My Heart To A Starship Trooper	1978
SARAH BRIGHTMAN & ANDREA BOCELLI		
	Time To Say Goodbye (Con Te Partiro)	1997
SARAH BRIGHTMAN & PAUL MILES-KINGSTON		
	Pie Jesu	1985
SARAH BRIGHTMAN & STEVE HARLEY		
	The Phantom Of The Opera	1986
	(CLIFF RICHARD & SARAH BRIGHTMAN)	
	All I Ask Of You	1986
	(JOSE CARRERAS & SARAH BRIGHTMAN)	
	Amigos Para Siempre (Friends For Life)	1992
	(MICHAEL CRAWFORD/SARAH BRIGHTMAN)	
	The Music Of The Night/Wishing You	
	Were Somehow Here Again	1987
MARTIN BRILEY	The Salt In My Tears	1983
JOHNNY BRISTOL	Hang On In There Baby	1974
	(AMII STEWART & JOHNNY BRISTOL)	
	My Guy/My Girl (Medley)	1980

ARTIST	SONG TITLE	DATE
BRITISH SEA POWER		
	Carrion/Apologies To Insect Life	2003
	Remember Me	2003
ANDREA BRITTON/JURGEN VRIES		
	Take My Hand	2004
	(OXYGEN featuring ANDREA BRITTON)	
	Am I On Your Mind	2003
CHAD BROCK	Ordinary Life	1999
	Yes!	2000
BROKEN ENGLISH	Comin' On Strong	1987
BRONSKI BEAT	Come On, Come On	1986
	Hit That Perfect Beat	1985
	It Ain't Necessarily So	1984
	Smalltown Boy	1984
	Why?	1984
BRONSKI BEAT & MARC ALMOND		
	I Feel Love (Medley)	1985
	(EARTHA KITT & BRONSKI BEAT)	
	Cha Cha Heels	1989
HERMAN BROOD	Saturday Night	1979
BROOK BROTHERS	Trouble Is My Middle Name	1963
BROOKLYN BRIDGE		
	Worst That Could Happen	1968
BROOKS & DUNN	Ain't Nothing 'Bout You	2001
	Husbands And Wives	1998
	The Long Goodbye	2001

ARTIST	SONG TITLE	DATE
	Only In America	2001
	Red Dirt Road	2003
	You Can't Take The Honky Tonk Out Of The Girl	2003
ELKIE BROOKS	Don't Cry Out Loud	1978
	Fool If You Think It's Over	1982
	Lilac Wine	1978
	Nights In White Satin	1982
	No More The Fool	1986
	Pearl's A Singer	1977
	Sunshine After The Rain	1977
GARTH BROOKS	The Dance/Friends In Low Places	1995
	The Red Strokes/Ain't Going Down (Til The Sun Comes Up)	1994
	Standing Outside The Fire	1994
GARTH BROOKS AS CHRIS GAINES		
	Lost In You	1999
MEL BROOKS	To Be Or Not To Be (The Hitler Rap)	1984
MEREDITH BROOKS		
	Bitch	1997
	I Need	1997
BROS	Are You Mine?	1991
	Cat Among The Pigeons/Silent Night	1988
	Chocolate Box	1989
	Drop The Boy	1988
	I Owe You Nothing	1988

ARTIST	SONG TITLE	DATE
	I Quit	1988
	Madly In Love	1990
	Sister	1989
	Too Much	1989
	Try	1991
	When Will I Be Famous?	1987
BROTHER BEYOND	Be My Twin	1989
	Drive On	1989
	The Girl I Used To Know	1990
	The Harder I Try	1988
	He Ain't No Competition	1988
BROTHER BROWN featuring FRANK'EE		
	Under The Water	1999
BROTHERHOOD OF MAN		
	Angelo	1977
	Beautiful Lover	1978
	Figaro	1978
	My Sweet Rosalie	1976
	Oh Boy (The Mood I'm In)	1977
	Save Your Kisses For Me	1976
	United We Stand	1970
	Where Are You Going To My Love	1970
BROTHERS	Sing Me	1977
BROTHERS IN RHYTHM		
	Such A Good Feeling	1991

ARTIST	SONG TITLE	DATE
BROTHERS JOHNSON		
	Get The Funk Out Ma Face	1976
	I'll Be Good To You	1976
	Stomp!	1980
	Strawberry Letter 23	1977
EDGAR BROUGHTON BAND		
	Apache Dropout	1971
	Out Demons Out	1970
BROWN SAUCE	I Wanna Be A Winner	1981
CRAZY WORLD OF ARTHUR BROWN		
	Fire	1968
BOBBY BROWN	Don't Be Cruel	1988
	Every Little Step	1989
	Feelin' Inside	1997
	The Free Style Mega-Mix	1990
	Get Away	1993
	Good Enough	1992
	Humpin' Around	1992
	My Prerogative	1988
	On Our Own	1989
	Rock Wit'cha	1989
	Roni	1989
	Two Can Play That Game	1994
BOBBY BROWN & WHITNEY HOUSTON		
	Something In Common	1994

ARTIST	SONG TITLE	DATE
	(GLENN MEDEIROS featuring BOBBY BROWN)	
	She Ain't Worth It	1990
	(JA RULE featuring BOBBY BROWN)	
	Thug Lovin'	2002
DENNIS BROWN	Money In My Pocket	1979
DIANA BROWN & BARRIE K. SHARPE		
	The Masterplan	1990
ERROL BROWN	Personal Touch	1987
FOXY BROWN	Hot Spot	1999
	Oh Yeah	2001
FOXY BROWN featuring BLACKSTREET		
	Get Me Home	1997
FOXY BROWN featuring DRU HILL		
	Big Bad Mamma	1997
FOXY BROWN featuring JAY-Z		
	I'll Be	1997
	(CASE featuring FOXY BROWN)	
	Touch Me Tease Me	1996
	(JAY-Z featuring BABYFACE & FOXY BROWN)	
	Sunshine	1997
	(JAY-Z featuring FOXY BROWN)	
	Ain't No Playa	1997
HORACE BROWN	One For The Money	1996
	Things We Do For Love	1996
IAN BROWN	Can't See Me	1998
	Corpses	1998

ARTIST	SONG TITLE	DATE
	Dolphins Were Monkeys	2000
	F.E.A.R.	2001
	Golden Gaze	2000
	Keep What Ya Got	2004
	Love Like A Fountain	1999
	My Star	1998
	Whispers	2002
	(UNKLE featuring IAN BROWN)	
	Be There	1999
JAMES BROWN	Ain't It Funky Now (Part 1)	1969
	Body Heat	1977
	Bring It Up	1967
	Brother Rapp (Parts 1 & 2)	1970
	Cold Sweat (Part 1)	1967
	Escape-Ism (Part 1)	1971
	Funk On Ah Roll	1999
	Get It Together (Part 1)	1967
	Get On The Good Foot (Part 1)	1972
	Get Up (I Feel Like Being A Sex Machine)	1970
	Get Up Offa That Thing	1976
	Get Up, Get Into It, Get Involved (Part 1)	1971
	Give It Up Or Turn It A Loose	1969
	Goodbye My Love	1968
	Hot Pants (She Got To Use What She Got To Get What She Wants)	1971
	I Can't Stand Myself (When You Touch Me)	1967

ARTIST	SONG TITLE	DATE
	I Don't Want Nobody To Give Me Nothing	1969
	I Got Ants In My Pants (Part 1)	1973
	I Got The Feelin'	1968
	I Got You (I Feel Good)	1965
	I'm A Greedy Man (Part 1)	1971
	It's A Man's Man's Man's World	1966
	It's A New Day (Parts 1 & 2)	1970
	King Heroin	1972
	Let A Man Come In And Do The Popcorn (Part 1)	1969
	Licking Stick-Licking Stick	1968
	Living In America	1985
	Make It Funky	1971
	Mother Popcorn (You Got To Have A Mother For Me)	1969
	My Thang	1974
	Oh Baby Don't You Weep (Part 1)	1964
	Out Of Sight	1964
	Papa Don't Take No Mess (Part 1)	1974
	Papa's Got A Brand New Bag	1965
	The Payback (Part 1)	1974
	The Popcorn	1969
	Rapp Payback (Where Iz Moses?)	1981
	Say It Loud — I'm Black And I'm Proud	1968
	Soul Power (Part 2)	1971

ARTIST	SONG TITLE	DATE
	Super Bad (Parts 1 & 2)	1970
	Talking Loud And Saying Nothing (Part 1)	1972
	There Was A Time	1968
	World (Part 1)	1969
JAMES BROWN featuring FULL FORCE		
	I'm Real	1988
JOCELYN BROWN	Ain't No Mountain High Enough	1998
	Somebody Else's Guy	1984
(DA MOB featuring JOCELYN BROWN)		
	Fun	1998
(INCOGNITO featuring JOCELYN BROWN)		
	Always There	1991
(KYM MAZELLE & JOCELYN BROWN)		
	Gimme All Your Lovin'	1994
	No More Tears (Enough Is Enough)	1994
(NUYORICAN SOUL featuring JOCELYN BROWN)		
	I Am The Black Gold Of The Sun	1997
	It's Alright, I Feel It!	1997
(RIGHT SAID FRED/JOCELYN BROWN)		
	Don't Talk Just Kiss	1991
(TODD TERRY featuring MARTHA WASH & JOCELYN BROWN)		
	Keep On Jumpin'	1996
JOE BROWN	Hey Mama	1973
	Nature's Time For Love	1963

ARTIST	SONG TITLE	DATE
	Sally Ann	1963
	With A Little Help From My Friends	1967
JOE BROWN & THE BRUVVERS		
	That's What Love Will Do	1963
KATHY BROWN/J. MAJIK		
	Love Is Not A Game	2001
(PRAXIS featuring KATHY BROWN)		
	Turn Me Out (Turn To Sugar)	1997
MAXINE BROWN	Oh No Not My Baby	1964
PETER BROWN	Dance With Me	1978
	Do Ya Wanna Get Funky With Me	1977
POLLY BROWN	Up In A Puff Of Smoke	1975
ROY CHUBBY BROWN/SMOKIE		
	Living Next Door To Alice (Who The F**k Is Alice?)	1995
SAM BROWN	Can I Get A Witness	1989
	Kissing Gate	1990
	Stop	1989
SHARON BROWN	I Specialize In You	1982
SHIRLEY BROWN	Woman To Woman	1974
SLEEPY BROWN featuring OUTKAST		
	I Can't Wait	2004
(LUDACRIS featuring SLEEPY BROWN)		
	Saturday (Oooh! Ooooh!)	2002
DUNCAN BROWNE	Journey	1972

ARTIST	SONG TITLE	DATE
JACKSON BROWNE	Boulevard	1980
	Doctor My Eyes	1972
	For America	1986
	Here Comes Those Tears Again	1977
	Lawyers In Love	1983
	Runnin' On Empty	1978
	Somebody's Baby	1982
	Stay	1978
	Stay/The Load-Out	1978
	Tender Is The Night	1983
	That Girl Could Sing	1980
	(CLARENCE CLEMONS & JACKSON BROWNE)	
	You're A Friend Of Mine	1985
TOM BROWNE	Funkin' For Jamaica (N.Y.)	1980
BROWNSTONE	5 Miles To Empty	1997
	Grapevyne	1995
	I Can't Tell You Why	1995
	If You Love Me	1994
	Kiss And Tell	1997
BROWNSVILLE STATION		
	Kings Of The Party	1974
	Smokin' In The Boys Room	1973
BRUISERS	Blue Girl	1963
FRANK BRUNO	Eye Of The Tiger	1995
DORA BRYAN	All I Want For Christmas Is A Beatle	1963
KELLE BRYAN	Higher Than Heaven	1999

ARTIST	SONG TITLE	DATE
SHARON BRYANT	Let Go	1989
PEABO BRYSON	If Ever You're In My Arms Again	1984
PEABO BRYSON & REGINA BELLE		
	A Whole New World (Aladdin's Theme)	1992
PEABO BRYSON & ROBERTA FLACK		
	Tonight I Celebrate My Love	1983
	(CELINE DION & PEABO BRYSON)	
	Beauty And The Beast	1992
	(KENNY G WITH PEABO BRYSON)	
	By The Time This Night Is Over	1993
B.T. EXPRESS	Do It ('Til You're Satisfied)	1974
	Express	1975
	Give It What You Got	1975
	Peace Pipe	1975
BT	Embracing The Sunshine	1995
	Flaming June	1997
	Mercury And Solace	1999
	Remember	1998
BT featuring KIRSTY HAWKSHAW		
	Dreaming	2000
BT featuring TORI AMOS		
	Blue Skies	1996
BT featuring VINCENT COVELLO		
	Loving You More	1996
	(TIESTO featuring BT)	
	Love Comes Again	2004

ARTIST	SONG TITLE	DATE
BUBBLE PUPPY	Hot Smoke & Sasafrass	1969
BUCHANAN BROTHERS		
	Medicine Man (Part I)	1969
ROY BUCHANAN	Sweet Dreams	1973
BUCKETHEADS	The Bomb! (These Sounds Fall Into My Mind)	1995
	Get Myself Together	1996
LINDSEY BUCKINGHAM		
	Go Insane	1984
	Trouble	1981
BUCKINGHAMS	Don't You Care	1967
	Hey Baby (They're Playing Our Song)	1967
	Kind Of A Drag	1966
	Mercy, Mercy, Mercy	1967
	Susan	1967
BUCKNER & GARCIA		
	Pac-Man Fever	1982
BUCKS FIZZ	I Hear Talk	1984
	If You Can't Stand The Heat	1982
	Land Of Make Believe	1981
	London Town	1983
	Making Your Mind Up	1981
	My Camera Never Lies	1982
	New Beginning (Mamba Sayra)	1986
	Now Those Days Are Gone	1982
	One Of Those Nights	1981

ARTIST	SONG TITLE	DATE
	Piece Of The Action	1981
	Run For Your Life	1983
	Talking In Your Sleep	1984
	When We Were Young	1983
JOE BUDDEN	Pump It Up	2003
(CHRISTINA MILIAN featuring JOE BUDDEN)		
	Whatever U Want	2004
(MARQUES HOUSTON featuring JOE BUDDEN & PIED PIPER)		
	Clubbin	2003
BUFFALO G	We're Really Saying Something	2000
BUFFALO SPRINGFIELD		
	For What It's Worth (Stop, Hey What's That Sound)	1967
BUFFALO TOM: LIAM GALLAGHER & STEVE CRADOCK		
	Going Underground/Carnation	1999
JIMMY BUFFETT	Changes In Latitude, Changes In Attitude	1977
	Cheeseburgers In Paradise	1978
	Come Monday	1974
	Fins	1979
	Margaritaville	1977
BUGGLES	Clean, Clean	1980
	The Plastic Age	1980
	Video Killed The Radio Star	1979
BULL & THE MATADORS		
	The Funky Judge	1968

ARTIST	SONG TITLE	DATE
BULLET	White Lies, Blue Eyes	1971
B. BUMBLE & THE STINGERS		
	Nut Rocker	1962
BUMP	I'm Rushing	1992
EMMA BUNTON	Crickets Sings For Anamaria	2004
	Free Me	2003
	I'll Be There	2004
	Maybe	2003
	Take My Breath Away	2001
	We're Not Gonna Sleep Tonight	2001
	What Took You So Long?	2001
	(TIN TIN OUT featuring EMMA BUNTON)	
	What I Am	1999
BUOYS	Timothy	1971
ERIC BURDON & THE ANIMALS		
	Ring Of Fire	1969
	Sky Pilot	1968
ERIC BURDON & WAR		
	Spill The Wine	1970
SOLOMON BURKE	Goodbye Baby (Baby Goodbye)	1964
	Got To Get You Off My Mind	1965
	Tonight's The Night	1965
HANK C. BURNETTE		
	Spinning Rock Boogie	1976
ROCKY BURNETTE	Tired Of Toein' The Line	1980

ARTIST	SONG TITLE	DATE
MALANDRA BURROWS		
	Just This Side Of Love	1990
BURUNDI STEIPHENSON BLACK		
	Burundi Black	1971
BUS STOP	Jump	1999
BUS STOP featuring CARL DOUGLAS		
	Kung Fu Fighting	1998
BUS STOP featuring RANDY BACHMAN		
	You Ain't Seen Nothin' Yet	1998
BUSH	Comedown	1995
	Glycerine	1996
	Greedy Fly	1997
	Swallowed	1997
KATE BUSH	And So Is Love	1994
	Army Dreamers	1980
	Babooshka	1980
	The Big Sky	1986
	Breathing	1980
	Cloudbusting	1985
	December Will Be Magic Again	1980
	Experiment IV	1986
	Hounds Of Love	1986
	Kate Bush On Stage (EP)	1979
	Love And Anger	1990
	The Man With The Child In His Eyes	1978
	Moments Of Pleasure	1993

ARTIST	SONG TITLE	DATE
	The Red Shoes	1994
	Rocket Man (I Think It's Going To Be A Long Long Time)	1991
	Rubberband Girl	1993
	Running Up That Hill	1985
	Sat In Your Lap	1981
	The Sensual World	1989
	This Woman's Work	1989
	Wow	1979
	Wuthering Heights	1978
KATE BUSH AND LARRY ADLER		
	The Man I Love	1994
	(PETER GABRIEL & KATE BUSH)	
	Don't Give Up	1986
BUSTED	Air Hostess	2004
	Crashed The Wedding	2003
	Sleeping With The Light On	2003
	Thunderbirds/3 A.M.	2004
	What I Go To School For	2002
	Who's David	2004
	Year 3000	2003
	You Said No	2003
PRINCE BUSTER	Al Capone	1967
	Whine And Grine	1998
BERNARD BUTLER	Not Alone	1998
	Stay	1998

ARTIST	SONG TITLE	DATE
JERRY BUTLER	Are You Happy	1968
	Hey, Western Union Man	1968
	Moody Woman	1969
	Mr. Dream Merchant	1967
	Never Give You Up	1968
	Only The Strong Survive	1969
	What's The Use Of Breaking Up?	1969
JERRY BUTLER & BETTY EVERETT		
	Let It Be Me	1964
JERRY BUTLER & BRENDA LEE EAGER		
	Ain't Understanding Mellow	1971
JONATHAN BUTLER		
	If You're Ready (Come Go With Me)	1986
	Lies	1987
BUTTERSCOTCH	Don't You Know	1970
BUZZCOCKS	Ever Fallen In Love With Someone (You Shouldn't've Fallen In Love With)?	1978
	Everybody's Happy Nowadays	1979
	Harmony In My Head	1979
	Love You More	1978
	Promises	1978
	Spiral Scratch (EP)	1979
	What Do I Get?	1978
MAX BYGRAVES	Deck Of Cards	1973
	You're My Everything	1969

ARTIST	SONG TITLE	DATE
GARY BYRD & THE GB EXPERIENCE		
	The Crown	1983
TRACY BYRD	Ten Rounds With Jose Cuervo	2002
BYRDS	All I Really Want To Do	1965
	Chestnut Mare	1971
	Eight Miles High	1966
	Mr. Spaceman	1966
	Mr. Tambourine Man	1965
	My Back Pages	1967
	So You Want To Be A Rock 'n' Roll Star	1967
	Turn! Turn! Turn!	1965
DAVID BYRNE/X-PRESS 2		
	Lazy	2002
C COMPANY featuring TERRY NELSON		
	Battle Hymn Of Lt. Calley	1971
C&C MUSIC FACTORY		
	Do You Wanna Get Funky	1994
	I Found Love/Take A Toke	1995
	Just A Touch Of Love (Everyday)	1991
C&C MUSIC FACTORY featuring FREEDOM WILLIAMS		
	Gonna Make You Sweat	1990
	Here We Go	1991
	Things That Make You Go Hmmmm...	1991
C&C MUSIC FACTORY featuring Q UNIQUE & DEBORAH COOPER	Keep It Comin' (Dance Till You Can't Dance No More)	1992

ARTIST	SONG TITLE	DATE
FANTASTIC JOHNNY C		
	Boogaloo Down Broadway	1967
	Hitch It To The Horse	1968
MELANIE C	Here It Comes Again	2003
	I Turn To You	2000
	If That Were Me	2000
	Melt/Yeh Yeh Yeh	2003
	On The Horizon	2003
MELANIE C/LISA 'LEFT EYE' LOPES		
	Never Be The Same Again	2000
C.C.S.	The Band Played The Boogie	1973
	Brother	1972
	Tap Turns On The Water	1971
	Walkin'	1971
	Whole Lotta Love	1970
C.J. & CO.	Devil's Gun	1977
MONSERRAT CABALLE/FREDDIE MERCURY		
	Barcelona	1992
RYAN CABRERA	On The Way Down	2004
FLASH CADILLAC & THE CONTINENTAL KIDS		
	Did You Boogie (With Your Baby)	1976
SUSAN CADOGAN	Hurt So Good	1975
	Love Me Baby	1975
JOHN CAFFERTY	Tough All Over	1985
JOHN CAFFERTY & THE BEAVER BROWN BAND		
	C-I-T-Y	1985

ARTIST	SONG TITLE	DATE
	On The Dark Side	1984
	Tender Years	1984
CHRIS CAGLE	I Breathe In, I Breathe Out	2002
TANE CAIN	Holdin' On	1982
CAKE	The Distance	1997
	I Will Survive	1997
BOBBY CALDWELL	What You Won't Do For Love	1978
J.J. CALE	Crazy Mama	1972
CALLING	Adrienne	2002
	Our Lives	2004
	Things Will Go My Way	2004
	Wherever You Will Go	2001
CALLOWAY	I Wanna Be Rich	1990
CAM'RON featuring JUELZ SANTANA		
	Hey Ma	2003
	Oh Boy	2002
CAM'RON featuring MASE		
	Horse & Carriage	1998
	(MARIAH CAREY featuring CAM'RON)	
	Boy (I Need You)	2003
CAMEO	Back And Forth	1987
	Candy	1986
	She's Mine	1987
	She's Strange	1985
	Single Life	1985
	Word Up	1986

ARTIST	SONG TITLE	DATE
	(MARIAH featuring CAMEO)	
	Loverboy	2001
ANDY CAMERON	Ally's Tartan Army	1978
TONY CAMILLO'S BAZUKA		
	Dynomite (Part 1)	1975
CAMISRA	Clap Your Hands	1999
	Feel The Beat	1998
	Let Me Show You	1998
ALI CAMPBELL	Let Your Yeah Be Yeah	1995
	That Look In Your Eye	1995
ALI & KIBIBI CAMPBELL		
	Somethin' Stupid	1995
ELLIE CAMPBELL	So Many Ways	1999
ETHNA CAMPBELL	The Old Rugged Cross	1975
GLEN CAMPBELL	By The Time I Get To Phoenix	1967
	Can You Fool	1978
	Country Boy (You Got Your Feet In L.A.)	1975
	Don't Pull Your Love/Then You Can Tell Me Goodbye	1976
	Dream Baby (How Long Must I Dream)	1971
	Dreams Of The Everyday Housewife	1968
	Everything A Man Could Ever Need	1970
	Galveston	1969
	Gentle Of My Mind	1968
	Honey Come Back	1970
	I Wanna Love	1968

ARTIST	SONG TITLE	DATE
	It's Only Make Believe	1970
	Oh Happy Day	1970
	Rhinestone Cowboy	1975
	Southern Nights	1977
	Sunflower	1977
	True Grit	1969
	Try A Little Kindness	1969
	Where's The Playground Susie?	1969
	Wichita Lineman	1968
GLEN CAMPBELL & BOBBIE GENTRY		
	Let It Be Me	1969
	All I Have To Do Is Dream	1969
(RIKKI & DAZ featuring GLEN CAMPBELL		
	Rhinestone Cowboy (Giddy Up Giddy Up)	2002
JUNIOR CAMPBELL	Hallelujah Freedom	1972
	Sweet Illusion	1973
NAOMI CAMPBELL	Love And Tears	1994
PAT CAMPBELL	The Deal	1969
TEVIN CAMPBELL	Always In My Heart	1994
	Can We Talk	1993
	I'm Ready	1994
	Round And Round	1990
	Tell Me What You Want Me To Do	1991
CAN	I Want More	1976
CANDLEBOX	Far Behind	1994

ARTIST	SONG TITLE	DATE
CANDLEWICK GREEN		
	Who Do You Think You Are?	1974
CANDY FLIP	Strawberry Fields Forever	1990
CANDY GIRLS	Fee Fi Fo Fum	1995
	I Want Candy	1996
CANDY GIRLS featuring SWEET PUSSY PAULINE		
	Wham Bam	1996
CANDYMAN	Knockin' Boots	1990
CANDYSKINS	Monday Morning	1997
CANIBUS	Second Round K.O.	1998
CANNED HEAT	Going Up The Country	1968
	Let's Work Together	1970
	On The Road Again	1968
CANNIBAL AND THE HEADHUNTERS		
	Land Of 1000 Dances	1965
FREDDY CANNON	Abigail Beecher	1964
	Action	1965
NICK CANNON featuring R. KELLY		
	Gigolo	2003
BLU CANTRELL	Hit 'Em Up Style (Oops!)	2001
	Make Me Wanna Scream	2003
BLU CANTRELL featuring SEAN PAUL		
	Breathe	2003
JIM CAPALDI	It's All Up To You	1974
	Love Hurts	1975
	That's Love	1983

ARTIST	SONG TITLE	DATE
CAPERCAILLIE	A Prince Amongst Islands (EP)	1992
CAPITOLS	Cool Jerk	1968
CAPPELLA	Helyom Halib (Acid Acid Acid)	1989
	Move It Up/Big Beat	1994
	Move On Baby	1994
	Tell Me The Way	1995
	U & Me	1994
	U Got 2 Know	1993
	U Got 2 Let The Music	1993
CAPPELLA featuring LOLEATTA HOLLOWAY		
	Take Me Away	1992
CAPRICE	Oh Yeah	1999
	Once Around The Sun	2001
TONY CAPSTICK	Capstick Comes Home/Sheffield Grinder	1981
CAPTAIN & TENNILLE		
	Can't Stop Dancin'	1977
	Do That To Me One More Time	1979
	Lonely Night (Angel Face)	1976
	Love Will Keep Us Together	1975
	Muskrat Love	1976
	Shop Around	1976
	The Way I Want To Touch You	1975
	You Need A Woman Tonight	1978
	You Never Done It Like That	1978
CAPTAIN HOLLYWOOD PROJECT		
	Impossible	1994

ARTIST	SONG TITLE	DATE
	More And More	1993
CAPTAIN SENSIBLE	Glad It's All Over/Damned On 45	1984
	Happy Talk	1982
	Wot!	1982
IRENE CARA	Breakdance	1984
	The Dream (Hold On To Your Dream)	1983
	Fame	1980
	Flashdance... What A Feeling	1983
	Out Here On My Own	1980
	Why Me?	1983
CARAVELLES	You Don't Have To Be A Baby To Cry	1963
CARDIGANS	Carnival	1995
	Erase/Rewind	1999
	For What It's Worth	2003
	Hanging Around	1999
	Lovefool	1997
	My Favourite Game	1998
	Rise & Shine	1996
	Sick & Tired	1995
	Your New Cuckoo	1997
	(TOM JONES & THE CARDIGANS)	
	Burning Down The House	1999
CAREFREES	We Love You Beatles	1964
MARIAH CAREY	All I Want For Christmas Is You	1994
	Always Be My Baby	1996
	Anytime You Need A Friend	1994

ARTIST	SONG TITLE	DATE
	Butterfly	1997
	Can't Let Go	1991
	Dreamlover	1993
	Emotions	1991
	Fantasy	1995
	Hero	1993
	Honey	1997
	I Don't Wanna Cry	1991
	I Still Believe	1999
	I'll Be There	1992
	Love Takes Time	1990
	Make It Happen	1992
	My All	1998
	Never Too Far/Don't Stop (Funkin' 4 Jamaica)	2001
	Open Arms	1996
	Someday	1991
	Through The Rain	2002
	Vision Of Love	1990
	Without You/Never Forget You	1994
MARIAH CAREY & BOYZ II MEN		
	One Sweet Day	1995
MARIAH CAREY & WESTLIFE		
	Against All Odds	2000
MARIAH CAREY & WHITNEY HOUSTON		
	When You Believe	1998

ARTIST	SONG TITLE	DATE
MARIAH CAREY featuring CAM'RON		
	Boy (I Need You)	2003
MARIAH CAREY featuring JAY-Z		
	Heartbreaker	1999
MARIAH CAREY featuring JOE & 98 DEGREES		
	Thank God I Found You	1999
MARIAH CAREY featuring SNOOP DOGG		
	Crybaby	2000
MARIAH featuring CAMEO		
	Loverboy	2001
(BUSTA RHYMES AND MARIAH CAREY featuring FLIPMODE SQUAD)		
	I Know What You Want	2003
(LUTHER VANDROSS & MARIAH CAREY)		
	Endless Love	1994
TONY CAREY	A Fine Fine Day	1984
	The First Day Of Summer	1984
HENSON CARGILL	Skip A Rope	1967
BELINDA CARLISLE	Always Breaking My Heart	1996
	Bigscaryanimal	1993
	California	1997
	Circle In The Sand	1988
	Do You Feel Like I Feel?	1991
	Half The World	1992
	Heaven Is A Place On Earth	1987
	I Get Weak	1988

ARTIST	SONG TITLE	DATE
	In Too Deep	1996
	La Luna	1989
	Lay Down Your Arms	1993
	Leave A Light On	1989
	Little Black Book	1992
	Live Your Life Be Free	1991
	Love In The Key Of C	1996
	Mad About You	1986
	Runaway Horses	1990
	Summer Rain	1990
	(We Want) The Same Thing	1990
	World Without You	1988
CARL CARLTON	Everlasting Love	1974
	She's A Bad Mama Jama (She's Built, She's Stacked)	1981
VANESSA CARLTON	Ordinary Day	2002
	A Thousand Miles	2002
(COUNTING CROWS featuring VANESSA CARLTON)		
	Big Yellow Taxi	2003
CARMEL	Bad Day	1983
	More, More, More	1984
ERIC CARMEN	All By Myself	1975
	Change Of Heart	1978
	Hungry Eyes	1987
	I Wanna Hear It From Your Lips	1985
	Make Me Lose Control	1988

ARTIST	SONG TITLE	DATE
	Never Gonna Fall In Love Again	1976
	She Did It	1977
	Sunrise	1976
KIM CARNES	Bette Davis Eyes	1981
	Crazy In The Night (Barking At Airplanes)	1985
	Does It Make You Remember	1982
	Draw Of The Cards	1981
	Invisible Hands	1983
	More Love	1980
	Voyeur	1982
(GENE COTTON WITH KIM CARNES)		
	You're A Part Of Me	1978
(KENNY ROGERS & KIM CARNES)		
	Don't Fall In Love With A Dreamer	1980
(KENNY ROGERS WITH KIM CARNES & JAMES INGRAM)		
	What About Me?	1984
MARY CHAPIN CARPENTER		
	Shut Up And Kiss Me	1995
(SHAWN COLVIN WITH MARY CHAPIN CARPENTER)		
	One Cool Remove	1995
CARPENTERS	All You Get From Love Is A Love Song	1977
	Calling Occupants Of Interplanetary Craft	1977
	Goodbye To Love/I Won't Last A Day Without You	1972
	Hurting Each Other	1972

ARTIST	SONG TITLE	DATE
	I Need To Be In Love	1976
	It's Going To Take Some Time	1972
	Jambalaya	1974
	Merry Christmas Darling	1990
	Only Yesterday	1975
	Please Mr. Postman	1974
	Rainy Days And Mondays	1971
	Santa Claus Is Comin' To Town	1975
	Sing	1973
	Solitaire	1975
	Superstar/For All You Know	1971
	Sweet, Sweet Smile	1978
	There's A Kind Of Hush (All Over The World)	1976
	(They Long To Be) Close To You	1970
	Top Of The World	1973
	Touch Me When We're Dancing	1981
	We've Only Just Begun	1970
	Yesterday Once More	1973
LINDA CARR & THE LOVE SQUAD		
	Highwire	1975
LUCY CARR	Missing You	2003
VIKKI CARR	It Must Be Him	1967
	The Lesson	1967
	With Pen In Hand	1969
RAFFAELLA CARRA	Do It, Do It Again	1978

ARTIST	SONG TITLE	DATE
PAUL CARRACK	Don't Shed A Tear	1987
	Eyes Of Blue	1996
	How Long?	1996
	I Live By The Groove	1989
	I Need You	1982
	One Good Reason	1988
KEITH CARRADINE	I'm Easy	1976
CARRERAS/DOMINGO/PAVAROTTI WITH MEHTA		
	Libiamo/La Donna E Mobile	1994
	You'll Never Walk Alone	1998
JOSE CARRERAS & SARAH BRIGHTMAN		
	Amigos Para Siempre (Friends For Life)	1992
TIA CARRERE	Ballroom Blitz	1992
JIM CARREY	Cuban Pete	1995
DINA CARROLL	Ain't No Man	1992
	Don't Be A Stranger	1993
	Escaping	1996
	Express	1993
	One, Two, Three	1998
	Only Human	1996
	The Perfect Year	1993
	So Close	1992
	Someone Like You	2001
	Special Kind Of Love	1992
	This Time	1993
	Without Love	1999

ARTIST	SONG TITLE	DATE
	(QUARTZ WITH DINA CARROLL)	
	It's Too Late	1991
	Naked Love (Just Say You Want Me)	1991
RONNIE CARROLL	Say Wonderful Things	1963
JASPER CARROTT	Funky Moped/Magic Roundabout	1975
CARS	Drive	1984
	Hello Again	1984
	I'm Not The One	1986
	Just What I Needed	1978
	Let's Go	1979
	Magic	1984
	My Best Friend's Girl	1978
	Shake It Up	1981
	Since You're Gone	1982
	Tonight She Comes	1985
	Touch And Go	1980
	Why Can't I Have You	1985
	You Are The Girl	1987
	You Might Think	1984
ALEX CARTANA	Hey Papi	2004
	(LEE-CABRERA featuring ALEX CARTANA)	
	Shake It (Move A Little Closer)	2003
CARTER THE UNSTOPPABLE SEX MACHINE		
	After The Watershed	1991
	Born On The 5th Of November	1995
	Do Re Me, So Far So Good	1992

ARTIST	SONG TITLE	DATE
	Glam Rock Cops	1994
	The Impossible Dream	1992
	Lean On Me I Won't Fall Over	1993
	Lenny And Terence	1993
	Let's Get Tattoos	1994
	The Only Living Boy In New Cross	1992
	Rubbish	1992
	Sheriff Fatman	1991
	The Young Offender's Mum	1995
AARON CARTER	Aaron's Party (Come Get It)	2000
	Crazy Little Party Girl	1998
	Crush On You	1997
	I Want Candy	2000
	I'm Gonna Miss You Forever	1998
	Leave It Up To Me	2002
	Surfin' USA	1998
CLARENCE CARTER	Patches	1970
	Slip Away	1968
	Snatching It Back	1969
	Too Weak To Fight	1968
JUNE CARTER/JOHNNY CASH		
	If I Were A Carpenter	1970
MEL CARTER	(All Of A Sudden) My Heart Sings	1965
	Band Of Gold	1966
	Hold Me Thrill Me Kiss Me	1965
NICK CARTER	Help Me	2002

ARTIST	SONG TITLE	DATE
CARTOONS	Aisy Waisy	1999
	Doodah!	1999
	Witch Doctor	1999
CARVELLS	The L.A. Run	1977
CASCADES	Rhythm Of The Rain	1963
CASE	Happily Ever After	1999
	Missing You	2001
CASE & JOE	Faded Pictures	1998
CASE featuring FOXY BROWN		
	Touch Me Tease Me	1996
	(JA RULE featuring CASE)	
	Livin' It Up	2001
ED CASE	Something In Your Eyes	2000
ED CASE & SWEETIE IRIE		
	Who?	2001
ALVIN CASH & THE CRAWLERS		
	Twine Time	1965
JOHNNY CASH	A Boy Named Sue	1969
	Folsom Prison Blues	1968
	Hurt/Personal Jesus	2003
	It Ain't Me Babe	1965
	One Piece At A Time	1976
	A Thing Called Love	1972
	Understand Your Man	1964
	What Is Truth?	1970

ARTIST	SONG TITLE	DATE
JOHNNY CASH & JUNE CARTER		
	If I Were A Carpenter	1970
ROSANNE CASH	Seven Year Ache	1981
CA$HFLOW	Mine All Mine/Party Freak	1986
CASHMAN & WEST	American City Suite	1972
CASHMERE	Can I	1985
CASINOS	Then You Can Tell Me Goodbye	1967
MAMA CASS	Dream A Little Dream Of Me	1968
	It's Getting Better	1969
CASSIDY featuring MASHONDA		
	Get No Better	2004
CASSIDY featuring R. KELLY		
	Hotel	2004
DAVID CASSIDY	Could It Be Forever/Cherish	1972
	Darlin'	1975
	Daydreamer/The Puppy Song	1973
	How Can I Be Sure	1972
	I Write The Songs/Get It Up For Love	1975
	I'm A Clown/Some Kind Of A Summer	1973
	If I Didn't Care	1974
	The Last Kiss	1985
	Lyin' To Myself	1990
	Please Please Me	1974
	Rock Me Baby	1972
SHAUN CASSIDY	Da Doo Ron Ron	1977
	Do You Believe In Magic	1978

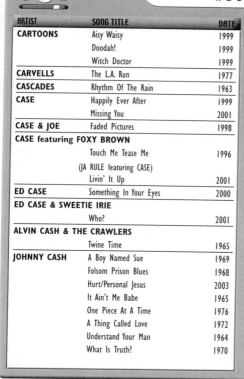

ARTIST	SONG TITLE	DATE
	Hey Deanie	1977
	That's Rock 'n' Roll	1977
CASSIUS	Cassius 1999	1999
	Feeling For You	1999
CAST	Alright	1995
	Beat Mama	1999
	Finetime	1995
	Flying	1996
	Free Me	1997
	Guiding Star	1997
	I'm So Lonely	1997
	Live The Dream	1997
	Magic Hour	1999
	Sandstorm	1996
	Walkaway	1996
CAST FROM CASUALTY		
	Everlasting Love	1998
CASTAWAYS	Liar, Liar	1965
BOOMER CASTLEMAN		
	Judy Mae	1975
JIMMY CASTOR	Hey, Leroy, Your Mama's Callin' You	1966
JIMMY CASTOR BUNCH		
	The Bertha Butt Boogie (Pt 1)	1975
	Troglodyte (Cave Man)	1972
CASUALS	Jesamine	1968
	Toy	1968

ARTIST	SONG TITLE	DATE
CAT	Tongue Tied	1993
CAT MOTHER & THE ALL NIGHT NEWS BOYS		
	Good Old Rock 'n' Roll	1969
CATATONIA	Dead From The Waist Down	1999
	Game On	1998
	I Am The Mob	1997
	Karaoke Queen	1999
	Londinium	1999
	Mulder And Scully	1998
	Road Rage	1998
	Stone By Stone	2001
	Strange Glue	1998
	You've Got A Lot To Answer For	1996
CATCH	Bingo	1997
CATE BROTHERS	Union Man	1976
CATHERINE WHEEL	I Want To Touch You	1992
CATS U.K.	Luton Airport	1979
CAUSE & EFFECT	You Think You Know Her	1992
FELIX CAVALIERE	Only A Lonely Heart Sees	1980
NICK CAVE & KYLIE MINOGUE		
	Where The Wild Roses Grow	1995
NICK CAVE & THE BAD SEEDS		
	Henry Lee	1996
	Nature Boy	2004
CELEBRATION/MIKE LOVE		
	Almost Summer	1978

ARTIST	SONG TITLE	DATE
CELETIA	Rewind	1998
CENTRAL LINE	Nature Boy	1983
CERRONE	Je Suis Music	1979
	Love In C Minor	1977
	Supernature	1978
PETER CETERA	Glory Of Love	1986
	One Good Woman	1988
	Restless Heart	1992
PETER CETERA & AMY GRANT		
	The Next Time I Fall	1986
	(AZ YET featuring PETER CETERA)	
	Hard To Say I'm Sorry	1997
	(CHER & PETER CETERA)	
	After All	1989
CEVIN FISHER'S BIG BREAK		
	The Freaks Come Out	1998
CHAD & JEREMY	Before And After	1965
	Distant Shores	1966
	I Don't Wanna Lose You Baby	1965
	If I Loved You	1965
	A Summer Song	1964
	Willow Weep For Me	1964
	Yesterday's Gone	1963
CHAIRMEN OF THE BOARD		
	Elmo James	1972
	Everything's Tuesday	1970

ARTIST	SONG TITLE	DATE
	Finders Keepers	1973
	Give Me Just A Little More Time	1970
	I'm On My Way To A Better Place	1973
	Pay To The Piper	1970
	Working On A Building Of Love	1972
	(You've Got Me) Dangling On A String	1970
CHAKACHAS	Jungle Fever	1972
CHAKRA	I Am	1997
RICHARD CHAMBERLAIN		
	Hi-Lili, Hi-Lo	1963
	True Love	1963
CHAMBERS BROTHERS		
	I Can't Turn You Loose	1968
	Time Has Come Today	1968
CHAMELEON	The Way It Is	1996
CHAMPAIGN	How 'Bout Us	1981
	Try Again	1983
GENE CHANDLER	Bless Our Love	1964
	Does She Have A Friend?	1980
	Get Down	1979
	Groovy Situation	1970
	Just Be True	1964
	Nothing Can Stop Me	1965
	What Now	1964
CHANELLE	One Man	1989

ARTIST	SONG TITLE	DATE
CHANGE	Change Of Heart	1984
	Let's Go Together	1985
	A Lovers Holiday/The Glow Of Love	1980
	Searching	1980
CHANGING FACES	Foolin' Around	1994
	G.H.E.T.T.O.U.T.	1997
	Stroke You Up	1994
	Time After Time	1998
BRUCE CHANNEL	Keep On	1968
CHANSON	Don't Hold Back	1978
CHANTAYS	Pipeline	1963
HARRY CHAPIN	Cat's In The Cradle	1974
	Sequel	1980
	Taxi	1972
	W.O.L.D.	1974
TRACY CHAPMAN	Fast Car	1988
	Give Me One Reason	1996
CHARLATANS	Can't Get Out Of Bed	1994
	Crashin' In	1995
	Forever	1999
	How High	1997
	I Never Want An Easy Life If Me And He Were Ever To Get There	1994
	Impossible	2000
	Just Lookin'/Bullet Comes	1995
	Just When You're Thinkin' Things Over	1995

ARTIST	SONG TITLE	DATE
	Love Is The Key	2001
	A Man Needs To Be Told	2001
	Me. In Time	1991
	My Beautiful Friend	1999
	North Country Boy	1997
	One To Another	1996
	The Only One I Know	1990
	Over Rising	1991
	Tellin' Stories	1997
	Then	1990
	Try Again Today	2004
	Up At The Lake	2004
	Weirdo	1992
CHARLENE	I've Never Been To Me	1982
CHARLES & EDDIE	House Is Not A Home	1993
	N.Y.C. (Can You Believe This City)	1993
	24-7-365	1995
	Would I Lie To You?	1992
RAY CHARLES	Baby Don't You Cry (The New Swingova Rhythm)	1964
	Booty Butt	1971
	Busted	1963
	Crying Time	1965
	Don't Change On Me	1971
	Don't Set Me Free	1963
	Eleanor Rigby	1968

ARTIST	SONG TITLE	DATE
	Here We Go Again	1967
	I Choose To Sing The Blues	1966
	In The Heat Of The Night	1967
	Let's Go Get Stoned	1966
	My Heart Cries For You	1964
	No One	1963
	No One To Cry To	1964
	Take These Chains From My Heart	1963
	Together Again	1966
	Yesterday	1967
	(QUINCY JONES featuring RAY CHARLES & CHAKA KHAN)	
	I'll Be Good To You	1990
RAY CHARLES SINGERS		
	Al-Di-La	1964
	Love Me With All Your Heart	1964
	One More Time	1964
SONNY CHARLES	Put It In A Magazine	1982
SONNY CHARLES & THE CHECKMATES, LTD.		
	Black Pearl	1969
TINA CHARLES	Dance Little Lady Dance	1976
	Dr. Love	1976
	I Love To Love (But My Baby Loves To Dance)	1976
	I'll Go Where Your Music Takes Me	1978

ARTIST	SONG TITLE	DATE
	Love Bug — Sweets For My Sweet (Medley)	1977
	Love Me Like A Lover	1976
	Rendezvous	1977
CHARLIE	It's Inevitable	1983
CHARTBUSTERS	She's The One	1964
CHAS & DAVE	Ain't No Pleasing You	1982
	Gertcha	1979
	Rabbit	1980
	Stars Over 45	1981
	(MATCHROOM MOB WITH CHAS & DAVE)	
	Snooker Loopy	1986
CHASE	Get It On	1971
JC CHASEZ	Blowin' Me Up (With Her Love)	2003
	Some Girls (Dance With Women)/Blowin' Me Up (With Her Love)	2004
	(BASEMENT JAXX featuring JC CHASEZ)	
	Plug It In	2004
CHEAP TRICK	Ain't That A Shame	1979
	Can't Stop Falling Into Love	1990
	Don't Be Cruel	1977
	Dream Police	1979
	The Flame	1988
	Ghost Town	1988
	I Want You To Want Me	1979
	Voices	1979

ARTIST	SONG TITLE	DATE
OLIVER CHEATHAM	Get Down Saturday Night	1983
	(ROOM 5 featuring OLIVER CHEATHAM)	
	Make Luv	2003
	Music & You	2003
CHUBBY CHECKER	Hey, Bobba Needle	1964
	Lazy Elsie Molly	1964
	Let's Do The Freddie	1965
	Let's Twist Again	1962
	What Do You Say	1963
	(FAT BOYS & CHUBBY CHECKER)	
	The Twist (Yo, Twist)	1988
CHECKMATES LTD.	Proud Mary	1969
CHEECH & CHONG	Basketball Jones featuring Tyrone	
	Shoelaces	1973
	Earache My Eye (featuring Alice Bowie)	1974
	Sister Mary Elephant (Shudd-Up!)	1973
JUDY CHEEKS	Reach	1994
	So In Love (The Real Deal)	1993
	This Time/Respect	1995
	You're The Story Of My Life/As Long	
	As You're Good To Me	1995
CHEEKY GIRLS	Cheeky Flamenco	2004
	Cheeky Song (Touch My Bum)	2002
	Have A Cheeky Christmas	2003
	Hooray Hooray (It's A Cheeky Holiday)	2003
	Take Your Shoes Off	2003

ARTIST	SONG TITLE	DATE
CHEETAHS	Mecca	1964
	Soldier Boy	1965
CHEF	Chocolate Salty Balls (PS I Love You)	1998
CHELSEA F.C.	Blue Is The Colour	1972
	Blue Tomorrow	2000
	No One Can Stop Us Now	1994
	(SUGGS & CO featuring CHELSEA TEAM)	
	Blue Day	1997
CHEMICAL BROTHERS		
	Block Rockin' Beats	1997
	Come With Us/The Test	2002
	Elektrobank	1997
	Hey Boy Hey Girl	1999
	It Began In Afrika	2001
	Leave Home	1995
	Let Forever Be	1999
	Life Is Sweet	1995
	Loops Of Fury EP	1996
	Out Of Control	1999
	Setting Sun	1996
	Star Guitar	2002
CHEQUERS	Hey Miss Payne	1976
	Rock On Brother	1975
CHER	Alfie	1966
	All I Really Want To Do	1965
	All Or Nothing	1999

ARTIST	SONG TITLE	DATE
	Bang Bang (My Baby Shot Me Down)	1966
	Believe	1998
	Could've Been You	1992
	Dark Lady	1974
	Dove L'Amore	1999
	Gypsys, Tramps And Thieves	1971
	Half-Breed	1973
	Heart Of Stone	1990
	I Found Someone	1987
	If I Could Turn Back Time	1989
	Just Like Jesse James	1989
	Living In A House Divided	1972
	Love And Understanding	1991
	The Music's No Good Without You	2001
	Not Enough Love In The World	1996
	Oh No Not My Baby	1992
	One By One	1996
	Save Up All Your Tears	1991
	The Shoop Shoop Song (It's In His Kiss)	1990
	Strong Enough	1999
	The Sun Ain't Gonna Shine Anymore	1996
	Sunny	1966
	Take Me Home	1979
	Too Many Rivers To Cross	1993
	Train Of Thought	1974
	Walking In Memphis	1995

ARTIST	SONG TITLE	DATE
	The Way Of Love	1972
	We All Sleep Alone	1988
	Where Do You Go	1965
	You Better Sit Down Kids	1967
CHER & PETER CETERA		
	After All	1989
CHER WITH BEAVIS & BUTT-HEAD		
	I Got You Babe	1994
CHER, CHRISSIE HYNDE & NENEH CHERRY with		
ERIC CLAPTON	Love Can Build A Bridge	1995
CHERI	Murphy's Law	1982
CHEROKEES	Seven Daffodils	1964
CHERELLE	Never Knew Love Like This	1988
CHERELLE WITH ALEXANDER O'NEAL		
	Saturday Love	1986
EAGLE-EYE CHERRY		
	Are You Still Having Fun	2000
	Falling In Love Again	1998
	Save Tonight	1998
NENEH CHERRY	Buddy X	1993
	Buffalo Stance	1989
	I've Got You Under My Skin	1990
	Inna City Mamma	1989
	Kisses On The Wind	1989
	Kootchi	1996
	Manchild	1989

ARTIST	SONG TITLE	DATE
	Money Love	1992
	Woman	1996
(CHER, CHRISSIE HYNDE & NENEH CHERRY with ERIC CLAPTON)		
	Love Can Build A Bridge	1995
(DREEM TEEM vs NENEH CHERRY)		
	Buddy X 99	1999
(YOUSSOU N'DOUR featuring NENEH CHERRY)		
	7 Seconds	1994
KENNY CHESNEY	Big Star	2002
	Don't Happen Twice	2001
	The Good Stuff	2002
	How Forever Feels	1999
	I Go Back	2004
	I Lost It	2000
	No Shoes, No Shirt, No Problems	2003
	There Goes My Life	2003
	You Had Me From Hello	1999
	Young	2002
KENNY CHESNEY & UNCLE KRACKER		
	When The Sun Goes Down	2004
MARK CHESNUT	I Don't Want To Miss A Thing	1998
CHIC	Dance, Dance, Dance (Yowsah, Yowsah, Yowsah)	1977
	Everybody Dance	1978
	Good Times	1979

ARTIST	SONG TITLE	DATE
	I Want Your Love	1979
	Jack Le Freak	1987
	Le Freak	1978
	My Feet Keep Dancing	1979
	My Forbidden Lover	1979
CHICAGO LOOP	(When She Needs Good Lovin') She Comes To Me	1966
CHICAGO	Alive Again	1978
	Along Comes A Woman	1985
	Another Rainy Day In New York City	1976
	Baby What A Big Surprise	1977
	Beginnings/Colour My World	1971
	Call On Me	1974
	Chasin' The Wind	1991
	Dialogue (Part I & Part II)	1972
	Does Anybody Really Know What Time It Is?	1970
	Feelin' Stronger Every Day	1973
	Free	1971
	Hard Habit To Break	1984
	Hard To Say I'm Sorry	1982
	Harry Truman	1975
	I Don't Wanna Live Without Your Love	1988
	I'm A Man	1970
	(I've Been) Searchin' So Long	1974
	If She Would Have Been Faithful	1987

ARTIST	SONG TITLE	DATE
	If You Leave Me Now	1976
	Just You 'n' Me	1973
	Look Away	1988
	Love Me Tomorrow	1982
	Lowdown	1971
	Make Me Smile	1970
	No Tell Lover	1978
	Old Days	1975
	Questions 67 And 68	1971
	Saturday In The Park	1972
	Stay The Night	1984
	25 Or 6 To 4	1970
	What Kind Of Man Would I Be?	1989
	Will You Still Love Me?	1986
	Wishing You Were Here	1974
	You're Not Alone	1989
	You're The Inspiration	1984
CHICANE	Lost You Somewhere	1997
	No Ordinary Morning/Halcyon	2000
	Offshore	1996
	Strong In Love	1998
	Sunstroke	1997
CHICANE featuring BRYAN ADAMS		
	Don't Give Up	2000

ARTIST	SONG TITLE	DATE
CHICANE featuring MAIRE BRENNAN OF CLANNAD		
	Saltwater	1999
CHICANE featuring PETER CUNNAH		
	Love On The Run	2003
CHICANE WITH POWER CIRCLE		
	Offshore '97	1997
CHICKEN SHACK	I'd Rather Go Blind	1969
CHICKEN SHED	I Am In Love With The World	1997
CHICORY TIP	Good Grief Christina	1973
	Son Of My Father	1972
	What's Your Name	1972
CHIEFTAINS featuring THE CORRS		
	I Know My Love	1999
CHIFFONS	He's So Fine	1963
	One Fine Day	1963
	Sweet Talkin' Guy	1966
CHILD	It's Only Make Believe	1978
	Only You (And You Alone)	1979
	When You Walk In The Room	1978
DESMOND CHILD	Love On A Rooftop	1991
JANE CHILD	Don't Wanna Fall In Love	1990
CHILDREN OF TANSLEY SCHOOL		
	My Mum Is One In A Million	1981
CHILDLINERS	The Gift Of Christmas	1995
CHILI HI FLY	Is It Love?	2000

ARTIST	SONG TITLE	DATE
CHI-LITES	(For God's Sake) Give More Power To	
	The People	1971
	Have You Seen Her/Oh Girl	1975
	Homely Girl	1974
	I Found Sunshine	1974
	It's Time For Love	1975
	A Letter To Myself	1973
	Stoned Out Of My Mind	1973
	Too Good To Be Forgotten	1974
	You Don't Have To Go	1976
CHILL FAC-TORR	Twist (Round 'n' Round)	1983
CHILLIWACK	I Believe	1982
	My Girl (Gone, Gone, Gone)	1981
CHIMES	Heaven	1990
	I Still Haven't Found What I'm Looking	
	For	1990
CHINA BLACK	Almost See You (Somewhere)	1995
	Searching	1994
	Stars	1994
	(LADYSMITH BLACK MAMBAZO featuring	
	CHINA BLACK)	
	Swing Low Sweet Chariot	1995
CHINA CRISIS	Best Kept Secret	1987
	Black Man Ray	1985
	Christian	1983
	King In A Catholic Style (Wake Up)	1985

ARTIST	SONG TITLE	DATE
	Wishful Thinking	1984
CHINGY	Balla Baby	2004
	Holidae Inn	2004
	Right Thurr	2003
CHINGY featuring J. WEAV		
	One Call Away	2004
CHIPPENDALES	Give Me Your Body	1992
CHOCOLATE PUMA	I Wanna Be U	2001
CHOO CHOO PROJECT		
	Phazin' & Phazin'	2000
CHORDS	Maybe Tomorrow	1980
CHRIS CHRISTIAN	I Want You, I Need You	1981
NEIL CHRISTIAN	That's Nice	1966
CHRISTIANS	Born Again	1988
	The Bottle	1993
	Forgotten Town	1987
	Harvest For The World	1988
	Hooverville (They Promised Us The World)	1987
	Ideal World	1988
	What's In A Word	1992
	When The Fingers Point	1987
	Words	1989
	(MARSDEN/MCCARTNEY/JOHNSON/CHRISTIANS)	
	Ferry 'Cross The Mersey	1989
CHRISTIE	San Bernadino	1970
	Yellow River	1970

ARTIST	SONG TITLE	DATE
DAVID CHRISTIE	Saddle Up	1982
JOHN CHRISTIE	Here's To Love (Auld Lang Syne)	1976
LOU CHRISTIE	I'm Gonna Make You Mine	1969
	Lightnin' Strikes	1965
	Rhapsody In The Rain	1966
	She Sold Me Magic	1969
TONY CHRISTIE	Avenues And Alleyways	1973
	Drive Safely Darlin'	1976
	I Did What I Did For Maria	1971
	(Is This The Way To) Amarillo	1971
	Las Vegas	1971
	(ALL SEEING I featuring TONY CHRISTIE)	
	Walk Like A Panther '98	1999
GAVIN CHRISTOPHER		
	One Step Closer To You	1986
SHAWN CHRISTOPHER		
	Don't Lose The Magic	1992
CHUCKS	Loo-Be-Loo	1963
CHUMBAWAMBA	Amnesia	1998
	Top Of The World (Ole, Ole, Ole)	1998
	Tubthumping	1997
CHURCH	Under The Milky Way	1988
CHARLOTTE CHURCH		
	Just Wave Hello	1999
	(JURGEN VRIES featuring CMC)	
	The Opera Song (Brave New World)	2003

ARTIST	SONG TITLE	DATE
CIARA featuring PETEY PABLO		
	Goodies	2004
CICERO	Love Is Everywhere	1992
CINDERELLA	Coming Home	1989
	Don't Know What You Got (Till It's Gone)	1988
	The Last Mile	1989
	Nobody's Fool	1986
	Shelter Me	1990
GIGLIOLA CINQUETTI		
	Go (Before You Break My Heart)	1974
	Non Ho L'Eta Per Amarti	1964
CITIZEN KING	Better Days (And The Bottom Drops Out)	1999
CITY BOY	5.7.0.5	1978
	What A Night	1978
CITY HIGH	What Would You Do?	2001
CITY HIGH featuring EVE		
	Caramel	2001
CK & SUPREME DREAM TEAM		
	Dreamer	2003
	(JAIMESON featuring ANGEL BLU AND CK)	
	Take Control	2004
GARY CLAIL ON-U SOUND SYSTEM		
	Human Nature	1991
GARY CLAIL ON-U SOUND SYSTEM featuring		
BIM SHERMAN	Who Pays The Piper?	1992

ARTIST	SONG TITLE	DATE
CLAIRE & FRIENDS	It's 'Orrible Being In Love (When You're	
	8½)	1986
CLANNAD	In A Lifetime	1989
	Theme From Harry's Game	1982
ERIC CLAPTON	After Midnight	1970
	Bad Love	1990
	Behind The Mask	1987
	Change The World	1996
	Circus	1998
	Forever Man	1985
	Hello Old Friend	1976
	I Can't Stand It	1981
	I Shot The Sheriff	1974
	I've Got A Rock 'n' Roll Heart	1983
	Knockin' On Heaven's Door	1975
	Lay Down Sally	1978
	Layla	1992
	My Father's Eyes	1998
	Promises	1978
	Swing Low Sweet Chariot	1975
	Tears In Heaven	1992
	Tulsa Time	1980
	Watch Out For Lucy	1979
	Willie And The Hand Jive	1974
	Wonderful Tonight	1978
	Wonderful Tonight (Live)	1991

ARTIST	SONG TITLE	DATE
	(BEATCHUGGERS featuring ERIC CLAPTON)	
	Forever Man (How Many Times)	2000
	(CHER, CHRISSIE HYNDE & NENEH CHERRY	
	with ERIC CLAPTON)	
	Love Can Build A Bridge	1995
	(ELTON JOHN & ERIC CLAPTON)	
	Runaway Train	1992
	(STING WITH ERIC CLAPTON)	
	It's Probably Me	1992
DAVE CLARK FIVE	Any Way You Want It	1964
	At The Scene	1966
	Because	1964
	Bits And Pieces	1964
	Can't You See That She's Mine	1964
	Catch Us If You Can	1965
	Come Home	1965
	Do You Love Me	1964
	Everybody Get Together	1970
	Everybody Knows (I Still Love You)	1967
	Glad All Over	1964
	Good Old Rock 'n' Roll	1969
	I Like It Like That	1965
	Live In The Sky	1968
	More Good Old Rock 'n' Roll	1970
	No One Can Break A Heart Like You	1968
	Over And Over	1965

ARTIST	SONG TITLE	DATE
	Please Tell Me Why	1966
	Put A Little Love In Your Heart	1969
	The Red Balloon	1968
	Reelin' And Rockin'	1965
	Thinking Of You Baby	1964
	Try Too Hard	1966
	You Got What It Takes	1967
	You Must Have Been A Beautiful Baby	1967
DEE CLARK	Ride A Wild Horse	1975
GARY CLARK	We Sail On The Stormy Waters	1993
LONI CLARK	Rushing	1993
	U	1994
PETULA CLARK	Casanova/Chariot	1963
	The Cat In The Window	1967
	Color My World	1966
	Don't Give Up	1968
	Don't Sleep In The Subway	1967
	Downtown	1964
	I Couldn't Live Without Your Love	1966
	I Know A Place	1965
	Kiss Me Goodbye	1968
	My Love	1965
	The Other Man's Grass Is Always Greener	1967
	Round Every Corner	1965
	A Sign Of The Times	1966

ARTIST	SONG TITLE	DATE
	The Song Of My Life	1971
	This Is My Song	1967
	Who Am I	1966
	You'd Better Come Home	1965
	You're The One	1965
ROY CLARK	Yesterday, When I Was Young	1969
TERRI CLARK	Girls Lie Too	2004
	I Just Wanna Be Mad	2002
	I Wanna Do It All	2003
	You're Easy On The Eyes	1998
DAVE CLARKE	No One's Driving	1996
	Southside	1996
JOHN COOPER CLARKE		
	Gimmix! Play Loud	1979
STANLEY CLARKE & GEORGE DUKE		
	Sweet Baby	1981
TONY CLARKE	The Entertainer	1965
KELLY CLARKSON	Breakaway	2004
	Low/The Trouble With Us	2003
	Miss Independent	2003
	A Moment Like This	2002
CLASH	Bank Robber	1980
	The Call Up	1980
	Clash City Rockers	1978
	Complete Control	1977
	The Cost Of Living (EP)	1979

ARTIST	SONG TITLE	DATE
	English Civil War (Johnny Comes Marching Home)	1979
	I Fought The Law	1988
	London Calling	1979
	The Magnificent Seven	1981
	Rock The Casbah	1982
	Should I Stay Or Should I Go?/Straight To Hell	1982
	This Is England	1985
	Tommy Gun	1978
	Train In Vain (Stand By Me)	1980
	(White Man) At Hammersmith Palais	1978
	White Riot	1977
CLASSICS IV	Everyday With You Girl	1969
	Traces	1969
CLASSICS IV	What Am I Crying For?	1972
CLASSIX NOUVEAUX		
	Is It A Dream	1982
JUDY CLAY & WILLIAM BELL		
	Private Number	1968
TOM CLAY	What The World Needs Now Is Love/ Abraham, Martin & John	1971
ADAM CLAYTON & LARRY MULLEN		
	Theme From 'Mission: Impossible'	1996
CLEA	Download It	2003
	Stuck In The Middle	2004
CLARENCE CLEMONS & JACKSON BROWNE		
	You're A Friend Of Mine	1985
CLEOPATRA	Cleopatra's Theme	1998
	Come And Get Me	2000
	I Want You Back	1998
	Life Ain't Easy	1998
	A Touch Of Love	1999
CLEPTOMANIACS featuring BRYAN CHAMBERS		
	All I Do	2001
JIMMY CLIFF	I Can See Clearly Now	1993
	Wild World	1970
	Wonderful World, Beautiful People	1969
LINDA CLIFFORD	Bridge Over Troubled Water	1979
CLIMAX	Precious And Few	1972
CLIMAX BLUES BAND		
	Couldn't Get It Right	1977
	I Love You	1981
CLIMIE FISHER	I Won't Bleed For You	1988
	Love Changes (Everything)	1988
	Love Like A River	1988
	Rise To The Occasion	1987
	This Is Me	1988
PATSY CLINE	Crazy	1961
CLIPSE	Grindin'	2002
	When The Last Time	2002

ARTIST	SONG TITLE	DATE
CLIPSE featuring FAITH EVANS		
	Ma, I Don't Love Her	2003
CLIQUE	Sugar On Sunday	1969
CLIVILLES & COLE	A Deeper Love	1992
	Pride (In The Name Of Love)	1992
CLOCK	Axel F/Keep Pushin'	1995
	Blame It On The Boogie	1998
	Everybody	1995
	Holding On 4 U	1996
	In My House	1995
	It's Over	1997
	Keep The Fires Burning	1994
	Oh What A Night	1996
	The Rhythm	1994
	Rock Your Body	1998
	That's The Way (I Like It)	1998
	U Sexy Thing	1997
	Whoomph! (There It Is)	1995
CLOUT	Substitute	1978
CLUB 69	Let Me Be Your Underwear	1992
CLUB NOUVEAU	Lean On Me	1987
	Why You Treat Me So Bad?	1987
CLUBHOUSE	Do It Again/Billie Jean (Medley)	1983
CLUBHOUSE featuring CARL		
	Light My Fire	1994
	Living In The Sunshine	1994

ARTIST	SONG TITLE	DATE
COAST TO COAST	(Do) The Hucklebuck	1981
	Let's Jump The Broomstick	1981
ODIA COATES/PAUL ANKA		
	I Believe There's Nothing Stronger Than Our Love	1975
	I Don't Like To Sleep Alone	1975
	One Man Woman/One Woman Man	1974
	(You're) Having My Baby	1974
EDDIE COCHRAN	C'mon Everybody	1958
	My Way	1963
	Summertime Blues	1958
TOM COCHRANE	Life Is A Highway	1992
COCK ROBIN	The Promise You Made	1986
	When Your Heart Is Weak	1985
BRUCE COCKBURN		
	Wondering Where The Lions Are	1980
JOE COCKER	(All I Know) Feels Like Forever	1992
	Cry Me A River	1970
	Delta Lady	1969
	Feeling Alright	1972
	High Time We Went/Black-Eyed Blues	1971
	Let The Healing Begin	1994
	The Letter	1970
	Midnight Rider	1972
	Now That The Music Has Gone	1992

ARTIST	SONG TITLE	DATE
	She Came In Through The Bathroom Window	1969
	The Simple Things	1994
	Unchain My Heart	1992
	When The Night Comes	1989
	With A Little Help From My Friends	1968
	You Are So Beautiful	1975
JOE COCKER & JENNIFER WARNES		
	Up Where We Belong	1982
COCKEREL CHORUS	Nice One Cyril	1973
COCKNEY REJECTS	The Greatest Cockney Rip-Off	1980
	I'm Forever Blowing Bubbles	1980
COCO	Bad Old Days	1978
	I Need A Miracle	1997
COCTEAU TWINS	Bluebeard	1994
	Evangeline	1993
	Iceblink Luck	1990
	Pearly-Dewdrops Drops	1984
	Tishbite	1996
CODE RED	Can We Talk	1997
	Is There Someone Out There?	1997
COMMANDER CODY & HIS LOST PLANET AIRMEN		
	Hot Rod Lincoln	1972
COFFEE	Casanova	1980
DENNIS COFFEY & THE DETROIT GUITAR BAND		
	Scorpio	1971

ARTIST	SONG TITLE	DATE
	Taurus	1972
IZHAR COHEN & ALPHABETA		
	A-Ba-Ni-Bi	1978
MARC COHN	Walk Through This World	1993
	Walking In Memphis	1991
COLA BOY	7 Ways To Love	1991
COLDCUT	More Beats & Pieces	1997
	Stop This Crazy Thing	1988
COLDCUT featuring LISA STANSFIELD		
	People Hold On	1989
COLDCUT featuring YAZZ & THE PLASTIC POPULATION		
	Doctorin' The House	1988
COLDPLAY	Clocks	2003
	In My Place	2002
	The Scientist	2002
	Shiver	2000
	Trouble	2000
	Yellow	2000
JUDE COLE	Baby, It's Tonight	1990
	Time For Letting Go	1990
LLOYD COLE	Cut Me Down	1986
	Jennifer She Said	1988
	Like Lovers Do	1995
LLOYD COLE & THE COMMOTIONS		
	Brand New Friend	1985
	Lost Weekend	1985

ARTIST	SONG TITLE	DATE
	Perfect Skin	1984
MJ COLE	Crazy Love	2000
	Sincere	1998
	Wondering Why	2003
MJ COLE featuring ELISABETH TROY		
	Hold On To Me	2000
NAT 'KING' COLE	I Don't Want To Be Hurt Anymore	1964
	I Don't Want To See Tomorrow	1964
	Let's Face The Music And Dance	1994
	When I Fall In Love	1987
	(NATALIE COLE & NAT 'KING' COLE)	
	Unforgettable	1991
NATALIE COLE	Everlasting	1988
	I Live For Your Love	1987
	I've Got Love On My Mind	1977
	Inseparable	1975
	Jump Start	1987
	Miss You Like Crazy	1989
	Our Love	1978
	Pink Cadillac	1988
	Someone That I Used To Love	1980
	Sophisticated Lady (She's A Different Lady)	1976
	This Will Be	1975
	Wild Women Do	1990

ARTIST	SONG TITLE	DATE
NATALIE COLE & NAT 'KING' COLE		
	Unforgettable	1991
PAULA COLE	I Don't Want To Wait	1997
	Where Have All The Cowboys Gone?	1997
COLLAPSED LUNG	London Tonight/Eat My Goal	1996
COLLECTIVE SOUL	December	1995
	Shine	1994
	The World I Know	1995
DAVE & ANSIL COLLINS		
	Double Barrel	1971
	Monkey Spanner	1971
EDWYN COLLINS	A Girl Like You	1995
	The Magic Piper (Of Love)	1997
JEFF COLLINS	Only You	1972
JUDY COLLINS	Amazing Grace	1970
	Both Sides Now	1968
	Cook With Honey	1973
	Send In The Clowns	1977
MICHELLE COLLINS	Sunburn	1999
PHIL COLLINS	Against All Odds (Take A Look At Me Now)	1984
	Another Day In Paradise	1989
	Both Sides Of The Story	1993
	Can't Stop Loving You	2002
	Dance Into The Light	1996
	Do You Remember?	1990

ARTIST	SONG TITLE	DATE
	Don't Lose My Number	1985
	Everyday	1994
	Groovy Kind Of Love	1988
	Hang In Long Enough	1990
	I Don't Care Anymore	1983
	I Missed Again	1981
	I Wish It Would Rain Down	1990
	If Leaving Me Is Easy	1981
	In The Air Tonight	1981
	It's In Your Eyes	1996
	One More Night	1985
	Something Happened On The Way To Heaven	1990
	Sussudio	1985
	Take Me Home	1986
	That's Just The Way It Is	1990
	True Colours	1998
	Two Hearts	1988
	You Can't Hurry Love	1982
	You'll Be In My Heart	1999
PHIL COLLINS & MARILYN MARTIN		
	Separate Lives	1985
(BONE THUGS-N-HARMONY featuring PHIL COLLINS)		
	Home	2003
(LIL' KIM featuring PHIL COLLINS)		
	In The Air Tonite	2001

ARTIST	SONG TITLE	DATE
(PHILIP BAILEY & PHIL COLLINS)		
	Easy Lover	1984
RODGER COLLINS	You Sexy Sugar Plumb (But I Like It)	1976
TYLER COLLINS	Girls Nite Out	1990
COLOR ME BADD	All 4 Love	1991
	Choose	1994
	The Earth, The Sun, The Rain	1996
	Forever Love	1992
	I Adore Mi Amor	1991
	I Wanna Sex You Up	1991
	Slow Motion	1992
	Thinkin' Back	1992
	Time And Chance	1993
COLOUR FIELD	Thinking Of You	1985
COLOUR GIRL	Can't Get Used To Losing You	2000
JESSI COLTER	I'm Not Lisa	1975
CHI COLTRANE	Thunder And Lightning	1972
SHAWN COLVIN	Sunny Came Home	1997
SHAWN COLVIN WITH MARY CHAPIN CARPENTER		
	One Cool Remove	1995
COMMENTATORS	N-N-Nineteen Not Out	1985
COMMODORES	Easy	1977
	Fancy Dancer	1977
	Flying High	1978
	Just To Be Close To You	1976
	Lady You Bring Me Up	1981

ARTIST	SONG TITLE	DATE
	Machine Gun	1974
	Nightshift	1985
	Oh No	1981
	Old-Fashioned Love	1980
	Sail On	1979
	Slippery When Wet	1975
	Still	1979
	Sweet Love/Brick House	1977
	Three Times A Lady	1978
	Too Hot Ta Trot/Zoom	1978
	Wonderland	1979
COMMON/ERYKAH		
	Love Of My Life (An Ode To Hip Hop)	2002
	(MARY J. BLIGE featuring COMMON)	
	Dance For Me	2002
COMMUNARDS	Disenchanted	1986
	Don't Leave Me This Way	1986
	For A Friend	1988
	Never Can Say Goodbye	1987
	So Cold The Night	1986
	There's More To Love	1988
	Tomorrow	1987
	You Are My World	1985
PERRY COMO	And I Love You So	1973
	Dream On Little Dreamer	1965
	For The Good Times	1973

ARTIST	SONG TITLE	DATE
	I Think Of You	1971
	I Want To Give	1974
	It's Impossible	1970
	Seattle	1969
	Walk Right Back	1973
COMPANY B	Fascinated	1987
CON FUNK SHUN	Ffun	1977
	Too Tight	1981
CONCEPT	Mr. DJ	1985
CONCRETE BLONDE		
	Joey	1990
CONDUCTOR & THE COWBOY		
	Feeling This Way	2000
CONGREGATION	Softly Whispering I Love You	1971
CONGRESS	40 Miles	1991
ARTHUR CONLEY	Funky Street	1968
	Shake, Rattle & Roll	1967
	Sweet Soul Music	1967
CONNELLS	'74-'75	1995
HARRY CONNICK JR.		
	Recipe For Love/It Had To Be You	1991
RAY CONNIFF & THE SINGERS		
	Somewhere, My Love	1966
BILLY CONNOLLY	D.I.V.O.R.C.E.	1975
	In The Brownies	1979
	No Chance (No Change)	1976

ARTIST	SONG TITLE	DATE
	Super Gran	1985
SARAH CONNOR	Bounce	2004
SARAH CONNOR featuring TQ		
	Let's Get Back To Bed... Boy	2001
NORMAN CONNORS	You Are My Starship	1976
CONSORTIUM	All The Love In The World	1969
BILL CONTI	Gonna Fly Now (Theme From 'Rocky')	1977
CONTOURS	Do You Love Me	1988
	Just A Little Misunderstanding	1970
CONTROL	Dance With Me (I'm Your Ecstasy)	1991
CONVERT	Nightbird	1992
CONWAY BROTHERS		
	Turn It Up	1985
NORMAN COOK featuring BILLY BRAGG/MC WILDSKI		
	Won't Talk About It/Blame It On The	
	Bass	1989
PETER COOK	The Ballad Of Spotty Muldoon	1965
PETER COOK & DUDLEY MOORE		
	Goodbye-Ee	1965
SAM COOKE	Another Saturday Night	1963
	A Change Is Gonna Come	1965
	Cousin Of Mine	1964
	Frankie And Johnny	1963
	Good News	1964
	Good Times	1964
	Shake	1965

ARTIST	SONG TITLE	DATE
	Sugar Dumpling	1965
	Tennessee Waltz	1964
	Wonderful World	1960
COOKIE CREW	Born This Way (Let's Dance)	1989
	Got To Keep On	1989
(BEATMASTERS featuring THE COOKIE CREW)		
	Rok Da House	1988
RITA COOLIDGE	All Time High	1983
	I'd Rather Leave While I'm In Love	1979
	The Way You Do The Things You Do	1978
	We're All Alone	1977
	Words	1978
	You	1978
	(Your Love Has Lifted Me) Higher And	
	Higher	1977
COOLIO	Fantastic Voyage	1994
	It's All The Way Live (Now)	1996
	1, 2, 3, 4 (Sumpin' New)	1996
	Ooh La La	1997
	Too Hot	1995
COOLIO featuring 40 THEVZ		
	C U When U Get There	1997
COOLIO featuring LV		
	Gangsta's Paradise	1995
(B REAL/BUSTA RHYMES/COOLIO/LL COOL J/		

ARTIST	SONG TITLE	DATE
	METHOD MAN)	
	Hit 'Em High (The Monstars' Anthem)	1997
COOLNOTES	In Your Car	1985
	Spend The Night	1985
COOPER TEMPLE CLAUSE		
	Blind Pilots	2003
	Film Maker/Been Training Dogs	2002
	Promises Promises	2003
	Who Needs Enemies?	2002
ALICE COOPER	Bed Of Nails	1989
	Clones (We're All)	1980
	Eighteen	1971
	Elected	1972
	Feed My Frankenstein	1992
	Hello Hurray	1973
	Hey Stupid	1991
	How You Gonna See Me Now	1978
	I Never Cry	1976
	It's Me	1994
	Lost In America	1994
	Love's A Loaded Gun	1991
	No More Mr. Nice Guy	1973
	Only Women	1975
	Poison	1989
	School's Out	1972
	Teenage Lament '74	1974

ARTIST	SONG TITLE	DATE
	You And Me	1977
JULIAN COPE	Beautiful Love	1991
	Charlotte Anne	1988
	I Come From Another Planet, Baby	1996
	Planetary Sit-In	1996
	Shut Your Mouth	1986
	Trampolene	1987
	Try Try Try	1995
IMANI COPPOLA	Legend Of A Cowgirl	1997
CORAL	Bill McCai	2003
	Don't Think You're The First	2003
	Dreaming Of You	2002
	Goodbye	2002
	Pass It On	2003
	Secret Kiss	2003
CORINA	Temptation	1991
CORNELIUS BROTHERS & SISTER ROSE		
	Don't Ever Be Lonely (A Poor Little Fool Like Me)	1972
	I'm Never Gonna Be Alone Anymore	1972
	Too Late To Turn Back Now	1972
	Treat Her Like A Lady	1971
CORNERSHOP	Brimful Of Asha	1998
	Lessons Learned From Rocky I To Rocky III	2002
	Sleep On The Left Side	1998

ARTIST	SONG TITLE	DATE
CORONA	Baby Baby	1995
	I Don't Wanna Be A Star	1995
	Megamix	1997
	The Rhythm Of The Night	1994
	Try Me Out	1995
CORONATION STREET CAST – BARRIE/BRIGGS		
	Always Look On The Bright Side Of Life/	
	Something Stupid	1995
CORRS	Angel	2004
	Breathless	2001
	Dreams	1998
	Give Me A Reason	2001
	Irresistible	2000
	Radio	1999
	Runaway	1999
	So Young	1998
	Summer Sunshine	2004
	What Can I Do?	1998
	Would You Be Happier?	2001
	(THE CHIEFTAINS featuring THE CORRS)	
	I Know My Love	1999
FERRY CORSTEN	Punk	2002
	Rock Your Body Rock	2004
BILL COSBY	Little Ole Man (Uptight — Everything's	
	Alright)	1967
COSMIC GATE	Exploration Of Space	2002

ARTIST	SONG TITLE	DATE
	Fire Wire	2001
COSMIC ROUGH RIDERS		
	Because You	2003
	Justify The Rain	2003
	The Pain Inside	2001
	Revolution (In The Summertime)	2001
COSMOS	Take Me With You	2002
ELVIS COSTELLO	Accidents Will Happen	1979
	Don't Let Me Be Misunderstood	1986
	Everyday I Write The Book	1983
	A Good Year For The Roses	1981
	High Fidelity	1980
	I Can't Stand Up For Falling Down	1980
	(I Don't Wanna Go To) Chelsea	1978
	I Wanna Be Loved/Turning The Town	
	Red	1984
	New Amsterdam	1980
	Oliver's Army	1979
	Pump It Up	1978
	Radio Radio	1978
	She	1999
	Sulky Girl	1994
	Veronica	1989
	Watchin' The Detectives	1977
GENE COTTON	Before My Heart Finds Out	1978
	Like A Sunday In Salem (The Amos &	

ARTIST	SONG TITLE	DATE
	Andy Show)	1978
	You Got Me Runnin'	1976
GENE COTTON with KIM CARNES		
	You're A Part Of Me	1978
MIKE COTTON'S JAZZMEN		
	Swing That Hammer	1963
COUGARS	Saturday Nite At The Duck-Pond	1963
COUNCIL COLLECTIVE		
	Soul Deep	1984
COUNT FIVE	Psychotic Reaction	1966
COUNTING CROWS	Accidentally In Love	2004
	American Girls	2002
	Hanginaround	1999
COUNTING CROWS featuring VANESSA CARLTON		
	Big Yellow Taxi	2003
COURSE	Ain't Nobody	1997
	Ready Or Not	1997
TINA COUSINS	Killin' Time	1999
	Pray	1998
	(SASH! featuring TINA COUSINS)	
	Mysterious Times	1998
DON COVAY	I Was Checkin' Out She Was Checkin' In	1973
	It's Better To Have (And Don't Need)	1974
	Mercy Mercy	1964
COVEN	One Tin Soldier	1971
COVER GIRLS	Because Of You	1987

ARTIST	SONG TITLE	DATE
	My Heart Skips A Beat	1989
	Promise Me	1988
	We Can't Go Wrong	1989
	Wishing On A Star	1992
COVERDALE PAGE	Take Me For A Little While	1993
JULIE COVINGTON	Don't Cry For Me Argentina	1976
	Only Women Bleed	1977
COWSILLS	Hair	1969
	Indian Lake	1968
	The Rain, The Park & Other Things	1967
	We Can Fly	1968
CARL COX	Does It Feel Good To You	1992
	Phuture 2000	1999
	Sensual Sophis-Ti-Cat/The Player	1996
	Two Paintings And A Drum	1996
DEBORAH COX	Nobody's Supposed To Be Here	1998
	Sentimental	1995
	Who Do U Love	1996
DEBORAH COX WITH R.L.		
	We Can't Be Friends	1999
DJ CARL COX	I Want You (Forever)	1991
PETER COX	Ain't Gonna Cry Again	1997
	If You Walk Away	1997
	What A Fool Believes	1998
GRAHAM COXON	Bittersweet Bundle Of Misery	2004
	Freakin' Out/All Over Me	2004

ARTIST	SONG TITLE	DATE
	Spectacular	2004
JIMMY COZIER	She's All I Got	2001
SARAH CRACKNELL	Anymore	1996
BILLY 'CRASH' CRADDOCK		
	Rub It In	1974
	Ruby Baby	1974
CRADLE OF FILTH	Babalon A.D. (So Glad For The Madness)	2003
CRAIG	At This Time Of Year	2000
CRAMPS	Bikini Girls With Machine Guns	1990
CRANBERRIES	Dreams	1994
	Free To Decide/When You're Gone	1996
	Linger	1993
	Ode To My Family	1994
	Promises	1999
	Ridiculous Thoughts	1995
	Salvation	1996
	Zombie	1994
LES CRANE	Desiderata	1971
CRANES	Jewel	1993
CRASH TEST DUMMIES		
	Afternoons & Coffeespoons	1994
	The Ballad Of Peter Pumpkinhead	1995
	Mmm Mmm Mmm Mmm	1994
BEVERLEY CRAVEN	Holding On	1991
	Love Scenes	1993

ARTIST	SONG TITLE	DATE
	Promise Me	1991
	Woman To Woman	1991
BILLY CRAWFORD	Trackin'	2003
	You Didn't Expect That	2003
MICHAEL CRAWFORD/SARAH BRIGHTMAN		
	The Music Of The Night/Wishing You Were Somehow Here Again	1987
RANDY CRAWFORD	Almaz	1986
	One Day I'll Fly Away	1980
	Rainy Night In Georgia	1981
	You Might Need Somebody	1981
ROBERT CRAY BAND		
	Smoking Gun	1987
CRAZY ELEPHANT	Gimme Gimme Good Lovin'	1969
CRAZY TOWN	Butterfly	2001
	Revolving Door	2001
CREAM	Anyone For Tennis (The Savage Seven Theme)	1968
	Badge	1969
	Crossroads	1969
	I Feel Free	1966
	Strange Brew	1967
	Sunshine Of Your Love	1968
	White Room	1968
	Wrapping Paper	1966
CREATION	Painter Man	1966

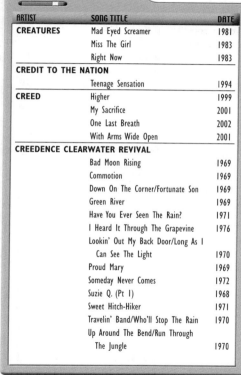

ARTIST	SONG TITLE	DATE
CREATURES	Mad Eyed Screamer	1981
	Miss The Girl	1983
	Right Now	1983
CREDIT TO THE NATION		
	Teenage Sensation	1994
CREED	Higher	1999
	My Sacrifice	2001
	One Last Breath	2002
	With Arms Wide Open	2001
CREEDENCE CLEARWATER REVIVAL		
	Bad Moon Rising	1969
	Commotion	1969
	Down On The Corner/Fortunate Son	1969
	Green River	1969
	Have You Ever Seen The Rain?	1971
	I Heard It Through The Grapevine	1976
	Lookin' Out My Back Door/Long As I Can See The Light	1970
	Proud Mary	1969
	Someday Never Comes	1972
	Suzie Q. (Pt 1)	1968
	Sweet Hitch-Hiker	1971
	Travelin' Band/Who'll Stop The Rain	1970
	Up Around The Bend/Run Through The Jungle	1970

ARTIST	SONG TITLE	DATE
MARSHALL CRENSHAW		
	Someday, Someway	1982
KID CREOLE & THE COCONUTS		
	Annie I'm Not Your Daddy	1982
	Dear Addy	1982
	I'm A Wonderful Thing (Baby)	1982
	Me No Pop I	1981
	The Sex Of It	1990
	Stool Pigeon	1982
	There's Something Wrong In Paradise	1983
CRESCENDO	Are You Out There	1995
BOB CREWE GENERATION		
	Music To Watch Girls By	1966
CRICKETS	Don't Try To Change Me	1963
	My Little Girl	1963
	(They Call Her) La Bamba	1964
	(BUDDY HOLLY & THE CRICKETS)	
	You've Got Love	1964
CRIMINAL ELEMENT ORCH/WENDELL WILLIAMS		
	Everybody (Rap)	1990
CRISPY AND CO.	Get It Together	1975
	Brazil	1975
CRITTERS	Don't Let The Rain Fall Down On Me	1967
	Mr. Dieingly Sad	1966
	Younger Girl	1966

ARTIST	SONG TITLE	DATE
JIM CROCE	Bad, Bad Leroy Brown	1973
	I Got A Name	1973
	I'll Have To Say I Love You In A Song	1974
	One Less Set Of Footprints	1973
	Operator (That's Not The Way It Feels)	1972
	Time In A Bottle	1973
	Workin' At The Car Wash Blues	1974
	You Don't Mess Around With Jim	1972
CROOKLYN CLAN/FATMAN SCOOP		
	Be Faithful	2003
	It Takes Scoop	2004
BING CROSBY	White Christmas	1977
(DAVID BOWIE & BING CROSBY)		
	Peace On Earth/Little Drummer Boy	1982
DAVID CROSBY	Immigration Man	1972
CROSBY, STILLS & NASH		
	Just A Song Before I Go	1977
	Marrakesh Express	1969
	Southern Cross	1982
	Wasted On The Way	1982
CROSBY, STILLS, NASH & YOUNG		
	Ohio	1970
	Our House	1970
	Suite: Judy Blue Eyes	1969
	Teach Your Children	1970
	Woodstock	1972

ARTIST	SONG TITLE	DATE
CROSS COUNTRY	In The Midnight Hour	1973
CHRISTOPHER CROSS		
	All Right	1983
	Arthur's Theme (Best That You Can Do)	1981
	Never Be The Same	1980
	No Time For Talk	1983
	Ride Like The Wind	1980
	Sailing	1980
	Say You'll Be Mine	1981
	Think Of Laura	1983
CROW	Evil Woman Don't Play Your Games With Me	1969
SHERYL CROW	All I Wanna Do	1994
	Anything But Down	1999
	Can't Cry Anymore	1995
	A Change Would Do You Good	1997
	Everyday Is A Winding Road	1997
	The First Cut Is The Deepest	2003
	Hard To Make A Stand	1997
	Home	1997
	If It Makes You Happy	1996
	My Favorite Mistake	1998
	Run, Baby, Run	1995
	Soak Up The Sun	2002
	Strong Enough	1994
	Sweet Child O' Mine	1999

ARTIST	SONG TITLE	DATE
	There Goes The Neighbourhood	1998
	Tomorrow Never Dies	1997
CROWD	You'll Never Walk Alone	1985
CROWDED HOUSE	Distant Sun	1993
	Don't Dream It's Over	1987
	Fall At Your Feet	1991
	Fingers Of Love	1994
	Four Seasons In One Day	1992
	Instinct	1996
	It's Only Natural	1992
	Locked Out	1994
	Nails In My Feet	1993
	Not The Girl You Think You Are	1996
	Pineapple Head	1994
	Something So Strong	1987
	Weather With You	1992
RODNEY CROWELL		
	Ashes By Now	1980
CROWN HEIGHTS AFFAIR		
	Galaxy Of Love	1978
	You Gave Me Love	1980
CRUCIAL CONFLICT	Hay	1996
JULEE CRUISE	Falling	1990
CRUSADERS	Street Life	1979
BOBBY CRUSH	Borsalino	1972
CRW	I Feel Love	2000

ARTIST	SONG TITLE	DATE
CRYIN' SHAMES	Please Stay	1966
CRYSTALS	Da Doo Ron Ron	1963
	I Wonder	1964
	Then He Kissed Me	1963
CUBAN BOYS	Cognoscenti Vs Intelligentsia	1999
CUBIC 22	Night In Motion	1991
CUD	Neurotica	1994
	Purple Love Balloon	1992
	Rich And Strange	1992
CUFF LINKS	Tracy	1969
	When Julie Comes Around	1970
JAMIE CULLUM	These Are The Days/Frontin'	2004
CULT	Fire Woman	1989
	Lil' Devil	1987
	Love Removal Machine	1987
	Rain	1985
	Revolution	1985
	She Sells Sanctuary	1985
	Sun King/Edie (Ciao Baby)	1989
	Wild Flower	1987
	Wild Hearted Son	1991
CULTURE BEAT	Anything	1994
	Crying In The Rain	1996
	Got To Get It	1993
	Inside Out	1996
	Mr. Vain	1993

ARTIST	SONG TITLE	DATE
	World In Our Hands	1994
CULTURE CLUB	Church Of The Poison Mind	1983
	Do You Really Want To Hurt Me	1982
	God Thank You Woman	1986
	I Just Wanna Be Loved	1998
	I'll Tumble 4 Ya	1983
	It's A Miracle	1984
	Karma Chameleon	1983
	The Medal Song	1984
	Miss Me Blind	1984
	Mistake No. 3	1984
	Move Away	1986
	Time (Clock Of The Heart)	1983
	Victims	1983
	The War Song	1984
	Your Kisses Are Charity	1999
SMILEY CULTURE	Police Officer	1984
BURTON CUMMINGS		
	Stand Tall	1976
	You Saved My Soul	1981
LARRY CUNNINGHAM & THE MIGHTY AVONS		
	A Tribute To Jim Reeves	1964
CUPID'S INSPIRATION		
	Yesterday Has Gone	1968
CUPIDS	Brenda	1976

ARTIST	SONG TITLE	DATE
MIKE CURB CONGREGATION		
	Burning Bridges	1970
CURE	Boys Don't Cry	1986
	Catch	1987
	The Caterpillar	1984
	Close To Me	1990
	The End Of The World	2004
	A Forest	1980
	Friday, I'm In Love	1992
	Hanging Garden	1982
	High	1992
	In Between Days	1985
	Just Like Heaven	1987
	A Letter To Elise	1992
	The Love Cats	1983
	Lovesong	1989
	Lullaby	1989
	Mint Car	1996
	Never Enough	1990
	Pictures Of You	1990
	Primary	1981
	Talking Off	2004
	The 13th	1996
	The Walk	1983
	Why Can't I Be You?	1987

ARTIST	SONG TITLE	DATE
CURIOSITY KILLED THE CAT		
	Down To Earth	1987
	Misfit	1987
	Name And Number	1989
	Ordinary Day	1987
(CURIOSITY)		
	Hang On In There Baby	1992
CURVE	Blackerthreetracker (EP)	1993
	Clipped	1991
	Coast Is Clear	1991
	Fait Accompli	1992
	Horror Head (EP)	1992
CURVED AIR	Back Street Luv	1971
JON CUTLER featuring E-MAN		
	It's Yours	2002
CUTTING CREW	(I Just) Died In Your Arms	1987
	I've Been In Love Before	1987
	One For The Mockingbird	1987
CYGNUS X	Superstring	2001
CYMARRON	Rings	1971
JOHNNY CYMBAL	Mr. Bass Man	1963
CYPRESS HILL	Dr. Greenthumb	1999
	Highlife/Can't Get The Best Of Me	2000
	I Ain't Goin' Out Like That	1993
	Illusions	1996
	Insane In The Brain	1993
	Lick A Shot	1994
	Lowrider/Trouble	2001
	(Rap) Superstar/(Rock) Superstar	2000
	Tequila Sunrise	1998
	Throw Your Set In The Air	1995
	When The Sh.. Goes Down	1993
CYRKLE	Red Rubber Ball	1966
	Turn-Down Day	1966
BILLY RAY CYRUS	Achy Breaky Heart	1992
	Could've Been Me	1992
D TRAIN	Music Part I	1983
	You're The One For Me	1982
BOBBY D'AMBROSIO featuring MICHELLE WEEKS		
	Moment Of My Life	1997
D'ANGELO	Brown Sugar	1995
	Cruisin'	1996
	Lady	1996
	Untitled (How Does It Feel)	2000
(GENIUS/GZA featuring D'ANGELO)		
	Cold World	1996
(METHOD MAN featuring D'ANGELO)		
	Break Ups 2 Make Ups	1999
D'BORA	Going Round	1995
D'INFLUENCE	Hypnotize	1997
	Rock With You	1998
D'MENACE	Deep Menace (Spank)	1998

ARTIST	SONG TITLE	DATE
CHUCK D/ANTHRAX		
	Bring The Noise	1991
	(PUBLIC DOMAIN featuring CHUCK D)	
	Rock Da Funky Beats	2001
DIMPLES D	Sucker DJ	1990
MAXWELL D	Serious	2001
D-SHAKE	Yaah/Techno Trance	1990
D-SIDE	Invisible	2003
	Pushin' Me Out	2004
	Real World	2003
	Speechless	2003
D. MOB featuring CATHY DENNIS		
	C'mon And Get My Love	1989
	Why	1994
D. MOB featuring GARY HAISMAN		
	We Call It Acieed	1988
D. MOB featuring LRS		
	It Is Time To Get Funky	1989
D. MOB featuring NUFF JUICE		
	Put Your Hands Together	1990
D.B.M. AND T	Mr. President	1970
D.J. JAZZY JEFF & THE FRESH PRINCE		
	Boom! Shake That Room	1993
	Can't Wait To Be With You	1994
	I'm Looking For The One (To Be With Me)	1993
	Girls Ain't Nothing But Trouble	1986

ARTIST	SONG TITLE	DATE
	Lovely Daze	1998
	A Nightmare On My Street	1988
	Parents Just Don't Understand	1988
	Ring My Bell	1991
	Summertime	1991
D.J.H. featuring STEFY		
	I Like It	1991
	Think About...	1991
D12	Fight Music	2001
	How Come	2004
	My Band	2004
	Purple Hills	2001
	Shit On You	2001
D:REAM	Blame It On Me	1994
	Party Up The World	1995
	The Power (Of All The Love In The World)	1995
	Shoot Me With Your Love	1995
	Star/I Like It	1993
	Take Me Away	1994
	Things Can Only Get Better	1994
	U R The Best Thing	1994
	Unforgiven	1993
AZZIDO DA BASS	Dooms Night	2000
DA BRAT	Fa All Y'all	1994
	Funkdafied	1994

ARTIST	SONG TITLE	DATE
	Give It 2 You	1995
	Sittin' On Top Of The World	1996
DA BRAT featuring T-BOZ		
	Ghetto Love	1997
DA BRAT featuring TYRESE		
	What'chu Like	2000
	(JD featuring DA BRAT)	
	The Party Continues	1998
	(LIL' KIM featuring DA BRAT, LEFT EYE, MISSY ELLIOTT)	
	Not Tonight	1997
	(MISSY 'MISDEMEANOR' ELLIOTT featuring DA BRAT)	
	Sock It 2 Me	1997
DA CLICK	Good Rhymes	1999
	We Are Da Click	1999
DA FOOL	No Good	1999
DA HOOL	Bora Bora	1998
	Meet Her At The Love Parade	1998
DA MOB featuring JOCELYN BROWN		
	Fun	1998
DA MUTTZ	Wassuup	2000
RUI DA SILVA featuring CASSANDRA		
	Touch Me	2001
PAUL DA VINCI	Your Baby Ain't Your Baby Anymore	1974

ARTIST	SONG TITLE	DATE
TERRY DACTYL & THE DINOSAURS		
	Seaside Shuffle	1972
DADDY DEWDROP	Chick-A-Boom	1971
DAFT PUNK	Around The World	1997
	Burnin'	1997
	Da Funk/Musique	1997
	Digital Love	2001
	Harder Better Faster Stronger	2001
	One More Time	2000
DAISY CHAINSAW	Love Your Money	1992
DAKATOS	The Cruel Sea	1963
DALE & GRACE	Stop And Think It Over	1964
ROGER DALTREY	Free Me	1980
	Giving It All Away	1973
	I'm Free	1973
	Without Your Love	1980
DAMAGE	Forever	1996
	Ghetto Romance	2000
	Love Guaranteed	1997
	Love II Love	1996
	Love Lady	1997
	Rumours	2000
	So What If I	2001
	Still Be Lovin' You	2001
	Wonderful Tonight	1997
DAMIAN	The Time Warp (Saw Remix)	1989

ARTIST	SONG TITLE	DATE
MICHAEL DAMIAN	Cover Of Love	1989
	Rock On	1989
	Was It Nothing At All	1989
DAMN YANKEES	High Enough	1990
	Where You Goin' Now	1992
DAMNED	Alone Again Or	1987
	Anything	1986
	Eloise	1986
	Gigolo	1987
	Grimly Fiendish	1985
	Is It A Dream	1985
	Love Song	1979
	The Shadow Of Love	1985
	Smash It Up	1979
LIZ DAMON'S ORIENT EXPRESS		
	1900 Yesterday	1970
VIC DAMONE	You Were Only Fooling	1965
RICHIE DAN	Call It Fate	2000
DAN-I	Monkey Chop	1979
DANA	All Kinds Of Everything	1970
	Fairytale	1976
	It's Gonna Be A Cold Cold Christmas	1975
	Never Gonna Fall In Love Again	1976
	Please Tell Him I Said Hello	1975
	Who Put The Lights Out	1971

ARTIST	SONG TITLE	DATE
DANA INTERNATIONAL		
	Diva	1998
VIC DANA	I Love You Drops	1966
	Red Roses For A Blue Lady	1965
	Shangri-La	1964
DANCE 2 TRANCE	P.Ower Of A.Merican N.Atives	1993
	Take A Free Fall	1993
EVAN DANDO	Stop My Head	2003
DANDY WARHOLS	Bohemian Like You	2001
	Boys Better	1998
	Every Day Should Be A Holiday	1998
	Get Off	2002
	Not If You Were The Last Junkie On Earth	1998
	We Used To Be Friends	2003
	You Were The Last High	2003
CHARLIE DANIELS BAND		
	The Devil Went Down To Georgia	1979
	In America	1980
	The Legend Of Wooley Swamp	1980
	The South's Gonna Do It	1975
	Still In Saigon	1982
	Uneasy Rider	1973
DANNY & THE JUNIORS		
	At The Hop	1976
DANNY WILSON	Mary's Prayer	1987
	The Second Summer Of Love	1989

ARTIST	SONG TITLE	DATE
STEVEN DANTE	I'm Too Scared	1988
	(JELLYBEAN featuring STEVEN DANTE)	
	The Real Thing	1987
DANZEL	Pump It Up	2004
DAPHNE & CELESTE		
	Ooh Stick You!	2000
	School's Out	2000
	Ugly	2000
TERENCE TRENT D'ARBY		
	Dance Little Sister	1988
	Delicate	1993
	Do You Love Me Like You Say?	1993
	Holding On To You	1995
	If You Let Me Stay	1987
	Let Her Down Easy	1993
	She Kissed Me	1993
	Sign Your Name	1988
	Wishing Well	1988
MATT DAREY & MARCELLA WOODS		
	U Shine On	2002
MATT DAREY presents DSP		
	From Russia With Love	2000
MATT DAREY presents MASH UP		
	Liberation (Temptation – Fly Like An Angel)	1999

ARTIST	SONG TITLE	DATE
MATT DAREY'S MASH UP presents MARCELLA WOODS		
	Beautiful	2000
BOBBY DARIN	Eighteen Yellow Roses	1963
	If I Were A Carpenter	1966
	Lovin' You	1967
DARIUS	Colourblind	2002
	Girl In The Moon	2003
	Incredible (What I Meant To Say)	2003
	Kinda Love	2004
	Rushes	2002
DARK STAR	Graceadelica	2000
	I Am The Sun	2000
DARKMAN	Yabba Dabba Doo	1994
DARKNESS	Christmas Time (Don't Let The Bells End)	2003
	Growing On Me	2003
	I Believe In A Thing Called Love	2003
	Love Is Only A Feeling	2004
DARLING BUDS	Hit The Ground	1989
GUY DARRELL	I've Been Hurt	1973
JAMES DARREN	All	1967
DARTS	The Boy From New York City	1978
	Come Back My Love	1978
	Daddy Cool/The Girl Can't Help It	1977
	Don't Let It Fade Away	1978
	Duke Of Earl	1979
	Get It	1979

ARTIST	SONG TITLE	DATE
	It's Raining	1978
	Let's Hang On	1980
DARUDE	Feel The Beat	2000
	Out Of Control (Back For More)	2001
	Sandstorm	2000
DAS EFX	They Want Efx	1992
	(ICE CUBE featuring DAS EFX)	
	Check Yo Self	1993
THE DATSUNS	Harmonic Generator	2003
	In Love	2002
DAVID & DAVID	Welcome To The Boomtown	1986
DAVID & JONATHAN		
	Lovers Of The World Unite	1966
	Michelle	1966
ANN-MARIE DAVID	Wonderful Dream	1973
CRAIG DAVID	Fill Me In	2001
	Hidden Agenda	2003
	Rendezvous	2001
	7 Days	2001
	Spanish	2003
	Walking Away	2000
	What's Your Flava?	2002
	World Filled With Love	2003
CRAIG DAVID featuring STING		
	Rise & Fall	2003

ARTIST	SONG TITLE	DATE
	(ARTFUL DODGER & ROBBIE CRAIG featuring CRAIG DAVID)	
	Woman Trouble	2000
	(ARTFUL DODGER featuring CRAIG DAVID)	
	Re-Rewind The Crowd Say Bo Selecta	1999
F.R. DAVID	Words	1983
PAUL DAVIDSON	Midnight Rider	1975
DAVE DAVIES	Death Of A Clown	1967
	Susannah's Still Alive	1967
WINDSOR DAVIES & DON ESTELLE		
	Whispering Grass	1975
ALANA DAVIS	32 Flavors	1997
BILLIE DAVIS	He's The One	1963
	I Want You To Be My Baby	1968
	Tell Him	1963
MAC DAVIS	Baby Don't Get Hooked On Me	1972
	It's Hard To Be Humble	1980
	One Hell Of A Woman	1974
	Rock 'n' Roll (I Gave You The Best Years Of My Life)	1974
	Stop And Smell The Roses	1974
PAUL DAVIS	Cool Night	1981
	Do Right	1980
	I Go Crazy	1977
	Love Or Let Me Be Lonely	1982
	Ride 'Em Cowboy	1974

ARTIST	SONG TITLE	DATE
	'65 Love Affair	1982
	Superstar	1976
	Sweet Life	1978
ROY DAVIS JR. featuring PEVEN EVERETT		
	Gabriel	1997
SAMMY DAVIS JR.	Don't Blame The Children	1967
	I've Gotta Be Me	1968
SKEETER DAVIS	The End Of The World	1963
SPENCER DAVIS GROUP		
	Gimme Some Lovin'	1966
	I'm A Man	1967
	Keep On Runnin'	1965
	Mr Second Class	1968
	Somebody Help Me	1966
	Time Seller	1967
	When I Come Home	1966
TYRONE DAVIS	Can I Change My Mind	1968
	Give It Up (Turn It Loose)	1976
	Is It Something You've Got	1969
	There It Is	1973
	Turn Back The Hands Of Time	1970
DAWN	See Tony Orlando	
DANA DAWSON	Got To Give Me Love	1995
	Show Me	1996
	3 Is Family	1995
DARREN DAY	Summer Holiday Medley	1996

ARTIST	SONG TITLE	DATE
DORIS DAY	Move Over Darling	1964
MORRIS DAY	Fishnet	1988
TAYLOR DAYNE	Can't Get Enough Of Your Love	1993
	Don't Rush Me	1988
	Heart Of Stone	1990
	I'll Always Love You	1988
	I'll Be Your Shelter	1990
	I'll Wait	1994
	Love Will Lead You Back	1990
	Prove Your Love	1988
	Tell It To My Heart	1987
	With Every Beat Of My Heart	1989
DAZZ BAND	Let It All Blow	1984
	Let It Whip	1982
DB BOULEVARD	Point Of View	2002
DC TALK	Just Between You And Me	1996
DE LA SOUL	Breakadawn	1993
	Eye Know	1989
	The Magic Number/Buddy	1989
	Me Myself And I	1989
	Ring Ring Ring (Ha Ha Hey)	1991
	A Rolling Skating Jam Named Saturdays	1991
	Say No Go	1989
DE LA SOUL featuring CHAKA KHAN		
	All Good	2000

ARTIST	SONG TITLE	DATE
DE LA SOUL featuring REDMAN		
	Oooh	2000
	(QUEEN LATIFAH & DE LA SOUL)	
	Mamma Gave Birth To The Soul Children	1990
VINCENT DE MOOR		
	Fly Away	2001
DE NADA	Bring It On To My Love	2002
	Love You Anyway	2001
DE NUIT	All That Mattered (Love You Down)	2002
WILLIAM DEVAUGHN		
	Be Thankful For What You've Got	1974
TONY DE VIT	Burning Up	1995
	(99TH FLOOR ELEVATORS featuring TONY DE VIT)	
	Hooked	1995
	I'll Be There	1996
DE'LACY	Hideaway	1995
	That Look	1996
DEACON BLUE	Cover From The Sky	1991
	Dignity	1994
	Fergus Sings The Blues	1989
	Four Bacharach & David Songs (EP)	1990
	Hang Your Head (EP)	1993
	I Was Right And You Were Wrong	1994
	Love And Regret	1989
	Only Tender Love	1993
	Queen Of The New Year	1990

ARTIST	SONG TITLE	DATE
	Real Gone Kid	1988
	Twist & Shout	1991
	Wages Day	1989
	When Will You Make My Telephone Ring	1988
	Will We Be Lovers	1993
	Your Swaying Arms	1991
	Your Town	1992
DEAD 60S	Riot Radio	2004
DEAD END KIDS	Have I The Right?	1977
DEAD KENNEDYS	Too Drunk To Fuck	1981
DEAD OR ALIVE	Brand New Lover	1987
	In Too Deep	1985
	Lover Come Back To Me	1985
	My Heart Goes Bang (Get Me To The Doctor)	1985
	Something In My House	1987
	That's The Way (I Like It)	1984
	You Spin Me Round (Like A Record)	1985
DEADEYE DICK	New Age Girl	1994
BILL DEAL & THE RHONDELS		
	I've Been Hurt	1969
	May I	1969
	What Kind Of Fool Do You Think I Am	1969
DEAN & JEAN	Hey Jean, Hey Dean	1964
HAZELL DEAN	Maybe (We Should Call It A Day)	1988
	Searchin'	1984

ARTIST	SONG TITLE	DATE
	Turn It Into Love	1988
	Whatever I Do (Wherever I Go)	1984
	Who's Leaving Who	1988
JIMMY DEAN	I.O.U.	1976
LETITIA DEAN & PAUL MEDFORD		
	Something Outa Nothing	1986
DEATH IN VEGAS	Aisha	2000
	Dirge	2000
	Hands Around My Throat	2002
DEATH IN VEGAS WITH LIAM GALLAGHER		
	Scorpio Rising	2002
DEBARGE	All This Love	1983
	I Like It	1983
	Rhythm Of The Night	1985
	Time Will Reveal	1983
	Who's Holding Donna Now	1985
CHICO DEBARGE	Talk To Me	1986
EL DEBARGE	Who's Johnny	1986
	(QUINCY JONES featuring AL B. SURE!, JAMES INGRAM, EL DEBARGE)	
	Secret Garden	1990
CHRIS DE BURGH	Don't Pay The Ferryman	1983
	Lady In Red	1987
	Missing You	1988
	Separate Tables	1992
	The Simple Truth	1991

ARTIST	SONG TITLE	DATE
	So Beautiful	1997
	A Spaceman Came Travelling/The Ballroom Of Romance	1986
DECLAN featuring YOUNG VOICES CHOIR		
	Tell Me Why	2002
DEE DEE	Forever	2002
	The One	2003
DAVE DEE, DOZY, BEAKY, MICK & TICH		
	Bend It!	1966
	Don Juan	1969
	Hideaway	1966
	Hold Tight!	1966
	Last Night In Soho	1968
	The Legend Of Xanadu	1968
	Okay!	1967
	Save Me	1966
	Snake In The Grass	1969
	Touch Me, Touch Me	1967
	The Wreck Of The 'Antoinette'	1968
	You Make It Move	1965
	Zabadak!	1967
KIKI DEE	Chicago	1977
	First Thing In The Morning	1977
	I've Got The Music In Me	1974
	Loving And Free/Amoureuse	1973
	Star	1981

ARTIST	SONG TITLE	DATE
	(You Don't Know) How Glad I Am	1975
	(ELTON JOHN & KIKI DEE)	
	Don't Go Breaking My Heart	1976
	True Love	1993
DEEE-LITE	Groove Is In The Heart	1990
	Power Of Love/Deee-Lite Theme	1990
DEELE	Two Occasions	1988
DEEP BLUE SOMETHING		
	Breakfast At Tiffany's	1995
	Josey	1996
DEEP DISH	Flashdance	2004
DEEP DISH WITH EBTG		
	The Future Of The Future	1998
DEEP FEELING	Do You Love Me	1970
DEEP FOREST	Deep Forest	1994
	Marta's Song	1995
	Savanna Dance	1994
	Sweet Lullaby	1994
DEEP PURPLE	Black Night	1970
	Fireball	1971
	Hush	1968
	Kentucky Woman	1968
	Never Before	1972
	New Live And Rare (EP)	1977
	Smoke On The Water	1973
	Strange Kind Of Woman	1971

ARTIST	SONG TITLE	DATE
DEEPEST BLUE	Deepest Blue	2003
	Give It Away	2004
	Is It A Sin	2004
RICK DEES & HIS CAST OF IDIOTS		
	Disco Duck	1976
DEETAH	El Paradiso Rico	1999
	Relax	1998
	(RICHARD BLACKWOOD featuring DEETAH)	
	1-2-3-4 Get With The Wicked	2000
DEF LEPPARD	Action	1994
	All I Want Is Everything	1996
	Animal	1987
	Armageddon It	1988
	Foolin'	1983
	Have You Ever Needed Someone So Bad	1992
	Heaven Is	1993
	Hysteria	1988
	Let's Get Rocked	1992
	Long Long Way To Go	2003
	Love Bites	1988
	Make Love Like A Man	1992
	Miss You In A Heartbeat	1993
	Now	2002
	Photograph	1983
	Pour Some Sugar On Me	1988
	Rock Of Ages	1983

ARTIST	SONG TITLE	DATE
	Rocket	1989
	Slang	1996
	Stand Up (Kick Love Into Motion)	1992
	Tonight	1993
	Two Steps Behind	1993
	When Love & Hate Collide	1995
	Work It Out	1996
DEFAULT	Wasting My Time	2002
DEFINITION OF SOUND		
	Moira Jane's Cafe	1992
	Pass The Vibes	1995
	Wear Your Love Like Heaven	1991
DEFRANCO FAMILY	Abra-Ca-Dabra	1973
DEFRANCO FAMILY featuring TONY DEFRANCO		
	Heartbeat — It's A Lovebeat	1973
	Save The Last Dance For Me	1974
DEFTONES	Minerva	2003
	My Own Summer (Shove It)	1998
DEGREES OF MOTION		
	Do You Want It Right Now	1994
DEGREES OF MOTION featuring BITI		
	Do You Want It Right Now	1992
	Shine On	1994
DESMOND DEKKER & THE ACES		
	Israelites	1969
	It Mek	1969

ARTIST	SONG TITLE	DATE
	007 (Shanty Town)	1967
	Sing A Little Song	1975
	You Can Get It If You Really Want	1970
DEL AMITRI	Always The Last To Know	1992
	Be My Downfall	1992
	Cry To Be Found	1998
	Don't Come Home Too Soon	1998
	Driving With The Brakes On	1995
	Here And Now	1995
	Just Before You Leave	2002
	Just Like A Man	1992
	Kiss This Thing Goodbye	1990
	Move Away Jimmy Blue	1990
	Not Where It's At	1997
	Nothing Ever Happens	1990
	Roll To Me	1995
	Spit In The Rain	1990
	Tell Her This	1995
	When You Were Young	1993
DELANEY & BONNIE		
	Comin' Home	1969
	Only You Know & I Know	1971
DELANEY & BONNIE & FRIENDS		
	Never Ending Song Of Love	1971
DELAYS	Hey Girl	2003
	Long Time Coming	2004

ARTIST	SONG TITLE	DATE
	Nearer Than Heaven	2004
DELEGATES	Convention '72	1972
DELEGATION	Where Is The Love (We Used To Know)	1977
DELERIUM featuring LEIGH NASH		
	Innocente (Falling In Love)	2001
DELERIUM featuring RANI		
	Underwater	2001
DELERIUM featuring SARAH MCLACHLAN		
	Silence	2000
DELFONICS	Break Your Promise	1968
	Didn't I (Blow Your Mind This Time)	1970
	La-La Means I Love You	1968
	Ready Or Not Here I Come (Can't Hide From Love)	1968
	Trying To Make A Fool Of Me	1970
	You Got Yours And I'll Get Mine	1969
DELINQUENT HABITS		
	Tres Delinquentes	1996
DELIRIOUS?	Deeper	1997
	I Could Sing Of Your Love Forever	2001
	It's OK	2000
	Promise	1997
	See The Star	1999
	Waiting For The Summer	2001
DELLS	Always Together	1968
	Does Anybody Know I'm Here	1968

ARTIST	SONG TITLE	DATE
	Give Your Baby A Standing Ovation	1973
	I Can Sing A Rainbow/Love Is Blue	1969
	The Love We Had (Stays On My Mind)	1971
	Oh What A Nite	1969
	Stay In My Corner	1968
	There Is	1968
TIM DELUXE featuring SAM OBERNIK		
	It Just Won't Do	2002
CHAKA DEMUS & PLIERS		
	Gal Wine	1994
	I Wanna Be Your Man	1994
	Murder She Wrote	1994
	She Don't Let Nobody	1993
	Tease Me	1993
CHAKA DEMUS & PLIERS/JACK RADICS/TAXI GANG		
	Twist And Shout	1993
DENISE & JOHNNY	Especially For You	1998
CATHY DENNIS	Everybody Move	1991
	Falling (The P.M. Dawn Version)	1993
	Irresistible	1992
	Just Another Dream	1990
	Too Many Walls	1991
	Touch Me (All Night Long)	1991
	Waterloo Sunset	1997
	West End Pad	1996
	You Lied To Me	1992

ARTIST	SONG TITLE	DATE
(D. MOB featuring CATHY DENNIS)		
	C'mon And Get My Love	1989
	Why	1994
STEFAN DENNIS	Don't It Make You Feel Good	1989
DENNISONS	Walking The Dog	1964
RICHARD DENTON & MARTIN COOK		
	Theme From 'Hong Kong Beat'	1978
JOHN DENVER	Annie's Song	1974
	Back Home Again	1974
	Fly Away	1975
	I'm Sorry/Calypso	1975
	Like A Sad Song	1976
	Looking For Space	1976
	My Sweet Lady	1977
	Rocky Mountain High	1972
	Shanghai Breezes	1982
	Some Days Are Diamonds (Some Days Are Stone)	1981
	Sunshine On My Shoulders	1974
	Sweet Surrender	1974
	Take Me Home, Country Roads	1971
	Thank God I'm A Country Boy	1975
KARL DENVER	Can You Forgive Me	1963
	Indian Love Call	1963
	Love Me With All Your Heart	1964
	My World Of Blue	1964

ARTIST	SONG TITLE	DATE
	Still	1963
DEODATO	Also Sprach Zarathustra (2001)	1973
DEPARTMENT S	Is Vic There?	1981
DEPARTURE	All Mapped Out	2004
LYNSEY DE PAUL	Getting A Drag	1972
	My Man And Me	1975
	No Honestly	1974
	Ooh I Do	1974
	Sugar Me	1972
	Won't Somebody Dance With Me	1973
LYNSEY DE PAUL & MIKE MORAN		
	Rock Bottom	1977
DEPECHE MODE	Barrel Of A Gun	1997
	Behind The Wheel	1988
	Blasphemous Rumours/Someday	1984
	Condemnation (EP)	1993
	Dream On	2001
	Enjoy The Silence	1990
	Enjoy The Silence 04	2004
	Everything Counts	1983
	Freelove	2001
	Get The Balance Right	1983
	Home	1997
	I Feel Loved	2001
	I Feel You	1993
	In Your Room	1994

ARTIST	SONG TITLE	DATE
	It's Called A Heart	1985
	It's No Good	1997
	Just Can't Get Enough	1981
	Leave In Silence	1982
	Love In Itself	1983
	Master And Servant	1984
	The Meaning Of Love	1982
	Never Let Me Down Again	1987
	New Life	1981
	Only When I Lose Myself	1998
	People Are People	1985
	Personal Jesus	1989
	Policy Of Truth	1990
	A Question Of Lust	1986
	A Question Of Time	1986
	See You	1982
	Shake The Disease	1985
	Strangelove	1987
	Stripped	1986
	Useless	1997
	Walking In My Shoes	1993
	World In My Eyes	1990
DEREK	Cinnamon	1968
DEREK & THE DOMINOS		
	Layla	1972
RICK DERRINGER	Rock And Roll Hoochie Koo	1974

ARTIST	SONG TITLE	DATE
DES'REE	Feel So High	1992
	Life	1998
	What's Your Sign	1998
	You Gotta Be	1994
TERI DESARIO WITH K.C.		
	Yes, I'm Ready	1979
JACKIE DESHANNON	Love Will Find A Way	1969
	Put A Little Love In Your Heart	1969
	What The World Needs Now Is Love	1965
DESIRELESS	Voyage Voyage	1988
DESTINY'S CHILD	Bills, Bills, Bills	1999
	Bootylicious	2001
	Bug A Boo	1999
	Emotion	2001
	Independent Women Part I	2000
	Jumpin, Jumpin	2000
	Lose My Breath	2004
	No, No, No	1997
	Say My Name	1999
	Survivor	2001
	With Me	1998
DESTINY'S CHILD featuring TIMBALAND		
	Get On The Bus	1999
(MATTHEW MARSDEN featuring DESTINY'S CHILD)		
	She's Gone	1998

ARTIST	SONG TITLE	DATE
STEPHANIE DE SYKES		
	Born With A Smile On My Face	1974
	We'll Find Our Day	1975
DETERGENTS	Leader Of The Laundromat	1964
DETROIT EMERALDS		
	Baby Let Me Take You In My Arms	1972
	Feel The Need In Me	1973
	I Think Of You	1973
	You Want It, You Got It	1972
DETROIT GRAND PU BAHS		
	Sandwiches	2000
MARCELLA DETROIT		
	I Believe	1994
	I'm No Angel	1994
MARCELLA DETROIT & ELTON JOHN		
	Ain't Nothing Like The Real Thing	1994
DETROIT SPINNERS		
	See The Spinners	
DEUCE	Call It Love	1995
	I Need You	1995
	No Surrender	1996
	On The Bible	1995
WILLIAM DEVAUGHN		
	Be Thankful For What You Got	1974
DEVICE	Hanging On A Heart Attack	1986
DEVO	Whip It	1980

ARTIST	SONG TITLE	DATE
BARRY DEVORZON & PERRY BOTKIN		
	Nadia's Theme (The Young & The Restless)	1976
DEVOTIONS	Rip Van Winkle	1964
DEXY'S MIDNIGHT RUNNERS		
	Because Of You	1986
	Celtic Soul Brothers	1983
	Come On Eileen	1983
	Dance Stance	1980
	Geno	1980
	Jackie Wilson Said	1982
	Let's Get This Straight (From The Start)	1982
	Show Me	1981
	There There My Dear	1980
CLIFF DEYOUNG	My Sweet Lady	1974
DENNIS DEYOUNG	Desert Moon	1984
TONY DI BART	Do It	1994
	The Real Thing	1994
SHY FX & T-POWER featuring DI		
	Shake Ur Body	2002
SHY FX & T-POWER featuring DI & SKIBADEE		
	Don't Wanna Know	2002
DIAMOND RIO	Beautiful Mess	2002
	I Believe	2003
	One More Day	2001
	Unbelievable	1998

ARTIST	SONG TITLE	DATE
JIM DIAMOND	Hi Ho Silver	1986
	I Should Have Known Better	1984
NEIL DIAMOND	America	1981
	Be	1973
	Be Mine Tonight	1982
	Beautiful Noise	1976
	Brother Love's Travelling Salvation Show	1969
	Cherry Cherry	1966
	Cracklin' Rosie	1970
	Desiree	1977
	Do It	1970
	Forever In Blue Jeans	1979
	Girl, You'll Be A Woman Soon	1967
	He Ain't Heavy, He's My Brother	1970
	Heartlight	1982
	Hello Again	1981
	Holly Holy	1969
	I Am... I Said	1971
	I Got The Feelin' (Oh No No)	1966
	I'm Alive	1983
	I've Been This Way Before	1975
	If You Know What I Mean	1976
	Kentucky Woman	1967
	Longfellow Serenade	1974
	Love On The Rocks	1980
	Morning Has Broken	1992

ARTIST	SONG TITLE	DATE
	Play Me	1972
	September Morn	1979
	Shilo	1970
	Solitary Man	1970
	Song Sung Blue	1972
	Soolaimon (African Trilogy II)	1970
	Stones	1971
	Sweet Caroline	1969
	Thank The Lord For The Night Time	1967
	Walk On Water	1972
	Yesterday's Songs	1981
	You Got To Me	1967
	(BARBRA & NEIL)	
	You Don't Bring Me Flowers	1978
MANU DIBANGO	Soul Makossa	1973
DICK & DEEDEE	Thou Shalt Not Steal	1964
CHARLES DICKENS	That's The Way Love Goes	1965
LITTLE JIMMY DICKENS		
	May The Bird Of Paradise Fly Up Your Nose	1965
GWEN DICKEY/JAY-Z		
	Wishing On A Star	1998
	(KWS & GWEN DICKEY)	
	Ain't Nobody (Loves Me Better)	1994
	(ROSE ROYCE featuring GWEN DICKEY)	
	Car Wash	1998

ARTIST	SONG TITLE	DATE
NEVILLE DICKIE	Robin's Return	1969
DICKIES	Banana Splits (The Tra La La Song)	1979
	Nights In White Satin	1979
BRUCE DICKINSON	All The Young Dudes	1990
	Shoot All The Clowns	1994
	Tattooed Millionaire	1990
	Tears Of The Dragon	1994
	(MR. BEAN & SMEAR CAMPAIGN featuring	
	BRUCE DICKINSON)	
	(I Want To Be) Elected	1992
BARBARA DICKSON	Another Suitcase In Another Hall	1977
	Answer Me	1976
	January February	1980
	(ELAINE PAIGE & BARBARA DICKSON)	
	I Know Him So Well	1985
BO DIDDLEY	Hey Good Lookin'	1965
	Pretty Thing	1963
DIDDY	Give Me Love	1997
DIDO	Don't Leave Home	2004
	Here With Me	2001
	Hunter	2001
	Life For Rent	2003
	Sand In My Shoes	2004
	Thank You	2001
	White Flag	2003

ARTIST	SONG TITLE	DATE
	(FAITHLESS featuring DIDO)	
	One Step Too Far	2002
DIFFERENT GEAR vs THE POLICE		
	When The World Is Running Down	2000
JOE DIFFIE	A Night To Remember	1999
DIGABLE PLANETS	Rebirth Of Slick (Cool Like Dat)	1993
DIGITAL EXCITATION		
	Pure Pleasure	1992
DIGITAL ORGASM	Running Out Of Time	1991
	Startouchers	1992
DIGITAL UNDERGROUND		
	The Humpty Dance	1990
	Kiss You Back	1991
DILATED PEOPLES	This Way	2004
	Worst Comes To Worst	2002
DILLINJA featuring SKIBADEE		
	Twist 'Em Out	2003
DINO	Gentle	1990
	I Like It	1989
	Ooh Child	1993
	Romeo	1990
	Sunshine	1989
DINO, DESI & BILLY		
	I'm A Fool	1965
	Not The Lovin' Kind	1965

ARTIST	SONG TITLE	DATE
DINOSAUR JR.	Feel The Pain	1994
	Start Choppin	1993
DIO	Mystery	1984
	Rock 'n' Roll Children	1985
DION	Abraham, Martin And John	1968
	The Wanderer	1961
CELINE DION	All By Myself	1997
	Because You Loved Me	1996
	Call The Man	1997
	Falling Into You	1996
	The First Time Ever I Saw Your Face	2000
	Goodbye's (The Saddest Word)	2002
	I'm Alive	2002
	(If There Was) Any Other Way	1991
	If You Asked Me To	1992
	It's All Coming Back To Me Now	1996
	Love Can Move Mountains	1992
	Misled	1994
	My Heart Will Go On	1998
	A New Day Has Come	2002
	Nothing Broken But My Heart	1992
	One Heart	2003
	Only One Road	1995
	The Power Of Love	1993
	The Reason	1997
	That's The Way It Is	1999

ARTIST	SONG TITLE	DATE
	Think Twice	1994
	Treat Her Like A Lady	1999
	Tu M'aimes Encore (To Love Me Again)	1995
	Where Does My Heart Beat Now	1990
CELINE DION & CLIVE GRIFFIN		
	When I Fall In Love	1993
CELINE DION & PEABO BRYSON		
	Beauty & The Beast	1992
CELINE DION & R. KELLY		
	I'm Your Angel	1998
CELINE DION WITH THE BEE GEES		
	Immortality	1998
	(BARBRA STREISAND & CELINE DION)	
	Tell Him	1997
DIRE STRAITS	Brothers In Arms	1985
	Calling Elvis	1991
	Encores (EP)	1993
	Money For Nothing	1985
	Private Investigations	1982
	Romeo And Juliet	1981
	Skateaway	1981
	So Far Away	1986
	Sultans Of Swing	1979
	Twisting By The Pool	1983
	Walk Of Life	1985
	Your Latest Trick	1986

ARTIST	SONG TITLE	DATE
DIRECKT	Two Fatt Guitars (Revisited)	1994
SENATOR EVERETT DIRKSEN		
	Gallant Men	1966
DIRT DEVILS	The Drill	2002
DIRTY VEGAS	Days Go By	2002
	Ghosts	2002
DISCO CITIZENS	Footprint	1997
	Right Here Right Now	1995
DISCO TEX presents CLOUDBURST		
	I Can Cast A Spell	2001
DISCO TEX & THE SEX-O-LETTES		
	Get Dancin'	1974
	I Wanna Dance Wit' Choo (Doo Dat Dance), Part I	1975
DISHWALLA	Counting Blue Cars	1996
DISTANT SOUNDZ	Time After Time	2002
SACHA DISTEL	Raindrops Keep Fallin' On My Head	1970
DISTURBED	Prayer	2002
DIVA SURPRISE featuring GEORGIA JONES		
	On Top Of The World	1998
DIVE	Boogie	1998
DIVERSIONS	Fattie Bum Bum	1975
DIVINE	Lately	1998
	One More Try	1999
DIVINE COMEDY	Absent Friends	2004
	Bad Ambassador	2001

ARTIST	SONG TITLE	DATE
	Becoming More Like Alfie	1996
	Come Home Billy Bird	2004
	Everybody Knows (Except You)	1997
	The Frog Princess	1996
	Generation Sex	1998
	Gin Soaked Boy	1999
	Love What You Do	2001
	National Express	1999
	The Pop Singer's Fear Of The Pollen Count	1999
	Something For The Weekend	1996
DIVINE INSPIRATION		
	The Way (Put Your Hand In My Hand)	2003
DIVINE	Walk Like A Man	1985
	You Think You're A Man	1984
DIVINYLS	I Touch Myself	1991
DIXIE CHICKS	Cowboy Take Me Away	1999
	Goodbye Earl	2000
	If I Fall You're Going Down With Me	2001
	Long Time Gone	2002
	Ready To Run	1999
	There's Your Trouble	1998
	Travelin' Soldier	2003
	Without You	2000
	You Were Mine	1999
DIXIEBELLES	Southtown U.S.A.	1964

ARTIST	SONG TITLE	DATE
DIXIE CUPS	Chapel Of Love	1964
	Iko Iko	1965
	People Say	1964
	You Should Have Seen The Way He Looked At Me	1964
DIZZEE RASCAL	Fix Up Look Sharp	2003
	I Luv U	2003
	Jus' A Rascal	2003
	Stand Up Tall	2004
	(BASEMENT JAXX featuring DIZZEE RASCAL) Lucky Star	2003
DJ ALIGATOR PROJECT	The Whistle Song (Blow My Whistle Bitch)	2002
DJ BOBO	Chihuahua	2003
DJ CASPER	Cha Cha Slide	2004
DJ CASPER featuring THE GAP BAND	Oops Upside Your Head	2004
DJ DADO	X-Files	1996
DJ DEE KLINE	I Don't Smoke	2000
DJ DUKE	Blow Your Whistle	1994
	Turn It Up (Say Yeah)	1994
DJ ERIC	We Are Love	1999
DJ FLAVOURS	Your Caress (All I Need)	1997
DJ GARRY	Dream Universe	2002
DJ JEAN	The Launch	1999

ARTIST	SONG TITLE	DATE
DJ JURGEN presents ALICE DEEJAY	Better Off Alone	1999
DJ KOOL	Let Me Clear My Throat	1997
DJ LUCK & MC NEAT	Irie	2002
	A Little Bit Of Luck	1999
	Piano Loco	2001
DJ LUCK & MC NEAT featuring ARI GOLD	I'm All About You	2001
DJ LUCK & MC NEAT featuring JJ	Ain't No Stoppin' Us	2000
	Masterblaster 2000	2000
DJ MARKY & XRS featuring STAMINA MC	LK (Carolina Carol Bela)	2002
DJ MIKO	What's Up	1994
DJ MILANO featuring SAMANTHA FOX	Santa Maria	1998
DJ MISJAH AND DJ TIM	Access	1996
DJ OTZI	Do Wah Diddy	2001
	Hey Baby (Uhh, Ahh)	2001
DJ PIED PIPER and THE MASTERS OF CEREMONIES	Do You Really Like It	2001
DJ QUICKSILVER	Belissima	1997
	Free	1997
	Planet Love	1998

ARTIST	SONG TITLE	DATE
DJ RAP	Bad Girl	1998
	Good To Be Alive	1998
DJ SAKIN & FRIENDS		
	Nomansland (David's Song)	1999
	Protect Your Mind (For The Love Of A Princess)	1999
DJ SAMMY	The Boys Of Summer	2003
	Sunlight	2003
DJ SAMMY & YANOU featuring DO		
	Heaven	2002
DJ SANDY vs HOUSETRAP		
	Overdrive	2000
DJ SCOTT featuring LORNA B		
	Do You Wanna Party	1995
	Sweet Dreams	1995
DJ SEDUCTION	Come On	1992
	Hardcore Heaven/You And Me	1992
DJ SHADOW	High Noon	1997
	Six Days	2002
	You Can't Go Home Again	2002
DJ SHOG	This Is My Sound	2002
DJ SNEAK featuring BEAR WHO?		
	Fix My Sink	2003
DJ SUPREME	Tha Horns Of Jericho	1998
	Tha Wild Style	1997

ARTIST	SONG TITLE	DATE
(PORN KINGS vs DJ SUPREME)		
	Up To The Wildstyle	1999
DJ TIESTO	Lethal Industry	2002
DJ TIESTO featuring KIRSTY HAWKSHAW		
	Urban Train	2001
DJ TIESTO featuring SUZANNE PALMER		
	643 (Love's On Fire)	2002
TIESTO featuring BT		
	Love Comes Again	2004
DJ ZINC	138 Trek	2000
BORIS DLUGOSCH	Hold Your Head Up High	1997
BORIS DLUGOSCH featuring ROISIN MURPHY		
	Never Enough	2001
DMAC	The World She Knows	2002
DMX	Party Up (Up In Here)	2000
	Slippin'	1999
	Where The Hood At?	2003
	Who We Be	2001
	X Gon' Give It To Ya	2003
DMX featuring SHEEK OF THE LOX		
	Get At Me Dog	1998
DMX featuring SWIZZ BEATZ		
	Get It On The Floor	2004
(LOX featuring DMX & LIL' KIM)		
	Money, Power & Respect	1998
DNA	La Serenissima	1990

ARTIST	SONG TITLE	DATE
DNA featuring SHARON REDD		
	Can You Handle It	1992
DNA featuring SUZANNE VEGA		
	Tom's Diner	1990
DO OR DIE featuring TWISTA		
	Po Pimp	1996
ANITA DOBSON	Anyone Can Fall In Love	1986
DOCTOR & THE MEDICS		
	Burn	1986
	Spirit In The Sky	1986
DR. ALBAN	It's My Life	1992
	Sing Hallelujah!	1993
DR. DRE	Keep Their Heads Ringin'	1995
	Nuthin' But A 'G' Thang/Let Me Ride	1994
DR. FEELGOOD	As Long As The Price Is Right	1979
	Milk And Alcohol	1979
	She's A Wind Up	1977
DR. HOOK	Baby Makes Her Blue Jeans Talk	1982
	Better Love Next Time	1979
	The Cover Of 'Rolling Stone'	1972
	Girls Can Get It	1980
	If Not You	1976
	A Little Bit More	1976
	More Like The Movies	1978
	Only Sixteen	1976
	Sexy Eyes	1980

ARTIST	SONG TITLE	DATE
	Sharing The Night Together	1978
	Sylvia's Mother	1972
	When You're In Love With A Beautiful Woman	1979
DR. JOHN	Right Place Wrong Time	1973
DOCTOR SPIN	Tetris	1992
KEN DODD	Broken Hearted	1970
	Eight By Ten	1964
	Happiness	1964
	It's Love	1966
	Just Out Of Reach (Of My Two Empty Arms)	1972
	Let Me Cry On Your Shoulder	1967
	More Than Love	1966
	Promises	1966
	The River (Le Colline Sono In Fiore)	1965
	So Deep Is The Night	1964
	Still	1963
	Tears	1965
	Tears Won't Wash Away These Heartaches	1969
	Think Of Me (Wherever You Are)	1975
	When Love Comes Around	1971
DODGY	Every Single Day	1998
	Found You	1997
	Good Enough	1996

ARTIST	SONG TITLE	DATE
	If You're Thinking Of Me	1996
	In A Room	1996
	So Let Me Go Far	1995
	Staying Out For The Summer	1994
DOG EAT DOG	No Fronts – The Remixes	1996
NATE DOGG/50 CENT		
	21 Questions	2003
NATE DOGG featuring SNOOP DOGGY DOGG		
	Never Leave Me Alone	1996
NATE DOGG featuring WARREN G		
	Nobody Does It Better	1998
(FABOLOUS featuring NATE DOGG)		
	Can't Deny It	2001
(LUDACRIS featuring NATE DOGG)		
	Area Codes	2001
(MARK RONSON featuring GHOSTFACE KILLAH & NATE DOGG)		
	Ooh Wee	2003
(MOS DEF & NATE DOGG featuring PHAROAH E MONCH)		
	Oh No	2001
(OBIE TRICE featuring NATE DOGG)		
	The Set Up (You Don't Know)	2004
(SHADE SHEIST featuring NATE DOGG & KURUPT)		
	Where I Wanna Be	2001

ARTIST	SONG TITLE	DATE
(WARREN G & NATE DOGG)		
	Regulate	1994
(WESTSIDE CONNECTION featuring NATE DOGG)		
	Gangsta Nation	2003
DOGS D'AMOUR	Satellite Kid	1989
	Victims Of Success	1990
DOGS DIE IN HOT CARS		
	Godhopping	2004
	I Love You 'Cause I Have To	2004
KEN DOH	Nakasakai (EP) (I Need A Lover Tonight)	1996
PETER DOHERTY	Babyshambles	2004
(WOLFMAN featuring PETER DOHERTY)		
	For Lovers	2004
JOE DOLAN	Make Me An Island	1969
	Teresa	1969
	You're Such A Good Looking Woman	1970
THOMAS DOLBY	Close But No Cigar	1992
	Hyperactive	1984
	Hyperactive!	1994
	I Love You Goodbye	1992
	She Blinded Me With Science	1983
	Windpower	1982
JOE DOLCE	Shaddap You Face	1981
DOLL	Desire Me	1979
DOLLAR	Give Me Back My Heart	1982
	Give Me Some Kinda Magic	1982

ARTIST	SONG TITLE	DATE
	Hand Held In Black & White	1981
	I Want To Hold Your Hand	1979
	Love's Gotta Hold On Me	1979
	Mirror Mirror (Mon Amour)	1981
	Oh L'Amour	1987
	Shooting Star	1978
	Videotheque	1982
	Who Were You With In The Moonlight	1979
PLACIDO DOMINGO & JENNIFER RUSH		
	Till I Loved You	1989
(CARRERAS/DOMINGO/PAVAROTTI WITH MEHTA)		
	Libiamo/La Donna E Mobile	1994
	You'll Never Walk Alone	1998
DOMINO	Getto Jam	1993
	Sweet Potatoe Pie	1994
FATS DOMINO	Red Sails In The Sunset	1963
DON-E	Love Makes The World Go Round	1992
SIOBHAN DONAGHY		
	Overrated	2003
ANDRU DONALDS	Mishale	1994
BO DONALDSON & THE HEYWOODS		
	Billy, Don't Be A Hero	1974
	The Heartbreak Kid	1974
	Who Do You Think You Are	1974
DONNAS	Take It Off	2003

ARTIST	SONG TITLE	DATE
DONOVAN	Atlantis	1969
	Catch The Wind	1965
	Colours	1965
	Epistle To Dippy	1967
	Hurdy Gurdy Man	1968
	Jennifer Juniper	1968
	Lalena	1968
	Mellow Yellow	1966
	Sunshine Superman	1966
	There Is A Mountain	1967
	To Susan On The West Coast Waiting	1969
	Turquoise	1965
	Wear Your Love Like Heaven	1967
DONOVAN WITH JEFF BECK GROUP		
	Goo Goo Barabajagal	1969
	Goo Goo Barabajagal (Love Is Hot)	1969
JASON DONOVAN	Another Night	1990
	Any Dream Will Do	1991
	As Time Goes By	1992
	Every Day (I Love You More)	1989
	Hang On To Your Love	1990
	Happy Together	1991
	I'm Doing Fine	1990
	Joseph Mega-Remix	1991
	Mission Of Love	1992

ARTIST	SONG TITLE	DATE
	Nothing Can Divide Us	1988
	R.S.V.P.	1991
	Rhythm Of The Rain	1990
	Sealed With A Kiss	1989
	Too Many Broken Hearts	1989
	When You Come Back To Me	1989
(KYLIE MINOGUE & JASON DONOVAN)		
	Especially For You	1988
DOOBIE BROTHERS	Another Park, Another Sunday	1974
	Black Water	1974
	China Grove	1973
	Dependin' On You	1979
	The Doctor	1989
	It Keeps You Runnin'	1976
	Jesus Is Just Alright	1972
	Listen To The Music	1972
	Long Train Runnin'	1993
	Minute By Minute	1979
	One Step Closer	1980
	Real Love	1980
	Sweet Maxine	1975
	Take Me In Your Arms (Rock Me A Little While)	1975
	Takin' It To The Streets	1976
	What A Fool Believes	1979

ARTIST	SONG TITLE	DATE
DOOLALLY	Straight From The Heart	1999
DOOLEYS	The Chosen Few	1979
	Honey I'm Lost	1979
	Love Of My Life	1977
	Love Patrol	1980
	A Rose Has To Die	1978
	Think I'm Gonna Fall In Love With You	1977
	Wanted	1979
VAL DOONICAN	Elusive Butterfly	1966
	Heaven Is My Woman's Love	1973
	If I Knew Then What I Know Now	1968
	If The Whole World Stopped Lovin'	1967
	Memories Are Made Of This	1967
	Morning	1971
	The Special Years	1965
	Two Streets	1967
	Walk Tall	1964
	What Would I Be	1966
	You're The Only One	1968
DOOP	Doop	1994
DOORS	Hello, I Love You	1968
	Light My Fire	1967
	Love Her Madly	1971
	Love Me Two Times	1967
	People Are Strange	1967

ARTIST	SONG TITLE	DATE
	Riders On The Storm	1971
	Touch Me	1968
	The Unknown Soldier	1968
DOPE SMUGGLAZ	Double Double Dutch	1999
CHARLIE DORE	Pilot Of The Airwaves	1980
DOROTHY	What's That Tune? (Doo-Doo-Doo-Doo-Doo-Doo-Doo-Doo-Doo-Doo)	1995
LEE DORSEY	Confusion	1966
	Get Out Of My Life, Woman	1966
	Holy Cow	1966
	Ride Your Pony	1965
	Working In The Coal Mine	1966
DOUBLE	The Captain Of Her Heart	1986
DOUBLE 99	Ripgroove	1997
DOUBLE DEE featuring DANY		
	Found Love	1995
DOUBLE TROUBLE	Love Don't Live Here Anymore	1990
DOUBLE TROUBLE & REBEL M.C.		
	Just Keep Rockin'	1989
	(REBEL MC/DOUBLE TROUBLE)	
	Street Tuff	1989
ROB DOUGAN	Clubbed To Death	2002
CARL DOUGLAS	Dance The Kung Fu	1974
	Kung Fu Fighting	1974
	Run Back	1978

ARTIST	SONG TITLE	DATE
	(BUS STOP featuring CARL DOUGLAS)	
	Kung Fu Fighting	1998
CAROL DOUGLAS	Doctor's Orders	1974
CRAIG DOUGLAS	Town Crier	1963
MIKE DOUGLAS	The Men In My Little Girl's Life	1969
DOVE	Don't Dream	1999
PATTY DUKE	Say Something Funny	1965
RONNIE DOVE	Cry	1966
	Happy Summer Days	1966
	I Really Don't Want To Know	1966
	I'll Make All Your Dreams Come True	1965
	Kiss Away	1965
	Let's Start All Over Again	1966
	A Little Bit Of Heaven	1965
	One Kiss For Old Time's Sake	1965
	Right Or Wrong	1964
	Say You	1964
	When Liking Turns To Loving	1966
DOVES	Catch The Sun	2000
	Caught By The River	2002
	The Cedar Room	2000
	The Man Who Told Everything	2000
	Pounding	2002
	There Goes The Fear	2002
DOWLANDS	All My Loving	1964
DON DOWNING	Lonely Days, Lonely Nights	1973

ARTIST	SONG TITLE	DATE
WILL DOWNING	In My Dreams	1988
	A Love Supreme	1988
(MICA PARIS & WILL DOWNING)		
	Where Is The Love	1989
JASON DOWNS featuring MILK		
	White Boy With A Feather	2001
LAMONT DOZIER	Fish Ain't Bitin'	1974
	Trying To Hold On To My Woman	1973
DR. BUZZARD'S ORIGINAL 'SAVANNAH' BAND		
	Whispering/Cherchez La Femme/	
	Se Si Bon	1976
DR. DRE	Dre Day	1993
	Keep Their Heads Ringin'	1995
	Let Me Ride	1993
DR. DRE & LL COOL J		
	Zoom	1998
DR. DRE featuring EMINEM		
	Forget About Dre	2000
DR. DRE featuring KNOC-TURN'AL		
	Bad Intentions	2002
DR. DRE featuring SNOOP DOGG		
	The Next Episode	2001
	Still D.R.E.	2000
(EMINEM featuring DR. DRE)		
	Guilty Conscience	1999

ARTIST	SONG TITLE	DATE
(2PAC featuring DR. DRE & ROGER TROUTMAN)		
	California Love/How Do U Want It	1996
(BLACKSTREET featuring DR. DRE)		
	No Diggity	1996
NICK DRAKE	Magic	2004
PETE DRAKE	Forever	1964
DRAMATICS	In The Rain	1973
	Whatcha See Is Whatcha Get	1971
DREADZONE	Little Britain	1996
DREAM	He Loves U Not	2001
	This Is Me	2001
DREAM ACADEMY	Life In A Northern Town	1985
DREAM FREQUENCY		
	Take Me	1992
DREAM FREQUENCY/DEBBIE SHARP		
	Feel So Real	1992
DREAM WARRIORS	Ludi	1991
	My Definition Of A Bombastic Jazz Style	1990
	Wash Your Face In My Sink	1990
DREAMCATCHER	I Don't Wanna Lose My Way	2002
DREEM TEEM	The Theme	1997
DREEM TEEM vs ARTFUL DODGER featuring MZ MAY & MC ALISTAIR	It Ain't Enough	2001
DREEM TEEM vs NENEH CHERRY		
	Buddy X 99	1999

ARTIST	SONG TITLE	DATE
EDDIE DRENNON & B.B.S. UNLIMITED		
	Let's Do The Latin Hustle	1976
DRIFTERS	At The Club/Saturday Night At The Movies	1972
	Can I Take You Home Little Girl?	1975
	Come On Over To My Place	1972
	Down On The Beach Tonight	1974
	Every Night's A Saturday Night With You	1976
	Hello Happiness	1976
	I'll Take You Home	1963
	I've Got Sand In My Shoes	1964
	Kissin' In The Back Row Of The Movies	1974
	Like Sister And Brother	1973
	Love Games	1975
	There Goes My First Love	1975
	Under The Boardwalk	1964
	You're More Than A Number In My Little Red Book	1976
DRIFTWOOD	Freeloader	2003
JULIE DRISCOLL, BRIAN AUGER & THE TRINITY		
	This Wheel's On Fire	1968
DRIVER 67	Car 67	1978
MINNIE DRIVER	Everything I've Got In My Pocket	2004
DRIZA BONE	Pressure	1994
	Real Love	1991

ARTIST	SONG TITLE	DATE
DROWNING POOL	Bodies	2002
DRS	Gangsta Lean	1993
DRU HILL	5 Steps	1997
	How Deep Is Your Love	1998
	I Should Be...	2002
	In My Bed	1997
	Never Make A Promise	1997
	Tell Me	1996
	These Are The Times	1998
	We're Not Making Love No More	1997
	(FOXY BROWN featuring DRU HILL) Big Bad Mamma	1997
	(WILL SMITH featuring DRU HILL) Wild Wild West	1999
DRUGSTORE	El President	1998
DRUPI	Vado Via	1973
DT8 featuring ROXANNE WILDE		
	Destination	2003
DT8 PROJECT	The Sun Is Shining (Down On Me)	2004
JOHN DU CANN	Don't Be A Dummy	1979
DUALERS	Kiss On The Lips	2004
DUBLINERS	Black Velvet Band	1967
	Seven Drunken Nights	1967
	(POGUES & THE DUBLINERS) The Irish Rover	1987

ARTIST	SONG TITLE	DATE
DUBSTAR	Anywhere	1995
	Elevator Song	1996
	I Will Be Your Girlfriend	1998
	No More Talk	1997
	Not So Manic Now	1996
	I (Friday Night)	2000
	Stars	1996
HILARY DUFF	Come Clean	2004
	So Yesterday	2003
STEPHEN 'TIN TIN' DUFFY		
	Icing On The Cake	1985
	Kiss Me	1985
DUICE	Dazzey Duks	1993
DUKE	So In Love With You	1996
GEORGE DUKE	Brazilian Love Affair	1980
	(STANLEY CLARKE & GEORGE DUKE)	
	Sweet Baby	1981
PATTY DUKE	Don't Just Stand There	1965
DUM DUMS	Army Of Two	2001
	Can't Get You Out Of My Thoughts	2000
	Everything	2000
	You Do Something To Me	2000
DUMONDE	Never Look Back	2001
DUNBLANE	Knockin' On Heaven's Door/Throw These Guns Away	1996

ARTIST	SONG TITLE	DATE
DAVID DUNDAS	Another Funny Honeymoon	1977
	Jeans On	1976
ERROLL DUNKLEY	O.K. Fred	1979
CLIVE DUNN	Grandad	1970
ROBBIE DUPREE	Hot Rod Hearts	1980
	Steal Away	1980
SIMON DUPREE & THE BIG SOUND		
	Kites	1967
JERMAINE DUPRI & LUDACRIS		
	Welcome To Atlanta	2001
	(MARQUES HOUSTON featuring JERMAINE DUPRI)	
	Pop That Booty	2004
DURAN DURAN	All She Wants Is	1988
	Burning The Ground	1989
	Careless Memories	1981
	Come Undone	1993
	Do You Believe In Shame	1989
	Electric Barbarella	1999
	Girls On Film	1981
	Hungry Like The Wolf	1982
	I Don't Want Your Love	1988
	Is There Something I Should Know	1983
	Meet El Presidente	1987
	My Own Way	1981
	New Moon On Monday	1984
	Notorious	1986

ARTIST	SONG TITLE	DATE
	Ordinary World	1993
	Out Of My Mind	1997
	Perfect Day	1995
	Planet Earth	1981
	(Reach Up For The) Sunrise	2004
	The Reflex	1984
	Rio	1983
	Save A Prayer	1985
	Skin Trade	1987
	Too Much Information	1993
	Union Of The Snake	1983
	A View To Kill	1985
	Violence Of Summer (Love's Taking Over)	1990
	White Lines (Don't Do It)	1995
	The Wild Boys	1984
JUDITH DURHAM	The Olive Tree	1967
IAN DURY	I Want To Be Straight	1980
IAN DURY & THE BLOCKHEADS		
	Hit Me With Your Rhythm Stick	1978
	Reasons To Be Cheerful (Pt 3)	1979
	What A Waste!	1978
DUST JUNKYS	What Time Is It?	1998
DUSTED	Always Remember To Respect And Honour Your Mother	2001
DUTCH FORCE	Deadline	2000

ARTIST	SONG TITLE	DATE
DUTCH featuring CRYSTAL WATERS		
	My Time	2003
DYKE & THE BLAZERS		
	Let A Woman Be A Woman — Let A Man Be A Man	1969
	We Got More Soul	1969
BOB DYLAN	Baby Stop Crying	1978
	Can You Please Crawl Out Your Window	1966
	Dignity	1995
	George Jackson	1971
	Gotta Serve Somebody	1979
	Hurricane (Part 1)	1975
	I Want You	1966
	Just Like A Woman	1966
	Knockin' On Heaven's Door	1973
	Lay Lady Lay	1969
	Like A Rolling Stone	1965
	Positively 4th Street	1965
	Rainy Day Women #12 & 35	1966
	Subterranean Homesick Blues	1965
	Tangled Up In Blue	1975
	Times They Are A-Changin'	1965
	Watching The River Flow	1971
DYNASTY	I Don't Want To Be A Freak (But I Can't Help Myself)	1979

ARTIST	SONG TITLE	DATE
RONNIE DYSON	(If You Let Me Make Love To You Then)	
	Why Can't I Touch You?	1970
	One Man Band (Plays All Alone)	1973
	When You Get Right Down To It	1971
E'VOKE	Arms Of Loren	1996
	Runaway	1995
SHEILA E	The Belle Of St. Mark	1984
	The Glamorous Life	1984
	A Love Bizarre	1985
E-40 FEATURING BO-ROCK		
	Things'll Never Change/Rapper's Ball	1997
E-MOTION	The Naughty North & The Sexy South	1996
E-Z ROLLERS	Walk This Land	1999
E-ZEE POSSEE	Everything Starts With An 'E'	1990
E.U.	Da'butt	1988
EAGLES	Already Gone	1974
	Best Of My Love	1974
	Get Over It	1994
	Heartache Tonight	1979
	Hotel California	1977
	I Can't Tell You Why	1980
	Life In The Fast Lane	1977
	The Long Run	1979
	Lyin' Eyes	1975
	New Kid In Town	1976
	One Of These Nights	1975

ARTIST	SONG TITLE	DATE
	Peaceful Easy Feeling	1972
	Please Come Home For Christmas	1978
	Seven Bridges Road	1980
	Take It Easy	1972
	Take It To The Limit	1975
	Witchy Woman	1972
EAMON	F**k It (I Don't Want You Back)	2004
EAMON featuring GHOSTFACE		
	Love Them	2004
STACY EARL	Love Me All Up	1991
	Romeo & Juliet	1992
EARL-JEAN	I'm Into Somethin' Good	1964
EARTH, WIND & FIRE		
	After The Love Has Gone	1979
	Can't Hide Love	1976
	Devotion	1974
	Fall In Love With Me	1983
	Fantasy	1978
	Getaway	1976
	Got To Get You Into My Life	1978
	I've Had Enough	1982
	Let Me Talk	1980
	Let's Groove	1981
	Mighty Mighty	1974
	Saturday Nite	1976
	September	1978

ARTIST	SONG TITLE	DATE
	Serpentine Fire	1977
	Shining Star	1975
	Sing A Song	1975
	Star	1979
	That's The Way Of The World	1975
EARTH, WIND & FIRE WITH THE EMOTIONS		
	Boogie Wonderland	1979
EAST 17	Around The World	1994
	Betcha Can't Wait	1999
	Deep	1993
	Do U Still?	1996
	Each Time	1998
	Gold	1992
	Hey Child	1997
	Hold My Body Tight	1995
	House Of Love	1992
	It's Alright	1993
	Let It Rain	1995
	Slow It Down	1993
	Someone To Love	1996
	Stay Another Day	1994
	Steam	1994
	Thunder	1995
	West End Girls	1993
EAST 17 featuring GABRIELLE		
	If You Ever	1996

ARTIST	SONG TITLE	DATE
EAST 57TH STREET featuring DONNA ALLEN		
	Saturday	1997
EAST OF EDEN	Jig-A-Jig	1971
EAST SIDE BEAT	Alive & Kicking	1992
	Ride Like The Wind	1991
SHEENA EASTON	Almost Over You	1983
	Do It For Love	1985
	For Your Eyes Only	1981
	Just Another Broken Heart	1981
	The Lover In Me	1988
	Machinery	1982
	Modern Girl	1981
	Morning Train (A.K.A. 9 To 5)	1981
	9 To 5 (A.K.A. Morning Train)	1980
	One Man Woman	1980
	Strut	1984
	Sugar Walls	1984
	Telefone (Long Distance Love Affair)	1983
	What Comes Naturally	1991
	When He Shines	1982
	You Could Have Been With Me	1981
SHEENA EASTON & KENNY ROGERS		
	We've Got Tonight	1983
	(PRINCE WITH SHEENA EASTON)	
	The Arms Of Orion	1989
EASYBEATS	Friday On My Mind	1967

ARTIST	SONG TITLE	DATE
	Hello, How Are You	1968
EASYWORLD	Junkies	2003
	'Til The Day	2004
CLEVELAND EATON	Bama Boogie Woogie	1978
EAZY-E	Just Tah Let U Know	1996
ECHO & THE BUNNYMEN		
	The Back Of Love	1982
	Bring On The Dancing Horses	1985
	The Cutter	1983
	The Game	1987
	I Want To Be There When You Come	1997
	The Killing Moon	1984
	Lips Like Sugar	1987
	Never Stop	1983
	Nothing Lasts Forever	1997
	People Are Strange	1988
	Rust	1999
	Seven Seas	1984
	Shine So Hard (EP)	1981
	Silver	1984
ECHOBEATZ	Mas Que Nada	1998
ECHOBELLY	Dark Therapy	1996
	Great Things	1995
	I Can't Imagine The World Without Me	1994
	King Of The Kerb	1995
	The World Is Flat	1997

ARTIST	SONG TITLE	DATE
BILLY ECKSTINE & SARAH VAUGHAN		
	Passing Strangers	1969
ECLIPSE	Makes Me Love You	1999
EDDIE & THE HOTRODS		
	Quit This Town	1978
	Teenage Depression	1976
EDDY & THE SOUL BAND		
	Theme From Shaft	1985
DUANE EDDY & THE REBELETTES		
	Boss Guitar	1963
	Lonely Boy Lonely Guitar	1963
	Play Me Like You Play Your Guitar	1975
	(ART OF NOISE featuring DUANE EDDY)	
	Peter Gunn	1986
RANDY EDELMAN	Concrete And Clay	1976
	Uptown Uptempo Woman	1976
EDELWEISS	Bring Me Edelweiss	1989
EDEN'S CRUSH	Get Over Yourself	2001
EDISON LIGHTHOUSE		
	Love Grows (Where My Rosemary Goes)	1970
DAVE EDMUNDS	Baby I Love You	1973
	Born To Be With You	1973
	Girls Talk	1979
	I Hear You Knocking	1973
	I Knew The Bride	1977
	Queen Of Hearts	1979

ARTIST	SONG TITLE	DATE
	The Race Is On	1981
	Singing The Blues	1980
	Slipping Away	1983
KEVON EDMUNDS	24/7	1999
EDWARD BEAR	Close Your Eyes	1973
	Last Song	1972
ALTON EDWARDS	I Just Wanna (Spend Some Time With You)	1982
JONATHAN EDWARDS		
	Sunshine	1971
RUPIE EDWARDS	Ire Feelings (Skanga)	1974
	Lego Skanga	1975
EELS	Last Stop: This Town	1998
	Mr. E's Beautiful Blues	2000
	Novocaine For The Soul	1997
	Souljacker Part I	2001
	Susan's House	1997
	Your Lucky Day In Hell	1997
WALTER EGAN	Magnet And Steel	1978
EIFFEL 65	Blue (Da Ba Dee)	1999
	Move Your Body	2000
808 STATE	Cubik/Olympic	1990
	In Yer Face	1991
	Lift/Open Your Mind	1991
	Lopez	1997
	One In Ten	1992

ARTIST	SONG TITLE	DATE
	Pacific	1989
	(MC TUNES VERSUS 808 STATE)	
	The Only Rhyme That Bites	1990
EIGHTH DAY	She's Not Just Another Woman	1971
	You've Got To Crawl (Before You Walk)	1971
EIGHTH WONDER	Cross My Heart	1988
	I'm Not Scared	1988
EIGHTIES MATCHBOX B-LINE DISASTER		
	Chicken	2003
	I Could Be An Angle	2004
	Mister Mental	2004
	Psychosis Safari	2003
	Rise Of The Eagles	2004
EL CHICANO	Viva Tirado (Part I)	1970
EL COCO	Cocomotion	1978
EL MARIACHI	Cuba	1996
ELASTICA	Connection	1994
	Line Up	1994
	Waking Up	1995
ELATE	Somebody Like You	1997
DONNIE ELBERT	I Can't Help Myself	1972
	A Little Piece Of Leather	1972
	Where Did Our Love Go	1971
ELBOW	Asleep In The Back/Coming Second	2002
	Fallen Angel	2003
	Not A Job	2004

ARTIST	SONG TITLE	DATE
	Red	2001
ELECTRAFIXION	Sister Pain	1996
ELECTRASY	Morning Afterglow	1998
ELECTRIBE 101	Talking With Myself	1990
	Tell Me When The Fever Ended	1989
ELECTRIC INDIAN	Keem-O-Sabe	1969
ELECTRIC LIGHT ORCHESTRA		
	All Over The World	1980
	Calling America	1986
	Can't Get It Out Of My Head	1974
	Confusion/Last Train To London	1979
	The Diary Of Horace Wimp	1979
	Do Ya	1977
	Don't Bring Me Down	1979
	Don't Walk Away	1980
	The ELO EP	1978
	Evil Woman	1975
	Hold On Tight	1981
	I'm Alive	1980
	Livin' Thing	1976
	Ma-Ma-Ma-Belle	1974
	Mr. Blue Sky	1978
	10538 Overture	1972
	Rock 'n' Roll Is King	1983
	Rockaria	1977
	Roll Over Beethoven	1973

ARTIST	SONG TITLE	DATE
	Shine A Little Love	1979
	Showdown	1973
	Strange Magic	1976
	Sweet Talkin' Woman	1978
	Telephone Line	1977
	Ticket To The Moon/Here Is The News	1982
	Turn To Stone	1977
	Twilight	1978
	Wild West Hero	1978
	(OLIVIA NEWTON-JOHN & ELECTRIC LIGHT ORCHESTRA)	
	Xanadu	1980
ELECTRIC PRUNES	Get Me To The World On Time	1967
	I Had Too Much To Dream (Last Night)	1967
ELECTRIC SIX	Dance Commander	2003
	Danger! High Voltage	2003
	Gay Bar	2003
ELECTRIC SOFT PARADE		
	Empty At The End/This Given Line	2002
	Silent To The Dark II	2002
ELECTRIQUE BOUTIQUE		
	Revelation	2000
ELECTRONIC	Disappointed	1992
	Feel Every Beat	1991
	For You	1996
	Forbidden City	1996

ARTIST	SONG TITLE	DATE
	Get The Message	1991
	Getting Away With It	1990
	Second Nature	1997
	Vivid	1999
ELECTRONICAS	Original Bird Dance	1981
ELECTROSET	How Does It Feel?	1992
ELEMENT FOUR	Big Brother UK TV Theme	2000
ELEPHANT MAN	Pon De River, Pon De Bank	2003
ELEVATORMAN	Funk & Drive	1995
LARRY ELGART	Hooked On Swing	1982
ELGINS	Heaven Must Have Sent You	1971
	Put Yourself In My Place	1971
YVONNE ELLIMAN	Hello Stranger	1977
	I Can't Get You Out Of My Mind	1977
	I Don't Know How To Love Him	1971
	If I Can't Have You	1978
	Love Me	1976
	Love Pains	1979
BERN ELLIOTT & THE FENMAN		
	New Orleans	1964
	Money	1963
MISSY 'MISDEMEANOR' ELLIOTT		
	Beep Me 911	1998
	4 My People	2002
	Get Ur Freak On	2001
	The Rain (Supa Dupa Fly)	1997

ARTIST	SONG TITLE	DATE
MISSY ELLIOTT	I'm Really Hot	2004
	Pass That Dutch	2003
	Work It	2002
MISSY 'MISDEMEANOR' ELLIOTT featuring DA BRAT		
	Sock It 2 Me	1997
MISSY 'MISDEMEANOR' ELLIOTT featuring NAS, EVE & Q-TI	Hot Boyz	2000
MISSY 'MISDEMEANOR' ELLIOTT featuring LIL' KIM		
	Hit 'Em Wit Da Hee	1998
MISSY 'MISDEMEANOR' ELLIOTT featuring LUDACRIS		
	One Minute Man	2001
MISSY 'MISDEMEANOR' ELLIOTT featuring MC SOLAAR		
	All N My Grill	1999
MISSY ELLIOTT featuring LUDACRIS		
	Gossip Folks	2003
(GHOSTFACE featuring MISSY ELLIOTT)		
	Push	2004
(JANET featuring MISSY ELLIOTT, P. DIDDY & CARLY SIMON)		
	Son Of A Gun	2001
(LIL' KIM featuring DA BRAT, LEFT EYE, MISSY ELLIOTT)		
	Not Tonight	1997
(MELANIE B featuring MISSY ELLIOTT)		
	I Want You Back	1998
(NICOLE featuring MISSY 'MISDEMEANOR'		

ARTIST	SONG TITLE	DATE
	ELLIOTT & MOCHA)	
	Make It Hot	1998
	(TIMBALAND & MAGOO featuring MISSY ELLIOTT)	
	Cop That Shit	2004
	(TOTAL featuring MISSY ELLIOTT)	
	Trippin'	1998
SHIRLEY ELLIS	The Clapping Song	1965
	The Name Game	1964
SOPHIE ELLIS-BEXTOR		
	Get Over You/Move This Mountain	2002
	I Won't Change You	2004
	Mixed Up World	2003
	Murder On The Dancefloor	2001
	Music Gets The Best Of Me	2002
	Take Me Home (A Girl Like Me)	2001
JENNIFER ELLISON	Baby I Don't Care	2003
	Bye Bye Boy	2004
EMBRACE	All You Good Good People (EP)	1997
	Come Back To What You Know	1998
	Fireworks (EP)	1997
	Gravity	2004
	Hooligan	1999
	I Wouldn't Wanna Happpen To You	2000
	Make It Last	2001
	My Weakness Is None Of Your Business	1998

ARTIST	SONG TITLE	DATE
	One Big Family (EP)	1997
	Save Me	2000
	Wonder	2001
	You're Not Alone	2000
EMERSON DRIVE	Fall Into Me	2002
	I Should Be Sleeping	2002
KEITH EMERSON	Honky Tonk Train Blues	1976
EMERSON, LAKE & PALMER		
	Fanfare For The Common Man	1977
	From The Beginning	1972
DICK EMERY	If You Love Her	1969
EMF	Children	1991
	I Believe	1991
	It's You	1992
	Lies	1991
	Perfect Day	1995
	They're Here	1992
	Unbelievable	1991
	Unexplained EP	1992
EMF/REEVES AND MORTIMER		
	I'm A Believer	1995
EMILIA	Big Big World	1998
EMINEM	Business	2003
	Cleanin' Out My Closet	2002
	Just Lose It	2004
	Lose Yourself	2002

ARTIST	SONG TITLE	DATE
	My Name Is	1999
	The Real Slim Shady	2000
	Sing For The Moment	2003
	Stan	2000
	The Way I Am	2000
	Without Me	2002
EMINEM featuring DR. DRE		
	Guilty Conscience	1999
(DR. DRE featuring EMINEM)		
	Forgot About Dre	2000
EMMA	Give A Little Love Back To The World	1990
EMMIE	More Than This	1999
EMOTIONS	Best Of My Love	1977
	I Don't Wanna Lose Your Love	1977
	So I Can Love You	1969
(EARTH, WIND & FIRE WITH THE EMOTIONS)		
	Boogie Wonderland	1979
EN VOGUE	Don't Let Go (Love)	1996
	Free Your Mind/Giving Him Something	
	He Can Feel	1992
	Give It Up, Turn It Loose	1992
	Hold On	1990
	Lies	1990
	Love Don't Love You	1993
	My Lovin' (You're Never Gonna Get It)	1992
	Riddle	2000

ARTIST	SONG TITLE	DATE
	Runaway Love	1993
	Too Gone, Too Long	1997
	Whatever	1997
(SALT 'N 'PEPA featuring EN VOGUE)		
	Whatta Man	1994
EN-CORE	Le Disc Jockey	1998
EN-CORE featuring STEPHEN EMMANUEL & ESKA		
	Coochy Coo	2000
ENCHANTMENT	Gloria	1977
	It's You That I Need	1978
ENERGY 52	Cafe Del Mar	1998
HARRY ENFIELD	Loadsamoney (Doin' Up The House)	1988
ENGLAND BOYS	Go England	2002
ENGLAND DAN & JOHN FORD COLEY		
	Gone Too Far	1977
	I'd Really Love To See You Tonight	1976
	It's Sad To Belong	1977
	Love Is The Answer	1979
	Nights Are Forever Without You	1976
	We'll Never Have To Say Goodbye	
	Again	1978
ENGLAND SUPPORTERS' BAND		
	The Great Escape 2000	2000
ENGLAND UNITED	(How Does It Feel To Be) On Top Of	
	The World	1998

ARTIST	SONG TITLE	DATE
ENGLAND WORLD CUP SQUAD		
	Back Home	1970
	This Time (We'll Get It Right)/England, We'll Fly The Flag	1982
ENGLANDNEWORDER		
	World In Motion	1990
ENGLISH CONGREGATION		
	Softly Whispering I Love You	1972
KIM ENGLISH	Nite Life	1994
SCOTT ENGLISH	Brandy	1971
ENIGMA	Ain't No Stoppin'	1981
	Age Of Loneliness	1994
	Beyond The Invisible	1997
	The Eyes Of Truth	1994
	I Love Music	1981
	Return To Innocence	1994
	Sadeness (Part 1)	1991
ENYA	Anywhere Is	1995
	Book Of Days	1992
	Caribbean Blue	1991
	The Celts	1992
	Evening Falls	1988
	How Can I Keep From Singing?	1991
	On My Way Home	1996
	Only Time	2001
	Orinoco Flow (Sail Away)	1989

ARTIST	SONG TITLE	DATE
	(MARIO WINANS featuring ENYA & P. DIDDY)	
	I Don't Wanna Know	2004
	(PIRATES featuring ENYA, SHOLA AMA, NAILA BOSS & ISHANI)	
	You Should Really Know	2004
EQUALS	Baby, Come Back	1968
	Black Skin Blue Eyed Boys	1970
	Laurel And Hardy	1968
	Michael And The Slipper Tree	1969
	Rub A Dub Dub	1969
	Viva Bobbie Joe	1969
ERASURE	Abba-Esque (EP)	1992
	Always	1994
	Am I Right?	1991
	Blue Savannah	1990
	Breath Of Life	1992
	Chains Of Love	1988
	Chorus (Fishes In The Sea)	1991
	The Circus	1987
	Crackers International (EP)	1988
	Don't Say Your Love Is Killing Me	1997
	Drama!	1989
	Fingers & Thumbs (Cold Summer's Day)	1995
	Freedom	2000
	I Love Saturday	1994
	In My Arms	1997

ARTIST	SONG TITLE	DATE
	It Doesn't Have To Be Me	1987
	A Little Respect	1989
	Love To Hate You	1991
	Make Me Smile (Come Up And See Me)	2003
	Oh L'Amour	2003
	Run To The Sun	1994
	Ship Of Fools	1988
	Solsbury Hill	2003
	Sometimes	1986
	Star	1990
	Stay With Me	1995
	Victim Of Love	1987
	Who Needs Love (Like That)	1992
	You Surround Me	1989
ERNIE	Rubber Duckie	1970
ERUPTION	One Way Ticket	1979
ERUPTION featuring PRECIOUS WILSON		
	I Can't Stand The Rain	1978
ESCAPE CLUB	I'll Be There	1991
	Shake For The Sheik	1988
	Wild Wild West	1988
ESCRIMA	Deeper	1995
	Train Of Thought	1995
ESPN PRESENTS	The Jock Jam	1997
ESQUIRES	And Get Away	1967
	Get On Up	1967

ARTIST	SONG TITLE	DATE
ESSENCE	The Promise	1998
DAVID ESSEX	America	1974
	City Lights	1976
	Coming Home	1976
	Cool Out Tonight	1977
	Falling Angels Riding	1985
	Gonna Make You A Star	1974
	Hold Me Close	1975
	If I Could	1975
	Imperial Wizard	1979
	Lamplight	1973
	Me And My Girl (Night-Clubbing)	1982
	Oh What A Circus	1978
	Rock On	1973
	Rollin' Stone	1975
	Silver Dream Machine (Pt 1)	1980
	Stardust	1974
	Tahiti (From 'Mutiny On The Bounty')	1983
	A Winter's Tale	1982
DAVID ESSEX & CATHERINE ZETA-JONES		
	True Love Ways	1994
GLORIA ESTEFAN	Always Tomorrow	1992
	Coming Out Of The Dark	1991
	Don't Let This Moment End	1999
	Don't Wanna Lose You	1989
	Everlasting Love	1995

ARTIST	SONG TITLE	DATE
	Get On Your Feet	1989
	Go Away	1993
	Heaven's What I Feel	1998
	Here We Are	1989
	Hold Me, Thrill Me, Kiss Me	1994
	I'm Not Giving You Up	1996
	If We Were Lovers/Con Los Anos Que	
	Me Quedan	1993
	Live For Loving You	1991
	Mi Tierra	1993
	Miami Hit Mix/Christmas Through Your	
	Eyes	1992
	Oye	1998
	Oye Mi Canto (Hear My Voice)	1989
	Reach	1996
	Remember Me With Love	1991
	Rhythm Is Gonna Get You	1988
	Seal Our Fate	1991
	Turn The Beat Around	1994
	You'll Be Mine (Party Time)	1996
GLORIA ESTEFAN & THE MIAMI SOUND MACHINE		
	Anything For You	1988
	Betcha Say That	1987
	Can't Stay Away From You	1987
	1-2-3	1988

ARTIST	SONG TITLE	DATE
	(MIAMI SOUND MACHINE)	
	Bad Boy	1986
	Conga	1985
	Dr. Beat	1984
	Falling In Love (Uh-Oh)	1986
	Words Get In The Way	1986
	*NSYNC/GLORIA ESFEFAN)	
	Music Of My Heart	2000
ESTELLE	Free	2004
	1980	2004
DEON ESTUS	Heaven Help Me	1989
ETA	Casual Sub (Burning Spear)	1997
ETERNAL	Angel Of Mine	1997
	Crazy	1994
	Don't You Love Me	1997
	Good Thing	1996
	I Am Blessed	1995
	Just A Step From Heaven	1994
	Oh Baby I...	1994
	Power Of A Woman	1995
	Save Our Love	1994
	Secrets	1996
	So Good	1994
	Someday	1996
	Stay	1994
	What'cha Gonna Do	1999

ARTIST	SONG TITLE	DATE
ETERNAL featuring BEBE WINANS		
	I Wanna Be The Only One	1997
MELISSA ETHERIDGE		
	Come To My Window	1994
	I Want To Come Over	1996
	I'm The Only One	1994
	If I Wanted To/Like The Way I Do	1995
	Nowhere To Go	1996
ETHICS	To The Beat Of The Drum (La Luna)	1995
ETHIOPIANS	Train To Skaville	1967
TONY ETORIA	I Can Prove It	1977
EUROGROOVE	Dive To Paradise	1995
	It's On You (Scan Me)	1995
	Move Your Body	1995
EUROPE	Carrie	1987
	The Final Countdown	1987
	I'll Cry For You	1992
	Rock The Night	1987
	Superstitious	1988
EURYTHMICS	Angel	1990
	Beethoven (I Love To Listen To)	1987
	Don't Ask Me Why	1989
	Here Comes The Rain Again	1984
	I Need A Man	1988
	I Saved The World Today	1999
	It's Alright (Baby's Coming Back)	1986

ARTIST	SONG TITLE	DATE
	The King And Queen Of America	1990
	Love Is A Stranger	1983
	The Miracle Of Love	1986
	Missionary Man	1986
	Revival	1989
	Right By Your Side	1984
	17 Again	2000
	Sexcrime (Nineteen Eighty Four)	1984
	Sweet Dreams (Are Made Of This)	1983
	There Must Be An Angel (Playing With My Heart)	1985
	Thorn In My Side	1986
	When Tomorrow Comes	1986
	Who's That Girl?	1984
	Would I Lie To You?	1985
	You Have Placed A Chill In My Heart	1988
EURYTHMICS & ARETHA FRANKLIN		
	Sisters Are Doin' It For Themselves	1985
EUSEBE	Summertime Healing	1995
EVANESCENCE	Bring Me To Life	2003
	Everybody's Fool	2004
	Going Under	2003
	My Immortal	2003
FAITH EVANS	I Love You	2002
	Love Like This	1998
	Never Gonna Let You Go	1999

ARTIST	SONG TITLE	DATE
	Soon As I Get Home	1995
	You Gets No Love	2001
FAITH EVANS featuring PUFF DADDY		
	All Night Long	1999
(CLIPSE featuring FAITH EVANS)		
	Ma, I Don't Love Her	2003
(ERIC BENET featuring FAITH EVANS)		
	Georgy Porgy	1999
(EVE featuring FAITH EVANS)		
	Love Is Blind	2000
(PUFF DADDY & FAITH EVANS featuring 112)		
	I'll Be Missing You	1997
(WHITNEY HOUSTON featuring FAITH EVANS & KELLY PRICE)		
	Heartbreak Hotel	2000
MAUREEN EVANS	I Love How You Love Me	1964
PAUL EVANS	Hello, This Is Joannie (The Telephone Answering Machine Song)	1978
SARA EVANS	Born To Fly	2000
	I Could Not Ask For More	2001
	I Keep Looking	2002
	No Place That Far	1998
	Suds In The Bucket	2004
EVASIONS	Wikka Wrap	1981
EVE	Good Life	1995
	Gotta Man	1999

ARTIST	SONG TITLE	DATE
	Groove Of Love	1994
	Satisfaction	2002
	Who's That Girl	2001
EVE featuring ALICIA KEYS		
	Gangsta Lovin'	2002
EVE featuring FAITH EVANS		
	Love Is Blind	2000
EVE featuring GWEN STEFANI		
	Let Me Blow Ya Mind	2001
(MARY J. BLIGE featuring EVE)		
	Not Today	2003
(MISSY 'MISDEMEANOR' ELLIOTT featuring NAS, EVE & Q-TI)		
	Hot Boyz	2000
(ANGIE STONE featuring ALICIA KEYS & EVE)		
	Brotha Part II	2002
(CITY HIGH featuring EVE)		
	Caramel	2001
EVE 6	Here's To The Night	2001
	Inside Out	1998
EVE & NOKIO	What Ya Want	1999
EVERCLEAR	Santa Monica (Watch The World Die)	1996
	Wonderful	2000
BETTY EVERETT	Getting Mighty Crowded	1965
	It's In His Kiss (The Shoop Shoop Song)	1968
	Shoop Shoop Song (It's In His Kiss)	1964

ARTIST	SONG TITLE	DATE
	There'll Come A Time	1969
	(JERRY BUTLER & BETTY EVERETT)	
	Let It Be Me	1964
KENNY EVERETT	Captain Kremmen (Retribution)	1977
	Snot Rap	1983
EVERLAST	Black Jesus	2001
	What It's Like	1998
EVERLY BROTHERS	Bowling Green	1967
	Ferris Wheel	1964
	The Girl Sang The Blues	1963
	Gone, Gone, Gone	1964
	I'll Never Get Over You	1965
	It's Been Nice (Goodnight)	1963
	It's My Time	1968
	Love Is Strange	1965
	The Price Of Love	1965
	(So It Is... So It Was) So It Will Always Be	1963
	That'll Be The Day	1965
PHIL EVERLY & CLIFF RICHARD		
	All I Have To Do Is Dream/Miss You Nights	1994
	She Means Nothing To Me	1983
EVERTON 1985	Here We Go	1985
EVERTON FC	All Together Now	1995
EVERY MOTHERS' SON		
	Come On Down To My Boat	1967

ARTIST	SONG TITLE	DATE
EBTG vs SOUL VISION		
	Tracey In My Room	2001
EVERYTHING BUT THE GIRL		
	Before Today	1997
	Covers (EP)	1992
	Driving	1996
	Each And Every One	1984
	Five Fathoms	1999
	I Don't Want To Talk About It	1988
	Missing	1995
	Single	1996
	Walking Wounded	1996
	Wrong	1996
	(DEEP DISH WITH EBTG)	
	The Future Of The Future	1998
EVOLUTION	Everybody Dance	1993
	Love Thing	1993
EXCITERS	Reaching For The Best	1975
EXILE	Kiss You All Over	1978
	You Thrill Me	1978
EXPLOITED	Dead Cities	1981
EXPOSE	Come Go With Me	1987
	I Wish The Phone Would Ring	1992
	I'll Never Get Over You (Getting Over Me)	1993
	Let Me Be The One	1987
	Point Of No Return	1987

ARTIST	SONG TITLE	DATE
	Seasons Change	1987
	Tell Me Why	1989
	What You Don't Know	1989
	When I Looked At Him	1989
	Your Baby Never Looked Good In Blue	1990
EXTREME	Decadence Dance	1991
	Get The Funk Out	1991
	Hole Hearted	1991
	More Than Words	1991
	Rest In Peace	1992
	Song For Love	1992
	Stop The World	1992
	Tragic Comic	1993
EYC	Black Book	1994
	Feelin' Alright	1993
	Number One	1994
	One More Chance	1994
	Ooh-Ah-Aa (I Feel It)	1995
	The Way You Work It	1994
EYE TO EYE	Nice Girls	1982
EYE TO EYE featuring TAKA BOOM		
	Just Can't Get Enough (No No No No)	2001
ADAM F	Circles	1997
	Music In My Mind	1998
ADAM F featuring LIL' MO		
	Where's My...?	2002

ARTIST	SONG TITLE	DATE
(REDMAN featuring ADAM F)		
	Smash Sumthin'	2001
FAB featuring MC PARKER		
	Thunderbirds Are Go	1990
FAB FOR featuring ROBERT OWENS		
	Last Night A DJ Blew My Mind	2003
LARA FABIAN	I Will Love Again	2000
FABOLOUS	Breathe	2004
	Young'n (Holla Back)	2001
FABOLOUS featuring MIKE SHOREY & LIL' MO		
	Can't Let You Go	2003
FABOLOUS featuring NATE DOGG		
	Can't Deny It	2001
FABOLOUS featuring P. DIDDY & JAGGED EDGE		
	Trade It All	2002
FABOLOUS featuring TAMIA		
	Into You	2003
(LIL' MO featuring FABOLOUS)		
	4 Ever	2003
	Superwoman Pt II	2001
(B2K featuring FABOLOUS)		
	Badaboom	2004
FABULOUS BAKER BOYS		
	Oh Boy	1997
FABULOUS THUNDERBIRDS		
	Tuff Enuff	1986

ARTIST	SONG TITLE	DATE
FACE TO FACE	10-9-8	1984
FACES	Cindy Incidentally	1973
	(I Know) I'm Losing You	1971
	Pool Hall Richard/I Wish It Would Rain	1973
	Stay With Me	1972
	ROD STEWART & THE FACES	
	You Can Make Me Dance Sing Or	
	Anything	1974
FACTS OF LIFE	Sometimes	1977
DONALD FAGEN	I.G.Y. (What A Beautiful World)	1982
JOE FAGIN	That's Living (Alright)	1984
YVONNE FAIR	It Should Have Been Me	1976
BARBARA FAIRCHILD		
	Teddy Bear Song	1973
FAIRGROUND ATTRACTION		
	Find My Love	1988
	Perfect	1988
FAIRPORT CONVENTION		
	Si Tu Dois Partir	1969
FAIRWEATHER	Natural Sinner	1970
ANDY FAIRWEATHER-LOW		
	Reggae Tune	1974
	Wide Eyed And Legless	1975
FAITH	You Used To Love Me	1995
FAITH, HOPE AND CHARITY		
	Just One Look	1976

ARTIST	SONG TITLE	DATE
FAITH NO MORE	Ashes To Ashes	1997
	Digging The Grave	1995
	Epic	1990
	Everything's Ruined	1992
	Evidence	1995
	From Out Of Nowhere	1990
	I'm Easy/Be Aggressive	1993
	Midlife Crisis	1992
	Ricochet	1995
	A Small Victory	1992
FAITH NO MORE/BOO-YAA TRIBE		
	Another Body Murdered	1993
	(SPARKS vs FAITH NO MORE)	
	This Town Ain't Big Enough For Both Of	
	Us	1997
ADAM FAITH	The First Time	1963
	I Love Being In Love With You	1964
	If He Tells You	1964
	It's Alright	1965
	A Message To Martha (Kentucky	
	Bluebird)	1964
	Someone's Taken Maria Away	1965
	Stop Feeling Sorry For Yourself	1965
	Walkin' Tall	1963
	We Are In Love	1963
	What Now	1963

ARTIST	SONG TITLE	DATE
HORACE FAITH	Black Pearl	1970
MARIANNE FAITHFULL		
	As Tears Go By	1964
	Come And Stay With Me	1965
	Summer Nights	1965
	This Little Bird	1965
	Yesterday	1965
FAITHLESS	Bring My Family Back	1999
	Don't Leave	1997
	God Is A DJ	1998
	I Want More	2004
	Insomnia	1996
	Mass Destruction	2004
	Muhammad Ali	2001
	Reverence	1997
	Salva Mea	1996
	Take The Long Way Home	1998
	Tarantula	2001
	We Come I	2001
FAITHLESS featuring DIDO		
	One Step Too Far	2002
FALCO	Rock Me Amadeus	1960
	Vienna Calling	1986
BILLY FALCON	Power Windows	1991
CHRISTIAN FALK featuring DEMETREUS		
	Make It Right	2000

ARTIST	SONG TITLE	DATE
FALL	Free Range	1992
	There's A Ghost In My House	1987
	Victoria	1988
HAROLD FALTERMEYER		
	Axel F	1985
AGNETHA FALTSKOG		
	Can't Shake Loose	1983
	The Heat Is On	1983
	If I Thought You'd Ever Change Your Mind	2004
	When You Walk In The Room	2004
FAME AND PRICE TOGETHER		
	Rosetta	1971
GEORGIE FAME	The Ballad Of Bonnie & Clyde	1967
	Because I Love You	1967
	Get Away	1966
	In The Meantime	1965
	Like We Used To Be	1965
	Peaceful	1969
	Seventh Son	1969
	Sittin' In The Park	1966
	Something	1965
	Sunny	1966
	Try My World	1967
	Yeh, Yeh	1965
FAMILY	Burlesque	1972

ARTIST	SONG TITLE	DATE
	In My Own Time	1971
	No Mule's Fool	1969
	Strange Band	1970
FAMILY DOGG	A Way Of Life	1969
FAMILY STAND	Ghetto Heaven	1990
FANCY	Touch Me	1974
	Wild Thing	1974
FANNY	Butter Boy	1975
	Charity Ball	1971
FANTASTICS	Something Old, Something New	1971
FAR CORPORATION	Stairway To Heaven	1985
DON FARDON	Belfast Boy	1970
	Indian Reservation	1970
	(The Lament Of The Cherokee) Indian Reservation	1968
FARGETTA and ANNE-MARIE SMITH		
	Music	1993
DONNA FARGO	Funny Face	1972
	The Happiest Girl In The Whole U.S.A.	1972
CHRIS FARLOWE	Handbags And Gladrags	1967
	Out Of Time	1966
	Ride On Baby	1966
	Think	1966
FARM	All Together Now	1990
	Don't Let Me Down	1991
	Don't You Want Me	1992

ARTIST	SONG TITLE	DATE
	Groovy Train	1990
	Love See No Colour	1993
	Mind	1991
FARM featuring SFX BOYS CHOIR, LIVERPOOL		
	All Together Now 2004	2004
JOHN FARNHAM	You're The Voice	1987
JOANNE FARRELL	All I Wanna Do	1995
DIONNE FARRIS	I Know	1995
GENE FARROW & THE G.F. BAND		
	Move Your Body	1978
FASCINATIONS	Girls Are Out To Get You	1971
SUSAN FASSBENDER		
	Twilight Cafe	1981
FAST FOOD ROCKERS		
	Fast Food Song	2003
	I Love Christmas	2003
	Say Cheese (Smile Please)	2003
FASTBALL	Out Of My Head	1999
	The Way	1998
FASTER PUSSYCAT	House Of Pain	1990
FAT BOYS & CHUBBY CHECKER		
	The Twist (Yo, Twist)	1988
FAT BOYS & THE BEACH BOYS		
	Wipeout	1987
FAT JOE featuring ASHANTI		
	What's Luv?	2002

ARTIST	SONG TITLE	DATE
FAT JOE featuring R. KELLY		
	We Thuggin'	2001
	(JENNIFER LOPEZ featuring BIG PUN & FAT JOE)	
	Feelin' So Good	2000
	(TERROR SQUAD featuring FAT JOE & REMY)	
	Lean Back	2004
	(THALIA featuring FAT JOE)	
	I Want You	2003
FAT LARRY'S BAND	Center City	1977
	Zoom	1982
FAT LES	Naughty Christmas (Goblin In The Office)	1998
	Vindaloo	1998
FAT LES 2000	Jerusalem	2000
FATBACK BAND	(Are You Ready) Do The Bus Stop	1975
	(Do The) Spanish Hustle	1976
	Double Dutch	1977
	I Found Lovin'	1987
	Night Fever	1976
	Yum, Yum (Gimme Some)	1975
FATBOY SLIM	Everybody Needs A 303	1997
	Gangster Trippin	1998
	Praise You	1999
	Right Here Right Now	1999
	The Rockafeller Skank	1998
	Slash Dot Dash	2004

ARTIST	SONG TITLE	DATE
	Slashdotdash	2004
	Star 69	2001
	Sunset (Bird Of Prey)	2000
	Ya Mama/Song For Shelter	2001
FATBOY SLIM featuring MACY GRAY		
	Demons	2001
	(FREDDY FRESH featuring FATBOY SLIM)	
	Badder Badder Schwing	1999
FATHER M.C.	Everything's Gonna Be Alright	1992
	I'll Do 4 You	1991
FATIMA MANSION	Everything I Do	1992
FATMAN SCOOP featuring THE CROOKLYN CLAN		
	Be Faithful	2003
	It Takes Scoop	2004
PHIL FEARON	I Can Prove It	1986
PHIL FEARON & GALAXY		
	Everybody's Laughing	1984
	What Do I Do	1984
GALAXY featuring PHIL FEARON		
	Dancing Tight	1983
	Wait Until Tonight (My Love)	1983
FEEDER	Buck Rogers	2001
	Come Back Around	2002
	Day In Day Out	1999
	Find The Colour	2003
	Forget About Tomorrow	2003

ARTIST	SONG TITLE	DATE
	High	1997
	Insomnia	1999
	Just A Day (EP)	2001
	Just The Way I'm Feeling	2003
	Seven Days In The Sun	2001
	Suffocate	1998
	Turn	2001
	Yesterday Went Too Soon	1999
WILTON FELDER	Inherit The Wind	1980
JOSE FELICIANO	And The Sun Will Shine	1969
	Hi-Heel Sneakers	1968
	Light My Fire	1968
FELIX	Don't You Want Me	1992
	It Will Make Me Crazy	1992
	Stars	1993
FELIX DA HOUSECAT		
	Silver Screen Shower Scene	2002
JULIE FELIX	Heaven Is Here	1970
	If I Could (El Condor Pasa)	1970
FELON	Get Out	2002
FREDDY FENDER	Before The Next Teardrop Falls	1975
	Secret Love	1975
	Wasted Days And Wasted Nights	1975
	You'll Lose A Good Thing	1976
JAY FERGUSON	Shakedown Cruise	1979
	Thunder Island	1977

ARTIST	SONG TITLE	DATE
MAYNARD FERGUSON		
	Gonna Fly Now	1977
LUISA FERNANDEZ	Lay Love On You	1978
FERRANTE & TEICHER		
	Midnight Cowboy	1969
FERRY AID	Let It Be	1987
BRYAN FERRY	Don't Stop The Dance	1985
	Extended Play E.P.	1976
	A Hard Rain's A-Gonna Fall	1973
	I Put A Spell On You	1993
	The In Crowd	1974
	Is Your Love Strong Enough?	1986
	Kiss And Tell	1988
	Let's Stick Together	1976
	The Right Stuff	1987
	Sign Of The Times	1978
	Slave To Love	1985
	Smoke Gets In Your Eyes	1974
	This Is Tomorrow	1977
	Tokyo Joe	1977
	Will You Love Me Tomorrow	1993
	You Go To My Head	1975
LENA FIAGBE	Gotta Get It Right	1993
KAREL FIALKA	Hey Matthew	1987
FICTION FACTORY	(Feels Like) Heaven	1984

ARTIST	SONG TITLE	DATE
FIDDLER'S DRAM	Daytrip To Bangor (Didn't We Have A Lovely Time)	1979
FIELDS OF THE NEPHILIM		
	Moonchild	1988
	Psychonaut	1989
	Sumerland (Dreamed)	1990
FIERCE	Dayz Like That	1999
	Right Here Right Now	1999
	So Long	1999
	Sweet Love 2k	2000
FIESTAS	So Fine	1969
5TH DIMENSION	Aquarius/Let The Sunshine In (Medley)	1969
	Blowing Away	1970
	California Soul	1968
	Carpet Man	1968
	Go Where You Wanna Go	1967
	If I Could Reach You	1972
	(Last Night) I Didn't Get To Sleep At All	1972
	Living Together, Growing Together	1973
	Love's Lines, Angles And Rhymes	1971
	Never My Love	1971
	One Less Bell To Answer	1970
	Paper Cup	1967
	Puppet Man	1970
	Save The Country	1970
	Stoned Soul Picnic	1968

ARTIST	SONG TITLE	DATE
	Sweet Blindness	1968
	Together Let's Find Love	1972
	Up Up & Away	1967
	Wedding Bell Blues	1969
	Workin' On A Groovy Thing	1969
FIFTH ESTATE	Ding Dong The Witch Is Dead	1967
50 CENT	In Da Club	2003
	P.I.M.P.	2003
50 CENT & G-UNIT	If I Can't/...Them Thangs	2004
50 CENT featuring NATE DOGG		
	21 Questions	2003
FILTER	Take A Picture	1999
FILTER AND THE CRYSTAL METHOD		
	(Can't You) Trip Like I Do	1997
FINCH	Letters To You	2003
FINE YOUNG CANNIBALS		
	Don't Look Back	1989
	Ever Fallen In Love	1987
	The Flame	1996
	Good Thing	1989
	I'm Not The Man I Used To Be	1989
	Johnny Come Home	1985
	She Drives Me Crazy	1989
	Suspicious Minds	1986
FINGER ELEVEN	One Thing	2004
FINN	Suffer Never	1995

ARTIST	SONG TITLE	DATE
FINN BROTHERS	Won't Give In	2004
NEIL FINN	She Will Have Her Way	1998
	Sinner	1998
	Wherever You Are	2001
ELISA FIORILLO	On The Way Up	1990
	(JELLYBEAN featuring ELISA FIORILLO)	
	Who Found Who	1987
FIRE ISLAND	There But For The Grace Of God	1994
FIRE ISLAND featuring LOLEATTA HOLLOWAY		
	Shout To The Top	1998
FIREBALLS	Bottle Of Wine	1967
FIREFALL	Cinderella	1977
	Headed For A Fall	1980
	Just Remember I Love You	1977
	Staying With It	1981
	Strange Way	1978
	You Are The Woman	1976
FIREHOUSE	Don't Treat Me Bad	1991
	I Live My Life For You	1995
	Love Of A Lifetime	1991
	When I Look Into Your Eyes	1992
FIRM	Arthur Daley ('E's Alright)	1982
	Star Trekkin'	1987
FIRM	Radioactive	1985
FIRM featuring DAWN ROBINSON		
	Firm Biz	1997

ARTIST	SONG TITLE	DATE
FIRST CHOICE	Armed & Extremely Dangerous	1973
	Smarty Pants	1973
FIRST CLASS	Beach Baby	1974
LISA FISCHER	How Can I Ease The Pain	1991
FISCHERSPOONER	Emerge	2002
FISH	Big Wedge	1990
	A Gentleman's Excuse Me	1990
	Internal Exile	1991
	State Of Mind	1989
CEVIN FISHER/LOLEATTA HOLLOWAY		
	(You Got Me) Burning Up	1999
ELLA FITZGERALD	Can't Buy Me Love	1964
SCOTT FITZGERALD & YVONNE KEELEY		
	If I Had Words	1978
5IVE	Closer To Me	2001
	Don't Wanna Let You Go	2000
	Everybody Get Up	1998
	Got The Feelin'	1998
	If Ya Gettin' Down	1999
	Keep On Movin'	1999
	Let's Dance	2001
	Slam Dunk (Da Funk)	1997
	Until The Time Is Through	1998
	When The Lights Go Out	1998
5IVE & QUEEN	We Will Rock You	2000
FIVE AMERICANS	I See The Light	1966

ARTIST	SONG TITLE	DATE
	Sound Of Love	1967
	Western Union	1967
	Zip Code	1967
FIVE FLIGHTS UP	Do What You Wanna Do	1970
FIVE FOR FIGHTING		
	100 Years	2004
	Superman (It's Not Easy)	2001
FIVE MAN ELECTRICAL BAND		
	Absolutely Right	1971
	Signs	1971
504 BOYZ	Wobble Wobble	2000
5.6.7.8.'S	Woo Hoo	2004
FIVE STAIRSTEPS	O-O-O Child	1970
FIVE STAR	All Fall Down	1985
	Another Weekend	1988
	Can't Wait Another Minute	1986
	Find The Time	1986
	If I Say Yes	1986
	Let Me Be The One	1985
	Love Take Over	1985
	Rain Or Shine	1986
	Rock My World	1988
	The Slightest Touch	1987
	Somewhere Somebody	1987
	Stay Out Of My Life	1987
	Strong As Steel	1987

ARTIST	SONG TITLE	DATE
	System Addict	1986
	Whenever You're Ready	1987
5000 VOLTS	Doctor Kiss-Kiss	1976
	I'm On Fire	1975
FIXX	Are We Ourselves?	1984
	How Much Is Enough	1991
	One Thing Leads To Another	1983
	Saved By Zero	1983
	Secret Separation	1986
	The Sign Of Fire	1983
FKW	Jingo	1994
ROBERTA FLACK	Feel Like Makin' Love	1974
	The First Time Ever I Saw Your Face	1974
	If I Ever See You Again	1978
	Jesse	1973
	Killing Me Softly With His Song	1973
	Making Love	1982
	You've Got A Friend	1971
ROBERTA FLACK & DONNY HATHAWAY		
	Back Together Again	1980
	The Closer I Get To You	1978
	Where Is The Love	1972
ROBERTA FLACK with MAXI PRIEST		
	Set The Night To Music	1991
(PEABO BRYSON & ROBERTA FLACK)		
	Tonight I Celebrate My Love	1983

ARTIST	SONG TITLE	DATE
FLAMING EMBER	I'm Not My Brother's Keeper	1970
	Mind, Body And Soul	1969
	Westbound No. 9	1970
FLAMING LIPS	Do You Realize??	2002
	Fight Test	2003
	Race For The Prize	1999
	Yoshimi Battles The Pink Robots Pt I	2003
FLAMINGOS	The Boogaloo Party	1969
FLASH	Small Beginnings	1972
FLASH AND THE PAN		
	Waiting For A Train	1983
FLEETWOOD MAC	Albatross	1968
	Big Love	1987
	Black Magic Woman	1968
	Don't Stop	1977
	Dreams	1977
	Everywhere	1987
	Go Your Own Way	1977
	The Green Manalishi	1970
	Gypsy	1982
	Hold Me	1982
	Little Lies	1987
	Love In Store	1982
	Man Of The World	1969
	Need Your Love So Bad	1968
	Oh Diane	1982

ARTIST	SONG TITLE	DATE
	Oh Well	1969
	Over My Head	1975
	Rhiannon (Will You Ever Win)	1976
	Sara	1979
	Save Me	1990
	Say You Love Me	1976
	Seven Wonders	1987
	Think About Me	1980
	Tusk	1979
	You Make Lovin' Fun	1977
FLICKMAN	The Sound Of Bamboo	2000
BERNI FLINT	I Don't Want To Put A Hold On You	1977
FLINTLOCK	Dawn	1976
FLIP & FILL	I Wanna Dance With Somebody	2003
	Shooting Star	2002
FLIP & FILL featuring JO JAMES		
	Field Of Dreams	2003
FLIP & FILL featuring JUNIOR		
	Irish Blue	2004
FLIP & FILL featuring KAREN PARRY		
	Discoland	2004
FLIP & FILL featuring KELLY LLORENNA		
	True Love Never Dies	2002
	(PORN KINGS vs FLIP & FILL featuring 740 BOYS)	
	Shake Ya Shimmy	2003
FLIRTATIONS	Nothing But A Heartache	1969

ARTIST	SONG TITLE	DATE
FLOATERS	Float On	1977
FLOCK OF SEAGULLS		
	I Ran (So Far Away)	1982
	The More You Live, The More You Love	1984
	Space Age Love Song	1982
	Transfer Affection	1983
	Wishing (If I Had A Photograph Of You)	1982
FLOETRY	Say Yes	2003
FLOWERED UP	It's On/Egg Rush	1991
	Take It	1991
	Weekender	1992
FLOWERPOT MEN	Let's Go To San Francisco	1967
MIKE FLOWERS POPS		
	Don't Cry For Me Argentina	1996
	Light My Fire/Please Release Me	1996
	Wonderwall	1995
EDDIE FLOYD	Bring It On Home To Me	1968
	I've Never Found A Girl (To Love Me Like You Do)	1968
	Knock On Wood	1966
	Things Get Better	1967
FLUKE	Absurd	1997
	Atom Bomb	1996
	Bubble	1994
	Bullet	1995
	Tosh	1995

ARTIST	SONG TITLE	DATE
FLYING LIZARDS	Money	1979
FLYING MACHINE	Smile A Little Smile For Me	1969
FLYING PICKETS	Only You	1983
	When You're Young And In Love	1984
FOCUS	Hocus Pocus	1973
	Sylvia	1973
FOG	Been A Long Time	1998
DAN FOGELBERG	Hard To Say	1981
	Heart Hotels	1980
	The Language Of Love	1984
	Leader Of The Band	1981
	Longer	1979
	Make Love Stay	1983
	Missing You	1982
	Part Of The Plan	1975
	Run For The Roses	1982
	Same Old Lang Syne	1980
DAN FOGELBERG/TIM WEISBERG		
	The Power Of Gold	1978
JOHN FOGERTY	The Old Man Down The Road	1984
	Rock And Roll Girls	1985
	Rockin' All Over The World	1975
FOGHAT	Drivin' Wheel	1976
	I Just Want To Make Love To You	1977
	Slow Ride	1975
	Stone Blue	1978

ARTIST	SONG TITLE	DATE
	Third Time Lucky (First Time I Was A Fool)	1979
BEN FOLDS FIVE	Army	1999
	Battle Of Who Could Care Less	1997
	Brick	1998
	Kate	1997
	Underground	1996
FOLK IMPLOSION	Natural One	1995
LENNY FONTANA & DJ SHORTY		
	Chocolate Sensation	2000
WAYNE FONTANA	Come On Home	1966
	It Was Easier To Hurt Her	1965
	Pamela, Pamela	1966
WAYNE FONTANA & THE MINDBENDERS		
	Game Of Love	1965
	Just A Little Bit Too Late	1965
	She Needs Love	1965
	Stop Look And Listen	1964
	Um, Um, Um, Um, Um, Um	1964
FOO FIGHTERS	All My Life	2002
	Big Me	1996
	Breakout	2000
	Everlong	1997
	For All The Cows	1995
	Have It All	2003
	I'll Stick Around	1995

ARTIST	SONG TITLE	DATE
	Learn To Fly	1999
	Low	2003
	Monkey Wrench	1997
	My Hero	1998
	This Is A Call	1995
	Times Like These	2003
FOO FIGHTERS/WEEN		
	Walking After You/Beacon Light	1998
FOOL'S GARDEN	Lemon Tree	1996
STEVE FORBERT	Romeo's Tune	1979
FORCE M.D.'S	Tender Love	1986
CLINTON FORD	Run To The Door	1967
LITA FORD	Kiss Me Deadly	1988
LITA FORD & OZZY OSBOURNE		
	Close My Eyes Forever	1989
MARTYN FORD ORCHESTRA		
	Let Your Body Go Downtown	1977
WILLA FORD	I Wanna Be Bad	2001
JULIA FORDHAM	Happy Ever After	1988
	Love Moves (In Mysterious Ways)	1992
FOREIGNER	Blue Morning, Blue Day	1978
	Break It Up	1982
	Cold As Ice	1977
	Dirty White Boy	1978
	Double Vision	1978
	Feels Like The First Time	1977

ARTIST	SONG TITLE	DATE
	Head Games	1979
	Hot Blooded	1978
	I Don't Want To Live Without You	1988
	I Want To Know What Love Is	1984
	Juke Box Hero	1982
	Long, Long Way From Home	1977
	Say You Will	1987
	That Was Yesterday	1985
	Urgent	1981
	Waiting For A Girl Like You	1981
FORMATIONS	At The Top Of The Stairs	1971
FORREST	Feel The Need In Me	1983
	Rock The Boat	1983
FORTUNES	Freedom Come, Freedom Go	1971
	Here Comes That Rainy Day Feeling Again	1971
	Here It Comes Again	1965
	Storm In A Teacup	1972
	This Golden Ring	1966
	You've Got Your Troubles	1965
49ERS	Don't You Love Me	1990
	Girl To Girl	1990
	Touch Me	1989
49ERS featuring ANNE-MARIE SMITH		
	Rockin' My Body	1995

ARTIST	SONG TITLE	DATE
FOSTER AND ALLEN		
	A Bunch Of Thyme	1982
	Maggie	1983
DAVID FOSTER	Love Theme From St. Elmo's Fire	1985
FOUNDATION featuring NATALIE ROSSI		
	All Out Of Love	2003
FOUNDATIONS	Baby, Now That I've Found You	1967
	Back On My Feet Again	1968
	Build Me Up Buttercup	1969
	In The Bad Bad Old Days	1969
FOUNTAINS OF WAYNE		
	I Want An Alien For Christmas	1997
	Radiation Vibe	1997
	Stacy's Mom	2003
FOUR BUCKETEERS	The Bucket Of Water Song	1980
4-4-2	Come On England	2004
FOUR JACKS & A JILL		
	Master Jack	1968
4 NON BLONDES	What's Up	1993
4 OF US	She Hits Me	1993
411	Dumb	2004
411 featuring GHOSTFACE KILLAH		
	On My Knees	2004
4 P.M.	Sukiyaki	1994
FOUR PENNIES	Black Girl	1964
	I Found Out The Hard Way	1964

ARTIST	SONG TITLE	DATE
	Juliet	1964
	Troble Is My Middle Name	1966
	Until It's Time For You To Go	1965
FOUR SEASONS	Alone	1964
	Beggin'	1967
	Big Girls Don't Cry	1962
	Big Man In Town	1964
	Bye, Bye, Baby (Baby Goodbye)	1965
	C'mon Marianne	1967
	Dawn (Go Away)	1964
	December '63 (Oh What A Night)	1975
	Down The Hall	1977
	I've Got You Under My Skin	1966
	Let's Hang On!	1965
	Opus 17 (Don't You Worry 'Bout Me)	1966
	Rag Doll	1964
	Rhapsody	1977
	Ronnie	1964
	Save It For Me	1964
	Silver Star	1976
	Stay	1964
	Tell It To The Rain	1966
	Walk Like A Man	1963
	Watch The Flowers Grow	1967
	We Can Work It Out	1976
	Who Loves You	1975

ARTIST	SONG TITLE	DATE
	Will You Love Me Tomorrow	1968
	Working My Way Back To You	1966
(FRANKIE VALLI & THE FOUR SEASONS)		
	The Night	1975
(WONDER WHO?)		
	Don't Think Twice	1965
4 STRINGS	Diving	2002
	(Take Me Away) Into The Night	2002
4 THE CAUSE	Stand By Me	1998
FOUR TOPS	Ain't No Woman (Like The One I've Got)	1973
	Are You Man Enough	1973
	Ask The Lonely	1965
	Baby I Need Your Loving	1964
	Bernadette	1967
	Do What You Gotta Do	1969
	Don't Walk Away	1981
	I Can't Help Myself	1965
	I'm In A Different World	1968
	If I Were A Carpenter	1968
	It's All In The Game	1970
	It's The Same Old Song	1965
	Just Seven Numbers (Can Straighten Out My Life)	1971
	Keeper Of The Castle	1972
	Loco In Acapulco	1988
	Loving You Is Sweeter Than Ever	1966

ARTIST	SONG TITLE	DATE
	Macarthur Park (Part II)	1971
	Reach Out I'll Be There	1966
	Seven Rooms Of Gloom	1967
	Shake Me Wake Me (When It's Over)	1966
	Simple Game	1971
	Something About You	1965
	Standing In The Shadows Of Love	1966
	Still Water (Love)	1970
	Sweet Understanding Love	1973
	Walk Away Renee	1968
	Walk With Me Talk With Me Darling	1972
	What Is A Man	1969
	When She Was My Girl	1981
	Yesterday's Dreams	1968
	You Keep Running Away	1967
FOUR TOPS featuring SMOKEY ROBINSON		
	Indestructible	1989
	(SUPREMES & FOUR TOPS)	
	River Deep Mountain High	1970
	You Gotta Have Love In Your Heart	1971
FOURMOST	Baby I Need Your Lovin'	1964
	Girls, Girls, Girls	1965
	Hello Little Girl	1963
	How Can I Tell Her	1964
	I'm In Love	1963
	A Little Loving	1964

ARTIST	SONG TITLE	DATE
14-18	Goodbye-Ee	1975
FOX	Imagine Me, Imagine You	1975
	Only You Can	1975
	S-S-S-Single Bed	1976
GEMMA FOX featuring MC LYTE		
	Girlfriend's Story	2004
JAMES FOX	Hold Onto Our Love	2004
NOOSHA FOX	Georgina Bailey	1977
SAMANTHA FOX	Do Ya Do Ya (Wanna Please Me)	1986
	Hold On Tight	1986
	I Only Wanna Be With You	1989
	I Surrender (To The Spirit Of The Night)	1987
	I Wanna Have Some Fun	1988
	Love House	1988
	Nothing's Gonna Stop Me Now	1987
	Touch Me (I Want Your Body)	1986
SAMANTHA FOX featuring FULL FORCE		
	Naughty Girls (Need Love Too)	1988
	(DJ MILANO featuring SAMANTHA FOX)	
	Santa Maria	1998
BRUCE FOXTON	Freak	1983
INEZ FOXX	Hurt By Love	1964
INEZ & CHARLIE FOXX		
	Mockinbird	1969
JOHN FOXX	Burning Car	1980
	Europe (After The Rain)	1981

ARTIST	SONG TITLE	DATE
	No-One Driving (Double Single)	1980
	Underpass	1980
FOXY	Get Off	1978
	Hot Number	1979
FPI PROJECT	Going Back To My Roots	1989
FRAGGLES	'Fraggle Rock' Theme	1984
FRAGMA	Say That You're Here	2001
	Toca Me	1999
	Toca's Miracle	2000
	You Are Alive	2001
FRAGMA featuring MARIA RUBIA		
	Everytime You Need Me	2001
PETER FRAMPTON	Baby, I Love Your Way	1976
	Do You Feel Like We Do	1976
	I Can't Stand It No More	1979
	I'm In You	1977
	Show Me The Way	1976
	Signed, Sealed, Delivered (I'm Yours)	1977
CONNIE FRANCIS	Be Anything (But Be Mine)	1964
	Blue Winter	1964
	My Child	1965
	Vacation	1992
CLAUDE FRANCOIS	Tears On The Telephone	1976
FRANK AND WALTERS		
	After All	1993

ARTIST	SONG TITLE	DATE
FRANKE & THE KNOCKOUTS		
	Sweetheart	1981
	Without You (Not Another Lonely Night)	1982
	You're My Girl	1981
FRANKEE	F.U.R.B. (F U Right Back)	2004
FRANKIE GOES TO HOLLYWOOD		
	The Power Of Love	1984
	Rage Hard	1986
	Relax	1985
	Two Tribes	1984
	Warriors (Of The Wasteland)	1986
	Watching The Wildlife	1987
	Welcome To The Pleasuredome	1985
ARETHA FRANKLIN	Ain't No Way	1968
	All The King's Horses	1972
	Angel	1973
	Another Night	1986
	Baby I Love You	1967
	Border Song (Holy Moses)	1970
	Bridge Over Troubled Water/Brand New Me	1971
	Call Me/Son Of A Preacher Man	1970
	Chain Of Fools	1967
	Day Dreaming	1972
	A Deeper Love	1994
	Don't Play That Song	1970

ARTIST	SONG TITLE	DATE
	Eleanor Rigby	1969
	Freeway Of Love	1985
	The House That Jack Built	1968
	I Can't See Myself Leaving You	1969
	I Never Loved A Man (The Way I Love You)	1967
	I Say A Little Prayer	1968
	I'm In Love	1974
	Jimmy Lee	1986
	Jump To It	1982
	Jumpin' Jack Flash	1986
	Master Of Eyes (The Deepness Of Your Eyes)	1973
	My Song	1968
	A Natural Woman (You Make Me Feel Like)	1967
	Respect	1967
	Rock Steady	1971
	A Rose Is Still A Rose	1998
	Satisfaction	1968
	See Saw	1968
	Share Your Love With Me	1969
	Something He Can Feel	1976
	Spanish Harlem	1971
	Spirit In The Dark	1970

ARTIST	SONG TITLE	DATE
	(Sweet Sweet Baby) Since You've Been Gone	1968
	Think	1968
	Until You Come Back To Me (That's What I'm Gonna Do)	1973
	The Weight	1969
	Who's Zoomin' Who	1985
	Willing To Forgive	1994
	You're All I Need To Get By	1971
ARETHA FRANKLIN & ELTON JOHN		
	Through The Storm	1989
ARETHA FRANKLIN & GEORGE MICHAEL		
	I Knew You Were Waiting (For Me)	1987
ARETHA FRANKLIN/WHITNEY HOUSTON		
	It Isn't, It Wasn't, It Ain't Ever Gonna Be	1989
	(EURYTHMICS & ARETHA FRANKLIN) Sisters Are Doin' It For Themselves	1985
ERMA FRANKLIN	(Take A Little) Piece Of My Heart	1992
RODNEY FRANKLIN	The Groove	1980
FRANTIQUE	Strut Your Funky Stuff	1979
FRANZ FERDINAND	Matinee	2004
	Michael	2004
	Take Me Out	2004
FREAK NASTY	Da' Dip	1997
FREAK POWER	No Way	1998
	Turn On, Tune In, Cop Out	1995

ARTIST	SONG TITLE	DATE
FRED & ROXY	Something For The Weekend	2000
JOHN FRED & HIS PLAYBOY BAND		
	Judy In Disguise (With Glasses)	1967
FREDDIE & THE DREAMERS		
	Do The Freddie	1965
	I Love You Baby	1964
	I Understand	1965
	I'm Telling You Now	1965
	If You Gotta Make A Fool Of Somebody	1963
	A Little You	1965
	Over You	1964
	You Were Made For Me	1965
FREE	All Right Now	1970
	Free (EP)	1978
	Little Bit Of Love	1972
	My Brother Jake	1971
	Wishing Well	1973
FREEEZ	Flying High	1981
	I.O.U.	1983
	Pop Goes My Love	1983
	Southern Freeez	1981
FREEFALL featuring JAN JOHNSTON		
	Skydive (I Feel Wonderful)	2001
FREELAND	We Want Your Soul	2003
BOBBY FREEMAN	C'mon And Swim	1964
FREE MOVEMENT	I've Found Someone Of My Own	1971

ARTIST	SONG TITLE	DATE
FREESTYLERS	Push Up	2004
FREESTYLERS featuring TENOR FLY		
	B-Boy Stance	1998
ACE FREHLEY	New York Groove	1976
FREIHEIT	Keeping The Dream Alive	1988
NICKI FRENCH	Don't Play That Song Again	2000
	Total Eclipse Of The Heart	1995
FRESH 4	Wishing On A Star	1989
DOUG E. FRESH & THE GET FRESH CREW		
	The Show	1985
FREDDY FRESH featuring FATBOY SLIM		
	Badder Badder Schwing	1999
GLENN FREY	The Heat Is On	1984
	I Found Somebody	1982
	The One You Love	1982
	Sexy Girl	1984
	Smuggler's Blues	1985
	True Love	1988
	You Belong To The City	1985
FRIDA	I Know There's Something Going On	1982
RALPH FRIDGE	Angel	2000
DEAN FRIEDMAN	Ariel	1977
	Lucky Stars	1978
	Lydia	1978
FRIEND AND LOVER		
	Reach Out Of The Darkness	1968

ARTIST	SONG TITLE	DATE
FRIENDS OF DISTINCTION		
	Going In Circles	1969
	Grazin' In The Grass	1969
	Love Or Let Me Be Lonely	1970
FRIJID PINK	The House Of The Rising Sun	1970
MAX FROST & THE TROOPERS		
	Shape Of Things To Come	1968
FU-SCHNICKENS WITH SHAQUILLE O'NEAL		
	What's Up Doc? (Can We Rock)	1993
FUEL	Hemorrhage (In My Hands)	2000
FUGEES	Fu-Gee-La	1995
	Killing Me Softly	1996
	No Woman No Cry	1996
	Ready Or Not	1996
	Rumble In The Jungle	1997
FULL FORCE	Alice I Want You Just For Me	1985
	(JAMES BROWN featuring FULL FORCE)	
	I'm Real	1988
	(SAMANTHA FOX featuring FULL FORCE)	
	Naughty Girls (Need Love Too)	1988
FULL INTENTION	America (I Love America)	1996
	Shake Your Body (Down To The Ground)	1997
BOBBY FULLER FOUR		
	I Fought The Law	1966
	Love's Made A Fool Of You	1966

ARTIST	SONG TITLE	DATE
FUN BOY THREE	The Lunatics Have Taken Over The Asylum	1981
	Our Lips Are Sealed	1983
	Summertime	1982
	The Telephone Always Rings	1982
	The Tunnel Of Love	1983
FUN BOY THREE & BANANARAMA		
	It Ain't What You Do It's The Way That You Do It	1982
	(BANANARAMA with FUN BOY THREE)	
	Really Saying Something	1982
FUN LOVIN' CRIMINALS		
	Big Night Out	1998
	The Fun Lovin' Criminal	1996
	I'm Not In Love/Scooby Snacks	1997
	King Of New York	1997
	Korean Bodega	1999
	Loco	2001
	Love Unlimited	1998
	Scooby Snacks	1996
FUNERAL FOR A FRIEND		
	Escape Artists Never Die	2004
	Juneau	2003
	She Drove Me To Daytime Television	2003
FARLEY 'JACKMASTER' FUNK featuring DARYL PANDY		
	Love Can't Turn Around	1986
FUNKADELIC	One Nation Under A Groove (Pt I)	1978

ARTIST	SONG TITLE	DATE
FUNKDOOBIEST	Bow Wow Wow	1994
	Wopbabalubop	1993
FUNK MASTERS	It's Over	1983
FUNKSTAR DE LUXE/BOB MARLEY		
	Rainbow Country	2000
	Sun Is Shining	1999
FUNKY GREEN DOGS		
	Fired Up!	1997
FUNKY WORM	Hustle! (To The Music...)	1988
RICHIE FURAY	I Still Have Dreams	1979
FUREYS & DAVIE ARTHUR		
	When You Were Sweet Sixteen	1981
FURNITURE	Brilliant Mind	1986
NELLY FURTADO	Forca	2004
	I'm Like A Bird	2001
	... On The Radio (Remember The Days)	2002
	Powerless (Say What You Want)	2003
	Try	2004
	Turn Off The Light	2001
BILLY FURY	Do You Really Love Me Too	1964
	Give Me Your Word	1966
	I Will	1964
	I'll Never Quite Get Over You	1966
	I'm Lost Without You	1965
	In Summer	1963
	In Thoughts Of You	1965

ARTIST	SONG TITLE	DATE
	It's Only Make Believe	1964
	Like I've Never Been Gone	1963
	Run To My Lovin' Arms	1965
	Somebody Else's Girl	1963
	When Will You Say I Love You	1963
FUTURE BREEZE	Temple Of Dreams	2002
FUTURE SOUND OF LONDON		
	Cascade	1993
	Far Out Son Of Lung And The Ramblings Of A Madman	1995
	Lifeforms	1994
	My Kingdom	1996
	Papua New Guinea	1992
	We Have Explosive	1997
FUTUREHEADS	Decent Days And Nights	2004
FUZZ	I Love You For All Seasons	1971
FUZZBOX	International Rescue	1989
	Pink Sunshine	1989
	Self!	1989
	(WE'VE GOT A FUZZBOX AND WE'RE GONNA USE IT) Love Is The Slug	1986
FYA featuring SMUJJI		
	Must Be Love	2004
ALI G & SHAGGY	Me Julie	2002
DARIO G	Carnaval 2002	2002

ARTIST	SONG TITLE	DATE
	Carnaval De Paris	1998
	Dream To Me	2001
	Heaven Is Closer (Feels Like Heaven)	2003
	Sunchyme	1997
	Sunmachine	1998
	Voices	2000
GINA G	Fresh	1997
	Gimme Some Love	1997
	I Belong To You	1996
	Ooh Aah... Just A Little Bit	1996
	Ti Amo	1997
KENNY G	Auld Lang Syne	1999
	Don't Make Me Wait For Love	1987
	Forever In Love	1992
	Silhouette	1988
	Songbird	1987
KENNY G WITH PEABO BRYSON		
	By The Time This Night Is Over	1993
(TONI BRAXTON WITH KENNY G)		
	How Could An Angel Break My Heart	1997
WARREN G	Do You See	1995
	I Shot The Sheriff	1997
	This D.J.	1994
WARREN G & NATE DOGG		
	Regulate	1994

ARTIST	SONG TITLE	DATE
WARREN G featuring ADINA HOWARD		
	What's Love Got To Do With It	1996
WARREN G featuring MACK 10		
	I Want It All	1999
WARREN G featuring RON ISLEY		
	Smokin' Me Out	1997
WARREN G featuring SISSEL		
	Prince Igor	1998
(NATE DOGG featuring WARREN G)		
	Nobody Does It Better	1998
(PETER ANDRE featuring WARREN G)		
	All Night All Right	1998
G-UNIT	Stunt 101	2003
	Wanna Get To Know You	2004
(50 CENT & G-UNIT)		
	If I Can't/... Them Thangs	2004
(JOE featuring G-UNIT)		
	Ride Wit U/More & More	2004
G.O.S.H.	The Wishing Well	1987
PETER GABRIEL	Big Time	1987
	Biko	1980
	Digging In The Dirt	1992
	Games Without Frontiers	1980
	In Your Eyes	1986
	No Self Control	1980
	Shock The Monkey	1982

ARTIST	SONG TITLE	DATE
	Sledgehammer	1986
	Solsbury Hill	1977
	Steam	1992
	SW Live (EP)	1994
PETER GABRIEL & KATE BUSH		
	Don't Give Up	1986
GABRIELLE	Because Of You	1994
	Don't Need The Sun To Shine (To Make	
	Me Smile)	2001
	Dreams	1993
	Forget About The World	1996
	Give Me A Little More Time	1996
	Going Nowhere	1993
	I Wish	1993
	If You Really Cared	1996
	Out Of Reach	2001
	Rise	2000
	Should I Stay	2000
	Stay The Same	2004
	Sunshine	1999
	Walk On By	1997
	When A Woman	2000
	(EAST 17 featuring GABRIELLE)	
	If You Ever	1996
DAVE GAHAN	Bottle Living	2003
	Dirty Sticky Floors	2003

ARTIST	SONG TITLE	DATE
	I Need You	2003
ROSIE GAINES	Closer Than Close	1997
	I Surrender	1997
GALA	Come Into My Life	1998
	Freed From Desire	1997
	Let A Boy Cry	1997
GALLAGHER & LYLE	Breakaway	1976
	Every Little Teardrop	1977
	Heart On My Sleeve	1976
	I Wanna Stay With You	1976
LIAM GALLAGHER/DEATH IN VEGAS		
	Scorpio Rising	2002
	(BUFFALO TOM: LIAM GALLAGHER & STEVE	
	CRADOCK)	
	Going Underground/Carnation	1999
PATSY GALLANT	From New York To L.A.	1977
GALLEON	So I Begin	2002
GALLERY	Big City Miss Ruth Ann	1972
	I Believe In Music	1972
	Nice To Be With You	1972
GALLIANO	Long Time Gone	1994
	Twyford Down	1994
FRANK GALLUP	The Ballad Of Irving	1966
JAMES GALWAY	Annie's Song	1978
GAP BAND	Big Fun	1986

ARTIST	SONG TITLE	DATE
	Burn Rubber On Me (Why You Wanna Hurt Me)	1981
	Early In The Morning	1982
	Humpin'	1981
	Oops Upside Your Head	1980
	Party Lights	1980
	Someday	1984
	You Dropped A Bomb On Me	1982
GARBAGE	Androgyny	2001
	Breaking Up The Girl	2002
	Cherry Lips (Go Baby Go!)	2002
	I Think I'm Paranoid	1998
	Milk	1996
	Only Happy When It Rains	1995
	Push It	1998
	Queer	1995
	Shut Your Mouth	2002
	Special	1998
	Stupid Girl	1996
	When I Grow Up	1999
	The World Is Not Enough	1999
	You Look So Fine	1999
ADAM GARCIA	Night Fever	1998
SCOTT GARCIA featuring MC STYLES		
	A London Thing	1997
BORIS GARDINER	Elizabethan Reggae	1970

ARTIST	SONG TITLE	DATE
	I Want To Wake Up With You	1986
	You're Everything To Me	1986
ART GARFUNKEL	All I Know (As Garfunkel)	1973
	Break Away	1975
	Bright Eyes	1979
	I Only Have Eyes For You	1975
	I Shall Sing	1973
	Second Avenue	1974
	Since I Don't Have You	1979
ART GARFUNKEL, JAMES TAYLOR & PAUL SIMON		
	(What A) Wonderful World	1978
JESSICA GARLICK	Come Back	2002
GALE GARNETT	We'll Sing In The Sunshine	1964
LAURENT GARNIER		
	Greed/The Man With The Red Face	2000
LEE GARRETT	You're My Everything	1976
LEIF GARRETT	Feel The Need	1979
	I Was Made For Dancin'	1978
	Runaround Sue	1977
	Surfin' U.S.A.	1977
LESLEY GARRETT & AMANDA THOMPSON		
	Ave Maria	1993
DAVID GARRICK	Dear Mrs. Applebee	1966
	Lady Jane	1966
GARY'S GANG	Keep On Dancin'	1979
GAT DECOR	Passion	1996

ARTIST	SONG TITLE	DATE
STEPHEN GATELY	I Believe	2000
	New Beginning/Bright Eyes	2000
	Stay	2001
DAVID GATES	Goodbye Girl	1977
	Never Let Her Go	1975
	Took The Last Train	1978
GARETH GATES	Anyone Of Us (Stupid Mistake)	2002
	Say It Isn't So	2003
	Unchained Melody	2002
	What My Heart Wants To Say	2002
GARETH GATES featuring THE KUMARS		
	Spirit In The Sky	2003
(WILL YOUNG & GARETH GATES)		
	The Long And Winding Road/Suspicious Minds	2002
GAY DAD	Joy!	1999
	To Earth With Love	1999
MARVIN GAYE	Abraham, Martin & John	1970
	Ain't That Peculiar	1965
	Baby Don't You Do It	1964
	Chained	1968
	Come Get To This	1973
	Distant Lover	1974
	The End Of Our Road	1970
	Got To Give It Up	1977

ARTIST	SONG TITLE	DATE
	How Sweet It Is To Be Loved By You	1964
	I Heard It Through The Grapevine	1968
	I Want You	1976
	I'll Be Doggone	1965
	Inner City Blues (Makes Me Wanna Holler)	1971
	Let's Get It On	1973
	Mercy Mercy Me	1971
	My Love Is Waiting	1983
	One More Heartache	1966
	Pretty Little Baby	1965
	(Sexual) Healing	1982
	That's The Way Love Is	1969
	Too Busy Thinking About My Baby	1969
	Trouble Man	1972
	Try It Baby	1964
	What's Going On	1971
	You	1968
	You're A Wonderful One	1964
	Your Unchanging Love	1967
MARVIN GAYE & DIANA ROSS		
	My Mistake (Was To Love You)	1974
	You're A Special Part Of Me	1973
MARVIN GAYE & KIM WESTON		
	It Takes Two	1967

ARTIST	SONG TITLE	DATE
MARVIN GAYE & MARY WELLS		
	Once Upon A Time	1964
	What's The Matter With You Baby	1964
MARVIN GAYE & TAMMI TERRELL		
	Ain't No Mountain High Enough	1967
	Ain't Nothing Like The Real Thing	1968
	Good Lovin' Ain't Easy To Come By	1969
	If I Could Build My Whole World Around You	1967
	Keep On Lovin' Me Honey	1968
	Onion Song	1969
	You Ain't Livin' Till You're Lovin'	1969
	You're All I Need To Get By	1968
	Your Precious Love	1967
	(DIANA ROSS & MARVIN GAYE)	
	Stop Look Listen (To Your Heart)	1974
	You Are Everything	1974
	(ERICK SERMON featuring MARVIN GAYE)	
	Music	2001
CRYSTAL GAYLE	Don't It Make My Brown Eyes Blue	1977
	Half The Way	1979
	Talking In Your Sleep	1978
	(EDDIE RABBITT WITH CRYSTAL GAYLE)	
	You And I	1982
MICHELLE GAYLE	Do You Know	1997
	Freedom	1995

ARTIST	SONG TITLE	DATE
	Happy Just To Be With You	1995
	I'll Find You	1994
	Looking Up	1993
	Sensational	1997
	Sweetness	1994
GLORIA GAYNOR	How High The Moon	1976
	I Am What I Am	1983
	I Will Survive	1978
	Let Me Know (I Have A Right)	1979
	Never Can Say Goodbye	1974
	Reach Out, I'll Be There	1975
GAZZA	Geordie Boys (Gazza Rap)	1990
GAZZA and LINDISFARNE		
	Fog On The Tyne (Revisited)	1990
DAVID GEDDES	The Last Game Of The Season (A Blind Man In The Bleachers)	1975
	Run Joey Run	1975
J. GEILS BAND	Angel In Blue	1982
	Centerfold	1981
	Come Back	1980
	Freeze-Frame	1982
	Give It To Me	1973
	I Do	1982
	Looking For A Love	1971
	Love Stinks	1980
	Must Of Got Lost	1974

ARTIST	SONG TITLE	DATE
	One Last Kiss	1978
BOB GELDOF	The Great Song Of Indifference	1990
	This Is The World Calling	1986
GEMINI	Could It Be Forever	1996
	Even Though You Broke My Heart	1995
	Steal Your Love Away	1996
GEMS FOR JEM	Lifting Me Higher	1995
GENE & DEBBE	Playboy	1968
GENE	As Good As It Gets	1999
	Fighting Fit	1996
	Fill Her Up	1999
	For The Dead	1996
	Haunted By You	1995
	Olympian	1995
	Sleep Well Tonight	1994
	Speak To Me Someone	1997
	We Could Be Kings	1997
	Where Are They Now?	1997
GENERAL PUBLIC	I'll Take You There	1994
	Tenderness	1984
GENERATION X	King Rocker	1979
	Valley Of The Dolls	1979
	Your Generation	1977
GENESIS	Abacab	1981
	Congo	1997
	Follow You Follow Me	1978

ARTIST	SONG TITLE	DATE
	Hold On My Heart	1992
	I Can't Dance	1992
	I Know What I Like (In Your Wardrobe)	1974
	In Too Deep	1987
	Invisible Touch	1986
	Jesus He Knows Me	1992
	Keep It Dark	1981
	Land Of Confusion	1986
	Mama	1983
	Man On The Corner	1982
	Misunderstanding	1980
	Never A Time	1992
	No Reply At All	1981
	No Son Of Mine	1991
	Paperlate	1982
	Spot The Pigeon (EP)	1977
	Tell Me Why	1993
	That's All!	1983
	3 X 3 (EP)	1982
	Throwing It All Away	1986
	Tonight Tonight Tonight	1987
	Turn It On Again	1980
GENEVA	Best Regrets	1997
	Into The Blue	1997
	No One Speaks	1996
	Tranquillizer	1997

ARTIST	SONG TITLE	DATE
GENIUS CRU	Boom Selection	2001
	Course Bruv	2001
GENIUS/GZA featuring D'ANGELO		
	Cold World	1996
BOBBIE GENTRY	Fancy	1969
	I'll Never Fall In Love Again	1969
	Ode To Billie Joe	1967
	Raindrops Keep Fallin' On My Head	1970
BOBBIE GENTRY & GLEN CAMPBELL		
	All I Have To Do Is Dream	1969
	Let It Be Me	1969
GENTRYS	Keep On Dancing	1965
GEORDIE	All Because Of You	1973
	Can You Do It	1973
	Don't Do That	1972
	Electric Lady	1973
SOPHIA GEORGE	Girlie Girlie	1985
GEORGIA SATELLITES		
	Keep Your Hands To Yourself	1986
GERARDO	Rico Suave	1991
	We Want The Funk	1991
DANYEL GERRARD	Butterfly	1971
GERRY & THE PACEMAKERS		
	Don't Let The Sun Catch You Crying	1964
	Ferry 'Cross The Mersey	1964
	Girl On A Swing	1966

ARTIST	SONG TITLE	DATE
	How Do You Do It?	1964
	I Like It	1964
	I'll Be There	1964
	I'm The One	1964
	It's Gonna Be All Right	1964
	Walk Hand In Hand	1965
	You'll Never Walk Alone	1963
GET WET	Just So Lonely	1981
GETO BOYS	Mind Playing Tricks On Me	1991
	Six Feet Deep	1993
STAN GETZ/ASTRUD GILBERTO		
	The Girl From Ipanema	1964
GHOST TOWN DJ'S		
	My Boo	1996
GHOSTFACE featuring MISSY ELLIOTT		
	Push	2004
GHOSTFACE KILLAH		
	All That I Got Is You	1997
	Cherchez Laghost	2000
GHOSTFACE KILLAH/411		
	On My Knees	2004
(ANOTHER LEVEL/GHOSTFACE KILLAH)		
	I Want You For Myself	1999
(EAMON featuring GHOSTFACE)		
	Love Them	2004

ARTIST	SONG TITLE	DATE
	(MARK RONSON featuring GHOSTFACE KILLAH & NATE DOGG)	
	Ooh Wee	2003
GIANT	I'll See You In My Dreams	1990
GIANT STEPS	Another Lover	1988
ANDY GIBB	Desire	1980
	An Everlasting Love	1978
	I Just Wanna Be Your Everything	1977
	(Love Is) Thicker Than Water	1977
	Me (Without You)	1981
	(Our Love) Don't Throw It All Away	1978
	Shadow Dancing	1978
	Time Is Time	1980
ANDY GIBB & OLIVIA NEWTON-JOHN		
	I Can't Help It	1980
BARRY GIBB	Shine Shine	1984
	(BARBRA STREISAND & BARRY GIBB)	
	Guilty	1980
	What Kind Of Fool	1981
ROBIN GIBB	Boys Do Fall In Love	1984
	Oh! Darling	1978
	Please	2003
	Saved By The Bell	1969
STEVE GIBBONS BAND		
	Tulane	1977

ARTIST	SONG TITLE	DATE
TERRI GIBBS	Somebody's Knockin'	1981
DEBBIE GIBSON	Anything Is Possible	1990
	Electric Youth	1989
	Foolish Beat	1988
	Lost In Your Eyes	1989
	No More Rhyme	1989
	Only In My Dreams	1987
	Out Of The Blue	1988
	Shake Your Love	1987
	Staying Together	1988
	We Could Be Together	1989
	(CRAIG MCLACHLAN & DEBBIE GIBSON)	
	You're The One That I Want	1993
WAYNE GIBSON	Under My Thumb	1974
GIBSON BROTHERS	Cuba/Better Do It Salsa	1980
	Mariana	1980
	Ooh! What A Life	1979
	Que Sera Mi Vida (If You Should Go)	1979
GIDEA PARK	Beach Boy Gold	1981
	Seasons Of Gold	1981
GIGOLO AUNTS	Where I Find My Heaven	1995
ASTRUD GILBERTO/STAN GETZ		
	The Girl From Ipanema	1964
NICK GILDER	Hot Child In The City	1978
DONNA GILES	And I'm Telling You I'm Not Going	1996
JOHNNY GILL	Fairweather Friend	1990

ARTIST	SONG TITLE	DATE
	My, My, My	1990
	Rub You The Right Way	1990
	(SHABBA RANKS featuring JOHNNY GILL)	
	Slow And Sexy	1992
VINCE GILL/AMY GRANT		
	House Of Love	1994
	(BARBRA STREISAND/VINCE GILL)	
	If You Ever Leave Me	1999
GILLAN	Mutually Assured Destruction	1981
	New Orleans	1981
	Nightmare	1981
	No Laughing In Heaven	1981
	Restless	1982
	Trouble	1980
MICKEY GILLEY	Stand By Me	1980
STUART GILLIES	Amanda	1973
BILLY GILMAN	One Voice	2000
THEA GILMORE	Juliet (Keep That In Mind)	2003
JAMES GILREATH	Little Band Of Gold	1963
JIM GILSTRAP	Swing Your Daddy	1975
GORDON GILTRAP	Heartsong	1978
GIN BLOSSOMS	Found Out About You	1993
	Hey Jealousy	1993
	Till I Hear It From You/Follow You Down	1996
GINUWINE	Differences	2001
	Hell Yeah	2003

ARTIST	SONG TITLE	DATE
	Holler	1998
	Pony	1996
	So Anxious	1999
	Stingy	2002
	Tell Me Do U Wanna	1997
	What's So Different?	1999
	When Doves Cry	1997
	(P. DIDDY & GINUWINE featuring LOON, MARIO WINANS)	
	I Need A Girl (Part Two)	2002
MARTINE GIRAULT	Revival	1993
GIRL THING	Girls On Top	2000
	Last One Standing	2000
GIRLS ALOUD	Jump	2003
	Life Got Cold	2003
	Love Machine	2004
	No Good Advice	2003
	The Show	2004
	Sound Of The Underground	2002
GIRLS AT PLAY	Airhead	2001
	Respectable	2001
GIRLS OF FHM	Da Ya Think I'm Sexy?	2004
GIRLSCHOOL	Hit And Run	1981
JUNIOR GISCOMBE	Then Came You	1992
GIUFFRIA	Call To The Heart	1984

ARTIST	SONG TITLE	DATE
GLADIATOR featuring IZZY		
	Now We Are Free	2004
GLAMMA KID	Bills 2 Pay	2000
	Why	1999
GLAMMA KID featuring SHOLA AMA		
	Taboo	1999
GLASS BOTTLE	I Ain't Got Time Anymore	1971
GLASS TIGER	Don't Forget Me (When I'm Gone)	1986
	I Will Be There	1987
	I'm Still Searching	1988
	Someday	1986
GLASS TIGER featuring ROD STEWART		
	My Town	1991
GLENN & CHRIS	Diamond Lights	1987
GARY GLITTER	Always Yours	1974
	And Then She Kissed Me	1981
	Another Rock And Roll Christmas	1984
	Dance Me Up	1984
	Do You Wanna Touch Me (Oh Yeah)	1973
	Doing Alright With The Boys	1975
	Hello! Hello! I'm Back Again	1973
	I Didn't Know I Loved You (Till I Saw You Rock And Roll)	1972
	I Love You Love Me Love	1973
	I'm The Leader Of The Gang (I Am)	1973
	It Takes All Night Long	1977

ARTIST	SONG TITLE	DATE
	A Little Boogie Woogie (In The Back Of My Mind)	1977
	Love Like You And Me	1975
	Oh Yes! You're Beautiful	1974
	Papa Oom Mow Mow	1975
	Remember Me This Way	1974
	Rock & Roll Part 2	1972
	You Belong To Me	1976
GLITTER BAND	Angel Face	1974
	Goodbye My Love	1975
	Just For You	1974
	Let's Get Together Again	1974
	Love In The Sun	1975
	People Like You And People Like Me	1976
	The Tears I Cried	1975
DANA GLOVER	Thinking Over	2003
GLOWORM	Carry Me Home	1994
	I Lift My Cup	1993
GO WEST	Call Me	1985
	Don't Look Down — The Sequel	1987
	Faithful	1992
	Goodbye Girl	1985
	The King Of Wishful Thinking	1990
	Tracks Of My Tears	1993
	We Close Our Eyes	1985
	What You Won't Do For Love	1993

ARTIST	SONG TITLE	DATE
GO-GO'S	Head Over Heels	1984
	Our Lips Are Sealed	1981
	Turn To You	1984
	Vacation	1982
	We Got The Beat	1982
	The Whole World Lost Its Head	1995
GODIEGO	The Water Margin	1977
GODLEY & CREME	Cry	1985
	Under Your Thumb	1981
	Wedding Bells	1981
GODSPELL	Day By Day	1972
ANDREW GOLD	How Can This Be Love	1978
	Lonely Boy	1977
	Never Let Her Slip Away	1978
	Thank You For Being A Friend	1978
BRIAN & TONY GOLD/RED DRAGON		
	Compliments On Your Kiss	1994
	(SHAGGY featuring BRIAN & TONY GOLD)	
	Hey Sexy Lady	2002
GOLDBUG	Whole Lotta Love	1996
GOLDEN EARRING	Radar Love	1974
	Twilight Zone	1982
GOLDEN GIRLS	Kinetic	1998
GOLDFRAPP	Black Cherry	2004
	Strict Machine	2004
	Train	2003

ARTIST	SONG TITLE	DATE
	Twist	2003
GOLDIE	Believe	1998
	Inner City Life	1995
	Making Up Again	1978
	Tempertemper	1998
GOLDIE featuring KRS ONE		
	Digital	1997
GOLDIE & THE GINGERBREADS		
	Can't You Hear My Heartbeat	1965
GOLDIE LOOKIN CHAIN		
	Guns Don't Kill People Rappers Do	2004
	Half Man Half Machine/Self Suicide	2004
	Your Mother's Got A Penis	2004
BOBBY GOLDSBORO		
	Autumn Of My Life	1968
	Blue Autumn	1966
	Hello, Summertime	1974
	Honey	1968
	It's Too Late	1966
	Little Things	1965
	See The Funny Little Clown	1964
	The Straight Life	1966
	Summer (The First Time)	1973
	Voodoo Woman	1965
	Watching Scotty Grow	1970
	Whenever He Holds You	1964

ARTIST	SONG TITLE	DATE
GLEN GOLDSMITH	Dreaming	1988
	I Won't Cry	1987
	What You See Is What You Get	1988
GOLDTRIX presents ANDREA BROWN		
	It's Love (Trippin')	2002
GOMEZ	Bring It On	1999
	Catch Me Up	2004
	Rhythm & Blues Alibi	1999
	Shot Shot	2002
	We Haven't Turned Around	1999
	Whippin' Piccadilly	1998
IAN GOMM	Hold On	1979
GOMPIE	Alice (Who The X Is Alice?)	1995
GONZALEZ	Haven't Stopped Dancing Yet	1979
GOO GOO DOLLS	Black Balloon	1999
	Broadway	2000
	Here Is Gone	2002
	Iris	1998
	Name	1995
	Slide	1998
GOOD CHARLOTTE	The Anthem	2003
	Girls And Boys	2003
	Lifestyles Of The Rich And Famous	2003
	Predictable	2004
	The Young And The Hopeless/Hold On	2003

ARTIST	SONG TITLE	DATE
GOODBYE MR MACKENZIE		
	The Rattler	1989
ROGER GOODE featuring TASHA BAXTER		
	In The Beginning	2002
GOODFELLAS	Sugar Honey Ice Tea	1997
GOODFELLAS featuring LISA MILLETT		
	Soul Heaven	2001
GOODIE MOBB	Cell Therapy	1995
GOODIES	Black Pudding Bertha	1975
	Funky Gibbon/Sick-Man Blues	1975
	The In Betweenies/Father Christmas Do Not Touch Me	1974
	Make A Daft Noise For Christmas	1975
	Nappy Love/Wild Thing	1975
DICKIE GOODMAN	Energy Crisis '74	1974
	Mr. Jaws	1975
GOODMEN	Give It Up	1993
DELTA GOODREM	Born To Try	2003
	Innocent Eyes	2003
	Lost Without You	2003
	Not Me Not I	2003
GOOMBAY DANCE BAND		
	Seven Tears	1982
GOONS	Ying Tong Song	1973
LONNIE GORDON	Gonna Catch You	1991
	Happenin' All Over Again	1990

ARTIST	SONG TITLE	DATE
(QUARTZ LOCK featuring LONNIE GORDON)		
	Love Eviction	1995
LESLEY GORE	California Nights	1967
	I Don't Wanna Be A Loser	1964
	It's My Party	1963
	Look Of Love	1964
	Maybe I Know	1964
	My Town, My Guy And Me	1965
	Sunshine, Lollipops & Roses	1965
	That's The Way Boys Are	1964
GORILLAZ	Clint Eastwood	2001
	19/2000	2001
	Rock The House	2001
	Tomorrow Comes Today	2002
EYDIE GORME	Blame It On The Bossa Nova	1963
(STEVE LAWRENCE & EYDIE GORME)		
	I Want To Stay Here	1963
MATT GOSS	Fly	2004
	I'm Coming With Ya	2003
	If You Were Here Tonight	1996
	The Key	1995
IRV GOTTI presents JA RULE, ASHANTI, CHARLI BALTIMORE		
	Down 4 U	2002
ROBERT GOULET	My Love, Forgive Me (Amore, Scusami)	1964
GOURYELLA	Gouryella	1999

ARTIST	SONG TITLE	DATE
	Walhalla	1999
G.Q.	Disco Nights (Rock Freak)	1979
	I Do Love You	1979
GRACE	Down To Earth	1996
	Hand In Hand	1997
	I Want To Live	1995
	If I Could Fly	1996
	Not Over Yet	1995
	Skin On Skin	1996
(PLANET PERFECTO featuring GRACE)		
	Not Over Yet 99	1999
GRAFITI	What Is The Problem?	2003
JAKI GRAHAM	Breaking Away	1986
	Round And Round	1985
	Set Me Free	1986
	Step Right Up	1986
(DAVID GRANT & JAKI GRAHAM)		
	Could It Be I'm Falling In Love	1985
	Mated	1985
LARRY GRAHAM	One In A Million You	1980
	Your Love	1975
MIKEY GRAHAM	You're My Angel	2000
LOU GRAMM	Just Between You And Me	1989
	Midnight Blue	1987
	True Blue Love	1990

ARTIST	SONG TITLE	DATE
GRAND FUNK	Bad Time	1975
	The Loco-Motion	1974
	Shinin' On	1974
	Some Kind Of Wonderful	1974
	Walk Like A Man	1973
	We're An American Band	1973
GRAND FUNK RAILROAD		
	Closer To Home	1970
	Footstompin' Music	1972
	Inside Looking Out	1971
	Rock 'n Roll Soul	1972
GRANDADDY	The Crystal Lake	2001
	Now It's On	2003
GRANDMASTER FLASH, MELLE MEL & THE FURIOUS FIVE		
	The Message	1982
	White Lines	1983
GRANDMASTER MELLE MEL & THE FURIOUS FIVE		
	Step Off (Pt 1)	1984
GRANGE HILL CAST		
	Just Say No	1986
AMY GRANT	Baby Baby	1991
	Big Yellow Taxi	1995
	Every Heartbeat	1991
	Find A Way	1985
	Good For Me	1992

ARTIST	SONG TITLE	DATE
	I Will Remember You	1992
	Lucky One	1994
	That's What Love Is For	1991
AMY GRANT WITH VINCE GILL		
	House Of Love	1994
	(PETER CETERA & AMY GRANT)	
	The Next Time I Fall	1986
DAVID GRANT	Love Will Find A Way	1983
	Stop And Go	1983
	Watching You Watching Me	1983
DAVID GRANT & JAKI GRAHAM		
	Could It Be I'm Falling In Love	1985
	Mated	1985
EDDY GRANT	Can't Get Enough Of You	1981
	Do You Feel My Love?	1980
	Electric Avenue	1983
	Gimme Hope Jo'anna	1988
	I Don't Wanna Dance	1982
	I Love You, Yes I Love You	1981
	Living On The Front Line	1979
	Romancing The Stone	1984
JULIE GRANT	Come To Me	1964
	Count On Me	1963
	Up On The Roof	1963
GRAPEFRUIT	C'mon Marianne	1968
	Dear Delilah	1968

ARTIST	SONG TITLE	DATE
GRASS ROOTS	Baby Hold On	1970
	Bella Linda	1968
	Glory Bound	1972
	Heaven Knows	1969
	I'd Wait A Million Years	1969
	Let's Live For Today	1967
	Midnight Confessions	1968
	The River Is Wide	1969
	The Runaway	1972
	Sooner Or Later	1971
	Temptation Eyes	1970
	Things I Should Have Said	1967
	Two Divided By Love	1971
	Where Were You When I Needed You	1966
GRATEFUL DEAD	Touch Of Grey	1987
DAVID GRAY	Babylon	2000
	Be Mine	2003
	The Other Side	2002
	Please Forgive Me	2000
	Sail Away	2001
	Say Hello Wave Goodbye	2001
	This Year's Love	2001
DOBIE GRAY	Drift Away	1973
	The 'In' Crowd	1965
	You Can Do It	1978
DORIAN GRAY	I've Got You On My Mind	1968

ARTIST	SONG TITLE	DATE
LES GRAY	A Groovy Kind Of Love	1977
	Demons	2001
MACY GRAY	I Try	1999
	Still	2000
	When I See You	2003
	Why Didn't You Call Me	2000
MACY GRAY featuring ERYKAH BADU		
	Sweet Baby	2001
	(BLACK EYED PEAS featuring MACY GRAY)	
	Request & Line	2001
	(FATBOY SLIM featuring MACY GRAY)	
	Demons	2001
CHARLES RANDOLPH GREAN SOUNDE		
	Quentin's Theme (From TV Series 'Dark Shadows')	1969
GREAT WHITE	The Angel Song	1989
	Once Bitten Twice Shy	1989
R.B. GREAVES	Always Something There To Remind Me	1970
	Take A Letter Maria	1969
CYNDI GRECCO	Making Our Dreams Come True	1976
GREEDIES	A Merry Jingle	1979
GREEN DAY	American Idiot	2004
	Basket Case	1995
	Brain Stew/Jaded	1996
	Geek Stink Breath	1995
	Hitchin' A Ride	1997

ARTIST	SONG TITLE	DATE
	Longview	1995
	Minority	2000
	Redundant	1998
	Stuck With Me	1996
	Time Of Your Life (Good Riddance)	1998
	Waiting	2001
	Warning	2000
	Welcome To Paradise	1994
	When I Come Around	1995
GREEN JELLY	Anarchy In The UK	1993
	Three Little Pigs	1993
	(HULK HOGAN WITH GREEN JELLY)	
	I'm The Leader Of The Gang	1993
GREEN VELVET	La La Land	2002
AL GREEN	Call Me (Come Back Home)	1973
	Full Of Fire	1975
	Here I Am (Come And Take Me)	1973
	I'm Still In Love With You	1972
	Keep Me Cryin'	1976
	L-O-V-E (Love)	1975
	Let's Get Married	1974
	Let's Stay Together	1971
	Livin' For You	1973
	Look What You Done For Me	1972
	Sha-La-La (Make Me Happy)	1974
	Tired Of Being Alone	1971

ARTIST	SONG TITLE	DATE
	You Ought To Be With Me	1972
	(ANNIE LENNOX & AL GREEN)	
	Put A Little Love In Your Heart	1988
	(ARTHUR BAKER /BACKBEAT DISCIPLES	
	featuring AL GREEN)	
	The Message Is Love	1989
GARLAND GREEN	Jealous Kind Of Fella	1969
JESSE GREEN	Come With Me	1977
	Flip	1976
	Nice And Slow	1976
PAT GREEN	Wave On Wave	2003
ROBSON GREEN & JEROME FLYNN		
	I Believe/Up On The Roof	1995
	Unchained Melody/White Cliffs Of Dover	1995
	What Becomes Of The Broken	
	Hearted/Saturday Night At The Movies	1996
VIVIAN GREEN	Emotional Rollercoaster	2003
NORMAN GREENBAUM		
	Spirit In The Sky	1970
LORNE GREENE	Ringo	1964
LEE GREENWOOD	God Bless The USA	2001
GREYHOUND	Black And White	1971
	I Am What I Am	1972
	Moon River	1972
GRID	Crystal Clear	1993
	Diablo	1995

ARTIST	SONG TITLE	DATE
	Rollercoaster	1994
	Swamp Thing	1994
	Texas Cowboys	1994
ALISTAIR GRIFFIN	Bring It On/My Lover's Prayer	2004
	You And Me (Tonight)	2004
BILLY GRIFFIN	Hold Me Tighter In The Rain	1983
ANDY GRIGGS	She's More	2000
	You Won't Ever Be Lonely	1999
LARRY GROCE	Junk Food Junkie	1976
GROOVE ARMADA	At The River	1999
	Easy	2003
	If Everybody Looked The Same	1999
	My Friend	2001
	Purple Haze	2002
	Superstylin'	2001
GROOVE ARMADA featuring GRAM'MA FUNK		
	I See You Baby	1999
GROOVE GENERATION featuring LEO SAYER		
	You Make Me Feel Like Dancing	1998
GROOVE THEORY	Tell Me	1995
GROOVERIDER	Rainbows Of Colour	1998
HENRY GROSS	Shannon	1976
	Springtime Mama	1976
GSP	The Banana Song	1992
GTR	When The Heart Rules The Mind	1986
GUESS WHO	Albert Flasher	1971

ARTIST	SONG TITLE	DATE
	American Woman/No Sugar Tonight	1970
	Clap For The Wolfman	1974
	Dancin' Fool	1974
	Hand Me Down World	1970
	Laughing	1969
	No Time	1969
	Rain Dance	1971
	Shakin' All Over	1965
	Share The Land	1970
	Star Baby	1974
	These Eyes	1969
	Undun	1969
DAVID GUETTA featuring CHRIS WILLIS		
	Just A Little More Love	2003
GREG GUIDRY	Goin' Down	1982
GUN	Race With The Devil	1968
GUN	Better Days	1989
	Crazy You	1997
	Don't Say It's Over	1994
	The Only One	1995
	Shame On You	1990
	Something Worthwhile	1995
	Steal Your Fire	1992
	Word Up	1994
GUNHILL ROAD	Back When My Hair Was Short	1973

ARTIST	SONG TITLE	DATE
GUNS N' ROSES	Ain't It Fun	1993
	The Civil War (EP)	1993
	Don't Cry	1991
	Knockin' On Heaven's Door	1992
	Live And Let Die	1991
	Paradise City	1989
	Patience	1989
	Since I Don't Have You	1994
	Sweet Child O' Mine	1988
	Sympathy For The Devil	1995
	Welcome To The Jungle/Nightrain	1988
	Yesterdays/November Rain	1992
	You Could Be Mine	1991
GUNTHER & THE SUNSHINE GIRLS		
	Ding Dong Song	2004
GURU	Feel The Music	1995
GURU featuring N'DEA DAVENPORT		
	Trust Me	1993
GURU featuring CHAKA KHAN		
	Watch What You Say	1995
GURU featuring DEE C. LEE		
	No Time To Play	1993
GURU JOSH	Infinity	1990
	Whose Law (Is It Anyway?)	1990
ADRIAN GURVITZ	Classic	1982
GUSTO	Disco's Revenge	1996

ARTIST	SONG TITLE	DATE
	Let's All Chant	1996
ARLO GUTHRIE	The City Of New Orleans	1972
GWEN GUTHRIE	Ain't Nothing Goin' On But The Rent	1986
	Good To Go Lover/Outside In The Rain	1987
	(They Long To Be) Close To You	1986
GUY	Dancin'	1999
JASMINE GUY	Just Want To Hold You	1991
A GUY CALLED GERALD		
	Voodoo Ray (EP)	1989
GUYS & DOLLS	Here I Go Again	1975
	Stoney Ground	1976
	There's A Whole Lot Of Loving	1975
	You Don't Have To Say You Love Me	1976
GYPSYMEN	Babarabatiri	2001
H & CLAIRE	All Out Of Love	2002
	DJ	2002
	Half A Heart	2002
H-TOWN	Knockin' Da Boots	1993
	They Like It Slow	1997
	A Thin Line Between Love & Hate	1996
H2O	Dream To Sleep	1983
	Just Outside Of Heaven	1983
H2O FEATURING BILLIE		
	Nobody's Business	1996
HADDAWAY	Catch A Fire	1995
	Fly Away	1995

ARTIST	SONG TITLE	DATE
	I Miss You	1993
	Life	1993
	Rock My Heart	1994
	What Is Love	1993
SAMMY HAGAR	Give To Live	1987
	I Can't Drive 55	1984
	I've Done Everything For You	1980
	Two Sides To Love	1984
	Your Love Is Driving Me Crazy	1982
MERLE HAGGARD	If We Can Make It Through December	1973
K-CI HAILEY OF JODECI		
	If You Think You're Lonely Now	1995
HAIRCUT 100	Fantastic Day	1982
	Favourite Shirts (Boy Meets Girl)	1981
	Love Plus One	1982
	Nobody's Fool	1982
CURTIS HAIRSTON	I Want Your Lovin' (Just A Little Bit)	1985
HAL featuring GILLIAN ANDERSON		
	Extremis	1997
HALE & PACE	The Stonk	1991
BILL HALEY & HIS COMETS		
	Rock Around The Clock	1974
AARON HALL	All The Places (I Will Kiss You)	1998
	I Miss You	1994
AUDREY HALL	One Dance Won't Do	1986
	Smile	1986

ARTIST	SONG TITLE	DATE
DARYL HALL	Dreamtime	1986
	Foolish Pride	1986
	Stop Loving Me, Stop Loving You	1994
DARYL HALL & JOHN OATES		
	Adult Education	1984
	Back Together Again	1977
	Did It In A Minute	1982
	Do What You Want, Be What You Are	1976
	Downtown Life	1988
	Everything Your Heart Desires	1988
	Family Man	1983
	How Does It Feel To Be Back	1980
	I Can't Go For That (No Can Do)	1981
	It's A Laugh	1978
	Kiss On My List	1981
	Maneater	1982
	Method Of Modern Love	1984
	Missed Opportunity	1988
	One On One	1983
	Out Of Touch	1984
	Possession Obsession	1985
	Private Eyes	1981
	Rich Girl	1977
	Sara Smile	1976
	Say It Isn't So	1983
	She's Gone	1976

ARTIST	SONG TITLE	DATE
	So Close	1990
	Some Things Are Better Left Unsaid	1985
	Wait For Me	1979
	The Way You Do The Things You Do/My Girl	1985
	You Make My Dreams	1981
	You've Lost That Lovin' Feeling	1980
	Your Imagination	1982
DARYL HALL/SOUNDS OF BLACKNESS		
	Gloryland	1994
JIMMY HALL	I'm Happy That Love Has Found You	1980
LYNDEN DAVID HALL		
	Do I Qualify?	1998
	Forgive Me	2000
	Sexy Cinderella	1998
TOM T. HALL	I Love	1973
GERI HALLIWELL	Bag It Up	2000
	Calling	2001
	It's Raining Men	2001
	Lift Me Up	1999
	Look At Me	1999
	Mi Chico Latino	1999
	Scream If You Wanna Go Faster	2001
HALO JAMES	Could Have Told You So	1989
ANTHONY HAMILTON		
	Charlene	2004

ARTIST	SONG TITLE	DATE
(NAPPY ROOTS featuring ANTHONY HAMILTON)		
	Po' Folks	2002
(TWISTA featuring ANTHONY HAMILTON)		
	Sunshine	2004
ASHLEY HAMILTON	Wimmin'	2003
HAMILTON, JOE FRANK & REYNOLDS		
	Don't Pull Your Love	1971
	Fallin' In Love	1975
	Winners And Losers	1975
LYNNE HAMILTON	On The Inside (Theme from 'Prisoner Cell Block H')	1989
MARVIN HAMLISCH	The Entertainer	1974
M.C. HAMMER	Addams Groove	1991
	Do Not Pass Me By	1992
	(Hammer Hammer) They Put Me In The Mix	1991
	Have You Seen Her	1990
	Here Comes The Hammer	1991
	Pray	1990
	Pumps And A Bump	1994
	2 Legit 2 Quit	1991
	U Can't Touch This	1990
	Yo!!! Sweetness	1991
JAN HAMMER	Crockett's Theme	1987
	Miami Vice Theme	1985
ALBERT HAMMOND	Free Electric Band	1973

ARTIST	SONG TITLE	DATE
	I'm A Train	1974
	It Never Rains In Southern California	1972
HAMPENBERG	Ducktoy	2002
HERBIE HANCOCK	Autodrive	1983
	I Thought It Was You	1978
	Rockit	1983
	You Bet Your Love	1979
HANDLEY FAMILY	Wam Bam	1973
HANSON	I Will Come To You	1997
	If Only	2000
	Mmmbop	1997
	Thinking Of You	1998
	This Time Around	2000
	Weird	1998
	Where's The Love	1997
HAPPENINGS	Go Away Little Girl	1966
	I Got Rhythm	1967
	My Mammy	1967
	See You In September	1966
HAPPY CLAPPERS	Can't Help It	1996
	Hold On	1995
	I Believe	1995
HAPPY MONDAYS	The Boys Are Back In Town	1999
	Judge Fudge	1991
	Kinky Afro	1990
	Loose Fit	1991

ARTIST	SONG TITLE	DATE
	Madchester Rave On (EP)	1989
	Step On	1990
	Stinkin Thinkin	1992
ED HARCOURT	All Of Your Days Will Be Blessed	2003
PAUL HARDCASTLE	Don't Waste My Time	1986
	Just For Money	1985
	19	1985
	The Wizard	1986
DUANE HARDEN/ARMAND VAN HELDEN		
	You Don't Know Me	1999
	(POWERHOUSE featuring DUANE HARDEN)	
	What You Need	1999
MIKE HARDING	Rochdale Cowboy	1975
FRANCOISE HARDY	All Over The World	1965
	Et Meme	1965
	Tous Les Garcons Et Les Filles	1964
STEVE HARLEY	Here Comes The Sun	1976
STEVE HARLEY & COCKNEY REBEL		
	Make Me Smile (Come Up And See Me)	1975
	Mr Raffles (Man, It Was Mean)	1975
	(COCKNEY REBEL)	
	Judy Teen	1974
	Mr. Soft	1974
	(SARAH BRIGHTMAN & STEVE HARLEY)	
	The Phantom Of The Opera	1986
HARLEY QUINNE	New Orleans	1972

ARTIST	SONG TITLE	DATE
HARMONIX	Landslide	1996
HARMONY GRASS	Move In A Little Closer Baby	1969
JIMMY HARNEN WITH SYNC		
	Where Are You Now	1989
HARPERS BIZARRE	Anything Goes	1967
	Come To The Sunshine	1967
	The 59th Street Bridge Song (Feelin' Groovy)	1967
HARPO	Movie Star	1976
SLIM HARPO	Baby Scratch My Back	1966
HARRIET	Temple Of Love	1991
ANITA HARRIS	Anniversary Waltz	1968
	Dream A Little Dream Of Me	1968
	Just Loving You	1967
EMMYLOU HARRIS	Here, There & Everywhere	1976
	Mister Sandman	1981
JET HARRIS & TONY MEEHAN		
	Applejack	1963
	Diamonds	1963
	Scarlett O'Hara	1963
KEITH HARRIS & ORVILLE		
	Orville's Song	1982
	White Christmas	1985
MAJOR HARRIS	Love Won't Let Me Wait	1975
NIKI HARRIS/SNAP!		
	Exterminate!	1993

ARTIST	SONG TITLE	DATE
	Do You See The Light (Looking For)	1993
RICHARD HARRIS	Macarthur Park	1968
ROLF HARRIS	Bluer Than Blue	1969
	Fine Day	2000
	Stairway To Heaven	1993
	Sun Arise	1962
	Two Little Boys	1969
SAM HARRIS	Sugar Don't Bite	1984
SIMON HARRIS	Bass (How Low Can You Go)	1988
	Here Comes That Sound	1988
GEORGE HARRISON		
	All Those Years Ago	1981
	Any Road	2003
	Bangla Desh	1971
	Blow Away	1979
	Crackerbox Palace	1977
	Dark Horse	1974
	Ding Dong	1974
	Give Me Love (Give Me Peace On Earth)	1973
	Got My Mind Set On You	1987
	My Sweet Lord/Isn't It A Pity	1970
	This Song	1976
	What Is Life	1971
	When We Was Fab	1988
	You	1975
NOEL HARRISON	The Windmills Of Your Mind	1969

ARTIST	SONG TITLE	DATE
WILBERT HARRISON		
	Let's Work Together (Part 1)	1969
HARRY J. & THE ALL STARS		
	Liquidator	1969
DEBBIE HARRY	French Kissin' In The USA	1986
DEBORAH HARRY	Backfired	1981
	I Can See Clearly	1993
	I Want That Man	1989
COREY HART	Boy In The Box	1985
	Can't Help Falling In Love	1986
	Everything In My Heart	1985
	I Am By Your Side	1986
	In Your Soul	1988
	It Ain't Enough	1984
	A Little Love	1990
	Never Surrender	1985
	Sunglasses At Night	1984
FREDDIE HART	Easy Loving	1971
RICHARD HARTLEY/MICHAEL REED ORCHESTRA		
	The Music Of Torvill & Dean (EP)	1984
DAN HARTMAN	I Can Dream About You	1984
	Instant Replay	1978
	Second Nature	1985
	This Is It	1979
	We Are The Young	1984
HARVEY	Get Up And Move	2002

ARTIST	SONG TITLE	DATE
SENSATIONAL ALEX HARVEY BAND		
	The Boston Tea Party	1976
	Delilah	1975
	Gamblin' Bar Room Blues	1975
BRIAN HARVEY	Straight Up No Bends	2001
BRIAN HARVEY AND THE REFUGEE CREW		
	Loving You (Ole Ole Ole)	2001
	(TRUE STEPPERS featuring BRIAN HARVEY & DONELL JONES)	
	True Step Tonight	2000
PJ HARVEY	C'mon Billy	1995
	Down By The Water	1995
	The Letter	2004
	A Perfect Day Elise	1998
	Send His Love To Me	1995
	The Wind	1999
GORDON HASKELL	How Wonderful You Are	2001
DAVID HASSELHOFF		
	If I Could Only Say Goodbye	1993
DONNY HATHAWAY		
	You've Got A Friend	1971
	(ROBERTA FLACK & DONNY HATHAWAY)	
	Back Together Again	1980
	The Closer I Get To You	1978
	Where Is The Love	1972

ARTIST	SONG TITLE	DATE
CHARLOTTE HATHERLEY		
	Summer	2004
HATIRAS featuring SLARTA JOHN		
	Spaced Invader	2001
HAVEN	Say Something	2002
	Til The End	2002
RICHIE HAVENS	Here Comes The Sun	1971
CHESNEY HAWKES	I'm A Man Not A Boy	1991
	The One And Only	1991
EDWIN HAWKINS SINGERS		
	Oh Happy Day	1969
	(MELANIE WITH THE EDWIN HAWKINS SINGERS)	
	Lay Down (Candles In The Rain)	1970
SOPHIE B. HAWKINS		
	As I Lay Me Down	1995
	Damn I Wish I Was Your Lover	1992
	Don't Don't Tell Me No	1994
	Right Beside You	1994
KIRSTY HAWKSHAW/BT		
	Dreaming	2000
	(DJ TIESTO featuring KIRSTY HAWKSHAW)	
	Urban Train	2001
HAWKWIND	Silver Machine	1972
	Urban Guerrilla	1973
DARREN HAYES	Crush	2003
	I Miss You	2002

ARTIST	SONG TITLE	DATE
	Insatiable	2002
	Pop!ular	2004
	Strange Relationship	2002
ISAAC HAYES	By The Time I Get To Phoenix	1969
	Disco Connection	1976
	Do Your Thing	1972
	Don't Let Go	1979
	Joy (Part I)	1973
	Never Can Say Goodbye	1971
	Theme From 'Shaft'	1971
	Theme From 'The Men'	1972
	Walk On By	1969
HAYSI FANTAYZEE	John Wayne Is Big Leggy	1982
	Shiny Shiny	1983
JUSTIN HAYWARD	Forever Autumn	1978
JUSTIN HAYWARD & JOHN LODGE		
	Blue Guitar	1975
LEON HAYWOOD	Don't Push It Don't Force It	1980
	I Want'a Do Something Freaky To You	1975
HAYWOODE	Roses	1986
OFRA HAZA	Im Nin'alu	1988
LEE HAZLEWOOD/NANCY SINATRA		
	Did You Ever	1971
	Some Velvet Morning	1968
MURRAY HEAD	One Night In Bangkok	1985
	Superstar	1971

ARTIST	SONG TITLE	DATE
ROY HEAD	Just A Little Bit	1965
	Treat Her Right	1965
ROY HEAD & THE TRAITS		
	Apple Of My Eye	1965
HEADGIRL	St. Valentine's Day Massacre (EP)	1981
HEADSWIM	Tourniquet	1998
JEFF HEALEY BAND		
	Angel Eyes	1989
JEREMY HEALY & AMOS		
	Argentina	1997
	Stamp!	1996
HEAR 'N' AID	Stars	1986
HEAR'SAY	Everybody	2001
	Lovin' Is Easy	2002
	Pure And Simple	2001
	The Way To Your Love	2001
HEART	All I Wanna Do Is Make Love To You	1990
	Alone	1987
	Barracuda	1977
	Crazy On You	1976
	Dog & Butterfly	1979
	Even It Up	1980
	Heartless	1978
	I Didn't Want To Need You	1990
	Magic Man	1976
	Never/These Dreams	1988

ARTIST	SONG TITLE	DATE
	Nothin' At All	1986
	Straight On	1978
	Stranded	1990
	Tell It Like It Is	1980
	There's The Girl	1987
	This Man Is Mine	1982
	What About Love?	1985
	Who Will You Run To	1987
	Will You Be There (In The Morning)	1993
HEARTBEAT	Tears From Heaven	1987
HEARTISTS	Belo Horizonti	1998
HEARTLESS CREW	The Heartless Theme Aka 'The Superglue Riddim'	2002
JOEY HEATHERTON	Gone	1972
HEATWAVE	Always And Forever	1978
	Boogie Nights	1977
	Gangsters Of The Groove	1981
	The Groove Line	1978
	Jitterbuggin'	1981
	Mind Blowing Decisions	1978
	Too Hot To Handle/Slip Your Disc To This	1977
HEAVEN 17	Come Live With Me	1983
	Crushed By The Wheels Of Industry	1983
	Sunset Now	1984
	Temptation	1983
	This Is Mine	1984

ARTIST	SONG TITLE	DATE
	(We Don't Need This) Fascist Groove Thang	1993
HEAVY D.	Big Daddy	1997
HEAVY D. & THE BOYZ		
	Got Me Waiting	1994
	Is It Good To You	1991
	Now That We Found Love	1991
	Nuttin' But Love	1994
	This Is Your Night	1994
BOBBY HEBB	Love Love Love	1972
	A Satisfied Mind	1966
	Sunny	1966
SHARLENE HECTOR WITH THE NEW INSPIRATIONAL CHOIR	I Wish I Knew How It Would Feel To Be Free	2004
HED BOYS	Girls & Boys	1994
HEDGEHOPPERS ANONYMOUS		
	It's Good News Week	1965
NEIL HEFTI	Batman Theme	1966
HEIGHTS	How Do You Talk To An Angel	1992
HEINZ	Country Boy	1963
	Just Like Eddie	1963
	Questions I Can't Answer	1964
	You Were There	1964
HELICOPTER	On Ya Way	1994

ARTIST	SONG TITLE	DATE
HELIOTROPIC featuring VERNA V		
	Alive	1999
HELL IS FOR HEROES		
	Night Vision	2002
	Retreat	2003
	You Drove Me To It	2003
HELLER AND FARLEY PROJECT		
	Ultra Flava	1996
PETE HELLER	Big Love	1999
HELLO	New York Groove	1975
	Tell Him	1974
JIMMY HELMS	Gonna Make You An Offer You Can't Refuse	1973
JIMI HENDRIX	Gipsy Eyes/Remember	1971
	Johnny B. Goode	1972
JIMI HENDRIX EXPERIENCE		
	All Along The Watchtower	1968
	Burning Of The Midnight Lamp	1967
	Hey Joe	1966
	Purple Haze	1967
	Voodoo Chile	1970
	The Wind Cries Mary	1967
AINSLIE HENDERSON		
	Keep Me A Secret	2003
DON HENLEY	All She Wants To Do Is Dance	1985
	The Boys Of Summer	1984

ARTIST	SONG TITLE	DATE
	Dirty Laundry	1982
	The End Of The Innocence	1989
	The Heart Of The Matter	1990
	The Last Worthless Eveing	1989
	Not Enough Love In The World	1985
	Sunset Grill	1985
	(PATTY SMYTH WITH DON HENLEY)	
	Sometimes Love Just Ain't Enough	1992
CASSIUS HENRY	Broke	2002
PAUL HENRY & THE MAYSON GLEN ORCHESTRA		
	Benny's Theme	1978
PAULINE HENRY	Can't Take Your Love	1994
	Feel Like Making Love	1993
	Love Hangover	1995
	Too Many People	1993
PAULINE HENRY featuring WAYNE MARSHALL		
	Never Knew Love Like This	1996
JIM HENSON/KERMIT		
	Rainbow Connection	1979
HEPBURN	Bugs	1999
	Deep Deep Down	2000
	I Quit	1999
HERD	From The Underworld	1967
	I Don't Want Our Loving To Die	1968
	Paradise Lost	1967

ARTIST	SONG TITLE	DATE
HERMAN'S HERMITS		
	Bet Yer Life I Do	1970
	Can't You Hear My Heartbeat	1965
	Dandy	1966
	Don't Go Out Into The Rain (You're Going To Melt)	1967
	East West	1966
	Here Comes The Star	1969
	I Can Take Or Leave Your Loving	1968
	I'm Henry VIII I Am	1965
	I'm Into Something Good	1964
	Just A Little Bit Better	1965
	Lady Barbara	1970
	Leaning On The Lamp Post	1966
	Listen People	1966
	Mrs. Brown You've Got A Lovely Daughter	1965
	Museum	1967
	A Must To Avoid	1965
	My Sentimental Friend	1969
	No Milk Today	1967
	Show Me Girl	1964
	Silhouettes	1965
	Sleepy Joe	1968
	Something's Happening	1968
	Sunshine Girl	1968
	There's A Kind Of Hush	1967

ARTIST	SONG TITLE	DATE
	This Door Swings Both Ways	1966
	Wonderful World	1965
	Years May Come, Years May Go	1970
	You Won't Be Leavin'	1966
HERMES HOUSE BAND		
	Country Roads	2001
PATRICK HERNANDEZ		
	Born To Be Alive	1979
TY HERNDON	It Must Be Love	1998
HESITATIONS	Born Free	1968
NICK HEYWARD	Blue Hat For A Blue Day	1983
	Love All Day	1984
	Rollerblade	1996
	Take That Situation	1983
	Warning Sign	1984
	Whistle Down The Wind	1983
HI GLOSS	You'll Never Know	1981
HI TEK 3 featuring YA KID K		
	Spin That Wheel (Turtles Get Real)	1990
HI TENSION	British Hustle/Peace On Earth	1978
	Hi Tension	1978
HI-FIVE	I Can't Wait Another Minute	1991
	I Like The Way (The Kissing Game)	1991
	Never Should've Let You Go	1993
	Quality Time	1992
	She's Playing Hard To Get	1992

ARTIST	SONG TITLE	DATE
HI-GATE	Gonna Work It Out	2001
	I Can Hear Voices/Caned And Unable	2000
	Pitchin' (In Every Direction)	2000
HINDA HICKS	I Wanna Be Your Lady	1998
	If You Want Me	1998
	Truly	1998
	You Think You Own Me	1998
BERTIE HIGGINS	Key Largo	1981
HIGH	Box Set Go	1991
HIGH INERGY	You Can't Turn Me Off (In The Middle Of Turning Me On)	1977
HIGHLY LIKELY	Whatever Happened To You ('Likely Lads' Theme)	1973
BENNY HILL	Ernie (The Fastest Milk Man In The West)	1971
	Harvest Of Love	1963
CHRIS HILL	Bionic Santa	1976
	Renta Santa	1975
DAN HILL	Sometimes When We Touch	1977
DAN HILL (DUET WITH VONDA SHEPARD)		
	Can't We Try	1987
FAITH HILL	Breathe	1999
	Cry	2002
	If My Heart Had Wings	2001
	Let Me Let Go	1998
	There You'll Be	2001
	This Kiss	1998

ARTIST	SONG TITLE	DATE
	The Way You Love Me	2001
	(TIM McGRAW WITH FAITH HILL)	
	It's Your Love	1997
LAURYN HILL	Doo Wop (That Thing)	1998
	Everything Is Everything	1999
	Ex-Factor	1999
	(BOB MARLEY featuring LAURYN HILL)	
	Turn Your Lights Down Low	1999
	(REFUGEE ALLSTARS/LAURYN HILL)	
	The Sweetest Thing	1997
RONI HILL	You Keep Me Hangin' On/Stop In The	
	Name Of Love	1977
VINCE HILL	Edelweiss	1967
	Heartaches	1966
	The Importance Of Your Love	1968
	Look Around (And You'll Find Me	
	There)	1971
	Love Letters In The Sand	1967
	Merci Cheri	1966
	Roses Of Picardy	1967
	Take Me To Your Heart Again	1966
HILLSIDE SINGERS	I'd Like To Teach The World To Sing	1971
RONNIE HILTON	Don't Let The Rain Come Down	1964
	A Windmill In Old Amsterdam	1965
HIM	Buried Alive By Love	2003
	The Funeral Of Hearts	2004

ARTIST	SONG TITLE	DATE
	The Sacrament	2003
	Solitary Man	2004
DENI HINES	I Like The Way	1997
	It's Alright	1997
JOE HINTON	Funny	1964
HIPSWAY	The Honey Thief	1987
AL HIRT	Cotton Candy	1964
	Java	1964
	Sugar Lips	1964
HITHOUSE	Jack To The Sound Of The Underground	1988
THE HIVES	Hate To Say I Told You So	2002
	Main Offender	2002
	Walk Idiot Walk	2004
SUSANNA HOFFS	All I Want	1996
	My Side Of The Bed	1991
HULK HOGAN with GREEN JELLY		
	I'm The Leader Of The Gang (I Am!)	1993
HOKU	Another Dumb Blonde	2000
DEMI HOLBORN	I'd Like To Teach The World To Sing	2002
HOLE	Celebrity Skin	1998
	Doll Parts	1995
	Malibu	1999
	Violet	1995
HOLE IN ONE	Life's Too Short	1997
AMY HOLLAND	How Do I Survive	1980

ARTIST	SONG TITLE	DATE
JOOLS HOLLAND & JAMIROQUAI		
	I'm In The Mood For Love	2001
HOLLAND-DOZIER featuring LAMONT DOZIER		
	Why Can't We Be Lovers	1972
JENNIFER HOLLIDAY		
	And I'm Telling You I'm Not Going	1982
HOLLIES	The Air That I Breathe	1974
	The Baby	1972
	Bus Stop	1966
	Carrie-Anne	1967
	The Day That Curly Bill Shot Down Crazy Sam McGhee	1973
	Gasoline Alley Bred	1970
	He Ain't Heavy, He's My Brother	1969
	Here I Go Again	1964
	Hey Willy	1971
	Holliedaze (Medley)	1981
	I Can't Let Go	1966
	I Can't Tell The Bottom From The Top	1970
	I'm Alive	1965
	If I Needed Someone	1965
	Jennifer Eccles	1968
	Just Like Me	1963
	Just One Look	1964
	King Midas In Reverse	1967
	Listen To Me	1968

ARTIST	SONG TITLE	DATE
	Long Cool Woman (In A Black Dress)	1972
	Long Dark Road	1972
	Look Through Any Window	1965
	On A Carousel	1967
	Pay You Back With Interest	1967
	Searchin'	1963
	Sorry Suzanne	1969
	Stay	1963
	Stop In The Name Of Love	1983
	Stop Stop Stop	1966
	We're Through	1964
	Yes I Will	1965
DAVE HOLLISTER	My Favorite Girl	1999
BRENDA HOLLOWAY		
	Every Little Bit Hurts	1964
	When I'm Gone	1965
	You've Made Me So Very Happy	1967
LOLEATTA HOLLOWAY/FIRE ISLAND		
	Shout To The Top	1998
	(CAPPELLA featuring LOLEATTA HOLLOWAY)	
	Take Me Away	1992
	(CEVIN FISHER/LOLEATTA HOLLOWAY)	
	(You Got Me) Burning Up	1999
HOLLY & THE IVYS		
	Christmas On 45	1981

ARTIST	SONG TITLE	DATE
BUDDY HOLLY	Bo Diddley	1963
	Brown Eyed Handsome Man	1963
	Love's Made A Fool Of You	1964
	Peggy Sue	1957
	What To Do	1963
	Wishing	1963
BUDDY HOLLY & THE CRICKETS		
	You've Got Love	1964
HOLLYWOOD BEYOND		
	What's The Colour Of Money ?	1986
EDDIE HOLMAN	Hey There Lonely Girl	1969
CLINT HOLMES	Playground In My Mind	1973
DAVID HOLMES	Don't Die Just Yet	1998
	My Mate Paul	1998
RUPERT HOLMES	Answering Machine	1980
	Escape (The Pina Colada Song)	1979
	Him	1980
JOHN HOLT	Help Me Make It Through The Night	1974
STEVE HOLY	Good Morning Beautiful	2001
HOMBRES	Let It Out (Let It All Hang Out)	1967
HONDELLS	Little Honda	1964
HONDY	Hondy (No Access)	1997
HONEY CONE	The Day I Found Myself	1972
	One Monkey Don't Stop No Show (Pt 1)	1971
	Stick-Up	1971
	Want Ads	1971

ARTIST	SONG TITLE	DATE
HONEYBUS	I Can't Let Maggie Go	1968
HONEYCOMBS	Have I The Right?	1964
	Is It Because	1964
	Something Better Beginning	1965
	That's The Way	1965
HONEYCRACK	King Of Misery	1996
	Sitting At Home	1996
HONEYDRIPPERS	Rockin' At Midnight	1985
	Sea Of Love	1964
HONEYMOON SUITE	Feel It Again	1986
HONEYZ	End Of The Line	1998
	Finally Found	1998
	I Don't Know	2001
	Love Of A Lifetime	1999
	Never Let You Down	1999
	Not Even Gonna Trip	2000
	Won't Take It Lying Down	2000
HONKY	Join The Party	1977
HOOBASTANK	The Reason	2004
JOHN LEE HOOKER	Boom Boom	1992
	Dimples	1964
	(VAN MORRISON & JOHN LEE HOOKER)	
	Gloria	1993
HOOTERS	And We Danced	1985
	Day By Day	1985
	Satellite	1987

ARTIST	SONG TITLE	DATE
	Where Do The Children Go	1986
HOOTIE & THE BLOWFISH		
	Hold My Hand	1994
	Let Her Cry	1995
	Old Man & Me (When I Get To Heaven)	1996
	Only Wanna Be With You	1995
	Time	1995
	Tucker's Town	1996
HOPE OF THE STATES		
	Enemies/Friends	2003
	Nehemiah	2004
	The Red The White The Black The Blue	2004
MARY HOPKIN	Goodbye	1969
	If You Love Me (I Won't Care)	1976
	Knock Knock Who's There	1970
	Temma Harbour	1970
	Think About Your Children	1970
	Those Were The Days	1968
JIMMY 'BO' HORNE	Dance Across The Floor	1978
BRUCE HORNSBY & THE RANGE		
	Across The River	1990
	Every Little Kiss	1987
	Look Out Any Window	1988
	Mandolin Rain	1987
	The Valley Road	1988
	The Way It Is	1986

ARTIST	SONG TITLE	DATE
HOT	Angel In Your Arms	1977
HOT BLOOD	Soul Dracula	1976
HOT BUTTER	Popcorn	1972
HOT CHOCOLATE	Are You Getting Enough Of What Makes You Happy	1980
	Brother Louie	1973
	Chances	1982
	Cheri Babe	1974
	A Child's Prayer	1975
	Disco Queen	1975
	Don't Stop It Now	1976
	Emma	1975
	Every 1's A Winner	1978
	Girl Crazy	1982
	Heaven Is In The Back Seat Of My Cadillac	1976
	I Believe (In Love)	1971
	I Gave You My Heart (Didn't I)	1984
	I'll Put You Together Again (From Dear Anyone)	1978
	It Started With A Kiss	1982
	Love Is Life	1970
	Man To Man	1976
	No Doubt About It	1980
	Put Your Love In Me	1977
	So You Win Again	1977

ARTIST	SONG TITLE	DATE
	Tears On The Telephone	1983
	What Kinda Boy You Looking For (Girl)	1983
	You Could Have Been A Lady	1971
	You Sexy Thing	1975
	You'll Always Be A Friend	1972
HOT HOT HEAT	Bandages	2003
	No, Not Now	2003
HOT STREAK	Body Work	1983
HOTHOUSE FLOWERS		
	Don't Go	1988
	Emotional Time	1993
	Give It Up	1990
	I Can See Clearly Now	1990
HOTLEGS	Neanderthal Man	1970
HOTSHOTS	Snoopy Vs. The Red Baron	1973
STEVEN HOUGHTON		
	Truly	1998
	Wind Beneath My Wings	1997
HOUSE OF LOVE	Beatles And The Stones	1990
	Shine On	1990
HOUSE OF PAIN	It Ain't A Crime	1994
	Jump Around/Top O' The Morning To Ya	1993
	On Point	1994
	Over There (I Don't Care)	1995
	Shamrocks & Shenanigans/Who's The Man	1993

ARTIST	SONG TITLE	DATE
HOUSE OF VIRGINISM		
	I'll Be There For You (Doya Dododo Doya)	1993
	Reachin	1994
HOUSE TRAFFIC	Every Day Of My Life	1997
HOUSEMARTINS	Build	1987
	Caravan Of Love	1986
	Five Get Over Excited	1987
	Happy Hour	1986
	Me And The Farmer	1987
	There Is Always Something There To Remind Me	1988
	Think For A Minute	1986
HOUSEMASTER BOYZ & THE RUDE BOY OF HOUSE		
	House Nation	1987
HOUSTON	I Like That	2004
DAVID HOUSTON	Almost Persuaded	1966
MARQUES HOUSTON featuring JERMAINE 'JD' DUPRI		
	Pop That Booty	2004
MARQUES HOUSTON featuring JOE BUDDEN & PIED PIPER	Clubbin	2003
THELMA HOUSTON	Don't Leave Me This Way	1976
	Saturday Night, Sunday Morning	1979
WHITNEY HOUSTON		
	All The Man That I Need	1990
	Didn't We Almost Have It All	1987
	Exhale (Shoop Shoop)	1995

ARTIST	SONG TITLE	DATE
	Greatest Love Of All	1986
	How Will I Know	1985
	I Believe In You And Me	1996
	I Have Nothing	1993
	I Learned From The Best	1999
	I Wanna Dance With Somebody (Who Loves Me)	1987
	I Will Always Love You	1992
	I'm Every Woman	1993
	I'm Your Baby Tonight	1990
	It's Not Right But It's Okay	1999
	Love Will Save The Day	1988
	Miracle	1991
	My Love Is Your Love	1999
	My Name Is Not Susan	1991
	One Moment In Time	1988
	Queen Of The Night	1993
	Run To You	1993
	Saving All My Love For You	1985
	So Emotional	1987
	The Star Spangled Banner	2001
	Step By Step	1997
	Whatchulookinat	2002
	Where Do Broken Hearts Go	1988
	Why Does It Hurt So Bad	1996
	You Give Good Love	1985

ARTIST	SONG TITLE	DATE
WHITNEY HOUSTON & CE CE WINANS		
	Count On Me	1996
WHITNEY HOUSTON & ENRIQUE IGLESIAS		
	Could I Have This Kiss Forever	2000
WHITNEY HOUSTON featuring FAITH EVANS & KELLY PRICE	Heartbreak Hotel	2000
WHITNEY HOUSTON/GEORGE MICHAEL		
	If I Told You That	2000
(ARETHA FRANKLIN/WHITNEY HOUSTON)		
	It Isn't, It Wasn't, It Ain't Ever Gonna Be	1989
(BOBBY BROWN & WHITNEY HOUSTON)		
	Something In Common	1994
(MARIAH CAREY & WHITNEY HOUSTON)		
	When You Believe	1998
ADINA HOWARD	Freak Like Me	1995
(WARREN G featuring ADINA HOWARD)		
	What's Love Got To Do With It	1996
BILLY HOWARD	King Of The Cops	1975
ROBERT HOWARD & KYM MAZELLE		
	Wait	1989
DANNY HOWELLS & DICK TREVOR featuring ERIRE		
	Dusk Til Dawn	2004
HUDSON BROTHERS		
	So You Are A Star	1974
AL HUDSON & THE SOUL PARTNERS		
	You Can Do It	1979

ARTIST	SONG TITLE	DATE
HUDSON-FORD	Burn Baby Burn	1974
	Floating In The Wind	1974
	Pick Up The Pieces	1973
HUE AND CRY	Labour Of Love	1993
	Looking For Linda	1989
	Violently (EP)	1989
HUES CORPORATION		
	Rock The Boat	1974
	Rockin' Soul	1974
HUFF & HERB	Feeling Good	1997
HUFF & PUFF	Help Me Make It	1996
GRAYSON HUGH	Talk It Over	1989
FRED HUGHES	Oo Wee Baby, I Love You	1965
JIMMY HUGHES	Steal Away	1964
HUMAN BEINZ	Nobody But Me	1967
HUMAN LEAGUE	Bein' Boiled	1982
	Don't You Want Me	1982
	Filling Up With Heaven	1995
	Heart Like A Wheel	1990
	Human	1986
	(Keep Feeling) Fascination	1983
	The Lebanon	1984
	Life On Your Own	1984
	Louise	1984
	Love Action (I Believe In Love)	1981
	Mirror Man	1983

ARTIST	SONG TITLE	DATE
	One Man In My Heart	1995
	Open Your Heart	1981
	The Sound Of The Crowd	1981
	Stay With Me Tonight	1996
	Tell Me When	1995
HUMAN NATURE	He Don't Love You	2001
HUMAN RESOURCE	The Complete Dominator	1991
	Dominator	1991
HUMANOID	Stakker Humanoid	1988
HUMATE	Love Stimulation	1999
HUMBLE PIE	Natural Born Bugie	1969
ENGELBERT HUMPERDINCK		
	After The Lovin'	1976
	Am I That Easy To Forget	1967
	Another Time, Another Place	1971
	I'm A Better Man	1969
	The Last Waltz	1967
	Les Bicyclettes De Belsize	1968
	A Man Without Love	1968
	My Marie	1970
	Quando Quando Quando	1999
	Release Me (And Let Me Love Again)	1967
	Sweetheart	1970
	There Goes My Everything	1967
	Too Beautiful To Last	1972
	The Way It Used To Be	1969

ARTIST	SONG TITLE	DATE
	Winter World Of Love	1969
PAUL HUMPHREY & HIS COOL AID CHEMISTS		
	Cool Aid	1971
HUNDRED REASONS		
	EP Three	2001
	Falter	2002
	The Great Test	2003
	If I Could	2002
	Silver	2002
	What You Get	2004
TOMMY HUNT	Crackin' Up	1975
	Loving On The Losing Side	1976
ALFONZO HUNTER	Just The Way	1997
IAN HUNTER	Once Bitten Twice Shy	1975
JOHN HUNTER	Tragedy	1984
HURLEY & TODD	Sunstorm	2000
STEVE 'SILK' HURLEY		
	Jack Your Body	1987
HURRICANE #1	Chain Reaction	1997
	Just Another Illusion	1997
	Only The Strongest Will Survive	1998
	Step Into My World	1997
PHIL HURTT	Giving It Back	1978
HWA featuring SONIC THE HEDGEHOG		
	Supersonic	1992

ARTIST	SONG TITLE	DATE
HYBRID featuring CHRISSIE HYNDE		
	Kid 2000	2000
BRIAN HYLAND	Gypsy Woman	1970
	The Joker Went Wild	1966
	Run, Run, Look And See	1966
	Sealed With A Kiss	1962
SHEILA HYLTON	The Bed's Too Big Without You	1981
DICK HYMAN & HIS ELECTRIC ECLECTICS		
	The Minotaur	1969
CHRISSIE HYNDE/UB40		
	I Got You Babe	1985
	(CHER, CHRISSIE HYNDE & NENEH CHERRY with ERIC CLAPTON)	
	Love Can Build A Bridge	1995
	(HYBRID featuring CHRISSIE HYNDE)	
	Kid 2000	2000
	(TUBE & BERGER featuring CHRISSIE HYNDE)	
	Straight Ahead	2004
HYPER GO GO	High	1992
	Raise	1994
HYPERLOGIC	Only Me	1995
HYSTERIC EGO	Ministry Of Love	1997
	Want Love	1996
HYSTERIX	Must Be The Music	1994
I MONSTER	Daydream In Blue	2001

ARTIST	SONG TITLE	DATE
IAN VAN DAHL	Believe	2004
	Castles In The Sky	2001
	I Can't Let You Go	2003
	Reason	2002
	Try	2002
	Will I	2001
JANIS IAN	At Seventeen	1975
	Society's Child (Baby I've Been Thinking)	1967
ICE CUBE	It Was A Good Day	1993
	You Know How We Do It	1994
ICE CUBE featuring GEORGE CLINTON		
	Bop Gun (One Nation)	1994
ICE CUBE featuring DAS EFX		
	Check Yo Self	1993
ICE CUBE featuring MACK 10 & MS. TOI		
	You Can Do It	1999
ICE CUBE featuring MR. SHORT KHOP		
	Pushin' Weight	1998
	(YO-YO featuring ICE CUBE)	
	You Can't Play With My Yo-Yo	1991
ICE HOUSE	Crazy	1987
	Hey Little Girl	1983
ICE MC	Bom Digi Bom (Think About The Way)	1996
ICE-T	Gotta Lotta Love	1994
	I Must Stand	1996

ARTIST	SONG TITLE	DATE
	The Lane	1996
	That's How I'm Livin'	1993
ICEBURG SLIMM	Nursery Rhymes	2000
ICEHOUSE	Crazy	1987
	Electric Blue	1988
ICICLE WORKS	Love Is A Wonderful Colour	1983
	Whisper To A Scream (Birds Fly)	1984
IDEAL	Get Gone	1999
IDEAL US featuring LIL' MO		
	Whatever	2000
IDES OF MARCH	Vehicle	1970
IDLEWILD	Actually It's Darkness	2000
	American English	2002
	Little Discourage	1999
	Live In A Hiding Place	2002
	A Modern Way Of Letting Go	2003
	Roseability	2000
	These Wooden Ideas	2000
	When I Argue I See Shapes	1999
	You Held The World In Your Arms	2002
BILLY IDOL	Cradle Of Love	1990
	Don't Need A Gun	1987
	Eyes Without A Face	1984
	Flesh For Fantasy	1984
	Hot In The City	1982
	Mony Mony	1987

ARTIST	SONG TITLE	DATE
	Rebel Yell	1985
	Shock To The System	1993
	Sweet Sixteen	1987
	To Be A Lover	1986
	White Wedding	1983
IDOLS	Happy Xmas (War Is Over)	2003
FRANK IFIELD	Angry At The Big Oak Tree	1964
	Call Her Your Sweetheart	1966
	Confessin' (That I Love You)	1963
	Don't Blame Me	1964
	I Should Care	1964
	Mule Train	1963
	No One Will Ever Know	1966
	Nobody's Darlin' But Mine	1963
	Paradise	1965
	Summer Is Over	1964
	Wayward Wind	1963
FRANK IFIELD/BACKROOM BOYS		
	She Taught Me How To Yodel	1991
ENRIQUE IGLESIAS	Addicted	2003
	Bailamos	1999
	Be With You	2000
	Escape	2002
	Hero	2001
	Love To See You Cry	2002
	Maybe	2002

ARTIST	SONG TITLE	DATE
	Rhythm Divine	1999
ENRIQUE IGLESIAS featuring KELIS		
	Not In Love	2004
(LIONEL RICHIE featuring ENRIQUE IGLESIAS)		
	To Love A Woman	2003
(WHITNEY HOUSTON & ENRIQUE IGLESIAS)		
	Could I Have This Kiss Forever	2000
JULIO IGLESIAS	Amor	1982
	Begin The Beguine (Volver A Empezar)	1981
	Hey!	1983
	Quiereme Mucho (Yours)	1982
JULIO IGLESIAS & DIANA ROSS		
	All Of You	1984
JULIO IGLESIAS & WILLIE NELSON		
	To All The Girls I've Loved Before	1984
JULIO IGLESIAS featuring STEVIE WONDER		
	My Love	1988
IIO	At The End	2003
	Rapture	2001
IKETTES	Peaches 'n' Cream	1965
ILLUSION	Did You See Her Eyes	1969
IMAANI	Where Are You	1998
IMAGINATION	Body Talk	1981
	Changes	1982
	Flashback	1981
	In And Out Of Love	1981

ARTIST	SONG TITLE	DATE
	In The Heat Of The Night	1982
	Just An Illusion	1982
	Looking At Midnight	1983
	Music And Lights	1982
	Thank You My Love	1984
IMAJIN featuring KEITH MURRAY		
	Shorty (You Keep Playin' With My Mind)	1998
NATALIE IMBRUGLIA		
	Beauty On The Fire	2002
	Big Mistake	1998
	Smoke	1998
	That Day	2001
	Torn	1997
	Wishing I Was There	1998
	Wrong Impression	2002
IMMATURE	Constantly	1994
	Never Lie	1994
	Please Don't Go	1996
IMMATURE featuring SMOOTH		
	We Got It	1996
IMMATURE featuring SMOOTH AND ED FROM GOOD		
BURGER	Watch Me Do My Thing	1997
IMPERIALS	Who's Gonna Love Me	1977
IMPOSTER	Pills & Soap	1983
IMPRESSIONS	Amen	1964
	Check Out Your Mind	1970

ARTIST	SONG TITLE	DATE
	Choice Of Colors	1969
	Finally Got Myself Together (I'm A Changed Man)	1974
	First Impressions	1975
	Fool For You	1968
	I'm So Proud	1964
	Keep On Pushing	1964
	People Get Ready	1965
	Talking About My Baby	1964
	This Is My Country	1968
	We're A Winner	1967
	Woman's Got Soul	1965
	You Must Believe Me	1964
	You've Been Cheatin'	1965
IMX	Stay The Night	1999
INCANTATION	Cacharpaya (Andes Pumpsa Daesi)	1982
INCOGNITO	Don't You Worry 'Bout A Thing	1992
	Everyday	1995
	Jump To My Love/Always There	1996
	Pieces Of A Dream	1994
INCOGNITO featuring JOCELYN BROWN		
	Always There	1991
INCUBUS	Are You In?	2002
	Drive	2001
	Megalomaniac	2004
	Wish You Were Here	2002

ARTIST	SONG TITLE	DATE
INDECENT OBSESSION		
	Tell Me Something	1990
INDEEP	Last Night A D.J. Saved My Life	1983
INDEPENDENTS	Leaving Me	1973
INDIA/MAW	To Be In Love	1999
	(NUYORICAN SOUL featuring INDIA)	
	Runaway	1997
INDIA.ARIE	Brown Skin	2001
	Video	2001
LOS INDIOS TABAJARAS		
	Maria Elena	1963
INDO	R U Sleeping	1998
INDUSTRY STANDARD		
	Volume 1 (What You Want What You Need)	1998
INFORMATION SOCIETY		
	Think	1990
	Walking Away	1989
	What's On Your Mind (Pure Energy)	1988
JAMES INGRAM	I Don't Have The Heart	1990
JAMES INGRAM & MICHAEL MCDONALD		
	Yah Mo B There	1983
	(KENNY ROGERS WITH KIM CARNES & JAMES INGRAM)	
	What About Me?	1984

ARTIST	SONG TITLE	DATE
	(LINDA RONSTADT AND JAMES INGRAM)	
	Somewhere Out There	1987
	(PATTI AUSTIN & JAMES INGRAM)	
	Baby Come To Me	1982
	(QUINCY JONES featuring AL B. SURE, JAMES INGRAM, EL DEBARGE)	
	Secret Garden	1990
	(QUINCY JONES featuring JAMES INGRAM)	
	Just Once	1981
	One Hundred Ways	1981
LUTHER INGRAM	I'll Be Your Shelter (In Time Of Storm)	1972
	(If Loving You Is Wrong) I Don't Wanna Be Right	1972
JOHN INMAN	Are You Being Served Sir?	1975
INMATES	The Walk	1979
INME	Crushed Like Fruit	2003
	Faster The Chase	2004
INNER CIRCLE	Bad Boys	1993
	Everything Is Great	1979
	Sweat (A La La La La Long)	1993
INNER CITY	Ain't Nobody Better	1989
	Big Fun	1988
	Do You Love What You Feel	1989
	Good Life	1988
	Good Life (Buena Vida)	1999
	Hallelujah '92	1992

ARTIST	SONG TITLE	DATE
	Pennies From Heaven	1992
	Whatcha Gonna Do With My Lovin'	1989
	Your Love	1996
INNOCENCE	I'll Be There	1992
	Let's Push It	1990
	A Matter Of Fact	1990
	Natural Thing	1990
	One Love In My Lifetime	1992
	Silent Voice	1990
INOJ	Love You Down	1998
	Time After Time	1998
INSPIRAL CARPETS	Bitches Brew	1992
	Caravan	1991
	Dragging Me Down	1992
	Generations	1992
	I Want You	1994
	Island Head (EP)	1990
	Joe	1995
	Saturn 5	1994
	She Comes In The Fall	1990
	This Is How It Feels	1990
	Two Worlds Collide	1992
INSPIRATIONAL CHOIR		
	Abide With Me	1985
INSTANT FUNK	I Got My Mind Made Up (You Can Get It Girl)	1979

ARTIST	SONG TITLE	DATE
INTENSO PROJECT	Luv Da Sunshine	2002
INTENSO PROJECT featuring LAURA JAYE		
	Your Music	2003
INTERACTIVE	Forever Young	1996
INTERPOL	Slow Hands	2004
INTRIGUES	In A Moment	1969
INTRO	Come Inside	1993
INTRUDERS	Cowboys To Girls	1968
	I'll Always Love My Mama	1974
	(Love Is Like A) Baseball Game	1968
	Win Place Or Show (She's A Winner)	1974
INXS	Baby Don't Cry	1992
	Beautiful Girl	1993
	Bitter Tears	1991
	Devil Inside	1988
	Disappear	1990
	Elegantly Wasted	1997
	The Gift	1993
	Heaven Sent	1992
	Mystify	1989
	Need You Tonight	1987
	Never Tear Us Apart	1988
	New Sensation	1988
	Not Enough Time	1992
	The One Thing	1983
	Shining Star (EP)	1991

ARTIST	SONG TITLE	DATE
	The Strangest Party (These Are The Times)	1994
	Suicide Blonde	1990
	Taste It	1992
	What You Need	1986
(JIMMY BARNES & INXS)		
	Good Times	1991
(PAR-T-ONE vs INXS)		
	I'm So Crazy	2001
(TALL PAUL vs INXS)		
	Precious Heart	2001
TIPPA IRIE	Hello Darling	1986
DONNIE IRIS	Ah! Leah!	1980
	Love Is Like A Rock	1981
	My Girl	1982
IRISH ROVERS	The Unicorn	1968
	Wasn't That A Party	1981
IRON BUTTERFLY	In-A-Gada-Da-Vida	1968
IRON MAIDEN	Aces High	1984
	The Angel And The Gambler	1998
	Be Quick Or Be Dead	1992
	Bring Your Daughter... To The Slaughter	1991
	Can I Play With Madness	1988
	The Clairvoyant	1988
	The Evil That Men Do	1988

ARTIST	SONG TITLE	DATE
	Fear Of The Dark (Live)	1993
	Flight Of Icarus	1983
	From Here To Eternity	1992
	Hallowed Be Thy Name	1993
	Holy Smoke	1990
	Infinite Dreams	1989
	Man On The Edge	1995
	The Number Of The Beast	1982
	Out Of The Silent Planet	2000
	Rainmaker	2003
	Run To The Hills	1982
	Running Free	1980
	Sanctuary	1980
	Stranger In A Strange Land	1986
	The Trooper	1983
	Twilight Zone/Wrath Child	1981
	2 Minutes To Midnight	1984
	Virus	1996
	Wasted Years	1986
	The Wicker Man	2000
	Wildest Dreams	2003
	Women In Uniform	1980
IRONHORSE	Sweet Lui-Louise	1979
BIG DEE IRWIN	Swinging On A Star	1963
RUSS IRWIN	My Heart Belongs To You	1991
CHRIS ISAAK	Blue Hotel	1991

ARTIST	SONG TITLE	DATE
	Can't Do A Thing (To Stop Me)	1993
	Wicked Game	1990
ISHA-D	Stay (Tonight)	1995
ISLEY BROTHERS	Behind A Painted Smile	1969
	Don't Say Goodnight (It's Time For Love)	
	(Pts 1 & 2)	1980
	Fight The Power (Pt 1)	1975
	For The Love Of You (Pts 1 & 2)	1975
	Harvest For The World	1976
	Highways Of My Life	1974
	I Guess I'll Always Love You	1969
	I Turned You On	1969
	It's A Disco Night (Rock Don't Stop)	1979
	It's Your Thing	1969
	Livin' In The Life	1977
	Love The One You're With	1971
	Pop That Thang	1972
	Put Yourself In My Place	1969
	Summer Breeze	1974
	That Lady	1973
	This Old Heart Of Mine	1966
ISLEY BROTHERS featuring RONALD ISLEY AKA		
MR. BIGGS	Contagious	2001
RON ISLEY/WARREN G		
	(R. KELLY featuring RONALD ISLEY)	
	Down Low (Nobody Has To Know)	1996

ARTIST	SONG TITLE	DATE
	(ROD STEWART WITH RONALD ISLEY)	
	This Old Heart Of Mine	1990
	(WARREN G featuring RONALD ISLEY)	
	Smokin' Me Out	1997
ISOTONIK	Different Strokes	1992
	Everywhere I Go/Let's Get Down	1992
IT BITES	Calling All The Heroes	1986
IT'S IMMATERIAL	Driving Away From Home (Jim's Tune)	1986
ITTY BITTY BOOZY WOOZY		
	Tempo Fiesta (Party Time)	1995
IVY LEAGUE	Funny How Love Can Be	1965
	That's Why I'm Crying	1965
	Tossing And Turning	1965
RAY J	Let It Go	1997
RAY J featuring LIL' KIM		
	Wait A Minute	2001
	(BRANDY & RAY J)	
	Another Day In Paradise	2001
J-KWON	Tipsy	2004
J-SHIN featuring LATOCHA SCOTT		
	One Night Stand	1999
J.J. FAD	Supersonic	1988
JA RULE	Clap Back/Reigns	2003
	Holla Holla	1999
JA RULE featuring ASHANTI		
	Always On Time	2001

ARTIST	SONG TITLE	DATE
	Mesmerize	2003
JA RULE featuring BOBBY BROWN		
	Thug Lovin'	2002
JA RULE featuring CASE		
	Livin' It Up	2001
JA RULE featuring CHARLI 'CHUCK' BALTIMORE		
	Down Ass Chick	2002
JA RULE featuring CHRISTINA MILIAN		
	Between Me And You	2001
JA RULE featuring LIL' MO		
	I Cry	2001
JA RULE featuring LIL' MO & VITA		
	Put It On Me	2000
JA RULE featuring R. KELLY & ASHANTI		
	Wonderful	2004
(IRV GOTTI presents JA RULE, ASHANTI, CHARLI BALTIMORE)		
	Down 4 U	2002
(JAY-Z featuring AMIL & JA RULE)		
	Can I Get A...	1999
(JENNIFER LOPEZ featuring JA RULE)		
	Ain't It Funny	2001
(MARY J. BLIGE featuring JA RULE)		
	Rainy Dayz	2002
JACK 'N' CHILL	The Jack That House Built	1988
TERRY JACKS	If You Go Away	1974

ARTIST	SONG TITLE	DATE
	Seasons In The Sun	1974
ALAN JACKSON	Drive (For Daddy Gene)	2002
	It Must Be Love	2000
	Little Man	1999
	Remember When	2003
	That'd Be Alright	2003
	Where I Come From	2001
	Where Were You (When The World Stopped Turning)	2001
	Work In Progress	2002
CHAD JACKSON	Hear The Drummer (Get Wicked)	1990
DEE D. JACKSON	Automatic Lover	1978
DEON JACKSON	Love Makes The World Go Round	1966
FREDDIE JACKSON	Have You Ever Loved Somebody	1987
	He'll Never Love You (Like I Do)	1985
	Jam Tonight	1987
	Me & Mrs. Jones	1992
	Rock Me Tonight (For Old Times Sake)	1985
	You Are My Lady	1985
J.J. JACKSON	But It's Alright	1966
JANET JACKSON	Again	1993
	All For You	2001
	Alright	1990
	Any Time, Any Place/And On And On	1994
	Because Of Love	1994
	Black Cat	1990

ARTIST	SONG TITLE	DATE
	Come Back To Me	1990
	Control	1986
	Doesn't Really Matter	2000
	Escapade	1990
	Go Deep	1998
	I Get Lonely	1998
	If	1993
	Let's Wait Awhile	1987
	Love Will Never Do (Without You)	1990
	Miss You Much	1989
	Nasty	1986
	Pleasure Principal	1987
	Rhythm Nation	1989
	Runaway	1995
	Someone To Call My Lover	2001
	That's The Way Love Goes	1993
	Together Again	1997
	Twenty Foreplay	1996
	What Have You Done For Me Lately	1986
	When I Think Of You	1986
	Whoops Now/What'll I Do	1995
	You Want This/70's Love Groove	1994
JANET	All Nite (Don't Stop)/ I Want You	2004
	Just A Little While	2004
JANET featuring MISSY ELLIOTT, P. DIDDY & CARLY SIMON	Son Of A Gun	2001

ARTIST	SONG TITLE	DATE
JANET featuring Q-TIP AND JONI MITCHELL		
	Got 'Til It's Gone	1997
(BEENIE MAN featuring JANET)		
	Feel It Boy	2002
(BLACKSTREET WITH JANET)		
	Girlfriend/Boyfriend	1999
(BUSTA RHYMES featuring JANET)		
	What's It Gonna Be?!	1999
(LUTHER VANDROSS AND JANET JACKSON)		
	The Best Things In Life Are Free	1992
(MICHAEL JACKSON & JANET JACKSON)		
	Scream/Childhood	1995
JERMAINE JACKSON		
	Burnin' Hot	1980
	Daddy's Home	1972
	Do What You Do	1984
	Dynamite	1984
	I Think It's Love	1986
	Let Me Tickle Your Fancy	1982
	Let's Get Serious	1980
	You're Supposed To Keep Your Love For Me	1980
JOE JACKSON	Breaking Us In Two	1983
	Is She Really Going Out With Him?	1979
	It's Different For Girls	1980
	Steppin' Out	1982

ARTIST	SONG TITLE	DATE
	You Can't Get What You Want (Till You Know What You Want)	1984
(SUZANNE VEGA featuring JOE JACKSON)		
	Left Of Center	1986
MICHAEL JACKSON	Ain't No Sunshine	1972
	Another Part Of Me	1988
	Bad	1987
	Beat It	1983
	Ben	1972
	Billie Jean	1983
	Black Or White	1991
	Blood On The Dance Floor	1997
	Butterflies	2001
	Cry	2001
	Dirty Diana	1988
	Don't Stop Till You Get Enough	1979
	Earth Song	1995
	Farewell My Summer Love	1984
	Girl You're So Together	1984
	Give In To Me	1993
	Gone Too Soon	1993
	Got To Be There	1971
	Heal The World	1992
	History/Ghosts	1997
	Human Nature	1983
	I Wanna Be Where You Are	1972

ARTIST	SONG TITLE	DATE
	In The Closet	1992
	Jam	1992
	Just A Little Bit Of You	1975
	Leave Me Alone	1989
	Liberian Girl	1989
	Man In The Mirror	1988
	Off The Wall	1980
	One Day In Your Life	1981
	One More Chance	2003
	P.Y.T. (Pretty Young Thing)	1983
	Remember The Time	1992
	Rock With You	1979
	Rockin' Robin	1972
	She's Out Of My Life	1980
	Smooth Criminal	1988
	Stranger In Moscow	1996
	They Don't Care About Us	1996
	Thriller	1984
	Wanna Be Startin' Something	1983
	The Way You Make Me Feel	1987
	Who Is It	1993
	Will You Be There	1993
	You Are Not Alone	1995
	You Rock My World	2001
MICHAEL JACKSON & JANET JACKSON		
	Scream/Childhood	1995

ARTIST	SONG TITLE	DATE
MICHAEL JACKSON & PAUL McCARTNEY		
	The Girl Is Mine	1982
MICHAEL JACKSON (DUET WITH SIEDAH GARRETT)		
	I Just Can't Stop Loving You	1987
MICHAEL JACKSON WITH THE JACKSON 5		
	I Want You Back '88	1988
	(PAUL McCARTNEY & MICHAEL JACKSON)	
	Say Say Say	1983
	(STEVIE WONDER & MICHAEL JACKSON)	
	Get It	1988
	(3T featuring MICHAEL JACKSON)	
	Why	1996
MICK JACKSON	Blame It On The Boogie	1978
	Weekend	1979
MILLIE JACKSON	Ask Me What You Want	1972
	Hurts So Good	1973
	(ELTON JOHN & MILLIE JACKSON)	
	Act Of War	1985
REBBIE JACKSON	Centipede	1984
TONY JACKSON & THE VIBRATIONS		
	Bye Bye Baby	1964
JACKSON 5	ABC	1970
	Corner Of The Sky	1972
	Dancing Machine	1974
	Doctor My Eyes	1973
	Get It Together	1973

ARTIST	SONG TITLE	DATE
	Hallelujah Day	1973
	I Am Love (Pts 1 & 2)	1975
	I Want You Back	1969
	I'll Be There	1970
	Little Bitty Pretty One	1972
	Lookin' Through The Windows	1972
	The Love You Save	1970
	Mama's Pearl	1971
	Maybe Tomorrow	1971
	Never Can Say Goodbye	1971
	Skywriter	1973
	Sugar Daddy	1971
	Whatever You Got, I Want	1974
JACKSONS	Blame It On The Boogie	1978
	Can You Feel It	1981
	Destiny	1979
	Dreamer	1977
	Enjoy Yourself	1976
	Even Though You've Gone	1978
	Goin' Places	1977
	Heartbrreak Hotel	1980
	Lovely One	1980
	Nothin (That Compares 2 U)	1989
	Shake Your Body (Down To The Ground)	1979
	Show You The Way To Go	1977
	State Of Shock	1984

ARTIST	SONG TITLE	DATE
	Torture	1984
	Walk Right Now	1981
JACKY	White Horses	1968
JENNIFER LOPEZ featuring JADAKISS & STYLES		
	Jenny From The Block	2002
JADE	Don't Walk Away	1992
	Every Day Of The Week	1994
	I Wanna Love You	1992
	One Woman	1993
	(POV featuring JADE)	
	All Thru The Nite	1994
JAGGED EDGE	Gotta Be	1998
	He Can't Love U	1999
	Let's Get Married	2000
	Promise	2000
	Walked Outta Heaven	2004
JAGGED EDGE featuring NELLY		
	Where The Party At?	2001
	(FABOLOUS featuring P. DIDDY & JAGGED EDGE)	
	Trade It All	2002
MICK JAGGER	Just Another Night	1985
	Let's Work	1987
	Lucky In Love	1985
	Memo From Turner	1970
	Sweet Thing	1993

ARTIST	SONG TITLE	DATE
MICK JAGGER & DAVID BOWIE		
	Dancing In The Street	1985
JAGGERZ	The Rapper	1970
JAGS	Back Of My Hand	1979
JAHEIM	Could It Be	2001
	Just In Case	2001
JAHEIM featuring NEXT		
	Anything	2002
JAIMESON	Complete	2003
JAIMESON featuring ANGEL BLU		
	True	2003
JAIMESON featuring ANGEL BLU AND CK		
	Take Control	2004
JAKATTA	American Dream	2001
	One Fine Day	2003
	So Lonely	2002
JAKATTA featuring SEAL		
	My Vision	2002
JALN BAND	Disco Music/I Like It	1976
	I Got To Sing	1977
JAM & SPOON featuring REA		
	Be Angeled	2002
JAM & SPOON featuring PLAVKA		
	Angel (Ladadi O-Heyo)	1995
	Find Me (Odyssey To Anyoona)	1994

ARTIST	SONG TITLE	DATE
	Right In The Night (Fall In Love With Music)	1994
JAM TRONIK	Another Day In Paradise	1990
JAM	Absolute Beginners	1981
	All Around The World	1977
	Beat Surrender	1982
	The Bitterest Pill (I Ever Had To Swallow)	1982
	David Watts/'A' Bomb In Wardour Street	1978
	Down In The Tube Station At Midnight	1978
	The Eton Rifles	1979
	Funeral Pyre	1981
	Going Underground/Dreams Of Children	1980
	In The City	2002
	Just Who Is The Five O'Clock Hero	1982
	The Modern World	1977
	News Of The World	1978
	Start	1980
	Strange Town	1979
	Town Called Malice/Precious	1982
	When You're Young	1979
JAMELIA	Call Me	2000
	I Do	1999
	See It In A Boy's Eyes	2004
	Superstar	2003

ARTIST	SONG TITLE	DATE
JAMELIA featuring BEENIE MAN		
	Money	2000
JAMELIA featuring RAH DIGGA		
	Bout	2003
JAMES BOYS	Over And Over	1973
JAMES	Born Of Frustration	1992
	Come Home	1990
	Destiny Calling	1998
	Getting Away With It (All Messed Up)	2001
	How Was It For You?	1990
	I Know What I'm Here For	1999
	Jam J/Say Something	1994
	Just Like Fred Astaire	1999
	Laid	1993
	Lose Control	1990
	Ring The Bells	1992
	Runaground	1998
	She's A Star	1997
	Sit Down	1991
	Sometimes	1993
	Sound	1991
	Tomorrow	1997
	Waltzing Along	1997
DUNCAN JAMES & KEEDIE		
	I Believe My Heart	2004

ARTIST	SONG TITLE	DATE
ETTA JAMES	I Just Want To Make Love To You	1996
	Security	1968
	Tell Mama	1967
JIMMY JAMES & THE VAGABONDS		
	I'll Go Where The Music Takes Me	1976
	Now Is The Time	1976
	Red Red Wine	1968
JONI JAMES	My Last Date (With You)	1969
RICK JAMES	Cold Blooded	1983
	Give It To Me Baby	1981
	17	1984
	Super Freak (Pt 1)	1981
	You And I	1978
TOMMY JAMES	Draggin' The Line	1971
	I'm Comin' Home	1971
	Three Times In Love	1980
TOMMY JAMES & THE SHONDELLS		
	Ball Of Fire	1969
	Crimson & Clover	1968
	Crystal Blue Persuasion	1969
	Do Something To Me	1968
	Gettin' Together	1967
	Hanky Panky	1966
	I Like The Way	1967
	I Think We're Alone Now	1967
	It's Only Love	1966

ARTIST	SONG TITLE	DATE
	Mirage	1967
	Mony Mony	1968
	Say I Am (What I Am)	1966
	She	1969
	Sweet Cherry Wine	1969
WENDY JAMES	The Nameless One	1993
JAMIROQUAI	Alright	1997
	Blow Your Mind	1993
	Canned Heat	1999
	Corner Of The Earth	2002
	Cosmic Girl	1996
	Deeper Underground	1998
	Emergency On Planet Earth	1993
	Half The Man	1994
	High Times	1997
	King For A Day	1999
	Little L	2001
	Love Foolosophy	2002
	Space Cowboy	1994
	Stillness In Time	1995
	Supersonic	1999
	Too Young To Die	1993
	Virtual Insanity	1996
	When You Gonna Learn?	1993
	You Give Me Something	2001

ARTIST	SONG TITLE	DATE
	(JOOLS HOLLAND & JAMIROQUAI)	
	I'm In The Mood For Love	2001
	(M-BEAT featuring JAMIROQUAI)	
	Do U Know Where You're Coming From	1996
JAMX & DELEON	Can U Dig It	2002
JAN & DEAN	Dead Man's Curve	1964
	I Found A Girl	1965
	The Little Old Lady (From Pasadena)	1964
	The New Girl In School	1964
	Popsicle	1966
	Ride The Wild Surf	1964
	Sidewalk Surfin'	1964
	Surf City	1963
	You Really Know How To Hurt A Guy	1965
JANE'S ADDICTION	Been Caught Stealing	1991
	Just Because	2003
HORST JANKOWSKI		
	A Walk In The Black Forest	1965
SAMANTHA JANUS	A Message To Your Heart	1991
JAPAN	All Tomorrow's Parties	1983
	Cantonese Boy	1982
	European Son	1982
	Ghosts	1982
	I Second That Emotion	1982
	Life In Tokyo	1982
	Night Porter	1982

ARTIST	SONG TITLE	DATE
	Quiet Life	1981
	Visions Of China	1981
JEAN-MICHEL JARRE		
	Oxygene 10	1997
	Oxygene 8	1997
	Oxygene Part IV	1977
JEAN MICHEL JARRE & APOLLO 440		
	Rendez-Vous '98	1998
JEAN MICHEL JARRE featuring NATACHA ATLAS		
	C'est La Vie	2000
AL JARREAU	Moonlighting (Theme)	1987
	Mornin'	1983
	Trouble In Paradise	1983
	We're In This Love Together	1981
JARS OF CLAY	Flood	1996
JAVELLS featuring NOSMO KING		
	Goodbye Nothing To Say	1974
JAVINE	Best Of My Love	2004
	Don't Walk Away	2004
	Real Things	2003
	Surrender (Your Love)	2003
JAY & THE AMERICANS		
	Cara Mia	1965
	Come A Little Bit Closer	1964
	Crying	1966

ARTIST	SONG TITLE	DATE
	Let's Lock The Door (And Throw Away The Key)	1964
	Some Enchanted Evening	1965
	Sunday And Me	1965
	This Magic Moment	1968
	Walkin' In The Rain	1969
JAY & THE TECHNIQUES		
	Apples Peaches Pumpkin Pie	1967
	Keep The Ball Rollin'	1967
	Strawberry Shortcake	1968
CANDEE JAY	If I Were You	2004
JAY-Z	Anything	2000
	Change Clothes	2003
	Excuse Me Miss	2003
	Girls, Girls, Girls	2001
	Hard Knock Life (Ghetto Anthem)	1998
	I Just Wanna Love U (Give It 2 Me)	2000
	Izzo (H.O.V.A.)	2001
	Jigga My Nigga	1999
	99 Problems/Dirt Off Your Shoulder	2004
JAY-Z featuring UGK		
	Big Pimpin'	2000
JAY-Z featuring AMIL & JA RULE		
	Can I Get ...	1999
JAY-Z featuring BABYFACE & FOXY BROWN		
	Sunshine	1997

ARTIST	SONG TITLE	DATE
JAY-Z featuring BEYONCE KNOWLES		
	'03 Bonnie & Clyde	2003
JAY-Z featuring BLACKSTREET		
	The City Is Mine	1998
JAY-Z featuring FOXY BROWN		
	Ain't No Playa	1997
JAY-Z featuring GWEN DICKEY		
	Wishing On A Star	1998
JAY-Z featuring MARY J. BLIGE		
	Can't Knock The Hustle	1997
	(ANOTHER LEVEL featuring JAY-Z) Be Alone No More	1999
	(FOXY BROWN featuring JAY-Z) I'll Be	1997
	(MARIAH CAREY featuring JAY-Z) Heartbreaker	1999
	(PANJABI MC featuring JAY-Z) Beware Of The Boys (Mundian To Bach Ke)	2003
	(PHARRELL WILLIAMS featuring JAY-Z) Frontin'	2003
	(R. KELLY & JAY-Z) Fiesta	2001
	Honey	2002
JAYDEE	Plastic Dreams	1997
JERRY JAYE	My Girl Josephine	1967

ARTIST	SONG TITLE	DATE
JD featuring DA BRAT		
	The Party Continues	1998
	(SNOOP DOGGY DOGG featuring JD)	
	We Just Wanna Party With You	1997
WYCLEF JEAN	Gone Till November	1998
	Perfect Gentleman	2001
	Wish You Were Here	2001
WYCLEF JEAN and THE REFUGEE ALLSTARS		
	Guantanamera	1997
	We Trying To Stay Alive	1997
WYCLEF JEAN featuring BONO		
	New Day	1999
WYCLEF JEAN featuring CLAUDETTE ORTIZ		
	Two Wrongs (Don't Make A Right)	2002
WYCLEF JEAN featuring MARY J. BLIGE		
	911	2000
WYCLEF JEAN featuring THE ROCK & MELKY SEDECK		
	It Doesn't Matter	2000
	(QUEEN WITH WYCLEF JEAN featuring PRAS	
	MICHEL & FREE)	
	Another One Bites The Dust	1998
JEFFERSON AIRPLANE		
	Be My Lady	1982
	Find Your Way Back	1981
	No Way Out	1984
	Somebody To Love	1967

ARTIST	SONG TITLE	DATE
	White Rabbit	1967
	Winds Of Change	1983
JEFFERSON STARSHIP		
	Count On Me	1978
	Jane	1979
	Miracles	1975
	Runaway	1978
	With Your Love	1976
STARSHIP	Tomorrow Doesn't Matter Tonight	1986
JEFFERSON	Baby Take Me In Your Arms	1969
	The Colour Of My Love	1969
JOE JEFFREY GROUP		
	My Pledge Of Love	1969
JELLY BEANS	I Wanna Love Him So Bad	1964
JELLYBEAN	Jingo	1987
	Sidewalk Talk	1985
JELLYBEAN featuring ADELE BERTEI		
	Just A Mirage	1988
JELLYBEAN featuring ELISA FIORILLO		
	Who Found Who	1987
JELLYBEAN featuring STEVEN DANTE		
	The Real Thing	1987
JELLYFISH	The King Is Half Undressed	1991
JEMINI	Cry Baby	2003
WAYLON JENNINGS		
	Good Hearted Woman	1976

ARTIST	SONG TITLE	DATE
	Luckenbach, Texas (Back To The Basics Of Love)	1977
	Theme From 'The Dukes Of Hazzard' (Good Ol' Boys)	1980
JENTINA	Bad Ass Strippa	2004
	French Kisses	2004
JESSY	Look At Me Now	2003
JESUS & MARY CHAIN		
	April Skies	1987
	Blues From A Gun	1989
	Cracking Up	1998
	Darklands	1987
	Far Gone And Out	1992
	Happy When It Rains	1987
	Iloverocknroll	1998
	Reverence	1992
	Sidewalking	1988
	Some Candy Talking	1986
	Sometimes Always	1994
	Sound Of Speed (EP)	1993
JESUS JONES	The Devil You Know	1993
	International Bright Young Thing	1991
	Real Real Real	1991
	The Right Decision	1993
	Right Here, Right Now	1991
	Who? Where? Why?	1991

ARTIST	SONG TITLE	DATE
	Zeroes And Ones	1993
JESUS LIZARD/NIRVANA		
	Puss/Oh, The Guilt	1993
JESUS LOVES YOU	Bow Down Mister	1991
	Generations Of Love	1991
JET	Are You Gonna Be My Girl?	2003
	Cold Hard Bitch	2004
	Look What You've Done	2004
	Rollover DJ	2003
JETHRO TULL	Bungle In The Jungle	1974
	Life Is A Long Song/Up The Pool	1971
	Living In The Past	1972
	Love Story	1969
	Ring Our Solstice Bells (EP)	1976
	Sweet Dream	1969
	The Witch's Promise/Teacher	1970
JETS	Love Makes The World Go Round	1982
	Yes Tonight Josephine	1981
JETS	Cross My Broken Heart	1987
	Crush On You	1986
	I Do You	1987
	Make It Real	1988
	Rocket 2 U	1988
	You Got It All	1986
JOAN JETT	Dirty Deeds	1990
	Everyday People	1983

ARTIST	SONG TITLE	DATE
	Fake Friends	1983
JOAN JETT & THE BLACKHEARTS		
	Crimson And Clover	1982
	Do You Wanna Touch Me (Oh Yeah)	1982
	I Hate Myself For Loving You	1988
	I Love Rock 'n' Roll	1982
	Little Liar	1988
	BARBUSTERS (JOAN JETT & THE BLACKHEARTS)	
	Light Of Day	1987
JEWEL	Down So Long	1999
	Foolish Games/You Were Meant For Me	1997
	Hands	1998
	Standing Still	2001
	Who Will Save Your Soul	1996
BUDDY JEWELL	Help Pour Out The Rain (Lacey's Song)	2003
	Sweet Southern Comfort	2004
JEZ & CHOOPIE	Yim	1998
JIGSAW	If I Have To Go Away	1977
	Love Fire	1976
	Sky High	1975
JILTED JOHN	Jilted John	1978
JIMMY EAT WORLD	The Middle	2002
	Pain	2004
	Sweetness	2002

ARTIST	SONG TITLE	DATE
JIMMY THE HOOVER		
	Tantalise (Wo Wo Ee Yeh Yeh)	1983
JINGLE BELLES	Christmas Spectre	1983
JINNY	Keep Warm	1995
	Wanna Be With You	1995
JIVE BUNNY & THE MASTERMIXERS		
	Can Can You Party	1990
	Crazy Party Mixes	1990
	Let's Party	1989
	Let's Swing Again	1990
	Over To You John (Here We Go...)	1991
	Swing The Mood	1989
	That Sounds Good To Me	1990
	That's What I Like	1989
JIVE FIVE	I'm A Happy Man	1965
JJ72	Formulae	2002
	October Swimmer	2000
	Oxygen	2000
	Snow	2001
SAMI JO	Tell Me A Lie	1974
JOBOXERS	Boxer Beat	1983
	Johnny Friendly	1983
	Just Got Lucky	1983
JODECI	Come & Talk To Me	1992
	Cry For You	1993
	Feenin'	1994

ARTIST	SONG TITLE	DATE
	Forever My Lady	1991
	Freek'n You	1995
	Get On Up	1996
	Lately	1993
	Love U 4 Life	1995
JOE	All The Things (Your Man Won't Do)	1996
	Don't Wanna Be A Player	1997
	Good Girls	1998
	I Wanna Know	2001
	I'm In Luv	1994
	Let's Stay Home Tonight	2002
	The Love Scene	1997
	The One For Me	1994
JOE featuring G-UNIT		
	Ride Wit U/More & More	2004
JOE featuring MYSTIKAL		
	Stutter	2001
	(BIG PUNISHER featuring JOE)	
	Still Not A Player	1998
	(CASE & JOE)	
	Faded Pictures	1998
	(MARIAH CAREY featuring JOE & 98 DEGREES)	
	Thank God I Found You	1999
JOE PUBLIC	Live And Learn	1992
BILLY JOEL	All About Soul	1993
	All For Leyna	1980

ARTIST	SONG TITLE	DATE
	All Shook Up	1992
	Allentown	1982
	And So It Goes	1990
	Big Shot	1979
	Don't Ask Me Why	1980
	The Entertainer	1974
	Honesty	1979
	I Go To Extremes	1990
	An Innocent Man	1983
	It's Still Rock And Roll To Me	1980
	Just The Way You Are	1977
	Keeping The Faith	1985
	Leave A Tender Moment/Goodnight Saigon	1984
	The Longest Time	1984
	A Matter Of Trust	1986
	Modern Woman	1986
	Movin' Out (Anthony's Song)	1978
	My Life	1978
	The Night Is Still Young	1985
	Only The Good Die Young	1978
	Piano Man	1974
	Pressure	1982
	The River Of Dreams	1993
	Say Goodbye To Hollywood	1981
	She's Always A Woman	1978

ARTIST	SONG TITLE	DATE
	She's Got A Way	1981
	Sometimes A Fantasy	1980
	Tell Her About It	1983
	This Is The Time	1986
	Uptown Girl	1983
	We Didn't Start The Fire	1989
	You May Be Right	1980
	You're Only Human (Second Wind)	1985
JOHN & ERNEST	Super Fly Meets Shaft	1973
ELTON JOHN	Are You Ready For Love?	2003
	Believe	1995
	Bennie And The Jets	1974
	The Bitch Is Back	1974
	Bite Your Lip (Get Up And Dance!)	1977
	Blessed	1995
	Blue Eyes	1982
	Can You Feel The Love Tonight?	1994
	Candle In The Wind	1974
	Candle In The Wind 1997/Something About The Way You Look Tonight	1997
	Chloe	1981
	Circle Of Life	1994
	Club At The End Of The Street	1990
	Cold As Christmas	1983
	Crazy Water	1977
	Crocodile Rock	1972

ARTIST	SONG TITLE	DATE
	Daniel	1973
	Don't Let The Sun Go Down On Me	1974
	Don't Ya Wanna Play This Game No More?	1980
	Ego	1978
	Empty Garden (Hey Hey Johnny)	1982
	Friends	1971
	Goodbye Yellow Brick Road	1973
	Grow Some Funk Of Your Own/I Feel Like A Bullet	1976
	Honky Cat	1972
	I Don't Wanna Go On With You Like That	1988
	I Guess That's Why They Call It The Blues	1983
	I Want Love	2001
	I'm Still Standing	1983
	If The River Can Bend	1998
	In Neon	1984
	Island Girl	1975
	Kiss The Bride	1983
	The Last Song	1992
	Levon	1971
	Little Jeannie	1980
	Lucy In The Sky With Diamonds	1974
	Made In England	1995

ARTIST	SONG TITLE	DATE
	Mama Can't Buy You Love	1979
	Nikita	1986
	Nobody Wins	1981
	The One	1992
	Original Sin	2002
	Part-Time Love	1978
	Passengers	1984
	Philadelphia Freedom	1975
	Pinball Wizard	1976
	Please	1996
	Recover Your Soul	1998
	Rocket Man	1972
	Sacrifice/Healing Hands	1990
	Sad Songs (Say So Much)	1984
	Saturday Night's Alright For Fighting	1973
	Simple Life	1993
	Someone Saved My Life Tonight	1975
	Song For Guy	1978
	Sorry Seems To Be The Hardest Word	1976
	Step Into Christmas	1973
	This Train Don't Stop There Anymore	2002
	Victim Of Love	1979
	Who Wears These Shoes?	1984
	A Word In Spanish	1988
	Wrap Her Up	1985
	You Gotta Love Somebody	1990

ARTIST	SONG TITLE	DATE
	Your Song	1970
ELTON JOHN & ERIC CLAPTON		
	Runaway Train	1992
ELTON JOHN & KIKI DEE		
	Don't Go Breaking My Heart	1976
	True Love	1993
ELTON JOHN & LEANN RIMES		
	Written In The Stars	1999
ELTON JOHN & LUCIANO PAVAROTTI		
	Live Like Horses	1996
ELTON JOHN & MILLIE JACKSON		
	Act Of War	1985
ELTON JOHN featuring JOHN LENNON		
	I Saw Her Standing There	1981
(ARETHA FRANKLIN & ELTON JOHN)		
	Through The Storm	1989
(JENNIFER RUSH WITH ELTON JOHN)		
	Flames Of Paradise	1987
(MARCELLA DETROIT & ELTON JOHN)		
	Ain't Nothing Like The Real Thing	1994
LITTLE WILLIE JOHN		
	Sleep	1980
ROBERT JOHN	Hey There Lonely Girl	1980
	The Lion Sleeps Tonight	1972
	Sad Eyes	1979

ARTIST	SONG TITLE	DATE
JOHNNY HATES JAZZ		
	Heart Of Gold	1988
	I Don't Want To Be A Hero	1988
	Shattered Dreams	1988
	Turn Back The Clock	1987
SAMMY JOHNS	Chevy Van	1975
ANDREAS JOHNSON	Glorious	2000
CAREY JOHNSON	Real Fashion (Reggae Style)	1987
DON JOHNSON	Heartbeat	1986
	(BARBRA STREISAND & DON JOHNSON)	
	Till I Loved You (Love Theme From	
	'Goya')	1988
HOLLY JOHNSON	Americanos	1989
	Atomic City	1989
	Love Train	1989
	(MARSDEN/MCCARTNEY/JOHNSON/CHRISTIANS)	
	Ferry 'Cross The Mersey	1989
BANDWAGON	Breakin' Down The Walls Of Heartache	1968
JOHNNY JOHNSON & THE BANDWAGON		
	(Blame It) On The Pony Express	1970
	Let's Hang On	1969
	Sweet Inspiration	1970
	You	1969
KEVIN JOHNSON	Rock 'n' Roll (I Gave You The Best Years	
	Of My Life)	1975

ARTIST	SONG TITLE	DATE
LAURIE JOHNSON'S LONDON BIG BAND		
	Theme From 'The Professionals'	1997
LJ JOHNSON	Your Magic Put A Spell On Me	1976
LOU JOHNSON	Message To Martha (Kentucky Bluebird)	1964
MARV JOHNSON	I Miss You Baby	1969
	I'll Pick A Rose For My Rose	1969
MICHAEL JOHNSON		
	Almost Like Being In Love	1978
	Bluer Than Blue	1978
	This Night Won't Last Forever	1979
PAUL JOHNSON	Get Get Down	1999
PUFF JOHNSON	Forever More	1997
	Over And Over	1997
SABRINA JOHNSON	Peace	1991
SYLEENA JOHNSON	Tonight I'm Gonna Let Go	2002
	(KANYE WEST featuring SYLEENA JOHNSON)	
	All Falls Down	2004
ANA JOHNSSON	We Are	2004
BRUCE JOHNSTON	Pipeline	1977
JAN JOHNSTON	Flesh	2001
	(FREEFALL featuring JAN JOHNSTON)	
	Skydive (I Feel Wonderful)	2001
	(SUB MERGE featuring JAN JOHNSTON)	
	Take Me By The Hand	1997
	(TOMSKI featuring JAN JOHNSTON)	
	Love Will Come	2000

ARTIST	SONG TITLE	DATE
TOM JOHNSTON	Savannah Nights	1979
JO JO GUNNE	Run Run Run	1972
JOJO	Leave (Get Out)	2004
FRANCE JOLI	Come To Me	1979
JOLLY ROGER	Acid Man	1988
JOMANDA	Got A Love For You	1991
	Never	1993
JON & ROBIN & THE IN CROWD		
	Do It Again A Little Bit Slower	1967
JON & VANGELIS	I Hear You Now	1980
	I'll Find My Way Home	1981
JON OF THE PLEASED WIMMIN		
	Passion	1995
	Give Me Strength	1996
JONAH	Sssst (Listen)	2000
JONES GIRLS	You Gonna Make Me Love Somebody	
	Else	1979
ALED JONES	Walking In The Air	1985
BARBARA JONES	Just When I Needed You Most	1981
DONELL JONES	Shorty (Got Her Eyes On Me)	2000
	U Know What's Up	2000
	Where I Wanna Be	2000
	(TRUE STEPPERS featuring BRIAN HARVEY &	
	DONELL JONES)	
	True Step Tonight	2000

ARTIST	SONG TITLE	DATE
GEORGIA JONES/DIVA SURPRISE		
	On Top Of The World	1998
	(PLUX featuring GEORGIA JONES)	
	Over & Over	1996
GRACE JONES	Love Is The Drug	1986
	Private Life	1980
	Pull Up To The Bumper/La Vie En Rose	1986
	Slave To The Rhythm	1985
HOWARD JONES	All I Want	1986
	Everlasting Love	1989
	Hide And Seek	1984
	Life In One Day	1985
	Lift Me Up	1992
	Like To Get To Know You Well	1984
	Look Mama	1985
	New Song	1984
	No One Is To Blame	1986
	Pearl In The Shell	1984
	The Prisoner	1989
	Things Can Only Get Better	1985
	What Is Love?	1983
	You Know I Love You... Don't You?	1986
JACK JONES	Dear Heart	1964
	The Impossible Dream (The Quest)	1966
	Lady	1967
	The Race Is On	1965

ARTIST	SONG TITLE	DATE
JUGGY JONES	Inside America	1976
LINDA JONES	Hypnotized	1967
NORAH JONES	Don't Know Why	2002
	Sunrise	2004
ORAN 'JUICE' JONES		
	The Rain	1986
PAUL JONES	High Time	1966
	I've Been A Bad, Bad Boy	1967
	Thinkin' Ain't For Me	1967
QUINCY JONES	Ai No Corrida	1981
	Razzamatazz	1981
	The Secret Garden	1990
	Stomp — The Remixes	1996
	Stuff Like That	1978
QUINCY JONES featuring AL B. SURE!, J. INGRAM,		
E. DEBARGE	Secret Garden	1990
QUINCY JONES featuring RAY CHARLES & CHAKA KHAN		
	I'll Be Good To You	1990
QUINCY JONES featuring JAMES INGRAM		
	Just Once	1981
	One Hundred Ways	1981
RICKIE LEE JONES	Chuck E.'s In Love	1979
TAMMY JONES	Let Me Try Again	1975
TOM JONES	All You Need Is Love	1993
	A Boy From Nowhere	1987
	Can't Stop Loving You	1970

ARTIST	SONG TITLE	DATE
	Daughter Of Darkness	1970
	Delilah	1968
	Detroit City	1967
	Funny Familiar Forgotten Feeling	1967
	Green, Green Grass Of Home	1966
	Help Yourself	1968
	I (Who Have Nothing)	1970
	I'll Never Fall In Love Again	1969
	I'm Comin' Home	1967
	If I Only Knew	1994
	It's Not Unusual	1965
	Letter To Lucille	1973
	Love Me Tonight	1969
	A Minute Of Your Time	1968
	Once Upon A Time/Not Responsible	1966
	Puppet Man	1971
	Resurrection Shuffle	1971
	Say You'll Stay Until Tomorrow	1977
	She's A Lady	1971
	Something 'Bout You Baby I Like	1974
	Thunderball	1965
	Till	1971
	Tom Jones International	2002
	What's New Pussycat?	1965
	With These Hands	1965
	Without Love (There Is Nothing)	1969

ARTIST	SONG TITLE	DATE
	The Young New Mexican Puppeteer	1972
TOM JONES & CERYS MATTHEWS		
	Baby, It's Cold Outside	1999
TOM JONES & HEATHER SMALL		
	You Need Love Like I Do	2000
TOM JONES & MOUSSE T		
	Sex Bomb	2000
TOM JONES & STEREOPHONICS		
	Mama Told Me Not To Come	2000
TOM JONES & THE CARDIGANS		
	Burning Down The House	1999
	(ART OF NOISE featuring TOM JONES)	
	Kiss	1988
JANIS JOPLIN	Me And Bobby McGee	1971
ALISON JORDAN	Boy From New York City	1992
JEREMY JORDAN	The Right Kind Of Love	1992
	Wannagirl	1993
MONTELL JORDAN	Falling	1996
	Get It On Tonite	1999
	I Can Do That	1998
	I Like	1996
	Let's Ride	1998
	Somethin' 4 Da Honeyz	1995
	This Is How We Do It	1995
	What's On Tonight	1997

ARTIST	SONG TITLE	DATE
MONTELL JORDAN featuring SLICK RICK		
	I Like It	1996
RONNY JORDAN	So What!	1992
DAVID JOSEPH	Let's Live It Up (Nite People)	1983
	You Can't Hide (Your Love From Me)	1983
MARK JOSEPH	Bringing Back Those Memories	2004
	Fly	2003
	Get Through	2003
MARTYN JOSEPH	Dolphins Make Me Cry	1992
JOURNEY	After The Fall	1983
	Any Way You Want It	1980
	Be Good To Yourself	1986
	Don't Stop Believing	1981
	Faithfully	1983
	Girl Can't Help It	1986
	I'll Be Alright Without You	1986
	Lovin', Touchin', Squeezin'	1979
	Only The Young	1985
	Open Arms	1982
	The Party's Over (Hopelessly In Love)	1981
	Send Her My Love	1983
	Separate Ways (Worlds Apart)	1983
	Still They Ride	1982
	Suzanne	1986
	Walks Like A Lady	1980

ARTIST	SONG TITLE	DATE
	When You Love A Woman	1996
	Who's Crying Now	1981
JOY DIVISION	Atmosphere	1988
	Love Will Tear Us Apart	1980
JOY STRINGS	It's An Open Secret	1964
	A Starry Night	1964
JOYRIDER	Rush Hour	1996
JT AND THE BIG FAMILY		
	Moments In Soul	1990
JT MONEY featuring SOLE		
	Who Dat	1999
JT PLAYAZ	Just Playin'	1997
JTQ WITH NOEL MCKOY		
	Love The Life	1993
JUDAS PRIEST	Breaking The Law	1980
	Living After Midnight	1980
	Take On The World	1979
	United	1980
JUDGE DREAD	Big Eight	1973
	Big Seven	1972
	Big Six	1972
	Big Ten	1975
	Christmas In Dreadland/Come Outside	1975
	5th Anniversary (EP)	1977
	Je T'Aime (Moi Non Plus)	1975

ARTIST	SONG TITLE	DATE
	The Winkle Man	1976
	Y Viva Suspenders	1976
JUICE	Best Days	1998
JUICY LUCY	Who Do You Love	1970
JULIA & COMPANY	Breakin' Down (Sugar Samba)	1984
JUMP 'N THE SADDLE		
	The Curly Shuffle	1983
WALLY JUMP JR & THE CRIMINAL ELEMENT		
	Tighten Up (I Just Can't Stop Dancin')	1987
JUNGLE BOOK	The Jungle Book Groove	1993
JUNGLE BOYS	Jungle Rock	2004
JUNGLE BROTHERS	Because I Got It Like That	1998
	Doin' Our Own Dang	1990
	I'll House You	1988
	Jungle Brother	1998
	V.I.P.	1999
	What 'U' Waitin' '4'	1990
	(MR ON vs THE JUNGLE BROTHERS)	
	Breathe Don't Stop	2004
JUNIOR	Mama Used To Say	1982
	Too Late	1982
	(KIM WILDE & JUNIOR)	
	Another Step (Closer To You)	1987
JUNIOR JACK	E Samba	2003
	My Feeling	2000

ARTIST	SONG TITLE	DATE
	Stupidisco	2004
	Thrill Me	2002
JUNIOR JACK featuring ROBERT SMITH		
	Da Hype	2004
JUNIOR M.A.F.I.A.	Player's Anthem	1995
JUNIOR M.A.F.I.A. featuring THE NOTORIOUS B.I.G.		
	Get Money	1996
JUNIOR SENIOR	Move Your Feet	2003
	Rhythm Bandits	2003
JURASSIC 5	Concrete Schoolyard	1998
JUST LUIS	American Pie	1995
JUST US	I Can't Grow Peaches On A Cherry	
	Tree	1966
JUSTIN	It's All About You	1999
	Let It Be Me	2000
	Over You	1999
	This Boy	1998
JUVENILE/WACKO/SKIP		
	Nolia Clap	2004
JUVENILE featuring FRESH & LIL' WAYNE		
	Back That Thang Up	1999
(B.G. featuring BABY, TURK, MANNIE FRESH, JUVENILE)		
	Bling Bling	1999
PATRICK JUVET	Got A Feeling	1978
	I Love America	1978

ARTIST	SONG TITLE	DATE
JX	Close To Your Heart	1997
	Restless	2004
	Son Of A Gun	1995
	There's Nothing I Won't Do	1996
	You Belong To Me	1995
ELVIS vs JXL	A Little Less Conversation	2002
K-CI & JOJO	All My Life	1998
	Crazy	2001
	Don't Rush (Take Love Slowly)	1998
	Tell Me It's Real	1999
	You Bring Me Up	1997
(2PAC featuring KC AND JOJO)		
	How Do You Want It?	1996
(WILL SMITH featuring K-CI)		
	Will 2K	1999
K-GEE	I Don't Really Care	2000
K-KLASS	Don't Stop	1992
	Let Me Show You	1993
	Rhythm Is A Mystery	1991
	So Right	1992
	What You're Missing	1994
K-WARREN featuring LEE-O		
	Coming Home	2001
K2 FAMILY	Bouncing Flow	2001
K7	Come Baby Come	1993

ARTIST	SONG TITLE	DATE
K7 & THE SWING KIDS		
	Hi De Ho	1994
KACI	I Think I Love You	2002
	Paradise	2001
	Tu Amor	2001
JOSHUA KADISON	Beautiful In My Eyes	1994
	Jessie	1993
KADOC	The Night Train	1996
	Rock The Bells	1997
BERT KAEMPFERT	Red Roses For A Blue Lady	1965
	Three O'Clock In The Morning	1965
BERT KAEMPFERT & HIS ORCHESTRA		
	Bye Bye Blues	1966
KAJAGOOGOO	Big Apple	1983
	Hang On Now	1983
	The Lion's Mouth	1984
	Ooh To Be Ah	1983
	Too Shy	1983
KALEEF	Golden Brown	1996
	Sands Of Time	1998
PREEYA KALIDAS	Shakalaka Baby	2002
KALIPHZ featuring PRINCE NASEEM		
	Walk Like A Champion	1996
NICK KAMEN	Each Time You Break My Heart	1986
	Loving You Is Sweeter Than Ever	1987
	Tell Me	1988

ARTIST	SONG TITLE	DATE
INI KAMOZE	Here Comes The Hotstepper	1994
KANDI	Don't Think I'm Not	2000
	(SOLE featuring J.T. MONEY AND KANDI)	
	4, 5, 6	1999
KANDIDATE	Girls Girls Girls	1979
	I Don't Wanna Lose You	1979
KANE	Rain Down On Me	2004
BIG DADDY KANE	Very Special	1993
EDEN KANE	Boys Cry	1964
KANE GANG	Closest Thing To Heaven	1984
	Motortown	1987
	Respect Yourself	1984
KANSAS	All I Wanted	1986
	Carry On Wayward Son	1976
	Dust In The Wind	1978
	People Of The South Wind	1979
	Play This Game Tonight	1982
	Point Of Know Return	1977
MORY KANTE	Yeke Yeke	1988
KAOMA	Lambada	1989
KASABIAN	Club Foot	2004
	L.S.F.	2004
	Processed Beats	2004
KASENENTZ-KATZ SINGING ORCHESTRAL CIRCUS		
	Quick Joey Small (Run Joey Run)	1968

ARTIST	SONG TITLE	DATE
KATRINA & THE WAVES		
	Do You Want Crying	1985
	Love Shine A Light	1997
	Sun Street	1986
	That's The Way	1989
	Walking On Sunshine	1985
KAVANA	Crazy Chance	1996
	Funky Love	1998
	I Can Make You Feel Good	1997
	MFEO	1997
	Special Kind Of Something	1998
	Where Are You	1996
	Will You Wait For Me	1999
NIAMH KAVANAGH	In Your Eyes	1993
D KAY & EPSILON featuring STAMINA MC		
	Barcelona	2003
JANET KAY	Silly Games	1979
	(LINDY LAYTON/JANET KAY)	
	Silly Games	1990
SAMMY KAYE	Charade	1964
KC & THE SUNSHINE BAND		
	Boogie Shoes	1978
	Get Down Tonight	1975
	Give It Up	1983
	I Like To Do It	1976
	I'm So Crazy ('Bout You)	1975

ARTIST	SONG TITLE	DATE
	I'm Your Boogie Man	1977
	It's The Same Old Song	1978
	Keep It Comin' Love	1977
	Please Don't Go	1979
	Queen Of Clubs	1974
	(Shake, Shake, Shake) Shake Your Booty	1976
	Sound Your Funky Horn	1974
	That's The Way (I Like It)	1975
	(TERI DESARIO WITH K.C.)	
	Yes, I'm Ready	1979
KEANE	Bedshaped	2004
	Everybody's Changing	2004
	Somewhere Only We Know	2004
RONAN KEATING	I Hope You Dance	2004
	I Love It When We Do	2002
	If Tomorrow Never Comes	2002
	Life Is A Rollercoaster	2000
	The Long Goodbye	2003
	Lost For Words	2003
	Lovin' Each Day	2001
	She Believes (In Me)	2004
	The Way You Make Me Feel	2000
	When You Say Nothing At All	1999
RONAN KEATING & LEANN RIMES		
	Last Thing On My Mind	2004

ARTIST	SONG TITLE	DATE
RONAN KEATING featuring LULU		
	We've Got Tonight	2002
KEEDY	Save Some Love	1991
KEVIN KEEGAN	Head Over Heels In Love	1979
KEITH	Ain't Gonna Lie	1966
	98.6	1966
	Tell Me To My Face	1967
KEITH'N'SHANE	Girl You Know It's True	2000
LISA KEITH	Better Than You	1993
TOBY KEITH	American Soldier	2003
	Courtesy Of The Red, White And Blue (The Angry American)	2002
	How Do You Like Me Now?	2000
	I Love This Bar	2003
	I Wanna Talk About Me	2001
	I'm Just Talkin' About Tonight	2001
	My List	2002
	Whiskey Girl	2004
	Who's Your Daddy	2002
	You Shouldn't Kiss Me Like This	2000
TOBY KEITH (DUET WITH WILLIE NELSON)		
	Beer For My Horses	2003
KELIS	Caught Out There	2000
	Good Stuff	2000
	Milkshake	2004
	Trick Me	2004

ARTIST	SONG TITLE	DATE
	Young Fresh N' New	2001
KELIS featuring ANDRE 3000		
	Millionaire	2004
(ENRIQUE featuring KELIS)		
	Not In Love	2004
(OL' DIRTY BASTARD featuring KELIS)		
	Got Your Money	1999
(P. DIDDY featuring KELIS)		
	Let's Get Ill	2003
(RICHARD X featuring KELIS)		
	Finest Dreams	2003
FRANK KELLY	Christmas Countdown	1984
R. KELLY	Bump N' Grind	1994
	Did You Ever Think	1999
	Feelin' On You Booty	2001
	Fiesta	2001
	The 4 Play (EP)	1995
	Gotham City	1997
	Half On A Baby	1998
	Happy People/U Saved Me	2004
	I Believe I Can Fly	1996
	I Can't Sleep Baby (If I)	1996
	I Wish	2000
	If I Could Turn Back The Hands Of Time	1999
	Ignition	2002

ARTIST	SONG TITLE	DATE
	Only The Loot Can Make Me Happy	
	When A Woman's Fed Up/I Can't Sleep	2000
	Sex Me	1993
	She's Got That Vibe	1994
	Step In The Name Of Love/Thoia	
	Thoing	2003
	The Storm Is Over Now	2001
	Summer Bunnies	1994
	Thank God It's Friday	1996
	When A Woman's Fed Up	1998
	The World's Greatest	2001
	You Remind Me Of Something	1995
	Your Body's Callin'	1994
R. KELLY & JAY-Z	Honey	2002
R. KELLY & PUBLIC ANNOUNCEMENT		
	Dedicated	1993
	Honey Love	1992
R. KELLY featuring BIG TIGGER		
	Snake	2003
R. KELLY featuring KEITH MURRAY		
	Home Alone	1998
R. KELLY featuring RONALD ISLEY		
	Down Low (Nobody Has To Know)	1996
	(CASSIDY featuring R. KELLY)	
	Hotel	2004
	(CELINE DION & R. KELLY)	
	I'm Your Angel	1998
	(FAT JOE featuring R. KELLY)	
	We Thuggin'	2001
	(JA RULE featuring R. KELLY & ASHANTI)	
	Wonderful	2004
	(MARQUES HOUSTON featuring JOE BUDDEN	
	& PIED PIPER)	
	Clubbin	2003
	(NICK CANNON featuring R. KELLY)	
	Gigolo	2003
	(PUFF DADDY featuring R. KELLY)	
	Satisfy You	1999
	(SPARKLE featuring R. KELLY)	
	Be Careful	1998
	(TWISTA featuring R. KELLY)	
	So Sexy	2004
JOHNNY KEMP	Birthday Suit	1989
	Just Got Paid	1988
TARA KEMP	Hold You Tight	1991
	Piece Of My Heart	1991
EDDIE KENDRICKS	Boogie Down	1974
	He's A Friend	1976
	Keep On Truckin'	1973
	Shoeshine Boy	1975
	Son Of Sagittarius	1974

ARTIST	SONG TITLE	DATE
KENICKIE	I Would Fix You	1998
	In Your Car	1997
	Nightlife	1997
	Punka	1997
BRIAN KENNEDY	A Better Man	1996
	Life, Love & Happiness	1996
	Put The Message In The Box	1997
JOYCE KENNEDY & JEFFREY OSBORNE		
	The Last Time I Made Love	1984
KENNY	Baby I Love You, Ok!	1975
	The Bump	1974
	Fancy Pants	1975
	Give It To Me Now	1973
	Heart Of Stone	1973
	Julie Anne	1975
GERARD KENNY	Fantasy	1980
KERBDOG	Dummy Crusher	1994
NIK KERSHAW	Dancing Girls	1984
	Don Quixote	1985
	Human Racing	1984
	I Won't Let The Sun Go Down On Me	1984
	The Riddle	1984
	When A Heart Beats	1985
	Wide Boy	1985
	Wouldn't It Be Good	1984

ARTIST	SONG TITLE	DATE
ALICIA KEYS	Fallin'	2001
	Girlfriend	2002
	How Come You Don't Call Me	2002
	If I Ain't Got You	2004
	A Woman's Worth	2001
	You Don't Know My Name	2003
ALICIA KEYS featuring TONY TONI TONE		
	Diary	2004
(ANGIE STONE featuring ALICIA KEYS & EVE)		
	Brotha Part II	2002
(EVE featuring ALICIA KEYS)		
	Gangsta Lovin'	2002
CHAKA KHAN	Eye To Eye	1985
	I Feel For You	1984
	I'm Every Woman	1978
	This Is My Night	1985
(BRANDY, TAMIA, GLADYS KNIGHT & CHAKA KHAN)		
	Missing You	1996
(DE LA SOUL featuring CHAKA KHAN)		
	All Good	2000
(GURU featuring CHAKA KHAN)		
	Watch What You Say	1995
(QUINCY JONES featuring RAY CHARLES & CHAKA KHAN)		
	I'll Be Good To You	1990

ARTIST	SONG TITLE	DATE
(RUFUS & CHAKA KHAN)		
	Ain't Nobody	1989
	At Midnight (My Love Will Lift You Up)	1977
	Dance Wit Me	1976
	Do You Love What You Feel	1979
	Hollywood	1977
	Once You Get Started	1975
	Stay	1978
	Sweet Thing	1976
	You Got The Love	1974
PRAGA KHAN	Rave Alert	1992
PRAGA KHAN featuring JADE 4 U		
	Free Your Body/Injected With A Poison	1992
KHIA	My Neck My Back (Lick It)	2004
MARY KIANI	I Give It All To You/I Imagine	1995
	Let The Music Play	1996
	100%	1997
	When I Call Your Name	1995
KICKS LIKE A MULE		
	The Bouncer	1992
KID CREME featuring CHARLISE		
	Hypnotising	2003
KID ROCK	American Bad Ass	2000
	Cowboy	1999
	Only God Knows Why	2000

ARTIST	SONG TITLE	DATE
JOHNNY KIDD & THE PIRATES		
	Hungry For Love	1963
	I'll Never Get Over You	1963
NICOLE KIDMAN & EWAN MCGREGOR		
	Come What May	2001
(ROBBIE WILLIAMS & NICOLE KIDMAN)		
	Somethin' Stupid	2001
KIDS FROM 'FAME'	Friday Night (Live Version)	1983
	Hi-Fidelity (featuring Valerie Landsberg)	1982
	Starmaker	1982
GREG KIHN	Lucky	1985
GREG KIHN BAND	The Breakup Song (They Don't Write	
	'Em)	1981
	Jeopardy	1983
KILLER MIKE featuring BIG BOI		
	A.D.I.D.A.S.	2003
(BONECRUSHER featuring KILLER MIKE & T.I.)		
	Never Scared	2003
(OUTKAST featuring KILLER MIKE)		
	The Whole World	2001
THE KILLERS	All These Things That I've Done	2004
	Mr Brightside	2004
	Somebody Told Me	2004
KILLING JOKE	Democracy	1996
	Loose Cannon	2003
	Love Like Blood	1985

ARTIST	SONG TITLE	DATE
	Millennium	1994
	The Pandemonium Single	1994
ANDY KIM	Baby I Love You	1969
	Be My Baby	1970
	Fire, Baby I'm On Fire	1974
	How'd We Ever Get This Way	1968
	Rock Me Gently	1974
	Shoot'em Up Baby	1968
	So Good Together	1969
KING ADORA	Bionic	2001
	Suffocate	2001
KING CURTIS	Memphis Soul Stew	1967
	Ode To Billie Joe	1967
KING FLOYD	Baby Let Me Kiss You	1971
	Groove Me	1970
KING HARVEST	Dancing In The Moonlight	1972
KING KURT	Destination Zululand	1983
KING	Alone Without You	1985
	Love And Pride	1985
	The Taste Of Your Tears	1985
	Torture	1986
	Won't You Hold My Hand Now	1985
B.B. KING	Ask Me No Questions	1971
	I Like To Live The Love	1973
	Paying The Cost To Be Boss	1968
	Rock Me Baby	1964

ARTIST	SONG TITLE	DATE
	The Thrill Is Gone	1969
	To Know You Is To Love You	1973
	(U2 WITH B.B. KING)	
	When Love Comes To Town	1989
BEN E. KING	I (Who Have Nothing)	1983
	Stand By Me	1986
	Supernatural Thing (Part I)	1975
CAROLE KING	Been To Canaan	1972
	Believe In Humanity	1973
	Corazon	1973
	Hard Rock Cafe	1977
	It's Too Late/I Feel The Earth Move	1971
	Jazzman	1974
	Nightingale	1975
	One Fine Day	1980
	Only Love Is Real	1976
	So Far Away/Smackwater Jack	1971
	Sweet Seasons	1972
DIANA KING	Ain't Nobody	1995
	I Say A Little Prayer	1997
	Shy Guy	1995
EVELYN 'CHAMPAGNE' KING		
	Back To Love	1982
	I Don't Know If It's Right	1979
	I'm In Love	1981
	Love Come Down	1982

ARTIST	SONG TITLE	DATE
	Shame	1978
	Your Personal Touch	1985
JONATHAN KING	Everyone's Gone To The Moon	1965
	Flirt!	1972
	Hooked On A Feeling	1971
	Lazy Bones	1971
	Let It All Hang Out	1970
	One For You, One For Me	1978
	Una Paloma Blanca (White Dove)	1975
(53RD AND 3RD featuring THE SOUND OF SHAG)		
	Chick-A-Boom (Don't Ya Jes Love It)	1975
(BUBBLEROCK)		
	(I Can't Get No) Satisfaction	1974
SOLOMON KING	She Wears My Ring	1968
	When We Were Young	1968
KINGMAKER	Eat Yourself Whole	1992
	Idiots At The Wheel (EP)	1992
	Queen Jane	1993
	10 Years Asleep	1993
	You And I Will Never See Things Eye	
	To Eye	1995
KINGS OF LEON	The Bucket	2004
	Molly's Chambers	2003
	What I Saw	2003
KINGS OF TOMORROW featuring JULIE MCKNIGHT		
	Finally	2001

ARTIST	SONG TITLE	DATE
KINGSMEN	The Jolly Green Giant	1965
	Louie Louie	1963
	Money	1964
KINKS	All Day And All Of The Night	1964
	Ape Man	1970
	Autumn Almanac	1967
	Come Dancing	1983
	Days	1968
	The Days (EP)	1997
	Dead End Street	1966
	Dedicated Follower Of Fashion	1966
	Don't Forget To Dance	1983
	Everybody's Gonna Be Happy	1965
	Lola	1970
	Plastic Man	1969
	A Rock 'n' Roll Fantasy	1978
	See My Friend	1965
	Set Me Free	1965
	Sunny Afternoon	1966
	Supersonic Rocket Ship	1972
	Till The End Of The Day	1965
	Tired Of Waiting For You	1965
	Victoria	1970
	Waterloo Sunset	1967
	A Well Respected Man	1965
	Who'll Be The Next In Line	1965

ARTIST	SONG TITLE	DATE
	Wonderboy	1968
	You Really Got Me	1964
FERN KINNEY	Together We Are Beautiful	1980
KIRA	I'll Be Your Angel	2003
KATHY KIRBY	Dance On	1963
	I Belong	1965
	Let Me Go, Lover!	1964
	Secret Love	1963
	You're The One	1964
BO KIRKLAND & RUTH DAVIS		
	You're Gonna Get Next To Me	1977
KISS	Beth	1976
	Calling Dr. Love	1977
	Christine Sixteen	1977
	Crazy Crazy Nights	1987
	Creatures Of The Night	1983
	Forever	1990
	God Gave Rock & Roll To You II	1992
	Hard Luck Woman	1976
	I Was Made For Lovin' You	1979
	Lick It Up	1983
	Reason To Live	1987
	Rock And Roll All Nite	1975
	Rocket Ride	1978
	Shout It Out Loud	1976
	Unholy	1992

ARTIST	SONG TITLE	DATE
KISSING THE PINK	Last Film	1983
MAC & KATIE KISSOON		
	Chirpy Chirpy Cheep Cheep	1971
	Don't Do It Baby	1975
	Like A Butterfly	1975
	Sugar Candy Kisses	1975
EARTHA KITT	Where Is My Man	1983
EARTHA KITT & BRONSKI BEAT		
	Cha Cha Heels	1989
KIX	Don't Close Your Eyes	1989
KLESHAY	Reasons	1998
	Rush	1999
KLF	America: What Time Is Love?	1992
	Last Train To Trancentral	1991
	3 A.M. Eternal	1991
KLF/CHILDREN OF THE REVOLUTION		
	What Time Is Love?	1990
KLF/TAMMY WYNETTE		
	Justified And Ancient	1991
	(JUSTIFIED ANCIENTS OF MU MU)	
	It's Grim Up North	1991
	(1300 DRUMS featuring UNJUSTIFIED ANCIENTS	
	OF MU MU)	
	Ooh! Aah! Cantona	1996
KLUBBHEADS	Discohopping	1997
	Kickin' Hard	1998

ARTIST	SONG TITLE	DATE
	Klubbhopping	1996
KLYMAXX	I Miss You	1985
	I'd Still Say Yes	1987
	Man Size Love	1986
KMC featuring DHANY		
	I Feel So Fine	2002
KNACK	Baby Talks Dirty	1980
	Good Girls Don't	1979
	My Sharona	1979
KNICKERBOCKERS	Lies	1966
BEVERLEY KNIGHT	Come As You Are	2004
	Flavour Of The Old School	1995
	Get Up	2001
	Gold	2002
	Greatest Day	1999
	Made It Back 99	1999
	Not Too Late For Love	2004
	Rewind (Find A Way)	1998
	Shoulda Woulda Coulda	2002
	Sista Sista	1999
BEVERLEY KNIGHT featuring REDMAN		
	Made It Back	1998
FREDERICK KNIGHT	I've Been Lonely So Long	1972
GLADYS KNIGHT	Licence To Kill	1989
GLADYS KNIGHT & THE PIPS		
	Baby Don't Change Your Mind	1977

ARTIST	SONG TITLE	DATE
	The Best Thing That Ever Happened	1975
	Bourgie, Bourgie	1980
	Come Back And Finish What You Started	1978
	Daddy Could Swear, I Declare	1973
	The End Of Our Road	1968
	Everybody Needs Love	1967
	Friendship Train	1969
	Giving Up	1964
	Help Me Make It Through The Night	1972
	Home Is Where The Heart Is	1977
	I Don't Want To Do Wrong	1971
	I Feel A Song (In My Heart)	1974
	I Heard It Through The Grapevine	1967
	I've Got To Use My Imagination	1973
	If I Were Your Woman	1970
	It Should Have Been Me	1968
	Just Walk In My Shoes	1972
	The Look Of Love	1973
	Love Overboard	1988
	Make Me The Woman That You Go Home To	1971
	Make Yours A Happy Home	1976
	Midnight Train To Georgia	1973
	Neither One Of Us (Wants To Be The First To Say Goodbye)	1973
	The Nitty Gritty	1969

ARTIST	SONG TITLE	DATE
	Nobody But You	1977
	On And On	1974
	The One And Only	1978
	Part Time Love	1975
	So Sad The Song	1976
	Taste Of Bitter Love	1980
	The Way We Were/Try To Remember (Medley)	1975
	You Need Love Like I Do (Don't You)	1970
	(BRANDY, TAMIA, GLADYS KNIGHT & CHAKA KHAN)	
	Missing You	1996
JEAN KNIGHT	Mr. Big Stuff	1971
JORDAN KNIGHT	Give It To You	1999
ROBERT KNIGHT	Everlasting Love	1967
	Love On A Mountain Top	1973
FRED KNOBLOCK	Why Not Me	1980
FRED KNOBLOCK & SUSAN ANTON		
	Killin' Time	1980
MARK KNOPFLER	Boom, Like That	2004
	Darling Pretty	1996
FRANKIE KNUCKLES	The Whistle Song	1991
FRANKIE KNUCKLES featuring ADEVA		
	Too Many Fish	1995
	Whadda U Want (From Me)	1995
MIKE KOGLIN	The Silence	1998

ARTIST	SONG TITLE	DATE
MIKE KOGLIN featuring BEATRICE		
	On My Way	1999
KON KAN	I Beg Your Pardon	1989
JOHN KONGOS	He's Gonna Step On You Again	1971
	Tokoloshe Man	1971
KONTAKT	Show Me A Sign	2003
KOOL & THE GANG		
	Big Fun	1982
	Celebration	1980
	Cherish	1985
	Emergency	1985
	Fresh	1985
	Funky Stuff	1973
	Get Down On It	1982
	Hi De Hi, Hi De Ho	1982
	Higher Plane	1994
	Hollywood Swinging	1974
	Joanna/Tonight	1984
	Jones Vs Jones/Summer Madness	1981
	Jungle Boogie	1973
	Ladies Night	1979
	Misled	1984
	Ooh La La La (Let's Go Dancin')	1982
	Spirit Of The Boogie	1975
	Steppin' Out	1981
	Stone Love	1987

ARTIST	SONG TITLE	DATE
	Straight Ahead	1983
	Take It To The Top	1981
	Take My Heart (You Can Have It If You Want It)	1981
	Too Hot	1980
	Victory	1986
	(When You Say You Love Somebody) In The Heart	1984
KORGIS	Everybody's Gotta Learn Sometime	1980
	If I Had You	1979
KORN	A.D.I.D.A.S.	1997
	Did My Time	2003
	Falling Away From Me	2000
	Freak On A Leash	1999
	Good God	1997
	Got The Life	1998
	Here To Stay	2002
	Make Me Bad	2000
	No Place To Hide	1996
	Thoughtless	2002
KOSHEEN	All In My Head	2003
	Catch	2001
	Hide U	2001
	Hungry	2002
KP & ENVYI	Swing My Way	1997
KRAFTWERK	Aerodynamik	2004

ARTIST	SONG TITLE	DATE
	Autobahn	1975
	Expo 2000	2000
	The Model/Computer Love	1981
	Pocket Calculator	1981
	The Robots	1991
	Showroom Dummies	1982
	Tour De France	1983
BILLY J. KRAMER & THE DAKOTAS		
	Bad To Me	1964
	Do You Want To Know A Secret	1963
	From A Window	1964
	I'll Keep You Satisfied	1964
	Little Children	1964
	Trains And Boats And Planes	1965
LENNY KRAVITZ	Again	2000
	Are You Gonna Go My Way?	1993
	Believe	1993
	Dig In	2001
	Fly Away	1998
	Heaven Help	1993
	It Ain't Over 'Til It's Over	1991
	Let Love Rule	1990
	Rock And Roll Is Dead	1995
LENNY KRAVITZ/P. DIDDY/LOON/PHARRELL WILLIAMS		
	Show Me Your Soul	2004
KRAZE	The Party	1988

ARTIST	SONG TITLE	DATE
KRIS KROSS	Alright	1993
	It's A Shame	1992
	Jump	1992
	Tonite's Tha Night	1995
	Warm It Up	1992
KRIS KRISTOFFERSON		
	Loving Her Was Easier (Than Anything I'll Ever Do Again)	1971
	Why Me	1973
CHAD KROEGER & JOSEY SCOTT		
	Hero	2002
KRS ONE	Step Into A World	1997
	(GOLDIE featuring KRS ONE)	
	Digital	1997
KRUSH	House Arrest	1987
BOB KUBAN & THE IN-MEN		
	The Cheater	1966
KULA SHAKER	Govinda	1996
	Hey Dude	1996
	Hush	1997
	Mystical Machine Gun	1999
	Shower Your Love	1999
	Sound Of Drums	1998
	Tattva	1996
KURSAAL FLYERS	Little Does She Know	1976
KURUPT	It's Over	2001

ARTIST	SONG TITLE	DATE
	(SHADE SHEIST featuring NATE DOGG & KURUPT)	
	Where I Wanna Be	2001
KUT KLOSE	I Like	1995
KWS	Please Don't Go/Game Boy	1992
	Rock Your Baby	1992
KWS & GWEN DICKEY		
	Ain't Nobody (Loves Me Better)	1994
KWS featuring TEDDY PENDERGRASS		
	The More I Get, The More I Want	1994
KWS/THE TRAMMPS		
	Hold Back The Night	1992
KYPER	Tic-Tac-Toe	1990
L.A. GUNS	The Ballad Of Jayne	1990
L.A. MIX	Check This Out	1988
L.A. MIX featuring JAZZI P		
	Get Loose	1989
LL COOL J	Ain't Nobody	1997
	Around The Way Girl	1991
	Doin' It	1996
	Father	1998
	Going Back To Cali/Jack The Ripper	1988
	Headsprung	2004
	Hey Lover	1995
	How I'm Comin'	1993
	I Need Love	1987
	I'm That Type Of Guy	1989

ARTIST	SONG TITLE	DATE
	Loungin'	1996
	Luv U Better	2002
	Mama Said Knock You Out	1991
	Phenomenon	1997
LL COOL J featuring 7 AURELIUS		
	Hush	2004
LL COOL J featuring AMERIE		
	Paradise	2002
	(B REAL/BUSTA RHYMES/COOLIO/LL COOL J/ METHOD MAN)	
	Hit 'Em High (The Monstars' Anthem)	1997
	(BABYFACE featuring LL COOL J, SHALAMAR)	
	This Is For The Lover In You	1996
	(DR. DRE & LL COOL J)	
	Zoom	1998
	(JENNIFER LOPEZ featuring LL COOL J)	
	All I Have	2003
L7	Andres	1994
	Everglade	1992
	Monster	1992
	Pretend We're Dead	1992
L.T.D.	(Every Time I Turn Around) Back In Love Again	1977
	Love Ballad	1976
	Shine On	1980

ARTIST	SONG TITLE	DATE
LA BELLE EPOQUE	Black Is Black	1977
LA BOUCHE	Be My Lover	1995
	Sweet Dreams	1996
LA'S	There She Goes	1990
LABELLE	Lady Marmalade (Voulez-Vous Coucher Avec Moi Ce Soir?)	1975
PATTI LABELLE	New Attitude	1985
	Oh, People	1986
PATTI LABELLE & HER BLUE BELLES		
	You'll Never Walk Alone	1964
PATTI LABELLE & MICHAEL MCDONALD		
	On My Own	1986
CHERYL LADD	Think It Over	1978
LADIES FIRST	I Can't Wait	2002
	Messin'	2001
LADY FLASH	Street Singer	1976
LADY SAW/VITAMIN C		
	Smile	1999
	(NO DOUBT featuring LADY SAW)	
	Underneath It All	2002
	(UB40 featuring LADY SAW)	
	Since I Met You Lady/Sparkle Of My Eyes	2001
LADYSMITH BLACK MAMBAZO		
	Inkanyezi Nezazi (The Star & The Wiseman)	1997

ARTIST	SONG TITLE	DATE
LADYSMITH BLACK MAMBAZO featuring CHINA BLACK		
	Swing Low Sweet Chariot	1995
	(B*WITCHED featuring LADYSMITH BLACK MAMBAZO)	
	I Shall Be There	1999
LAGUNA	Spiller From Rio (Do It Easy)	1997
LAID BACK	White Horse	1984
LAIN/WOOKIE	Back Up (To Me)	2001
	Battle	2000
FRANKIE LAINE	I'll Take Care Of Your Cares	1967
	Making Memories	1967
	You Gave Me A Mountain	1969
GREG LAKE	I Believe In Father Christmas	1975
LAMB	Gorecki	1997
ANNABEL LAMB	Riders On The Storm	1983
LAMBRETTAS	D-a-a-a-ance	1980
	Poison Ivy	1980
GEORGE LAMOND	Bad Of The Heart	1990
MAJOR LANCE	Come See	1965
	The Matador	1964
	Rhythm	1964
	Um, Um, Um, Um, Um, Um	1964
LANDSCAPE	Einstein A Go-Go	1981
	Norman Bates	1981
MICKEY LEE LANE	Shaggy Dog	1964

ARTIST	SONG TITLE	DATE
RONNIE LANE & SLIM CHANCE		
	How Come?	1974
	The Poacher	1974
K.D. LANG	Constant Craving	1993
	(ROY ORBISON & K.D. LANG)	
	Crying	1992
LANGE featuring SKYE		
	Drifting Away	2002
LARKS	The Jerk	1964
LARSEN-FEITEN BAND		
	Who'll Be The Fool Tonight	1980
NICOLETTE LARSON	Let Me Go, Love	1980
	Lotta Love	1978
DENISE LA SALLE	My Toot Toot	1985
	Trapped By A Thing Called Love	1971
LASGO	Alone	2002
	Pray	2002
	Something	2002
	Surrender	2004
DAVID LASLEY	If I Had My Wish Tonight	1982
JAMES LAST BAND	The Seduction (Love Theme)	1980
LATE SHOW	Bristol Stomp	1979
LATIMORE	Let's Straighten It Out	1974
	Somethin' 'Bout 'Cha	1977
LATIN QUARTER	Radio Africa	1986
LATINO RAVE	Deep Heat '89	1989

ARTIST	SONG TITLE	DATE
GINO LATINO	Welcome	1990
LATOUR	People Are Still Having Sex	1991
KENNY LATTIMORE	For You	1997
STACY LATTISAW	Jump To The Beat	1980
	Let Me Be Your Angel	1980
	Love On A Two Way Street	1981
	Miracles	1983
CYNDI LAUPER	All Through The Night	1984
	Change Of Heart	1986
	Come On Home	1995
	Girls Just Want To Have Fun	1983
	The Goonies 'R' Good Enough	1985
	Hey Now (Girls Just Want To Have Fun)	1994
	I Drove All Night	1989
	I'm Gonna Be Strong	1995
	Money Changes Everything	1984
	She Bop	1984
	That's What I Think	1993
	Time After Time	1984
	True Colors	1986
	What's Going On	1987
	Who Let In The Rain	1994
	The World Is Stone	1992
	You Don't Know	1997
LAUREL & HARDY	The Trail Of The Lonesome Pine	1975
LAURNEA	Days Of Youth	1997

ARTIST	SONG TITLE	DATE
AVRIL LAVIGNE	Complicated	2002
	Don't Tell Me	2004
	I'm With You	2003
	Losing Grip	2003
	My Happy Ending	2004
	Sk8er Boi	2002
JOEY LAWRENCE	I Can't Help Myself	1993
	Nothin' My Love Can't Fix	1993
SOPHIE LAWRENCE	Love's Unkind	1991
STEVE LAWRENCE & EYDIE GORME		
	I Want To Stay Here	1963
TRACY LAWRENCE	Lesson Learned	2000
VICKI LAWRENCE	The Night The Lights Went Out In Georgia	1973
LAYO & BUSHWACKA		
	Love Story	2002
	Love Story (Vs Finally)	2003
	It's Up To You (Shining Through)	2003
LINDY LAYTON	We Got The Love	1993
LINDY LAYTON/JANET KAY		
	Silly Games	1990
LCD	Zorba's Dance	1998
LE CLICK	Call Me	1997
KELE LE ROC	Little Bit Of Lovin'	1998
	My Love	1999

ARTIST	SONG TITLE	DATE
	(SHY FX & T-POWER featuring KELE LE ROC)	
	Feelin' U	2003
LE ROUX	Nobody Said It Was Easy (Lookin' For	
	The Lights)	1982
VICKY LEANDROS	Come What May	1972
	The Love In Your Eyes	1972
LEAVES	Hey Joe	1966
LEBLANC & CARR	Falling	1977
LED ZEPPELIN	Black Dog	1971
	D'Yer Mak'er	1973
	Fool In The Rain	1979
	Immigrant Song	1970
	Trampled Under Foot	1975
	Whole Lotta Love	1969
ANGEL LEE	What's Your Name?	2000
ANN LEE	2 Times	1999
	Voices	2000
BRENDA LEE	All Alone Am I	1962
	As Usual	1963
	Christmas Will Be Just Another Lonely	
	Day	1964
	Coming On Strong	1966
	I Wonder	1963
	Is It True	1964
	Losing You	1963
	Ride Ride Ride	1967

ARTIST	SONG TITLE	DATE
	Rusty Bells	1965
	Sweet Impossible You	1963
	Think	1964
	Too Many Rivers	1965
DEE C. LEE	See The Day	1985
	(GURU featuring DEE C. LEE)	
	No Time To Play	1993
DICKEY LEE	Laurie (Strange Things Happen)	1965
JACKIE LEE	The Duck	1965
	Rupert	1971
JOHNNY LEE	Lookin' For Love	1980
LAURA LEE	Women's Love Rights	1971
LEAPY LEE	Good Morning	1969
	Little Arrows	1968
PEGGY LEE	Is That All There Is	1969
LEE-CABRERA featuring ALEX CARTANA		
	Shake It (Move A Little Closer)	2003
LEEDS UNITED F.C.	Leeds United	1972
LEFT BANKE	Pretty Ballerina	1967
	Walk Away Renee	1966
LEFTFIELD	Release The Pressure	1996
LEFTFIELD featuring DJUM DJUM		
	The Afro-Left EP	1995
LEFTFIELD featuring TONI HALLIDAY		
	Original	1995
LEFTFIELD LYDON	Open Up	1993

ARTIST	SONG TITLE	DATE
LEFTFIELD/BAMBAATAA		
	Afrika Shox	1999
LEFTFIELD/ROOTS MANUVA		
	Dusted	1999
JODY LEI	Showdown	2003
LEILA K	Open Sesame	1993
LEILANI	Do You Want Me?	1999
	Madness Thing	1999
LEMAR	Another Day	2004
	Dance (With U)	2003
	50:50/Lullaby	2003
LEMON JELLY	Nice Weather For Ducks	2003
	Space Walk	2002
LEMON PIPERS	Green Tambourine	1967
LEMONESCENT	All Right Now	2004
	Cinderella	2003
	Help Me Mama	2003
LEMONHEADS	If I Could Talk I'd Tell You	1996
	Into Your Arms	1993
	It's A Shame About Ray	1993
	Mrs. Robinson/Bein' Around	1992
LEN	Cryptik Souls Crew	2000
	Steal My Sunshine	1999
JOHN LENNON	Borrowed Time	1984
	Imagine	1971
	(Just Like) Starting Over	1980

ARTIST	SONG TITLE	DATE
	Mind Games	1973
	No. 9 Dream	1975
	Nobody Told Me	1984
	Stand By Me	1976
	Watching The Wheels	1981
	Whatever Gets You Thru' The Night	1974
	Woman	1981
JOHN LENNON & THE PLASTIC ONO BAND		
	Power To The People	1971
JOHN LENNON WITH THE PLASTIC ONO NUCLEAR BAND		
	Whatever Gets You Thru The Night	1974
LENNON, ONO & THE PLASTIC ONO BAND		
	Instant Karma	1970
(ELTON JOHN featuring JOHN LENNON)		
	I Saw Her Standing There	1981
(JOHN AND YOKO & THE PLASTIC ONO BAND)		
	Happy Xmas (War Is Over)	1980
(PLASTIC ONO BAND)		
	Cold Turkey	1969
	Give Peace A Chance	1969
JULIAN LENNON	Because	1985
	Saltwater	1991
	Say You're Wrong	1985
	Stick Around	1986
	Too Late For Goodbyes	1985
	Valotte	1984

ARTIST	SONG TITLE	DATE
ANNIE LENNOX	Cold	1992
	Little Bird/Love Song For A Vampire	1993
	No More 'I Love Yous'	1995
	Precious	1992
	Waiting In Vain	1995
	Walking On Broken Glass	1992
	A Whiter Shade Of Pale	1995
	Why	1992
ANNIE LENNOX & AL GREEN		
	Put A Little Love In Your Heart	1988
KRISTIAN LEONTIOU		
	Shining	2004
	Story Of My Life	2004
LESS THAN JAKE	She's Gonna Break Soon	2003
LET LOOSE	Best In Me	1995
	Crazy For You	1994
	Everybody See Everybody Do	1995
	Make It With You	1996
	One Night Stand	1995
	Seventeen	1994
	Take It Easy	1996
LETTERMEN	Goin' Out Of My Head/Can't Take My Eyes Off You	1967
	Hurt So Bad	1969
	Theme From 'A Summer Place'	1965

ARTIST	SONG TITLE	DATE
LEVEL 42	All Over You	1994
	Children Say	1987
	The Chinese Way	1983
	Forever Now	1994
	Guaranteed	1991
	Heaven In My Hands	1988
	Hot Water	1984
	It's Over	1987
	Leaving Me Now	1985
	Lessons In Love	1987
	Love Games	1981
	Love In A Peaceful World	1994
	Micro Kid	1983
	Running In The Family	1987
	Something About You	1986
	The Sun Goes Down (Living It Up)	1983
	Take A Look	1988
	Take Care Of Yourself	1989
	To Be With You Again	1987
	Tracie	1989
LEVELLERS	Belaruse	1993
	Celebrate	1997
	Dog Train	1997
	Exodus — Live	1996
	Fantasy	1995
	15 Years (EP)	1992

ARTIST	SONG TITLE	DATE
	Hope St	1995
	Julie (EP)	1994
	Just The One	1995
	One Way	1999
	This Garden	1993
	What A Beautiful Day	1997
	Wild As Angels (EP)	2003
LEVERT	Casanova	1987
GERALD LEVERT	Baby Hold On To Me	1992
	I'd Give Anything	1994
	Taking Everything	1999
	Thinkin' About It	1998
BARRINGTON LEVY/REBEL M.C./TENOR FLY		
	Tribal Base	1991
	(TALISMAN P featuring BARRINGTON LEVY)	
	Here I Come (Sing DJ)	2001
JONA LEWIE	Stop The Cavalry	1980
	You'll Always Find Me In The Kitchen At	
	Parties	1980
BARBARA LEWIS	Baby, I'm Yours	1965
	Make Me Belong To You	1966
	Make Me Your Baby	1965
	Puppy Love	1964
CJ LEWIS	Best Of My Life	1994
	Dollars	1994
	Everything Is Alright (Uptight)	1994

ARTIST	SONG TITLE	DATE
	R To The A	1995
	Sweets For My Sweet	1994
DANNY J LEWIS	Spend The Night	1998
DONNA LEWIS	I Love You Always Forever	1996
	Without Love	1997
GARY LEWIS & THE PLAYBOYS		
	Count Me In	1965
	Everybody Loves A Clown	1965
	Girls In Love	1967
	Green Grass	1966
	My Heart's Symphony	1966
	Save Your Heart For Me	1965
	Sealed With A Kiss	1968
	She's Just My Style	1965
	Sure Gonna Miss Her	1966
	This Diamond Ring	1965
	Where Will The Words Come From	1966
	(You Don't Have To) Paint Me A	
	Picture	1966
GLENN LEWIS	Don't You Forget It	2001
HUEY LEWIS & THE NEWS		
	Couple Days Off	1991
	Doing It All For My Baby	1987
	Heart And Soul	1983
	The Heart Of Rock 'n' Roll	1984
	Hip To Be Square	1986

ARTIST	SONG TITLE	DATE
	Hope You Love Me Like I Say You Do	1982
	I Know What I Like	1987
	I Want A New Drug	1984
	If This Is It	1984
	It Hit Me Like A Hammer	1991
	Jacob's Ladder	1987
	Perfect World	1988
	The Power Of Love/Do You Believe In Love?	1986
	Small World	1988
	Stuck With You	1986
	Walking On A Thin Line	1984
JERRY LEE LEWIS	Chantilly Lace	1972
	Good Golly Miss Molly	1963
	Me And Bobby McGee	1971
LINDA LEWIS	Baby I'm Yours	1976
	It's In His Kiss	1975
	Rock-A-Doodle-Doo	1973
RAMSEY LEWIS TRIO		
	A Hard Day's Night	1966
	Hang On Sloopy	1965
	The 'In' Crowd	1965
	Wade In The Water	1972
SHAZNAY LEWIS	Never Felt Like This Before	2004
JOHN LEYTON	Cupboard Love	1963
	I'll Cut Your Tail Off	1963

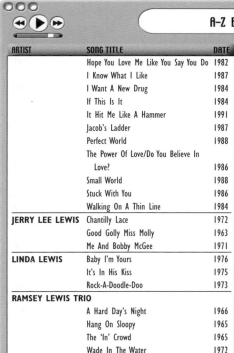

ARTIST	SONG TITLE	DATE
LFO	Girl On TV	1999
	LFO	1990
	Summer Girls	1999
LIBERATION	Liberation	1992
LIBERTINES	Can't Stand Me Now	2004
	Don't Look Back Into The Sun	2003
	Time For Heroes	2003
	Up The Bracket	2002
	What A Waster	2002
	What Became Of The Likely Lads	2004
LIBERTY	Doin' It	2001
	Thinking It Over	2001
LIBERTY X	Everybody Cries	2004
	Got To Have Your Love	2002
	Holding On For You	2002
	Jumpin'	2003
	Just A Little	2002
	(RICHARD X vs LIBERTY X)	
	Being Nobody	2003
LIEUTENANT PIGEON		
	Desperate Dan	1972
	Mouldy Old Dough	1972
LIFEHOUSE	Hanging By A Moment	2001
LIGHT OF THE WORLD		
	I Shot The Sheriff	1981
	I'm So Happy/Time	1981

ARTIST	SONG TITLE	DATE
LIGHTER SHADE OF BROWN		
	Hey D.J.	1994
	On A Sunday Afternoon	1991
GORDON LIGHTFOOT		
	Carefree Highway	1974
	The Circle Is Small (I Can See It In Your Eyes)	1978
	If You Could Read My Mind	1970
	Rainy Day People	1975
	Sundown	1974
	The Wreck Of The Edmund Fitzgerald	1976
LIGHTHOUSE	One Fine Morning	1971
	Sunny Days	1972
LIGHTHOUSE FAMILY		
	Goodbye Heartbreak	1996
	High	1998
	(I Wish I Knew How It Would Feel To Be) Free	2001
	Lifted	1996
	Lost In Space	1998
	Loving Every Minute	1996
	Ocean Drive	1996
	Postcard From Heaven	1999
	Question Of Faith	1998
	Raincloud	1997
	Run	2002

ARTIST	SONG TITLE	DATE
LIGHTNING SEEDS	Change	1995
	The Life Of Riley	1992
	Life's Too Short	1999
	Lucky You	1995
	Marvellous	1995
	Perfect	1995
	Pure	1990
	Ready Or Not	1996
	Sense	1992
	Sugar Coated Iceberg	1997
	What If...	1996
	You Showed Me	1997
	(BADDIEL & SKINNER & LIGHTNING SEEDS)	
	Three Lions (The Official Song Of The England Football Team)	1996
LIL BOW WOW	Bow Wow (That's My Name)	2001
LIL BOW WOW featuring XSCAPE		
	Bounce With Me	2000
LIL LOUIS	French Kiss	1989
	I Called You	1990
	(JOSH WINK & LIL LOUIS)	
	How's Your Evening So Far	2000
LITTLE LOUIE & MARC ANTHONY		
	Ride On The Rhythm	1998
LIL MO' YIN YANG	Reach	1996
LIL SCRAPPY	No Problem	2004

ARTIST	SONG TITLE	DATE
LIL WAYNE	Go D.J.	2004
LIL' FLIP	Sunshine	2004
LIL' KIM	Crush On You	1997
	No Matter What They Say	2000
	Not Tonight	1997
LIL' KIM featuring MR. CHEEKS		
	The Jump Off	2003
LIL' KIM featuring PHIL COLLINS		
	In The Air Tonite	2001
LIL' KIM featuring PUFF DADDY		
	No Time	1996
(CHRISTINA AGUILERA featuring LIL' KIM)		
	Can't Hold Us Down	2003
(CHRISTINA AGUILERA, LIL' KIM, MYA & PINK)		
	Lady Marmalade	2001
(LOX featuring DMX & LIL' KIM)		
	Money, Power & Respect	1998
(MISSY 'MISDEMEANOR' ELLIOTT featuring LIL' KIM)		
	Hit 'Em Wit Da Hee	1998
(NOTORIOUS B.I.G. featuring PUFF DADDY & LIL' KIM)		
	Notorious B.I.G.	2000
(RAY J featuring LIL' KIM)		
	Wait A Minute	2001

ARTIST	SONG TITLE	DATE
LIL' MO/ADAM F	Where's My...?	2002
LIL' MO featuring FABOLOUS		
	4 Ever	2003
	Superwoman Pt. II	2001
(ANGIE MARTINEZ featuring LIL' MO & SACARIO)		
	If I Could Go!	2002
(FABOLOUS featuring MIKE SHOREY & LIL' MO)		
	Can't Let You Go	2003
(IDEAL featuring LIL' MO)		
	Whatever	2000
(JA RULE featuring LIL' MO)		
	I Cry	2001
(JA RULE featuring LIL' MO & VITA)		
	Put It On Me	2000
LIL' ROMEO	My Baby	2001
LIL' ZANE featuring 112		
	Callin' Me	2000
LILYS	A Nanny In Manhattan	1998
LIMAHL	Never Ending Story	1985
	Only For Love	1983
ALISON LIMERICK	Love Come Down	1994
	Make It On My Own	1992
	Time Of Our Lives	1994
	Where Love Lives (Come On In)	1991
LIMIT	Say Yeah	1985

ARTIST	SONG TITLE	DATE
LIMMIE & THE FAMILY COOKIN'		
	Dreamboat	1973
	A Walkin' Miracle	1974
	You Can Do Magic	1973
LIMP BIZKIT	Behind Blue Eyes	2003
	Boiler	2001
	My Generation	2000
	My Way	2001
	Rollin'	2001
	Take A Look Around (Theme From M:I2)	2000
BOB LIND	Elusive Butterfly	1966
LINDA & THE FUNKY BOYS		
	Sold My Rock 'n' Roll (Gave It For Funky Soul)	1976
LINDISFARNE	All Fall Down	1972
	Lady Eleanor	1972
	Meet Me On The Corner	1972
	Run For Home	1978
	(GAZZA AND LINDISFARNE)	
	Fog On The Tyne (Revisited)	1990
LINDSAY	No Dream Impossible	2001
MARK LINDSAY	Arizona	1969
	Silver Bird	1970
LINEAR	Sending All My Love	1990
	T.L.C.	1992
AARON LINES	You Can't Hide Beautiful	2002

ARTIST	SONG TITLE	DATE
LAURIE LINGO & THE DIPSTICKS		
	Convoy GB	1976
LINK	Whatcha Gone Do?	1998
LINKIN PARK	Breaking The Habit	2004
	Crawling	2001
	Faint	2003
	H! Vltg3/Pts.Of.Athrty	2002
	In The End	2001
	Numb	2003
	One Step Closer	2001
	Papercut	2001
	Somewhere I Belong	2003
LINUS LOVES featuring SAM OBERNIK		
	Stand Back	2003
LINX	Intuition	1981
	So This Is Romance	1981
	Throw Away The Key	1981
	You're Lying	1980
LIONROCK	Carnival	1993
	Rude Boy Rock	1998
	Straight At Yer Head	1996
LIPPS INC.	Funkytown	1980
LIQUID CHILD	Diving Faces	1999
LIQUID	Sweet Harmony/One Love Family	1995
LIQUID GOLD	Dance Yourself Dizzy	1980
	The Night The Wine And The Roses	1980

ARTIST	SONG TITLE	DATE
	Substitute	1980
LISA LISA	Skip To My Lu	1994
LISA LISA & CULT JAM		
	Head To Toe	1987
	I Wonder If I Take You Home	1985
	Let The Beat Hit 'Em	1991
	Little Jackie Wants To Be A Star	1989
	Lost In Emotion	1987
LISA LISA & CULT JAM WITH FULL FORCE		
	All Cried Out	1986
LISA MARIE EXPERIENCE		
	Do That To Me	1996
	Keep On Jumpin'	1996
LISBON LIONS featuring MARTIN O'NEILL & THE CELTIC		
	The Best Day Of Our Lives	2002
LIT	My Own Worst Enemy	1999
	Over My Head	2000
LITHIUM and SONYA MADAN		
	Ride A Rocket	1997
LITTLE ANGELS	Boneyard	1991
	I Ain't Gonna Cry	1991
	Product Of The Working Class	1991
	Radical Your Lover	1990
	She's A Little Angel	1990
	Soapbox	1993
	Ten Miles High	1994

ARTIST	SONG TITLE	DATE
	Too Much Too Young	1992
	Womankind	1993
	Young Gods	1991
LITTLE ANTHONY & THE IMPERIALS		
	Goin' Out Of My Head	1964
	Hurt So Bad	1965
	I Miss You So	1965
	I'm On The Outside (Looking In)	1964
	Take Me Back	1965
LITTLE BENNY & THE MASTERS		
	Who Comes To Boogie	1985
LITTLE EVA	Keep Your Hands Off My Baby	1962
	Let's Turkey Trot	1963
	The Loco-Motion	1962
LITTLE MILTON	We're Gonna Make It	1965
LITTLE RICHARD	Bama Lama Bama Loo	1964
	Good Golly Miss Molly	1958
LITTLE RIVER BAND		
	Cool Change	1979
	Happy Anniversary	1977
	Help Is On Its Way	1977
	It's A Long Way There	1976
	Lady	1979
	Lonesome Loser	1979
	Man On Your Mind	1982
	The Night Owls	1981

ARTIST	SONG TITLE	DATE
	The Other Guy	1982
	Reminiscing	1978
	Take It Easy On Me	1981
	We Two	1983
	You're Driving Me Out Of My Mind	1983
LITTLE SISTER	Somebody's Watching You	1970
	You're The One (Pt 2)	1970
LITTLE TREES	Help! I'm A Fish	2001
DE ETTA LITTLE & NELSON PIGFOOT		
	You Take My Heart Away	1977
LIVE ELEMENT	Be Free	2002
LIVE	Lakini's Juice	1997
	Lightning Crashes	1996
	Selling The Drama	1995
LIVERPOOL EXPRESS		
	Dreamin'	1977
	Every Man Must Have A Dream	1976
	You Are My Love	1976
LIVERPOOL F.C.	Anfield Rap (Red Machine In Full Effect)	1988
	We Can Do It	1977
LIVERPOOL F.C. & THE BOOT ROOM BOYS		
	Pass & Move (It's The Liverpool Groove)	1996
LIVIN' JOY	Deep In You	1997
	Don't Stop Movin'	1996
	Dreamer	1995

ARTIST	SONG TITLE	DATE
	Follow The Rules	1996
	Where Can I Find Love	1997
LIVING COLOUR	Cult Of Personality	1989
	Glamour Boys	1989
	Leave It Alone	1993
	Love Rears It's Ugly Head	1991
	Solace Of You	1991
LIVING IN A BOX	Blow The House Down	1989
	Gatecrashing	1989
	Living In A Box	1987
	Room In Your Heart	1989
	Scales Of Justice	1987
LIVING IN A BOX featuring BOBBY WOMACK		
	So The Story Goes	1987
DANDY LIVINGSTONE		
	Big City/Think About That	1973
	Suzanne Beware Of The Devil	1972
KELLY LLORENNA	Heart Of Gold	2002
	Tell It To My Heart	2002
	This Time I Know It's For Real	2004
	(FLIP & FILL featuring KELLY LLORENNA)	
	True Love Never Dies	2002
LLOYD featuring ASHANTI		
	Southside	2004
LMC vs U2	Take Me To The Clouds Above	2004

ARTIST	SONG TITLE	DATE
LO FIDELITY ALLSTARS		
	Battleflag	1998
	Vision Incision	1998
LO-KEY?	I Got A Thang 4 Ya!	1992
LOBO	Caribbean Disco	1981
	Don't Expect Me To Be Your Friend	1972
	Don't Tell Me Goodnight	1975
	How Can I Tell Her?	1973
	I'd Love You To Want Me	1972
	It Sure Took A Long, Long Time	1973
	Me And You And A Dog Named Boo	1971
	Standing At The End Of The Line	1974
	Where Were You When I Was Falling In Love?	1979
LOS LOBOS	Come On Let's Go	1987
	La Bamba	1987
LOCK 'N' LOAD	Blow Ya Mind	2000
HANK LOCKLIN	I Feel A Cry Coming On	1966
LOCOMOTIVE	Rudi's In Love	1968
LODGER	I'm Leaving	1998
LISA LOEB	I Do	1997
LISA LOEB & NINE STORIES		
	Do You Sleep?	1995
	Stay	1994
JOHNNY LOGAN	Hold Me Now	1987
	What's Another Year	1980

ARTIST	SONG TITLE	DATE
LOGGINS & MESSINA		
	My Music	1973
	Thinking Of You	1973
	Your Mama Don't Dance	1972
DAVE LOGGINS	Please Come To Boston	1974
KENNY LOGGINS	Danger Zone	1986
	Footloose	1984
	Forever	1985
	Heart To Heart	1982
	I'm Alright	1980
	I'm Free (Heaven Helps The Man)	1984
	Keep The Fire	1980
	Meet Me Half Way	1987
	Nobody's Fool	1988
	This Is It	1979
	Vox Humana	1985
	Welcome To Heartland	1983
	Whenever I Call You 'Friend'	1978
KENNY LOGGINS & STEVE PERRY		
	Don't Fight It	1952
LOLLY	Big Boys Don't Cry/Rockin' Robin	1999
	Girls Just Wanna Have Fun	2000
	Mickey	1999
	Per Sempre Amore (Forever In Love)	2000
	Viva La Radio	1999
LONDON BOYS	Harlem Desire	1989

ARTIST	SONG TITLE	DATE
	London Nights	1989
	Requiem	1989
LONDON STRING CHORALE		
	Galloping Home	1973
LONDON SYMPHONY ORCHESTRA		
	Theme From 'Superman' (Main Title)	1979
LONDONBEAT	A Better Love	1991
	I've Been Thinking About You	1991
	9 A.M. (The Comfort Zone)	1988
	You Bring On The Sun	1992
LONESTAR	Amazed	1999
	I'm Already There	2001
	Let's Be Us Again	2004
	My Front Porch Looking In	2003
	Not A Day Goes By	2002
	Smile	1999
	Tell Her	2000
	What About Now	2000
LONG AND THE SHORT		
	The Letter	1964
SHORTY LONG	Here Comes The Judge	1968
LONGPIGS	Blue Skies	1999
	Far	1996
	Lost Myself	1996
	On And On	1996
	She Said	1996

ARTIST	SONG TITLE	DATE
JOE LONGTHORNE & LIZ DAWN		
	Passing Strangers	1994
LONGVIEW	Further	2003
	In A Dream	2004
LONYO	Summer Of Love	2000
LONYO featuring MC ONYX STONE		
	Garage Girls	2001
LOOK	I Am The Beat	1980
LOOKING GLASS	Brandy (You're A Fine Girl)	1972
	Jimmy Loves Mary-Anne	1973
LOON/TONI BRAXTON		
	Hit The Freeway	2003
	(LENNY KRAVITZ/P. DIDDY/LOON/PHARRELL WILLIAMS)	
	Show Me Your Soul	2004
	(P. DIDDY & GINUWINE featuring LOON, MARIO WINANS)	
	I Need A Girl (Part Two)	2002
	(P. DIDDY featuring USHER & LOON)	
	I Need A Girl (Part One)	2002
LOOP DA LOOP	Hazel	1999
LOOSE ENDS	Don't Be A Fool	1990
	Hangin' On A String (Contemplating)	1985
	Magic Touch	1985
	Slow Down	1986

ARTIST	SONG TITLE	DATE
LISA 'LEFT EYE' LOPES		
	The Block Party	2001
(MELANIE C/LISA 'LEFT EYE' LOPES)		
	Never Be The Same Again	2000
DENISE LOPEZ	Sayin' Sorry (Doesn't Make It Right)	1988
JENNIFER LOPEZ	Ain't It Funny	2001
	Baby I Love U	2004
	I'm Glad	2003
	I'm Real	2001
	If You Had My Love	1999
	Jenny From The Block	2002
	Love Don't Cost A Thing	2001
	Play	2001
	Waiting For Tonight	1999
JENNIFER LOPEZ featuring BIG PUN & FAT JOE		
	Feelin' So Good	2000
JENNIFER LOPEZ featuring LL COOL J		
	All I Have	2003
JENNIFER LOPEZ featuring NAS		
	I'm Gonna Be Alright	2002
TRINI LOPEZ	I'm Comin' Home Cindy	1966
	If I Had A Hammer	1963
	Kansas City	1963
	Lemon Tree	1965
A'ME LORAIN	Whole Wide World	1990

ARTIST	SONG TITLE	DATE
JEFF LORBER featuring KARYN WHITE		
	Facts Of Love	1986
LORD TARIQ & PETER GUNZ		
	Deja Vu	1997
TREY LORENZ	Photograph Of Mary	1993
	Someone To Hold	1992
GLORIA LORING & CARL ANDERSON		
	Friends And Lovers	1986
LOS DEL RIO	Macarena	1996
LOS POP TOPS	Mamy Blue	1971
JOE LOSS & HIS ORCHESTRA		
	March Of The Mods	1964
LOST BOYZ	Renee	1996
LOST BROTHERS featuring G TOM MAC		
	Cry Little Sister	2003
LOST GENERATION	The Sly, Slick, And The Wicked	1970
LOST TRIBE	Gamemaster	1999
LOST WITNESS	Did I Dream (Song To The Siren)	2002
	Happiness Happening	1999
	Red Sun Rising	1999
	7 Colours	2000
LOSTPROPHETS	Burn Burn	2003
	The Fake Sound Of Progress	2002
	Last Summer	2004
	Last Train Home	2004
	Wake Up (Make A Move)	2004

ARTIST	SONG TITLE	DATE
LOTUS EATERS	First Picture Of You	1983
LOUCHIE LOU & MICHIE ONE		
	Good Sweet Lovin'	1996
	Shout	1993
	(SUGGS featuring LOUCHIE LOU & MICHIE ONE)	
	No More Alcohol	1996
LOUIE LOUIE	Sittin' In The Lap Of Luxury	1990
	The Thought Of It	1992
LOUISE	All That Matters	1998
	Arms Around The World	1997
	Beautiful Inside	2000
	In Walked Love	1996
	Let's Go Round Again	1997
	Light Of My Life	1995
	Naked	1996
	One Kiss From Heaven	1996
	Pandora's Kiss	2003
	Stuck In The Middle With You	2001
	2 Faced	2000
	Undivided Love	1996
LOVE	7 And 7 Is	1966
LOVE AFFAIR	Bringing On Back The Good Times	1969
	A Day Without Love	1968
	Everlasting Love	1968
	One Road	1969
	Rainbow Valley	1968

ARTIST	SONG TITLE	DATE
LOVE AND KISSES	Thank God It's Friday	1978
LOVE AND ROCKETS		
	So Alive	1989
LOVE CITY GROOVE		
	Love City Groove	1995
LOVE DECADE	I Feel You	1992
	Is This A Dream?	1996
	So Real	1991
LOVE INC.	Broken Bones	2003
	Into The Night	2004
	You're A Superstar	2002
LOVE SCULPTURE	Sabre Dance	1968
LOVE TO INFINITY	Keep Love Together	1995
LOVE TRIBE	Stand Up	1996
LOVE UNLIMITED	I Belong To You	1974
	It May Be Winter Outside (But In My Heart It's Spring)	1975
	Walkin' In The Rain With The One I Love	1972
LOVE UNLIMITED ORCHESTRA		
	Love's Theme	1973
	Satin Soul	1975
DARLENE LOVE	All Alone On Christmas	1992
MONIE LOVE	Born 2 B.R.E.E.D.	1993
	Down To Earth	1990
	Full Term Love	1992
	Grandpa's Party	1989

ARTIST	SONG TITLE	DATE
	I Can Do This	1989
	In A Word Or 2/The Power	1993
	Slice Of Da Pie	2000
MONIE LOVE featuring TRUE IMAGE		
	It's A Shame (My Sister)	1990
MONIE LOVE vs ADEVA		
	Ring My Bell	1991
LOVE/HATE	Wasted In America	1992
LOVEBUG	Who's The Daddy	2003
LOVEBUG STARSKI	Amityville (The House On The Hill)	1986
LOVEDEEJAY AKEMI/YOSH		
	It's What's Upfront That Counts	1995
	The Screamer	1996
LOVEHAPPY	Message Of Love	1995
BILL LOVELADY	Reggae For It Now	1979
LOVELAND featuring RACHEL MCFARLANE		
	Don't Make Me Wait	1995
	I Need Somebody	1995
	(Keep On) Shining/Hope (Never Give Up)	1994
LOVELAND vs DARLENE LEWIS		
	Let The Music Lift You Up	1994
LOVERBOY	Heaven In Your Eyes	1986
	Hot Girls In Love	1983
	Lovin' Every Minute Of It	1985
	Notorious	1987

ARTIST	SONG TITLE	DATE
	Queen Of Broken Hearts	1983
	This Could Be The Night	1986
	Turn Me Loose	1981
	When It's Over	1982
	Working For The Weekend	1981
LOVESTATION	Sensuality	1998
	Teardrops	1998
LENE LOVICH	Bird Song	1979
	Lucky Number	1979
	Say When	1979
LOVIN' SPOONFUL	Darling Be Home Soon	1967
	Daydream	1966
	Did You Ever Have To Make Up Your Mind	1966
	Do You Believe In Magic	1965
	Nashville Cats	1966
	Rain On The Roof	1966
	She Is Still A Mystery	1967
	Six O'Clock	1967
	Summer In The City	1966
	You Didn't Have To Be So Nice	1965
NICK LOWE	Cracking Up	1979
	Cruel To Be Kind	1979
NICK LOWE & HIS COWBOY OUTFIT		
	I Love The Sound Of Breaking Glass	1978

ARTIST	SONG TITLE	DATE
LOWGOLD	Beauty Dies Young	2001
LOWRELL	Mellow Mellow Right On	1979
LOX	If You Think I'm Jiggy	1998
LOX featuring DMX & LIL' KIM		
	Money, Power & Respect	1998
LSG (LEVERT.SWEAT.GILL)		
	Curious	1998
	My Body	1998
LUCAS	Lucas With The Lid Off	1994
CARRIE LUCAS	Dance With You	1979
LUCID	Crazy	1999
	I Can't Help Myself	1998
	Stay With Me Till Dawn	1999
LUCY PEARL	Dance Tonight	2000
	Don't Mess With My Man	2000
LUDACRIS	Act A Fool	2003
	Rollout (My Business)	2002
	Southern Hospitality	2001
	Stand Up	2003
	What's Your Fantasy	2001
LUDACRIS featuring NATE DOGG		
	Area Codes	2001
LUDACRIS featuring SLEEPY BROWN		
	Saturday (Oooh! Ooooh!)	2002
LUDACRIS featuring MYSTIKAL & INFAMOUS 2.0		
	Move Bitch	2002

ARTIST	SONG TITLE	DATE
(AMERIE featuring LUDACRIS)		
	Why Don't We Fall In Love	2002
(JERMAINE DUPRI & LUDACRIS)		
	Welcome To Atlanta	2001
(MISSY 'MISDEMEANOR' ELLIOTT featuring LUDACRIS)		
	Gossip Folks	2003
	One Minute Man	2001
(USHER featuring LIL' JON & LUDACRIS)		
	Yeah!	2004
BAZ LUHRMANN	Everybody's Free (To Wear Sunscreen)	1999
LUKE featuring NO GOOD BUT SO GOOD		
	Raise The Roof	1998
LUKE featuring THE 2 LIVE CREW		
	Banned In The USA	1990
LULU	Best Of Both Worlds	1967
	The Boat That I Row	1967
	Boom Bang-A-Bang	1969
	Boy	1968
	Goodbye Baby And Amen	1994
	I Could Never Miss You (More Than I Do)	1981
	I'm A Tiger	1968
	Independence	1993
	Leave A Little Love	1965
	Let's Pretend	1967

ARTIST	SONG TITLE	DATE
	Love Loves To Love Love	1967
	The Man Who Sold The World	1974
	Me, The Peaceful Heart	1968
	Oh Me Oh My (I'm A Fool For You Baby)	1969
	Shout	1964
	Take Your Mama For A Ride	1975
	To Sir With Love	1967
	Try To Understand	1965
	Where The Poor Boys Dance	2000
LULU and BOBBY WOMACK		
	I'm Back For More	1993
(RONAN KEATING featuring LULU)		
	We've Got Tonight	2002
(TAKE THAT featuring LULU)		
	Relight My Fire	1993
LUMIDEE	Never Leave You (Oh Oooh, Uh Oooh)	2003
VICTOR LUNDBERG	An Open Letter To My Teenage Son	1967
LUNIZ	I Got 5 On It	1995
	Playa Hata	1996
LUSCIOUS JACKSON		
	Naked Eye	1996
LUSH	500 (Shake Baby Shake)	1996
	For Love (EP)	1992
	Ladykillers	1996
	Single Girl	1996
LUSTRAL	Everytime	1999

ARTIST	SONG TITLE	DATE
LV	Throw Your Hands Up/Gangsta's Paradise	1995
	(COOLIO featuring LV)	
	Gangsta's Paradise	1995
KENNY LYNCH	I'll Stay By You	1965
	Stand By Me	1964
	What Am I To You	1964
	You Can Never Stop Me Loving You	1963
LIAM LYNCH	United States Of Whatever	2002
CHERYL LYNN	Got To Be Real	1978
TAMI LYNN	I'm Gonna Run Away From You	1971
GLORIA LYNNE	I Wish You Love	1964
PHILIP LYNOTT	Dear Miss Lonely Hearts	1980
	King's Call	1980
	Yellow Pearl	1981
	(GARY MOORE & PHIL LYNOTT)	
	Out In The Fields	1985
LYNYRD SKYNYRD	Free Bird	1976
	Saturday Night Special	1975
	Sweet Home Alabama/Double Trouble	1976
	What's Your Name	1977
LYTE FUNKIE ONES		
	Every Other Time	2002
	Girl On TV	2000
	Summer Girls	1999
KEVIN LYTTLE	Last Drop	2004

ARTIST	SONG TITLE	DATE
	Turn Me On	2003
M	Moonlight And Muzak	1979
	Pop Muzik	1979
M FACTOR	Mother	2002
M PEOPLE	Angel St	1998
	Colour My Life	1992
	Don't Look Any Further	1993
	Dreaming	1999
	Elegantly American: One Night In	
	Heaven/Moving On Up	1994
	Excited	1992
	Fantasy Island	1997
	How Can I Love You More?	1993
	Itchycoo Park	1995
	Just For You	1997
	Love Rendezvous	1995
	Moving On Up	1994
	One Night In Heaven	1993
	Open Your Heart	1995
	Renaissance	1994
	Search For The Hero	1995
	Sight For Sore Eyes	1994
	Someday	1992
	Testify	1998
M&S presents GIRL NEXT DOOR		
	Salsoul Nugget (If U Wanna)	2001

ARTIST	SONG TITLE	DATE
M-BEAT featuring GENERAL LEVY		
	Incredible	1994
M-BEAT featuring JAMIROQUAI		
	Do U Know Where You're Coming From	1996
M-BEAT featuring NAZLYN		
	Sweet Love	1994
M. & O. BAND	Let's Do The Latin Hustle	1976
M.C. BRAINS	Oochie Coochie	1992
M.C. MIKER 'G' & DEEJAY SVEN		
	Holiday Rap	1986
M.O.P.	Cold As Ice	2001
M.O.P. featuring BUSTA RHYMES		
	Ante Up	2001
M/A/R/R/S	Pump Up The Volume	1987
M2M	Don't Say You Love Me	2000
M3	Bailamos	1999
TIMO MAAS	To Get Down	2002
TIMO MAAS featuring MARTIN BETTINGHAUS		
	Ubik	2000
TIMO MAAS featuring MC CHICKABOO		
	Shifter	2002
MOMS MABLEY	Abraham, Martin & John	1969
MAC BAND featuring THE MCCAMPBELL BROTHERS		
	Roses Are Red	1988
	Stalemate	1988
PETE MAC JR.	The Water Margin	1977

ARTIST	SONG TITLE	DATE
NEIL MACARTHUR	She's Not There	1969
KIRSTY MACCOLL	Days	1989
	A New England	1985
	There's A Guy Works Down The Chipshop	
	Swears He's Elvis	1981
	Walking Down Madison	1991
	(THE POGUES featuring KIRSTY MACCOLL)	
	Fairytale Of New York	1987
SHANE MACGOWAN	My Way	1996
SHANE MACGOWAN & SINEAD O'CONNOR		
	Haunted	1995
SHANE MACGOWAN AND THE POPES		
	That Woman's Got Me Drinking	1994
BYRON MACGREGOR		
	Americans	1974
MARY MACGREGOR		
	Good Friend	1979
	Torn Between Two Lovers	1976
MACK 10	Backyard Boogie	1997
MACK 10 & THA DOGG POUND		
	Nothin' But The Cavi Hit	1996
	(ICE CUBE featuring MACK 10 & MS. TOI)	
	You Can Do It	1999
	(WARREN G featuring MACK 10)	
	I Want It All	1999
BILLY MACK	Christmas Is All Around	2003

ARTIST	SONG TITLE	DATE
CRAIG MACK	Flava In Ya Ear	1994
	Get Down	1994
PATRICK MACNEE & HONOR BLACKMAN		
	Kinky Boots	1990
MAD COBRA	Flex	1992
MAD DONNA	The Wheels On The Bus	2002
MAD STUNTMAN/REEL 2 REAL		
	Can You Feel It?	1994
	I Like To Move It	1994
	Raise Your Hands	1994
MAD'HOUSE	Holiday	2002
	Like A Prayer	2002
MADASUN	Don't You Worry	2000
	Feel Good	2000
	Walking On Water	2000
MADDOG/STRETCH 'N' VERN		
	Get Up! Go Insane!	1997
	I'm Alive	1996
MADE IN LONDON	Dirty Water	2000
MADISON AVENUE	Don't Call Me Baby	1999
	Everything You Need	2001
	Who The Hell Are You	2000
MADNESS	Baggy Trousers	1980
	Cardiac Arrest	1982
	Driving My Car	1982
	Embarrassment	1980

ARTIST	SONG TITLE	DATE
	Grey Day	1981
	House Of Fun	1982
	It Must Be Love	1983
	Lovestruck	1999
	Michael Caine	1984
	My Girl	1980
	One Better Day	1984
	One Step Beyond...	1979
	Our House	1983
	The Prince	1979
	Return Of The Los Palmas 7	1981
	Shut Up	1981
	The Sun And The Rain	1983
	Sweetest Girl	1986
	Tomorrow's (Just Another Day)/Madness (Is All In The Mind)	1983
	Uncle Sam	1985
	(Waiting For) The Ghost Train	1986
	Wings Of A Dove	1983
	Work Rest & Play E.P.	1980
	Yesterday's Men	1985
	(SPECIAL AKA/MADNESS/SELECTER/BEAT) The 2 Tone EP	1993
MADONNA	American Life	2003
	American Pie	2000
	Angel	1985

ARTIST	SONG TITLE	DATE
	Another Suitcase In Another Hall	1997
	Bad Girl	1993
	Beautiful Stranger	1999
	Bedtime Story	1995
	Borderline	1984
	Causing A Commotion	1987
	Cherish	1989
	Crazy For You	1985
	Dear Jessie	1989
	Deeper And Deeper	1992
	Die Another Day	2002
	Don't Cry For Me Argentina	1997
	Don't Tell Me	2000
	Dress You Up	1985
	Drowned World (Substitute For Love)	1998
	Erotica	1992
	Express Yourself	1989
	Fever	1993
	Frozen	1998
	Gambler	1985
	Hanky Panky	1990
	Holiday	1983
	Hollywood	2003
	Human Nature	1995
	I'll Remember	1994
	Into The Groove	1985

ARTIST	SONG TITLE	DATE
	Justify My Love	1990
	Keep It Together	1990
	La Isla Bonita	1987
	Like A Prayer	1989
	Like A Virgin	1984
	Live To Tell	1986
	The Look Of Love	1987
	Love Profusion	2003
	Lucky Star	1964
	Material Girl	1985
	Music	2000
	Nothing Really Matters	1999
	Oh Father	1989
	One More Chance	1996
	Open Your Heart	1986
	Papa Don't Preach	1986
	The Power Of Goodbye/Little Star	1998
	Rain	1993
	Ray Of Light	1998
	Rescue Me	1991
	Secret	1994
	Take A Bow	1994
	This Used To Be My Playground	1992
	True Blue	1986
	Vogue	1990
	What It Feels Like For A Girl	2001

ARTIST	SONG TITLE	DATE
	Who's That Girl	1987
	You Must Love Me	1996
	You'll See	1995
	(BRITNEY SPEARS featuring MADONNA)	
	Me Against The Music	2003
LISA MAFFIA	All Over	2003
	In Love	2003
	(OXIDE & NEUTRINO featuring MEGAMAN, ROMEO & LISA MAFFIA)	
	No Good 4 Me	2000
CLEDUS MAGGARD & THE CITIZEN'S BAND		
	The White Knight	1975
MAGIC AFFAIR	Give Me All Your Love	1994
	In The Middle Of The Night	1994
	Omen III	1994
MAGIC LANTERNS	Shame Shame	1968
MAGNUM	Days Of No Trust	1988
	It Must Have Been Love	1988
	Rockin' Chair	1990
	Start Talking Love	1988
MAGOO AND TIMBALAND		
	Up Jumps Da Boogie	1997
	(TIMBALAND & MAGOO featuring MISSY ELLIOTT)	
	Cop That Shit	2004
	(TIMBALAND AND MAGOO)	
	Clock Strikes	1998

ARTIST	SONG TITLE	DATE
SEAN MAGUIRE	Don't Pull Your Love	1996
	Good Day	1996
	Now That I've Found You	1995
	Someone To Love	1994
	Suddenly	1995
	Take This Time	1994
	Today's The Day	1997
	You To Me Are Everything	1995
MAI TAI	Body And Soul	1985
	History	1985
MAIN INGREDIENT	Everybody Plays The Fool	1972
	Happiness Is Just Around The Bend	1974
	Just Don't Want To Be Lonely	1974
MAISONETTES	Heartache Avenue	1982
J. MAJIK featuring KATHY BROWN		
	Love Is Not A Game	2001
MIRIAM MAKEBA	Pata Pata	1967
CARL MALCOLM	Fattie Bum-Bum	1975
MALO	Suavecito	1972
MAMA CASS	Dream A Little Dream Of Me	1968
	Make Your Own Kind Of Music	1969
MAMAS & THE PAPAS		
	California Dreamin'	1966
	Creeque Alley	1967
	Dedicated To The One I Love	1967
	Glad To Be Unhappy	1967

ARTIST	SONG TITLE	DATE
	I Saw Her Again	1966
	Look Through Any Window	1966
	Monday Monday	1966
	Twelve Thirty (Young Girls Are Coming To The Canyon)	1967
	Words Of Love	1966
MAN 2 MAN MEET MAN PARRISH		
	Male Stripper	1987
1999 MANCHESTER UNITED SQUAD		
	Lift It High (All About Belief)	1999
MANCHESTER UNITED & THE CHAMPIONS		
	United (We Love You)	1993
MANCHESTER UNITED		
1995 FOOTBALL SQUAD featuring STRYKER		
	We're Gonna Do It Again	1995
MANCHESTER UNITED FA CUP SQUAD		
	Move Move Move (The Red Tribe)	1996
MANCHESTER UNITED FOOTBALL CLUB		
	Glory Glory Man. United	1983
	We All Follow Man. United	1985
MANCHESTER UNITED FOOTBALL SQUAD		
	Come On You Reds	1994
MELISSA MANCHESTER		
	Don't Cry Out Loud	1978
	Fire In The Morning	1980
	Just Too Many People	1975

ARTIST	SONG TITLE	DATE
	Just You And I	1976
	Midnight Blue	1975
	Pretty Girls	1979
	You Should Hear How She Talks About You	1982
MANCHILD	Nothing Without Me	2001
HENRY MANCINI	Main Theme From 'The Thorn Birds'	1984
	The Pink Panther Theme	1964
HENRY MANCINI & HIS ORCHESTRA		
	How Soon	1964
	Love Theme From 'Romeo & Juliet'	1969
	Theme From 'Love Story'	1971
BARBARA MANDRELL		
	(If Loving You Is Wrong) I Don't Want To Be Right	1979
MANFRED MANN	Come Tomorrow	1965
	Do Wah Diddy Diddy	1964
	5-4-3-2-1	1964
	Fox On The Run	1968
	Ha! Ha! Said The Clown	1967
	Hubble Bubble (Toil And Trouble)	1964
	If You Gotta Go, Go Now	1965
	Just Like A Woman	1966
	Mighty Quinn	1968
	My Name Is Jack	1968
	Oh No, Not My Baby	1965

ARTIST	SONG TITLE	DATE
	Pretty Flamingo	1966
	Ragamuffin Man	1969
	Semi-Detached Suburban Mr. James	1966
	Sha La La	1964
	Sweet Pea	1967
	You Gave Me Somebody To Love	1966
MANFRED MANN'S EARTH BAND		
	Blinded By The Light	1976
	Davy's On The Road Again	1978
	Joybringer	1973
	Runner	1984
	Spirit In The Night	1977
CHUCK MANGIONE	Feels So Good	1978
	Give It All You Got	1980
MANHATTAN TRANSFER		
	Boy From New York City	1981
	Chanson D'Amour	1977
	Don't Let Go	1977
	On A Little Street In Singapore	1978
	Operator	1975
	Spice Of Life	1983
	Tuxedo Junction	1976
	Twilight Zone/Twilight Tone	1980
	Walk In Love	1978
	Where Did Our Love Go/Je Voulais (Te Dire Que Je T'Attends)	1978

ARTIST	SONG TITLE	DATE
MANHATTANS	Don't Take Your Love	1975
	Hurt	1976
	Kiss And Say Goodbye	1976
	Shining Star	1980
MANIA	Looking For A Place	2004
MANIC MC'S featuring SARA CARLSON		
	Mental	1989
MANIC STREET PREACHERS		
	Australia	1996
	A Design For Life	1996
	The Everlasting	1998
	Everything Must Go	1996
	Faster/PCP	1994
	Found That Soul	2001
	From Despair To Where	1993
	If You Tolerate This Your Children Will Be Next	1998
	Kevin Carter	1996
	La Tristesse Durera (Scream To A Sigh)	1993
	Let Robeson Sing	2001
	Life Becoming A Landslide	1994
	Little Baby Nothing	1992
	The Love Of Richard Nixon	2004
	Love's Sweet Exile/Repeat	1991
	The Masses Against The Classes	2000
	Motorcycle Emptiness	1992

ARTIST	SONG TITLE	DATE
	Ocean Spray	2001
	Revol	1994
	Roses In The Hospital	1993
	She Is Suffering	1994
	Slash 'n' Burn	1992
	So Why So Sad	2001
	Stay Beautiful	1991
	There By The Grace Of God	2002
	Tsunami	1999
	You Love Us	1992
	You Stole The Sun From My Heart	1999
MANIC STREET PREACHERS/FATIMA MANSION		
	Theme From M.A.S.H./Everything I Do	1992
BARRY MANILOW	Bermuda Triangle	1981
	Can't Smile Without You	1978
	Copacabana (At The Copa)	1978
	Could It Be Magic	1975
	Daybreak	1977
	Even Now	1978
	I Don't Want To Walk Without You	1980
	I Made It Through The Rain	1980
	I Wanna Do It With You	1982
	I Write The Songs	1975
	I'm Gonna Sit Right Down And Write Myself A Letter	1982
	It's A Miracle	1975

ARTIST	SONG TITLE	DATE
	Let's Hang On	1982
	Lonely Together	1980
	Looks Like We Made It	1977
	Mandy	1974
	Memory	1982
	Oh Julie	1982
	The Old Songs	1981
	Please Don't Be Scared	1989
	Read 'Em And Weep	1983
	Ready To Take A Chance Again	1978
	Ships	1979
	Some Kind Of Friend	1983
	Somewhere Down The Road	1981
	Somewhere In The Night	1978
	Stay	1982
	This One's For You	1976
	Tryin' To Get The Feeling Again	1976
	Weekend In New England	1976
	When I Wanted You	1979
MANKIND	Dr. Who	1978
HERBIE MANN	Hijack	1975
	Superman	1979
JOHNNY MANN SINGERS		
	Up-Up And Away	1967
MANSUN	Being A Girl (Part One) (EP)	1998
	Closed For Business	1997

ARTIST	SONG TITLE	DATE
	Electric Man	2000
	Fool	2001
	I Can Only Disappoint U	2000
	Legacy (EP)	1998
	Negative	1998
	One (EP)	1996
	She Makes My Nose Bleed	1997
	Six	1999
	Taxloss	1997
	Three (EP)	1996
	Two (EP)	1996
	Wide Open Space	1996
KURTIS MANTRONIK presents CHAMONIX		
	How Did You Know	2003
MANTRONIX	Bassline	1986
	Don't Go Messin' With My Heart	1991
	Who Is It	1987
MANTRONIX featuring WONDRESS		
	Got To Have Your Love	1990
	Take Your Time	1990
MANUEL & THE MUSIC OF THE MOUNTAINS		
	Rodrigo's Guitar Concerto De Aranjuez	1976
MARATHON	Movin'	1992
MARBLES	Only One Woman	1968
MARC ET CLAUDE	I Need Your Lovin' (Like The Sunshine)	2000
	La	1998

ARTIST	SONG TITLE	DATE
	Loving You '03	2003
	Tremble	2002
LITTLE PEGGY MARCH		
	Hello Heartache, Goodbye Love	1963
MARCY PLAYGROUND		
	Sex And Candy	1998
MARDI GRAS	Too Busy Thinking About My Baby	1972
BENNY MARDONES		
	Into The Night	1989
KELLY MARIE	Feels Like I'm In Love	1980
	Hot Love	1981
	Loving Just For Fun	1980
TEENA MARIE	Behind The Groove	1980
	I Need Your Lovin'	1980
	Lovergirl	1984
MARILLION	Assassing	1984
	Beautiful	1995
	Cover My Eyes (Pain And Heaven)	1991
	Don't Hurt Yourself	2004
	Dry Land	1991
	Easter	1990
	Freaks (Live)	1988
	Garden Party	1983
	He Knows You Know	1983
	Heart Of Lothian	1985
	The Hollow Man	1994

ARTIST	SONG TITLE	DATE
	Hooks In You	1989
	Incommunicado	1987
	Kayleigh	1985
	Lavender	1985
	No One Can	1992
	Punch And Judy	1984
	Sugar Mice	1987
	Sympathy	1992
	Warm Wet Circles	1987
	You're Gone	2004
MARILYN	Calling Your Name	1983
	Cry And Be Free	1984
	You Don't Love Me	1984
MARILYN MANSON	The Beautiful People	1997
	Disposable Teens	2000
	The Dope Show	1998
	The Fight Song	2001
	Mobscene	2003
	The Nobodies	2001
	Personal Jesus	2004
	Rock Is Dead	1999
	Tainted Love	2002
	This Is The New Shit	2003
	Torniquet	1997
MARIO	C'mon	2003
	Just A Friend	2002

ARTIST	SONG TITLE	DATE
MARION	Let's All Go Together	1995
	Sleep	1996
	Time	1996
MARK' OH	Tears Don't Lie	1995
MARKY MARK & THE FUNKY BUNCH		
	Good Vibrations	1991
	Wildside	1991
MARKETTS	Batman Theme	1966
PIGMEAT MARKHAM		
	Here Comes The Judge	1968
YANNIS MARKOPOULOS		
	Who Pays The Ferryman?	1977
GUY MARKS	Loving You Has Made Me Bananas	1978
BOB MARLEY	No Woman No Cry	1975
	Satisfy My Soul	1978
	Waiting In Vain	1977
BOB MARLEY & THE WAILERS		
	Buffalo Soldier	1983
	Could You Be Loved	1980
	Exodus	1977
	Iron Lion Zion	1992
	Is This Love	1978
	Jamming/Punky Reggae Party	1977
	Keep On Moving	1995
	One Love/People Get Ready	1984
	Three Little Birds	1980

ARTIST	SONG TITLE	DATE
BOB MARLEY featuring LAURYN HILL		
	Turn Your Lights Down Low	1999
BOB MARLEY vs FUNKSTAR DE LUXE		
	Rainbow Country	2000
	Sun Is Shining	1999
ZIGGY MARLEY & THE MELODY MAKERS		
	Tomorrow People	1988
LENE MARLIN	Sitting Down Here	2000
	Unforgivable Sinner	2000
	Where I'm Headed	2001
MARLY	You Never Know	2004
MARMALADE	Baby Make It Soon	1969
	Back On The Road	1971
	Cousin Norman	1971
	Falling Apart At The Seams	1976
	Lovin' Things	1968
	My Little One	1971
	Ob-La-Di, Ob-La-Da	1968
	Radancer	1972
	Rainbow	1970
	Reflections Of My Life	1970
	Wait For Me Marianne	1968
MAROON5	Harder To Breathe	2004
	She Will Be Loved	2004
	This Love	2004
MARRADONA	Out Of My Head	1994

ARTIST	SONG TITLE	DATE
MATTHEW MARSDEN		
	The Heart's Lone Desire	1998
MATTHEW MARSDEN featuring DESTINY'S CHILD		
	She's Gone	1998
MARSDEN/MCCARTNEY/JOHNSON/CHRISTIANS		
	Ferry 'Cross The Mersey	1989
KYM MARSH	Come On Over	2003
	Cry	2003
	Sentimental	2003
MARSHALL HAIN	Coming Home	1978
	Dancing In The City	1978
MARSHALL TUCKER BAND		
	Fire On The Mountain	1975
	Heard It In A Love Song	1977
JOY MARSHALL	The More I See You	1966
KEITH MARSHALL	Only Crying	1981
WAYNE MARSHALL	Ooh Aah (G-Spot)	1994
MARTAY featuring ZZ TOP		
	Gimme All Your Lovin' 2000	1999
LENA MARTELL	One Day At A Time	1979
MARTHA & THE MUFFINS		
	Echo Beach	1980
MARTHA & THE VANDELLAS		
	Bless You	1972
	Dancing In The Street	1964
	Forget Me Not	1971

ARTIST	SONG TITLE	DATE
	Honey Chile	1967
	I'm Ready For Love	1966
	Jimmy Mack	1967
	Love Bug Leave My Heart Alone	1967
	My Baby Loves Me	1966
	Nowhere To Run	1965
	Wild One	1964
	You've Been On Love Too Long	1965
MARTIKA	I Feel The Earth Move	1989
	Love... Thy Will Be Done	1991
	Martika's Kitchen	1991
	More Than You Know	1989
	Toy Soldiers	1989
BILLIE RAY MARTIN		
	Imitation Of Life	1996
	Running Around Town	1995
	Your Loving Arms	1995
BOBBI MARTIN	Don't Forget I Still Love You	1964
	For The Love Of Him	1970
DEAN MARTIN	Come Running Back	1966
	The Door Is Still Open To My Heart	1964
	Everybody Loves Somebody	1964
	Gentle On My Mind	1969
	Houston	1965
	I Will	1965
	In The Chapel In The Moonlight	1967

ARTIST	SONG TITLE	DATE
	Little Ole Wine Drinker Me	1967
	(Remember Me) I'm The One Who Loves You	1965
	Send Me The Pillow That You Dream On	1965
	Somewhere There's A Someone	1966
	You're Nobody Till Somebody Loves You	1964
JUAN MARTIN	Love Theme From 'The Thorn Birds'	1984
MARILYN MARTIN	Night Moves	1986
(PHIL COLLINS & MARILYN MARTIN)		
	Separate Lives	1985
MOON MARTIN	Rolene	1979
RICKY MARTIN	The Cup Of Life	1998
	Livin' La Vida Loca	1999
	Loaded	2001
	Shake Your Bon-Bon	1999
	She Bangs	2000
	She's All I Ever Had	1999
	(Un, Dos, Tres) Maria	1997
RICKY MARTIN & CHRISTINA AGUILERA		
	Nobody Wants To Be Lonely	2001
RICKY MARTIN featuring MEJA		
	Private Emotion	2000
STEVE MARTIN	King Tut	1978
WINK MARTINDALE		
	Deck Of Cards	1959

ARTIST	SONG TITLE	DATE
ANGIE MARTINEZ featuring LIL' MO & SACARIO		
	If I Could Go!	2002
NANCY MARTINEZ	For Tonight	1986
AL MARTINO	Always Together	1964
	I Love You More And More Every Day	1964
	Mary In The Morning	1967
	Spanish Eyes	1965
	Tears And Roses	1964
	Think I'll Go Somewhere And Cry Myself To Sleep	1966
	To The Door Of The Sun (Alle Porte Del Sole)	1974
	Volare	1975
MARVELETTES	Don't Mess With Bill	1966
	The Hunter Gets Captured By The Game	1967
	I'll Keep Holding On	1965
	My Baby Must Be A Magician	1966
	Too Many Fish In The Sea	1964
	When You're Young And In Love	1976
MARVELOWS	I Do	1965
MARVIN AND TAMARA		
	Groove Machine	1999
	North, South, East, West	1999
HANK MARVIN	Joy Of Living	1970
(CLIFF & HANK)		
	Throw Down A Line	1969

ARTIST	SONG TITLE	DATE
LEE MARVIN	Wand'rin' Star	1970
RICHARD MARX	Angelia	1989
	Chains Around My Heart	1992
	Children Of The Night	1990
	Don't Mean Nothing	1987
	Endless Summer Nights	1988
	Hazard	1992
	Hold On To The Nights	1988
	Keep Coming Back	1991
	Now And Forever	1994
	Right Here Waiting	1989
	Satisfied	1989
	Should've Known Better	1987
	Silent Scream	1994
	Take This Heart	1992
	Too Late To Say Goodbye	1990
	The Way She Loves Me	1994
MARXMAN	All About Eve	1993
MARY JANE GIRLS	All Night Long	1983
	In My House	1985
MARY MARY	I Sings	2000
	Shackles (Praise You)	2000
MASE	Feel So Good	1997
	Welcome Back	2004
MASE featuring BLACKSTREET		
	Get Ready	1999

ARTIST	SONG TITLE	DATE
MASE featuring P. DIDDY		
	Breathe, Stretch, Shake	2004
MASE featuring PUFF DADDY		
	Lookin' At Me	1998
MASE featuring TOTAL		
	What You Want	1998
	(112 featuring MASE)	
	Love Me	1998
	(BLACKSTREET & MYA featuring MASE &	
	BLINKY BLINK)	
	Take Me There	1998
	(BRANDY featuring MASE)	
	Top Of The World	1998
	(BRIAN MCKNIGHT featuring MASE)	
	You Should Be Mine (Don't Waste Your	
	Time)	1997
	(CAM'RON featuring MASE)	
	Horse & Carriage	1998
	(NOTORIOUS B.I.G. featuring PUFF DADDY & MASE)	
	Mo Money Mo Problems	1997
	(PUFF DADDY featuring MASE)	
	Can't Nobody Hold Me Down	1997
HUGH MASEKELA	Grazing In The Grass	1968
MASH!	U Don't Have To Say U Love Me	1994
MASH	Theme From M*A*S*H* (Suicide Is	
	Painless)	1980

ARTIST	SONG TITLE	DATE
MASHMAKHAN	As The Years Go By	1970
BARBARA MASON	From His Woman To You	1974
	Give Me Your Love	1973
	Sad, Sad Girl	1965
	Yes, I'm Ready	1965
DAVE MASON	We Just Disagree	1977
	Will You Still Love Me Tomorrow	1978
MARY MASON	Angel Of The Morning/Any Way That	
	You Want Me (Medley)	1977
MASS ORDER	Lift Every Voice (Take Me Away)	1992
MASSIVE	Unfinished Sympathy	1991
MASSIVE ATTACK	Angel	1998
	Karmacoma	1995
	Massive Attack (EP)	1992
	Protection	1995
	Risingson	1997
	Safe From Harm	1991
	Sly	1994
	Special Cases	2003
	Teardrop	1998
MASSIVO featuring TRACY		
	Loving You	1990
MASTA ACE INCORPORATED		
	Born To Roll	1994
MASTER P featuring FIEND, SILKK THE SHOCKER, MIA X	Make Em' Say Uhh!	1998

ARTIST	SONG TITLE	DATE
MASTER P featuring SILKK THE SHOCKER, SONS OF FUNK	Goodbye To My Homies	1998
MASTER P featuring PIMP C AND THE SHOCKER	I Miss My Homies	1997
MASTER P featuring SONS OF FUNK	I Got The Hook Up!	1998
(MONTELL JORDAN featuring MASTER P & SILKK THE SHOCKER)		
	Let's Ride	1998
MASTER SINGERS	Highway Code	1966
PAUL MASTERSON presents SUSHI		
	The Earthshaker	2002
MATCHBOX	Buzz Buzz A Diddle It	1980
	Midnite Dynamos	1980
	Over The Rainbow/You Belong To Me	
	(Medley)	1980
	Rockabilly Rebel	1979
	When You Ask About Love	1980
MATCHBOX TWENTY		
	Back 2 Good	1998
	Bent	2000
	Bright Lights	2003
	Disease	2002
	If You're Gone	2000
	Push	1998
	Real World	1998

ARTIST	SONG TITLE	DATE
MATCHROOM MOB WITH CHAS & DAVE		
	Snooker Loopy	1986
MIREILLE MATHIEU		
	La Derniere Valse	1967
JOHNNY MATHIS	Gone, Gone, Gone	1979
	I'm Stone In Love With You	1975
	When A Child Is Born (Soleado)	1976
JOHNNY MATHIS & DENIECE WILLIAMS		
	Too Much, Too Little, Too Late	1978
	(DIONNE WARWICK & JOHNNY MATHIS)	
	Friends In Love	1982
MATT BIANCO	Don't Blame It On That Girl/Wap Bam	
	Boogie	1988
	Get Out Of Your Lazy Bed	1984
	Half A Minute	1984
	Yeh Yeh	1985
MATTHEWS' SOUTHERN COMFORT		
	Woodstock	1970
AL MATTHEWS	Fool	1975
CERYS MATTHEWS/TOM JONES		
	Baby, It's Cold Outside	1999
	(SPACE WITH CERYS OF CATATONIA)	
	The Ballad Of Tom Jones	1998
DAVE MATTHEWS BAND		
	The Space Between	2001
	Where Are You Going	2002

ARTIST	SONG TITLE	DATE
IAN MATTHEWS	Shake It	1978
SUMMER MATTHEWS		
	Little Miss Perfect	2004
MATUMBI	Point Of View (Squeeze A Little Lovin)	1979
MAUREEN	Thinking Of You	1990
PAUL MAURIAT & HIS ORCHERSTRA		
	Love Is Blue (L'amour Est Bleu)	1968
MAVERICKS	Dance The Night Away	1998
	I've Got This Feeling	1998
MAW presents INDIA		
	To Be In Love	1999
MAXIM	Carmen Queasy	2000
MAXWELL	Ascension (Don't Ever Wonder)	1996
	Fortunate	1999
	Lifetime	2001
	Sumthin' Sumthin' The Mantra	1997
ROBERT MAXWELL, HIS HARP & HIS ORCHESTRA		
	Shangri-La	1964
MAXX	Get-A-Way	1994
	No More (I Can't Stand It)	1994
	You Can Get It	1994
BRIAN MAY	Back To The Light	1992
	Driven By You	1991
	Too Much Love Will Kill You	1992
BRIAN MAY WITH COZY POWELL		
	Resurrection	1993

ARTIST	SONG TITLE	DATE
SIMON MAY	The Summer Of My Life	1976
SIMON MAY ORCHESTRA		
	Howard's Way	1985
MAYA/TAMPERER	Feel It	1998
	Hammer To The Heart	2000
	If You Buy This Record Your Life Will	
	Be Better	1998
JOHN MAYER	Bigger Than My Body	2003
	No Such Thing	2002
	Your Body Is A Wonderland	2002
CURTIS MAYFIELD	(Don't Worry) If There's A Hell Below	
	We're All Going To Go	1970
	Freddie's Dead	1972
	Future Shock	1973
	Kung Fu	1974
	Move On Up	1971
	Superfly	1972
	(BRAN VAN 3000 featuring CURTIS MAYFIELD)	
	Astounded	2001
MAZE featuring FRANKIE BEVERLY		
	Too Many Games	1985
KYM MAZELLE	Got To Get You Back	1989
	Was That All It Was	1990
	Young Hearts Run Free	1997
KYM MAZELLE & JOCELYN BROWN		
	Gimme All Your Lovin'	1994

ARTIST	SONG TITLE	DATE
	No More Tears (Enough Is Enough)	1994
	(MOTIV 8 WITH KYM MAZELLE)	
	Searching For The Golden Eye	1995
	(RAPINATION/KYM MAZELLE)	
	Love Me The Right Way	1992
	(ROBERT HOWARD & KYM MAZELLE)	
	Wait	1989
MAZZY STAR	Flowers In December	1996
MC JIG	Cha-Cha Slide	2004
MC LYTE	Cold Rock A Party	1996
	Ruffneck	1993
MC LYTE featuring GINA THOMPSON		
	It's All Yours	1998
MC LYTE featuring XSCAPE		
	Keep On, Keepin' On	1996
	(GEMMA FOX featuring MC LYTE)	
	Girlfriend's Story	2004
MC NEAT/DJ LUCK	Ain't No Stoppin' Us	2000
	I'm All About You	2001
	Irie	2002
	Masterblaster 2000	2000
	Piano Loco	2001
MC TUNES VERSUS 808 STATE		
	The Only Rhyme That Bites	1990
	Tunes Splits The Atom	1990

ARTIST	SONG TITLE	DATE	ARTIST	SONG TITLE	DATE
MCALMONT & BUTLER				Arrow Through Me	1979
	Bring It Back	2002		Band On The Run	1974
	Falling	2002		Beautiful Night	1997
	Yes	1995		Birthday	1990
	You Do	1995		Coming Up	1980
DAVID MCALMONT	Look At Yourself	1997		Getting Closer	1979
DAVID MCALMONT/DAVID ARNOLD				Give Ireland Back To The Irish	1972
	Diamonds Are Forever	1997		Goodnight Tonight	1979
MAC MCANALLY	It's A Crazy World	1977		Helen Wheels	1973
FRANKIE MCBRIDE	Five Little Fingers	1967		Hi, Hi, Hi/C Moon	1972
MARTINA MCBRIDE				Hope Of Deliverance	1993
	Blessed	2002		I've Had Enough	1978
	I Love You	1999		Jet	1974
	In My Daughter's Eyes	2004		Junior's Farm /Sally G	1974
	This One's For The Girls	2003		Let 'Em In	1976
	Whatever You Say	1999		Letting Go	1975
	Wrong Again	1998		Listen To What The Man Said	1975
EDWIN MCCAIN	I Could Not Ask For More	1999		Live And Let Die	1973
	I'll Be	1998		London Town	1978
C.W. MCCALL	Convoy	1975		Mary Had A Little Lamb/Little Woman	
	Wolf Creek Pass	1975		Love	1972
DAVID MCCALLUM	Communication	1966		Maybe I'm Amazed	1977
PETER MCCANN	Do You Wanna Make Love	1977		Mull Of Kintyre/Girls' School	1977
PAUL MCCARTNEY	All My Trials	1990		My Brave Face	1989
	Another Day/Oh Woman Oh Why Oh			My Love	1973
	Why	1971		No More Lonely Nights	1984

ARTIST	SONG TITLE	DATE
	Old Siam Sir	1979
	Once Upon A Long Ago	1987
	Only Love Remains	1986
	Pipes Of Peace	1983
	Press	1986
	Put It There	1990
	Silly Love Songs	1976
	So Bad	1983
	Spies Like Us	1985
	Take It Away	1982
	This One	1989
	Tropic Island Hum	2004
	Venus And Mars Rock Show	1975
	Waterfalls	1980
	We All Stand Together	1984
	With A Little Luck	1978
	Wonderful Christmastime	1979
	The World Tonight	1997
	Young Boy	1997
PAUL MCCARTNEY & MICHAEL JACKSON		
	Say Say Say	1983
PAUL MCCARTNEY & STEVIE WONDER		
	Ebony And Ivory	1982
PAUL & LINDA MCCARTNEY		
	Back Seat Of My Car	1971
	Uncle Albert/Admiral Halsey	1971

ARTIST	SONG TITLE	DATE
(MARSDEN/MCCARTNEY/JOHNSON/CHRISTIANS)		
	Ferry 'Cross The Mersey	1989
(MICHAEL JACKSON & PAUL MCCARTNEY)		
	The Girl Is Mine	1982
ALTON MCCLAIN & DESTINY		
	It Must Be Love	1979
DELBERT MCCLINTON		
	Giving It Up For Your Love	1980
MARILYN MCCOO & BILLY DAVIS JR.		
	You Don't Have To Be A Star (To Be In My Show)	1977
	Your Love	1977
VAN MCCOY	Change With The Times	1975
	The Hustle	1975
	The Shuffle	1977
	Soul Cha Cha	1977
MCCOYS	Come On Let's Go	1966
	Fever	1965
	Hang On Sloopy	1965
GEORGE MCCRAE	Honey I	1976
	I Ain't Lyin'	1975
	I Can't Leave You Alone	1974
	I Get Lifted	1975
	It's Been So Long	1975
	Rock Your Baby	1974
	Sing A Happy Song	1975

ARTIST	SONG TITLE	DATE
	You Can Have It All	1974
GWEN MCCRAE	Rockin' Chair	1975
(MUSIC & MYSTERY/GWEN MCCRAE)		
	All This Love I'm Giving	1993
MARTINE MCCUTCHEON		
	I'm Over You	2000
	I've Got You	1999
	On The Radio	2001
	Perfect Moment	1999
	Talking In Your Sleep/Love Me	1999
JULIE MCDERMOTT/AWESOME 3		
	Don't Go (96 Remix)	1996
(THIRD DIMENSION featuring JULIE MCDERMOTT)		
	Don't Go	1996
JANE MCDONALD	Cruise Into Christmas Medley	1998
MICHAEL MCDONALD		
	I Keep Forgettin' (Everytime You're Near)	1982
	No Lookin' Back	1985
	Sweet Freedom	1986
(JAMES INGRAM & MICHAEL MCDONALD)		
	Yah Mo B There	1983
(PATTI LABELLE & MICHAEL MCDONALD)		
	On My Own	1986
RONNIE MCDOWELL		
	The King Is Gone	1977

ARTIST	SONG TITLE	DATE
REBA MCENTIRE	Somebody	2004
	What Do You Say	1999
MCFADDEN & WHITEHEAD		
	Ain't No Stoppin' Us Now	1979
BRIAN MCFADDEN	Real To Me	2004
RACHELLE MCFARLANE		
	Lover	1998
BOBBY MCFERRIN	Don't Worry Be Happy	1988
MCFLY	5 Colours In Her Hair	2004
	Obviously	2004
	That Girl	2004
MIKE MCGEAR	Leave It	1974
MAUREEN MCGOVERN		
	The Continental	1976
	Different Worlds	1979
	The Morning After	1973
TIM MCGRAW	Angry All The Time	2001
	The Cowboy In Me	2002
	Don't Take The Girl	1994
	For A Little While	1998
	Grown Men Don't Cry	2001
	I Like It, I Love It	1995
	Indian Outlaw	1994
	Live Like You Were Dying	2004
	My Best Friend	1999
	My Next Thirty Years	2000

ARTIST	SONG TITLE	DATE
	Please Remember Me	1999
	Real Good Man	2003
	Red Rag Top	2002
	She's My Kind Of Rain	2003
	Something Like That	1999
	Unbroken	2002
	Watch The Wind Blow By	2003
TIM MCGRAW (WITH FAITH HILL)		
	It's Your Love	1997
	(JO DEE MESSINA WITH TIM MCGRAW)	
	Bring On The Rain	2001
FREDDIE MCGREGOR		
	Just Don't Want To Be Lonely	1987
MCGUINN, CLARK & HILLMAN		
	Don't You Write Her Off	1979
MCGUINNESS FLINT		
	Malt And Barley Blues	1971
	When I'm Dead And Gone	1970
BARRY MCGUIRE	Eve Of Destruction	1965
JOEY MCINTYRE	Stay The Same	1999
MARIA MCKEE	I'm Gonna Soothe You	1993
	Show Me Heaven	1990
KENNETH MCKELLAR		
	A Man Without Love	1966
LOREENA MCKENNITT		
	The Mummer's Dance	1998

ARTIST	SONG TITLE	DATE
BOB & DOUG MCKENZIE		
	Take Off	1982
SCOTT MCKENZIE	Like An Old Time Movie	1967
	San Francisco (Be Sure To Wear Flowers In Your Hair)	1967
BRIAN MCKNIGHT	Back At One	1999
	One Last Cry	1993
	You Should Be Mine	1998
BRIAN MCKNIGHT featuring TONE & KOBE BRYANT		
	Hold Me	1998
BRIAN MCKNIGHT featuring MASE		
	You Should Be Mine (Don't Waste Your Time)	1997
	(VANESSA WILLIAMS & BRIAN MCKNIGHT)	
	Love Is	1993
CRAIG MCLACHLAN	One Reason Why	1992
CRAIG MCLACHLAN & CHECK 1-2		
	Amanda	1990
	Mona	1990
CRAIG MCLACHLAN & DEBBIE GIBSON		
	You're The One That I Want	1993
SARAH MCLACHLAN		
	Adia	1998
	Angel	1998
	Building A Mystery	1997
	I Will Remember You (Live)	1999

ARTIST	SONG TITLE	DATE
	Sweet Surrender	1998
	(DELERIUM featuring SARAH MCLACHLAN)	
	Silence	2000
TOMMY MCLAIN	Sweet Dreams	1966
MALCOLM MCLAREN		
	Double Dutch	1983
	Madame Butterfly	1984
	Something's Jumpin' In Your Shirt	1989
	Soweto	1983
	Waltz Darling	1989
MALCOLM MCLAREN & THE MCLARENETTES		
	Soweto	1983
MALCOLM MCLAREN & THE WORLD'S FAMOUS		
SUPREME TEAM	Buffalo Gals	1982
BITTY MCLEAN	Dedicated To The One I Love	1994
	Here I Stand	1994
	It Keeps Rainin' (Tears From My Eyes)	1993
	Over The River	1995
	Pass It On	1993
	We've Only Just Begun	1995
	What Goes Around	1994
DON MCLEAN	American Pie (Pts 1 & 2)	1971
	Crying	1981
	Dreidel	1972
	Everyday	1973
	Since I Don't Have You	1981

ARTIST	SONG TITLE	DATE
	Vincent/Castles In The Air	1972
ROBIN MCNAMARA		
	Lay A Little Lovin' On Me	1970
LUTRICIA MCNEAL	Ain't That Just	1997
	The Greatest Love You'll Never Know	1998
	Someone Loves You Honey	1998
	Stranded	1998
RITA MCNEIL	Working Man	1990
RALPH MCTELL	Dreams Of You	1975
	Streets Of London	1974
CHRISTINE MCVIE	Got A Hold On Me	1984
	Love Will Show Us How	1984
ME AND YOU featuring WE THE PEOPLE BAND		
	You Never Know What You've Got	1979
ME ME ME	Hanging Around	1996
ABIGAIL MEAD & NIGEL GOULDING		
	Full Metal Jacket (I Wanna Be Your Drill	
	Instructor)	1987
SISTER JANET MEAD		
	The Lord's Prayer	1974
MEAT LOAF	Bat Out Of Hell	1993
	Couldn't Have Said It Better	2003
	Dead Ringer For Love	1981
	I'd Do Anything For Love (But I Won't	
	Do That)	1993
	I'd Lie For You (And That's The Truth)	1995

ARTIST	SONG TITLE	DATE
	Man Of Steel	2003
	Midnight At The Lost And Found	1983
	Modern Girl	1984
	Not A Dry Eye In The House	1996
	Objects In The Rear View Mirror May Appear Closer Than They Are	1994
	Paradise By The Dashboard Light	1978
	Rock And Roll Dreams Come Through	1994
	Runnin' For The Red Light (I Gotta Life)	1996
	Two Out Of Three Ain't Bad	1978
	You Took The Words Right Out Of My Mouth	1978
MEAT LOAF featuring JOHN PARR		
	Rock 'n' Roll Mercenaries	1986
MEAT LOAF featuring PATTI RUSSO		
	Is Nothing Sacred	1999
MECO	Empire Strikes Back (Medley)	1980
	Pop Goes The Movies (Part 1)	1982
	Star Wars Theme/Cantina Band	1977
	Theme From Close Encounters	1978
	Theme From The Wizard Of Oz	1978
GLENN MEDEIROS	Nothing's Gonna Change My Love For You	1987
GLENN MEDEIROS & RAY PARKER JR		
	All I'm Missing Is You	1990

ARTIST	SONG TITLE	DATE
GLENN MEDEIROS featuring BOBBY BROWN		
	She Ain't Worth It	1990
MEDICINE HEAD	(And The) Pictures In The Sky	1971
	One And One Is One	1973
	Rising Sun	1973
	Slip And Slide	1974
BILL MEDLEY	He Ain't Heavy, He's My Brother	1988
BILL MEDLEY & JENNIFER WARNES		
	(I've Had) The Time Of My Life	1987
TONY MEEHAN	Song Of Mexico	1964
	(JET HARRIS & TONY MEEHAN)	
	Applejack	1963
	Diamonds	1963
	Scarlett O'Hara	1963
MEGA CITY FOUR	Shivering Sand	1992
	Stop	1992
MEGABASS	Time To Make The Floor Burn	1990
MEGADETH	Hangar 18	1991
	Holywars... The Punishment Due	1990
	No More Mr. Nice Guy	1990
	Skin O' My Teeth	1992
	Sweating Bullets	1993
	Symphony Of Destruction	1992
	Train Of Consequences	1995
RANDY MEISNER	Deep Inside My Heart	1980
	Hearts On Fire	1981

ARTIST	SONG TITLE	DATE
	Never Been In Love	1982
MEJA	All 'Bout The Money	1998
	(RICKY MARTIN featuring MEJA)	
	Private Emotion	2000
MEL & KIM	F.L.M.	1987
	Respectable	1987
	Showing Out	1986
	That's The Way It Is	1988
MEL & TIM	Backfield In Motion	1969
	Starting All Over Again	1972
MELANIE	Bitter Bad	1973
	Brand New Key	1971
	The Nickel Song	1972
	Peace Will Come (According To Plan)	1970
	Ring The Living Bell	1972
	Ruby Tuesday	1970
	What Have They Done To My Song Ma	1971
	Will You Love Me Tomorrow	1974
MELANIE B	Feels So Good	2001
	Lullaby	2001
	Tell Me	2000
MELANIE B featuring MISSY ELLIOTT		
	I Want You Back	1998
MELANIE G	Word Up	1999
MELANIE C	Goin' Down	1999
	Northern Star	1999

ARTIST	SONG TITLE	DATE
	(BRYAN ADAMS featuring MELANIE C)	
	When You're Gone	1998
MELANIE WITH THE EDWIN HAWKINS SINGERS		
	Lay Down (Candles In The Rain)	1970
LISETTE MELENDEZ		
	Together Forever	1991
JOHN COUGAR MELLENCAMP		
	Again Tonight	1992
	Authority Song	1984
	Check It Out	1988
	Cherry Bomb	1987
	Crumblin' Down	1983
	Dance Naked	1994
	Get A Leg Up	1991
	Jack & Diane	1982
	Key West Intermezzo (I Saw You First)	1996
	Lonely Ol' Night	1985
	Paper In Fire	1987
	Pink Houses	1983
	Pop Singer	1989
	Rain On The Scarecrow	1986
	R.O.C.K. In The U.S.A. (A Salute To 60's Rock)	1986
	Rumbleseat	1986
	Small Town	1985

ARTIST	SONG TITLE	DATE
(JOHN COUGAR)	Ain't Even Done With The Night	1981
	Hand To Hold On To	1982
	Hurts So Good	1982
	I Need A Lover	1979
	This Time	1980
JOHN MELLENCAMP featuring ME'SHELL NDEGEOCELLO		
	Wild Night	1994
WILL MELLOR	No Matter What I Do	1998
	When I Need You	1998
MELLOW MAN ACE	Mentirosa	1990
KATIE MELUA	Call Off The Search	2004
	The Closest Thing To Crazy	2003
HAROLD MELVIN & THE BLUE NOTES		
	Bad Luck (Pt 1)	1975
	Don't Leave Me This Way	1977
	Get Out (And Let Me Cry)	1975
	If You Don't Know Me By Now	1972
	The Love I Lost (Pt 1)	1973
	Satisfaction Guaranteed (Or Take Your Love Back)	1974
	Wake Up Everybody (Pt 1)	1975
MEMBERS	Offshore Banking Business	1979
	Sound Of The Suburbs	1979

ARTIST	SONG TITLE	DATE
MEMBERS OF MAYDAY		
	10 In 01	2001
MEN AT LARGE	So Alone	1993
MEN AT WORK	Down Under	1982
	Dr. Heckyll & Mr. Jive	1983
	It's A Mistake	1983
	Overkill	1983
	Who Can It Be Now?	1982
MEN OF VIZION	Do You Feel Me? (...Freak You)	1999
MEN WITHOUT HATS		
	Pop Goes The World	1987
	The Safety Dance	1983
SERGIO MENDES	Alibis	1984
	Never Gonna Let You Go	1983
SERGIO MENDES & BRASIL '66		
	The Fool On The Hill	1968
	The Look Of Love	1968
	Scarborough Fair	1968
MENSWEAR	Being Brave	1996
	Daydreamer	1995
	Sleeping In	1995
	Stardust	1995
	We Love You	1996
MENTAL AS ANYTHING		
	Live It Up	1987

ARTIST	SONG TITLE	DATE
NATALIE MERCHANT		
	Carnival	1995
	Jealousy	1996
	Wonder	1995
MERCURY REV	The Dark Is Rising	2002
	Delta Sun Bottleneck Stomp	1999
	Goddess On A Hiway	1999
	Opus 40	1999
FREDDIE MERCURY	The Great Pretender	1987
	I Was Born To Love You	1985
	In My Defence	1992
	Living On My Own	1993
	Love Kills	1984
	Time	1986
FREDDIE MERCURY & MONSERRAT CABALLE		
	Barcelona	1992
MERCY	Love (Can Make You Happy)	1969
MERO	It Must Be Love	2000
MERSEYBEATS	Don't Turn Around	1964
	I Love You, Yes I Do	1965
	I Stand Accused	1966
	I Think Of You	1964
	It's Love That Really Counts	1963
	Last Night	1964
	Wishin' And Hopin'	1964
MERSEYS	Sorrow	1966

ARTIST	SONG TITLE	DATE
MERTON PARKAS	You Need Wheels	1979
MESSIAH	Temple Of Dreams	1992
	Thunderdome	1993
MESSIAH/PRECIOUS WILSON		
	I Feel Love	1992
JO DEE MESSINA	Lesson In Leavin'	1999
	Stand Beside Me	1998
	That's The Way	2000
JO DEE MESSINA with TIM MCGRAW		
	Bring On The Rain	2001
METALLICA	Enter Sandman	1991
	The $5.98 EP – Garage Days	
	Re-Revisited	1987
	Frantic	2003
	Fuel	1998
	Harvester Of Sorrow	1988
	Hero Of The Day	1996
	I Disappear	2000
	Mama Said	1996
	The Memory Remains	1997
	Nothing Else Matters	1992
	One	1989
	Sad But True	1993
	St Anger	2003
	The Unforgiven II	1998
	The Unforgiven	1991

ARTIST	SONG TITLE	DATE
	Until It Sleeps	1996
	Wherever I May Roam	1992
	Whiskey In The Jar	1999
METERS	Cissy Strut	1969
	Sophisticated Cissy	1969
METHOD MAN featuring BUSTA RHYMES		
	What's Happenin'	2004
METHOD MAN featuring D'ANGELO		
	Break Ups 2 Make Ups	1999
METHOD MAN/MARY J. BLIGE		
	I'll Be There For You/You're All I Need	
	To Get By	1995
	(B REAL/BUSTA RHYMES/COOLIO/LL COOL J/	
	METHOD MAN)	
	Hit 'Em High (The Monstars' Anthem)	1997
	(MARY J. BLIGE featuring METHOD MAN)	
	Love At 1st Sight	2003
	(REDMAN/METHOD MAN)	
	How High	1995
MEZZOFORTE	Garden Party	1983
MFSB	Sexy	1975
MFSB featuring THE THREE DEGREES		
	TSOP (The Sound Of Philadelphia)	1974
GEORGE MICHAEL	Amazing	2004
	Careless Whisper	1984
	A Different Corner	1986

ARTIST	SONG TITLE	DATE
	Faith	1987
	Fastlove	1996
	Father Figure	1988
	Flawless (Go To The City)	2004
	Freedom!	1990
	Freeek!	2002
	Heal The Pain	1991
	I Want Your Sex	1987
	Jesus To A Child	1996
	Kissing A Fool	1988
	Monkey	1988
	Older/I Can't Make You Love Me	1997
	One More Try	1988
	Outside	1998
	Praying For Time	1990
	Shoot The Dog	2002
	Spinning The Wheel	1996
	Star People '97	1997
	Too Funky	1992
	Waiting For That Day	1991
	You Have Been Loved/The Strangest	
	Thing '97	1997
GEORGE MICHAEL & MARY J. BLIGE		
	As	1999
GEORGE MICHAEL/ELTON JOHN		
	Don't Let The Sun Go Down On Me	1991

ARTIST	SONG TITLE	DATE
GEORGE MICHAEL AND QUEEN		
	Five Live (EP)	1993
	Somebody To Love	1993
(TOBY BOURKE WITH GEORGE MICHAEL)		
	Waltz Away Dreaming	1997
(ARETHA FRANKLIN & GEORGE MICHAEL)		
	I Knew You Were Waiting (For Me)	1987
(WHITNEY HOUSTON/GEORGE MICHAEL)		
	If I Told You That	2000
LEE MICHAELS	Can I Get A Witness	1971
	Do You Know What I Mean	1971
MICHEL'LE	Nicety	1990
	No More Lies	1989
	Something In My Heart	1991
KEITH MICHEL	Captain Beaky/Wilfred The Weasel	1980
	I'll Give You The Earth	1971
PRAS MICHEL	Blue Angels	1998
PRAS MICHEL featuring OL' DIRTY BASTARD & MYA		
	Ghetto Superstar (That Is What You Are)	1998
(QUEEN WITH WYCLEF JEAN FEAT PRAS MICHEL & FREE)		
	Another One Bites The Dust	1998
(DANTE THOMAS featuring PRAS)		
	Miss California	2001

ARTIST	SONG TITLE	DATE
(REFUGEE CAMP ALL STARS featuring PRAS WITH KY-MANI)		
	Avenues	1997
MICHELLE	All This Time	2004
YVETTE MICHELLE	I'm Not Feeling You	1997
MICROBE	Groovy Baby	1969
MIDDLE OF THE ROAD		
	Chirpy Chirpy Cheep Cheep	1971
	Sacramento (A Wonderful Town)	1972
	Samson And Delilah	1972
	Soley Soley	1971
	Tweedle Dee, Tweedle Dum	1971
BETTE MIDLER	Boogie Woogie Bugle Boy	1973
	Do You Want To Dance	1972
	Friends/Chapel Of Love (2 Weeks)	1973
	From A Distance	1990
	Married Man	1979
	My Mother's Eyes	1980
	The Rose	1980
	When A Man Loves A Woman	1980
	Wind Beneath My Wings	1989
MIDNIGHT OIL	Beds Are Burning	1988
	Truganini	1993
MIDNIGHT STAR	Headlines	1986
	Midas Touch	1986
	Operator	1984

ARTIST	SONG TITLE	DATE
MIGHTY DUB KATZ	Magic Carpet Ride	1997
MIGHTY MIGHTY BOSSTONES		
	The Impression That I Get	1998
MIGHTY MORPH'N POWER RANGERS		
	Power Rangers	1994
MIGIL FIVE	Mockingbird Hill	1964
	Near You	1964
MIKAILA	So In Love With Two	2000
MIKE & THE MECHANICS		
	All I Need Is A Miracle	1986
	A Beggar On A Beach Of Gold	1995
	The Living Years	1989
	Now That You've Gone	1999
	Over My Shoulder	1995
	Silent Running (On Dangerous Ground)	1985
	Taken In	1986
	Word Of Mouth	1991
MIKE	Twangling Three Fingers In A Box	1994
MIKI & GRIFF	I Wanna Stay Here	1963
JOHN MILES	Highfly	1975
	Music	1976
	Remember Yesterday	1976
	Slowdown	1977
ROBERT MILES	Children	1996
	Fable	1996

ARTIST	SONG TITLE	DATE
ROBERT MILES featuring KATHY SLEDGE		
	Freedom	1997
ROBERT MILES featuring MARIA NAYLER		
	One & One	1996
MILESTONE	I Care 'Bout You	1997
CHRISTINA MILIAN	Am To Pm	2001
	Dip It Low	2004
	When You Look At Me	2002
CHRISTINA MILIAN featuring JOE BUDDEN		
	Whatever U Want	2004
	(JA RULE featuring CHRISTINA MILIAN)	
	Between Me And You	2001
	(ROMEO featuring CHRISTINA MILIAN)	
	It's All Gravy	2002
MILK & HONEY	Hallelujah	1979
MILK & SUGAR vs JOHN PAUL YOUNG		
	Love Is In The Air	2002
MILK & SUGAR/LIZZY PATTINSON		
	Let The Sunshine In	2003
MILK INC.	In My Eyes	2002
	Land Of The Living	2003
	Walk On Water	2002
MILK INCORPORATED		
	Good Enough (La Vache)	1998
MILKY	Just The Way You Are	2002

ARTIST	SONG TITLE	DATE
FRANKIE MILLER	Be Good To Yourself	1977
	Darlin'	1978
GLENN MILLER & HIS ORCHESTRA		
	Moonlight Serenade/Little Brown Jug/In The Mood	1976
JODY MILLER	Home Of The Brave	1965
	Queen Of The House	1965
NED MILLER	From A Jack To A King	1962
ROGER MILLER	Chug-A-Lug	1964
	Dang Me	1964
	Do-Wacka-Do	1964
	Engine Engine #9	1965
	England Swings	1965
	Husbands And Wives	1966
	Kansas City Star	1965
	King Of The Road	1965
	Little Green Apples	1968
	One Dyin' And A Buryin'	1965
	Walkin' In The Sunshine	1967
	You Can't Roller Skate In A Buffalo Herd	1966
STEVE MILLER BAND		
	Abracadabra	1982
	Fly Like An Eagle	1976
	Heart Like A Wheel	1981
	Jet Airliner	1977

ARTIST	SONG TITLE	DATE
	The Joker	1973
	Jungle Love	1977
	Rock'n Me	1976
	Swingtown	1977
	Take The Money And Run	1976
LISA MILLETT/A.T.F.C.		
	Sleep Talk	2002
	(A.T.F.C. presents ONEPHATDEEVA featuring LISA MILLETT)	
	Bad Habit	2000
	(GOODFELLAS featuring LISA MILLETT)	
	Soul Heaven	2001
MILLI VANILLI	All Or Nothing	1990
	Baby Don't Forget My Number	1989
	Blame It On The Rain	1989
	Girl I'm Gonna Miss You	1989
MILLICAN & NESBITT		
	For Old Time's Sake	1974
	Vaya Con Dios (May God Be With You)	1973
MILLIE	My Boy Lollipop	1964
	Sweet William	1964
MILLS BROTHERS	Cab Driver	1968
FRANK MILLS	Music Box Dancer	1979
STEPHANIE MILLS	The Medicine Song	1984
	Never Knew Love Like This Before	1980
	What Cha Gonna Do With My Lovin'	1979

ARTIST	SONG TITLE	DATE
STEPHANIE MILLS WITH TEDDY PENDERGRASS		
	Two Hearts	1981
MILLTOWN BROTHERS		
	Which Way Should I Jump?	1991
RONNIE MILSAP	Any Day Now	1982
	I Wouldn't Have Missed It For The World	1981
	It Was Almost Like A Song	1977
	Smoky Mountain Rain	1980
	Stranger In My House	1983
	(There's) No Gettin' Over Me	1981
C.B. MILTON	It's A Loving Thing	1995
GARNET MIMMS	I'll Take Good Care Of You	1966
MINDBENDERS	Ashes To Ashes	1966
	Can't Live With You, Can't Live Without	
	You	1966
	A Groovy Kind Of Love	1966
	(WAYNE FONTANA & THE MINDBENDERS)	
	She Needs Love	1965
	Stop Look And Listen	1964
MARCELLO MINERBI		
	Zorba's Dance	1965
MINI POPS	Songs For Christmas (EP)	1987
MINIMALISTIX	Close Cover	2002
	Magic Fly	2003
MINK DEVILLE	Spanish Stroll	1977
LIZA MINNELLI	Losing My Mind	1989

ARTIST	SONG TITLE	DATE
DANNII	All I Wanna Do	1997
	Disremembrance	1998
	Everything I Wanted	1997
DANNII MINOGUE	Baby Love	1991
	Don't Wanna Lose This Feeling	2003
	Get Into You	1994
	I Begin To Wonder	2003
	I Don't Wanna Take This Pain	1991
	Jump To The Beat	1991
	Love & Kisses	1991
	Put The Needle On It	2002
	Show You The Way To Go	1992
	Success	1991
	This Is It	1993
	This Is The Way	1993
DANNII MINOGUE vs FLOWER POWER		
	You Won't Forget About Me	2004
	(RIVA featuring DANNII MINOGUE)	
	Who Do You Love Now? (Stringer)	2001
KYLIE MINOGUE	Better The Devil You Know	1990
	Breathe	1998
	Can't Get You Out Of My Head	2002
	Celebration	1992
	Chocolate	2004
	Come Into My World	2002
	Confide In Me	1994

ARTIST	SONG TITLE	DATE
	Did It Again	1997
	Finer Feelings	1992
	Give Me Just A Little More Time	1992
	Got To Be Certain	1988
	Hand On Your Heart	1989
	I Should Be So Lucky	1988
	In Your Eyes	2002
	It's No Secret	1988
	Je Ne Sais Pas Pourquoi	1988
	The Loco-Motion	1988
	Love At First Sight	2002
	Never Too Late	1989
	On A Night Like This	2000
	Please Stay	2000
	Put Yourself In My Place	1994
	Red Blooded Woman	2004
	Shocked	1991
	Slow	2003
	Some Kind Of Bliss	1997
	Spinning Around	2000
	Step Back In Time	1990
	Tears On My Pillow	1990
	What Do I Have To Do	1991
	What Kind Of Fool	1992
	Where Is The Feeling?	1995
	Word Is Out	1991

ARTIST	SONG TITLE	DATE
	Wouldn't Change A Thing	1989
KYLIE MINOGUE & JASON DONOVAN		
	Especially For You	1988
KYLIE MINOGUE/KEITH WASHINGTON		
	If You Were With Me Now	1991
(NICK CAVE & KYLIE MINOGUE)		
	Where The Wild Roses Grow	1995
(ROBBIE WILLIAMS/KYLIE MINOGUE)		
	Kids	2000
SUGAR MINOTT	Good Thing Going (We've Got A Good Thing Going)	1981
MINT CONDITION	Breakin' My Heart (Pretty Brown Eyes)	1992
	If You Love Me	1999
	U Send Me Swingin'	1994
	What Kind Of Man Would I Be	1996
	You Don't Have To Hurt No More	1997
MINT ROYALE	Blue Song	2003
	Sexiest Man In Jamaica	2002
MINT ROYALE featuring LAUREN LAVERNE		
	Don't Falter	2000
SMOKEY ROBINSON & THE MIRACLES		
	Abraham, Martin And John	1969
	Baby, Baby Don't You Cry	1969
	(Come 'Round Here) I'm The One You Need	1971
	Do It Baby	1974
	Doggone Right	1969

ARTIST	SONG TITLE	DATE
	Going To A Go-Go	1965
	Here I Go Again	1969
	I Don't Blame You At All	1971
	I Like It Like That	1964
	I Second That Emotion	1967
	If You Can Want	1968
	The Love I Saw In You Was Just A Mirage	1967
	Love Machine	1975
	More Love	1967
	My Girl Has Gone	1965
	Ooh Baby Baby	1965
	Point It Out	1969
	Special Occasion	1968
	The Tears Of A Clown	1970
	That's What Love Is Made Of	1964
	The Tracks Of My Tears	1969
	Yester Love	1968
MIRAGE	Jack Mix II	1987
	Jack Mix IV	1987
DANNY MIRROR	I Remember Elvis Presley (The King Is Dead)	1977
MIRRORBALL	Given Up	1999
MIS-TEEQ	All I Want	2001
	B With Me	2002
	Can't Get It Back	2003

ARTIST	SONG TITLE	DATE
	One Night Stand	2001
	Roll On/This Is How We Do It	2002
	Scandalous	2004
	Style	2003
	Why	2001
MISHKA	Give You All The Love	1999
MISS SHIVA	Dreams	2001
MISS X	Christine	1963
MISSION	Beyond The Pale	1988
	Butterfly On A Wheel	1990
	Deliverance	1990
	Hands Across The Ocean	1990
	Into The Blue	1990
	Like A Child Again	1992
	Never Again	1992
	Severina	1987
	Stay With Me	1986
	Tower Of Strength	1988
	Wasteland	1987
MR MISTER	Broken Wings	1985
	Is It Love	1986
	Kyrie	1986
	Something Real (Inside Me/Inside You)	1987
MISTURA featuring LLOYD MICHELS		
	The Flasher	1976
DES MITCHELL	(Welcome) To The Dance	2000

ARTIST	SONG TITLE	DATE
JONI MITCHELL	Big Yellow Taxi	1974
	Free Man In Paris	1974
	Help Me	1974
	You Turn Me On, I'm A Radio	1972
(JANET featuring Q-TIP AND JONI MITCHELL)		
	Got 'Til It's Gone	1997
WILLIE MITCHELL	Soul Serenade	1968
	20-75	1964
MIXMASTER	Grand Piano	1989
MIXTURES	The Pushbike Song	1971
HANK MIZELL	Jungle Rock	1976
MN8	Baby It's You	1995
	Dreaming	1996
	Happy	1995
	I've Got A Little Something For You	1995
	If You Only Let Me In	1995
	Pathway To The Moon	1996
	Tuff Act To Follow	1996
MO THUGS FAMILY featuring BONE THUGS-N-HARMONY		
	Ghetto Cowboy	1998
MOBILES	Drowning In Berlin	1982
MOBY	Bodyrock	1999
	Every Time You Touch Me	1995
	Extreme Ways	2002
	Feel It	1993
	Feeling So Real	1994

ARTIST	SONG TITLE	DATE
	Go	1991
	Honey	1998
	Hymn	1994
	In This World	2002
	Into The Blue	1995
	James Bond Theme	1997
	Move	1993
	Natural Blues	2000
	Porcelain	2000
	Run On	1999
	We Are All Made Of Stars	2002
	Why Does My Heart Feel So Bad	1999
MOBY featuring GWEN STEFANI		
	South Side	2000
MOCEDADES	Eres Tu (Touch The Wind)	1974
MOCK TURTLES	Can You Dig It?	1991
MODELS	Out Of Sight Out Of Mind	1986
MODERN ROMANCE		
	Ay Ay Ay Ay Moosey	1981
	Best Years Of Our Lives	1982
	Cherry Pink And Apple Blossom White	1982
	Don't Stop That Crazy Rhythm	1983
	Everybody Salsa	1981
	High Life	1983
	Queen Of The Rapping Scene (Nothing Ever Goes The Way You Plan)	1982

ARTIST	SONG TITLE	DATE
	Walking In The Rain	1983
MODERN TALKING	Brother Louie	1986
MODJO	Chillin'	2001
	Lady (Hear Me Tonight)	2000
MOFFATTS	Crazy	1999
	Until You Loved Me	1999
MOIST	Push	1995
MOJO MEN	Sit Down, I Think I Love You	1967
MOJOS	Everything's Alright	1964
	Seven Daffodils	1964
	Why Not Tonight	1964
MOKENSTEF	He's Mine	1995
MOLELLA featuring THE OUTHERE BROTHERS		
	If You Wanna Party	1995
MOLOKO	Familiar Feeling	2003
	Forever More	2003
	Fun For Me	1996
	Pure Pleasure Seeker	2000
	Sing It Back	1999
	The Time Is Now	2000
MOMENTS	Dolly My Love	1975
	Jack In The Box	1977
	Look At Me (I'm In Love)	1975
	Love On A Two-Way Street	1970
	Sexy Mama	1974

ARTIST	SONG TITLE	DATE
MOMENTS AND WHATNAUTS		
	Girls	1975
MONACO	Sweet Lips	1997
	What Do You Want From Me?	1997
PHAROAHE MONCH	Got You	2001
	Simon Says	2000
	(MOS DEF & NATE DOGG featuring	
	PHAROAHE MONCH)	
	Oh No	2001
MONEY MARK	Hand In Your Head	1998
EDDIE MONEY	Baby Hold On	1978
	Endless Nights	1987
	I Wanna Go Back	1987
	I'll Get By	1991
	The Love In Your Eyes	1989
	Maybe I'm A Fool	1979
	Peace In Our Time	1989
	Take Me Home Tonight	1986
	Think I'm In Love	1982
	Two Tickets To Paradise	1978
	Walk On Water	1988
ZOOT MONEY & THE BIG ROLL BAND		
	Big Time Operator	1966
MONICA	Angel Of Mine	1998
	Before You Walk Out Of My Life/Like	
	This And Like That	1995

ARTIST	SONG TITLE	DATE
	Don't Take It Personal (Just One Of Dem Days)	1995
	The First Night	1998
	For You I Will	1997
	Why I Love You So Much/Ain't Nobody	1996
	(BRANDY & MONICA)	
	The Boy Is Mine	1998
MONIFAH	Touch It	1998
	You	1996
MONKEES	Alternate Title	1967
	D.W. Washburn	1968
	Daydream Believer	1967
	The Girl I Knew Somewhere	1967
	I'm A Believer	1966
	(I'm Not Your) Steppin' Stone	1966
	Last Train To Clarksville	1966
	A Little Bit Me, A Little Bit You	1967
	The Monkees (EP)	1989
	Pleasant Valley Sunday	1967
	Tapioca Tundra	1968
	That Was Then, This Is Now	1986
	Valleri	1968
	Words	1967
MONKS	Nice Legs Shame About Her Face	1979
MATT MONRO	And You Smiled	1973
	For Mama	1965
	From Russia With Love	1963
	Walk Away	1964
	Without You	1965
	Yesterday	1965
GERRY MONROE	Cry	1970
	It's A Sin To Tell A Lie	1971
	Little Drops Of Silver	1971
	My Prayer	1970
	Sally	1970
MONSOON	Ever So Lonely	1982
MONSTA BOY featuring DENZIE		
	Sorry (I Didn't Know)	2000
MONSTER MAGNET	Powertrip	1999
HUGO MONTENEGRO & HIS ORCHESTRA		
	The Good, The Bad & The Ugly	1968
CHRIS MONTEZ	Call Me	1966
	Let's Dance	1962
	The More I See You	1966
	Some Kinda Fun	1963
	There Will Never Be Another You	1966
	Time After Time	1966
MONTGOMERY GENTRY		
	If You Ever Stop Loving Me	2004
	My Town	2002
	She Couldn't Change Me	2001

ARTIST	SONG TITLE	DATE
JOHN MICHAEL MONTGOMERY		
	Hold On To Me	1998
	Letters From Home	2004
	The Little Girl	2000
MELBA MONTGOMERY		
	No Charge	1974
MONTROSE AVENUE		
	Where Do I Stand?	1998
MONYAKA	Go Deh Yaka (Go To The Top)	1983
MOODY BLUES	Blue World	1983
	From The Bottom Of My Heart	1965
	Gemini Dream	1981
	Go Now!	1965
	I Know You're Out There Somewhere	1988
	I'm Just A Singer (In A Rock 'n' Roll Band)	1973
	Isn't Life Strange	1972
	Nights In White Satin	1972
	Question	1970
	Sitting At The Wheel	1983
	Steppin' In A Slide Zone	1978
	The Story In Your Eyes	1971
	Tuesday Afternoon (Forever Afternoon)	1968
	The Voice	1981
	Voices In The Sky	1968
	Your Wildest Dreams	1986

ARTIST	SONG TITLE	DATE
MICHAEL MOOG	That Sound	1999
MOONY	Dove (I'll Be Loving You)	2002
BOBBY MOORE & THE RHYTHM ACES		
	Searching For My Love	1966
CHANTE MOORE	Chante's Got A Man	1999
	Straight Up	2001
DOROTHY MOORE	Funny How Time Slips Away	1976
	I Believe You	1977
	Misty Blue	1976
DUDLEY MOORE/PETER COOK		
	Goodbye-Ee	1965
GARY MOORE	After The War	1989
	Cold Day In Hell	1992
	Empty Rooms	1985
	Friday On My Mind	1987
	Over The Hills And Far Away	1986
	Parisienne Walkways	1979
	Still Got The Blues (For You)	1990
	Story Of The Blues	1992
	Wild Frontier	1987
GARY MOORE & PHIL LYNOTT		
	Out In The Fields	1985
JACKIE MOORE	Precious Precious	1970
MANDY MOORE	Candy	2000
	I Wanna Be With You	2000
MELBA MOORE	Love's Comin' At Ya	1982

ARTIST	SONG TITLE	DATE
	Mind Up Tonight	1983
	This Is It	1976
RAY MOORE	O' My Father Had A Rabbit	1986
SAM MOORE & LOU REED		
	Soul Man	1987
TINA MOORE	Never Gonna Let You Go	1997
	Nobody Better	1998
LISA MOORISH	I'm Your Man	1995
	Love For Life	1996
	Mr Friday Night	1996
DAVID MORALES & THE BAD YARD CLUB		
	Gimme Luv (Eenie Meenie Miny Mo)	1993
	In De Ghetto	1996
DAVID MORALES presents THE FACE featuring		
JULIET ROBERTS	Needin' U II	2001
MICHAEL MORALES	What I Like About You	1989
	Who Do You Give Your Love To	1989
MORCHEEBA	Part Of The Process	1998
	Rome Wasn't Built In A Day	2000
	Trigger Hippie	1996
DEBELAH MORGAN	Dance With Me	2001
JAMIE J. MORGAN	Walk On The Wild Side	1990
RAY MORGAN	The Long And Winding Road	1970
ALANIS MORISSETTE		
	Everything	2004
	Hand In My Pocket	1995

ARTIST	SONG TITLE	DATE
	Hands Clean	2002
	Head Over Feet	1996
	Ironic	1996
	Joining You	1999
	So Pure	1999
	Thank U	1998
	You Learn	1996
ALANIS MORISSETTE		
	You Oughta Know	1995
MORJAC featuring RAZ CONWAY		
	Stars	2003
GIORGIO MORODER		
	Chase	1979
	From Here To Eternity	1977
GIORGIO MORODER & PHIL OAKEY		
	Together In Electric Dreams	1984
ENNIO MORRICONE		
	Chi Mai Theme (From 'The Life And Times Of David Lloyd George')	1981
MORRIS MINOR & THE MAJORS		
	Stutter Rap (No Sleep 'Til Bedtime)	1987
MARK MORRISON	Crazy	1996
	Horny	1996
	Let's Get Down	1995
	Moan & Groan	1997
	Return Of The Mack	1997

ARTIST	SONG TITLE	DATE
	Trippin'	1996
	Who's The Mack!	1997
MARK MORRISON & CONNER REEVES		
	Best Friend	1999
VAN MORRISON	Blue Money	1971
	Brown Eyed Girl	1967
	Come Running	1970
	Domino	1970
	Precious Time	1999
	Wild Night	1971
VAN MORRISON & JOHN LEE HOOKER		
	Gloria	1993
VAN MORRISON with CLIFF RICHARD		
	Whenever God Shines His Light	1989
MORRISSEY	Alma Matters	1997
	Boxers	1995
	The Boy Racer	1995
	Certain People I Know	1992
	Dagenham Dave	1995
	Everyday Is Like Sunday	1988
	First Of The Gang To Die	2004
	Interesting Drug	1989
	Irish Blood, English Heart	2004
	Last Of The Famous International Playboys	1989
	Let Me Kiss You	2004

ARTIST	SONG TITLE	DATE
	The More You Ignore Me, The Closer I Get	1994
	My Love Life	1991
	November Spawned A Monster	1990
	Ouija Board, Ouija Board	1989
	Our Frank	1991
	Piccadilly Palare	1990
	Pregnant For The Last Time	1991
	Satan Rejected My Soul	1998
	Sing Your Life	1991
	Suedehead	1988
	We Hate It When Our Friends Become Successful	1992
	You're The One For Me, Fatty	1992
MORRISSEY & SIOUXSIE		
	Interlude	1994
MOS DEF & NATE DOGG featuring PHAROAHE MONCH		
	Oh No	2001
MOTELS	Only The Lonely	1982
	Remember The Nights	1983
	Shame	1985
	Suddenly Last Summer	1983
WENDY MOTEN	Come In Out Of The Rain	1994
	So Close To Love	1994
MOTHER	All Funked Up	1993
MOTHERLODE	When I Die	1969

ARTIST	SONG TITLE	DATE
MOTIV 8	Break The Chain	1995
	Rockin' For Myself	1994
MOTIV 8 WITH KYM MAZELLE		
	Searching For The Golden Eye	1995
MOTLEY CRUE	Don't Go Away Mad (Just Go Away)	1990
	Dr. Feelgood	1989
	Girls, Girls, Girls	1987
	Home Sweet Home	1991
	Hooligan's Holiday	1994
	Kickstart My Heart	1989
	Primal Scream	1991
	Smokin' In The Boys Room	1985
	Without You	1990
	You're All I Need/Wild Side	1988
MOTORCYCLE	As The Rush Comes	2004
MOTORHEAD	Ace Of Spades	1980
	Bomber	1979
	The Golden Years (EP)	1980
	Iron Fist	1982
	Motorhead Live	1981
	Overkill	1979
MOTORS	Airport	1978
	Forget About You	1978
MOTT THE HOOPLE	All The Way From Memphis	1973
	All The Young Dudes	1972
	Foxy, Foxy	1974

ARTIST	SONG TITLE	DATE
	The Golden Age Of Rock And Roll	1974
	Honaloochie Boogie	1973
	Roll Away The Stone	1973
MOUNTAIN	Mississippi Queen	1970
NANA MOUSKOURI	Only Love	1986
MOUSSE T featuring EMMA LANFORD		
	Is It Cos I'm Cool?	2004
MOUSSE T vs HOT'N'JUICY		
	Horny	1998
	(TOM JONES & MOUSSE T)	
	Sex Bomb	2000
MOUTH & MCNEAL		
	How Do You Do?	1972
	I See A Star	1974
MOVE	Blackberry Way	1968
	Brontosaurus	1970
	California Man	1972
	Chinatown	1971
	Curly	1969
	Fire Brigade	1968
	Flowers In The Rain	1967
	I Can Hear The Grass Grow	1967
	Night Of Fear	1967
	Tonight	1971

ARTIST	SONG TITLE	DATE
MOVEMENT 98/CARROLL THOMPSON		
	Joy And Heartbreak	1990
MOVING PICTURES	What About Me	1982
ALISON MOYET	All Cried Out	1984
	Invisible	1985
	Is This Love?	1986
	Love Letters	1987
	Love Resurrection	1984
	That Ole Devil Called Love	1985
	This House	1991
	Weak In The Presence Of Beauty	1987
	Whispering Your Name	1994
MOZAIC	Rays Of The Rising Sun	1996
	Sing It (The Hallelujah Song)	1995
MR OIZO	Flat Beat	1999
MR ON vs THE JUNGLE BROTHERS		
	Breathe Don't Stop	2004
MR ROY	Saved	1995
MR V	Give Me Life	1994
MR. BEAN & SMEAR CAMPAIGN (featuring BRUCE DICKINSON)		
	(I Want To Be) Elected	1992
MR. BIG	Feel Like Calling Home	1977
	Just Take My Heart	1992
	Romeo	1977
	To Be With You	1991
	Wild World	1993

ARTIST	SONG TITLE	DATE
MR. BLOBBY	Christmas In Blobbyland	1995
	Mr. Blobby	1993
MR. BLOE	Groovin' With Mr. Bloe	1970
MR. CHEEKS	Lights, Camera, Action!	2001
	(LIL' KIM featuring MR. CHEEKS) The Jump Off	2003
	(X-ECUTIONERS featuring MIKE SHINODA & MR. HAHN OF LINKIN PARK) It's Goin' Down	2002
MR. HANKEY	Mr. Hankey The Christmas Poo	1999
MR. JACK	Wiggly World	1997
MR PINK presents THE PROGRAM		
	Love & Affection	2002
MR. PRESIDENT	Coco Jamboo	1997
MR. REDS vs DJ SKRIBBLE		
	Everybody Come On (Can U Feel It)	2003
MR. VEGAS	Heads High	1999
MRS WOOD	Joanna	1997
MS. DYNAMITE	Dy-Na-Mi-Tee	2002
	It Takes More	2002
	Put Him Out	2002
	(STICKY featuring MS. DYNAMITE) Booo!	2001
MTM	Don't Say You Love Me	1999

ARTIST	SONG TITLE	DATE
MTUME	Juicy Fruit	1983
MUD	The Cat Crept In	1974
	Crazy	1973
	Dyna-Mite	1973
	Hypnosis	1973
	L'L'Lucy	1975
	Lean On Me	1976
	Lonely This Christmas	1974
	Moonshine Sally	1975
	Oh Boy	1975
	One Night	1975
	Rocket	1974
	The Secrets That You Keep	1975
	Shake It Down	1976
	Show Me You're A Woman	1975
	Tiger Feet	1974
MARIA MULDAUR	I'm A Woman	1974
	Midnight At The Oasis	1974
MULL HISTORICAL SOCIETY		
	The Final Arrears	2003
	How 'Bout I Love You More	2004
	Watching Xanadu	2002
LARRY MULLEN/ADAM CLAYTON		
	Theme From Mission: Impossible	1996
SHAWN MULLINS	Lullabye	1998
SAMANTHA MUMBA	Always Come Back To Your Love	2001

ARTIST	SONG TITLE	DATE
	Baby Come On Over	2001
	Body II Body	2000
	Gotta Tell You	2000
	I'm Right Here	2002
	Lately	2001
MUNGO JERRY	Alright, Alright, Alright	1973
	Baby Jump	1971
	In The Summertime	1970
	Lady Rose	1971
	Long Legged Woman Dressed In Black	1974
	Open Up	1972
	Wild Love	1973
	You Don't Have To Be In The Army To Fight In The War	1971
MUPPETS	Halfway Down The Stairs	1977
	The Muppet Show Music Hall (EP)	1977
MURDERDOLLS	White Wedding	2003
LYDIA MURDOCK	Superstar	1983
SHIRLEY MURDOCK	As We Lay	1987
MICHAEL MURPHEY	Carolina In The Pines	1975
	Geronimo's Cadillac	1972
	Renegade	1976
	What's Forever For	1982
	Wildfire	1975
EDDIE MURPHY	Party All The Time	1985
	Put Your Mouth On Me	1989

ARTIST	SONG TITLE	DATE
ROISIN MURPHY/BORIS DLUGOSCH		
	Never Enough	2001
	(PSYCHEDELIC WALTONS featuring	
	ROISIN MURPHY)	
	Wonderland	2002
WALTER MURPHY & THE BIG APPLE BAND		
	A Fifth Of Beethoven	1976
ANNE MURRAY	Blessed Are The Believers	1981
	Broken Hearted Me	1979
	Could I Have This Dance	1980
	Danny's Song	1973
	Daydream Believer	1979
	I Just Fall In Love Again	1979
	Love Song	1973
	Shadows In The Moonlight	1979
	Snowbird	1970
	You Needed Me	1978
	You Won't See Me	1974
KEITH MURRAY/IMAJIN		
	Shorty (You Keep Playin' With My Mind)	1998
	(R. KELLY featuring KEITH MURRAY)	
	Home Alone	1998
JUNIOR MURVIN	Police And Thieves	1980
MUSE	Bliss	2001
	Butterflies & Hurricanes	2004
	Dead Star/In Your World	2002

ARTIST	SONG TITLE	DATE
	Hyper Music/Feeling Good	2001
	Hysteria	2003
	Muscle Museum	2000
	Newborn	2001
	Plug In Baby	2001
	Sing For Absolution	2004
	Sunburn	2000
	Unintended	2000
MUSIC	Freedom Fighters	2004
	Getaway	2002
	Take The Long Road And Walk It	2002
	The Truth Is No Words	2003
MUSIC & MYSTERY/GWEN MCCRAE		
	All This Love I'm Giving	1993
MUSIC EXPLOSION	Little Bit O' Soul	1967
MUSIC MACHINE	Talk Talk	1966
MUSICAL YOUTH	Never Gonna Give You Up	1983
	007	1983
	Pass The Dutchie	1982
	Sixteen	1984
	Tell Me Why	1983
	Youth Of Today	1982
MUSIQ	Dontchange	2002
	Halfcrazy	2002
	Just Friends (Sunny)	2000
MUSIQ SOULCHILD	Love	2001

ARTIST	SONG TITLE	DATE
MUSIQUE	In The Bush	1978
MUSIQUE vs U2	New Year's Dub	2001
MY BLOODY VALENTINE		
	To Here Knows When	1991
MY LIFE STORY	Duchess	1997
	It's A Girl Thing	1999
	The King Of Kissingdom	1997
	Sparkle	1996
	Strumpet	1997
	12 Reasons Why I Love Her	1996
MY VITRIOL	Always Your Way	2001
	Grounded	2001
	Moodswings/The Gentle Art Of Choking	2002
MYA	Case Of The Ex (Whatcha Gonna Do)	2000
	Free	2001
	My First Night With You	1999
	My Love Is Like... Wo	2003
MYA featuring SILKK THE SHOCKER		
	Movin' On	1998
MYA WITH SPECIAL GUEST SISQO		
	It's All About Me	1998
	(BEENIE MAN featuring MYA)	
	Girls Dem Sugar	2001
	(BLACKSTREET & MYA featuring MASE & BLINKY BLIN)	
	Take Me There	1998

ARTIST	SONG TITLE	DATE
	(CHRISTINA AGUILERA, LIL' KIM, MYA & PINK)	
	Lady Marmalade	2001
	(PRAS MICHEL featuring OL' DIRTY BASTARD & introducing MYA)	
	Ghetto Superstar (That Is What You Are)	1998
BILLIE MYERS	Kiss The Rain	1997
	Tell Me	1998
RICHARD MYHILL	It Takes Two To Tango	1978
ALANNAH MYLES	Black Velvet	1990
	Love Is	1990
MYLO	Drop The Pressure	2004
MYSTIC MERLIN	Just Can't Give You Up	1980
MYSTIKAL	Bouncin' Back (Bumpin' Me Against The Wall)	2001
	Shake Ya Ass	2000
MYSTIKAL featuring NIVEA		
	Danger (Been So Long)	2001
	(LUDACRIS featuring MYSTIKAL & INFAMOUS 2.0)	
	Move Bitch	2002
	(JOE featuring MYSTIKAL)	
	Stutter	2001
	(SILKK THE SHOCKER featuring MYSTIKAL)	
	It Ain't My Fault 1 & 2	1999
MYTOWN	Party All Night	1999
N II U	I Miss You	1994
N E R D	Maybe	2004

ARTIST	SONG TITLE	DATE
	Provider/Lapdance	2003
	Rock Star	2002
	She Wants To Move	2004
N E R D featuring LEE HARVEY & VITA		
	Lapdance	2001
*NSYNC	Bye Bye Bye	2000
	(God Must Have Spent) A Little More Time On You	1998
	Gone	2001
	I Want You Back	1998
	I'll Never Stop	2000
	It's Gotta Be Me	2000
	Pop	2001
	Tearin' Up My Heart	1999
	This I Promise You	2000
*NSYNC featuring NELLY		
	Girlfriend	2002
*NSYNC/GLORIA ESTEFAN		
	Music Of My Heart	2000
	(ALABAMA featuring *NSYNC) (God Must Have Spent) A Little More Time On You	1999
YOUSSOU N'DOUR featuring NENEH CHERRY		
	7 Seconds	1994
N'N'G featuring KALLAGHAN		
	Right Before My Eyes	2000

ARTIST	SONG TITLE	DATE
N-JOI	Adrenalin (EP)	1991
	Anthem	1991
	The Drumstick (EP)	1993
	Live In Manchester (Pts 1 & 2)	1992
N-TRANCE	D.I.S.C.O.	1997
	Destiny	2003
	Electronic Pleasure	1996
	Forever	2002
	The Mind Of The Machine	1997
	Paradise City	1998
	Shake Ya Body	2000
	Turn Up The Power	1994
N-TRANCE featuring KELLY LLORENNA		
	Set You Free	1994
N-TRANCE featuring RICARDO DA FORCE		
	Stayin' Alive	1995
N-TRANCE featuring ROD STEWART		
	Do Ya Think I'm Sexy?	1997
N-TYCE	Boom Boom	1998
	Hey DJ! (Play That Song)	1997
	Telefunkin'	1998
	We Come To Party	1997
N.O.R.E.	Nothin'	2002
N.O.R.E. FEATURING DADDY YANKEE, NINA SKY		
	Oye Mi Canto	2004
N.W.A.	Express Yourself	1990

ARTIST	SONG TITLE	DATE
	100 Miles And Runnin'	1990
N2DEEP	Back To The Hotel	1992
JIMMY NAIL	Ain't No Doubt	1992
	Big River	1995
	Country Boy	1996
	Cowboy Dreams	1995
	Crocodile Shoes	1994
	Love	1995
	Love Don't Live Here Anymore	1985
NAKATOMI	Children Of The Night	2002
NAKED EYES	Promises, Promises	1983
	There's Always Something There To Remind Me	1983
	(What) In The Name Of Love	1984
	When The Lights Go Out	1983
NALIN & KANE	Beachball	1998
NAPOLEON XIV	They're Coming To Take Me Away, Ha-Haaa!	1966
NAPPY ROOTS featuring ANTHONY HAMILTON		
	Po' Folks	2002
NARADA	Divine Emotions	1988
NARADA MICHAEL WALDEN		
	I Shoulda Loved Ya	1980
	Tonight I'm Alright	1980
NARCOTIC THRUST	I Like It	2004
	Safe From Harm	2002

ARTIST	SONG TITLE	DATE
NAS	Got Ur Self A...	2002
	I Can	2003
	If I Ruled The World	1996
	Made You Look	2002
	Nastradamus	2000
	Street Dreams	1996
NAS featuring PUFF DADDY		
	Hate Me Now	1999
(ALLURE featuring NAS)		
	Head Over Heels	1997
(JENNIFER LOPEZ featuring NAS)		
	I'm Gonna Be Alright	2002
(MISSY 'MISDEMEANOR' ELLIOTT featuring NAS, EVE & Q-TIP)		
	Hot Boyz	2000
(QB FINEST featuring NAS & BRAVEHEARTS)		
	Oochie Wally	2001
GRAHAM NASH	Chicago	1971
	Immigration Man	1972
JOHNNY NASH	Cupid	1969
	Hold Me Tight	1968
	I Can See Clearly Now	1972
	Stir It Up	1973
	Tears On My Pillow	1975
	There Are More Questions Than Answers	1972
	(What A) Wonderful World	1976

ARTIST	SONG TITLE	DATE
	You Got Soul	1969
NASHVILLE TEENS	Find My Way Back Home	1965
	Google Eye	1964
	This Little Bird	1965
	Tobacco Road	1964
NATASHA	Iko Iko	1982
ULTRA NATE	Desire	2000
	Free (The Mixes)	1998
NATURAL	Put Your Arms Around Me	2002
NATURAL BORN CHILLERS		
	Rock The Funky Beat	1997
NATURAL BORN GROOVES		
	Groovebird	1997
NATURAL FOUR	Can This Be Real	1974
NATURAL SELECTION		
	Do Anything	1991
	Hearts Don't Think They Feel	1991
NATURALS	I Should Have Known Better	1964
DAVID NAUGHTON	Makin' It	1979
NAUGHTY BY NATURE		
	Feel Me Flow	1995
	Hip Hop Hooray	1993
	O.P.P.	1991
NAUGHTY BY NATURE featuring ZHANE		
	Jamboree	1999
MARIA NAYLER	Naked And Sacred	1998

ARTIST	SONG TITLE	DATE
(ROBERT MILES featuring MARIA NAYLER)		
	One & One	1996
NAZARETH	Bad Bad Boy	1973
	Broken Down Angel	1973
	Holy Roller	1975
	Hot Tracks (EP)	1977
	Love Hurts	1975
	May The Sunshine	1979
	My White Bicycle	1975
	This Flight Tonight	1973
NEARLY GOD	Poems	1996
NED'S ATOMIC DUSTBIN		
	All I Ask Of Myself Is That I Hold Together	1995
	Happy	1991
	Intact	1992
	Not Sleeping Around	1992
	Trust	1991
SAM NEELY	Loving You Just Crosssed My Mind	1972
	You Can Have Her	1974
JOEY NEGRO	Do What You Feel	1991
	Enter Your Fantasy (EP)	1992
JOEY NEGRO featuring TAKA BOOM		
	Must Be The Music	2000
NEIGHBORHOOD	Big Yellow Taxi	1970
NEIL	Hole In My Shoe	1984

ARTIST	SONG TITLE	DATE
NELLY	E.I.	2000
	Hot In Herre	2002
	(Hot Shit) Country Grammar	2000
	Iz U	2003
	My Place/Flap Your Wings	2004
	No. 1	2001
NELLY & ST. LUNATICS		
	Batter Up	2001
NELLY featuring CITY SPUD		
	Ride Wit Me	2001
NELLY featuring JUSTIN TIMBERLAKE		
	Work It	2003
NELLY featuring KELLY ROWLAND		
	Dilemma	2002
NELLY featuring TIM MCGRAW		
	Over And Over	2004
(*NSYNC featuring NELLY)		
	Girlfriend	2002
(JAGGED EDGE featuring NELLY)		
	Where The Party At?	2001
NELSON	After The Rain	1990
	(Can't Live Without Your) Love And	
	Affection	1990
	More Than Ever	1991
	Only Time Will Tell	1991
MARC NELSON	15 Minutes	1999

ARTIST	SONG TITLE	DATE
PHYLLIS NELSON	Move Closer	1985
RICK NELSON	Fools Rush In	1963
	For You	1963
	Garden Party	1972
	It's Up To You	1963
	She Belongs To Me	1969
	The Very Thought Of You	1964
SHARA NELSON	Inside Out/Down That Road	1994
	One Goodbye In Ten	1993
	Rough With The Smooth	1995
	Uptight	1994
SHELLEY NELSON/TIN TIN OUT		
	Here's Where The Story Ends	1998
	Sometimes	1998
WILLIE NELSON	Always On My Mind	1982
	Blue Eyes Crying In The Rain	1975
	Good Hearted Woman	1976
	Let It Be Me	1982
	On The Road Again	1980
(JULIO IGLESIAS & WILLIE NELSON)		
	To All The Girls I've Loved Before	1984
(TOBY KEITH DUET WITH WILLIE NELSON)		
	Beer For My Horses	2003
NENA	99 Luftballons	1983
	99 Red Balloons	1984

ARTIST	SONG TITLE	DATE
NEON PHILHARMONIC		
	Morning Girl	1969
NEPTUNES/P. DIDDY		
	Diddy	2002
FRANCES NERO	Footsteps Following Me	1991
PETER NERO	Theme From 'Summer Of '42'	1971
MICHAEL NESMITH	Rio	1977
MICHAEL NESMITH & THE FIRST NATIONAL BAND		
	Joanne	1970
ROBBIE NEVIL	Back On Holiday	1988
	C'est La Vie	1986
	Dominoes	1987
	Just Like You	1991
	Wot's It To Ya	1987
AARON NEVILLE	Everybody Plays The Fool	1991
	Tell It Like It Is	1966
	(LINDA RONSTADT featuring AARON NEVILLE)	
	All My Life	1990
	Don't Know Much	1989
IVAN NEVILLE	Not Just Another Girl	1988
JASON NEVINS presents UKNY/HOLLY JAMES		
	I'm In Heaven	2003
JASON NEVINS vs CYPRESS HILL		
	Insane In The Brain	1999
	(RUN-DMC vs JASON NEVINS)	
	It's Like That	1998

ARTIST	SONG TITLE	DATE
NEW ATLANTIC	I Know	1992
	The Sunshine After The Rain	1994
NEW BIRTH	Dream Merchant	1975
	I Can Understand It	1973
NITE-LITERS	K-Jee	1971
NEW CHRISTY MINSTRELS		
	Today	1964
NEW COLONY SIX	I Will Always Think About You	1968
	Things I'd Like To Say	1968
NEW EDITION	Candy Girl	1983
	Cool It Now	1984
	Earth Angel	1986
	Hit Me Off	1996
	I'm Still In Love With You	1996
	If It Isn't Love	1988
	A Little Bit Of Love (Is All It Takes)	1986
	Lost In Love	1985
	Mr. Telephone Man	1984
	Something About You	1997
NEW ENGLAND	Don't Ever Wanna Lose Ya	1979
NEW FOUND GLORY		
	My Friends Over You	2002
NEW GENERATION	Smokey Blues Away	1968
NEW KIDS ON THE BLOCK		
	Call It What You Want	1991
	Cover Girl	1989

ARTIST	SONG TITLE	DATE
	Games	1991
	Hangin' Tough	1989
	I'll Be Loving You (Forever)	1989
	If You Go Away	1991
	Let's Try Again/Didn't I Blow Your Mind	1990
	Please Don't Go Girl	1988
	Step By Step	1990
	This One's For The Children	1989
	Tonight	1990
	You Got It (The Right Stuff)	1988
(NKOTB)		
	Dirty Dawg	1994
NEW MODEL ARMY	Get Me Out	1990
	Green And Grey	1989
	Here Comes The War	1993
	No Rest	1985
	Space	1991
	Stupid Question	1989
	Vagabonds	1989
NEW MUSIK	Living By Numbers	1980
	Sanctuary	1980
	The World Of Water	1980
NEW ORDER	Blue Monday	1983
	Ceremony	1981
	Confusion	1983
	Crystal	2001

ARTIST	SONG TITLE	DATE
	Fine Time	1988
	Here To Stay	2002
	1963	1995
	Procession/Everything's Gone Green	1981
	Regret	1993
	Round & Round	1989
	Ruined In A Day	1993
	Shellshock	1986
	60 Miles An Hour	2001
	Spooky	1993
	State Of The Nation	1986
	Temptation	1982
	Thieves Like Us	1984
	Touched By The Hand Of God	1987
	True Faith	1987
	True Faith — 94	1994
	World (The Price Of Love)	1993
(ENGLANDNEWORDER)		
	World In Motion	1990
NEW POWER GENERATION		
	Get Wild	1995
	The Good Life	1997
NEW RADICALS	You Get What You Give	1998
NEW SEEKERS	Anthem (One Day In Every Week)	1978
	Beg, Steal Or Borrow	1972
	Circles	1972

ARTIST	SONG TITLE	DATE
	Come Softly To Me	1972
	Goodbye Is Just Another Word	1973
	I Get A Little Sentimental Over You	1974
	I Wanna Go Back	1977
	I'd Like To Teach The World To Sing (In Perfect Harmony)	1971
	Never Ending Song Of Love	1971
	Nevertheless (I'm In Love With You)	1973
	Pinball Wizard/See Me, Feel Me (Medley)	1973
	You Won't Find Another Fool Like Me	1973
NEW SEEKERS featuring EVE GRAHAM		
	Look What They've Done To My Song Ma	1970
NEW VAUDEVILLE BAND		
	Finchley Central	1967
	Green Street Green	1967
	Peek-A-Boo	1967
	Winchester Cathedral	1966
NEW VISION	(Just) You And Me	2000
NEW WORLD	Kara, Kara	1971
	Rose Garden	1971
	Sister Jane	1972
	Tom-Tom Turnaround	1971
NEW YORK CITY	I'm Doin' Fine Now	1973
NEWBEATS	Bread And Butter	1964
	Break Away (From That Boy)	1965
	Everything's Alright	1964

ARTIST	SONG TITLE	DATE
	Run Baby Run (Back Into My Arms)	1965
BOOKER NEWBERRY III		
	Love Town	1983
MICKEY NEWBURY	An American Trilogy	1971
DAVE NEWMAN	The Lion Sleeps Tonight (Wimoweh)	1972
RANDY NEWMAN	Short People	1977
NEWTON	Sometimes When We Touch	1997
JUICE NEWTON	Angel Of The Morning	1981
	Break It To Me Gently	1982
	Heart Of The Night	1982
	Love's Been A Little Bit Hard On Me	1982
	Queen Of Hearts	1981
	The Sweetest Thing (I've Ever Known)	1981
	Tell Her No	1983
WAYNE NEWTON	Daddy Don't You Walk So Fast	1972
	Red Roses For A Blue Lady	1965
	Years	1980
OLIVIA NEWTON-JOHN		
	Banks Of The Ohio	1971
	Come On Over	1976
	Deeper Than The Night	1979
	Don't Stop Believin'	1976
	Have You Never Been Mellow	1975
	Heart Attack	1982
	Hopelessly Devoted To You	1978
	I Honestly Love You	1974

ARTIST	SONG TITLE	DATE
	If Not For You	1971
	If You Love Me (Let Me Know)	1974
	Jet	1980
	Landslide	1982
	Let It Shine/He Ain't Heavy He's My Brother	1975
	Let Me Be There	1973
	A Little More Love	1978
	Livin' In Desperate Times	1984
	Long Live Love	1974
	Magic	1980
	Make A Move On Me	1982
	Physical	1981
	Please Mr. Please	1975
	Sam	1977
	Something Better To Do	1975
	Soul Kiss	1985
	Take Me Home, Country Roads	1973
	Tied Up	1983
	Totally Hot	1979
	Twist Of Fate	1983
	What Is Life	1972
OLIVIA NEWTON-JOHN & CLIFF RICHARD		
	Had To Be	1995
	Suddenly	1980

ARTIST	SONG TITLE	DATE
OLIVIA NEWTON-JOHN & ELECTRIC LIGHT ORCHESTRA		
	Xanadu	1980
(ANDY GIBB & OLIVIA NEWTON-JOHN)		
	I Can't Help It	1980
(JOHN TRAVOLTA & OLIVIA NEWTON-JOHN)		
	Summer Nights	1978
	The Grease Megamix	1990
	You're The One That I Want	1978
NEXT OF KIN	More Love	1999
	24 Hours From You	1999
NEXT	Butta Love	1997
	I Still Love You	1998
	Too Close	1998
	Wifey	2000
(JAHEIM featuring NEXT)		
	Anything	2002
NICE	America	1968
PAUL NICHOLAS	Dancing With The Captain	1976
	Grandma's Party	1976
	Heaven On The 7th Floor	1977
	Reggae Like It Used To Be	1976
SUE NICHOLLS	Where Will You Be	1968
JOE NICHOLS	Brokenheartsville	2003
	The Impossible	2002
NICKELBACK	Feelin' Way Too Damn Good	2004
	How You Remind Me	2001

ARTIST	SONG TITLE	DATE
	Never Again	2002
	Someday	2003
	Too Bad	2002
STEVIE NICKS	After The Glitter Fades	1982
	Edge Of Seventeen (Just Like The White	
	Winged Dove)	1982
	I Can't Wait	1986
	If Anyone Falls	1983
	Leather And Lace	1981
	Rooms On Fire	1989
	Sometimes It's A Bitch	1991
	Stand Back	1983
	Talk To Me	1985
STEVIE NICKS WITH SANDY STEWART		
	Nightbird	1983
STEVIE NICKS WITH TOM PETTY & THE		
HEARTBREAKERS	Needles And Pins	1986
	Stop Draggin' My Heart Around	1981
NICOLE featuring MISS 'MISDEMEANOR' ELLIOTT		
& MOCHA	Make It Hot	1998
NICOLE	A Little Peace	1982
NIELSEN/PEARSON	If You Should Sail	1980
NIGEL & MARVIN	Follow Da Leader	2002
NIGHT RANGER	Don't Tell Me You Love Me	1983
NIGHT	Hot Summer Nights	1979

ARTIST	SONG TITLE	DATE
	(CHRIS THOMPSON & NIGHT)	
	If You Remember Me	1979
NIGHTCRAWLERS	Push The Feeling On	1995
NIGHTCRAWLERS featuring JOHN REID		
	Don't Let The Feeling Go	1995
	Let's Push It	1996
	Should I Ever (Fall In Love)	1996
	Surrender Your Love	1995
NIGHTCRAWLERS featuring JOHN REID & ALYSHA		
WARREN	Keep On Pushing Our Love	1996
MAXINE NIGHTINGALE		
	Lead Me On	1979
	Love Hit Me	1977
	Right Back Where We Started From	1976
NIGHTMARES ON WAX		
	Aftermath/I'm For Real	1990
NIGHT RANGER	Don't Tell Me You Love Me	1983
	Four In The Morning (I Can't Take Any	
	More)	1985
	Goodbye	1985
	Sentimental Street	1985
	Sister Christian	1984
	When You Close Your Eyes	1984
NIKKI	Notice Me	1990
KURT NILSEN	She's So High	2004

ARTIST	SONG TITLE	DATE
NILSSON	Coconut	1972
	Daybreak	1974
	Everybody's Talkin'	1969
	I Guess The Lord Must Be In New York City	1969
	Jump Into The Fire	1972
	Me And My Arrow	1971
	Spaceman	1972
	Without You	1971
CHARLOTTE NILSSON		
	Take Me To Your Heaven	1999
NINA SKY	Move Ya Body	2004
NINE DAYS	Absolutely (Story Of A Girl)	2000
NINE INCH NAILS	Closer	1994
	The Day The World Went Away	1999
	Sin	1991
	We're In This Together	1999
999	Homicide	1978
911	All I Want Is You	1998
	Bodyshakin'	1997
	The Day We Find Love	1997
	Don't Make Me Wait	1996
	How Do You Want Me To Love You?	1998
	The Journey	1997
	A Little Bit More	1999
	Love Sensation	1996
	More Than A Woman	1998

ARTIST	SONG TITLE	DATE
	Night To Remember	1996
	Party People... Friday Night	1997
	Private Number	1999
	Wonderland	1999
1910 FRUITGUM CO.		
	Goody Goody Gumdrops	1968
	Indian Giver	1969
	1,2,3, Red Light	1968
	Simon Says	1968
	Special Delivery	1969
98 DEGREES	Because Of You	1998
	Give Me Just One Night (Una Noche)	2000
	The Hardest Thing	1999
	I Do (Cherish You)	1999
	Invisible Man	1997
	My Everything	2000
	Thank God I Found You (With Mariah Carey featuring Joe)	1999
95 SOUTH	Whoot, There It Is	1993
99TH FLOOR ELEVATORS featuring TONY DE VIT		
	Hooked	1995
	I'll Be There	1996
NIRVANA	All Apologies/Rape Me	1993
	Come As You Are	1992
	Heart-Shaped Box	1993
	In Bloom	1992

ARTIST	SONG TITLE	DATE
	Lithium	1992
	Rainbow Chaser	1969
	Smells Like Teen Spirit	1991
	(NIRVANA/JESUS LIZARD)	
	Puss/Oh, The Guilt	1993
NITEFLYTE	If You Want It	1979
NITRO DELUXE	Let's Get Brutal	1988
NITTY GRITTY DIRT BAND		
	An American Dream	1979
	Make A Little Magic	1980
	Mr. Bojangles	1970
NIVEA	Laundromat/Don't Mess With My Man	2003
NIVEA featuring MYSTIKAL		
	Danger (Been So Long)	2001
NO DOUBT	Don't Speak	1997
	Ex-Girlfriend	2000
	Hella Good	2002
	Hey Baby	2002
	It's My Life/Bathwater	2004
	Just A Girl	1995
	New	1999
	Simple Kind Of Life	2000
	Spiderwebs	1997
	Underneath It All	2002
NO DOUBT featuring BOUNTY KILLER		
	Hey Baby	2001

ARTIST	SONG TITLE	DATE
NO MERCY	Kiss You All Over	1997
	Please Don't Go	1997
	Where Do You Go	1996
NO WAY SIS	I'd Like To Teach The World To Sing	1996
CLIFF NOBLES & CO.		
	The Horse	1968
NODDY	Make Way For Noddy	2003
NOISE NEXT DOOR	Lock Up Ya Daughters/Ministry Of Mayhem	2004
BERNIE NOLAN	Macushla	2004
KENNY NOLAN	I Like Dreamin'	1976
	Love's Grown Deep	1977
NOLANS	Attention To Me	1981
	Chemistry	1981
	Don't Love Me Too Hard	1982
	Don't Make Waves	1980
	Gotta Pull Myself Together	1980
	I'm In The Mood For Dancing	1979
	Spirit, Body And Soul	1979
	Who's Gonna Rock You	1980
NOMAD	Just A Groove	1991
NOMAD featuring MC MIKEE FREEDOM		
	(I Wanna Give You) Devotion	1991
NONCHALANT	5 O'Clock	1996
PETER NOONE	Oh You Pretty Thing	1971
NOREAGA	Superthug	1998

ARTIST	SONG TITLE	DATE
CHRIS NORMAN/SUZI QUATRO		
	Stumblin' In	1979
NORTH AND SOUTH		
	Breathing	1997
	I'm A Man Not A Boy	1997
	No Sweat '98	1998
	Tarantino's New Star	1997
FREDDIE NORTH	She's All I Got	1971
NORTHERN HEIGHTZ		
	Look At Us	2004
NORTHERN LINE	All Around The World	2000
	Love On The Northern Line	2000
	Run For Your Life	1999
NORTHERN UPROAR		
	Any Way You Look	1997
	From A Window/This Morning	1996
	Livin' It Up	1996
NORTHSIDE	My Rising Star	1990
	Take 5	1991
NOTORIOUS B.I.G.	Big Poppa/Warning	1995
	Hypnotize	1997
	Juicy	1994
	One More Chance/Stay With Me	1995
NOTORIOUS B.I.G. featuring 112		
	Sky's The Limit/Going Back To Cali	1997

ARTIST	SONG TITLE	DATE
NOTORIOUS B.I.G. featuring PUFF DADDY & LIL' KIM		
	Notorious B.I.G.	2000
NOTORIOUS B.I.G. featuring PUFF DADDY & MASE		
	Mo Money Mo Problems	1997
	(112 featuring THE NOTORIOUS B.I.G.)	
	Only You	1996
	(2PAC & THE NOTORIOUS B.I.G.)	
	Runnin'	1998
	(JUNIOR M.A.F.I.A. featuring THE NOTORIOUS B.I.G.)	
	Get Money	1996
	(PUFF DADDY & FAMILY featuring THE NOTORIOUS B.I.G.)	
	Victory	1998
	(TOTAL featuring THE NOTORIOUS B.I.G.)	
	Can't You See	1995
	(TUPAC featuring THE NOTORIOUS B.I.G.)	
	Runnin' (Dying To Live)	2004
NOTTINGHAM FOREST WITH PAPER LACE		
	We Got The Whole World In Our Hands	1978
ALDO NOVA	Fantasy	1982
NOVASPACE	Time After Time	2003
NOVY vs ENIAC	Pumpin	2000
	Superstar	1998
NU COLOURS	Desire	1996
	Power	1993

ARTIST	SONG TITLE	DATE
	Special Kind Of Lover	1996
NU FLAVOR	Heaven	1997
NU GENERATION	In Your Arms (Rescue Me)	2000
NU SHOOZ	I Can't Wait	1986
	Point Of No Return	1986
NU SOUL featuring KELLI RICH		
	Hide-A-Way	1996
TED NUGENT	Cat Scratch Fever	1977
NUKLEUZ DJ S	DJ Nation	2002
	DJ Nation — Bootleg Edition	2003
GARY NUMAN	Berserker	1984
	Cars	1980
	Complex	1979
	I Can't Stop	1986
	I Die: You Die	1980
	The Live EP	1985
	Music For Chameleons	1982
	No More Lies	1988
	Rip	2002
	She's Got Claws	1981
	Sister Surprise	1983
	This Is Love	1986
	This Wreckage	1980
	Warriors	1983
	We Are Glass	1980
	We Take Mystery (To Bed)	1982

ARTIST	SONG TITLE	DATE
	White Boys And Heroes	1982
GARY NUMAN & DRAMATIS		
	Love Needs No Disguise	1981
GARY NUMAN vs RICO		
	Crazier	2003
	(RADIO HEART featuring GARY NUMAN)	
	Radio Heart	1987
	(SHARPE & NUMAN)	
	Change Your Mind	1985
NUSH	U Girls (Look So Sexy)	1995
NUYORICAN SOUL featuring INDIA		
	Runaway	1997
NUYORICAN SOUL featuring JOCELYN BROWN		
	I Am The Black Gold Of The Sun	1997
	It's Alright, I Feel It!	1997
NYCC	Fight For Your Right (To Party)	1998
NYLONS	Kiss Him Goodbye	1987
O-TOWN	All Or Nothing	2001
	Liquid Dreams	2001
	Love Should Be A Crime	2002
	These Are The Days	2003
	We Fit Together	2001
O-ZONE	Dragostea Din Tei	2004
O.R.G.A.N.	To The World	1998
OAK RIDGE BOYS	Bobbie Sue	1982
	Elvira	1981

ARTIST	SONG TITLE	DATE
(RICK PINETTE AND OAK)		
	King Of The Hill	1980
OAKENFOLD	The Harder They Come	2003
	Southern Sun/Ready Steady Go	2002
	Starry Eyed Surprise	2002
PHIL OAKEY/GIORGIO MORODER		
	Together In Electric Dreams	1984
OASIS	All Around The World	1998
	Cigarettes & Alcohol	1994
	D'You Know What I Mean?	1997
	Don't Look Back In Anger	1996
	Go Let It Out	2000
	The Hindu Times	2002
	Little By Little/She Is Love	2002
	Live Forever	1994
	Roll With It	1995
	Shakermaker	1994
	Some Might Say	1995
	Songbird	2003
	Stand By Me	1997
	Stop Crying Your Heart Out	2002
	Sunday Morning Call	2000
	Supersonic	1994
	Whatever	1994
	Who Feels Love?	2000
	Wonderwall	1996

ARTIST	SONG TITLE	DATE
JOHN O'BANION	Love You Like I Never Loved Before	1981
RIC OCASEK	Emotion In Motion	1986
OCEAN	Put Your Hand In The Hand	1971
OCEAN COLOUR SCENE		
	Better Day	1997
	The Circle	1996
	The Day We Caught The Train	1996
	Golden Gate Bridge	2004
	Hundred Mile High City	1997
	I Just Need Myself	2003
	It's A Beautiful Thing	1998
	July/I Am The News	2000
	Make The Deal	2003
	Profit In Peace	1999
	The Riverboat Song	1996
	So Low	1999
	Travellers Tune	1997
	Up On The Down Side	2001
	You've Got It Bad	1996
BILLY OCEAN	Calypso Crazy	1988
	Caribbean Queen (No More Love On The Run)	1984
	The Colour Of Love	1988
	Get Outta My Dreams Get Into My Car	1988
	L.O.D. (Love On Delivery)	1976
	License To Chill	1989

ARTIST	SONG TITLE	DATE
	Love Is Forever	1986
	Love Really Hurts Without You	1976
	Love Zone	1986
	Loverboy	1984
	Red Light Spells Danger	1977
	Stop Me (If You've Heard It All Before)	1976
	Suddenly	1985
	There'll Be Sad Songs (To Make You Cry)	1986
	When The Going Gets Tough, The Tough Get Going	1985
OCEANIC	Controlling Me	1992
	Insanity	1991
	Wicked Love	1991
OCEANLAB	Satellite	2004
DES O'CONNOR	Careless Hands	1967
	Dick-A-Dum-Dum (Kings Road)	1969
	I Pretend	1968
	I'll Go On Hoping	1970
	Loneliness	1969
	One, Two, Three O'Leary	1968
	The Tip Of My Fingers	1970
	(ROGER WHITTAKER & DES O'CONNOR)	
	The Skye Boat Song	1986
HAZEL O'CONNOR	D-Days	1981
	Eighth Day	1980
	Will You	1981

ARTIST	SONG TITLE	DATE
SINEAD O'CONNOR	The Emperor's New Clothes	1990
	Gospel Oak (EP)	1997
	Mandinka	1988
	Nothing Compares 2 U	1990
	Success Has Made A Failure Of Our Home	1992
	Thank You For Hearing Me	1994
	(SHANE MACGOWAN & SINEAD O'CONNOR)	
	Haunted	1995
OCTOPUS	Saved	1996
ALAN O'DAY	Undercover Angel	1977
KENNY O'DELL	Beautiful People	1967
DANIEL O'DONNELL		
	A Christmas Kiss	1999
	Footsteps	1996
	Give A Little Love	1998
	I Just Want To Dance With You	1992
	Light A Candle	2000
	The Love Songs (EP)	1997
	The Magic Is There	1998
	Morning Has Broken	2000
	Singing The Blues	1994
	Timeless	1996
	Uno Mas	1999
	The Way Dreams Are	1999
	What Ever Happened To Old Fashioned Love	1993

ARTIST	SONG TITLE	DATE
	You Raise Me Up	2003
DANIEL O'DONNELL & MARY DUFF		
	Secret Love	1995
ODYSSEY	Going Back To My Roots	1981
	Hang Together	1981
	If You're Lookin' For A Way Out	1980
	Inside Out	1982
	Native New Yorker	1977
	Use It Up And Wear It Out	1980
ESTHER & ABI OFARIM		
	Cinderella Rockafella	1968
	One More Dance	1968
OFF-SHORE	I Can't Take The Power	1990
OFFSPRING	All I Want	1997
	Hit That	2004
	The Kids Aren't Alright	1999
	Million Miles Away	2001
	Original Prankster	2000
	Pretty Fly (For A White Guy)	1999
	Self Esteem	1995
	Want You Bad	2001
	Why Don't You Get A Job?	1999
OH WELL	Oh Well	1989
OHIO EXPRESS	Beg, Borrow Or Steal	1967
	Chewy Chewy	1968
	Down At Lulu's	1968

ARTIST	SONG TITLE	DATE
	Mercy	1969
	Yummy Yummy Yummy	1969
OHIO PLAYERS	Ecstasy	1973
	Fire	1984
	Fopp	1976
	Funky Worm	1973
	Love Rollercoaster	1975
	Skin Tight	1974
	Sweet Sticky Thing	1975
	Who'd She Coo?	1976
O'JAYS	Back Stabbers	1972
	Brandy	1978
	Darlin' Darlin' Baby (Sweet, Tender, Love)	1977
	For The Love Of Money	1974
	Forever Mine	1979
	I Love Music	1976
	Livin' For The Weekend	1976
	Love Train	1973
	Put Your Hands Together	1973
	Sing A Happy Song	1979
	Time To Get Down	1973
	Used Ta Be My Girl	1978
OK GO	Get Over It	2003
O'KAYSIONS	Girl Watcher	1968
DANNY O'KEEFE	Goodtime Charlie's Got The Blues	1972

ARTIST	SONG TITLE	DATE
OL' DIRTY BASTARD featuring KELIS		
	Got Your Money	1999
	(PRAS MICHEL featuring OL' DIRTY BASTARD & introducing MYA)	
	Ghetto Superstar (That Is What You Are)	1998
OL' SKOOL (featuring KEITH SWEAT & XSCAPE		
	Am I Dreaming	1998
MIKE OLDFIELD	Blue Peter	1979
	Guilty	1979
	In Dulce Jubilo/On Horseback	1975
	Moonlight Shadow	1983
	Portsmouth	1976
	Sentinel	1992
	Tattoo	1992
	Tubular Bells	1974
SALLY OLDFIELD	Mirrors	1978
OLIVE	Outlaw	1997
	You're Not Alone	1997
OLIVER	Good Morning Starshine	1969
	Jean	1979
	Sunday Mornin'	1969
OLIVIA	Bizounce	2001
OLLIE & JERRY	Breakin'... There's No Stopping Us	1984
NIGEL OLSSON	Dancin' Shoes	1978
	Little Bit Of Soap	1979

ARTIST	SONG TITLE	DATE
OLYMPIC ORCHESTRA		
	Reilly	1983
OLYMPIC RUNNERS	The Bitch	1979
	Get It While You Can	1978
	Sir Dancealot	1979
OMAR	Golden Brown	1997
	Say Nothin'	1997
	There's Nothing Like This	1991
OMC	How Bizarre	1996
FRANK O'MOIRAGHI featuring AMNESIA		
	Feel My Body	1996
ONE	One More Chance	1997
I GIANT LEAP	My Culture	2002
112	Come See Me	1996
	Cupid	1997
	Dance With Me	2001
	It's Over Now	2001
	Peaches & Cream	2001
112 featuring LIL'Z		
	Anywhere	1999
112 featuring MASE		
	Love Me	1998
112 featuring THE NOTORIOUS B.I.G.		
	Only You	1996
	(ALLURE featuring 112)	
	All Cried Out	1997

ARTIST	SONG TITLE	DATE
	(LIL' ZANE featuring 112)	
	Callin' Me	2000
	(THE NOTORIOUS B.I.G. featuring 112)	
	Sky's The Limit/Going Back To Cali	1997
	(PUFF DADDY & FAITH EVANS featuring 112)	
	I'll Be Missing You	1997
ONE 2 MANY	Downtown	1989
ONE DOVE	Breakdown	1993
	Why Don't You Take Me?	1994
187 LOCKDOWN	The Don	1998
	Gunman	1997
	Kung-Fu	1998
100 PROOF AGED IN SOUL		
	Somebody's Been Sleeping	1970
ONE HUNDRED TON & A FEATHER		
	It Only Takes A Minute	1976
1000 CLOWNS	(Not The) Greatest Rapper	1999
ONE TRUE VOICE	Sacred Trust/After You're Gone (I'll Still	
	Be Loving You)	2002
	Shakespeare's (Way With) Words	2003
ALEXANDER O'NEAL		
	All True Man	1991
	Criticize	1987
	Fake	1987
	Hitmix (Official Bootleg Mega-Mix)	1989
	If You Were Here Tonight	1986

ARTIST	SONG TITLE	DATE
	In The Middle	1993
	Let's Get Together	1996
	Love Makes No Sense	1993
	Never Knew Love Like This	1988
	(CHERRELLE WITH ALEXANDER O'NEAL)	
	Saturday Love	1986
JAMIE O'NEAL	There Is No Arizona	2000
	When I Think About Angels	2001
SHAQUILLE O'NEAL		
	(I Know I Got) Skillz	1993
	You Can't Stop The Reign	1997
	(FU-SCHNICKENS WITH SHAQUILLE O'NEAL)	
	What's Up Doc? (Can We Rock)	1993
ONEPHATDEEVA/A.T.F.C.		
	In And Out Of My Life	1999
	(A.T.F.C. presents ONEPHATDEEVA featuring	
	LISA MILLETT)	
	Bad Habit	2000
THE ONES	Flawless	2001
YOKO ONO	Walking On Thin Ice	1981
	(JOHN & YOKO & THE PLASTIC ONO BAND)	
	Happy Xmas (War Is Over)	2003
ONYX	Slam	1993
	Throw Ya Gunz	1993
OOBERMAN	Blossoms Falling	1999
OPM	El Capitan	2002

ARTIST	SONG TITLE	DATE
	Heaven Is A Halfpipe	2001
OPTIMYSTIC	Nothing But Love	1994
OPUS	Live Is Life	1986
OPUS III	It's A Fine Day	1992
ORANGE JUICE	Rip It Up	1983
ORB	Assassin	1992
	Asylum	1997
	Blue Room	1992
	Little Fluffy Clouds	1993
	Once More	2001
	Oxbow Lakes	1995
	Perpetual Dawn	1994
	Toxygene	1997
ROY ORBISON	Blue Bayou/Mean Woman Blues	1963
	Borne On The Wind	1964
	Breakin' Up Is Breakin' My Heart	1966
	Crawling Back	1965
	Falling	1963
	Goodnight	1965
	Heartbreak Radio	1992
	I Drove All Night	1992
	In Dreams	1963
	It's Over	1964
	Lana	1966
	My Friend	1969
	Oh, Pretty Woman	1964

ARTIST	SONG TITLE	DATE
	Penny Arcade	1969
	Pretty Paper	1963
	Ride Away	1965
	(Say) You're My Girl	1965
	She's A Mystery To Me	1989
	So Good	1967
	There Won't Be Many Coming Home	1966
	Too Soon To Know	1966
	Twinkle Toes	1966
	Walk On	1968
	You Got It	1989
ROY ORBISON & K.D. LANG		
	Crying	1992
WILLIAM ORBIT	Barber's Adagio For Strings	1999
	Ravel's Pavane Pour Une Infante Defunte	2000
	(PINK featuring WILLIAM ORBIT)	
	Feel Good Time	2003
ORBITAL	Are We Here?	1994
	The Box	1996
	Chime	1990
	Funny Break (One Is Enough)	2001
	Mutations (EP)	1992
	Nothing Left	1999
	One Perfect Sunrise	2004
	Radiccio (EP)	1992
	Rest & Play (EP)	2002

ARTIST	SONG TITLE	DATE
	The Saint	1997
	Satan	1997
	Style	1999
ORBITAL & ANGELO BADALAMENTI		
	Beached	2000
ORCHESTRA ON THE HALF SHELL		
	Turtle Rhapsody	1990
ORCHESTRAL MANOEUVRES IN THE DARK (OMD)		
	Dream Of Me (Based On Love's Theme)	1993
	Dreaming	1988
	Enola Gay	1980
	(Forever) Live And Die	1986
	Genetic Engineering	1983
	If You Leave	1986
	Joan Of Arc	1981
	Locomotion	1984
	Maid Of Orleans (The Waltz Joan Of Arc)	1982
	Messages	1980
	Pandora's Box	1991
	Sailing On The Seven Seas	1991
	The OMD Remixes	1998
	Secret	1985
	So In Love	1985
	Souvenir	1981
	Stand Above Me	1993
	Talking Loud And Clear	1984

ARTIST	SONG TITLE	DATE
	Tesla Girls	1984
	Walking On The Milky Way	1996
ORDINARY BOYS	Seaside	2004
	Talk Talk Talk	2004
	Week In Week Out	2004
RAUL ORELLANA	The Real Wild House	1989
ORIGINAL	B 2 Gether	1995
	I Luv U Baby	1995
ORIGINAL CASTE	One Tin Soldier	1969
ORIGINALS	Baby, I'm For Real	1969
	The Bells	1970
ORION	Eternity	2000
TONY ORLANDO & DAWN		
	Candida	1970
	Cupid	1976
	He Don't Love You (Like I Love You)	1975
	I Play And Sing	1971
	Knock Three Times	1970
	Look In My Eyes Pretty Woman	1974
	Mornin' Beautiful	1975
	Say, Has Anybody Seen My Sweet Gypsy Rose	1973
	Steppin' Out (Gonna Boogie Tonight)	1974
	Summer Sand	1971
	Tie A Yellow Ribbon Round The Old Oak Tree	1973

ARTIST	SONG TITLE	DATE
	What Are You Doing Sunday	1971
	Who's In The Strawberry Patch With Sally	1974
	You're All I Need To Get By	1975
ORLEANS	Dance With Me	1975
	Love Takes Time	1979
	Still The One	1976
BENJAMIN ORR	Stay The Night	1986
ROBERT ELLIS ORRALL WITH CARLENE CARTER		
	I Couldn't Say No	1983
STACIE ORRICO	I Could Be The One	2004
	I Promise	2004
	Stuck	2003
	(There's Gotta Be) More To Life	2003
BETH ORTON	Best Bit (EP)	1997
	Central Reservation	1999
	She Cries Your Name	1997
	Stolen Car	1999
JEFFREY OSBORNE	The Borderlines	1985
	Don't You Get So Mad	1983
	I Really Don't Need No Light	1982
	On The Wings Of Love	1982
	Stay With Me Tonight	1983
	You Should Be Mine (The Woo Woo Song)	1986
	(JOYCE KENNEDY & JEFFREY OSBORNE)	
	The Last Time I Made Love	1984

ARTIST	SONG TITLE	DATE
	(DIONNE WARWICK & JEFFREY OSBORNE)	
	Love Power	1987
JOAN OSBORNE	One Of Us	1995
	St. Teresa	1996
KELLY OSBOURNE	Papa Don't Preach	2002
	Shut Up	2003
	(OZZY & KELLY OSBOURNE)	
	Changes	2003
OZZY OSBOURNE	Bark At The Moon	1983
	Dreamer/Gets Me Through	2002
	Mama, I'm Coming Home	1992
	No More Tears	1991
	Perry Mason	1995
	Shot In The Dark	1986
	So Tired	1984
	(LITA FORD & OZZY OSBOURNE)	
	Close My Eyes Forever	1989
OZZY & KELLY OSBOURNE		
	Changes	2003
OSIBISA	Dance The Body Music	1976
	Sunshine Day	1976
DONNY OSMOND	Are You Lonesome Tonight/When I Fall In Love	1973
	Breeze On By	2004
	C'mon Marianne	1976
	Go Away Little Girl	1971

ARTIST	SONG TITLE	DATE
	Hey Girl/I Knew You When	1971
	A Million To One	1973
	My Love Is A Fire	1990
	Puppy Love	1972
	Sacred Emotion	1989
	Soldier Of Love	1989
	Sweet And Innocent	1971
	Too Young	1972
	The Twelfth Of Never	1973
	Where Did All The Good Times Go	1974
	Why/Lonely Boy	1972
	Young Love	1973
DONNY & MARIE OSMOND		
	Ain't Nothing Like The Real Thing	1976
	Deep Purple	1975
	I'm Leaving It (All) Up To You	1974
	Make The World Go Away	1975
	Morning Side Of The Mountain	1974
	On The Shelf	1978
	(You're My) Soul And Inspiration	1977
LITTLE JIMMY OSMOND		
	I'm Gonna Knock On Your Door	1974
	Long Haired Lover From Liverpool	1972
	Tweedlee Dee	1973
MARIE OSMOND	Paper Roses	1973
	This Is The Way That I Feel	1977

ARTIST	SONG TITLE	DATE
	Who's Sorry Now	1975
OSMONDS	Crazy Horses	1972
	Double Lovin'	1971
	Down By The Lazy River	1972
	Goin' Home	1973
	Having A Party	1975
	Hold Her Tight	1972
	I Can't Live A Dream	1976
	I Can't Stop	1974
	I'm Still Gonna Need You	1975
	Let Me In	1973
	Love Me For A Reason	1974
	One Bad Apple	1971
	The Proud One	1975
	Yo-Yo	1971
GILBERT O'SULLIVAN		
	Alone Again (Naturally)	1972
	Christmas Song	1974
	Clair	1972
	Get Down	1973
	Happiness Is Me And You	1974
	I Don't Love You But I Think I Like You	1975
	No Matter How I Try	1971
	Nothing Rhymed	1970
	Ooh Baby	1973
	Ooh-Wakka-Doo-Wakka-Day	1972

ARTIST	SONG TITLE	DATE
	Out Of The Question	1973
	Underneath The Blanket	1971
	We Will	1971
	What's In A Kiss	1980
	Why, Oh Why, Oh Why	1973
OT QUARTET	Hold That Sucker Down	1994
OTHER ONES	Holiday	1987
THE OTHERS	Stan Bowles	2004
OTT	All Out Of Love	1997
	Forever Girl	1997
	Let Me In	1997
	The Story Of Love	1998
OTTAWAN	D.I.S.C.O.	1980
	Hands Up (Give Me Your Heart)	1981
JOHN OTWAY	Bunsen Burner	2002
JOHN OTWAY & WILD WILLY BARRETT		
	Really Free	1977
OUI 3	Break From The Old Routine	1993
	Fact Of Life	1994
	For What It's Worth	1993
OUR KID	You Just Might See Me Cry	1976
OUTFIELD	All The Love In The World	1986
	For You	1990
	Since You've Been Gone	1987
	Voices Of Babylon	1989
	Your Love	1986

ARTIST	SONG TITLE	DATE
OUTHERE BROTHERS		
	Boom Boom Boom	1995
	Don't Stop (Wiggle Wiggle)	1995
	La La La Hey Hey	1995
	Let Me Hear You Say 'Ole Ole'	1997
(MOLELLA featuring THE OUTHERE BROTHERS)		
	If You Wanna Party	1995
OUTKAST	ATLiens	1996
	Elevators (Me & You)	1996
	Hey Ya!	2003
	Ms. Jackson	2000
	Player's Ball	1994
	Roses	2004
	So Fresh, So Clean	2001
OUTKAST featuring KILLER MIKE		
	The Whole World	2001
OUTLANDISH	Gunatanamo	2003
OUTLAWS	(Ghost) Riders In The Sky	1980
	There Goes Another Love Song	1975
OUTSIDERS	Girl In Love	1966
	Help Me Girl	1966
	Respectable	1966
	Time Won't Let Me	1966
OVERLANDERS	Michelle	1966
MARK OWEN	Alone Without You	2003
	Child	1996

ARTIST	SONG TITLE	DATE
	Clementine	1997
	Four Minute Warning	2003
	I Am What I Am	1997
	Makin' Out	2004
SID OWEN	Good Thing Going	2000
BUCK OWENS	I've Got A Tiger By The Tail	1965
ROBERT OWENS	I'll Be Your Friend	1997
	(FAB FOR featuring ROBERT OWENS)	
	Last Night A DJ Blew My Mind	2003
OXIDE & NEUTRINO	Bound 4 Da Reload (Casualty)	2000
	Devil's Nightmare	2001
	Rap Dis/Only Wanna Know U Cos Ure	
	Famous	2001
	Up Middle Finger	2001
OXIDE & NEUTRINO featuring MEGAMAN, ROMEO &		
LISA MAFFI	No Good 4 Me	2000
OXIDE & NEUTRINO featuring KOWDEAN		
	Dem Girlz (I Don't Know Why)	2002
OXO	Whirly Girl	1983
OXYGEN featuring ANDREA BRITTON		
	Am I On Your Mind	2003
OZARK MOUNTAIN DAREDEVILS		
	If You Wanna Get To Heaven	1974
	Jackie Blue	1975
P.M. DAWN	I'd Die Without You	1992

ARTIST	SONG TITLE	DATE
	Looking Through Patient Eyes	1993
	More Than Likely	1993
	Paper Doll	1992
	Reality Used To Be A Friend Of Mine	1992
	Set Adrift On Memory Bliss	1991
	A Watcher's Point Of View	1991
P.O.D.	Alive	2002
	Youth Of The Nation	2002
PABLO CRUISE	Cool Love	1981
	Don't Want To Live Without It	1978
	I Want You Tonight	1979
	Love Will Find A Way	1978
	Whatcha Gonna Do	1977
DON PABLO'S ANIMALS		
	Venus	1990
PETEY PABLO	Raise Up	2001
THOM PACE	Maybe	1979
PACIFIC GAS & ELECTRIC		
	Are You Ready	1970
PAFFENDORF	Be Cool	2002
JIMMY PAGE & ROBERT PLANT		
	Gallows Pole	1994
	Most High	1998
	(PUFF DADDY featuring JIMMY PAGE)	
	Come With Me	1998
MARTIN PAGE	In The House Of Stone And Light	1994

ARTIST	SONG TITLE	DATE
PATTI PAGE	Hush, Hush Sweet Charlotte	1964
TOMMY PAGE	I'll Be Your Everything	1990
	A Shoulder To Cry On	1989
PAGLIARO	Lovin' You Ain't Easy	1972
ELAINE PAIGE	Memory	1981
ELAINE PAIGE & BARBARA DICKSON		
	I Know Him So Well	1985
JENNIFER PAIGE	Crush	1998
KEVIN PAIGE	Anything I Want	1990
	Don't Shut Me Out	1989
BRAD PAISLEY	Celebrity	2003
	He Didn't Have To Be	1999
	I'm Gonna Miss Her (The Fishin' Song)	2002
	Little Moments	2003
	We Danced	2000
	Wrapped Around	2001
ROBERT PALMER	Addicted To Love	1986
	Bad Case Of Loving You (Doctor, Doctor)	1979
	Change His Ways	1989
	Early In The Morning	1988
	Every Kinda People	1978
	Hyperactive	1986
	I Didn't Mean To Turn You On	1986
	Know By Now	1994
	Looking For Clues	1980

ARTIST	SONG TITLE	DATE
	Mercy Mercy Me (The Ecology)/	
	I Want You	1991
	She Makes My Day	1988
	Simply Irresistible	1988
	Some Guys Have All The Luck	1982
	You Blow Me Away	1994
	You're Amazing	1990
ROBERT PALMER AND UB40		
	I'll Be Your Baby Tonight	1990
SUZANNE PALMER/ABSO*UTE		
	I Believe	1997
	(DJ TIESTO featuring SUZANNE PALMER)	
	643 (Love's On Fire)	2002
PANJABI MC	Mundian To Bach Ke	2003
PANJABI MC featuring JAY-Z		
	Jogi/Beware Of The Boys	2003
PANTERA	I'm Broken	1994
	Planet Caravan	1994
	Walk	1993
PAPA ROACH	Between Angels & Insects	2001
	Last Resort	2001
	She Loves Me Not	2002
PAPER DOLLS	Something Here In My Heart (Keeps	
	A-Tellin' Me No)	1968
PAPER LACE	Billy, Don't Be A Hero	1974
	The Black Eyed Boys	1974

ARTIST	SONG TITLE	DATE
	The Night Chicago Died	1974
	(NOTTINGHAM FOREST WITH PAPER LACE)	
	We Got The Whole World In Our Hands	1978
PAPERBOY	Ditty	1992
PAR-T-ONE vs INXS		
	I'm So Crazy	2001
PARADE	Sunshine Girl	1967
VANESSA PARADIS	Be My Baby	1992
	Joe Le Taxi	1988
PARAMOUNTS	Poison Ivy	1964
PARCHMENT	Light Up The Fire	1972
PARIS	Guerilla Funk	1995
MICA PARIS	Breathe Life Into Me	1988
	Contribution	1990
	I Never Felt Like This Before	1993
	I Wanna Hold On To You	1993
	Like Dreamers Do	1988
	My One Temptation	1988
	One	1995
	Stay	1998
MICA PARIS & WILL DOWNING		
	Where Is The Love	1989
RYAN PARIS	Dolce Vita	1983
SIMON PARK ORCHESTRA		
	Eye Level	1973
GRAHAM PARKER	The Pink Panther (EP)	1977

ARTIST	SONG TITLE	DATE
GRAHAM PARKER & THE SHOT		
	Wake Up (Next To You)	1985
RAY PARKER JR.	Bad Boy	1982
	Ghostbusters	1984
	Girls Are More Fun	1985
	I Don't Think That Man Should Sleep Alone	1987
	I Still Can't Get Over You	1983
	Jamie	1984
	Let Me Go	1982
	The Other Woman	1982
RAY PARKER JR. & RAYDIO		
	Jack And Jill	1978
	That Old Song	1981
	Two Places At The Same Time	1980
	A Woman Needs Love (Just Like You Do)	1981
	You Can't Change That	1979
	(GLENN MEDEIROS & RAY PARKER JR.)	
	All I'm Missing Is You	1990
ROBERT PARKER	Barefootin'	1966
SARA PARKER	My Love Is Deep	1997
ALEX PARKS	Cry	2004
	Maybe That's What It Takes	2003
MICHAEL PARKS	Long Lonesome Highway	1970
PARLIAMENT	Flash Light	1978

ARTIST	SONG TITLE	DATE
	Tear The Roof Off The Sucker (Give Up The Funk)	1976
PARLIAMENTS	(I Wanna) Testify	1967
JOHN PARR	Naughty Naughty	1984
	St. Elmo's Fire (Man In Motion)	1985
	(MEAT LOAF featuring JOHN PARR)	
	Rock 'n' Roll Mercenaries	1986
DEAN PARRISH	I'm On My Way	1975
KAREN PARRY/FLIP & FILL		
	Discoland	2004
	(PASCAL featuring KAREN PARRY)	
	I Think We're Alone Now	2002
ALAN PARSONS	Damned If I Do	1979
	Prime Time	1984
ALAN PARSONS PROJECT		
	Don't Answer Me	1984
	Eye In The Sky	1982
	Games People Play	1980
	I Wouldn't Want To Be Like You	1977
	(The System Of) Doctor Tarr And Professor Fether	1976
	Time	1981
PARTIZAN	Drive Me Crazy	1997
PARTLAND BROTHERS		
	Soul City	1987

ARTIST	SONG TITLE	DATE
PARTNERS IN KRYME		
	Turtle Power	1990
DAVID PARTON	Isn't She Lovely	1977
DOLLY PARTON	Baby I'm Burnin'	1978
	Heartbreaker	1978
	Here You Come Again	1977
	Jolene	1976
	9 To 5	1980
	Starting Over Again	1980
	Two Doors Down	1978
	(KENNY ROGERS & DOLLY PARTON)	
	Islands In The Stream	1983
STELLA PARTON	The Danger Of A Stranger	1977
PARTRIDGE FAMILY		
	Breaking Up Is Hard To Do	1972
	Doesn't Somebody Want To Be Wanted	1971
	I Think I Love You	1970
	I Woke Up In Love This Morning	1971
	I'll Meet You Halfway	1971
	It's One Of Those Nights (Yes Love)	1971
	Lookin' Thru The Eyes Of Love	1973
	Walking In The Rain	1973
DON PARTRIDGE	Blue Eyes	1968
	Breakfast On Pluto	1969
	Rosie	1968
PARTY	In My Dreams	1991

ARTIST	SONG TITLE	DATE
ALEX PARTY	Don't Give Me Your Life	1995
	Read My Lips	1996
	Saturday Night Party (Read My Lips)	1994
	Wrap Me Up	1995
PASADENAS	Enchanted Lady	1988
	I Believe In Miracles	1992
	I'm Doing Fine Now	1992
	Let's Stay Together	1992
	Love Thing	1990
	Make It With You	1992
	Riding On A Train	1988
	Tribute (Right On)	1988
PASCAL featuring KAREN PARRY		
	I Think We're Alone Now	2002
PASSENGERS	Miss Sarajevo	1995
PASSIONS	I'm In Love With A German Film Star	1981
PAT & MICK	I Haven't Stopped Dancing Yet	1989
	Let's All Chant	1988
	Use It Up And Wear It Out	1990
ROBBIE PATTON	Don't Give It Up	1981
PATTY & THE EMBLEMS		
	Mixed-Up, Shook-Up, Girl	1964
PAUL & PAULA	Hey Paula	1962
	Young Lovers	1963
BILLY PAUL	Let 'Em In	1977
	Let's Make A Baby	1976

ARTIST	SONG TITLE	DATE
	Me And Mrs. Jones	1972
	Only The Strong Survive	1977
	Thanks For Saving My Life	1974
	Your Song	1977
LYN PAUL	It Oughta Sell A Million	1975
OWEN PAUL	My Favourite Waste Of Time	1986
SEAN PAUL	Get Busy	2003
	Gimme The Light	2002
	Like Glue	2003
SEAN PAUL featuring SASHA		
	I'm Still In Love With You	2004
	(BEYONCE featuring SEAN PAUL)	
	Baby Boy	2003
	(BLU CANTRELL featuring SEAN PAUL)	
	Breathe	2003
LUCIANO PAVAROTTI		
	Nessun Dorma	1990
	(CARRERAS/DOMINGO/PAVAROTTI WITH MEHTA)	
	Libiamo/La Donna E Mobile	1994
	You'll Never Walk Alone	1998
	(ELTON JOHN & LUCIANO PAVAROTTI)	
	Live Like Horses	1996
	(ZUCCHERO WITH LUCIANO PAVAROTTI)	
	Miserere	1992
PAVEMENT	Carrot Rope	1999
	Shady Lane	1997

ARTIST	SONG TITLE	DATE
RITA PAVONE	Heart	1966
	Remember Me	1964
	You Only You	1967
PAY AS U GO	Champagne Dance	2002
FREDA PAYNE	Band Of Gold	1970
	Bring The Boys Home	1971
	Deeper And Deeper	1970
PEACH UNION	On My Own	1997
PEACHES	Set It Off	2002
PEACHES featuring IGGY POP		
	Kick It	2004
PEACHES & HERB	Close Your Eyes	1967
	For Your Love	1967
	I Pledge My Love	1980
	Let's Fall In Love	1966
	Love Is Strange	1967
	Reunited	1979
	Shake Your Groove Thing	1978
	Two Little Kids	1967
PEARL JAM	Alive	1992
	Daughter	1994
	Dissident	1994
	Even Flow	1992
	Given To Fly	1998
	I Am Mine	2002
	I Got ID/Long Road	1995

ARTIST	SONG TITLE	DATE
	Jeremy	1992
	Last Kiss	1999
	Merkinball	1995
	Not For You	1995
	Nothing As It Seems	2000
	Tremor Christ/Spin The Black Circle	1994
	Who You Are	1996
	Wishlist	1998
LESLIE PEARL	If The Love Fits Wear It	1982
PEARLS	Guilty	1974
	Third Finger Left Hand	1972
	You Came, You Saw, You Conquered	1972
JOHNNY PEARSON ORCHESTRA		
	Sleepy Shores	1971
PEBBLES	Girlfriend	1988
	Giving You The Benefit	1990
	Love Makes Things Happen	1990
	Mercedes Boy	1988
PEDDLERS	Birth	1969
	Girlie	1970
ANN PEEBLES	I Can't Stand The Rain	1973
NIA PEEPLES	Street Of Dreams	1991
	Trouble	1988
DONALD PEERS	Give Me One More Chance	1972
	Please Don't Go	1968
MARTI PELLOW	Close To You	2001

ARTIST	SONG TITLE	DATE
	I've Been Around The World	2001
TEDDY PENDERGRASS		
	Close The Door	1978
	(KWS featuring TEDDY PENDERGRASS)	
	The More I Get, The More I Want	1994
	(STEPHANIE MILLS WITH TEDDY PENDERGRASS)	
	Two Hearts	1981
CE CE PENISTON	Finally	1991
	Hit By Love	1994
	I'm In The Mood	1994
	Keep Givin' Me Your Love	1994
	Keep On Walkin'	1992
	Somebody Else's Guy	1998
	We Got A Love Thang	1992
DAWN PENN	You Don't Love Me (No, No, No)	1994
MICHAEL PENN	No Myth	1990
PEOPLE	I Love You	1968
PEOPLE'S CHOICE	Do It Any Way You Wanna	1975
	I Likes To Do It	1971
	Jam, Jam, Jam (All Night Long)	1978
PEPE DELUXE	Before You Leave	2001
PEPPERMINT RAINBOW		
	Will You Be Staying After Sunday	1969
PEPPERS	Pepper Box	1974
PEPSI & SHIRLIE	Goodbye Stranger	1987
	Heartache	1987

ARTIST	SONG TITLE	DATE
PERAN	Good Time	2002
LANCE PERCIVAL	Shame And Scandal In The Family	1965
PERFECT GENTLEMEN		
	Ooh La La (I Can't Get Over You)	1990
PERFECT PHASE	Horny Horns	1999
PERFECTO ALLSTARZ		
	Reach Up (Papa's Got A Brand New Pig Bag)	1995
PERPETUAL MOTION		
	Keep On Dancin' (Let's Go)	1998
STEVE PERRY	Foolish Heart	1984
	Oh, Sherrie	1984
	She's Mine	1984
	Strung Out	1994
	You Better Wait	1994
PERSUADERS	Some Guys Have All The Luck	1973
	Thin Line Between Love And Hate	1971
JON PERTWEE	Worzel's Song	1980
PET SHOP BOYS	Always On My Mind	1988
	Before	1996
	Being Boring	1990
	Can You Forgive Her?	1993
	DJ Culture	1991
	Domino Dancing	1988
	Flamboyant	2004
	Go West	1993

ARTIST	SONG TITLE	DATE
	Heart	1988
	Home And Dry	2002
	I Don't Know What You Want But I Can't Give It Anymore	1999
	I Get Along	2002
	I Wouldn't Normally Do This Kind Of Thing	1993
	It's A Sin	1987
	It's Alright	1989
	Jealousy	1991
	Left To My Own Devices	1988
	Liberation	1994
	Love Comes Quickly	1986
	Miracles	2003
	New York City Boy	1999
	Opportunities (Let's Make Lots Of Money)	1986
	Paninaro '95	1995
	A Red Letter Day	1997
	Rent	1987
	Se A Vida E (That's The Way Life Is)	1996
	Single	1996
	So Hard	1990
	Somewhere	1997
	Suburbia	1986
	Was It Worth It	1991
	West End Girls	1986

ARTIST	SONG TITLE	DATE
	Where The Streets Have No Name/ Can't Take My Eyes Off You	1991
	Yesterday, When I Was Mad	1994
	You Only Tell Me You Love Me When You're Drunk	2000
PET SHOP BOYS & DUSTY SPRINGFIELD		
	What Have I Done To Deserve This?	1987
PETER & GORDON	Baby, I'm Yours	1965
	I Don't Want To See You Again	1964
	I Go To Pieces	1965
	Knight In Rusty Armour	1966
	Lady Godiva	1966
	Nobody I Know	1964
	Sunday For Tea	1967
	To Know You Is To Love You	1965
	True Love Ways	1965
	Woman	1966
	A World Without Love	1964
PETER, PAUL & MARY		
	Blowin' In The Wind	1963
	Day Is Done	1969
	For Lovin' Me	1965
	I Dig Rock And Roll Music	1967
	Leaving On A Jet Plane	1969
	Tell It On The Mountain	1964
	Too Much Of Nothing	1967

ARTIST	SONG TITLE	DATE
PETERS & LEE	By Your Side	1973
	Don't Stay Away Too Long	1974
	Hey Mr. Music Man	1976
	Rainbow	1974
	Welcome Home	1973
BERNADETTE PETERS		
	Gee Whiz	1980
TOM PETTY	Free Fallin'	1989
	I Won't Back Down	1989
	Runnin' Down A Dream	1989
	You Don't Know How It Feels	1994
TOM PETTY & THE HEARTBREAKERS		
	American Girl	1977
	Anything That's Rock'n'Roll	1977
	Breakdown	1977
	Change Of Heart	1983
	Don't Come Around Here No More	1985
	Don't Do Me Like That	1979
	Jammin' Me	1987
	Learning To Fly	1991
	Mary Jane's Last Dance	1993
	Refugee	1980
	Too Good To Be True	1992
	The Waiting	1981
	You Got Lucky	1982

ARTIST	SONG TITLE	DATE
TOM PETTY & THE HEARTBREAKERS WITH STEVIE NICKS	Needles And Pins	1986
	Stop Draggin' My Heart Around	1981
PF PROJECT featuring EWAN MCGREGOR		
	Choose Life	1997
LIZ PHAIR	Why Can't I	2003
PHARCYDE	Runnin'	1996
PHARRELL WILLIAMS featuring JAY-Z		
	Frontin'	2003
	(BUSTA RHYMES featuring P. DIDDY & PHARRELL)	
	Pass The Courvoisier — Part II	2002
	(SNOOP DOGG featuring PHARRELL)	
	Beautiful	2003
PHATS & SMALL	Feel Good	1999
	This Time Around	2001
	Tonite	1999
PHATS & SMALL PRESENT MUTANT DISCO		
	Turn Around	1999
PHD	I Won't Let You Down	1982
PHILADELPHIA INTERNATIONAL ALL-STARS		
	Let's Clean Up The Ghetto	1977
PHILHARMONIC ORCHESTRA		
	Thus Spake Zarathustra	1969
ESTHER PHILLIPS	What A Diff'rence A Day Makes	1975
JOHN PHILLIPS	Mississippi	1970

ARTIST	SONG TITLE	DATE
PHIXX	Hold On Me	2003
	Love Revolution	2004
	Wild Boys	2004
PHOEBE ONE	Get On It	1999
PHOTEK	Ni-Ten-Ichi-Ryu	1997
JIM PHOTOGLO	Fool In Love With You	1981
	We Were Meant To Be Lovers	1980
PHUNKY PHANTOM		
	Get Up Stand Up	1998
PIANOHEADZ	It's Over (Distortion)	1998
PIANOMAN	Blurred	1996
MARK PICCHIOTTI presents BASSTOY featuring DANA		
	Runnin'	2002
BOBBY 'BORIS' PICKETT & THE CRYPT KICKERS		
	Monster Mash	1962
WILSON PICKETT	Don't Fight It	1965
	Don't Knock My Love (Pt 1)	1971
	Don't Let The Green Grass Fool You	1971
	Engine Number 9	1970
	Everybody Needs Somebody To Love	1967
	Fire And Water	1971
	Funky Broadway	1967
	Hey Jude	1968
	I Found A Love (Pt 1)	1967
	I'm A Midnight Mover	1968
	In The Midnight Hour	1965

ARTIST	SONG TITLE	DATE
	Land Of 1000 Dances	1966
	Mustang Sally	1966
	She's Lookin' Good	1968
	634-5789	1966
	Stag-O-Lee	1967
	Sugar Sugar	1970
PICKETTYWITCH	Baby I Won't Let You Down	1970
	(It's Like A) Sad Old Kinda Movie	1970
	That Same Old Feeling	1970
MAURO PICOTTO	Gonna Get Ya Lizard	1999
	Iguana	2000
	Komodo (Save A Soul)	2001
	Like This Like That	2001
	Lizard (Gonna Get You)	1999
	Pulsar 2002	2002
PIGBAG	The Big Bean	1982
	Papa's Got A Brand New Pigbag	1982
PIGLETS	Johnny Reggae	1971
PILOT	Call Me Round	1975
	January	1975
	Just A Smile	1975
	Magic	1975
COURTNEY PINE	Like Dreamers Do	1988
PINK	Don't Let Me Get Me	2002
	Family Portrait	2002
	Get The Party Started	2001

ARTIST	SONG TITLE	DATE
	God Is A DJ	2004
	Just Like A Pill	2002
	Last To Know	2004
	Most Girls	2000
	There You Go	2000
	Trouble	2003
	You Make Me Sick	2001
PINK featuring WILLIAM ORBIT		
	Feel Good Time	2003
(CHRISTINA AGUILERA, LIL' KIM, MYA & PINK)		
	Lady Marmalade	2001
PINK FLOYD	Another Brick In The Wall	1980
	Arnold Layne	1967
	High Hopes/Keep Talking	1994
	Money	1973
	Not Now John	1983
	See Emily Play	1967
	Take It Back	1994
	When The Tigers Broke Free	1982
PINK LADY	Kiss In The Dark	1979
PINKEES	Danger Games	1982
PINKERTON'S ASSORTED COLOURS		
	Mirror Mirror	1966
PIONEERS	Give And Take	1972
	Let Your Yeah Be Yeah	1971
	Long Shot Kick De Bucket	1969

ARTIST	SONG TITLE	DATE
PIPKINS	Gimme Dat Ding	1970
PIRANHAS	Tom Hark	1980
	Zambezi	1982
PIRATES featuring ENYA, SHOLA AMA, NAILA BOSS & ISHANI	You Should Really Know	2004
PITBULL featuring LIL JON		
	Culo	2004
GENE PITNEY	Backstage	1966
	Blue Angel	1974
	I Must Be Seeing Things	1965
	I'm Gonna Be Strong	1964
	(In The) Cold Light Of Day	1967
	It Hurts To Be In Love	1964
	Just One Smile	1966
	Last Chance To Turn Around	1965
	Looking Thru The Eyes Of Love	1965
	Maria Elena	1969
	Nobody Needs Your Love	1966
	Princess In Rags	1965
	Shady Lady	1970
	She's A Heartbreaker	1968
	Something's Gotten Hold Of My Heart	1967
	Somewhere In The Country	1968
	A Street Called Hope	1970
	That Girl Belongs To Yesterday	1964
	Twenty Four Hours From Tulsa	1963

ARTIST	SONG TITLE	DATE
	24 Sycamore	1973
	Yours Until Tomorrow	1968
MARIO PIU	Communication (Somebody Answer The Phone)	1999
MARIO PIU presents DJ ARABESQUE		
	The Vision	2001
PIXIES	Debaser	1997
	Planet Of Sound	1991
	Velouria	1990
PIZZAMAN	Happiness	1995
	Sex On The Streets	1995
	Trippin On Sunshine	1994
ANT & DEC	Better Watch Out	1996
	Falling	1997
	Shout	1997
	We're On The Ball	2002
	When I Fall In Love	1996
	(PJ AND DUNCAN)	
	Eternal Love	1994
	If I Give You My Number	1994
	Let's Get Ready To Rumble	1994
	Our Radio Rocks	1995
	Perfect	1995
	Stepping Stone	1996
	Stuck On U	1995
	U Krazy Katz	1995

ARTIST	SONG TITLE	DATE
	Why Me?	1994
PJB featuring HANNAH AND HER SISTERS		
	Bridge Over Troubled Water	1991
PLACEBO	The Bitter End	2003
	Bruise Pristine	1997
	English Summer Rain	2004
	Every You Every Me	1999
	Nancy Boy	1997
	Pure Morning	1998
	Slave To The Wage	2000
	Special Needs	2003
	Taste In Men	2000
	Teenage Angst	1996
	This Picture	2003
	Twenty Years	2004
	You Don't Care About Us	1998
PLANET FUNK	Chase The Sun	2001
	Who Said (Stuck In The UK)	2003
PLANET PERFECTO	Bullet In The Gun	1999
PLANET PERFECTO featuring GRACE		
	Not Over Yet 99	1999
PLANET SOUL	Set U Free	1995
PLANETS	Lines	1979
ROBERT PLANT	Big Log	1983
	Heaven Knows	1988
	In The Mood	1983

ARTIST	SONG TITLE	DATE
	Little By Little	1985
	Tall Cool One	1988
	29 Palms	1993
	(JIMMY PAGE & ROBERT PLANT)	
	Gallows Pole	1994
	Most High	1998
PLASTIC BERTRAND	Ca Plane Pour Moi	1978
	Sha La La La Lee	1978
PLASTIC ONO BAND		
	Cold Turkey	1969
PLASTIC PENNY	Everything I Am	1968
PLATINUM 45 featuring MORE FIRE CREW		
	Oi!	2002
PLATTERS	I Love You 1,000 Times	1966
	With This Ring	1967
PLAYA	Cheers 2 U	1998
PLAYER	Baby Come Back	1977
	Prisoner Of Your Love	1978
	This Time I'm In It For Love	1978
PLAYERS ASSOCIATION		
	Turn The Music Up!	1979
PLUMMET	Cherish The Day	2004
	Damaged	2003
PLUS ONE featuring SIRRON		
	It's Happenin'	1990

ARTIST	SONG TITLE	DATE
PLUX featuring GEORGIA JONES		
	Over & Over	1996
POCO	Call It Love	1989
	Crazy Love	1979
	Heart Of The Night	1979
	Nothin' To Hide	1989
POETS	Now We're Thru	1964
POGUES	Fiesta	1988
	Poguetry In Motion (EP)	1986
	Tuesday Morning	1993
POGUES & THE DUBLINERS		
	The Irish Rover	1987
POGUES featuring KIRSTY MACCOLL		
	Fairytale Of New York	1987
POINT BLACK	Nicole	1981
POINT BREAK	Do We Rock	1999
	Freakytime	2000
	Stand Tough	2000
	What About Us	2000
	You	2000
POINTER SISTERS	American Music	1982
	Automatic	1984
	Dare Me	1985
	Fairytale	1974
	Fire	1978
	Goldmine	1986

ARTIST	SONG TITLE	DATE
	Happiness	1979
	He's So Shy	1980
	How Long (Betcha' Got A Chick On The Side)	1975
	I Need You	1984
	I'm So Excited	1984
	Jump (For My Love)	1984
	Neutron Dance	1984
	Should I Do It	1982
	Slow Hand	1981
	Yes We Can Can	1973
BONNIE POINTER	Heaven Must Have Sent You	1979
	I Can't Help Myself (Sugar Pie, Honey Bunch)	1979
POISON	Every Rose Has Its Thorn	1988
	Fallen Angel	1988
	I Won't Forget You	1987
	Life Goes On	1991
	Nothin' But A Good Time	1988
	Ride The Wind	1991
	So Tell Me Why	1991
	Something To Believe In	1990
	Stand	1993
	Talk Dirty To Me	1987
	Unskinny Bop	1990
	Until You Suffer Some (Fire And Ice)	1993

ARTIST	SONG TITLE	DATE
	Your Mama Don't Dance	1989
POLECATS	John I'm Only Dancing/Big Green Car	1981
	Rockabilly Guy	1981
POLICE	Can't Stand Losing You	1979
	De Do Do Do, De Da Da Da	1980
	Don't Stand So Close To Me	1981
	Every Breath You Take	1983
	Every Little Thing She Does Is Magic	1981
	Invisible Sun	1981
	King Of Pain	1983
	Message In A Bottle	1979
	Roxanne	1979
	Six Pack	1980
	So Lonely	1980
	Spirits In The Material World	1982
	Synchronicity II	1983
	Walking On The Moon	1979
	Wrapped Around Your Finger	1984
	(STING AND THE POLICE)	
	Roxanne '97	1997
	(DIFFERENT GEAR vs THE POLICE)	
	When The World Is Running Down	2000
SU POLLARD	Starting Together	1986
POLOROID	So Damn Beautiful	2003
POLTERGEIST	Vicious Circles	1996

ARTIST	SONG TITLE	DATE
PETER POLYCARPOU		
	Love Hurts	1993
THE POLYPHONIC SPREE		
	Hanging Around	2002
	Light And Day	2003
	Soldier Girl	2003
BRIAN POOLE & THE TREMELOES		
	Candy Man	1964
	Do You Love Me	1963
	I Can Dance	1963
	I Want Candy	1965
	Someone, Someone	1964
	Three Bells	1965
	Twelve Steps To Love	1964
	Twist And Shout	1963
GLYN POOLE	Milly Molly Mandy	1973
POP!	Can't Say Goodbye	2004
	Heaven And Earth	2004
POP WILL EAT ITSELF		
	Bulletproof!	1992
	Can U Dig It?	1989
	Dance Of The Mad	1990
	Everything's Cool	1994
	Get The Girl! Kill The Baddies!	1993
	Ich Bin Ein Auslander	1994
	Karmadrome/Eat Me Drink Me...	1992

ARTIST	SONG TITLE	DATE
	92 Degrees	1991
	RSVP/Familus Horribilus	1993
	Touched By The Hand Of Cicciolina	1990
	X, Y + Zee	1991
IGGY POP	Lust For Life	1996
	The Passenger	1998
	Real Wild Child (Wild One)	1986
IGGY POP WITH KATE PIERSON		
	Candy	1990
	(PEACHES featuring IGGY POP)	
	Kick It	2004
POPPY FAMILY	That's Where I Went Wrong	1970
	Which Way You Goin' Billy?	1970
POPPYFIELDS	45 RPM	2004
PORN KINGS	Amour (C'mon)	1997
	Up To No Good	1996
PORN KINGS vs DJ SUPREME		
	Up To The Wildstyle	1999
PORN KINGS vs FLIP & FILL featuring 740 BOYS		
	Shake Ya Shimmy	2003
PORTISHEAD	All Mine	1997
	Glory Box	1995
	Only You	1998
	Over	1997
	Sour Times	1995
PORTRAIT	Here We Go Again!	1992

ARTIST	SONG TITLE	DATE
PORTSMOUTH SINFONIA		
	Classical Muddly	1981
SANDY POSEY	Born A Woman	1966
	I Take It Back	1967
	Single Girl	1966
	What A Woman In Love Won't Do	1967
POSITIVE FORCE	We Got The Funk	1979
POSITIVE GANG	Sweet Freedom	1993
POSITIVE K	I Got A Man	1992
MIKE POST	The Rockford Files	1975
	Theme From Magnum P.I.	1982
MIKE POST featuring LARRY CARLTON		
	Theme From 'Hill Street Blues'	1982
POTTERS	We'll Be With You	1972
POV featuring JADE		
	All Thru The Nite	1994
COZY POWELL	Dance With The Devil	1973
	The Man In Black	1974
	Na Na Na	1974
	(BRIAN MAY WITH COZY POWELL)	
	Resurrection	1993
JESSE POWELL	You	1999
POWER STATION	Communication	1985
	Get It On (Bang A Gong)	1985
	Some Like It Hot	1985
POWERHOUSE	Rhythm Of The Night	1997

ARTIST	SONG TITLE	DATE
POWERHOUSE featuring DUANE HARDEN		
	What You Need	1999
WILL POWERS	Kissing With Confidence	1983
POZO-SECO SINGERS		
	I Can Make It With You	1966
	Look What You've Done	1966
PPK	Reload	2002
	Resurrection	2001
PEREZ 'PREZ' PRADO & HIS ORCHESTRA		
	Guaglione	1995
PRAISE	Only You	1991
PRATT AND MCCLAIN WITH BROTHERLOVE		
	Happy Days	1977
PRAXIS featuring KATHY BROWN		
	Turn Me Out (Turn To Sugar)	1997
PRECIOUS	It's Gonna Be My Way	2000
	Rewind	2000
	Say It Again	1999
PRECOCIOUS BRATS featuring KEVIN & PERRY		
	Big Girl	2000
PREFAB SPROUT	If You Don't Love Me	1992
	Jordan: The EP	1991
	The King Of Rock 'n' Roll	1988
	Life Of Surprises	1993
	A Prisoner Of The Past	1997
	The Sound Of Crying	1992

ARTIST	SONG TITLE	DATE
	When Love Breaks Down	1985
PRELUDE	After The Goldrush	1974
PREMIERS	Farmer John	1964
PRESIDENTS	5-10-15-20 (25-30 Years Of Love)	1970
PRESIDENTS OF THE UNITED STATES		
	Dune Buggy	1996
	Lump	1996
	Mach 5	1996
	Peaches	1996
ELVIS PRESLEY	Ain't That Loving You Baby	1964
	All That I Am	1966
	Always On My Mind	1972
	An American Trilogy	1972
	Are You Lonesome Tonight (Live)	1982
	Ask Me	1964
	Big Boss Man	1967
	Blue Christmas	1964
	Blue River	1966
	Bossa Nova Baby	1963
	Burning Love	1972
	Clean Up Your Own Back Yard	1969
	Crying In The Chapel	1965
	Do The Clam	1965
	Don't Be Cruel	1956
	Don't Cry Daddy	1969
	Fool	1973

ARTIST	SONG TITLE	DATE
	Frankie And Johnny	1966
	The Girl Of My Best Friend	1976
	Green Green Grass Of Home	1975
	Guitar Man	1981
	Heartbreak Hotel/Hound Dog	1971
	Hurt/For The Heart	1976
	I Can Help	1983
	I Just Can't Help Believing	1971
	I Really Don't Want To Know/There Goes My Everything	1970
	I'm Leavin'	1971
	I'm Yours	1965
	I've Got A Thing About You Baby/Take Good Care Of You	1974
	I've Lost You/The Next Step Is Love	1970
	If Every Day Was Like Christmas	1966
	If I Can Dream	1968
	If You Talk In Your Sleep	1974
	In The Ghetto	1969
	Indescribably Blue	1967
	It Hurts Me	1964
	It Won't Seem Like Christmas (Without You)	1979
	It's Now Or Never	1960
	It's Only Love/Beyond The Reef	1980
	Jailhouse Rock	1983

ARTIST	SONG TITLE	DATE
	Kentucky Rain	1970
	Kiss Me Quick	1964
	Kissin' Cousins	1964
	Love Letters	1966
	Memories	1969
	Moody Blue/She Thinks I Still Care	1976
	My Boy	1975
	My Way	1977
	One Broken Heart For Sale	1963
	Polk Salad Annie	1973
	Promised Land	1974
	Puppet On A String	1965
	Rags To Riches	1971
	Raised On Rock	1973
	Rubberneckin'	2003
	Separate Ways	1972
	Spinout	1966
	Steamroller Blues	1973
	Such A Night	1964
	(Such An) Easy Question	1965
	Suspicion	1976
	Suspicious Minds	1969
	T.R.O.U.B.L.E.	1975
	Tell Me Why	1966
	That's All Right	2004
	The Twelfth Of Never	1995

ARTIST	SONG TITLE	DATE
	U.S. Male	1968
	Until It's Time For You To Go	1972
	Viva Las Vegas	1964
	Way Down	1977
	What'd I Say	1964
	Where Did They Go, Lord	1971
	The Wonder Of You/Mama Liked The Roses	1970
	You Don't Have To Say You Love Me/ Patch It Up	1970
	You Gotta Stop/The Love Machine	1967
	(You're The) Devil In Disguise	1963
	Your Time Hasn't Come Yet Baby	1968
ELVIS vs JXL	A Little Less Conversation	2002
LISA MARIE PRESLEY		
	Lights Out	2003
PRESSHA	Splackavellie	1998
BILLY PRESTON	Nothing From Nothing	1974
	Outa-Space	1972
	Space Race	1973
	Struttin'	1974
	That's The Way God Planned It	1969
	Will It Go Round In Circles	1973
BILLY PRESTON & SYREETA		
	With You I'm Born Again	1979
	(THE BEATLES WITH BILLY PRESTON)	
	Don't Let Me Down	1969

ARTIST	SONG TITLE	DATE
	Get Back	1969
PRETENDERS	Back On The Chain Gang	1982
	Brass In Pocket	1979
	Don't Get Me Wrong	1986
	Human	1999
	Hymn To Her	1986
	I Go To Sleep	1981
	I'll Stand By You	1994
	Kid	1979
	Message Of Love	1981
	Middle Of The Road	1983
	Night In My Veins	1994
	Show Me	1984
	Stop Your Sobbing	1979
	Talk Of The Town	1980
	2000 Miles	1983
PRETTY POISON	Catch Me I'm Falling	1987
	Nightime	1988
PRETTY THINGS	Cry To Me	1965
	Don't Bring Me Down	1964
	Honey I Need	1965
ALAN PRICE	Baby Of Mine/Just For You	1979
	Jarrow Song	1974
ALAN PRICE SET	Don't Stop The Carnival	1968
	Hi-Lili, Hi-Lo	1966
	The House That Jack Built	1967

ARTIST	SONG TITLE	DATE
	I Put A Spell On You	1966
	Simon Smith & His Amazing Dancing Bear	1967
(FAME AND PRICE TOGETHER)		
	Rosetta	1971
KELLY PRICE	Friend Of Mine	1998
	Secret Love	1999
(WHITNEY HOUSTON featuring FAITH EVANS & KELLY PRICE)		
	Heartbreak Hotel	2000
RAY PRICE	For The Good Times	1970
CHARLEY PRIDE	Kiss An Angel Good Mornin'	1971
MAXI PRIEST	Close To You	1990
	Just Wanna Know/Fe Real	1992
	One More Chance	1993
	Some Guys Have All The Luck	1987
	Strollin' On	1986
	That Girl	1996
	Watching The World Go By	1996
	Wild World	1988
(ROBERTA FLACK WITH MAXI PRIEST)		
	Set The Night To Music	1991
(SHABBA RANKS featuring MAXI PRIEST)		
	Housecall	1993
PRIMAL SCREAM	Accelerator	2000
	Burning Wheel	1997
	Come Together	1990

ARTIST	SONG TITLE	DATE
	Dixie-Narco (EP)	1992
	Higher Than The Sun	1991
	Jailbird	1994
	Kill All Hippies	2000
	Kowalski	1997
	Loaded	1990
	Miss Lucifer	2002
	Rocks/Funky Jam	1994
	Star	1997
	Swastika Eyes	1999
PRIMAL SCREAM, IRVINE WELSH & ON-U SOUND		
	The Big Man And The Scream Team	
	Meet The Barmy Army Uptown	1996
PRIMITIVES	Crash	1988
	Out Of Reach	1988
	Sick Of It	1989
	Way Behind Me	1988
PRINCE	Alphabet Street	1988
	Anotherloverholenyohead	1986
	Batdance	1989
	Controversy	1993
	Diamonds And Pearls	1991
	Gett Off	1991
	Glam Slam	1988
	I Could Never Take The Place Of Your	
	Man	1987

ARTIST	SONG TITLE	DATE
	I Wanna Be Your Lover	1979
	I Wish U Heaven	1988
	If I Was Your Girlfriend	1987
	Letitgo	1994
	Money Don't Matter 2 Night	1992
	Mountains	1986
	New Power Generation	1990
	Partyman	1989
	Peach	1993
	Purple Medley	1995
	Sexy MF/Strollin'	1992
	Sign 'O' The Times	1987
	Thieves In The Temple	1990
	U Got The Look	1987
PRINCE & THE NEW POWER GENERATION		
	Cream	1991
	My Name Is Prince	1992
	7	1992
	Thunder	1992
PRINCE & THE REVOLUTION		
	Delirious	1983
	Girls And Boys	1986
	I Would Die 4 U	1984
	Kiss	1986
	Let's Go Crazy/Take Me With U	1985
	1999/Little Red Corvette	1985

ARTIST	SONG TITLE	DATE
	Paisley Park	1985
	Pop Life	1985
	Purple Rain	1984
	Raspberry Beret	1985
	When Doves Cry	1984
PRINCE WITH SHEENA EASTON		
	The Arms Of Orion	1989
	(TAFKAP)	
	The Beautiful Experience	1994
	Dinner With Delores	1996
	Eye Hate U	1995
	Gold	1995
	The Most Beautiful Girl In The World	1994
	(THE ARTIST)	
	Betcha By Golly Wow!	1996
	The Holy River	1997
PRINCESS	After The Love Has Gone	1985
	I'll Keep On Loving You	1986
	Say I'm Your No. 1	1985
	Tell Me Tomorrow	1986
PRINCESS SUPERSTAR		
	Bad Babysitter	2002
PRISM	Don't Let Him Know	1982
PRIZNA featuring DEMOLITION MAN		
	Fire	1995
P.J. PROBY	Hold Me	1964

ARTIST	SONG TITLE	DATE
	I Apologise	1965
	I Can't Make It Alone	1966
	It's Your Day Today	1968
	Let The Water Run Down	1965
	Maria	1965
	Niki Hoeky	1967
	Somewhere	1964
	That Means A Lot	1965
	To Make A Big Man Cry	1966
	Together	1964
	You've Come Back	1966
PROCLAIMERS	I'm Gonna Be (500 Miles)	1993
	King Of The Road	1990
	Let's Get Married	1994
	Letter From America	1987
	What Makes You Cry	1994
PROCOL HARUM	Conquistador	1972
	Homburg	1967
	Pandora's Box	1975
	A Whiter Shade Of Pale	1967
PRODIGY	Baby's Got A Temper	2002
	Breathe	1996
	Charly	1991
	Everybody In The Place (EP)	1992
	Fire/Jericho	1992
	Firestarter	1997

ARTIST	SONG TITLE	DATE
	Girls	2004
	No Good (Start The Dance)	1994
	One Love	1993
	Out Of Space/Ruff In The Jungle	1992
	Poison	1995
	Smack My Bitch Up	1997
	Voodoo People	1994
	Wind It Up (Rewound)	1993
PROFYLE	Liar	2000
PROGRESS presents THE BOY WUNDA		
	Everybody	1999
PROPAGANDA	Dr. Mabuse	1984
	Duel	1985
	Heaven Give Me Words	1990
PROPELLERHEADS	Spybreak!	1997
PROPELLERHEADS featuring SHIRLEY BASSEY		
	History Repeating	1997
PROPELLERHEADS/DAVID ARNOLD		
	On Her Majesty's Secret Service	1997
BRIAN PROTHEROE	Pinball	1974
JEANNE PRUETT	Satin Sheets	1973
ERIC PRYDZ	Call On Me	2004
PSEUDO ECHO	Funky Town	1987
PSYCHEDELIC FURS	Heartbreak Beat	1987
	Heaven	1984
	Pretty In Pink	1986

ARTIST	SONG TITLE	DATE
PSYCHEDELIC WALTONS featuring ROISIN MURPHY		
	Wonderland	2002
PUBLIC ANNOUNCEMENT		
	Body Bumpin' (Yippie-Yi-Yo)	1998
	Mamacita	2000
PUBLIC DOMAIN	Operation Blade (Bass In The Place)	2000
	Too Many MC's/Let Me Clear My Throat	2002
PUBLIC DOMAIN featuring CHUCK D		
	Rock Da Funky Beats	2001
PUBLIC ENEMY	Bring The Noise	1988
	Can't Truss It	1991
	Don't Believe The Hype	1988
	Fight The Power	1989
	Give It Up	1994
	He Got Game	1998
	Rebel Without A Pause	1987
	Shut 'Em Down	1992
	Welcome To The Terrordome	1990
PUBLIC IMAGE LTD		
	Death Disco (Pts 1 & 2)	1979
	Disappointed	1989
	Don't Ask Me	1990
	Flowers Of Romance	1981
	Public Image	1978
	Rise	1986
	This Is Not A Love Song	1983

ARTIST	SONG TITLE	DATE
GARY PUCKETT & THE UNION GAP		
	Don't Give In To Him	1969
	Lady Willpower	1968
	Over You	1968
	This Girl Is A Woman Now	1969
	Young Girl	1968
	(UNION GAP featuring GARY PUCKETT)	
	Woman, Woman	1967
PUDDLE OF MUDD	Blurry	2001
	Control	2002
	She Hates Me	2002
TITO PUENTE JR & THE LATIN RHYTHM		
	Oye Como Va	1996
P. DIDDY & GINUWINE featuring LOON, MARIO WINANS		
	I Need A Girl (Part Two)	2002
P. DIDDY featuring KELIS		
	Let's Get Ill	2003
P. DIDDY featuring THE NEPTUNES		
	Diddy	2002
P. DIDDY featuring USHER & LOON		
	I Need A Girl (Part One)	2002
P. DIDDY, BLACK ROB & MARK CURRY		
	Bad Boy For Life	2001
PUFF DADDY & FAITH EVANS featuring 112		
	I'll Be Missing You	1997

ARTIST	SONG TITLE	DATE
PUFF DADDY & FAMILY		
	It's All About The Benjamins/Been Around	
	The World	1997
PUFF DADDY & FAMILY featuring THE NOTORIOUS B.I.G. & BUSTA RHYMES		
	Victory	1998
PUFF DADDY & THE FAMILY		
	Been Around The World	1997
PUFF DADDY featuring HURRICANE G		
	P.E. 2000	1999
PUFF DADDY featuring JIMMY PAGE		
	Come With Me	1998
PUFF DADDY featuring MARIO WINANS		
	Best Friend	1999
PUFF DADDY featuring MASE		
	Can't Nobody Hold Me Down	1997
PUFF DADDY featuring R. KELLY		
	Satisfy You	1999
	(SWV featuring PUFF DADDY)	
	Someone	1997
	(B2K featuring P. DIDDY)	
	Bump, Bump, Bump	2003
	(BABY featuring P. DIDDY)	
	Do That ...	2002

ARTIST	SONG TITLE	DATE
(BUSTA RHYMES featuring P. DIDDY & PHARRELL)		
	Pass The Courvoisier – Part II	2002
(FABOLOUS featuring P. DIDDY & JAGGED EDGE)		
	Trade It All	2002
(FAITH EVANS featuring PUFF DADDY)		
	All Night Long	1999
(JANET featuring MISSY ELLIOTT, P. DIDDY & CARLY SIMON)		
	Son Of A Gun	2001
(LENNY KRAVITZ/P. DIDDY/LOON/PHARRELL WILLIAMS)		
	Show Me Your Soul	2004
(LIL' KIM featuring PUFF DADDY)		
	No Time	1996
(MARIO WINANS featuring ENYA & P. DIDDY)		
	I Don't Wanna Know	2004
(MASE featuring P. DIDDY)		
	Breathe, Stretch, Shake	2004
	Lookin' At Me	1998
(NAS featuring PUFF DADDY)		
	Hate Me Now	1999
(NOTORIOUS B.I.G. featuring PUFF DADDY & LIL' KIM)		
	Notorious B.I.G.	2000

ARTIST	SONG TITLE	DATE
(NOTORIOUS B.I.G. featuring PUFF DADDY & MASE)		
	Mo Money Mo Problems	1997
PULP	Bad Cover Version	2002
	Common People	1995
	Disco 2000	1995
	Do You Remember The First Time?	1994
	Help The Aged	1997
	A Little Soul	1998
	Mis-Shapes/Sorted For Es & Wizz	1995
	Party Hard	1998
	The Sisters (EP)	1994
	Something Changed	1996
	Sunrise/The Trees	2001
	This Is Hardcore	1998
PULSE featuring ANTOINETTE ROBERSON		
	The Lover That You Are	1996
PUPPIES	Funky Y-2-C	1994
PURE PRAIRIE LEAGUE		
	Amie	1975
	I'm Almost Ready	1980
	Let Me Love You Tonight	1980
	Still Right Here In My Heart	1981
PURESSENCE	All I Want	1998
	This Feeling	1998
	Walking Dead	2002

ARTIST	SONG TITLE	DATE
PURETONE	Addicted To Bass	2002
	Stuck In A Groove	2003
JAMES & BOBBY PURIFY		
	I'm Your Puppet	1966
	Let Love Come Between Us	1987
	Morning Glory	1976
	Shake A Tail Feather	1967
	Wish You Didn't Have To Go	1967
PURPLE KINGS	That's The Way You Do It	1994
PUSH	The Legacy	2001
	Strange World	2001
	Tranzy State Of Mind	2002
	Universal Nation	1999
	(SUNSCREEM vs PUSH)	
	Please Save Me	2001
PUSSYCAT	Mississippi	1976
	Smile	1976
PYRAMIDS	Penetration	1964
	Train Tour To Rainbow City	1967
PYTHON LEE JACKSON		
	In A Broken Dream	1972
MONTY PYTHON	Always Look On The Bright Side	1991
Q	Dancin' Man	1977
Q TEE	Gimme That Body	1996
STACEY Q	Two Of Hearts	1986
	We Connect	1986

ARTIST	SONG TITLE	DATE
Q-CLUB	Tell It To My Heart	1996
Q-TEX	Let The Love	1996
Q-TIP	Breathe And Stop	2000
	Vivrant Thing	1999
	(RAPHAEL SAADIQ & Q-TIP)	
	Get Involved	1999
	(JANET featuring Q-TIP AND JONI MITCHELL)	
	Got 'Til It's Gone	1997
	(MISSY 'MISDEMEANOR' ELLIOTT featuring	
	NAS, EVE & Q-TIP)	
	Hot Boyz	2000
QATTARA	Come With Me	1997
QB FINEST featuring NAS & BRAVEHEARTS		
	Oochie Wally	2001
QFX	Everytime You Touch Me	1996
	Freedom 2	1997
	Say You'll Be Mine	1999
	You Got The Power	1996
QUAD CITY DJ'S	C'mon 'n Ride It (The Train)	1996
	Space Jam	1996
QUADROPHONIA	Quadrophonia	1991
	The Wave Of The Future	1991
QUANTUM JUMP	The Lone Ranger	1979
QUARTERFLASH	Find Another Fool	1982
	Harden My Heart	1981
	Take Me To Heart	1983

ARTIST	SONG TITLE	DATE
QUARTZ LOCK featuring LONNIE GORDON		
	Love Eviction	1995
QUARTZ introducing DINA CARROLL		
	It's Too Late	1991
QUARTZ WITH DINA CARROLL		
	Naked Love (Just Say You Want Me)	1991
SUZI QUATRO	Can The Can	1973
	Daytona Demon	1973
	Devil Gate Drive	1974
	48 Crash	1973
	If You Can't Give Me Love	1978
	Mama's Boy	1980
	She's In Love With You	1979
	Tear Me Apart	1977
	Too Big	1974
	The Wild One	1974
	Your Mamma Won't Like Me	1975
SUZI QUATRO & CHRIS NORMAN		
	Stumblin' In	1979
FINLEY QUAYE	Even After All	1997
	It's Great When We're Together	1997
	Spiritualized	2000
	Sunday Shining	1997
	Your Love Gets Sweeter	1998
QUEEN	Another One Bites The Dust	1980
	Backchat	1982

ARTIST	SONG TITLE	DATE
	Bicycle Race/Fat Bottomed Girls	1978
	Body Language	1982
	Bohemian Rhapsody/These Are The Days Of Our Lives	1991
	Breakthru'	1989
	Crazy Little Thing Called Love	1979
	Don't Stop Me Now	1979
	Flash	1980
	Friends Will Be Friends	1986
	Hammer To Fall	1984
	Headlong	1991
	Heaven For Everyone	1995
	I Want It All	1989
	I Want To Break Free	1984
	I'm Going Slightly Mad	1991
	Innuendo	1991
	The Invisible Man	1989
	It's A Hard Life	1984
	Killer Queen	1975
	A Kind Of Magic	1986
	Las Palabras De Amor	1982
	Let Me Live	1996
	The Miracle	1989
	No-One But You/Tie Your Mother Down	1998
	Now I'm Here	1975
	One Vision	1985

ARTIST	SONG TITLE	DATE
	Play The Game	1980
	Queen's First (EP)	1977
	Radio GaGa	1984
	Save Me	1980
	Scandal	1989
	Seven Seas Of Rhye	1974
	The Show Must Go On	1991
	Somebody To Love	1976
	Spread Your Wings	1978
	Thank God It's Christmas	1984
	Too Much Love Will Kill You	1996
	We Are The Champions	1977
	Who Wants To Live Forever	1986
	A Winter's Tale	1995
	You Don't Fool Me	1996
	You're My Best Friend	1976
QUEEN & DAVID BOWIE		
	Under Pressure	1981
(5IVE & QUEEN)		
	We Will Rock You	2000
(GEORGE MICHAEL & QUEEN)		
	Five Live (EP)	1993
	Somebody To Love	1993
QUEEN LATIFAH	U.N.I.T.Y.	1993
QUEEN LATIFAH & DE LA SOUL		
	Mamma Gave Birth To The Soul Children	1990

ARTIST	SONG TITLE	DATE
QUEEN LATIFAH, SHADES & FREE		
	Mr. Big Stuff	1997
(SHABBA RANKS featuring QUEEN LATIFAH)		
	What'cha Gonna Do?	1993
QUEEN PEN	It's True	1998
	Man Behind The Music	1998
QUEEN PEN featuring ERIC WILLIAMS		
	All My Love	1998
QUEENS OF THE STONE AGE		
	First It Giveth	2003
	Go With The Flow	2003
	The Lost Art Of Keeping A Secret	2000
	No One Knows	2002
QUEENSRYCHE	Best I Can	1991
	Bridge	1995
	I Am I	1995
	Jet City Woman	1991
	Silent Lucidity	1991
QUENTIN & ASH	Tell Him	1996
QUESTION MARK & THE MYSTERIONS		
	I Need Somebody	1966
	96 Tears	1966
TOMMY QUICKLY & THE REMO FOUR		
	Wild Side Of Life	1964
QUIET RIOT	Bang Your Head (Metal Health)	1984
	Cum On Feel The Noize	1983

ARTIST	SONG TITLE	DATE
EIMEAR QUINN	The Voice	1996
SINEAD QUINN	I Can't Break Down	2003
	What You Need Is ...	2003
QUIREBOYS	Brother Louie	1993
	Hey You	1990
	I Don't Love You Anymore	1990
	7 O'Clock	1989
	There She Goes Again/Misled	1990
R.A.F.	We've Got To Live Together	1992
R.E.M.	All The Way To Reno	2001
	Animal	2004
	At My Most Beautiful	1999
	Bad Day	2003
	Bang And Blame	1994
	Bittersweet Me	1996
	Crush With Eyeliner	1995
	Daysleeper	1998
	Drive	1992
	E-Bow The Letter	1996
	Electrolite	1996
	Everybody Hurts	1993
	The Great Beyond	2000
	Imitation Of Life	2001
	It's The End Of The World As We Know It	1991
	Leaving New York	2004

ARTIST	SONG TITLE	DATE
	Losing My Religion	1991
	Lotus	1998
	Man On The Moon	1992
	Near Wild Heaven	1991
	Nightswimming	1993
	The One I Love	1987
	Orange Crush	1989
	Radio Song	1991
	Shiny Happy People	1991
	The Sidewinder Sleeps Tonite	1993
	Stand	1989
	Strange Currencies	1995
	Tongue	1995
	What's The Frequency, Kenneth?	1994
EDDIE RABBITT	Drivin' My Life Away	1980
	Every Which Way But Loose	1979
	I Don't Know Where To Start	1982
	I Love A Rainy Night	1980
	Someone Could Lose A Heart Tonight	1981
	Step By Step	1981
	Suspicions	1979
EDDIE RABBITT WITH CRYSTAL GAYLE		
	You And I	1982
STEVE RACE	Pied Piper (The Beeje)	1963
RACEY	Boy Oh Boy	1979
	Lay Your Love On Me	1978

ARTIST	SONG TITLE	DATE
	Runaround Sue	1980
	Some Girls	1979
RACING CARS	They Shoot Horses Don't They?	1977
JIMMY RADCLIFFE	Long After Tonight Is All Over	1965
RADHA KRISHNA TEMPLE		
	Govinda	1970
	Hare Krishna	1969
RADIO HEART featuring GARY NUMAN		
	Radio Heart	1987
RADIO STARS	Nervous Wreck	1978
RADIOHEAD	Anyone Can Play Guitar	1993
	Creep	1993
	Fake Plastic Trees	1995
	Go To Sleep	2003
	High & Dry/Planet Telex	1995
	Just	1995
	Karma Police	1997
	Knives Out	2001
	My Iron Lung (EP)	1994
	No Surprises	1998
	Paranoid Android	1997
	Pyramid Song	2001
	Street Spirit (Fade Out)	1996
	There There	2003
	2 + 2 = 5	2003
RADISH	Little Pink Stars	1997

ARTIST	SONG TITLE	DATE
CHEF RAEKWON	Ice Cream	1995
GERRY RAFFERTY	Baker Street	1978
	Days Gone Down	1979
	Get It Right Next Time	1979
	Home And Dry	1978
	Night Owl	1979
	Right Down The Line	1978
RAGE	Run To You	1992
RAGE AGAINST THE MACHINE		
	Bombtrack	1993
	Bullet In The Head	1993
	Bulls On Parade	1996
	Guerrilla Radio	1999
	Killing In The Name	1993
	People Of The Sun	1996
RAGHAV	Can't Get Enough	2004
RAGHAV featuring JAHAZIEL		
	Let's Work It Out	2004
	(2PLAY featuring RAGHAV & JUCXI)	
	So Confused	2004
	(2PLAY featuring RAGHAV & NAILA BOSS)	
	It Can't Be Right	2004
RAGTIMERS	The Sting	1974
RAH BAND	Clouds Across The Moon	1985
	The Crunch	1977
	Falcon	1980

ARTIST	SONG TITLE	DATE
RAILWAY CHILDREN		
	Every Beat Of My Heart	1991
RAINBOW	It's A Rainbow	2002
RAINBOW	All Night Long	1980
	Can't Happen Here	1981
	I Surrender	1981
	L.A. Connection	1978
	Long Live Rock'n'Roll	1978
	Since You've Been Gone	1979
	Stone Cold	1982
RAINBOW COTTAGE		
	Seagull	1976
RAINMAKERS	Let My People Go-Go	1987
BONNIE RAITT	I Can't Make You Love Me	1991
	Love Sneakin' Up On You	1994
	Not The Only One	1992
	Something To Talk About	1991
	You	1994
	You Got It	1995
RAKIM	Guess Who's Back	1997
	(TRUTH HURTS featuring RAKIM)	
	Addictive	2002
TONY RALLO & THE MIDNITE BAND		
	Holdin' On	1980
RAM JAM	Black Betty	1977
EDDIE RAMBEAU	Concrete And Clay	1965

ARTIST	SONG TITLE	DATE
RAMBLERS	The Sparrow	1979
KAREN RAMIREZ	If We Try	1998
	Looking For Love	1998
RAMMSTEIN	Amerika	2004
	Feuer Frei	2002
	Ich Will	2002
RAMONES	Baby, I Love You	1980
	Don't Come Close	1978
	Sheena Is A Punk Rocker	1977
	Swallow My Pride	1977
RAMPAGE featuring BILLY LAWRENCE		
	Take It To The Streets	1997
RANK 1	Airwave	2000
SHABBA RANKS	Family Affair	1993
	Let's Get It On	1995
	Mr. Loverman	1992
SHABBA RANKS featuring JOHNNY GILL		
	Slow And Sexy	1992
SHABBA RANKS featuring MAXI PRIEST		
	Housecall	1993
SHABBA RANKS featuring QUEEN LATIFAH		
	What'cha Gonna Do?	1993
	(SCRITTI POLITTI featuring SHABBA RANKS)	
	She's A Woman	1991
RAPINATION/KYM MAZELLE		
	Love Me The Right Way	1992

ARTIST	SONG TITLE	DATE
RAPPIN' 4-TAY	Playaz Club	1994
RAPPIN' 4-TAY featuring THE SPINNERS		
	I'll Be Around	1995
THE RAPTURE	House Of Jealous Lovers	2003
	Love Is All	2004
RARE BIRD	Sympathy	1970
RARE EARTH	Born To Wander	1970
	Get Ready	1970
	Hey Big Brother	1971
	I Just Want To Celebrate	1971
	(I Know) I'm Losing You	1970
	Warm Ride	1978
RASCAL FLATTS	I Melt	2003
	Love You Out Loud	2003
	Mayberry	2004
	Prayin' For Daylight	2000
	These Days	2002
RASCALS	A Beautiful Morning	1968
	Carry Me Back	1969
	Heaven	1969
	People Got To Be Free	1968
	A Ray Of Hope	1968
	See	1969
	(YOUNG RASCALS)	
	A Girl Like You	1967
	Good Lovin'	1966

ARTIST	SONG TITLE	DATE
	Groovin'	1967
	How Can I Be Sure	1967
	I've Been Lonely Too Long	1967
	It's Wonderful	1967
	You Better Run	1966
RASMUS	Guilty	2004
	In The Shadows	2004
RASPBERRIES	Go All The Way	1972
	I Wanna Be With You	1972
	Let's Pretend	1973
	Overnight Sensation (Hit Record)	1974
ROLAND RAT SUPERSTAR		
	Love Me Tender	1984
	Rat Rapping	1983
RATT	Lay It Down	1985
	Round And Round	1984
RATTLES	The Witch	1970
RAVEN MAIZE	Fascinated	2002
	The Real Life	2001
THE RAVEONETTES	That Great Love Sound	2003
RAW SILK	Do It To The Music	1982
LOU RAWLS	Dead End Street	1967
	Lady Love	1978
	Love Is A Hurtin' Thing	1966
	A Natural Man	1971
	Your Good Thing (Is About To End)	1969

ARTIST	SONG TITLE	DATE
	You'll Never Find Another Love Like Mine	1976
RAY, GOODMAN & BROWN		
	Special Lady	1980
JIMMY RAY	Are You Jimmy Ray?	1998
RAYBON BROTHERS		
	Butterfly Kisses	1997
RAYDIO	Is This A Love Thing	1978
	Jack And Jill	1978
COLLIN RAYE	Anyone Else	1999
	Someone You Used To Know	1998
RAYVON/SHAGGY		
	Angel	2001
	In The Summertime	1995
RAZE	Break 4 Love	1988
	Jack The Groove	1987
RAZE featuring LADY J AND SECRETARY OF ENTERTAINMENT	All 4 Love (Break 4 Love 1990)	1990
RAZE presents DOUG LAZY		
	Let It Roll	1989
RAZORLIGHT	Golden Touch	2004
	Stumble & Fall	2004
	Vice	2004
RE-FLEX	The Politics Of Dancing	1983
CHRIS REA	Auberge	1991
	Fool (If You Think It's Over)	1978

ARTIST	SONG TITLE	DATE
	God's Great Banana Skin	1992
	Julia	1993
	Let's Dance	1987
	Nothing To Fear	1992
	On The Beach Summer 88	1988
	The Road To Hell (Pt 2)	1989
	Stainsby Girls	1985
	Tell Me There's A Heaven	1990
	Winter Song	1991
	You Can Go Your Own Way	1994
EDDI READER	Patience Of Angels	1994
	Town Without Pity	1996
READY FOR THE WORLD		
	Digital Display	1985
	Love You Down	1986
	Oh Sheila	1985
REAL LIFE	Catch Me I'm Falling	1984
	Send Me An Angel	1983
REAL MCCOY	Come And Get Your Love	1995
	One More Time	1997
	(MC SAR & THE REAL MCCOY)	
	Another Night	1994
	Run Away	1995
	Love & Devotion	1995
REAL PEOPLE	Believer	1992

ARTIST	SONG TITLE	DATE
REAL ROXANNE WITH HITMAN HOWIE		
	(Bang Zoom) Let's Go Go	1986
REAL THING	Boogie Down (Get Funky Now)	1979
	Can You Feel The Force	1979
	Can't Get By Without You	1976
	Let's Go Disco	1978
	Love's Such A Wonderful Thing	1977
	Rainin' Through My Sunshine	1978
	Whenever You Want My Love	1978
	You To Me Are Everything	1976
	You'll Never Know What You're Missing	1977
REBEL MC	Better World	1990
REBEL MC/TENOR FLY/BARRINGTON LEVY		
	Tribal Base	1991
REBEL MC/DOUBLE TROUBLE		
	Just Keep Rockin'	1989
	Street Tuff	1989
RED 'N' WHITE MACHINES		
	Southampton Boys	2003
RED BOX	For America	1986
	Lean On Me (Ah-Li-Ayo)	1985
RED DRAGON/BRIAN & TONY GOLD		
	Compliments On Your Kiss	1994
RED 5	I Love You... Stop!	1997
	Lift Me Up	1997

ARTIST	SONG TITLE	DATE
RED HILL CHILDREN		
	When Children Rule The World	1996
RED HOT CHILI PEPPERS		
	Aeroplane	1996
	Around The World	1999
	By The Way	2002
	Californication	2000
	Can't Stop	2003
	Fortune Faded	2003
	Give It Away	1994
	Love Rollercoaster	1997
	My Friends	1995
	Otherside	2000
	Road Trippin'	2001
	Scar Tissue	1999
	Soul To Squeeze	1993
	Taste The Pain	1990
	Under The Bridge	1992
	Universally Speaking	2003
	Warped	1995
	The Zephyr Song	2002
REDBONE	Come And Get Your Love	1974
	The Witch Queen Of New Orleans	1971
SHARON REDD	In The Name Of Love	1983
	Love How You Feel	1983
	Never Give You Up	1982

ARTIST	SONG TITLE	DATE
(DNA featuring SHARON REDD)		
	Can You Handle It	1992
GENE REDDING	This Heart	1974
OTIS REDDING	Amen	1968
	Fa-Fa-Fa-Fa-Fa (Sad Songs)	1966
	The Happy Song (Dum-Dum)	1968
	Hard To Handle	1968
	(I Can't Get No) Satisfaction	1966
	I Can't Turn You Loose	1966
	I've Been Loving You Too Long (To Stop Now)	1965
	My Girl	1965
	My Lover's Prayer	1966
	Papa's Got A Brand New Bag	1968
	Respect	1965
	Satisfaction	1966
	Shake	1967
	(Sittin' On) The Dock Of The Bay	1968
	Try A Little Tenderness	1966
OTIS REDDING & CARLA THOMAS		
	Knock On Wood	1967
	Tramp	1967
HELEN REDDY	Ain't No Way To Treat A Lady	1975
	Angie Baby	1974
	Bluebird	1975
	Delta Dawn	1973
	Emotion	1975
	I Am Woman	1972
	I Can't Hear You No More/Music Is My Life	1976
	I Don't Know How To Love Him	1971
	Keep On Singing	1974
	Leave Me Alone (Ruby Red Dress)	1973
	Peaceful	1973
	Somewhere In The Night	1975
	You And Me Against The World	1974
	You're My World	1977
REDEYE	Games	1970
REDHEAD KINGPIN & THE FBI		
	Do The Right Thing	1989
REDMAN featuring ADAM F		
	Smash Sumthin'	2001
REDMAN/METHOD MAN		
	How High	1995
(BEVERLEY KNIGHT featuring REDMAN)		
	Made It Back	1998
(CHRISTINA AGUILERA featuring REDMAN)		
	Dirrty	2002
(DE LA SOUL featuring REDMAN)		
	Oooh	2000
(DRU HILL featuring REDMAN)		
	How Deep Is Your Love	1998

ARTIST	SONG TITLE	DATE
	(ERICK SERMON featuring REDMAN)	
	React	2002
REDNEX	Cotton Eye Joe	1995
	Old Pop In An Oak	1995
REDS UNITED	Sing Up For The Champions	1997
	United Calypso '98	1998
REDSKINS	Bring It Down (The Insane Thing)	1985
ALEX REECE	Candles	1996
	Feel The Sunshine	1996
DAN REED NETWORK		
	Ritual	1988
	Stardate	1990
	Rainbow Child	1990
JERRY REED	Amos Moses	1970
	When You're Hot, You're Hot	1971
LOU REED	Satellite Of Love '04	2004
	Walk On The Wild Side	1973
	(SAM MOORE & LOU REED)	
	Soul Man	1987
REEF	Come Back Brighter	1997
	Consideration	1997
	Good Feeling	1995
	I've Got Something To Say	1999
	Naked	1995
	Place Your Hands	1996
	Set The Record Straight	2000

ARTIST	SONG TITLE	DATE
	Weird	1995
	Yer Old	1997
REEL	Lift Me Up	2001
	You Take Me Away	2002
REEL 2 REAL	Are You Ready For Some More?	1996
	Go On Move	1994
	Jazz It Up	1996
REEL 2 REAL featuring THE MAD STUNTMAN		
	Can You Feel It?	1994
	Conway	1995
	I Like To Move It	1994
	Raise Your Hands	1994
REELISTS	Freak Mode	2002
CONNER REEVES	Earthbound	1997
	My Father's Son	1997
	Read My Mind	1998
	Searching For A Soul	1998
	(MARK MORRISON & CONNER REEVES)	
	Best Friend	1999
JIM REEVES	Angels Don't Lie	1970
	But You Love Me, Daddy	1969
	Distant Drums	1966
	Guilty	1963
	I Heard A Heart Break Last Night	1967
	I Love You Because/He'll Have To Go/	
	Moonlight & Roses	1971

ARTIST	SONG TITLE	DATE
	I Won't Come In While He's There	1967
	I Won't Forget You	1964
	Is It Really Over	1965
	It Hurts So Much (To See You Go)	1965
	Nobody's Fool	1970
	Not Until The Next Time	1965
	Pretty Brown Eyes	1968
	There's A Heartache Following Me	1964
	This World Is Not My Home	1965
	Trying To Forget	1967
	Welcome To My World	1963
	When Two Worlds Collide	1969
VIC REEVES & THE WONDER STUFF		
	Dizzy	1991
VIC REEVES/THE ROMAN NUMERALS		
	Born Free	1991
	(EMF/REEVES AND MORTIMER)	
	I'm A Believer	1995
REFLECTIONS	(Just Like) Romeo & Juliet	1964
REFUGEE ALLSTARS/LAURYN HILL		
	The Sweetest Thing	1997
	(WYCLEF JEAN AND THE REFUGEE ALLSTARS)	
	Guantanamera	1997
	We Trying To Stay Alive	1997
REFUGEE CAMP ALLSTARS featuring PRAS		
WITH KY-MANI	Avenues	1997

ARTIST	SONG TITLE	DATE
	(BRIAN HARVEY AND THE REFUGEE CREW)	
	Loving You (Ole Ole Ole)	2001
REGENTS	7 Teen	1979
REGGAE PHILHARMONIC ORCHESTRA		
	Minnie The Moocher	1988
REGINA	Baby Love	1986
CLARENCE REID	Nobody But You Babe	1969
MIKE REID	The Ugly Duckling	1975
NEIL REID	Mother Of Mine	1972
REMBRANDTS	I'll Be There For You/This House Is Not	
	A Home	1995
	Just The Way It Is, Baby	1991
RENAISSANCE	Northern Lights	1978
DIANE RENAY	Kiss Me Sailor	1964
	Navy Blue	1964
RENE & ANGELA	I'll Be Good	1985
RENE & RENE	Lo Mucho Que Te Quiero (The More I	
	Love You)	1968
RENEE AND RENATO		
	Save Your Love	1982
RENEGADE SOUNDWAVE		
	Probably A Robbery	1990
MIKE RENO & ANN WILSON		
	Almost Paradise... Love Theme From	
	Footloose	1984

ARTIST	SONG TITLE	DATE
REO SPEEDWAGON		
	Can't Fight This Feeling	1985
	Don't Let Him Go	1981
	Here With Me	1988
	I Do' Wanna Know	1984
	In My Dreams	1987
	In Your Letter	1981
	Keep On Loving You	1980
	Keep The Fire Burnin'	1982
	Live Every Moment	1985
	One Lonely Night	1985
	Sweet Time	1982
	Take It On The Run	1981
	That Ain't Love	1987
REPERATA & THE DELRONS		
	Captain Of Your Ship	1968
REPUBLICA	Drop Dead Gorgeous	1997
	From Rush Hour With Love	1998
	Ready To Go	1997
REST ASSURED	Treat Infamy	1998
RESTLESS HEART	I'll Still Be Loving You	1987
	When She Cries	1992
REUNION	Life Is A Rock (But The Radio Rolled Me)	1974
REVELATION	Just Be Dub To Me	2003

ARTIST	SONG TITLE	DATE
PAUL REVERE & THE RAIDERS		
	Don't Take It So Hard	1968
	Good Thing	1966
	The Great Airplane Strike	1966
	Him Or Me — What's It Gonna Be	1967
	Hungry	1966
	I Had A Dream	1967
	Just Like Me	1965
	Kicks	1966
	Let Me	1969
	Mr. Sun, Mr. Moon	1969
	Too Much Talk	1968
	Ups And Downs	1967
RAIDERS	Birds Of A Feather	1971
	Indian Reservation (The Lament Of The Cherokee Reservation)	1971
REYNOLDS GIRLS	I'd Rather Jack	1989
LAWRENCE REYNOLDS		
	Jesus Is A Soul Man	1969
REZILLOS	Top Of The Pops	1978
REZONANCE Q	Someday	2003
RHIANNA	Oh Baby	2002
RHODA WITH SEPCIAL A.K.A.		
	The Boiler	1982
BUSTA RHYMES	Break Ya Neck	2001
	Dangerous	1998

ARTIST	SONG TITLE	DATE
	Do My Thing	1997
	Gimme Some More	1999
	Put Your Hands Where My Eyes Could See	1997
	Turn It Up/Fire It Up	1998
	Woo-Hah!! Got You All In Check	1996
BUSTA RHYMES AND MARIAH CAREY featuring FLIPMODE SQUAD	I Know What You Want	2003
BUSTA RHYMES featuring ERYKAH BADU	One	1998
BUSTA RHYMES featuring JANET	What's It Gonna Be?	1999
BUSTA RHYMES featuring P. DIDDY & PHARRELL	Pass The Courvoisier — Part II	2002
BUSTA RHYMES featuring SPLIFF STAR	Make It Clap	2003
BUSTA RHYMES featuring ZHANE	It's A Party	1996
(B REAL/BUSTA RHYMES/COOLIO/LL COOL J/METHOD MAN)	Hit 'Em High (The Monstars' Anthem)	1997
(M.O.P. featuring BUSTA RHYMES)	Ante Up	2001
(METHOD MAN featuring BUSTA RHYMES)	What's Happenin'	2004

ARTIST	SONG TITLE	DATE
(PUFF DADDY & THE FAMILY featuring THE NOTORIOUS B.I.G. & BUSTA RHYMES)	Victory	1998
RHYTHM HERITAGE	Barretta's Theme (Keep Your Eye On The Sparrow)	1976
	Theme From S.W.A.T.	1974
RHYTHM OF LIFE	You Put Me In Heaven With Your Touch	2000
RHYTHM ON THE LOOSE	Break Of Dawn	1995
RHYTHMKILLAZ	Wack Ass Mf	2001
RIALTO	Dream Another Dream	1998
	Monday Morning 5:19	1997
	Untouchable	1998
ROSIE RIBBONS	Blink	2002
	A Little Bit	2003
DAMIEN RICE	Cannonball	2004
RICH KIDS	Rich Kids	1978
CHARLIE RICH	Behind Closed Doors	1973
	Every Time You Touch Me (I Get High)	1975
	I Love My Friend	1974
	Mohair Sam	1965
	The Most Beautiful Girl	1973
	There Won't Be Anymore	1974
	A Very Special Love Song	1974
	We Love Each Other	1975
RICHIE RICH	I'll House You	1988

ARTIST	SONG TITLE	DATE
RISHI RICH PROJECT featuring JAY SEAN & JUGGY D		
	Dance With You (Nachna Tere Naal)	2003
	(JAY SEAN featuring RISHI RICH PROJECT)	
	Eyes On You	2004
TONY RICH PROJECT		
	Like A Woman	1996
	Nobody Knows	1995
RICHARD X featuring KELIS		
	Finest Dreams	2003
RICHARD X vs LIBERTY X		
	Being Nobody	2003
CLIFF RICHARD	All My Love	1967
	Baby You're Dynamite/Ocean Deep	1984
	The Best Of Me	1989
	Big Ship	1969
	Blue Turns To Grey	1966
	Can't Keep This Feeling In	1998
	Carrie	1980
	Congratulations	1968
	Constantly	1964
	Daddy's Home	1982
	The Day I Met Marie	1967
	Devil Woman	1976
	Don't Forget To Catch Me	1968
	Don't Talk To Him	1963
	Dreaming	1980

ARTIST	SONG TITLE	DATE
	Flying Machine	1971
	From A Distance	1990
	Good Times (Better Times)	1969
	Goodbye Sam, Hello Samantha	1970
	Healing Love	1993
	Help It Along/Tomorrow Rising	1973
	Hey Mr Dream Maker	1976
	Human Work Of Art	1993
	I Ain't Got Time Any More	1970
	I Can't Ask For Any More Than You	1976
	I Could Easily Fall	1964
	I Just Don't Have The Heart	1989
	I Still Believe In You	1992
	I'll Come Runnin'	1967
	I'll Love You Forever Today	1968
	I'm The Lonely One	1964
	In The Country	1966
	It's All In The Game	1963
	It's All Over	1967
	Jesus	1972
	The Joy Of Living	1970
	Lean On You	1989
	Let Me Be The One	2002
	A Little In Love	1980
	Little Town	1982
	Living In Harmony	1972

ARTIST	SONG TITLE	DATE
	Lucky Lips	1963
	Marianne	1968
	The Millennium Prayer	1999
	The Minute You're Gone	1965
	The Miracle	1999
	Miss You Nights	1976
	Mistletoe And Wine	1988
	Misunderstood Man	1995
	More To Life	1991
	My Kinda Life	1977
	My Pretty One	1987
	Never Let Go	1993
	Never Say Die (Give A Little Bit More)	1983
	On My Word	1965
	On The Beach	1964
	The Only Way Out	1982
	Peace In Our Time	1993
	Please Don't Fall In Love	1983
	Power To All Our Friends	1973
	Remember Me	1987
	Santa's List	2003
	Saviour's Day	1990
	She's So Beautiful	1985
	Silhouettes	1990
	Silvery Rain	1971
	Sing A Song Of Freedom	1971

ARTIST	SONG TITLE	DATE
	Some People	1987
	Somethin' Is Goin' On	2004
	Somewhere Over The Rainbow/	
	What A Wonderful World	2001
	Stronger Than That	1990
	Summer Holiday	1963
	Sunny Honey Girl	1971
	Take Me High	1973
	This New Year	1992
	Time Drags By	1966
	The Time In Between	1965
	True Love Ways	1983
	The Twelfth Of Never	1964
	Two Hearts	1988
	Visions	1966
	We Don't Talk Anymore	1979
	We Should Be Together	1991
	When Two Worlds Drift Apart	1977
	Wind Me Up (Let Me Go)	1965
	Wired For Sound	1981
	With The Eyes Of A Child	1969
	(You Keep Me) Hangin' On	1974
CLIFF RICHARD & OLIVIA NEWTON-JOHN		
	Had To Be	1995
CLIFF RICHARD & SARAH BRIGHTMAN		
	All I Ask Of You	1986

ARTIST	SONG TITLE	DATE
CLIFF RICHARD & THE YOUNG ONES		
	Living Doll	1986
CLIFF RICHARD featuring HELEN HOBSON		
	The Wedding	1996
CLIFF RICHARD/PHIL EVERLY		
	All I Have To Do Is Dream/Miss You Nights	1994
CLIFF & HANK	Throw Down A Line	1969
(OLIVIA NEWTON-JOHN & CLIFF RICHARD)		
	Suddenly	1980
(PHIL EVERLY & CLIFF RICHARD)		
	She Means Nothing To Me	1983
(VAN MORRISON WITH CLIFF RICHARD)		
	Whenever God Shines His Light	1989
LIONEL RICHIE	All Night Long (All Night)	1983
	Angel	2000
	Ballerina Girl	1986
	Closest Thing To Heaven	1998
	Dancing On The Ceiling	1986
	Do It To Me	1992
	Don't Stop The Music	2000
	Don't Wanna Lose You	1996
	Hello	1984
	I Forgot	2001
	Just For You	2004
	Love Will Conquer All	1986
	My Destiny	1992
	My Love	1983
	Penny Lover	1984
	Running With The Night	1983
	Say You, Say Me	1985
	Se La	1987
	Stuck On You	1984
	Tender Heart	2001
	Truly	1982
	You Are	1983
LIONEL RICHIE featuring ENRIQUE IGLESIAS		
	To Love A Woman	2003
(DIANA ROSS & LIONEL RICHIE)		
	Endless Love	1981
SHANE RICHIE	I'm Your Man	2003
JONATHAN RICHMAN & THE MODERN LOVERS		
	Egyptian Reggae	1977
	The Morning Of Our Lives	1978
	Roadrunner	1977
ADAM RICKITT	Best Thing	2000
	Everything My Heart Desires	1999
	I Breathe Again	1999
RIDE	Birdman	1994
	Fall (EP)	1990
	Leave Them All Behind	1992
	Play (EP)	1990

ARTIST	SONG TITLE	DATE
	Today Forever (EP)	1991
	Twisterella	1992
STAN RIDGWAY	Camouflage	1986
RIFF	My Heart Is Failing Me	1991
RIGHT SAID FRED	Bumped	1993
	Deeply Dippy	1992
	I'm Too Sexy	1991
	Stick It Out	1993
	Those Simple Things/Daydream	1992
	You're My Mate	2001
RIGHT SAID FRED/JOCELYN BROWN		
	Don't Talk Just Kiss	1991
RIGHTEOUS BROTHERS		
	Dream On	1974
	Ebb Tide	1965
	Give It To The People	1974
	Go Ahead And Cry	1966
	He	1966
	Island In The Sun	1966
	Just Once In My Life	1965
	Rock And Roll Heaven	1974
	Unchained Melody	1990
	The White Cliffs Of Dover	1966
	(You're My) Soul And Inspiration	1966
	You've Lost That Lovin' Feelin'	1964

ARTIST	SONG TITLE	DATE
RIKKI & DAZ featuring GLEN CAMPBELL		
	Rhinestone Cowboy (Giddy Up Giddy Up)	2002
CHERYL 'PEPSII' RILEY		
	Thanks For My Child	1988
JEANNIE C. RILEY	Harper Valley P.T.A.	1968
LEANN RIMES	Big Deal	1999
	Blue	1996
	But I Do Love You	2002
	Can't Fight The Moonlight	2001
	Crazy	1999
	How Do I Live	1997
	I Need You	2001
	Life Goes On	2002
	Looking Through Your Eyes/Commitment	1998
	We Can	2003
	(ELTON JOHN & LEANN RIMES)	
	Written In The Stars	1999
	(RONAN KEATING & LEANN RIMES)	
	Last Thing On My Mind	2004
RIMSHOTS	7-6-5-4-3-2-1 (Blow Your Whistle)	1975
MIGUEL RIOS	Song Of Joy	1970
WALDO DE LOS RIOS		
	Mozart Symphony No. 40 In G Minor	1971
RIP CHORDS	Three Window Coupe	1964
MINNIE RIPERTON	Lovin' You	1975

ARTIST	SONG TITLE	DATE
RITCHIE FAMILY	The Best Disco In Town	1976
	Brazil	1975
LEE RITENOUR	Is It You	1981
RIVA featuring DANNII MINOGUE		
	Who Do You Love Now? (Stringer)	2001
RIVER CITY PEOPLE		
	California Dreamin'/Carry The Blame	1990
	Standing In The Need Of Love	1992
	(What's Wrong With) Dreaming?	1990
ROBBIE RIVERA presents RHYTHM BANGERS		
	Bang	2000
JOHNNY RIVERS	Baby I Need Your Lovin'	1967
	Blue Suede Shoes	1973
	Help Me Rhonda	1975
	(I Washed My Hands In) Muddy Water	1966
	Maybelline	1964
	Memphis	1964
	Midnight Special	1965
	Mountain Of Love	1964
	Poor Side Of Town	1966
	Rockin' Pneumonia & The Boogie Woogie Flu	1972
	Secret Agent Man	1966
	Seventh Son	1965
	Summer Rain	1967
	Swayin' To The Music (Slow Dancin')	1977

ARTIST	SONG TITLE	DATE
	The Tracks Of My Tears	1967
	Under Your Spell Again	1965
	Where Have All The Flowers Gone?	1965
RIVIERAS	California Sun	1964
ROACHFORD	Cuddly Toy (Feel For Me)	1989
	Family Man	1989
	Get Ready!	1991
	How Could I? (Insecurity)	1998
	Lay Your Love On Me	1994
	Only To Be With You	1994
	This Generation	1994
	The Way I Feel	1997
ROAD APPLES	Let's Live Together	1975
ROB 'N' RAZ featuring LEILA K		
	Got To Get	1989
KATE ROBBINS	More Than In Love	1981
MARTY ROBBINS	Ruby Ann	1962
AUSTIN ROBERTS	Rocky	1975
	Something's Wrong With Me	1972
JOE ROBERTS	Back In My Life	1994
	Lover	1994
	(MELANIE WILLIAMS & JOE ROBERTS)	
	You Are Everything	1995
JULIET ROBERTS	Again/I Want You	1994
	Bad Girls/I Like	1999
	Caught In The Middle	1994

ARTIST	SONG TITLE	DATE
	Free Love	1993
	So Good/Free Love 98	1998
(DAVID MORALES presents THE FACE featuring JULIET ROBERTS)		
	Needin' U II	2001
KANE ROBERTS	Does Anybody Really Fall In Love Anymore	1991
MALCOLM ROBERTS		
	Love Is All	1969
	May I Have The Next Dream With You	1968
B.A. ROBERTSON	Bang Bang	1979
	Knocked It Off	1979
	Kool In The Kaftan	1980
	To Be Or Not To Be	1980
B.A. ROBERTSON & MAGGIE BELL		
	Hold Me	1981
ROBBIE ROBERTSON		
	Somewhere Down The Crazy River	1988
SMOKEY ROBINSON		
	The Agony And The Ecstasy	1975
	Baby Come Close	1973
	Bay That's Backatcha	1975
	Being With You	1981
	Cruisin'	1979
	Just My Soul Responding	1974
	Just To See Her	1987

ARTIST	SONG TITLE	DATE
	Let Me Be The Block	1980
	One Heartbeat	1987
	Tell Me Tomorrow (Part 1)	1982
SMOKEY ROBINSON & THE MIRACLES		
	The Tears Of A Clown	1970
(FOUR TOPS featuring SMOKEY ROBINSON)		
	Indestructible	1989
TOM ROBINSON	Listen To The Radio (Atmospherics)	1983
	Rising Free (EP)	1978
	2-4-6-8 Motorway	1977
	Up Against The Wall	1978
	War Baby	1983
VICKI SUE ROBINSON		
	Turn The Beat Around	1976
ROBYN	Do You Know (What It Takes)	1997
	Do You Really Want Me	1998
	Show Me Love	1997
ERIN ROCHA	Can't Do Right For Doing Wrong	2003
ROCHELLE	My Magic Man	1986
ROCK AID ARMENIA		
	Smoke On The Water	1989
ROCK FOLLIES	O.K.	1977
ROCKERS REVENGE		
	Walking On Sunshine	1982
ROCKERS REVENGE featuring DONNIE CALVIN		
	The Harder They Come	1983

ARTIST	SONG TITLE	DATE
ROCKET FROM THE CRYPT		
	On A Rope	1996
ROCKETS	Oh Well	1979
ROCKFORD FILES	You Sexy Dancer	1995
ROCKIN' BERRIES	He's In Town	1964
	Poor Man's Son	1965
	What In The World's Come Over You	1965
	You're My Girl	1965
ROCKSTEADY CREW	(Hey You) The Rocksteady Crew	1983
ROCKWELL	Obscene Phone Caller	1984
	Somebody's Watching Me	1984
ROCKY V/JB ELLIS & T HARE		
	Go For It! (Heart And Fire)	1991
CLODAGH RODGERS		
	Biljo	1969
	Come Back And Shake Me	1969
	Goodnight Midnight	1969
	Jack In The Box	1971
	Lady Love Bug	1971
JIMMIE RODGERS	Child Of Clay	1967
	It's Over	1966
RODS	Do Anything You Wanna Do	1977
TOMMY ROE	Come On	1964
	Dizzy	1969
	Everybody	1963
	The Folk Singer	1963

ARTIST	SONG TITLE	DATE
	Heather Honey	1969
	Hooray For Hazel	1966
	It's Now Winters Day	1966
	Jam Up Jelly Tight	1969
	Stagger Lee	1971
	Susie Darlin'	1962
	Sweet Pea	1966
ROGER	I Want To Be Your Man	1987
	(2PAC featuring DR. DRE & ROGER TROUTMAN)	
	California Love/How Do U Want It	1996
JULIE ROGERS	Hawaiian Wedding Song	1965
	Like A Child	1964
	The Wedding	1964
KENNY ROGERS	All My Life	1983
	Coward Of The County	1979
	Daytime Friends	1977
	The Gambler	1978
	I Don't Need You	1981
	Lady	1980
	Love Or Something Like That	1978
	Love The World Away	1980
	Love Will Turn You Around	1982
	Lucille	1977
	Share Your Love	1981
	She Believes In Me	1979

ARTIST	SONG TITLE	DATE
	This Woman	1984
	Through The Years	1981
	You Decorated My Life	1979
KENNY ROGERS & DOLLY PARTON		
	Islands In The Stream	1983
KENNY ROGERS & KIM CARNES		
	Don't Fall In Love With A Dreamer	1980
KENNY ROGERS & THE FIRST EDITION		
	Heed The Call	1970
	Ruben James	1969
	Ruby, Don't Take Your Love To Town	1969
	Something's Burning	1970
	Tell It All Brother	1970
KENNY ROGERS WITH ALISON KRAUSS & BILLY DEAN		
	Buy Me A Rose	2000
KENNY ROGERS WITH KIM CARNES & JAMES INGRAM		
	What About Me?	1984
(DOTTIE WEST & KENNY ROGERS)		
	What Are We Doin' In Love	1981
(FIRST EDITION)		
	But You Know I Love You	1969
	Just Dropped In (To See What Condition My Condition Was In)	1968
(SHEENA EASTON & KENNY ROGERS)		
	We've Got Tonight	1983
ROKOTTO	Boogie On Up	1977

ARTIST	SONG TITLE	DATE
ROLLERGIRL	Dear Jessie	2000
ROLLING STONES	Ain't Too Proud To Beg	1974
	Almost Hear You Sigh	1990
	Angie	1973
	Anybody Seen My Baby?	1997
	As Tears Go By	1965
	Beast Of Burden	1978
	Brown Sugar	1971
	Come On	1963
	Dandelion	1967
	Don't Stop	2002
	Doo Doo Doo Doo Doo (Heartbreaker)	1974
	Emotional Rescue	1980
	Fool To Cry	1976
	Get Off Of My Cloud	1965
	Going To A Go-Go	1982
	Hang Fire	1982
	Happy	1972
	Harlem Shuffle	1986
	Have You Seen Your Mother Baby Standing In The Shadow?	1966
	Heart Of Stone	1965
	Highwire	1991
	Honky Tonk Women	1969
	(I Can't Get No) Satisfaction	1965
	I Go Wild	1995

ARTIST	SONG TITLE	DATE
	I Wanna Be Your Man	1963
	It's All Over Now	1964
	It's Only Rock 'n Roll (But I Like It)	1974
	Jumpin' Jack Flash	1968
	Lady Jane	1966
	The Last Time	1965
	Let's Spend The Night Together/Ruby Tuesday	1967
	Like A Rolling Stone	1995
	Little Red Rooster	1964
	Love Is Strong	1994
	Miss You	1978
	Mixed Emotions	1989
	Mother's Little Helper	1966
	19th Nervous Breakdown	1966
	Not Fade Away	1964
	One Hit (To The Body)	1986
	Out Of Tears	1994
	Paint It Black	1966
	Respectable	1978
	Rock And A Hard Place	1989
	Saint Of Me	1998
	Shattered	1978
	She's A Rainbow	1967
	She's So Cold	1980
	Start Me Up	1981

ARTIST	SONG TITLE	DATE
	Street Fighting Man	1971
	Sympathy For The Devil	2003
	Tell Me (You're Coming Back)	1964
	Time Is On My Side	1964
	Tumbling Dice	1972
	Undercover Of The Night	1983
	Waiting On A Friend	1981
	We Love You/Dandelion	1967
	Wild Horses	1971
	You Got Me Rocking	1994
ROLLINS BAND	Liar/Disconnect	1994
ROLLO GOES MYSTIC		
	Love, Love, Love — Here I Come	1995
ROLLO GOES SPIRITUAL WITH PAULINE TAYLOR		
	Let This Be A Prayer	1996
ROMAN HOLLIDAY	Don't Try To Stop It	1983
	Motormania	1983
ROMANTICS	One In A Million	1984
	Talking In Your Sleep	1983
ROME	Do You Like This	1997
	I Belong To You (Every Time I See Your Face)	1997
ROMEO	Romeo Dunn	2002
ROMEO featuring CHRISTINA MILIAN		
	It's All Gravy	2002

ARTIST	SONG TITLE	DATE
	(OXIDE & NEUTRINO featuring MEGAMAN, ROMEO & LISA MAFFIA)	
	No Good 4 Me	2000
ROMEO VOID	A Girl In Trouble (Is A Temporary Thing)	1984
MAX ROMEO	Wet Dream	1969
HARRY 'CHOO CHOO' ROMERO presents INAYA DAY		
	Just Can't Get Enough	1999
RONALDO'S REVENGE		
	Mas Que Mancada	1998
RONETTES	Baby, I Love You	1964
	Be My Baby	1963
	Do I Love You	1964
	(The Best Part Of) Breakin' Up	1964
	Walking In The Rain	1964
RONNY & THE DAYTONAS		
	G.T.O.	1964
	Sandy	1965
MARK RONSON featuring GHOSTFACE KILLAH & NATE DOGG		
	Ooh Wee	2003
LINDA RONSTADT	Back In The U.S.A.	1978
	Blue Bayou	1977
	Get Closer	1982
	Heat Wave/Love Is A Rose	1975
	How Do I Make You	1980
	Hurt So Bad	1980
	I Can't Let Go	1980

ARTIST	SONG TITLE	DATE
	I Knew You When	1982
	It's So Easy	1977
	Long Long Time	1970
	Ooh Baby Baby	1978
	Poor Poor Pitiful Me	1978
	That'll Be The Day	1976
	Tracks Of My Tears	1975
	Tumbling Dice	1978
	When Will I Be Loved	1975
	You're No Good	1974
LINDA RONSTADT featuring AARON NEVILLE		
	All My Life	1990
	Don't Know Much	1989
LINDA RONSTADT AND JAMES INGRAM		
	Somewhere Out There	1987
ROOFTOP SINGERS	Walk Right In	1963
ROOM 5 featuring OLIVER CHEATHAM		
	Make Luv	2003
	Music & You	2003
ROOSTER	Come Get Some	2004
ROOTS	What They Do	1997
ROOTS featuring CODY CHESNUTT		
	The Seed (2.0)	2003
ROOTS featuring ERYKAH BADU		
	You Got Me	1999
ROSE GARDEN	Next Plane To London	1967

ARTIST	SONG TITLE	DATE
ROSE ROYCE	Car Wash/Is It Love You're After	1988
	Do Your Dance	1977
	I Wanna Get Next To You	1977
	It Makes You Feel Like Dancin'	1978
	Love Don't Live Here Anymore	1978
	Wishing On A Star	1978
DIANA ROSS	Ain't No Mountain High Enough	1970
	All Of My Life	1974
	The Best Years Of My Life	1994
	The Boss	1979
	Chain Reaction	1986
	Doobedood'ndoobe Doobedood'ndoobe	1972
	The Force Behind The Power	1992
	Gettin' Ready For Love	1977
	Good Morning Heartache	1973
	Heart (Don't Change My Mind)	1993
	I Thought It Took A Little Time (But Today I Fell In Love)	1976
	I Will Survive	1996
	I'm Coming Out	1980
	I'm Gone	1995
	I'm Still Waiting	1971
	If We Hold On Together	1992
	In The Ones You Love	1996
	It's My House	1979
	It's My Turn	1980

ARTIST	SONG TITLE	DATE
	Last Time I Saw Him	1974
	Love Hangover	1976
	Love Me	1974
	Mirror Mirror	1982
	Missing You	1984
	Muscles	1982
	My Old Piano	1980
	Not Over You Yet	1999
	One Love In A Lifetime	1976
	One Shining Moment	1992
	Pieces Of Ice	1983
	Reach Out And Touch (Somebody's Hand)	1970
	Reach Out I'll Be There	1971
	Remember Me	1970
	So Close	1983
	Sorry Doesn't Always Make It Right	1975
	Surrender	1971
	Swept Away	1984
	Take Me Higher	1995
	Theme From Mahogany (Do You Know Where You're Going To)	1975
	Touch Me In The Morning	1973
	Upside Down	1980
	When You Tell Me That You Love Me	1991
	Why Do Fools Fall In Love	1981
	Work That Body	1982

ARTIST	SONG TITLE	DATE
	Workin' Overtime	1989
	Your Love	1993
DIANA ROSS & LIONEL RICHIE		
	Endless Love	1981
DIANA ROSS & MARVIN GAYE		
	Stop, Look, Listen (To Your Heart)	1974
	You Are Everything	1974
(JULIO IGLESIAS & DIANA ROSS)		
	All Of You	1984
(MARVIN GAYE & DIANA ROSS)		
	My Mistake (Was To Love You)	1974
	You're A Special Part Of Me	1973
JACKIE ROSS	Selfish One	1964
RICKY ROSS	Radio On	1996
NINI ROSSO	Il Silenzio	1965
DAVID LEE ROTH	California Girls	1985
	Just A Gigolo/I Ain't Got Nobody	1985
	Just Like Paradise	1988
	A Lil' Ain't Enough	1991
	Yankee Rose	1986
ROTTERDAM TERMINATION SOURCE		
	Poing	1992
DEMIS ROUSSOS	Because	1977
	Can't Say How Much I Love You	1976
	Happy To Be On An Island In The Sun	1975
	Kyrila (EP)	1977

ARTIST	SONG TITLE	DATE
	The Roussos Phenomenon (EP)	1976
	When Forever Has Gone	1976
KELLY ROWLAND	Can't Nobody	2003
	Stole	2002
	Train On A Track	2003
(NELLY featuring KELLY ROWLAND)		
	Dilemma	2002
JOHN ROWLES	Hush... Not A Word To Mary	1968
	If I Only Had Time	1968
LISA ROXANNE	No Flow	2001
ROXETTE	Almost Unreal	1993
	The Big L	1991
	Church Of Your Heart	1992
	Crash! Boom! Bang!	1994
	Dangerous	1989
	Dressed For Success	1989
	Fading Like A Flower (Every Time You Leave)	1991
	Fireworks	1994
	How Do You Do!	1992
	It Must Have Been Love	1990
	Joyride	1991
	Listen To Your Heart/Dangerous	1990
	The Look	1989
	Queen Of Rain	1992
	Run To You	1994

ARTIST	SONG TITLE	DATE
	Sleeping In My Car	1994
	Spending My Time	1991
	Wish I Could Fly	1999
ROXY MUSIC	All I Want Is You	1974
	Angel Eyes	1979
	Avalon	1982
	Both Ends Burning	1975
	Dance Away	1979
	Jealous Guy	1981
	Love Is The Drug	1975
	More Than This	1982
	Oh Yeah (On The Radio)	1980
	Over You	1980
	Pyjamarama	1973
	The Same Old Scene	1980
	Street Life	1973
	Take A Chance With Me	1982
	Trash	1979
	Virginia Plain	1972
ROY 'C'	Shotgun Wedding	1966
ROYAL GUARDSMEN		
	Return Of The Red Baron	1967
	Snoopy Vs. The Red Baron	1966
ROYAL HOUSE	Can You Party	1988
	Yeah! Buddy	1989

ARTIST	SONG TITLE	DATE
ROYAL PHILHARMONIC ORCHESTRA		
	Hooked On Classics	1981
ROYAL SCOTS DRAGOON GUARDS		
	Amazing Grace	1972
	Heykens Serenade (Standchen)/The Day Is Ended	1972
	Little Drummer Boy	1972
BILLY JOE ROYAL	Cherry Hill Park	1969
	Down In The Boondocks	1965
	I Knew You When	1965
	I've Got To Be Somebody	1965
ROYKSOPP	Eple	2003
	Poor Leno	2002
	Remind Me/So Easy	2002
ROZALLA	Are You Ready To Fly	1992
	Baby	1995
	Everybody's Free (To Feel Good)	1992
	Faith (In The Power Of Love)	1991
	I Love Music	1994
	This Time I Found Love	1994
	You Never Love The Same Way Twice	1994
RTZ	Until Your Love Comes Back Around	1992
RUBETTES	Baby I Know	1977
	Foe-Dee-O-Dee	1975
	I Can Do It	1975
	Juke Box Jive	1974

ARTIST	SONG TITLE	DATE
	Little Darling	1975
	Sugar Baby Love	1974
	Tonight	1974
	Under One Roof	1976
	You're The Reason Why	1976
MARIA RUBIA	Say It	2001
	(FRAGMA featuring MARIA RUBIA)	
	Everytime You Need Me	2001
RUBICON	I'm Gonna Take Care Of Everything	1978
RUBY & THE ROMANTICS		
	Our Day Will Come	1963
RUDE BOYS	Written All Over Your Face	1991
DANNY LA RUE	On Mother Kelly's Doorstep	1968
RUFF DRIVERZ	Deeper Love	1998
	Don't Stop	1998
	Dreaming	1998
	Waiting For The Sun	1999
RUFF DRIVERZ presents ARROLA		
	La Musica	1999
RUFF ENDZ	No More	2000
FRANCES RUFFELLE	Lonely Symphony	1994
BRUCE RUFFIN	Mad About You	1972
	Rain	1971
DAVID RUFFIN	My Whole World Ended (The Moment You Left Me)	1969
	Walk Away From Love	1975

ARTIST	SONG TITLE	DATE
JIMMY RUFFIN	Farewell Is A Lonely Sound	1970
	Gonna Give Her All The Love I've Got	1967
	Hold On To My Love	1980
	I'll Say Forever My Love	1970
	I've Passed This Way Before	1966
	It's Wonderful	1970
	Tell Me What You Want	1974
	What Becomes Of The Brokenhearted	1966
RUFFNECK featuring YAVAHN		
	Everybody Be Somebody	1995
RUFUS	Tell Me Something Good	1974
RUFUS & CHAKA KHAN		
	Ain't Nobody	1989
	Do You Love What You Feel	1979
	Stay	1978
RUFUS featuring CHAKA KHAN		
	At Midnight (My Love Will Lift You Up)	1977
	Dance Wit Me	1976
	Hollywood	1977
	Once You Get Started	1975
	Sweet Thing	1976
	You Got The Love	1974
RUGBYS	You, I	1969
RUN DMC	Down With The King	1993
	It's Tricky	1987
	Run's House	1988

ARTIST	SONG TITLE	DATE
	Walk This Way	1986
	You Be Illin'	1986
RUN DMC featuring JACKNIFE LEE		
	It's Tricky 2003	2003
RUN DMC vs JASON NEVINS		
	It's Like That	1998
TODD RUNDGREN	Can We Still Be Friends	1978
	Good Vibrations	1976
	Hello It's Me	1973
	I Saw The Light	1972
RUNRIG	An Abhal As Airde (The Highest Apple)	1995
	The Greatest Flame	1997
	Hearthammer	1991
	Rhythm Of My Heart	1996
	Things That Are	1995
	This Time Of Year	1995
	Wonderful	1993
RUNT	We Gotta Get You A Woman	1970
RUPAUL	House Of Love/Back To My Roots	1993
	Supermodel (You Better Work)	1993
(ELTON JOHN & RUPAUL)		
	Don't Go Breaking My Heart	1994
(MARTHA WASH featuring RUPAUL)		
	It's Raining Men... The Sequel	1998
RUSH	Closer To The Heart	1978
	Countdown/New World Man	1983

ARTIST	SONG TITLE	DATE
	The Spirit Of The Radio	1980
	Tom Sawyer	1981
JENNIFER RUSH	The Power Of Love	1985
	Ring Of Ice	1985
JENNIFER RUSH (DUET WITH ELTON JOHN)		
	Flames Of Paradise	1987
(PLACIDO DOMINGO & JENNIFER RUSH)		
	Till I Loved You	1989
MERRILEE RUSH	Angel Of The Morning	1968
PATRICE RUSHEN	Forget Me Nots	1982
	I Was Tired Of Being Alone	1982
BOBBY RUSSELL	1432 Franklin Pike Circle Hero	1968
	Saturday Morning Confusion	1971
BRENDA RUSSELL	Piano In The Dark	1988
	So Good, So Right	1979
LEON RUSSELL	Lady Blue	1975
	Tight Rope	1972
RUTLES	I Must Be In Love	1978
RUTS	Babylon's Burning	1979
	Something That I Said	1979
	Staring At The Rude Boys	1980
BARRY RYAN	Can't Let You Go	1972
	Eloise	1968
	The Hunt	1969
	Kitsch	1970
	Love Is Love	1969

ARTIST	SONG TITLE	DATE
JOSHUA RYAN	Pistol Whip	2001
PAUL & BARRY RYAN		
	Don't Bring Me Your Heartaches	1965
	Have Pity On The Boy	1966
	I Love Her	1966
	I Love How You Love Me	1966
	Keep It Out Of Sight	1967
REBEKAH RYAN	You Life Me Up	1996
BOBBY RYDELL	Forget Him	1963
MARK RYDER	Joy	2001
MITCH RYDER	What Now My Love	1967
MITCH RYDER & THE DETROIT WHEELS		
	Devil With A Blue Dress On & Good	
	Golly Miss Molly	1966
	Jenny Take A Ride!	1965
	Little Latin Lupe Lu	1966
	Sock It To Me Baby!	1967
	Too Many Fish In The Sea & Three	
	Little Fishes	1967
RYTHM SYNDICATE		
	Hey Donna	1991
	P.A.S.S.I.O.N.	1991
S CLUB	Alive	2002
	Say Goodbye/Love Ain't Gonna Wait For	
	You	2003
S CLUB 7	Bring It All Back	1999

ARTIST	SONG TITLE	DATE
	Don't Stop Movin'	2001
	Have You Ever	2001
	Natural	2000
	Never Had A Dream Come True	2001
	Reach	2000
	S Club Party	1999
	Two In A Million/You're My Number One	1999
	You	2002
S CLUB 8	Don't Tell Me You're Sorry	2004
	Fool No More	2003
	Sundown	2003
S CLUB JUNIORS	Automatic High	2002
	New Direction	2002
	One Step Closer	2002
	Puppy Love/Sleigh Ride	2002
S'EXPRESS	Hey Music Lover	1989
	Mantra For A State Of Mind	1989
	Nothing To Lose	1990
	Superfly Guy	1988
	Theme From S'Express	1988
S-J	I Feel Divine	1998
ROBIN S	It Must Be Love	1997
	Luv 4 Luv	1993
	Show Me Love	1993
S.M.A.S.H	(I Want To Kill) Somebody	1994

ARTIST	SONG TITLE	DATE
S.O.A.P.	This Is How We Party	1998
S.O.S. BAND	The Finest	1986
	Just Be Good To Me	1984
	Just The Way You Like It	1984
	Take Your Time (Do It Right) (Pt 1)	1980
S.O.U.L. S.Y.S.T.E.M. featuring MICHELLE VISAGE		
	It's Gonna Be A Lovely Day	1993
RAPHAEL SAADIQ	Ask Of You	1995
RAPHAEL SAADIQ & Q-TIP		
	Get Involved	1999
SABRES OF PARADISE		
	Wilmot	1994
SABRINA	All Of Me	1988
	Boys (Summertime Love)	1988
SACRED SPIRIT	Wishes Of Happiness & Prosperity	
	(Yeha-Noha)	1995
SAD CAFE	Every Day Hurts	1979
	I'm In Love Again	1980
	My Oh My	1980
	Strange Little Girl	1980
SADE	By Your Side	2000
	Never As Good As The First Time	1986
	No Ordinary Love	1992
	Paradise	1988
	Smooth Operator	1985
	The Sweetest Taboo	1985

ARTIST	SONG TITLE	DATE
	When Am I Gonna Make A Living	1984
	Your Love Is King	1984
S/SGT. BARRY SADLER		
	The 'A' Team	1966
	The Ballad Of The Green Berets	1966
SAFFRON HILL featuring BEN ONONO		
	My Love Is Always	2002
SA-FIRE	Thinking Of You	1989
SAFRI DUO	Played-A-Live (The Bongo Song)	2001
SAGA	On The Loose	1982
SAGAT	Funk Dat	1993
CAROLE BAYER SAGER		
	Stronger Than Before	1981
	You're Moving Out Today	1977
BALLY SAGOO	Dil Cheez (My Heart...)	1996
	Tum Bin Jiya	1997
SAIGON KICK	Love Is On The Way	1992
SAILCAT	Motorcycle Mama	1972
SAILOR	Girls Girls Girls	1976
	Glass Of Champagne	1975
	One Drink Too Many	1977
ST. CECILIA	Leap Up And Down (Wave Your Knickers	
	In The Air)	1971
SAINT ETIENNE	Avenue	1992
	The Bad Photographer	1998
	Boy Is Crying	2001

ARTIST	SONG TITLE	DATE
	He's On The Phone	1995
	Hobart Paving/Who Do You Think You Are	1993
	Hug My Soul	1994
	I Was Born On Christmas Day	1993
	Join Our Club/People Get Real	1992
	Only Love Can Break Your Heart/Filthy	1991
	Pale Movie	1994
	Soft Like Me	2003
	Sylvie	1998
	You're In A Bad Way	1993
(PAUL VAN DYK featuring SAINT ETIENNE)		
	Tell Me Why (The Riddle)	2000
ST. LOUIS UNION	Girl	1966
CRISPIAN ST. PETERS		
	The Pied Piper	1966
	You Were On My Mind	1967
ST. WINIFRED'S SCHOOL		
	There's No One Quite Like Grandma	1980
SAINT featuring SUZANNA DEE		
	Show Me Heaven	2003
BUFFY SAINTE-MARIE		
	The Big Ones Get Away	1992
	I'm Gonna Be A Country Girl Again	1972
	Mister Can't You See	1972
	Soldier Blue	1971
SAINTS	The Perfect Day	1977

ARTIST	SONG TITLE	DATE
KYU SAKAMOTO	Sukiyaki	1963
SAKKARIN	Sugar Sugar	1971
SALSOUL ORCHESTRA		
	Nice 'n' Tasty	1976
	Tangerine	1976
SALT TANK	Eugina	1996
SALT 'N' PEPA	Push It/Tramp	1988
	Twist And Shout	1988
SALT-N-PEPA	Ain't Nuthin' But A She Thing	1995
	The Brick Track Versus Gitty Up	1999
	Champagne	1996
	Do You Want Me	1991
	Expression	1990
	Let's Talk About Sex	1991
	None Of Your Business	1994
	R U Ready	1997
	Shake Your Thang (It's Your Thang)	1988
	Shoop	1993
	Start Me Up	1992
	Whatta Man	1994
	You Showed Me	1991
SAM & DAVE	Hold On! I'm Comin'	1966
	I Thank You	1968
	Soothe Me	1967
	Soul Man	1967
	Soul Sister Brown Sugar	1969

ARTIST	SONG TITLE	DATE
SAM & MARK	The Sun Has Come Your Way	2004
	With A Little Help From My Friends/	
	Measure Of A Man	2004
SAM THE SHAM & THE PHARAOHS		
	The Hair On My Chinny Chin Chin	1966
	How Do You Catch A Girl	1966
	Ju Ju Hand	1965
	Lil' Red Riding Hood	1966
	Ring Dang Doo	1965
	Wooly Bully	1965
RICHIE SAMBORA	Hard Times Come Easy	1998
MICHAEL SAMMES SINGERS		
	Somewhere My Love	1967
SAMMIE	I Like It	2000
SAN JOSE	Argentine Melody (Cancion De Argentina)	1978
SAN REMO GOLDEN STRINGS		
	Festival Time	1971
	Hungry For Love	1965
JUNIOR SANCHEZ featuring DAJAE		
	B With U	1999
ROGER SANCHEZ	Another Chance	2001
ROGER SANCHEZ featuring ARMAND VAN HELDEN		
	You Can't Change Me	2001
ROGER SANCHEZ featuring COOLY'S HOT BOX		
	I Never Knew	2000

ARTIST	SONG TITLE	DATE
ROGER SANCHEZ presents TWILIGHT		
	I Want Your Love	1999
CHRIS SANDFORD	Not Too Little — Not Too Much	1963
SANDPEBBLES	Love Power	1967
SANDPIPERS	Come Saturday Morning	1969
	Guantanamera	1966
	Hang On Sloopy	1976
	Kumbaya	1969
	Louie, Louie	1966
	Quando M'innamororo (A Man Without	
	Love)	1968
SANDY B	Make The World Go Round	1998
SANFORD/TOWNSEND BAND		
	Smoke From A Distant Fire	1977
SAMANTHA SANG	Emotion	1977
SANTA CLAUS & THE CHRISTMAS TREES		
	Singalong-A-Santa	1982
	Singalong-A-Santa Again	1983
SANTA ESMERALDA	Don't Let Me Be Misunderstood	1977
MONGO SANTAMARIA		
	Cloud Nine	1969
SANTANA	Black Magic Woman	1970
	Everybody's Everything	1971
	Evil Ways	1970
	Hold On	1982
	No One To Depend On	1972

ARTIST	SONG TITLE	DATE
	Oye Como Va	1971
	Samba Pa Ti	1974
	She's Not There	1977
	Stormy	1979
	Winning	1981
	You Know That I Love You	1979
SANTANA featuring MICHELLE BRANCH		
	The Game Of Love	2002
SANTANA featuring ROB THOMAS		
	Smooth	1999
SANTANA featuring THE PRODUCT G&B		
	Maria Maria	2000
(CAM'RON featuring JUELZ SANTANA)		
	Hey Ma	2003
	Oh Boy	2002
LINA SANTIAGO	Feels So Good (Show Me Your Love)	1996
SANTOS	Camels	2001
LARRY SANTOS	We Can't Hide It Anymore	1976
SAPPHIRES	Who Do You Love	1964
MIKE SARNE	Code Of Love	1963
	Just For Kicks	1963
JOY SARNEY	Naughty Naughty Naughty	1977
PETER SARSTEDT	Frozen Orange Juice	1969
	Where Do You Go To (My Lovely)	1969
ROBIN SARSTEDT	My Resistance Is Low	1976
SASH!	Adelante	2000

ARTIST	SONG TITLE	DATE
	Colour The World	1999
	Encore Une Fois	1997
	Just Around The Hill	2000
	La Primavera	1998
	With My Own Eyes	2000
SASH! featuring LA TREC		
	Stay	1997
SASH! featuring RODRIGUEZ		
	Ecuador	1997
SASH! featuring SHANNON		
	Move Mania	1998
SASH! featuring TINA COUSINS		
	Mysterious Times	1998
SASHA	Higher Ground	1994
SASHA & MARIA	Be As One	1996
SASHA with SAM MOLLISON		
	Magic	1994
SASHA/EMERSON	Scorchio	2000
(SEAN PAUL featuring SASHA)		
	I'm Still In Love With You	2004
SATURDAY NIGHT BAND		
	Come On Dance, Dance	1978
SAVAGE GARDEN	Affirmation	2000
	The Animal Song	1999
	The Best Thing	2001
	Crash And Burn	2000

ARTIST	SONG TITLE	DATE
	Hold Me	2000
	I Knew I Loved You	1999
	I Want You	1997
	To The Moon And Back	1997
	Truly Madly Deeply	1997
CHANTAY SAVAGE	I Will Survive	1996
TELLY SAVALAS	If	1975
SAW DOCTORS	Small Bit Of Love	1994
	This Is Me	2002
	To Win Just Once	1996
	World Of Good	1996
SAXON	And The Bands Played On	1981
	Never Surrender	1981
	Power And The Glory	1983
	747 (Strangers In The Night)	1980
	Wheels Of Steel	1980
LEO SAYER	Easy To Love	1977
	Have You Ever Been In Love	1982
	Heart (Stop Beating In Time)	1982
	How Much Love	1977
	I Can't Stop Loving You (Though I Try)	1978
	Living In A Fantasy	1981
	Long Tall Glasses (I Can Dance)	1975
	Moonlighting	1975
	More Than I Can Say	1980
	One Man Band	1974

ARTIST	SONG TITLE	DATE
	Orchard Road	1983
	Raining In My Heart	1978
	The Show Must Go On	1973
	Thunder In My Heart	1977
	When I Need You	1977
	You Make Me Feel Like Dancing	1976
(GROOVE GENERATION featuring LEO SAYER)		
	You Make Me Feel Like Dancing	1998
ALEXEI SAYLE	'Ullo John Got A New Motor?	1984
SCAFFOLD	Do You Remember	1968
	Gin Gan Goolie	1969
	Lily The Pink	1968
	Liverpool Lou	1974
	Thank U Very Much	1967
BOZ SCAGGS	Breakdown Dead Ahead	1980
	Heart Of Mine	1988
	Hollywood	1977
	It's Over	1976
	Jojo	1980
	Lido Shuffle	1977
	Look What You've Done To Me	1980
	Lowdown	1976
	Miss Sun	1980
	What Can I Say	1977
SCANDAL featuring PATTY SMYTH		
	The Warrior	1984

ARTIST	SONG TITLE	DATE
SCANTY SANDWICH	Because Of You	2000
JOEY SCARBURY	Theme From 'Greatest American Hero'	
	(Believe It Or Not)	1981
SCARFACE	Game Over	1997
	I Never Seen A Man Cry (Aka I Seen A	
	Man Die)	1994
SCARFACE featuring 2PAC & JOHNNY P		
	Smile	1997
SCARLET	I Wanna Be Free (To Be With Him)	1995
	Independent Love Song	1995
SCARLET FANTASTIC		
	No Memory	1987
SCARLETT AND BLACK		
	You Don't Know	1988
SCATMAN JOHN	Scatman (Ski-Ba-Bop-Ba-Dop-Bop)	1995
	Scatman's World	1995
SCENT	Up & Down	2004
LALO SCHIFRIN	Bullitt	1997
	Jaws	1976
SCHILLER	Das Glockenspiel	2001
PETER SCHILLING	Major Tom (Coming Home)	1983
TIMOTHY B. SCHMIT		
	Boys Night Out	1987
JOHN SCHNEIDER	It's Now Or Never	1981
PHILLIP SCHOFIELD		
	Close Every Door	1992

ARTIST	SONG TITLE	DATE
EDDIE SCHWARTZ	All Out Tomorrows	1981
SCISSOR SISTERS	Comfortably Numb	2004
	Laura	2004
	Mary	2004
	Take Your Mama	2004
SCOOCH	The Best Is Yet To Come	2000
	For Sure	2000
	More Than I Needed To Know	2000
	When My Baby	1999
SCOOTER	Back In The UK	1996
	I'm Raving	1996
	The Logical Song	2002
	The Move Your Ass (EP)	1995
	Nessaja	2002
	The Night	2003
	Posse (I Need You On The Floor)	2002
	Rebel Yell	1996
	Weekend!	2003
SCOOTER vs MARC ACARDIPANE & DICK RULES		
	Maria (I Like It Loud)	2003
SCORPIONS	Is There Anybody There?/Another Piece	
	Of Meat	1979
	Rock You Like A Hurricane	1984
	Send Me An Angel	1991
	Wind Of Change	1991

ARTIST	SONG TITLE	DATE
SCOTLAND WORLD CUP SQUAD		
	Easy, Easy	1974
	We Have A Dream	1982
	(ROD STEWART WITH THE SCOTTISH EURO '96 SQUAD)	
	Purple Heather	1996
SCOTT & LEON	Shine On	2001
	You Used To Hold Me	2000
FREDDIE SCOTT	Are You Lonely For Me	1966
JAMIE SCOTT	Just	2004
JILL SCOTT	Gettin' In The Way	2000
PEGGY SCOTT & JO JO BENSON		
	Lover's Holiday	1968
	Pickin' Wild Mountain Berries	1968
	Soul Shake	1969
SIMON SCOTT & THE LEROYS		
	Move It Baby	1964
LISA SCOTT-LEE	Lately	2003
	Too Far Gone	2003
SCREAMING BLUE MESSIAHS		
	I Wanna Be A Flintstone	1988
SCRITTI POLITTI	Absolute	1984
	Oh Patti (Don't Feel Sorry For Loverboy)	1988
	Perfect Way	1985
	Wood Beez (Pray Like Aretha Franklin)	1984
	The Word Girl (featuring Ranking Ann)	1985
SCRITTI POLITTI featuring SHABBA RANKS		
	She's A Woman	1991
JOHNNY SEA	Day For Decision	1966
SEAHORSES	Blinded By The Sun	1997
	Love Is The Law	1997
	Love Me And Leave Me	1997
	You Can Talk To Me	1997
SEAL	The Beginning	1991
	Crazy	1991
	Don't Cry	1996
	Fly Like An Eagle	1996
	Future Love (EP)	1991
	Get It Together	2003
	Killer (EP)	1991
	Kiss From A Rose/I'm Alive	1995
	Prayer For The Dying	1994
	Violet	1992
	(JAKATTA featuring SEAL)	
	My Vision	2002
SEALS & CROFTS	Diamond Girl	1973
	Hummingbird	1973
	I'll Play For You	1975
	My Fair Share	1977
	Summer Breeze	1972
	We May Never Pass This Way (Again)	1973
	You're The Love	1978

ARTIST	SONG TITLE	DATE
SEALS & CROFTS featuring CAROLYN WILLIS		
	Get Closer	1976
JAY SEAN	Stolen	2004
JAY SEAN featuring RISHI RICH PROJECT		
	Eyes On You	2004
	(RISHI RICH PROJECT featuring JAY SEAN)	
	Dance With You (Nachna Tere Naal)	2003
SEARCHERS	Bumble Bee	1965
	Don't Throw Your Love Away	1964
	Goodbye My Love	1965
	He's Got No Love	1965
	Love Potion Number Nine	1964
	Needles And Pins	1964
	Someday We're Gonna Love Again	1964
	Sugar And Spice	1963
	Sweets For My Sweet	1963
	Take It Or Leave It	1966
	Take Me For What I'm Worth	1965
	What Have They Done To The Rain	1965
	When I Get Home	1965
	When You Walk In The Room	1964
SEASHELLS	Maybe I Know	1972
SEBADOH	Flame	1999
JOHN SEBASTIAN	Welcome Back	1976
JON SECADA	Angel	1993
	Do You Believe In Us	1992

ARTIST	SONG TITLE	DATE
	Do You Really Want Me	1993
	I'm Free	1993
	If You Go	1994
	Just Another Day	1992
	Mental Picture	1994
HARRY SECOMBE	If I Ruled The World	1963
	This Is My Song	1967
SECOND CITY SOUND		
	Tchaikovsky One	1966
SECRET AFFAIR	Let Your Heart Dance	1979
	My World	1980
	Time For Action	1979
SECRET LIFE	Love So Strong	1995
NEIL SEDAKA	Bad Blood	1975
	Breaking Up Is Hard To Do	1975
	The Immigrant	1975
	Laughter In The Rain	1974
	A Little Lovin'	1974
	Love In The Shadows	1976
	Oh! Carol (EP)	1972
	Our Last Song Together	1973
	The Queen Of 1964	1975
	Standing On The Inside	1973
	Steppin' Out	1976
	That's When The Music Takes Me	1975

ARTIST	SONG TITLE	DATE
NEIL SEDAKA & DARA SEDAKA		
	Should've Never Let You Go	1980
MAX SEDGLEY	Happy	2004
SEDUCTION	Could This Be Love	1990
	Heartbeat	1990
	Two To Make It Right	1989
	You're My One And Only (True Love)	1989
SEEDS	Pushin' Too Hard	1966
SEEKERS	The Carnival Is Over	1965
	Georgy Girl	1966
	I'll Never Find Another You	1965
	Morningtown Ride	1966
	Someday One Day	1966
	Walk With Me	1966
	When Will The Good Apples Fall	1967
	A World Of Our Own	1965
SEETHER featuring AMY LEE		
	Broken	2004
BOB SEGER	Old Time Rock & Roll	1979
	Roll Me Away	1983
BOB SEGER & THE SILVER BULLET BAND		
	Against The Wind	1980
	American Storm	1986
	Even Now	1983
	Fire Lake	1980
	Hollywood Nights	1978

ARTIST	SONG TITLE	DATE
	Like A Rock	1986
	Mainstreet	1977
	Night Moves	1976
	The Real Love	1991
	Shakedown	1987
	Shame On The Moon	1982
	Still The Same	1978
	Tryin' To Live My Life Without You	1981
	Understanding	1984
	We've Got Tonite	1978
	You'll Accomp'ny Me	1980
BOB SEGER SYSTEM		
	Ramblin' Gamblin' Man	1968
SELECTER	Missing Words	1980
	On My Radio	1979
	Three Minute Hero	1980
	The Whisper	1980
(SPECIAL AKA/MADNESS/SELECTER/BEAT)		
	The 2 Tone EP	1993
SELENA	Dreaming Of You	1995
MARILYN SELLARS	One Day At A Time	1974
PETER SELLERS	A Hard Day's Night	1965
MICHAEL SEMBELLO		
	Automatic Man	1983
	Maniac	1983
SEMISONIC	Chemistry	2001

ARTIST	SONG TITLE	DATE
	Closing Time	1999
	Secret Smile	1999
	Singing In My Sleep	2000
SENATOR BOBBY	Wild Thing	1967
SENSELESS THINGS	Easy To Smile	1992
	Hold It Down	1992
SENSER	Switch	1994
SEPULTURA	Ratamahatta	1996
	Roots Bloody Roots	1996
SERENDIPITY SINGERS		
	Beans In My Ears	1964
	Don't Let The Rain Come Down (Crooked Little Man)	1964
SERIOUS DANGER	Deeper	1997
ERICK SERMON featuring MARVIN GAYE		
	Music	2001
ERICK SERMON featuring REDMAN		
	React	2002
SETTLERS	The Lightning Tree	1971
BRIAN SETZER ORCHESTRA		
	Jump Jive An' Wail	1999
TAJA SEVELLE	Love Is Contagious	1988
702	All I Want	1997
	Get It Together	1997
	Steelo	1996
	Where My Girls At?	1999

ARTIST	SONG TITLE	DATE
	You Don't Know	1999
(SUBWAY featuring 702)		
	This Lil' Game We Play	1995
SEVEN MARY THREE		
	Cumbersome	1996
SEVERINE	Un Banc, Un Abre, Une Rue	1971
SEX PISTOLS	Anarchy In The UK	1992
	C'mon Everybody	1979
	God Save The Queen	1977
	The Great Rock'n'Roll Swindle/Rock Around The Clock	1979
	Holidays In The Sun	1977
	(I'm Not Your) Stepping Stone	1980
	No One Is Innocent (A Punk Prayer By Ronald Biggs)/My Way	1978
	Pretty Vacant	1977
	Silly Thing/Who Killed Bambi	1979
	Something Else/Friggin' In The Riggin'	1979
SEX-O-SONIQUE	I Thought It Was You	1997
CHARLIE SEXTON	Beat's So Lonely	1985
PHIL SEYMOUR	Precious To Me	1981
SHADES OF BLUE	Oh How Happy	1966
SHADES OF RHYTHM		
	Extacy	1991
	The Sound Of Eden	1991

ARTIST	SONG TITLE	DATE
SHADOWS	Atlantis	1963
	Don't Cry For Me Argentina	1978
	Don't Make My Baby Blue	1965
	Foot Tapper	1963
	Genie With The Light Brown Lamp	1964
	Geronimo	1963
	I Met A Girl	1966
	Let Me Be The One	1975
	Maroc 7	1967
	Mary Anne	1965
	A Place In The Sun	1966
	Rhythm And Greens	1964
	Riders In The Sky	1980
	The Rise & Fall Of Flingel Bunt	1964
	Shindig	1963
	Stingray	1965
	Theme For Young Lovers	1964
	Theme From The Deer Hunter (Cavatina)	1979
	The War Lord	1965
SHADOWS OF KNIGHT	Gloria	1966
	Oh Yeah	1966
SHAFT	Mambo Italiano	2000
	(Mucho Mambo) Sway	1999
	Roobarb & Custard	1991
SHAG	Loop Di Love	1972

ARTIST	SONG TITLE	DATE
SHAGGY	Boombastic/In The Summertime	1995
	Dance And Shout/Hope	2001
	It Wasn't Me	2001
	Luv Me Luv Me	2001
	Oh Carolina	1993
	Something Different/The Train Is Coming	1996
SHAGGY featuring BRIAN & TONY GOLD	Hey Sexy Lady	2002
SHAGGY featuring GRAND PUBA	Why You Treat Me So Bad	1996
SHAGGY featuring MARSHA	Piece Of My Heart	1997
SHAGGY featuring RAYVON	Angel	2001
(ALI G & SHAGGY)	Me Julie	2002
(MAXI PRIEST featuring SHAGGY)	That Girl	1996
SHAI	Baby I'm Yours	1993
	Comforter	1993
	If I Ever Fall In Love	1992
	The Place Where You Belong	1994
SHAKATAK	Dark Is The Night	1983
	Down On The Street	1984
	Easier Said Than Done	1981
	Invitations	1982

ARTIST	SONG TITLE	DATE
	Night Birds	1982
	Streetwalkin'	1982
SHAKEDOWN	At Night	2002
SHAKESPEAR'S SISTER		
	Goodbye Cruel World	1992
	Hello (Turn Your Radio On)	1992
	I Can Drive	1996
	I Don't Care	1992
	Stay	1992
	You're History	1989
SHAKIRA	Objection (Tango)	2002
	Underneath Your Clothes	2002
	Whenever, Wherever	2001
SHALAMAR	Dancing In The Sheets	1984
	Dead Giveaway	1983
	Disappearing Act	1983
	Friends	1982
	I Can Make You Feel Good	1982
	I Owe You One	1980
	Make That Move	1981
	A Night To Remember	1982
	Over And Over	1983
	The Second Time Around	1979
	Take That To The Bank	1978
	There It Is	1982
	Uptown Festival (Part I)	1977

ARTIST	SONG TITLE	DATE
SHAM ROCK	Tell Me Ma	1998
SHAM 69	Angels With Dirty Faces	1978
	Hersham Boys	1979
	Hurry Up Harry	1978
	If The Kids Are United	1978
	Questions And Answers	1979
SHAMEN	Boss Drum	1992
	Destination Eschaton	1995
	Ebeneezer Goode	1992
	Heal	1996
	Hyperreal	1991
	L.S.I.	1992
	Move Any Mountain	1991
	Phorever People	1992
	The SOS EP	1993
	Transamazonia	1995
SHAMEN/TERENCE MCKENNA		
	Re:evolution	1993
SHAMPOO	Delicious	1995
	Girl Power	1996
	Trouble	1994
	Viva La Megababes	1994
SHANA	I Want You	1989
PAUL SHANE & THE YELLOWCOATS		
	Hi-De-Hi (Holiday Rock)	1981

ARTIST	SONG TITLE	DATE
SHANGRI-LAS	Give Him A Great Big Kiss	1964
	Give Us Your Blessing	1965
	I Can Never Go Home Anymore	1965
	Leader Of The Pack	1964
	Long Live Our Love	1966
	Remember (Walkin' In The Sand)	1964
SHANICE	I Love Your Smile	1991
	Saving Forever For You	1992
	Silent Prayer	1992
	When I Close My Eyes	1999
SHANKS & BIGFOOT		
	Sing-A-Long	2000
	Sweet Like Chocolate	1999
SHANNON	Give Me Tonight	1984
	Let The Music Play	1983
	Sweet Somebody	1984
	(SASH! featuring SHANNON)	
	Move Mania	1998
	(TODD TERRY presents SHANNON)	
	It's Over Love	1997
DEL SHANNON	Handy Man	1964
	Keep Searchin' (We'll Follow The Sun)	1964
	Little Town Flirt	1962
	Mary Jane	1964
	Sea Of Love	1981
	Stranger In Town	1965

ARTIST	SONG TITLE	DATE
	Sue's Gotta Be Mine	1963
	Two Kinds Of Teardrops	1963
	Two Silhouettes	1963
SHAPESHIFTERS	Lola's Theme	2004
HELEN SHAPIRO	Fever	1964
	Queen For Tonight	1963
	Woe Is Me	1963
SHARADA HOUSE GANG		
	Keep It Up	1995
FEARGAL SHARKEY	A Good Heart	1985
	I've Got News For You	1991
	Listen To Your Father	1984
	Loving You	1985
	You Little Thief	1986
SHARONETTES	Papa Oom Mow Mow	1975
SHARPE & NUMAN	Change Your Mind	1985
	No More Lies	1988
ROCKY SHARPE & THE REPLAYS		
	Imagination	1979
	Rama Lama Ding Dong	1978
	Shout Shout (Knock Yourself Out)	1982
SANDIE SHAW	Girl Don't Come	1964
	Hand In Glove	1984
	How Can You Tell	1965
	I'll Stop At Nothing	1965
	Long Live Love	1965

ARTIST	SONG TITLE	DATE
	Message Understood	1965
	Monsieur Dupont	1969
	Nothing Comes Easy	1966
	Puppet On A String	1967
	Run	1966
	(There's) Always Something There To Remind Me	1964
	Think Sometimes About Me	1966
	Today	1968
	Tomorrow	1966
	Tonight In Tokyo	1967
	You've Not Changed	1967
TOMMY SHAW	Girls With Guns	1984
SHE MOVES	Breaking All The Rules	1997
GARY SHEARSTON	I Get A Kick Out Of You	1974
SHED SEVEN	Bully Boy	1996
	Chasing Rainbows	1996
	Cry For Help	2001
	Devil In Your Shoes (Walking All Over)	1998
	Disco Down	1999
	Dolphin	1994
	Getting Better	1996
	Going For Gold	1996
	The Heroes	1998
	Ocean Pie	1994
	On Standby	1996

ARTIST	SONG TITLE	DATE
	She Left Me On Friday	1998
	Speakeasy	1994
	Where Have You Been Tonight?	1995
	Why Can't I Be You?	2003
SHEEP ON DRUGS	From A To H And Back Again	1993
SHEER ELEGANCE	Life Is Too Short Girl	1976
	Milky Way	1975
DUNCAN SHEIK	Barely Breathing	1996
SHEILA AND B. DEVOTION		
	Spacer	1979
SHEILA B. DEVOTION		
	Singin' In The Rain (Pt. 1)	1978
SHADE SHEIST featuring NATE DOGG & KURUPT		
	Where I Wanna Be	2001
DOUG SHELDON	I Saw Linda Yesterday	1963
PETER SHELLEY	Gee Baby	1974
	Love Me Love My Dog	1975
BLAKE SHELTON	Austin	2001
	The Baby	2002
SHENA	Let The Beat Hit 'Em	1997
	(JURGEN VRIES featuring SHENA) Wilderness	2003
VONDA SHEPARD	Searchin' My Soul	1998
T.G. SHEPPARD	I Loved 'Em Every One	1981
SHERBET	Howzat	1976
SHERIFF	When I'm With You	1988

ARTIST	SONG TITLE	DATE
ALLAN SHERMAN	Crazy Downtown	1965
	Hello Mudduah! Hello Fadduh!	1963
BOBBY SHERMAN	Cried Like A Baby	1971
	The Drum	1971
	Easy Come, Easy Go	1970
	Hey, Mister Sun	1970
	Julie, Do Ya Love Me	1970
	La La La (If I Had You)	1969
	Little Woman	1969
SHERRICK	Just Call	1987
PLUTO SHERVINGTON		
	Dat	1976
	Your Honour	1982
HOLLY SHERWOOD		
	Day By Day	1972
SHIFTY	Slide Along Side	2004
SHINEHEAD	Jamaican In New York	1993
SHIRELLES	Foolish Little Girl	1963
SHIRLEY AND COMPANY		
	Shame, Shame, Shame	1975
SHIVA	Freedom	1995
	Work It Out	1995
SHOCKING BLUE	Venus	1969
SHORTIE vs BLACK LEGEND		
	Somebody	2001
SHOWADDYWADDY	Blue Moon	1980

ARTIST	SONG TITLE	DATE
	Dancin' Party	1977
	Footsteps	1981
	Heartbeat	1975
	Heavenly	1975
	Hey Mr. Christmas	1974
	Hey Rock And Roll	1974
	I Wonder Why	1978
	A Little Bit Of Soap	1978
	Multiplication	1981
	A Night At Daddy Gees	1979
	Pretty Little Angel Eyes	1978
	Remember Then	1979
	Rock 'n' Roll Lady	1974
	Sweet Little Rock 'n' Roller	1979
	Sweet Music	1975
	Three Steps To Heaven	1975
	Trocadero	1976
	Under The Moon Of Love	1976
	When	1977
	Who Put The Bomp (In The Bomp-A-Bomp-A-Bomp)	1982
	Why Do Lovers Break Each Other's Hearts?	1980
	You Got What It Takes	1977
SHOWSTOPPERS	Ain't Nothin' But A House Party	1968
	Eeny Meeny	1968

ARTIST	SONG TITLE	DATE
SHRINK	Are You Ready To Party	2000
SHUT UP AND DANCE		
	Raving I'm Raving	1992
	Save It 'Til The Mourning After	1995
SHY FX & T-POWER featuring DI		
	Shake Ur Body	2002
SHY FX & T-POWER featuring DI & SKIBADEE		
	Don't Wanna Know	2002
SHY FX & T-POWER featuring KELE LE ROC		
	Feelin' U	2003
SHYSTIE	One Wish	2004
SIA	Taken For Granted	2000
	(ZERO 7 featuring SIA & SOPHIE)	
	Destiny	2001
LABI SIFFRE	Crying Laughing Loving Lying	1972
	It Must Be Love	1971
	(Something Inside) So Strong	1987
	Watch Me	1972
BUNNY SIGLER	Let The Good Times Roll & Feel So	
	Good	1967
SIGNUM	What Ya Got 4 Me	2002
SIGUE SIGUE SPUTNIK		
	Love Missile F1-11	1986
	Success	1988
	Twenty First Century Boy	1986

ARTIST	SONG TITLE	DATE
SILICONE SOUL featuring LOUISE CLARE MARSHALL		
	Right On!	2001
SILK	Freak Me	1993
	Girl U For Me/Lose Control	1993
	If You (Lovin' Me)	1999
SILKIE	You've Got To Hide Your Love Away	1965
SILKK THE SHOCKER featuring MYSTIKAL		
	It Ain't My Fault 1 & 2	1999
	(MASTER P featuring FIEND, SILKK THE SHOCKER, MIA X)	
	Make Em' Say Uhh!	1998
	(MASTER P featuring SILKK THE SHOCKER, SONS OF FUNK)	
	Goodbye To My Homies	1998
	(MONTELL JORDAN featuring MASTER P & SILKK THE SHOCKER)	
	Let's Ride	1998
	(MYA featuring SILKK THE SHOCKER)	
	Movin' On	1998
LUCIE SILVAS	What You're Made Of	2004
SILVER	Wham Bam (Shang-A-Lang)	1976
SILVER BULLET	20 Seconds To Comply	1989
	Undercover Anarchist	1991
SILVER CONDOR	You Could Take My Heart Away	1981
SILVER CONVENTION		
	Everybody's Talkin' 'Bout Love	1977

ARTIST	SONG TITLE	DATE
	Fly Robin Fly	1975
	Get Up And Boogie (That's Right)	1976
	Save Me	1975
SILVER SUN	Golden Skin	1997
	I'll See You Around	1998
	Lava	1997
	Too Much, Too Little, Too Late	1998
JOHN SILVER	Come On Over	2003
SILVERCHAIR	Abuse Me	1997
	Freak	1997
SILVETTI	Spring Rain	1977
GENE SIMMONS	Haunted House	1964
PATRICK SIMMONS	So Wrong	1983
SIMON	Free At Last	2001
SIMON & GARFUNKEL		
	America	1972
	At The Zoo	1967
	The Boxer	1969
	Bridge Over Troubled Water	1970
	Cecilia	1970
	The Dangling Conversation	1966
	El Condor Pasa	1970
	Fakin' It	1967
	A Hazy Shade Of Winter	1966
	Homeward Bound	1966
	I Am A Rock	1966

ARTIST	SONG TITLE	DATE
	Mrs. Robinson	1968
	My Little Town	1975
	Scarborough Fair/Canticle	1968
	Seven O'Clock News/Silent Night	1991
	The Sounds Of Silence	1965
	Wake Up Little Susie	1982
CARLY SIMON	Anticipation	1971
	Attitude Dancing	1975
	Coming Around Again	1986
	Haven't Got Time For The Pain	1974
	Jesse	1980
	Nobody Does It Better	1977
	The Right Thing To Do	1973
	That's The Way I've Always Heard It Should Be	1971
	Why	1982
	You Belong To Me	1978
	You're So Vain	1972
CARLY SIMON & JAMES TAYLOR		
	Devoted To You	1978
	Mockingbird	1974
	(JANET featuring MISSY ELLIOTT, P. DIDDY & CARLY SIMON)	
	Son Of A Gun	2001
JOE SIMON	The Chokin' Kind	1969
	Drowning In The Sea Of Love	1971

ARTIST	SONG TITLE	DATE
	Get Down, Get Down (Get On The Floor)	1975
	Power Of Love	1972
	Step By Step	1973
	(You Keep Me) Hangin' On	1968
	Your Turn To Cry	1970
JOE SIMON featuring THE MAIN STREETERS		
	Theme From Cleopatra Jones	1973
PAUL SIMON	American Tune	1973
	The Boy In The Bubble	1986
	50 Ways To Leave Your Lover	1975
	Kodachrome	1973
	Late In The Evening	1980
	Loves Me Like A Rock	1973
	Me And Julio Down By The Schoolyard	1972
	Mother And Child Reunion	1972
	The Obvious Child	1990
	One Trick Pony	1980
	Slip Slidin' Away	1977
	Still Crazy After All These Years	1976
	Take Me To The Mardi Gras	1973
	You Can Call Me Al	1986
PAUL SIMON/PHOEBE SNOW		
	Gone At Last	1975
	(ART GARFUNKEL, JAMES TAYLOR & PAUL SIMON)	
	(What A) Wonderful World	1978

ARTIST	SONG TITLE	DATE
NINA SIMONE	Ain't Got No/I Got Life/Do What You Gotta Do	1968
	Feeling Good	1994
	I Put A Spell On You	1969
	My Baby Just Cares For Me	1987
	To Love Somebody	1969
SIMPLE KID	Truck On	2004
SIMPLE MINDS	All The Things She Said	1986
	The Amsterdam EP	1989
	Belfast Child	1989
	Don't You (Forget About Me)	1985
	Ghost Dancing	1986
	Glitterball	1998
	Glittering Prize	1982
	Hypnotised	1995
	Kick It In	1989
	Let There Be Love	1991
	Love Song/Alive And Kicking	1992
	Promised You A Miracle	1982
	Real Life	1991
	Sanctify Yourself	1986
	See The Lights	1991
	She's A River	1995
	Someone Somewhere (In Summertime)	1982
	Speed Your Love To Me	1984
	Stand By Love	1991

ARTIST	SONG TITLE	DATE
	This Is Your Land	1989
	Up On The Catwalk	1984
	Waterfront	1983
SIMPLE PLAN	Perfect	2003
SIMPLICIOUS	Let Her Feel It	1985
SIMPLY RED	Ain't That A Lot Of Love	1999
	The Air That I Breathe	1998
	Angel	1996
	Ev'ry Time We Say Goodbye	1987
	Fairground	1995
	Fake	2003
	For Your Babies	1992
	Ghetto Girl	1998
	Holding Back The Years	1986
	Home	2004
	If You Don't Know Me By Now	1989
	Infidelity	1987
	It's Only Love	1989
	Money's Too Tight (To Mention)	1986
	Montreux EP	1992
	Never Never Love	1996
	A New Flame	1989
	The Real Thing	1987
	Remembering The First Time	1995
	The Right Thing	1987
	Say You Love Me	1998

ARTIST	SONG TITLE	DATE
	Something Got Me Started	1991
	Stars	1991
	Sunrise	2003
	Thrill Me	1992
	We're In This Together	1996
	You Make Me Feel Brand New	2003
	Your Eyes	2000
	Your Mirror	1992
	(SLY AND ROBBIE featuring SIMPLY RED)	
	Night Nurse	1997
ASHLEE SIMPSON	Pieces Of Me	2004
JESSICA SIMPSON	I Think I'm In Love With You	2000
	I Wanna Love You Forever	1999
	Irresistible	2001
	With You	2004
PAUL SIMPSON featuring ADEVA		
	Musical Freedom (Moving On Up)	1989
SIMPSONS	Deep, Deep Trouble	1991
	Do The Bartman	1991
JOYCE SIMS	All And All	1986
	Come Into My Life	1988
	Lifetime Love	1987
	Looking For A Love	1989
	Walk Away	1988
KYM SIMS	A Little Bit More	1992
	Take My Advice	1992

ARTIST	SONG TITLE	DATE
	Too Blind To See It	1991
FRANK SINATRA	Cycles	1968
	I Believe I'm Gonna Love You	1975
	I Will Drink The Wine	1971
	It Was A Very Good Year	1965
	Love's Been Good To Me	1969
	My Kind Of Girl	1964
	My Way	1969
	Softly, As I Leave You	1964
	Somewhere In Your Heart	1964
	Strangers In The Night	1966
	Summer Wind	1966
	That's Life	1966
	Theme From New York, New York	1980
	The World We Knew (Over And Over)	1967
	(NANCY & FRANK SINATRA)	
	Somethin' Stupid	1967
NANCY SINATRA	Friday's Child	1966
	The Highway Song	1969
	How Does That Grab You, Darlin'?	1966
	Lightning's Girl	1967
	Love Eyes	1967
	Sugar Town	1966
	These Boots Are Made For Walkin'	1966
	You Only Live Twice/Jackson	1967

ARTIST	SONG TITLE	DATE
NANCY SINATRA & LEE HAZLEWOOD		
	Did You Ever	1971
	Jackson	1967
	Lady Bird	1967
	Some Velvet Morning	1968
NANCY & FRANK SINATRA		
	Somethin' Stupid	1967
SINCLAIR	Ain't No Casanova	1993
GORDON SINCLAIR	The Americans (A Canadian's Opinion)	1974
BOB SINCLAR	The Beat Goes On	2003
	I Feel For You	2000
SINE	Just Let Me Do My Thing	1978
SINGING NUN	Dominique	1963
SINITTA	Cross My Broken Heart	1988
	G.T.O.	1987
	Hitchin' A Ride	1990
	I Don't Believe In Miracles	1988
	Love On A Mountain Top	1989
	Right Back Where We Started From	1989
	Shame Shame Shame	1992
	So Macho/Cruising	1986
	Toy Boy	1987
SIOUXSIE & THE BANSHEES		
	Arabian Knights	1981
	Candyman	1986
	Christine	1980

ARTIST	SONG TITLE	DATE
	Cities In The Dust	1985
	Dazzle	1984
	Dear Prudence	1983
	Face To Face	1992
	Fire Works	1982
	Happy House	1980
	Hong Kong Garden	1978
	Kiss Them For Me	1991
	O Baby	1995
	Peek-A-Boo	1988
	Playground Twist	1979
	Spellbound	1981
	The Staircase (Mystery)	1979
	Swimming Horses	1984
	This Wheel's On Fire	1987
	(MORRISSEY & SIOUXSIE)	
	Interlude	1994
SIR DOUGLAS QUINTET		
	Mendocino	1969
	The Rains Came	1966
	She's About A Mover	1965
SIR MIX-A-LOT	Baby Got Back	1992
SISQO	Dance For Me	2001
	Got To Get It	2000
	Incomplete	2000
	Thong Song	2000

ARTIST	SONG TITLE	DATE
	Unleash The Dragon	2000
	(MYA WITH SPECIAL GUEST SISQO)	
	It's All About Me	1998
SISTER 2 SISTER	Sister	2000
SISTER BLISS	Sister Sister	2000
SISTER BLISS featuring JOHN MARTYN		
	Deliver Me	2001
SISTER BLISS WITH COLETTE		
	Cantgetaman, Cantgetajob (Life's A Bitch)	1994
	Oh! What A World	1995
SISTER HAZEL	All For You	1997
SISTER SLEDGE	Frankie	1985
	Got To Love Somebody	1980
	He's The Greatest Dancer	1979
	Lost In Music	1984
	Mama Never Told Me	1975
	My Guy	1982
	Thinking Of You	1984
	We Are Family	1979
SISTERS OF MERCY		
	Doctor Jeep	1990
	Dominion	1988
	Lucretia My Reflection	1988
	More	1990
	Temple Of Love	1992
	This Corrosion	1987

ARTIST	SONG TITLE	DATE
	Under The Gun	1993
666	Devil	2000
SIXPENCE NONE THE RICHER		
	Kiss Me	1999
	There She Goes	1999
60FT DOLLS	Happy Shopper	1996
	Talk To Me	1996
69 BOYZ	Tootsie Roll	1994
	Woof Woof	1998
SIZE 9	I'm Ready	1995
RONI SIZE/REPRAZENT		
	Brown Paper Bag	1997
	Dirty Beats	2001
	Heroes	1997
	Share The Fall	1997
	Watching Windows	1998
	Who Told You	2000
SKATALITES	Guns Of Navarone	1967
SKEE-LO	I Wish	1995
	Top Of The Stairs	1996
PETER SKELLERN	Hold On To Love	1975
	You're A Lady	1972
SKIBADEE/DILLINJA		
	Twist 'Em Out	2003

ARTIST	SONG TITLE	DATE
	(SHY FX & T-POWER featuring DI & SKIBADEE)	
	Don't Wanna Know	2002
SKID ROW	18 And Life	1989
	I Remember You	1989
	Monkey Business	1991
	Wasted Time	1991
	Youth Gone Wild/Delivering The Goods	1992
SKIDS	Charade	1979
	Circus Games	1980
	Into The Valley	1979
	Masquerade	1979
	Working For The Yankee Dollar	1979
SKIN	Trashed	2003
SKIN	How Lucky You Are	1996
	Look But Don't Touch (EP)	1994
	The Money EP	1994
	Perfect Day	1996
	Take Me To The River	1995
	Tower Of Strength	1994
SKIN UP	A Juicy Red Apple	1992
SKINNY	Failure	1998
SKIPWORTH & TURNER		
	Thinking About Your Love	1985
SKUNK ANANSIE	All I Want	1996
	Brazen 'Weep'	1997

ARTIST	SONG TITLE	DATE
	Charity	1996
	Charlie Big Potato	1999
	Hedonism (Just Because You Feel Good)	1997
	Lately	1999
	Secretly	1999
	Twisted (Everyday Hurts)	1996
	Weak	1996
SKY	Toccata	1980
SKYLARK	Wildflower	1973
SKYY	Call Me	1982
SL2	DJ's Take Control/Way In My Brain	1991
	On A Ragga Tip	1992
	Drumbeats	1992
SLACKER	Scared	1997
	Your Face	1997
SLADE	All Join Hands	1984
	The Bangin' Man	1974
	Coz I Luv You	1971
	Cum On Feel The Noize	1973
	Everyday	1974
	Far Far Away	1974
	Get Down And Get With It	1971
	Gudbuy T'Jane	1972
	How Does It Feel?	1975
	In For A Penny	1975
	Let's Call It Quits	1976

ARTIST	SONG TITLE	DATE
	Lock Up Your Daughters	1981
	Look Wot You Dun	1972
	Mama Weer All Crazee Now	1972
	Merry Xmas Everybody	1973
	My Baby Left Me But That's Alright Mama	1977
	My Friend Stan	1973
	My Oh My	1984
	Radio Wall Of Sound	1991
	Run, Runaway	1984
	Skweeze Me, Pleeze Me	1973
	Take Me Bak 'Ome	1972
	Thanks For The Memory (Wham Bam Thank You Mam)	1975
	We'll Bring The House Down	1981
SLADE vs FLUSH	Merry Christmas Everybody '98 Remix	1998
SLAUGHTER	Fly To The Angels	1990
	Spend My Life	1990
	Up All Night	1990
SLAVE	Slide	1977
PERCY SLEDGE	It Tears Me Up	1966
	Love Me Tender	1967
	Take Time To Know Her	1968
	Warm And Tender Love	1966
	When A Man Loves A Woman	1966

ARTIST	SONG TITLE	DATE
SLEEPER	Inbetweener	1995
	Nice Guy Eddie	1996
	Romeo Me	1997
	Sale Of The Century	1996
	She's A Good Girl	1997
	Statuesque	1996
	Vegas	1995
	What Do I Do Now?	1995
SLICK	Space Bass	1979
SLIK	Forever & Ever	1976
	Requiem	1976
SLIPKNOT	Duality	2004
	Left Behind	2001
	Spit It Out	2000
	Vermilion	2004
	Wait And Bleed	2000
SLIPSTREEM	We Are Raving — The Anthem	1992
SLO-MOSHUN	Bells Of Ny	1994
P.F. SLOAN	Sins Of The Family	1965
SLUSNIK LUNA	Sun	2001
SLY & THE FAMILY STONE		
	Dance To The Music	1968
	Everyday People	1968
	Family Affair	1971
	Hot Fun In The Summertime	1969
	I Want To Take You Higher	1970

ARTIST	SONG TITLE	DATE
	If You Want Me To Stay	1973
	M'lady	1968
	Runnin' Away	1972
	Stand	1969
	Thank You (Falettinme Be Mice Elf Agin)/	
	Everybody Is A Star	1970
	Time For Livin'	1974
SLY AND ROBBIE	Boops (Here To Go)	1987
SLY AND ROBBIE featuring SIMPLY RED		
	Night Nurse	1997
SLY FOX	Let's Go All The Way	1985
SMALL FACES	Afterglow Of Your Love	1969
	All Or Nothing	1966
	Here Come The Nice	1967
	Hey Girl	1966
	I Can't Make It	1967
	Itchycoo Park	1968
	Lazy Sunday	1968
	My Mind's Eye	1966
	Sha-La-La-La-Lee	1966
	Tin Soldier	1967
	Universal	1968
	What Cha Gonna Do About It	1965
HEATHER SMALL	Proud	2000
	(TOM JONES & HEATHER SMALL)	
	You Need Love Like I Do	2000

ARTIST	SONG TITLE	DATE
SMART E'S	Sesame's Treet	1992
SMASH MOUTH	All Star	1999
	I'm A Believer	2001
	Then The Morning Comes	1999
	Walkin' On The Sun	1997
SMASHING PUMPKINS		
	Ava Adore	1998
	Bullet With Butterfly Wings	1995
	Cherub Rock	1993
	Disarm	1994
	The End Is The Beginning Is The End	1997
	1979	1996
	Perfect	1998
	Stand Inside Your Love	2000
	Thirty-Three	1996
	Tonight, Tonight	1996
SMILEZ & SOUTHSTAR		
	Tell Me (What's Goin' On)	2003
SMITH	Baby It's You	1969
FRANKIE SMITH	Double Dutch Bus	1981
HURRICANE SMITH	Don't Let It Die	1971
	Oh Babe, What Would You Say	1972
	Who Was It	1972
KEELY SMITH	You're Breakin' My Heart	1965
MICHAEL W. SMITH		
	I Will Be Here For You	1992

ARTIST	SONG TITLE	DATE
	Place In This World	1991
O.C. SMITH	Daddy's Little Man	1969
	Little Green Apples	1968
	The Son Of Hickory Holler's Tramp	1968
	Together	1977
PATTI SMITH GROUP		
	Because The Night	1978
REX SMITH	You Take My Breath Away	1979
REX SMITH & RACHEL SWEET		
	Everlasting Love	1981
SAMMI SMITH	Help Me Make It Through The Night	1971
VERDELLE SMITH	Tar And Cement	1966
WHISTLING JACK SMITH		
	I Was Kaiser Bill's Batman	1967
WILL SMITH	Freakin' It	2000
	Gettin' Jiggy Wit It	1998
	Just Cruisin'	1997
	Just The Two Of Us	1998
	Men In Black	1997
	Miami	1998
	Will 2k	1999
WILL SMITH featuring DRU HILL		
	Wild Wild West	1999
WILL SMITH featuring TRA-KNOX		
	Black Suits Comin' (Nod Ya Head)	2002

ARTIST	SONG TITLE	DATE
	(TATYANA ALI featuring WILL SMITH)	
	Boy You Knock Me Out	1999
SMITHEREREENS	A Girl Like You	1989
	Too Much Passion	1992
SMITHS	Ask	1986
	Big Mouth Strikes Again	1986
	The Boy With The Thorn In His Side	1985
	Girlfriend In A Coma	1987
	Heaven Knows I'm Miserable Now	1984
	How Soon Is Now	1985
	I Started Something I Couldn't Finish	1987
	Last Night I Dreamt That Somebody Loved Me	1987
	Panic	1986
	Shakespeare's Sister	1985
	Sheila Take A Bow	1987
	Shoplifters Of The World Unite	1987
	There Is A Light That Never Goes Out	1992
	This Charming Man	1992
	What Difference Does It Make	1984
	William It Was Really Nothing	1984
SMOKE 2 SEVEN	Been There Done That	2002
SMOKEY	Don't Play Your Rock 'n' Roll To Me	1975
	If You Think You Know How To Love Me	1975
SMOKE CITY	Underwater Love	1997
SMOKIE	For A Few Dollars More	1978

ARTIST	SONG TITLE	DATE
	I'll Meet You At Midnight	1976
	It's Your Life	1977
	Lay Back In The Arms Of Someone	1977
	Living Next Door To Alice	1976
	Mexican Girl	1978
	Needles And Pins	1977
	Oh Carol	1978
	Something's Been Making Me Blue	1976
	Take Good Care Of My Baby	1980
SMOKIE featuring ROY CHUBBY BROWN		
	Living Next Door To Alice (Who The F**k Is Alice?)	1995
SMOKIN BEATS featuring LYN EDEN		
	Dreams	1998
SMOKIN' MOJO FILTERS		
	Come Together	1995
SMOOTH	Mind Blowin'	1995
	(IMMATURE featuring SMOOTH)	
	Watch Me Do My Thing	1997
	We Got It	1995
JEAN JACQUES SMOOTHIE		
	2 People	2001
SMURFS	I've Got A Little Puppy	1996
	Your Christmas Wish	1996
	(FATHER ABRAHAM & THE SMURFS)	
	Christmas In Smurfland	1978

ARTIST	SONG TITLE	DATE
	Dippety Day	1978
	The Smurf Song	1978
PATTY SMYTH	No Mistakes	1992
PATTY SMYTH WITH DON HENLEY		
	Sometimes Love Just Ain't Enough	1992
SNAKEBITE	The Bit Goes On	1997
SNAP!	Cult Of Snap	1990
	Mary Had A Little Boy	1990
	Oops Up	1990
	The Power	1990
	Rhythm Is A Dancer	1992
	Snap Mega Mix	1991
SNAP!/NIKI HARRIS	Do You See The Light (Looking For)	1993
	Exterminate!	1993
SNAP! featuring SUMMER		
	The First The Last Eternity	1995
	Welcome To Tomorrow	1994
SNAP! vs PLAYTHING		
	Do You See The Light	2002
SNAP! vs MOTIVO	The Power (Of Bhangra)	2003
SNEAKER	More Than Just The Two Of Us	1981
SNEAKER PIMPS	Low Five	1999
	Post Modern Sleaze	1997
	6 Underground	1996
	Spin Spin Sugar	1997
DAVID SNEDDON	Baby Get Higher	2003

ARTIST	SONG TITLE	DATE
	Best Of Order	2003
	Don't Let Go	2003
	Stop Living The Lie	2003
SNIFF 'N' THE TEARS		
	Drivers Seat	1979
SNOOP DOGG	From Tha Chuuuch To Da Palace	2002
	Snoop Dogg	2001
SNOOP DOGG featuring PHARRELL		
	Beautiful	2003
	Drop It Like It's Hot	2004
SNOOP DOGGY DOGG		
	Doggy Dogg World	1994
	Gin And Juice	1994
	Still A G Thing	1998
	Tha Doggfather	1998
	Vapors	1997
	What's My Name?	1993
SNOOP DOGGY DOGG featuring CHARLIE WILSON		
	Snoop's Upside Ya Head	1996
SNOOP DOGGY DOGG featuring JD		
	We Just Wanna Party With You	1997
	(2PAC AND SNOOP DOGGY DOGG)	
	Wanted Dead Or Alive	1997
	(ANGIE STONE featuring SNOOP DOGG)	
	I Wanna Thank Ya	2004

ARTIST	SONG TITLE	DATE
(DR. DRE featuring SNOOP DOGG)		
	The Next Episode	2001
	Still D.R.E.	2000
(KEITH SWEAT featuring SNOOP DOGG)		
	Come And Get With Me	1998
(MARIAH CAREY featuring SNOOP DOGG)		
	Crybaby	2000
(XZIBIT featuring SNOOP DOGG)		
	X	2001
SNOW PATROL	Chocolate	2004
	How To Be Dead	2004
	Run	2004
	Spitting Games	2004
SNOW	Girl, I've Been Hurt	1993
	Informer	1993
MARK SNOW	The X Files	1996
PHOEBE SNOW	Every Night	1979
	Poetry Man	1975
(PAUL SIMON/PHOEBE SNOW)		
	Gone At Last	1975
SNOWMEN	Hokey Cokey	1981
SO SOLID CREW	Broken Silence	2003
	Ride Wid Us	2002
	They Don't Know	2001
	21 Seconds	2001

ARTIST	SONG TITLE	DATE
SO SOLID CREW presents MR. SHABZ		
	Haters	2002
SOAPY	Horny As Funk	1996
SODA CLUB featuring ANDREA ANATOLA		
	Keep Love Together	2003
SODA CLUB featuring ASHLEY JADE		
	Ain't No Love (Ain't No Use)	2004
SODA CLUB featuring HANNAH ALETHEA		
	Heaven Is A Place On Earth	2003
	Take My Breath Away	2002
SOFT CELL	Bedsitter	1981
	Down In The Subway	1984
	The Night	2003
	Numbers/Barriers	1983
	Say Hello Wave Goodbye	1982
	Soul Inside	1983
	Tainted Love	1982
	Torch	1982
	What	1982
	Where The Heart Is	1982
SOFT CELL/MARC ALMOND		
	Say Hello Wave Goodbye '91	1991
SOHO	Hippychick	1990
SOLAR STONE	Seven Cities	1999
SOLE/JT MONEY	Who Dat	1999

ARTIST	SONG TITLE	DATE
SOLE featuring JT MONEY AND KANDI		
	4, 5, 6	1999
SOLID HARMONIE	I Wanna Love You	1998
	I Want You To Want Me	1998
	I'll Be There For You	1998
SOLO (US)	Heaven	1996
SAL SOLO	San Damiano (Heart And Soul)	1984
MARTIN SOLVEIG	Rocking Music	2004
BELOUIS SOME	Imagination	1986
	Some People	1986
JIMMY SOMERVILLE	Heartbeat	1995
	Hurt So Good	1995
	Read My Lips (Enough Is Enough)	1990
	Smalltown Boy (1991 Remix)	1991
	To Love Somebody	1990
	You Make Me Feel (Mighty Real)	1990
JIMMY SOMERVILLE/JUNE MILES KINGSTON		
	Comment Te Dire Adieu	1989
SOMETHIN' FOR THE PEOPLE featuring TRINA & TAMARA		
	My Love Is The Shhh!	1997
SOMETHING CORPORATE		
	Punk Rock Princess	2003
SOMORE featuring DAMON TRUEITT		
	I Refuse (What You Want)	1998
SON BY FOUR	Purest Of Pain (A Puro Dolor)	2000

ARTIST	SONG TITLE	DATE
SON'Z OF A LOOP DA LOOP ERA		
	Far Out	1992
SONIA	Be Young, Be Foolish, Be Happy	1991
	Better The Devil You Know	1993
	Boogie Nights	1992
	Can't Forget You	1989
	Counting Every Minute	1990
	End Of The World	1990
	Listen To Your Heart	1989
	Only Fools (Never Fall In Love)	1991
	You To Me Are Everything	1991
	You'll Never Stop Me Loving You	1989
	(BIG FUN & SONIA)	
	You've Got A Friend	1990
SONIC YOUTH	Bull In The Heather	1994
	100%	1992
	Sugar Kane	1993
SONIQUE	Can't Make Up My Mind	2003
	I Put A Spell On You	1998
	It Feels So Good	1998
	Sky	2000
SONNY	Laugh At Me	1965
SONNY & CHER	All I Ever Need Is You	1971
	Baby Don't Go	1965
	The Beat Goes On	1967
	But You're Mine	1965

ARTIST	SONG TITLE	DATE
	A Cowboy's Work Is Never Done	1972
	I Got You Babe	1965
	Just You	1965
	Little Man	1966
	What Now My Love	1966
	When You Say Love	1972
SOPWITH CAMEL	Hello Hello	1966
SORROWS	Take A Heart	1965
SOUL ASYLUM	Black Gold	1994
	Misery	1995
	Runaway Train	1993
	Somebody To Shove	1993
SOUL CHILDREN	I'll Be The Other Woman	1974
SOUL CONTROL	Chocolate (Choco Choco)	2004
SOUL FOR REAL	Candy Rain	1995
	Every Little Thing I Do	1995
SOUL II SOUL	Back To Life	1989
	A Dream's A Dream	1990
	Get A Life	1989
	I Care	1995
	Joy	1992
	Just Right	1992
	Keep On Movin'	1989
	Love Enuff	1995
	Missing You	1990
	Move Me No Mountain	1992

ARTIST	SONG TITLE	DATE
	Represent	1997
	Wish	1993
SOUL II SOUL/CARON WHEELER		
	Back To Life (However Do You Want Me)	1989
SOUL SURVIVORS	Explosion In Your Soul	1967
	Expressway To Your Heart	1967
AARON SOUL	Ring Ring Ring	2001
DAVID SOUL	Don't Give Up On Us	1977
	Going In With My Eyes Open	1977
	It Sure Brings Out The Love In Your Eyes	1978
	Let's Have A Quiet Night In	1977
	Silver Lady	1977
JIMMY SOUL	If You Wanna Be Happy	1963
SOULDECISION featuring THRUST		
	Faded	2000
SOULSEARCHER	Can't Get Enough	1999
	Do It To Me Again	2000
SOULWAX	Any Minute Now	2004
	Too Many DJ's	2000
SOUND BLUNTZ	Billie Jean	2002
SOUND-DE-ZIGN	Happiness	2001
SOUNDGARDEN	Black Hole Sun	1994
	Blow Up The Outside World	1996
	Burden In My Hand	1996
	Fell On Black Days	1995
	Jesus Christ Pose	1992

ARTIST	SONG TITLE	DATE
	Pretty Noose	1996
	Spoonman	1994
SOUNDS INCORPORATED		
	Spanish Harlem	1964
	The Spartans	1964
SOUNDS NICE	Love At First Sight (Je T'aime... Moi Non	
	Plus)	1969
SOUNDS OF BLACKNESS		
	Everything Is Gonna Be Alright	1994
	I Believe	1994
	I'm Going All The Way	1995
	Optimistic	1992
	Spirit	1997
(DARYL HALL/SOUNDS OF BLACKNESS)		
	Gloryland	1994
SOUNDS OF SUNSHINE		
	Love Means (You Never Have To Say	
	You're Sorry)	1971
SOUNDS ORCHESTRAL		
	Cast Your Fate To The Wind	1965
SOUP DRAGONS	Divine Thing	1992
	I'm Free	1990
	Mother Universe	1990
SOURCE	Clouds	1997
SOURCE featuring CANDI STATON		
	You Got The Love	1997

ARTIST	SONG TITLE	DATE
JOE SOUTH	Games People Play	1969
	Walk A Mile In My Shoes	1970
SOUTHER HILLMAN FURAY BAND		
	Fallin' In Love	1974
J.D. SOUTHER	You're Only Lonely	1979
(JAMES TAYLOR & J. D. SOUTHER)		
	Her Town Too	1981
SOUTHSIDE SPINNERS		
	Luvstruck	2000
SOUVLAKI	Inferno	1997
SOVEREIGN COLLECTION		
	Mozart 40	1971
RED SOVINE	Teddy Bear	1976
SPACE	Avenging Angels	1998
	The Bad Days (EP)	1998
	Begin Again	1998
	Dark Clouds	1997
	Female Of The Species	1996
	Magic Fly	1977
	Me And You Versus The World	1996
	Neighbourhood	1996
SPACE with CERYS OF CATATONIA		
	The Ballad Of Tom Jones	1998
SPACE BROTHERS	Forgiven (I Feel Your Love)	1997
	Heaven Will Come	1999
	Legacy (Show Me Love)	1999

ARTIST	SONG TITLE	DATE
	Shine	1997
SPACE MANOEUVRES		
	Stage One	2000
SPACEDUST	Gym And Tonic	1998
	Let's Get Down	1999
SPACEHOG	In The Meantime	1996
SPAGNA	Call Me	1987
	Every Girl And Boy	1988
SPANDAU BALLET	Chant No. I (I Don't Need This Pressure On)	1981
	Communication	1983
	Fight For Ourselves	1986
	The Freeze	1981
	Gold	1983
	Highly Strung	1984
	How Many Lies	1987
	I'll Fly For You	1984
	Instinction	1982
	Lifeline	1982
	Musclebound/Glow	1981
	Only When You Leave	1984
	Paint Me Down	1981
	Round And Round	1984
	Through The Barricades	1986
	To Cut A Long Story Short	1980
	True	1983

ARTIST	SONG TITLE	DATE
SPANKY & OUR GANG		
	Lazy Day	1967
	Like To Get To Know You	1968
	Making Every Minute Count	1967
	Sunday Morning	1968
	Sunday Will Never Be The Same	1967
SPARKLE	Time To Move On	1998
SPARKLE featuring R. KELLY		
	Be Careful	1998
SPARKS	Amateur Hour	1974
	Beat The Clock	1979
	Get In The Swing	1975
	Looks, Looks, Looks	1975
	Never Turn Your Back On Mother Earth	1974
	The Number One Song In Heaven	1979
	Something For The Girl With Everything	1975
	This Town Ain't Big Enough For Both Of Us	1974
	When Do I Get To Sing 'My Way'	1995
SPARKS vs FAITH NO MORE		
	This Town Ain't Big Enough For Both Of Us	1997
BUBBA SPARXXX	Lovely	2002
	Ugly	2001

ARTIST	SONG TITLE	DATE
SPEAR OF DESTINY		
	Never Take Me Alive	1987
	So In Love With You	1988
BILLIE JO SPEARS	Blanket On The Ground	1975
	Sing Me An Old Fashioned Song	1976
	What I've Got In Mind	1976
BRITNEY SPEARS	... Baby One More Time	1998
	Born To Make You Happy	2000
	Don't Let Me Be The Last To Know	2001
	Everytime	2004
	From The Bottom Of My Broken Heart	2000
	I Love Rock 'n' Roll	2002
	I'm A Slave 4 U	2001
	I'm Not A Girl, Not Yet A Woman	2002
	Lucky	2000
	Oops!... I Did It Again	2000
	Overprotected	2002
	Sometimes	1999
	Stronger	2000
	Toxic	2004
	(You Drive Me) Crazy	1999
BRITNEY SPEARS featuring MADONNA		
	Me Against The Music	2003
BRITNEY SPEARS featuring PHARRELL WILLIAMS		
	Boys	2002
SPECIAL D	Come With Me	2004

ARTIST	SONG TITLE	DATE
SPECIALS	Do Nothing/Maggie's Farm	1980
	Ghost Town	1981
	Rat Race/Rude Boys Outa Jail	1980
	Special AKA Live! (EP)	1980
	Stereotype/International Jet Set	1980
SPECIALS featuring RICO		
	A Message To You Rudy/Nite Klub	1979
SPECIAL AKA	Gangsters	1979
	Nelson Mandela	1984
	(RHODA WITH SPECIAL AKA)	
	The Boiler	1982
CHRIS SPEDDING	Motor Bikin'	1975
SPEECH	Like Marvin Gaye Said (What's Going On)	1996
SPEEDWAY	Can't Turn Back	2004
	Genie In A Bottle/Save Yourself	2003
	In & Out	2004
JUDSON SPENCE	Yeah,yeah,yeah	1988
DON SPENCER	Fireball	1963
TRACIE SPENCER	It's All About You (Not About Me)	1999
	Symptoms Of True Love	1988
	This House	1990
SPICE GIRLS	Goodbye	1998
	Holler/Let Love Lead The Way	2000
	Mama/Who Do You Think You Are	1997
	Say You'll Be There	1997
	Spice Up Your Life	1997

ARTIST	SONG TITLE	DATE
	Stop	1998
	Too Much	1998
	2 Become 1	1997
	Viva Forever	1998
	Wannabe	1997
SPIDER	New Romance (It's A Mystery)	1980
SPILLER	Cry Baby	2002
	Groovejet (If This Ain't Love)	2000
SPIN CITY	Landslide	2000
SPIN DOCTORS	Cleopatra's Cat	1994
	Jimmy Olsen's Blues	1993
	Little Miss Can't Be Wrong	1992
	Two Princes	1993
SPINAL TAP	Bitch School	1992
SPINNERS (AKA DETROIT SPINNERS)		
	Body Language	1980
	Could It Be I'm Falling In Love	1973
	Cupid — I've Loved You For A Long Time (Medley)	1980
	Ghetto Child	1973
	I'll Always Love You	1965
	I'm Coming Home	1974
	Living A Little, Laughing A Little	1975
	Love Don't Love Nobody (Pt 1)	1974
	Love Or Leave	1975
	Mighty Love (Pt 1)	1974

ARTIST	SONG TITLE	DATE
	One Of A Kind (Love Affair)	1973
	The Rubberband Man	1976
	They Just Can't Stop It The (Games People Play)	1975
	Wake Up Susan	1977
	Working My Way Back To You/Forgive Me, Girl	1980
(DIONNE WARWICK & THE SPINNERS)		
	Then Came You	1974
(THE SPINNERS)		
	It's A Shame	1970
(RAPPIN' 4-TAY featuring THE SPINNERS)		
	I'll Be Around	1995
SPIRAL STAIRCASE	More Today Than Yesterday	1969
SPIRIT	I Got A Line On You	1969
SPIRITS	Don't Bring Me Down	1994
	Spirit Inside	1995
SPIRITUALIZED	The Abbey Road EP	1998
	Do It All Over Again	2002
	Electricity	1997
	I Think I'm In Love	1998
	She Kissed Me (It Felt Like A Hit)	2003
	Stop Your Crying	2001
SPIRITUALIZED ELECTRIC MAINLINE		
	Let It Flow	1995
SPIRO AND WIX	Tara's Theme	1996

ARTIST	SONG TITLE	DATE
SPITTING IMAGE	The Chicken Song	1986
	Santa Claus Is On The Dole/First Atheist	
	Tabernacle Choir	1986
SPLINTER	Costafine Town	1974
SPLIT ENZ	I Got You	1980
SPLODGENESSABOUNDS		
	Simon Templer/Two Pints Of Lager And	
	A Packet Of Crisps Please	1980
	Two Little Boys/Horse	1980
SPOILED & ZIGO	More & More	2000
SPOKESMEN	The Dawn Of Correction	1965
SPOOKS	Karma Hotel	2001
	Things I've Seen	2001
SPORTY THIEVZ	No Pigeons	1999
SPOTNICKS	Hava Nagila	1963
	Just Listen To My Heart	1963
DUSTY SPRINGFIELD		
	All I See Is You	1966
	A Brand New Me	1969
	Give Me Time	1967
	Goin' Back	1966
	How Can I Be Sure	1970
	I Close My Eyes And Count To Ten	1968
	I Just Don't Know What To Do With	
	Myself	1964
	I Only Want To Be With You	1964

ARTIST	SONG TITLE	DATE
	I'll Try Anything	1967
	In Private	1989
	In The Middle Of Nowhere	1965
	Little By Little	1966
	The Look Of Love	1967
	Losing You	1964
	Nothing Has Been Proved	1989
	Reputation	1990
	Some Of Your Lovin'	1965
	Son Of A Preacher Man	1968
	Stay Awhile	1964
	The Windmills Of Your Mind	1969
	Wishin' And Hopin'	1964
	You Don't Have To Say You Love Me	1966
	Your Hurtin' Kinda Love	1965
	(PET SHOP BOYS & DUSTY SPRINGFIELD)	
	What Have I Done To Deserve This?	1987
RICK SPRINGFIELD	Affair Of The Night	1983
	Bop 'Til You Drop	1984
	Bruce	1984
	Celebrate Youth	1985
	Don't Talk To Strangers	1982
	Don't Walk Away	1984
	Human Touch	1983
	I Get Excited	1982
	I've Done Everything For You	1981

ARTIST	SONG TITLE	DATE
	Jessie's Girl	1981
	Love Is Alright Tonite	1981
	Love Somebody	1984
	Rock Of Life	1988
	Souls	1983
	Speak To The Sky	1972
	State Of The Heart	1985
	What Kind Of Fool Am I	1982
SPRINGFIELDS	Come On Home	1963
	Say I Won't Be There	1963
BRUCE SPRINGSTEEN		
	Better Days	1992
	Born To Run	1975
	Brilliant Disguise	1987
	Cover Me	1984
	Dancing In The Dark	1984
	Fade Away	1981
	57 Channels (And Nothin' On)	1992
	The Ghost Of Tom Joad	1996
	Glory Days	1985
	Human Touch/Better Days	1992
	Hungry Heart	1980
	I'm Goin' Down	1985
	I'm On Fire/Born In The U.S.A.	1985
	Lonesome Day	2002
	My Hometown	1985

ARTIST	SONG TITLE	DATE
	One Step Up	1988
	Prove It All Night	1978
	The River	1981
	Santa Claus Is Comin' To Town	1985
	Secret Garden	1997
	Spare Parts	1988
	Streets Of Philadelphia	1994
	Tougher Than The Rest	1988
	Tunnel Of Love	1987
	War	1986
SPRINGWATER	I Will Return	1971
SPUNGE	Jump On Demand	2002
SPYRO GYRA	Morning Dance	1979
SQUEEZE	Another Nail In My Heart	1980
	Cool For Cats	1979
	853-5937	1987
	Heaven Knows	1996
	Hourglass	1987
	Is That Love	1981
	Labelled With Love	1981
	Slap & Tickle	1979
	Take Me I'm Yours	1978
	Third Rail	1993
	This Summer	1996
	Up The Junction	1979

ARTIST	SONG TITLE	DATE
BILLY SQUIER	Everybody Wants You	1982
	In The Dark	1981
	Rock Me Tonite	1984
	The Stroke	1981
DOROTHY SQUIRES	For Once In My Life	1969
	My Way	1970
	Till	1970
ST. ANDREWS CHORALE		
	Cloud 99	1976
ST. JOHN'S COLLEGE CHOIR & BAND GRENADIER		
GUARDS	The Queen's Birthday Song	1986
WARREN STACY	My Girl My Girl	2002
JIM STAFFORD	I Got Stoned And I Missed It	1975
	My Girl Bill	1974
	Spiders & Snakes	1973
	Swamp Witch	1973
	Wildwood Weed	1974
	Your Bulldog Drinks Champagne	1974
TERRY STAFFORD	I'll Touch A Star	1964
	Suspicion	1964
STAIND	It's Been Awhile	2001
	Outside	2001
	Price To Play	2003
	So Far Away	2003
STAKKA BO	Here We Go	1993
STALLION	Old Fashioned Boy (You're The One)	1977

ARTIST	SONG TITLE	DATE
FRANK STALLONE	Far From Over	1983
STAMFORD AMP	Anything For You	2002
STAMPEDERS	Hit The Road Jack	1976
	Sweet City Woman	1971
JOE STAMPLEY	Soul Song	1973
STAN	Suntan	1993
STANDELLS	Dirty Water	1966
THE STANDS	Here She Comes Again	2004
	I Need You	2003
	When The River Rolls Over You	2003
MICHAEL STANLEY BAND		
	He Can't Love You	1980
	My Town	1983
LISA STANSFIELD	All Around The World	1990
	All Woman	1991
	Change	1991
	In All The Right Places	1993
	Little Bit Of Heaven	1993
	Live Together	1990
	Never, Never Gonna Give You Up	1997
	The Real Thing	1997
	Set Your Loving Free	1992
	So Natural	1993
	Someday (I'm Coming Back)	1992
	This Is The Right Time	1990
	Time To Make You Mine	1992

ARTIST	SONG TITLE	DATE
	What Did I Do To You? (EP)	1990
	You Can't Deny It	1990
LISA STANSFIELD vs THE DIRTY ROTTEN SCOUNDRELS		
	People Hold On (The Bootleg Mixes)	1997
(COLDCUT featuring LISA STANSFIELD)		
	People Hold On	1989
STAPLE SINGERS	Heavy Makes You Happy	1971
	I'll Take You There	1972
	If You're Ready (Come Go With Me)	1974
	Let's Do It Again	1975
	Oh La De Da	1973
	Respect Yourself	1971
	This World	1972
	Touch A Hand Make A Friend	1974
STARBUCK	Everybody Be Dancin'	1977
	Moonlight Feels Right	1976
STARCHASER	Love Will Set You Free (Jambe Myth)	2002
BUDDY STARCHER	History Repeats Itself	1966
STARDUST	Music Sounds Better With You	1998
ALVIN STARDUST	Good Love Can Never Die	1975
	I Feel Like Buddy Holly	1984
	I Won't Run Away	1984
	Jealous Mind	1974
	My Coo-Ca-Choo	1973
	Pretend	1981
	Red Dress	1974

ARTIST	SONG TITLE	DATE
	So Near To Christmas	1984
	Sweet Cheatin' Rita	1975
	Tell Me Why	1974
	You You You	1974
STARFIGHTER	Apache	2000
STARGARD	Theme Song From 'Which Way Is Up'	1978
	What You Waitin' For	1978
STARLAND VOCAL BAND		
	Afternoon Delight	1976
STARLIGHT	Numero Uno	1989
STARPARTY	I'm In Love	2000
STARPOINT	Object Of My Desire	1985
BRENDA K. STARR	I Still Believe	1988
	What You See Is What You Get	1988
EDWIN STARR	Agent Double-O-Soul	1965
	Contact	1979
	H.A.P.P.Y. Radio	1979
	Stop Her On Sight (SOS)/Headline News	1968
	Stop The War Now	1970
	25 Miles	1969
	War	1970
FREDDIE STARR	It's You	1974
RINGO STARR	Back Off Boogaloo	1972
	It Don't Come Easy	1971
	It's All Down To Goodnight Vienna/	
	Oo-Wee	1975

ARTIST	SONG TITLE	DATE
	No No Song/Snookeroo	1975
	Oh My My	1974
	Only You	1974
	Photograph	1973
	Wrack My Brain	1981
	You're Sixteen	1973
STARS ON 45/STARSOUND		
	Stars On 45 (Medley)	1981
	Stars On 45 (Vol 2)	1981
	Stars On 45 (Vol 3)	1981
	Stars On Stevie	1982
STARS ON 54	If You Could Read My Mind	1998
STARSAILOR	Alcoholic	2001
	Born Again	2003
	Fever	2001
	Four To The Floor	2004
	Good Souls	2001
	Lullaby	2001
	Poor Misguided Fool	2002
	Silence Is Easy	2003
STARSHIP	It's Not Enough	1989
	It's Not Over ('Til It's Over)	1987
	Jane	1980
	Nothing's Gonna Stop Us Now	1987
	Sara	1985
	We Built This City	1985

ARTIST	SONG TITLE	DATE
STARSOUND	See Stars on 45	
STARTRAX	Startrax Club Disco	1981
STAR TURN ON 45 PINTS		
	Pump Up The Bitter	1988
STARVATION	Starvation/Tam-Tam Pour L'ethiope	1985
STARZ	Cherry Baby	1977
STATE OF MIND	This Is It	1998
STATIC REVENGER	Happy People	2001
STATLER BROTHERS		
	Flowers On The Wall	1965
CANDI STATON	Love On Love	1999
	Nights On Broadway	1977
	Stand By Your Man	1970
	Suspicious Minds	1982
	Young Hearts Run Free	1976
	(SOURCE featuring CANDI STATON)	
	You Got The Love	1997
STATUS QUO	Accident Prone	1978
	Again And Again	1978
	Ain't Complaining	1988
	The Anniversary Waltz — Part 1	1990
	Break The Rules	1974
	Burning Bridges (On And Off And On Again)	1988
	Can't Give You More	1991
	Caroline	1973

ARTIST	SONG TITLE	DATE
	Dear John	1982
	Don't Stop	1996
	Down Down	1974
	Down The Dustpipe	1970
	Dreamin'	1986
	Going Down Town Tonight	1984
	I Didn't Mean It	1994
	Ice In The Sun	1968
	In My Chair	1970
	In The Army Now	1986
	Jam Side Down	2002
	Lies/Don't Drive My Car	1980
	Living On An Island	1979
	Marguerita Time	1983
	Mean Girl	1973
	A Mess Of The Blues	1983
	Mystery Song	1976
	Ol' Rag Blues	1983
	Paper Plane	1973
	Pictures Of Matchstick Men	1968
	Rain	1976
	Red Sky	1986
	Restless	1994
	Roadhouse Medley (Anniversary Waltz Part 25)	1992
	Rock 'n' Roll	1981

ARTIST	SONG TITLE	DATE
	Rock 'Til You Drop	1992
	Rockin' All Over The World	1977
	Roll Over Lay Down	1975
	Rolling Home	1986
	Runnin' All Over The World	1988
	She Don't Fool Me	1982
	Sherri Don't Fail Me Now!	1994
	Something 'Bout You Baby	1981
	The Wanderer	1984
	The Way It Goes	1999
	What You're Proposing	1980
	Whatever You Want	1979
	When You Walk In The Room	1995
	Who Gets The Love	1988
	Wild Side Of Life	1976
	You'll Come 'Round	2004
STATUS QUO WITH THE BEACH BOYS		
	Fun Fun Fun	1996
STAXX	Joy	1993
STEALER'S WHEEL	Everything Will Turn Out Fine	1973
	Star	1974
	Stuck In The Middle With You	1973
STEAM	Na Na Hey Hey Kiss Him Goodbye	1969
STEEL BREEZE	Dreamin' Is Easy	1983
	You Don't Want Me Anymore	1982
STEEL PULSE	Prodigal Son	1978

ARTIST	SONG TITLE	DATE
STEELEYE SPAN	All Around My Hat	1975
	Gaudette	1973
STEELHEART	I'll Never Let You Go	1991
STEELY DAN	Black Friday	1975
	Deacon Blues	1978
	Do It Again	1972
	FM (No Static At All)	1978
	Haitian Divorce	1976
	Hey Nineteen	1980
	Josie	1978
	Peg	1977
	Reeling In The Years	1973
	Rikki Don't Lose That Number	1974
	Time Out Of Mind	1981
GWEN STEFANI/EVE		
	Let Me Blow Ya Mind	2001
(MOBY featuring GWEN STEFANI)		
	South Side	2000
TOMMY SHANE STEINER		
	What If She's An Angel	2002
JIM STEINMAN	Rock And Roll Dreams Come Through	1981
STELLAR PROJECT featuring BRANDI EMMA		
	Get Up Stand Up	2004
VAN STEPHENSON	Modern Day Delilah	1984
STEPPENWOLF	Born To Be Wild	1968
	Hey Lawdy Mama	1970

ARTIST	SONG TITLE	DATE
	Magic Carpet Ride	1968
	Monster	1969
	Move Over	1969
	Rock Me	1969
	Straight Shootin' Woman	1974
STEPS	After The Love Has Gone	1999
	Better Best Forgotten	1999
	Chain Reaction/One For Sorrow	2001
	Deeper Shade Of Blue	2000
	5,6,7,8	1997
	Heartbeat/Tragedy	1998
	Here And Now/You'll Be Sorry	2001
	It's The Way You Make Me Feel/Too Busy Thinking 'Bout My Baby	2001
	Last Thing On My Mind	1998
	Love's Got A Hold On My Heart	1999
	Say You'll Be Mine/Better The Devil You Know	1999
	Stomp	2000
	When I Said Goodbye/Summer Of Love	2000
	Words Are Not Enough/I Know Him So Well	2001
STEREO MCS	Connected	1993
	Creation	1993
	Deep Down And Dirty	2001
	Elevate My Mind	1991

ARTIST	SONG TITLE	DATE
	Ground Level	1993
	Step It Up	1992
	Un-Connected	1992
STEREOPHONICS	The Bartender And The Thief	1998
	Handbags And Gladrags	2001
	Have A Nice Day	2001
	Hurry Up And Wait	1999
	I Wouldn't Believe Your Radio	1999
	Just Looking	1999
	Local Boy In The Photograph	1998
	Madame Helga	2003
	Maybe Tomorrow	2003
	More Life In A Tramp's Vest	1997
	Moviestar	2004
	Mr Writer	2001
	Pick A Part That's News	1999
	Since I Told You It's Over	2003
	Step On My Old Size Nines	2001
	A Thousand Trees	1997
	Traffic	1997
	Vegas Two Times	2002
	(TOM JONES & STEREOPHONICS)	
	Mama Told Me Not To Come	2000
STEREOPOL featuring NEVADA		
	Dancin' Tonight	2003

ARTIST	SONG TITLE	DATE
CAT STEVENS	Another Saturday Night	1974
	A Bad Night	1967
	Can't Keep It In	1972
	The Hurt	1973
	I Love My Dog	1966
	I'm Gonna Get Me A Gun	1967
	Lady D'Arbanville	1970
	Matthew And Son	1967
	Moon Shadow	1971
	Morning Has Broken	1972
	Oh Very Young	1974
	Peace Train	1971
	Ready	1974
	(Remember The Days Of The) Old Schoolyard	1977
	Sitting	1972
	Two Fine People	1975
	Wild World	1971
RACHEL STEVENS	Funky Dory	2003
	More More More	2004
	Some Girls	2004
	Sweet Dreams My L.A. Ex	2003
RAY STEVENS	Along Came Jones	1969
	Bridget The Midget (The Queen Of The Blues)	1971
	Everything Is Beautiful	1970

ARTIST	SONG TITLE	DATE
	Gitarzan	1969
	In The Mood	1977
	Indian Love Call	1975
	Misty	1975
	Mr. Businessman	1968
	The Streak	1974
	Turn Your Radio On	1972
SHAKIN' STEVENS	Because I Love You	1986
	The Best Christmas Of Them All	1990
	Breakin' Up My Heart	1985
	Come See About Me	1987
	Cry Just A Little Bit	1983
	Feel The Need In Me	1988
	Give Me Your Heart Tonight	1982
	Green Door	1981
	Hot Dog	1980
	I Might	1990
	I'll Be Home This Christmas	1991
	I'll Be Satisfied	1982
	It's Late	1983
	It's Raining	1981
	A Letter To You	1984
	Lipstick Powder & Paint	1985
	A Little Boogie Woogie (In The Back Of My Mind)	1987
	Love Attack	1989

ARTIST	SONG TITLE	DATE
	A Love Worth Waiting For	1984
	Marie Marie	1980
	Merry Christmas Everyone	1985
	Oh Julie	1982
	The Shakin' Stevens (EP)	1982
	Shirley	1982
	Teardrops	1984
	This Ole House	1981
	True Love	1988
	Turning Away	1986
	What Do You Want To Make Those Eyes At Me For	1987
	You Drive Me Crazy	1981
SHAKY & BONNIE	A Rockin' Good Way	1984
SHAKY featuring ROGER TAYLOR		
	Radio	1992
STEVENSON'S ROCKET		
	Alright Baby	1975
B.W. STEVENSON	My Maria	1973
AL STEWART	Midnight Rocks	1980
	Song On The Radio	1979
	Time Passages	1978
	Year Of The Cat	1976
AMII STEWART	Friends	1984
	Knock On Wood/Light My Fire	1985
	The Letter/Paradise Bird	1980

ARTIST	SONG TITLE	DATE
	Light My Fire — 137 Disco Heaven	1979
AMII STEWART & JOHNNY STEWART		
	My Guy/My Girl (Medley)	1980
ANDY STEWART	Donald Where's Your Troosers	1989
BILLY STEWART	I Do Love You	1965
	Secret Love	1966
	Sitting In The Park	1965
	Summertime	1966
DAVE STEWART	Heart Of Stone	1994
DAVE STEWART & BARBARA GASKIN		
	It's My Party	1981
DAVE STEWART: GUEST VOCALS COLIN BLUNSTONE		
	What Becomes Of The Brokenhearted	1981
DAVID A. STEWART featuring CANDY DULFER		
	Lily Was Here	1990
JERMAINE STEWART		
	Get Lucky	1988
	Say It Again	1988
	We Don't Have To Take Our Clothes Off	1986
JOHN STEWART	Gold	1979
	Lost Her In The Sun	1979
	Midnight Wind	1979
ROD STEWART	Ain't Love A Bitch	1979
	Angel/What Made Milwaukee Famous	1972
	Baby Jane	1983
	Broken Arrow	1991

ARTIST	SONG TITLE	DATE
	Crazy About Her	1989
	Da Ya Think I'm Sexy	1978
	Downtown Train	1989
	Every Beat Of My Heart	1986
	Farewell/Bring It On Home To Me	1974
	Forever Young	1988
	Get Back	1976
	Have I Told You Lately	1993
	Having A Party	1994
	Hotlegs/I Was Only Joking	1978
	I Can't Deny It	2001
	I Don't Want To Talk About It/First Cut Is The Deepest	1977
	(I Know) I'm Losing You	1971
	I've Been Drinkin'	1973
	If Loving You Is Wrong (I Don't Want To Be Right)	1980
	Infatuation	1984
	The Killing Of Georgie (Parts I & II)	1977
	Lost In You	1988
	Love Touch	1986
	Maggie May/Reason To Believe	1971
	The Motown Song	1991
	My Girl	1980
	My Heart Can't Tell You No	1989
	Oh! No Not My Baby	1973

ARTIST	SONG TITLE	DATE
	Ole Ola (Muhler Brasileira)	1978
	Ooh La La	1998
	Passion	1980
	Rhythm Of My Heart	1991
	Ruby Tuesday	1993
	Sailing	1975
	Shotgun Wedding	1993
	Some Guys Have All The Luck	1984
	Sweet Surrender	1983
	This Old Heart Of Mine	1975
	Tom Traubert's Blues (Waltzing Matilda)	1992
	Tonight I'm Yours (Don't Hurt Me)	1982
	Tonight's The Night (Gonna Be Alright)	1976
	What Am I Gonna Do (I'm So In Love With You)	1983
	You Wear It Well	1972
	You're In My Heart (The Final Acclaim)	1977
	You're The Star	1995
	Young Turks	1981
ROD STEWART & TINA TURNER		
	It Takes Two	1990
ROD STEWART WITH THE SCOTTISH EURO '96 SQUAD		
	Purple Heather	1996
(BRYAN ADAMS/ROD STEWART/STING)		
	All For Love	1993

ARTIST	SONG TITLE	DATE
(GLASS TIGER featuring ROD STEWART)		
	My Town	1991
(N-TRANCE featuring ROD STEWART)		
	Do Ya Think I'm Sexy?	1997
STICKY featuring MS. DYNAMITE		
	Booo!	2001
STIFF LITTLE FINGERS		
	At The Edge	1980
	Listen (EP)	1982
	Nobody's Hero/Tin Soldiers	1980
CURTIS STIGERS	I Wonder Why	1991
	Never Saw A Miracle	1992
	This Time	1995
	You're All That Matters To Me	1992
THE STILLS	Lola Stars And Stripes	2004
STEPHEN STILLS	Love The One You're With	1970
	Sit Yourself Down	1971
STILTSKIN	Footsteps	1994
	Inside	1994
STING	After The Rain Has Fallen	2000
	All This Time	1991
	Be Still My Beating Heart	1988
	Brand New Day	1999
	Demolition Man	1993
	Englishman In New York	1990

ARTIST	SONG TITLE	DATE
	Fields Of Gold	1993
	Fortress Around Your Heart	1985
	I Was Brought To My Senses	1996
	If I Ever Lose My Faith In You	1993
	If You Love Somebody Set Them Free	1965
	Let Your Soul Be Your Pilot	1996
	Love Is The Seventh Wave	1985
	Nothing 'Bout Me	1994
	Russians	1986
	Send Your Love	2003
	Seven Days	1993
	Spread A Little Happiness	1982
	This Cowboy Song	1995
	We'll Be Together	1987
	When We Dance	1994
	You Still Touch Me	1996
STING AND THE POLICE		
	Roxanne '97	1997
STING featuring CHEB MAMI		
	Desert Rose	2000
STING WITH ERIC CLAPTON		
	It's Probably Me	1992
(BRYAN ADAMS/ROD STEWART/STING)		
	All For Love	1993
(CRAIG DAVID featuring STING)		
	Rise & Fall	2003

ARTIST	SONG TITLE	DATE
(PATO BANTON WITH STING)		
	Spirits In A Material World	1996
BYRON STINGILY	Get Up (Everybody)	1997
	Sing A Song	1997
	That's The Way Love Is	2000
	You Make Me Feel (Mighty Real)	1998
STIX 'N' STONED	Outrageous	1996
STOCK AITKEN WATERMAN		
	Roadblock	1987
CATHERINE STOCK	To Have And To Hold	1986
STONE PONEYS	Different Drum	1967
STONE ROSES	Begging You	1995
	Elephant Stone	1990
	Fool's Gold/What The World Is Waiting For	1989
	I Am The Resurrection	1992
	I Wanna Be Adored	1991
	Love Spreads	1994
	Made Of Stone	1990
	One Love	1990
	She Bangs The Drums	1989
	Ten Storey Love Song	1995
	Waterfall	1992
STONE SOUR	Bother	2003
STONE TEMPLE PILOTS		
	Plush	1993

ARTIST	SONG TITLE	DATE
ANGIE STONE	Life Story	2000
	Wish I Didn't Miss You	2002
ANGIE STONE featuring ALICIA KEYS & EVE		
	Brotha Part II	2002
ANGIE STONE featuring SNOOP DOGG		
	I Wanna Thank Ya	2004
	(BLUE featuring STEVIE WONDER & ANGIE STONE)	
	Signed, Sealed, Delivered, I'm Yours	2003
JOSS STONE	Fell In Love With A Boy	2004
	Super Duper Love (Are You Diggin On Me?)	2004
	You Had Me	2004
R & J STONE	We Do It	1976
STONEBOLT	I Will Still Love You	1978
STONEBRIDGE featuring THERESE		
	Put 'Em High	2004
PAUL STOOKEY	Wedding Song (This Is Love)	1971
STORIES	Brother Louie	1973
STORM	It's My House	1979
STORM	I've Got A Lot To Learn About Love	1991
	Storm	1998
	Storm Animal	2000
	Time To Burn	2000
REBECCA STORM	The Show (Theme From 'Connie')	1985
GEORGE STRAIT	The Best Day	2000

ARTIST	SONG TITLE	DATE
	Cowboys Like Us	2003
	Go On	2000
	I Hate Everything	2004
	Living And Living Well	2002
	Meanwhile	1999
	Run	2001
	She'll Leave You With A Smile	2002
	Write This Down	1999
NICK STRAKER BAND		
	A Walk In The Park	1980
PETER STRAKER & THE HANDS OF DR TELENY		
	The Spirit Is Willing	1972
STRANGELOVE	Beautiful Alone	1996
	The Greatest Show On Earth	1997
STRANGELOVES	Cara-Lin	1965
	I Want Candy	1965
	Night Time	1966
STRANGLERS	All Day And All Of The Night	1988
	Always The Sun	1991
	Bear Cage	1980
	Big Thing Coming	2004
	Duchess	1979
	European Female	1983
	5 Minutes	1978
	Golden Brown	1982
	Grip '89 (Get A) Grip (On Yourself)	1989

ARTIST	SONG TITLE	DATE
	Midnight Summer Dream	1983
	Nice 'n' Sleazy	1978
	Nice In Nice	1986
	96 Tears	1990
	No Mercy	1984
	No More Heroes	1977
	Nuclear Device (The Wizard Of Aus)	1979
	Peaches/Go Buddy Go	1977
	Skin Deep	1984
	Something Better Change/Straighten Out	1977
	Strange Little Girl	1982
	Walk On By	1978
	Who Wants The World	1980
STRAW	The Aeroplane Song	1999
STRAWBERRY ALARM CLOCK		
	Incense And Peppermints	1967
	Tomorrow	1967
STRAWBERRY SWITCHBLADE		
	Since Yesterday	1984
STRAWBS	Lay Down	1972
	Part Of The Union	1973
	Shine On Silver Sun	1973
STRAY CATS	I Won't Stand In Your Way	1983
	The Race Is On	1981
	Rock This Town	1982
	Runaway Boys	1980

ARTIST	SONG TITLE	DATE
	(She's) Sexy + 17	1983
	Stray Cat Strut	1982
STREET PEOPLE	Jennifer Tomkins	1970
STREETBAND	Toast/Hold On	1978
STREETS	Blinded By The Lights	2004
	Don't Mug Yourself	2002
	Dry Your Eyes	2004
	Fit But You Know It	2004
	Has It Come To This	2001
	Let's Push Things Forward	2002
	Weak Become Heroes	2002
BARBRA STREISAND		
	As If We Never Said Goodbye	1994
	Comin' In And Out Of Your Life	1981
	Evergreen (Love Theme From 'A Star Is Born')	1976
	Kiss Me In The Rain	1980
	Love Theme From 'Eyes Of Laura Mars' (Prisoner)	1978
	The Main Event/Fight	1979
	Memory	1982
	My Heart Belongs To Me	1977
	People	1964
	Places That Belong To You	1992
	Second Hand Rose	1965
	Songbird	1978

ARTIST	SONG TITLE	DATE
	Stoney End	1970
	Sweet Inspiration/Where You Lead	1972
	The Way He Makes Me Feel	1983
	The Way We Were	1973
	With One Look	1993
	Woman In Love	1980
BARBRA STREISAND & BARRY GIBB		
	Guilty	1980
	What Kind Of Fool	1981
BARBRA STREISAND & BRYAN ADAMS		
	I Finally Found Someone	1996
BARBRA STREISAND & CELINE DION		
	Tell Him	1997
BARBRA STREISAND & DON JOHNSON		
	Till I Loved You (Love Theme From 'Goya')	1988
BARBRA STREISAND/VINCE GILL		
	If You Ever Leave Me	1999
	(DONNA SUMMER & BARBRA STREISAND)	
	No More Tears (Enough Is Enough)	1979
BARBRA & NEIL	You Don't Bring Me Flowers	1978
STRETCH	Why Did You Do It	1975
STRETCH 'N' VERN presents 'MADDOG'		
	Get Up! Go Insane!	1997
	I'm Alive	1996
STRIKE	I Have Peace	1997
	Inspiration	1996

ARTIST	SONG TITLE	DATE
	The Morning After (Free At Last)	1995
	My Love Is For Real	1996
	U Sure Do	1995
STROKES	Hard To Explain/New York City Cops	2001
	Last Nite	2001
	Reptilia	2004
	Someday	2002
	12:51	2003
JOE STRUMMER & THE MESCALEROS		
	Coma Girl	2003
	(BLACK GRAPE featuring JOE STRUMMER & KEITH ALLEN)	
	England's Irie	1996
JUD STRUNK	Daisy A Day	1973
STRYPER	Honestly	1987
STUDIO 2	Travelling Man	1998
STUDIO 45	Freak It!	1999
AMY STUDT	All I Wanna Do	2004
	Just A Little Girl	2002
	Misfit	2003
	Under The Thumb	2003
STUNTMASTERZ	The Ladyboy Is Mine	2001
STUTZ BEARCATS & THE DENIS KING ORCHESTRA		
	The Song That I Sing (Theme From 'We'll Meet Again')	1982

ARTIST	SONG TITLE	DATE
STYLE COUNCIL	Come To Milton Keynes	1985
	Groovin' (You're The Best Thing/Big Boss Groove)	1984
	Have You Ever Had It Blue	1986
	It Didn't Matter	1987
	Life At A Top People's Health Farm	1988
	The Lodgers	1985
	Long Hot Summer	1983
	Money Go Round (Pt.1)	1983
	My Ever Changing Moods	1984
	Promised Land	1989
	Shout To The Top	1984
	Solid Bond In Your Heart	1983
	Speak Like A Child	1983
	Walls Come Tumbling Down!	1985
	Wanted	1987
STYLES	Good Times	2002
	(JENNIFER LOPEZ featuring JADAKISS & STYLES)	
	Jenny From The Block	2002
STYLES & BREEZE	You're Shining	2004
STYLISTICS	Betcha By Golly, Wow	1972
	Break Up To Make Up	1973
	Can't Give You Anything (But My Love)	1975
	Can't Help Falling In Love	1976
	Funky Weekend	1976
	I'm Stone In Love With You	1972

ARTIST	SONG TITLE	DATE
	Let's Put It All Together	1974
	Na Na Is The Saddest Word	1975
	Peek-A-Boo	1973
	People Make The World Go Round	1972
	Rockin' Roll Baby	1973
	$7000 And You	1977
	Sing Baby Sing	1975
	Sixteen Bars	1976
	Star On A TV Show	1975
	Stop, Look, Listen (To Your Heart)	1971
	You Are Everything	1971
	You Make Me Feel Brand New	1974
	You'll Never Get To Heaven (If You Break My Heart)	1973
STYX	Babe	1979
	The Best Of Times	1981
	Blue Collar Man (Long Nights)	1978
	Come Sail Away	1977
	Don't Let It End	1983
	Fooling Yourself (The Angry Young Man)	1978
	Lady	1974
	Lorelei	1976
	Love At First Sight	1991
	Mademoiselle	1976
	Mr. Roboto	1983
	Music Time	1984

ARTIST	SONG TITLE	DATE
	Renegade	1979
	Show Me The Way	1990
	Too Much Time On My Hands	1981
	Why Me	1979
SUAVE	My Girl	1988
SUB MERGE featuring JAN JOHNSTON		
	Take Me By The Hand	1997
SUB SUB featuring MELANIE WILLIAMS		
	Ain't No Love (Ain't No Use)	1993
SUBLIMINAL CUTS	Le Voie Le Soleil	1996
SUBWAY featuring 702		
	This Lil' Game We Play	1995
SUEDE	Animal Nitrate	1993
	Attitude/Golden Gun	2003
	Beautiful Ones	1996
	Can't Get Enough	1999
	Electricity	1999
	Everything Will Flow	1999
	Filmstar	1997
	Lazy	1997
	Metal Mickey	1992
	New Generation	1995
	Obsessions	2002
	Positivity	2002
	Saturday Night	1997
	She's In Fashion	1999

ARTIST	SONG TITLE	DATE
	So Young	1993
	Stay Together	1994
	Trash	1996
	We Are The Pigs	1994
	The Wild Ones	1994
SUGABABES	Caught In A Moment	2004
	Freak Like Me	2002
	Hole In The Head	2003
	New Year	2000
	Overload	2000
	Round Round	2002
	Run For Cover	2001
	Shape	2003
	Soul Sound	2001
	Stronger/Angels With Dirty Faces	2002
	Too Lost In You	2003
SUGAR	If I Can't Change Your Mind	1993
	Your Favourite Thing	1994
SUGAR RAY	Every Morning	1999
	Falls Apart	2000
	Someday	1999
	When It's Over	2001
SUGARCUBES	Hit	1992
SUGARHILL GANG	Rapper's Delight	1979
SUGARLOAF	Green Eyed Lady	1970

ARTIST	SONG TITLE	DATE
SUGARLOAF/JERRY CORBETTA		
	Don't Call Us We'll Call You	1974
SUGGS	Camden Town	1995
	Cecilia	1996
	I Am	1998
	I'm Only Sleeping/Off On Holiday	1995
	The Tune	1995
SUGGS featuring LOUCHIE LOU & MICHIE ONE		
	No More Alcohol	1996
SUGGS & CO featuring CHELSEA TEAM		
	Blue Day	1997
SULTANS OF PING F.C.		
	You Talk Too Much	1993
SUM 41	Fat Lip	2001
	The Hell Song	2003
	In Too Deep	2001
	It's What We're All About	2002
	Motivation	2002
	Still Waiting	2002
SUMMER/SNAP!	The First The Last Eternity	1995
	Welcome To Tomorrow	1994
DONNA SUMMER	Back In Love Again	1978
	Bad Girls	1979
	Cold Love	1980
	Could It Be Magic	1976
	Deep Down Inside	1977

ARTIST	SONG TITLE	DATE
	Dim All The Lights	1979
	Dinner With Gershwin	1987
	Heaven Knows	1979
	Hot Stuff	1979
	I Don't Wanna Get Hurt	1989
	I Feel Love	1977
	I Love You	1977
	I Remember Yesterday	1977
	Last Dance	1978
	Love Is In Control (Finger On The Trigger)	1982
	Love To Love You Baby	1975
	Love's About To Change My Heart	1989
	Love's Unkind	1977
	Macarthur Park	1978
	Melody Of Love (Wanna Be Loved)	1994
	On The Radio	1980
	Rumour Has It	1978
	She Works Hard For The Money	1983
	State Of Independence	1996
	There Goes My Baby	1984
	This Time I Know It's For Real	1989
	Unconditional Love	1983
	Walk Away	1980
	The Wanderer	1980
	Who Do You Think You're Foolin'	1981

ARTIST	SONG TITLE	DATE
	Winter Melody	1976
	The Woman In Me	1982
DONNA SUMMER & BARBRA STREISAND		
	No More Tears (Enough Is Enough)	1979
HENRY LEE SUMMER		
	Hey Baby	1989
	I Wish I Had A Girl	1988
MARK SUMMERS	Summers Magic	1991
SUNDANCE	Sundance	1997
	Won't Let This Feeling Go	2000
SUNDAYS	Goodbye	1992
	Summertime	1997
SUNFIRE	Young, Free And Single	1983
SUNNY	Doctor's Orders	1974
SUNSCREEM	Broken English	1993
	Exodus	1995
	Love U More	1993
	Perfect Motion	1992
	Pressure Us	1993
	Secrets	1996
	White Skies	1996
SUNSCREEM vs PUSH		
	Please Save Me	2001
SUNSHINE COMPANY		
	Back On The Street Again	1967

ARTIST	SONG TITLE	DATE
SUPER CAT featuring JACK RADICS		
	My Girl Josephine	1995
SUPER FURRY ANIMALS		
	Demons	1997
	Do Or Die	2000
	(Drawing) Rings Around The World	2001
	Fire In My Heart	1999
	God! Show Me Music	1996
	Golden Retriever	2003
	Hello Sunshine	2003
	Hermann Loves Pauline	1997
	Ice Hockey Hair	1998
	If You Don't Want Me To Destroy You	1996
	The International Language Of Screaming	1997
	It's Not The End Of The World?	2002
	Juxtaposed With U	2001
	The Man Don't Give A Fuck	2004
	Northern Lites	1999
	Play It Cool	1997
	Something 4 The Weekend	1996
SUPERCAR	Tonite	1999
SUPERGRASS	Alright/Time	1995
	Going Out	1996
	Grace	2002
	Kiss Of Life	2004
	Late In The Day	1997

ARTIST	SONG TITLE	DATE
	Lenny	1995
	Mansize Rooster	1995
	Mary	1999
	Moving	1999
	Pumping On Your Stereo	1999
	Richard III	1997
	Seen The Light	2003
	Sun Hits The Sky	1997
SUPERMEN LOVERS		
	Starlight	2001
SUPERNATURALS	The Day Before Yesterday's Man	1997
	I Wasn't Built To Get Up	1998
	Lazy Lover	1996
	Love Has Passed Away	1997
	Smile	1997
SUPERSISTER	Coffee	2000
	Shopping	2001
SUPERTRAMP	Bloody Well Right	1975
	Breakfast In America	1979
	Dreamer	1980
	Give A Little Bit	1977
	Goodbye Stranger	1979
	It's Raining Again	1982
	The Logical Song	1979
	My Kind Of Lady	1983
	Take The Long Way Home	1979

ARTIST	SONG TITLE	DATE
DIANA ROSS & THE SUPREMES		
	I'm Livin' In Shame	1969
	In And Out Of Love	1967
	Love Child	1968
	Reflections	1967
	Someday We'll Be Together	1969
DIANA ROSS & THE SUPREMES & THE TEMPTATIONS		
	I Second That Emotion	1969
	I'm Gonna Make You Love Me	1969
	Why (Must We Fall In Love)	1970
SUPREMES	Automatically Sunshine	1972
	Baby Love	1964
	Back In My Arms Again	1965
	Bad Weather	1973
	Come See About Me	1964
	The Composer	1969
	Everybody's Got The Right To Love	1970
	Floy Joy	1972
	Forever Came Today	1968
	The Happening	1967
	I Hear A Symphony	1965
	I'll Try Something New	1969
	I'm Gonna Let My Heart Do The Walking	1976
	Love Is Here And Now You're Gone	1967
	Love Is Like An Itching In My Heart	1966
	My World Is Empty Without You	1966

ARTIST	SONG TITLE	DATE
	Nathan Jones	1971
	No Matter What Sign You Are	1969
	Nothing But Heartaches	1965
	Some Things You Never Get Used To	1968
	Stoned Love	1970
	Stop! In The Name Of Love	1965
	Up The Ladder To The Roof	1970
	Where Did Our Love Go	1964
	You Can't Hurry Love	1966
	You Keep Me Hangin' On	1966
SUPREMES & FOUR TOPS		
	River Deep Mountain High	1970
	You Gotta Have Love In Your Heart	1971
AL B. SURE!	Nite And Day	1988
	(QUINCY JONES featuring AL B. SURE, JAMES INGRAM, EL DEBARGE)	
	Secret Garden	1990
SUREAL	You Take My Breath Away	2000
SURFACE	The First Time	1990
	Happy	1987
	Never Gonna Let You Down	1991
	Shower Me With Your Love	1989
SURFACE NOISE	The Scratch	1980
SURFARIS	Wipe Out	1966
SURPRISE SISTERS	La Booga Rooga	1976

ARTIST	SONG TITLE	DATE
SURVIVOR	American Heartbeat	1982
	Burning Heart	1985
	Eye Of The Tiger	1982
	High On You	1985
	I Can't Hold Back	1984
	Is This Love	1986
	Poor Man's Son	1981
	The Search Is Over	1985
SUTHERLAND BROTHERS AND QUIVER		
	Arms Of Mary	1976
	Secrets	1976
BILLY SWAN	I Can Help	1974
BETTYE SWANN	Don't Touch Me	1969
	Make Me Yours	1967
SWANS WAY	Soul Train	1984
PATRICK SWAYZE featuring WENDY FRASER		
	She's Like The Wind	1988
KEITH SWEAT	I Want Her	1988
	I'll Give All My Love To You	1990
	I'm Not Ready	1999
	Just A Touch	1996
	Keep It Comin'	1991
	Make You Sweat	1990
	Twisted	1996
KEITH SWEAT featuring ATHENA CAGE		
	Nobody	1996

ARTIST	SONG TITLE	DATE
KEITH SWEAT featuring SNOOP DOGG		
	Come And Get With Me	1998
	(OL' SKOOL featuring KEITH SWEAT & XSCAPE)	
	Am I Dreaming	1998
SWEATHOG	Hallelujah	1971
SWEET DREAMS	Honey Honey	1974
SWEET DREAMS	I'm Never Giving Up	1983
SWEET FEMALE ATTITUDE		
	Flowers	2000
SWEET INSPIRATIONS		
	Sweet Inspiration	1968
SWEET PEOPLE	Et Les Oiseaux Chantaient (And The	
	Birds Were Singing)	1980
SWEET SENSATION	Hooked On You	1989
	If Wishes Came True	1990
	Love Child	1990
	Purely By Coincidence	1975
	Sad Sweet Dreamer	1975
SWEET SENSATIONS WITH ROMEO J.D		
	Sincerely Yours	1989
SWEET	Action	1976
	Alexander Graham Bell	1971
	Ballroom Blitz	1975
	Blockbuster!	1973
	Co-Co	1971
	Fox On The Run	1975

ARTIST	SONG TITLE	DATE
	Funny Funny	1971
	Hell Raiser	1973
	The Lies In Your Eyes	1976
	Little Willy	1973
	Love Is Like Oxygen	1978
	Poppa Joe	1972
	The Six Teens	1974
	Teenage Rampage	1974
	Wig Wam Bam	1972
SWEET TEE	It's Like That Y'all/I Got Da Feelin'	1988
RACHEL SWEET	B-A-B-Y	1978
	(REX SMITH & RACHEL SWEET)	
	Everlasting Love	1981
SWEETBOX	Everything's Gonna Be Alright	1998
SWING OUT SISTER		
	Am I The Same Girl?	1992
	Breakout	1987
	La La (Means I Love You)	1994
	Surrender	1987
	Twilight World	1987
	You On My Mind	1989
SWINGIN' MEDALLIONS		
	Double Shot (Of My Baby's Love)	1966
SWINGING BLUE JEANS		
	Don't Make Me Over	1966
	Good Golly Miss Molly	1964

ARTIST	SONG TITLE	DATE
	Hippy Hippy Shake	1964
	It's Too Late Now	1963
	You're No Good	1964
SWITCH	There'll Never Be	1978
SWITCHFOOT	Meant To Live	2004
SWV	Anything	1994
	Can We	1997
	It's All About U	1996
	Downtown	1994
	I'm So Into You	1993
	Rain	1998
	Right Here (Human Nature)	1993
	Use Your Heart	1996
	Weak	1993
	You're The One	1996
SWV FEATURING PUFF DADDY		
	Someone	1997
SYBIL	Don't Make Me Over	1989
	Let Yourself Go	1987
	Walk On By	1990
	When I'm Good And Ready	1993
	(WEST END featuring SYBIL)	
	The Love I Lost	1993
SYLK 130	Last Night A DJ Saved My Life	1998
SYLK-E. FYNE featuring CHILL		
	Romeo And Juliet	1998

ARTIST	SONG TITLE	DATE
SYLVERS	Boogie Fever	1976
	High School Dance	1977
	Hot Line	1976
FOSTER SYLVERS	Misdemeanor	1973
SYLVESTER	Dance (Disco Heat)	1978
	I (Who Have Nothing)	1979
	You Make Me Feel (Mighty Real)	1979
SYLVESTER & PATRICK COWLEY		
	Do You Wanna Funk	1982
SYLVIA	Hasta La Vista	1975
	Nobody	1982
	Pillow Talk	1973
	Y Viva Espana	1974
DAVID SYLVIAN	Bamboo Houses/Bamboo Music	1982
	I Surrender	1999
	The Ink In The Well	1984
	Red Guitar	1984
DAVID SYLVIAN & RIUICHI SAKAMOTO		
	Forbidden Colours	1983
SYMBOLS	Best Part Of Breaking Up	1968
SYMPOSIUM	The Answer To Why I Hate You	1997
	Fairweather Friend	1997
	Farewell To Twilight	1997
SYNDICATE OF SOUND		
	Little Girl	1966
SYNTAX	Pray	2003

ARTIST	SONG TITLE	DATE
SYREETA	Harmour Love	1975
	Your Kiss Is Sweet	1975
	(BILLY PRESTON & SYREETA)	
	With You I'm Born Again	1979
SYSTEM	Don't Disturb The Groove	1987
SYSTEM F	Cry	2000
	Out Of The Blue	1999
SYSTEM 7	7:7 Expansion	1993
SYSTEM OF A DOWN		
	Aerials	2002
	Chop Suey	2001
	Toxicity	2002
T-BOZ	Touch Myself	1996
	(DA BRAT featuring T-BOZ)	
	Ghetto Love	1997
T-BONES	No Matter What Shape (Your Stomach's	
	In)	1965
T-CONNECTION	Do What You Wanna Do	1977
	On Fire	1978
T-EMPO	Saturday Night, Sunday Morning	1994
T-POWER/SHY FX featuring DI		
	Shake Ur Body	2002
	(SHY FX & T-POWER featuring KELE LE ROC)	
	Feelin' U	2003
T-SPOON	Sex On The Beach	1998
	Tom's Party	1999

ARTIST	SONG TITLE	DATE
T. REX	Bang A Gong (Get It On)	1972
	Children Of The Revolution	1972
	Debora/One Inch Rock	1972
	Dreamy Lady	1975
	Get It On	1971
	The Groover	1973
	Hot Love	1971
	I Love To Boogie	1976
	Jeepster	1971
	Light Of Love	1974
	London Boys	1976
	Metal Guru	1972
	New York City	1975
	One Inch Rock	1968
	Ride A White Swan	1970
	Solid Gold Easy Action	1972
	Telegram Sam	1972
	Truck On (Tyke)	1973
	20th Century Boy	1973
	(MARC BOLAN & T. REX)	
	Teenage Dream	1974
T.A.T.U.	All The Things She Said	2003
	Not Gonna Get Us	2003
T.I.	Let's Get Away	2004
	Rubber Band Man	2004

ARTIST	SONG TITLE	DATE
(BONECRUSHER featuring KILLER MIKE & T.I.)		
	Never Scared	2003
T99	Anasthasia	1991
	Nocturne	1991
TA MARA & THE SEEN		
	Everybody Dance	1985
TACO	Puttin' On The Ritz	1983
TAFFY	I Love My Radio	1987
TAG TEAM	Whoomp! (There It Is)	1993
TAK TIX	Feel Like Singing	1996
TAKE 5	Never Had It So Good	1999
TAKE THAT	Babe	1993
	Back For Good	1995
	Could It Be Magic	1992
	Everything Changes	1994
	How Deep Is Your Love	1996
	I Found Heaven	1992
	It Only Takes A Minute	1992
	Love Ain't Here Anymore	1994
	A Million Love Songs (EP)	1992
	Never Forget	1995
	Once You've Tasted Love	1992
	Pray	1993
	Promises	1991
	Sure	1994
	Why Can't I Wake Up With You?	1993

ARTIST	SONG TITLE	DATE
TAKE THAT featuring LULU		
	Relight My Fire	1993
TALI	Lyric On My Lip	2004
TALISMAN P featuring BARRINGTON LEVY		
	Here I Come (Sing DJ)	2001
TALK TALK	It's My Life	1984
	Life's What You Make It	1986
	Talk Talk	1982
	Today	1982
TALKING HEADS	And She Was	1986
	Burning Down The House	1983
	Once In A Lifetime	1981
	Road To Nowhere	1985
	Take Me To The River	1978
	Wild Wild Life	1986
TALL PAUL	Rock Da House	1997
TALL PAUL vs INXS		
	Precious Heart	2001
TAMBA TRIO	Mas Que Nada	1998
TAMI SHOW	The Truth	1991
TAMIA	Imagination	1998
	So Into You	1998
	Stranger In My House	2001
(BRANDY, TAMIA, GLADYS KNIGHT & CHAKA KHAN)		
	Missing You	1996

ARTIST	SONG TITLE	DATE
(ERIC BENET featuring TAMIA)		
	Spend My Life With You	1999
(FABOLOUS featuring TAMIA)		
	Into You	2003
TAMPERER featuring MAYA		
	Feel It	1998
	Hammer To The Heart	2000
	If You Buy This Record Your Life Will	
	Be Better	1998
TAMS	Be Young, Be Foolish, Be Happy	1970
	Hey Girl Don't Bother Me	1971
	There Ain't Nothing Like Shaggin'	1987
NORMA TANEGA	Walkin' My Cat Named Dog	1966
TANK	Maybe I Deserve	2001
BILL TARMEY	One Voice	1993
	Wind Beneath My Wings	1994
TASTE OF HONEY	Boogie Oogie Oogie	1978
	Sukiyaki	1981
TATJANA	Santa Maria	1996
TAVARES	Check It Out	1973
	Don't Take Away The Music	1976
	The Ghost Of Love	1978
	Heaven Must Be Missing An Angel	1976
	It Only Takes A Minute	1975
	The Mighty Power Of Love	1977
	More Than A Woman	1977

ARTIST	SONG TITLE	DATE
	One Step Away	1977
	A Penny For Your Thoughts	1982
	Remember What I Told You To Forget/	
	My Ship	1975
	Whodunit	1977
ANDY TAYLOR	Take It Easy	1986
BOBBY TAYLOR & THE VANCOUVERS		
	Does Your Mama Know About Me	1968
FELICE TAYLOR	I Feel Love Comin' On	1967
JAMES TAYLOR	Country Road	1971
	Don't Let Me Be Lonely Tonight	1972
	Fire And Rain	1970
	Handy Man	1977
	How Sweet It Is (To Be Loved By You)	1975
	Long Ago And Far Away	1971
	Shower The People	1976
	Up On The Roof	1979
	You've Got A Friend	1971
	Your Smiling Face	1977
JAMES TAYLOR & J. D. SOUTHER		
	Her Town Too	1981
(ART GARFUNKEL, JAMES TAYLOR & PAUL SIMON)		
	(What A) Wonderful World	1978
(CARLY SIMON & JAMES TAYLOR)		
	Devoted To You	1978
	Mockingbird	1974

ARTIST	SONG TITLE	DATE
JOHN TAYLOR	I Do What I Do... (Theme From '9½ Weeks'	1986
JOHNNIE TAYLOR	Cheaper To Keep Her	1973
	Disco Lady	1976
	I Am Somebody Part II	1970
	I Believe In You (You Believe In Me)	1973
	Jody's Got Your Girl And Gone	1971
	Somebody's Gettin' It	1976
	Steal Away	1970
	Take Care Of Your Homework	1969
	Testify (I Wonna)	1969
	We're Getting Careless With Our Love	1974
	Who's Making Love	1968
LIVINGSTON TAYLOR	First Time Love	1980
	I Will Be In Love With You	1978
R. DEAN TAYLOR	Gotta See Jane	1968
	Indiana Wants Me	1970
	There's A Ghost In My House	1974
	Window Shopping	1974
ROGER TAYLOR	Happiness?	1994
	Nazis	1994
	Surrender	1999
ROGER TAYLOR & YOSHIKI	Foreign Sand	1994
TC 1992	Funky Guitar	1992

ARTIST	SONG TITLE	DATE
KIRI TE KANAWA	World In Union	1991
TEACH-IN	Ding-A-Dong	1975
TEARDROP EXPLODES		
	Passionate Friend	1981
	Reward	1981
	Treason (It's Just A Story)	1981
TEARS FOR FEARS	Advice For The Young At Heart	1990
	Break It Down Again	1993
	Change	1983
	Everybody Wants To Rule The World	1985
	Everybody Wants To Run The World	1986
	Head Over Heels	1985
	I Believe (A Soulful Re-Recording)	1985
	Laid So Low (Tears Roll Down)	1992
	Mad World	1982
	Mothers Talk	1986
	Pale Shelter	1983
	Raoul And The Kings Of Spain	1995
	Shout	1985
	Sowing The Seeds Of Love	1989
	The Way You Are	1983
	Woman In Chains	1989
TECHNOCAT featuring TOM WILSON		
	Technocat	1995
TECHNOHEAD	Happy Birthday	1996
	I Wanna Be A Hippy	1996

ARTIST	SONG TITLE	DATE
TECHNOTRONIC	Get Up! (Before The Night Is Over)	1990
	Megamix	1990
	Pump Up The Jam '96	1996
TECHNOTRONIC featuring FELLY		
	Pump Up The Jam	1989
TECHNOTRONIC featuring MC ERIC		
	This Beat Is Technotronic	1990
TECHNOTRONIC featuring REGGIE		
	Move That Body	1991
	Work	1991
TECHNOTRONIC featuring YA KID K		
	Get Up (Before The Night Is Over)	1990
	Move This	1992
	Rockin' Over The Beat	1990
TEE SET	Ma Belle Amie	1970
TEEGARDEN & VAN WINKLE		
	God, Love And Rock & Roll	1970
TEENAGE FANCLUB	Ain't That Enough	1997
	Mellow Doubt	1995
	Radio	1993
	Sparky's Dream	1995
	What You Do To Me (EP)	1992
TELETUBBIES	Teletubbies Say Eh-Oh!	1997
TELEVISION	Foxhole	1978
	Marquee Moon	1977
	Prove It	1977

ARTIST	SONG TITLE	DATE
TELEX	Rock Around The Clock	1979
NINO TEMPO & APRIL STEVENS		
	All Strung Out	1966
	Deep Purple	1963
	Whispering	1963
TEMPTATIONS	Ain't Too Proud To Beg	1966
	All I Need	1967
	Ball Of Confusion (That's What The World Is Today)	1970
	Beauty Is Only Skin Deep	1966
	Cloud Nine	1968
	Don't Let The Joneses Get You Down	1969
	Get Ready	1966
	Girl (Why You Wanna Make Me Blue)	1964
	Glasshouse	1975
	Happy People	1974
	Hey Girl (I Like Your Style)	1973
	I Can't Get Next To You	1969
	I Could Never Love Another (After Loving You)	1968
	(I Know) I'm Losing You	1966
	I Wish It Would Rain	1968
	I'll Be In Trouble	1964
	I'll Try Something New	1969
	It's Growing	1965

ARTIST	SONG TITLE	DATE
	Just My Imagination (Running Away With Me)	1971
	(Loneliness Made Me Realize) It's You That I Need	1967
	Let Your Hair Down	1973
	Masterpiece	1973
	My Baby	1965
	My Girl	1965
	Papa Was A Rollin' Stone	1972
	The Plastic Man	1973
	Please Return Your Love To Me	1968
	Psychedelic Shack	1970
	Run Away Child, Running Wild	1969
	Shakey Ground	1975
	Since I Lost My Baby	1965
	Superstar (Remember How You Got Where You Are)	1971
	Take A Look Around	1972
	Treat Her Like A Lady	1984
	Ungena Za Ulimwengu (Unite The World)	1970
	The Way You Do The Things You Do	1964
	You're My Everything	1967
(DIANA ROSS & THE SUPREMES & THE TEMPTATIONS)	I Second That Emotion	1969

ARTIST	SONG TITLE	DATE
	I'm Gonna Make You Love Me	1969
	Why (Must We Fall In Love)	1970
10CC	Art For Art's Sake	1975
	The Dean And I	1973
	Donna	1972
	Dreadlock Holiday	1978
	Good Morning Judge	1977
	I'm Mandy Fly Me	1976
	I'm Not In Love	1975
	Life Is A Minestone	1975
	People In Love	1977
	Rubber Bullets	1973
	Silly Love	1974
	Things We Do For Love	1977
	The Wall Street Shuffle	1974
TEN CITY	Devotion	1989
	That's The Way Love Is	1989
TEN POLE TUDOR	Rock Around The Clock	1979
	Swords Of A Thousand Men	1981
	Wunderbar	1981
TEN SHARP	You	1992
10,000 MANIACS	Because The Night	1993
	More Than This	1997
TEN YEARS AFTER	I'd Love To Change The World	1971
	Love Like A Man	1970
TENACIOUS D	Wonderboy	2002

ARTIST	SONG TITLE	DATE
DANNY TENAGLIA & CELEDA		
	Music Is The Answer (Dancin' & Prancin')	1998
TENOR FLY/FREESTYLERS		
	B-Boy Stance	1998
	(REBEL M.C./TENOR FLY/BARRINGTON LEVY)	
	Tribal Base	1991
ROBERT TEPPER	No Easy Way Out	1986
TAMMI TERRELL/MARVIN GAYE		
	Ain't No Mountain High Enough	1967
	Ain't Nothin' Like The Real Thing	1968
	Good Lovin' Ain't Easy To Come By	1969
	If I Could Build My Whole World Around You	1967
	Keep On Lovin' Me Honey	1968
	Onion Song	1969
	You Ain't Livin' Till You're Lovin'	1969
	You're All I Need To Get By	1968
	Your Precious Love	1967
TERROR SQUAD featuring FAT JOE & REMY		
	Lean Back	2004
TERRORVISION	Alice, What's The Matter?	1994
	Bad Actress	1996
	Celebrity Hit List	1996
	D'Ya Wanna Go Faster	2001
	Easy	1997
	Josephine	1998

ARTIST	SONG TITLE	DATE
	Middleman	1994
	My House	1994
	Oblivion	1994
	Perseverance	1996
	Pretend Best Friend	1994
	Some People Say	1995
	Tequila	1999
HELEN TERRY	Love Lies Lost	1984
TODD TERRY	Ready For A New Day	1998
	Something Goin' On	1997
TODD TERRY featuring MARTHA WASH & JOCELYN BROWN	Keep On Jumpin'	1996
TODD TERRY presents SHANNON		
	It's Over Love	1997
TODD TERRY PROJECT		
	Weekend	1995
TONY TERRY	With You	1991
TESLA	Love Song	1989
	Signs	1991
JOE TEX	Ain't Gonna Bump No More (With No Big Fat Woman)	1977
	Hold What You've Got	1964
	I Gotcha	1972
	I Want To Do Everything For You	1965
	Men Are Gettin' Scarce	1968
	S.Y.S.L.J.F.M. (The Letter Song)	1966

ARTIST	SONG TITLE	DATE
	Show Me	1967
	Skinny Legs And All	1967
	A Sweet Woman Like You	1965
TEXAS	Alone With You	1992
	Black Eyed Boy	1997
	Halo	1997
	I Don't Want A Lover	1989
	I'll See It Through	2003
	In Demand	2000
	In Our Lifetime	1999
	Inner Smile	2001
	Put Your Arms Around Me	1997
	So Called Friend	1993
	So In Love With You	1994
	Summer Son	1999
	Tired Of Being Alone	1992
	When We Are Together	1999
	You Owe It All To Me	1993
TEXAS featuring KARDINAL OFFISHALL		
	Carnival Girl	2003
TEXAS featuring WU TANG CLAN		
	Say What You Want/Insane	1998
THALIA featuring FAT JOE		
	I Want You	2003
THE THE	The Beat(en) Generation	1989
	Dis-Infected (EP)	1994

ARTIST	SONG TITLE	DATE
	Dogs Of Lust	1993
	Heartland	1986
	I Saw The Light	1995
	Love Is Stronger Than Death	1993
	Slow Emotion Replay	1993
THEATRE OF HATE	Do You Believe In The Westworld	1982
THEAUDIENCE	I Know Enough (I Don't Get Enough)	1998
	A Pessimist Is Never Disappointed	1998
THEM	Baby Please Don't Go	1965
	Here Comes The Night	1965
	Mystic Eyes	1965
THEN JERICHO	Big Area	1989
	The Motive (Living Without You)	1987
	Sugar Box	1989
	What Does It Take	1989
THERAPY?	Church Of Noise	1998
	Diane	1995
	Die Laughing	1994
	Face The Strange (EP)	1993
	Lonely, Cryin' Only	1998
	Loose	1995
	Nowhere	1994
	Opal Mantra	1993
	Shortsharpshock (EP)	1993
	Stories	1995
	Teethgrinder	1992

ARTIST	SONG TITLE	DATE
	Trigger Inside	1994
THEY MIGHT BE GIANTS		
	Birdhouse In Your Soul	1990
	Boss Of Me	2001
THICK D	Insatiable	2002
THIN LIZZY	The Boys Are Back In Town	1976
	Chinatown	1980
	Cold Sweat	1983
	Dancin' In The Moonlight (It's Caught Me In The Spotlight)	1977
	Dedication	1991
	Do Anything You Want To	1979
	Don't Believe A Word	1977
	Jailbreak	1976
	Killer On The Loose	1980
	Killers Live (EP)	1981
	Rosalie (Cowgirls' Song) (Medley)	1978
	Sarah	1979
	Thunder And Lightning	1983
	Waiting For An Alibi	1979
	Whisky In The Jar	1973
THINK	Once You Understand	1971
3RD BASS	Pop Goes The Weasel	1991
THIRD DIMENSION featuring JULIE MCDERMOTT		
	Don't Go	1996
3RD EDGE	In And Out	2002

ARTIST	SONG TITLE	DATE
	Know You Wanna	2003
THIRD EYE BLIND	How's It Going To Be	1997
	Jumper	1998
	Never Let You Go	2000
	Semi-Charmed Life	1997
THIRD WORLD	Cool Meditation	1979
	Dancing On The Floor (Hooked On Love)	1981
	Now That We've Found Love	1978
1300 DRUMS featuring UNJUSTIFIED ANCIENTS OF MU MU	Ooh! Aah! Cantona	1996
THIRTEEN SENSES	Do No Wrong	2004
	Into The Fire	2004
38 SPECIAL	Back Where You Belong	1984
	Caught Up In You	1982
	Hold On Loosely	1981
	If I'd Been The One	1983
	Like No Other Night	1986
	Second Chance	1989
	The Sound Of Your Voice	1991
	Teacher Teacher	1984
	You Keep Runnin' Away	1982
B.J. THOMAS	Billy And Sue	1966
	Don't Worry Baby	1977
	Everybody's Out Of Town	1970
	The Eyes Of A New York Woman	1968

ARTIST	SONG TITLE	DATE
	(Hey Won't You Play) Another Somebody Done Somebody Wrong So	1975
	Hooked On A Feeling	1968
	I Just Can't Help Believing	1970
	Mama	1966
	Mighty Clouds Of Joy	1971
	Most Of All	1970
	No Love At All	1971
	Raindrops Keep Fallin' On My Head	1969
	Rock And Roll Lullaby	1972
B.J. THOMAS & THE TRIUMPHS		
	I'm So Lonesome I Could Cry	1966
CARL THOMAS	I Wish	2000
CARLA THOMAS	B-A-B-Y	1966
	(OTIS REDDING & CARLA THOMAS)	
	Knock On Wood	1967
	Tramp	1967
DANTE THOMAS featuring PRAS		
	Miss California	2001
EVELYN THOMAS	High Energy	1984
	Weak Spot	1976
IAN THOMAS	Painted Ladies	1973
IRMA THOMAS	Wish Someone Would Care	1964
KENNY THOMAS	Best Of You	1991
	Outstanding	1991
	Piece By Piece	1993

ARTIST	SONG TITLE	DATE
	Stay	1993
	Tender Love	1991
	Thinking About Your Love	1991
	Trippin' On Your Love	1993
	When I Think Of You	1995
LILLO THOMAS	Sexy Girl	1987
NICKY THOMAS	Love Of The Common People	1970
RUFUS THOMAS	The Breakdown	1971
	Do The Funky Chicken	1970
	(Do The) Push And Pull Part 1	1970
TIMMY THOMAS	Why Can't We Live Together	1972
THOMPSON TWINS	Doctor! Doctor!	1984
	Don't Mess With Doctor Dream	1985
	Get That Love	1987
	Hold Me Now	1984
	King For A Day	1986
	Lay Your Hands On Me	1985
	Lies	1983
	Love On Your Side	1983
	Sister Of Mercy	1984
	Sugar Daddy	1989
	Watching	1983
	We Are Detective	1983
	You Take Me Up	1984
CHRIS THOMPSON & NIGHT		
	If You Remember Me	1979

ARTIST	SONG TITLE	DATE
SUE THOMPSON	Paper Tiger	1965
ALI THOMSON	Take A Little Rhythm	1980
CYNDI THOMSON	What I Really Meant To Say	2001
DAVID THORNE	The Alley Cat Song	1963
KEN THORNE & HIS ORCHESTRA		
	Theme From 'The Legion's Last Patrol'	1963
THOSE 2 GIRLS	All I Want	1995
THOUSAND YARD STARE		
	Comeuppance (EP)	1992
THREE 'N ONE presents JOHNNY SHAKER featuring		
SERIAL D	Pearl River	1999
THREE AMIGOS	Louie Louie	1999
	25 Miles 2001	2001
3 COLOURS RED	Beautiful Day	1999
	Copper Girl	1997
	Nuclear Holiday	1997
	Pure	1997
	Sixty Mile Smile	1997
	This Is My Time	1999
THREE DEGREES	Get Your Love Back	1974
	Giving Up, Giving In	1978
	Long Lost Lover	1975
	Maybe	1970
	My Simple Heart	1979
	The Runner	1979
	Take Good Care Of Yourself	1975

ARTIST	SONG TITLE	DATE
	Toast Of Love	1976
	When Will I See You Again	1974
	Woman In Love	1979
	Year Of Decision	1974
	(MFSB featuring THE THREE DEGREES)	
	TSOP (The Sound Of Philadelphia)	1974
THREE DOG NIGHT		
	Black & White	1972
	Celebrate	1970
	Easy To Be Hard	1969
	Eli's Coming	1969
	The Family Of Man	1972
	Joy To The World	1971
	Let Me Serenade You	1973
	Liar	1971
	Mama Told Me (Not To Come)	1970
	Never Been To Spain	1971
	An Old Fashioned Love Song	1971
	One	1969
	One Man Band	1970
	Out In The Country	1970
	Pieces Of April	1972
	Play Something Sweet (Brickyard Blues)	1974
	Shambala	1973
	The Show Must Go On	1974
	Sure As I'm Sittin' Here	1974

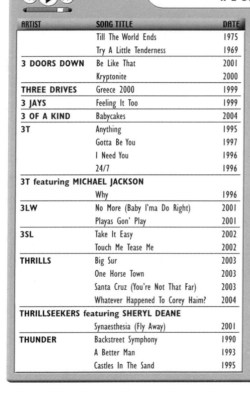

ARTIST	SONG TITLE	DATE
	Till The World Ends	1975
	Try A Little Tenderness	1969
3 DOORS DOWN	Be Like That	2001
	Kryptonite	2000
THREE DRIVES	Greece 2000	1999
3 JAYS	Feeling It Too	1999
3 OF A KIND	Babycakes	2004
3T	Anything	1995
	Gotta Be You	1997
	I Need You	1996
	24/7	1996
3T featuring MICHAEL JACKSON		
	Why	1996
3LW	No More (Baby I'ma Do Right)	2001
	Playas Gon' Play	2001
3SL	Take It Easy	2002
	Touch Me Tease Me	2002
THRILLS	Big Sur	2003
	One Horse Town	2003
	Santa Cruz (You're Not That Far)	2003
	Whatever Happened To Corey Haim?	2004
THRILLSEEKERS featuring SHERYL DEANE		
	Synaesthesia (Fly Away)	2001
THUNDER	Backstreet Symphony	1990
	A Better Man	1993
	Castles In The Sand	1995

ARTIST	SONG TITLE	DATE
	Dirty Love	1990
	Don't Wait Up	1997
	Everybody Wants Her	1992
	Gimme Some Lovin'	1990
	In A Broken Dream	1995
	Like A Satellite (EP)	1993
	Love Walked In	1991
	Low Life In High Places	1992
	The Only One	1998
	Play That Funky Music	1998
	River Of Pain	1995
	She's So Fine	1990
	Stand Up	1995
THUNDERBUGS	Friends Forever	1999
THUNDERCLAP NEWMAN		
	Something In The Air	1969
THUNDERTHIGHS	Central Park Arrest	1974
BOBBY THURSTON	Check Out The Groove	1980
TIERRA	Together	1980
TIFFANY	All This Time	1988
	Could've Been	1987
	I Saw Him Standing There	1988
	I Think We're Alone Now	1987
	Radio Romance	1989
TIGA AND ZYNTHERIUS		
	Sunglasses At Night	2002

ARTIST	SONG TITLE	DATE
TIGER	Race	1996
TIGHT FIT	Back To The Sixties	1981
	Fantasy Island	1982
	The Lion Sleeps Tonight	1982
TANITA TIKARAM	Good Tradition	1988
	Twist In My Sobriety	1988
'TIL TUESDAY	Voices Carry	1985
	What About Love	1986
JOHNNY TILLOTSON		
	Heartaches By The Number	1965
	I Rise, I Fall	1964
	It Keeps Right On A-Hurtin'	1966
	Out Of My Mind	1963
	She Understands Me	1964
	Worried Guy	1964
TILT	Invisible	1999
TIMBALAND & MAGOO		
	Clock Strikes	1998
	(AALIYAH featuring TIMBALAND)	
	We Need A Resolution	2001
	(DESTINY'S CHILD featuring TIMBALAND)	
	Get On The Bus	1999
	(MAGOO AND TIMBALAND)	
	Up Jumps Da Boogie	1997
TIMBALAND & MAGOO featuring MISSY ELLIOTT		
	Cop That Shit	2004

ARTIST	SONG TITLE	DATE
JUSTIN TIMBERLAKE		
	Cry Me A River	2003
	Like I Love You	2002
	Rock Your Body	2003
	Senorita	2003
	(NELLY featuring JUSTIN TIMBERLAKE)	
	Work It	2003
TIMBRUK 3	The Future's So Bright I Gotta Wear Shades	1986
TIME	The Bird	1985
	Jerk Out	1990
	Jungle Love	1984
TIME FREQUENCY	Dreamscape '94	1994
	New Emotion (EP)	1993
	The Power Zone (EP)	1993
	Real Love '93	1993
	Such A Phantasy (EP)	1994
TIMEBOX	Beggin'	1968
TIMELORDS	Doctorin' The Tardis	1988
TIMES TWO	Strange But True	1988
TIMEX SOCIAL CLUB		
	Rumors	1986
TIMMY T	One More Try	1990
	Time After Time	1990
TIN MACHINE	You Belong In Rock N' Roll	1991
TIN TIN	Toast And Marmalade For Tea	1971

ARTIST	SONG TITLE	DATE
TIN TIN OUT	All I Wanna Do	1997
	Strings For Yasmin	1997
TIN TIN OUT featuring EMMA BUNTON		
	What I Am	1999
TIN TIN OUT featuring ESPIRITU		
	Always Something There To Remind Me	1995
TIN TIN OUT featuring SHELLEY NELSON		
	Here's Where The Story Ends	1998
	Sometimes	1998
TIN TIN OUT featuring TONY HADLEY		
	Dance With Me	1997
TIN TIN OUT featuring WENDY PAGE		
	Eleven To Fly	1999
TIN TIN OUT featuring SWEET TEE		
	The Feeling	1994
TINDERSTICKS	Bathtime	1997
TINMAN	Eighteen Strings	1994
TINY TIM	Tip Toe Thru The Tulips With Me	1968
AARON TIPPIN	Where The Stars And Stripes And The Eagle Fly	2001
TITANIC	Sultana	1971
TJR featuring XAVIER		
	Just Gets Better	1997
TLC	Ain't Too Proud 2 Beg	1992
	Baby-Baby-Baby	1992
	Creep	1994

ARTIST	SONG TITLE	DATE
	Creep '96	1996
	Dear Lie	1999
	Diggin' On You	1995
	Girl Talk	2002
	Hat 2 Da Back	1993
	No Scrubs	1999
	Red Light Special	1995
	Unpretty	1999
	Waterfalls	1995
	What About Your Friends	1992
TOAD THE WET SPROCKET		
	All I Want	1992
	Fall Down	1994
	Walk On The Ocean	1992
TOBY BEAU	My Angel Baby	1978
TOGETHER	Hardcore Uproar	1990
TOKENS	I Hear Trumpets Blow	1966
	Portrait Of My Love	1967
TOKYO GHETTO PUSSY		
	Everybody On The Floor (Pump Up)	1995
TOM TOM CLUB	Genius Of Love	1982
	Under The Boardwalk	1982
	Wordy Rappinghood	1981
TOMCRAFT	Loneliness	2003
RICKY TOMLINSON	Are You Lookin' At Me?	2001
TOMMI	Like What	2003

ARTIST	SONG TITLE	DATE
TOMMY TUTONE	Angels Say No	1980
	867-5309/Jenny	1982
TOMSKI featuring JAN JOHNSTON		
	Love Will Come	2000
TONE LOC	Funky Cold Medina/On Fire	1989
	Wild Thing/Loc'ed After Dark	1989
OSCAR TONEY JR.	For Your Precious Love	1967
TONGUE 'N' CHEEK		
	Forget Me Nots	1991
	Nobody	1990
	Tomorrow	1990
TONIGHT	Drummer Man	1978
TONY TONI TONE featuring DJ QUIK		
	Let's Get Down	1997
TONY TONI TONE		
	Anniversary	1993
	Feels Good	1990
	If I Had No Loot	1993
	It Never Rains (In Southern California)	1990
	(Lay Your Head On My) Pillow	1994
	Thinking Of You	1997
TOPLOADER	Achilles Heel	2000
	Dancing In The Moonlight	2000
	Just Hold On	2000
	Only For A While	2001
	Time Of My Life	2002

ARTIST	SONG TITLE	DATE
TOPOL	If I Were A Rich Man	1967
MEL TORME	Comin' Home Baby	1962
TORNADOS	Globetrotter	1963
	The Ice Cream Man	1963
	Robot	1963
TOTAL	Kissin' You	1996
	No One Else	1995
	What About Us	1997
TOTAL featuring MISSY ELLIOTT		
	Trippin'	1998
TOTAL featuring THE NOTORIOUS B.I.G.		
	Can't You See	1995
	(MASE featuring TOTAL)	
	What You Want	1998
TOTAL CONTRAST	Takes A Little Time	1985
TOTO	Africa	1982
	Hold The Line	1978
	I Won't Hold You Back	1983
	I'll Be Over You	1986
	Make Believe	1982
	99	1979
	Pamela	1988
	Rosanna	1982
	Stranger In Town	1984
	Without Your Love	1986
TOTO COELO	I Eat Cannibals (Pt 1)	1982

ARTIST	SONG TITLE	DATE
TOTTENHAM HOTSPUR F.A. CUP FINAL SQUAD		
	Hot Shot Tottenham!	1987
	Ossie's Dream (Spurs Are On Their Way To Wembley)	1981
	Tottenham Tottenham	1982
TOUCH & GO	Would You...?	1998
TOURISTS	Don't Say I Told You So	1980
	I Only Want To Be With You	1979
	The Loneliest Man In The World	1979
	So Good To Be Back Home Again	1980
TOWER OF POWER	Don't Change Horses (In The Middle Of A Stream)	1974
	So Very Hard To Go	1973
	You're Still A Young Man	1972
LIDELL TOWNSELL	Nu Nu	1992
PETE TOWNSHEND	Face The Face	1985
	Let My Love Open The Door	1980
	Rough Boys	1980
TOXIC TWO	Rave Generator	1992
TOY DOLLS	Nellie The Elephant	1984
TOYA	I Do!!	2001
TOYAH	Be Loud Be Proud (Be Heard)	1982
	Brave New World	1982
	Don't Fall In Love (I Said)	1985
	Four From Toyah (EP)	1981
	Four More From Toyah (EP)	1981

ARTIST	SONG TITLE	DATE
	I Want To Be Free	1981
	Rebel Run	1983
	Thunder In Mountains	1981
TOYS	Attack	1965
	A Lover's Concerto	1965
FAYE TOZER/RUSSELL WATSON		
	Someone Like You	2002
T'PAU	China In Your Hand	1987
	Heart And Soul	1987
	I Will Be With You	1988
	Only The Lonely	1989
	Secret Garden	1988
	Sex Talk (Live)	1988
	Valentine	1988
	Whenever You Need Me	1991
TQ	Better Days	1999
	Bye Bye Baby	1999
	Daily	2000
	Westside	1998
	(ANOTHER LEVEL featuring TQ)	
	Summertime	1999
	(SARAH CONNOR featuring TQ)	
	Let's Get Back To Bed... Boy	2001
TRACIE	Give It Some Emotion	1983
	The House That Jack Built	1983
TRADE WINDS	New York's A Lonely Town	1965

ARTIST	SONG TITLE	DATE
TRAFFIC	Here We Go Round The Mulberry Bush	1967
	Hole In My Shoe	1967
	No Face, No Name, No Number	1968
	Paper Sun	1967
TRAIN	Drops Of Jupiter (Tell Me)	2001
	Meet Virginia	1999
TRAMMPS	Disco Inferno	1978
	Hold Back The Night	1975
	Sixty Minute Man	1975
	That's Where The Happy People Go	1976
	Zing Went The Strings Of My Heart	1974
	(KWS/THE TRAMMPS)	
	Hold Back The Night	1992
TRANSPLANTS	Diamonds And Guns	2003
TRANSVISION VAMP		
	Baby I Don't Care	1989
	Born To Be Sold	1989
	(I Just Wanna) B With U	1991
	I Want Your Love	1988
	Landslide Of Love	1989
	The Only One	1989
	Revolution Baby	1988
TRANS-X	Living On Video	1985
TRASH	Golden Slumbers/Carry That Weight	1969
TRASHMEN	Bird Dance Beat	1964

ARTIST	SONG TITLE	DATE
TRAVELING WILBURYS		
	Handle With Care	1988
TRAVIS	All I Want To Do Is Rock	1997
	Coming Around	2000
	Driftwood	1999
	Flowers In The Window	2002
	Happy	1997
	Love Will Come Through	2004
	More Than Us EP	1998
	Re-Offender	2003
	Side	2001
	Sing	2001
	Tied To The 90's	1997
	Turn	1999
	U16 Girls	1997
	Walking In The Sun	2004
	Why Does It Always Rain On Me?	1999
	Writing To Reach You	1999
RANDY TRAVIS	Three Wooden Crosses	2003
JOHN TRAVOLTA	All Strung Out On You	1977
	Greased Lightning	1978
	Let Her In	1976
	Sandy	1978
	Whenever I'm Away From You	1976
JOHN TRAVOLTA & OLIVIA NEWTON-JOHN		
	The Grease Megamix	1990

ARTIST	SONG TITLE	DATE
	Summer Nights	1978
	You're The One That I Want	1978
TREMELOES	Be Mine	1967
	By The Way	1970
	(Call Me) Number One	1969
	Even The Bad Times Are Good	1967
	Hello Buddy	1971
	Hello World	1969
	Helule Helule	1968
	Here Comes My Baby	1967
	I Shall Be Released	1968
	Me And My Life	1970
	My Little Lady	1968
	Silence Is Golden	1967
	Suddenly You Love Me	1968
JACKIE TRENT	I'll Be There	1969
	When The Summertime Is Over	1965
	Where Are You Now (My Love)	1965
RALPH TRESVANT	Sensitivity	1990
	Stone Cold Gentleman	1991
TREVOR & SIMON	Hands Up	2000
TRIBE CALLED QUEST		
	Can I Kick It?	1991
	Ince Again	1996
	Stressed Out	1996
TRIBE OF TOFFS	John Kettley (Is A Weatherman)	1988

ARTIST	SONG TITLE	DATE
OBIE TRICE	Got Some Teeth	2003
OBIE TRICE featuring NATE DOGG		
	The Set Up (You Don't Know)	2004
TRICK DADDY	I'm A Thug	2001
TRICK DADDY featuring LIL JON & TWISTA		
	Let's Go	2004
	(YING YANG TWINS featuring TRICK DADDY)	
	Whats Happnin!	2004
TRICKSTER	Move On Up	1998
TRICKY	Black Steel	1995
	Christiansands	1996
	Makes Me Wanna Die	1997
	Money Greedy/Broken Homes	1998
	Overcome	1995
	Pumpkin	1995
	Tricky Kid	1997
TRICKY vs THE GRAVEDIGGAZ		
	The Hell EP	1995
TRICKY DISCO	Tricky Disco	1990
TRINIDAD OIL COMPANY		
	The Calendar Song (January, February, March, April, May)	1977
TRINITY-X	Forever	2002
TRIO	Da Da Da	1982
TRIPLE EIGHT	Give Me A Reason	2003
	Knock Out	2003

ARTIST	SONG TITLE	DATE
TRIPLE X	Feel The Same	1999
TRIPLETS	You Don't Have To Go Home Tonight	1991
TRISCO	Musak	2001
TRAVIS TRITT	Best Of Intentions	2000
	It's A Great Day To Be Alive	2001
	Love Of A Woman	2001
TRIUMPH	Hold On	1979
	Somebody's Out There	1986
KATHY TROCCOLI	Everything Changes	1992
TROGGS	Any Way That You Want Me	1966
	Give It To Me	1967
	I Can't Control Myself	1966
	Little Girl	1968
	Love Is All Around	1968
	Night Of The Long Grass	1967
	Wild Thing	1966
	With A Girl Like You	1966
TROUBADOURS DU ROI BAUDOUIN		
	Sanctus (Missa Luba)	1969
DORIS TROY	Whatcha Gonna Do About It	1964
TRU FAITH & DUB CONSPIRACY		
	Freak Like Me	2000
TRUBBLE	Dancing Baby (Ooga-Chaka)	1998
TRUCE	Eyes Don't Lie	1998
TRUCKS	It's Just Porn Mum	2002
TRUE PARTY	Whazzup	2000

ARTIST	SONG TITLE	DATE
TRUE STEPPERS & DANE BOWERS featuring VICTORIA BECKHAM	Out Of Your Mind	2000
TRUE STEPPERS featuring BRIAN HARVEY & DONNELL JONES	True Step Tonight	2000
TRUE STEPPERS featuring DANE BOWERS		
	Buggin	2000
ANDREA TRUE CONNECTION		
	More, More, More	1976
	N.Y., You Got Me Dancing	1977
	What's Your Name, What's Your Number	1978
TRUTH	Confusion (Hits Us Every Time)	1983
	A Step In The Right Direction	1983
TRUTH HURTS featuring RAKIM		
	Addictive	2002
TRUTH	Girl	1966
TUBE & BERGER featuring CHRISSIE HYNDE		
	Straight Ahead	2004
TUBES	Don't Want To Wait Anymore	1981
	Prime Time	1979
	She's A Beauty	1983
	White Punks On Dope	1977
TUBEWAY ARMY	Are 'Friends' Electric?	1979
BARBARA TUCKER	Beautiful People	1994
	Everybody Dance (The Horn Song)	1998
	I Get Lifted	1994

ARTIST	SONG TITLE	DATE
BARBARA TUCKER featuring DARRYL D'BONNEAU		
	Stop Playing With My Mind	2000
TANYA TUCKER	Lizzie & The Rainman	1975
TOMMY TUCKER	Hi-Heel Sneakers	1964
TUKAN	Light A Rainbow	2001
TURIN BRAKES	Average Man	2003
	5 Mile (These Are The Days)	2003
	Long Distance	2002
	Mind Over Money	2001
	Pain Killer	2003
	Underdog (Save Me)	2001
IKE & TINA TURNER		
	I Want To Take You Higher	1970
	A Love Like Yours	1966
	Nutbush City Limits	1973
	Proud Mary	1971
	River Deep Mountain High	1966
RUBY TURNER	I'd Rather Go Blind	1987
	If You're Ready (Come Go With Me)	1986
	Stay With Me Baby	1994
SPYDER TURNER	Stand By Me	1966
TINA TURNER	Be Tender With Me Baby	1990
	The Best	1989
	Better Be Good To Me	1984
	Disco Inferno	1993
	Goldeneye	1995

ARTIST	SONG TITLE	DATE
	Help	1984
	I Don't Wanna Fight	1993
	I Don't Wanna Lose You	1989
	I Want You Near Me	1992
	Let's Stay Together	1984
	Look Me In The Heart	1990
	Love Thing	1992
	Missing You	1996
	Nutbush City Limits (The 90s Version)	1991
	On Silent Wings	1996
	One Of The Living	1985
	Open Arms	2004
	Private Dancer	1985
	Show Some Respect	1985
	Something Beautiful Remains	1996
	Steamy Windows	1989
	Two People	1986
	Typical Male	1986
	Way Of The World	1991
	We Don't Need Another Hero (Thunderdome)	1985
	What You Get Is What You See	1987
	What's Love Got To Do With It	1984
	Whatever You Want	1996
	Why Must We Wait Until Tonight	1993

ARTIST	SONG TITLE	DATE
TINA TURNER featuring BARRY WHITE		
	In Your Wildest Dreams	1996
(BRYAN ADAMS & TINA TURNER)		
	It's Only Love	1985
(ROD STEWART & TINA TURNER)		
	It Takes Two	1990
(TINA)		
	Whatever You Need	2000
	When The Heartache Is Over	1999
TURTLES	Elenore	1968
	Happy Together	1967
	It Ain't Me Babe	1965
	Let Me Be	1965
	She'd Rather Be With Me	1967
	She's My Girl	1967
	You Baby	1966
	You Know What I Mean	1967
	You Showed Me	1969
TUXEDO JUNCTION	Chattanooga Choo Choo	1978
SHANIA TWAIN	Any Man Of Mine/Whose Bed Have Your Boots Been Under	1995
	Don't Be Stupid (You Know I Love You)	1997
	Forever And For Always	2003
	From This Moment On	1998
	I'm Gonna Getcha Good!	2002
	Ka-Ching!	2003

ARTIST	SONG TITLE	DATE
	Love Gets Me Every Time	1997
	Man! I Feel Like A Woman!	1999
	Thank You Baby	2003
	That Don't Impress Me Much	1999
	When	1998
	When You Kiss Me/Up!	2003
	You're Still The One	1998
TWEENIES	Best Friends Forever	2001
	Do The Lollipop	2001
	Have Fun Go Mad	2002
	I Believe In Christmas	2001
	Number 1	2000
TWEET	Call Me	2002
	Oops (Oh My)	2002
TWEETS	The Birdie Song (Birdie Dance)	1981
12 GAUGE	Dunkie Butt	1994
TWENTY 4 SEVEN	Are You Dreaming?	1990
	I Can't Stand It	1990
20 FINGERS featuring GILLETTE		
	Short Dick Man	1994
21ST CENTURY GIRLS		
	21st Century Girls	1999
22-20S	Shoot Your Gun	2004
	22 Days	2004
TWICE AS MUCH	Sittin' On A Fence	1966
TWIGGY	Here I Go Again	1976

ARTIST	SONG TITLE	DATE
DWIGHT TWILLEY	Girls	1984
DWIGHT TWILLEY BAND		
	I'm On Fire	1975
TWINKLE	Golden Lights	1965
	Terry	1964
TWISTA	Overnight Celebrity	2004
	Slow Jamz	2004
TWISTA featuring ANTHONY HAMILTON		
	Sunshine	2004
TWISTA featuring R. KELLY		
	So Sexy	2004
TWISTED SISTER	I Am (I'm Me)	1983
	The Kids Are Back	1983
	We're Not Gonna Take It	1984
TWISTED X	Born In England	2004
CONWAY TWITTY	You've Never Been This Far Before	1973
TWO COWBOYS	Everybody Gonfi Gon	1994
2 EIVISSA	Oh La La La	1997
2 FUNKY 2 featuring KATHRYN DION		
	Brothers & Sisters	1996
2 IN A ROOM	El Trago (The Drink)	1994
	Wiggle It	1990
2 IN A TENT	When I'm Cleaning Windows (Turned	
	Out Nice Again)	1994
2 LIVE CREW	Me So Horny	1989

ARTIST	SONG TITLE	DATE
	(LUKE featuring THE 2 LIVE CREW)	
	Banned In The USA	1990
TWO MEN, A DRUM MACHINE AND A TRUMPET		
	Heat It Up	1988
	I'm Tired Of Getting Pushed Around	1988
2TWO THIRD3	I Want The World	1994
	I Want To Be Alone	1994
2 UNLIMITED	Do What's Good For Me	1995
	Faces	1993
	Get Ready For This	1994
	Here I Go	1995
	Let The Beat Control Your Body	1994
	Magic Friend	1992
	Maximum Overdrive	1993
	No Limit	1993
	No One	1994
	The Real Thing	1994
	Tribal Dance	1993
	Twilight Zone	1992
	Wanna Get Up	1998
	Workaholic	1992
2K	Fuck The Millennium	1997
2PAC	Changes	1998
	Dear Mama/Old School	1995
	Do For Love	1998
	Happy Home	1998

ARTIST	SONG TITLE	DATE
	I Ain't Mad At Cha	1996
	I Get Around	1993
	I Wonder If Heaven Got A Ghetto	1998
	Keep Ya Head Up	1993
	Letter 2 My Unborn	2001
	Thugz Mansion	2003
	Until The End Of Time	2001
2PAC& NOTORIOUS B.I.G.		
	Runnin'	1998
	Runnin' (Dying To Live)	2004
2PAC AND SNOOP DOGGY DOGG		
	Wanted Dead Or Alive	1997
2PAC featuring DR DRE		
	California Love	1996
2PAC featuring DR. DRE & ROGER TROUTMAN		
	California Love/How Do U Want It	1996
2PAC featuring KC AND JOJO		
	How Do You Want It?	1996
	(MAKAVELI)	
	To Live & Die In L.A.	1997
	Toss It Up	1997
	(SCARFACE featuring 2PAC & JOHNNY P)	
	Smile	1997
2PLAY featuring RAGHAV & JUCXI		
	So Confused	2004

ARTIST	SONG TITLE	DATE
2PLAY featuring RAGHAV & NAILA BOSS		
	It Can't Be Right	2004
TYCOON	Such A Woman	1979
BONNIE TYLER	Holding Out For A Hero	1984
	It's A Heartache	1978
	Lost In France	1976
	Married Men	1979
	More Than A Lover	1977
	Total Eclipse Of The Heart	1983
	(SHAKY & BONNIE)	
	A Rockin' Good Way	1984
TYMES	Ms Grace	1974
	People	1968
	So Much In Love	1963
	You Little Trustmaker	1974
TYMES 4	Bodyrock	2001
	She Got Game	2001
TYPICALLY TROPICAL		
	Barbados	1975
TYREE featuring KOOL ROCK STEADY		
	Turn Up The Bass	1989
TYRELL CORPORATION		
	Better Days Ahead	1995
TYRESE	How You Gonna Act Like That	2003
	Nobody Else	1998
	Sweet Lady	1999

ARTIST	SONG TITLE	DATE
	(DA BRAT featuring TYRESE)	
	What'chu Like	2000
TZANT	Bounce With The Massive	1998
	Hot & Wet (Believe It)	1996
	Sounds Of Wickedness	1998
JUDIE TZUKE	Stay With Me Till Dawn	1979
U-KREW	If U Were Mine	1990
U.N.V.	Something's Goin' On	1993
U.S.U.R.A.	Open Your Mind	1993
	Sweat	1993
UB40	Breakfast In Bed	1988
	Bring Me Your Cup	1993
	C'est La Vie	1994
	Can't Help Falling In Love	1993
	Cherry Oh Baby	1984
	Come Back Darling	1998
	Don't Break My Heart	1985
	Don't Let It Pass You By/Don't Slow Down	1981
	The Earth Dies Screaming/Dream A Lie	1980
	Here I Am (Come And Take Me)	1991
	Higher Ground	1993
	Holly Holy	1998
	Homely Girl	1989
	(I Can't Help) Falling In Love With You	1993
	I Got You Babe	1985

ARTIST	SONG TITLE	DATE
	I Won't Close My Eyes	1982
	If It Happens Again	1984
	King/Food For Thought	1980
	Kingston Town	1990
	Love Is All Is Alright	1982
	Many Rivers To Cross	1983
	Maybe Tomorrow	1987
	My Way Of Thinking/I Think It's Going To Rain	1980
	One In Ten	1981
	Please Don't Make Me Cry	1983
	Rat In Mi Kitchen	1987
	Red Red Wine	1988
	Reggae Music	1994
	Sing Our Own Song	1986
	So Here I Am	1982
	Tell Me Is It True	1997
	The Train Is Coming	1999
	Until My Dying Day	1995
	Watchdogs	1987
	The Way You Do The Things You Do	1990
	Wear You To The Ball	1990
	Where Did I Go Wrong	1988
UB40 featuring LADY SAW	Since I Met You Lady/Sparkle Of My Eyes	2001

ARTIST	SONG TITLE	DATE
UB40 featuring UNITED COLOURS OF SOUND		
	Swing Low	2003
	(AFRIKA BAMBAATAA AND FAMILY featuring UB40)	
	Reckless	1988
	(ROBERT PALMER AND UB40)	
	I'll Be Your Baby Tonight	1990
UD PROJECT	Saturday Night	2004
UD PROJECT vs SUNCLUB		
	Summer Jam	2003
UFO	Doctor Doctor	1979
	Young Blood	1980
UGLY KID JOE	Busy Bee	1993
	Cat's In The Cradle	1993
	Everything About You	1992
	Milkman's Son	1995
	Neighbor	1992
TILLMAN UHRMACHER		
	On The Run	2002
UK APACHI WITH SHY FX		
	Original Nuttah	1994
UK MIXMASTERS	The Bare Necessities Megamix	1991
	The Night Fever Megamix	1991
UK SUBS	Party In Paris	1980
	She's Not There/Kicks (EP)	1979
	Stranglehold	1979
	Teenage	1980

ARTIST	SONG TITLE	DATE
	Tomorrow's Girls	1979
	Warhead	1980
TRACEY ULLMAN	Breakaway	1983
	Move Over Darling	1983
	My Guy	1984
	Sunglasses	1984
	They Don't Know	1984
ULTIMATE KAOS	Casanova	1997
	Hoochie Booty	1995
	Right Here	1995
	Show A Little Love	1995
	Some Girls	1994
ULTRA	Rescue Me	1999
	The Right Time	1998
	Say It Once	1998
	Say You Do	1998
ULTRA HIGH	Stay With Me	1995
ULTRA NATE	Found A Cure	1998
	Free	1997
	New Kind Of Medicine	1998
ULTRABEAT	Better Than Life	2004
	Feelin' Fine	2003
	Pretty Green Eyes	2003
ULTRASOUND	Floodlit World	1999
	Stay Young	1998

ARTIST	SONG TITLE	DATE
ULTRAVOX	All Fall Down	1986
	All Stood Still	1981
	Dancing With Tears In My Eyes	1984
	Hymn	1982
	Lament	1984
	Love's Great Adventure	1984
	One Small Day	1984
	Reap The Wild Wind	1982
	Same Old Story	1986
	Sleepwalk	1980
	Slow Motion	1981
	The Thin Wall	1981
	Vienna	1981
	Visions In Blue	1983
	The Voice	1981
	We Came To Dance	1983
UMBOZA	Sunshine	1996
LOS UMBRELLOS	No Tengo Dinero	1998
UMBOZA	Cry India	1995
PIERO UMILIANI	Mah-Na, Mah-Na	1977
UN-CUT	Midnight	2003
UNBELIEVABLE TRUTH		
	Higher Than Reason	1998
	Solved	1998
UNCANNY ALLIANCE		
	I Got My Education	1992

ARTIST	SONG TITLE	DATE
UNCLE KRACKER	Follow Me	2001
	(KENNY CHESNEY & UNCLE KRACKER)	
	When The Sun Goes Down	2004
UNCLE SAM	I Don't Ever Want To See You Again	1997
UNDERCOVER	Baker Street	1992
	I Wanna Stay With You	1993
	Never Let Her Slip Away	1992
UNDERGROUND SUNSHINE		
	Birthday	1969
UNDERTONES	Here Comes The Summer	1979
	It's Going To Happen!	1981
	Jimmy Jimmy	1979
	My Perfect Cousin	1980
	Teenage Kicks	1978
	Wednesday Week	1980
	You've Got My Number (Why Don't You Use It!)	1979
UNDERWORLD	Born Slippy	1996
	Cowgirl	2000
	Dinosaur Adventure 3D	2003
	Jumbo	1999
	King Of Snake	1999
	Pearl's Girl	1996
	Push Upstairs	1999
	Two Months Off	2002

ARTIST	SONG TITLE	DATE
UNDISPUTED TRUTH		
	Smiling Faces Sometime	1971
UNIFICS	The Beginning Of The End	1968
	Court Of Love	1968
U96	Das Boot	1992
UNION featuring ENGLAND RUGBY WORLD CUP SQUAD		
	Swing Low (Run With The Ball)	1991
UNIQUE	What I Got Is What You Need	1983
UNIQUE 3	Musical Melody/Weight For The Bass	1990
UNIT FOUR PLUS TWO		
	Concrete And Clay	1965
	(You've) Never Been In Love Like This Before	1965
UNIVERSAL	Make It With You	1997
	Rock Me Good	1997
UNKLE	Eye For An Eye	2003
UNKLE featuring IAN BROWN		
	Be There	1999
UNTOUCHABLES	Free Yourself	1985
UP YER RONSON	Are You Gonna Be There?	1996
	I Will Be Released	1997
UP YER RONSON featuring MARY PEARCE		
	Lost In Love	1995
PHIL UPCHURCH COMBO		
	You Can't Sit Down	1966

ARTIST	SONG TITLE	DATE
UPSETTERS	The Return Of DJ Ango/Dollar In The Teeth	1969
UPSIDE DOWN	Change Your Mind	1996
	Everytime I Fall In Love	1996
	If You Leave Me Now	1996
	Never Found A Love Like This Before	1996
URBAN HYPE	A Trip To Trumpton	1992
URBAN COOKIE COLLECTIVE		
	Feels Like Heaven	1993
	High On A Happy Vibe	1994
	The Key The Secret	1993
	Sail Away	1994
URBAN DANCE SQUAD		
	Deeper Shade Of Soul	1990
URBAN SHAKEDOWN		
	Some Justice	1992
URBAN SPECIES	Brother	1994
	Spiritual Love	1994
KEITH URBAN	But For The Grace Of God	2000
	Days Go By	2004
	Raining On Sunday	2003
	Somebody Like You	2002
	Where The Blacktop Ends	2001
	Who Wouldn't Want To Be Me	2003
	You'll Think Of Me	2004

ARTIST	SONG TITLE	DATE
MIDGE URE	Call Of The Wild	1986
	Cold, Cold Heart	1991
	If I Was	1985
	No Regrets	1982
	That Certain Smile	1985
MIDGE URE & MICK KARN		
	After A Fashion	1983
URGE OVERKILL	Girl, You'll Be A Woman Soon	1994
URIAH HEEP	Easy Livin'	1972
URUSEI YATSURA	Hello Tiger	1998
US3	Cantaloop (Flip Fantasia)	1993
	Come On Everybody (Get Down)	1997
US3 featuring RASHAAN		
	Cantaloop	1993
US3 featuring TUKKA YOOT		
	Riddum	1993
USA FOR AFRICA	We Are The World	1985
USHER	Burn	2004
	My Way	1998
	Nice & Slow	1998
	Pop Ya Collar	2001
	U Don't Have To Call	2002
	U Got It Bad	2001
	U Remind Me	2001
	U-Turn	2002
	You Make Me Wanna	1997

ARTIST	SONG TITLE	DATE
USHER & ALICIA KEYS		
	My Boo	2004
USHER featuring LIL' JON & LUDACRIS		
	Yeah!	2004
	(P. DIDDY featuring USHER & LOON)	
	I Need A Girl (Part One)	2002
UTAH SAINTS	Believe In Me	1993
	Funky Music	2000
	I Still Think Of You	1994
	I Want You	1993
	Love Song	2000
	Something Good	1992
	What Can You Do For Me	1991
UTOPIA	Set Me Free	1980
U2	All I Want Is You	1989
	Angel Of Harlem	1989
	Beautiful Day	2000
	Desire	1988
	Discotheque	1997
	Electrical Storm	2002
	Elevation	2001
	Even Better Than The Real Thing	1992
	Fire	1981
	The Fly	1991
	Hold Me, Thrill Me, Kiss Me, Kill Me	1995

ARTIST	SONG TITLE	DATE
	I Still Haven't Found What I'm Looking For	1987
	If God Will Send His Angels	1997
	Last Night On Earth	1997
	Mysterious Ways	1991
	New Year's Day	1983
	One	1992
	Please	1997
	Pride (In The Name Of Love)	1984
	Staring At The Sun	1997
	Stay (Faraway, So Close!)/I've Got You Under My Skin	1993
	Stuck In A Moment You Can't Get Out Of	2001
	Sweetest Thing	1998
	Two Hearts Beat As One	1983
	The Unforgettable Fire	1985
	Vertigo	2004
	Walk On	2001
	Where The Streets Have No Name	1987
	Who's Gonna Ride Your Wild Horses	1992
	With Or Without You	1987
U2 WITH B.B. KING		
	When Love Comes To Town	1989
(LMC vs U2)		
	Take Me To The Clouds Above	2004

ARTIST	SONG TITLE	DATE
(MUSIQUE vs U2)		
	New Year's Dub	2001
V	Blood Sweat And Tears	2004
	Hip To Hip/Can You Feel It?	2004
HOLLY VALANCE	Down Boy	2002
	Kiss Kiss	2002
	Naughty Girl	2002
	State Of Mind	2003
JERRY VALE	Have You Looked Into Your Heart	1964
JOHN VALENTI	Anything You Want	1976
FRANKIE VALLI	Can't Take My Eyes Off You	1967
	Fallen Angel	1976
	Grease	1978
	I Make A Fool Of Myself	1967
	My Eyes Adored You	1974
	Our Day Will Come	1975
	Swearin' To God	1975
	To Give (The Reasons I Live)	1967
	(You're Gonna) Hurt Yourself	1966
	You're Ready Now	1970
PAUL VAN DYK	Another Way/Avenue	1999
	For An Angel	1998
	We Are Alive	2000
PAUL VAN DYK featuring HEMSTOCK		
	Nothing But You	2003

ARTIST	SONG TITLE	DATE
PAUL VAN DYK featuring SAINT ETIENNE		
	Tell Me Why (The Riddle)	2000
PAUL VAN DYK featuring VEGA 4		
	Time Of Our Lives/Connected	2003
VAN HALEN	Black And Blue	1988
	Can't Stop Lovin' You	1995
	Dance The Night Away	1979
	Dancing In The Street	1982
	Don't Tell Me	1995
	Dreams	1986
	Feels So Good	1989
	Finish What Ya Started	1988
	I'll Wait	1984
	Jump	1984
	Love Walks In	1986
	(Oh) Pretty Woman	1982
	Panama	1984
	Top Of The World	1991
	When It's Love	1988
	Why Can't This Be Love	1986
	You Really Got Me	1978
ARMAND VAN HELDEN		
	The Funk Phenomena	1997
	Koochy	2000
	My My My	2004
	Why Can't You Free Some Time	2001

ARTIST	SONG TITLE	DATE
ARMAND VAN HELDEN featuring DUANE HARDEN		
	You Don't Know Me	1999
ARMAND VAN HELDEN featuring ROLAND CLARK		
	Flowerz	1999
ARMAND VAN HELDEN featuring SPALDING ROCKWELL		
	Hear My Name	2004
	(ROGER SANCHEZ featuring ARMAND VAN HELDEN)	
	You Can't Change Me	2001
VANDENBERG	Burning Heart	1983
LUTHER VANDROSS	Ain't No Stopping Us Now	1995
	Always And Forever	1995
	Any Love	1988
	Dance With My Father	2003
	Don't Want To Be A Fool	1991
	Give Me The Reason	1988
	Heaven Knows	1993
	Here And Now	1989
	I Gave It Up (When I Fell In Love)	1988
	I Really Didn't Mean It	1987
	Little Miracles (Happen Every Day)	1993
	Love Is On The Way	1993
	Love The One You're With	1994
	Never Too Much	1981
	Power Of Love/Love Power	1991
	She Won't Talk To Me	1989

ARTIST	SONG TITLE	DATE
	So Amazing	1987
	Stop To Love	1986
	Take You Out	2001
	'Til My Baby Gets Home	1985
	Your Secret Love	1996
LUTHER VANDROSS & MARIAH CAREY		
	Endless Love	1994
LUTHER VANDROSS AND JANET JACKSON		
	The Best Things In Life Are Free	1992
	(DIONNE WARWICK & LUTHER VANDROSS)	
	How Many Times Can We Say Goodbye	1983
VANESSA-MAE	I'm A-Doun For Lack O'Johnnie (A Little	
	Scottish Fantasy)	1996
	Red Hot	1995
	Toccata & Fugue	1995
VANGELIS	Chariots Of Fire	1981
VANILLA	No Way No Way	1997
	True To Us	1998
VANILLA FUDGE	Take Me For A Little While	1968
	You Keep Me Hangin' On	1967
VANILLA ICE	Ice Ice Baby	1990
	Play That Funky Music	1990
	Rollin' In My 5.0	1991
	Satisfaction	1991
VANITY FARE	Early In The Morning	1969
	Hitchin' A Ride	1970

ARTIST	SONG TITLE	DATE
	I Live For The Sun	1968
GINO VANNELLI	I Just Wanna Stop	1978
	Living Inside Myself	1981
	People Gotta Move	1974
RANDY VANWARMER		
	Just When I Needed You Most	1979
VAPORS	Turning Japanese	1980
VARIOUS	Perfect Day	1997
VARIOUS ARTISTS	The Brits 1990	1990
	Thank Abba For The Music	1999
SPECIAL AKA/MADNESS/SELECTER/BEAT		
	The 2 Tone EP	1993
JUNIOR VASQUEZ	Get Your Hands Off My Man!	1995
	If Madonna Calls	1996
PHIL VASSAR	Just Another Day In Paradise	2000
	That's When I Love You	2002
FRANKIE VAUGHAN	Hello, Dolly!	1964
	Hey Mama	1963
	Loop De Loop	1963
	Nevertheless	1968
	So Tired	1967
	There Must Be A Way	1967
SARAH VAUGHAN/BILLY ECKSTINE		
	Passing Strangers	1969
VBIRDS	Virtuality	2003
BOBBY VEE	Beautiful People	1967

ARTIST	SONG TITLE	DATE
	Bobby Tomorrow	1963
	My Girl/Hey Girl (Medley)	1968
	The Night Has A Thousand Eyes	1962
BOBBY VEE & THE STRANGERS		
	Come Back When You Grow Up	1967
SUZANNE VEGA	Luka	1987
	Marlene On The Wall	1986
	No Cheap Thrill	1997
SUZANNE VEGA featuring JOE JACKSON		
	Left Of Center	1986
	(DNA featuring SUZANNE VEGA)	
	Tom's Diner	1990
VEGAS	Possessed	1992
ROSIE VELA	Magic Smile	1987
VELVELETTES	These Things Will Keep Me Loving You	1971
VELVET REVOLVER	Fall To Pieces	2004
	Slither	2004
VENGABOYS	Boom, Boom, Boom, Boom!!	1999
	Cheekah Bow Bow (That Computer Song)	2000
	Forever As One	2001
	Kiss (When The Sun Don't Shine)	1999
	Shalala Lala	2000
	Uncle John From Jamaica	2000
	Up And Down	1998
	We Like To Party! (The Vengabus)	1999
	We're Going To Ibiza!	1999

ARTIST	SONG TITLE	DATE
VENTURES	Hawaii Five-O	1969
	Slaughter On Tenth Avenue	1964
	Walk-Don't Run '64	1964
VIK VENUS	Moonflight	1969
BILLY VERA	I Can Take Care Of Myself	1981
BILLY VERA & BEATERS		
	At This Moment	1986
BILLY VERA & JUDY CLAY		
	Country Girl City Man	1968
VERACOCHA	Carte Blanche	1999
VERNONS GIRLS	Funny All Over	1963
VERTICAL HORIZON		
	Everything You Want	2000
	You're A God	2000
VERVE	Bitter Sweet Symphony	1998
	The Drugs Don't Work	1997
	History	1995
	Lucky Man	1997
	On Your Own	1995
	This Is Music	1995
VERVE PIPE	The Freshman	1997
VIBRATIONS	My Girl Sloopy	1964
VIBRATORS	Automatic Lover	1978
MARIA VIDAL	Body Rock	1985
VIENNA PHILHARMONIC ORCHESTRA		
	Theme From 'The Onedin Line'	1971

ARTIST	SONG TITLE	DATE
VILLAGE PEOPLE	Can't Stop The Music	1980
	Go West	1979
	In The Navy	1979
	Macho Man	1978
	Y.M.C.A.	1978
VINES	Get Free	2002
	Highly Evolved	2002
	Outtathaway	2002
	Ride	2004
BOBBY VINTON	Beer Barrel Polka/Dick And Jane	1975
	Blue Velvet	1963
	Clinging Vine	1964
	Coming Home Soldier	1966
	The Days Of Sand And Shovels	1969
	Dum-De-Da	1966
	Every Day Of My Life	1972
	Halfway To Paradise	1968
	I Love How You Love Me	1968
	Just As Much As Ever	1967
	L-O-N-E-L-Y	1965
	Long Lonely Nights	1965
	Mr. Lonely	1964
	My Heart Belongs To Only You	1964
	My Melody Of Love	1974
	Please Love Me Forever	1967
	Roses Are Red	1990

ARTIST	SONG TITLE	DATE
	Satin Pillows	1965
	Sealed With A Kiss	1972
	Take Good Care Of My Baby	1968
	Tell Me Why	1964
	There! I've Said It Again	1963
	To Know You Is To Love You	1969
	What Color (Is A Man)	1965
VIOLENT DELIGHT	All You Ever Do	2003
	I Wish I Was A Girl	2003
VIOLINSKI	Clog Dance	1979
VIRTUES	Guitar Boogie Shuffle	1969
VIRUS	Moon	1997
VISAGE	Damned Don't Cry	1982
	Fade To Grey	1980
	Mind Of A Toy	1981
	Night Train	1982
	Visage	1981
VISCOUNTS	Harlem Nocturne	1959
VITA/IRV GOTTI/JA RULE/ASHANTI/CHARLI BALTIMORE		
	Down 4 U	2002
	(JA RULE featuring LIL' MO & VITA)	
	Put It On Me	2000
	(NERD featuring LEE HARVEY & VITA)	
	Lapdance	2001
VITAMIN C	Graduation (Friends Forever)	2000

ARTIST	SONG TITLE	DATE
VITAMIN C featuring LADY SAW		
	Smile	1999
VIXEN	Cryin'	1989
	Edge Of A Broken Heart	1988
	How Much Love	1990
	Love Made Me	1989
	Not A Minute Too Soon	1991
VOGGUE	Dancin' The Night Away	1981
VOGUES	Five O'Clock World	1965
	The Land Of Milk And Honey	1966
	Magic Town	1966
	My Special Angel	1968
	No Not Much	1969
	Till	1968
	Turn Around Look At Me	1968
	You're The One	1965
VOICE OF THE BEEHIVE		
	Don't Call Me Baby	1988
	I Say Nothing	1988
	I Think I Love You	1991
	Monsters And Angels	1991
	Perfect Place	1992
VOICES OF LIFE	The Word Is Love (Say The Word)	1998
VOICES OF THEORY		
	Say It	1998
	Wherever You Go	1998

ARTIST	SONG TITLE	DATE
VOICES THAT CARE	Voices That Care	1991
VOLCANO	More To Love	1994
VON BONDIES	C'mon C'mon	2004
VOODOO & SERANO		
	Blood Is Pumpin'	2001
	Overload	2003
ROGER VOUDOURIS	Get Used To It	1979
VOYAGE	From East To West/Scots Machine	1978
	Let's Fly Away	1979
VOYAGER	Halfway Hotel	1979
JURGEN VRIES	The Theme	2002
JURGEN VRIES featuring ANDREA BRITTON		
	Take My Hand	2004
JURGEN VRIES featuring CMC		
	The Opera Song (Brave New World)	2003
JURGEN VRIES featuring SHENA		
	Wilderness	2003
VS	Call U Sexy	2004
	Love You Like Mad	2004
	Make It Hot	2004
KRISTINE W	Feel What You Want	1994
W.A.S.P	Chainsaw Charlie (Murders In The New Morgue)	1992
	Forever Free	1989
	I Don't Need No Doctor (Live)	1987
	Mean Man	1989

ARTIST	SONG TITLE	DATE
	The Real Me	1989
	Scream Until You Like It	1987
	Sunset & Babylon	1993
WA WA NEE	Sugar Free	1987
WADSWORTH MANSION		
	Sweet Mary	1970
JACK WAGNER	All I Need	1984
WAH!	Hope (I Wish You'd Believe Me)	1983
	The Story Of The Blues	1982
	(MIGHTY WAH!)	
	Come Back	1984
WAIKIKIS	Hawaii Tattoo	1964
WAILERS	Tall Cool One	1964
LOUDON WAINWRIGHT III		
	Dead Skunk	1973
JOHN WAITE	Every Step Of The Way	1985
	Missing You	1984
	Tears	1984
JOHNNY WAKELIN	In Zaire	1976
JOHNNY WAKELIN & THE KINSHASA BAND		
	Black Superman (Muhammad Ali)	1975
WALKER BROTHERS		
	Another Tear Falls	1966
	(Baby) You Don't Have To Tell Me	1966
	Deadlier Than The Male	1966
	Love Her	1965

ARTIST	SONG TITLE	DATE
	Make It Easy On Yourself	1965
	My Ship Is Coming In	1965
	No Regrets	1976
	Stay With Me Baby	1967
	The Sun Ain't Gonna Shine (Anymore)	1966
	Walking In The Rain	1967
CHRIS WALKER	Take Time	1992
CLAY WALKER	The Chain Of Love	2000
	You're Beginning To Get To Me	1998
GARY WALKER	Twinkie-Lee	1966
	You Don't Love Me	1966
JOHN WALKER	Annabella	1967
JR. WALKER & THE ALL STARS		
	Come See About Me	1967
	Do The Boomerang	1965
	Do You See My Love (For You Growing)	1970
	Gotta Hold On To This Feeling	1970
	Hip City (Part 2)	1968
	How Sweet It Is (To Be Loved By You)	1966
	(I'm A) Road Runner	1969
	Pucker Up Buttercup	1967
	Shake And Fingerpop	1965
	Shotgun	1965
	Take Me Girl I'm Ready	1973
	These Eyes	1969
	Walk In The Night	1972

ARTIST	SONG TITLE	DATE
	Way Back Home	1973
	What Does It Take (To Win Your Love)	1969
SCOTT WALKER	Jackie	1967
	Joanna	1968
	Lights Of Cincinnati	1969
TERRI WALKER	Ching Ching (Lovin' You Still)	2003
JERRY WALLACE	If You Leave Me Tonight I'll Cry	1972
	In The Misty Moonlight	1964
RIK WALLER	I Will Always Love You	2002
	(Something Inside) So Strong	2002
JOE WALSH	All Night Long	1980
	A Life Of Illusion	1981
	Life's Been Good	1978
	Rocky Mountain Way	1973
STEVE WALSH	I Found Lovin'	1987
JAMIE WALTERS	Hold On	1995
TREVOR WALTERS	Love Me Tonight	1981
	Stuck On You	1984
WAMDUE PROJECT	King Of The Castle	1999
	You're The Reason	2000
TRAVIS WAMMACK	(Shu-Doo-Pa-Poo-Poop) Love Being Your	
	Fool	1975
WALTER WANDERLEY		
	Summer Samba (So Nice)	1966
WANG CHUNG	Dance Hall Days	1984
	Don't Let Go	1984

ARTIST	SONG TITLE	DATE
	Everybody Have Fun Tonight	1986
	Hypnotize Me (From 'Innerspace')	1987
	Let's Go	1987
WANNADIES	Hit	1997
	Someone Somewhere	1996
	You & Me Song	1996
WAR	All Day Music	1971
	Ballero	1974
	The Cisco Kid	1973
	Galaxy	1978
	Gypsy Man	1973
	Hey Senorita	1978
	Low Rider	1975
	Me And Baby Brother	1973
	Slippin' Into Darkness	1972
	Summer	1976
	Why Can't We Be Friends?	1975
	The World Is A Ghetto	1972
	(ERIC BURDON & WAR)	
	Spill The Wine	1970
WARD BROTHERS	Cross That Bridge	1987
ANITA WARD	Ring My Bell	1979
CLIFFORD T. WARD	Gaye	1973
	Scullery	1974
MICHAEL WARD	Let There Be Peace On Earth (Let It	
	Begin With Me)	1973

ARTIST	SONG TITLE	DATE
STEVE WARINER	Two Teardrops	1999
WARM JETS	Hurricane	1998
	Never Never	1998
WARM SOUNDS	Birds And Bees	1967
JENNIFER WARNES	I Know A Heartache When I See One	1979
	Right Time Of The Night	1977
	(BILL MEDLEY & JENNIFER WARNES)	
	(I've Had) The Time Of My Life	1987
	(JOE COCKER & JENNIFER WARNES)	
	Up Where We Belong	1982
WARP BROTHERS	Blast The Speakers	2001
	We Will Survive	2001
WARP BROTHERS vs AQUAGEN		
	Phatt Bass	2000
WARRANT	Cherry Pie	1990
	Down Boys	1989
	Heaven	1989
	I Saw Red	1990
	Sometimes She Cries	1990
ALYSHA WARREN	I Thought I Meant The World To You	1995
WARRIOR	Voodoo	2001
	Warrior	2000
DIONNE WARWICK	Alfie	1967
	All The Love In The World	1982
	The April Fools	1969
	Are You There (With Another Girl)	1965

ARTIST	SONG TITLE	DATE
	Deja Vu	1979
	Do You Know The Way To San Jose	1968
	Heartbreaker	1982
	I Just Don't Know What To Do With Myself	1966
	I Say A Little Prayer	1967
	I'll Never Fall In Love Again	1969
	I'll Never Love This Way Again	1979
	Let Me Go To Him	1970
	Make It Easy On Yourself	1970
	Message To Michael	1966
	No Night So Long	1980
	Promises Promises	1968
	Reach Out For Me	1964
	(Theme From) Valley Of The Dolls	1968
	This Girl's In Love With You	1969
	Trains And Boats And Planes	1966
	Walk On By	1964
	Who Is Gonna Love Me?	1968
	The Windows Of The World	1967
	You Can Have Him	1965
	You'll Never Get To Heaven (If You Break My Heart)	1964
	You've Lost That Lovin' Feeling	1969
DIONNE WARWICK & FRIENDS		
	That's What Friends Are For	1985

ARTIST	SONG TITLE	DATE
DIONNE WARWICK & JEFFREY OSBORNE		
	Love Power	1987
DIONNE WARWICK & JOHNNY MATHIS		
	Friends In Love	1982
DIONNE WARWICK & LUTHER VANDROSS		
	How Many Times Can We Say Goodbye	1983
DIONNE WARWICK & THE SPINNERS		
	Then Came You	1974
WAS (NOT WAS)	Papa Was A Rolling Stone	1990
	Shake Your Head	1992
	Spy In The House Of Love	1988
	Walk The Dinosaur	1989
MARTHA WASH	Give It To You	1993
MARTHA WASH featuring RUPAUL		
	It's Raining Men... The Sequel	1998
	(TODD TERRY featuring MARTHA WASH &	
	JOCELYN BROWN)	
	Keep On Jumpin'	1996
GENO WASHINGTON & THE RAM JAM BAND		
	Michael (The Lover)	1967
	Water	1966
GROVER WASHINGTON JR.		
	Just The Two Of Us	1981
KEITH WASHINGTON		
	Kissing You	1991

ARTIST	SONG TITLE	DATE
	(KYLIE MINOGUE/KEITH WASHINGTON)	
	If You Were With Me Now	1991
SARAH WASHINGTON		
	Everything	1996
	Heaven	1996
	I Will Always Love You	1993
WATERBOYS	Fisherman's Blues	1989
	Glastonbury Song	1993
	The Return Of Pan	1993
	The Whole Of The Moon	1991
WATERFRONT	Cry	1989
WATERGATE	Heart Of Asia	2000
DENNIS WATERMAN		
	I Could Be So Good For You	1980
DENNIS WATERMAN & GEORGE COLE		
	What Are We Gonna Get 'Er Indoors	1983
CRYSTAL WATERS	Ghetto Day/What I Need	1994
	Gypsy Woman	1991
	Makin' Happy	1991
	Megamix	1992
	100% Pure Love	1994
	Relax	1995
	Say... If You Feel Alright	1997
CRYSTAL WATERS/SABRINA JOHNSON		
	Gypsy Woman/Peace	1992

ARTIST	SONG TITLE	DATE
	(DUTCH featuring CRYSTAL WATERS)	
	My Fault	2003
	My Time	2003
ROGER WATERS	What God Wants (Part I)	1992
LAUREN WATERWORTH		
	Baby Now That I've Found You	2002
JODY WATLEY	Don't You Want Me	1987
	Everything	1989
	I'm The One You Need	1992
	Looking For A New Love	1987
	Real Love	1989
	Some Kind Of Lover	1988
	When A Man Loves A Woman	1994
JODY WATLEY WITH ERIC B & RAKIM		
	Friends	1989
	(BABYFACE featuring LL COOL J, JODY WATLEY, JEFFREY DANIELS)	
	This Is For The Lover In You	1996
JOHNNY 'GUITAR' WATSON		
	I Need It	1976
RUSSELL WATSON	Nothing Sacred — A Song For Kirsty	2002
	Swing Low '99	1999
RUSSELL WATSON & FAYE TOZER		
	Someone Like You	2002
WAVELENGTH	Hurry Home	1982
WAX	Bridge To Your Heart	1987

ARTIST	SONG TITLE	DATE
WAY OUT WEST	Ajare	1997
	Domination	1996
WAY OUT WEST featuring TRICIA LEE KELSHALL		
	Mindcircus	2002
WAY OUT WEST/MISS JOANNA LAW		
	The Gift	1996
JAN WAYNE	Because The Night	2002
	Total Eclipse Of The Heart	2003
JEFF WAYNE	Eve Of The War	1978
JIMMY WAYNE	Stay Gone	2003
WE FIVE	Let's Get Together	1965
	You Were On My Mind	1965
WEATHER GIRLS	It's Raining Men	1984
JIM WEATHERLY	The Need To Be	1974
WEATHERMEN	It's The Same Old Song	1971
MARTI WEBB	Always There	1986
	Ben	1985
	Take That Look Off Your Face	1980
WEDDING PRESENT		
	Blue Eyes	1992
	Boing!	1992
	Brassneck	1990
	California	1992
	Come Play With Me	1992
	Dalliance	1991
	Flying Saucer	1992

ARTIST	SONG TITLE	DATE
	Go-Go Dancer	1992
	Kennedy	1989
	Love Slave	1992
	Montreal	1997
	No Christmas	1992
	The Queen Of Outer Space	1992
	Silver Shorts	1992
	Sticky	1992
	Three	1992
	3 Songs (EP)	1990
FRED WEDLOCK	Oldest Swinger In Town	1981
WEDNESDAY	Last Kiss	1973
WEE PAPA GIRL RAPPERS		
	Heat It Up	1988
	Wee Rule	1988
WEEKEND PLAYERS		
	21st Century	2001
MICHELLE WEEKS	Don't Give Up	1997
	(BOBBY D'AMBROSIO featuring MICHELLE WEEKS)	
	Moment Of My Life	1997
WEEN/FOO FIGHTERS		
	Walking After You/Beacon Light	1998
WEEZER	Buddy Holly	1995
	Hash Pipe	2001
	Island In The Sun	2001
	Keep Fishin'	2002

ARTIST	SONG TITLE	DATE
	Say It Isn't So	1995
	Undone — The Sweater Song	1995
ERIC WEISSBERG & STEVE MANDELL		
	Dueling Banjos	1973
BOB WELCH	Ebony Eyes	1978
	Hot Love, Cold World	1978
	Precious Love	1979
	Sentimental Lady	1977
DENISE WELCH	You Don't Have To Say You Love Me/Cry	
	Me A River	1995
LENNY WELCH	Breaking Up Is Hard To Do	1970
	Ebb Tide	1964
PAUL WELLER	The Bottle	2004
	Brand New Start	1998
	Broken Stones	1995
	Brushed	1997
	The Changingman	1995
	Friday Street	1997
	Hung Up	1994
	It's Written In The Stars	2002
	Leafy Mysteries	2002
	Mermaids	1997
	Out Of The Sinking	1996
	Peacock Suit	1996
	Sunflower	1993
	Uh Huh Oh Yeh	1992

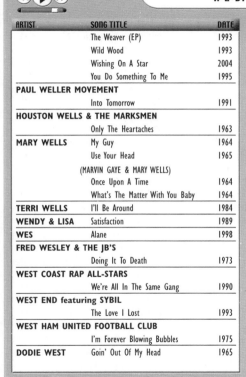

ARTIST	SONG TITLE	DATE
	The Weaver (EP)	1993
	Wild Wood	1993
	Wishing On A Star	2004
	You Do Something To Me	1995
PAUL WELLER MOVEMENT		
	Into Tomorrow	1991
HOUSTON WELLS & THE MARKSMEN		
	Only The Heartaches	1963
MARY WELLS	My Guy	1964
	Use Your Head	1965
	(MARVIN GAYE & MARY WELLS)	
	Once Upon A Time	1964
	What's The Matter With You Baby	1964
TERRI WELLS	I'll Be Around	1984
WENDY & LISA	Satisfaction	1989
WES	Alane	1998
FRED WESLEY & THE JB'S		
	Doing It To Death	1973
WEST COAST RAP ALL-STARS		
	We're All In The Same Gang	1990
WEST END featuring SYBIL		
	The Love I Lost	1993
WEST HAM UNITED FOOTBALL CLUB		
	I'm Forever Blowing Bubbles	1975
DODIE WEST	Goin' Out Of My Head	1965

ARTIST	SONG TITLE	DATE
DOTTIE WEST & KENNY ROGERS		
	What Are We Doin' In Love	1981
KANYE WEST	Jesus Walks	2004
KANYE WEST featuring SYLEENA JOHNSON		
	All Falls Down	2004
	(BRANDY featuring KANYE WEST)	
	Talk About Our Love	2004
KEITH WEST	Excerpt From 'A Teenage Opera'	1967
	Sam	1967
WESTBAM	Wizards Of The Sonic	1995
WESTLIFE	Bop Bop Baby	2002
	Flying Without Wings	1999
	Fool Again	2000
	Hey Whatever	2003
	I Have A Dream/Seasons In The Sun	1999
	If I Let You Go	1999
	Mandy	2003
	My Love	2000
	Obvious	2004
	Queen Of My Heart	2001
	Swear It Again	1999
	Tonight/Miss You Nights	2003
	Unbreakable	2002
	Uptown Girl	2001
	What Makes A Man	2000
	World Of Our Own	2002

ARTIST	SONG TITLE	DATE
	(MARIAH CAREY & WESTLIFE)	
	Against All Odds	2000
WESTSIDE CONNECTION		
	Bow Down	1996
	Gangstas Make The World Go Round	1997
WESTSIDE CONNECTION featuring NATE DOGG		
	Gangsta Nation	2003
WESTWORLD	Ba-Na-Na-Bam-Boo	1987
	Sonic Boom Boy	1987
WET WET WET	Angel Eyes (Home And Away)	1987
	Blue For You/This Time (Live)	1993
	Broke Away	1989
	Cold Cold Heart	1994
	Don't Want To Forgive Me Now	1995
	Goodnight Girl	1992
	Hold Back The River	1990
	If I Never See You Again	1997
	Julia Says	1995
	Lip Service	1992
	Love Is All Around	1994
	Make It Tonight	1991
	More Than Love	1992
	Morning	1996
	She's All On My Mind	1995
	Shed A Tear	1993
	Somewhere Somehow	1995

ARTIST	SONG TITLE	DATE
	Stay With Me Heartache/I Feel Fine	1990
	Strange	1997
	Sweet Little Mystery	1987
	Sweet Surrender	1989
	Temptation	1988
	Wishing I Was Lucky	1987
	Yesterday	1997
WET WET WET/BILLY BRAGG WITH CARA TIVEY		
	With A Little Help From My Friends/	
	She's Leaving Home	1988
WET WILLIE	Keep On Smilin'	1974
	Street Corner Serenade	1977
	Weekend	1979
WHALE	Hobo Humpin' Slobo Babe	1995
WHAM!	Bad Boys	1983
	Careless Whisper	1984
	Club Fantastic (Megamix)	1983
	Club Tropicana	1983
	The Edge Of Heaven/Where Did Your	
	Heart Go	1986
	Freedom	1985
	I'm Your Man	1985
	Last Christmas/Everything She Wants	1984
	Wake Me Up Before You Go-Go	1984
	Wham Rap	1983
	Young Guns (Go For It)	1982

ARTIST	SONG TITLE	DATE
SARAH WHATMORE	Automatic	2003
	When I Lost You	2002
REBECCA WHEATLEY		
	Stay With Me (Baby)	2000
WHEATUS	A Little Respect	2001
	Teenage Dirtbag	2001
	Wannabe Gangster/Leroy	2002
CARON WHEELER	Livin' In The Light	1990
	UK Blak	1990
	(SOUL II SOUL featuring CARON WHEELER)	
	Back To Life (However Do You Want Me)	1989
	Keep On Movin'	1989
BILL WHELAN	Riverdance	1994
WHEN IN ROME	The Promise	1988
WHIGFIELD	Another Day	1994
	Close To You	1995
	Last Christmas/Big Time	1995
	Saturday Night	1994
	Think Of You	1995
WHISPERS	And The Beat Goes On	1980
	It's A Love Thing	1981
	Lady	1980
	My Girl	1980
	Rock Steady	1987
WHISTLE	Always And Forever	1990
	(Nothin' Serious) Just Buggin'	1986

ARTIST	SONG TITLE	DATE
IAN WHITCOMB	You Turn Me On	1965
WHITE LION	Wait	1988
	When The Children Cry	1988
WHITE STRIPES	Dead Leaves And The Dirty Ground	2002
	Fell In Love With A Girl	2002
	The Hardest Button To Button	2003
	Hotel Yorba	2001
	I Just Don't Know What To Do With Myself	2003
	7 Nation Army	2003
WHITE TOWN	Your Woman	1997
WHITE ZOMBIE	Electric Head Pt 2 (The Ecstasy)	1996
BARRY WHITE	Baby We Better Try And Get It Together	1976
	Can't Get Enough Of Your Love, Babe	1974
	Don't Make Me Wait Too Long	1976
	I Only Want To Be With You	1995
	I'll Do Anything You Want Me To	1975
	I'm Gonna Love You Just A Little More Baby	1973
	I'm Qualified To Satisfy You	1977
	I've Got So Much To Give	1973
	It's Ecstasy When You Lay Down Next To Me	1977
	Just The Way You Are	1978
	Let The Music Play	1975
	Never, Never Gonna Give Ya Up	1973

ARTIST	SONG TITLE	DATE
	Oh What A Night For Dancing	1978
	Practice What You Preach/Love Is The Icon	1995
	Sho' You Right	1987
	What Am I Gonna Do With You	1975
	You See The Trouble With Me	1976
	You're The First, The Last, My Everything	1974
(QUINCY JONES featuring AL B. SURE, BARRY WHITE, JAMES INGRAM)		
	Secret Garden	1990
(TINA TURNER featuring BARRY WHITE)		
	In Your Wildest Dreams	1996
CHRIS WHITE	Spanish Wine	1976
KARYN WHITE	Romantic	1991
	Secret Rendezvous	1989
	Superwoman	1989
	The Way I Feel About You	1991
	The Way You Love Me	1988
(JEFF LORBER featuring KARYN WHITE)		
	Facts Of Love	1986
SNOWY WHITE	Bird Of Paradise	1983
TAM WHITE	What In The World's Come Over You	1975
TONY JOE WHITE	Groupie Girl	1970
	Polk Salad Annie	1969
WHITEHEAD BROS.	Forget I Was A G	1995
	Your Love Is A 187	1995
WHITE PLAINS	I've Got You On My Mind	1970

ARTIST	SONG TITLE	DATE
	Julie, Do Ya Love Me	1970
	My Baby Loves Lovin'	1970
	Step Into A Dream	1973
	When You Are A King	1971
WHITESNAKE	The Deeper The Love	1990
	Don't Break My Heart Again	1981
	Fool For Your Loving	1989
	Give Me All Your Love	1988
	Give Me More Time	1984
	Guilty Of Love	1983
	Here I Go Again/Bloody Luxury	1982
	Is This Love/Sweet Lady Luck	1994
	Now You're Gone	1990
	Still Of The Night	1987
	Would I Lie To You	1981
MARGARET WHITING		
	The Wheel Of Hurt	1966
SLIM WHITMAN	Happy Anniversary	1974
ROGER WHITTAKER		
	Durham Town (The Leavin')	1969
	I Don't Believe In If Anymore	1970
	The Last Farewell	1975
	Mammy Blue	1971
	New World In The Morning	1970
ROGER WHITTAKER & DES O'CONNOR		
	The Skye Boat Song	1986

ARTIST	SONG TITLE	DATE
WHO DA FUNK featuring JESSICA EVE		
	Shiny Disco Balls	2002
WHO DA FUNK featuring TERRA DEVA		
	Sting Me Red (You Think You're So Clever)	2003
WHO	Anyway Anyhow Anywhere	1965
	Athena	1982
	Behind Blue Eyes	1971
	Call Me Lightning	1968
	5:15	1973
	Happy Jack	1967
	I Can See For Miles	1967
	I Can't Explain	1965
	I'm A Boy	1966
	I'm Free	1969
	Join Together	1972
	Let's See Action	1971
	Magic Bus	1968
	My Generation	1965
	Pictures Of Lily	1967
	Pinball Wizard	1969
	Relay	1973
	The Relay	1972
	See Me, Feel Me	1970
	The Seeker	1970
	Squeeze Box	1975

ARTIST	SONG TITLE	DATE
	Substitute	1966
	Summertime Blues	1970
	Who Are You	1978
	Won't Get Fooled Again	1971
	You Better You Bet	1981
WIDEBOYS featuring DENNIS G		
	Sambuca	2001
JANE WIEDLIN	Rush Hour	1988
WIGAN'S CHOSEN FEW		
	Footsee	1975
WIGAN'S OVATION	Per-So-Nal-Ly	1975
	Skiing In The Snow	1975
HARLOW WILCOX	Groovy Grubworm	1969
WILD CHERRY	Play That Funky Music	1976
WILD COLOUR	Dreams	1995
WILDCHILD	Jump To My Beat	1996
	Legends Of The Dark Black (Pt 2)	1995
	Renegade Master	1995
WILDCHILD featuring JOMALSKI		
	Bad Boy	1998
EUGENE WILDE	Gotta Get You Home Tonight	1984
	Personality	1985
KIM WILDE	Cambodia	1981
	Chequered Love	1981
	Four Letter Word	1988
	Heart Over Mind	1992

ARTIST	SONG TITLE	DATE
	Hey Mister Heartache	1988
	If I Can't Have You	1993
	Kids In America	1982
	Love Blonde	1983
	Love In The Natural Way	1989
	Love Is Holy	1992
	Never Trust A Stranger	1988
	Rage To Love	1985
	Say You Really Want Me	1987
	The Second Time	1984
	View From A Bridge	1982
	Water On Glass/Boys	1981
	You Came	1988
	You Keep Me Hangin' On	1987
KIM WILDE & JUNIOR		
	Another Step (Closer To You)	1987
KIM WILDE & MEL SMITH		
	Rockin' Around The Christmas Tree	1987
MATTHEW WILDER	Break My Stride	1983
	The Kid's American	1984
WILDHEARTS	Anthem	1997
	Caffeine Bomb	1994
	I Wanna Go Where The People Go	1995
	If Life Is Like A Love Bank.../Geordie In Wonderland	1995
	Just In Lust	1995

ARTIST	SONG TITLE	DATE
	Red Light Green Light (EP)	1996
	Sick Of Drugs	1996
	So Into You	2003
	Stormy In The North — Karma In The South	2003
	Suckerpunch	1994
	Top Of The World	2003
	Urge	1997
	Vanilla Radio	2002
WILEY	Wot Do U Call It?	2004
JONATHAN WILKES	Just Another Day	2001
SUE WILKINSON	You Gotta Be A Hustler If You Wanna Get On	1980
WILL TO POWER	Baby I Love Your Way/Freebird Medley	1988
	I'm Not In Love	1990
ALYSON WILLIAMS	I Need Your Lovin'	1989
	Sleep Talk	1989
ALYSON WILLIAMS featuring NIKKI-D		
	My Love Is So Raw	1989
ANDY WILLIAMS	Ain't It True	1965
	Almost There	1965
	....And Roses And Roses	1965
	Battle Hymn Of The Republic	1968
	Can't Get Used To Losing You	1963
	Can't Help Falling In Love	1970
	Can't Take My Eyes Off You	1968

ARTIST	SONG TITLE	DATE
	Dear Heart	1964
	A Fool Never Learns	1964
	Getting Over You	1974
	Happy Heart	1969
	Home Lovin' Man	1970
	In The Arms Of Love	1966
	It's So Easy	1970
	Love Theme From 'The Godfather' (Speak Softly Love)	1972
	May Each Day	1966
	Music To Watch Girls By	1967
	On The Street Where You Live	1964
	Solitaire	1973
	(Where Do I Begin) Love Story	1971
	Wrong For Each Other	1964
	You Lay So Easy On My Mind	1975
ANDY & DAVID WILLIAMS	I Don't Know Why (I Just Do)	1973
DANNY WILLIAMS	Dancin' Easy	1977
	White On White	1964
DENIECE WILLIAMS	Baby, Baby My Love's All For You	1977
	Free	1976
	It's Gonna Take A Miracle	1982
	Let's Hear It For The Boy	1984
	That's What Friends Are For	1977

ARTIST	SONG TITLE	DATE
	(JOHNNY MATHIS & DENIECE WILLIAMS) Too Much, Too Little, Too Late	1978
DON WILLIAMS	I Believe In You	1980
	I Recall A Gypsy Woman	1976
	You're My Best Friend	1976
ERIC WILLIAMS/2PAC	Do For Love	1998
	(QUEEN PEN featuring ERIC WILLIAMS) All My Love	1998
FREEDOM WILLIAMS/C&C MUSIC FACTORY	Gonna Make You Sweat	1990
	Here We Go	1991
	Things That Make You Go Hmmmm...	1991
IRIS WILLIAMS	He Was Beautiful (Cavatina)	1979
JOHN WILLIAMS	Cavatina	1979
	Main Title (Theme From 'Jaws')	1975
	Theme From 'Close Encounters Of The Third Kind'	1977
	Theme From 'E.T.'	1982
	Star Wars	1977
KENNY WILLIAMS	(You're) Fabulous Babe	1977
LENNY WILLIAMS	Shoo Doo Fu Fu Ooh!	1977
MASON WILLIAMS	Classical Gas	1968
MELANIE WILLIAMS	Everyday Thang	1994

ARTIST	SONG TITLE	DATE
MELANIE WILLIAMS & JOE ROBERTS		
	You Are Everything	1995
(SUB SUB featuring MELANIE WILLIAMS)		
	Ain't No Love (Ain't No Use)	1993
PHARRELL WILLIAMS/BRITNEY SPEARS		
	Boys	2002
(LENNY KRAVITZ/P.DIDDY/LOON/		
PHARRELL WILLIAMS)		
	Show Me Your Soul	2004
ROBBIE WILLIAMS	Angels	1997
	Come Undone	2003
	Eternity/The Road To Mandalay	2001
	Feel	2002
	Freedom	1996
	Lazy Days	1997
	Let Love Be Your Energy	2001
	Let Me Entertain You	1998
	Millennium	1998
	No Regrets/Antmusic	1998
	Old Before I Die	1997
	Radio	2004
	Rock DJ	2000
	Sexed Up	2003
	She's The One/It's Only Us	1999
	Something Beautiful	2003
	South Of The Border	1997

ARTIST	SONG TITLE	DATE
	Strong	1999
	Supreme	2000
ROBBIE WILLIAMS & NICOLE KIDMAN		
	Somethin' Stupid	2001
ROBBIE WILLIAMS/KYLIE MINOGUE		
	Kids	2000
ROGER WILLIAMS	Born Free	1966
VANESSA WILLIAMS		
	Colors Of The Wind	1995
	Dreamin'	1989
	Just For Tonight	1992
	Running Back To You	1991
	Save The Best For Last	1992
	The Sweetest Days	1994
VANESSA WILLIAMS & BRIAN MCKNIGHT		
	Love Is	1993
VESTA WILLIAMS	Once Bitten Twice Shy	1986
BRUCE WILLIS	Respect Yourself	1987
	Under The Boardwalk	1987
MARK WILLS	Back At One	2000
	19 Somethin'	2002
	Wish You Were Here	1999
VIOLA WILLS	Both Sides Now/Dare To Dream	1986
	Gonna Get Along Without You Now	1979
MARIA WILLSON	Chooza Looza	2003
WILSON PHILLIPS	The Dream Is Still Alive	1991

ARTIST	SONG TITLE	DATE
	Give It Up	1992
	Hold On	1990
	Impulsive	1990
	Release Me	1990
	You Won't See Me Cry	1992
	You're In Love	1991
AL WILSON	I've Got A Feeling (We'll Be Seeing Each Other Again)	1976
	La La Peace Song	1974
	Show And Tell	1973
	The Snake	1968
ANN WILSON & ROBIN ZANDER		
	Surrender To Me	1989
(MIKE RENO & ANN WILSON)		
	Almost Paradise... Love Theme From Footloose	1984
BRIAN WILSON	Caroline, No	1966
	Wonderful	2004
DOOLEY WILSON	As Time Goes By	1977
GRETCHEN WILSON		
	Here For The Party	2004
	Redneck Woman	2004
J. FRANK WILSON & THE CAVALIERS		
	Last Kiss	1964
JACKIE WILSON	I Get The Sweetest Feeling/Higher And Higher	1975

ARTIST	SONG TITLE	DATE
	Reet Petite	1986
	Since You Showed Me How To Be Happy	1967
	Whispers (Gettin' Louder)	1966
MARI WILSON	Cry Me A River	1983
	Just What I Always Wanted	1982
MERI WILSON	Telephone Man	1977
NANCY WILSON	Face It Girl, It's Over	1968
	(You Don't Know) How Glad I Am	1964
PRECIOUS WILSON/ERUPTION		
	I Can't Stand The Rain	1978
(MESSIAH/PRECIOUS WILSON)		
	I Feel Love	1992
WILTON PLACE STREET BAND		
	Disco Lucy ('I Love Lucy' Theme)	1977
WIMBLEDON CHORAL SOCIETY		
	World Cup '98 — Pavane	1998
MARIO WINANS featuring ENYA & P. DIDDY		
	I Don't Wanna Know	2004
(P. DIDDY & GINUWINE featuring LOON, MARIO WINANS)		
	I Need A Girl (Part Two)	2002
(PUFF DADDY featuring MARIO WINANS)		
	Best Friend	1999
JESSE WINCHESTER		
	Say What	1981
WIND	Make Believe	1969

ARTIST	SONG TITLE	DATE
WINDJAMMER	Tossing And Turning	1984
WING & A PRAYER FIFE & DRUM CORPS		
	Baby Face	1975
WINGER	Headed For A Heartbreak	1989
	Miles Away	1990
	Seventeen	1989
PETE WINGFIELD	Eighteen With A Bullet	1975
WINK	Higher State Of Consciousness '96	1996
JOSH WINK	Higher State Of Consciousness	1995
JOSH WINK & LIL LOUIS		
	How's Your Evening So Far	2000
WINX	Don't Laugh	1995
	Hypnotizin'	1996
KATE WINSLET	What If	2001
WINSTONS	Color Him Father	1969
EDGAR WINTER	River's Risin'	1974
EDGAR WINTER GROUP		
	Frankenstein	1973
	Free Ride	1973
RUBY WINTERS	Come To Me!	1978
	I Will!	1977
STEVE WINWOOD	Back In The High Life Again	1987
	Don't You Know What The Night Can Do	1988
	The Finer Things	1987
	Freedom Overspill	1986
	Higher Love	1986

ARTIST	SONG TITLE	DATE
	Holding On	1988
	One And Only Man	1990
	Roll With It	1988
	Valerie	1987
	While You See A Chance	1981
WISDOME	Off The Wall	2000
WISEGUYS	Ooh La La	1999
	Start The Commotion	2001
BILL WITHERS	Ain't No Sunshine	1971
	Kissing My Love	1973
	Lean On Me	1972
	Lovely Day	1977
	Use Me	1972
WIZZARD	Angel Fingers (A Teen Ballad)	1973
	Are You Ready To Rock	1974
	Ball Park Incident	1972
	I Wish It Could Be Christmas Every Day	1973
	Rock 'n Roll Winter (Loony's Tune)	1974
	See My Baby Jive	1973
	This Is The Story Of My Love (Baby)	1974
ANDREW W.K.	Party Hard	2001
JAH WOBBLE'S INVADERS OF THE HEART		
	Becoming More Like God	1994
	Visions Of You	1992
TERRY WOGAN	The Floral Dance	1978
PETER WOLF	Come As You Are	1987

ARTIST	SONG TITLE	DATE
	I Need You Tonight	1984
	Lights Out	1984
WOLFMAN featuring PETER DOHERTY		
	For Lovers	2004
WOMACK & WOMACK		
	Celebrate The World	1989
	Life Is Just A Ballgame	1988
	Love Wars	1984
	Teardrops	1988
BOBBY WOMACK	Harry Hippie	1972
	Lookin' For A Love	1974
	Nobody Wants You When You're Down	
	And Out	1973
	That's The Way I Feel About Cha	1971
	(LIVING IN A BOX featuring BOBBY WOMACK)	
	So The Story Goes	1987
	(LULU AND BOBBY WOMACK)	
	I'm Back For More	1993
LEE ANN WOMACK	I Hope You Dance	2001
	I'll Think Of A Reason Later	1999
WOMBLES	Banana Rock	1974
	Let's Womble To The Party Tonight	1975
	Minuetto Allegretto	1974
	Remember You're A Womble	1974
	Super Womble	1975
	Wombling Merry Christmas	1974

ARTIST	SONG TITLE	DATE
	The Wombling Song	1974
	Wombling White Tie And Tails (Fox Trot)	1975
WOMBLES WITH ROY WOOD		
	I Wish It Could Be A Wombling Merry	
	Christmas Every Day	2000
WONDER DOG	Ruff Mix	1982
WONDER STUFF	Caught In My Shadow	1991
	Circlesquare	1990
	Don't Let Me Down Gently	1989
	Full Of Life (Happy Now)	1993
	Golden Green/Get Together	1989
	Hot Love Now! (EP)	1994
	It's Yer Money I'm After Baby	1988
	On The Ropes (EP)	1993
	The Size Of A Cow	1991
	Unbearable	1994
	Welcome To The Cheap Seats (EP)	1992
	Who Wants To Be The Disco King	1989
	(VIC REEVES & THE WONDER STUFF)	
	Dizzy	1991
STEVIE WONDER	Another Star	1977
	As	1977
	Blowin' In The Wind	1966
	Boogie On Reggae Woman	1974
	Castles In The Sand	1964
	Do I Do	1982

ARTIST	SONG TITLE	DATE
	Don't You Worry 'Bout A Thing	1974
	For Once In My Life	1968
	For Your Love	1995
	Go Home	1985
	Happy Birthday	1981
	He's Misstra Know-It-All	1974
	Heaven Help Us All	1970
	Hey Harmonica Man	1964
	Higher Ground	1973
	I Ain't Gonna Stand For It	1980
	I Don't Know Why	1969
	I Just Called To Say I Love You	1984
	I Was Made To Love Her	1967
	I Wish	1976
	I'm Wondering	1967
	If You Really Love Me	1971
	Lately	1981
	Living For The City	1973
	Love Light In Flight	1984
	Master Blaster (Jammin')	1980
	My Cherie Amour	1969
	Never Had A Dream Come True	1970
	Nothing's Too Good For My Baby	1966
	Overjoyed	1986
	Part Time Lover	1985
	A Place In The Sun	1966

ARTIST	SONG TITLE	DATE
	Send One Your Love	1979
	Shoo-Be-Doo-Be-Doo-Da-Day	1968
	Signed, Sealed, Delivered, I'm Yours	1970
	Sir Duke	1977
	Skeletons	1987
	Superstition	1972
	Superwoman (Where Were You When I Needed You)	1972
	That Girl	1982
	Travlin' Man	1967
	Uptight (Everything's Alright)	1965
	We Can Work It Out	1971
	Yester-Me, Yester-You, Yesterday	1969
	You Are The Sunshine Of My Life	1973
	You Haven't Done Nothin'	1974
	You Met Your Match	1968
STEVIE WONDER & MICHAEL JACKSON		
	Get It	1988
	(BABYFACE featuring STEVIE WONDER) How Come, How Long	1997
	(BLUE featuring STEVIE WONDER & ANGIE STONE Signed, Sealed, Delivered, I'm Yours	2003
	(JULIO IGLESIAS featuring STEVIE WONDER) My Love	1988

ARTIST	SONG TITLE	DATE
	(PAUL McCARTNEY & STEVIE WONDER)	
	Ebony And Ivory	1982
WAYNE WONDER	Bounce Along	2003
	No Letting Go	2003
WONDERS	That Thing You Do!	1997
WONDRESS/MANTRONIX		
	Got To Have Your Love	1990
	Take Your Time	1990
BRENTON WOOD	Baby You Got It	1967
	Gimme Little Sign	1967
	The Oogum Boogum Song	1967
LAUREN WOOD	Please Don't Leave	1979
ROY WOOD	Dear Elaine	1973
	Forever	1973
	Going Down The Road	1974
	Oh What A Shame	1975
	(WOMBLES WITH ROY WOOD)	
	I Wish It Could Be A Wombling Merry	
	Christmas Every Day	2000
MARCELLA WOODS/MATT DAREY		
	U Shine On	2002
	(MATT DAREY'S MASH UP presents	
	MARCELLA WOODS)	
	Beautiful	2000
STEVIE WOODS	Just Can't Win 'Em All	1982
	Steal The Night	1981

ARTIST	SONG TITLE	DATE
WOOKIE featuring LAIN		
	Back Up (To Me)	2001
	Battle	2000
WOOLPACKERS	Hillbilly Rock Hillbilly Roll	1996
	Line Dance Party	1997
WORLD PARTY	All I Gave	1993
	Beautiful Dream	1997
	Is It Like Today?	1993
	Message In The Box	1990
	Ship Of Fools(Save Me From Tomorrow)	1987
WORLDS APART	Beggin' To Be Written	1994
	Could It Be I'm Falling In Love	1994
	Everlasting Love	1993
	Heaven Must Be Missing An Angel	1993
DARRYL WORLEY	Have You Forgotten?	2003
	I Miss My Friend	2002
WRECKX-N-EFFECT	Juicy	1990
	Rump Shaker	1992
	Wreckx Shop	1994
BETTY WRIGHT	Clean Up Woman	1971
	Girls Can't Do What The Guys Do	1968
	Shoorah! Shoorah!	1975
	Where Is The Love	1975
CHARLES WRIGHT & THE WATTS 103 STREET		
RHYTHM BAND	Do Your Thing	1969
	Express Yourself	1970

ARTIST	SONG TITLE	DATE
	Love Land	1970
CHELY WRIGHT	Single White Female	1999
GARY WRIGHT	Dream Weaver	1976
	Love Is Alive	1976
	Really Wanna Know You	1981
STEVE WRIGHT & THE AFTERNOON BOYS		
	I'm Alright	1982
WU-TANG CLAN	Gravel Pit	2000
(TEXAS featuring WU-TANG CLAN)		
	Say What You Want/Insane	1998
WURZELS	The Combine Harvester (Brand New Key)	1976
	Farmer Bill's Cowman (I Was Kaiser Bill's Batman)	1977
	I Am A Cider Drinker (Paloma Blanca)	1976
WWF SUPERSTARS	Slam Jam	1992
	Wrestlemania	1993
KEKE WYATT featuring AVANT		
	Nothing In This World	2002
ROBERT WYATT	I'm A Believer	1974
	Shipbuilding	1983
PETE WYLIE	Sinful	1986
BILL WYMAN	A New Fashion	1982
	(Si Si) Je Suis Un Rock Star	1981
TAMMY WYNETTE	D.I.V.O.R.C.E.	1975
	I Don't Wanna Play House	1976
	Stand By Your Man	1968

ARTIST	SONG TITLE	DATE
(KLF/TAMMY WYNETTE)		
	Justified And Ancient	1991
MARK WYNTER	It's Almost Tomorrow	1963
	Only You (And You Alone)	1964
	Shy Girl	1963
X-ECUTIONERS featuring MIKE SHINODA & MR. HAHN		
OF LINKIN PARK	It's Goin' Down	2002
X-PRESS 2	Say What!	1993
	The Sound	1996
X-PRESS 2 featuring DAVID BYRNE		
	Lazy	2002
X-RAY SPEX	The Day The World Turned Dayglo	1978
	Germ Free Adolescence	1978
	Identity	1978
XPANSIONS	Move Your Body (Elevation)	1991
XSCAPE	The Arms Of The One Who Loves You	1998
	Feels So Good	1995
	Just Kickin' It	1993
	My Little Secret	1998
	Understanding	1993
	Who Can I Run To	1995
(LIL BOW WOW featuring XSCAPE)		
	Bounce With Me	2000
(MC LYTE featuring XSCAPE)		
	Keep On, Keepin' On	1996

ARTIST	SONG TITLE	DATE
	(OL' SKOOL featuring KEITH SWEAT & XSCAPE)	
	Am I Dreaming	1998
XTC	The Disappointed	1992
	Generals And Majors/Don't Lose Your Temper	1980
	Making Plans For Nigel	1979
	Senses Working Overtime	1982
	Sgt Rock (Is Going To Help Me)	1981
	Towers Of London	1980
XTM & DJ CHUCKY presents ANNIA		
	Fly On The Wings Of Love	2003
XZIBIT	Multiply	2002
XZIBIT featuring SNOOP DOGG		
	X	2001
YA KID K/HI TEK 3		
	Spin That Wheel (Turtles Get Real)	1990
	(TECHNOTRONIC featuring YA KID K)	
	Get Up (Before The Night Is Over)	1990
	Move This	1992
	Rockin' Over The Beat	1990
'WEIRD AL' YANKOVIC		
	Eat It	1984
	Smells Like Nirvana	1992
YARBROUGH & PEOPLES		
	Don't Stop The Music	1981

ARTIST	SONG TITLE	DATE
GLENN YARBROUGH		
	Baby The Rain Must Fall	1965
YARDBIRDS	Evil Hearted You/Still I'm Sad	1965
	For Your Love	1965
	Happenings Ten Years Time Ago	1966
	Heart Full Of Soul	1965
	I'm A Man	1965
	Over Under Sideways Down	1966
	Shapes Of Things	1966
YAZOO	Don't Go	1982
	Nobody's Diary	1983
	Only You	1982
	The Other Side Of Love	1982
	Situation	1990
YAZZ	Fine Time	1989
	Stand Up For Your Love Rights	1988
	Treat Me Good	1990
	Where Has All The Love Gone	1989
YAZZ & ASWAD	How Long	1993
YAZZ & THE PLASTIC POPULATION		
	The Only Way Is Up	1988
	(COLDCUT featuring YAZZ & THE PLASTIC POPULATION)	
	Doctorin' The House	1988
YEAH YEAH YEAHS		
	Date With The Night	2003

ARTIST	SONG TITLE	DATE
	Machine	2002
	Maps	2003
	Pin	2003
TRISHA YEARWOOD		
	How Do I Live	1997
YELL!	Instant Replay	1990
YELLO	Of Course I'm Lying	1989
	The Race	1988
YELLOW BALLOON	Yellow Balloon	1967
YELLOW DOG	Just One More Night	1978
YELLOW MAGIC ORCHESTRA		
	Computer Game (Theme From The Invaders)	1980
YELLOWCARD	Ocean Avenue	2004
YEOVIL TOWN FC	Yeovil True	2004
YES	Don't Kill The Whale	1978
	Going For The One	1977
	Leave It	1984
	Love Will Find A Way	1987
	Owner Of A Lonely Heart	1983
	Rhythm Of Love	1987
	Roundabout	1972
	Wonderous Stories	1977
	Your Move	1971
YIN & YAN	If	1975

ARTIST	SONG TITLE	DATE
YING YANG TWINS featuring TRICK DADDY		
	Whats Happnin!	2004
YO-YO featuring ICE CUBE		
	You Can't Play With My Yo-Yo	1991
YOMANDA	On The Level	2000
	Sunshine	2000
	Synth & Strings	1999
	You're Free	2003
YORK	The Awakening	1999
	Farewell To The Moon	2000
	On The Beach	2000
	(ATB featuring YORK) The Fields Of Love	2001
YOSH presents LOVEDEEJAY AKEMI		
	It's What's Upfront That Counts	1995
	The Screamer	1996
YOUNG BLACK TEENAGERS		
	Tap The Bottle	1994
YOUNG BUCK	Let Me In	2004
YOUNG DISCIPLES	Apparently Nothin'	1991
YOUNG GUNZ featuring RELL		
	No Better Love	2004
YOUNG M.C.	Bust A Move	1989
	Principal's Office	1989
YOUNG & CO	I Like (What You're Doing To Me)	1980

ARTIST	SONG TITLE	DATE
BARRY YOUNG	One Has My Name (The Other Has My Heart)	1965
FARON YOUNG	It's Four In The Morning	1972
JIMMY YOUNG	Miss You	1963
JOHN PAUL YOUNG	Love Is In The Air	1978
	(MILK & SUGAR vs JOHN PAUL YOUNG)	
	Love Is In The Air	2002
KAREN YOUNG	Hot Shot	1978
	Nobody's Child	1969
NEIL YOUNG	Harvest Moon	1993
	Heart Of Gold	1972
	Old Man	1972
	Only Love Can Break Your Heart	1970
PAUL YOUNG	Come Back And Stay	1984
	Don't Dream It's Over	1991
	Everything Must Change	1984
	Everytime You Go Away	1985
	I Wish You Love	1997
	I'm Gonna Tear Your Playhouse Down	1985
	It Will Be You	1994
	Love Of The Common People	1983
	Now I Know What Made Otis Blue	1993
	Oh Girl	1990
	Softly Whispering I Love You	1990
	Tomb Of Memories	1985
	What Becomes Of The Brokenhearted	1992

ARTIST	SONG TITLE	DATE
	Wherever I Lay My Hat (That's My Home)	1983
	Wonderland	1986
	(ZUCCHERO/PAUL YOUNG)	
	Senza Una Donna (Without A Woman)	1991
RETTA YOUNG	Sending Out An S.O.S.	1975
WILL YOUNG	Don't Let Me Down/You And I	2002
	Evergreen/Anything Is Possible	2002
	Friday's Child	2004
	Leave Right Now	2003
	Light My Fire	2002
	Your Game	2004
WILL YOUNG & GARETH GATES	The Long And Winding Road/Suspicious Minds	2002
YOUNG-HOLT UNLIMITED	Soulful Strut	1968
	Wack Wack	1966
SYDNEY YOUNGBLOOD	If Only I Could	1989
	Sit And Wait	1989
YOUNGBLOODS	Get Together	1969
YOUNG IDEA	With A Little Help From My Friends	1967
HELMUT ZACHARIAS ORCHESTRA	Tokyo Melody	1964
PIA ZADORA	The Clapping Song	1982

ARTIST	SONG TITLE	DATE
ZAGER & EVANS	In The Year 2525 (Exordium & Terminus)	1969
MICHAEL ZAGER BAND		
	Let's All Chant	1978
GEORGHE ZAMFIR	(Light Of Experience) Doina De Jale	1976
FRANK ZAPPA	Valley Girl	1982
LENA ZAVARONI	Ma! (He's Making Eyes At Me)	1974
	(You've Got) Personality	1974
ZED BIAS	Neighbourhood	2000
ZEE	Dreamtime	1996
	Say My Name	1997
ZERO 7 featuring SIA & SOPHIE		
	Destiny	2001
ZERO B	The EP (Brand New Mixes)	1992
CATHERINE ZETA-JONES		
	For All Time	1992
WARREN ZEVON	Werewolves Of London	1978
ZHANE	Groove Thang	1994
	Hey Mr. D.J.	1993
	Request Line	1997
	Sending My Love	1994
	Shame	1994
	(BUSTA RHYMES featuring ZHANE)	
	It's A Party	1996
	(NAUGHTY BY NATURE featuring ZHANE)	
	Jamboree	1999
ZIG AND ZAG	Hands Up! Hands Up!	1995

ARTIST	SONG TITLE	DATE
	Them Girls Them Girls	1994
ZODIAC MINDWARP		
	Prime Mover	1987
ZOE	Lightning	1991
	Sunshine On A Rainy Day	1991
ZOMBIE NATION	Kernkraft 400	2000
ZOMBIES	She's Not There	1964
	Tell Her No	1965
	Time Of The Season	1969
ZUCCHERO WITH LUCIANO PAVAROTTI		
	Miserere	1992
ZUCCHERO/PAUL YOUNG		
	Senza Una Donna (Without A Woman)	1991
ZUTONS	Don't Ever Think (Too Much)	2004
	Pressure Point	2004
	Remember Me	2004
	You Will You Won't	2004
ZWAN	Honestly	2003
ZZ TOP	Doubleback	1990
	Gimme All Your Lovin'	1983
	I Thank You	1980
	Legs	1984
	My Head's In Mississippi	1991
	Pincushion	1994
	Rough Boy	1986
	Sharp Dressed Man	1984

ARTIST	SONG TITLE	DATE	ARTIST	SONG TITLE	DATE
	Sleeping Bag	1985			
	Stages	1986			
	Tush	1975			
	Velcro Fly	1986			
	Viva Las Vegas	1992			
(MARTAY featuring ZZ TOP)					
	Gimme All Your Lovin' 2000	1999			

ARTIST	SONG TITLE	DATE
THE 'A' TEAM	S/Sgt. Barry Sadler	1966
A-BA-NI-BI	Izhar Cohen & Alphabeta	1978
A.D.I.D.A.S.	Korn	1997
A.D.I.D.A.S.	Killer Mike featuring Big Boi	2003
A9	Ariel	2000
AARON'S PARTY (COME GET IT)		
	Aaron Carter	2000
ABACAB	Genesis	1981
ABBA-ESQUE (EP)	Erasure	1992
THE ABBEY ROAD EP	Spiritualized	1998
ABC	Jackson Five	1970
ABC AND D	Blue Bamboo	1994
AN ABHAL AS AIRDE (THE HIGHEST APPLE)		
	Runrig	1995
ABIDE WITH ME	Inspirational Choir	1985
ABIGAIL BEECHER	Freddy Cannon	1964
ABRA-CA-DABRA	Defranco Family	1973
ABRACADABRA	Steve Miller Band	1982
ABRAHAM, MARTIN & JOHN		
	Moms Mabley	1969
ABRAHAM, MARTIN & JOHN		
	Marvin Gaye	1970
ABRAHAM, MARTIN & JOHN		
	Smokey Robinson & The Miracles	1969

ARTIST	SONG TITLE	DATE
ABRAHAM, MARTIN & JOHN		
	Dion	1968
ABSENT FRIENDS	Divine Comedy	2004
ABSOLUTE	Scritti Politti	1984
ABSOLUTE BEGINNERS	David Bowie	1986
ABSOLUTE BEGINNERS	Jam	1981
ABSOLUTE REALITY	Alarm	1985
ABSOLUTELY (STORY OF A GIRL)		
	Nine Days	2000
ABSOLUTELY EVERYBODY	Vanessa Amorosi	2000
ABSOLUTELY FABULOUS	Absolutely Fabulous	1994
ABSOLUTELY RIGHT	Five Man Electrical Band	1971
ABSURD	Fluke	1997
ABUSE ME	Silverchair	1997
ACAPULCO 1922	Kenny Ball	1963
ACCELERATOR	Primal Scream	2000
ACCESS	DJ Misjah And DJ Tim	1996
ACCIDENT PRONE	Status Quo	1978
ACCIDENT WAITING TO HAPPEN (EP)		
	Billy Bragg	1992
ACCIDENTALLY IN LOVE	Counting Crows	2004
ACCIDENTS WILL HAPPEN	Elvis Costello	1979
ACE OF SPADES	Motorhead	1980
ACE OF SPADES (CCN REMIX)		
	Motorhead	1993
ACES HIGH	Iron Maiden	1984

ARTIST	SONG TITLE	DATE
ACHILLES HEEL	Toploader	2000
ACHY BREAKY HEART	Billy Ray Cyrus	1992
ACID MAN	Jolly Roger	1988
ACROSS THE RIVER	Bruce Hornsby & The Range	1990
ACT A FOOL	Ludacris	2003
ACT OF WAR	Elton John & Millie Jackson	1985
ACTION	Def Leppard	1994
ACTION	Sweet	1976
ACTION	Freddy Cannon	1965
ACTIV 8 (COME WITH ME)	Altern 8	1991
ACTUALLY IT'S DARKNESS	Idlewild	2000
ADDAMS GROOVE	Hammer	1991
ADDICTED	Enrique Iglesias	2003
ADDICTED TO BASS	Puretone	2002
ADDICTED TO LOVE	Robert Palmer	1986
ADDICTION	Almighty	1993
ADDICTIVE	Truth Hurts featuring Rakim	2002
ADELANTE	Sash!	2000
ADIA	Sarah McLachlan	1998
ADORED AND EXPLORED	Marc Almond	1995
ADRENALIN (EP)	N-Joi	1991
ADRIENNE	Calling	2002
ADULT EDUCATION	Daryl Hall & John Oates	1984
ADVICE FOR THE YOUNG AT HEART		
	Tears For Fears	1990
AERIALS	System Of A Down	2002

SONG TITLE	ARTIST	DATE
AERODYNAMIK	Kraftwerk	2004
AEROPLANE	Red Hot Chili Peppers	1996
THE AEROPLANE SONG	Straw	1999
AFFAIR OF THE NIGHT	Rick Springfield	1983
AFFIRMATION	Savage Garden	2000
AFRICA	Toto	1982
AFRIKA SHOX	Leftfield/Bambaataa	1999
THE AFRO-LEFT EP	Leftfield featuring DJum DJum	1995
AFRODISIAC	Brandy	2004
AFTER A FASHION	Midge Ure & Mick Karn	1983
AFTER ALL	Frank And Walters	1993
AFTER ALL	Cher & Peter Cetera	1989
AFTER HOURS	Bluetones	2002
AFTER MIDNIGHT	Eric Clapton	1970
AFTER THE FALL	Journey	1983
AFTER THE GLITTER FADES		
	Stevie Nicks	1982
AFTER THE GOLDRUSH	Prelude	1974
AFTER THE LOVE HAS GONE		
	Steps	1999
AFTER THE LOVE HAS GONE		
	Princess	1985
AFTER THE LOVE HAS GONE		
	Earth, Wind & Fire	1979
AFTER THE LOVIN'	Engelbert Humperdinck	1976
AFTER THE RAIN	Nelson	1990

SONG TITLE	ARTIST	DATE
AFTER THE RAIN HAS FALLEN	Sting	2000
AFTER THE WAR	Gary Moore	1989
AFTER THE WATERSHED	Carter The Unstoppable Sex Machine	1991
AFTERGLOW OF YOUR LOVE	Small Faces	1969
AFTERMATH/I'M FOR REAL	Nightmares On Wax	1990
AFTERNOON DELIGHT	Starland Vocal Band	1976
AFTERNOONS & COFFEESPOONS	Crash Test Dummies	1994
AGADOO	Black Lace	1984
AGAIN	Janet Jackson	1993
AGAIN	Lenny Kravitz	2000
AGAIN	Juliet Roberts	1994
AGAIN AND AGAIN	Status Quo	1978
AGAIN TONIGHT	John Mellencamp	1992
AGAINST ALL ODDS	Mariah Carey & Westlife	2000
AGAINST ALL ODDS (TAKE A LOOK AT ME NOW)	Phil Collins	1984
AGAINST THE WIND	Bob Seger & The Silver Bullet Band	1980
AGE OF LONELINESS	Enigma	1994
THE AGE OF LOVE	Age Of Love	1998
AGENT DOUBLE-O-SOUL	Edwin Starr	1965

SONG TITLE	ARTIST	DATE
THE AGONY AND THE ECSTASY	Smokey Robinson	1975
AH! LEAH!	Donnie Iris	1980
AI NO CORRIDA	Quincy Jones	1981
AIN'T 2 PROUD 2 BEG	TLC	1992
AIN'T COMPLAINING	Status Quo	1988
AIN'T EVEN DONE WITH THE NIGHT	John Cougar	1981
AIN'T GOIN' TO GOA	Alabama 3	1998
AIN'T GONNA BUMP NO MORE (WITH NO BIG FAT WOMAN)	Joe Tex	1977
AIN'T GONNA CRY AGAIN	Peter Cox	1997
AIN'T GONNA LIE	Keith	1966
AIN'T GOT NO/I GOT LIFE/DO WHAT YOU GOTTA DO	Nina Simone	1968
AIN'T IT FUN	Guns N' Roses	1993
AIN'T IT FUNKY NOW (PART 1)	James Brown	1969
AIN'T IT FUNNY	Jennifer Lopez	2001
AIN'T IT TRUE	Andy Williams	1965
AIN'T LOVE A BITCH	Rod Stewart	1979
AIN'T NO CASANOVA	Sinclair	1993
AIN'T NO DOUBT	Jimmy Nail	1992
AIN'T NO LOVE (AIN'T NO USE)	Sub Sub featuring Melanie Williams	1993

SONG TITLE	ARTIST	DATE
AIN'T NO LOVE (AIN'T NO USE)		
	Soda Club featuring Ashley Jade	2004
AIN'T NO MAN	Dina Carroll	1992
AIN'T NO MOUNTAIN HIGH ENOUGH		
	Jocelyn Brown	1998
AIN'T NO MOUNTAIN HIGH ENOUGH		
	Diana Ross	1970
AIN'T NO MOUNTAIN HIGH ENOUGH		
	Marvin Gaye & Tammi Terrell	1967
AIN'T NO PLAYA	Jay-Z featuring Foxy Brown	1997
AIN'T NO PLEASING YOU	Chas & Dave	1982
AIN'T NO STOPPIN'	Enigma	1981
AIN'T NO STOPPIN' US	DJ Luck & MC Neat featuring Jj	2000
AIN'T NO STOPPIN' US NOW		
	McFadden & Whitehead	1979
AIN'T NO STOPPING US NOW		
	Luther Vandross	1995
AIN'T NO SUNSHINE	Michael Jackson	1972
AIN'T NO SUNSHINE	Bill Withers	1971
AIN'T NO WAY	Aretha Franklin	1968
AIN'T NO WAY TO TREAT A LADY		
	Helen Reddy	1975
AIN'T NO WOMAN (LIKE THE ONE I'VE GOT)		
	Four Tops	1973
AIN'T NOBODY	Course	1997
AIN'T NOBODY	Rufus & Chaka Khan	1989

SONG TITLE	ARTIST	DATE
AIN'T NOBODY	Diana King	1995
AIN'T NOBODY	LL Cool J	1997
AIN'T NOBODY (LOVES ME BETTER)		
	KWS & Gwen Dickey	1994
AIN'T NOBODY BETTER	Inner City	1989
AIN'T NOTHIN' BUT A HOUSE PARTY		
	Showstoppers	1968
AIN'T NOTHIN' LIKE THE REAL THING		
	Marvin Gaye & Tammi Terrell	1968
AIN'T NOTHING 'BOUT YOU		
	Brooks & Dunn	2001
AIN'T NOTHING GOIN' ON BUT THE RENT		
	Gwen Guthrie	1986
AIN'T NOTHING LIKE THE REAL THING		
	Marcella Detroit & Elton John	1994
AIN'T NOTHING LIKE THE REAL THING		
	Donny & Marie Osmond	1976
AIN'T NOTHING YOU CAN DO		
	Bobby Bland	1964
AIN'T NUTHIN' BUT A SHE THING		
	Salt 'N 'Pepa	1995
AIN'T SHE SWEET	Beatles	1964
AIN'T TALKIN' 'BOUT DUB	Apollo 440	1997
AIN'T THAT A LOT OF LOVE		
	Simply Red	1999
AIN'T THAT A SHAME	Cheap Trick	1979

SONG TITLE	ARTIST	DATE
AIN'T THAT ENOUGH	Teenage Fanclub	1997
AIN'T THAT JUST	Lutricia McNeal	1997
AIN'T THAT LOVING YOU BABY		
	Elvis Presley	1964
AIN'T THAT PECULIAR	Marvin Gaye	1965
AIN'T 2 PROUD 2 BEG	TLC	1992
AIN'T 2 PROUD 2 BEG	Temptations	1966
AIN'T 2 PROUD 2 BEG	Rolling Stones	1974
AIN'T UNDERSTANDING MELLOW		
	Jerry Butler & Brenda Lee Eager	1971
AIN'T WHAT YOU DO	Big Brovaz	2003
AIR HOSTESS	Busted	2004
THE AIR THAT I BREATHE	Hollies	1974
THE AIR THAT I BREATHE	Simply Red	1998
AIR WE BREATHE	Alisha's Attic	1997
AIRHEAD	Girls At Play	2001
AIRPORT	Motors	1978
AIRPORT LOVE THEME (GWEN AND VERN)		
	Vincent Bell	1970
AIRWAVE	Rank 1	2000
AISHA	Death In Vegas	2000
AISY WAISY	Cartoons	1999
AJARE	Way Out West	1997
AL CAPONE	Prince Buster	1967
AL-DI-LA	Ray Charles Singers	1964
ALABAMA SONG	David Bowie	1980

SONG TITLE	ARTIST	DATE
ALANE	Wes	1998
ALARM CALL	Bjork	1998
ALBATROSS	Fleetwood Mac	1968
ALBERT FLASHER	Guess Who	1971
ALCOHOLIC	Starsailor	2001
ALEXANDER GRAHAM BELL		
	Sweet	1971
ALFIE	Cilla Black	1966
ALFIE	Cher	1966
ALFIE	Dionne Warwick	1967
ALIBIS	Sergio Mendes	1984
ALICE (WHO THE X IS ALICE?)		
	Gompie	1995
ALICE I WANT YOU JUST FOR ME		
	Full Force	1985
ALICE LONG	Tommy Boyce & Bobby Hart	1968
ALICE, WHAT'S THE MATTER?		
	Terrorvision	1994
ALIEN	Atlanta Rhythm Section	1981
ALISHA RULES THE WORLD		
	Alisha's Attic	1996
ALIVE	Heliotropic featuring Verna V	1999
ALIVE	Beastie Boys	1999
ALIVE	Pearl Jam	1992
ALIVE	P.O.D.	2002
ALIVE	S Club	2002

SONG TITLE	ARTIST	DATE
ALIVE	Bee Gees	1972
ALIVE & KICKING	East Side Beat	1992
ALIVE & KICKING	Simple Minds	1985
ALIVE AGAIN	Chicago	1978
ALL	James Darren	1967
ALL 'BOUT THE MONEY	Meja	1998
ALL 4 LOVE	Color Me Badd	1991
ALL 4 LOVE (BREAK 4 LOVE 1990)		
	Raze/Lady J	1990
ALL ABOUT EVE	Marxman	1993
ALL ABOUT LOVIN' YOU	Bon Jovi	2003
ALL ABOUT SOUL	Billy Joel	1993
ALL ABOUT US	Peter Andre	1997
ALL ALONE AM I	Brenda Lee	1962
ALL ALONE ON CHRISTMAS		
	Darlene Love	1992
ALL ALONG THE WATCHTOWER		
	Jimi Hendrix Experience	1968
ALL AND ALL	Joyce Sims	1986
ALL APOLOGIES/RAPE ME	Nirvana	1993
ALL AROUND MY HAT	Steeleye Span	1975
ALL AROUND THE TOWN (2ND RE-ENTRY)		
	Jam	1983
ALL AROUND THE WORLD	Northern Line	2000
ALL AROUND THE WORLD	Jam	1977
ALL AROUND THE WORLD	Lisa Stansfield	1990

SONG TITLE	ARTIST	DATE
ALL AROUND THE WORLD	Oasis	1998
ALL BECAUSE OF YOU	Geordie	1973
ALL BY MYSELF	Eric Carmen	1975
ALL BY MYSELF	Celine Dion	1997
ALL CRIED OUT	Allure	1998
ALL CRIED OUT	Alison Moyet	1984
ALL CRIED OUT	Lisa Lisa & Cult Jam With Full Force	1986
ALL DAY AND ALL OF THE NIGHT		
	Kinks	1964
ALL DAY AND ALL OF THE NIGHT		
	Stranglers	1988
ALL DAY MUSIC	War	1971
ALL FALL DOWN	Five Star	1985
ALL FALL DOWN	Lindisfarne	1972
ALL FALL DOWN	Ultravox	1986
ALL FALLS DOWN	Kanye West featuring Syleena Johnson	2004
ALL FIRED UP	Pat Benatar	1988
ALL FOR LEYNA	Billy Joel	1980
ALL FOR LOVE	Bryan Adams/Rod Stewart/Sting	1993
ALL FOR LOVE	Color Me Badd	1991
ALL FOR YOU	Janet Jackson	2001
ALL FOR YOU	Sister Hazel	1997
ALL FUNKED UP	Mother	1

SONG TITLE	ARTIST	DATE
ALL GOOD	De La Soul featuring Chaka Khan	2000
ALL HOOKED UP	All Saints	2001
ALL I ASK OF MYSELF IS THAT I HOLD TOGETHER	Ned's Atomic Dustbin	1995
ALL I ASK OF YOU	Cliff Richard & Sarah Brightman	1986
ALL I DO	Cleptomaniacs featuring Bryan Chambers	2001
ALL I EVER NEED IS YOU	Sonny & Cher	1971
ALL I GAVE	World Party	1993
ALL I HAVE	Jennifer Lopez featuring LL Cool J	2003
ALL I HAVE TO DO IS DREAM	Bobbie Gentry & Glen Campbell	1969
ALL I HAVE TO DO IS DREAM/MISS YOU NIGHTS	Cliff Richard/Phil Everly	1994
ALL I HAVE TO GIVE	Backstreet Boys	1999
ALL I KNOW	Art Garfunkel	1973
(ALL I KNOW) FEELS LIKE FOREVER	Joe Cocker	1992
ALL I NEED	Air	1998
ALL I NEED	Temptations	1967
ALL I NEED	Jack Wagner	1984
ALL I NEED IS A MIRACLE	Mike & The Mechanics	1986

SONG TITLE	ARTIST	DATE
ALL I NEED IS EVERYTHING/JUMP	Aztec Camera	1984
ALL I REALLY WANT TO DO	Byrds	1965
ALL I REALLY WANT TO DO	Cher	1965
ALL I SEE IS YOU	Dusty Springfield	1966
ALL I WANNA DO	Joanne Farrell	1995
ALL I WANNA DO	Tin Tin Out	1997
ALL I WANNA DO	Sheryl Crow	1994
ALL I WANNA DO	Dannii	1997
ALL I WANNA DO	Amy Studt	2004
ALL I WANNA DO IS MAKE LOVE TO YOU	Heart	1990
ALL I WANT	Those 2 Girls	1995
ALL I WANT	Susanna Hoffs	1996
ALL I WANT	Offspring	1997
ALL I WANT	Puressence	1998
ALL I WANT	Skunk Anansie	1996
ALL I WANT	Mis-Teeq	2001
ALL I WANT	Howard Jones	1986
ALL I WANT	702	1997
ALL I WANT	Toad The Wet Sprocket	1992
ALL I WANT FOR CHRISTMAS IS A BEATLE	Dora Bryan	1963

SONG TITLE	ARTIST	DATE
ALL I WANT FOR CHRISTMAS IS YOU		
	Mariah Carey	1994
ALL I WANT IS EVERYTHING		
	Def Leppard	1996
ALL I WANT IS YOU	Bryan Adams	1992
ALL I WANT IS YOU	Roxy Music	1974
ALL I WANT IS YOU	U2	1989
ALL I WANT IS YOU	911	1998
ALL I WANT IS YOU	Bellefire	2002
ALL I WANT TO DO IS ROCK		
	Travis	1997
ALL I WANTED	Kansas	1986
ALL I'M MISSING IS YOU	Glenn Medeiros & Ray Parker Jr.	1990
ALL IN MY HEAD	Kosheen	2003
ALL IS FULL OF LOVE	Bjork	1999
ALL JOIN HANDS	Slade	1984
ALL KINDS OF EVERYTHING		
	Dana	1970
ALL MAPPED OUT	The Departure	2004
ALL MINE	Portishead	1997
ALL MY LIFE	K-Ci & Jojo	1998
ALL MY LIFE	Foo Fighters	2002
ALL MY LIFE	Kenny Rogers	1983
ALL MY LIFE	Linda Ronstadt featuring	
	Aaron Neville	1990

SONG TITLE	ARTIST	DATE
ALL MY LOVE	Cliff Richard	1967
ALL MY LOVE	Queen Pen featuring	
	Eric Williams	1998
ALL MY LOVING	Dowlands	1964
ALL MY TRIALS	Paul McCartney	1990
ALL N MY GRILL	Missy 'Misdemeanor' Elliott/	
	MC Solaar	1999
ALL NIGHT ALL RIGHT	Peter Andre featuring Warren G	1998
ALL NIGHT HOLIDAY	Russ Abbot	1985
ALL NIGHT LONG	Faith Evans featuring	
	Puff Daddy	1999
ALL NIGHT LONG	Mary Jane Girls	1983
ALL NIGHT LONG	Rainbow	1980
ALL NIGHT LONG	Joe Walsh	1980
ALL NIGHT LONG (ALL NIGHT)		
	Lionel Richie	1983
ALL NITE (DON'T STOP)/I WANT YOU		
	Janet	2004
(ALL OF A SUDDEN) MY HEART SINGS		
	Mel Carter	1965
ALL OF ME	Sabrina	1988
ALL OF ME LOVES ALL OF YOU		
	Bay City Rollers	1974
ALL OF MY HEART	ABC	1982
ALL OF MY LIFE	Diana Ross	1974

SONG TITLE	ARTIST	DATE
ALL OF YOU	Julio Iglesias & Diana Ross	1984
ALL OF YOUR DAYS WILL BE BLESSED		
	Ed Harcourt	2003
ALL OR NOTHING	Cher	1999
ALL OR NOTHING	Small Faces	1966
ALL OR NOTHING	O-Town	2001
ALL OR NOTHING	Milli Vanilli	1990
ALL OUT OF LOVE	Air Supply	1980
ALL OUT OF LOVE	OTT	1997
ALL OUT OF LOVE	H & Claire	2002
ALL OUT OF LOVE	Foundation featuring Natalie Rossi	2003
ALL OUT TOMORROWS	Eddie Schwartz	1981
ALL OVER	Lisa Maffia	2003
ALL OVER THE WORLD	Electric Light Orchestra	1980
ALL OVER THE WORLD	Francoise Hardy	1965
ALL OVER YOU	Level 42	1994
ALL POSSIBILITIES	Badly Drawn Boy	2003
ALL RIGHT	Christopher Cross	1983
ALL RIGHT NOW	Free	1970
ALL RIGHT NOW	Lemonescent	2004
ALL RISE	Blue	2001
ALL SHE WANTS IS	Duran Duran	1988
ALL SHE WANTS TO DO IS DANCE		
	Don Henley	1985
ALL SHOOK UP	Billy Joel	1992

SONG TITLE	ARTIST	DATE
ALL STAR	Smash Mouth	1999
ALL STOOD STILL	Ultravox	1981
ALL STRUNG OUT	Nino Tempo & April Stevens	1966
ALL STRUNG OUT ON YOU	John Travolta	1977
ALL SUSSED OUT	Almighty	1996
ALL THAT I AM	Elvis Presley	1966
ALL THAT I CAN SAY	Mary J. Blige	1999
ALL THAT I GOT IS YOU	Ghostface Killah	1997
ALL THAT I NEED	Boyzone	1998
ALL THAT MATTERED (LOVE YOU DOWN)		
	De Nuit	2002
ALL THAT MATTERS	Louise	1998
ALL THAT SHE WANTS	Ace Of Base	1993
ALL THE KING'S HORSES	Aretha Franklin	1972
ALL THE LOVE IN THE WORLD		
	Consortium	1969
ALL THE LOVE IN THE WORLD		
	Dionne Warwick	1982
ALL THE LOVE IN THE WORLD		
	Outfield	1986
ALL THE MAN THAT I NEED		
	Whitney Houston	1990
ALL THE PLACES (I WILL KISS YOU)		
	Aaron Hall	1998
ALL THE SMALL THINGS	Blink-182	1999

SONG TITLE	ARTIST	DATE
ALL THE THINGS (YOUR MAN WON'T DO)		
	Joe	1996
ALL THE THINGS SHE SAID	Simple Minds	1986
ALL THE THINGS SHE SAID	t.A.T.u.	2003
ALL THE WAY FROM MEMPHIS		
	Mott The Hoople	1973
ALL THE WAY TO RENO	R.E.M.	2001
ALL THE YOUNG DUDES	Bruce Dickinson	1990
ALL THE YOUNG DUDES	Mott The Hoople	1972
ALL THESE THINGS THAT I'VE DONE		
	The Killers	2004
ALL THIS LOVE	Debarge	1983
ALL THIS LOVE I'M GIVING		
	Music & Mystery/Gwen McCrae	1993
ALL THIS TIME	Sting	1991
ALL THIS TIME	Michelle	2004
ALL THIS TIME	Tiffany	1988
ALL THOSE YEARS AGO	George Harrison	1981
ALL THROUGH THE NIGHT	Cyndi Lauper	1984
ALL THRU THE NITE	POV featuring Jade	1994
ALL TIME HIGH	Rita Coolidge	1983
ALL TOGETHER NOW	Everton FC	1995
ALL TOGETHER NOW	Farm	1990
ALL TOGETHER NOW 2004	Farm featuring SFX Boys Choir,	
	Liverpool	2004

SONG TITLE	ARTIST	DATE
ALL TOMORROW'S PARTIES	Japan	1983
ALL TRUE MAN	Alexander O'Neal	1991
ALL WOMAN	Lisa Stansfield	1991
ALL YOU EVER DO	Violent Delight	2003
ALL YOU GET FROM LOVE IS A LOVE SONG		
	Carpenters	1977
ALL YOU GOOD GOOD PEOPLE (EP)		
	Embrace	1997
ALL YOU NEED IS LOVE	Beatles	1967
ALL YOU NEED IS LOVE	Tom Jones	1993
ALL YOU WANTED	Michelle Branch	2002
ALLENTOWN	Billy Joel	1982
THE ALLEY CAT SONG	David Thorne	1963
ALLY'S TARTAN ARMY	Andy Cameron	1978
ALMA MATTERS	Morrissey	1997
ALMAZ	Randy Crawford	1986
ALMOST DOESN'T COUNT	Brandy	1999
ALMOST HEAR YOU SIGH	Rolling Stones	1990
ALMOST LIKE BEING IN LOVE		
	Michael Johnson	1978
ALMOST OVER YOU	Sheena Easton	1983
ALMOST PARADISE... LOVE THEME FROM FOOTLOOSE		
	Mike Reno/Ann Wilson	1984
ALMOST PERSUADED	David Houston	1966
ALMOST SEE YOU (SOMEWHERE)		
	China Black	1995

SONG TITLE	ARTIST	DATE
ALMOST SUMMER	Celebration/Mike Love	1978
ALMOST THERE	Andy Williams	1965
ALMOST UNREAL	Roxette	1993
ALONE	Big Country	1993
ALONE	Bee Gees	1997
ALONE	Heart	1987
ALONE	Lasgo	2002
ALONE	Four Seasons	1964
ALONE AGAIN (NATURALLY)		
	Gilbert O'Sullivan	1972
ALONE AGAIN OR	Damned	1987
ALONE WITH YOU	Texas	1992
ALONE WITHOUT YOU	King	1985
ALONE WITHOUT YOU	Mark Owen	2003
ALONG CAME JONES	Ray Stevens	1969
ALONG COMES A WOMAN	Chicago	1985
ALONG COMES MARY	Association	1966
ALPHABET STREET	Prince	1988
ALREADY GONE	Eagles	1974
ALRIGHT	Cast	1995
ALRIGHT	Janet Jackson	1990
ALRIGHT	Jamiroquai	1997
ALRIGHT	Kris Kross	1993
ALRIGHT BABY	Stevenson's Rocket	1975
ALRIGHT, ALRIGHT, ALRIGHT		
	Mungo Jerry	1973

SONG TITLE	ARTIST	DATE
ALRIGHT/TIME	Supergrass	1995
ALSO SPRACH ZARATHUSTRA (2001)		
	Deodato	1973
ALTERNATE TITLE	Monkees	1967
ALWAYS	Atlantic Starr	1987
ALWAYS	Bon Jovi	1994
ALWAYS	Erasure	1994
ALWAYS AND FOREVER	Luther Vandross	1995
ALWAYS AND FOREVER	Whistle	1990
ALWAYS AND FOREVER	Heatwave	1978
ALWAYS BE MY BABY	Mariah Carey	1996
ALWAYS BREAKING MY HEART		
	Belinda Carlisle	1996
ALWAYS COME BACK TO YOUR LOVE		
	Samantha Mumba	2001
ALWAYS HAVE, ALWAYS WILL		
	Ace Of Base	1998
ALWAYS IN MY HEART	Tevin Campbell	1994
ALWAYS LOOK ON THE BRIGHT SIDE		
	Monty Python	1991
ALWAYS LOOK ON THE BRIGHT SIDE OF LIFE/		
SOMETHING STUPID	Coronation Street Cast – Barrie/Briggs	1995
ALWAYS ON MY MIND	Pet Shop Boys	1988
ALWAYS ON MY MIND	Elvis Presley	1972
ALWAYS ON MY MIND	Willie Nelson	1982

SONG TITLE	ARTIST	DATE
ALWAYS ON TIME	Ja Rule featuring Ashanti	2001
ALWAYS REMEMBER TO RESPECT AND HONOUR YOUR		
MOTHER	Dusted	2001
ALWAYS SOMETHING THERE TO REMIND ME		
	Tin Tin Out/Espiritu	1995
ALWAYS SOMETHING THERE TO REMIND ME		
	R.B. Greaves	1970
ALWAYS THE LAST TO KNOW		
	Del Amitri	1992
ALWAYS THE SUN	Stranglers	1991
ALWAYS THERE	Marti Webb	1986
ALWAYS THERE	Incognito featuring	
	Jocelyn Brown	1991
ALWAYS TOGETHER	Dells	1968
ALWAYS TOGETHER	Al Martino	1964
ALWAYS TOMORROW	Gloria Estefan	1992
ALWAYS YOUR WAY	My Vitriol	2001
ALWAYS YOURS	Gary Glitter	1974
AM I DREAMING	Ol' Skool (featuring Keith Sweat	
	& Xscape)	1998
AM I ON YOUR MIND	Oxygen featuring	
	Andrea Britton	2003
AM I RIGHT?	Erasure	1991
AM I THAT EASY TO FORGET		
	Engelbert Humperdinck	1967
AM I THE SAME GIRL?	Swing Out Sister	1992

SONG TITLE	ARTIST	DATE
AM TO PM	Christina Milian	2001
AMANDA	Stuart Gillies	1973
AMANDA	Craig McLachlan & Check 1-2	1990
AMANDA	Boston	1986
AMATEUR HOUR	Sparks	1974
AMAZED	Lonestar	1999
AMAZING	George Michael	2004
AMAZING	Aerosmith	1993
AMAZING GRACE	Judy Collins	1970
AMAZING GRACE	Royal Scots Dragoon Guards	1972
AMEN	Impressions	1964
AMEN	Otis Redding	1968
AMERICA	Nice	1968
AMERICA	David Essex	1974
AMERICA	Simon & Garfunkel	1972
AMERICA	Neil Diamond	1981
AMERICA (I LOVE AMERICA)		
	Full Intention	1996
AMERICA: WHAT TIME IS LOVE?		
	KLF	1992
AMERICAN BAD ASS	Kid Rock	2000
AMERICAN CITY SUITE	Cashman & West	1972
AMERICAN DREAM	Jakatta	2001
AN AMERICAN DREAM	Nitty Gritty Dirt Band	1979
AMERICAN ENGLISH	Idlewild	2002

SONG TITLE	ARTIST	DATE
AMERICAN GIRL	Tom Petty & The Heartbreakers	1977
AMERICAN GIRLS	Counting Crows	2002
AMERICAN HEARTBEAT	Survivor	1982
AMERICAN IDIOT	Green Day	2004
AMERICAN LIFE	Madonna	2003
AMERICAN MUSIC	Pointer Sisters	1982
AMERICAN PIE	Just Luis	1995
AMERICAN PIE	Madonna	2000
AMERICAN PIE (PTS 1 & 2)	Don McLean	1971
AMERICAN SOLDIER	Toby Keith	2003
AMERICAN STORM	Bob Seger & The Silver Bullet Band	1986
AN AMERICAN TRILOGY	Elvis Presley	1972
AN AMERICAN TRILOGY	Mickey Newbury	1971
AMERICAN TUNE	Paul Simon	1973
AMERICAN WOMAN/NO SUGAR TONIGHT	Guess Who	1970
AMERICANOS	Holly Johnson	1989
AMERICANS	Byron Macgregor	1974
THE AMERICANS (A CANADIAN'S OPINION)	Gordon Sinclair	1974
AMERIKA	Rammstein	2004
AMIE	Pure Prairie League	1975
AMIGO	Black Slate	1980

SONG TITLE	ARTIST	DATE
AMIGOS PARA SIEMPRE	Jose Carreras & Sarah Brightman	1992
AMITYVILLE (THE HOUSE ON THE HILL)	Lovebug Starski	1986
AMNESIA	Chumbawamba	1998
AMOR	Julio Iglesias	1982
AMOS MOSES	Jerry Reed	1970
AMOUR (C'MON)	Porn Kings	1997
THE AMSTERDAM EP	Simple Minds	1989
ANARCHY IN THE UK	Sex Pistols	1992
ANARCHY IN THE UK	Green Jelly	1993
ANASTHASIA	T99	1991
AND GET AWAY	Esquires	1967
AND I LOVE HER	Beatles	1964
AND I LOVE YOU SO	Perry Como	1973
AND I'M TELLING YOU I'M NOT GOING	Donna Giles	1996
AND I'M TELLING YOU I'M NOT GOING	Jennifer Holliday	1982
AND OUR FEELINGS	Babyface	1994
... AND ROSES AND ROSES	Andy Williams	1965
AND SHE WAS	Talking Heads	1986
AND SO IS LOVE	Kate Bush	1994
AND SO IT GOES	Billy Joel	1990
AND THE BANDS PLAYED ON	Saxon	1981

SONG TITLE	ARTIST	DATE
AND THE BEAT GOES ON	Whispers	1980
AND THE SUN WILL SHINE	Jose Feliciano	1969
(AND THE) PICTURES IN THE SKY		
	Medicine Head	1971
AND THEN SHE KISSED ME		
	Gary Glitter	1981
AND WE DANCED	Hooters	1985
AND WHEN I DIE	Blood Sweat & Tears	1969
AND YOU SMILED	Matt Monro	1973
ANDRES	L7	1994
ANDROGYNY	Garbage	2001
ANFIELD RAP (RED MACHINE IN FULL EFFECT)		
	Liverpool F.C.	1988
ANGEL	Eurythmics	1990
ANGEL	Jon Secada	1993
ANGEL	Massive Attack	1998
ANGEL	Sarah McLachlan	1998
ANGEL	Madonna	1985
ANGEL	Simply Red	1996
ANGEL	Ralph Fridge	2000
ANGEL	Lionel Richie	2000
ANGEL	Shaggy featuring Rayvon	2001
ANGEL	Aretha Franklin	1973
ANGEL	Corrs	2004
ANGEL	Aerosmith	1988
ANGEL	Rod Stewart	1972

SONG TITLE	ARTIST	DATE
ANGEL (LADADI O-HEYO)	Jam & Spoon featuring Plavka	1995
THE ANGEL AND THE GAMBLER		
	Iron Maiden	1998
ANGEL BABY	Angelica	1991
ANGEL EYES	Roxy Music	1979
ANGEL EYES	Jeff Healey Band	1989
ANGEL EYES (HOME AND AWAY)		
	Wet Wet Wet	1987
ANGEL EYES/VOULEZ VOUS	ABBA	1979
ANGEL FACE	Glitter Band	1974
ANGEL FINGERS (A TEEN BALLAD)		
	Wizzard	1973
ANGEL IN BLUE	J. Geils Band	1982
ANGEL IN YOUR ARMS	Hot	1977
ANGEL INTERCEPTOR	Ash	1995
ANGEL OF HARLEM	U2	1989
ANGEL OF MINE	Eternal	1997
ANGEL OF MINE	Monica	1998
ANGEL OF THE MORNING	P.P. Arnold	1968
ANGEL OF THE MORNING	Juice Newton	1981
ANGEL OF THE MORNING	Merrilee Rush	1968
ANGEL OF THE MORNING – ANY WAY THAT YOU WANT ME (MEDLEY)	Mary Mason	1977
THE ANGEL SONG	Great White	1989
ANGEL ST	M People	1998

SONG TITLE	ARTIST	DATE
ANGEL/WHAT MADE MILWAUKEE FAMOUS		
	Rod Stewart	1972
ANGELIA	Richard Marx	1989
ANGELO	Brotherhood Of Man	1977
ANGELS	Robbie Williams	1997
ANGELS DON'T LIE	Jim Reeves	1970
ANGELS GO BALD: TOO	Howie B	1997
ANGELS SAY NO	Tommy Tutone	1980
ANGELS WITH DIRTY FACES		
	Sham 69	1978
ANGIE	Rolling Stones	1973
ANGIE BABY	Helen Reddy	1974
ANGRY ALL THE TIME	Tim McGraw	2001
ANGRY AT THE BIG OAK TREE		
	Frank Ifield	1964
ANGRY CHAIR	Alice In Chains	1993
ANIMAL	Def Leppard	1987
ANIMAL	R.E.M.	2004
ANIMAL ARMY	Babylon Zoo	1996
ANIMAL NITRATE	Suede	1993
THE ANIMAL SONG	Savage Garden	1999
ANNABELLA	John Walker	1967
ANNIE I'M NOT YOUR DADDY		
	Kid Creole & The Coconuts	1982
ANNIE'S SONG	John Denver	1974
ANNIE'S SONG	James Galway	1978

SONG TITLE	ARTIST	DATE
ANNIVERSARY	Tony Toni Tone	1993
ANNIVERSARY WALTZ	Anita Harris	1968
THE ANNIVERSARY WALTZ	Status Quo	1990
ANOTHER BODY MURDERED		
	Faith No More/Boo-Yaa Tribe	1993
ANOTHER BRICK IN THE WALL		
	Pink Floyd	1980
ANOTHER CHANCE	Roger Sanchez	2001
ANOTHER DAY	Whigfield	1994
ANOTHER DAY	Lemar	2004
ANOTHER DAY IN PARADISE		
	Phil Collins	1989
ANOTHER DAY IN PARADISE		
	Brandy & Ray J	2001
ANOTHER DAY IN PARADISE		
	Jam Tronik	1990
ANOTHER DAY/OH WOMAN OH WHY OH WHY		
	Paul McCartney	1971
ANOTHER DUMB BLONDE	Hoku	2000
ANOTHER FUNNY HONEYMOON		
	David Dundas	1977
ANOTHER LOVER	Dane Bowers	2001
ANOTHER LOVER	Giant Steps	1988
ANOTHER NAIL IN MY HEART		
	Squeeze	1980
ANOTHER NIGHT	Jason Donovan	1990

SONG TITLE	ARTIST	DATE
ANOTHER NIGHT	(MC Sar &) The Real McCoy	1994
ANOTHER NIGHT	Aretha Franklin	1986
ANOTHER ONE BITES THE DUST	Queen	1980
ANOTHER PARK, ANOTHER SUNDAY	Doobie Brothers	1974
ANOTHER PART OF ME	Michael Jackson	1988
ANOTHER RAINY DAY IN NEW YORK CITY	Chicago	1976
ANOTHER ROCK AND ROLL CHRISTMAS	Gary Glitter	1984
ANOTHER SAD LOVE SONG	Toni Braxton	1993
ANOTHER SATURDAY NIGHT	Sam Cooke	1963
ANOTHER SATURDAY NIGHT	Cat Stevens	1974
ANOTHER STAR	Stevie Wonder	1977
ANOTHER STEP (CLOSER TO YOU)	Kim Wilde & Junior	1987
ANOTHER SUITCASE IN ANOTHER HALL	Barbara Dickson	1977
ANOTHER SUITCASE IN ANOTHER HALL	Madonna	1997
ANOTHER TEAR FALLS	Walker Brothers	1966
ANOTHER TIME, ANOTHER PLACE	Engelbert Humperdinck	1971

SONG TITLE	ARTIST	DATE
ANOTHER WAY/AVENUE	Paul Van Dyk	1999
ANOTHER WEEKEND	Five Star	1988
ANOTHERLOVERHOLENYOHEAD	Prince	1986
ANSWER ME	Barbara Dickson	1976
THE ANSWER TO WHY I HATE YOU	Symposium	1997
ANSWERING BELL	Ryan Adams	2002
ANSWERING MACHINE	Rupert Holmes	1980
ANT RAP	Adam & The Ants	1981
ANTE UP	M.O.P. featuring Busta Rhymes	2001
ANTHEM	Wildhearts	1997
ANTHEM	N-Joi	1991
ANTHEM (ONE DAY IN EVERY WEEK)	New Seekers	1978
THE ANTHEM	Good Charlotte	2003
ANTICIPATION	Carly Simon	1971
ANTMUSIC	Adam & The Ants	1980
ANY DAY NOW	Ronnie Milsap	1982
ANY DREAM WILL DO	Jason Donovan	1991
ANY LOVE	Luther Vandross	1988
ANY MAN OF MINE/WHOSE BED HAVE YOUR BOOTS BEEN UNDER	Shania Twain	1995
ANY MINUTE NOW	Soulwax	2004
ANY ROAD	George Harrison	2003

SONG TITLE	ARTIST	DATE
ANY TIME, ANY PLACE/AND ON AND ON		
	Janet Jackson	1994
ANY WAY THAT YOU WANT ME		
	Troggs	1966
ANY WAY YOU LOOK	Northern Uproar	1997
ANY WAY YOU WANT IT	Dave Clark Five	1964
ANY WAY YOU WANT IT	Journey	1980
ANYBODY SEEN MY BABY?	Rolling Stones	1997
ANYMORE	Sarah Cracknell	1996
ANYONE CAN FALL IN LOVE		
	Anita Dobson	1986
ANYONE CAN PLAY GUITAR		
	Radiohead	1993
ANYONE ELSE	Collin Raye	1999
ANYONE FOR TENNIS (THE SAVAGE SEVEN THEME)		
	Cream	1968
ANYONE OF US (STUPID MISTAKE)		
	Gareth Gates	2002
ANYONE WHO HAD A HEART		
	Cilla Black	1964
ANYTHING	SWV	1994
ANYTHING	Damned	1986
ANYTHING	Culture Beat	1994
ANYTHING	3T	1995
ANYTHING	Jay-Z	2000
ANYTHING	Jaheim featuring Next	2002

SONG TITLE	ARTIST	DATE
ANYTHING BUT DOWN	Sheryl Crow	1999
ANYTHING FOR YOU	Gloria Estefan & The Miami	
	Sound Machine	1988
ANYTHING FOR YOU	Stamford Amp	2002
ANYTHING GOES	Harpers Bizarre	1967
ANYTHING I WANT	Kevin Paige	1990
ANYTHING IS POSSIBLE	Debbie Gibson	1990
ANYTHING THAT'S ROCK'N'ROLL		
	Tom Petty & The Heartbreakers	1977
ANYTHING YOU WANT	John Valenti	1976
ANYTIME (I'LL BE THERE)	Paul Anka	1976
ANYTIME YOU NEED A FRIEND		
	Mariah Carey	1994
ANYWAY ANYHOW ANYWHERE		
	Who	1965
ANYWAY YOU WANT IT	Dave Clark Five	1964
ANYWHERE	Dubstar	1995
ANYWHERE	112 featuring Lil'z	1999
ANYWHERE FOR YOU	Backstreet Boys	1997
ANYWHERE IS	Enya	1995
APACHE	Starfighter	2000
APACHE DROPOUT	Edgar Broughton Band	1971
APE MAN	Kinks	1970
APOLLO 9	Adam Ant	1984
APPARENTLY NOTHIN'	Young Disciples	1991
APPARENTLY NOTHING	Brand New Heavies	2000

SONG TITLE	ARTIST	DATE
APPLE OF MY EYE	Roy Head & The Traits	1965
APPLEJACK	Jet Harris & Tony Meehan	1963
APPLES PEACHES PUMPKIN PIE		
	Jay & The Techniques	1967
THE APRIL FOOLS	Dionne Warwick	1969
APRIL SKIES	Jesus And Mary Chain	1987
AQUARIUS/LET THE SUNSHINE IN (MEDLEY)		
	5th Dimension	1969
ARABIAN KNIGHTS	Siouxsie & The Banshees	1981
ARE 'FRIENDS' ELECTRIC?	Tubeway Army	1979
ARE U STILL DOWN	Jon B.	1998
ARE WE HERE?	Orbital	1994
ARE WE OURSELVES?	Fixx	1984
ARE YOU BEING SERVED SIR?		
	John Inman	1975
ARE YOU BLUE OR ARE YOU BLIND?		
	Bluetones	1995
ARE YOU DREAMING?	Twenty 4 Seven	1990
ARE YOU GETTING ENOUGH OF WHAT MAKES YOU		
HAPPY	Hot Chocolate	1980
ARE YOU GONNA BE MY GIRL?		
	Jet	2003
ARE YOU GONNA BE THERE?		
	Up Yer Ronson	1996
ARE YOU GONNA GO MY WAY		
	Lenny Kravitz	1993

SONG TITLE	ARTIST	DATE
ARE YOU HAPPY	Jerry Butler	1968
ARE YOU HAPPY NOW?	Michelle Branch	2003
ARE YOU IN?	Incubus	2002
ARE YOU JIMMY RAY?	Jimmy Ray	1998
ARE YOU LONELY FOR ME	Freddie Scott	1966
ARE YOU LONESOME TONIGHT (LIVE)		
	Elvis Presley	1982
ARE YOU LONESOME TONIGHT/WHEN I FALL IN LOVE		
	Donny Osmond	1973
ARE YOU LOOKIN' AT ME?	Ricky Tomlinson	2001
ARE YOU MAN ENOUGH	Four Tops	1973
ARE YOU MINE?	Bros	1991
ARE YOU OUT THERE	Crescendo	1995
ARE YOU READY	Break Machine	1984
ARE YOU READY	Pacific Gas & Electric	1970
ARE YOU READY FOR LOVE?		
	Elton John	2003
ARE YOU READY FOR SOME MORE?		
	Reel 2 Real	1996
ARE YOU READY TO FLY	Rozalla	1992
ARE YOU READY TO PARTY		
	Shrink	2000
ARE YOU READY TO ROCK	Wizzard	1974
(ARE YOU READY) DO THE BUS STOP		
	Fatback Band	1975
ARE YOU READY?	AC/DC	1991

SONG TITLE	ARTIST	DATE
ARE YOU STILL HAVING FUN		
	Eagle-Eye Cherry	2000
ARE YOU THAT SOMEBODY?		
	Aaliyah	1998
ARE YOU THERE (WITH ANOTHER GIRL)		
	Dionne Warwick	1965
AREA CODES	Ludacris featuring Nate Dogg	2001
ARGENTINA	Jeremy Healy & Amos	1997
ARGENTINE MELODY (CANCION DE ARGENTINA)		
	San Jose	1978
ARIA	Acker Bilk	1976
ARIEL	Dean Friedman	1977
ARIENNE	Tasmin Archer	1993
ARIZONA	Mark Lindsay	1969
ARMAGEDDON IT	Def Leppard	1988
ARMED & EXTREMELY DANGEROUS		
	First Choice	1973
ARMS AROUND THE WORLD		
	Louise	1997
ARMS OF LOREN	E'voke	1996
ARMS OF MARY	Sutherland Brothers And Quiver	1976
THE ARMS OF ORION	Prince With Sheena Easton	1989
THE ARMS OF THE ONE WHO LOVES YOU		
	Xscape	1998
ARMY	Ben Folds Five	1999

SONG TITLE	ARTIST	DATE
ARMY DREAMERS	Kate Bush	1980
ARMY OF ME	Bjork	1995
ARMY OF TWO	Dum Dums	2001
ARNOLD LAYNE	Pink Floyd	1967
AROUND THE WAY GIRL	LL Cool J	1991
AROUND THE WORLD	Red Hot Chili Peppers	1999
AROUND THE WORLD	Aqua	2000
AROUND THE WORLD	East 17	1994
AROUND THE WORLD	Daft Punk	1997
AROUND THE WORLD (LA LA LA LA LA)		
	ATC	2001
ARRANGED MARRIAGE	Apache Indian	1993
ARROW THROUGH ME	Paul McCartney	1979
ART FOR ART'S SAKE	10cc	1975
ARTHUR DALEY ('E'S ALRIGHT)		
	Firm	1982
ARTHUR'S THEME (BEST THAT YOU CAN DO)		
	Christopher Cross	1981
AS	George Michael & Mary J. Blige	1999
AS	Stevie Wonder	1977
AS GOOD AS IT GETS	Gene	1999
AS I LAY ME DOWN	Sophie B. Hawkins	1995
AS IF WE NEVER SAID GOODBYE		
	Barbra Streisand	1994

SONG TITLE	ARTIST	DATE
AS LONG AS THE PRICE IS RIGHT		
	Dr. Feelgood	1979
AS LONG AS YOU LOVE ME		
	Backstreet Boys	1997
AS TEARS GO BY	Marianne Faithfull	1964
AS TEARS GO BY	Rolling Stones	1965
AS THE RUSH COMES	Motorcycle	2004
AS THE YEARS GO BY	Mashmakhan	1970
AS TIME GOES BY	Jason Donovan	1992
AS TIME GOES BY	Dooley Wilson	1977
AS USUAL	Brenda Lee	1963
AS WE LAY	Shirley Murdock	1987
ASCENSION (DON'T EVER WONDER)		
	Maxwell	1996
ASHES BY NOW	Rodney Crowell	1980
ASHES TO ASHES	Faith No More	1997
ASHES TO ASHES	David Bowie	1980
ASHES TO ASHES	Mindbenders	1966
ASK	Smiths	1986
ASK ME	Elvis Presley	1964
ASK ME NO QUESTIONS	B.B. King	1971
ASK ME WHAT YOU WANT		
	Millie Jackson	1972
ASK OF YOU	Raphael Saadiq	1995
ASK THE LONELY	Four Tops	1965

SONG TITLE	ARTIST	DATE
ASLEEP IN THE BACK/COMING SECOND		
	Elbow	2002
ASSASSIN	Orb	1992
ASSASSING	Marillion	1984
ASSESSMENT	Beta Band	2004
ASTOUNDED	Bran Van 3000 featuring	
	Curtis Mayfield	2001
ASTRAL AMERICA	Apollo 440	1994
ASYLUM	Orb	1997
AT MIDNIGHT (MY LOVE WILL LIFT YOU UP)		
	Rufus/Chaka Khan	1977
AT MY MOST BEAUTIFUL	R.E.M.	1999
AT NIGHT	Shakedown	2002
AT SEVENTEEN	Janis Ian	1975
AT THE CLUB	Drifters	1972
AT THE EDGE	Stiff Little Fingers	1980
AT THE END	110	2003
AT THE HOP	Danny & The Juniors	1976
AT THE RIVER	Groove Armada	1999
AT THE SCENE	Dave Clark Five	1966
AT THE TOP OF THE STAIRS		
	Formations	1971
AT THE ZOO	Simon & Garfunkel	1967
AT THIS MOMENT	Billy Vera & The Beaters	1986
AT THIS TIME OF YEAR	Craig	2000

SONG TITLE	ARTIST	DATE
AT YOUR BEST (YOU ARE LOVE)		
	Aaliyah	1994
ATHENA	Who	1982
ATLANTA LADY (SOMETHING ABOUT YOUR LOVE)		
	Marty Balin	1981
ATLANTIS	Donovan	1969
ATLANTIS	Shadows	1963
ATLIENS	Outkast	1996
ATMOSPHERE	Russ Abbot	1984
ATMOSPHERE	Joy Division	1988
ATOM BOMB	Fluke	1996
ATOMIC	Blondie	1980
ATOMIC CITY	Holly Johnson	1989
ATTACK	Toys	1965
ATTENTION TO ME	Nolans	1981
ATTITUDE/GOLDEN GUN	Suede	2003
ATTITUDE DANCING	Carly Simon	1975
AUBERGE	Chris Rea	1991
AUBREY	Bread	1973
AULD LANG SYNE	Kenny G	1999
AUSTIN	Blake Shelton	2001
AUSTRALIA	Manic Street Preachers	1996
AUTHORITY SONG	John Cougar Mellencamp	1984
AUTOBAHN	Kraftwerk	1975
AUTODRIVE	Herbie Hancock	1983
AUTOMATIC	Pointer Sisters	1984

SONG TITLE	ARTIST	DATE
AUTOMATIC	Sarah Whatmore	2003
AUTOMATIC HIGH	S Club Juniors	2002
AUTOMATIC LOVER	Dee D. Jackson	1978
AUTOMATIC LOVER	Vibrators	1978
AUTOMATIC MAN	Michael Sembello	1983
AUTOMATICALLY SUNSHINE		
	Supremes	1972
AUTOPHILIA	Bluetones	2000
AUTUMN ALMANAC	Kinks	1967
AUTUMN OF MY LIFE	Bobby Goldsboro	1968
AVA ADORE	Smashing Pumpkins	1998
AVALON	Roxy Music	1982
AVE MARIA	Lesley Garrett & Amanda Thompson	1993
AVENGING ANGELS	Space	1998
AVENUE	Saint Etienne	1992
AVENUES	Refugee Camp Allstars featuring Pras (With Ky-Mani)	1997
AVENUES AND ALLEYWAYS		
	Tony Christie	1973
AVERAGE MAN	Turin Brakes	2003
THE AWAKENING	York	1999
AXEL F	Harold Faltermeyer	1985
AXEL F/KEEP PUSHIN'	Clock	1995
AY AY AY AY MOOSEY	Modern Romance	1981
AYLA	Ayla	1999

SONG TITLE	ARTIST	DATE
B 2 GETHER	Original	1995
B WITH ME	Mis-Teeq	2002
B WITH U	Junior Sanchez featuring Dajae	1999
B-A-B-Y	Rachel Sweet	1978
B-A-B-Y	Carla Thomas	1966
B-BOY STANCE	Freestylers featuring Tenor Fly	1998
B.B.D. (I THOUGHT IT WAS ME)	Bell Biv Devoe	1990
BA-NA-NA-BAM-BOO	Westworld	1987
BAAL'S HYMN (EP)	David Bowie	1982
BABALON A.D. (SO GLAD FOR THE MADNESS)	Cradle Of Filth	2003
BABARABATIRI	Gypsymen	2001
BABE	Styx	1979
BABE	Take That	1993
BABOOSHKA	Kate Bush	1980
BABY	Rozalla	1995
BABY	Ashanti	2002
BABY	Brandy	1995
THE BABY	Hollies	1972
THE BABY	Blake Shelton	2002
BABY BABY	Corona	1995
BABY BABY	Amy Grant	1991
BABY-BABY-BABY	TLC	1992
BABY, BABY DON'T YOU CRY	Smokey Robinson & The Miracles	1969

SONG TITLE	ARTIST	DATE
BABY, BABY MY LOVE'S ALL FOR YOU	Deniece Williams	1977
BABY BE MINE	Blackstreet featuring Teddy Riley	1993
BABY BLUE	Badfinger	1972
BABY BOY	Big Brovaz	2003
BABY BOY	Beyonce featuring Sean Paul	2003
BABY CAN I HOLD YOU/SHOOTING STAR	Boyzone	1997
BABY COME BACK	Equals	1968
BABY COME BACK	Pato Banton	1994
BABY COME BACK	Player	1977
BABY, COME TO ME	Patti Austin & James Ingram	1983
BABY COME CLOSE	Smokey Robinson	1973
BABY COME ON OVER	Samantha Mumba	2001
BABY COME TO ME	Patti Austin (with James Ingram)	1982
BABY DON'T CHANGE YOUR MIND	Gladys Knight & The Pips	1977
BABY DON'T CRY	INXS	1992
BABY DON'T FORGET MY NUMBER	Milli Vanilli	1989
BABY DON'T GET HOOKED ON ME	Mac Davis	1972
BABY DON'T GO	Sonny & Cher	1965
BABY DON'T YOU CRY (THE NEW SWINGOVA RHYTHM)	Ray Charles	1964

SONG TITLE	ARTIST	DATE
BABY DON'T YOU DO IT	Marvin Gaye	1964
BABY FACE	Wing & A Prayer Fife & Drum Corps	1975
BABY GET HIGHER	David Sneddon	2003
BABY GOT BACK	Sir Mix-A-Lot	1992
BABY HOLD ON	Grass Roots	1970
BABY HOLD ON	Eddie Money	1978
BABY HOLD ON TO ME	Gerald Levert	1992
BABY I DON'T CARE	Transvision Vamp	1989
BABY I DON'T CARE	Jennifer Ellison	2003
BABY I KNOW	Rubettes	1977
BABY I LIED	Deborah Allen	1983
BABY I LOVE U	Jennifer Lopez	2004
BABY I LOVE YOU	Aretha Franklin	1967
BABY I LOVE YOU	Dave Edmunds	1973
BABY I LOVE YOU	Andy Kim	1969
BABY, I LOVE YOU	Ramones	1980
BABY, I LOVE YOU	Ronettes	1964
BABY I LOVE YOU, OK!	Kenny	1975
BABY I LOVE YOUR WAY	Big Mountain	1994
BABY, I LOVE YOUR WAY	Peter Frampton	1976
BABY I LOVE YOUR WAY/FREEBIRD MEDLEY	Will To Power	1988
BABY I NEED YOUR LOVIN'	Fourmost	1964
BABY I NEED YOUR LOVIN'	Johnny Rivers	1967
BABY I NEED YOUR LOVING	Four Tops	1964
BABY I WON'T LET YOU DOWN	Pickettywitch	1970
BABY I'M BURNIN'	Dolly Parton	1978
BABY, I'M FOR REAL	Originals	1969
BABY I'M YOURS	Linda Lewis	1976
BABY I'M YOURS	Shai	1993
BABY, I'M YOURS	Peter & Gordon	1965
BABY, I'M YOURS	Barbara Lewis	1965
BABY I'M-A WANT YOU	Bread	1971
BABY, IT'S COLD OUTSIDE	Tom Jones & Cerys Matthews	1999
BABY, IT'S TONIGHT	Jude Cole	1990
BABY IT'S YOU	MN8	1995
BABY IT'S YOU	Dave Berry	1964
BABY IT'S YOU	Beatles	1995
BABY IT'S YOU	Smith	1969
BABY JANE	Rod Stewart	1983
BABY JUMP	Mungo Jerry	1971
BABY LET ME KISS YOU	King Floyd	1971
BABY LET ME TAKE YOU HOME	Animals	1964
BABY LET ME TAKE YOU IN MY ARMS	Detroit Emeralds	1972

SONG TITLE	ARTIST	DATE
BABY LOVE	Supremes	1964
BABY LOVE	Dannii Minogue	1991
BABY LOVE	Regina	1986
BABY MAKE IT SOON	Marmalade	1969
BABY MAKES HER BLUE JEANS TALK		
	Dr. Hook	1982
BABY NOW THAT I'VE FOUND YOU		
	Lauren Waterworth	2002
BABY, NOW THAT I'VE FOUND YOU		
	Foundations	1967
BABY OF MINE/JUST FOR YOU		
	Alan Price	1979
...BABY ONE MORE TIME	Britney Spears	1998
BABY PLEASE DON'T GO	Them	1965
BABY SCRATCH MY BACK	Slim Harpo	1966
BABY STOP CRYING	Bob Dylan	1978
BABY TAKE ME IN YOUR ARMS		
	Jefferson	1969
BABY TALKS DIRTY	Knack	1980
BABY THE RAIN MUST FALL		
	Glenn Yarbrough	1965
BABY WE BETTER TRY AND GET IT TOGETHER		
	Barry White	1976
BABY WE CAN'T GO WRONG		
	Cilla Black	1974

SONG TITLE	ARTIST	DATE
BABY WHAT A BIG SURPRISE		
	Chicago	1977
(BABY) YOU DON'T HAVE TO TELL ME		
	Walker Brothers	1966
BABY YOU GOT IT	Brenton Wood	1967
BABY YOU'RE A RICH MAN	Beatles	1967
BABY YOU'RE DYNAMITE/OCEAN DEEP		
	Cliff Richard	1984
BABY'S GOT A TEMPER	Prodigy	2002
BABYCAKES	3 Of A Kind	2004
BABYLON	David Gray	2000
BABYLON'S BURNING	Ruts	1979
BABYSHAMBLES	Peter Doherty	2004
BACHELORETTE	Bjork	1997
BACK 2 GOOD	Matchbox Twenty	1998
BACK AND FORTH	Aaliyah	1994
BACK AND FORTH	Cameo	1987
BACK AT ONE	Brian McKnight	1999
BACK AT ONE	Mark Wills	2000
BACK FOR GOOD	Take That	1995
BACK HERE	Bbmak	2001
BACK HOME	England World Cup Squad	1970
BACK HOME AGAIN	John Denver	1974
BACK IN BLACK	AC/DC	1980
BACK IN LOVE AGAIN	Donna Summer	1978
BACK IN MY ARMS AGAIN	Supremes	1965

SONG TITLE	ARTIST	DATE
BACK IN MY LIFE	Joe Roberts	1994
BACK IN MY LIFE	Alice Deejay	1999
BACK IN THE DAY	Ahmad!	1994
BACK IN THE HIGH LIFE AGAIN		
	Steve Winwood	1987
BACK IN THE SADDLE	Aerosmith	1977
BACK IN THE U.S.A.	Linda Ronstadt	1978
BACK IN THE U.S.S.R.	Beatles	1976
BACK IN THE UK	Scooter	1996
THE BACK OF LOVE	Echo & The Bunnymen	1982
BACK OF MY HAND	Jags	1979
BACK OFF BOOGALOO	Ringo Starr	1972
BACK ON HOLIDAY	Robbie Nevil	1988
BACK ON MY FEET AGAIN	Foundations	1968
BACK ON MY FEET AGAIN	Babys	1980
BACK ON THE CHAIN GANG		
	Pretenders	1982
BACK ON THE ROAD	Marmalade	1971
BACK ON THE STREET AGAIN		
	Sunshine Company	1967
BACK SEAT OF MY CAR	Paul & Linda McCartney	1971
BACK STABBERS	O'Jays	1972
BACK STREET LUV	Curved Air	1971
BACK THAT THANG UP	Juvenile featuring Fresh & Lil' Wayne	1999
BACK TO LIFE	Soul II Soul/Caron Wheeler	1989

SONG TITLE	ARTIST	DATE
BACK TO LOVE	Brand New Heavies	1994
BACK TO LOVE	Evelyn 'Champagne' King	1982
BACK TO THE HOTEL	N2Deep	1992
BACK TO THE LIGHT	Brian May	1992
BACK TO THE OLD SCHOOL		
	Bassheads	1992
BACK TO THE SIXTIES	Tight Fit	1981
BACK TO YOU	Bryan Adams	1997
BACK TOGETHER	Babybird	1999
BACK TOGETHER AGAIN	Roberta Flack & Donny Hathaway	1980
BACK TOGETHER AGAIN	Daryl Hall & John Oates	1977
BACK UP (TO ME)	Wookie featuring Lain	2001
BACK WHEN MY HAIR WAS SHORT		
	Gunhill Road	1973
BACK WHEN/GOING ALL THE WAY		
	Allstars	2002
BACK WHERE YOU BELONG		
	38 Special	1984
BACKCHAT	Queen	1982
BACKFIELD IN MOTION	Mel & Tim	1969
BACKFIRED	Deborah Harry	1981
BACKSTAGE	Gene Pitney	1966
BACKSTREET SYMPHONY	Thunder	1990
BACKYARD BOOGIE	Mack 10	1997
BAD	Michael Jackson	1987

SONG TITLE	ARTIST	DATE
BAD ACTRESS	Terrorvision	1996
BAD AMBASSADOR	Divine Comedy	2001
BAD ASS STRIPPA	Jentina	2004
BAD BABYSITTER	Princess Superstar	2002
BAD BAD BOY	Nazareth	1973
BAD, BAD LEROY BROWN	Jim Croce	1973
BAD BLOOD	Neil Sedaka	1975
BAD BOY	Wildchild featuring Jomalski	1998
BAD BOY	Miami Sound Machine	1986
BAD BOY	Ray Parker Jr.	1982
BAD BOY FOR LIFE	P. Diddy, Black Rob & Mark Curry	2001
BAD BOYS	Wham!	1983
BAD BOYS	Inner Circle	1993
BAD CASE OF LOVING YOU (DOCTOR, DOCTOR)	Robert Palmer	1979
BAD COVER VERSION	Pulp	2002
BAD DAY	Carmel	1983
BAD DAY	R.E.M.	2003
THE BAD DAYS (EP)	Space	1998
BAD GIRL	DJ Rap	1998
BAD GIRL	Madonna	1993
BAD GIRLS	Donna Summer	1979
BAD GIRLS/I LIKE	Juliet Roberts	1999
BAD HABIT	A.T.F.C. presents Onephatdeeva featuring Lisa Millett	2000
BAD INTENTIONS	Dr. Dre featuring Knoc-Turn'al	2002
BAD LOVE	Eric Clapton	1990
BAD LUCK (PT 1)	Harold Melvin & The Blue Notes	1975
BAD MEDICINE	Bon Jovi	1988
BAD MOON RISING	Creedence Clearwater Revival	1969
A BAD NIGHT	Cat Stevens	1967
BAD OF THE HEART	George Lamond	1990
BAD OLD DAYS	Coco	1978
BAD OLD MAN	Babybird	1998
THE BAD PHOTOGRAPHER	Saint Etienne	1998
BAD TIME	Grand Funk	1975
BAD TO ME	Billy J. Kramer & The Dakotas	1964
THE BAD TOUCH	Bloodhound Gang	2000
BAD WEATHER	Supremes	1973
BAD YOUNG BROTHER	Derek B	1988
BADABOOM	B2K featuring Fabolous	2004
BADDER BADDER SCHWING	Freddy Fresh featuring Fatboy Slim	1999
BADDEST RUFFEST	Backyard Dog	2001
BADGE	Cream	1969
BAG IT UP	Geri Halliwell	2000
BAG LADY	Erykah Badu	2000
BAGGY TROUSERS	Madness	1980
BAILAMOS	M3	1999

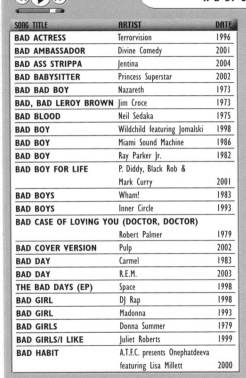

SONG TITLE	ARTIST	DATE
BAILAMOS	Enrique Iglesias	1999
BAKER STREET	Gerry Rafferty	1978
BAKER STREET	Undercover	1992
BALL OF CONFUSION	Temptations	1970
BALL OF FIRE	Tommy James & The Shondells	1969
BALL PARK INCIDENT	Wizzard	1972
BALLA BABY	Chingy	2004
THE BALLAD OF BONNIE & CLYDE	Georgie Fame	1967
THE BALLAD OF CHASEY LAIN	Bloodhound Gang	2000
THE BALLAD OF JAYNE	L.A. Guns	1990
BALLAD OF JOHN AND YOKO	Beatles	1969
THE BALLAD OF PETER PUMPKINHEAD	Crash Test Dummies	1995
THE BALLAD OF SPOTTY MULDOON	Peter Cook	1965
THE BALLAD OF THE GREEN BERETS	Ssgt. Barry Sadler	1966
THE BALLAD OF TOM JONES	Space With Cerys Of Catatonia	1998
THE BALLAD OF IRVING	Frank Gallup	1966
BALLERINA GIRL	Lionel Richie	1986
BALLERO	War	1974
BALLROOM BLITZ	Tia Carrere	1992

SONG TITLE	ARTIST	DATE
BALLROOM BLITZ	Sweet	1975
BAMA BOOGIE WOOGIE	Cleveland Eaton	1978
BAMA LAMA BAMA LOO	Little Richard	1964
BAMBOO HOUSES/BAMBOO MUSIC	David Sylvian	1982
BAMBOOGIE	Bamboo	1998
BANANA REPUBLIC	Boomtown Rats	1980
BANANA ROCK	Wombles	1974
THE BANANA SONG	GSP	1992
BANANA SPLITS (THE TRA LA LA SONG)	Dickies	1979
BAND OF GOLD	Freda Payne	1970
BAND OF GOLD	Mel Carter	1966
BAND ON THE RUN	Paul McCartney	1974
THE BAND PLAYED THE BOOGIE	C.C.S.	1973
A BANDA	Herb Alpert & The Tijuana Brass	1967
BANDAGES	Hot Hot Heat	2003
BANG	Blur	1991
BANG	Robbie Rivera presents Rhythm Bangers	2000
BANG A GONG (GET IT ON)	T. Rex	1972
BANG AND BLAME	R.E.M.	1994
BANG BANG	B.A. Robertson	1979

SONG TITLE	ARTIST	DATE
BANG BANG (MY BABY SHOT ME DOWN)		
	Cher	1966
BANG YOUR HEAD (METAL HEALTH)		
	Quiet Riot	1984
(BANG ZOOM) LET'S GO GO		
	Real Roxanne with Hitman Howie	1986
BANG-SHANG-A-LANG	Archies	1968
BANGIN' MAN	Slade	1974
BANGLA-DESH	George Harrison	1971
BANK ROBBER	Clash	1980
BANKROBBER	Audioweb	1997
BANKS OF THE OHIO	Olivia Newton-John	1971
BANNED IN THE USA	Luke featuring The 2 Live Crew	1990
BANNER MAN	Blue Mink	1971
BARBADOS	Typically Tropical	1975
BARBARA ANN	Beach Boys	1966
BARBARELLA	Alisha's Attic	1999
BARBER'S ADAGIO FOR STRINGS		
	William Orbit	1999
BARBIE GIRL	Aqua	1997
BARCELONA	Freddie Mercury & Monserrat Caballe	1992
BARCELONA	D Kay & Epsilon featuring Stamina MC	2003

SONG TITLE	ARTIST	DATE
THE BARE NECESSITIES MEGAMIX		
	UK Mixmasters	1991
BAREFOOTIN'	Robert Parker	1966
BARELY BREATHING	Duncan Sheik	1996
BARK AT THE MOON	Ozzy Osbourne	1983
BARRACUDA	Heart	1977
BARREL OF A GUN	Depeche Mode	1997
BARRETTA'S THEME	Rhythm Heritage	1976
THE BARTENDER AND THE THIEF		
	Stereophonics	1998
BASKET CASE	Green Day	1995
BASKETBALL JONES featuring TYRONE SHOELACES		
	Cheech & Chong	1973
BASS (HOW LOW CAN YOU GO)		
	Simon Harris	1988
BASSLINE	Mantronix	1986
BAT OUT OF HELL	Meat Loaf	1993
BATDANCE	Prince	1989
BATHTIME	Tindersticks	1997
BATMAN THEME	Neil Hefti	1966
BATMAN THEME	Marketts	1966
BATTER UP	Nelly & St. Lunatics	2001
BATTLE	Wookie featuring Lain	2000
BATTLE HYMN OF LT. CALLEY		
	C Company featuring Terry Nelson	1971

SONG TITLE	ARTIST	DATE
BATTLE HYMN OF THE REPUBLIC		
	Andy Williams	1968
BATTLE OF WHO COULD CARE LESS		
	Ben Folds Five	1997
BATTLEFLAG	Lo Fidelity Allstars	1998
BAY THAT'S BACKATCHA	Smokey Robinson	1975
BE	Neil Diamond	1973
BE ALONE NO MORE	Another Level	1998
BE ANGELED	Jam & Spoon featuring Rea	2002
BE ANYTHING (BUT BE MINE)		
	Connie Francis	1964
BE AS ONE	Sasha & Maria	1996
BE CAREFUL	Sparkle featuring R. Kelly	1998
BE COOL	Paffendorf	2002
BE FAITHFUL	Fatman Scoop featuring	
	The Crooklyn Clan	2003
BE FREE	Live Element	2002
BE GOOD TO YOURSELF	Frankie Miller	1977
BE GOOD TO YOURSELF	Journey	1986
BE HAPPY	Mary J. Blige	1994
BE LIKE THAT	3 Doors Down	2001
BE LOUD BE PROUD (BE HEARD)		
	Toyah	1982
BE MINE	Tremeloes	1967
BE MINE	David Gray	2003
BE MINE TONIGHT	Neil Diamond	1982

SONG TITLE	ARTIST	DATE
BE MY BABY	Ronettes	1963
BE MY BABY	Vanessa Paradis	1992
BE MY BABY	Andy Kim	1970
BE MY DOWNFALL	Del Amitri	1992
BE MY LADY	Jefferson Airplane	1982
BE MY LOVER	La Bouche	1995
BE MY TWIN	Brother Beyond	1989
BE NEAR ME	ABC	1985
BE QUICK OR BE DEAD	Iron Maiden	1992
BE STILL MY BEATING HEART		
	Sting	1988
BE TENDER WITH ME BABY		
	Tina Turner	1990
BE THANKFUL FOR WHAT YOU'VE GOT		
	William Devaughn	1974
BE THE FIRST TO BELIEVE		
	A1	1999
BE THERE	Unkle featuring Ian Brown	1999
BE WITH YOU	Bangles	1989
BE WITH YOU	Enrique Iglesias	2000
BE YOUNG, BE FOOLISH, BE HAPPY		
	Sonia	1991
BE YOUNG, BE FOOLISH, BE HAPPY		
	Tams	1970
BEACH BABY	First Class	1974
BEACH BOY GOLD	Gidea Park	1981

SONG TITLE	ARTIST	DATE
THE BEACH BOYS MEDLEY		
	Beach Boys	1981
BEACHBALL	Nalin & Kane	1998
BEACHED	Orbital & Angelo Badalamenti	2000
BEANS IN MY EARS	Serendipity Singers	1964
BEAR CAGE	Stranglers	1980
BEAST OF BURDEN	Rolling Stones	1978
BEAT DIS	Bomb The Bass	1988
BEAT GOES ON	All Seeing I	1998
THE BEAT GOES ON	Sonny & Cher	1967
THE BEAT GOES ON	Bob Sinclar	2003
BEAT IT	Michael Jackson	1983
BEAT MAMA	Cast	1999
BEAT SURRENDER	Jam	1982
BEAT THE CLOCK	Sparks	1979
BEAT'S SO LONELY	Charlie Sexton	1985
THE BEAT(EN) GENERATION		
	The The	1989
BEATLES AND THE STONES		
	House Of Love	1990
THE BEATLES MOVIE MEDLEY		
	Beatles	1982
BEAUTIFUL	Marillion	1995
BEAUTIFUL	Matt Darey's Mash Up presents Marcella Woods	2000
BEAUTIFUL	Snoop Dogg featuring Pharrell	2003

SONG TITLE	ARTIST	DATE
BEAUTIFUL	Christina Aguilera	2003
BEAUTIFUL ALONE	Strangelove	1996
BEAUTIFUL DAY	3 Colours Red	1999
BEAUTIFUL DAY	U2	2000
BEAUTIFUL DREAM	World Party	1997
THE BEAUTIFUL EXPERIENCE		
	TAFKAP	1994
BEAUTIFUL GIRL	INXS	1993
BEAUTIFUL IN MY EYES	Joshua Kadison	1994
BEAUTIFUL INSIDE	Louise	2000
BEAUTIFUL LIFE	Ace Of Base	1995
BEAUTIFUL LOVE	Julian Cope	1991
BEAUTIFUL LOVER	Brotherhood Of Man	1978
BEAUTIFUL MESS	Diamond Rio	2002
A BEAUTIFUL MORNING	Rascals	1968
BEAUTIFUL NIGHT	Paul McCartney	1997
BEAUTIFUL NOISE	Neil Diamond	1976
BEAUTIFUL ONES	Suede	1996
BEAUTIFUL PEOPLE	Barbara Tucker	1994
BEAUTIFUL PEOPLE	Kenny O'Dell	1967
BEAUTIFUL PEOPLE	Bobby Vee	1967
THE BEAUTIFUL PEOPLE	Marilyn Manson	1997
BEAUTIFUL STRANGER	Madonna	1999
BEAUTIFUL SUNDAY	Daniel Boone	1972
BEAUTY AND THE BEAST	David Bowie	1978
BEAUTY AND THE BEAST	Celine Dion & Peabo Bryson	1992

SONG TITLE	ARTIST	DATE
BEAUTY DIES YOUNG	Lowgold	2001
BEAUTY IS ONLY SKIN DEEP	Temptations	1966
BEAUTY ON THE FIRE	Natalie Imbruglia	2002
BEAUTY'S ONLY SKIN DEEP	Aswad	1989
BECAUSE	Julian Lennon	1985
BECAUSE	Demis Roussos	1977
BECAUSE	Dave Clark Five	1964
BECAUSE I GOT HIGH	Afroman	2001
BECAUSE I GOT IT LIKE THAT	Jungle Brothers	1998
BECAUSE I LOVE YOU	Georgie Fame	1967
BECAUSE I LOVE YOU	Shakin' Stevens	1986
BECAUSE I LOVE YOU (THE POSTMAN SONG)	Stevie B	1990
BECAUSE OF LOVE	Janet Jackson	1994
BECAUSE OF YOU	Gabrielle	1994
BECAUSE OF YOU	98 Degrees	1998
BECAUSE OF YOU	Dexy's Midnight Runners	1986
BECAUSE OF YOU	Scanty Sandwich	2000
BECAUSE OF YOU	Cover Girls	1987
BECAUSE THE NIGHT	Patti Smith Group	1978
BECAUSE THE NIGHT	Jan Wayne	2002
BECAUSE THE NIGHT	10,000 Maniacs	1993
BECAUSE WE WANT TO	Billie	1998
BECAUSE YOU	Cosmic Rough Riders	2003
BECAUSE YOU LOVED ME	Celine Dion	1996
BECOMING MORE LIKE ALFIE	Divine Comedy	1996
BECOMING MORE LIKE GOD	Jah Wobble's Invaders Of The Heart	1994
BED OF NAILS	Alice Cooper	1989
BED OF ROSES	Bon Jovi	1993
BEDSITTER	Soft Cell	1981
THE BED'S TOO BIG WITHOUT YOU	Sheila Hylton	1981
BEDS ARE BURNING	Midnight Oil	1988
BEDSHAPED	Keane	2004
BEDTIME STORY	Madonna	1995
BEEN A LONG TIME	Fog	1998
BEEN AROUND THE WORLD	Puff Daddy & The Family	1997
BEEN CAUGHT STEALING	Jane's Addiction	1991
BEEN THERE DONE THAT	Smoke 2 Seven	2002
BEEN TO CANAAN	Carole King	1972
BEEP ME 911	Missy 'Misdemeanor' Elliott	1998
BEER BARREL POLKA/DICK AND JANE	Bobby Vinton	1975
BEER FOR MY HORSES	Toby Keith Duet With Willie Nelson	2003

SONG TITLE	ARTIST	DATE
BEETHOVEN (I LOVE TO LISTEN TO)		
	Eurythmics	1987
BEETLEBUM	Blur	1997
BEFORE	Pet Shop Boys	1996
BEFORE AND AFTER	Chad & Jeremy	1965
BEFORE I LET YOU GO	Blackstreet	1994
BEFORE MY HEART FINDS OUT		
	Gene Cotton	1978
BEFORE THE NEXT TEARDROP FALLS		
	Freddy Fender	1975
BEFORE TODAY	Everything But The Girl	1997
BEFORE YOU LEAVE	Pepe Deluxe	2001
BEFORE YOU LOVE ME	Alsou	2001
BEFORE YOU WALK OUT OF MY LIFE		
	Monica	1995
BEG, BORROW OR STEAL	Ohio Express	1967
BEG, STEAL OR BORROW	New Seekers	1972
A BEGGAR ON A BEACH OF GOLD		
	Mike & The Mechanics	1995
BEGGIN'	Timebox	1968
BEGGIN'	Four Seasons	1967
BEGGIN' TO BE WRITTEN	Worlds Apart	1994
BEGGING YOU	Stone Roses	1995
BEGIN AGAIN	Space	1998
BEGIN THE BEGUINE (VOLVER A EMPEZAR)		
	Julio Iglesias	1981

SONG TITLE	ARTIST	DATE
THE BEGINNING OF THE END		
	Unifics	1968
THE BEGINNING	Seal	1991
BEGINNINGS/COLOUR MY WORLD		
	Chicago	1971
BEHIND A PAINTED SMILE		
	Isley Brothers	1969
BEHIND BLUE EYES	Limp Bizkit	2003
BEHIND BLUE EYES	Who	1971
BEHIND CLOSED DOORS	Charlie Rich	1973
BEHIND THE GROOVE	Teena Marie	1980
BEHIND THE MASK	Eric Clapton	1987
BEHIND THE WHEEL	Depeche Mode	1988
BEIN' BOILED	Human League	1982
BEING A GIRL (PART ONE) (EP)		
	Mansun	1998
BEING BORING	Pet Shop Boys	1990
BEING BRAVE	Menswear	1996
BEING NOBODY	Richard X vs Liberty X	2003
BEING WITH YOU	Smokey Robinson	1981
BEL AMOUR	Bel Amour	2001
BELARUSE	Levellers	1993
BELFAST	Boney M	1977
BELFAST BOY	Don Fardon	1970
BELFAST CHILD	Simple Minds	1989
BELIEVE	Lenny Kravitz	1993

SONG TITLE	ARTIST	DATE
BELIEVE	Goldie	1998
BELIEVE	Cher	1998
BELIEVE	Elton John	1995
BELIEVE	Ian Van Dahl	2004
BELIEVE IN HUMANITY	Carole King	1973
BELIEVE IN ME	Utah Saints	1993
BELIEVER	Real People	1992
BELIEVERS	Baz	2001
BELISSIMA	DJ Quicksilver	1997
BELL BOTTOMED TEAR	Beautiful South	1992
BELLA LINDA	Grass Roots	1968
BELLE & SEBASTIAN PRESENT 'BOOKS'	Belle & Sebastian	2004
THE BELLE OF ST. MARK	Sheila E	1984
BELLS OF NY	Slo-Moshun	1994
THE BELLS	Originals	1970
BELO HORIZONTI	Heartists	1998
BEN	Michael Jackson	1972
BEN	Marti Webb	1985
BEND IT!	Dave Dee, Dozy, Beaky, Mick & Tich	1966
BEND ME, SHAPE ME	American Breed	1967
BEND ME, SHAPE ME	Amen Corner	1968
BENEDICTUS/NIGHTMARE	Brainbug	1997
BENNIE AND THE JETS	Elton John	1974

SONG TITLE	ARTIST	DATE
BENNY'S THEME	Paul Henry & Mayson Glen Orchestra	1978
BENT	Matchbox Twenty	2000
BENTLEYS GONNA SORT YOU OUT!	Bentley Rhythm Ace	1997
BERMUDA TRIANGLE	Barry Manilow	1981
BERNADETTE	Four Tops	1967
BERSERKER	Gary Numan	1984
THE BERTHA BUTT BOOGIE (PT I)	Jimmy Castor Bunch	1975
THE BEST	Tina Turner	1989
BEST BIT (EP)	Beth Orton	1997
THE BEST CHRISTMAS OF THEM ALL	Shakin' Stevens	1990
THE BEST DAY OF OUR LIVES	Lisbon Lions featuring Martin O'Neill	2002
THE BEST DAY	George Strait	2000
BEST DAYS	Juice	1998
THE BEST DISCO IN TOWN	Ritchie Family	1976
BEST FRIEND	Mark Morrison & Conner Reeves	1999
BEST FRIEND	Puff Daddy featuring Mario Winans	1999
BEST FRIEND	Brandy	1995

SONG TITLE	ARTIST	DATE
BEST FRIEND/STAND DOWN MARGARET (DUB)		
	Beat	1980
BEST FRIENDS	Allstars	2001
BEST FRIENDS FOREVER	Tweenies	2001
BEST I CAN	Queensryche	1991
BEST IN ME	Let Loose	1995
THE BEST IS YET TO COME		
	Scooch	2000
BEST KEPT SECRET	China Crisis	1987
BEST OF BOTH WORLDS	Lulu	1967
BEST OF INTENTIONS	Travis Tritt	2000
THE BEST OF LOVE	Michael Bolton	1997
THE BEST OF ME	Cliff Richard	1989
BEST OF MY LIFE	CJ Lewis	1994
BEST OF MY LOVE	Emotions	1977
BEST OF MY LOVE	Javine	2004
BEST OF MY LOVE	Eagles	1974
BEST OF ORDER	David Sneddon	2003
THE BEST OF TIMES	Styx	1981
BEST OF YOU	Kenny Thomas	1991
BEST PART OF BREAKING UP		
	Symbols	1968
BEST REGRETS	Geneva	1997
BEST THING	Adam Rickitt	2000
THE BEST THING THAT EVER HAPPENED		
	Gladys Knight & The Pips	1975

SONG TITLE	ARTIST	DATE
THE BEST THING	Savage Garden	2001
THE BEST THINGS IN LIFE ARE FREE		
	Luther Vandross/Janet Jackson	1992
THE BEST YEARS OF MY LIFE		
	Diana Ross	1994
BEST YEARS OF OUR LIVES		
	Modern Romance	1982
BET YER LIFE I DO	Herman's Hermits	1970
BETCHA BY GOLLY WOW	Stylistics	1972
BETCHA BY GOLLY WOW!	The Artist	1996
BETCHA CAN'T WAIT	East 17	1999
BETCHA SAY THAT	Gloria Estefan & The Miami Sound Machine	1987
BETH	Kiss	1976
BETTE DAVIS EYES	Kim Carnes	1981
BETTER BE GOOD TO ME	Tina Turner	1984
BETTER BEST FORGOTTEN	Steps	1999
BETTER DAY	Ocean Colour Scene	1997
BETTER DAYS	Gun	1989
BETTER DAYS	Bruce Springsteen	1992
BETTER DAYS	TQ	1999
BETTER DAYS (AND THE BOTTOM DROPS OUT)		
	Citizen King	1999
BETTER DAYS AHEAD	Tyrell Corporation	1995
A BETTER LOVE	Londonbeat	1991
BETTER LOVE NEXT TIME	Dr. Hook	1979

SONG TITLE	ARTIST	DATE
A BETTER MAN	Brian Kennedy	1996
A BETTER MAN	Thunder	1993
BETTER OFF ALONE	DJ Jurgen presents Alice Deejay	1999
BETTER THAN LIFE	Ultrabeat	2004
BETTER THAN YOU	Lisa Keith	1993
BETTER THE DEVIL YOU KNOW		
	Kylie Minogue	1990
BETTER THE DEVIL YOU KNOW		
	Sonia	1993
BETTER WATCH OUT	Ant & Dec	1996
BETTER WORLD	Rebel M.C.	1990
BETWEEN ANGELS & INSECTS		
	Papa Roach	2001
BETWEEN ME AND YOU	Ja Rule featuring	
	Christina Milian	2001
BETWEEN THE WARS (EP)	Billy Bragg	1985
BEWARE OF THE BOYS (MUNDIAN TO BACH KE)		
	Panjabi MC featuring Jay-Z	2003
BEYOND THE INVISIBLE	Enigma	1997
BEYOND THE PALE	Mission	1988
BICYCLE RACE/FAT BOTTOMED GIRLS		
	Queen	1978
BIG APPLE	Kajagoogoo	1983
BIG AREA	Then Jericho	1989
BIG BAD MAMMA	Foxy Brown featuring Dru Hill	1997
THE BIG BEAN	Pigbag	1982

SONG TITLE	ARTIST	DATE
BIG BIG WORLD	Emilia	1998
BIG BOSS MAN	Elvis Presley	1967
BIG BOYS DON'T CRY/ROCKIN' ROBIN		
	Lolly	1999
BIG BROTHER UK TV THEME		
	Element Four	2000
BIG CITY MISS RUTH ANN		
	Gallery	1972
BIG CITY/THINK ABOUT THAT		
	Dandy Livingstone	1973
BIG DADDY	Heavy D	1997
BIG DEAL	Leann Rimes	1999
BIG EIGHT	Judge Dread	1973
BIG FUN	Gap Band	1986
BIG FUN	Inner City	1988
BIG FUN	Kool & The Gang	1982
BIG GIRL	Precocious Brats featuring	
	Kevin & Perry	2000
BIG GIRLS DON'T CRY	Four Seasons	1962
BIG GUN	AC/DC	1993
BIG IN JAPAN	Alphaville	1984
THE BIG L	Roxette	1991
BIG LOG	Robert Plant	1983
BIG LOVE	Fleetwood Mac	1987
BIG LOVE	Pete Heller	1999

SONG TITLE	ARTIST	DATE
THE BIG MAN AND THE SCREAM TEAM MEET THE BARMY ARMY UPTOWN	Primal Scream, Irvine Welsh & On-U Sound	1996
BIG MAN IN TOWN	Four Seasons	1964
BIG ME	Foo Fighters	1996
BIG MISTAKE	Natalie Imbruglia	1998
BIG MOUTH STRIKES AGAIN	Smiths	1986
BIG NIGHT OUT	Fun Lovin' Criminals	1998
THE BIG ONES GET AWAY	Buffy Sainte-Marie	1992
BIG PANTY WOMAN	Barefoot Man	1998
BIG PIMPIN'	Jay-Z (featuring UGK)	2000
BIG POPPA/WARNING	Notorious B.I.G.	1995
BIG RIVER	Jimmy Nail	1995
BIG SEVEN	Judge Dread	1972
BIG SHIP	Cliff Richard	1969
BIG SHOT	Billy Joel	1979
BIG SIX	Judge Dread	1972
THE BIG SKY	Kate Bush	1986
BIG SPENDER	Shirley Bassey	1967
BIG STAR	Kenny Chesney	2002
BIG SUR	Thrills	2003
BIG TEN	Judge Dread	1975
BIG THING COMING	Stranglers	2004
BIG TIME	Peter Gabriel	1987

SONG TITLE	ARTIST	DATE
BIG TIME OPERATOR	Zoot Money & The Big Roll Band	1966
BIG TIME SENSUALITY	Bjork	1993
BIG WEDGE	Fish	1990
BIG YELLOW TAXI	Joni Mitchell	1974
BIG YELLOW TAXI	Amy Grant	1995
BIG YELLOW TAXI	Counting Crows featuring Vanessa Carlton	2003
BIG YELLOW TAXI	Neighborhood	1970
BIGGER THAN MY BODY	John Mayer	2003
BIGGEST PART OF ME	Ambrosia	1980
BIGSCARYANIMAL	Belinda Carlisle	1993
BIKINI GIRLS WITH MACHINE GUNS	Cramps	1990
BIKO	Peter Gabriel	1980
BILJO	Clodagh Rodgers	1969
BILL MCCAI	Coral	2003
BILLIE JEAN	Michael Jackson	1983
BILLIE JEAN	Sound Bluntz	2002
BILLS 2 PAY	Glamma Kid	2000
BILLS, BILLS, BILLS	Destiny's Child	1999
BILLY AND SUE	B.J. Thomas	1966
BILLY, DON'T BE A HERO	Paper Lace	1974
BILLY, DON'T BE A HERO	Bo Donaldson & The Heywoods	1974
BINGO	Catch	1997
BINGO BANGO	Basement Jaxx	2000

SONG TITLE	ARTIST	DATE
BIONIC	King Adora	2001
BIONIC SANTA	Chris Hill	1976
THE BIRD	Time	1985
BIRD DANCE BEAT	Trashmen	1964
BIRD OF PARADISE	Snowy White	1983
BIRD SONG	Lene Lovich	1979
BIRDHOUSE IN YOUR SOUL		
	They Might Be Giants	1990
THE BIRDIE SONG (BIRDIE DANCE)		
	Tweets	1981
BIRDMAN	Ride	1994
BIRDS AND BEES	Warm Sounds	1967
THE BIRDS AND THE BEES	Jewel Akens	1965
BIRDS OF A FEATHER	Raiders	1971
BIRTH	Peddlers	1969
BIRTHDAY	Paul McCartney	1990
BIRTHDAY	Underground Sunshine	1969
BIRTHDAY SUIT	Johnny Kemp	1989
THE BIT GOES ON	Snakebite	1997
BITCH	Meredith Brooks	1997
THE BITCH	Olympic Runners	1979
THE BITCH IS BACK	Elton John	1974
BITCH SCHOOL	Spinal Tap	1992
BITCHES BREW	Inspiral Carpets	1992
BITE YOUR LIP (GET UP AND DANCE!)		
	Elton John	1977

SONG TITLE	ARTIST	DATE
BITS AND PIECES	Dave Clark Five	1964
BITTER BAD	Melanie	1973
THE BITTER END	Placebo	2003
BITTER SWEET	Marc Almond	1988
BITTER SWEET SYMPHONY		
	Verve	1998
BITTER TEARS	INXS	1991
THE BITTEREST PILL (I EVER HAD TO SWALLOW)		
	Jam	1982
BITTERSWEET BUNDLE OF MISERY		
	Graham Coxon	2004
BITTERSWEET ME	R.E.M.	1996
BIZOUNCE	Olivia	2001
BLACK & WHITE	Three Dog Night	1972
BLACK & WHITE ARMY	Black & White Army	1998
BLACK AND BLUE	Van Halen	1988
BLACK AND WHITE	Greyhound	1971
BLACK BALLOON	Goo Goo Dolls	1999
BLACK BETTY	Ram Jam	1977
BLACK BOOK	EYC	1994
BLACK CAT	Janet Jackson	1990
BLACK CHERRY	Goldfrapp	2004
BLACK COFFEE	All Saints	2000
BLACK DOG	Led Zeppelin	1971
BLACK EYED BOY	Texas	1997
THE BLACK EYED BOYS	Paper Lace	1974

SONG TITLE	ARTIST	DATE
BLACK FRIDAY	Steely Dan	1975
BLACK GIRL	Four Pennies	1964
BLACK GOLD	Soul Asylum	1994
BLACK HOLE SUN	Soundgarden	1994
BLACK IS BLACK	Los Bravos	1966
BLACK IS BLACK	La Belle Epoque	1977
BLACK JESUS	Everlast	2001
BLACK MAGIC WOMAN	Fleetwood Mac	1968
BLACK MAGIC WOMAN	Santana	1970
BLACK MAN RAY	China Crisis	1985
BLACK NIGHT	Deep Purple	1970
BLACK OR WHITE	Michael Jackson	1991
BLACK PEARL	Horace Faith	1970
BLACK PEARL	Sonny Charles & The Checkmates, Ltd.	1969
BLACK PUDDING BERTHA	Goodies	1975
BLACK SKIN BLUE EYED BOYS	Equals	1970
BLACK STEEL	Tricky	1995
BLACK SUITS COMIN'	Will Smith featuring Tra-Knox	2002
BLACK SUPERMAN (MUHAMMAD ALI)	Johnny Wakelin	1975
BLACK TIE WHITE NOISE	David Bowie featuring Al B. Sure!	1993
BLACK VELVET	Alannah Myles	1990
BLACK VELVET BAND	Dubliners	1967

SONG TITLE	ARTIST	DATE
BLACK WATER	Doobie Brothers	1974
BLACKBERRY WAY	Move	1968
BLACKBIRD ON THE WIRE	Beautiful South	1997
BLACKERTHREETRACKER (EP)	Curve	1993
BLAME IT ON ME	D:ream	1994
BLAME IT ON THE BOOGIE	Big Fun	1989
BLAME IT ON THE BOOGIE	Clock	1998
BLAME IT ON THE BOOGIE	Mick Jackson	1978
BLAME IT ON THE BOOGIE	Jacksons	1978
BLAME IT ON THE BOSSA NOVA	Eydie Gorme	1963
BLAME IT ON THE RAIN	Milli Vanilli	1989
BLAME IT ON THE WEATHERMAN	B*Witched	1999
(BLAME IT) ON THE PONY EXPRESS	Johnny Johnson & The Bandwagon	1970
BLANKET ON THE GROUND	Billie Jo Spears	1975
BLASPHEMOUS RUMOURS/SOMEDAY	Depeche Mode	1984

SONG TITLE	ARTIST	DATE
BLAST THE SPEAKERS	Warp Brothers	2001
BLAZE OF GLORY	Jon Bon Jovi	1990
BLESS OUR LOVE	Gene Chandler	1964
BLESS YOU	Martha Reeves & The Vandellas	1972
BLESSED	Elton John	1995
BLESSED	Martina McBride	2002
BLESSED ARE THE BELIEVERS	Anne Murray	1981
BLIND PILOTS	Cooper Temple Clause	2003
BLIND VISION	Blancmange	1983
BLINDED BY THE LIGHT	Manfred Mann's Earth Band	1976
BLINDED BY THE LIGHTS	The Streets	2004
BLINDED BY THE SUN	Seahorses	1997
BLING BLING	B.G. featuring Baby, Turk, Mannie Fresh, Juvenile	1999
BLINK	Rosie Ribbons	2002
BLISS	Muse	2001
THE BLOCK PARTY	Lisa 'Left Eye' Lopes	2001
BLOCK ROCKIN' BEATS	Chemical Brothers	1997
BLOCKBUSTER!	Sweet	1973
BLOOD IS PUMPIN'	Voodoo & Serano	2001
BLOOD ON THE DANCE FLOOR	Michael Jackson	1997
BLOOD SWEAT AND TEARS V		2004
THE BLOOD THAT MOVES THE BODY	A-Ha	1988

SONG TITLE	ARTIST	DATE
BLOODY WELL RIGHT	Supertramp	1975
BLOSSOMS FALLING	Ooberman	1999
BLOW AWAY	George Harrison	1979
BLOW THE HOUSE DOWN	Living In A Box	1989
BLOW UP THE OUTSIDE WORLD	Soundgarden	1996
BLOW YA MIND	Lock 'n' Load	2000
BLOW YOUR MIND	Jamiroquai	1993
BLOW YOUR WHISTLE	DJ Duke	1994
BLOWIN' IN THE WIND	Stevie Wonder	1966
BLOWIN' IN THE WIND	Peter, Paul & Mary	1963
BLOWIN' ME UP (WITH HER LOVE)	JC Chasez	2003
BLOWING AWAY	5th Dimension	1970
BLOWING KISSES IN THE WIND	Paula Abdul	1991
BLUE	Leann Rimes	1996
BLUE (DA BA DEE)	Eiffel 65	1999
BLUE ANGEL	Gene Pitney	1974
BLUE ANGELS	Pras	1998
BLUE AUTUMN	Bobby Goldsboro	1966
BLUE BAYOU	Linda Ronstadt	1977
BLUE BAYOU/MEAN WOMAN BLUES	Roy Orbison	1963
BLUE CHRISTMAS	Elvis Presley	1964

SONG TITLE	ARTIST	DATE
BLUE COLLAR MAN (LONG NIGHTS)		
	Styx	1978
BLUE DAY	Suggs & Co featuring	
	Chelsea Team	1997
BLUE EYES	Wedding Present	1992
BLUE EYES	Elton John	1982
BLUE EYES	Don Partridge	1968
BLUE EYES CRYING IN THE RAIN		
	Willie Nelson	1975
BLUE FOR YOU/THIS TIME (LIVE)		
	Wet Wet Wet	1993
BLUE GIRL	Bruisers	1963
BLUE GUITAR	Justin Hayward & John Lodge	1975
BLUE HAT FOR A BLUE DAY		
	Nick Heyward	1983
BLUE HOTEL	Chris Isaak	1991
BLUE IS THE COLOUR	Chelsea F.C.	1972
BLUE JEAN	David Bowie	1984
BLUE MONDAY	New Order	1983
BLUE MONEY	Van Morrison	1971
BLUE MOON	Showaddywaddy	1980
BLUE MOON/ONLY YOU	John Alford	1996
BLUE MORNING, BLUE DAY		
	Foreigner	1978
BLUE PETER	Mike Oldfield	1979
BLUE RIVER	Elvis Presley	1966

SONG TITLE	ARTIST	DATE
BLUE ROOM	Orb	1992
BLUE SAVANNAH	Erasure	1990
BLUE SKIES	BT featuring Tori Amos	1996
BLUE SKIES	Longpigs	1999
BLUE SONG	Mint Royale	2003
BLUE SUEDE SHOES	Johnny Rivers	1973
BLUE TOMORROW	Chelsea Football Club	2000
BLUE TURNS TO GREY	Cliff Richard	1966
BLUE VELVET	Bobby Vinton	1963
BLUE WINTER	Connie Francis	1964
BLUE WORLD	Moody Blues	1983
BLUE'S THEME	Davie Allan & The Arrows	1967
BLUEBEARD	Cocteau Twins	1994
BLUEBIRD	Helen Reddy	1975
BLUEBIRDS OVER THE MOUNTAIN		
	Beach Boys	1968
BLUER THAN BLUE	Rolf Harris	1969
BLUER THAN BLUE	Michael Johnson	1978
BLUES FROM A GUN	Jesus & Mary Chain	1989
BLUETONIC	Bluetones	1995
BLURRED	Pianoman	1996
BLURRY	Puddle Of Mudd	2001
BO DIDDLEY	Buddy Holly	1963
BOOM, LIKE THAT	Mark Knopfler	2004
THE BOAT THAT I ROW	Lulu	1967
BOBBIE SUE	Oak Ridge Boys	1982

SONG TITLE	ARTIST	DATE
BOBBY TOMORROW	Bobby Vee	1963
BODIES	Drowning Pool	2002
BODY & SOUL	Anita Baker	1994
BODY AND SOUL	Mai Tai	1985
BODY BUMPIN' (YIPPIE-YI-YO)		
	Public Announcement	1998
BODY GROOVE	Architechs featuring Nana	2000
BODY HEAT	James Brown	1977
BODY IN MOTION	Atlantic Ocean	1994
BODY LANGUAGE	Adventures Of Stevie V	1990
BODY LANGUAGE	Spinners	1980
BODY LANGUAGE	Queen	1982
BODY MOVIN'	Beastie Boys	1998
BODY ROCK	Maria Vidal	1985
BODY TALK	Imagination	1981
BODY II BODY	Samantha Mumba	2000
BODY WORK	Hot Streak	1983
BODYROCK	Moby	1999
BODYROCK	Tymes 4	2001
BODYSHAKIN'	911	1997
BOHEMIAN LIKE YOU	Dandy Warhols	2001
BOHEMIAN RHAPSODY	Braids	1996
BOHEMIAN RHAPSODY/THESE ARE THE DAYS OF OUR LIVES	Queen	1991
BOILER	Limp Bizkit	2001
THE BOILER	Rhoda With Special AKA	1982

SONG TITLE	ARTIST	DATE
BOING!	Wedding Present	1992
BOM DIGI BOM (THINK ABOUT THE WAY)		
	Ice MC	1996
THE BOMB! (THESE SOUNDS FALL INTO MY MIND)		
	Bucketheads	1995
BOMB DIGGY	Another Level	1999
BOMBER	Motorhead	1979
BOMBTRACK	Rage Against The Machine	1993
BONEY M MEGAMIX	Boney M	1992
BONEYARD	Little Angels	1991
BOOGALOO DOWN BROADWAY		
	Fantastic Johnny C	1967
THE BOOGALOO PARTY	Flamingos	1969
BOOGIE	Dive	1998
BOOGIE CHILD	Bee Gees	1977
BOOGIE DOWN	Eddie Kendricks	1974
BOOGIE DOWN (GET FUNKY NOW)		
	Real Thing	1979
BOOGIE FEVER	Sylvers	1976
BOOGIE NIGHTS	Sonia	1992
BOOGIE NIGHTS	Heatwave	1977
BOOGIE ON REGGAE WOMAN		
	Stevie Wonder	1974
BOOGIE ON UP	Rokotto	1977
BOOGIE OOGIE OOGIE	Taste Of Honey	1978
BOOGIE SHOES	KC & The Sunshine Band	1978

SONG TITLE	ARTIST	DATE
BOOGIE WONDERLAND	Earth, Wind & Fire with The Emotions	1979
BOOGIE WOOGIE BUGLE BOY	Bette Midler	1973
BOOK OF DAYS	Enya	1992
BOOM BANG-A-BANG	Lulu	1969
BOOM BOOM	John Lee Hooker	1992
BOOM BOOM	N-Tyce	1998
BOOM BOOM BOOM	Outhere Brothers	1995
BOOM SELECTION	Genius Cru	2001
BOOM! SHAKE THAT ROOM	D.J. Jazzy Jeff & The Fresh Prince	1993
BOOM, BOOM, BOOM, BOOM!!	Vengaboys	1999
BOOMBASTIC	Shaggy	1995
BOOO!	Sticky featuring Ms. Dynamite	2001
BOOPS (HERE TO GO)	Sly And Robbie	1987
BOOTI CALL	Blackstreet	1994
BOOTIE CALL	All Saints	1998
BOOTY BUTT	Ray Charles	1971
BOOTYLICIOUS	Destiny's Child	2001
BOP BOP BABY	Westlife	2002
BOP GUN (ONE NATION)	Ice Cube featuring George Clinton	1994
BOP 'TIL YOU DROP	Rick Springfield	1984

SONG TITLE	ARTIST	DATE
BORA BORA	Da Hool	1998
THE BORDER	America	1983
BORDER SONG (HOLY MOSES)	Aretha Franklin	1970
BORDERLINE	Madonna	1984
THE BORDERLINES	Jeffrey Osborne	1985
BORN 2 B.R.E.E.D.	Monie Love	1993
BORN A WOMAN	Sandy Posey	1966
BORN AGAIN	Christians	1988
BORN AGAIN	Badly Drawn Boy	2003
BORN AGAIN	Starsailor	2003
BORN DEAD	Body Count	1994
BORN FREE	Vic Reeves/The Roman Numerals	1991
BORN FREE	Hesitations	1968
BORN FREE	Roger Williams	1966
BORN IN ENGLAND	Twisted X	2004
BORN IN THE U.S.A.	Bruce Springsteen	1984
BORN OF FRUSTRATION	James	1992
BORN ON THE 5TH OF NOVEMBER	Carter The Unstoppable Sex Machine	1995
BORN SLIPPY	Underworld	1996
BORN SLIPPY NUXX	Underworld	2003
BORN THIS WAY (LET'S DANCE)	Cookie Crew	1989

SONG TITLE	ARTIST	DATE
BORN TO BE ALIVE	Patrick Hernandez	1979
BORN TO BE MY BABY	Bon Jovi	1988
BORN TO BE SOLD	Transvision Vamp	1989
BORN TO BE WILD	Steppenwolf	1968
BORN TO BE WITH YOU	Dave Edmunds	1973
BORN TO FLY	Sara Evans	2000
BORN TO MAKE YOU HAPPY		
	Britney Spears	2000
BORN TO ROLL	Masta Ace Incorporated	1994
BORN TO RUN	Bruce Springsteen	1975
BORN TO TRY	Delta Goodrem	2003
BORN TO WANDER	Rare Earth	1970
BORN WITH A SMILE ON MY FACE		
	Stephanie De Sykes	1974
BORNE ON THE WIND	Roy Orbison	1964
BORROWED TIME	John Lennon	1984
BORSALINO	Bobby Crush	1972
BOSS DRUM	Shamen	1992
BOSS GUITAR	Duane Eddy & The Rebelettes	1963
BOSS OF ME	They Might Be Giants	2001
THE BOSS	Braxtons	1997
THE BOSS	Diana Ross	1979
BOSSA NOVA BABY	Elvis Presley	1963
THE BOSTON TEA PARTY	Sensational Alex Harvey Band	1976
BOTH ENDS BURNING	Roxy Music	1975
BOTH SIDES NOW	Judy Collins	1968

SONG TITLE	ARTIST	DATE
BOTH SIDES NOW/DARE TO DREAM		
	Viola Wills	1986
BOTH SIDES OF THE STORY		
	Phil Collins	1993
BOTHER	Stone Sour	2003
BOTTLE LIVING	Dave Gahan	2003
BOTTLE OF WINE	Fireballs	1967
THE BOTTLE	Christians	1993
THE BOTTLE	Paul Weller	2004
BOULEVARD	Jackson Browne	1980
BOUNCE	Sarah Connor	2004
BOUNCE ALONG	Wayne Wonder	2003
BOUNCE WITH ME	Lil Bow Wow featuring Xscape	2000
BOUNCE WITH THE MASSIVE		
	Tzant	1998
THE BOUNCER	Kicks Like A Mule	1992
BOUNCIN' BACK (BUMPIN' ME AGAINST THE WALL)		
	Mystikal	2001
BOUNCING FLOW	K2 Family	2001
BOUND 4 DA RELOAD (CASUALTY)		
	Oxide & Neutrino	2000
BOURGIE, BOURGIE	Gladys Knight & The Pips	1980
BOUT	Jamelia featuring Rah Digga	2003
BOW DOWN	Westside Connection	1996
BOW DOWN MISTER	Jesus Loves You	1991

SONG TITLE	ARTIST	DATE
BOW WOW (THAT'S MY NAME)		
	Lil Bow Wow	2001
BOW WOW WOW	Funkdoobiest	1994
BOWLING GREEN	Everly Brothers	1967
THE BOX	Orbital	1996
BOX SET GO	High	1991
THE BOXER	Simon & Garfunkel	1969
BOXER BEAT	Joboxers	1983
BOXERS	Morrissey	1995
BOY	Lulu	1968
BOY (I NEED YOU)	Mariah Carey featuring Cam'ron	2003
BOY FROM NEW YORK CITY		
	Alison Jordan	1992
BOY FROM NEW YORK CITY		
	Manhattan Transfer	1981
THE BOY FROM NEW YORK CITY		
	Darts	1978
THE BOY FROM NEW YORK CITY		
	Ad Libs	1965
A BOY FROM NOWHERE	Tom Jones	1987
BOY IN THE BOX	Corey Hart	1985
THE BOY IN THE BUBBLE	Paul Simon	1986
BOY IS CRYING	Saint Etienne	2001
THE BOY IS MINE	Brandy & Monica	1998
A BOY NAMED SUE	Johnny Cash	1969
BOY OH BOY	Racey	1979

SONG TITLE	ARTIST	DATE
THE BOY RACER	Morrissey	1995
THE BOY WITH THE THORN IN HIS SIDE		
	Smiths	1985
THE BOY WITH THE X-RAY EYES		
	Babylon Zoo	1996
BOY YOU KNOCK ME OUT	Tatyana Ali featuring Will Smith	1999
BOYS	Bon	2001
BOYS	Britney Spears featuring	
	Pharrell Williams	2002
BOYS (SUMMERTIME LOVE)		
	Sabrina	1988
THE BOYS ARE BACK IN TOWN		
	Happy Mondays	1999
THE BOYS ARE BACK IN TOWN		
	Thin Lizzy	1976
BOYS BETTER	Dandy Warhols	1998
BOYS CRY	Eden Kane	1964
BOYS DO FALL IN LOVE	Robin Gibb	1984
BOYS DON'T CRY	Cure	1986
BOYS KEEP SWINGIN'	David Bowie	1979
BOYS NIGHT OUT	Timothy B. Schmit	1987
THE BOYS OF SUMMER	Don Henley	1984
THE BOYS OF SUMMER	DJ Sammy	2003
BRAIN STEW/JADED	Green Day	1996
BRAND NEW DAY	Sting	1999
BRAND NEW FRIEND	Lloyd Cole & The Commotions	1985

SONG TITLE	ARTIST	DATE
BRAND NEW KEY	Melanie	1971
BRAND NEW LOVER	Dead Or Alive	1987
A BRAND NEW ME	Dusty Springfield	1969
BRAND NEW START	Paul Weller	1998
BRANDY	Scott English	1971
BRANDY	O'Jays	1978
BRANDY (YOU'RE A FINE GIRL)		
	Looking Glass	1972
BRASS IN POCKET	Pretenders	1979
	Pretenders	1980
BRASSNECK	Wedding Present	1990
BRAVE NEW WORLD	Toyah	1982
BRAZEN 'WEEP'	Skunk Anansie	1997
BRAZIL	Crispy And Company	1975
BRAZIL	Ritchie Family	1975
BRAZILIAN LOVE AFFAIR	George Duke	1980
BREAD AND BUTTER	Newbeats	1964
BREAK AWAY	Beach Boys	1969
BREAK AWAY	Art Garfunkel	1975
BREAK AWAY (FROM THAT BOY)		
	Newbeats	1965
BREAK 4 LOVE	Raze	1988
BREAK DANCE PARTY	Break Machine	1984
BREAK FROM THE OLD ROUTINE		
	Oui 3	1993
BREAK IT DOWN AGAIN	Tears For Fears	1993

SONG TITLE	ARTIST	DATE
BREAK IT TO ME GENTLY	Juice Newton	1982
BREAK IT UP	Foreigner	1982
BREAK MY STRIDE	Matthew Wilder	1983
BREAK OF DAWN	Rhythm On The Loose	1995
BREAK THE CHAIN	Motiv 8	1995
BREAK THE RULES	Status Quo	1974
BREAK UP TO MAKE UP	Stylistics	1973
BREAK UPS 2 MAKE UPS	Method Man featuring D'Angelo	1999
BREAK YA NECK	Busta Rhymes	2001
BREAK YOUR PROMISE	Delfonics	1968
BREAKADAWN	De La Soul	1993
BREAKAWAY	Tracey Ullman	1983
BREAKAWAY	Gallagher & Lyle	1976
BREAKAWAY	Kelly Clarkson	2004
BREAKBEAT ERA	Breakbeat Era	1998
BREAKDANCE	Irene Cara	1984
BREAKDOWN	One Dove	1993
BREAKDOWN	Tom Petty & The Heartbreakers	1977
THE BREAKDOWN	Rufus Thomas	1971
BREAKDOWN DEAD AHEAD	Boz Scaggs	1980
BREAKFAST AT TIFFANY'S	Deep Blue Something	1995
BREAKFAST IN AMERICA	Supertramp	1979
BREAKFAST IN BED	UB40	1988
BREAKFAST ON PLUTO	Don Partridge	1969
BREAKIN' DOWN (SUGAR SAMBA)		
	Julia & Company	1984

SONG TITLE	ARTIST	DATE
BREAKIN' DOWN THE WALLS OF HEARTACHE		
	Bandwagon	1968
BREAKIN' MY HEART (PRETTY BROWN EYES)		
	Mint Condition	1992
BREAKIN' UP IS BREAKIN' MY HEART		
	Roy Orbison	1966
BREAKIN' UP MY HEART	Shakin' Stevens	1985
BREAKIN'... THERE'S NO STOPPING US		
	Ollie & Jerry	1984
BREAKING ALL THE RULES	She Moves	1997
BREAKING AWAY	Jaki Graham	1986
BREAKING AWAY	Balance	1981
BREAKING THE HABIT	Linkin Park	2004
BREAKING THE LAW	Judas Priest	1980
BREAKING UP IS HARD TO DO		
	Partridge Family	1972
BREAKING UP IS HARD TO DO		
	Neil Sedaka	1975
BREAKING UP IS HARD TO DO		
	Lenny Welch	1970
BREAKING UP THE GIRL	Garbage	2002
BREAKING US IN TWO	Joe Jackson	1983
BREAKOUT	Foo Fighters	2000
BREAKOUT	Swing Out Sister	1987
BREAKTHRU'	Queen	1989

SONG TITLE	ARTIST	DATE
THE BREAKUP SONG (THEY DON'T WRITE 'EM)		
	Greg Kihn Band	1981
BREATH OF LIFE	Erasure	1992
BREATHE	Faith Hill	1999
BREATHE	Prodigy	1996
BREATHE	Kylie Minogue	1998
BREATHE	Blu Cantrell featuring	
	Sean Paul	2003
BREATHE	Michelle Branch	2003
BREATHE	Fabolous	2004
BREATHE (A LITTLE DEEPER)		
	Blameless	1996
BREATHE AGAIN	Toni Braxton	1993
BREATHE AND STOP	Q-Tip	2000
BREATHE DON'T STOP	Mr On vs The Jungle Brothers	2004
BREATHE EASY	Blue	2004
BREATHE LIFE INTO ME	Mica Paris	1988
BREATHE, STRETCH, SHAKE	Mase featuring P. Diddy	2004
BREATHING	North And South	1997
BREATHING	Kate Bush	1980
BREATHLESS	Corrs	2001
BREEZE ON BY	Donny Osmond	2004
BRENDA	Cupids	1976
BRICK	Ben Folds Five	1998
BRICK HOUSE	Commodores	1977

SONG TITLE	ARTIST	DATE
THE BRICK TRACK VERSUS GITTY UP		
	Salt 'N 'Pepa	1999
BRIDGE	Queensryche	1995
BRIDGE OVER TROUBLED WATER		
	PJB featuring Hannah And	
	Her Sisters	1991
BRIDGE OVER TROUBLED WATER		
	Linda Clifford	1979
BRIDGE OVER TROUBLED WATER		
	Simon & Garfunkel	1970
BRIDGE OVER TROUBLED WATER/BRAND NEW ME		
	Aretha Franklin	1971
BRIDGE TO YOUR HEART	Wax	1987
BRIDGET THE MIDGET (THE QUEEN OF THE BLUES)		
	Ray Stevens	1971
BRIGHT EYES	Art Garfunkel	1979
BRIGHT LIGHTS	Matchbox Twenty	2003
BRIGHTER THAN SUNSHINE	Aqualung	2003
BRILLIANT DISGUISE	Bruce Springsteen	1987
BRILLIANT MIND	Furniture	1986
BRIMFUL OF ASHA	Cornershop	1998
BRING IT ALL BACK	S Club 7	1999
BRING IT ALL TO ME	Blaque	1999
BRING IT BACK	McAlmont & Butler	2002
BRING IT DOWN (THE INSANE THING)		
	Redskins	1985

SONG TITLE	ARTIST	DATE
BRING IT ON	Gomez	1999
BRING IT ON HOME TO ME	Animals	1965
BRING IT ON HOME TO ME	Eddie Floyd	1968
BRING IT ON TO MY LOVE	De Nada	2002
BRING IT ON/MY LOVER'S PRAYER		
	Alistair Griffin	2004
BRING IT UP	James Brown	1967
BRING ME CLOSER	Altered Images	1983
BRING ME EDELWEISS	Edelweiss	1989
BRING ME TO LIFE	Evanescence	2003
BRING ME YOUR CUP	UB40	1993
BRING MY FAMILY BACK	Faithless	1999
BRING ON THE DANCING HORSES		
	Echo & The Bunnymen	1985
BRING ON THE RAIN	Jo Dee Messina with	
	Tim McGraw	2001
BRING THE BOYS HOME	Freda Payne	1971
BRING THE NOISE	Anthrax featuring Chuck D	1991
BRING THE NOISE	Public Enemy	1988
BRING YOUR DAUGHTER... TO THE SLAUGHTER		
	Iron Maiden	1991
BRINGING BACK THOSE MEMORIES		
	Mark Joseph	2004
BRINGING ON BACK THE GOOD TIMES		
	Love Affair	1969
BRISTOL STOMP	Late Show	1979

SONG TITLE	ARTIST	DATE
BRITISH HUSTLE/PEACE ON EARTH		
	Hi Tension	1978
THE BRITS 1990	Various Artists	1990
BROADWAY	Goo Goo Dolls	2000
BROKE	Cassius Henry	2002
BROKE AWAY	Wet Wet Wet	1989
BROKE/WON	Beta Band	2001
BROKEN	Seether featuring Amy Lee	2004
BROKEN ARROW	Rod Stewart	1991
BROKEN BONES	Love Inc.	2003
BROKEN DOWN ANGEL	Nazareth	1973
BROKEN ENGLISH	Sunscreem	1993
BROKEN HEARTED	Ken Dodd	1970
BROKEN HEARTED ME	Anne Murray	1979
BROKEN LAND	Adventures	1988
BROKEN SILENCE	So Solid Crew	2003
BROKEN STONES	Paul Weller	1995
BROKEN WINGS	Mr Mister	1985
BROKENHEARTED	Brandy	1995
BROKENHEARTSVILLE	Joe Nichols	2003
BRONTOSAURUS	Move	1970
BROTHA PART II	Angie Stone featuring Alicia Keys	
	& Eve	2002
BROTHER	Urban Species	1994
BROTHER	C.C.S.	1972
BROTHER LOUIE	Quireboys	1993

SONG TITLE	ARTIST	DATE
BROTHER LOUIE	Hot Chocolate	1973
BROTHER LOUIE	Modern Talking	1986
BROTHER LOUIE	Stories	1973
BROTHER LOVE'S TRAVELLING SALVATION SHOW		
	Neil Diamond	1969
BROTHER RAPP (PTS 1 & 2)		
	James Brown	1970
BROTHERS & SISTERS	2 Funky 2 featuring	
	Kathryn Dion	1996
BROTHERS IN ARMS	Dire Straits	1985
BROWN EYED GIRL	Van Morrison	1967
BROWN EYED HANDSOME MAN		
	Buddy Holly	1963
BROWN GIRL IN THE RING ('93)		
	Boney M	1993
BROWN PAPER BAG	Roni Size & Reprazent	1997
BROWN SKIN	India.Arie	2001
BROWN SUGAR	D'Angelo	1995
BROWN SUGAR	Rolling Stones	1971
BRUCE	Rick Springfield	1984
BRUISE PRISTINE	Placebo	1997
BRUSHED	Paul Weller	1997
BUBBLE	Fluke	1994
BUBBLIN'	Blue	2004
BUBBLING HOT	Pato Banton with	
	Ranking Roger	1995

PAGE 556

SONG TITLE	ARTIST	DATE
BUCK ROGERS	Feeder	2001
THE BUCKET	Kings Of Leon	2004
THE BUCKET OF WATER SONG	Four Bucketeers	1980
BUDDHA OF SUBURBIA	David Bowie	1993
BUDDY HOLLY	Weezer	1995
BUDDY X	Neneh Cherry	1993
BUFFALO GALS	Malcolm McLaren/World's Famous Supreme Team	1982
BUFFALO SOLDIER	Bob Marley & The Wailers	1983
BUFFALO STANCE	Neneh Cherry	1989
BUG A BOO	Destiny's Child	1999
BUG POWDER DUST	Bomb The Bass featuring Justin Warfield	1994
BUGGIN	True Steppers featuring Dane Bowers	2000
BUGS	Hepburn	1999
BUILD	Housemartins	1987
BUILD ME UP BUTTERCUP	Foundations	1969
BUILDING A MYSTERY	Sarah McLachlan	1997
BULL IN THE HEATHER	Sonic Youth	1994
BULLET	Fluke	1995
BULLET IN THE GUN	Planet Perfecto	1999
BULLET IN THE HEAD	Rage Against The Machine	1993
BULLET WITH BUTTERFLY WINGS	Smashing Pumpkins	1995
BULLETPROOF!	Pop Will Eat Itself	1992
BULLITT	Lalo Schifrin	1997
BULLS ON PARADE	Rage Against The Machine	1996
BULLY BOY	Shed Seven	1996
BUMBLE BEE	Searchers	1965
BUMP N' GRIND	R. Kelly	1994
THE BUMP	Kenny	1974
BUMP, BUMP, BUMP	B2K featuring P.DIDDY	2003
BUMPED	Right Said Fred	1993
A BUNCH OF THYME	Foster And Allen	1982
BUNGLE IN THE JUNGLE	Jethro Tull	1974
BUNSEN BURNER	John Otway	2002
BUONA SERA	Bad Manners	1981
BURDEN IN MY HAND	Soundgarden	1996
BURIED ALIVE BY LOVE	Him	2003
BURLESQUE	Family	1972
BURN	Doctor & The Medics	1986
BURN	Usher	2004
BURN BABY BURN	Ash	2001
BURN BABY BURN	Hudson-Ford	1974
BURN BURN	Lostprophets	2003
BURN IT UP	Beatmasters With P.P. Arnold	1988
BURN RUBBER ON ME (WHY YOU WANNA HURT ME)	Gap Band	1981
BURNIN'	Daft Punk	1997
BURNIN' FOR YOU	Blue Oyster Cult	1981

SONG TITLE	ARTIST	DATE
BURNIN' HOT	Jermaine Jackson	1980
BURNING	Baby Bumps	1998
BURNING BRIDGES	Mike Curb Congregation	1970
BURNING BRIDGES (ON AND OFF AND ON AGAIN)	Status Quo	1988
BURNING CAR	John Foxx	1980
BURNING DOWN THE HOUSE	Tom Jones & The Cardigans	1999
BURNING DOWN THE HOUSE	Talking Heads	1983
BURNING HEART	Survivor	1985
BURNING HEART	Vandenberg	1983
BURNING LOVE	Elvis Presley	1972
BURNING OF THE MIDNIGHT LAMP	Jimi Hendrix Experience	1967
BURNING THE GROUND	Duran Duran	1989
BURNING UP	Tony De Vit	1995
BURNING WHEEL	Primal Scream	1997
BURUNDI BLACK	Burundi Steiphenson Black	1971
BUS STOP	Hollies	1966
BUSINESS	Eminem	2003
BUST A MOVE	Young M.C.	1989
BUSTED	Ray Charles	1963
BUSY BEE	Ugly Kid Joe	1993
BUT FOR THE GRACE OF GOD	Keith Urban	2000

SONG TITLE	ARTIST	DATE
BUT I DO LOVE YOU	Leann Rimes	2002
BUT IT'S ALRIGHT	J.J. Jackson	1966
BUT YOU KNOW I LOVE YOU	First Edition	1969
BUT YOU LOVE ME, DADDY	Jim Reeves	1969
BUT YOU'RE MINE	Sonny & Cher	1965
BUTTA LOVE	Next	1997
BUTTER BOY	Fanny	1975
BUTTERFLIES	Michael Jackson	2001
BUTTERFLIES & HURRICANES	Muse	2004
BUTTERFLY	Mariah Carey	1997
BUTTERFLY	Crazy Town	2001
BUTTERFLY	Danyel Gerrard	1971
BUTTERFLY KISSES	Raybon Brothers	1997
BUTTERFLY ON A WHEEL	Mission	1990
BUY IT IN BOTTLES	Richard Ashcroft	2003
BUY ME A ROSE	Kenny Rogers with Alison Krauss & Billy Dean	2000
BUZZ BUZZ A DIDDLE IT	Matchbox	1980
BUZZIN'	Asian Dub Foundation	1998
BY THE DEVIL (I WAS TEMPTED)	Blue Mink	1973
BY THE TIME I GET TO PHOENIX	Glen Campbell	1967

SONG TITLE	ARTIST	DATE
BY THE TIME I GET TO PHOENIX		
	Isaac Hayes	1969
BY THE TIME THIS NIGHT IS OVER		
	Kenny G With Peabo Bryson	1993
BY THE WAY	Big Three	1963
BY THE WAY	Tremeloes	1970
BY THE WAY	Red Hot Chili Peppers	2002
BY YOUR SIDE	Sade	2000
BY YOUR SIDE	Peters & Lee	1973
BYE BYE BABY	Tony Jackson & The Vibrations	1964
BYE BYE BABY	Bay City Rollers	1975
BYE BYE BABY	TQ	1999
BYE, BYE, BABY (BABY GOODBYE)		
	Four Seasons	1965
BYE BYE BLUES	Bert Kaempfert & His Orchestra	1966
BYE BYE BOY	Jennifer Ellison	2004
BYE BYE BYE	*NSYNC	2000
C U WHEN U GET THERE	Coolio featuring 40 Thevz	1997
C'30, C'60, C'90 GO	Bow Wow Wow	1980
C'EST LA VIE	UB40	1994
C'EST LA VIE	Jean Michel Jarre featuring Natacha Atlas	2000
C'EST LA VIE	B*Witched	1999
C'EST LA VIE	Robbie Nevil	1986
C'MON	Mario	2003

SONG TITLE	ARTIST	DATE
C'MON 'N RIDE IT (THE TRAIN)		
	Quad City DJ's	1996
C'MON AND GET MY LOVE		
	D. Mob featuring Cathy Dennis	1989
C'MON AND SWIM	Bobby Freeman	1964
C'MON BILLY	PJ Harvey	1995
C'MON C'MON	The Von Bondies	2004
C'MON EVERYBODY	Eddie Cochran	1958
C'MON EVERYBODY	Sex Pistols	1979
C'MON KIDS	Boo Radleys	1996
C'MON MARIANNE	Grapefruit	1968
C'MON MARIANNE	Four Seasons	1967
C'MON MARIANNE	Donny Osmond	1976
C'MON PEOPLE (WE'RE MAKING IT NOW)		
	Richard Ashcroft	2000
C-I-T-Y	John Cafferty & The Beaver Brown Band	1985
CA PLANE POUR MOI	Plastic Bertrand	1978
CAB DRIVER	Mills Brothers	1968
CACHARPAYA (ANDES PUMPSA DAESI)		
	Incantation	1982
CAFE DEL MAR	Energy 52	2002
CAFE DEL MAR '98	Energy 52	1998
CAFFEINE BOMB	Wildhearts	1994
THE CALENDAR SONG (JANUARY, FEBRUARY, MARCH, APRIL, MAY)	Trinidad Oil Company	1977

SONG TITLE	ARTIST	DATE
CALIFORNIA	Belinda Carlisle	1997
CALIFORNIA	Wedding Present	1992
CALIFORNIA DREAMIN'	Mamas & The Papas	1966
CALIFORNIA DREAMIN'/CARRY THE BLAME		
	River City People	1990
CALIFORNIA GIRLS	Beach Boys	1965
CALIFORNIA GIRLS	David Lee Roth	1985
CALIFORNIA LOVE/HOW DO U WANT IT		
	2pac/Dr. Dre/Roger Troutman	1996
CALIFORNIA MAN	Move	1972
CALIFORNIA NIGHTS	Lesley Gore	1967
CALIFORNIA SAGA	Beach Boys	1973
CALIFORNIA SOUL	5th Dimension	1968
CALIFORNIA SUN	Rivieras	1964
CALIFORNICATION	Red Hot Chili Peppers	2000
THE CALL	Backstreet Boys	2001
CALL HER YOUR SWEETHEART		
	Frank Ifield	1966
CALL IT FATE	Richie Dan	2000
CALL IT LOVE	Deuce	1995
CALL IT LOVE	Poco	1989
CALL IT WHAT YOU WANT	New Kids On The Block	1991
CALL ME	Le Click	1997
CALL ME	Blondie	1980
CALL ME	Go West	1985
CALL ME	Spagna	1987

SONG TITLE	ARTIST	DATE
CALL ME	Jamelia	2000
CALL ME	Tweet	2002
CALL ME	Chris Montez	1966
CALL ME	Skyy	1982
CALL ME (COME BACK HOME)		
	Al Green	1973
CALL ME LIGHTNING	Who	1968
(CALL ME) NUMBER ONE	Tremeloes	1969
CALL ME ROUND	Pilot	1975
CALL ME/SON OF A PREACHER MAN		
	Aretha Franklin	1970
CALL OF THE WILD	Midge Ure	1986
CALL OFF THE SEARCH	Katie Melua	2004
CALL ON ME	Chicago	1974
CALL ON ME	Eric Prydz	2004
CALL THE MAN	Celine Dion	1997
CALL TO THE HEART	Giuffria	1984
CALL U SEXY	Vs	2004
THE CALL UP	Clash	1980
CALL UP THE GROUPS	Barron Knights	1964
CALLIN' ME	Lil' Zane featuring 112	2000
CALLING	Geri Halliwell	2001
CALLING ALL GIRLS	ATL	2004
CALLING ALL THE HEROES	It Bites	1986
CALLING AMERICA	Electric Light Orchestra	1986
CALLING DR. LOVE	Kiss	1977

SONG TITLE	ARTIST	DATE
CALLING ELVIS	Dire Straits	1991
CALLING OCCUPANTS OF INTERPLANETARY CRAFT		
	Carpenters	1977
CALLING YOUR NAME	Marilyn	1983
CALYPSO CRAZY	Billy Ocean	1988
CAMBODIA	Kim Wilde	1981
CAMDEN TOWN	Suggs	1995
CAMELS	Santos	2001
CAMOUFLAGE	Stan Ridgway	1986
CAN CAN	Bad Manners	1981
CAN CAN YOU PARTY	Jive Bunny & The Mastermixers	1990
CAN I	Cashmere	1985
CAN I CHANGE MY MIND	Tyrone Davis	1968
CAN I GET A ...	Jay-Z featuring Amil & Ja Rule	1999
CAN I GET A WITNESS	Sam Brown	1989
CAN I GET A WITNESS	Lee Michaels	1971
CAN I KICK IT?	A Tribe Called Quest	1991
CAN I PLAY WITH MADNESS		
	Iron Maiden	1988
CAN I TAKE YOU HOME LITTLE GIRL?		
	Drifters	1975
CAN I TOUCH YOU... THERE?		
	Michael Bolton	1995
CAN I TRUST YOU	Bachelors	1966
CAN THE CAN	Suzi Quatro	1973
CAN THIS BE REAL	Natural Four	1974

SONG TITLE	ARTIST	DATE
CAN U DIG IT?	Pop Will Eat Itself	1989
CAN U DIG IT	Jamx & Deleon	2002
CAN WE	SWV	1997
CAN WE FIX IT	Bob The Builder	2000
CAN WE STILL BE FRIENDS	Todd Rundgren	1978
CAN WE TALK	Code Red	1997
CAN WE TALK	Tevin Campbell	1993
CAN YOU DIG IT?	Mock Turtles	1991
CAN YOU DO IT	Geordie	1973
CAN YOU FEEL IT	Jacksons	1981
CAN YOU FEEL IT?	Reel 2 Real featuring The Mad Stuntman	1994
CAN YOU FEEL THE FORCE		
	Real Thing	1979
CAN YOU FEEL THE FORCE ('86 REMIX)		
	Real Thing	1986
CAN YOU FEEL THE LOVE TONIGHT?		
	Elton John	1994
CAN YOU FOOL	Glen Campbell	1978
CAN YOU FORGIVE HER?	Pet Shop Boys	1993
CAN YOU FORGIVE ME	Karl Denver	1963
CAN YOU HANDLE IT	Sharon Redd	1981
CAN YOU HANDLE IT	DNA featuring Sharon Redd	1992
CAN YOU PARTY	Royal House	1988
CAN YOU PLEASE CRAWL OUT YOUR WINDOW		
	Bob Dylan	1966

SONG TITLE	ARTIST	DATE
(CAN YOU) FEEL THE PASSION		
	Blue Pearl	1992
CAN'T BE WITHOUT YOU TONIGHT		
	Judy Boucher	1987
CAN'T BUY ME LOVE	Ella Fitzgerald	1964
CAN'T BUY ME LOVE	Beatles	1964
CAN'T CRY ANYMORE	Sheryl Crow	1995
CAN'T DENY IT	Fabolous featuring Nate Dogg	2001
CAN'T DO A THING (TO STOP ME)		
	Chris Isaak	1993
CAN'T DO RIGHT FOR DOING WRONG		
	Erin Rocha	2003
CAN'T FIGHT THE MOONLIGHT		
	Leann Rimes	2001
CAN'T FIGHT THIS FEELING		
	REO Speedwagon	1985
CAN'T FORGET YOU	Sonia	1989
CAN'T GET BY WITHOUT YOU		
	Real Thing	1976
CAN'T GET BY WITHOUT YOU (THE 2ND DECADE REMIX)	Real Thing	1986
CAN'T GET ENOUGH	Suede	1999
CAN'T GET ENOUGH	Bad Company	1974
CAN'T GET ENOUGH	Soulsearcher	1999
CAN'T GET ENOUGH	Raghav	2004

SONG TITLE	ARTIST	DATE
CAN'T GET ENOUGH OF YOU		
	Eddy Grant	1981
CAN'T GET ENOUGH OF YOUR LOVE		
	Taylor Dayne	1993
CAN'T GET ENOUGH OF YOUR LOVE, BABE		
	Barry White	1974
CAN'T GET IT BACK	Mis-Teeq	2003
CAN'T GET IT OUT OF MY HEAD		
	Electric Light Orchestra	1974
CAN'T GET OUT OF BED	Charlatans	1994
CAN'T GET USED TO LOSING YOU		
	Colour Girl	2000
CAN'T GET USED TO LOSING YOU		
	Beat	1983
CAN'T GET USED TO LOSING YOU		
	Andy Williams	1963
CAN'T GET YOU OUT OF MY HEAD		
	Kylie Minogue	2002
CAN'T GET YOU OUT OF MY THOUGHTS		
	Dum Dums	2000
CAN'T GIVE YOU ANYTHING (BUT MY LOVE)		
	Stylistics	1975
CAN'T GIVE YOU MORE	Status Quo	1991
CAN'T HAPPEN HERE	Rainbow	1981
CAN'T HELP FALLING IN LOVE		
	Stylistics	1976

SONG TITLE	ARTIST	DATE
CAN'T HELP FALLING IN LOVE	Andy Williams	1970
CAN'T HELP FALLING IN LOVE	Corey Hart	1986
CAN'T HELP FALLING IN LOVE	UB40	1993
CAN'T HELP IT	Happy Clappers	1996
CAN'T HIDE LOVE	Earth, Wind & Fire	1976
CAN'T HOLD US DOWN	Christina Aguilera featuring Lil' Kim	2003
CAN'T KEEP IT IN	Cat Stevens	1972
CAN'T KEEP ME SILENT	Angelic	2001
CAN'T KEEP THIS FEELING IN	Cliff Richard	1998
CAN'T KNOCK THE HUSTLE	Jay-Z featuring Mary J. Blige	1997
CAN'T LET GO	Mariah Carey	1991
CAN'T LET HER GO	Boyz II Men	1998
CAN'T LET YOU GO	Barry Ryan	1972
CAN'T LET YOU GO	Fabolous featuring Mike Shorey & Lil' Mo	2003
CAN'T LIVE WITH YOU, CAN'T LIVE WITHOUT YOU	Mindbenders	1966
(CAN'T LIVE WITHOUT YOUR) LOVE AND AFFECTION	Nelson	1990
CAN'T MAKE UP MY MIND	Sonique	2003

SONG TITLE	ARTIST	DATE
CAN'T NOBODY	Kelly Rowland	2003
CAN'T NOBODY HOLD ME DOWN	Puff Daddy featuring Mase	1997
CAN'T SAY GOODBYE	Pop!	2004
CAN'T SAY HOW MUCH I LOVE YOU	Demis Roussos	1976
CAN'T SEE ME	Ian Brown	1998
CAN'T SHAKE LOOSE	Agnetha Faltskog	1983
CAN'T SHAKE THE FEELING	Big Fun	1989
CAN'T SMILE WITHOUT YOU	Barry Manilow	1978
CAN'T STAND LOSING YOU	Police	1979
CAN'T STAND ME NOW	Libertines	2004
CAN'T STAY AWAY FROM YOU	Gloria Estefan/Miami Sound Machine	1987
CAN'T STOP	Red Hot Chili Peppers	2003
CAN'T STOP	After 7	1990
CAN'T STOP DANCIN'	Captain & Tennille	1977
CAN'T STOP FALLING INTO LOVE	Cheap Trick	1990
CAN'T STOP LOVIN' YOU	Van Halen	1995
CAN'T STOP LOVING YOU	Phil Collins	2002
CAN'T STOP LOVING YOU	Tom Jones	1970
CAN'T STOP THE MUSIC	Village People	1980

SONG TITLE	ARTIST	DATE
CAN'T STOP THIS THING WE STARTED		
	Bryan Adams	1991
CAN'T TAKE MY EYES OFF YOU		
	Boystown Gang	1982
CAN'T TAKE MY EYES OFF YOU		
	Andy Williams	1968
CAN'T TAKE MY EYES OFF YOU		
	Frankie Valli	1967
CAN'T TAKE YOUR LOVE	Pauline Henry	1994
CAN'T TRUSS IT	Public Enemy	1991
CAN'T TURN BACK	Speedway	2004
CAN'T WAIT ANOTHER MINUTE		
	Five Star	1986
CAN'T WAIT TO BE WITH YOU		
	D.J. Jazzy Jeff & The Fresh	
	Prince	1994
CAN'T WE TRY	Dan Hill (Duet with	
	Vonda Shepard)	1987
CAN'T YOU HEAR MY HEARTBEAT		
	Goldie & The Gingerbreads	1965
CAN'T YOU HEAR MY HEARTBEAT		
	Herman's Hermits	1965
CAN'T YOU SEE	Total featuring The Notorious	
	B.I.G.	1995
CAN'T YOU SEE THAT SHE'S MINE		
	Dave Clark Five	1964

SONG TITLE	ARTIST	DATE
(CAN'T YOU) TRIP LIKE I DO		
	Filter And The Crystal Method	1997
CAN'TCHA SAY (YOU BELIEVE IN ME)/STILL IN LOVE		
	Boston	1987
CANDIDA	Dawn	1970
CANDLE IN THE WIND	Elton John	1974
CANDLE IN THE WIND 1997		
	Elton John	1997
CANDLES	Alex Reece	1996
CANDY	Cameo	1986
CANDY	Ash	2001
CANDY	Mandy Moore	2000
CANDY	Iggy Pop With Kate Pierson	1990
CANDY GIRL	Babybird	1997
CANDY GIRL	New Edition	1983
CANDY MAN	Brian Poole & The Tremeloes	1964
CANDY RAIN	Soul For Real	1995
CANDYMAN	Siouxsie & The Banshees	1986
CANNED HEAT	Jamiroquai	1999
CANNONBALL	Breeders	1993
CANNONBALL	Damien Rice	2004
CANTALOOP	US3 featuring Rashaan	1993
CANTALOOP (FLIP FANTASIA)		
	US3	1993
CANTGETAMAN, CANTGETAJOB (LIFE'S A BITCH)		
	Sister Bliss	1994

SONG TITLE	ARTIST	DATE
CANTO DELLA TERRA	Andrea Bocelli	1999
CANTONESE BOY	Japan	1982
CAPSTICK COMES HOME/SHEFFIELD GRINDER		
	Tony Capstick	1981
CAPTAIN BEAKY/WILFRED THE WEASEL		
	Keith Michel	1980
CAPTAIN KREMMEN (RETRIBUTION)		
	Kenny Everett	1977
THE CAPTAIN OF HER HEART		
	Double	1986
CAPTAIN OF YOUR SHIP	Reperata & The Delrons	1968
CAR 67	Driver 67	1978
CAR WASH	Rose Royce	1988
CARA MIA	Jay & The Americans	1965
CARA-LIN	Strangeloves	1965
CARAMEL	City High featuring Eve	2001
CARAVAN	Inspiral Carpets	1991
CARAVAN OF LOVE	Housemartins	1986
CARDIAC ARREST	Madness	1982
CAREFREE HIGHWAY	Gordon Lightfoot	1974
CARELESS HANDS	Des O'Connor	1967
CARELESS MEMORIES	Duran Duran	1981
CARELESS WHISPER	Wham!	1984
CARIBBEAN BLUE	Enya	1991
CARIBBEAN DISCO	Lobo	1981

SONG TITLE	ARTIST	DATE
CARIBBEAN QUEEN (NO MORE LOVE ON THE RUN)		
	Billy Ocean	1984
CARMEN QUEASY	Maxim	2000
CARNAVAL 2002	Dario G	2002
CARNAVAL DE PARIS	Dario G	1998
CARNIVAL	Lionrock	1993
CARNIVAL	Cardigans	1995
CARNIVAL	Natalie Merchant	1995
CARNIVAL GIRL	Texas featuring Kardinal Offishall	2003
THE CARNIVAL IS OVER	Seekers	1965
CAROLINA IN THE PINES	Michael Murphey	1975
CAROLINE	Status Quo	1973
CAROLINE, NO	Brian Wilson	1966
CARPET MAN	5th Dimension	1968
CARRIE	Europe	1987
CARRIE	Cliff Richard	1980
CARRIE-ANNE	Hollies	1967
CARRION/APOLOGIES TO INSECT LIFE		
	British Sea Power	2003
CARROT ROPE	Pavement	1999
CARRY ME BACK	Rascals	1969
CARRY ME HOME	Gloworm	1994
CARRY ON WAYWARD SON		
	Kansas	1976
CARS	Gary Numan	1980

SONG TITLE	ARTIST	DATE
CARS (E REG MODEL)/ARE 'FRIENDS' ELECTRIC?		
	Gary Numan	1987
CARTE BLANCHE	Veracocha	1999
CARTOON HEROES	Aqua	2000
CARTROUBLE	Adam & The Ants	1981
CASABLANCA	Kenny Ball	1963
CASANOVA	Ultimate Kaos	1997
CASANOVA	Coffee	1980
CASANOVA	Levert	1987
CASANOVA/CHARIOT	Petula Clark	1963
CASCADE	Future Sound Of London	1993
CASE OF THE EX (WHATCHA GONNA DO)		
	Mya	2000
CASINO ROYALE	Herb Alpert & The Tijuana Brass	1967
CASSIUS 1999	Cassius	1999
CAST YOUR FATE TO THE WIND		
	Sounds Orchestral	1965
CASTLES IN THE AIR	Don McLean	1981
CASTLES IN THE SAND	Thunder	1995
CASTLES IN THE SAND	Stevie Wonder	1964
CASTLES IN THE SKY	Ian Van Dahl	2001
CASUAL SUB (BURNING SPEAR)		
	ETA	1997
CAT AMONG THE PIGEONS/SILENT NIGHT		
	Bros	1988
THE CAT CREPT IN	Mud	1974
THE CAT IN THE WINDOW	Petula Clark	1967
CAT SCRATCH FEVER	Ted Nugent	1977
CAT'S IN THE CRADLE	Ugly Kid Joe	1993
CAT'S IN THE CRADLE	Harry Chapin	1974
CAT'S PEOPLE (PUTTING OUT FIRE)		
	David Bowie	1982
CATCH	Cure	1987
CATCH	Kosheen	2001
CATCH A FIRE	Haddaway	1995
CATCH ME I'M FALLING	Pretty Poison	1987
CATCH ME I'M FALLING	Real Life	1984
CATCH ME UP	Gomez	2004
CATCH THE SUN	Doves	2000
CATCH THE WIND	Donovan	1965
CATCH US IF YOU CAN	Dave Clark Five	1965
THE CATERPILLAR	Cure	1984
CATH	Bluebells	1984
CAUGHT A LITE SNEEZE	Tori Amos	1996
CAUGHT BY THE RIVER	Doves	2002
CAUGHT IN A MOMENT	Sugababes	2004
CAUGHT IN MY SHADOW	Wonder Stuff	1991
CAUGHT IN THE MIDDLE	Juliet Roberts	1994
CAUGHT IN THE MIDDLE	Al	2002
CAUGHT OUT THERE	Kelis	2000

SONG TITLE	ARTIST	DATE
CAUGHT UP IN THE RAPTURE		
	Anita Baker	1986
CAUGHT UP IN YOU	38 Special	1982
CAUSING A COMMOTION	Madonna	1987
CAVATINA	John Williams	1979
CECILIA	Suggs	1996
CECILIA	Simon & Garfunkel	1970
THE CEDAR ROOM	Doves	2000
CELEBRATE	Levellers	1997
CELEBRATE	Three Dog Night	1970
CELEBRATE OUR LOVE	Alice Deejay	2001
CELEBRATE THE WORLD	Womack & Womack	1989
CELEBRATE YOUTH	Rick Springfield	1985
CELEBRATION	Kool & The Gang	1980
CELEBRATION	Kylie Minogue	1992
CELEBRITY	Brad Paisley	2003
CELEBRITY HIT LIST	Terrorvision	1996
CELEBRITY SKIN	Hole	1998
CELL THERAPY	Goodie Mobb	1995
CELTIC SOUL BROTHERS	Kevin Rowland & Dexy's	
	Midnight Runners	1983
THE CELTS	Enya	1992
CENTER CITY	Fat Larry's Band	1977
CENTERFOLD	J. Geils Band	1981
CENTIPEDE	Rebbie Jackson	1984
CENTRAL PARK ARREST	Thunderthighs	1974

SONG TITLE	ARTIST	DATE
CENTRAL RESERVATION	Beth Orton	1999
CEREMONY	New Order	1981
CERTAIN PEOPLE I KNOW		
	Morrissey	1992
CH-CHECK IT OUT	Beastie Boys	2004
CHA CHA HEELS	Eartha Kitt & Bronski Beat	1989
CHA CHA SLIDE	DJ Casper	2004
CHA-CHA SLIDE	MC Jig	2004
CHAIN OF FOOLS	Aretha Franklin	1967
THE CHAIN OF LOVE	Clay Walker	2000
CHAIN REACTION	Hurricane #1	1997
CHAIN REACTION	Diana Ross	1986
CHAIN REACTION	Steps	2001
CHAINED	Marvin Gaye	1968
CHAINS	Tina Arena	1996
CHAINS AROUND MY HEART		
	Richard Marx	1992
CHAINS OF LOVE	Erasure	1988
CHAINSAW CHARLIE (MURDERS IN THE NEW MORGUE)		
	W.A.S.P	1992
CHALK DUST – THE UMPIRE STRIKES BACK		
	The Brat	1982
CHAMPAGNE	Salt 'N 'Pepa	1996
CHAMPAGNE DANCE	Pay As U Go	2002
CHANCE	Big Country	1983
CHANCES	Hot Chocolate	1982

SONG TITLE	ARTIST	DATE
CHANGE	Blind Melon	1994
CHANGE	Tears For Fears	1983
CHANGE	Lisa Stansfield	1991
CHANGE	Lightning Seeds	1995
CHANGE CLOTHES	Jay-Z	2003
CHANGE HIS WAYS	Robert Palmer	1989
A CHANGE IS GONNA COME		
	Sam Cooke	1965
CHANGE OF HEART	Change	1984
CHANGE OF HEART	Eric Carmen	1978
CHANGE OF HEART	Cyndi Lauper	1986
CHANGE OF HEART	Tom Petty & The Heartbreakers	1983
CHANGE THE WORLD	Eric Clapton	1996
CHANGE WITH THE TIMES	Van McCoy	1975
A CHANGE WOULD DO YOU GOOD		
	Sheryl Crow	1997
CHANGE YOUR MIND	Sharpe & Numan	1985
CHANGE YOUR MIND	Upside Down	1996
CHANGES	2Pac	1998
CHANGES	Imagination	1982
CHANGES	Ozzy & Kelly Osbourne	2003
CHANGES IN LATITUDE, CHANGES IN ATTITUDE		
	Jimmy Buffett	1977
THE CHANGINGMAN	Paul Weller	1995
CHANSON D'AMOUR	Manhattan Transfer	1977

SONG TITLE	ARTIST	DATE
CHANT NO. I (I DON'T NEED THIS PRESSURE ON)		
	Spandau Ballet	1981
CHANTE'S GOT A MAN	Chante Moore	1999
CHANTILLY LACE	Jerry Lee Lewis	1972
CHAPEL IN THE MOONLIGHT		
	Bachelors	1965
CHAPEL OF LOVE	Dixie Cups	1964
CHARADE	Skids	1979
CHARADE	Sammy Kaye	1964
CHARIOTS OF FIRE	Vangelis	1981
CHARITY	Skunk Anansie	1996
CHARITY BALL	Fanny	1971
CHARLENE	Anthony Hamilton	2004
CHARLIE BIG POTATO	Skunk Anansie	1999
CHARLIE'S ANGELS 2000	Apollo 440	2000
CHARLOTTE ANNE	Julian Cope	1988
CHARLY	Prodigy	1991
CHARMAINE	Bachelors	1963
CHARMLESS MAN	Blur	1996
CHASE	Giorgio Moroder	1979
CHASE THE SUN	Planet Funk	2001
CHASIN' THE WIND	Chicago	1991
CHASING RAINBOWS	Shed Seven	1996
CHATTANOOGA CHOO CHOO		
	Tuxedo Junction	1978

SONG TITLE	ARTIST	DATE
CHEAPER TO KEEP HER	Johnnie Taylor	1973
THE CHEATER	Bob Kuban & The In-Men	1966
CHECK IT OUT	John Cougar Mellencamp	1988
CHECK IT OUT	Tavares	1973
CHECK IT OUT (EVERYBODY)		
	B.M.R featuring Felicia	1999
CHECK OUT THE GROOVE	Bobby Thurston	1980
CHECK OUT YOUR MIND	Impressions	1970
CHECK THE MEANING	Richard Ashcroft	2002
CHECK THIS OUT	L.A. Mix	1988
CHECK YO SELF	Ice Cube featuring Das Efx	1993
CHEEKAH BOW BOW (THAT COMPUTER SONG)		
	Vengaboys	2000
CHEEKY	Boniface	2002
CHEEKY FLAMENCO	Cheeky Girls	2004
CHEEKY SONG (TOUCH MY BUM)		
	Cheeky Girls	2002
CHEERS 2 U	Playa	1998
CHEESEBURGERS IN PARADISE		
	Jimmy Buffett	1978
CHEMICAL WORLD	Blur	1993
CHEMISTRY	Semisonic	2001
CHEMISTRY	Nolans	1981
CHEQUERED LOVE	Kim Wilde	1981
CHERCHEZ LAGHOST	Ghostface Killah	2000
CHERI BABE	Hot Chocolate	1974

SONG TITLE	ARTIST	DATE
CHERISH	Kool & The Gang	1985
CHERISH	Madonna	1989
CHERISH	Association	1966
CHERISH	David Cassidy	1971
CHERISH THE DAY	Plummet	2004
CHERRY BABY	Starz	1977
CHERRY BOMB	John Cougar Mellencamp	1987
CHERRY CHERRY	Neil Diamond	1966
CHERRY HILL PARK	Billy Joe Royal	1969
CHERRY LIPS (GO BABY GO!)		
	Garbage	2002
CHERRY OH BABY	UB40	1984
CHERRY PIE	Warrant	1990
CHERRY PINK AND APPLE BLOSSOM WHITE		
	Modern Romance	1982
CHERUB ROCK	Smashing Pumpkins	1993
CHESTNUT MARE	Byrds	1971
CHEVY VAN	Sammy Johns	1975
CHEWING GUM	Annie	2004
CHEWY CHEWY	Ohio Express	1968
CHI MAI THEME	Ennio Morricone	1981
CHICAGO	Kiki Dee	1977
CHICAGO	Graham Nash	1971
CHICK-A-BOOM	Daddy Dewdrop	1971
CHICK-A-BOOM	53rd And 3rd featuring The Sound Of Shag	1975

SONG TITLE	ARTIST	DATE
CHICKEN	Eighties Matchbox B-Line Disaster	2003
THE CHICKEN SONG	Spitting Image	1986
CHIHUAHUA	DJ Bobo	2003
CHILD	Mark Owen	1996
CHILD OF CLAY	Jimmie Rodgers	1967
A CHILD'S PRAYER	Hot Chocolate	1975
CHILDREN	EMF	1991
CHILDREN	Robert Miles	1996
CHILDREN OF THE NIGHT	Nakatomi	2002
CHILDREN OF THE NIGHT	Richard Marx	1990
CHILDREN OF THE REVOLUTION	T. Rex	1972
CHILDREN SAY	Level 42	1987
CHILLIN'	Modjo	2001
CHIME	Orbital	1990
CHINA GIRL	David Bowie	1983
CHINA GROVE	Doobie Brothers	1973
CHINA IN YOUR HAND	T'Pau	1987
CHINATOWN	Move	1971
CHINATOWN	Thin Lizzy	1980
THE CHINESE WAY	Level 42	1983
CHING CHING (LOVIN' YOU STILL)	Terri Walker	2003
CHIQUITITA	ABBA	1979

SONG TITLE	ARTIST	DATE
CHIRPY CHIRPY CHEEP CHEEP	Middle Of The Road	1971
CHIRPY CHIRPY CHEEP CHEEP	Mac & Katie Kissoon	1971
CHLOE	Elton John	1981
CHOCOLATE	Snow Patrol	2004
CHOCOLATE	Kylie Minogue	2004
CHOCOLATE (CHOCO CHOCO)	Soul Control	2004
CHOCOLATE BOX	Bros	1989
CHOCOLATE SALTY BALLS (PS I LOVE YOU)	Chef	1998
CHOCOLATE SENSATION	Lenny Fontana & DJ Shorty	2000
CHOICE OF COLORS	Impressions	1969
CHOICE?	Blow Monkeys/Sylvia Tella	1989
CHOK THERE	Apache Indian	1993
THE CHOKIN' KIND	Joe Simon	1969
CHOO CHOO TRAIN	Box Tops	1968
CHOOSE	Color Me Badd	1994
CHOOSE LIFE	PF Project featuring Ewan McGregor	1997
CHOOZA LOOZA	Maria Willson	2003
CHOP SUEY	System Of A Down	2001
CHORUS (FISHES IN THE SEA)	Erasure	1991
THE CHOSEN FEW	Dooleys	1979

SONG TITLE	ARTIST	DATE
CHRISTIAN	China Crisis	1983
CHRISTIANSANDS	Tricky	1996
CHRISTINE	Miss X	1963
CHRISTINE	Siouxsie & The Banshees	1980
CHRISTINE SIXTEEN	Kiss	1977
CHRISTMAS COUNTDOWN	Frank Kelly	1984
CHRISTMAS IN BLOBBYLAND		
	Mr. Blobby	1995
CHRISTMAS IN DREADLAND/COME OUTSIDE		
	Judge Dread	1975
CHRISTMAS IN SMURFLAND		
	Father Abraham & The Smurfs	1978
CHRISTMAS IS ALL AROUND		
	Billy Mack	2003
A CHRISTMAS KISS	Daniel O'Donnell	1999
CHRISTMAS ON 45	Holly & The Ivys	1981
CHRISTMAS RAPPIN'	Kurtis Blow	1979
CHRISTMAS SONG	Gilbert O'Sullivan	1974
THE CHRISTMAS SONG (CHESTNUTS ROASTING ON AN		
OPEN FIRE)	Christina Aguilera	1999
CHRISTMAS SPECTRE	Jingle Belles	1983
CHRISTMAS TIME (DON'T LET THE BELLS END)		
	The Darkness	2003
CHRISTMAS WILL BE JUST ANOTHER LONELY DAY		
	Brenda Lee	1964
CHUCK E.'S IN LOVE	Rickie Lee Jones	1979

SONG TITLE	ARTIST	DATE
CHUG-A-LUG	Roger Miller	1964
CHURCH OF NOISE	Therapy?	1998
CHURCH OF THE POISON MIND		
	Culture Club	1983
CHURCH OF YOUR HEART	Roxette	1992
CIGARETTES & ALCOHOL	Oasis	1994
CINDERELLA	Lemonescent	2003
CINDERELLA	Firefall	1977
CINDERELLA ROCKAFELLA	Esther & Abi Ofarim	1968
CINDY INCIDENTALLY	Faces	1973
CINNAMON	Derek	1968
THE CIRCLE	Ocean Colour Scene	1996
CIRCLE IN THE SAND	Belinda Carlisle	1988
THE CIRCLE IS SMALL (I CAN SEE IT IN YOUR EYES)		
	Gordon Lightfoot	1978
CIRCLE OF LIFE	Elton John	1994
CIRCLES	New Seekers	1972
CIRCLES	Adam F	1997
CIRCLES	Atlantic Starr	1982
CIRCLESQUARE	Wonder Stuff	1990
CIRCUS	Eric Clapton	1998
THE CIRCUS	Erasure	1987
CIRCUS GAMES	Skids	1980
THE CISCO KID	War	1973
CISSY STRUT	Meters	1969
CITIES IN THE DUST	Siouxsie & The Banshees	1985

SONG TITLE	ARTIST	DATE
THE CITY IS MINE	Jay-Z featuring Blackstreet	1998
CITY LIGHTS	David Essex	1976
THE CITY OF NEW ORLEANS	Arlo Guthrie	1972
THE CIVIL WAR (EP)	Guns N' Roses	1993
CLAIR	Gilbert O'Sullivan	1972
THE CLAIRVOYANT	Iron Maiden	1988
CLAP BACK/REIGNS	Ja Rule	2003
CLAP FOR THE WOLFMAN	Guess Who	1974
CLAP YOUR HANDS	Camisra	1999
THE CLAPPING SONG	Belle Stars	1982
THE CLAPPING SONG	Shirley Ellis	1965
THE CLAPPING SONG	Pia Zadora	1982
CLASH CITY ROCKERS	Clash	1978
CLASSIC	Adrian Gurvitz	1982
CLASSICAL GAS	Mason Williams	1968
CLASSICAL MUDDLY	Portsmouth Sinfonia	1981
CLEAN UP WOMAN	Betty Wright	1971
CLEAN UP YOUR OWN BACK YARD	Elvis Presley	1969
CLEAN, CLEAN	Buggles	1980
CLEANIN' OUT MY CLOSET	Eminem	2002
CLEMENTINE	Mark Owen	1997
CLEOPATRA'S CAT	Spin Doctors	1994
CLEOPATRA'S THEME	Cleopatra	1998

SONG TITLE	ARTIST	DATE
CLINGING VINE	Bobby Vinton	1964
CLINT EASTWOOD	Gorillaz	2001
CLIPPED	Curve	1991
CLOCK STRIKES	Timbaland And Magoo	1998
CLOCKS	Coldplay	2003
CLOG DANCE	Violinski	1979
CLONES (WE'RE ALL)	Alice Cooper	1980
CLOSE (TO THE EDIT)	Art Of Noise	1984
CLOSE BUT NO CIGAR	Thomas Dolby	1992
CLOSE COVER	Minimalistix	2002
CLOSE EVERY DOOR	Phillip Schofield	1992
CLOSE MY EYES FOREVER	Lita Ford & Ozzy Osbourne	1989
CLOSE THE DOOR	Teddy Pendergrass	1978
CLOSE TO ME	Cure	1990
CLOSE TO YOU	Maxi Priest	1990
CLOSE TO YOU	Whigfield	1995
CLOSE TO YOU	Marti Pellow	2001
CLOSE TO YOUR HEART	JX	1997
CLOSE YOUR EYES	Edward Bear	1973
CLOSE YOUR EYES	Peaches & Herb	1967
CLOSED FOR BUSINESS	Mansun	1997
CLOSER	Nine Inch Nails	1994
THE CLOSER I GET TO YOU	Roberta Flack & Donny Hathaway	1978
CLOSER THAN CLOSE	Rosie Gaines	1997

SONG TITLE	ARTIST	DATE
CLOSER THAN MOST	Beautiful South	2000
CLOSER TO FREE	Bodeans	1996
CLOSER TO HOME	Grand Funk Railroad	1970
CLOSER TO ME	5ive	2001
CLOSER TO THE HEART	Rush	1978
THE CLOSER YOU GET	Alabama	1983
THE CLOSEST THING TO CRAZY	Katie Melua	2003
CLOSEST THING TO HEAVEN	Lionel Richie	1998
CLOSEST THING TO HEAVEN	Kane Gang	1984
CLOSING TIME	Semisonic	1999
CLOUD NINE	Temptations	1968
CLOUD NINE	Mongo Santamaria	1969
CLOUD 99	St. Andrews Chorale	1976
CLOUD NUMBER 9	Bryan Adams	1999
CLOUDBUSTING	Kate Bush	1985
CLOUDS	Source	1997
CLOUDS ACROSS THE MOON	Rah Band	1985
CLUB AT THE END OF THE STREET	Elton John	1990
CLUB COUNTRY	Associates	1982
CLUB FANTASTIC (MEGAMIX)	Wham!	1983

SONG TITLE	ARTIST	DATE
CLUB FOOT	Kasabian	2004
CLUB TROPICANA	Wham!	1983
CLUBBED TO DEATH	Rob Dougan	2002
CLUBBIN	Marques Houston featuring Joe Budden & Pied Piper	2003
CO-CO	Sweet	1971
COAST IS CLEAR	Curve	1991
COCHISE	Audioslave	2003
COCO JAMBOO	Mr. President	1997
COCOMOTION	El Coco	1978
COCONUT	Nilsson	1972
COCOON	Bjork	2002
CODE OF LOVE	Mike Sarne	1963
COFFEE	Supersister	2000
COFFEE + TV	Blur	1999
COGNOSCENTI vs INTELLIGENTSIA	Cuban Boys	1999
COLD	Annie Lennox	1992
COLD AS CHRISTMAS	Elton John	1983
COLD AS ICE	Foreigner	1977
COLD AS ICE	M.O.P.	2001
COLD BLOODED	Rick James	1983
COLD COLD HEART	Wet Wet Wet	1994
COLD, COLD HEART	Midge Ure	1991
COLD DAY IN HELL	Gary Moore	1992
COLD HARD BITCH	Jet	2004

SONG TITLE	ARTIST	DATE
COLD HEARTED	Paula Abdul	1989
COLD LOVE	Donna Summer	1980
COLD ROCK A PARTY	MC Lyte	1996
COLD SWEAT	Thin Lizzy	1983
COLD SWEAT (PART 1)	James Brown	1967
COLD TURKEY	Plastic Ono Band	1969
COLD WORLD	Genius/GZA featuring D'Angelo	1996
COLOR HIM FATHER	Winstons	1969
COLOR MY WORLD	Petula Clark	1966
COLORS OF THE WIND	Vanessa Williams	1995
COLOUR MY LIFE	M People	1992
THE COLOUR OF LOVE	Billy Ocean	1988
THE COLOUR OF MY LOVE	Jefferson	1969
COLOUR THE WORLD	Sash!	1999
COLOURBLIND	Darius	2002
COLOURS	Donovan	1965
COLOURS OF THE WIND	Vanessa Williams	1995
COMA GIRL	Joe Strummer & The Mescaleros	2003
THE COMBINE HARVESTER (BRAND NEW KEY)	Wurzels	1976
COMBINE HARVESTER 2001 REMIX	Wurzels	2001
COME & TALK TO ME	Jodeci	1992
COME A LITTLE BIT CLOSER	Jay & The Americans	1964

SONG TITLE	ARTIST	DATE
COME AND GET IT	Badfinger	1970
COME AND GET ME	Cleopatra	2000
COME AND GET WITH ME	Keith Sweat featuring Snoop Dogg	1998
COME AND GET YOUR LOVE	Real McCoy	1995
COME AND GET YOUR LOVE	Redbone	1974
COME AND STAY WITH ME	Marianne Faithfull	1965
COME AS YOU ARE	Nirvana	1992
COME AS YOU ARE	Beverley Knight	2004
COME AS YOU ARE	Peter Wolf	1987
COME BABY COME	K7	1993
COME BACK	Mighty Wah!	1984
COME BACK	Jessica Garlick	2002
COME BACK	J. Geils Band	1980
COME BACK AND FINISH WHAT YOU STARTED	Gladys Knight & The Pips	1978
COME BACK AND SHAKE ME	Clodagh Rodgers	1969
COME BACK AND STAY	Paul Young	1984
COME BACK AROUND	Feeder	2002
COME BACK BRIGHTER	Reef	1997
COME BACK DARLING	UB40	1998
COME BACK MY LOVE	Darts	1978

SONG TITLE	ARTIST	DATE
COME BACK TO ME	Janet Jackson	1990
COME BACK TO WHAT YOU KNOW		
	Embrace	1998
COME BACK WHEN YOU GROW UP		
	Bobby Vee & The Strangers	1967
COME CLEAN	Hilary Duff	2004
COME DANCING	Kinks	1983
COME GET SOME	Rooster	2004
COME GET TO THIS	Marvin Gaye	1973
COME GO WITH ME	Beach Boys	1981
COME GO WITH ME	Expose	1987
COME HOME	James	1990
COME HOME	Dave Clark Five	1965
COME HOME BILLY BIRD	Divine Comedy	2004
COME IN OUT OF THE RAIN		
	Wendy Moten	1994
COME INSIDE	Intro	1993
COME INTO MY LIFE	Gala	1998
COME INTO MY LIFE	Joyce Sims	1988
COME INTO MY WORLD	Kylie Minogue	2002
COME LIVE WITH ME	Heaven 17	1983
COME MONDAY	Jimmy Buffett	1974
COME ON	Rolling Stones	1963
COME ON	DJ Seduction	1992
COME ON	Tommy Roe	1964
COME ON, COME ON	Bronski Beat	1986

SONG TITLE	ARTIST	DATE
COME ON DANCE, DANCE	Saturday Night Band	1978
COME ON DOWN TO MY BOAT		
	Every Mothers' Son	1967
COME ON EILEEN	Dexy's Midnight Runners	1983
COME ON ENGLAND	4-4-2	2004
COME ON EVERYBODY (GET DOWN)		
	US3	1997
COME ON HOME	Cyndi Lauper	1995
COME ON HOME	Springfields	1963
COME ON HOME	Wayne Fontana	1966
COME ON LET'S GO	Los Lobos	1987
COME ON LET'S GO	McCoys	1966
COME ON OVER	John Silver	2003
COME ON OVER	Kym Marsh	2003
COME ON OVER	Olivia Newton-John	1976
COME ON OVER BABY (ALL I WANT IS YOU)		
	Christina Aguilera	2000
COME ON OVER TO MY PLACE		
	Drifters	1972
COME ON YOU REDS	Manchester United Football Squad	1994
COME OVER	Aaliyah	2003
COME PLAY WITH ME	Wedding Present	1992
COME RUNNING	Van Morrison	1970
COME RUNNING BACK	Dean Martin	1966
COME SAIL AWAY	Styx	1977

SONG TITLE	ARTIST	DATE
COME SATURDAY MORNING		
	Sandpipers	1969
COME SEE	Major Lance	1965
COME SEE ABOUT ME	Supremes	1964
COME SEE ABOUT ME	Shakin' Stevens	1987
COME SEE ABOUT ME	Jr. Walker & The All Stars	1967
COME SEE ME	112	1996
COME SOFTLY TO ME	New Seekers	1972
COME TO DADDY	Aphex Twins	1997
COME TO ME	Julie Grant	1964
COME TO ME	France Joli	1979
COME TO ME!	Ruby Winters	1978
COME TO MILTON KEYNES		
	Style Council	1985
COME TO MY WINDOW	Melissa Etheridge	1994
COME TO THE SUNSHINE	Harpers Bizarre	1967
COME TOGETHER	Primal Scream	1990
COME TOGETHER	Smokin' Mojo Filters	1995
COME TOGETHER	Aerosmith	1978
COME TOGETHER	Beatles	1969
COME TOMORROW	Manfred Mann	1965
COME UNDONE	Duran Duran	1993
COME UNDONE	Robbie Williams	2003
COME WHAT MAY	Nicole Kidman & Ewan McGregor	2001
COME WHAT MAY	Vicky Leandros	1972

SONG TITLE	ARTIST	DATE
COME WITH ME	Qattara	1997
COME WITH ME	Puff Daddy featuring Jimmy Page	1998
COME WITH ME	Jesse Green	1977
COME WITH ME	Special D	2004
COME WITH US/THE TEST	Chemical Brothers	2002
COMEDOWN	Bush	1995
COMEUPPANCE (EP)	Thousand Yard Stare	1992
COMFORTABLY NUMB	Scissor Sisters	2004
COMFORTER	Shai	1993
COMIN' HOME	Delaney & Bonnie	1969
COMIN' HOME BABY	Mel Torme	1962
COMIN' IN AND OUT OF YOUR LIFE		
	Barbra Streisand	1981
COMIN' ON STRONG	Broken English	1987
COMING AROUND	Travis	2000
COMING AROUND AGAIN	Carly Simon	1986
COMING HOME	K-Warren featuring Lee-O	2001
COMING HOME	David Essex	1976
COMING HOME	Marshall Hain	1978
COMING HOME	Cinderella	1989
COMING HOME NOW	Boyzone	1996
COMING HOME SOLDIER	Bobby Vinton	1966
COMING ON STRONG	Brenda Lee	1966
COMING OUT OF THE DARK		
	Gloria Estefan	1991

SONG TITLE	ARTIST	DATE
COMING UP	Paul McCartney	1980
COMING UP (LIVE AT GLASGOW)		
	Paul McCartney	1980
COMMENT TE DIRE ADIEU		
	Jimmy Somerville/June Miles Kingston	1989
COMMON PEOPLE	Pulp	1995
COMMOTION	Creedence Clearwater Revival	1969
COMMUNICATION	David McCallum	1966
COMMUNICATION	Armin	2000
COMMUNICATION	Spandau Ballet	1983
COMMUNICATION	Power Station	1985
COMMUNICATION (SOMEBODY ANSWER THE PHONE)		
	Mario Piu	1999
COMPLETE	Jaimeson	2003
COMPLETE CONTROL	Clash	1977
THE COMPLETE DOMINATOR		
	Human Resource	1991
COMPLETELY	Michael Bolton	1994
COMPLEX	Gary Numan	1979
COMPLICATED	Avril Lavigne	2002
COMPLIMENTS ON YOUR KISS		
	Red Dragon With Brian & Tony Gold	1994
THE COMPOSER	Supremes	1969

SONG TITLE	ARTIST	DATE
COMPUTER GAME (THEME FROM THE INVADERS)		
	Yellow Magic Orchestra	1980
COMPUTER LOVE	Kraftwerk	1981
CONCRETE AND CLAY	Randy Edelman	1976
CONCRETE AND CLAY	Unit Four Plus Two	1965
CONCRETE AND CLAY	Eddie Rambeau	1965
CONCRETE SCHOOLYARD	Jurassic 5	1998
CONDEMNATION (EP)	Depeche Mode	1993
CONFESSIN' (THAT I LOVE YOU)		
	Frank Ifield	1963
CONFIDE IN ME	Kylie Minogue	1994
CONFUSION	Lee Dorsey	1966
CONFUSION	New Order	1983
CONFUSION	Electric Light Orchestra	1979
CONFUSION (HITS US EVERY TIME)		
	Truth	1983
CONGA	Miami Sound Machine	1985
CONGO	Genesis	1997
CONGRATULATIONS	Cliff Richard	1968
CONNECTED	Stereo MC's	1993
CONNECTION	Elastica	1994
CONQUISTADOR	Procol Harum	1972
CONSIDERATION	Reef	1997
CONSTANT CRAVING	K.D. Lang	1993
CONSTANTLY	Cliff Richard	1964
CONSTANTLY	Immature	1994

SONG TITLE	ARTIST	DATE
CONTACT	Edwin Starr	1979
CONTAGIOUS	Isley Brothers featuring Ronald Isley Aka Mr. Biggs	2001
THE CONTINENTAL	Maureen McGovern	1976
CONTRIBUTION	Mica Paris	1990
CONTROL	Puddle Of Mudd	2002
CONTROL	Janet Jackson	1986
CONTROLLING ME	Oceanic	1992
CONTROVERSY	Prince	1993
CONVENTION '72	Delegates	1972
CONVERSATIONS	Cilla Black	1969
CONVOY	C.W. McCall	1975
CONVOY GB	Laurie Lingo & The Dipsticks	1976
CONWAY	Reel 2 Real featuring The Mad Stuntman	1995
COOCHY COO	En-Core featuring Stephen Emmanuel & Eska	2000
COOK WITH HONEY	Judy Collins	1973
COOL AID	Paul Humphrey & His Cool Aid Chemists	1971
COOL CHANGE	Little River Band	1979
COOL FOR CATS	Squeeze	1979
COOL IT NOW	New Edition	1984
COOL JERK	Capitols	1968
COOL LOVE	Pablo Cruise	1981
COOL MEDITATION	Third World	1979

SONG TITLE	ARTIST	DATE
COOL NIGHT	Paul Davis	1981
COOL OUT TONIGHT	David Essex	1977
COP THAT SHIT	Timbaland & Magoo featuring Missy Elliott	2004
COPACABANA (AT THE COPA)	Barry Manilow	1978
COPPER GIRL	3 Colours Red	1997
CORAZON	Carole King	1973
CORNER OF THE EARTH	Jamiroquai	2002
CORNER OF THE SKY	Jackson Five	1972
CORNERSHOP	Babybird	1997
CORNFLAKE GIRL	Tori Amos	1994
CORPSES	Ian Brown	1998
COSMIC GIRL	Jamiroquai	1996
THE COST OF LIVING (EP)	Clash	1979
COSTAFINE TOWN	Splinter	1974
COTTON CANDY	Al Hirt	1964
COTTON EYE JOE	Rednex	1995
COTTONFIELDS	Beach Boys	1970
COULD HAVE TOLD YOU SO	Halo James	1989
COULD I HAVE THIS DANCE	Anne Murray	1980
COULD I HAVE THIS KISS FOREVER	Whitney Houston/Enrique Iglesias	2000

SONG TITLE	ARTIST	DATE
COULD IT BE	Jaheim	2001
COULD IT BE FOREVER	Gemini	1996
COULD IT BE FOREVER/CHERISH		
	David Cassidy	1972
COULD IT BE I'M FALLING IN LOVE		
	David Grant & Jaki Graham	1985
COULD IT BE I'M FALLING IN LOVE		
	Spinners	1973
COULD IT BE I'M FALLING IN LOVE		
	Worlds Apart	1994
COULD IT BE MAGIC	Take That	1992
COULD IT BE MAGIC	Barry Manilow	1975
COULD IT BE MAGIC	Donna Summer	1976
COULD THIS BE LOVE	Seduction	1990
COULD YOU BE LOVED	Bob Marley & The Wailers	1980
COULD'VE BEEN	Tiffany	1987
COULD'VE BEEN ME	Billy Ray Cyrus	1992
COULD'VE BEEN YOU	Cher	1992
COULDN'T GET IT RIGHT	Climax Blues Band	1977
COULDN'T HAVE SAID IT BETTER		
	Meat Loaf	2003
COUNT ME IN	Gary Lewis & The Playboys	1965
COUNT ON ME	Julie Grant	1963
COUNT ON ME	Whitney Houston & Ce Ce Winans	1996
COUNT ON ME	Jefferson Starship	1978

SONG TITLE	ARTIST	DATE
COUNTDOWN/NEW WORLD MAN (LIVE)		
	Rush	1983
COUNTING BLUE CARS	Dishwalla	1996
COUNTING EVERY MINUTE	Sonia	1990
COUNTING SHEEP	Airhead	1991
COUNTRY BOY	Jimmy Nail	1996
COUNTRY BOY	Heinz	1963
COUNTRY BOY (YOU GOT YOUR FEET IN L.A.)		
	Glen Campbell	1975
COUNTRY GIRL CITY MAN	Billy Vera & Judy Clay	1968
COUNTRY HOUSE	Blur	1995
COUNTRY ROAD	James Taylor	1971
COUNTRY ROADS	Hermes House Band	2001
COUPLE DAYS OFF	Huey Lewis & The News	1991
COURSE BRUV	Genius Cru	2001
COURT OF LOVE	Unifics	1968
COURTESY OF THE RED, WHITE AND BLUE		
	Toby Keith	2002
COUSIN NORMAN	Marmalade	1971
COUSIN OF MINE	Sam Cooke	1964
COVER FROM THE SKY	Deacon Blue	1991
COVER GIRL	New Kids On The Block	1989
COVER ME	Bruce Springsteen	1984
COVER MY EYES (PAIN AND HEAVEN)		
	Marillion	1991

SONG TITLE	ARTIST	DATE
THE COVER OF 'ROLLING STONE'		
	Dr. Hook	1972
COVER OF LOVE	Michael Damian	1989
COVERS (EP)	Everything But The Girl	1992
COWARD OF THE COUNTY		
	Kenny Rogers	1979
COWBOY	Kid Rock	1999
COWBOY DREAMS	Jimmy Nail	1995
THE COWBOY IN ME	Tim McGraw	2002
COWBOY TAKE ME AWAY	Dixie Chicks	1999
COWBOYS & KISSES	Anastacia	2001
COWBOYS LIKE US	George Strait	2003
COWBOYS TO GIRLS	Intruders	1968
A COWBOY'S WORK IS NEVER DONE		
	Sonny & Cher	1972
COWGIRL	Underworld	2000
COZ I LUV YOU	Slade	1971
CRACKERBOX PALACE	George Harrison	1977
CRACKERS INTERNATIONAL (EP)		
	Erasure	1988
CRACKIN' UP	Tommy Hunt	1975
CRACKING UP	Jesus And Mary Chain	1998
CRACKING UP	Nick Lowe	1979
CRACKLIN' ROSIE	Neil Diamond	1970
CRADLE OF LOVE	Billy Idol	1990
CRASH	Primitives	1988

SONG TITLE	ARTIST	DATE
CRASH AND BURN	Savage Garden	2000
CRASH! BOOM! BANG!	Roxette	1994
CRASHED THE WEDDING	Busted	2003
CRASHIN' IN	Charlatans	1995
CRAWLING	Linkin Park	2001
CRAWLING BACK	Roy Orbison	1965
CRAYZY MAN	Blast featuring VDC	1994
CRAZIER	Gary Numan vs Rico	2003
CRAZY	Leann Rimes	1999
CRAZY	K-Ci & Jojo	2001
CRAZY	Patsy Cline	1961
CRAZY	Eternal	1994
CRAZY	Mud	1973
CRAZY	Seal	1991
CRAZY	Mark Morrison	1996
CRAZY	Moffatts	1999
CRAZY	Lucid	1999
CRAZY	Aerosmith	1994
CRAZY	Boys	1990
CRAZY	Icehouse	1987
CRAZY/BLIND MAN	Aerosmith	1994
CRAZY ABOUT HER	Rod Stewart	1989
CRAZY BEAT	Blur	2003
CRAZY CHANCE	Kavana	1996
CRAZY CHANCE 97	Kavana	1997
CRAZY CRAZY NIGHTS	Kiss	1987

SONG TITLE	ARTIST	DATE
CRAZY DOWNTOWN	Allan Sherman	1965
CRAZY FOR YOU	Madonna	1985
CRAZY FOR YOU	Let Loose	1994
CRAZY HORSES	Osmonds	1972
CRAZY IN LOVE	Beyonce	2003
CRAZY IN THE NIGHT (BARKING AT AIRPLANES)		
	Kim Carnes	1985
CRAZY LITTLE PARTY GIRL		
	Aaron Carter	1998
CRAZY LITTLE THING CALLED LOVE		
	Queen	1979
CRAZY LOVE	MJ Cole	2000
CRAZY LOVE	Allman Brothers Band	1979
CRAZY LOVE	Poco	1979
CRAZY MAMA	J.J. Cale	1972
CRAZY ON YOU	Heart	1976
CRAZY PARTY MIXES	Jive Bunny & The	
	Mastermixers	1990
CRAZY RAP	Afroman	2002
CRAZY WATER	Elton John	1977
CRAZY YOU	Gun	1997
CREAM	Blank & Jones	1999
CREAM	Prince & The New Power	
	Generation	1991
CREATION	Stereo MC's	1993

SONG TITLE	ARTIST	DATE
CREATURES OF THE NIGHT		
	Kiss	1983
CREEP	TLC	1994
CREEP	Radiohead	1993
CREEQUE ALLEY	Mamas & The Papas	1967
CRICKETS SING FOR ANAMARIA		
	Emma Bunton	2004
CRIED LIKE A BABY	Bobby Sherman	1971
CRIMINAL	Fiona Apple	1997
CRIMSON & CLOVER	Tommy James & The Shondells	1968
CRIMSON AND CLOVER	Joan Jett & The Blackhearts	1982
CRITICIZE	Alexander O'Neal	1987
CROCKETT'S THEME	Jan Hammer	1987
CROCODILE ROCK	Elton John	1972
CROCODILE SHOES	Jimmy Nail	1994
CROSS MY BROKEN HEART		
	Sinitta	1988
CROSS MY BROKEN HEART		
	Jets	1987
CROSS MY HEART	Eighth Wonder	1988
CROSS THAT BRIDGE	Ward Brothers	1987
CROSSROADS	Blazin' Squad	2002
CROSSROADS	Cream	1969
THE CROWN	Gary Byrd & The GB	
	Experience	1983
CRUCIFIED	Army Of Lovers	1992

SONG TITLE	ARTIST	DATE
CRUCIFY	Tori Amos	1992
THE CRUEL SEA	Dakatos	1963
CRUEL SUMMER	Ace Of Base	1998
CRUEL SUMMER	Bananarama	1984
CRUEL TO BE KIND	Nick Lowe	1979
CRUISE INTO CHRISTMAS MEDLEY		
	Jane McDonald	1998
CRUISIN'	D'Angelo	1996
CRUISIN'	Smokey Robinson	1979
CRUISING FOR BRUISING	Basia	1990
CRUMBLIN' DOWN	John Cougar Mellencamp	1983
THE CRUNCH	Rah Band	1977
CRUSH	Jennifer Paige	1998
CRUSH	Darren Hayes	2003
CRUSH ON YOU	Lil' Kim	1997
CRUSH ON YOU	Aaron Carter	1997
CRUSH ON YOU	Jets	1986
CRUSH WITH EYELINER	R.E.M.	1995
CRUSHED BY THE WHEELS OF INDUSTRY		
	Heaven 17	1983
CRUSHED LIKE FRUIT	InMe	2003
CRY	Michael Jackson	2001
CRY	Godley & Creme	1985
CRY	Waterfront	1989
CRY	System F	2000
CRY	Gerry Monroe	1970

SONG TITLE	ARTIST	DATE
CRY	Faith Hill	2002
CRY	Kym Marsh	2003
CRY	Alex Parks	2004
CRY	Ronnie Dove	1966
CRY AND BE FREE	Marilyn	1984
CRY BABY	Spiller	2002
CRY BABY	Jemini	2003
CRY BOY CRY	Blue Zoo	1982
CRY FOR HELP	Shed Seven	2001
CRY FOR HELP	Rick Astley	1991
CRY FOR YOU	Jodeci	1993
CRY INDIA	Umboza	1995
CRY JUST A LITTLE BIT	Shakin' Stevens	1983
CRY LIKE A BABY	Box Tops	1968
CRY LITTLE SISTER	Lost Brothers featuring	
	G Tom Mac	2003
CRY ME A RIVER	Mari Wilson	1983
CRY ME A RIVER	Justin Timberlake	2003
CRY ME A RIVER	Joe Cocker	1970
CRY TO BE FOUND	Del Amitri	1998
CRY TO ME	Pretty Things	1965
CRY WOLF	A-Ha	1986
CRYBABY	Mariah Carey featuring	
	Snoop Dogg	2000
CRYIN'	Vixen	1989
CRYIN'	Aerosmith	1993

SONG TITLE	ARTIST	DATE
CRYING	Don McLean	1981
CRYING	Roy Orbison & K.D. Lang	1992
CRYING	Jay & The Americans	1966
CRYING AT THE DISCOTEQUE		
	Alcazar	2001
THE CRYING GAME	Boy George	1993
THE CRYING GAME	Dave Berry	1964
CRYING IN THE CHAPEL	Elvis Presley	1965
CRYING IN THE RAIN	Culture Beat	1996
CRYING IN THE RAIN	A-Ha	1990
CRYING LAUGHING LOVING LYING		
	Labi Siffre	1972
CRYING OVER YOU	Ken Boothe	1974
CRYING TIME	Ray Charles	1965
CRYPTIK SOULS CREW	Len	2000
CRYSTAL	New Order	2001
CRYSTAL BLUE PERSUASION		
	Tommy James & The Shondells	1969
CRYSTAL CLEAR	Grid	1993
THE CRYSTAL LAKE	Grandaddy	2001
CUBA	El Mariachi	1996
CUBA/BETTER DO IT SALSA		
	Gibson Brothers	1980
CUBAN PETE	Jim Carrey	1995
CUBIK/OLYMPIC	808 State	1990
CUDDLY TOY	Roachford	1989

SONG TITLE	ARTIST	DATE
CULO	Pitbull featuring Lil Jon	2004
CULT OF PERSONALITY	Living Colour	1989
CULT OF SNAP!	Snap!	1990
CUM ON FEEL THE NOIZE	Slade	1973
CUM ON FEEL THE NOIZE	Quiet Riot	1983
CUMBERSOME	Seven Mary Three	1996
THE CUP OF LIFE	Ricky Martin	1998
CUPBOARD LOVE	John Leyton	1963
CUPID	Johnny Nash	1969
CUPID	112	1997
CUPID	Tony Orlando & Dawn	1976
CUPID/I'VE LOVED YOU FOR A LONG TIME (MEDLEY)		
	Spinners	1980
CURIOUS	LSG (Levert.Sweat.Gill)	1998
CURLY	Move	1969
THE CURLY SHUFFLE	Jump 'N The Saddle	1983
CUT ME DOWN	Lloyd Cole	1986
CUT SOME RUG/CASTLE ROCK		
	Bluetones	1996
CUT THE CAKE	Average White Band	1975
CUTS LIKE A KNIFE	Bryan Adams	1983
THE CUTTER	Echo & The Bunnymen	1983
CYCLES	Frank Sinatra	1968
D'YA WANNA GO FASTER	Terrorvision	2001
D'YER MAK'ER	Led Zeppelin	1973

SONG TITLE	ARTIST	DATE
D'YOU KNOW WHAT I MEAN?		
	Oasis	1997
DA-A-ANCE!	Lambrettas	1980
D-DAYS	Hazel O'Connor	1981
D.I.S.C.O.	Ottawan	1980
D.I.S.C.O.	N-Trance	1997
D.I.V.O.R.C.E.	Billy Connolly	1975
D.I.V.O.R.C.E.	Tammy Wynette	1975
D.J.	David Bowie	1979
D.O.A.	Bloodrock	1971
D.W. WASHBURN	Monkees	1968
DA DA DA	Trio	1982
DA DOO RON RON	Crystals	1963
DA DOO RON RON	Shaun Cassidy	1977
DA FUNK/MUSIQUE	Daft Punk	1997
DA HYPE	Junior Jack featuring Robert Smith	2004
DA YA THINK I'M SEXY	Rod Stewart	1978
DA YA THINK I'M SEXY?	Girls Of FHM	2004
DA' DIP	Freak Nasty	1997
DA'BUTT	E.U.	1988
DADDY COOL	Boney M	1976
DADDY COOL/THE GIRL CAN'T HELP IT		
	Darts	1977
DADDY COULD SWEAR, I DECLARE		
	Gladys Knight & The Pips	1973

SONG TITLE	ARTIST	DATE
DADDY DON'T YOU WALK SO FAST		
	Daniel Boone	1971
DADDY DON'T YOU WALK SO FAST		
	Wayne Newton	1972
DADDY'S HOME	Cliff Richard	1982
DADDY'S HOME	Jermaine Jackson	1972
DADDY'S LITTLE MAN	O.C. Smith	1969
DAGENHAM DAVE	Morrissey	1995
DAILY	TQ	2000
DAISY A DAY	Jud Strunk	1973
DAISY JANE	America	1975
DALLIANCE	Wedding Present	1991
DAMAGED	Plummet	2003
DAMN I WISH I WAS YOUR LOVER		
	Sophie B. Hawkins	1992
DAMNED DON'T CRY	Visage	1982
DAMNED IF I DO	Alan Parsons	1979
THE DANCE/FRIENDS IN LOW PLACES		
	Garth Brooks	1995
DANCE (DISCO HEAT)	Sylvester	1978
DANCE (WITH U)	Lemar	2003
DANCE ACROSS THE FLOOR		
	Jimmy 'Bo' Horne	1978
DANCE AND SHOUT/HOPE	Shaggy	2001
DANCE AWAY	Roxy Music	1979
DANCE COMMANDER	Electric Six	2003

SONG TITLE	ARTIST	DATE
DANCE, DANCE, DANCE	Beach Boys	1964
DANCE, DANCE, DANCE (YOWSAH, YOWSAH, YOWSAH)		
	Chic	1977
DANCE FOR ME	Sisqo	2001
DANCE FOR ME	Mary J. Blige featuring Common	2002
DANCE HALL DAYS	Wang Chung	1984
DANCE INTO THE LIGHT	Phil Collins	1996
DANCE LITTLE LADY DANCE		
	Tina Charles	1976
DANCE LITTLE SISTER	Terence Trent D'Arby	1988
DANCE ME UP	Gary Glitter	1984
DANCE NAKED	John Mellencamp	1994
DANCE OF THE CUCKOOS	Band Of The Black Watch	1975
DANCE OF THE MAD	Pop Will Eat Itself	1990
DANCE ON	Kathy Kirby	1963
DANCE STANCE	Dexy's Midnight Runners	1980
DANCE THE BODY MUSIC	Osibisa	1976
DANCE THE KUNG FU	Carl Douglas	1974
DANCE THE NIGHT AWAY	Mavericks	1998
DANCE THE NIGHT AWAY	Van Halen	1979
DANCE TO THE MUSIC	Sly & The Family Stone	1968
DANCE TONIGHT	Lucy Pearl	2000
DANCE WIT ME	Rufus featuring Chaka Khan	1976
DANCE WITH ME	Tin Tin Out featuring Tony Hadley	1997
DANCE WITH ME	Debelah Morgan	2001
DANCE WITH ME	Peter Brown	1978
DANCE WITH ME	112	2001
DANCE WITH ME	Orleans	1975
DANCE WITH ME (I'M YOUR ECSTASY)		
	Control	1991
DANCE WITH MY FATHER	Luther Vandross	2003
DANCE WITH THE DEVIL	Cozy Powell	1973
DANCE WITH YOU	Carrie Lucas	1979
DANCE WITH YOU	Rishi Rich Project featuring Jay Sean & Juggy D	2003
DANCE YOURSELF DIZZY	Liquid Gold	1980
DANCIN'	Guy	1999
DANCIN' (ON A SATURDAY NIGHT)		
	Barry Blue	1973
DANCIN' EASY	Danny Williams	1977
DANCIN' FOOL	Guess Who	1974
DANCIN' IN THE KEY OF LIFE		
	Steve Arrington	1985
DANCIN' IN THE MOONLIGHT (IT'S CAUGHT ME IN THE SPOTLIGHT)	Thin Lizzy	1977
DANCIN' MAN	Q	1977
DANCIN' PARTY	Showaddywaddy	1977
DANCIN' SHOES	Nigel Olsson	1978
DANCIN' THE NIGHT AWAY		
	Voggue	1981

SONG TITLE	ARTIST	DATE
DANCIN' TONIGHT	Stereopol featuring Nevada	2003
DANCING BABY (OOGA–CHAKA)		
	Trubble	1998
DANCING GIRLS	Nik Kershaw	1984
DANCING IN THE CITY	Marshall Hain	1978
DANCING IN THE DARK	Bruce Springsteen	1984
DANCING IN THE DARK	Big Daddy	1985
DANCING IN THE MOONLIGHT		
	Toploader	2000
DANCING IN THE MOONLIGHT		
	King Harvest	1972
DANCING IN THE SHEETS	Shalamar	1984
DANCING IN THE STREET	Martha & The Vandellas	1964
DANCING IN THE STREET	David Bowie & Mick Jagger	1985
DANCING IN THE STREET	Van Halen	1982
DANCING MACHINE	Jackson 5	1974
DANCING ON THE CEILING		
	Lionel Richie	1986
DANCING ON THE FLOOR (HOOKED ON LOVE)		
	Third World	1981
DANCING QUEEN	ABBA	1976
DANCING TIGHT	Galaxy featuring Phil Fearon	1983
DANCING WITH TEARS IN MY EYES		
	Ultravox	1984
DANCING WITH THE CAPTAIN		
	Paul Nicholas	1976

SONG TITLE	ARTIST	DATE
DANDELION	Rolling Stones	1967
DANDY	Herman's Hermits	1966
DANG ME	Roger Miller	1964
DANGER (BEEN SO LONG)	Mystikal featuring Nivea	2001
DANGER GAMES	Pinkees	1982
DANGER! HIGH VOLTAGE	Electric Six	2003
THE DANGER OF A STRANGER		
	Stella Parton	1977
DANGER ZONE	Kenny Loggins	1986
DANGEROUS	Busta Rhymes	1998
DANGEROUS	Roxette	1989
DANGEROUS MINDS (EP)	Various	1996
THE DANGLING CONVERSATION		
	Simon & Garfunkel	1966
DANIEL	Elton John	1973
DANNY'S SONG	Anne Murray	1973
DARE ME	Pointer Sisters	1985
DARE TO FALL IN LOVE	Brent Bourgeois	1990
DARK CLOUDS	Space	1997
DARK HORSE	George Harrison	1974
THE DARK IS RISING	Mercury Rev	2002
DARK IS THE NIGHT	A-Ha	1993
DARK IS THE NIGHT	Shakatak	1983
DARK LADY	Cher	1974
DARK THERAPY	Echobelly	1996
DARKHEART	Bomb The Bass featuring	

SONG TITLE	ARTIST	DATE
	Spikey Tee	1994
DARKLANDS	Jesus & Mary Chain	1987
DARLIN'	Beach Boys	1967
DARLIN'	David Cassidy	1975
DARLIN'	Frankie Miller	1978
DARLIN' DARLIN' BABY (SWEET, TENDER, LOVE)		
	O'Jays	1977
DARLING BE HOME SOON	Lovin' Spoonful	1967
DARLING PRETTY	Mark Knopfler	1996
DAS BOOT	U96	1992
DAS GLOCKENSPIEL	Schiller	2001
DAT	Pluto Shervington	1976
DATE WITH THE NIGHT	The Yeah Yeah Yeahs	2003
DAUGHTER	Pearl Jam	1994
DAUGHTER OF DARKNESS	Tom Jones	1970
DAVID WATTS/'A' BOMB IN WARDOUR STREET		
	Jam	1978
DAVY'S ON THE ROAD AGAIN		
	Manfred Mann's Earth Band	1978
DAWN	Flintlock	1976
DAWN (GO AWAY)	Four Seasons	1964
THE DAWN OF CORRECTION		
	Spokesmen	1965
DAY & NIGHT	Billie Piper	2000
DAY AFTER DAY	Badfinger	1971

SONG TITLE	ARTIST	DATE
THE DAY BEFORE YESTERDAY'S MAN		
	Supernaturals	1997
THE DAY BEFORE YOU CAME		
	ABBA	1982
THE DAY BEFORE YOU CAME		
	Blancmange	1984
DAY BY DAY	Holly Sherwood	1972
DAY BY DAY	Godspell	1972
DAY BY DAY	Hooters	1985
DAY DREAMING	Aretha Franklin	1972
DAY FOR DECISION	Johnny Sea	1966
THE DAY I FOUND MYSELF		
	Honey Cone	1972
THE DAY I MET MARIE	Cliff Richard	1967
DAY IN DAY OUT	Feeder	1999
DAY IS DONE	Peter, Paul & Mary	1969
THE DAY IT RAINED FOREVER		
	Aurora	2002
THE DAY THAT CURLY BILL SHOT DOWN CRAZY SAM		
MCGHEE	Hollies	1973
THE DAY THE WORLD TURNED DAYGLO		
	X-Ray Spex	1978
THE DAY THE WORLD WENT AWAY		
	Nine Inch Nails	1999
DAY TRIPPER	Beatles	1965

SONG TITLE	ARTIST	DATE
THE DAY WE CAUGHT THE TRAIN		
	Ocean Colour Scene	1996
THE DAY WE FIND LOVE	911	1997
A DAY WITHOUT LOVE	Love Affair	1968
DAY-IN DAY-OUT	David Bowie	1987
DAYBREAK	Barry Manilow	1977
DAYBREAK	Nilsson	1974
DAYDREAM	Lovin' Spoonful	1966
DAYDREAM BELIEVER	Monkees	1967
DAYDREAM BELIEVER	Anne Murray	1979
DAYDREAM IN BLUE	I Monster	2001
DAYDREAMER	Menswear	1995
DAYDREAMER/THE PUPPY SONG		
	David Cassidy	1973
DAYDREAMIN'	Tatyana Ali	1998
DAYS	Kinks	1968
DAYS	Kirsty MacColl	1989
DAYS GO BY	Dirty Vegas	2002
DAYS GO BY	Keith Urban	2004
DAYS GONE DOWN	Gerry Rafferty	1979
DAYS OF NO TRUST	Magnum	1988
DAYS OF OUR LIVEZ	Bone Thugs-N-Harmony	1997
THE DAYS OF PEARLY SPENCER		
	Marc Almond	1992
THE DAYS OF SAND AND SHOVELS		
	Bobby Vinton	1969

SONG TITLE	ARTIST	DATE
DAYS OF YOUTH	Laurnea	1997
DAYSLEEPER	R.E.M.	1998
DAYTIME FRIENDS	Kenny Rogers	1977
DAYTONA DEMON	Suzi Quatro	1973
DAYTRIP TO BANGOR	Fiddler's Dram	1979
DAYZ LIKE THAT	Fierce	1999
DAZZ	Brick	1976
DAZZEY DUKS	Duice	1993
DAZZLE	Siouxsie & The Banshees	1984
DE DO DO DO, DE DA DA DA		
	Police	1980
DEACON BLUES	Steely Dan	1978
DEAD CITIES	Exploited	1981
DEAD END STREET	Kinks	1966
DEAD END STREET	Lou Rawls	1967
DEAD FROM THE WAIST DOWN		
	Catatonia	1999
DEAD GIVEAWAY	Shalamar	1983
DEAD LEAVES AND THE DIRTY GROUND		
	White Stripes	2002
DEAD MAN WALKING	David Bowie	1997
DEAD MAN'S CURVE	Jan & Dean	1964
DEAD RINGER FOR LOVE	Meat Loaf	1981
DEAD SKUNK	Loudon Wainwright III	1973
DEAD STAR/IN YOUR WORLD		
	Muse	2002

SONG TITLE	ARTIST	DATE
DEADBEAT CLUB	B-52's	1990
DEADLIER THAN THE MALE		
	Walker Brothers	1966
DEADLINE	Dutch Force	2000
DEADWEIGHT	Beck	1997
THE DEAL	Pat Campbell	1969
THE DEAN AND I	10cc	1973
DEAR ADDY	Kid Creole & The Coconuts	1982
DEAR DELILAH	Grapefruit	1968
DEAR ELAINE	Roy Wood	1973
DEAR HEART	Jack Jones	1964
DEAR HEART	Andy Williams	1964
DEAR JESSIE	Rollergirl	2000
DEAR JESSIE	Madonna	1989
DEAR JOHN	Status Quo	1982
DEAR LIE	TLC	1999
DEAR MAMA/OLD SCHOOL	2Pac	1995
DEAR MISS LONELY HEARTS		
	Philip Lynott	1980
DEAR MRS. APPLEBEE	David Garrick	1966
DEAR PRUDENCE	Siouxsie & The Banshees	1983
DEATH DISCO (PTS 1 & 2)	Public Image Ltd	1979
DEATH OF A CLOWN	Dave Davies	1967
DEBASER	Pixies	1997
DEBORA/ONE INCH ROCK	T. Rex	1972
DECADENCE DANCE	Extreme	1991

SONG TITLE	ARTIST	DATE
DECEMBER	All About Eve	1989
DECEMBER	Collective Soul	1995
DECEMBER '63 (OH WHAT A NIGHT)		
	Four Seasons	1975
DECEMBER WILL BE MAGIC AGAIN		
	Kate Bush	1980
DECENT DAYS AND NIGHTS		
	The Futureheads	2004
DECK OF CARDS	Max Bygraves	1973
DECK OF CARDS	Wink Martindale	1959
DEDICATED	R. Kelly & Public Announcement	1993
DEDICATED FOLLOWER OF FASHION		
	Kinks	1966
DEDICATED TO THE ONE I LOVE		
	Mamas & The Papas	1967
DEDICATED TO THE ONE I LOVE		
	Bitty McLean	1994
DEDICATION	Thin Lizzy	1991
DEEP	East 17	1993
DEEP DEEP DOWN	Hepburn	2000
DEEP, DEEP TROUBLE	Simpsons	1991
DEEP DOWN AND DIRTY	Stereo MC's	2001
DEEP DOWN INSIDE	Donna Summer	1977
DEEP FOREST	Deep Forest	1994
DEEP HEAT '89	Latino Rave	1989
DEEP IN YOU	Livin' Joy	1997

SONG TITLE	ARTIST	DATE
DEEP INSIDE MY HEART	Randy Meisner	1980
DEEP MENACE (SPANK)	D'Menace	1998
DEEP PURPLE	Nino Tempo & April Stevens	1963
DEEP PURPLE	Donny & Marie Osmond	1975
DEEPER	Escrima	1995
DEEPER	Delirious?	1997
DEEPER	Serious Danger	1997
DEEPER AND DEEPER	Madonna	1992
DEEPER AND DEEPER	Freda Payne	1970
DEEPER LOVE	Ruff Driverz	1998
DEEPER LOVE (SYMPHONIC PARADISE)	BBE	1998
A DEEPER LOVE	Clivilles & Cole	1992
A DEEPER LOVE	Aretha Franklin	1994
DEEPER SHADE OF BLUE	Steps	2000
DEEPER SHADE OF SOUL	Urban Dance Squad	1990
DEEPER THAN THE NIGHT	Olivia Newton-John	1979
THE DEEPER THE LOVE	Whitesnake	1990
DEEPER UNDERGROUND	Jamiroquai	1998
DEEPEST BLUE	Deepest Blue	2003
DEEPLY DIPPY	Right Said Fred	1992
DEJA VU	Lord Tariq & Peter Gunz	1997
DEJA VU	Dionne Warwick	1979
DELICATE	Terence Trent D'Arby	1993
DELICIOUS	Shampoo	1995

SONG TITLE	ARTIST	DATE
DELILAH	Sensational Alex Harvey Band	1975
DELILAH	Tom Jones	1968
DELIRIOUS	Prince & The Revolution	1983
DELIVER ME	Sister Bliss featuring John Martyn	2001
DELIVERANCE	Mission	1990
DELTA DAWN	Helen Reddy	1973
DELTA LADY	Joe Cocker	1969
DELTA SUN BOTTLENECK STOMP	Mercury Rev	1999
DEM GIRLZ	Oxide & Neutrino featuring Kowdean	2002
DEMOCRACY	Killing Joke	1996
DEMOLITION MAN	Sting	1993
DEMONS	Super Furry Animals	1997
DEMONS	Fatboy Slim featuring Macy Gray	2001
DENIS	Blondie	1978
DEPENDIN' ON YOU	Doobie Brothers	1979
DER KOMMISSAR	After The Fire	1983
DESERT MOON	Dennis DeYoung	1984
DESERT ROSE	Sting featuring Cheb Mami	2000
DESIDERATA	Les Crane	1971
A DESIGN FOR LIFE	Manic Street Preachers	1996
DESIRE	Nu Colours	1996
DESIRE	Ultra Nate	2000

SONG TITLE	ARTIST	DATE
DESIRE	BBE	1998
DESIRE	U2	1988
DESIRE	Andy Gibb	1980
DESIRE ME	Doll	1979
DESIREE	Neil Diamond	1977
DESPERATE BUT NOT SERIOUS		
	Adam Ant	1982
DESPERATE DAN	Lieutenant Pigeon	1972
DESTINATION	DT8 featuring Roxanne Wilde	2003
DESTINATION ESCHATON	Shamen	1995
DESTINATION SUNSHINE	Balearic Bill	1999
DESTINATION ZULULAND	King Kurt	1983
DESTINY	Zero 7 featuring Sia & Sophie	2001
DESTINY	Jacksons	1979
DESTINY	N-Trance	2003
DESTINY CALLING	James	1998
DETROIT CITY	Tom Jones	1967
DEUTSCHER GIRLS	Adam & The Ants	1982
DEVIL	666	2000
DEVIL GATE DRIVE	Suzi Quatro	1974
DEVIL IN YOUR SHOES (WALKING ALL OVER)		
	Shed Seven	1998
DEVIL INSIDE	INXS	1988
THE DEVIL WENT DOWN TO GEORGIA		
	Charlie Daniels Band	1979

SONG TITLE	ARTIST	DATE
DEVIL WITH A BLUE DRESS ON/GOOD GOLLY MISS MOLLY	Mitch Ryder	1966
DEVIL WOMAN	Cliff Richard	1976
THE DEVIL YOU KNOW	Jesus Jones	1993
DEVIL'S ANSWER	Atomic Rooster	1971
DEVIL'S GUN	C.J. & Co.	1977
DEVIL'S HAIRCUT	Beck	1996
DEVIL'S NIGHTMARE	Oxide & Neutrino	2001
DEVIL'S TOY	Almighty	1991
DEVOTED TO YOU	Carly Simon & James Taylor	1978
DEVOTION	Ten City	1989
DEVOTION	Earth, Wind & Fire	1974
DIABLO	Grid	1995
DIAL MY HEART	Boys	1989
DIALOGUE (PART I & PART II)		
	Chicago	1972
DIAMOND DOGS	David Bowie	1974
DIAMOND GIRL	Seals & Crofts	1973
DIAMOND LIGHTS	Glenn & Chris	1987
DIAMOND SMILES	Boomtown Rats	1979
DIAMONDS	Herb Alpert	1987
DIAMONDS	Jet Harris & Tony Meehan	1963
DIAMONDS & PEARLS	Prince & The New Power Generation	1991
DIAMONDS AND GUNS	Transplants	2003
DIAMONDS AND PEARLS	Prince	1991

SONG TITLE	ARTIST	DATE
DIAMONDS AND RUST	Joan Baez	1975
DIAMONDS ARE FOREVER	David McAlmont/David Arnold	1997
DIANA	Paul Anka	1957
DIANE	Therapy?	1995
DIANE	Bachelors	1964
DIARY	Bread	1972
DIARY	Alicia Keys featuring Tony Toni Tone	2004
THE DIARY OF HORACE WIMP	Electric Light Orchestra	1979
DICK-A-DUM-DUM (KINGS ROAD)	Des O'Connor	1969
DID I DREAM (SONG TO THE SIREN)	Lost Witness	2002
DID IT AGAIN	Kylie Minogue	1997
DID IT IN A MINUTE	Daryl Hall & John Oates	1982
DID MY TIME	Korn	2003
DID YOU BOOGIE (WITH YOUR BABY)	Flash Cadillac & The Continental Kids	1976
DID YOU EVER	Nancy Sinatra & Lee Hazlewood	1971
DID YOU EVER HAVE TO MAKE UP YOUR MIND	Lovin' Spoonful	1966
DID YOU EVER THINK	R. Kelly	1999
DID YOU SEE HER EYES	Illusion	1969

SONG TITLE	ARTIST	DATE
DIDDY	P. Diddy featuring The Neptunes	2002
DIDN'T I (BLOW YOUR MIND THIS TIME)	Delfonics	1970
DIDN'T I (BLOW YOUR MIND)	New Kids On The Block	1989
DIDN'T WE ALMOST HAVE IT ALL	Whitney Houston	1987
DIE ANOTHER DAY	Madonna	2002
DIE LAUGHING	Therapy?	1994
DIFFERENCES	Ginuwine	2001
A DIFFERENT BEAT	Boyzone	1996
A DIFFERENT CORNER	George Michael	1986
DIFFERENT DRUM	Stone Poneys	1967
DIFFERENT STROKES	Isotonik	1992
DIFFERENT WORLDS	Maureen McGovern	1979
DIG IN	Lenny Kravitz	2001
DIGGIN' ON YOU	TLC	1995
DIGGING IN THE DIRT	Peter Gabriel	1992
DIGGING THE GRAVE	Faith No More	1995
DIGGING YOUR SCENE	Blow Monkeys	1986
DIGITAL	Goldie featuring KRS One	1997
DIGITAL DISPLAY	Ready For The World	1985
DIGITAL LOVE	Daft Punk	2001
DIGNITY	Bob Dylan	1995
DIGNITY	Deacon Blue	1994

SONG TITLE	ARTIST	DATE
DIL CHEEZ (MY HEART...)	Bally Sagoo	1996
DILEMMA	Nelly featuring Kelly Rowland	2002
DIM ALL THE LIGHTS	Donna Summer	1979
DIMPLES	John Lee Hooker	1964
DING DONG	George Harrison	1974
DING DONG SONG	Gunther & The Sunshine Girls	2004
DING DONG THE WITCH IS DEAD		
	Fifth Estate	1967
DING-A-DONG	Teach-In	1975
DINNER WITH DELORES	TAFKAP	1996
DINNER WITH GERSHWIN	Donna Summer	1987
DINOSAUR ADVENTURE 3D	Underworld	2003
DIP IT LOW	Christina Milian	2004
DIPPETY DAY	Father Abraham & The Smurfs	1978
DIRGE	Death In Vegas	2000
DIRRTY	Christina Aguilera featuring	
	Redman	2002
DIRTY BEATS	Roni Size/Reprazent	2001
DIRTY CASH (MONEY TALKS)		
	Adventures Of Stevie V	1990
DIRTY DAWG	NKOTB	1994
DIRTY DEEDS	Joan Jett	1990
DIRTY DIANA	Michael Jackson	1988
DIRTY LAUNDRY	Don Henley	1982
DIRTY LOVE	Thunder	1990
DIRTY STICKY FLOORS	Dave Gahan	2003

SONG TITLE	ARTIST	DATE
DIRTY WATER	Made In London	2000
DIRTY WATER	Standells	1966
DIRTY WHITE BOY	Foreigner	1978
THE DISADVANTAGES OF YOU		
	Brass Ring	1967
DIS-INFECTED (EP)	The The	1994
DISAPPEAR	INXS	1990
DISAPPEARING ACT	Shalamar	1983
DISAPPOINTED	Public Image Ltd	1989
DISAPPOINTED	Electronic	1992
THE DISAPPOINTED	XTC	1992
DISARM	Smashing Pumpkins	1994
DISCO 2000	Pulp	1995
DISCO BABES FROM OUTER SPACE		
	Babe Instinct	1999
DISCO CONNECTION	Isaac Hayes	1976
DISCO COP	Blue Adonis featuring	
	Lil' Miss Max	1998
DISCO DOWN	Shed Seven	1999
DISCO DUCK	Rick Dees & His Cast Of Idiots	1976
DISCO INFERNO	Trammps	1978
DISCO INFERNO	Tina Turner	1993
DISCO LADY	Johnnie Taylor	1976
DISCO LUCY (I LOVE LUCY THEME)		
	Wilton Place Street Band	1977
DISCO MUSIC/I LIKE IT	Jaln Band	1976

SONG TITLE	ARTIST	DATE
DISCO NIGHTS (ROCK FREAK)	G.Q.	1979
DISCO QUEEN	Hot Chocolate	1975
DISCO STOMP	Hamilton Bohannon	1975
DISCO'S REVENGE	Gusto	1996
DISCOHOPPING	Klubbheads	1997
DISCOLAND	Flip & Fill featuring Karen Parry	2004
DISCOTHEQUE	U2	1997
DISEASE	Matchbox Twenty	2002
DISENCHANTED	Communards	1986
DISILLUSION	Badly Drawn Boy	2000
DISPOSABLE TEENS	Marilyn Manson	2000
DISREMEMBRANCE	Dannii	1998
DISSIDENT	Pearl Jam	1994
THE DISTANCE	Cake	1997
DISTANT DRUMS	Jim Reeves	1966
DISTANT LOVER	Marvin Gaye	1974
DISTANT SHORES	Chad & Jeremy	1966
DISTANT SUN	Crowded House	1993
DITTY	Paperboy	1992
DIVA	Dana International	1998
DIVE TO PARADISE	Eurogroove	1995
DIVINE EMOTIONS	Narada	1988
DIVINE THING	Soup Dragons	1992
DIVING	4 Strings	2002

SONG TITLE	ARTIST	DATE
DIVING FACES	Liquid Child	1999
DIXIE-NARCO (EP)	Primal Scream	1992
DIZZY	Tommy Roe	1969
DIZZY	Vic Reeves & The Wonder Stuff	1991
DJ	H & Claire	2002
DJ CULTURE	Pet Shop Boys	1991
DJ NATION	Nukleuz DJ s	2002
DJ NATION – BOOTLEG EDITION	Nukleuz DJ s	2003
DJS TAKE CONTROL	SL2	1991
DO ANYTHING	Natural Selection	1991
DO ANYTHING YOU WANNA DO	Rods	1977
DO ANYTHING YOU WANT TO	Thin Lizzy	1979
DO FOR LOVE	2Pac	1998
DO I DO	Stevie Wonder	1982
DO I HAVE TO SAY THE WORDS?	Bryan Adams	1992
DO I LOVE YOU	Ronettes	1964
DO I QUALIFY?	Lynden David Hall	1998
DO IT	Tony Di Bart	1994
DO IT	Neil Diamond	1970
DO IT ('TIL YOU'RE SATISFIED)	B.T. Express	1974
DO IT AGAIN	Steely Dan	1972

SONG TITLE	ARTIST	DATE
DO IT AGAIN	Beach Boys	1968
DO IT AGAIN A LITTLE BIT SLOWER		
	Jon & Robin & The In Crowd	1967
DO IT AGAIN/BILLIE JEAN (MEDLEY)		
	Clubhouse	1983
DO IT ALL OVER AGAIN	Spiritualized	2002
DO IT ANY WAY YOU WANNA		
	People's Choice	1975
DO IT BABY	Miracles	1974
DO IT FOR LOVE	Sheena Easton	1985
DO IT OR DIE	Atlanta Rhythm Section	1979
DO IT TO ME	Lionel Richie	1992
DO IT TO ME AGAIN	Soulsearcher	2000
DO IT TO THE MUSIC	Raw Silk	1982
DO IT WITH MADONNA	Androids	2003
DO IT, DO IT AGAIN	Raffaella Carra	1978
DO ME	Bell Biv Devoe	1990
DO ME WRONG	Mel Blatt	2003
DO MY THING	Busta Rhymes	1997
DO NO WRONG	Thirteen Senses	2004
DO NOT DISTURB	Bananarama	1985
DO NOT PASS ME BY	Hammer	1992
DO NOTHING/MAGGIE'S FARM		
	Specials	1980
DO OR DIE	Super Furry Animals	2000

SONG TITLE	ARTIST	DATE
DO RE ME, SO FAR SO GOOD		
	Carter The Unstoppable Sex Machine	1992
DO RIGHT	Paul Davis	1980
DO SOMETHING TO ME	Tommy James & The Shondells	1968
DO THAT TO ME	Lisa Marie Experience	1996
DO THAT TO ME ONE MORE TIME		
	Captain & Tennille	1979
DO THE BARTMAN	Simpsons	1991
DO THE BOOMERANG	Jr. Walker & The All Stars	1965
DO THE CLAM	Elvis Presley	1965
DO THE CONGA	Black Lace	1984
DO THE FREDDIE	Freddie & The Dreamers	1965
DO THE FUNKY CHICKEN	Rufus Thomas	1970
(DO) THE HUCKLEBUCK	Coast To Coast	1981
DO THE LOLLIPOP	Tweenies	2001
DO THE RIGHT THING	Redhead Kingpin & The FBI	1989
(DO THE) PUSH AND PULL PART I		
	Rufus Thomas	1970
(DO THE) SPANISH HUSTLE		
	Fatback Band	1976
DO THEY KNOW IT'S CHRISTMAS?		
	Band Aid	1984
DO THEY KNOW IT'S CHRISTMAS?		
	Band Aid II	1989

SONG TITLE	ARTIST	DATE
DO U KNOW WHERE YOU'RE COMING FROM	M-Beat featuring Jamiroquai	1996
DO U STILL?	East 17	1996
DO WAH DIDDY	DJ Otzi	2001
DO WAH DIDDY DIDDY	Manfred Mann	1964
DO WE ROCK	Point Break	1999
DO WHAT YOU DO	Jermaine Jackson	1984
DO WHAT YOU FEEL	Joey Negro	1991
DO WHAT YOU GOTTA DO	Four Tops	1969
DO WHAT YOU WANNA DO	T-Connection	1977
DO WHAT YOU WANNA DO	Five Flights Up	1970
DO WHAT YOU WANT, BE WHAT YOU ARE	Daryl Hall & John Oates	1976
DO WHAT'S GOOD FOR ME	2 Unlimited	1995
DO YA	Electric Light Orchestra	1977
DO YA DO YA (WANNA PLEASE ME)	Samantha Fox	1986
DO YA THINK I'M SEXY?	N-Trance featuring Rod Stewart	1997
DO YA WANNA GET FUNKY WITH ME	Peter Brown	1977
DO YOU BELIEVE IN LOVE	Huey Lewis & The News	1982
DO YOU BELIEVE IN MAGIC	Shaun Cassidy	1978

SONG TITLE	ARTIST	DATE
DO YOU BELIEVE IN MAGIC	Lovin' Spoonful	1965
DO YOU BELIEVE IN SHAME	Duran Duran	1989
DO YOU BELIEVE IN THE WESTWORLD	Theatre Of Hate	1982
DO YOU BELIEVE IN US	Jon Secada	1992
DO YOU FEEL LIKE I FEEL?	Belinda Carlisle	1991
DO YOU FEEL LIKE WE DO	Peter Frampton	1976
DO YOU FEEL ME? (... FREAK YOU)	Men Of Vizion	1999
DO YOU FEEL MY LOVE?	Eddy Grant	1980
DO YOU KNOW	Michelle Gayle	1997
DO YOU KNOW (I GO CRAZY)	Angel City	2004
DO YOU KNOW (WHAT IT TAKES)	Robyn	1997
DO YOU KNOW THE WAY TO SAN JOSE	Dionne Warwick	1968
DO YOU KNOW WHAT I MEAN	Lee Michaels	1971
DO YOU LIKE THIS	Rome	1997
DO YOU LOVE ME	Dave Clark Five	1964
DO YOU LOVE ME	Deep Feeling	1970

SONG TITLE	ARTIST	DATE
DO YOU LOVE ME	Brian Poole & The Tremeloes	1963
DO YOU LOVE ME	Contours	1988
DO YOU LOVE ME LIKE YOU SAY?	Terence Trent D'Arby	1993
DO YOU LOVE WHAT YOU FEEL	Inner City	1989
DO YOU LOVE WHAT YOU FEEL	Rufus And Chaka Khan	1979
DO YOU REALIZE??	Flaming Lips	2002
DO YOU REALLY LIKE IT	DJ Pied Piper & Masters Of Ceremonies	2001
DO YOU REALLY LOVE ME TOO	Billy Fury	1964
DO YOU REALLY WANT ME	Jon Secada	1993
DO YOU REALLY WANT ME	Robyn	1998
DO YOU REALLY WANT TO HURT ME	Culture Club	1982
DO YOU REMEMBER	Scaffold	1968
DO YOU REMEMBER?	Phil Collins	1990
DO YOU REMEMBER THE FIRST TIME?	Pulp	1994
DO YOU SEE	Warren G	1995
DO YOU SEE MY LOVE	Jr. Walker & The All Stars	1970
DO YOU SEE THE LIGHT?	Snap! vs Plaything	2002

SONG TITLE	ARTIST	DATE
DO YOU SEE THE LIGHT (LOOKING FOR)	Snap! featuring Niki Harris	1993
DO YOU SLEEP?	Lisa Loeb & Nine Stories	1995
DO YOU UNDERSTAND	Almighty	1996
DO YOU WANNA DANCE?	Barry Blue	1973
DO YOU WANNA DANCE?	Beach Boys	1965
DO YOU WANNA FUNK	Sylvester & Patrick Cowley	1982
DO YOU WANNA GET FUNKY	C&C Music Factory	1994
DO YOU WANNA MAKE LOVE	Peter McCann	1977
DO YOU WANNA PARTY	DJ Scott (featuring Lorna B)	1995
DO YOU WANNA TOUCH ME (OH YEAH)	Gary Glitter	1973
DO YOU WANNA TOUCH ME (OH YEAH)	Joan Jett & The Blackhearts	1982
DO YOU WANT CRYING	Katrina & The Waves	1985
DO YOU WANT IT RIGHT NOW	Degrees Of Motion featuring Biti	1992
DO YOU WANT ME	Salt 'N 'Pepa	1991
DO YOU WANT ME?	Leilani	1999
DO YOU WANT TO DANCE	Bette Midler	1972
DO YOU WANT TO KNOW A SECRET	Billy J. Kramer & The Dakotas	1963

SONG TITLE	ARTIST	DATE
DO YOU WANT TO KNOW A SECRET		
	Beatles	1964
DO YOUR DANCE	Rose Royce	1977
DO YOUR THING	Isaac Hayes	1972
DO YOUR THING	Watts 103rd Street Band	1969
DO-WACKA-DO	Roger Miller	1964
THE DOCTOR	Doobie Brothers	1989
DOCTOR DOCTOR	Thompson Twins	1984
DOCTOR DOCTOR	UFO	1979
DOCTOR JEEP	Sisters Of Mercy	1990
DOCTOR JONES	Aqua	1998
DOCTOR KISS-KISS	5000 Volts	1976
DOCTOR MY EYES	Jackson 5	1973
DOCTOR MY EYES	Jackson Browne	1972
DOCTOR'S ORDERS	Sunny	1974
DOCTOR'S ORDERS	Carol Douglas	1974
DOCTORIN' THE HOUSE	Coldcut/Yazz & The Plastic	
	Population	1988
DOCTORIN' THE TARDIS	Timelords	1988
DOES ANYBODY KNOW I'M HERE		
	Dells	1968
DOES ANYBODY REALLY FALL IN LOVE ANYMORE		
	Kane Roberts	1991
DOES ANYBODY REALLY KNOW WHAT TIME IT IS?		
	Chicago	1970

SONG TITLE	ARTIST	DATE
DOES IT FEEL GOOD TO YOU		
	Carl Cox	1992
DOES IT MAKE YOU REMEMBER		
	Kim Carnes	1982
DOES SHE HAVE A FRIEND?	Gene Chandler	1980
DOES SHE LOVE THAT MAN?		
	Breathe	1990
DOES YOUR MAMA KNOW ABOUT ME		
	Bobby Taylor & The Vancouvers	1968
DOES YOUR MOTHER KNOW		
	ABBA	1979
DOESN'T REALLY MATTER	Janet Jackson	2000
DOESN'T SOMEBODY WANT TO BE WANTED		
	Partridge Family	1971
DOG & BUTTERFLY	Heart	1979
DOG EAT DOG	Adam & The Ants	1980
DOG TRAIN	Levellers	1997
DOGGONE RIGHT	Smokey Robinson & The	
	Miracles	1969
DOGGY DOGG WORLD	Snoop Doggy Dogg	1994
DOGS OF LUST	The The	1993
DOIN IT	LL Cool J	1996
DOIN' IT	Liberty	2001
DOIN' OUR OWN DANG	Jungle Brothers	1990
DOIN' THE DOO	Betty Boo	1990

SONG TITLE	ARTIST	DATE
DOING ALRIGHT WITH THE BOYS		
	Gary Glitter	1975
DOING IT ALL FOR MY BABY		
	Huey Lewis & The News	1987
DOING IT TO DEATH	Fred Wesley & The JB's	1973
DOLCE VITA	Ryan Paris	1983
DOLL PARTS	Hole	1995
DOLLARS	CJ Lewis	1994
DOLLY MY LOVE	Moments	1975
DOLPHIN	Shed Seven	1994
DOLPHINS MAKE ME CRY	Martyn Joseph	1992
DOLPHINS WERE MONKEYS		
	Ian Brown	2000
DOMINATION	Way Out West	1996
DOMINATOR	Human Resource	1991
DOMINION	Sisters Of Mercy	1988
DOMINIQUE	Singing Nun	1963
DOMINO	Van Morrison	1970
DOMINO DANCING	Pet Shop Boys	1988
DOMINOES	Robbie Nevil	1987
DON JUAN	Dave Dee, Dozy, Beaky, Mick & Tich	1969
DON QUIXOTE	Nik Kershaw	1985
THE DON	187 Lockdown	1998
DON'T ANSWER ME	Cilla Black	1966
DON'T ANSWER ME	Alan Parsons Project	1984

SONG TITLE	ARTIST	DATE
DON'T ASK ME	Public Image Ltd	1990
DON'T ASK ME WHY	Eurythmics	1989
DON'T ASK ME WHY	Billy Joel	1980
DON'T BE A DUMMY	John Du Cann	1979
DON'T BE A FOOL	Loose Ends	1990
DON'T BE A STRANGER	Dina Carroll	1993
DON'T BE CRUEL	Bobby Brown	1988
DON'T BE CRUEL	Elvis Presley	1956
DON'T BE CRUEL	Cheap Trick	1977
DON'T BE STUPID (YOU KNOW I LOVE YOU)		
	Shania Twain	1997
DON'T BELIEVE A WORD	Thin Lizzy	1977
DON'T BELIEVE THE HYPE	Public Enemy	1988
DON'T BLAME IT ON THAT GIRL/WAP BAM BOOGIE		
	Matt Bianco	1988
DON'T BLAME ME	Frank Ifield	1964
DON'T BLAME THE CHILDREN		
	Sammy Davis Jr.	1967
DON'T BREAK MY HEART	UB40	1985
DON'T BREAK MY HEART AGAIN		
	Whitesnake	1981
DON'T BRING ME DOWN	Spirits	1994
DON'T BRING ME DOWN	Animals	1966
DON'T BRING ME DOWN	Electric Light Orchestra	1979
DON'T BRING ME DOWN	Pretty Things	1964

SONG TITLE	ARTIST	DATE
DON'T BRING ME YOUR HEARTACHES		
	Paul & Barry Ryan	1965
DON'T CALL ME BABY	Madison Avenue	1999
DON'T CALL ME BABY	Voice Of The Beehive	1988
DON'T CALL US WE'LL CALL YOU		
	Sugarloaf/Jerry Corbetta	1974
DON'T CHANGE HORSES	Tower Of Power	1974
DON'T CHANGE ON ME	Ray Charles	1971
DON'T CLOSE YOUR EYES	Kix	1989
DON'T COME AROUND HERE NO MORE		
	Tom Petty & The Heartbreakers	1985
DON'T COME CLOSE	Ramones	1978
DON'T COME HOME TOO SOON		
	Del Amitri	1998
DON'T CROSS THE RIVER	America	1973
DON'T CRY	Asia	1983
DON'T CRY	Guns N' Roses	1991
DON'T CRY	Seal	1996
DON'T CRY DADDY	Elvis Presley	1969
DON'T CRY FOR ME ARGENTINA		
	Mike Flowers Pops	1996
DON'T CRY FOR ME ARGENTINA		
	Julie Covington	1976
DON'T CRY FOR ME ARGENTINA		
	Shadows	1978

SONG TITLE	ARTIST	DATE
DON'T CRY FOR ME ARGENTINA		
	Madonna	1997
DON'T CRY OUT LOUD	Elkie Brooks	1978
DON'T CRY OUT LOUD	Melissa Manchester	1978
DON'T DIE JUST YET	David Holmes	1998
DON'T DISTURB THE GROOVE		
	System	1987
DON'T DO IT	Band	1972
DON'T DO IT BABY	Mac & Katie Kissoon	1975
DON'T DO ME LIKE THAT	Tom Petty & The Heartbreakers	1979
DON'T DO THAT	Geordie	1972
DON'T DON'T TELL ME NO	Sophie B. Hawkins	1994
DON'T DREAM	Dove	1999
DON'T DREAM IT'S OVER	Crowded House	1987
DON'T DREAM IT'S OVER	Paul Young	1991
DON'T EVER BE LONELY	Cornelius Brothers & Sister	
	Rose	1972
DON'T EVER THINK (TOO MUCH)		
	Zutons	2004
DON'T EVER WANNA LOSE YA		
	New England	1979
DON'T EXPECT ME TO BE YOUR FRIEND		
	Lobo	1972
DON'T FALL IN LOVE (I SAID)		
	Toyah	1985

SONG TITLE	ARTIST	DATE
DON'T FALL IN LOVE WITH A DREAMER	Kenny Rogers & Kim Carnes	1980
DON'T FALTER	Mint Royale featuring Lauren Laverne	2000
(DON'T FEAR) THE REAPER	Apollo 440	1995
(DON'T FEAR) THE REAPER	Blue Oyster Cult	1976
DON'T FIGHT IT	Wilson Pickett	1965
DON'T FIGHT IT	Kenny Loggins & Steve Perry	1952
DON'T FORGET I STILL LOVE YOU	Bobbi Martin	1964
DON'T FORGET ME (WHEN I'M GONE)	Glass Tiger	1986
DON'T FORGET TO CATCH ME	Cliff Richard	1968
DON'T FORGET TO DANCE	Kinks	1983
DON'T FORGET TO REMEMBER	Bee Gees	1969
DON'T GET ME WRONG	Pretenders	1986
DON'T GIVE IN TO HIM	Gary Puckett & The Union Gap	1969
DON'T GIVE IT UP	Robbie Patton	1981
DON'T GIVE ME YOUR LIFE	Alex Party	1995
DON'T GIVE UP	Michelle Weeks	1997
DON'T GIVE UP	Chicane featuring Bryan Adams	2000

SONG TITLE	ARTIST	DATE
DON'T GIVE UP	Peter Gabriel & Kate Bush	1986
DON'T GIVE UP	Petula Clark	1968
DON'T GIVE UP ON US	David Soul	1977
DON'T GO	Third Dimension featuring Julie McDermott	1996
DON'T GO	Hothouse Flowers	1988
DON'T GO	Yazoo	1982
DON'T GO	Awesome 3 featuring Julie McDermott	1996
DON'T GO AWAY MAD (JUST GO AWAY)	Motley Crue	1990
DON'T GO BREAKING MY HEART	Elton John & Kiki Dee	1976
DON'T GO MESSIN' WITH MY HEART	Mantronix	1991
DON'T GO OUT INTO THE RAIN	Herman's Hermits	1967
DON'T HAPPEN TWICE	Kenny Chesney	2001
DON'T HOLD BACK	Chanson	1978
DON'T HURT YOURSELF	Marillion	2004
DON'T IT MAKE MY BROWN EYES BLUE	Crystal Gayle	1977
DON'T IT MAKE YOU FEEL GOOD	Stefan Dennis	1989
DON'T JUST STAND THERE	Patty Duke	1965
DON'T KILL THE WHALE	Yes	1978

SONG TITLE	ARTIST	DATE
DON'T KNOCK MY LOVE (PT 1)		
	Wilson Pickett	1971
DON'T KNOW MUCH	Linda Ronstadt featuring	
	Aaron Neville	1989
DON'T KNOW WHAT TO TELL YA		
	Aaliyah	2003
DON'T KNOW WHAT YOU GOT (TILL IT'S GONE)		
	Cinderella	1988
DON'T KNOW WHY	Norah Jones	2002
DON'T LAUGH	Winx	1995
DON'T LEAVE	Faithless	1997
DON'T LEAVE HOME	Dido	2004
DON'T LEAVE ME	Blackstreet	1997
DON'T LEAVE ME THIS WAY		
	Thelma Houston	1976
DON'T LEAVE ME THIS WAY		
	Communards	1986
DON'T LEAVE ME THIS WAY		
	Harold Melvin & The Blue Notes	1977
DON'T LET GO	Manhattan Transfer	1977
DON'T LET GO	David Sneddon	2003
DON'T LET GO	Isaac Hayes	1979
DON'T LET GO	Wang Chung	1984
DON'T LET GO (LOVE)	En Vogue	1996
DON'T LET HIM GO	REO Speedwagon	1981
DON'T LET HIM KNOW	Prism	1982

SONG TITLE	ARTIST	DATE
DON'T LET HIM TOUCH YOU		
	Angelettes	1972
DON'T LET IT DIE	Hurricane Smith	1971
DON'T LET IT END	Styx	1983
DON'T LET IT FADE AWAY	Darts	1978
DON'T LET IT GO TO YOUR HEAD		
	Brand New Heavies	1992
DON'T LET IT PASS YOU BY/DON'T SLOW DOWN		
	UB40	1981
DON'T LET IT SHOW ON YOUR FACE		
	Adeva	1992
DON'T LET ME BE LONELY TONIGHT		
	James Taylor	1972
DON'T LET ME BE MISUNDERSTOOD		
	Animals	1965
DON'T LET ME BE MISUNDERSTOOD		
	Elvis Costello	1986
DON'T LET ME BE MISUNDERSTOOD		
	Santa Esmeralda	1977
DON'T LET ME BE THE LAST TO KNOW		
	Britney Spears	2001
DON'T LET ME DOWN	Farm	1991
DON'T LET ME DOWN	Beatles With Billy Preston	1969
DON'T LET ME DOWN GENTLY		
	Wonder Stuff	1989

SONG TITLE	ARTIST	DATE
DON'T LET ME DOWN/YOU AND I		
	Will Young	2002
DON'T LET ME GET ME	Pink	2002
DON'T LET THE FEELING GO		
	Nightcrawlers featuring	
	John Reid	1995
DON'T LET THE GREEN GRASS FOOL YOU		
	Wilson Pickett	1971
DON'T LET THE JONESES GET YOU DOWN		
	Temptations	1969
DON'T LET THE RAIN COME DOWN		
	Ronnie Hilton	1964
DON'T LET THE RAIN COME DOWN (CROOKED		
LITTLE MAN)	Serendipity Singers	1964
DON'T LET THE RAIN FALL DOWN ON ME		
	Critters	1967
DON'T LET THE SUN CATCH YOU CRYING		
	Gerry & The Pacemakers	1964
DON'T LET THE SUN GO DOWN ON ME		
	Oleta Adams	1991
DON'T LET THE SUN GO DOWN ON ME		
	Elton John	1974
DON'T LET THE SUN GO DOWN ON ME		
	George Michael/Elton John	1991
DON'T LET THIS MOMENT END		
	Gloria Estefan	1999

SONG TITLE	ARTIST	DATE
DON'T LOOK ANY FURTHER		
	M People	1993
DON'T LOOK BACK	Fine Young Cannibals	1989
DON'T LOOK BACK	Boston	1978
DON'T LOOK BACK IN ANGER		
	Oasis	1996
DON'T LOOK BACK INTO THE SUN		
	Libertines	2003
DON'T LOOK DOWN – THE SEQUEL		
	Go West	1987
DON'T LOSE MY NUMBER	Phil Collins	1985
DON'T LOSE THE MAGIC	Shawn Christopher	1992
DON'T LOVE ME TOO HARD		
	Nolans	1982
DON'T MAKE ME OVER	Swinging Blue Jeans	1966
DON'T MAKE ME OVER	Sybil	1989
DON'T MAKE ME WAIT	Loveland featuring	
	Rachel McFarlane	1995
DON'T MAKE ME WAIT	911	1996
DON'T MAKE ME WAIT FOR LOVE		
	Kenny G	1987
DON'T MAKE ME WAIT TOO LONG		
	Barry White	1976
DON'T MAKE MY BABY BLUE		
	Shadows	1965
DON'T MAKE WAVES	Nolans	1980

SONG TITLE	ARTIST	DATE
DON'T MARRY HER	Beautiful South	1996
DON'T MEAN NOTHING	Richard Marx	1987
DON'T MESS UP A GOOD THING		
	Fontella Bass & Bobby McClure	1965
DON'T MESS WITH BILL	Marvelettes	1966
DON'T MESS WITH DOCTOR DREAM		
	Thompson Twins	1985
DON'T MESS WITH MY MAN		
	Lucy Pearl	2000
DON'T MISS THE PARTYLINE		
	Bizz Nizz	1990
DON'T MUG YOURSELF	Streets	2002
DON'T NEED A GUN	Billy Idol	1987
DON'T NEED THE SUN TO SHINE (TO MAKE ME SMILE)		
	Gabrielle	2001
DON'T PAY THE FERRYMAN		
	Chris De Burgh	1983
DON'T PLAY THAT SONG	Aretha Franklin	1970
DON'T PLAY THAT SONG AGAIN		
	Nicki French	2000
DON'T PLAY YOUR ROCK 'N' ROLL TO ME		
	Smokey	1975
DON'T PULL YOUR LOVE	Sean Maguire	1996
DON'T PULL YOUR LOVE	Hamilton, Joe Frank & Reynolds	1971
DON'T PULL YOUR LOVE/THEN YOU CAN TELL ME GOODBYE		
	Glen Campbell	1976

SONG TITLE	ARTIST	DATE
DON'T PUSH IT DON'T FORCE IT		
	Leon Haywood	1980
DON'T RUSH (TAKE LOVE SLOWLY)		
	K-Ci & Jojo	1998
DON'T RUSH ME	Taylor Dayne	1988
DON'T SAY GOODNIGHT (IT'S TIME FOR LOVE)		
	Isley Brothers	1980
DON'T SAY I TOLD YOU SO	Tourists	1980
DON'T SAY IT'S OVER	Gun	1994
DON'T SAY YOU DON'T REMEMBER		
	Beverly Bremmers	1971
DON'T SAY YOU LOVE ME	M2M	2000
DON'T SAY YOUR LOVE IS KILLING ME		
	Erasure	1997
DON'T SET ME FREE	Ray Charles	1963
DON'T SHED A TEAR	Paul Carrack	1987
DON'T SHUT ME OUT	Kevin Paige	1989
DON'T SLEEP IN THE SUBWAY		
	Petula Clark	1967
DON'T SPEAK	No Doubt	1997
DON'T STAND SO CLOSE TO ME		
	Police	1981
DON'T STAY AWAY TOO LONG		
	Peters & Lee	1974
DON'T STOP	K-Klass	1992
DON'T STOP	Status Quo	1996

SONG TITLE	ARTIST	DATE
DON'T STOP	Ruff Driverz	1998
DON'T STOP	ATB	1999
DON'T STOP	Fleetwood Mac	1977
DON'T STOP	Rolling Stones	2002
DON'T STOP (WIGGLE WIGGLE)		
	Outhere Brothers	1995
DON'T STOP BELIEVIN'	Olivia Newton-John	1976
DON'T STOP BELIEVING	Journey	1981
DON'T STOP IT NOW	Hot Chocolate	1976
DON'T STOP ME NOW	Queen	1979
DON'T STOP MOVIN'	Livin' Joy	1996
DON'T STOP MOVIN'	S Club 7	2001
DON'T STOP THAT CRAZY RHYTHM		
	Modern Romance	1983
DON'T STOP THE CARNIVAL		
	Alan Price Set	1968
DON'T STOP THE DANCE	Bryan Ferry	1985
DON'T STOP THE MUSIC	Lionel Richie	2000
DON'T STOP THE MUSIC	Yarbrough & Peoples	1981
DON'T STOP TILL YOU GET ENOUGH		
	Michael Jackson	1979
DON'T TAKE AWAY THE MUSIC		
	Tavares	1976
DON'T TAKE IT PERSONAL (JUST ONE OF DEM DAYS)		
	Monica	1995
DON'T TAKE IT SO HARD	Paul Revere & The Raiders	1968

SONG TITLE	ARTIST	DATE
DON'T TAKE THE GIRL	Tim McGraw	1994
DON'T TAKE YOUR LOVE	Manhattans	1975
DON'T TAKE YOUR LOVE AWAY		
	Avant	2004
DON'T TALK	Jon B	2001
DON'T TALK ABOUT LOVE	Bad Boys Inc	1993
DON'T TALK JUST KISS	Right Said Fred/Jocelyn Brown	1991
DON'T TALK TO HIM	Cliff Richard	1963
DON'T TALK TO ME ABOUT LOVE		
	Altered Images	1983
DON'T TALK TO STRANGERS		
	Rick Springfield	1982
DON'T TELL ME	Van Halen	1995
DON'T TELL ME	Blancmange	1984
DON'T TELL ME	Madonna	2000
DON'T TELL ME	Avril Lavigne	2004
DON'T TELL ME GOODNIGHT		
	Lobo	1975
DON'T TELL ME LIES	Breathe	1989
DON'T TELL ME YOU LOVE ME		
	Night Ranger	1983
DON'T TELL ME YOU'RE SORRY		
	S Club 8	2004
DON'T THINK I'M NOT	Kandi	2000
DON'T THINK TWICE	Wonder Who?	1965

SONG TITLE	ARTIST	DATE
DON'T THINK YOU'RE THE FIRST		
	Coral	2003
DON'T THROW IT ALL AWAY		
	Gary Benson	1975
DON'T THROW YOUR LOVE AWAY		
	Searchers	1964
DON'T TOUCH ME	Bettye Swann	1969
DON'T TREAT ME BAD	Firehouse	1991
DON'T TRY TO CHANGE ME		
	Crickets	1963
DON'T TRY TO STOP IT	Roman Holliday	1983
DON'T TURN AROUND	ASWAD	1988
DON'T TURN AROUND	Ace Of Base	1994
DON'T TURN AROUND	Merseybeats	1964
DON'T WAIT UP	Thunder	1997
DON'T WALK AWAY	Electric Light Orchestra	1980
DON'T WALK AWAY	Four Tops	1981
DON'T WALK AWAY	Jade	1992
DON'T WALK AWAY	Javine	2004
DON'T WALK AWAY	Rick Springfield	1984
DON'T WANNA BE A PLAYER		
	Joe	1997
DON'T WANNA FALL IN LOVE		
	Jane Child	1990
DON'T WANNA KNOW	Shy FX & T-Power featuring	
	Di & Skibadee	2002

SONG TITLE	ARTIST	DATE
DON'T WANNA LET YOU GO		
	Five	2000
DON'T WANNA LOSE THIS FEELING		
	Dannii Minogue	2003
DON'T WANNA LOSE YOU	Gloria Estefan	1989
DON'T WANNA LOSE YOU	Lionel Richie	1996
DON'T WANT TO BE A FOOL		
	Luther Vandross	1991
DON'T WANT TO FORGIVE ME NOW		
	Wet Wet Wet	1995
DON'T WANT TO LIVE WITHOUT IT		
	Pablo Cruise	1978
DON'T WANT TO WAIT ANYMORE		
	Tubes	1981
DON'T WASTE MY TIME	Paul Hardcastle	1986
DON'T WORRY	Kim Appleby	1990
DON'T WORRY	Appleton	2003
DON'T WORRY BABY	Beach Boys	1964
DON'T WORRY BABY	B.J. Thomas	1977
DON'T WORRY BE HAPPY	Bobby McFerrin	1988
(DON'T WORRY) IF THERE'S A HELL BELOW WE'RE		
ALL GOING TO GO	Curtis Mayfield	1970
DON'T YA WANNA PLAY THIS GAME NO MORE?		
	Elton John	1980
DON'T YOU (FORGET ABOUT ME)		
	Simple Minds	1985

SONG TITLE	ARTIST	DATE
DON'T YOU CARE	Buckinghams	1967
DON'T YOU FORGET IT	Glenn Lewis	2001
DON'T YOU GET SO MAD	Jeffrey Osborne	1983
DON'T YOU JUST KNOW IT	Amazulu	1985
DON'T YOU KNOW	Butterscotch	1970
DON'T YOU KNOW WHAT THE NIGHT CAN DO		
	Steve Winwood	1988
DON'T YOU LOVE ME	Eternal	1997
DON'T YOU LOVE ME	49ers	1990
DON'T YOU THINK IT'S TIME		
	Mike Berry	1963
DON'T YOU WANT ME	Human League	1982
DON'T YOU WANT ME	Felix	1992
DON'T YOU WANT ME	Farm	1992
DON'T YOU WANT ME	Jody Watley	1987
DON'T YOU WANT ME – REMIX		
	Felix	1995
DON'T YOU WORRY	Madasun	2000
DON'T YOU WORRY 'BOUT A THING		
	Incognito	1992
DON'T YOU WORRY 'BOUT A THING		
	Stevie Wonder	1974
DON'T YOU WRITE HER OFF		
	McGuinn, Clark & Hillman	1979
DONALD WHERE'S YOUR TROOSERS		
	Andy Stewart	1989

SONG TITLE	ARTIST	DATE
DONNA	10cc	1972
DONTCHANGE	Musiq	2002
DOO DOO DOO DOO DOO (HEARTBREAKER)		
	Rolling Stones	1974
DOO WOP (THAT THING)	Lauryn Hill	1998
DOOBEDOOD'NDOOBE DOOBEDOOD'NDOOBE		
	Diana Ross	1972
DOODAH!	Cartoons	1999
DOOMS NIGHT	Azzido Da Bass	2000
DOOP	Doop	1994
THE DOOR IS STILL OPEN TO MY HEART		
	Dean Martin	1964
DOORS OF YOUR HEART	Beat	1981
THE DOPE SHOW	Marilyn Manson	1998
DORAVILLE	Atlanta Rhythm Section	1974
DOUBLE BARREL	Dave & Ansil Collins	1971
DOUBLE DOUBLE DUTCH	Dope Smugglaz	1999
DOUBLE DUTCH	Fatback Band	1977
DOUBLE DUTCH	Malcolm McLaren	1983
DOUBLE DUTCH BUS	Frankie Smith	1981
DOUBLE LOVIN'	Osmonds	1971
DOUBLE SHOT (OF MY BABY'S LOVE)		
	Swingin' Medallions	1966
DOUBLE VISION	Foreigner	1978
DOUBLEBACK	ZZ Top	1990

SONG TITLE	ARTIST	DATE
DOVE (I'LL BE LOVING YOU)		
	Moony	2002
DOVE L'AMORE	Cher	1999
DOWN	Blink-182	2004
DOWN ASS CHICK	Ja Rule featuring Charli 'Chuck' Baltimore	2002
DOWN AT LULU'S	Ohio Express	1968
DOWN BOY	Holly Valance	2002
DOWN BOYS	Warrant	1989
DOWN BY THE LAZY RIVER		
	Osmonds	1972
DOWN BY THE WATER	PJ Harvey	1995
DOWN DOWN	Status Quo	1974
DOWN IN A HOLE	Alice In Chains	1993
DOWN IN THE BOONDOCKS		
	Billy Joe Royal	1965
DOWN IN THE SUBWAY	Soft Cell	1984
DOWN IN THE TUBE STATION AT MIDNIGHT		
	Jam	1978
DOWN 4 U	Irv Gotti presents Ja Rule, Ashanti, Charli Baltimore	2002
DOWN LOW (NOBODY HAS TO KNOW)		
	R. Kelly featuring Ronald Isley	1996
DOWN ON THE BEACH TONIGHT		
	Drifters	1974

SONG TITLE	ARTIST	DATE
DOWN ON THE CORNER/FORTUNATE SON		
	Creedence Clearwater Revival	1969
DOWN ON THE STREET	Shakatak	1984
DOWN SO LONG	Jewel	1999
DOWN THAT ROAD	Shara Nelson	1993
DOWN THE DUSTPIPE	Status Quo	1970
DOWN THE HALL	Four Seasons	1977
DOWN TO EARTH	Monie Love	1990
DOWN TO EARTH	Grace	1996
DOWN TO EARTH	Curiosity Killed The Cat	1987
DOWN UNDER	Men At Work	1982
DOWN WITH THE CLIQUE		
	Aaliyah	1995
DOWN WITH THE KING	Run DMC	1993
DOWNLOAD IT	Clea	2003
DOWNTOWN	Petula Clark	1964
DOWNTOWN	SWV	1994
DOWNTOWN	One 2 Many	1989
DOWNTOWN LIFE	Daryl Hall & John Oates	1988
DOWNTOWN TRAIN	Rod Stewart	1989
DR. BEAT	Miami Sound Machine	1984
DR. FEELGOOD	Motley Crue	1989
DR. GREENTHUMB	Cypress Hill	1999
DR. HECKYLL & MR. JIVE	Men At Work	1983
DR. LOVE	Tina Charles	1976
DR. MABUSE	Propaganda	1984

SONG TITLE	ARTIST	DATE
DR. WHO	Mankind	1978
DRAGGIN' THE LINE	Tommy James	1971
DRAGGING ME DOWN	Inspiral Carpets	1992
DRAGOSTEA DIN TEI	O-Zone	2004
DRAMA!	Erasure	1989
DRAW OF THE CARDS	Kim Carnes	1981
(DRAWING) RINGS AROUND THE WORLD		
	Super Furry Animals	2001
DRE DAY	Dr. Dre	1993
DREADLOCK HOLIDAY	10cc	1978
THE DREAM (HOLD ON TO YOUR DREAM)		
	Irene Cara	1983
DREAM A LITTLE DREAM OF ME		
	Anita Harris	1968
DREAM A LITTLE DREAM OF ME		
	Mama Cass	1968
DREAM ABOUT YOU/FUNKY MELODY		
	Stevie B	1995
DREAM ANOTHER DREAM	Rialto	1998
DREAM BABY (HOW LONG MUST I DREAM)		
	Glen Campbell	1971
DREAM COME TRUE	Brand New Heavies	1992
THE DREAM IS STILL ALIVE		
	Wilson Phillips	1991
DREAM MERCHANT	New Birth	1975
DREAM ON	Depeche Mode	2001
DREAM OF ME (BASED ON LOVE'S THEME)		
	OMD	1993
DREAM ON	Aerosmith	1976
DREAM ON	Righteous Brothers	1974
DREAM ON DREAMER	Brand New Heavies	1994
DREAM ON LITTLE DREAMER		
	Perry Como	1965
DREAM POLICE	Cheap Trick	1979
DREAM TO ME	Dario G	2001
DREAM TO SLEEP	H2O	1983
DREAM UNIVERSE	DJ Garry	2002
DREAM WEAVER	Gary Wright	1976
A DREAM'S A DREAM	Soul II Soul	1990
DREAMBOAT	Limmie & The Family Cookin'	1973
DREAMER	Supertramp	1980
DREAMER	Livin' Joy	1995
DREAMER	Jacksons	1977
DREAMER	CK & Supreme Dream Team	2003
DREAMER/GETS ME THROUGH		
	Ozzy Osbourne	2002
DREAMIN'	Status Quo	1986
DREAMIN'	Liverpool Express	1977
DREAMIN'	Vanessa Williams	1989
DREAMIN' IS EASY	Steel Breeze	1983
DREAMING	MN8	1996
DREAMING	BT featuring Kirsty Hawkshaw	2000

SONG TITLE	ARTIST	DATE
DREAMING	Blondie	1979
DREAMING	Glen Goldsmith	1988
DREAMING	Cliff Richard	1980
DREAMING	Ruff Driverz	1998
DREAMING	M People	1999
DREAMING	Aurora	2002
DREAMING	Orchestral Manoeuvres In The Dark	1988
DREAMING OF YOU	Coral	2002
DREAMING OF YOU	Selena	1995
DREAMLOVER	Mariah Carey	1993
DREAMS	Cranberries	1994
DREAMS	Wild Colour	1995
DREAMS	Smokin Beats featuring Lyn Eden	1998
DREAMS	Miss Shiva	2001
DREAMS	Fleetwood Mac	1977
DREAMS	Corrs	1998
DREAMS	Gabrielle	1993
DREAMS	Van Halen	1986
DREAMS OF THE EVERYDAY HOUSEWIFE	Glen Campbell	1968
DREAMS OF YOU	Ralph McTell	1975
DREAMSCAPE '94	Time Frequency	1994
DREAMTIME	Zee	1996
DREAMTIME	Daryl Hall	1986

SONG TITLE	ARTIST	DATE
DREAMY LADY	T-Rex	1975
DREIDEL	Don McLean	1972
DRESS YOU UP	Madonna	1985
DRESSED FOR SUCCESS	Roxette	1989
DRIFT AWAY	Michael Bolton	1992
DRIFT AWAY	Dobie Gray	1973
DRIFTING AWAY	Lange featuring Skye	2002
DRIFTWOOD	Travis	1999
THE DRILL	Dirt Devils	2002
DRINKING IN LA	Bran Van 3000	1999
DRIVE	Incubus	2001
DRIVE	Cars	1984
DRIVE	R.E.M.	1992
DRIVE (FOR DADDY GENE)	Alan Jackson	2002
DRIVE ME CRAZY	Partizan	1997
DRIVE ON	Brother Beyond	1989
DRIVE SAFELY DARLIN'	Tony Christie	1976
DRIVE-IN SATURDAY (SEATTLE – PHOENIX)	David Bowie	1973
DRIVEN BY YOU	Brian May	1991
DRIVERS SEAT	Sniff 'n' The Tears	1979
DRIVIN' MY LIFE AWAY	Eddie Rabbitt	1980
DRIVIN' WHEEL	Foghat	1976
DRIVING	Everything But The Girl	1996

SONG TITLE	ARTIST	DATE
DRIVING AWAY FROM HOME (JIM'S TUNE)		
	It's Immaterial	1986
DRIVING MY CAR	Madness	1982
DRIVING WITH THE BRAKES ON		
	Del Amitri	1995
DROP DEAD GORGEOUS	Republica	1997
DROP IT LIKE IT'S HOT	Snoop Dogg featuring Pharrell	2004
DROP THE BOY	Bros	1988
DROP THE PILOT	Joan Armatrading	1983
DROP THE PRESSURE	Mylo	2004
DROPS OF JUPITER (TELL ME)		
	Train	2001
DROWNED WORLD (SUBSTITUTE FOR LOVE)		
	Madonna	1998
DROWNING	Backstreet Boys	2001
DROWNING IN BERLIN	Mobiles	1982
DROWNING IN THE SEA OF LOVE		
	Joe Simon	1971
DROWNING/ALL OUT TO GET YOU		
	Beat	1981
THE DRUGS DON'T WORK	Verve	1997
THE DRUM	Bobby Sherman	1971
DRUMMER MAN	Tonight	1978
THE DRUMSTICK (EP)	N-Joi	1993
DRY COUNTY	Bon Jovi	1994
DRY LAND	Marillion	1991

SONG TITLE	ARTIST	DATE
DRY YOUR EYES	The Streets	2004
DRY YOUR EYES	Brenda & The Tabulations	1967
DUALITY	Slipknot	2004
DUB BE GOOD TO ME	Beats International	1990
DUCHESS	My Life Story	1997
DUCHESS	Stranglers	1979
THE DUCK	Jackie Lee	1965
DUCKTOY	Hampenberg	2002
DUDE	Beenie Man featuring Ms Thing	2004
DUDE (LOOKS LIKE A LADY)		
	Aerosmith	1987
DUEL	Propaganda	1985
DUELING BANJOS	Eric Weissberg & Steve Mandell	1973
DUKE OF EARL	Darts	1979
DUM-DE-DA	Bobby Vinton	1966
DUMB	Beautiful South	1998
DUMB	The 411	2004
DUMMY CRUSHER	Kerbdog	1994
DUNE BUGGY	Presidents Of The United States	1996
DUNKIE BUTT	12 Gauge	1994
DURHAM TOWN (THE LEAVIN')		
	Roger Whittaker	1969
DUSIC	Brick	1977
DUSK TIL DAWN	Danny Howells & Dick Trevor	
	featuring Erire	2004
DUST IN THE WIND	Kansas	1978

SONG TITLE	ARTIST	DATE
DUSTED	Leftfield/Roots Manuva	1999
DY-NA-MI-TEE	Ms Dynamite	2002
DYNA-MITE	Mud	1973
DYNAMITE	Jermaine Jackson	1984
DYNOMITE	Tony Camillo's Bazuka	1975
E SAMBA	Junior Jack	2003
E-BOW THE LETTER	R.E.M.	1996
E.I.	Nelly	2000
E=MC2	Big Audio Dynamite	1986
EACH AND EVERY ONE	Everything But The Girl	1984
EACH TIME	East 17	1998
EACH TIME YOU BREAK MY HEART		
	Nick Kamen	1986
EARACHE MY EYE featuring ALICE BOWIE		
	Cheech & Chong	1974
EARLY IN THE MORNING	Vanity Fare	1969
EARLY IN THE MORNING	Gap Band	1982
EARLY IN THE MORNING	Robert Palmer	1988
EARLY MORNING	Sugar Ray	1999
EARTH ANGEL	New Edition	1986
THE EARTH DIES SCREAMING/DREAM A LIE		
	UB40	1980
EARTH SONG	Michael Jackson	1995
THE EARTH, THE SUN, THE RAIN		
	Color Me Badd	1996
EARTHBOUND	Conner Reeves	1997

SONG TITLE	ARTIST	DATE
THE EARTHSHAKER	Paul Masterson presents Sushi	2002
EASE MY MIND	Arrested Development	1994
EASIER SAID THAN DONE	Shakatak	1981
EAST OF EDEN	Big Country	1984
EAST RIVER	Brecker Brothers	1978
EAST WEST	Herman's Hermits	1966
EASTER	Marillion	1990
EASY	Commodores	1977
EASY	Terrorvision	1997
EASY	Groove Armada	2003
EASY COME, EASY GO	Bobby Sherman	1970
EASY, EASY	Scotland World Cup Squad	1974
EASY LIVIN'	Uriah Heep	1972
EASY LOVER	Philip Bailey & Phil Collins	1984
EASY LOVING	Freddie Hart	1971
EASY TO BE HARD	Three Dog Night	1969
EASY TO LOVE	Leo Sayer	1977
EASY TO SMILE	Senseless Things	1992
EAT IT	Weird Al Yankovic	1984
EAT MY GOAL	Collapsed Lung	1998
EAT THE RICH	Aerosmith	1993
EAT YOURSELF WHOLE	Kingmaker	1992
EBB TIDE	Righteous Brothers	1965
EBB TIDE	Lenny Welch	1964
EBENEEZER GOODE	Shamen	1992

SONG TITLE	ARTIST	DATE
EBONY AND IVORY	Paul McCartney & Stevie Wonder	1982
EBONY EYES	Bob Welch	1978
ECHO BEACH	Martha & The Muffins	1980
ECHO PARK	Keith Barbour	1969
ECSTASY	Ohio Players	1973
ECUADOR	Sash! featuring Rodriguez	1997
EDELWEISS	Vince Hill	1967
EDGE OF A BROKEN HEART	Vixen	1988
THE EDGE OF HEAVEN/WHERE DID YOUR HEART GO	Wham!	1986
EDGE OF SEVENTEEN	Stevie Nicks	1982
EDIE (CIAO BABY)	Cult	1989
EENY MEENY	Showstoppers	1968
EGO	Elton John	1978
EGYPTIAN REGGAE	Jonathan Richman & The Modern Lovers	1977
EI	Nelly	2001
EIGHT BY TEN	Ken Dodd	1964
EIGHT DAYS A WEEK	Beatles	1965
853-5937	Squeeze	1987
808	Blaque Ivory	1999
EIGHT MILES HIGH	Byrds	1966
867-5309/JENNY	Tommy Tutone	1982
EIGHTEEN	Alice Cooper	1971

SONG TITLE	ARTIST	DATE
18 AND LIFE	Skid Row	1989
EIGHTEEN STRINGS	Tinman	1994
18 TIL I DIE	Bryan Adams	1997
EIGHTEEN WITH A BULLET	Pete Wingfield	1975
EIGHTEEN YELLOW ROSES	Bobby Darin	1963
EIGHTH DAY	Hazel O'Connor	1980
EINSTEIN A GO-GO	Landscape	1981
EL BIMBO	Bimbo Jet	1975
EL CAPITAN	OPM	2002
EL CONDOR PASA	Simon & Garfunkel	1970
EL NINO	Agnelli & Nelson	1998
EL PARADISO RICO	Deetah	1999
EL PRESIDENT	Drugstore	1998
EL SALVADOR	Athlete	2003
EL TRAGO (THE DRINK)	2 In A Room	1994
ELEANOR RIGBY	Ray Charles	1968
ELEANOR RIGBY	Beatles	1966
ELEANOR RIGBY	Aretha Franklin	1969
ELECTED	Alice Cooper	1972
ELECTION DAY	Arcadia	1985
ELECTRIC AVENUE	Eddy Grant	1983
ELECTRIC BARBARELLA	Duran Duran	1999
ELECTRIC BLUE	Icehouse	1988
ELECTRIC HEAD PT 2 (THE ECSTASY)	White Zombie	1996

SONG TITLE	ARTIST	DATE
ELECTRIC LADY	Geordie	1973
ELECTRIC MAN	Mansun	2000
ELECTRIC YOUTH	Debbie Gibson	1989
ELECTRICAL STORM	U2	2002
ELECTRICITY	Spiritualized	1997
ELECTRICITY	Suede	1999
ELECTROLITE	R.E.M.	1996
ELECTRONIC PLEASURE	N-Trance	1996
ELEGANTLY AMERICAN: ONE NIGHT IN HEAVEN/ MOVING ON UP	M People	1994
ELEGANTLY WASTED	INXS	1997
ELEKTROBANK	Chemical Brothers	1997
ELENORE	Turtles	1968
ELEPHANT STONE	Stone Roses	1990
THE ELEPHANT'S GRAVEYARD (GUILTY)	Boomtown Rats	1981
ELEVATE MY MIND	Stereo MC's	1991
ELEVATION	U2	2001
ELEVATOR SONG	Dubstar	1996
ELEVATORS (ME & YOU)	Outkast	1996
ELEVEN TO FLY	Tin Tin Out featuring Wendy Page	1999
ELI'S COMING	Three Dog Night	1969
ELIZABETHAN REGGAE	Boris Gardiner	1970
ELMO JAMES	Chairmen Of The Board	1972
THE ELO EP	Electric Light Orchestra	1978

SONG TITLE	ARTIST	DATE
ELOISE	Damned	1986
ELOISE	Barry Ryan	1968
ELUSIVE BUTTERFLY	Val Doonican	1966
ELUSIVE BUTTERFLY	Bob Lind	1966
ELVIRA	Oak Ridge Boys	1981
EMBARRASSMENT	Madness	1980
EMBRACE	Agnelli & Nelson	2000
EMBRACING THE SUNSHINE	BT	1995
EMERGE	Fischerspooner	2002
EMERGENCY	Kool & The Gang	1985
EMERGENCY ON PLANET EARTH	Jamiroquai	1993
EMMA	Hot Chocolate	1975
EMOTION	Destiny's Child	2001
EMOTION	Helen Reddy	1975
EMOTION	Samantha Sang	1977
EMOTION IN MOTION	Ric Ocasek	1986
EMOTIONAL RESCUE	Rolling Stones	1980
EMOTIONAL ROLLERCOASTER	Vivian Green	2003
EMOTIONAL TIME	Hothouse Flowers	1993
EMOTIONS	Mariah Carey	1991
EMOTIONS	Samantha Sang	1978
THE EMPEROR'S NEW CLOTHES	Sinead O'Connor	1990

SONG TITLE	ARTIST	DATE
EMPIRE STRIKES BACK (MEDLEY)		
	Meco	1980
EMPTY AT THE END/THIS GIVEN LINE		
	Electric Soft Parade	2002
EMPTY GARDEN (HEY HEY JOHNNY)		
	Elton John	1982
EMPTY ROOMS	Gary Moore	1985
ENCHANTED LADY	Pasadenas	1988
ENCORE UNE FOIS	Sash!	1997
ENCORES (EP)	Dire Straits	1993
THE END IS THE BEGINNING IS THE END		
	Smashing Pumpkins	1997
END OF A CENTURY	Blur	1994
THE END OF OUR ROAD	Marvin Gaye	1970
THE END OF OUR ROAD	Gladys Knight & The Pips	1968
THE END OF THE INNOCENCE		
	Don Henley	1989
END OF THE LINE	Honeyz	1998
END OF THE ROAD	Boyz II Men	1992
END OF THE WORLD	Sonia	1990
THE END OF THE WORLD	Skeeter Davis	1963
THE END OF THE WORLD	Cure	2004
ENDLESS LOVE	Diana Ross & Lionel Richie	1981
ENDLESS LOVE	Luther Vandross & Mariah Carey	1994
ENDLESS NIGHTS	Eddie Money	1987
ENDLESS SUMMER NIGHTS	Richard Marx	1988

SONG TITLE	ARTIST	DATE
ENEMIES/FRIENDS	Hope Of The States	2003
ENERGY CRISIS '74	Dickie Goodman	1974
ENGINE ENGINE #9	Roger Miller	1965
ENGINE NUMBER 9	Wilson Pickett	1970
ENGLAND SWINGS	Roger Miller	1965
ENGLAND'S IRIE	Black Grape/Joe Strummer & Keith Allen	1996
ENGLISH CIVIL WAR (JOHNNY COMES MARCHING HOME)		
	Clash	1979
ENGLISH SUMMER RAIN	Placebo	2004
ENGLISHMAN IN NEW YORK		
	Sting	1990
ENJOY THE SILENCE	Depeche Mode	1990
ENJOY YOURSELF	A+	1999
ENJOY YOURSELF	Jacksons	1976
ENOLA GAY	Orchestral Manoeuvres In The Dark	1980
ENTER SANDMAN	Metallica	1991
ENTER YOUR FANTASY (EP)		
	Joey Negro	1992
THE ENTERTAINER	Marvin Hamlisch	1974
THE ENTERTAINER	Tony Clarke	1965
THE ENTERTAINER	Billy Joel	1974
ENVY	Ash	2002
THE EP (BRAND NEW MIXES)		
	Zero B	1992

SONG TITLE	ARTIST	DATE
EP THREE	Hundred Reasons	2001
EPIC	Faith No More	1990
EPISTLE TO DIPPY	Donovan	1967
EPLE	Royksopp	2003
ERASE/REWIND	Cardigans	1999
ERASURE-ISH (A LITTLE RESPECT/STOP!)		
	Bjorn Again	1992
ERES TU (TOUCH THE WIND)		
	Mocedades	1974
ERNIE (THE FASTEST MILK MAN IN THE WEST)		
	Benny Hill	1971
EROTICA	Madonna	1992
ESCAPADE	Janet Jackson	1990
ESCAPE	Enrique Iglesias	2002
ESCAPE (THE PINA COLADA SONG)		
	Rupert Holmes	1979
ESCAPE ARTISTS NEVER DIE		
	Funeral For A Friend	2004
ESCAPE-ISM (PART 1)	James Brown	1971
ESCAPING	Dina Carroll	1996
ESPECIALLY FOR YOU	Denise & Johnny	1998
ESPECIALLY FOR YOU	Kylie Minogue &	
	Jason Donovan	1988
ET LES OISEAUX CHANTAIENT		
	Sweet People	1980
ET MEME	Francoise Hardy	1965

SONG TITLE	ARTIST	DATE
ETERNAL FLAME	Atomic Kitten	2001
ETERNAL FLAME	Bangles	1989
ETERNAL LOVE	PJ And Duncan	1994
ETERNITY	Orion	2000
ETERNITY/THE ROAD TO MANDALAY		
	Robbie Williams	2001
THE ETON RIFLES	Jam	1979
EUGINA	Salt Tank	1996
EURODISCO	Bis	1998
EUROPE (AFTER THE RAIN)		
	John Foxx	1981
EUROPEAN FEMALE	Stranglers	1983
EUROPEAN SON	Japan	1982
EV'RY TIME WE SAY GOODBYE		
	Simply Red	1987
EVANGELINE	Cocteau Twins	1993
EVAPOR 8	Altern 8	1992
EVE OF DESTRUCTION	Barry McGuire	1965
EVE OF THE WAR	Jeff Wayne	1978
EVEN AFTER ALL	Finley Quaye	1997
EVEN BETTER THAN THE REAL THING		
	U2	1992
EVEN FLOW	Pearl Jam	1992
EVEN IT UP	Heart	1980
EVEN NOW	Barry Manilow	1978

SONG TITLE	ARTIST	DATE
EVEN NOW	Bob Seger & The Silver Bullet Band	1983
EVEN THE BAD TIMES ARE GOOD	Tremeloes	1967
EVEN THE NIGHTS ARE BETTER	Air Supply	1982
EVEN THOUGH YOU BROKE MY HEART	Gemini	1995
EVEN THOUGH YOU'VE GONE	Jacksons	1978
EVENING FALLS	Enya	1988
EVER FALLEN IN LOVE	Fine Young Cannibals	1987
EVER FALLEN IN LOVE WITH SOMEONE (YOU SHOULDN'T'VE FALLEN IN LOVE WITH)?	Buzzcocks	1978
EVER SO LONELY	Monsoon	1982
EVERGLADE	L7	1992
EVERGREEN (LOVE THEME FROM 'A STAR IS BORN')	Barbra Streisand	1976
EVERGREEN/ANYTHING IS POSSIBLE	Will Young	2002
EVERLASTING	Natalie Cole	1988
AN EVERLASTING LOVE	Andy Gibb	1978
EVERLASTING LOVE	Robert Knight	1967
EVERLASTING LOVE	Gloria Estefan	1995
EVERLASTING LOVE	Cast From Casualty	1998

SONG TITLE	ARTIST	DATE
EVERLASTING LOVE	Love Affair	1968
EVERLASTING LOVE	Worlds Apart	1993
EVERLASTING LOVE	Rex Smith & Rachel Sweet	1981
EVERLASTING LOVE	Carl Carlton	1974
EVERLASTING LOVE	Howard Jones	1989
THE EVERLASTING	Manic Street Preachers	1998
EVERLONG	Foo Fighters	1997
EVERY 1'S A WINNER	Hot Chocolate	1978
EVERY ANGEL	All About Eve	1988
EVERY BEAT OF MY HEART	Railway Children	1991
EVERY BEAT OF MY HEART	Rod Stewart	1986
EVERY BREATH YOU TAKE	Police	1983
EVERY DAY (I LOVE YOU MORE)	Jason Donovan	1989
EVERY DAY HURTS	Sad Cafe	1979
EVERY DAY I LOVE YOU	Boyzone	1999
EVERY DAY OF MY LIFE	House Traffic	1997
EVERY DAY OF MY LIFE	Bobby Vinton	1972
EVERY DAY OF THE WEEK	Jade	1994
EVERY DAY SHOULD BE A HOLIDAY	Dandy Warhols	1998
EVERY GIRL AND BOY	Spagna	1988
EVERY HEARTBEAT	Amy Grant	1991
EVERY KINDA PEOPLE	Robert Palmer	1978
EVERY LITTLE BIT HURTS	Brenda Holloway	1964
EVERY LITTLE KISS	Bruce Hornsby & The Range	1987

SONG TITLE	ARTIST	DATE
EVERY LITTLE STEP	Bobby Brown	1989
EVERY LITTLE TEARDROP	Gallagher & Lyle	1977
EVERY LITTLE THING I DO	Soul For Real	1995
EVERY LITTLE THING SHE DOES IS MAGIC		
	Police	1981
EVERY LOSER WINS	Nick Berry	1986
EVERY MAN MUST HAVE A DREAM		
	Liverpool Express	1976
EVERY MORNING	Sugar Ray	1999
EVERY NIGHT	Phoebe Snow	1979
EVERY NIGHT'S A SATURDAY NIGHT WITH YOU		
	Drifters	1976
EVERY OTHER TIME	Lyte Funkie Ones	2002
EVERY ROSE HAS ITS THORN		
	Poison	1988
EVERY SINGLE DAY	Dodgy	1998
EVERY STEP OF THE WAY	John Waite	1985
EVERY TIME I THINK OF YOU		
	Babys	1979
(EVERY TIME I TURN AROUND) BACK IN LOVE AGAIN		
	L.T.D.	1977
EVERY TIME YOU TOUCH ME		
	Moby	1995
EVERY TIME YOU TOUCH ME (I GET HIGH)		
	Charlie Rich	1975

SONG TITLE	ARTIST	DATE
EVERY WHICH WAY BUT LOOSE		
	Eddie Rabbitt	1979
EVERY WOMAN IN THE WORLD		
	Air Supply	1980
EVERY YOU EVERY ME	Placebo	1999
EVERYBODY	Clock	1995
EVERYBODY	Tommy Roe	1963
EVERYBODY	Progress presents The Boy Wunda	1999
EVERYBODY	Hear'say	2001
EVERYBODY (BACKSTREET'S BACK)		
	Backstreet Boys	1998
EVERYBODY (RAP)	Criminal Element Orch/ Wendell Williams	1990
EVERYBODY BE DANCIN'	Starbuck	1977
EVERYBODY BE SOMEBODY		
	Ruffneck featuring Yavahn	1995
EVERYBODY COME ON (CAN U FEEL IT)		
	Mr. Reds vs DJ Skribble	2003
EVERYBODY CRIES	Liberty X	2004
EVERYBODY DANCE	Chic	1978
EVERYBODY DANCE	Evolution	1993
EVERYBODY DANCE	Ta Mara & The Seen	1985
EVERYBODY DANCE (THE HORN SONG)		
	Barbara Tucker	1998
EVERYBODY EVERYBODY	Black Box	1990

SONG TITLE	ARTIST	DATE
EVERYBODY GET TOGETHER	Dave Clark Five	1970
EVERYBODY GET UP	5ive	1998
EVERYBODY GONFI GON	Two Cowboys	1994
EVERYBODY HAVE FUN TONIGHT	Wang Chung	1986
EVERYBODY HURTS	R.E.M.	1993
EVERYBODY IN THE PLACE (EP)	Prodigy	1992
EVERYBODY KNOWS (I STILL LOVE YOU)	Dave Clark Five	1967
EVERYBODY KNOWS (EXCEPT YOU)	Divine Comedy	1997
EVERYBODY LOVES A CLOWN	Gary Lewis & The Playboys	1965
EVERYBODY LOVES SOMEBODY	Dean Martin	1964
EVERYBODY MOVE	Cathy Dennis	1991
EVERYBODY NEEDS A 303	Fatboy Slim	1997
EVERYBODY NEEDS LOVE	Stephen Bishop	1978
EVERYBODY NEEDS LOVE	Gladys Knight & The Pips	1967
EVERYBODY NEEDS SOMEBODY TO LOVE	Blues Brothers	1990
EVERYBODY NEEDS SOMEBODY TO LOVE	Wilson Pickett	1967

SONG TITLE	ARTIST	DATE
EVERYBODY ON THE FLOOR (PUMP UP)	Tokyo Ghetto Pussy	1995
EVERYBODY PLAYS THE FOOL	Main Ingredient	1972
EVERYBODY PLAYS THE FOOL	Aaron Neville	1991
EVERYBODY SALSA	Modern Romance	1981
EVERYBODY SEE EVERYBODY DO	Let Loose	1995
EVERYBODY WANTS HER	Thunder	1992
EVERYBODY WANTS TO RULE THE WORLD	Tears For Fears	1985
EVERYBODY WANTS TO RUN THE WORLD	Tears For Fears	1986
EVERYBODY WANTS YOU	Billy Squier	1982
EVERYBODY'S CHANGING	Keane	2004
EVERYBODY'S EVERYTHING	Santana	1971
EVERYBODY'S FOOL	Evanescence	2004
EVERYBODY'S FREE (TO FEEL GOOD)	Rozalla	1992
EVERYBODY'S FREE (TO WEAR SUNSCREEN)	Baz Luhrmann	1999
EVERYBODY'S GONNA BE HAPPY	Kinks	1965

SONG TITLE	ARTIST	DATE
EVERYBODY'S GOT SUMMER		
	Atlantic Starr	1994
EVERYBODY'S GOT THE RIGHT TO LOVE		
	Supremes	1970
(EVERYBODY'S GOT TO LEARN SOMETIME) I NEED		
YOUR LOVING	Baby D	1995
EVERYBODY'S GOTTA LEARN SOMETIME		
	Korgis	1980
EVERYBODY'S HAPPY NOWADAYS		
	Buzzcocks	1979
EVERYBODY'S LAUGHING	Phil Fearon & Galaxy	1984
EVERYBODY'S OUT OF TOWN		
	B.J. Thomas	1970
EVERYBODY'S TALKIN'	Nilsson	1969
EVERYBODY'S TALKIN'	Beautiful South	1994
EVERYBODY'S TALKIN' 'BOUT LOVE		
	Silver Convention	1977
(EVERYBODY) GET DANCIN'		
	Bombers	1979
EVERYDAY	Incognito	1995
EVERYDAY	Agnelli & Nelson	1999
EVERYDAY	Phil Collins	1994
EVERYDAY	Slade	1974
EVERYDAY	Don McLean	1973
EVERYDAY	Bon Jovi	2002

SONG TITLE	ARTIST	DATE
EVERYDAY I WRITE THE BOOK		
	Elvis Costello	1983
EVERYDAY IS A WINDING ROAD		
	Sheryl Crow	1997
EVERYDAY IS LIKE SUNDAY		
	Morrissey	1988
EVERYDAY PEOPLE	Sly & The Family Stone	1968
EVERYDAY PEOPLE	Joan Jett	1983
EVERYDAY THANG	Melanie Williams	1994
EVERYDAY WITH YOU GIRL		
	Classics IV	1969
EVERYONE SAYS 'HI'	David Bowie	2002
EVERYONE'S GONE TO THE MOON		
	Jonathan King	1965
EVERYTHING	Sarah Washington	1996
EVERYTHING	Dum Dums	2000
EVERYTHING	Mary J. Blige	1997
EVERYTHING	Alanis Morissette	2004
EVERYTHING	Jody Watley	1989
EVERYTHING A MAN COULD EVER NEED		
	Glen Campbell	1970
EVERYTHING ABOUT YOU	Ugly Kid Joe	1992
EVERYTHING CHANGES	Take That	1994
EVERYTHING CHANGES	Kathy Troccoli	1992
EVERYTHING COUNTS	Depeche Mode	1983

SONG TITLE	ARTIST	DATE
EVERYTHING EVENTUALLY		
	Appleton	2003
EVERYTHING I AM	Plastic Penny	1968
(EVERYTHING I DO) I DO IT FOR YOU		
	Bryan Adams	1991
EVERYTHING I OWN	Bread	1972
EVERYTHING I OWN	Ken Boothe	1974
EVERYTHING I OWN	Boy George	1987
EVERYTHING I WANTED	Dannii	1997
EVERYTHING I'VE GOT IN MY POCKET		
	Minnie Driver	2004
EVERYTHING IN MY HEART		
	Corey Hart	1985
EVERYTHING IS ALRIGHT (UPTIGHT)		
	CJ Lewis	1994
EVERYTHING IS BEAUTIFUL		
	Ray Stevens	1970
EVERYTHING IS EVERYTHING		
	Lauryn Hill	1999
EVERYTHING IS GONNA BE ALRIGHT		
	Sounds Of Blackness	1994
EVERYTHING IS GREAT	Inner Circle	1979
EVERYTHING MUST CHANGE		
	Paul Young	1984
EVERYTHING MUST GO	Manic Street Preachers	1996

SONG TITLE	ARTIST	DATE
EVERYTHING MY HEART DESIRES		
	Adam Rickitt	1999
EVERYTHING SHE WANTS	Wham!	1985
EVERYTHING STARTS WITH AN 'E'		
	E-Zee Possee	1990
EVERYTHING THAT TOUCHES YOU		
	Association	1968
EVERYTHING WILL FLOW	Suede	1999
EVERYTHING WILL TURN OUT FINE		
	Stealer's Wheel	1973
EVERYTHING YOU NEED	Madison Avenue	2001
EVERYTHING YOU WANT	Vertical Horizon	2000
EVERYTHING YOUR HEART DESIRES		
	Daryl Hall & John Oates	1988
EVERYTHING'S ALRIGHT	Mojos	1964
EVERYTHING'S ALRIGHT	Newbeats	1964
EVERYTHING'S COOL	Pop Will Eat Itself	1994
EVERYTHING'S GONNA BE ALRIGHT		
	Sweetbox	1998
EVERYTHING'S GONNA BE ALRIGHT		
	Father M.C.	1992
EVERYTHING'S RUINED	Faith No More	1992
EVERYTHING'S TUESDAY	Chairmen Of The Board	1970
EVERYTIME	Lustral	1999
EVERYTIME	Tatyana Ali	1999
EVERYTIME	Britney Spears	2004

SONG TITLE	ARTIST	DATE
EVERYTIME I CLOSE MY EYES	Babyface	1997
EVERYTIME I FALL IN LOVE	Upside Down	1996
EVERYTIME IT RAINS	Ace Of Base	1999
EVERYTIME YOU GO AWAY	Paul Young	1985
EVERYTIME YOU NEED ME	Fragma featuring Maria Rubia	2001
EVERYTIME YOU TOUCH ME	QFX	1996
EVERYTIME/READY OR NOT	A1	1999
EVERYWHERE	Fleetwood Mac	1987
EVERYWHERE	Michelle Branch	2001
EVERYWHERE I GO/LET'S GET DOWN	Isotonik	1992
EVIDENCE	Faith No More	1995
EVIL HEARTED YOU/STILL I'M SAD	Yardbirds	1965
THE EVIL THAT MEN DO	Iron Maiden	1988
EVIL WAYS	Santana	1970
EVIL WOMAN	Electric Light Orchestra	1975
EVIL WOMAN DON'T PLAY YOUR GAMES WITH ME	Crow	1969
EX-FACTOR	Lauryn Hill	1999
EX-GIRLFRIEND	No Doubt	2000

SONG TITLE	ARTIST	DATE
EXCERPT FROM 'A TEENAGE OPERA'	Keith West	1967
EXCITABLE	Amazulu	1985
EXCITED	M People	1992
EXCUSE ME MISS	Jay-Z	2003
EXHALE (SHOOP SHOOP)	Whitney Houston	1995
EXODUS	Sunscreem	1995
EXODUS	Bob Marley & The Wailers	1977
EXODUS – LIVE	Levellers	1996
EXPERIMENT IV	Kate Bush	1986
EXPLORATION OF SPACE	Cosmic Gate	2002
EXPLOSION IN YOUR SOUL	Soul Survivors	1967
EXPO 2000	Kraftwerk	2000
EXPRESS	BT Express	1975
EXPRESS	Dina Carroll	1993
EXPRESS YOUR FREEDOM	Anticappella	1995
EXPRESS YOURSELF	N.W.A.	1990
EXPRESS YOURSELF	Madonna	1989
EXPRESS YOURSELF	Charles Wright & The Watts 103rd Street	1970
EXPRESSION	Salt 'N 'Pepa	1990
EXPRESSWAY TO YOUR HEART	Soul Survivors	1967
EXTACY	Shades Of Rhythm	1991
EXTENDED PLAY EP	Bryan Ferry	1976

SONG TITLE	ARTIST	DATE
EXTERMINATE!	Snap! featuring Niki Harris	1993
EXTREME WAYS	Moby	2002
EXTREMIS	Hal featuring Gillian Anderson	1997
EYE FOR AN EYE	Unkle	2003
EYE HATE U	TAFKAP	1995
EYE IN THE SKY	Alan Parsons Project	1982
EYE KNOW	De La Soul	1989
EYE LEVEL	Simon Park Orchestra	1973
EYE OF THE TIGER	Frank Bruno	1995
EYE OF THE TIGER	Survivor	1982
EYE TO EYE	Chaka Khan	1985
EYES DON'T LIE	Truce	1998
THE EYES OF A NEW YORK WOMAN		
	B.J. Thomas	1968
EYES OF BLUE	Paul Carrack	1996
THE EYES OF TRUTH	Enigma	1994
EYES ON YOU	Jay Sean featuring The Rishi Rich Project	2004
EYES WITHOUT A FACE	Billy Idol	1984
THE F-WORD	Babybird	2000
F.E.A.R.	Ian Brown	2001
F.L.M.	Mel & Kim	1987
F.U.R.B. (F U RIGHT BACK)		
	Frankee	2004
FA ALL Y'ALL	Da Brat	1994

SONG TITLE	ARTIST	DATE
FA-FA-FA-FA-FA (SAD SONG)		
	Otis Redding	1966
FABLE	Robert Miles	1996
THE FACE	And Why Not?	1990
FACE IT GIRL, IT'S OVER	Nancy Wilson	1968
FACE THE FACE	Pete Townshend	1985
FACE THE STRANGE (EP)	Therapy?	1993
FACE TO FACE	Siouxsie & The Banshees	1992
FACES	2 Unlimited	1993
FACT OF LIFE	Oui 3	1994
THE FACTS OF LIFE	Black Box Recorder	2000
FACTS OF LOVE	Jeff Lorber featuring Karyn White	1986
FADE AWAY	Bruce Springsteen	1981
FADE TO GREY	Visage	1980
FADED	Souldecision featuring Thrust	2000
FADED PICTURES	Case & Joe	1998
FADING LIKE A FLOWER (EVERY TIME YOU LEAVE)		
	Roxette	1991
FAILURE	Skinny	1998
FAINT	Linkin Park	2003
FAIRGROUND	Simply Red	1995
FAIRWEATHER FRIEND	Symposium	1997
FAIRWEATHER FRIEND	Johnny Gill	1990
FAIRYTALE	Dana	1976
FAIRYTALE	Pointer Sisters	1974

SONG TITLE	ARTIST	DATE
FAIRYTALE OF NEW YORK	Pogues featuring Kirsty MacColl	1987
FAIT ACCOMPLI	Curve	1992
FAITH	George Michael	1987
FAITH (IN THE POWER OF LOVE)		
	Rozalla	1991
FAITHFUL	Go West	1992
FAITHFULLY	Journey	1983
FAKE	Alexander O'Neal	1987
FAKE	Simply Red	2003
FAKE FRIENDS	Joan Jett	1983
FAKE PLASTIC TREES	Radiohead	1995
THE FAKE SOUND OF PROGRESS		
	Lostprophets	2002
FAKIN' IT	Simon & Garfunkel	1967
FALCON	Rah Band	1980
FALL (EP)	Ride	1990
FALL AT YOUR FEET	Crowded House	1991
FALL DOWN	Toad The Wet Sprocket	1994
FALL IN LOVE WITH ME	Earth, Wind & Fire	1983
FALL INTO ME	Emerson Drive	2002
FALL TO PIECES	Velvet Revolver	2004
FALLEN ANGEL	Frankie Valli	1976
FALLEN ANGEL	Elbow	2003
FALLEN ANGEL	Poison	1988
FALLIN'	Alicia Keys	2001
FALLIN' IN LOVE	Hamilton, Joe Frank & Reynolds	1975

SONG TITLE	ARTIST	DATE
FALLIN' IN LOVE	Souther Hillman Furay Band	1974
FALLING	Julee Cruise	1990
FALLING	Boom!	2001
FALLING	Roy Orbison	1963
FALLING	Ant & Dec	1997
FALLING	McAlmont & Butler	2002
FALLING	Montell Jordan	1996
FALLING	Leblanc & Carr	1977
FALLING (THE P.M. DAWN VERSION)		
	Cathy Dennis	1993
FALLING ANGELS RIDING	David Essex	1985
FALLING APART AT THE SEAMS		
	Marmalade	1976
FALLING AWAY FROM ME	Korn	2000
FALLING IN LOVE (IS HARD ON THE KNEES)		
	Aerosmith	1997
FALLING IN LOVE (UH-OH)	Miami Sound Machine	1986
FALLING IN LOVE AGAIN	Eagle-Eye Cherry	1998
FALLING INTO YOU	Celine Dion	1996
FALLS APART	Sugar Ray	2000
FALTER	Hundred Reasons	2002
FAME	David Bowie	1975
FAME	Irene Cara	1980
FAME 90 (GASS MIX)	David Bowie	1990
FAMILIAR FEELING	Moloko	2003
FAMILY AFFAIR	BEF featuring Lalah Hathaway	1991

SONG TITLE	ARTIST	DATE
FAMILY AFFAIR	Mary J. Blige	2001
FAMILY AFFAIR	Sly & The Family Stone	1971
FAMILY AFFAIR	Shabba Ranks	1993
FAMILY MAN	Roachford	1989
FAMILY MAN	Daryl Hall & John Oates	1983
THE FAMILY OF MAN	Three Dog Night	1972
FAMILY PORTRAIT	Pink	2002
FANCY	Bobbie Gentry	1969
FANCY DANCER	Commodores	1977
FANCY PANTS	Kenny	1975
FANFARE FOR THE COMMON MAN		
	Emerson, Lake & Palmer	1977
FANNY (BE TENDER WITH MY LOVE)		
	Bee Gees	1975
FANTASTIC DAY	Haircut 100	1982
FANTASTIC VOYAGE	Coolio	1994
FANTASY	Black Box	1990
FANTASY	Earth, Wind & Fire	1978
FANTASY	Mariah Carey	1995
FANTASY	Levellers	1995
FANTASY	Gerard Kenny	1980
FANTASY	Appleton	2002
FANTASY	Aldo Nova	1982
FANTASY ISLAND	M People	1997
FANTASY ISLAND	Tight Fit	1982
FAR	Longpigs	1996

SONG TITLE	ARTIST	DATE
FAR BEHIND	Candlebox	1994
FAR FAR AWAY	Slade	1974
FAR FROM OVER	Frank Stallone	1983
FAR GONE AND OUT	Jesus & Mary Chain	1992
FAR OUT	Son'z Of A Loop Da Loop Era	1992
FAR-OUT SON OF LUNG & THE RAMBLINGS OF A		
MADMAN	Future Sound Of London	1995
FARAWAY PLACES	Bachelors	1963
FAREWELL/BRING IT ON HOME TO ME		
	Rod Stewart	1974
FAREWELL ANGELINA	Joan Baez	1965
FAREWELL IS A LONELY SOUND		
	Jimmy Ruffin	1970
FAREWELL MR. SORROW	All About Eve	1991
FAREWELL MY SUMMER LOVE		
	Michael Jackson	1984
FAREWELL TO THE MOON	York	2000
FAREWELL TO TWILIGHT	Symposium	1997
FARMER BILL'S COWMAN (I WAS KAISER BILL'S		
BATMAN)	Wurzels	1977
FARMER JOHN	Premiers	1964
FASCINATED	Lisa B	1993
FASCINATED	Raven Maize	2002
FASCINATED	Company B	1987
FASCINATING RHYTHM	Bass-O-Matic	1990
FASHION	David Bowie	1980

SONG TITLE	ARTIST	DATE
FAST AS YOU CAN	Fiona Apple	2000
FAST BOY/LIQUID LIPS	Bluetones	2003
FAST CAR	Tracy Chapman	1988
FAST FOOD SONG	Fast Food Rockers	2003
FASTER THE CHASE	InMe	2004
FASTER/PCP	Manic Street Preachers	1994
FASTLOVE	George Michael	1996
FAT LIP	Sum 41	2001
FAT NECK	Black Grape	1996
FATHER	LL Cool J	1998
FATHER AND SON	Boyzone	1995
FATHER FIGURE	George Michael	1988
FATTIE BUM BUM	Diversions	1975
FATTIE BUM-BUM	Carl Malcolm	1975
FAVOURITE SHIRTS (BOY MEETS GIRL)		
	Haircut 100	1981
FAVOURITE THINGS	Big Brovaz	2003
FEAR OF THE DARK (LIVE)	Iron Maiden	1993
FEE FI FO FUM	Candy Girls	1995
FEED MY FRANKENSTEIN	Alice Cooper	1992
FEED THE TREE	Belly	1993
FEEL	Robbie Williams	2002
FEEL EVERY BEAT	Electronic	1991
FEEL GOOD	Madasun	2000
FEEL GOOD	Phats & Small	1999
FEEL GOOD TIME	Pink featuring William Orbit	2003

SONG TITLE	ARTIST	DATE
FEEL IT	Moby	1993
FEEL IT	Tamperer featuring Maya	1998
FEEL IT AGAIN	Honeymoon Suite	1986
FEEL IT BOY	Beenie Man featuring Janet	2002
FEEL LIKE CALLING HOME	Mr. Big	1977
FEEL LIKE MAKIN' LOVE	George Benson	1983
FEEL LIKE MAKIN' LOVE	Roberta Flack	1974
FEEL LIKE MAKIN' LOVE	Bad Company	1975
FEEL LIKE MAKING LOVE	Pauline Henry	1993
FEEL LIKE SINGING	Tak Tix	1996
FEEL ME FLOW	Naughty By Nature	1995
FEEL MY BODY	Frank O'Moiraghi featuring Amnesia	1996
FEEL SO GOOD	Mase	1997
FEEL SO HIGH	Des'ree	1992
FEEL SO REAL	Dream Frequency/Debbie Sharp	1992
FEEL SO REAL	Steve Arrington	1985
FEEL THE BEAT	Camisra	1998
FEEL THE BEAT	Darude	2000
FEEL THE MUSIC	Guru	1995
FEEL THE NEED	Leif Garrett	1979
FEEL THE NEED IN ME	Detroit Emeralds	1973
FEEL THE NEED IN ME	Forrest	1983
FEEL THE NEED IN ME	Shakin' Stevens	1988
FEEL THE PAIN	Dinosaur Jr.	1994
FEEL THE SAME	Triple X	1999

SONG TITLE	ARTIST	DATE
FEEL THE SUNSHINE	Alex Reece	1996
FEEL WHAT YOU WANT	Kristine W	1994
FEELIN' ALRIGHT	EYC	1993
FEELIN' FINE	Ultrabeat	2003
FEELIN' INSIDE	Bobby Brown	1997
FEELIN' ON YOU BOOTY	R. Kelly	2001
FEELIN' SO GOOD	Jennifer Lopez featuring Big Pun & Fat Joe	2000
FEELIN' STRONGER EVERY DAY	Chicago	1973
FEELIN' U	Shy FX & T-Power featuring Kele Le Roc	2003
FEELIN' WAY TOO DAMN GOOD	Nickelback	2004
THE FEELING	Tin Tin Out featuring Sweet Tee	1994
FEELING ALRIGHT	Joe Cocker	1972
FEELING FOR YOU	Cassius	1999
FEELING GOOD	Nina Simone	1994
FEELING GOOD	Huff & Herb	1997
FEELING IT TOO	3 Jays	1999
FEELING SO REAL	Moby	1994
FEELING THIS	Blink-182	2003
FEELING THIS WAY	Conductor & The Cowboy	2000
FEELINGS	Morris Albert	1975
FEELS GOOD	Tony Toni Tone	1990
FEELS LIKE HEAVEN	Urban Cookie Collective	1993

SONG TITLE	ARTIST	DATE
FEELS LIKE I'M IN LOVE	Kelly Marie	1980
FEELS LIKE THE FIRST TIME	Foreigner	1977
(FEELS LIKE) HEAVEN	Fiction Factory	1984
FEELS SO GOOD	Xscape	1995
FEELS SO GOOD	Melanie B	2001
FEELS SO GOOD	Chuck Mangione	1978
FEELS SO GOOD	Van Halen	1989
FEELS SO GOOD (SHOW ME YOUR LOVE)	Lina Santiago	1996
FEELS SO RIGHT	Alabama	1981
FEENIN'	Jodeci	1994
FELL IN LOVE WITH A BOY	Joss Stone	2004
FELL IN LOVE WITH A GIRL	White Stripes	2002
FELL ON BLACK DAYS	Soundgarden	1995
FEMALE OF THE SPECIES	Space	1996
FERGUS SINGS THE BLUES	Deacon Blue	1989
FERNANDO	ABBA	1976
FERRIS WHEEL	Everly Brothers	1964
FERRY 'CROSS THE MERSEY	Marsden/McCartney/Johnson/Christians	1989
FERRY 'CROSS THE MERSEY	Gerry & The Pacemakers	1964

SONG TITLE	ARTIST	DATE
FESTIVAL TIME	San Remo Strings	1971
FEUER FREI	Rammstein	2002
FEVER	Helen Shapiro	1964
FEVER	Madonna	1993
FEVER	Starsailor	2001
FEVER	McCoys	1965
FFUN	Con Funk Shun	1977
FIELD OF DREAMS	Flip & Fill featuring Jo James	2003
FIELDS OF FIRE (400 MILES)		
	Big Country	1983
FIELDS OF GOLD	Sting	1993
THE FIELDS OF LOVE	ATB featuring YORK	2001
FIESTA	R. Kelly	2001
FIESTA	Pogues	1988
15 MINUTES	Marc Nelson	1999
15 YEARS (EP)	Levellers	1992
5TH ANNIVERSARY (EP)	Judge Dread	1977
A FIFTH OF BEETHOVEN	Walter Murphy & The Big	
	Apple Band	1976
50:50/LULLABY	Lemar	2003
THE 59TH STREET BRIDGE SONG (FEELIN' GROOVY)		
	Harpers Bizarre	1967
57 CHANNELS (AND NOTHIN' ON)		
	Bruce Springsteen	1992
50 WAYS TO LEAVE YOUR LOVER		
	Paul Simon	1975

SONG TITLE	ARTIST	DATE
FIGARO	Brotherhood Of Man	1978
FIGHT FOR OURSELVES	Spandau Ballet	1986
FIGHT FOR YOUR RIGHT (TO PARTY)		
	NYCC	1998
FIGHT MUSIC	D12	2001
THE FIGHT SONG	Marilyn Manson	2001
FIGHT TEST	Flaming Lips	2003
FIGHT THE POWER	Public Enemy	1989
FIGHT THE POWER PT I	Isley Brothers	1975
FIGHTER	Christina Aguilera	2003
FIGHTING FIT	Gene	1996
FILL HER UP	Gene	1999
FILL ME IN	Craig David	2001
FILLING UP WITH HEAVEN	Human League	1995
FILM MAKER/BEEN TRAINING DOGS		
	Cooper Temple Clause	2002
FILMSTAR	Suede	1997
THE FINAL ARREARS	Mull Historical Society	2003
THE FINAL COUNTDOWN	Europe	1987
FINALLY	Ce Ce Peniston	1991
FINALLY	Kings Of Tomorrow featuring	
	Julie McKnight	2001
FINALLY FOUND	Honeyz	1998
FINALLY GOT MYSELF TOGETHER (I'M A CHANGED		
MAN)	Impressions	1974
FINCHLEY CENTRAL	New Vaudeville Band	1967

SONG TITLE	ARTIST	DATE
FIND A WAY	Amy Grant	1985
FIND ANOTHER FOOL	Quarterflash	1982
FIND ME (ODYSSEY TO ANYOONA)		
	Jam & Spoon featuring Plavka	1994
FIND MY LOVE	Fairground Attraction	1988
FIND MY WAY BACK HOME		
	Nashville Teens	1965
FIND THE ANSWER WITHIN		
	Boo Radleys	1995
FIND THE COLOUR	Feeder	2003
FIND THE TIME	Five Star	1986
FIND YOUR WAY BACK	Jefferson Airplane	1981
FINDERS KEEPERS	Chairmen Of The Board	1973
FINE DAY	Rolf Harris	2000
A FINE FINE DAY	Tony Carey	1984
FINE TIME	New Order	1988
FINE TIME	Yazz	1989
FINER FEELINGS	Kylie Minogue	1992
THE FINER THINGS	Steve Winwood	1987
THE FINEST	S.O.S. Band	1986
FINEST DREAMS	Richard X featuring Kelis	2003
FINETIME	Cast	1995
FINGERS & THUMBS (COLD SUMMER'S DAY)		
	Erasure	1995
FINGERS OF LOVE	Crowded House	1994
FINISH WHAT YA STARTED	Van Halen	1988

SONG TITLE	ARTIST	DATE
FINS	Jimmy Buffett	1979
FIRE	U2	1981
FIRE	Prizna featuring Demolition Man	1995
FIRE	Crazy World Of Arthur Brown	1968
FIRE	Pointer Sisters	1978
FIRE	Crazy World Of Arthur	1968
FIRE	Ohio Players	1984
FIRE AND ICE	Pat Benatar	1981
FIRE AND RAIN	James Taylor	1970
FIRE AND WATER	Wilson Pickett	1971
FIRE, BABY I'M ON FIRE	Andy Kim	1974
FIRE BRIGADE	Move	1968
FIRE IN MY HEART	Super Furry Animals	1999
FIRE IN THE MORNING	Melissa Manchester	1980
FIRE LAKE	Bob Seger & The Silver Bullet Band	1980
FIRE ON THE MOUNTAIN	Marshall Tucker Band	1975
FIRE WIRE	Cosmic Gate	2001
FIRE WOMAN	Cult	1989
FIRE WORKS	Siouxsie & The Banshees	1982
FIRE/JERICHO	Prodigy	1992
FIREBALL	Don Spencer	1963
FIREBALL	Deep Purple	1971
FIRED UP!	Funky Green Dogs	1997
FIRESTARTER	Prodigy	1997

SONG TITLE	ARTIST	DATE
FIREWORKS	Roxette	1994
FIREWORKS EP	Embrace	1997
FIRM BIZ	Firm featuring Dawn Robinson	1997
FIRST CUT IS THE DEEPEST	P.P. Arnold	1967
THE FIRST CUT IS THE DEEPEST	Sheryl Crow	2003
THE FIRST CUT IS THE DEEPEST	Rod Stewart	1977
FIRST DATE	Blink-182	2001
THE FIRST DAY OF SUMMER	Tony Carey	1984
FIRST IMPRESSIONS	Impressions	1975
FIRST IT GIVETH	Queens Of The Stone Age	2003
1ST MAN IN SPACE	All Seeing I	1999
THE FIRST NIGHT	Monica	1998
FIRST OF MAY	Bee Gees	1969
1ST OF THA MONTH	Bone Thugs-N-Harmony	1995
FIRST OF THE GANG TO DIE	Morrissey	2004
FIRST PICTURE OF YOU	Lotus Eaters	1983
THE FIRST THE LAST ETERNITY	Snap! featuring Summer	1995
FIRST THING IN THE MORNING	Kiki Dee	1977

SONG TITLE	ARTIST	DATE
THE FIRST TIME EVER I SAW YOUR FACE	Celine Dion	2000
THE FIRST TIME EVER I SAW YOUR FACE	Roberta Flack	1974
FIRST TIME LOVE	Livingston Taylor	1980
THE FIRST TIME	Robin Beck	1988
THE FIRST TIME	Adam Faith	1963
THE FIRST TIME	Surface	1990
FISH AIN'T BITIN'	Lamont Dozier	1974
FISHERMAN'S BLUES	Waterboys	1989
FISHNET	Morris Day	1988
FIT BUT YOU KNOW IT	Streets	2004
5 COLOURS IN HER HAIR	McFly	2004
FIVE FATHOMS	Everything But The Girl	1999
5-4-3-2-1	Manfred Mann	1964
FIVE GET OVER EXCITED	Housemartins	1987
500 (SHAKE BABY SHAKE)	Lush	1996
FIVE LITTLE FINGERS	Frankie McBride	1967
FIVE LIVE (EP)	George Michael & Queen	1993
5 MILE (THESE ARE THE DAYS)	Turin Brakes	2003
5 MILES TO EMPTY	Brownstone	1997
5 MINUTES	Stranglers	1978
THE $5.98 EP – GARAGE DAYS RE-REVISITED	Metallica	1987
5 O'CLOCK	Nonchalant	1996

SONG TITLE	ARTIST	DATE
FIVE O'CLOCK WORLD	Vogues	1965
5.7.0.5	City Boy	1978
5 STEPS	Dru Hill	1997
5-10-15-20 (25-30 YEARS OF LOVE)		
	Presidents	1970
5,6,7,8	Steps	1997
5:15	Who	1973
FIX	Blackstreet	1997
FIX MY SINK	DJ Sneak featuring Bear Who?	2003
FIX UP LOOK SHARP	Dizzee Rascal	2003
FLAMBOYANT	Pet Shop Boys	2004
FLAME	Sebadoh	1999
THE FLAME	Fine Young Cannibals	1996
THE FLAME	Cheap Trick	1988
FLAMES OF PARADISE	Jennifer Rush (Duet With Elton John)	1987
FLAMINGO	Herb Alpert & The Tijuana Brass	1966
FLAMING JUNE	BT	1997
FLASH	BBE	1997
FLASH	Queen	1980
FLASH LIGHT	Parliament	1978
FLASHBACK	Imagination	1981
FLASHDANCE	Deep Dish	2004
FLASHDANCE... WHAT A FEELING	Irene Cara	1983
THE FLASHER	Mistura featuring Lloyd Michels	1976
FLAT BEAT	Mr Oizo	1999
FLAVA	Peter Andre	1996
FLAVA IN YA EAR	Craig Mack	1994
FLAVOR OF THE WEAK	American Hi-Fi	2001
FLAVOUR OF THE OLD SCHOOL		
	Beverley Knight	1995
FLAWLESS	The Ones	2001
FLAWLESS (GO TO THE CITY)		
	George Michael	2004
FLESH	Jan Johnston	2001
FLESH FOR FANTASY	Billy Idol	1984
FLEX	Mad Cobra	1992
FLIGHT OF ICARUS	Iron Maiden	1983
FLIP	Jesse Green	1976
FLIP REVERSE	Blazin' Squad	2003
FLIRT!	Jonathan King	1972
FLOAT ON	Floaters	1977
FLOATING IN THE WIND	Hudson-Ford	1974
FLOBBADANCE	Bill & Ben	2002
FLOOD	Jars Of Clay	1996
FLOODLIT WORLD	Ultrasound	1999
THE FLORAL DANCE	Brighouse And Rastrick	1977
THE FLORAL DANCE	Terry Wogan	1978
FLOWERS	Sweet Female Attitude	2000
FLOWERS IN DECEMBER	Mazzy Star	1996

SONG TITLE	ARTIST	DATE
FLOWERS IN THE RAIN	Move	1967
FLOWERS IN THE WINDOW	Travis	2002
FLOWERS OF ROMANCE	Public Image Ltd	1981
FLOWERS ON THE WALL	Statler Brothers	1965
FLOWERZ	Armand Van Helden featuring Roland Clark	1999
FLOY JOY	Supremes	1972
FLY	Mark Joseph	2003
FLY	Matt Goss	2004
THE FLY	U2	1991
FLY AWAY	Vincent De Moor	2001
FLY AWAY	Haddaway	1995
FLY AWAY	Lenny Kravitz	1998
FLY AWAY	John Denver	1975
FLY BY II	Blue	2002
FLY LIFE	Basement Jaxx	1997
FLY LIKE AN EAGLE	Seal	1996
FLY LIKE AN EAGLE	Steve Miller Band	1976
FLY ON THE WINGS OF LOVE	XTM & DJ Chucky presents Annia	2003
FLY ROBIN FLY	Silver Convention	1975
FLY TO THE ANGELS	Slaughter	1990
FLYING	Cast	1996
FLYING HIGH	Commodores	1978

SONG TITLE	ARTIST	DATE
FLYING HIGH	Freeez	1981
FLYING MACHINE	Cliff Richard	1971
FLYING SAUCER	Wedding Present	1992
FLYING WITHOUT WINGS	Westlife	1999
FM (NO STATIC AT ALL)	Steely Dan	1978
FOE-DEE-O-DEE	Rubettes	1975
FOG ON THE TYNE (REVISITED)	Gazza And Lindisfarne	1990
THE FOLK SINGER	Tommy Roe	1963
FOLLOW DA LEADER	Nigel & Marvin	2002
FOLLOW ME	Atomic Kitten	2000
FOLLOW ME	Uncle Kracker	2001
FOLLOW THE LEADER	Eric B. & Rakim	1988
FOLLOW THE RULES	Livin' Joy	1996
FOLLOW YOU DOWN	Gin Blossoms	1996
FOLLOW YOU FOLLOW ME	Genesis	1978
FOLLOWED THE WAVES	Auf Der Maur	2004
FOLSOM PRISON BLUES	Johnny Cash	1968
FOOL	Mansun	2001
FOOL	Al Matthews	1975
FOOL	Elvis Presley	1973
FOOL (IF YOU THINK IT'S OVER)	Chris Rea	1978
FOOL AGAIN	Westlife	2000
A FOOL AM I	Cilla Black	1966
FOOL FOR YOU	Impressions	1968

SONG TITLE	ARTIST	DATE
FOOL FOR YOUR LOVING	Whitesnake	1989
FOOL IF YOU THINK IT'S OVER		
	Elkie Brooks	1982
FOOL IN LOVE WITH YOU	Jim Photoglo	1981
FOOL IN THE RAIN	Led Zeppelin	1979
A FOOL NEVER LEARNS	Andy Williams	1964
FOOL NO MORE	S Club 8	2003
THE FOOL ON THE HILL	Sergio Mendes & Brasil '66	1968
FOOL TO CRY	Rolling Stones	1976
FOOL'S GOLD/WHAT THE WORLD IS WAITING FOR		
	Stone Roses	1989
FOOLED AROUND AND FELL IN LOVE		
	Elvin Bishop	1976
FOOLIN'	Def Leppard	1983
FOOLIN' AROUND	Changing Faces	1994
FOOLING YOURSELF (THE ANGRY YOUNG MAN)		
	Styx	1978
FOOLISH	Ashanti	2002
FOOLISH BEAT	Debbie Gibson	1988
FOOLISH GAMES	Jewel	1997
FOOLISH HEART	Steve Perry	1984
FOOLISH LITTLE GIRL	Shirelles	1963
FOOLISH PRIDE	Daryl Hall	1986
FOOLS GOLD	Stone Roses	1999
FOOLS RUSH IN	Rick Nelson	1963
FOOT STOMPIN' MUSIC	Hamilton Bohannon	1975

SONG TITLE	ARTIST	DATE
FOOT TAPPER	Shadows	1963
FOOTLOOSE	Kenny Loggins	1984
FOOTPRINT	Disco Citizens	1997
FOOTSEE	Wigan's Chosen Few	1975
FOOTSTEPS	Stiltskin	1994
FOOTSTEPS	Daniel O'Donnell	1996
FOOTSTEPS	Showaddywaddy	1981
FOOTSTEPS FOLLOWING ME		
	Frances Nero	1991
FOOTSTOMPIN' MUSIC	Grand Funk Railroad	1972
FOPP	Ohio Players	1976
FOR A FEW DOLLARS MORE		
	Smokie	1978
FOR A FRIEND	Communards	1988
FOR A LITTLE WHILE	Tim McGraw	1998
FOR ALL THAT YOU WANT	Gary Barlow	1999
FOR ALL THE COWS	Foo Fighters	1995
FOR ALL TIME	Catherine Zeta-Jones	1992
FOR ALL WE KNOW	Shirley Bassey	1971
FOR ALL WE KNOW	Carpenters	1971
FOR AMERICA	Red Box	1986
FOR AMERICA	Jackson Browne	1986
FOR AN ANGEL	Paul Van Dyk	1998
4 EVER	Lil' Mo featuring Fabolous	2003
FOR LOVE (EP)	Lush	1992

SONG TITLE	ARTIST	DATE
FOR LOVERS	Wolfman featuring Peter Doherty	2004
FOR LOVIN' ME	Peter, Paul & Mary	1965
FOR MAMA	Matt Monro	1965
FOR OLD TIME'S SAKE	Millican & Nesbitt	1974
FOR ONCE IN MY LIFE	Dorothy Squires	1969
FOR ONCE IN MY LIFE	Stevie Wonder	1968
FOR SURE	Scooch	2000
FOR THE DEAD	Gene	1996
FOR THE GOOD TIMES	Perry Como	1973
FOR THE GOOD TIMES	Ray Price	1970
FOR THE LOVE OF HIM	Bobbi Martin	1970
FOR THE LOVE OF MONEY	O'Jays	1974
FOR THE LOVE OF YOU (PTS 1 & 2)	Isley Brothers	1975
FOR THOSE ABOUT TO ROCK (WE SALUTE YOU)	AC/DC	1982
FOR TOMORROW	Blur	1993
FOR TONIGHT	Nancy Martinez	1986
FOR WHAT IT'S WORTH	Oui 3	1993
FOR WHAT IT'S WORTH	Cardigans	2003
FOR WHAT IT'S WORTH	Buffalo Springfield	1967
FOR WHAT YOU DREAM OF	Bedrock featuring Kyo	1996
FOR WHOM THE BELL TOLLS	Bee Gees	1993

SONG TITLE	ARTIST	DATE
FOR YOU	Electronic	1996
FOR YOU	Rick Nelson	1963
FOR YOU	Kenny Lattimore	1997
FOR YOU	Outfield	1990
FOR YOU I WILL	Monica	1997
FOR YOUR BABIES	Simply Red	1992
FOR YOUR EYES ONLY	Sheena Easton	1981
FOR YOUR LOVE	Stevie Wonder	1995
FOR YOUR LOVE	Yardbirds	1965
FOR YOUR LOVE	Peaches & Herb	1967
FOR YOUR PRECIOUS LOVE	Oscar Toney Jr.	1967
FORBIDDEN CITY	Electronic	1996
FORBIDDEN COLOURS	David Sylvian & Riuichi Sakamoto	1983
FORCA	Nelly Furtado	2004
THE FORCE BEHIND THE POWER	Diana Ross	1992
FOREIGN SAND	Roger Taylor & Yoshiki	1994
A FOREST	Cure	1980
FOREVER	Damage	1996
FOREVER	Charlatans	1999
FOREVER	Roy Wood	1973
FOREVER	Dee Dee	2002
FOREVER	N-Trance	2002
FOREVER	Trinity-X	2002

SONG TITLE	ARTIST	DATE
FOREVER	Pete Drake	1964
FOREVER	Kiss	1990
FOREVER	Kenny Loggins	1985
FOREVER & EVER	Slik	1976
FOREVER AND FOR ALWAYS		
	Shania Twain	2003
FOREVER AS ONE	Vengaboys	2001
FOREVER AUTUMN	Justin Hayward	1978
FOREVER CAME TODAY	Supremes	1968
FOREVER FREE	W.A.S.P.	1989
FOREVER GIRL	OTT	1997
FOREVER IN BLUE JEANS	Neil Diamond	1979
FOREVER IN LOVE	Kenny G	1992
FOREVER LOVE	Gary Barlow	1996
FOREVER LOVE	Color Me Badd	1992
FOREVER MAN	Eric Clapton	1985
FOREVER MAN (HOW MANY TIMES)		
	Beatchuggers/Eric Clapton	2000
FOREVER MINE	O'Jays	1979
FOREVER MORE	Puff Johnson	1997
FOREVER MORE	Moloko	2003
FOREVER MY LADY	Jodeci	1991
FOREVER NOW	Level 42	1994
FOREVER YOUNG	Interactive	1996
FOREVER YOUNG	Rod Stewart	1988
FOREVER YOUR GIRL	Paula Abdul	1989

SONG TITLE	ARTIST	DATE
(FOREVER) LIVE AND DIE	Orchestral Manoeuvres In The Dark	1986
FORGET ABOUT DRE	Dr. Dre featuring Eminem	2000
FORGET ABOUT THE WORLD		
	Gabrielle	1996
FORGET ABOUT TOMORROW		
	Feeder	2003
FORGET ABOUT YOU	Motors	1978
FORGET HIM	Bobby Rydell	1963
FORGET I WAS A G	Whitehead Bros.	1995
FORGET ME NOT	Martha & The Vandellas	1971
FORGET ME NOTS	Tongue 'n' Cheek	1991
FORGET ME NOTS	Patrice Rushen	1982
FORGIVE ME	Lynden David Hall	2000
FORGIVEN (I FEEL YOUR LOVE)		
	Space Brothers	1997
FORGOT ABOUT DRE	Dr. Dre featuring Eminem	2000
FORGOTTEN TOWN	Christians	1987
FORMULAE	JJ72	2002
FORTRESS AROUND YOUR HEART		
	Sting	1985
FORTUNATE	Maxwell	1999
FORTUNE FADED	Red Hot Chili Peppers	2003
48 CRASH	Suzi Quatro	1973
45 RPM	Poppyfields	2004
FOUND A CURE	Ultra Nate	1998

SONG TITLE	ARTIST	DATE
FOUND A CURE	Ashford & Simpson	1979
FOUND LOVE	Double Dee featuring Dany	1995
FOUND OUT ABOUT YOU	Gin Blossoms	1993
FOUND THAT SOUL	Manic Street Preachers	2001
FOUND YOU	Dodgy	1997
FOUR BACHARACH & DAVID SONGS (EP)		
	Deacon Blue	1990
FOUR FROM TOYAH (EP)	Toyah	1981
4, 5, 6	Sole featuring JT Money and Kandi	1999
FOUR IN THE MORNING (I CAN'T TAKE ANY MORE)		
	Night Ranger	1985
FOUR LETTER WORD	Kim Wilde	1988
FOUR MINUTE WARNING	Mark Owen	2003
FOUR MORE FROM TOYAH (EP)		
	Toyah	1981
4 MY PEOPLE	Missy 'Misdemeanor' Elliott	2002
4 PAGE LETTER	Aaliyah	1997
THE 4 PLAY EPS	R. Kelly	1995
FOUR SEASONS IN ONE DAY		
	Crowded House	1992
4 SEASONS OF LONELINESS		
	Boyz II Men	1997
FOUR TO THE FLOOR	Starsailor	2004
40 MILES	Congress	1991
FOX ON THE RUN	Manfred Mann	1968

SONG TITLE	ARTIST	DATE
FOX ON THE RUN	Sweet	1975
FOXHOLE	Television	1978
FOXY, FOXY	Mott The Hoople	1974
'FRAGGLE ROCK' THEME	Fraggles	1984
FRANKENSTEIN	Edgar Winter Group	1973
FRANKIE	Sister Sledge	1985
FRANKIE AND JOHNNY	Elvis Presley	1966
FRANKIE AND JOHNNY	Sam Cooke	1963
FRANTIC	Metallica	2003
FREAK	Silverchair	1997
FREAK	Bruce Foxton	1983
FREAK IT!	Studio 45	1999
FREAK LIKE ME	Adina Howard	1995
FREAK LIKE ME	Tru Faith & Dub Conspiracy	2000
FREAK LIKE ME	Sugababes	2002
FREAK ME	Another Level	1998
FREAK ME	Silk	1993
FREAK MODE	Reelists	2002
FREAK ON A LEASH	Korn	1999
FREAKIN' IT	Will Smith	2000
FREAKIN' OUT/ALL OVER ME		
	Graham Coxon	2004
FREAKS (LIVE)	Marillion	1988
THE FREAKS COME OUT	Cevin Fisher's Big Break	1998
FREAKYTIME	Point Break	2000
THE FRED EP	Various	1992

SONG TITLE	ARTIST	DATE
FREDDIE'S DEAD	Curtis Mayfield	1972
FREE	DJ Quicksilver	1997
FREE	Deniece Williams	1976
FREE	Ultra Nate	1997
FREE	Mya	2001
FREE	Estelle	2004
FREE	Chicago	1971
FREE (EP)	Free	1978
FREE (THE MIXES)	Ultra Nate	1998
FREE 'N' EASY	Almighty	1991
FREE AS A BIRD	Beatles	1995
FREE AT LAST	Simon	2001
FREE BIRD	Lynyrd Skynyrd	1976
FREE ELECTRIC BAND	Albert Hammond	1973
FREE FALLIN'	Tom Petty	1989
FREE LOVE	Juliet Roberts	1993
FREE MAN IN PARIS	Joni Mitchell	1974
FREE ME	Roger Daltrey	1980
FREE ME	Cast	1997
FREE ME	Emma Bunton	2003
FREE RANGE	Fall	1992
FREE RIDE	Edgar Winter Group	1973
THE FREE STYLE MEGA-MIX		
	Bobby Brown	1990
FREE TO DECIDE/WHEN YOU'RE GONE		
	Cranberries	1996

SONG TITLE	ARTIST	DATE
FREE YOUR BODY/INJECTED WITH A POISON		
	Praga Khan/Jade 4 U	1992
FREE YOUR MIND	En Vogue	1992
FREE YOURSELF	Untouchables	1985
FREED FROM DESIRE	Gala	1997
FREEDOM	Erasure	2000
FREEDOM	Wham!	1985
FREEDOM	Michelle Gayle	1995
FREEDOM	Shiva	1995
FREEDOM	Robbie Williams	1996
FREEDOM	Robert Miles featuring Kathy Sledge	1997
FREEDOM	QFX	2003
FREEDOM	George Michael	1990
FREEDOM 2	QFX	1997
FREEDOM COME, FREEDOM GO		
	Fortunes	1971
FREEDOM FIGHTERS	Music	2004
FREEDOM OVERSPILL	Steve Winwood	1986
FREEEK!	George Michael	2002
FREEK'N YOU	Jodeci	1995
FREELOADER	Driftwood	2003
FREELOVE	Depeche Mode	2001
FREESTYLER	Bomfunk MC's	2000
FREEWAY OF LOVE	Aretha Franklin	1985
THE FREEZE	Spandau Ballet	1981

SONG TITLE	ARTIST	DATE
FREEZE-FRAME	J. Geils Band	1982
FRENCH KISS	Lil Louis	1989
FRENCH KISSES	Jentina	2004
FRENCH KISSIN' IN THE USA	Debbie Harry	1986
FRESH	Kool & The Gang	1985
FRESH	Gina G	1997
THE FRESHMAN	Verve Pipe	1997
FRIDAY	Daniel Bedingfield	2003
FRIDAY, I'M IN LOVE	Cure	1992
FRIDAY NIGHT (LIVE VERSION)	Kids From 'Fame'	1983
FRIDAY ON MY MIND	Easybeats	1967
FRIDAY ON MY MIND	Gary Moore	1987
FRIDAY STREET	Paul Weller	1997
FRIDAY'S CHILD	Will Young	2004
FRIDAY'S CHILD	Nancy Sinatra	1966
FRIEND OF MINE	Kelly Price	1998
FRIEND OR FOE	Adam Ant	1982
FRIENDS	Jody Watley with Eric B & Rakim	1989
FRIENDS	Beach Boys	1968
FRIENDS	Arrival	1970
FRIENDS	Shalamar	1982
FRIENDS	Amii Stewart	1984
FRIENDS	Elton John	1971

SONG TITLE	ARTIST	DATE
FRIENDS/CHAPEL OF LOVE	Bette Midler	1973
FRIENDS AND LOVERS	Gloria Loring & Carl Anderson	1986
FRIENDS FOREVER	Thunderbugs	1999
FRIENDS IN LOVE	Dionne Warwick & Johnny Mathis	1982
FRIENDS WILL BE FRIENDS	Queen	1986
FRIENDSHIP TRAIN	Gladys Knight & The Pips	1969
THE FROG PRINCESS	Divine Comedy	1996
FROM A DISTANCE	Cliff Richard	1990
FROM A DISTANCE	Bette Midler	1990
FROM A JACK TO A KING	Ned Miller	1962
FROM A TO H AND BACK AGAIN	Sheep On Drugs	1993
FROM A WINDOW	Billy J. Kramer & The Dakotas	1964
FROM A WINDOW/THIS MORNING	Northern Uproar	1996
FROM DESPAIR TO WHERE	Manic Street Preachers	1993
FROM EAST TO WEST/SCOTS MACHINE	Voyage	1978
FROM HERE TO ETERNITY	Iron Maiden	1992
FROM HERE TO ETERNITY	Michael Ball	1994
FROM HERE TO ETERNITY	Giorgio Moroder	1977
FROM HIS WOMAN TO YOU	Barbara Mason	1974

SONG TITLE	ARTIST	DATE
FROM ME TO YOU	Beatles	1963
FROM NEW YORK TO L.A.	Patsy Gallant	1977
FROM OUT OF NOWHERE	Faith No More	1990
FROM RUSH HOUR WITH LOVE		
	Republica	1998
FROM RUSSIA WITH LOVE	Matt Darey presents DSP	2000
FROM RUSSIA WITH LOVE	John Barry	1963
FROM RUSSIA WITH LOVE	Matt Monro	1963
FROM THA CHUUUCH TO DA PALACE		
	Snoop Dogg	2002
FROM THE BEGINNING	Emerson, Lake & Palmer	1972
FROM THE BENCH AT BELVIDERE		
	Boo Radleys	1995
FROM THE BOTTOM OF MY BROKEN HEART		
	Britney Spears	2000
FROM THE BOTTOM OF MY HEART		
	Moody Blues	1965
FROM THE HEART	Another Level	1999
FROM THE UNDERWORLD	Herd	1967
FROM THIS MOMENT ON	Shania Twain	1998
FRONTIER PSYCHIATRIST	Avalanches	2001
FRONTIN'	Pharrell Williams featuring Jay-Z	2003
FROZEN	Madonna	1998
FROZEN ORANGE JUICE	Peter Sarstedt	1969
FU-GEE-LA	Fugees	1995

SONG TITLE	ARTIST	DATE
F**K IT (I DON'T WANT YOU BACK)		
	Eamon	2004
FUCK THE MILLENNIUM	2k	1997
FUEL	Metallica	1998
FULL METAL JACKET	Abigail Mead & Nigel Goulding	1987
FULL MOON	Brandy	2002
FULL OF FIRE	Al Green	1975
FULL OF LIFE (HAPPY NOW)		
	Wonder Stuff	1993
FULL TERM LOVE	Monie Love	1992
FUN	Da Mob featuring Jocelyn Brown	1998
FUN FOR ME	Moloko	1996
FUN FUN FUN	Status Quo With The Beach Boys	1996
FUN, FUN, FUN	Beach Boys	1964
THE FUN LOVIN' CRIMINAL		
	Fun Lovin' Criminals	1996
THE FUNERAL OF HEARTS	Him	2004
FUNERAL PYRE	Jam	1981
FUNK & DRIVE	Elevatorman	1995
FUNK DAT	Sagat	1993
FUNK ON AH ROLL	James Brown	1999
THE FUNK PHENOMENA	Armand Van Helden	1997
FUNKDAFIED	Da Brat	1994
FUNKIN' FOR JAMAICA (N.Y.)		
	Tom Browne	1980

SONG TITLE	ARTIST	DATE
FUNKY BROADWAY	Wilson Pickett	1967
FUNKY COLD MEDINA/ON FIRE		
	Tone Loc	1989
FUNKY DORY	Rachel Stevens	2003
FUNKY GIBBON/SICK-MAN BLUES		
	Goodies	1975
FUNKY GUITAR	TC 1992	1992
THE FUNKY JUDGE	Bull & The Matadors	1968
FUNKY LOVE	Kavana	1998
FUNKY MOPED/MAGIC ROUNDABOUT		
	Jasper Carrott	1975
FUNKY MUSIC	Utah Saints	2000
FUNKY NASSAU	Beginning Of The End	1971
FUNKY STREET	Arthur Conley	1968
FUNKY STUFF	Kool & The Gang	1973
FUNKY TOWN	Pseudo Echo	1987
FUNKY WEEKEND	Stylistics	1976
FUNKY WORM	Ohio Players	1973
FUNKY Y-2-C	Puppies	1994
FUNKYTOWN	Lipps Inc.	1980
FUNNY	Joe Hinton	1964
FUNNY ALL OVER	Vernons Girls	1963
FUNNY BREAK (ONE IS ENOUGH)		
	Orbital	2001
FUNNY FACE	Donna Fargo	1972

SONG TITLE	ARTIST	DATE
FUNNY FAMILIAR FORGOTTEN FEELING		
	Tom Jones	1967
FUNNY FUNNY	Sweet	1971
FUNNY HOW LOVE CAN BE		
	Ivy League	1965
FUNNY HOW TIME SLIPS AWAY		
	Dorothy Moore	1976
FURTHER	Longview	2003
FUTURE LOVE (EP)	Seal	1991
THE FUTURE OF THE FUTURE		
	Deep Dish With EBTG	1998
FUTURE SHOCK	Curtis Mayfield	1973
THE FUTURE'S SO BRIGHT I GOTTA WEAR SHADES		
	Timbruk 3	1986
G.H.E.T.T.O.U.T.	Changing Faces	1997
G.L.A.D.	Kim Appleby	1991
G.T.O.	Sinitta	1987
G.T.O.	Ronny & The Daytonas	1964
GABRIEL	Roy Davis Jr. featuring Peven Everett	1997
GAL WINE	Chaka Demus & Pliers	1994
GALAXIE	Blind Melon	1995
GALAXY	War	1978
GALAXY OF LOVE	Crown Heights Affair	1978
GALLANT MEN	Senator Everett Dirksen	1966

SONG TITLE	ARTIST	DATE
GALLOPING HOME	London String Chorale	1973
GALLOWS POLE	Jimmy Page & Robert Plant	1994
GALVESTON	Glen Campbell	1969
GAMBLER	Madonna	1985
THE GAMBLER	Kenny Rogers	1978
GAMBLIN' BAR ROOM BLUES		
	Sensational Alex Harvey Band	1975
THE GAME	Echo & The Bunnymen	1987
GAME OF LOVE	Wayne Fontana & The Mindbenders	1965
THE GAME OF LOVE	Santana featuring Michelle Branch	2002
GAME ON	Catatonia	1998
GAME OVER	Scarface	1997
GAMEMASTER	Lost Tribe	1999
GAMES	New Kids On The Block	1991
GAMES	Redeye	1970
GAMES PEOPLE PLAY	Joe South	1969
GAMES PEOPLE PLAY	Alan Parsons Project	1980
GAMES WITHOUT FRONTIERS		
	Peter Gabriel	1980
GANGSTA	Bell Biv Devoe	1992
GANGSTA LEAN	DRS	1993
GANGSTA LOVIN'	Eve featuring Alicia Keys	2002
GANGSTA NATION	Westside Connection featuring Nate Dogg	2003

SONG TITLE	ARTIST	DATE
GANGSTA'S PARADISE	Coolio featuring LV	1995
GANGSTAS MAKE THE WORLD GO ROUND		
	Westside Connection	1997
GANGSTER TRIPPIN	Fatboy Slim	1998
GANGSTERS	Special AKA	1979
GANGSTERS OF THE GROOVE		
	Heatwave	1981
GARAGE GIRLS	Lonyo featuring MC Onyx Stone	2001
GARDEN PARTY	Marillion	1983
GARDEN PARTY	Mezzoforte	1983
GARDEN PARTY	Rick Nelson	1972
GARY GILMOUR'S EYES	Adverts	1977
GASOLINE ALLEY BRED	Hollies	1970
GATECRASHING	Living In A Box	1989
GAUDETTE	Steeleye Span	1973
GAY BAR	Electric Six	2003
GAYE	Clifford T. Ward	1973
GEE BABY	Peter Shelley	1974
GEE WHIZ	Bernadette Peters	1980
GEEK STINK BREATH	Green Day	1995
GEMINI DREAM	Moody Blues	1981
GENERAL HOSPI-TALE	Afternoon Delights	1981
GENERALS AND MAJORS/DON'T LOSE YOUR TEMPER		
	XTC	1980
GENERATION SEX	Divine Comedy	1998

SONG TITLE	ARTIST	DATE
GENERATIONS	Inspiral Carpets	1992
GENERATIONS OF LOVE	Jesus Loves You	1991
GENETIC ENGINEERING	Orchestral Manoeuvres In	
	The Dark	1983
GENIE	B B & Q Band	1985
GENIE IN A BOTTLE	Christina Aguilera	1999
GENIE IN A BOTTLE/SAVE YOURSELF		
	Speedway	2003
GENIE WITH THE LIGHT BROWN LAMP		
	Shadows	1964
GENIUS OF LOVE	Tom Tom Club	1982
GENO	Dexy's Midnight Runners	1980
GENTLE	Dino	1990
GENTLE ON MY MIND	Glen Campbell	1968
GENTLE ON MY MIND	Dean Martin	1969
A GENTLEMAN'S EXCUSE ME		
	Fish	1990
GEORDIE BOYS (GAZZA RAP)		
	Gazza	1990
GEORGE JACKSON	Bob Dylan	1971
GEORGIA ON MY MIND	Michael Bolton	1990
GEORGINA BAILEY	Noosha Fox	1977
GEORGY GIRL	Seekers	1966
GEORGY PORGY	Eric Benet featuring Faith Evans	1999
GERM FREE ADOLESCENCE		
	X-Ray Spex	1978

SONG TITLE	ARTIST	DATE
GERONIMO	Shadows	1963
GERONIMO'S CADILLAC	Michael Murphey	1972
GERTCHA	Chas & Dave	1979
GET A LEG UP	John Mellencamp	1991
GET A LIFE	Soul II Soul	1989
GET AT ME DOG	DMX (featuring Sheek of	
	the Lox)	1998
GET AWAY	Georgie Fame	1966
GET AWAY	Bobby Brown	1993
GET BACK	Beatles With Billy Preston	1969
GET BACK	Rod Stewart	1976
GET BUSY	Sean Paul	2003
GET CLOSER	Linda Ronstadt	1982
GET CLOSER	Seals & Crofts (featuring	
	Carolyn Willis)	1976
GET DANCIN'	Disco Tex & The Sex-O-Lettes	1974
GET DOWN	Gene Chandler	1979
GET DOWN	Gilbert O'Sullivan	1973
GET DOWN	Craig Mack	1994
GET DOWN (YOU'RE THE ONE FOR ME)		
	Backstreet Boys	1996
GET DOWN AND GET WITH IT		
	Slade	1971
GET DOWN ON IT	Kool & The Gang	1982
GET DOWN SATURDAY NIGHT		
	Oliver Cheatham	1983

SONG TITLE	ARTIST	DATE
GET DOWN TONIGHT	KC & The Sunshine Band	1975
GET DOWN, GET DOWN (GET ON THE FLOOR)		
	Joe Simon	1975
GET FREE	Vines	2002
GET GET DOWN	Paul Johnson	1999
GET GONE	Ideal	1999
GET HERE	Oleta Adams	1990
GET HIGHER	Black Grape	1997
GET IN THE SWING	Sparks	1975
GET INTO YOU	Dannii Minogue	1994
GET INVOLVED	Raphael Saadiq & Q-Tip	1999
GET IT	Darts	1979
GET IT	Stevie Wonder & Michael Jackson	1988
GET IT ON	Power Station	1985
GET IT ON	T. Rex	1971
GET IT ON	Chase	1971
GET IT ON (BANG A GONG)		
	Power Station	1985
GET IT ON THE FLOOR	DMX featuring Swizz Beatz	2004
GET IT ON TONITE	Montell Jordan	1999
GET IT RIGHT NEXT TIME	Gerry Rafferty	1979
GET IT TOGETHER	Crispy And Co.	1975
GET IT TOGETHER	Seal	2003
GET IT TOGETHER	Jackson 5	1973
GET IT TOGETHER	702	1997

SONG TITLE	ARTIST	DATE
GET IT TOGETHER (PART 1)		
	James Brown	1967
GET IT TOGETHER/SABOTAGE		
	Beastie Boys	1994
GET IT WHILE YOU CAN	Olympic Runners	1978
GET LOOSE	L.A. Mix featuring Jazzi P	1989
GET LUCKY	Jermaine Stewart	1988
GET ME HOME	Foxy Brown featuring	
	Blackstreet	1997
GET ME OFF	Basement Jaxx	2002
GET ME OUT	New Model Army	1990
GET ME TO THE WORLD ON TIME		
	Electric Prunes	1967
GET MONEY	Junior M.A.F.I.A. featuring	
	The Notorious B.I.G.	1996
GET MYSELF TOGETHER	Bucketheads	1996
GET NO BETTER	Cassidy featuring Mashonda	2004
GET OFF	Dandy Warhols	2002
GET OFF	Foxy	1978
GET OFF OF MY CLOUD	Rolling Stones	1965
GET ON IT	Phoebe One	1999
GET ON THE BUS	Destiny's Child featuring	
	Timbaland	1999
GET ON THE DANCE FLOOR		
	Rob Base & D.J. E-Z Rock	1989

SONG TITLE	ARTIST	DATE
GET ON THE GOOD FOOT (PART 1)		
	James Brown	1972
GET ON UP	Jodeci	1996
GET ON UP	Esquires	1967
GET ON YOUR FEET	Gloria Estefan	1989
GET OUT	Felon	2002
GET OUT (AND LET ME CRY)		
	Harold Melvin & The Bluenotes	1975
GET OUT OF MY LIFE, WOMAN		
	Lee Dorsey	1966
GET OUT OF YOUR LAZY BED		
	Matt Bianco	1984
GET OUTTA MY DREAMS GET INTO MY CAR		
	Billy Ocean	1988
GET OVER IT	Ok Go	2003
GET OVER IT	Eagles	1994
GET OVER YOU/MOVE THIS MOUNTAIN		
	Sophie Ellis-Bextor	2002
GET OVER YOURSELF	Eden's Crush	2001
GET READY	Mase featuring Blackstreet	1999
GET READY	Temptations	1966
GET READY	Rare Earth	1970
GET READY!	Roachford	1991
GET READY FOR THIS	2 Unlimited	1994
GET THAT LOVE	Thompson Twins	1987
GET THE BALANCE RIGHT	Depeche Mode	1983

SONG TITLE	ARTIST	DATE
GET THE FUNK OUT	Extreme	1991
GET THE FUNK OUT MA FACE		
	Brothers Johnson	1976
GET THE GIRL! KILL THE BADDIES!		
	Pop Will Eat Itself	1993
GET THE MESSAGE	Electronic	1991
GET THE PARTY STARTED	Pink	2001
GET THROUGH	Mark Joseph	2003
GET TOGETHER	Youngbloods	1969
GET UP	Beverley Knight	2001
GET UP (BEFORE THE NIGHT IS OVER)		
	Technotronic/Ya Kid K	1990
GET UP (EVERYBODY)	Byron Stingily	1997
GET UP AND BOOGIE (THAT'S RIGHT)		
	Silver Convention	1976
GET UP AND MOVE	Harvey	2002
GET UP (I FEEL LIKE BEING A SEX MACHINE)		
	James Brown	1970
GET UP OFFA THAT THING		
	James Brown	1976
GET UP STAND UP	Phunky Phantom	1998
GET UP STAND UP	Stellar Project featuring	
	Brandi Emma	2004
GET UP! GO INSANE!	Stretch 'n' Vern presents	
	'Maddog'	1997

SONG TITLE	ARTIST	DATE
GET UP, GET INTO IT, GET INVOLVED (PT 1)		
	James Brown	1971
GET UR FREAK ON	Missy 'Misdemeanor' Elliott	2001
GET USED TO IT	Roger Voudouris	1979
GET WILD	New Power Generation	1995
GET YOUR HANDS OFF MY MAN!		
	Junior Vasquez	1995
GET YOUR LOVE BACK	Three Degrees	1974
GET-A-WAY	Maxx	1994
GETAWAY	The Music	2002
GETAWAY	Earth, Wind & Fire	1976
GETCHA BACK	Beach Boys	1985
GETT OFF	Prince	1991
GETTIN' IN THE WAY	Jill Scott	2000
GETTIN' JIGGY WIT IT	Will Smith	1998
GETTIN' READY FOR LOVE	Diana Ross	1977
GETTIN' TOGETHER	Tommy James & The Shondells	1967
GETTING A DRAG	Lynsey De Paul	1972
GETTING AWAY WITH IT	Electronic	1990
GETTING AWAY WITH IT (ALL MESSED UP)		
	James	2001
GETTING BETTER	Shed Seven	1996
GETTING CLOSER	Paul McCartney	1979
GETTING MIGHTY CROWDED		
	Betty Everett	1965
GETTING OVER YOU	Andy Williams	1974

SONG TITLE	ARTIST	DATE
GETTO JAM	Domino	1993
GHETTO CHILD	Spinners	1973
GHETTO COWBOY	Mo Thugs Family featuring	
	Bone Thugs-N-Harmony	1998
GHETTO DAY/WHAT I NEED		
	Crystal Waters	1994
GHETTO GIRL	Simply Red	1998
GHETTO HEAVEN	Family Stand	1990
GHETTO LOVE	Da Brat featuring T-Boz	1997
GHETTO ROMANCE	Damage	2000
GHETTO SUPERSTAR	Pras Michel featuring Ol' Dirty	
	Bastard & Mya	1998
GHOST DANCING	Simple Minds	1986
THE GHOST OF LOVE	Tavares	1978
THE GHOST OF TOM JOAD	Bruce Springsteen	1996
GHOST TOWN	Specials	1981
GHOST TOWN	Cheap Trick	1988
(GHOST) RIDERS IN THE SKY		
	Outlaws	1980
GHOSTBUSTERS	Ray Parker Jr.	1984
GHOSTS	Japan	1982
GHOSTS	Dirty Vegas	2002
THE GIFT OF CHRISTMAS	Childliners	1995
THE GIFT	INXS	1993
THE GIFT	Way Out West/Miss Joanna Law	1996
GIGOLO	Damned	1987

SONG TITLE	ARTIST	DATE
GIGOLO	Nick Cannon featuring R. Kelly	2003
GIMME ALL YOUR LOVIN'	ZZ Top	1983
GIMME ALL YOUR LOVIN'	Kym Mazelle & Jocelyn Brown	1994
GIMME ALL YOUR LOVIN' 2000		
	Martay featuring ZZ Top	1999
GIMME DAT BANANA	Black Gorilla	1977
GIMME DAT DING	Pipkins	1970
GIMME, GIMME, GIMME (A MAN AFTER MIDNIGHT)		
	ABBA	1979
GIMME GIMME GOOD LOVIN'		
	Crazy Elephant	1969
GIMME HOPE JO'ANNA	Eddy Grant	1988
GIMME LITTLE SIGN	Brenton Wood	1967
GIMME LOVE	Alexia	1998
GIMME LUV (EENIE MEENIE MINY MO)		
	David Morales/Bad Yard Club	1993
GIMME SHELTER (EP)	Various	1993
GIMME SOME	Brendon	1977
GIMME SOME LOVE	Gina G	1997
GIMME SOME LOVIN'	Thunder	1990
GIMME SOME LOVIN'	Blues Brothers	1980
GIMME SOME LOVING	Spencer Davis Group	1966
GIMME SOME MORE	Busta Rhymes	1999
GIMME THAT BODY	Q Tee	1996
GIMME THE LIGHT	Sean Paul	2002
GIMMIX! PLAY LOUD	John Cooper Clarke	1979

SONG TITLE	ARTIST	DATE
GIN AND JUICE	Snoop Doggy Dogg	1994
GIN GAN GOOLIE	Scaffold	1969
GIN HOUSE BLUES	Amen Corner	1967
GIN SOAKED BOY	Divine Comedy	1999
GIPSY EYES/REMEMBER	Jimi Hendrix	1971
GIRL	Truth	1966
GIRL	St. Louis Union	1966
GIRL (WHY YOU WANNA MAKE ME BLUE)		
	Temptations	1964
GIRL ALL THE BAD GUYS WANT		
	Bowling For Soup	2002
GIRL CAN'T HELP IT	Journey	1986
GIRL CRAZY	Hot Chocolate	1982
GIRL DON'T COME	Sandie Shaw	1964
THE GIRL FROM IPANEMA	Stan Getz, Joao Gilberto	1964
GIRL FROM MARS	Ash	1995
THE GIRL I KNEW SOMEWHERE		
	Monkees	1967
THE GIRL I USED TO KNOW		
	Brother Beyond	1990
GIRL I'M GONNA MISS YOU		
	Milli Vanilli	1989
GIRL IN LOVE	Outsiders	1966
GIRL IN THE MOON	Darius	2003
A GIRL IN TROUBLE (IS A TEMPORARY THING)		
	Romeo Void	1984

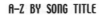
SONG TITLE	ARTIST	DATE
THE GIRL IS MINE	Michael Jackson & Paul McCartney	1982
A GIRL LIKE YOU	Edwyn Collins	1995
A GIRL LIKE YOU	Young Rascals	1967
A GIRL LIKE YOU	Smithereens	1989
THE GIRL OF MY BEST FRIEND	Elvis Presley	1976
GIRL OF MY DREAMS	Bram Tchaikovsky	1979
GIRL ON A SWING	Gerry & The Pacemakers	1966
GIRL ON TV	Lyte Funkie Ones	2000
GIRL ON TV	LFO	1999
GIRL POWER	Shampoo	1996
THE GIRL SANG THE BLUES	Everly Brothers	1963
GIRL TALK	TLC	2002
GIRL TO GIRL	49ers	1990
GIRL U FOR ME/LOSE CONTROL	Silk	1993
GIRL WATCHER	O'Kaysions	1968
GIRL YOU KNOW IT'S TRUE	Keith'n'Shane	2000
GIRL YOU KNOW IT'S TRUE	Milli Vanilli	1989
GIRL YOU'RE SO TOGETHER	Michael Jackson	1984
GIRL'S NOT GREY	AFI	2003

SONG TITLE	ARTIST	DATE
GIRL, I'VE BEEN HURT	Snow	1993
GIRL, YOU'LL BE A WOMAN SOON	Urge Overkill	1994
GIRL, YOU'LL BE A WOMAN SOON	Neil Diamond	1967
GIRLFRIEND	Billie	1998
GIRLFRIEND	Pebbles	1988
GIRLFRIEND	*NSYNC featuring Nelly	2002
GIRLFRIEND	Alicia Keys	2002
GIRLFRIEND	B2K	2003
GIRLFRIEND IN A COMA	Smiths	1987
GIRLFRIEND'S STORY	Gemma Fox featuring MC Lyte	2004
GIRLFRIEND/BOYFRIEND	Blackstreet With Janet	1999
GIRLIE	Peddlers	1970
GIRLIE GIRLIE	Sophia George	1985
GIRLS	Moments And Whatnauts	1975
GIRLS	Prodigy	2004
GIRLS	Dwight Twilley	1984
GIRLS/SHE'S CRAFTY	Beastie Boys	1987
GIRLS & BOYS	Hed Boys	1994
GIRLS AIN'T NOTHING BUT TROUBLE	D.J. Jazzy Jeff/Fresh Prince	1986
GIRLS AND BOYS	Blur	1994
GIRLS AND BOYS	Prince & The Revolution	1986
GIRLS AND BOYS	Good Charlotte	2003
GIRLS ARE MORE FUN	Ray Parker Jr.	1985

SONG TITLE	ARTIST	DATE
GIRLS ARE OUT TO GET YOU		
	Fascinations	1971
GIRLS CAN GET IT	Dr. Hook	1980
GIRLS CAN'T DO WHAT THE GUYS DO		
	Betty Wright	1968
GIRLS DEM SUGAR	Beenie Man featuring Mya	2001
GIRLS GIRLS GIRLS	Sailor	1976
GIRLS, GIRLS, GIRLS	Fourmost	1965
GIRLS, GIRLS, GIRLS	Motley Crue	1987
GIRLS, GIRLS, GIRLS	Jay-Z	2001
GIRLS GIRLS GIRLS	Kandidate	1979
GIRLS IN LOVE	Gary Lewis & Playboys	1967
GIRLS JUST WANNA HAVE FUN		
	Lolly	2000
GIRLS JUST WANT TO HAVE FUN		
	Cyndi Lauper	1983
GIRLS LIE TOO	Terri Clark	2004
GIRLS LIKE US	B15 featuring Chrissy D	
	& Lady G	2000
GIRLS NIGHT OUT	Alda	1998
GIRLS NITE OUT	Tyler Collins	1990
GIRLS ON FILM	Duran Duran	1981
GIRLS ON TOP	Girl Thing	2000
GIRLS TALK	Dave Edmunds	1979
GIRLS WITH GUNS	Tommy Shaw	1984
GIRLS' SCHOOL	Paul McCartney	1977

SONG TITLE	ARTIST	DATE
GITARZAN	Ray Stevens	1969
GIVE A LITTLE BIT	Supertramp	1977
GIVE A LITTLE LOVE	Aswad	1988
GIVE A LITTLE LOVE	Bay City Rollers	1975
GIVE A LITTLE LOVE	Daniel O'Donnell	1998
GIVE A LITTLE LOVE BACK TO THE WORLD		
	Emma	1990
GIVE AND TAKE	Pioneers	1972
GIVE HIM A GREAT BIG KISS		
	Shangri-Las	1964
GIVE IN TO ME	Michael Jackson	1993
GIVE IRELAND BACK TO THE IRISH		
	Paul McCartney	1972
GIVE IT 2 YOU	Da Brat	1995
GIVE IT ALL YOU GOT	Chuck Mangione	1980
GIVE IT AWAY	Red Hot Chili Peppers	1994
GIVE IT AWAY	Deepest Blue	2004
GIVE IT SOME EMOTION	Tracie	1983
GIVE IT TO ME	Troggs	1967
GIVE IT TO ME	J. Geils Band	1973
GIVE IT TO ME BABY	Rick James	1981
GIVE IT TO ME NOW	Kenny	1973
GIVE IT TO THE PEOPLE	Righteous Brothers	1974
GIVE IT TO YOU	Martha Wash	1993
GIVE IT TO YOU	Jordan Knight	1999
GIVE IT UP	Hothouse Flowers	1990

SONG TITLE	ARTIST	DATE
GIVE IT UP	Wilson Phillips	1992
GIVE IT UP	Goodmen	1993
GIVE IT UP	Public Enemy	1994
GIVE IT UP	KC	1983
GIVE IT UP (TURN IT LOOSE)		
	Tyrone Davis	1976
GIVE IT UP OR TURN IT A LOOSE		
	James Brown	1969
GIVE IT UP, TURN IT LOOSE		
	En Vogue	1992
GIVE IT WHAT YOU GOT	B.T. Express	1975
GIVE ME A LITTLE MORE TIME		
	Gabrielle	1996
GIVE ME A REASON	Corrs	2001
GIVE ME A REASON	Triple Eight	2003
GIVE ME ALL YOUR LOVE	Magic Affair	1994
GIVE ME ALL YOUR LOVE	Whitesnake	1988
GIVE ME BACK MY HEART		
	Dollar	1982
GIVE ME JUST A LITTLE MORE TIME		
	Chairmen Of The Board	1970
GIVE ME JUST A LITTLE MORE TIME		
	Kylie Minogue	1992
GIVE ME JUST ONE NIGHT (UNA NOCHE)		
	98 Degrees	2000
GIVE ME LIFE	Mr V	1994

SONG TITLE	ARTIST	DATE
GIVE ME LOVE	Diddy	1997
GIVE ME LOVE (GIVE ME PEACE ON EARTH)		
	George Harrison	1973
GIVE ME LUV	Alcatraz	1996
GIVE ME MORE TIME	Whitesnake	1984
GIVE ME ONE MORE CHANCE		
	Donald Peers	1972
GIVE ME ONE REASON	Tracy Chapman	1996
GIVE ME RHYTHM	Black Connection	1998
GIVE ME SOME KINDA MAGIC		
	Dollar	1982
GIVE ME STRENGTH	Jon Of The Pleased Wimmin	1996
GIVE ME THE NIGHT	George Benson	1980
GIVE ME THE REASON		
	Luther Vandross	1988
GIVE ME TIME	Dusty Springfield	1967
GIVE ME TONIGHT	Shannon	1984
GIVE ME YOU	Mary J. Blige	2000
GIVE ME YOUR BODY	Chippendales	1992
GIVE ME YOUR HEART TONIGHT		
	Shakin' Stevens	1982
GIVE ME YOUR LOVE	Barbara Mason	1973
GIVE ME YOUR WORD	Billy Fury	1966
(FOR GOD'S SAKE) GIVE MORE POWER TO THE PEOPLE		
	Chi-Lites	1971
GIVE PEACE A CHANCE	Plastic Ono Band	1969

SONG TITLE	ARTIST	DATE
GIVE TO LIVE	Sammy Hagar	1987
GIVE U MY HEART	Babyface (featuring Toni Braxton)	1992
GIVE US YOUR BLESSING	Shangri-Las	1965
GIVE YOU ALL THE LOVE	Mishka	1999
GIVE YOUR BABY A STANDING OVATION	Dells	1973
GIVEN TO FLY	Pearl Jam	1998
GIVEN UP	Mirrorball	1999
GIVING HIM SOMETHING HE CAN FEEL	En Vogue	1992
GIVING IT ALL AWAY	Roger Daltrey	1973
GIVING IT BACK	Phil Hurtt	1978
GIVING IT UP FOR YOUR LOVE	Delbert McClinton	1980
GIVING UP	Gladys Knight & The Pips	1964
GIVING UP ON LOVE	Rick Astley	1989
GIVING UP, GIVING IN	Three Degrees	1978
GIVING YOU THE BENEFIT	Pebbles	1990
GIVING YOU THE BEST THAT I GOT	Anita Baker	1988
GLAD ALL OVER	Dave Clark Five	1964
GLAD IT'S ALL OVER/DAMNED ON 45	Captain Sensible	1984
GLAD TO BE UNHAPPY	Mamas & The Papas	1967

SONG TITLE	ARTIST	DATE
GLAM ROCK COPS	Carter The Unstoppable Sex Machine	1994
GLAM SLAM	Prince	1988
THE GLAMOROUS LIFE	Sheila E	1984
GLAMOUR BOYS	Living Colour	1989
GLASS OF CHAMPAGNE	Sailor	1975
GLASSHOUSE	Temptations	1975
GLASTONBURY SONG	Waterboys	1993
GLITTER AND TRAUMA	Biffy Clyro	2004
GLITTERBALL	Simple Minds	1998
GLITTERING PRIZE	Simple Minds	1982
GLOBETROTTER	Tornados	1963
GLORIA	Van Morrison & John Lee Hooker	1993
GLORIA	Laura Branigan	1982
GLORIA	Enchantment	1977
GLORIA	Shadows Of Knight	1966
GLORIOUS	Andreas Johnson	2000
GLORY BOUND	Grass Roots	1972
GLORY BOX	Portishead	1995
GLORY DAYS	Bruce Springsteen	1985
GLORY GLORY MAN. UNITED	Manchester United Football Club	1983
GLORY OF LOVE	Peter Cetera	1986
GLORYLAND	Daryl Hall/Sounds Of Blackness	1994
GLYCERINE	Bush	1996

SONG TITLE	ARTIST	DATE
GO	Moby	1991
GO (BEFORE YOU BREAK MY HEART)		
	Gigliola Cinquetti	1974
GO AHEAD AND CRY	Righteous Brothers	1966
GO ALL THE WAY	Raspberries	1972
GO AWAY	Gloria Estefan	1993
GO AWAY LITTLE GIRL	Happenings	1966
GO AWAY LITTLE GIRL	Donny Osmond	1971
GO BACK	Crabby Appleton	1970
GO D.J.	Lil Wayne	2004
GO DEEP	Janet Jackson	1998
GO DEH YAKA (GO TO THE TOP)		
	Monyaka	1983
GO DOWN GAMBLIN'	Blood, Sweat & Tears	1971
GO ENGLAND	England Boys	2002
GO FOR IT! (HEART AND FIRE)		
	Rocky V/JB Ellis & T Hare	1991
GO GO GO	Chuck Berry	1963
GO HOME	Stevie Wonder	1985
GO INSANE	Lindsey Buckingham	1984
GO LET IT OUT	Oasis	2000
GO NORTH	Richard Barnes	1970
GO NOW!	Moody Blues	1965
GO ON	George Strait	2000
GO ON MOVE	Reel 2 Real	1994
GO THE DISTANCE	Michael Bolton	1997

SONG TITLE	ARTIST	DATE
GO TO SLEEP	Radiohead	2003
GO WEST	Village People	1979
GO WEST	Pet Shop Boys	1993
GO WHERE YOU WANNA GO		
	5th Dimension	1967
GO WILD IN THE COUNTRY		
	Bow Wow Wow	1982
GO WITH THE FLOW	Queens Of The Stone Age	2003
GO YOUR OWN WAY	Fleetwood Mac	1977
GO-GO DANCER	Wedding Present	1992
GOD BLESS THE USA	Lee Greenwood	2001
GOD GAVE ROCK & ROLL TO YOU II		
	Kiss	1992
GOD GAVE ROCK 'N' ROLL TO YOU		
	Argent	1973
GOD IS A DJ	Faithless	1998
GOD IS A DJ	Pink	2004
(GOD MUST HAVE SPENT) A LITTLE MORE TIME ON YOU		
	Alabama/*NSYNC	1999
GOD ONLY KNOWS	Beach Boys	1966
GOD SAVE THE QUEEN	Sex Pistols	1977
GOD THANK YOU WOMAN	Culture Club	1986
GOD! SHOW ME MUSIC	Super Furry Animals	1996
GOD'S GREAT BANANA SKIN		
	Chris Rea	1992

SONG TITLE	ARTIST	DATE
GOD, LOVE AND ROCK & ROLL		
	Teegarden & Van Winkle	1970
GODDESS ON A HIWAY	Mercury Rev	1999
GODHOPPING	Dogs Die In Hot Cars	2004
GOIN' BACK	Dusty Springfield	1966
GOIN' DOWN	Melanie C	1999
GOIN' DOWN	Greg Guidry	1982
GOIN' HOME	Osmonds	1973
GOIN' OUT OF MY HEAD	Dodie West	1965
GOIN' OUT OF MY HEAD	Little Anthony & The Imperials	1964
GOIN' OUT OF MY HEAD/CAN'T TAKE MY EYES OFF YOU		
	Lettermen	1967
GOIN' PLACES	Jacksons	1977
GOING BACK TO CALI/JACK THE RIPPER		
	LL Cool J	1988
GOING BACK TO MY ROOTS		
	FPI Project	1989
GOING BACK TO MY ROOTS		
	Odyssey	1981
GOING DOWN THE ROAD	Roy Wood	1974
GOING DOWN TOWN TONIGHT		
	Status Quo	1984
GOING FOR GOLD	Shed Seven	1996
GOING FOR THE ONE	Yes	1977
GOING GOING GONE	Brook Benton	1964
GOING IN CIRCLES	Friends Of Distinction	1969

SONG TITLE	ARTIST	DATE
GOING IN WITH MY EYES OPEN		
	David Soul	1977
GOING NOWHERE	Gabrielle	1993
GOING OUT	Supergrass	1996
GOING ROUND	D'Bora	1995
GOING TO A GO-GO	Rolling Stones	1982
GOING TO A GO-GO	Miracles	1965
GOING UNDER	Evanescence	2003
GOING UNDERGROUND/DREAMS OF CHILDREN		
	Jam	1980
GOING UNDERGROUND/CARNATION		
	Buffalo Tom: Liam Gallagher & Steve Cradock	1999
GOING UP THE COUNTRY	Canned Heat	1968
GOLD	East 17	1992
GOLD	Spandau Ballet	1983
GOLD	TAFKAP	1995
GOLD	Beverley Knight	2002
GOLD	John Stewart	1979
THE GOLDEN AGE OF ROCK AND ROLL		
	Mott The Hoople	1974
GOLDEN BROWN	Kaleef	1996
GOLDEN BROWN	Omar	1997
GOLDEN BROWN	Stranglers	1982
GOLDEN GATE BRIDGE	Ocean Colour Scene	2004
GOLDEN GAZE	Ian Brown	2000

SONG TITLE	ARTIST	DATE
GOLDEN GREEN/GET TOGETHER		
	Wonder Stuff	1989
GOLDEN LIGHTS	Twinkle	1965
GOLDEN RETRIEVER	Super Furry Animals	2003
GOLDEN SKIN	Silver Sun	1997
GOLDEN SLUMBERS/CARRY THAT WEIGHT		
	Trash	1969
GOLDEN TOUCH	Razorlight	2004
GOLDEN YEARS	David Bowie	1975
THE GOLDEN YEARS (EP)	Motorhead	1980
GOLDENBALLS (MR BECKHAM TO YOU)		
	Bell & Spurling	2002
GOLDENEYE	Tina Turner	1995
GOLDFINGER	Shirley Bassey	1965
GOLDFINGER	Ash	1996
GOLDMINE	Pointer Sisters	1986
GONE	*NSYNC	2001
GONE	Shirley Bassey	1964
GONE	Joey Heatherton	1972
GONE AT LAST	Paul Simon/Phoebe Snow	1975
GONE TILL NOVEMBER	Wyclef Jean	1998
GONE TOO FAR	England Dan & John Ford Coley	1977
GONE TOO SOON	Michael Jackson	1993
GONE, GONE, GONE	Everly Brothers	1964
GONE, GONE, GONE	Johnny Mathis	1979

SONG TITLE	ARTIST	DATE
GONNA CAPTURE YOUR HEART		
	Blue	1977
GONNA CATCH YOU	Lonnie Gordon	1991
GONNA FLY NOW	Maynard Ferguson	1977
GONNA FLY NOW (THEME FROM 'ROCKY')		
	Bill Conti	1977
GONNA GET ALONG WITHOUT YOU NOW		
	Viola Wills	1979
GONNA GET YA LIZARD	Mauro Picotto	1999
GONNA GIVE HER ALL THE LOVE I'VE GOT		
	Jimmy Ruffin	1967
GONNA MAKE YOU A STAR	David Essex	1974
GONNA MAKE YOU AN OFFER YOU CAN'T REFUSE		
	Jimmy Helms	1973
GONNA MAKE YOU SWEAT		
	C&C Music Factory featuring Freedom Williams	1990
GONNA WORK IT OUT	Hi-Gate	2001
GOO GOO BARABAJAGAL (LOVE IS HOT)		
	Donovan/Jeff Beck Group	1969
GOOD	Better Than Ezra	1995
GOOD AS GOLD	Beautiful South	1994
GOOD BOYS	Blondie	2003
GOOD DAY	Sean Maguire	1996
GOOD ENOUGH	Dodgy	1996
GOOD ENOUGH	Bobby Brown	1992

SONG TITLE	ARTIST	DATE
GOOD ENOUGH (LA VACHE)	Milk Incorporated	1998
GOOD FEELING	Reef	1995
GOOD FOR ME	Amy Grant	1992
GOOD FRIEND	Mary Macgregor	1979
GOOD GIRLS	Joe	1998
GOOD GIRLS DON'T	Knack	1979
GOOD GOD	Korn	1997
GOOD GOLLY MISS MOLLY	Little Richard	1958
GOOD GOLLY MISS MOLLY	Jerry Lee Lewis	1963
GOOD GOLLY MISS MOLLY	Swinging Blue Jeans	1964
GOOD GRIEF CHRISTINA	Chicory Tip	1973
A GOOD HEART	Feargal Sharkey	1985
GOOD HEARTED WOMAN	Waylon Jennings	1976
GOOD HEARTED WOMAN	Willie Nelson	1976
GOOD LIFE	Eve	1995
GOOD LIFE	Inner City	1988
GOOD LIFE (BUENA VIDA)	Inner City	1999
THE GOOD LIFE	New Power Generation	1997
THE GOOD LIFE	Tony Bennett	1963
GOOD LOVE CAN NEVER DIE	Alvin Stardust	1975
GOOD LOVIN'	Young Rascals	1966
GOOD LOVIN' AIN'T EASY TO COME BY	Marvin Gaye & Tammi Terrell	1969
GOOD LOVIN' GONE BAD	Bad Company	1975

SONG TITLE	ARTIST	DATE
GOOD LUCK	Basement Jaxx featuring Lisa Kekaula	2004
GOOD MORNING	Leapy Lee	1969
GOOD MORNING BEAUTIFUL	Steve Holy	2001
GOOD MORNING BRITAIN	Aztec Camera	1990
GOOD MORNING FREEDOM	Blue Mink	1970
GOOD MORNING HEARTACHE	Diana Ross	1973
GOOD MORNING JUDGE	10cc	1977
GOOD MORNING STARSHINE	Oliver	1969
GOOD MORNING SUNSHINE	Aqua	1998
GOOD NEWS	Sam Cooke	1964
GOOD OLD ARSENAL	Arsenal F.C. First Team Squad	1971
GOOD OLD ROCK 'N' ROLL	Dave Clark Five	1969
GOOD OLD ROCK 'N' ROLL	Cat Mother & The All Night News Boys	1969
GOOD RHYMES	Da Click	1999
GOOD SONG	Blur	2003
GOOD SOULS	Starsailor	2001
GOOD STUFF	B-52's	1992

SONG TITLE	ARTIST	DATE
GOOD STUFF	Kelis	2000
THE GOOD STUFF	Kenny Chesney	2002
GOOD SWEET LOVIN'	Louchie Lou & Michie One	1996
GOOD THING	Eternal	1996
GOOD THING	Fine Young Cannibals	1989
GOOD THING	Paul Revere & The Raiders	1966
GOOD THING GOING	Sid Owen	2000
GOOD THING GOING (WE'VE GOT A GOOD THING GOING)	Sugar Minott	1981
GOOD TIME	Peran	2002
GOOD TIME	A	2003
GOOD TIMES	Edie Brickell	1994
GOOD TIMES	Jimmy Barnes & INXS	1991
GOOD TIMES	Chic	1979
GOOD TIMES	Sam Cooke	1964
GOOD TIMES	Styles	2002
GOOD TIMES (BETTER TIMES)	Cliff Richard	1969
GOOD TIMIN'	Beach Boys	1979
GOOD TO BE ALIVE	DJ Rap	1998
GOOD TO GO LOVER/OUTSIDE IN THE RAIN	Gwen Guthrie	1987
GOOD TRADITION	Tanita Tikaram	1988
GOOD VIBRATIONS	Beach Boys	1966
GOOD VIBRATIONS	Marky Mark & The Funky Bunch	1991

SONG TITLE	ARTIST	DATE
GOOD VIBRATIONS	Todd Rundgren	1976
A GOOD YEAR FOR THE ROSES	Elvis Costello	1981
THE GOOD, THE BAD & THE UGLY	Hugo Montenegro & His Orchestra	1968
GOODBYE	Sundays	1992
GOODBYE	Mary Hopkin	1969
GOODBYE	Spice Girls	1998
GOODBYE	Coral	2002
GOODBYE	Night Ranger	1985
GOODBYE BABY (BABY GOODBYE)	Solomon Burke	1964
GOODBYE BABY AND AMEN	Lulu	1994
GOODBYE CRUEL WORLD	Shakespear's Sister	1992
GOODBYE EARL	Dixie Chicks	2000
GOODBYE GIRL	Go West	1985
GOODBYE GIRL	David Gates	1977
GOODBYE HEARTBREAK	Lighthouse Family	1996
GOODBYE IS JUST ANOTHER WORD	New Seekers	1973
GOODBYE MY LOVE	Glitter Band	1975
GOODBYE MY LOVE	Searchers	1965
GOODBYE MY LOVE	James Brown	1968

SONG TITLE	ARTIST	DATE
GOODBYE NOTHING TO SAY		
	Javells featuring Nosmo King	1974
GOODBYE SAM, HELLO SAMANTHA		
	Cliff Richard	1970
GOODBYE STRANGER	Pepsi & Shirlie	1987
GOODBYE STRANGER	Supertramp	1979
GOODBYE TO LOVE	Carpenters	1972
GOODBYE TO MY HOMIES		
	Master P featuring Silkk The Shocker	1998
GOODBYE TO YOU	Michelle Branch	2002
GOODBYE YELLOW BRICK ROAD		
	Elton John	1973
GOODBYE'S (THE SADDEST WORD)		
	Celine Dion	2002
GOODBYE-EE	14-18	1975
GOODBYE-EE	Peter Cook & Dudley Moore	1965
GOODGROOVE	Derek B	1988
GOODIES	Ciara featuring Petey Pablo	2004
GOODNIGHT	Babybird	1996
GOODNIGHT	Roy Orbison	1965
GOODNIGHT GIRL	Wet Wet Wet	1992
GOODNIGHT MIDNIGHT	Clodagh Rodgers	1969
GOODNIGHT MY LOVE	Paul Anka	1969
GOODNIGHT TONIGHT	Paul McCartney	1979

SONG TITLE	ARTIST	DATE
GOODTIME CHARLIE'S GOT THE BLUES		
	Danny O'Keefe	1972
GOODY GOODY GUMDROPS		
	1910 Fruitgum Co.	1968
GOODY TWO SHOES	Adam Ant	1982
GOOGLE EYE	Nashville Teens	1964
THE GOONIES 'R' GOOD ENOUGH		
	Cyndi Lauper	1985
GORECKI	Lamb	1997
GOSPEL OAK EP	Sinead O'Connor	1997
GOSSIP FOLKS	Missy Elliott featuring Ludacris	2003
GOT 'TIL IT'S GONE	Janet featuring Q-Tip and Joni Mitchell	1997
GOT A FEELING	Patrick Juvet	1978
GOT A HOLD ON ME	Christine McVie	1984
GOT A LOVE FOR YOU	Jomanda	1991
GOT ME WAITING	Heavy D. & The Boyz	1994
GOT MY MIND SET ON YOU		
	George Harrison	1987
GOT SOME TEETH	Obie Trice	2003
GOT THE FEELIN'	5ive	1998
GOT THE LIFE	Korn	1998
GOT THE TIME	Anthrax	1991
GOT TO BE CERTAIN	Kylie Minogue	1988
GOT TO BE REAL	Cheryl Lynn	1978
GOT TO BE THERE	Michael Jackson	1971

SONG TITLE	ARTIST	DATE
GOT TO GET	Rob 'n' Raz featuring Leila K	1989
GOT TO GET IT	Culture Beat	1993
GOT TO GET IT	Sisqo	2000
GOT TO GET UP	Afrika Bambaataa	1998
GOT TO GET YOU BACK	Kym Mazelle	1989
GOT TO GET YOU INTO MY LIFE	Earth, Wind & Fire	1978
GOT TO GET YOU INTO MY LIFE	Cliff Bennett & The Rebel Rousers	1966
GOT TO GET YOU INTO MY LIFE	Beatles	1976
GOT TO GET YOU OFF MY MIND	Solomon Burke	1965
GOT TO GIVE IT UP	Aaliyah	1996
GOT TO GIVE IT UP	Marvin Gaye	1977
GOT TO GIVE ME LOVE	Dana Dawson	1995
GOT TO HAVE YOUR LOVE	Mantronix featuring Wondress	1990
GOT TO HAVE YOUR LOVE	Liberty X	2002
GOT TO KEEP ON	Cookie Crew	1989
GOT TO LOVE SOMEBODY	Sister Sledge	1980
GOT UR SELF A...	Nas	2002
GOT YOU	Pharoahe Monch	2001
GOT YOUR MONEY	Ol' Dirty Bastard featuring Kelis	1999
GOTHAM CITY	R. Kelly	1997

SONG TITLE	ARTIST	DATE
GOTS TA BE	B2K	2002
GOTTA BE	Jagged Edge	1998
GOTTA BE YOU	3T	1997
GOTTA GET IT RIGHT	Lena Fiagbe	1993
GOTTA GET THRU THIS	Daniel Bedingfield	2002
GOTTA GET YOU HOME TONIGHT	Eugene Wilde	1984
GOTTA GO HOME/EL LUTE	Boney M	1979
GOTTA HOLD ON TO THIS FEELING	Jr. Walker & The All Stars	1970
GOTTA LOTTA LOVE	Ice-T	1994
GOTTA MAN	Eve	1999
GOTTA PULL MYSELF TOGETHER	Nolans	1980
GOTTA SEE JANE	R. Dean Taylor	1968
GOTTA SERVE SOMEBODY	Bob Dylan	1979
GOTTA TELL YOU	Samantha Mumba	2000
GOURYELLA	Gouryella	1999
GOVINDA	Kula Shaker	1996
GOVINDA	Radha Krishna Temple	1970
GRACE	Supergrass	2002
GRACEADELICA	Dark Star	2000
GRADUATION (FRIENDS FOREVER)	Vitamin C	2000
GRAND PIANO	Mixmaster	1989
GRANDAD	Clive Dunn	1970

SONG TITLE	ARTIST	DATE
GRANDMA'S PARTY	Paul Nicholas	1976
GRANDPA'S PARTY	Monie Love	1989
GRAPEVYNE	Brownstone	1995
GRAVEL PIT	Wu-Tang Clan	2000
GRAVITY	Embrace	2004
GRAZIN' IN THE GRASS	Friends Of Distinction	1969
GRAZING IN THE GRASS	Hugh Masekela	1968
GREASE	Frankie Valli	1978
THE GREASE MEGAMIX	John Travolta and Olivia Newton-John	1990
GREASED LIGHTNING	John Travolta	1978
THE GREAT AIRPLANE STRIKE	Paul Revere & The Raiders	1966
THE GREAT BEYOND	R.E.M.	2000
THE GREAT ESCAPE 2000	England Supporters' Band	2000
THE GREAT PRETENDER	Freddie Mercury	1987
THE GREAT ROCK'N'ROLL SWINDLE/ROCK AROUND THE CLOCK	Sex Pistols	1979
THE GREAT SONG OF INDIFFERENCE	Bob Geldof	1990
THE GREAT TEST	Hundred Reasons	2003
GREAT THINGS	Echobelly	1995
THE GREATEST COCKNEY RIP-OFF	Cockney Rejects	1980
GREATEST DAY	Beverley Knight	1999
THE GREATEST FLAME	Runrig	1997

SONG TITLE	ARTIST	DATE
GREATEST LOVE OF ALL	Whitney Houston	1986
THE GREATEST LOVE OF ALL	George Benson	1977
THE GREATEST LOVE YOU'LL NEVER KNOW	Lutricia McNeal	1998
THE GREATEST SHOW ON EARTH	Strangelove	1997
GREECE 2000	Three Drives	1999
GREED/THE MAN WITH THE RED FACE	Laurent Garnier	2000
GREEDY FLY	Bush	1997
GREEN AND GREY	New Model Army	1989
GREEN DOOR	Shakin' Stevens	1981
GREEN EYED LADY	Sugarloaf	1970
GREEN GRASS	Gary Lewis & The Playboys	1966
GREEN GREEN GRASS OF HOME	Elvis Presley	1975
GREEN GREEN GRASS OF HOME	Tom Jones	1966
GREEN LIGHT	American Breed	1968
THE GREEN MANALISHI	Fleetwood Mac	1970
GREEN ONIONS	Booker T. & The MG's	1979
GREEN RIVER	Creedence Clearwater Revival	1969
GREEN STREET GREEN	New Vaudeville Band	1967
GREEN TAMBOURINE	Lemon Pipers	1967

SONG TITLE	ARTIST	DATE
GREY DAY	Madness	1981
GRIMLY FIENDISH	Damned	1985
GRIND	Alice In Chains	1995
GRINDIN'	Clipse	2002
GRIP '89 (GET A) GRIP (ON YOURSELF)		
	Stranglers	1989
THE GROOVE	Rodney Franklin	1980
GROOVE IS IN THE HEART	Deee-Lite	1990
THE GROOVE LINE	Heatwave	1978
GROOVE MACHINE	Marvin And Tamara	1999
GROOVE ME	King Floyd	1970
GROOVE OF LOVE	Eve	1994
GROOVE THANG	Zhane	1994
GROOVEBIRD	Natural Born Grooves	1997
GROOVEJET (IF THIS AIN'T LOVE)		
	Spiller	2000
GROOVELINE	Blockster	1999
THE GROOVER	T. Rex	1973
GROOVIN'	Pato Banton & The Reggae Revolution	1996
GROOVIN'	Young Rascals	1967
GROOVIN'	Booker T. & The MG's	1967
GROOVIN' WITH MR. BLOE		
	Mr. Bloe	1970
GROOVIN' (YOU'RE THE BEST THING/BIG BOSS GROOVE)		
	Style Council	1984

SONG TITLE	ARTIST	DATE
GROOVY BABY	Microbe	1969
GROOVY GRUBWORM	Harlow Wilcox	1969
GROOVY KIND OF LOVE	Phil Collins	1988
A GROOVY KIND OF LOVE		
	Mindbenders	1966
A GROOVY KIND OF LOVE		
	Les Gray	1977
GROOVY SITUATION	Gene Chandler	1970
GROOVY TRAIN	Farm	1990
GROUND LEVEL	Stereo MC's	1993
GROUNDED	My Vitriol	2001
GROUPIE GIRL	Tony Joe White	1970
GROW SOME FUNK OF YOUR OWN/I FEEL LIKE A BULLET	Elton John	1976
GROWING ON ME	Darkness	2003
GROWN MEN DON'T CRY	Tim McGraw	2001
GUAGLIONE	Perez 'Prez' Prado & His Orchestra	1995
GUANTANAMERA	Wyclef Jean And The Refugee Allstars	1997
GUANTANAMERA	Sandpipers	1966
GUARANTEED	Level 42	1991
GUARDIANS OF THE LAND	George Bowyer	1998
GUDBUY T'JANE	Slade	1972
GUERILLA FUNK	Paris	1995
GUERRILLA RADIO	Rage Against The Machine	1999

SONG TITLE	ARTIST	DATE
GUESS I WAS A FOOL	Another Level	1998
GUESS WHO'S BACK	Rakim	1997
GUIDING STAR	Cast	1997
GUILTY	Mike Oldfield	1979
GUILTY	Jim Reeves	1963
GUILTY	Pearls	1974
GUILTY	Barbra Streisand & Barry Gibb	1980
GUILTY	Blue	2003
GUILTY	The Rasmus	2004
GUILTY CONSCIENCE	Eminem featuring Dr. Dre	1999
GUILTY OF LOVE	Whitesnake	1983
GUITAR BOOGIE SHUFFLE	Virtues	1969
GUITAR MAN	Bread	1972
GUITAR MAN	Elvis Presley	1981
GUNATANAMO	Outlandish	2003
GUNMAN	187 Lockdown	1997
GUNS DON'T KILL PEOPLE RAPPERS DO		
	Goldie Lookin Chain	2004
GUNS FOR HIRE	AC/DC	1983
GUNS OF NAVARONE	Skatalites	1967
GYM AND TONIC	Spacedust	1998
GYPSY	Fleetwood Mac	1982
GYPSY MAN	War	1973
GYPSY WOMAN	Brian Hyland	1970
GYPSY WOMAN	Crystal Waters	1991

SONG TITLE	ARTIST	DATE
GYPSYS, TRAMPS AND THIEVES		
	Cher	1971
H! VLTG3/PTS.OF.ATHRTY	Linkin Park	2002
H.A.P.P.Y. RADIO	Edwin Starr	1979
HA CHA CHA (FUNKTION)	Brass Construction	1977
HA! HA! SAID THE CLOWN	Manfred Mann	1967
HAD TO BE	Cliff Richard & Olivia Newton-John	1995
HAIR	Cowsills	1969
THE HAIR ON MY CHINNY CHIN CHIN		
	Sam The Sham & The Pharaohs	1966
HAITIAN DIVORCE	Steely Dan	1976
HALF A HEART	H & Claire	2002
HALF A MINUTE	Matt Bianco	1984
HALF MAN HALF MACHINE/SELF SUICIDE		
	Goldie Lookin Chain	2004
HALF ON A BABY	R. Kelly	1998
HALF THE MAN	Jamiroquai	1994
HALF THE WAY	Crystal Gayle	1979
HALF THE WORLD	Belinda Carlisle	1992
HALF-BREED	Cher	1973
HALFCRAZY	Musiq	2002
HALFWAY AROUND THE WORLD		
	A Teens	2001
HALFWAY DOWN THE STAIRS		
	Muppets	1977

SONG TITLE	ARTIST	DATE
HALFWAY HOTEL	Voyager	1979
HALFWAY TO PARADISE	Bobby Vinton	1968
HALLELUJAH	Milk & Honey	1979
HALLELUJAH	Sweathog	1971
HALLELUJAH '92	Inner City	1992
HALLELUJAH DAY	Jackson 5	1973
HALLELUJAH FREEDOM	Junior Campbell	1972
HALLO SPACEBOY	David Bowie	1996
HALLOWED BE THY NAME	Iron Maiden	1993
HALO	Texas	1997
(HAMMER HAMMER) THEY PUT ME IN THE MIX		
	M.C. Hammer	1991
HAMMER TO FALL	Queen	1984
HAMMER TO THE HEART	Tamperer featuring Maya	2000
HAND HELD IN BLACK & WHITE		
	Dollar	1981
HAND IN GLOVE	Sandie Shaw	1984
HAND IN HAND	Grace	1997
HAND IN MY POCKET	Alanis Morissette	1995
HAND IN YOUR HEAD	Money Mark	1998
HAND ME DOWN WORLD	Guess Who	1970
HAND ON YOUR HEART	Kylie Minogue	1989
HAND TO HOLD ON TO	John Cougar	1982
HANDBAGS AND GLADRAGS		
	Chris Farlowe	1967

SONG TITLE	ARTIST	DATE
HANDBAGS AND GLADRAGS		
	Stereophonics	2001
HANDFUL OF PROMISES	Big Fun	1990
HANDLE WITH CARE	Traveling Wilburys	1988
HANDS	Jewel	1998
HANDS ACROSS THE OCEAN		
	Mission	1990
HANDS AROUND MY THROAT		
	Death In Vegas	2002
HANDS CLEAN	Alanis Morissette	2002
HANDS OFF – SHE'S MINE	Beat	1980
HANDS TO HEAVEN	Breathe	1988
HANDS UP	Trevor & Simon	2000
HANDS UP (GIVE ME YOUR HEART)		
	Ottawan	1981
HANDS UP! HANDS UP!	Zig And Zag	1995
HANDY MAN	Del Shannon	1964
HANDY MAN	James Taylor	1977
HANG 'EM HIGH	Booker T. & The MG's	1968
HANG FIRE	Rolling Stones	1982
HANG IN LONG ENOUGH	Phil Collins	1990
HANG ON IN THERE BABY	Johnny Bristol	1974
HANG ON IN THERE BABY	Curiosity	1992
HANG ON NOW	Kajagoogoo	1983
HANG ON SLOOPY	McCoys	1965
HANG ON SLOOPY	Sandpipers	1976

SONG TITLE	ARTIST	DATE
HANG ON SLOOPY	Ramsey Lewis Trio	1965
HANG ON TO YOUR LOVE	Jason Donovan	1990
HANG TOGETHER	Odyssey	1981
HANG YOUR HEAD (EP)	Deacon Blue	1993
HANGAR 18	Megadeth	1991
HANGIN' ON A STRING	Loose Ends	1985
HANGIN' TOUGH	New Kids On The Block	1989
HANGINAROUND	Counting Crows	1999
HANGING AROUND	Cardigans	1999
HANGING AROUND	Me Me Me	1996
HANGING AROUND	The Polyphonic Spree	2002
HANGING BY A MOMENT	Lifehouse	2001
HANGING GARDEN	Cure	1982
HANGING ON A HEART ATTACK		
	Device	1986
HANGING ON THE TELEPHONE		
	Blondie	1978
HANKY PANKY	Tommy James & The Shondells	1966
HANKY PANKY	Madonna	1990
HAPPENIN' ALL OVER AGAIN		
	Lonnie Gordon	1990
THE HAPPENING	Supremes	1967
THE HAPPENING	Herb Alpert & The Tijuana Brass	1967
HAPPENINGS TEN YEARS TIME AGO		
	Yardbirds	1966

SONG TITLE	ARTIST	DATE
THE HAPPIEST GIRL IN THE WHOLE U.S.A.		
	Donna Fargo	1972
HAPPILY EVER AFTER	Case	1999
HAPPINESS	Ken Dodd	1964
HAPPINESS	Pizzaman	1995
HAPPINESS	Sound-De-Zign	2001
HAPPINESS?	Roger Taylor	1994
HAPPINESS	Pointer Sisters	1979
HAPPINESS HAPPENING	Lost Witness	1999
HAPPINESS IS JUST AROUND THE BEND		
	Main Ingredient	1974
HAPPINESS IS ME AND YOU		
	Gilbert O'Sullivan	1974
HAPPY	Travis	1997
HAPPY	Ned's Atomic Dustbin	1991
HAPPY	MN8	1995
HAPPY	Ashanti	2002
HAPPY	Max Sedgley	2004
HAPPY	Rolling Stones	1972
HAPPY	Surface	1987
HAPPY ANNIVERSARY	Slim Whitman	1974
HAPPY ANNIVERSARY	Little River Band	1977
HAPPY BIRTHDAY	Altered Images	1981
HAPPY BIRTHDAY	Stevie Wonder	1981
HAPPY BIRTHDAY	Technohead	1996

SONG TITLE	ARTIST	DATE
HAPPY DAYS	Pratt And McClain with Brotherlove	1977
HAPPY EVER AFTER	Julia Fordham	1988
HAPPY HEART	Andy Williams	1969
HAPPY HOME	2Pac	1998
HAPPY HOUR	Housemartins	1986
HAPPY HOUSE	Siouxsie & The Banshees	1980
HAPPY JACK	Who	1967
HAPPY JUST TO BE WITH YOU	Michelle Gayle	1995
HAPPY MUSIC	Blackbyrds	1976
HAPPY NATION	Ace Of Base	1994
HAPPY PEOPLE	Temptations	1974
HAPPY PEOPLE	Static Revenger	2001
HAPPY PEOPLE/U SAVED ME	R. Kelly	2004
HAPPY SHOPPER	60ft Dolls	1996
THE HAPPY SONG (DUM-DUM)	Otis Redding	1968
HAPPY SUMMER DAYS	Ronnie Dove	1966
HAPPY TALK	Captain Sensible	1982
HAPPY TO BE ON AN ISLAND IN THE SUN	Demis Roussos	1975
HAPPY TOGETHER	Jason Donovan	1991
HAPPY TOGETHER	Turtles	1967
HAPPY WHEN IT RAINS	Jesus & Mary Chain	1987

SONG TITLE	ARTIST	DATE
HAPPY XMAS (WAR IS OVER)	John And Yoko & The Plastic Ono Band	1980
HAPPY XMAS (WAR IS OVER)	Idols	2003
HARD AS A ROCK	AC/DC	1995
A HARD DAY'S NIGHT	Beatles	1964
A HARD DAY'S NIGHT	Peter Sellers	1965
A HARD DAY'S NIGHT	Ramsey Lewis	1966
HARD HABIT TO BREAK	Chicago	1984
HARD KNOCK LIFE (GHETTO ANTHEM)	Jay-Z	1998
HARD LUCK WOMAN	Kiss	1976
A HARD RAIN'S A-GONNA FALL	Bryan Ferry	1973
HARD ROAD	Black Sabbath	1978
HARD ROCK CAFE	Carole King	1977
HARD TIMES COME EASY	Richie Sambora	1998
HARD TO EXPLAIN/NEW YORK CITY COPS	Strokes	2001
HARD TO HANDLE	Black Crowes	1990
HARD TO HANDLE	Otis Redding	1968
HARD TO MAKE A STAND	Sheryl Crow	1997
HARD TO SAY	Dan Fogelberg	1981
HARD TO SAY I'M SORRY	Az Yet featuring Peter Cetera	1997
HARD TO SAY I'M SORRY	Chicago	1982

SONG TITLE	ARTIST	DATE
HARD TO SAY I'M SORRY	Aquagen	2003
HARDCORE HEAVEN/YOU AND ME		
	DJ Seduction	1992
HARDCORE UPROAR	Together	1990
HARDEN MY HEART	Quarterflash	1981
HARDER BETTER FASTER STRONGER		
	Daft Punk	2001
THE HARDER I TRY	Brother Beyond	1988
THE HARDER THEY COME	Rockers Revenge featuring	
	Donnie Calvin	1983
THE HARDER THEY COME	Oakenfold	2003
HARDER TO BREATHE	Maroon5	2004
THE HARDEST BUTTON TO BUTTON		
	White Stripes	2003
THE HARDEST THING	98 Degrees	1999
HARE KRISHNA	Radha Krishna Temple	1969
HARLEM DESIRE	London Boys	1989
HARLEM NOCTURNE	Viscounts	1959
HARLEM SHUFFLE	Bob & Earl	1969
HARLEM SHUFFLE	Rolling Stones	1986
HARMONIC GENERATOR	Datsuns	2003
HARMONICA MAN	Bravado	1994
HARMONY IN MY HEAD	Buzzcocks	1979
HARMOUR LOVE	Syreeta	1975
HARPER VALLEY P.T.A.	Jeannie C. Riley	1968
HARRY HIPPIE	Bobby Womack	1972

SONG TITLE	ARTIST	DATE
HARRY TRUMAN	Chicago	1975
HARVEST FOR THE WORLD		
	Christians	1988
HARVEST FOR THE WORLD		
	Isley Brothers	1976
HARVEST MOON	Neil Young	1993
HARVEST OF LOVE	Benny Hill	1963
HARVESTER OF SORROW	Metallica	1988
HAS IT COME TO THIS	Streets	2001
HASH PIPE	Weezer	2001
HASTA LA VISTA	Sylvia	1975
HAT 2 DA BACK	TLC	1993
HATE ME NOW	Nas featuring Puff Daddy	1999
HATE TO SAY I TOLD YOU SO		
	Hives	2002
HATERS	So Solid Crew presents	
	Mr. Shabz	2002
HAUNTED	Shane MacGowan &	
	Sinead O'Connor	1995
HAUNTED BY YOU	Gene	1995
HAUNTED HOUSE	Gene Simmons	1964
HAVA NAGILA	Spotnicks	1963
HAVE A CHEEKY CHRISTMAS		
	Cheeky Girls	2003
HAVE A NICE DAY	Stereophonics	2001
HAVE FUN GO MAD	Tweenies	2002

SONG TITLE	ARTIST	DATE
HAVE FUN, GO MAD!	Blair	1995
HAVE I THE RIGHT?	Dead End Kids	1977
HAVE I THE RIGHT?	Honeycombs	1964
HAVE I TOLD YOU LATELY	Rod Stewart	1993
HAVE IT ALL	Foo Fighters	2003
HAVE PITY ON THE BOY	Paul & Barry Ryan	1966
HAVE YOU EVER	S Club 7	2001
HAVE YOU EVER BEEN IN LOVE		
	Leo Sayer	1982
HAVE YOU EVER HAD IT BLUE		
	Style Council	1986
HAVE YOU EVER LOVED SOMEBODY		
	Freddie Jackson	1987
HAVE YOU EVER?	Brandy	1998
HAVE YOU EVER NEEDED SOMEONE SO BAD		
	Def Leppard	1992
HAVE YOU EVER REALLY LOVED A WOMAN?		
	Bryan Adams	1995
HAVE YOU EVER SEEN THE RAIN?		
	Creedence Clearwater Revival	1971
HAVE YOU FORGOTTEN?	Darryl Worley	2003
HAVE YOU LOOKED INTO YOUR HEART		
	Jerry Vale	1964
HAVE YOU NEVER BEEN MELLOW		
	Olivia Newton-John	1975
HAVE YOU SEEN HER	M.C. Hammer	1990

SONG TITLE	ARTIST	DATE
HAVE YOU SEEN HER	Chi-Lites	1975
HAVE YOU SEEN YOUR MOTHER BABY STANDING IN THE SHADOW?	Rolling Stones	1966
HAVEN'T GOT TIME FOR THE PAIN		
	Carly Simon	1974
HAVEN'T STOPPED DANCING YET		
	Gonzalez	1979
HAVING A PARTY	Osmonds	1975
HAVING A PARTY	Rod Stewart	1994
HAWAII FIVE-O	Ventures	1969
HAWAII TATTOO	Waikikis	1964
HAWAIIAN WEDDING SONG		
	Julie Rogers	1965
HAY	Crucial Conflict	1996
HAZARD	Richard Marx	1992
HAZEL	Loop Da Loop	1999
HAZELL	Maggie Bell	1978
HAZIN' & PHAZIN'	Choo Choo Project	2000
HAZY SHADE OF WINTER	Bangles	1987
A HAZY SHADE OF WINTER		
	Simon & Garfunkel	1966
HE	Righteous Brothers	1966
HE AIN'T HEAVY, HE'S MY BROTHER		
	Neil Diamond	1970
HE AIN'T HEAVY, HE'S MY BROTHER		
	Hollies	1969

SONG TITLE	ARTIST	DATE
HE AIN'T HEAVY, HE'S MY BROTHER		
	Bill Medley	1988
HE AIN'T NO COMPETITION		
	Brother Beyond	1988
HE CAN'T LOVE U	Jagged Edge	1999
HE CAN'T LOVE YOU	Michael Stanley Band	1980
HE DIDN'T HAVE TO BE	Brad Paisley	1999
HE DON'T LOVE YOU	Human Nature	2001
HE DON'T LOVE YOU (LIKE I LOVE YOU)		
	Tony Orlando & Dawn	1975
HE GOT GAME	Public Enemy	1998
HE KNOWS YOU KNOW	Marillion	1983
HE LOVES U NOT	Dream	2001
HE WAS BEAUTIFUL (CAVATINA)		
	Iris Williams	1979
HE WASN'T MAN ENOUGH	Toni Braxton	2000
HE'LL HAVE TO GO	Jim Reeves	1971
HE'LL NEVER LOVE YOU (LIKE I DO)		
	Freddie Jackson	1985
HE'S A FRIEND	Eddie Kendricks	1976
HE'S A LIAR	Bee Gees	1981
HE'S GONNA STEP ON YOU AGAIN		
	John Kongos	1971
HE'S GOT NO LOVE	Searchers	1965
HE'S IN TOWN	Rockin' Berries	1964
HE'S MINE	Mokenstef	1995

SONG TITLE	ARTIST	DATE
HE'S MISSTRA KNOW-IT-ALL		
	Stevie Wonder	1974
HE'S ON THE PHONE	Saint Etienne	1995
HE'S SO FINE	Chiffons	1963
HE'S SO SHY	Pointer Sisters	1980
HE'S THE GREATEST DANCER		
	Sister Sledge	1979
HE'S THE ONE	Billie Davis	1963
HEAD GAMES	Foreigner	1979
HEAD OVER FEET	Alanis Morissette	1996
HEAD OVER HEELS	ABBA	1982
HEAD OVER HEELS	Allure featuring Nas	1997
HEAD OVER HEELS	Tears For Fears	1985
HEAD OVER HEELS	Go-Go's	1984
HEAD OVER HEELS IN LOVE		
	Kevin Keegan	1979
HEAD TO TOE	Lisa Lisa & Cult Jam	1987
HEADED FOR A FALL	Firefall	1980
HEADED FOR A HEARTBREAK		
	Winger	1989
HEADLINE NEWS	Edwin Starr	1966
HEADLINES	Midnight Star	1986
HEADLONG	Queen	1991
HEADS HIGH	Mr. Vegas	1999
HEADSPRUNG	LL Cool J	2004
HEAL	Shamen	1996

SONG TITLE	ARTIST	DATE
HEAL THE PAIN	George Michael	1991
HEAL THE WORLD	Michael Jackson	1992
HEALING HANDS	Elton John	1989
HEALING LOVE	Cliff Richard	1993
HEAR MY NAME	Armand Van Helden featuring Spalding Rockwell	2004
HEAR THE DRUMMER (GET WICKED)	Chad Jackson	1990
HEAR YOU CALLING	Aurora	2000
HEARD IT ALL BEFORE	Sunshine Anderson	2001
HEARD IT IN A LOVE SONG	Marshall Tucker Band	1977
HEART	Rita Pavone	1966
HEART	Pet Shop Boys	1988
HEART (DON'T CHANGE MY MIND)	Diana Ross	1993
HEART (STOP BEATING IN TIME)	Leo Sayer	1982
HEART AND SOUL	T'Pau	1987
HEART AND SOUL	Huey Lewis & The News	1983
HEART ATTACK	Olivia Newton-John	1982
HEART FULL OF SOUL	Yardbirds	1965
HEART HOTELS	Dan Fogelberg	1980
HEART LIKE A WHEEL	Human League	1990
HEART LIKE A WHEEL	Steve Miller Band	1981
HEART OF ASIA	Watergate	2000

SONG TITLE	ARTIST	DATE
HEART OF GLASS	Blondie	1979
HEART OF GOLD	Johnny Hates Jazz	1988
HEART OF GOLD	Neil Young	1972
HEART OF GOLD	Kelly Llorenna	2002
HEART OF LOTHIAN	Marillion	1985
HEART OF MINE	Boz Scaggs	1988
THE HEART OF ROCK 'N' ROLL	Huey Lewis & The News	1984
HEART OF STONE	Dave Stewart	1994
HEART OF STONE	Kenny	1973
HEART OF STONE	Cher	1990
HEART OF STONE	Taylor Dayne	1990
HEART OF STONE	Rolling Stones	1965
THE HEART OF THE MATTER	Don Henley	1990
HEART OF THE NIGHT	Juice Newton	1982
HEART OF THE NIGHT	Poco	1979
HEART ON MY SLEEVE	Gallagher & Lyle	1976
HEART OVER MIND	Kim Wilde	1992
HEART TO HEART	Kenny Loggins	1982
THE HEART'S FILTHY LESSON	David Bowie	1995
THE HEART'S LONE DESIRE	Matthew Marsden	1998
HEART-SHAPED BOX	Nirvana	1993
HEARTACHE	Pepsi & Shirlie	1987

SONG TITLE	ARTIST	DATE
HEARTACHE AVENUE	Maisonettes	1982
HEARTACHE TONIGHT	Eagles	1979
HEARTACHES	Vince Hill	1966
HEARTACHES BY THE NUMBER		
	Johnny Tillotson	1965
HEARTBEAT	Jimmy Somerville	1995
HEARTBEAT	Nick Berry	1992
HEARTBEAT	Showaddywaddy	1975
HEARTBEAT	Don Johnson	1986
HEARTBEAT	Seduction	1990
HEARTBEAT/TRAGEDY	Steps	1998
HEARTBEAT – IT'S A LOVEBEAT		
	DeFranco Family/Tony DeFranco	1973
HEARTBREAK BEAT	Psychedelic Furs	1987
HEARTBREAK HOTEL	Whitney Houston/Faith Evans/	
	Kelly Price	2000
HEARTBREAK HOTEL/HOUND DOG		
	Elvis Presley	1971
THE HEARTBREAK KID	Bo Donaldson & The Heywoods	1974
HEARTBREAK RADIO	Roy Orbison	1992
HEARTBREAKER	Mariah Carey featuring Jay-Z	1999
HEARTBREAKER	Dionne Warwick	1982
HEARTBREAKER	Pat Benatar	1979
HEARTBREAKER	Dolly Parton	1978
HEARTBREAK HOTEL	Jacksons	1980
HEARTHAMMER	Runrig	1991

SONG TITLE	ARTIST	DATE
HEARTLAND	The The	1986
HEARTLESS	Heart	1978
THE HEARTLESS THEME AKA 'THE SUPERGLUE RIDDIM'		
	Heartless Crew	2002
HEARTLIGHT	Neil Diamond	1982
HEARTS DON'T THINK THEY FEEL		
	Natural Selection	1991
HEARTS OF STONE	Blue Ridge Rangers	1973
HEARTS ON FIRE	Bryan Adams	1987
HEARTS ON FIRE	Randy Meisner	1981
HEARTSONG	Gordon Giltrap	1978
THE HEAT IS ON	Agnetha Faltskog	1983
THE HEAT IS ON	Glenn Frey	1984
HEAT IT UP	Two Men, A Drum Machine and	
	A Trumpet	1988
HEAT IT UP	Wee Papa Girl Rappers	1988
HEAT OF THE MOMENT	After 7	1989
HEAT OF THE MOMENT	Asia	1982
HEAT OF THE NIGHT	Bryan Adams	1987
HEAT WAVE/LOVE IS A ROSE		
	Linda Ronstadt	1975
HEATHER HONEY	Tommy Roe	1969
HEATSEEKER	AC/DC	1988
HEAVEN	Chimes	1990
HEAVEN	Solo (US)	1996
HEAVEN	Sarah Washington	1996

SONG TITLE	ARTIST	DATE
HEAVEN	Bryan Adams	1985
HEAVEN	Psychedelic Furs	1984
HEAVEN	DJ Sammy & Yanou featuring Do	2002
HEAVEN	Nu Flavor	1997
HEAVEN	Rascals	1969
HEAVEN	Warrant	1989
HEAVEN AND EARTH	Pop!	2004
HEAVEN BESIDE YOU	Alice In Chains	1996
HEAVEN FOR EVERYONE	Queen	1995
HEAVEN GIVE ME WORDS	Propaganda	1990
HEAVEN HELP	Lenny Kravitz	1993
HEAVEN HELP ME	Deon Estus	1989
HEAVEN HELP MY HEART	Tina Arena	1995
HEAVEN HELP US ALL	Stevie Wonder	1970
HEAVEN IN MY HANDS	Level 42	1988
HEAVEN IN YOUR EYES	Loverboy	1986
HEAVEN IS	Def Leppard	1993
HEAVEN IS A HALFPIPE	OPM	2001
HEAVEN IS A PLACE ON EARTH	Belinda Carlisle	1987
HEAVEN IS A PLACE ON EARTH	Soda Club featuring Hannah Alethea	2003
HEAVEN IS CLOSER (FEELS LIKE HEAVEN)	Dario G	2003
HEAVEN IS HERE	Julie Felix	1970

SONG TITLE	ARTIST	DATE
HEAVEN IS IN THE BACK SEAT OF MY CADILLAC	Hot Chocolate	1976
HEAVEN IS MY WOMAN'S LOVE	Val Doonican	1973
HEAVEN KNOWS	Luther Vandross	1993
HEAVEN KNOWS	Squeeze	1996
HEAVEN KNOWS	Robert Plant	1988
HEAVEN KNOWS	Donna Summer	1979
HEAVEN KNOWS	Grass Roots	1969
HEAVEN KNOWS I'M MISERABLE NOW	Smiths	1984
HEAVEN MUST BE MISSING AN ANGEL	Worlds Apart	1993
HEAVEN MUST BE MISSING AN ANGEL	Tavares	1976
HEAVEN MUST HAVE SENT YOU	Elgins	1971
HEAVEN MUST HAVE SENT YOU	Bonnie Pointer	1979
HEAVEN ON THE 7TH FLOOR	Paul Nicholas	1977
HEAVEN SCENT	Bedrock	1999
HEAVEN SENT	INXS	1992
HEAVEN WILL COME	Space Brothers	1999
HEAVEN'S WHAT I FEEL	Gloria Estefan	1998
HEAVENLY	Showaddywaddy	1975

SONG TITLE	ARTIST	DATE
HEAVY MAKES YOU HAPPY	Bobby Bloom	1971
HEAVY MAKES YOU HAPPY	Staple Singers	1971
HEDONISM (JUST BECAUSE YOU FEEL GOOD)	Skunk Anansie	1997
HEED THE CALL	Kenny Rogers & The First Edition	1970
HELEN WHEELS	Paul McCartney	1973
HELICOPTER	Bloc Party	2004
THE HELL EP	Tricky Vs The Gravediggaz	1995
HELL RAISER	Sweet	1973
THE HELL SONG	Sum 41	2003
HELL YEAH	Ginuwine	2003
HELLA GOOD	No Doubt	2002
HELLO	Beloved	1990
HELLO	Lionel Richie	1984
HELLO (TURN YOUR RADIO ON)	Shakespear's Sister	1992
HELLO AGAIN	Cars	1984
HELLO AGAIN	Neil Diamond	1981
HELLO BUDDY	Tremeloes	1971
HELLO DARLING	Tippa Irie	1986
HELLO, DOLLY!	Bachelors	1966
HELLO, DOLLY!	Kenny Ball	1964
HELLO, DOLLY!	Louis Armstrong	1964

SONG TITLE	ARTIST	DATE
HELLO, DOLLY!	Frankie Vaughan	1964
HELLO GOODBYE	Beatles	1967
HELLO HAPPINESS	Drifters	1976
HELLO HEARTACHE, GOODBYE LOVE	Little Peggy March	1963
HELLO HELLO	Sopwith Camel	1966
HELLO! HELLO! I'M BACK AGAIN	Gary Glitter	1973
HELLO, HOW ARE YOU	Easybeats	1968
HELLO HURRAY	Alice Cooper	1973
HELLO IT'S ME	Todd Rundgren	1973
HELLO, I LOVE YOU	Doors	1968
HELLO LITTLE GIRL	Fourmost	1963
HELLO MUDDUAH! HELLO FADDUH!	Allan Sherman	1963
HELLO OLD FRIEND	Eric Clapton	1976
HELLO, SUMMERTIME	Bobby Goldsboro	1974
HELLO STRANGER	Yvonne Elliman	1977
HELLO SUNSHINE	Super Furry Animals	2003
HELLO SUSIE	Amen Corner	1969
HELLO, THIS IS JOANNIE (THE TELEPHONE ANSWERING MACHINE SONG)	Paul Evans	1978
HELLO TIGER	Urusei Yatsura	1998
HELLO WORLD	Tremeloes	1969
HELP	Bananarama/Lananeeneenoonoo	1989
HELP	Tina Turner	1984

SONG TITLE	ARTIST	DATE
HELP!	Beatles	1965
HELP! I'M A FISH	Little Trees	2001
HELP IS ON ITS WAY	Little River Band	1977
HELP IT ALONG/TOMORROW RISING		
	Cliff Richard	1973
HELP ME	Nick Carter	2002
HELP ME	Joni Mitchell	1974
HELP ME GIRL	Outsiders	1966
HELP ME MAKE IT	Huff & Puff	1996
HELP ME MAKE IT THROUGH THE NIGHT		
	John Holt	1974
HELP ME MAKE IT THROUGH THE NIGHT		
	Gladys Knight & The Pips	1972
HELP ME MAKE IT THROUGH THE NIGHT		
	Sammi Smith	1971
HELP ME MAMA	Lemonescent	2003
HELP ME RHONDA	Johnny Rivers	1975
HELP ME, RHONDA	Beach Boys	1965
HELP POUR OUT THE RAIN (LACEY'S SONG)		
	Buddy Jewell	2003
HELP THE AGED	Pulp	1997
HELP YOURSELF	Tom Jones	1968
HELULE HELULE	Tremeloes	1968
HELYOM HALIB (ACID ACID ACID)		
	Cappella	1989

SONG TITLE	ARTIST	DATE
HEMORRHAGE (IN MY HANDS)		
	Fuel	2000
HENRY LEE	Nick Cave & The Bad Seeds	1996
HER TOWN TOO	James Taylor & J. D. Souther	1981
HERE 4 ONE	Blazin' Squad	2004
HERE AND NOW	Del Amitri	1995
HERE AND NOW	Luther Vandross	1989
HERE AND NOW/YOU'LL BE SORRY		
	Steps	2001
HERE COME THE GOOD TIMES		
	A House	1994
HERE COME THE NICE	Small Faces	1967
HERE COMES MY BABY	Tremeloes	1967
HERE COMES THAT RAINY DAY FEELING AGAIN		
	Fortunes	1971
HERE COMES THAT SOUND		
	Simon Harris	1988
HERE COMES THE HAMMER		
	M.C. Hammer	1991
HERE COMES THE HOTSTEPPER		
	Ini Kamoze	1994
HERE COMES THE JUDGE	Shorty Long	1968
HERE COMES THE JUDGE	Pigmeat Markham	1968
HERE COMES THE NIGHT	Them	1965
HERE COMES THE RAIN AGAIN		
	Eurythmics	1984

SONG TITLE	ARTIST	DATE
HERE COMES THE STAR	Herman's Hermits	1969
HERE COMES THE SUMMER		
	Undertones	1979
HERE COMES THE SUN	Steve Harley	1976
HERE COMES THE SUN	Richie Havens	1971
HERE COMES THE WAR	New Model Army	1993
HERE COMES THOSE TEARS AGAIN		
	Jackson Browne	1977
HERE FOR THE PARTY	Gretchen Wilson	2004
HERE I AM	Bryan Adams	2002
HERE I AM (COME AND TAKE ME)		
	Al Green	1973
HERE I AM (COME AND TAKE ME)		
	UB40	1991
HERE I AM (JUST WHEN YOU THOUGHT I WAS OVER		
YOU)	Air Supply	1981
HERE I COME (SING DJ)	Talisman P featuring	
	Barrington Levy	2001
HERE I GO	2 Unlimited	1995
HERE I GO AGAIN	Archie Bell & The Drells	1972
HERE I GO AGAIN	Hollies	1964
HERE I GO AGAIN	Twiggy	1976
HERE I GO AGAIN	Guys And Dolls	1975
HERE I GO AGAIN	Smokey Robinson & The Miracles	1969
HERE I GO AGAIN/BLOODY LUXURY		
	Whitesnake	1982

SONG TITLE	ARTIST	DATE
HERE I STAND	Bitty McLean	1994
HERE IS GONE	Goo Goo Dolls	2002
HERE IT COMES AGAIN	Fortunes	1965
HERE IT COMES AGAIN	Melanie C	2003
HERE SHE COMES AGAIN	Stands	2004
HERE TO STAY	New Order	2002
HERE TO STAY	Korn	2002
HERE WE ARE	Gloria Estefan	1989
HERE WE GO	C&C Music Factory (featuring	
	Freedom Williams)	1991
HERE WE GO	Everton 1985	1985
HERE WE GO	Stakka Bo	1993
HERE WE GO AGAIN	Ray Charles	1967
HERE WE GO AGAIN!	Portrait	1992
HERE WE GO ROUND THE MULBERRY BUSH		
	Traffic	1967
HERE WITH ME	Dido	2001
HERE WITH ME	REO Speedwagon	1988
HERE YOU COME AGAIN	Dolly Parton	1977
HERE'S TO LOVE (AULD LANG SYNE)		
	John Christie	1976
HERE'S TO THE NIGHT	Eve 6	2001
HERE'S WHERE THE STORY ENDS		
	Tin Tin Out/Shelley Nelson	1998
HERE, THERE & EVERYWHERE		
	Emmylou Harris	1976

SONG TITLE	ARTIST	DATE
HERMANN LOVES PAULINE	Super Furry Animals	1997
HERO	Mariah Carey	1993
HERO	Enrique Iglesias	2001
HERO	Chad Kroeger & Josey Scott	2002
HERO OF THE DAY	Metallica	1996
HEROES	Roni Size/Reprazent	1997
HEROES	David Bowie	1977
THE HEROES	Shed Seven	1998
HEROES AND VILLAINS	Beach Boys	1967
HERSHAM BOYS	Sham 69	1979
HEY!	Julio Iglesias	1983
HEY BABY	No Doubt featuring Bounty Killer	2001
HEY BABY	Henry Lee Summer	1989
HEY BABY (THEY'RE PLAYING OUR SONG)	Buckinghams	1967
HEY BABY (UHH, AHH)	DJ Otzi	2001
HEY BABY (UNOFFICIAL WORLD CUP REMIX)	DJ Otzi	2002
HEY BIG BROTHER	Rare Earth	1971
HEY, BOBBA NEEDLE	Chubby Checker	1964
HEY BOY HEY GIRL	Chemical Brothers	1999
HEY CHILD	East 17	1997
HEY D.J.	Lighter Shade Of Brown	1994
HEY D.J. I CAN'T DANCE TO.../SKA TRAIN	Beatmasters/Betty Boo	1989

SONG TITLE	ARTIST	DATE
HEY DEANIE	Shaun Cassidy	1977
HEY DJ! (PLAY THAT SONG)	N-Tyce	1997
HEY DONNA	Rythm Syndicate	1991
HEY DUDE	Kula Shaker	1996
HEY GIRL	Small Faces	1966
HEY GIRL	Delays	2003
HEY GIRL (I LIKE YOUR STYLE)	Temptations	1973
HEY GIRL DON'T BOTHER ME	Tams	1971
HEY GIRL/I KNEW YOU WHEN	Donny Osmond	1971
HEY GOD	Bon Jovi	1996
HEY GOOD LOOKIN'	Bo Diddley	1965
HEY HARMONICA MAN	Stevie Wonder	1964
HEY JEALOUSY	Gin Blossoms	1993
HEY JEAN, HEY DEAN	Dean & Jean	1964
HEY JOE	Jimi Hendrix Experience	1966
HEY JOE	Leaves	1966
HEY JUDE	Beatles	1968
HEY JUDE	Wilson Pickett	1968
HEY JUPITER/PROFESSIONAL WIDOW	Tori Amos	1996
HEY LADIES	Beastie Boys	1989
HEY LAWDY MAMA	Steppenwolf	1970

SONG TITLE	ARTIST	DATE
HEY LEONARDO (SHE LIKES ME FOR ME)		
	Blessid Union Of Souls	1999
HEY, LEROY, YOUR MAMA'S CALLIN' YOU		
	Jimmy Castor	1966
HEY LITTLE GIRL	Ice House	1983
HEY LOVER	LL Cool J	1995
HEY MA	Cam'ron featuring Juelz Santana	2003
HEY MAMA	Frankie Vaughan	1963
HEY MAMA	Joe Brown	1973
HEY MAMA	Black Eyed Peas	2004
HEY MATTHEW	Karel Fialka	1987
HEY MISS PAYNE	Chequers	1976
HEY MISTER HEARTACHE	Kim Wilde	1988
HEY, MISTER SUN	Bobby Sherman	1970
HEY MR DREAM MAKER	Cliff Richard	1976
HEY MR. CHRISTMAS	Showaddywaddy	1974
HEY MR. D.J.	Zhane	1993
HEY MR. MUSIC MAN	Peters & Lee	1976
HEY MUSIC LOVER	S'express	1989
HEY NINETEEN	Steely Dan	1980
HEY NOW (GIRLS JUST WANT TO HAVE FUN)		
	Cyndi Lauper	1994
HEY PAPI	Alex Cartana	2004
HEY PAULA	Paul & Paula	1962
HEY ROCK AND ROLL	Showaddywaddy	1974
HEY SENORITA	War	1978

SONG TITLE	ARTIST	DATE
HEY SEXY LADY	Shaggy featuring Brian & Tony Gold	2002
HEY STUPID	Alice Cooper	1991
HEY THERE LONELY GIRL	Eddie Holman	1969
HEY THERE LONELY GIRL	Robert John	1980
HEY, WESTERN UNION MAN		
	Jerry Butler	1968
HEY WHATEVER	Westlife	2003
HEY WILLY	Hollies	1971
(HEY WON'T YOU PLAY) ANOTHER SOMEBODY DONE SOMEBODY WRONG SO	B.J. Thomas	1975
HEY YA!	Outkast	2003
HEY YOU	Quireboys	1990
HEY YOU	Bachman-Turner Overdrive	1975
(HEY YOU) THE ROCKSTEADY CREW		
	Rocksteady Crew	1983
HEYKENS SERENADE (STANDCHEN)/THE DAY IS ENDED		
	Royal Scots Dragoon Guards	1972
HI DE HI, HI DE HO	Kool & The Gang	1982
HI DE HO	K7 & The Swing Kids	1994
HI HO SILVER	Jim Diamond	1986
HI TENSION	Hi Tension	1978
HI, HI, HI/C MOON	Paul McCartney	1972
HI-DE-HI (HOLIDAY ROCK)	Paul Shane & The Yellowcoats	1981
HI-DE-HO	Blood, Sweat & Tears	1970

SONG TITLE	ARTIST	DATE
HI-FIDELITY (featuring VALERIE LANDSBERG)		
	Kids From 'Fame'	1982
HI-HEEL SNEAKERS	Tommy Tucker	1964
HI-HEEL SNEAKERS	Jose Feliciano	1968
HI-HO SILVER LINING	Jeff Beck	1967
HI-LILI, HI-LO	Richard Chamberlain	1963
HI-LILI, HI-LO	Alan Price Set	1966
HIDDEN AGENDA	Craig David	2003
HIDDEN PLACE	Bjork	2001
HIDE AND SEEK	Howard Jones	1984
HIDE U	Kosheen	2001
HIDE-A-WAY	Nu Soul featuring Kelli Rich	1996
HIDEAWAY	Dave Dee, Dozy, Beaky, Mick & Tich	1966
HIDEAWAY	De'lacy	1995
HIGH	Hyper Go Go	1992
HIGH	Feeder	1997
HIGH	Cure	1992
HIGH	Lighthouse Family	1998
HIGH & DRY/PLANET TELEX		
	Radiohead	1995
HIGH ENERGY	Evelyn Thomas	1984
HIGH ENOUGH	Damn Yankees	1990
HIGH FIDELITY	Elvis Costello	1980
HIGH HEAD BLUES/A CONSPIRACY		
	Black Crowes	1995

SONG TITLE	ARTIST	DATE
HIGH HOPES/KEEP TALKING		
	Pink Floyd	1994
HIGH IN THE SKY	Amen Corner	1968
HIGH LIFE	Modern Romance	1983
HIGH NOON	DJ Shadow	1997
HIGH ON A HAPPY VIBE	Urban Cookie Collective	1994
HIGH ON YOU	Survivor	1985
HIGH SCHOOL DANCE	Sylvers	1977
HIGH TIME	Paul Jones	1966
HIGH TIME WE WENT/BLACK-EYED BLUES		
	Joe Cocker	1971
HIGH TIMES	Jamiroquai	1997
HIGHER	Creed	1999
HIGHER AND HIGHER	Jackie Wilson	1969
HIGHER GROUND	UB40	1993
HIGHER GROUND	Sasha	1994
HIGHER GROUND	Stevie Wonder	1973
HIGHER LOVE	Steve Winwood	1986
HIGHER PLANE	Kool & The Gang	1994
HIGHER STATE OF CONSCIOUSNESS		
	Josh Wink	1995
HIGHER THAN HEAVEN	Kelle Bryan	1999
HIGHER THAN REASON	Unbelievable Truth	1998
HIGHER THAN THE SUN	Primal Scream	1991
HIGHFLY	John Miles	1975

SONG TITLE	ARTIST	DATE
HIGHLIFE/CAN'T GET THE BEST OF ME		
	Cypress Hill	2000
HIGHLY EVOLVED	Vines	2002
HIGHLY STRUNG	Spandau Ballet	1984
HIGHWAY 5 '92	Blessing	1992
HIGHWAY CODE	Master Singers	1966
HIGHWAY SONG	Blackfoot	1979
THE HIGHWAY SONG	Nancy Sinatra	1969
HIGHWAY TO HELL (LIVE)		
	AC/DC	1992
HIGHWAYS OF MY LIFE	Isley Brothers	1974
HIGHWIRE	Rolling Stones	1991
HIGHWIRE	Linda Carr & The Love Squad	1975
HIJACK	Herbie Mann	1975
HILLBILLY ROCK HILLBILLY ROLL		
	Woolpackers	1996
HIM	Rupert Holmes	1980
HIM OR ME – WHAT'S IT GONNA BE		
	Paul Revere & The Raiders	1967
THE HINDU TIMES	Oasis	2002
HIP CITY – PART 2	Jr. Walker & The All Stars	1968
HIP HOP HOORAY	Naughty By Nature	1993
HIP TO BE SQUARE	Huey Lewis & The News	1986
HIP TO HIP/CAN YOU FEEL IT?		
	V	2004
HIP-HUG-HER	Booker T. & The MG's	1967

SONG TITLE	ARTIST	DATE
HIPPY HIPPY SHAKE	Swinging Blue Jeans	1964
HIPPYCHICK	Soho	1990
HISTORY	Verve	1995
HISTORY	Mai Tai	1985
HISTORY REPEATING	Propellerheads featuring	
	Shirley Bassey	1997
HISTORY REPEATS ITSELF	Buddy Starcher	1966
HISTORY/GHOSTS	Michael Jackson	1997
HIT	Sugarcubes	1992
HIT	Wannadies	1997
HIT 'EM HIGH	B Real/Busta Rhymes/Coolio/	
	LL Cool J/Method Man	1997
HIT 'EM UP STYLE (OOPS!)		
	Blu Cantrell	2001
HIT 'EM WIT DA HEE	Missy 'Misdemeanor' Elliott	
	featuring Lil' Kim	1998
HIT AND RUN	Girlschool	1981
HIT BY LOVE	Ce Ce Peniston	1994
HIT ME OFF	New Edition	1996
HIT ME WITH YOUR BEST SHOT		
	Pat Benatar	1980
HIT ME WITH YOUR RHYTHM STICK		
	Ian Dury & The Blockheads	1978
HIT THAT	Offspring	2004
HIT THAT PERFECT BEAT	Bronski Beat	1985
HIT THE FREEWAY	Toni Braxton featuring Loon	2003

SONG TITLE	ARTIST	DATE
HIT THE GROUND	Darling Buds	1989
HIT THE ROAD JACK	Stampeders	1976
HITCH IT TO THE HORSE	Fantastic Johnny C	1968
HITCHIN' A RIDE	Sinitta	1990
HITCHIN' A RIDE	Green Day	1997
HITCHIN' A RIDE	Vanity Fare	1970
HITMIX (OFFICIAL BOOTLEG MEGA-MIX)		
	Alexander O'Neal	1989
HOBART PAVING/WHO DO YOU THINK YOU ARE		
	Saint Etienne	1993
HOBO HUMPIN' SLOBO BABE		
	Whale	1995
HOCUS POCUS	Focus	1973
HOKEY COKEY	Black Lace	1985
HOKEY COKEY	Snowmen	1981
HOLD BACK THE NIGHT	Trammps	1975
HOLD BACK THE NIGHT	KWS/Trammps	1992
HOLD BACK THE RIVER	Wet Wet Wet	1990
HOLD HER TIGHT	Osmonds	1972
HOLD IT DOWN	Senseless Things	1992
HOLD ME	P.J. Proby	1964
HOLD ME	B.A. Robertson & Maggie Bell	1981
HOLD ME	Savage Garden	2000
HOLD ME	Fleetwood Mac	1982
HOLD ME	Brian McKnight featuring Tone & Kobe Bryan)	1998

SONG TITLE	ARTIST	DATE
HOLD ME CLOSE	David Essex	1975
HOLD ME IN YOUR ARMS	Rick Astley	1989
HOLD ME NOW	Johnny Logan	1987
HOLD ME NOW	Thompson Twins	1984
HOLD ME THRILL ME KISS ME		
	Mel Carter	1965
HOLD ME TIGHT	Johnny Nash	1968
HOLD ME TIGHTER IN THE RAIN		
	Billy Griffin	1983
HOLD ME, THRILL ME, KISS ME		
	Gloria Estefan	1994
HOLD ME, THRILL ME, KISS ME, KILL ME		
	U2	1995
HOLD MY BODY TIGHT	East 17	1995
HOLD MY HAND	Hootie & The Blowfish	1994
HOLD ON	Happy Clappers	1995
HOLD ON	En Vogue	1990
HOLD ON	Wilson Phillips	1990
HOLD ON	Ian Gomm	1979
HOLD ON	Santana	1982
HOLD ON	Triumph	1979
HOLD ON	Jamie Walters	1995
HOLD ON LOOSELY	38 Special	1981
HOLD ON ME	Phixx	2003
HOLD ON MY HEART	Genesis	1992
HOLD ON TIGHT	Samantha Fox	1986

SONG TITLE	ARTIST	DATE
HOLD ON TIGHT	Electric Light Orchestra	1981
HOLD ON TO LOVE	Peter Skellern	1975
HOLD ON TO ME	MJ Cole featuring Elisabeth Troy	2000
HOLD ON TO ME	John Michael Montgomery	1998
HOLD ON TO MY LOVE	Jimmy Ruffin	1980
HOLD ON TO THE NIGHTS	Richard Marx	1988
HOLD ON! I'M COMIN'	Sam & Dave	1966
HOLD ONTO OUR LOVE	James Fox	2004
HOLD THAT SUCKER DOWN	OT Quartet	1994
HOLD THE LINE	Toto	1978
HOLD TIGHT!	Dave Dee, Dozy, Beaky, Mick & Tich	1966
HOLD WHAT YOU'VE GOT	Joe Tex	1964
HOLD YOU TIGHT	Tara Kemp	1991
HOLD YOUR HEAD UP	Argent	1972
HOLD YOUR HEAD UP HIGH	Boris Dlugosch	1997
HOLDIN' ON	Tony Rallo & The Midnite Band	1980
HOLDIN' ON	Tane Cain	1982
HOLDIN' ON TO YESTERDAY	Ambrosia	1975
HOLDING BACK THE YEARS	Simply Red	1986
HOLDING ON	Beverley Craven	1991

SONG TITLE	ARTIST	DATE
HOLDING ON	Steve Winwood	1988
HOLDING ON 4 U	Clock	1996
HOLDING ON FOR YOU	Liberty X	2002
HOLDING ON TO YOU	Terence Trent D'Arby	1995
HOLDING OUT FOR A HERO	Bonnie Tyler	1984
HOLE HEARTED	Extreme	1991
HOLE IN MY SHOE	Neil	1984
HOLE IN MY SHOE	Traffic	1967
HOLE IN MY SOUL	Aerosmith	1997
HOLE IN THE HEAD	Sugababes	2003
HOLIDAE INN	Chingy	2004
HOLIDAY	Madonna	1983
HOLIDAY	Mad'house	2002
HOLIDAY	Bee Gees	1967
HOLIDAY	Other Ones	1987
HOLIDAY RAP	M.C. Miker 'G' & Deejay Sven	1986
HOLIDAYS IN THE SUN	Sex Pistols	1977
HOLLA HOLLA	Ja Rule	1999
HOLLER	Ginuwine	1998
HOLLER/LET LOVE LEAD THE WAY	Spice Girls	2000
HOLLIEDAZE (MEDLEY)	Hollies	1981
THE HOLLOW MAN	Marillion	1994
HOLLY HOLY	UB40	1998
HOLLY HOLY	Neil Diamond	1969

SONG TITLE	ARTIST	DATE	SONG TITLE	ARTIST	DATE
HOLLYWOOD	Boz Scaggs	1977	HOMELY GIRL	Chi-Lites	1974
HOLLYWOOD	Madonna	2003	HOMELY GIRL	UB40	1989
HOLLYWOOD	Rufus featuring Chaka Khan	1977	HOMEWARD BOUND	Simon & Garfunkel	1966
HOLLYWOOD NIGHTS	Bob Seger & The Silver Bullet Band	1978	HOMICIDE	999	1978
HOLLYWOOD SWINGING	Kool & The Gang	1974	HONALOOCHIE BOOGIE	Mott The Hoople	1973
HOLY COW	Lee Dorsey	1966	HONDY (NO ACCESS)	Hondy	1997
THE HOLY RIVER	The Artist	1997	HONESTLY	Zwan	2003
HOLY ROLLER	Nazareth	1975	HONESTLY	Stryper	1987
HOLY SMOKE	Iron Maiden	1990	HONESTY	Billy Joel	1979
HOLYWARS... THE PUNISHMENT DUE	Megadeth	1990	HONEY	Moby	1998
HOMBURG	Procol Harum	1967	HONEY	Mariah Carey	1997
HOME	Depeche Mode	1997	HONEY	Bobby Goldsboro	1968
HOME	Sheryl Crow	1997	HONEY	R. Kelly & Jay-Z	2002
HOME	Bone Thugs-N-Harmony featuring Phil Collins	2003	HONEY CHILE	Martha & The Vandellas	1967
HOME	Simply Red	2004	HONEY COME BACK	Glen Campbell	1970
HOME ALONE	R. Kelly featuring Keith Murray	1998	HONEY HONEY	Sweet Dreams	1974
HOME AND DRY	Pet Shop Boys	2002	HONEY I	George McCrae	1976
HOME AND DRY	Gerry Rafferty	1978	HONEY I NEED	Pretty Things	1965
HOME IS WHERE THE HEART IS	Gladys Knight & The Pips	1977	HONEY I'M LOST	Dooleys	1979
HOME LOVIN' MAN	Andy Williams	1970	HONEY LOVE	R. Kelly & Public Announcement	1992
HOME OF THE BRAVE	Jody Miller	1965	THE HONEY THIEF	Hipsway	1987
HOME SWEET HOME	Motley Crue	1991	HONEY TO THE BEE	Billie	1999
			HONEY, HONEY	ABBA	1974
			HONG KONG GARDEN	Siouxsie & The Banshees	1978
			HONKY CAT	Elton John	1972

SONG TITLE	ARTIST	DATE
HONKY TONK TRAIN BLUES		
	Keith Emerson	1976
HONKY TONK WOMEN	Rolling Stones	1969
HOOCHIE BOOTY	Ultimate Kaos	1995
HOOK	Blues Traveler	1995
HOOKED	99th Floor Elevators featuring	
	Tony De Vit	1995
HOOKED ON A FEELING	Jonathan King	1971
HOOKED ON A FEELING	Blue Swede	1974
HOOKED ON A FEELING	B.J. Thomas	1968
HOOKED ON CLASSICS	Royal Philharmonic Orchestra	1981
HOOKED ON SWING	Larry Elgart	1982
HOOKED ON YOU	Sweet Sensation	1989
HOOKS IN YOU	Marillion	1989
HOOLIGAN	Embrace	1999
HOOLIGAN'S HOLIDAY	Motley Crue	1994
HOORAY FOR HAZEL	Tommy Roe	1966
HOORAY HOORAY (IT'S A CHEEKY HOLIDAY)		
	Cheeky Girls	2003
HOORAY HOORAY, IT'S A HOLI-HOLIDAY		
	Boney M	1979
HOOVERVILLE (THEY PROMISED US THE WORLD)		
	Christians	1987
HOPE (I WISH YOU'D BELIEVE ME)		
	Wah!	1983
HOPE OF DELIVERANCE	Paul McCartney	1993

SONG TITLE	ARTIST	DATE
HOPE ST	Levellers	1995
HOPE YOU LOVE ME LIKE YOU SAY YOU DO		
	Huey Lewis & The News	1982
HOPELESSLY	Rick Astley	1993
HOPELESSLY DEVOTED TO YOU		
	Olivia Newton-John	1978
HORNY	Mark Morrison	1996
HORNY	Mousse T vs Hot'n'juicy	1998
HORNY AS FUNK	Soapy	1996
HORNY HORNS	Perfect Phase	1999
HORROR HEAD (EP)	Curve	1992
THE HORSE	Cliff Nobles & Co.	1968
HORSE & CARRIAGE	Cam'ron featuring Mase	1998
A HORSE WITH NO NAME	America	1972
HOT & WET (BELIEVE IT)	Tzant	1996
HOT BLOODED	Foreigner	1978
HOT BOYZ	Missy 'Misdemeanor' Elliott	
	featuring Nas, Eve & Q-Ti	2000
HOT CHILD IN THE CITY	Nick Gilder	1978
HOT DOG	Shakin' Stevens	1980
HOT FUN IN THE SUMMERTIME		
	Sly & The Family Stone	1969
HOT GIRLS IN LOVE	Loverboy	1983
HOT HOT HOT	Arrow	1994
HOT IN HERRE	Nelly	2002
HOT IN THE CITY	Billy Idol	1982

SONG TITLE	ARTIST	DATE
HOT LEGS	Rod Stewart	1978
HOT LINE	Sylvers	1976
HOT LOVE	T. Rex	1971
HOT LOVE	Kelly Marie	1981
HOT LOVE NOW! (EP)	Wonder Stuff	1994
HOT LOVE, COLD WORLD	Bob Welch	1978
HOT NUMBER	Foxy	1979
HOT PANTS	James Brown	1971
HOT ROD HEARTS	Robbie Dupree	1980
HOT ROD LINCOLN	Commander Cody & His Lost Planet Airmen	1972
(HOT SHIT) COUNTRY GRAMMAR	Nelly	2000
HOT SHOT	Barry Blue	1974
HOT SHOT	Karen Young	1978
HOT SHOT TOTTENHAM!	Tottenham Hotspur F.A. Cup Final Squad	1987
HOT SMOKE & SASAFRASS	Bubble Puppy	1969
HOT SPOT	Foxy Brown	1999
HOT STUFF	Arsenal F.C.	1998
HOT STUFF	Donna Summer	1979
HOT SUMMER NIGHTS	Night	1979
HOT TRACK (EP)	Nazareth	1977
HOT VALVES (EP)	Be Bop Deluxe	1976
HOT WATER	Level 42	1984

SONG TITLE	ARTIST	DATE
HOTEL	Cassidy featuring R. Kelly	2004
HOTEL CALIFORNIA	Eagles	1977
HOTEL YORBA	White Stripes	2001
HOTLEGS/I WAS ONLY JOKING	Rod Stewart	1978
HOUNDS OF LOVE	Kate Bush	1986
HOURGLASS	Squeeze	1987
HOUSE ARREST	Krush	1987
HOUSE IS NOT A HOME	Charles & Eddie	1993
HOUSE MUSIC	Eddie Amador	1998
HOUSE NATION	Housemaster Boyz & The Rude Boy Of House	1987
HOUSE OF FUN	Madness	1982
HOUSE OF JEALOUS LOVERS	Rapture	2003
HOUSE OF LOVE	East 17	1992
HOUSE OF LOVE	Amy Grant With Vince Gill	1994
HOUSE OF LOVE/BACK TO MY ROOTS	Rupaul	1993
HOUSE OF PAIN	Faster Pussycat	1990
THE HOUSE OF THE RISING SUN	Animals	1964
THE HOUSE OF THE RISING SUN	Frijid Pink	1970
HOUSE ON FIRE	Arkarna	1997
HOUSE ON FIRE	Boomtown Rats	1982

SONG TITLE	ARTIST	DATE
THE HOUSE THAT JACK BUILT		
	Alan Price Set	1967
THE HOUSE THAT JACK BUILT		
	Tracie	1983
THE HOUSE THAT JACK BUILT		
	Aretha Franklin	1968
HOUSECALL	Shabba Ranks featuring	
	Maxi Priest	1993
HOUSTON	Dean Martin	1965
HOW 'BOUT I LOVE YOU MORE		
	Mull Historical Society	2004
HOW 'BOUT US	Champaign	1981
HOW ABOUT THAT	Bad Company	1992
HOW AM I SUPPOSED TO LIVE WITHOUT YOU		
	Michael Bolton	1989
HOW AM I SUPPOSED TO LIVE WITHOUT YOU		
	Laura Branigan	1983
HOW BIZARRE	OMC	1996
HOW CAN I BE SURE	Dusty Springfield	1970
HOW CAN I BE SURE	David Cassidy	1972
HOW CAN I BE SURE	Young Rascals	1967
HOW CAN I EASE THE PAIN		
	Lisa Fischer	1991
HOW CAN I FALL	Breathe	1988
HOW CAN I KEEP FROM SINGING?		
	Enya	1991

SONG TITLE	ARTIST	DATE
HOW CAN I LOVE YOU MORE?		
	M People	1993
HOW CAN I TELL HER	Fourmost	1964
HOW CAN I TELL HER?	Lobo	1973
HOW CAN THIS BE LOVE	Andrew Gold	1978
HOW CAN WE BE LOVERS	Michael Bolton	1990
HOW CAN YOU MEND A BROKEN HEART		
	Bee Gees	1971
HOW CAN YOU TELL	Sandie Shaw	1965
HOW COME	D12	2004
HOW COME?	Ronnie Lane & Slim Chance	1974
HOW COME, HOW LONG	Babyface featuring	
	Stevie Wonder	1997
HOW COME YOU DON'T CALL ME		
	Alicia Keys	2002
HOW COULD AN ANGEL BREAK MY HEART		
	Toni Braxton With Kenny G	1997
HOW COULD I? (INSECURITY)		
	Roachford	1998
HOW DEEP IS YOUR LOVE	Bee Gees	1977
HOW DEEP IS YOUR LOVE	Dru Hill	1998
HOW DEEP IS YOUR LOVE	Take That	1996
HOW DID YOU KNOW	Kurtis Mantronik presents	
	Chamonix	2003
HOW DO I LIVE	Leann Rimes	1997
HOW DO I LIVE	Trisha Yearwood	1997

SONG TITLE	ARTIST	DATE
HOW DO I MAKE YOU	Linda Ronstadt	1980
HOW DO I SURVIVE	Amy Holland	1980
HOW DO YOU CATCH A GIRL		
	Sam The Sham &	
	The Pharaohs	1966
HOW DO YOU DO?	Mouth & McNeal	1972
HOW DO YOU DO IT?	Gerry & The Pacemakers	1964
HOW DO YOU DO!	Roxette	1992
HOW DO YOU LIKE ME NOW?		
	Toby Keith	2000
HOW DO YOU TALK TO AN ANGEL		
	Heights	1992
HOW DO YOU WANT IT?	2Pac featuring KC And Jojo	1996
HOW DO YOU WANT ME TO LOVE YOU?		
	911	1998
HOW DOES IT FEEL TO BE BACK		
	Daryl Hall & John Oates	1980
(HOW DOES IT FEEL TO BE) ON TOP OF THE WORLD		
	England United	1998
HOW DOES IT FEEL?	Electroset	1992
HOW DOES IT FEEL?	Slade	1975
HOW DOES THAT GRAB YOU, DARLIN'?		
	Nancy Sinatra	1966
HOW FOREVER FEELS	Kenny Chesney	1999
HOW GEE	Black Machine	1994
HOW HIGH	Charlatans	1997

SONG TITLE	ARTIST	DATE
HOW HIGH	Redman/Method Man	1995
HOW HIGH THE MOON	Gloria Gaynor	1976
HOW I'M COMIN'	LL Cool J	1993
HOW LONG	Yazz & Aswad	1993
HOW LONG	Ace	1975
HOW LONG?	Paul Carrack	1996
HOW LONG (BETCHA' GOT A CHICK ON THE SIDE)		
	Pointer Sisters	1975
HOW LONG'S A TEAR TAKE TO DRY?		
	Beautiful South	1999
HOW LUCKY YOU ARE	Skin	1996
HOW MANY LIES	Spandau Ballet	1987
HOW MANY TIMES CAN WE SAY GOODBYE		
	Dionne Warwick/Luther Vandross	1983
HOW MEN ARE	Aztec Camera	1988
HOW MUCH I FEEL	Ambrosia	1978
HOW MUCH IS ENOUGH	Fixx	1991
HOW MUCH LOVE	Vixen	1990
HOW MUCH LOVE	Leo Sayer	1977
HOW SOON	Henry Mancini & His Orchestra	1964
HOW SOON IS NOW	Smiths	1985
HOW SWEET IT IS	Jr. Walker & The All-Stars	1966
HOW SWEET IT IS (TO BE LOVED BY YOU)		
	James Taylor	1975
HOW SWEET IT IS TO BE LOVED BY YOU		
	Marvin Gaye	1964

SONG TITLE	ARTIST	DATE
(HOW TO BE A) MILLIONAIRE		
	ABC	1986
HOW TO BE DEAD	Snow Patrol	2004
HOW TO DANCE	Bingo Boys	1991
HOW TO FALL IN LOVE (PART 1)		
	Bee Gees	1994
HOW U LIKE BASS	Norman Bass	2001
HOW WAS IT FOR YOU?	James	1990
HOW WILL I KNOW	Whitney Houston	1985
HOW WONDERFUL YOU ARE		
	Gordon Haskell	2001
HOW YOU GONNA ACT LIKE THAT		
	Tyrese	2003
HOW YOU GONNA SEE ME NOW		
	Alice Cooper	1978
HOW YOU REMIND ME	Nickelback	2001
HOW'D WE EVER GET THIS WAY		
	Andy Kim	1968
HOW'S IT GOING TO BE	Third Eye Blind	1997
HOW'S YOUR EVENING SO FAR		
	Josh Wink & Lil Louis	2000
HOWARD'S WAY	Simon May Orchestra	1985
HOWZAT	Sherbet	1976
HUBBLE BUBBLE (TOIL AND TROUBLE)		
	Manfred Mann	1964
HUDSON STREET	Agnelli & Nelson	2000

SONG TITLE	ARTIST	DATE
HUG MY SOUL	Saint Etienne	1994
HUMAN	Pretenders	1999
HUMAN	Human League	1986
HUMAN BEHAVIOR	Bjork	1993
HUMAN NATURE	Gary Clail On-U Sound System	1991
HUMAN NATURE	Madonna	1995
HUMAN NATURE	Michael Jackson	1983
HUMAN RACING	Nik Kershaw	1984
HUMAN TOUCH	Rick Springfield	1983
HUMAN TOUCH/BETTER DAYS		
	Bruce Springsteen	1992
HUMAN WORK OF ART	Cliff Richard	1993
HUMMINGBIRD	Seals & Crofts	1973
HUMPIN'	Gap Band	1981
HUMPIN' AROUND	Bobby Brown	1992
THE HUMPTY DANCE	Digital Underground	1990
HUNDRED MILE HIGH CITY		
	Ocean Colour Scene	1997
HUNG UP	Paul Weller	1994
HUNGRY	Kosheen	2002
HUNGRY	Paul Revere & The Raiders	1966
HUNGRY EYES	Eric Carmen	1987
HUNGRY FOR LOVE	Johnny Kidd & The Pirates	1963
HUNGRY FOR LOVE	San Remo Golden Strings	1965
HUNGRY HEART	Bruce Springsteen	1980
HUNGRY LIKE THE WOLF	Duran Duran	1982

SONG TITLE	ARTIST	DATE
THE HUNT	Barry Ryan	1969
HUNTER	Dido	2001
THE HUNTER GETS CAPTURED BY THE GAME	Marvelettes	1967
HUNTING HIGH AND LOW	A-Ha	1986
HURDY GURDY MAN	Donovan	1968
HURRICANE	Warm Jets	1998
HURRICANE (PART I)	Bob Dylan	1975
HURRY HOME	Wavelength	1982
HURRY UP AND WAIT	Stereophonics	1999
HURRY UP HARRY	Sham 69	1978
HURT	Manhattans	1976
THE HURT	Cat Stevens	1973
HURT/FOR THE HEART	Elvis Presley	1976
HURT/PERSONAL JESUS	Johnny Cash	2003
HURT BY LOVE	Inez Foxx	1964
HURT SO BAD	Lettermen	1969
HURT SO BAD	Little Anthony & The Imperials	1965
HURT SO BAD	Linda Ronstadt	1980
HURT SO GOOD	Susan Cadogan	1975
HURT SO GOOD	Jimmy Somerville	1995
HURTING EACH OTHER	Carpenters	1972
HURTS SO GOOD	Millie Jackson	1973
HURTS SO GOOD	John Cougar	1982
HUSAN	Bhangra Knights Vs Husan	2003

SONG TITLE	ARTIST	DATE
HUSBANDS AND WIVES	Brooks & Dunn	1998
HUSBANDS AND WIVES	Roger Miller	1966
HUSH	Kula Shaker	1997
HUSH	Deep Purple	1968
HUSH	LL Cool J featuring 7 Aurelius	2004
HUSH, HUSH SWEET CHARLOTTE	Patti Page	1964
HUSH... NOT A WORD TO MARY	John Rowles	1968
THE HUSTLE	Van McCoy featuring Soul City Symphony	1975
HUSTLE! (TO THE MUSIC...)	Funky Worm	1988
HYMN	Moby	1994
HYMN	Ultravox	1982
HYMN TO HER	Pretenders	1986
HYPER MUSIC/FEELING GOOD	Muse	2001
HYPERACTIVE	Robert Palmer	1986
HYPERACTIVE!	Thomas Dolby	1994
HYPERBALLAD	Bjork	1996
HYPERREAL	Shamen	1991
HYPNOSIS	Mud	1973
HYPNOTIC ST-8	Altern 8	1992
HYPNOTISED	Simple Minds	1995
HYPNOTISING	Kid Creme featuring Charlise	2003

SONG TITLE	ARTIST	DATE
HYPNOTIZE	D'Influence	1997
HYPNOTIZE	Notorious B.I.G.	1997
HYPNOTIZE ME Wang Chung 1987		
HYPNOTIZED	Linda Jones	1967
HYPNOTIZIN'	Winx	1996
HYSTERIA	Def Leppard	1988
HYSTERIA	Muse	2003
I (WHO HAVE NOTHING)	Shirley Bassey	1963
I (WHO HAVE NOTHING)	Tom Jones	1970
I (WHO HAVE NOTHING)	Ben E. King	1983
I (WHO HAVE NOTHING)	Sylvester	1979
I ADORE MI AMOR	Color Me Badd	1991
I AIN'T GOIN' OUT LIKE THAT		
	Cypress Hill	1993
I AIN'T GONNA CRY	Little Angels	1991
I AIN'T GONNA STAND FOR IT		
	Stevie Wonder	1980
I AIN'T GOT TIME ANYMORE		
	Cliff Richard	1970
I AIN'T GOT TIME ANY MORE		
	Glass Bottle	1971
I AIN'T LYIN'	George McCrae	1975
I AIN'T MAD AT CHA	2Pac	1996
I AM	Chakra	1997
I AM	Suggs	1998
I AM (I'M ME)	Twisted Sister	1983

SONG TITLE	ARTIST	DATE
I AM... I SAID	Neil Diamond	1971
I AM A CIDER DRINKER (PALOMA BLANCA)		
	Wurzels	1976
I AM A ROCK	Simon & Garfunkel	1966
I AM BLESSED	Eternal	1995
I AM BY YOUR SIDE	Corey Hart	1986
I AM I	Queensryche	1995
I AM, I FEEL	Alisha's Attic	1996
I AM IN LOVE WITH THE WORLD		
	Chicken Shed	1997
I AM LOVE (PTS 1 & 2)	Jackson 5	1975
I AM MINE	Pearl Jam	2002
I AM SOMEBODY (PART II)		
	Johnnie Taylor	1970
I AM THE BEAT	Look	1980
I AM THE BLACK GOLD OF THE SUN		
	Nuyorican Soul/Jocelyn Brown	1997
I AM THE LAW	Anthrax	1987
I AM THE MOB	Catatonia	1997
I AM THE RESURRECTION	Stone Roses	1992
I AM THE SUN	Dark Star	2000
I AM WHAT I AM	Mark Owen	1997
I AM WHAT I AM	Gloria Gaynor	1983
I AM WHAT I AM	Greyhound	1972
I AM WOMAN	Helen Reddy	1972
I APOLOGISE	P.J. Proby	1965

SONG TITLE	ARTIST	DATE
I BEG YOUR PARDON	Kon Kan	1989
I BEGIN TO WONDER	Dannii Minogue	2003
I BELIEVE	Happy Clappers	1995
I BELIEVE	Blessid Union Of Souls	1995
I BELIEVE	Booth And The Bad Angel	1996
I BELIEVE	Absolute featuring Suzanne Palmer	1997
I BELIEVE	Bachelors	1964
I BELIEVE	EMF	1991
I BELIEVE	Bon Jovi	1993
I BELIEVE	Marcella Detroit	1994
I BELIEVE	Sounds Of Blackness	1994
I BELIEVE	Stephen Gately	2000
I BELIEVE	Chilliwack	1982
I BELIEVE	Diamond Rio	2003
I BELIEVE (A SOULFUL RE-RECORDING)	Tears For Fears	1985
I BELIEVE (IN LOVE)	Hot Chocolate	1971
I BELIEVE 97	Happy Clappers	1997
I BELIEVE I CAN FLY	R. Kelly	1996
I BELIEVE/UP ON THE ROOF	Robson Green & Jerome Flynn	1995
I BELIEVE I'M GONNA LOVE YOU	Frank Sinatra	1975
I BELIEVE IN A THING CALLED LOVE	Darkness	2003

SONG TITLE	ARTIST	DATE
I BELIEVE IN CHRISTMAS	Tweenies	2001
I BELIEVE IN FATHER CHRISTMAS	Greg Lake	1975
I BELIEVE IN MIRACLES	Pasadenas	1992
I BELIEVE IN MUSIC	Gallery	1972
I BELIEVE IN YOU	Don Williams	1980
I BELIEVE IN YOU (YOU BELIEVE IN ME)	Johnnie Taylor	1973
I BELIEVE IN YOU AND ME	Whitney Houston	1996
I BELIEVE MY HEART	Duncan James & Keedie	2004
I BELIEVE THERE'S NOTHING STRONGER THAN OUR LOVE	Paul Anka/Odia Coates	1975
I BELIEVE YOU	Dorothy Moore	1977
I BELONG	Kathy Kirby	1965
I BELONG TO YOU	Gina G	1996
I BELONG TO YOU	Love Unlimited	1974
I BELONG TO YOU (EVERY TIME I SEE YOUR FACE)	Rome	1997
I BELONG TO YOU/HOW MANY WAYS	Toni Braxton	1994
I BREATHE AGAIN	Adam Rickitt	1999
I BREATHE IN, I BREATHE OUT	Chris Cagle	2002
I CALLED YOU	Lil Louis	1990
I CAN	Nas	2003

SONG TITLE	ARTIST	DATE
I CAN CAST A SPELL	Disco Tex presents Cloudburst	2001
I CAN DANCE	Brian Poole & The Tremeloes	1963
I CAN DO IT	Rubettes	1975
I CAN DO THAT	Montell Jordan	1998
I CAN DO THIS	Monie Love	1989
I CAN DREAM ABOUT YOU	Dan Hartman	1984
I CAN DRIVE	Shakespear's Sister	1996
I CAN HEAR MUSIC	Beach Boys	1969
I CAN HEAR THE GRASS GROW		
	Move	1967
I CAN HEAR VOICES/CANED AND UNABLE		
	Hi-Gate	2000
I CAN HELP	Billy Swan	1974
I CAN HELP	Elvis Presley	1983
I CAN LOVE YOU	Mary J. Blige	1997
I CAN LOVE YOU LIKE THAT		
	All-4-One	1995
I CAN MAKE IT WITH YOU	Pozo-Seco Singers	1966
I CAN MAKE YOU FEEL GOOD		
	Shalamar	1982
I CAN MAKE YOU FEEL GOOD		
	Kavana	1997
I CAN NEVER GO HOME ANYMORE		
	Shangri-Las	1965
I CAN ONLY DISAPPOINT U	Mansun	2000
I CAN PROVE IT	Tony Etoria	1977

SONG TITLE	ARTIST	DATE
I CAN PROVE IT	Phil Fearon	1986
I CAN SEE CLEARLY	Deborah Harry	1993
I CAN SEE CLEARLY NOW	Jimmy Cliff	1993
I CAN SEE CLEARLY NOW	Hothouse Flowers	1990
I CAN SEE CLEARLY NOW	Johnny Nash	1972
I CAN SEE FOR MILES	Who	1967
I CAN SING A RAINBOW/LOVE IS BLUE		
	Dells	1969
I CAN TAKE CARE OF MYSELF		
	Billy Vera	1981
I CAN TAKE OR LEAVE YOUR LOVING		
	Herman's Hermits	1968
I CAN UNDERSTAND IT	New Birth	1973
I CAN'T ASK FOR ANY MORE THAN YOU		
	Cliff Richard	1976
I CAN'T BREAK DOWN	Sinead Quinn	2003
I CAN'T CONTROL MYSELF	Troggs	1966
I CAN'T DANCE	Genesis	1992
I CAN'T DENY IT	Rod Stewart	2001
I CAN'T DRIVE 55	Sammy Hagar	1984
I CAN'T EXPLAIN	Who	1965
I CAN'T GET NEXT TO YOU	Temptations	1969
(I CAN'T GET NO) SATISFACTION		
	Otis Redding	1966
(I CAN'T GET NO) SATISFACTION		
	Rolling Stones	1965

SONG TITLE	ARTIST	DATE
(I CAN'T GET NO) SATISFACTION		
	Bubblerock	1974
I CAN'T GET YOU OUT OF MY MIND		
	Yvonne Elliman	1977
I CAN'T GO FOR THAT (NO CAN DO)		
	Daryl Hall & John Oates	1981
I CAN'T GROW PEACHES ON A CHERRY TREE		
	Just Us	1966
I CAN'T HEAR YOU NO MORE/MUSIC IS MY LIFE		
	Helen Reddy	1976
I CAN'T HELP IT	Bananarama	1988
I CAN'T HELP IT	Andy Gibb &	
	Olivia Newton-John	1980
I CAN'T HELP MYSELF	Joey Lawrence	1993
I CAN'T HELP MYSELF	Four Tops	1965
I CAN'T HELP MYSELF	Donnie Elbert	1972
I CAN'T HELP MYSELF	Lucid	1998
I CAN'T HELP MYSELF (SUGAR PIE, HONEY BUNCH)		
	Bonnie Pointer	1979
(I CAN'T HELP) FALLING IN LOVE WITH YOU		
	UB40	1993
I CAN'T HOLD BACK	Survivor	1984
I CAN'T IMAGINE THE WORLD WITHOUT ME		
	Echobelly	1994
I CAN'T LEAVE YOU ALONE		
	George McCrae	1974

SONG TITLE	ARTIST	DATE
I CAN'T LET GO	Hollies	1966
I CAN'T LET GO	Linda Ronstadt	1980
I CAN'T LET MAGGIE GO	Honeybus	1968
I CAN'T LET YOU GO	Ian Van Dahl	2003
I CAN'T LIVE A DREAM	Osmonds	1976
I CAN'T MAKE IT	Small Faces	1967
I CAN'T MAKE IT ALONE	P.J. Proby	1966
I CAN'T MAKE YOU LOVE ME		
	Bonnie Raitt	1991
I CAN'T READ YOU	Daniel Bedingfield	2003
I CAN'T SEE MYSELF LEAVING YOU		
	Aretha Franklin	1969
I CAN'T SLEEP BABY (IF I)	R. Kelly	1996
I CAN'T STAND IT	Twenty 4 Seven	1990
I CAN'T STAND IT	Eric Clapton	1981
I CAN'T STAND IT NO MORE		
	Peter Frampton	1979
I CAN'T STAND MYSELF (WHEN YOU TOUCH ME)		
	James Brown	1967
I CAN'T STAND THE RAIN	Eruption featuring	
	Precious Wilson	1978
I CAN'T STAND THE RAIN	Ann Peebles	1973
I CAN'T STAND UP FOR FALLING DOWN		
	Elvis Costello	1980
I CAN'T STOP	Osmonds	1974
I CAN'T STOP	Gary Numan	1986

SONG TITLE	ARTIST	DATE
I CAN'T STOP DANCING	Archie Bell & The Drells	1968
I CAN'T STOP LOVING YOU (THOUGH I TRY)		
	Leo Sayer	1978
I CAN'T TAKE THE POWER		
	Off-Shore	1990
I CAN'T TELL THE BOTTOM FROM THE TOP		
	Hollies	1970
I CAN'T TELL YOU WHY	Brownstone	1995
I CAN'T TELL YOU WHY	Eagles	1980
I CAN'T TURN YOU LOOSE	Otis Redding	1966
I CAN'T TURN YOU LOOSE	Chambers Brothers	1968
I CAN'T WAIT	Nu Shooz	1986
I CAN'T WAIT	Ladies First	2002
I CAN'T WAIT	Stevie Nicks	1986
I CAN'T WAIT	Sleepy Brown featuring	
	Outkast	2004
I CAN'T WAIT ANOTHER MINUTE		
	Hi-Five	1991
I CARE	Soul II Soul	1995
I CARE 'BOUT YOU	Milestone	1997
I CARE 4 YOU	Aaliyah	2002
I CHOOSE TO SING THE BLUES		
	Ray Charles	1966
I CLOSE MY EYES AND COUNT TO TEN		
	Dusty Springfield	1968

SONG TITLE	ARTIST	DATE
I COME FROM ANOTHER PLANET, BABY		
	Julian Cope	1996
I COULD BE AN ANGLE	Eighties Matchbox B-Line	
	Disaster	2004
I COULD BE HAPPY	Altered Images	1981
I COULD BE SO GOOD FOR YOU		
	Dennis Waterman	1980
I COULD BE THE ONE	Stacie Orrico	2004
I COULD EASILY FALL	Cliff Richard	1964
I COULD NEVER LOVE ANOTHER (AFTER LOVING YOU)		
	Temptations	1968
I COULD NEVER MISS YOU (MORE THAN I DO)		
	Lulu	1981
I COULD NEVER TAKE THE PLACE OF YOUR MAN		
	Prince	1987
I COULD NOT ASK FOR MORE		
	Sara Evans	2001
I COULD NOT ASK FOR MORE		
	Edwin McCain	1999
I COULD NOT LOVE YOU MORE		
	Bee Gees	1997
I COULD SING OF YOUR LOVE FOREVER		
	Delirious?	2001
I COULDN'T LIVE WITHOUT YOUR LOVE		
	Petula Clark	1966

SONG TITLE	ARTIST	DATE
I COULDN'T SAY NO	Robert Ellis Orrall with Carlene Carter	1983
I CRY	Ja Rule featuring Lil' Mo	2001
I DID WHAT I DID FOR MARIA	Tony Christie	1971
I DIDN'T KNOW I LOVED YOU (TILL I SAW YOU ROCK AND ROLL	Gary Glitter	1972
I DIDN'T MEAN IT	Status Quo	1994
I DIDN'T MEAN TO TURN YOU ON	Robert Palmer	1986
I DIDN'T WANT TO NEED YOU	Heart	1990
I DIE: YOU DIE	Gary Numan	1980
I DIG ROCK AND ROLL MUSIC	Peter, Paul & Mary	1967
I DISAPPEAR	Metallica	2000
I DO	Jamelia	1999
I DO	J. Geils Band	1982
I DO	Lisa Loeb	1997
I DO	Marvelows	1965
I DO (CHERISH YOU)	98 Degrees	1999
I DO!!	Toya	2001
I DO LOVE YOU	G.Q.	1979
I DO LOVE YOU	Billy Stewart	1965
I DO WHAT I DO... (THEME FROM 91/2 WEEKS)	John Taylor	1986

SONG TITLE	ARTIST	DATE
I DO YOU	Jets	1987
I DO'WANNA KNOW	REO Speedwagon	1984
I DO, I DO, I DO, I DO, I DO	ABBA	1976
I DON'T BELIEVE IN IF ANYMORE	Roger Whittaker	1970
I DON'T BELIEVE IN MIRACLES	Colin Blunstone	1972
I DON'T BELIEVE IN MIRACLES	Sinitta	1988
I DON'T CARE	Los Bravos	1966
I DON'T CARE	Shakespear's Sister	1992
I DON'T CARE ANYMORE	Phil Collins	1983
I DON'T EVER WANT TO SEE YOU AGAIN	Uncle Sam	1997
I DON'T HAVE THE HEART	James Ingram	1990
I DON'T HAVE TO BE ME ('TIL MONDAY)	Steve Azar	2002
I DON'T KNOW	Honeyz	2001
I DON'T KNOW ANYBODY ELSE	Black Box	1990
I DON'T KNOW HOW TO LOVE HIM	Yvonne Elliman	1971
I DON'T KNOW HOW TO LOVE HIM	Helen Reddy	1971

SONG TITLE	ARTIST	DATE
I DON'T KNOW IF IT'S RIGHT		
	Evelyn 'Champagne' King	1979
I DON'T KNOW WHAT YOU WANT BUT I CAN'T GIVE IT		
ANYMORE	Pet Shop Boys	1999
I DON'T KNOW WHERE TO START		
	Eddie Rabbitt	1982
I DON'T KNOW WHY	Stevie Wonder	1969
I DON'T KNOW WHY (I JUST DO)		
	Andy & David Williams	1973
I DON'T LIKE MONDAYS	Boomtown Rats	1979
I DON'T LIKE TO SLEEP ALONE		
	Paul Anka/Odia Coates	1975
I DON'T LOVE YOU ANYMORE		
	Quireboys	1990
I DON'T LOVE YOU BUT I THINK I LIKE YOU		
	Gilbert O'Sullivan	1975
I DON'T MIND AT ALL	Bourgeois Tagg	1987
I DON'T NEED NO DOCTOR (LIVE)		
	W.A.S.P.	1987
I DON'T NEED YOU	Kenny Rogers	1981
I DON'T REALLY CARE	K-Gee	2000
I DON'T SMOKE	DJ Dee Kline	2000
I DON'T THINK THAT MAN SHOULD SLEEP ALONE		
	Ray Parker Jr.	1987
I DON'T WANNA	Aaliyah	2000

SONG TITLE	ARTIST	DATE
I DON'T WANNA BE A LOSER		
	Lesley Gore	1964
I DON'T WANNA BE A STAR		
	Corona	1995
I DON'T WANNA CRY	Mariah Carey	1991
I DON'T WANNA DANCE	Eddy Grant	1982
I DON'T WANNA FIGHT	Tina Turner	1993
I DON'T WANNA GET HURT		
	Donna Summer	1989
I DON'T WANNA GO ON WITH YOU LIKE THAT		
	Elton John	1988
(I DON'T WANNA GO TO) CHELSEA		
	Elvis Costello & The Attractions	1978
I DON'T WANNA KNOW	Mario Winans featuring Enya	
	& P. Diddy	2004
I DON'T WANNA LIVE WITHOUT YOUR LOVE		
	Chicago	1988
I DON'T WANNA LOSE MY WAY		
	Dreamcatcher	2002
I DON'T WANNA LOSE YOU		
	Kandidate	1979
I DON'T WANNA LOSE YOU		
	Tina Turner	1989
I DON'T WANNA LOSE YOU BABY		
	Chad & Jeremy	1965

SONG TITLE	ARTIST	DATE
I DON'T WANNA LOSE YOUR LOVE		
	Emotions	1977
I DON'T WANNA PLAY HOUSE		
	Tammy Wynette	1976
I DON'T WANNA TAKE THIS PAIN		
	Dannii Minogue	1991
I DON'T WANT A LOVER	Texas	1989
I DON'T WANT NOBODY (TELLIN' ME WHAT TO DO)		
	Cherie Amore	2000
I DON'T WANT NOBODY TO GIVE ME NOTHING		
	James Brown	1969
I DON'T WANT OUR LOVING TO DIE		
	Herd	1968
I DON'T WANT TO	Toni Braxton	1997
I DON'T WANT TO BE A FREAK (BUT I CAN'T HELP MYSELF)	Dynasty	1979
I DON'T WANT TO BE A HERO		
	Johnny Hates Jazz	1988
I DON'T WANT TO BE HURT ANYMORE		
	Nat 'King' Cole	1964
I DON'T WANT TO DO WRONG		
	Gladys Knight & The Pips	1971
I DON'T WANT TO LIVE WITHOUT YOU		
	Foreigner	1988
I DON'T WANT TO MISS A THING		
	Aerosmith	1998

SONG TITLE	ARTIST	DATE
I DON'T WANT TO MISS A THING		
	Mark Chesnut	1998
I DON'T WANT TO PUT A HOLD ON YOU		
	Berni Flint	1977
I DON'T WANT TO SEE TOMORROW		
	Nat 'King' Cole	1964
I DON'T WANT TO SEE YOU AGAIN		
	Peter & Gordon	1964
I DON'T WANT TO SPOIL THE PARTY		
	Beatles	1965
I DON'T WANT TO TALK ABOUT IT		
	Everything But The Girl	1988
I DON'T WANT TO TALK ABOUT IT		
	Rod Stewart	1977
I DON'T WANT TO WAIT	Paula Cole	1997
I DON'T WANT TO WALK WITHOUT YOU		
	Barry Manilow	1980
I DON'T WANT YOUR LOVE		
	Duran Duran	1988
I DROVE ALL NIGHT	Cyndi Lauper	1989
I DROVE ALL NIGHT	Roy Orbison	1992
I EAT CANNIBALS (PT I)	Toto Coelo	1982
I FEEL A CRY COMING ON		
	Hank Locklin	1966
I FEEL A SONG (IN MY HEART)		
	Gladys Knight & The Pips	1974

SONG TITLE	ARTIST	DATE
I FEEL DIVINE	S-J	1998
I FEEL FINE	Beatles	1964
I FEEL FOR YOU	Chaka Khan	1984
I FEEL FOR YOU	Bob Sinclar	2000
I FEEL FREE	Cream	1966
I FEEL LIKE BUDDY HOLLY	Alvin Stardust	1984
I FEEL LOVE	CRW	2000
I FEEL LOVE	Donna Summer	1977
I FEEL LOVE	Messiah/Precious Wilson	1992
I FEEL LOVE (MEDLEY)	Bronski Beat & Marc Almond	1985
I FEEL LOVE COMIN' ON	Felice Taylor	1967
I FEEL LOVED	Depeche Mode	2001
I FEEL SO FINE	KMC featuring DHANY	2002
I FEEL THE EARTH MOVE	Martika	1989
I FEEL YOU	Love Decade	1992
I FEEL YOU	Peter Andre	1996
I FEEL YOU	Depeche Mode	1993
I FINALLY FOUND SOMEONE		
	Barbra Streisand &	
	Bryan Adams	1996
I FORGOT	Lionel Richie	2001
I FOUGHT THE LAW	Bobby Fuller Four	1966
I FOUGHT THE LAW	Clash	1988
I FOUND A GIRL	Jan & Dean	1965
I FOUND A LOVE (PART I)		
	Wilson Pickett	1967

SONG TITLE	ARTIST	DATE
I FOUND HEAVEN	Take That	1992
I FOUND LOVE/TAKE A TOKE		
	C&C Music Factory	1995
I FOUND LOVIN'	Fatback Band	1987
I FOUND LOVIN'	Steve Walsh	1987
I FOUND OUT THE HARD WAY		
	Four Pennies	1964
I FOUND SOMEBODY	Glenn Frey	1982
I FOUND SOMEONE	Cher	1987
I FOUND SUNSHINE	Chi-Lites	1974
I GAVE IT UP (WHEN I FELL IN LOVE)		
	Luther Vandross	1988
I GAVE YOU MY HEART (DIDN'T I)		
	Hot Chocolate	1984
I GET A KICK OUT OF YOU		
	Gary Shearston	1974
I GET A LITTLE SENTIMENTAL OVER YOU		
	New Seekers	1974
I GET ALONG	Pet Shop Boys	2002
I GET AROUND	Beach Boys	1964
I GET AROUND	2Pac	1993
I GET EXCITED	Rick Springfield	1982
I GET LIFTED	Barbara Tucker	1994
I GET LIFTED	George McCrae	1975
I GET LONELY	Janet Jackson	1998

SONG TITLE	ARTIST	DATE
I GET THE SWEETEST FEELING/HIGHER AND HIGHER		
	Jackie Wilson	1975
I GET WEAK	Belinda Carlisle	1988
I GIVE IT ALL TO YOU/I IMAGINE		
	Mary Kiani	1995
I GO BACK	Kenny Chesney	2004
I GO CRAZY	Paul Davis	1977
I GO TO EXTREMES	Billy Joel	1990
I GO TO PIECES	Peter & Gordon	1965
I GO TO SLEEP	Pretenders	1981
I GO WILD	Rolling Stones	1995
I GOT 5 ON IT	Luniz	1995
I GOT A LINE ON YOU	Spirit	1969
I GOT A MAN	Positive K	1992
I GOT A NAME	Jim Croce	1973
I GOT A THANG 4 YA!	Lo-Key?	1992
I GOT ANTS IN MY PANTS (PART 1)		
	James Brown	1973
I GOT ID/LONG ROAD	Pearl Jam	1995
I GOT MY EDUCATION	Uncanny Alliance	1992
I GOT MY MIND MADE UP (YOU CAN GET IT GIRL)		
	Instant Funk	1979
I GOT RHYTHM	Happenings	1967
I GOT STONED AND I MISSED IT		
	Jim Stafford	1975
I GOT THE FEELIN'	James Brown	1968

SONG TITLE	ARTIST	DATE
I GOT THE FEELIN' (OH NO NO)		
	Neil Diamond	1966
I GOT THE HOOK UP!	Master P featuring Sons Of	
	Funk	1998
I GOT THE VIBRATION/A POSITIVE VIBRATION		
	Black Box	1996
I GOT THIS FEELING	Baby Bumps	2000
I GOT TO SING	Jaln Band	1977
I GOT YOU	Split Enz	1980
I GOT YOU (I FEEL GOOD)		
	James Brown	1965
I GOT YOU BABE	Cher With Beavis & Butt-Head	1994
I GOT YOU BABE	Sonny & Cher	1965
I GOT YOU BABE	UB40	1985
I GOTCHA	Joe Tex	1972
I GUESS I'LL ALWAYS LOVE YOU		
	Isley Brothers	1969
I GUESS THAT'S WHY THEY CALL IT THE BLUES		
	Elton John	1983
I GUESS THE LORD MUST BE IN NEW YORK CITY		
	Nilsson	1969
I HAD A DREAM	Paul Revere & The Raiders	1967
I HAD TOO MUCH TO DREAM (LAST NIGHT)		
	Electric Prunes	1967
I HATE EVERYTHING	George Strait	2004

SONG TITLE	ARTIST	DATE
I HATE MYSELF FOR LOVING YOU		
	Joan Jett & The Blackhearts	1988
I HATE U	Tafkap	1995
I HAVE A DREAM	ABBA	1979
I HAVE A DREAM/SEASONS IN THE SUN		
	Westlife	1999
I HAVE NOTHING	Whitney Houston	1993
I HAVE PEACE	Strike	1997
I HAVEN'T STOPPED DANCING YET		
	Pat & Mick	1989
I HEAR A SYMPHONY	Supremes	1965
I HEAR TALK	Bucks Fizz	1984
I HEAR TRUMPETS BLOW	Tokens	1966
I HEAR YOU KNOCKING	Dave Edmunds	1973
I HEAR YOU NOW	Jon & Vangelis	1980
I HEARD A HEART BREAK LAST NIGHT		
	Jim Reeves	1967
I HEARD A RUMOUR	Bananarama	1987
I HEARD IT THROUGH THE GRAPEVINE		
	Creedence Clearwater Revival	1976
I HEARD IT THROUGH THE GRAPEVINE		
	Marvin Gaye	1968
I HEARD IT THROUGH THE GRAPEVINE		
	Gladys Knight & The Pips	1967
I HONESTLY LOVE YOU	Olivia Newton-John	1974
I HOPE YOU DANCE	Lee Ann Womack	2001

SONG TITLE	ARTIST	DATE
I HOPE YOU DANCE	Ronan Keating	2004
I JUST CALLED TO SAY I LOVE YOU		
	Stevie Wonder	1984
I JUST CAN'T HELP BELIEVING		
	Elvis Presley	1971
I JUST CAN'T HELP BELIEVING		
	B.J. Thomas	1970
I JUST CAN'T STOP LOVING YOU		
	Michael Jackson/Siedah Garrett	1987
I JUST DON'T HAVE THE HEART		
	Cliff Richard	1989
I JUST DON'T KNOW WHAT TO DO WITH MYSELF		
	Dusty Springfield	1964
I JUST DON'T KNOW WHAT TO DO WITH MYSELF		
	White Stripes	2003
I JUST DON'T KNOW WHAT TO DO WITH MYSELF		
	Dionne Warwick	1966
I JUST FALL IN LOVE AGAIN		
	Anne Murray	1979
I JUST NEED MYSELF	Ocean Colour Scene	2003
I JUST WANNA (SPEND SOME TIME WITH YOU)		
	Alton Edwards	1982
I JUST WANNA BE LOVED	Culture Club	1998
I JUST WANNA BE MAD	Terri Clark	2002
I JUST WANNA BE YOUR EVERYTHING		
	Andy Gibb	1977

SONG TITLE	ARTIST	DATE
I JUST WANNA LOVE U (GIVE IT 2 ME)	Jay-Z	2000
I JUST WANNA STOP	Gino Vannelli	1978
(I JUST WANNA) B WITH U	Transvision Vamp	1991
I JUST WANT TO BE YOUR EVERYTHING	Andy Gibb	1977
I JUST WANT TO CELEBRATE	Rare Earth	1971
I JUST WANT TO DANCE WITH YOU	Daniel O'Donnell	1992
I JUST WANT TO MAKE LOVE TO YOU	Foghat	1977
I JUST WANT TO MAKE LOVE TO YOU	Etta James	1996
(I JUST) DIED IN YOUR ARMS	Cutting Crew	1987
I KEEP FORGETTIN' (EVERYTIME YOU'RE NEAR)	Michael McDonald	1982
I KEEP LOOKING	Sara Evans	2002
I KNEW I LOVED YOU	Savage Garden	1999
I KNEW THE BRIDE	Dave Edmunds	1977
I KNEW YOU WERE WAITING (FOR ME)	Aretha Franklin/George Michael	1987
I KNEW YOU WHEN	Linda Ronstadt	1982
I KNEW YOU WHEN	Billy Joe Royal	1965
I KNOW	New Atlantic	1992

SONG TITLE	ARTIST	DATE
I KNOW	Dionne Farris	1995
I KNOW A HEARTACHE WHEN I SEE ONE	Jennifer Warnes	1979
I KNOW A PLACE	Petula Clark	1965
I KNOW ENOUGH (I DON'T GET ENOUGH)	Theaudience	1998
I KNOW HIM SO WELL	Elaine Paige & Barbara Dickson	1985
(I KNOW I GOT) SKILLZ	Shaquille O'Neal	1993
I KNOW MY LOVE	Chieftains featuring The Corrs	1999
I KNOW THERE'S SOMETHING GOING ON	Frida	1982
I KNOW WHAT I LIKE	Huey Lewis & The News	1987
I KNOW WHAT I LIKE (IN YOUR WARDROBE)	Genesis	1974
I KNOW WHAT I'M HERE FOR	James	1999
I KNOW WHAT YOU WANT	Busta Rhymes and Mariah Carey	2003
I KNOW WHERE IT'S AT	All Saints	1998
I KNOW YOU GOT SOUL	Eric B. & Rakim	1988
I KNOW YOU'RE OUT THERE SOMEWHERE	Moody Blues	1988
(I KNOW) I'M LOSING YOU	Faces	1971
(I KNOW) I'M LOSING YOU	Rare Earth	1970

SONG TITLE	ARTIST	DATE
(I KNOW) I'M LOSING YOU		
	Rod Stewart	1971
(I KNOW) I'M LOSING YOU		
	Temptations	1966
I LEARNED FROM THE BEST		
	Whitney Houston	1999
(I LEFT MY HEART) IN SAN FRANCISCO		
	Tony Bennett	1965
I LIFT MY CUP	Gloworm	1993
I LIKE	Montell Jordan	1996
I LIKE	Kut Klose	1995
I LIKE (WHAT YOU'RE DOING TO ME)		
	Young & Co	1980
I LIKE DREAMIN'	Kenny Nolan	1976
I LIKE IT	D.J.H. featuring Stefy	1991
I LIKE IT	Gerry & The Pacemakers	1964
I LIKE IT	Narcotic Thrust	2004
I LIKE IT	Blackout Allstars	1996
I LIKE IT	Debarge	1983
I LIKE IT	Dino	1989
I LIKE IT	Montell Jordan featuring Slick Rick	1996
I LIKE IT	Sammie	2000
I LIKE IT LIKE THAT	Dave Clark Five	1965
I LIKE IT LIKE THAT	Miracles	1964
I LIKE IT, I LOVE IT	Tim McGraw	1995

SONG TITLE	ARTIST	DATE
I LIKE THAT	Houston	2004
I LIKE THE WAY	Deni Hines	1997
I LIKE THE WAY	Tommy James & The Shondells	1967
I LIKE THE WAY (THE KISSING GAME)		
	Hi-Five	1991
I LIKE TO DO IT	KC & The Sunshine Band	1976
I LIKE TO LIVE THE LOVE	B.B. King	1973
I LIKE TO MOVE IT	Reel 2 Real featuring The Mad Stuntman	1994
I LIKES TO DO IT	People's Choice	1971
I LIVE BY THE GROOVE	Paul Carrack	1989
I LIVE FOR THE SUN	Vanity Fare	1968
I LIVE FOR YOUR LOVE	Natalie Cole	1987
I LIVE MY LIFE FOR YOU	Firehouse	1995
I LOST IT	Kenny Chesney	2000
I LOST MY HEART TO A STARSHIP TROOPER		
	Sarah Brightman and Hot Gossip	1978
I LOVE	Tom T. Hall	1973
I LOVE A RAINY NIGHT	Eddie Rabbitt	1980
I LOVE AMERICA	Patrick Juvet	1978
I LOVE BEING IN LOVE WITH YOU		
	Adam Faith	1964
I LOVE CHRISTMAS	Fast Food Rockers	2003
I LOVE HER	Paul & Barry Ryan	1966

SONG TITLE	ARTIST	DATE
I LOVE HOW YOU LOVE ME		
	Paul & Barry Ryan	1966
I LOVE HOW YOU LOVE ME		
	Maureen Evans	1964
I LOVE HOW YOU LOVE ME		
	Bobby Vinton	1968
I LOVE IT WHEN WE DO	Ronan Keating	2002
I LOVE MUSIC	Enigma	1981
I LOVE MUSIC	O'Jays	1976
I LOVE MUSIC	Rozalla	1994
I LOVE MY DOG	Cat Stevens	1966
I LOVE MY FRIEND	Charlie Rich	1974
I LOVE MY RADIO	Taffy	1987
I LOVE ROCK 'N' ROLL	Joan Jett & The Blackhearts	1982
I LOVE ROCK 'N' ROLL	Britney Spears	2002
I LOVE SATURDAY	Erasure	1994
I LOVE THE NIGHT LIFE (DISCO 'ROUND)		
	Alicia Bridges	1978
I LOVE THE SOUND OF BREAKING GLASS		
	Nick Lowe	1978
I LOVE THE WAY YOU LOVE ME		
	Boyzone	1998
I LOVE THIS BAR	Toby Keith	2003
I LOVE TO BOOGIE	T. Rex	1976
I LOVE TO LOVE (BUT MY BABY LOVES TO DANCE)		
	Tina Charles	1976

SONG TITLE	ARTIST	DATE
I LOVE YOU	Donna Summer	1977
I LOVE YOU	Climax Blues Band	1981
I LOVE YOU	Faith Evans	2002
I LOVE YOU	Martina McBride	1999
I LOVE YOU	People	1968
I LOVE YOU 'CAUSE I HAVE TO		
	Dogs Die In Hot Cars	2004
I LOVE YOU 1,000 TIMES	Platters	1966
I LOVE YOU ALWAYS FOREVER		
	Donna Lewis	1996
I LOVE YOU BABY	Freddie & The Dreamers	1964
I LOVE YOU BECAUSE	Jim Reeves	1971
I LOVE YOU DROPS	Vic Dana	1966
I LOVE YOU FOR ALL SEASONS		
	Fuzz	1971
I LOVE YOU FOREVER ALWAYS		
	Donna Lewis	1996
I LOVE YOU GOODBYE	Thomas Dolby	1992
I LOVE YOU LOVE ME LOVE		
	Gary Glitter	1973
I LOVE YOU MORE AND MORE EVERY DAY		
	Al Martino	1964
I LOVE YOU PERIOD	Dan Baird	1992
I LOVE YOU, YES I DO	Merseybeats	1965
I LOVE YOU, YES I LOVE YOU		
	Eddy Grant	1981

SONG TITLE	ARTIST	DATE
I LOVE YOU... STOP!	Red 5	1997
I LOVE YOUR SMILE	Shanice	1991
I LOVED 'EM EVERY ONE	T.G. Sheppard	1981
I LUV U	Dizzee Rascal	2003
I LUV U BABY	Original	1995
I MADE IT THROUGH THE RAIN		
	Barry Manilow	1980
I MAKE A FOOL OF MYSELF		
	Frankie Valli	1967
I MELT	Rascal Flatts	2003
I MET A GIRL	Shadows	1966
I MET HER IN CHURCH	Box Tops	1968
I MIGHT	Shakin' Stevens	1990
I MISS MY FRIEND	Darryl Worley	2002
I MISS MY HOMIES	Master P featuring Pimp C	
	and The Shocker	1997
I MISS YOU	Bjork	1997
I MISS YOU	Haddaway	1993
I MISS YOU	Darren Hayes	2002
I MISS YOU	Blink-182	2004
I MISS YOU	Aaron Hall	1994
I MISS YOU	Klymaxx	1985
I MISS YOU	N II U	1994
I MISS YOU BABY	Marv Johnson	1969
I MISS YOU SO	Little Anthony & The Imperials	1965
I MISSED AGAIN	Phil Collins	1981

SONG TITLE	ARTIST	DATE
I MUST BE IN LOVE	Rutles	1978
I MUST BE SEEING THINGS		
	Gene Pitney	1965
I MUST STAND	Ice-T	1996
I NEED	Meredith Brooks	1997
I NEED A GIRL (PART ONE)		
	P. Diddy featuring Usher	
	& Loon	2002
I NEED A GIRL (PART TWO)		
	P. Diddy & Ginuwine featuring	
	Loon	2002
I NEED A LOVER	John Cougar	1979
I NEED A MAN	Eurythmics	1988
I NEED A MIRACLE	Coco	1997
I NEED IT	Johnny 'Guitar' Watson	1976
I NEED LOVE	LL Cool J	1987
I NEED SOMEBODY	Loveland featuring	
	Rachel McFarlane	1995
I NEED SOMEBODY	Question Mark & The	
	Mysterions	1966
I NEED TO BE IN LOVE	Carpenters	1976
I NEED TO KNOW	Marc Anthony	1999
I NEED YOU	B.V.S.M.P.	1988
I NEED YOU	Deuce	1995
I NEED YOU	3T	1996
I NEED YOU	Leann Rimes	2001

SONG TITLE	ARTIST	DATE
I NEED YOU	Pointer Sisters	1984
I NEED YOU	Dave Gahan	2003
I NEED YOU	Stands	2003
I NEED YOU	America	1972
I NEED YOU	Paul Carrack	1982
I NEED YOU TONIGHT	Peter Wolf	1984
I NEED YOUR LOVIN'	Alyson Williams	1989
I NEED YOUR LOVIN'	Teena Marie	1980
I NEED YOUR LOVIN' (LIKE THE SUNSHINE)		
	Marc Et Claude	2000
I NEVER CRY	Alice Cooper	1976
I NEVER FELT LIKE THIS BEFORE		
	Mica Paris	1993
I NEVER KNEW	Roger Sanchez featuring	
	Cooly's Hot Box	2000
I NEVER LOVED A MAN (THE WAY I LOVE YOU)		
	Aretha Franklin	1967
I NEVER SEEN A MAN CRY (AKA I SEEN A MAN DIE)		
	Scarface	1994
I NEVER WANT AN EASY LIFE IF ME AND HE WERE		
EVER TO GET THERE	Charlatans	1994
I ONLY HAVE EYES FOR YOU		
	Art Garfunkel	1975
I ONLY LIVE TO LOVE YOU		
	Cilla Black	1967

SONG TITLE	ARTIST	DATE
I ONLY WANNA BE WITH YOU		
	Bay City Rollers	1976
I ONLY WANNA BE WITH YOU		
	Samantha Fox	1989
I ONLY WANT TO BE WITH YOU		
	Barry White	1995
I ONLY WANT TO BE WITH YOU		
	Dusty Springfield	1964
I ONLY WANT TO BE WITH YOU		
	Tourists	1979
I ONLY WANT TO BE WITH YOU		
	Bay City Rollers	1976
I ONLY WANT TO BE WITH YOU		
	Samantha Fox	1989
I OWE YOU NOTHING	Bros	1988
I OWE YOU ONE	Shalamar	1980
I PLAY AND SING	Dawn	1971
I PLEDGE MY LOVE	Peaches & Herb	1980
I PRETEND	Des O'Connor	1968
I PROMISE	Stacie Orrico	2004
I PUT A SPELL ON YOU	Sonique	1998
I PUT A SPELL ON YOU	Nina Simone	1969
I PUT A SPELL ON YOU	Alan Price Set	1966
I PUT A SPELL ON YOU	Bryan Ferry	1993
I QUIT	Bros	1988
I QUIT	Hepburn	1999

SONG TITLE	ARTIST	DATE
I RAN (SO FAR AWAY)	Flock Of Seagulls	1982
I REALLY DIDN'T MEAN IT	Luther Vandross	1987
I REALLY DON'T NEED NO LIGHT	Jeffrey Osborne	1982
I REALLY DON'T WANT TO KNOW	Ronnie Dove	1966
I REALLY DON'T WANT TO KNOW	Elvis Presley	1970
I RECALL A GYPSY WOMAN	Don Williams	1976
I REFUSE (WHAT YOU WANT)	Somore featuring Damon Trueitt	1998
I REMEMBER ELVIS PRESLEY (THE KING IS DEAD)	Danny Mirror	1977
I REMEMBER HOLDING YOU	Boys Club	1988
I REMEMBER YESTERDAY	Donna Summer	1977
I REMEMBER YOU	Skid Row	1989
I RISE, I FALL	Johnny Tillotson	1964
I SAVED THE WORLD TODAY	Eurythmics	1999
I SAW HER AGAIN	Mamas & The Papas	1966
I SAW HER STANDING THERE	Elton John featuring John Lennon	1981

SONG TITLE	ARTIST	DATE
I SAW HER STANDING THERE	Beatles	1964
I SAW HIM STANDING THERE	Tiffany	1988
I SAW LINDA YESTERDAY	Doug Sheldon	1963
I SAW RED	Warrant	1990
I SAW THE LIGHT	The The	1995
I SAW THE LIGHT	Todd Rundgren	1972
I SAY A LITTLE PRAYER	Aretha Franklin	1968
I SAY A LITTLE PRAYER	Diana King	1997
I SAY A LITTLE PRAYER	Dionne Warwick	1967
I SAY NOTHING	Voice Of The Beehive	1988
I SECOND THAT EMOTION	Miracles	1967
I SECOND THAT EMOTION	Japan	1982
I SECOND THAT EMOTION	Diana Ross & The Supremes & The Temptations	1969
I SEE A STAR	Mouth & McNeal	1974
I SEE THE LIGHT	Five Americans	1966
I SEE YOU BABY	Groove Armada featuring Gram'ma Funk	1999
I SHALL BE RELEASED	Tremeloes	1968
I SHALL BE THERE	B*Witched featuring Ladysmith Black Mambazo	1999
I SHALL SING	Garfunkel	1973
I SHOT THE SHERIFF	Eric Clapton	1974
I SHOT THE SHERIFF	Warren G	1997

SONG TITLE	ARTIST	DATE
I SHOT THE SHERIFF	Light Of The World	1981
I SHOULD BE SLEEPING	Emerson Drive	2002
I SHOULD BE SO LUCKY	Kylie Minogue	1988
I SHOULD BE...	Dru Hill	2002
I SHOULD CARE	Frank Ifield	1964
I SHOULD HAVE KNOWN BETTER	Naturals	1964
I SHOULD HAVE KNOWN BETTER	Jim Diamond	1984
I SHOULDA LOVED YA	Narada Michael Walden	1980
I SINGS	Mary Mary	2000
I SPECIALIZE IN YOU	Sharon Brown	1982
I STAND ACCUSED	Merseybeats	1966
I STARTED A JOKE	Bee Gees	1968
I STARTED SOMETHING I COULDN'T FINISH	Smiths	1987
I STILL BELIEVE	Mariah Carey	1999
I STILL BELIEVE	Brenda K. Starr	1988
I STILL BELIEVE IN YOU	Cliff Richard	1992
I STILL CAN'T GET OVER YOU	Ray Parker Jr.	1983
I STILL HAVE DREAMS	Richie Furay	1979
I STILL HAVEN'T FOUND WHAT I'M LOOKING FOR	Chimes	1990
I STILL HAVEN'T FOUND WHAT I'M LOOKING FOR	U2	1987

SONG TITLE	ARTIST	DATE
I STILL LOVE YOU	Next	1998
I STILL THINK OF YOU	Utah Saints	1994
I SURRENDER	Rosie Gaines	1997
I SURRENDER	David Sylvian	1999
I SURRENDER	Rainbow	1981
I SURRENDER (TO THE SPIRIT OF THE NIGHT)	Samantha Fox	1987
I SWEAR	All-4-One	1994
I TAKE IT BACK	Sandy Posey	1967
I THANK YOU	Adeva	1989
I THANK YOU	Sam & Dave	1968
I THANK YOU	ZZ Top	1980
I THINK I LOVE YOU	Voice Of The Beehive	1991
I THINK I LOVE YOU	Partridge Family	1970
I THINK I LOVE YOU	Kaci	2002
I THINK I'M IN LOVE	Spiritualized	1998
I THINK I'M IN LOVE WITH YOU	Jessica Simpson	2000
I THINK I'M PARANOID	Garbage	1998
I THINK IT'S LOVE	Jermaine Jackson	1986
I THINK OF YOU	Detroit Emeralds	1973
I THINK OF YOU	Perry Como	1971
I THINK OF YOU	Merseybeats	1964
I THINK WE'RE ALONE NOW	Tiffany	1987

SONG TITLE	ARTIST	DATE
I THINK WE'RE ALONE NOW	Pascal featuring Karen Parry	2002
I THINK WE'RE ALONE NOW	Tommy James & The Shondells	1967
I THOUGHT I MEANT THE WORLD TO YOU	Alysha Warren	1995
I THOUGHT IT TOOK A LITTLE TIME (BUT TODAY I FELL IN LOVE)	Diana Ross	1976
I THOUGHT IT WAS YOU	Sex-O-Sonique	1997
I THOUGHT IT WAS YOU	Herbie Hancock	1978
I TOUCH MYSELF	Divinyls	1991
I TRY	Macy Gray	1999
I TURN TO YOU	Christina Aguilera	2000
I TURN TO YOU	Melanie C	2000
I TURNED YOU ON	Isley Brothers	1969
I UNDERSTAND	Freddie & The Dreamers	1965
I WANNA BE A COWBOY	Boys Don't Cry	1986
I WANNA BE A FLINTSTONE	Screaming Blue Messiahs	1988
I WANNA BE A HIPPY	Technohead	1996
I WANNA BE A WINNER	Brown Sauce	1981
I WANNA BE ADORED	Stone Roses	1991
I WANNA BE BAD	Willa Ford	2001
I WANNA BE DOWN	Brandy	1994
I WANNA BE FREE (TO BE WITH HIM)	Scarlet	1995

SONG TITLE	ARTIST	DATE
I WANNA BE LOVED/TURNING THE TOWN RED	Elvis Costello	1984
I WANNA BE RICH	Calloway	1990
I WANNA BE THE ONE	Stevie B	1989
I WANNA BE THE ONLY ONE	Eternal featuring Bebe Winans	1997
I WANNA BE THERE	Blessid Union Of Souls	1997
I WANNA BE U	Chocolate Puma	2001
I WANNA BE WHERE YOU ARE	Michael Jackson	1972
I WANNA BE WITH YOU	Mandy Moore	2000
I WANNA BE WITH YOU	Raspberries	1972
I WANNA BE YOUR LADY	Hinda Hicks	1998
I WANNA BE YOUR LOVER	Prince	1979
I WANNA BE YOUR MAN	Chaka Demus & Pliers	1994
I WANNA BE YOUR MAN	Rolling Stones	1963
I WANNA DANCE WIT' CHOO (DOO DAT DANCE)	Disco Tex & The Sex-O-Lettes	1975
I WANNA DANCE WITH SOMEBODY	Flip & Fill	2003
I WANNA DANCE WITH SOMEBODY (WHO LOVES ME)	Whitney Houston	1987
I WANNA DO IT ALL	Terri Clark	2003
I WANNA DO IT WITH YOU	Barry Manilow	1982
I WANNA GET NEXT TO YOU	Rose Royce	1977

SONG TITLE	ARTIST	DATE
(I WANNA GIVE YOU) DEVOTION		
	Nomad featuring MC Mikee Freedom	1991
I WANNA GO BACK	New Seekers	1977
I WANNA GO BACK	Eddie Money	1987
I WANNA GO WHERE THE PEOPLE GO		
	Wildhearts	1995
I WANNA HAVE SOME FUN	Samantha Fox	1988
I WANNA HEAR IT FROM YOUR LIPS		
	Eric Carmen	1985
I WANNA HOLD ON TO YOU		
	Mica Paris	1993
I WANNA KNOW	Joe	2001
I WANNA LOVE	Glen Campbell	1968
I WANNA LOVE HIM SO BAD		
	Jelly Beans	1964
I WANNA LOVE YOU	Jade	1992
I WANNA LOVE YOU	Solid Harmonie	1998
I WANNA LOVE YOU FOREVER		
	Jessica Simpson	1999
I WANNA SEX YOU UP	Color Me Badd	1991
I WANNA STAY HERE	Miki & Griff	1963
I WANNA STAY WITH YOU	Undercover	1993
I WANNA STAY WITH YOU	Gallagher & Lyle	1976
I WANNA TALK ABOUT ME	Toby Keith	2001

SONG TITLE	ARTIST	DATE
I WANNA THANK YA	Angie Stone featuring Snoop Dogg	2004
(I WANNA) TESTIFY	Parliaments	1967
I WANT A NEW DRUG	Huey Lewis & The News	1984
I WANT AN ALIEN FOR CHRISTMAS		
	Fountains Of Wayne	1997
I WANT CANDY	Candy Girls	1996
I WANT CANDY	Aaron Carter	2000
I WANT CANDY	Brian Poole & The Tremeloes	1965
I WANT CANDY	Bow Wow Wow	1982
I WANT CANDY	Strangeloves	1965
I WANT HER	Keith Sweat	1988
I WANT IT ALL	Queen	1989
I WANT IT ALL	Warren G featuring Mack 10	1999
I WANT IT THAT WAY	Backstreet Boys	1999
I WANT LOVE	Elton John	2001
I WANT MORE	Can	1976
I WANT MORE	Faithless	2004
I WANT THAT MAN	Deborah Harry	1989
I WANT THE WORLD	2two Third3	1994
I WANT TO BE ALONE	2two Third3	1994
I WANT TO BE FREE	Toyah	1981
I WANT TO BE STRAIGHT	Ian Dury	1980
I WANT TO BE THERE WHEN YOU COME		
	Echo & The Bunnymen	1997
I WANT TO BE YOUR MAN	Roger	1987

SONG TITLE	ARTIST	DATE
I WANT TO BE YOUR PROPERTY		
	Blue Mercedes	1987
(I WANT TO BE) ELECTED	Mr. Bean & Smear Campaign	1992
I WANT TO BREAK FREE	Queen	1984
I WANT TO COME OVER	Melissa Etheridge	1996
I WANT TO DO EVERYTHING FOR YOU		
	Joe Tex	1965
I WANT TO GIVE	Perry Como	1974
I WANT TO GO WITH YOU	Eddy Arnold	1966
I WANT TO HOLD YOUR HAND		
	Beatles	1964
I WANT TO HOLD YOUR HAND		
	Dollar	1979
(I WANT TO KILL) SOMEBODY		
	S.M.A.S.H.	1994
I WANT TO KNOW WHAT LOVE IS		
	Foreigner	1984
I WANT TO LIVE	Grace	1995
I WANT TO STAY HERE	Steve Lawrence & Eydie Gorme	1963
I WANT TO TAKE YOU HIGHER		
	Sly & The Family Stone	1970
I WANT TO TAKE YOU HIGHER		
	Ike & Tina Turner	1970
I WANT TO TOUCH YOU	Catherine Wheel	1992
I WANT TO WAKE UP WITH YOU		
	Boris Gardiner	1986

SONG TITLE	ARTIST	DATE
I WANT YOU	Utah Saints	1993
I WANT YOU	Juliet Roberts	1994
I WANT YOU	Bob Dylan	1966
I WANT YOU	Inspiral Carpets	1994
I WANT YOU	Savage Garden	1997
I WANT YOU	Marvin Gaye	1976
I WANT YOU	Shana	1989
I WANT YOU	Thalia featuring Fat Joe	2003
I WANT YOU '98	Savage Garden	1998
I WANT YOU (FOREVER)	DJ Carl Cox	1991
I WANT YOU BACK	Bananarama	1988
I WANT YOU BACK	Cleopatra	1998
I WANT YOU BACK	Jackson 5	1969
I WANT YOU BACK	Melanie B featuring	
	Missy Elliott	1998
I WANT YOU BACK	*NSYNC	1998
I WANT YOU FOR MYSELF	Another Level/Ghostface Killah	1999
I WANT YOU NEAR ME	Tina Turner	1992
I WANT YOU TO BE MY BABY		
	Billie Davis	1968
I WANT YOU TO WANT ME		
	Cheap Trick	1979
I WANT YOU TO WANT ME		
	Solid Harmonie	1998
I WANT YOU TONIGHT	Pablo Cruise	1979
I WANT YOU, I NEED YOU	Chris Christian	1981

SONG TITLE	ARTIST	DATE
I WANT YOUR LOVE	Roger Sanchez presents Twilight	1999
I WANT YOUR LOVE	Atomic Kitten	2000
I WANT YOUR LOVE	Chic	1979
I WANT YOUR LOVE	Transvision Vamp	1988
I WANT YOUR LOVIN' (JUST A LITTLE BIT)	Curtis Hairston	1985
I WANT YOUR SEX	George Michael	1987
I WANT'A DO SOMETHING FREAKY TO YOU	Leon Haywood	1975
I WAS BORN ON CHRISTMAS DAY	Saint Etienne	1993
I WAS BORN TO LOVE YOU	Freddie Mercury	1985
I WAS BROUGHT TO MY SENSES	Sting	1996
I WAS CHECKIN' OUT SHE WAS CHECKIN' IN	Don Covay	1973
I WAS KAISER BILL'S BATMAN	Whistling Jack Smith	1967
I WAS MADE FOR DANCIN'	Leif Garrett	1978
I WAS MADE FOR LOVIN' YOU	Kiss	1979
I WAS MADE TO LOVE HER	Stevie Wonder	1967
I WAS ONLY JOKING	Rod Stewart	1978

SONG TITLE	ARTIST	DATE
I WAS RIGHT AND YOU WERE WRONG	Deacon Blue	1994
I WAS TIRED OF BEING ALONE	Patrice Rushen	1982
(I WASHED MY HANDS IN) MUDDY WATER	Johnny Rivers	1966
I WASN'T BUILT TO GET UP	Supernaturals	1998
I WILL	Billy Fury	1964
I WILL	Dean Martin	1965
I WILL!	Ruby Winters	1977
I WILL ALWAYS LOVE YOU	Whitney Houston	1992
I WILL ALWAYS LOVE YOU	Sarah Washington	1993
I WILL ALWAYS LOVE YOU	Rik Waller	2002
I WILL ALWAYS THINK ABOUT YOU	New Colony Six	1968
I WILL BE HERE FOR YOU	Michael W. Smith	1992
I WILL BE IN LOVE WITH YOU	Livingston Taylor	1978
I WILL BE RELEASED	Up Yer Ronson	1997
I WILL BE THERE	Glass Tiger	1987
I WILL BE WITH YOU	T'Pau	1988

SONG TITLE	ARTIST	DATE
I WILL BE YOUR GIRLFRIEND		
	Dubstar	1998
I WILL COME TO YOU	Hanson	1997
I WILL DRINK THE WINE	Frank Sinatra	1971
I WILL GET THERE	Boyz II Men	1999
I WILL LOVE AGAIN	Lara Fabian	2000
I WILL REMEMBER YOU	Amy Grant	1992
I WILL REMEMBER YOU (LIVE)		
	Sarah McLachlan	1999
I WILL RETURN	Springwater	1971
I WILL STILL LOVE YOU	Stonebolt	1978
I WILL SURVIVE	Cake	1997
I WILL SURVIVE	Arrival	1970
I WILL SURVIVE	Gloria Gaynor	1978
I WILL SURVIVE	Diana Ross	1996
I WILL SURVIVE	Chantay Savage	1996
I WISH	Gabrielle	1993
I WISH	Stevie Wonder	1976
I WISH	Skee-Lo	1995
I WISH	R. Kelly	2000
I WISH	Carl Thomas	2000
I WISH I HAD A GIRL	Henry Lee Summer	1988
I WISH I KNEW HOW IT WOULD FEEL TO BE FREE		
	Sharlene Hector	2004
(I WISH I KNEW HOW IT WOULD FEEL TO BE) FREE		
	Lighthouse Family	2001

SONG TITLE	ARTIST	DATE
I WISH I WAS A GIRL	Violent Delight	2003
I WISH IT COULD BE A WOMBLING MERRY CHRISTMAS		
EVERY DAY	Wombles With Roy Wood	2000
I WISH IT COULD BE CHRISTMAS EVERY DAY		
	Wizzard	1973
I WISH IT WOULD RAIN	Temptations	1968
I WISH IT WOULD RAIN DOWN		
	Phil Collins	1990
I WISH THE PHONE WOULD RING		
	Expose	1992
I WISH U HEAVEN	Prince	1988
I WISH YOU LOVE	Paul Young	1997
I WISH YOU LOVE	Gloria Lynne	1964
I WOKE UP IN LOVE THIS MORNING		
	Partridge Family	1971
I WON'T BACK DOWN	Tom Petty	1989
I WON'T BLEED FOR YOU	Climie Fisher	1988
I WON'T CHANGE YOU	Sophie Ellis-Bextor	2004
I WON'T CLOSE MY EYES	UB40	1982
I WON'T COME IN WHILE HE'S THERE		
	Jim Reeves	1967
I WON'T CRY	Glen Goldsmith	1987
I WON'T FORGET YOU	Jim Reeves	1964
I WON'T FORGET YOU	Poison	1987
I WON'T HOLD YOU BACK	Toto	1983

SONG TITLE	ARTIST	DATE
I WON'T LAST A DAY WITHOUT YOU		
	Carpenters	1974
I WON'T LET THE SUN GO DOWN ON ME		
	Nik Kershaw	1984
I WON'T LET YOU DOWN	PhD	1982
I WON'T RUN AWAY	Alvin Stardust	1984
I WON'T STAND IN YOUR WAY		
	Stray Cats	1983
I WONDER	Crystals	1964
I WONDER	Brenda Lee	1963
I WONDER IF HEAVEN GOT A GHETTO		
	2Pac	1998
I WONDER IF I TAKE YOU HOME		
	Lisa Lisa & Cult Jam	1985
I WONDER WHAT SHE'S DOING TONIGHT		
	Tommy Boyce & Bobby Hart	1967
I WONDER WHY	Showaddywaddy	1978
I WONDER WHY	Curtis Stigers	1991
I WOULD DIE 4 U	Prince & The Revolution	1984
I WOULD FIX YOU	Kenickie	1998
I WOULDN'T BELIEVE YOUR RADIO		
	Stereophonics	1999
I WOULDN'T HAVE MISSED IT FOR THE WORLD		
	Ronnie Milsap	1981
I WOULDN'T NORMALLY DO THIS KIND OF THING		
	Pet Shop Boys	1993

SONG TITLE	ARTIST	DATE
I WOULDN'T TRADE YOU FOR THE WORLD		
	Bachelors	1964
I WOULDN'T WANNA HAPPPEN TO YOU		
	Embrace	2000
I WOULDN'T WANT TO BE LIKE YOU		
	Alan Parsons Project	1977
I WRITE THE SONGS	Barry Manilow	1975
I WRITE THE SONGS/GET IT UP FOR LOVE		
	David Cassidy	1975
I'D DIE WITHOUT YOU	P.M. Dawn	1992
I'D DO ANYTHING FOR LOVE (BUT I WON'T DO THAT)		
	Meat Loaf	1993
I'D GIVE ANYTHING	Gerald Levert	1994
I'D LIE FOR YOU (AND THAT'S THE TRUTH)		
	Meat Loaf	1995
I'D LIKE TO TEACH THE WORLD TO SING		
	No Way Sis	1996
I'D LIKE TO TEACH THE WORLD TO SING		
	Demi Holborn	2002
I'D LIKE TO TEACH THE WORLD TO SING		
	Hillside Singers	1971
I'D LIKE TO TEACH THE WORLD TO SING		
	New Seekers	1971
I'D LOVE TO CHANGE THE WORLD		
	Ten Years After	1971

SONG TITLE	ARTIST	DATE
I'D LOVE YOU TO WANT ME	Lobo	1972
I'D RATHER GO BLIND	Chicken Shack	1969
I'D RATHER GO BLIND	Ruby Turner	1987
I'D RATHER JACK	Reynolds Girls	1989
I'D RATHER LEAVE WHILE I'M IN LOVE	Rita Coolidge	1979
I'D REALLY LOVE TO SEE YOU TONIGHT	England Dan & John Ford Coley	1976
I'D STILL SAY YES	Klymaxx	1987
I'D WAIT A MILLION YEARS	Grass Roots	1969
I'LL ALWAYS LOVE MY MAMA	Intruders	1974
I'LL ALWAYS LOVE YOU	Taylor Dayne	1988
I'LL ALWAYS LOVE YOU	Spinners	1965
I'LL BE	Foxy Brown featuring Jay-Z	1997
I'LL BE	Edwin McCain	1998
I'LL BE ALRIGHT WITHOUT YOU	Journey	1986
I'LL BE AROUND	Rappin' 4-Tay featuring The Spinners	1995
I'LL BE AROUND	Terri Wells	1984
I'LL BE BACK	Arnee & The Terminaters	1991
I'LL BE BY YOUR SIDE	Stevie B	1991
I'LL BE DOGGONE	Marvin Gaye	1965

SONG TITLE	ARTIST	DATE
I'LL BE GOOD	Rene & Angela	1985
I'LL BE GOOD TO YOU	Quincy Jones/Ray Charles & Chaka Khan	1990
I'LL BE GOOD TO YOU	Brothers Johnson	1976
I'LL BE HOME THIS CHRISTMAS	Shakin' Stevens	1991
I'LL BE IN TROUBLE	Temptations	1964
I'LL BE LOVING YOU (FOREVER)	New Kids On The Block	1989
I'LL BE MISSING YOU	Puff Daddy & Faith Evans featuring 112	1997
I'LL BE OVER YOU	Toto	1986
I'LL BE SATISFIED	Shakin' Stevens	1982
I'LL BE THE OTHER WOMAN	Soul Children	1974
I'LL BE THERE	Innocence	1992
I'LL BE THERE	99th Floor Elevators featuring Tony De Vit	1996
I'LL BE THERE	Jackie Trent	1969
I'LL BE THERE	Mariah Carey	1992
I'LL BE THERE	Gerry & The Pacemakers	1964
I'LL BE THERE	Jackson 5	1970
I'LL BE THERE	Emma Bunton	2004
I'LL BE THERE	Escape Club	1991
I'LL BE THERE FOR YOU	Bon Jovi	1989
I'LL BE THERE FOR YOU	Solid Harmonie	1998

SONG TITLE	ARTIST	DATE
I'LL BE THERE FOR YOU (DOYA DODODO DOYA)		
	House Of Virginism	1993
I'LL BE THERE FOR YOU/THIS HOUSE IS NOT A HOME		
	Rembrandts	1995
I'LL BE THERE FOR YOU/YOU'RE ALL I NEED TO GET BY		
	Method Man/Mary J. Blige	1995
I'LL BE YOUR ANGEL	Kira	2003
I'LL BE YOUR BABY TONIGHT		
	Robert Palmer And UB40	1990
I'LL BE YOUR EVERYTHING		
	Tommy Page	1990
I'LL BE YOUR FRIEND	Robert Owens	1997
I'LL BE YOUR SHELTER	Taylor Dayne	1990
I'LL BE YOUR SHELTER (IN TIME OF STORM)		
	Luther Ingram	1972
I'LL COME RUNNIN'	Cliff Richard	1967
I'LL CRY FOR YOU	Europe	1992
I'LL CRY INSTEAD	Beatles	1964
I'LL CUT YOUR TAIL OFF	John Leyton	1963
I'LL DO 4 YOU	Father M.C.	1991
I'LL DO ANYTHING YOU WANT ME TO		
	Barry White	1975
I'LL FIND MY WAY HOME	Jon & Vangelis	1981
I'LL FIND YOU	Michelle Gayle	1994
I'LL FLY FOR YOU	Spandau Ballet	1984
I'LL GET BY	Eddie Money	1991

SONG TITLE	ARTIST	DATE
I'LL GIVE ALL MY LOVE TO YOU		
	Keith Sweat	1990
I'LL GIVE YOU THE EARTH	Keith Michel	1971
I'LL GO ON HOPING	Des O'Connor	1970
I'LL GO WHERE THE MUSIC TAKES ME		
	Jimmy James & The Vagabonds	1976
I'LL GO WHERE YOUR MUSIC TAKES ME		
	Tina Charles	1978
I'LL HAVE TO SAY I LOVE YOU IN A SONG		
	Jim Croce	1974
I'LL HOUSE YOU	Jungle Brothers	1988
I'LL HOUSE YOU	Richie Rich	1988
I'LL HOUSE YOU '98	Jungle Brothers	1998
I'LL KEEP HOLDING ON	Marvelettes	1965
I'LL KEEP ON LOVING YOU		
	Princess	1986
I'LL KEEP YOU SATISFIED	Billy J. Kramer & The Dakotas	1964
I'LL LOVE YOU FOREVER TODAY		
	Cliff Richard	1968
I'LL MAKE ALL YOUR DREAMS COME TRUE		
	Ronnie Dove	1965
I'LL MAKE LOVE TO YOU	Boyz II Men	1994
I'LL MEET YOU AT MIDNIGHT		
	Smokie	1976
I'LL MEET YOU HALFWAY	Partridge Family	1971

SONG TITLE	ARTIST	DATE
I'LL NEVER BREAK YOUR HEART		
	Backstreet Boys	1998
I'LL NEVER FALL IN LOVE AGAIN		
	Bobbie Gentry	1969
I'LL NEVER FALL IN LOVE AGAIN		
	Tom Jones	1969
I'LL NEVER FALL IN LOVE AGAIN		
	Dionne Warwick	1969
I'LL NEVER FIND ANOTHER YOU		
	Seekers	1965
I'LL NEVER GET OVER YOU		
	Everly Brothers	1965
I'LL NEVER GET OVER YOU		
	Johnny Kidd & The Pirates	1963
I'LL NEVER GET OVER YOU (GETTING OVER ME)		
	Expose	1993
I'LL NEVER LET YOU GO	Steelheart	1991
I'LL NEVER LOVE THIS WAY AGAIN		
	Dionne Warwick	1979
I'LL NEVER QUITE GET OVER YOU		
	Billy Fury	1966
I'LL NEVER STOP	*NSYNC	2000
I'LL PICK A ROSE FOR MY ROSE		
	Marv Johnson	1969
I'LL PLAY FOR YOU	Seals & Crofts	1975

SONG TITLE	ARTIST	DATE
I'LL PUT YOU TOGETHER AGAIN (FROM DEAR ANYONE)		
	Hot Chocolate	1978
I'LL REMEMBER	Madonna	1994
I'LL SAIL THIS SHIP ALONE		
	Beautiful South	1989
I'LL SAY FOREVER MY LOVE		
	Jimmy Ruffin	1970
I'LL SEE IT THROUGH	Texas	2003
I'LL SEE YOU AROUND	Silver Sun	1998
I'LL SEE YOU IN MY DREAMS		
	Giant	1990
I'LL SLEEP WHEN I'M DEAD		
	Bon Jovi	1993
I'LL STAND BY YOU	Pretenders	1994
I'LL STAY BY YOU	Kenny Lynch	1965
I'LL STICK AROUND	Foo Fighters	1995
I'LL STILL BE LOVING YOU		
	Restless Heart	1987
I'LL STOP AT NOTHING	Sandie Shaw	1965
I'LL TAKE CARE OF YOUR CARES		
	Frankie Laine	1967
I'LL TAKE GOOD CARE OF YOU		
	Garnet Mimms	1966
I'LL TAKE YOU HOME	Drifters	1963
I'LL TAKE YOU THERE	Staple Singers	1972
I'LL TAKE YOU THERE	General Public	1994

SONG TITLE	ARTIST	DATE
I'LL THINK OF A REASON LATER		
	Lee Ann Womack	1999
I'LL TOUCH A STAR	Terry Stafford	1964
I'LL TRY ANYTHING	Dusty Springfield	1967
I'LL TRY SOMETHING NEW		
	Supremes	1969
I'LL TRY SOMETHING NEW		
	Temptations	1969
I'LL TUMBLE 4 YA	Culture Club	1983
I'LL WAIT	Taylor Dayne	1994
I'LL WAIT	Van Halen	1984
I'M A BELIEVER	EMF/Reeves And Mortimer	1995
I'M A BELIEVER	Monkees	1966
I'M A BELIEVER	Robert Wyatt	1974
I'M A BELIEVER	Smash Mouth	2001
I'M A BETTER MAN	Engelbert Humperdinck	1969
I'M A BOY	Who	1966
I'M A CLOWN/SOME KIND OF A SUMMER		
	David Cassidy	1973
I'M A CUCKOO	Belle & Sebastian	2004
I'M A-DOUN FOR LACK O'JOHNNIE (A LITTLE SCOTTISH		
FANTASY)	Vanessa-Mae	1996
I'M A FOOL	Dino, Desi & Billy	1965
I'M A GREEDY MAN (PART I)		
	James Brown	1971
I'M A HAPPY MAN	Jive Five	1965

SONG TITLE	ARTIST	DATE
I'M A MAN	Chicago	1970
I'M A MAN	Spencer Davis Group	1967
I'M A MAN	Yardbirds	1965
I'M A MAN NOT A BOY	Chesney Hawkes	1991
I'M A MAN NOT A BOY	North And South	1997
I'M A MIDNIGHT MOVER	Wilson Pickett	1968
I'M A SLAVE 4 U	Britney Spears	2001
I'M A THUG	Trick Daddy	2001
I'M A TIGER	Lulu	1968
I'M A TRAIN	Albert Hammond	1974
I'M A WOMAN	Maria Muldaur	1974
I'M A WONDERFUL THING (BABY)		
	Kid Creole & The Coconuts	1982
(I'M A) DREAMER	B B & Q Band	1986
(I'M A) ROAD RUNNER	Jr. Walker & The All-Stars	1969
I'M ALIVE	Electric Light Orchestra	1980
I'M ALIVE	Hollies	1965
I'M ALIVE	Stretch And Vern present	
	'Maddog'	1996
I'M ALIVE	Celine Dion	2002
I'M ALIVE	Neil Diamond	1983
I'M ALL ABOUT YOU	DJ Luck & MC Neat featuring	
	Ari Gold	2001
I'M ALMOST READY	Pure Prairie League	1980
I'M ALREADY THERE	Lonestar	2001

SONG TITLE	ARTIST	DATE
I'M ALRIGHT	Steve Wright & The Afternoon Boys	1982
I'M ALRIGHT	Kenny Loggins	1980
I'M ALWAYS TOUCHED (BY YOUR PRESENCE DEAR)	Blondie	1978
I'M AN UPSTART	Angelic Upstarts	1979
I'M BACK FOR MORE	Lulu And Bobby Womack	1993
I'M BORN AGAIN	Boney M	1979
I'M BROKEN	Pantera	1994
I'M COMIN' HOME	Tom Jones	1967
I'M COMIN' HOME	Tommy James	1971
I'M COMIN' HOME CINDY	Trini Lopez	1966
I'M COMING HOME	Spinners	1974
I'M COMING OUT	Diana Ross	1980
I'M COMING WITH YA	Matt Goss	2003
I'M CRYING	Animals	1964
I'M DOIN' FINE NOW	New York City	1973
I'M DOING FINE	Jason Donovan	1990
I'M DOING FINE NOW	Pasadenas	1992
I'M EASY	Keith Carradine	1976
I'M EASY/BE AGGRESSIVE	Faith No More	1993
I'M EVERY WOMAN	Chaka Khan	1978
I'M EVERY WOMAN	Whitney Houston	1993
I'M FALLING	Bluebells	1984
I'M FOREVER BLOWING BUBBLES	Cockney Rejects	1980

SONG TITLE	ARTIST	DATE
I'M FOREVER BLOWING BUBBLES	West Ham United Football Club	1975
I'M FREE	Roger Daltrey	1973
I'M FREE	Soup Dragons	1990
I'M FREE	Jon Secada	1993
I'M FREE	Who	1969
I'M FREE (HEAVEN HELPS THE MAN)	Kenny Loggins	1984
I'M GLAD	Jennifer Lopez	2003
I'M GOIN' DOWN	Mary J. Blige	1995
I'M GOIN' DOWN	Bruce Springsteen	1985
I'M GOING ALL THE WAY	Sounds Of Blackness	1995
I'M GOING SLIGHTLY MAD	Queen	1991
I'M GONE	Diana Ross	1995
I'M GONNA BE (500 MILES)	Proclaimers	1993
I'M GONNA BE A COUNTRY GIRL AGAIN	Buffy Sainte-Marie	1972
I'M GONNA BE ALRIGHT	Jennifer Lopez featuring Nas	2002
I'M GONNA BE STRONG	Cyndi Lauper	1995
I'M GONNA BE STRONG	Gene Pitney	1964
I'M GONNA GET ME A GUN	Cat Stevens	1967
I'M GONNA GET YOU	Bizarre Inc.	1992
I'M GONNA GETCHA GOOD!	Shania Twain	2002

SONG TITLE	ARTIST	DATE
I'M GONNA KNOCK ON YOUR DOOR		
	Little Jimmy Osmond	1974
I'M GONNA LET MY HEART DO THE WALKING		
	Supremes	1976
I'M GONNA LOVE YOU JUST A LITTLE MORE BABY		
	Barry White	1973
I'M GONNA MAKE YOU LOVE ME		
	Diana Ross & The Supremes	
	& The Temptations	1969
I'M GONNA MAKE YOU LOVE ME		
	Madeline Bell	1968
I'M GONNA MAKE YOU MINE		
	Lou Christie	1969
I'M GONNA MISS HER (THE FISHIN' SONG)		
	Brad Paisley	2002
I'M GONNA MISS YOU FOREVER		
	Aaron Carter	1998
I'M GONNA RUN AWAY FROM YOU		
	Tami Lynn	1971
I'M GONNA SIT RIGHT DOWN AND WRITE MYSELF		
A LETTER	Barry Manilow	1982
I'M GONNA SOOTHE YOU	Maria McKee	1993
I'M GONNA TAKE CARE OF EVERYTHING		
	Rubicon	1978
I'M GONNA TEAR YOUR PLAYHOUSE DOWN		
	Paul Young	1985

SONG TITLE	ARTIST	DATE
I'M HAPPY THAT LOVE HAS FOUND YOU		
	Jimmy Hall	1980
I'M HENRY VIII I AM	Herman's Hermits	1965
I'M IN A DIFFERENT WORLD		
	Four Tops	1968
I'M IN HEAVEN	Jason Nevins presents UKNY/	
	Holly James	2003
I'M IN LOVE	Starparty	2000
I'M IN LOVE	Fourmost	1963
I'M IN LOVE	Evelyn 'Champagne' King	1981
I'M IN LOVE	Aretha Franklin	1974
I'M IN LOVE AGAIN	Sad Cafe	1980
I'M IN LOVE WITH A GERMAN FILM STAR		
	Passions	1981
I'M IN LUV	Joe	1994
I'M IN THE MOOD	Ce Ce Peniston	1994
I'M IN THE MOOD FOR DANCING		
	Nolans	1979
I'M IN THE MOOD FOR LOVE		
	Jools Holland & Jamiroquai	2001
I'M IN YOU	Peter Frampton	1977
I'M INTO SOMETHIN' GOOD		
	Earl-Jean	1964
I'M INTO SOMETHING GOOD		
	Herman's Hermits	1964

SONG TITLE	ARTIST	DATE
I'M JUST A SINGER (IN A ROCK 'N' ROLL BAND)		
	Moody Blues	1973
I'M JUST TALKIN' ABOUT TONIGHT		
	Toby Keith	2001
I'M LEAVIN'	Elvis Presley	1971
I'M LEAVING	Lodger	1998
I'M LEAVING IT (ALL) UP TO YOU		
	Donny & Marie Osmond	1974
I'M LIKE A BIRD	Nelly Furtado	2001
I'M LIVIN' IN SHAME	Diana Ross & The Supremes	1969
I'M LOOKING FOR THE ONE (TO BE WITH ME)		
	D.J. Jazzy Jeff & The Fresh	
	Prince	1993
I'M LOST WITHOUT YOU	Billy Fury	1965
I'M MANDY FLY ME	10cc	1976
I'M NEVER GIVING UP	Sweet Dreams	1983
I'M NEVER GONNA BE ALONE ANYMORE		
	Cornelius Brothers & Sister Rose	1972
I'M NO ANGEL	Marcella Detroit	1994
I'M NOT A GIRL, NOT YET A WOMAN		
	Britney Spears	2002
I'M NOT FEELING YOU	Yvette Michelle	1997
I'M NOT GIVING YOU UP	Gloria Estefan	1996
I'M NOT GONNA LET IT BOTHER ME TONIGHT		
	Atlanta Rhythm Section	1978

SONG TITLE	ARTIST	DATE
I'M NOT GONNA LET YOU (GET THE BEST OF ME)		
	Colonel Abrams	1986
I'M NOT IN LOVE	Will To Power	1990
I'M NOT IN LOVE	10cc	1975
I'M NOT IN LOVE	Fun Lovin' Criminals	1997
I'M NOT LISA	Jessi Colter	1975
I'M NOT MY BROTHER'S KEEPER		
	Flaming Ember	1970
I'M NOT READY	Keith Sweat	1999
I'M NOT SCARED	Eighth Wonder	1988
I'M NOT THE MAN I USED TO BE		
	Fine Young Cannibals	1989
I'M NOT THE ONE	Cars	1986
(I'M NOT YOUR) STEPPIN' STONE		
	Monkees	1966
(I'M NOT YOUR) STEPPING STONE		
	Sex Pistols	1980
I'M ON FIRE	5000 Volts	1975
I'M ON FIRE	Dwight Twilley Band	1975
I'M ON FIRE	Bruce Springsteen	1985
I'M ON MY WAY	Dean Parrish	1975
I'M ON MY WAY TO A BETTER PLACE		
	Chairmen Of The Board	1973
I'M ON THE OUTSIDE (LOOKING IN)		
	Little Anthony & The Imperials	1964

SONG TITLE	ARTIST	DATE
I'M ONLY SLEEPING/OFF ON HOLIDAY		
	Suggs	1995
I'M OUTTA LOVE	Anastacia	2000
I'M OVER YOU	Martine McCutcheon	2000
I'M QUALIFIED TO SATISFY YOU		
	Barry White	1977
I'M RAVING	Scooter	1996
I'M READY	Size 9	1995
I'M READY	Bryan Adams	1998
I'M READY	Tevin Campbell	1994
I'M READY FOR LOVE	Martha & The Vandellas	1966
I'M REAL	James Brown featuring	
	Full Force	1988
I'M REAL	Jennifer Lopez	2001
I'M REALLY HOT	Missy Elliott	2004
I'M RIGHT HERE	Samantha Mumba	2002
I'M RUSHING	Bump	1992
I'M SO CRAZY	Par-T-One vs INXS	2001
I'M SO CRAZY ('BOUT YOU)		
	KC & The Sunshine Band	1975
I'M SO EXCITED	Pointer Sisters	1984
I'M SO HAPPY/TIME	Light Of The World	1981
I'M SO INTO YOU	SWV	1993
I'M SO LONELY	Cast	1997
I'M SO LONESOME I COULD CRY		
	B.J. Thomas & The Triumphs	1966

SONG TITLE	ARTIST	DATE
I'M SO PROUD	Impressions	1964
I'M SORRY/CALYPSO	John Denver	1975
I'M STILL GONNA NEED YOU		
	Osmonds	1975
I'M STILL IN LOVE WITH YOU		
	Al Green	1972
I'M STILL IN LOVE WITH YOU		
	Sean Paul featuring Sasha	2004
I'M STILL IN LOVE WITH YOU		
	New Edition	1996
I'M STILL SEARCHING	Glass Tiger	1988
I'M STILL STANDING	Elton John	1983
I'M STILL WAITING	Diana Ross	1971
I'M STONE IN LOVE WITH YOU		
	Johnny Mathis	1975
I'M STONE IN LOVE WITH YOU		
	Stylistics	1972
I'M TELLING YOU NOW	Freddie & The Dreamers	1965
I'M THAT TYPE OF GUY	LL Cool J	1989
I'M THE LEADER OF THE GANG (I AM!)		
	Hulk Hogan/Green Jelly	1993
I'M THE LEADER OF THE GANG (I AM)		
	Gary Glitter	1973
I'M THE LONELY ONE	Cliff Richard	1964
I'M THE MAN	Anthrax	1987
I'M THE ONE	Gerry & The Pacemakers	1964

SONG TITLE	ARTIST	DATE
I'M THE ONE YOU NEED	Jody Watley	1992
I'M THE ONLY ONE	Melissa Etheridge	1994
I'M THE URBAN SPACEMAN		
	Bonzo Dog Doo-Dah Band	1968
I'M TIRED OF GETTING PUSHED AROUND		
	2 Men A Drum Machine And A Trumpet	1988
I'M TOO SCARED	Steven Dante	1988
I'M TOO SEXY	Right Said Fred	1991
I'M WAKING UP TO US	Belle & Sebastian	2001
I'M WITH YOU	Avril Lavigne	2003
I'M WONDERING	Stevie Wonder	1967
I'M YOUR ANGEL	Celine Dion & R. Kelly	1998
I'M YOUR BABY TONIGHT	Whitney Houston	1990
I'M YOUR BOOGIE MAN	KC & The Sunshine Band	1977
I'M YOUR MAN	Lisa Moorish	1995
I'M YOUR MAN	Wham!	1985
I'M YOUR MAN	Shane Richie	2003
I'M YOUR PUPPET	James & Bobby Purify	1966
I'M YOURS	Elvis Presley	1965
I'VE BEEN A BAD, BAD BOY		
	Paul Jones	1967
I'VE BEEN AROUND THE WORLD		
	Marti Pellow	2001
I'VE BEEN DRINKIN'	Rod Stewart	1973
I'VE BEEN DRINKING	Jeff Beck	1973

SONG TITLE	ARTIST	DATE
I'VE BEEN HURT	Guy Darrell	1973
I'VE BEEN HURT	Bill Deal & The Rhondels	1969
I'VE BEEN IN LOVE BEFORE		
	Cutting Crew	1987
I'VE BEEN LONELY SO LONG		
	Frederick Knight	1972
I'VE BEEN LONELY TOO LONG		
	Young Rascals	1967
I'VE BEEN LOSING YOU	A-Ha	1986
I'VE BEEN LOVING YOU TOO LONG (TO STOP NOW)		
	Otis Redding	1965
I'VE BEEN THINKING ABOUT YOU		
	Londonbeat	1991
I'VE BEEN THIS WAY BEFORE		
	Neil Diamond	1975
I'VE BEEN WRONG BEFORE		
	Cilla Black	1965
(I'VE BEEN) SEARCHIN' SO LONG		
	Chicago	1974
I'VE DONE EVERYTHING FOR YOU		
	Sammy Hagar	1980
I'VE DONE EVERYTHING FOR YOU		
	Rick Springfield	1981
I'VE FOUND SOMEONE OF MY OWN		
	Free Movement	1971

SONG TITLE	ARTIST	DATE
I'VE GOT A FEELING (WE'LL BE SEEING EACH OTHER AGAIN)	Al Wilson	1976
I'VE GOT A LITTLE PUPPY	Smurfs	1996
I'VE GOT A LITTLE SOMETHING FOR YOU	MN8	1995
I'VE GOT A ROCK 'N' ROLL HEART	Eric Clapton	1983
I'VE GOT A THING ABOUT YOU BABY/TAKE GOOD CARE OF YOU	Elvis Presley	1974
I'VE GOT A TIGER BY THE TAIL	Buck Owens	1965
I'VE GOT A LOT TO LEARN ABOUT LOVE	Storm	1991
I'VE GOT LOVE ON MY MIND	Natalie Cole	1977
I'VE GOT NEWS FOR YOU	Feargal Sharkey	1991
I'VE GOT SAND IN MY SHOES	Drifters	1964
I'VE GOT SO MUCH TO GIVE	Barry White	1973
I'VE GOT SOMETHING TO SAY	Reef	1999
I'VE GOT THE MUSIC IN ME	Kiki Dee	1974
I'VE GOT THIS FEELING	Mavericks	1998

SONG TITLE	ARTIST	DATE
I'VE GOT TO BE SOMEBODY	Billy Joe Royal	1965
I'VE GOT TO USE MY IMAGINATION	Gladys Knight & The Pips	1973
I'VE GOT YOU	Martine McCutcheon	1999
I'VE GOT YOU ON MY MIND	Dorian Gray	1968
I'VE GOT YOU ON MY MIND	White Plains	1970
I'VE GOT YOU UNDER MY SKIN	Neneh Cherry	1990
I'VE GOT YOU UNDER MY SKIN	Four Seasons	1966
I'VE GOTTA BE ME	Sammy Davis Jr.	1968
I'VE GOTTA GET A MESSAGE TO YOU	Bee Gees	1968
I'VE HAD ENOUGH	Earth, Wind & Fire	1982
I'VE HAD ENOUGH	Paul McCartney	1978
(I'VE HAD) THE TIME OF MY LIFE	Bill Medley & Jennifer Warnes	1987
I'VE LOST YOU/THE NEXT STEP IS LOVE	Elvis Presley	1970
I'VE NEVER BEEN TO ME	Charlene	1982
I'VE NEVER FOUND A GIRL (TO LOVE ME LIKE YOU DO)	Eddie Floyd	1968

SONG TITLE	ARTIST	DATE
I'VE PASSED THIS WAY BEFORE		
	Jimmy Ruffin	1966
1-2-3	Len Barry	1965
I.G.Y. (WHAT A BEAUTIFUL WORLD)		
	Donald Fagen	1982
I.O.U.	Freeez	1983
I.O.U.	Jimmy Dean	1976
I'VE GOT A THING ABOUT YOU BABY		
	Elvis Presley	1974
ICE CREAM	Chef Raekwon	1995
THE ICE CREAM MAN	Tornados	1963
ICE HOCKEY HAIR	Super Furry Animals	1998
ICE ICE BABY	Vanilla Ice	1990
ICE IN THE SUN	Status Quo	1968
ICEBLINK LUCK	Cocteau Twins	1990
ICH BIN EIN AUSLANDER	Pop Will Eat Itself	1994
ICH WILL	Rammstein	2002
ICING ON THE CAKE	Stephen 'Tin Tin' Duffy	1985
IDEAL WORLD	Christians	1988
IDENTITY	X-Ray Spex	1978
IDIOTS AT THE WHEEL (EP)		
	Kingmaker	1992
IESHA	Another Bad Creation	1991
IF	Telly Savalas	1975
IF	Janet Jackson	1993
IF	Yin & Yan	1975

SONG TITLE	ARTIST	DATE
IF	Bread	1971
IF ANYONE FALLS	Stevie Nicks	1983
IF EVER YOU'RE IN MY ARMS AGAIN		
	Peabo Bryson	1984
IF EVERY DAY WAS LIKE CHRISTMAS		
	Elvis Presley	1966
IF EVERYBODY LOOKED THE SAME		
	Groove Armada	1999
IF GOD WILL SEND HIS ANGELS		
	U2	1997
IF HE TELLS YOU	Adam Faith	1964
IF I AIN'T GOT YOU	Alicia Keys	2004
IF I CAN DREAM	Elvis Presley	1968
IF I CAN'T CHANGE YOUR MIND		
	Sugar	1993
IF I CAN'T HAVE YOU	Yvonne Elliman	1978
IF I CAN'T HAVE YOU	Kim Wilde	1993
IF I CAN'T/ ... THEM THANGS		
	50 Cent & G-Unit	2004
IF I COULD	David Essex	1975
IF I COULD	Hundred Reasons	2002
IF I COULD (EL CONDOR PASA)		
	Julie Felix	1970
IF I COULD BUILD MY WHOLE WORLD AROUND YOU		
	Marvin Gaye & Tammi Terrell	1967
IF I COULD FLY	Grace	1996

SONG TITLE	ARTIST	DATE
IF I COULD GO!	Angie Martinez featuring Lil' Mo & Sacario	2002
IF I COULD ONLY MAKE YOU CARE	Mike Berry	1980
IF I COULD ONLY SAY GOODBYE	David Hasselhoff	1993
IF I COULD REACH YOU	5th Dimension	1972
IF I COULD TALK I'D TELL YOU	Lemonheads	1996
IF I COULD TEACH THE WORLD	Bone Thugs-N-Harmony	1997
IF I COULD TURN BACK THE HANDS OF TIME	R. Kelly	1999
IF I COULD TURN BACK TIME	Cher	1989
IF I DIDN'T CARE	David Cassidy	1974
IF I EVER FALL IN LOVE	Shai	1992
IF I EVER LOSE MY FAITH IN YOU	Sting	1993
IF I EVER LOSE THIS HEAVEN	Average White Band	1975
IF I EVER SEE YOU AGAIN	Roberta Flack	1978
IF I FALL YOU'RE GOING DOWN WITH ME	Dixie Chicks	2001
IF I GIVE YOU MY NUMBER	PJ And Duncan	1994

SONG TITLE	ARTIST	DATE
IF I HAD A HAMMER	Trini Lopez	1963
IF I HAD MY WISH TONIGHT	David Lasley	1982
IF I HAD NO LOOT	Tony Toni Tone	1993
IF I HAD WORDS	Scott Fitzgerald & Yvonne Keeley	1978
IF I HAD YOU	Korgis	1979
IF I HAVE TO GO AWAY	Jigsaw	1977
IF I KNEW THEN WHAT I KNOW NOW	Val Doonican	1968
IF I LET YOU GO	Westlife	1999
IF I LOVED YOU	Richard Anthony	1964
IF I LOVED YOU	Chad & Jeremy	1965
IF I NEEDED SOMEONE	Hollies	1965
IF I NEVER SEE YOU AGAIN	Wet Wet Wet	1997
IF I ONLY HAD TIME	John Rowles	1968
IF I ONLY KNEW	Tom Jones	1994
IF I RULED THE WORLD	Kurtis Blow	1986
IF I RULED THE WORLD	Tony Bennett	1965
IF I RULED THE WORLD	Harry Secombe	1963
IF I RULED THE WORLD	Nas	1996
IF I SAID YOU HAD A BEAUTIFUL BODY	Bellamy Brothers	1979
IF I SAY YES	Five Star	1986
IF I THOUGHT YOU'D EVER CHANGE YOUR MIND	Cilla Black	1969

SONG TITLE	ARTIST	DATE
IF I THOUGHT YOU'D EVER CHANGE YOUR MIND		
	Agnetha Faltskog	2004
IF I TOLD YOU THAT	Whitney Houston/	
	George Michael	2000
IF I WANTED TO/LIKE THE WAY I DO		
	Melissa Etheridge	1995
IF I WAS	Midge Ure	1985
IF I WAS YOUR GIRLFRIEND		
	Prince	1987
IF I WERE A CARPENTER	Bobby Darin	1966
IF I WERE A CARPENTER	Four Tops	1968
IF I WERE A CARPENTER	Johnny Cash & June Carter	1970
IF I WERE A RICH MAN	Topol	1967
IF I WERE YOU	Candee Jay	2004
IF I WERE YOUR WOMAN	Gladys Knight & The Pips	1970
IF I'D BEEN THE ONE	38 Special	1983
IF IT HAPPENS AGAIN	UB40	1984
IF IT ISN'T LOVE	New Edition	1988
IF IT MAKES YOU HAPPY	Sheryl Crow	1996
IF IT WASN'T FOR THE REASON THAT I LOVE YOU		
	Miki Anthony	1973
IF LEAVING ME IS EASY	Phil Collins	1981
IF LIFE IS LIKE A LOVE BANK.../GEORDIE IN		
WONDERLAND	Wildhearts	1995
IF LOVING YOU IS WRONG (I DON'T WANT TO BE		
RIGHT)	Rod Stewart	1980

SONG TITLE	ARTIST	DATE
(IF LOVING YOU IS WRONG) I DON'T WANT TO BE		
RIGHT	Barbara Mandrell	1979
(IF LOVING YOU IS WRONG) I DON'T WANNA BE RIGHT		
	Luther Ingram	1972
IF MADONNA CALLS	Junior Vasquez	1996
IF MY HEART HAD WINGS		
	Faith Hill	2001
IF NOT FOR YOU	Olivia Newton-John	1971
IF NOT YOU	Dr. Hook	1976
IF ONLY	Hanson	2000
IF ONLY I COULD	Sydney Youngblood	1989
(IF PARADISE IS) HALF AS NICE		
	Amen Corner	1969
IF SHE KNEW WHAT SHE WANTS		
	Bangles	1986
IF SHE WOULD HAVE BEEN FAITHFUL		
	Chicago	1987
IF THAT WERE ME	Melanie C	2000
IF THE KIDS ARE UNITED	Sham 69	1978
IF THE LOVE FITS WEAR IT	Leslie Pearl	1982
IF THE RIVER CAN BEND	Elton John	1998
IF THE WHOLE WORLD STOPPED LOVIN'		
	Val Doonican	1967
(IF THERE WAS) ANY OTHER WAY		
	Celine Dion	1991
IF THIS IS IT	Huey Lewis & The News	1984

SONG TITLE	ARTIST	DATE
IF TOMORROW NEVER COMES	Ronan Keating	2002
IF U WERE MINE	U-Krew	1990
IF WE CAN MAKE IT THROUGH DECEMBER	Merle Haggard	1973
IF WE HOLD ON TOGETHER	Diana Ross	1992
IF WE TRY	Karen Ramirez	1998
IF WE WERE LOVERS/CON LOS ANOS QUE ME QUEDAN	Gloria Estefan	1993
IF WISHES CAME TRUE	Sweet Sensation	1990
IF YA GETTIN' DOWN	5ive	1999
IF YOU (LOVIN' ME)	Silk	1999
IF YOU ASKED ME TO	Celine Dion	1992
IF YOU BUY THIS RECORD YOUR LIFE WILL BE BETTER	Tamperer/Maya	1998
IF YOU CAN WANT	Smokey Robinson & The Miracles	1968
IF YOU CAN'T GIVE ME LOVE	Suzi Quatro	1978
IF YOU CAN'T STAND THE HEAT	Bucks Fizz	1982
IF YOU COME BACK	Blue	2001
IF YOU COME TO ME	Atomic Kitten	2003
IF YOU COULD READ MY MIND	Stars On 54	1998

SONG TITLE	ARTIST	DATE
IF YOU COULD READ MY MIND	Gordon Lightfoot	1970
IF YOU DON'T KNOW ME BY NOW	Harold Melvin & The Blue Notes	1972
IF YOU DON'T KNOW ME BY NOW	Simply Red	1989
IF YOU DON'T LOVE ME	Prefab Sprout	1992
IF YOU DON'T WANT ME TO DESTROY YOU	Super Furry Animals	1996
IF YOU EVER	East 17 featuring Gabrielle	1996
IF YOU EVER LEAVE ME	Barbra Streisand/Vince Gill	1999
IF YOU EVER STOP LOVING ME	Montgomery Gentry	2004
IF YOU GO	Jon Secada	1994
IF YOU GO AWAY	Terry Jacks	1974
IF YOU GO AWAY	New Kids On The Block	1991
IF YOU GOTTA GO, GO NOW	Manfred Mann	1965
IF YOU GOTTA MAKE A FOOL OF SOMEBODY	Freddie & The Dreamers	1963
IF YOU HAD MY LOVE	Jennifer Lopez	1999
IF YOU KNOW WHAT I MEAN	Neil Diamond	1976
IF YOU LEAVE	Orchestral Manoeuvres In The Dark	1986
IF YOU LEAVE ME NOW	Upside Down	1996

SONG TITLE	ARTIST	DATE
IF YOU LEAVE ME NOW	Chicago	1976
IF YOU LEAVE ME TONIGHT I'LL CRY	Jerry Wallace	1972
(IF YOU LET ME MAKE LOVE TO YOU THEN) WHY CAN'T I TOUCH YOU?	Ronnie Dyson	1970
IF YOU LET ME STAY	Terence Trent D'Arby	1987
IF YOU LOVE HER	Dick Emery	1969
IF YOU LOVE ME	Brownstone	1994
IF YOU LOVE ME	Mint Condition	1999
IF YOU LOVE ME (I WON'T CARE)	Mary Hopkin	1976
IF YOU LOVE ME (LET ME KNOW)	Olivia Newton-John	1974
IF YOU LOVE SOMEBODY SET THEM FREE	Sting	1965
IF YOU NEEDED SOMEBODY	Bad Company	1990
IF YOU ONLY LET ME IN	MN8	1995
IF YOU REALLY CARED	Gabrielle	1996
IF YOU REALLY LOVE ME	Stevie Wonder	1971
IF YOU REMEMBER ME	Chris Thompson & Night	1979
IF YOU SHOULD SAIL	Nielsen/Pearson	1980
IF YOU TALK IN YOUR SLEEP	Elvis Presley	1974
IF YOU THINK I'M JIGGY	Lox	1998

SONG TITLE	ARTIST	DATE
IF YOU THINK YOU KNOW HOW TO LOVE ME	Smokey	1975
IF YOU THINK YOU'RE LONELY NOW	K-Ci Hailey Of Jodeci	1995
IF YOU TOLERATE THIS YOUR CHILDREN WILL BE NEXT	Manic Street Preachers	1998
IF YOU WALK AWAY	Peter Cox	1997
IF YOU WANNA BE HAPPY	Jimmy Soul	1963
IF YOU WANNA GET TO HEAVEN	Ozark Mountain Daredevils	1974
IF YOU WANNA PARTY	Molella featuring The Outhere Brothers	1995
IF YOU WANT IT	Niteflyte	1979
IF YOU WANT ME	Hinda Hicks	1998
IF YOU WANT ME TO STAY	Sly & The Family Stone	1973
IF YOU WERE HERE TONIGHT	Matt Goss	1996
IF YOU WERE HERE TONIGHT	Alexander O'Neal	1986
IF YOU WERE WITH ME NOW	Kylie Minogue/Keith Washington	1991
IF YOU'LL BE MINE	Babybird	1998
IF YOU'RE GONE	Matchbox Twenty	2000
IF YOU'RE LOOKIN' FOR A WAY OUT	Odyssey	1980

SONG TITLE	ARTIST	DATE
IF YOU'RE NOT THE ONE	Daniel Bedingfield	2002
IF YOU'RE READY (COME GO WITH ME)	Jonathan Butler	1986
IF YOU'RE READY (COME GO WITH ME)	Ruby Turner	1986
IF YOU'RE READY (COME GO WITH ME)	Staple Singers	1974
IF YOU'RE THINKING OF ME	Dodgy	1996
IF YOUR GIRL ONLY KNEW/ONE IN A MILLION	Aaliyah	1997
IF...	Bluetones	1998
IF/KEEP ON RUNNING	John Alford	1996
IGNITION	R. Kelly	2002
IGUANA	Mauro Picotto	2000
IKO IKO	Belle Stars	1989
IKO IKO	Dixie Cups	1965
IKO IKO	Natasha	1982
IL SILENZIO	Nini Rosso	1965
ILLUSIONS	Cypress Hill	1996
ILOVEROCKNROLL	Jesus And Mary Chain	1998
IM NIN'ALU	Ofra Haza	1988
IMAGINARY LOVER	Atlanta Rhythm Section	1978
IMAGINATION	Belouis Some	1986
IMAGINATION	Rocky Sharpe & The Replays	1979
IMAGINATION	Tamia	1998

SONG TITLE	ARTIST	DATE
IMAGINE	Shola Ama	2000
IMAGINE	John Lennon	1971
IMAGINE ME, IMAGINE YOU	Fox	1975
IMITATION OF LIFE	Billie Ray Martin	1996
IMITATION OF LIFE	R.E.M.	2001
THE IMMIGRANT	Neil Sedaka	1975
IMMIGRANT SONG	Led Zeppelin	1970
IMMIGRATION MAN	David Crosby	1972
IMMIGRATION MAN	Graham Nash	1972
IMMORTALITY	Celine Dion With The Bee Gees	1998
IMPERIAL WIZARD	David Essex	1979
THE IMPORTANCE OF YOUR LOVE	Vince Hill	1968
IMPOSSIBLE	Captain Hollywood Project	1994
IMPOSSIBLE	Charlatans	2000
THE IMPOSSIBLE	Joe Nichols	2002
THE IMPOSSIBLE DREAM (THE QUEST)	Jack Jones	1966
THE IMPOSSIBLE DREAM	Carter The Unstoppable Sex Machine	1992
THE IMPRESSION THAT I GET	Mighty Mighty Bosstones	1998
IMPULSIVE	Wilson Phillips	1990
IN & OUT	Speedway	2004
IN A BIG COUNTRY	Big Country	1983

SONG TITLE	ARTIST	DATE
IN A BROKEN DREAM	Thunder	1995
IN A BROKEN DREAM	Python Lee Jackson	1972
IN A DREAM	Longview	2004
IN A LIFETIME	Clannad	1989
IN A MOMENT	Intrigues	1969
IN A ROOM	Dodgy	1996
IN A WORD OR 2/THE POWER		
	Monie Love	1993
IN ALL THE RIGHT PLACES	Lisa Stansfield	1993
IN AMERICA	Charlie Daniels Band	1980
IN AND OUT	3rd Edge	2002
IN AND OUT OF LOVE	Imagination	1981
IN AND OUT OF LOVE	Diana Ross & The Supremes	1967
IN AND OUT OF MY LIFE	A.T.F.C. presents Onephatdeeva	1999
IN BETWEEN DAYS	Cure	1985
THE IN BETWEENIES/FATHER CHRISTMAS DO NOT		
TOUCH ME	Goodies	1974
IN BLOOM	Nirvana	1992
THE 'IN' CROWD	Dobie Gray	1965
THE 'IN' CROWD	Ramsey Lewis Trio	1965
THE IN CROWD	Bryan Ferry	1974
IN DA CLUB	50 Cent	2003
IN DE GHETTO	David Morales & The Bad Yard	
	Club	1996
IN DEMAND	Texas	2000
IN DREAMS	Roy Orbison	1963

SONG TITLE	ARTIST	DATE
IN DULCE JUBILO/ON HORSEBACK		
	Mike Oldfield	1975
IN FOR A PENNY	Slade	1975
IN LOVE	Datsuns	2002
IN LOVE	Lisa Maffia	2003
IN MY ARMS	Erasure	1997
IN MY BED	Dru Hill	1997
IN MY CHAIR	Status Quo	1970
IN MY DAUGHTER'S EYES	Martina McBride	2004
IN MY DEFENCE	Freddie Mercury	1992
IN MY DREAMS	Will Downing	1988
IN MY DREAMS	Party	1991
IN MY DREAMS	REO Speedwagon	1987
IN MY EYES	Milk Inc.	2002
IN MY EYES	Stevie B	1989
IN MY HOUSE	Clock	1995
IN MY HOUSE	Mary Jane Girls	1985
IN MY OWN TIME	Family	1971
IN MY PLACE	Coldplay	2002
IN MY WORLD	Anthrax	1990
IN NEON	Elton John	1984
IN OUR LIFETIME	Texas	1999
IN PRIVATE	Dusty Springfield	1989
IN SUMMER	Billy Fury	1963
IN THE AIR TONIGHT	Phil Collins	1981
IN THE AIR TONITE	Lil' Kim featuring Phil Collins	2001

SONG TITLE	ARTIST	DATE
IN THE ARMS OF LOVE	Andy Williams	1966
IN THE ARMY NOW	Status Quo	1986
IN THE BAD BAD OLD DAYS		
	Foundations	1969
IN THE BEGINNING	Roger Goode featuring	
	Tasha Baxter	2002
IN THE BROWNIES	Billy Connolly	1979
IN THE BUSH	Musique	1978
IN THE CHAPEL IN THE MOONLIGHT		
	Bachelors	1965
IN THE CHAPEL IN THE MOONLIGHT		
	Dean Martin	1967
IN THE CITY	Jam	2002
IN THE CLOSET	Michael Jackson	1992
IN THE COUNTRY	Cliff Richard	1966
IN THE DARK	Billy Squier	1981
IN THE END	Linkin Park	2001
IN THE GHETTO	Elvis Presley	1969
IN THE HEAT OF THE NIGHT		
	Imagination	1982
IN THE HEAT OF THE NIGHT		
	Ray Charles	1967
IN THE HOUSE OF STONE AND LIGHT		
	Martin Page	1994
IN THE MEANTIME	Spacehog	1996
IN THE MEANTIME	Georgie Fame	1965

SONG TITLE	ARTIST	DATE
IN THE MIDDLE	Alexander O'Neal	1993
IN THE MIDDLE OF NOWHERE		
	Dusty Springfield	1965
IN THE MIDDLE OF THE NIGHT		
	Magic Affair	1994
IN THE MIDNIGHT HOUR	Wilson Pickett	1965
IN THE MIDNIGHT HOUR	Cross Country	1973
IN THE MISTY MOONLIGHT		
	Jerry Wallace	1964
IN THE MOOD	Ray Stevens	1977
IN THE MOOD	Glenn Miller	1976
IN THE MOOD	Robert Plant	1983
IN THE NAME OF LOVE	Sharon Redd	1983
IN THE NAME OF THE FATHER		
	Black Grape	1995
IN THE NAVY	Village People	1979
IN THE NAVY (1994 REMIXES)		
	Village People	1994
IN THE ONES YOU LOVE	Diana Ross	1996
IN THE RAIN	Dramatics	1973
IN THE SHADOWS	The Rasmus	2004
IN THE STILL OF THE NIGHT (I'LL REMEMBER)		
	Boyz II Men	1992
IN THE SUMMERTIME	Mungo Jerry	1970
IN THE SUMMERTIME	Shaggy featuring Rayvon	1995

SONG TITLE	ARTIST	DATE
IN THE YEAR 2525 (EXORDIUM & TERMINUS)		
	Zager & Evans	1969
(IN THE) COLD LIGHT OF DAY		
	Gene Pitney	1967
IN THESE ARMS	Bon Jovi	1993
IN THIS WORLD	Moby	2002
IN THOUGHTS OF YOU	Billy Fury	1965
IN TOO DEEP	Dead Or Alive	1985
IN TOO DEEP	Belinda Carlisle	1996
IN TOO DEEP	Genesis	1987
IN TOO DEEP	Sum 41	2001
IN WALKED LOVE	Louise	1996
IN YER FACE	808 State	1991
IN YOUR ARMS (RESCUE ME)		
	Nu Generation	2000
IN YOUR CAR	Kenickie	1997
IN YOUR CAR	Coolnotes	1985
IN YOUR CARE	Tasmin Archer	1993
IN YOUR EYES	Niamh Kavanagh	1993
IN YOUR EYES	George Benson	1983
IN YOUR EYES	Kylie Minogue	2002
IN YOUR EYES	Peter Gabriel	1986
IN YOUR LETTER	REO Speedwagon	1981
IN YOUR ROOM	Bangles	1988
IN YOUR ROOM	Depeche Mode	1994
IN YOUR SOUL	Corey Hart	1988

SONG TITLE	ARTIST	DATE
IN YOUR WILDEST DREAMS		
	Tina Turner featuring Barry White	1996
IN ZAIRE	Johnny Wakelin	1976
IN-A-GADA-DA-VIDA	Iron Butterfly	1968
INBETWEENER	Sleeper	1995
INCE AGAIN	A Tribe Called Quest	1996
INCENSE AND PEPPERMINTS		
	Strawberry Alarm Clock	1967
THE INCIDENTALS	Alisha's Attic	1998
INCOMMUNICADO	Marillion	1987
INCOMPLETE	Sisqo	2000
INCREDIBLE	M-Beat featuring General Levy	1994
INCREDIBLE (WHAT I MEANT TO SAY)		
	Darius	2003
INDEPENDENCE	Lulu	1993
INDEPENDENT LOVE SONG		
	Scarlet	1995
INDEPENDENT WOMEN PART I		
	Destiny's Child	2000
INDESCRIBABLY BLUE	Elvis Presley	1967
INDESTRUCTIBLE	Four Tops featuring Smokey Robinson	1989
INDESTRUCTIBLE	Alisha's Attic	1997
INDIAN GIVER	1910 Fruitgum Co.	1969
INDIAN LAKE	Cowsills	1968

SONG TITLE	ARTIST	DATE
INDIAN LOVE CALL	Karl Denver	1963
INDIAN LOVE CALL	Ray Stevens	1975
INDIAN OUTLAW	Tim McGraw	1994
INDIAN RESERVATION	Don Fardon	1970
INDIAN RESERVATION (THE LAMENT OF THE CHEROKEE		
RESERVATION)	Raiders	1971
INDIANA WANTS ME	R. Dean Taylor	1970
INFATUATION	Rod Stewart	1984
INFECTED	Barthezz	2002
INFERNO	Souvlaki	1997
INFIDELITY	Simply Red	1987
INFILTRATE 202	Altern 8	1991
INFINITE DREAMS	Iron Maiden	1989
INFINITY	Guru Josh	1990
INFORMER	Snow	1993
INHERIT THE WIND	Wilton Felder	1980
THE INK IN THE WELL	David Sylvian	1984
INKANYEZI NEZAZI (THE STAR & THE WISEMAN)		
	Ladysmith Black Mambazo	1997
INNA CITY MAMMA	Neneh Cherry	1989
INNER CITY BLUES (MAKES ME WANNA HOLLER)		
	Marvin Gaye	1971
INNER CITY LIFE	Goldie	1995
INNER SMILE	Texas	2001
INNOCENT EYES	Delta Goodrem	2003
AN INNOCENT MAN	Billy Joel	1983

SONG TITLE	ARTIST	DATE
INNOCENTE (FALLING IN LOVE)		
	Delerium featuring Leigh Nash	2001
INNUENDO	Queen	1991
INSANE IN THE BRAIN	Cypress Hill	1993
INSANE IN THE BRAIN	Jason Nevins Vs Cypress Hill	1999
INSANIA	Peter Andre	2004
INSANITY	Oceanic	1991
INSATIABLE	Darren Hayes	2002
INSATIABLE	Thick D	2002
INSENSITIVE	Jann Arden	1996
INSEPARABLE	Natalie Cole	1975
INSIDE	Stiltskin	1994
INSIDE AMERICA	Juggy Jones	1976
INSIDE LOOKING OUT	Grand Funk Railroad	1971
INSIDE OUT	Culture Beat	1996
INSIDE OUT	Odyssey	1982
INSIDE OUT	Eve 6	1998
INSIDE OUT	Shara Nelson	1994
INSIDE LOOKING OUT	Animals	1966
INSOMNIA	Faithless	1996
INSOMNIA	Feeder	1999
INSPIRATION	Strike	1996
INSTANT KARMA	Lennon, Ono & The Plastic	
	Ono Band	1970
INSTANT REPLAY	Dan Hartman	1978
INSTANT REPLAY	Yell!	1990

SONG TITLE	ARTIST	DATE
INSTINCT	Crowded House	1996
INSTINCTION	Spandau Ballet	1982
INTACT	Ned's Atomic Dustbin	1992
INTERESTING DRUG	Morrissey	1989
INTERGALACTIC	Beastie Boys	1998
INTERLUDE	Morrissey & Siouxsie	1994
INTERNAL EXILE	Fish	1991
INTERNATIONAL BRIGHT YOUNG THING		
	Jesus Jones	1991
THE INTERNATIONAL LANGUAGE OF SCREAMING		
	Super Furry Animals	1997
INTERNATIONAL RESCUE	Fuzzbox	1989
INTO THE BLUE	Mission	1990
INTO THE BLUE	Moby	1995
INTO THE BLUE	Geneva	1997
INTO THE FIRE	Thirteen Senses	2004
INTO THE GROOVE	Madonna	1985
INTO THE NIGHT	Love Inc.	2004
INTO THE NIGHT	Benny Mardones	1989
INTO THE VALLEY	Skids	1979
INTO TOMORROW	Paul Weller Movement	1991
INTO YOU	Fabolous featuring Tamia	2003
INTO YOUR ARMS	Lemonheads	1993
INTRO	Alan Braxe & Fred Falke	2000
INTUITION	Linx	1981

SONG TITLE	ARTIST	DATE
INVINCIBLE (THEME FROM THE LEGEND OF BILLIE JEAN)	Pat Benatar	1985
INVISIBLE	Alison Moyet	1985
INVISIBLE	Tilt	1999
INVISIBLE	D-Side	2003
INVISIBLE	Clay Aiken	2003
INVISIBLE HANDS	Kim Carnes	1983
INVISIBLE MAN	98 Degrees	1997
THE INVISIBLE MAN	Queen	1989
INVISIBLE SUN	Police	1981
INVISIBLE TOUCH	Genesis	1986
INVITATIONS	Shakatak	1982
IRE FEELINGS (SKANGA)	Rupie Edwards	1974
IRIE	Luck & Neat	2002
IRIS	Goo Goo Dolls	1998
IRISH BLOOD, ENGLISH HEART	Morrissey	2004
IRISH BLUE	Flip & Fill featuring Junior	2004
THE IRISH ROVER	Pogues & The Dubliners	1987
IRON FIST	Motorhead	1982
IRON LION ZION	Bob Marley & The Wailers	1992
IRONIC	Alanis Morissette	1996
IRRESISTIBLE	Cathy Dennis	1992
IRRESISTIBLE	Corrs	2000
IRRESISTIBLE	Jessica Simpson	2001
IS IT A DREAM	Damned	1985

SONG TITLE	ARTIST	DATE
IS IT A DREAM	Classix Nouveaux	1982
IS IT A SIN	Deepest Blue	2004
IS IT BECAUSE	Honeycombs	1964
IS IT COS I'M COOL?	Mousse T featuring Emma Lanford	2004
IS IT GOOD TO YOU	Heavy D. & The Boyz	1991
IS IT LIKE TODAY?	World Party	1993
IS IT LOVE	Mr. Mister	1986
IS IT LOVE YOU'RE AFTER	Rose Royce	1979
IS IT LOVE?	Chili Hi Fly	2000
IS IT REALLY OVER	Jim Reeves	1965
IS IT SOMETHING YOU'VE GOT	Tyrone Davis	1969
IS IT TRUE	Brenda Lee	1964
IS IT YOU	Lee Ritenour	1981
IS NOTHING SACRED	Meat Loaf featuring Patti Russo	1999
IS SHE REALLY GOING OUT WITH HIM?	Joe Jackson	1979
IS THAT ALL THERE IS	Peggy Lee	1969
IS THAT LOVE	Squeeze	1981
IS THAT YOUR FINAL ANSWER?	Amoure	2000
IS THERE ANYBODY OUT THERE?	Bassheads	1991
IS THERE ANYBODY THERE?/ANOTHER PIECE OF MEAT		

SONG TITLE	ARTIST	DATE
	Scorpions	1979
IS THERE SOMEONE OUT THERE?	Code Red	1997
IS THERE SOMETHING I SHOULD KNOW	Duran Duran	1983
IS THIS A DREAM?	Love Decade	1996
IS THIS A LOVE THING	Raydio	1978
IS THIS LOVE	Bob Marley & The Wailers	1978
IS THIS LOVE	Alison Moyet	1986
IS THIS LOVE	Survivor	1986
IS THIS LOVE/SWEET LADY LUCK	Whitesnake	1994
(IS THIS THE WAY TO) AMARILLO	Tony Christie	1971
IS VIC THERE?	Department S	1981
IS YOUR LOVE STRONG ENOUGH?	Bryan Ferry	1986
ISLAND GIRL	Elton John	1975
ISLAND HEAD EP	Inspiral Carpets	1990
ISLAND IN THE SUN	Weezer	2001
ISLAND IN THE SUN	Righteous Brothers	1966
ISLAND OF LOST SOULS	Blondie	1982
ISLANDS IN THE STREAM	Kenny Rogers & Dolly Parton	1983
ISN'T IT A WONDER	Boyzone	1997
ISN'T IT TIME	Babys	1977
ISN'T LIFE STRANGE	Moody Blues	1972

SONG TITLE	ARTIST	DATE
ISN'T SHE LOVELY	David Parton	1977
ISOBEL	Bjork	1995
THE ISRAELITES	Desmond Dekker & The Aces	1969
IST OF THA MONTH	Bone Thugs-N-Harmony	1996
IT AIN'T A CRIME	House Of Pain	1994
IT AIN'T ENOUGH	Dreem Teem Vs Artful Dodger/MZ May/MC Alistair	2001
IT AIN'T ENOUGH	Corey Hart	1984
IT AIN'T GONNA BE ME	CJ Bolland	1999
IT AIN'T ME BABE	Johnny Cash	1965
IT AIN'T ME BABE	Turtles	1965
IT AIN'T MY FAULT 1 & 2	Silkk The Shocker featuring Mystikal	1999
IT AIN'T NECESSARILY SO	Bronski Beat	1984
IT AIN'T OVER 'TIL IT'S OVER	Lenny Kravitz	1991
IT AIN'T WHAT YOU DO IT'S THE WAY THAT YOU DO IT	Fun Boy Three & Bananarama	1982
IT BEGAN IN AFRIKA	Chemical Brothers	2001
IT CAN'T BE RIGHT	2Play featuring Raghav & Naila Boss	2004
IT DIDN'T MATTER	Style Council	1987
IT DOESN'T HAVE TO BE ME	Erasure	1987
IT DOESN'T HAVE TO BE THAT WAY	Blow Monkeys	1987

SONG TITLE	ARTIST	DATE
IT DOESN'T MATTER	Wyclef Jean/The Rock & Melky Sedeck	2000
IT DON'T COME EASY	Ringo Starr	1971
IT DON'T MATTER TO ME	Bread	1970
IT FEELS SO GOOD	Sonique	1998
IT HIT ME LIKE A HAMMER	Huey Lewis & The News	1991
IT HURTS ME	Elvis Presley	1964
IT HURTS SO MUCH (TO SEE YOU GO)	Jim Reeves	1965
IT HURTS TO BE IN LOVE	Gene Pitney	1964
IT IS TIME TO GET FUNKY	D. Mob featuring LRS	1989
IT ISN'T, IT WASN'T, IT AIN'T EVER GONNA BE	Aretha Franklin/ Whitney Houston	1989
IT JUST WON'T DO	Tim Deluxe featuring Sam Obernik	2002
IT KEEPS RAININ' (TEARS FROM MY EYES)	Bitty McLean	1993
IT KEEPS RIGHT ON A-HURTIN'	Johnny Tillotson	1966
IT KEEPS YOU RUNNIN'	Doobie Brothers	1976
IT MAKES YOU FEEL LIKE DANCIN'	Rose Royce	1978

SONG TITLE	ARTIST	DATE
IT MAY BE WINTER OUTSIDE (BUT IN MY HEART IT'S SPRING)	Love Unlimited	1975
IT MEK	Desmond Dekker & The Aces	1969
IT MIGHT BE YOU	Stephen Bishop	1983
IT MUST BE HIM	Vikki Carr	1967
IT MUST BE LOVE	Robin S	1997
IT MUST BE LOVE	Mero	2000
IT MUST BE LOVE	Madness	1983
IT MUST BE LOVE	Labi Siffre	1971
IT MUST BE LOVE	Ty Herndon	1998
IT MUST BE LOVE	Alan Jackson	2000
IT MUST BE LOVE	Alton McClain & Destiny	1979
IT MUST HAVE BEEN LOVE	Roxette	1990
IT MUST HAVE BEEN LOVE	Magnum	1988
IT NEVER RAINS (IN SOUTHERN CALIFORNIA)	Tony Toni Tone	1990
IT NEVER RAINS IN SOUTHERN CALIFORNIA	Albert Hammond	1972
IT ONLY TAKES A MINUTE	One Hundred Ton & A Feather	1976
IT ONLY TAKES A MINUTE	Take That	1992
IT ONLY TAKES A MINUTE	Tavares	1975
IT OUGHTA SELL A MILLION	Lyn Paul	1975
IT SHOULD HAVE BEEN ME	Yvonne Fair	1976

SONG TITLE	ARTIST	DATE
IT SHOULD HAVE BEEN ME	Gladys Knight & The Pips	1968
IT STARTED WITH A KISS	Hot Chocolate	1982
IT SURE BRINGS OUT THE LOVE IN YOUR EYES	David Soul	1978
IT SURE TOOK A LONG, LONG TIME	Lobo	1973
IT TAKES ALL NIGHT LONG	Gary Glitter	1977
IT TAKES MORE	Ms. Dynamite	2002
IT TAKES SCOOP	Fatman Scoop featuring The Crooklyn Clan	2004
IT TAKES TWO	Rob Base & D.J. E-Z Rock	1988
IT TAKES TWO	Marvin Gaye & Kim Weston	1967
IT TAKES TWO	Rod Stewart & Tina Turner	1990
IT TAKES TWO TO TANGO	Richard Myhill	1978
IT TEARS ME UP	Percy Sledge	1966
IT WAS A GOOD DAY	Ice Cube	1993
IT WAS A VERY GOOD YEAR	Frank Sinatra	1965
IT WAS ALMOST LIKE A SONG	Ronnie Milsap	1977
IT WAS EASIER TO HURT HER	Wayne Fontana	1965
IT WASN'T ME	Shaggy	2001
IT WILL BE YOU	Paul Young	1994

SONG TITLE	ARTIST	DATE
IT WILL MAKE ME CRAZY	Felix	1992
IT WON'T SEEM LIKE CHRISTMAS (WITHOUT YOU)		
	Elvis Presley	1979
IT WOULD TAKE A STRONG MAN		
	Rick Astley	1988
IT'S 'ORRIBLE BEING IN LOVE (WHEN YOU'RE 8½)		
	Claire & Friends	1986
IT'S A BEAUTIFUL THING	Ocean Colour Scene	1998
IT'S A CRAZY WORLD	Mac McAnally	1977
IT'S A DISCO NIGHT (ROCK DON'T STOP)		
	Isley Brothers	1979
IT'S A FINE DAY	Opus III	1992
IT'S A GAME	Bay City Rollers	1977
IT'S A GIRL THING	My Life Story	1999
IT'S A GREAT DAY TO BE ALIVE		
	Travis Tritt	2001
IT'S A HARD LIFE	Queen	1984
IT'S A HEARTACHE	Bonnie Tyler	1978
IT'S A LAUGH	Daryl Hall & John Oates	1978
IT'S A LONG WAY THERE	Little River Band	1976
IT'S A LOVE THING	Whispers	1981
IT'S A LOVING THING	C.B. Milton	1995
IT'S A MAN'S MAN'S MAN'S WORLD		
	James Brown	1966
IT'S A MIRACLE	Culture Club	1984
IT'S A MIRACLE	Barry Manilow	1975
IT'S A MISTAKE	Men At Work	1983
IT'S A NEW DAY (PART 1 & 2)		
	James Brown	1970
IT'S A PARTY	Busta Rhymes featuring Zhane	1996
IT'S A RAINBOW	Rainbow	2002
IT'S A SHAME	Kris Kross	1992
IT'S A SHAME	Spinners	1970
IT'S A SHAME (MY SISTER)	Monie Love featuring	
	True Image	1990
IT'S A SHAME ABOUT RAY	Lemonheads	1993
IT'S A SIN	Pet Shop Boys	1987
IT'S A SIN TO TELL A LIE	Gerry Monroe	1971
IT'S ALL ABOUT ME	Mya With Special Guest Sisqo	1998
IT'S ALL ABOUT THE BENJAMINS/BEEN AROUND THE		
WORLD	Puff Daddy & Family	1997
IT'S ALL ABOUT U	SWV	1996
IT'S ALL ABOUT YOU	Justin	1999
IT'S ALL ABOUT YOU (NOT ABOUT ME)		
	Tracie Spencer	1999
IT'S ALL BEEN DONE	Barenaked Ladies	1999
IT'S ALL COMING BACK TO ME NOW		
	Celine Dion	1996
IT'S ALL DOWN TO GOODNIGHT VIENNA/OO-WEE		
	Ringo Starr	1975
IT'S ALL GRAVY	Romeo featuring	
	Christina Milian	2002

SONG TITLE	ARTIST	DATE
IT'S ALL IN THE GAME	Four Tops	1970
IT'S ALL IN THE GAME	Cliff Richard	1963
IT'S ALL OVER	Cliff Richard	1967
IT'S ALL OVER NOW	Rolling Stones	1964
IT'S ALL OVER NOW, BABY BLUE		
	Joan Baez	1965
IT'S ALL THE WAY LIVE (NOW)		
	Coolio	1996
IT'S ALL UP TO YOU	Jim Capaldi	1974
IT'S ALL YOURS	MC Lyte featuring	
	Gina Thompson	1998
IT'S ALMOST TOMORROW	Mark Wynter	1963
IT'S ALRIGHT	Deni Hines	1997
IT'S ALRIGHT	East 17	1993
IT'S ALRIGHT	Pet Shop Boys	1989
IT'S ALRIGHT	Adam Faith	1965
IT'S ALRIGHT (BABY'S COMING BACK)		
	Eurythmics	1986
IT'S AN OPEN SECRET	Joy Strings	1964
IT'S BEEN AWHILE	Staind	2001
IT'S BEEN NICE (GOODNIGHT)		
	Everly Brothers	1963
IT'S BEEN SO LONG	George McCrae	1975
IT'S BETTER TO HAVE (AND DON'T NEED)		
	Don Covay	1974
IT'S CALLED A HEART	Depeche Mode	1985

SONG TITLE	ARTIST	DATE
IT'S DIFFERENT FOR GIRLS	Joe Jackson	1980
IT'S ECSTASY WHEN YOU LAY DOWN NEXT TO ME		
	Barry White	1977
IT'S FOR YOU	Cilla Black	1964
IT'S FOUR IN THE MORNING		
	Faron Young	1972
IT'S GETTING BETTER	Mama Cass	1969
IT'S GOIN' DOWN	X-Ecutioners featuring	
	Mike Shinoda & Mr. Hahn	2002
IT'S GOING TO HAPPEN!	Undertones	1981
IT'S GOING TO TAKE SOME TIME		
	Carpenters	1972
IT'S GONNA BE A COLD COLD CHRISTMAS		
	Dana	1975
IT'S GONNA BE A LOVELY DAY		
	S.O.U.L. S.Y.S.T.E.M.	1993
IT'S GONNA BE ALL RIGHT		
	Gerry & The Pacemakers	1964
IT'S GONNA BE ME	*NSYNC	2000
IT'S GONNA BE MY WAY	Precious	2000
IT'S GONNA BE... (A LOVELY DAY)		
	Brancaccio & Aisher	2002
IT'S GONNA TAKE A MIRACLE		
	Deniece Williams	1982
IT'S GOOD NEWS WEEK	Hedgehoppers Anonymous	1965
IT'S GOTTA BE ME	*NSYNC	2000

SONG TITLE	ARTIST	DATE
IT'S GREAT WHEN WE'RE TOGETHER		
	Finley Quaye	1997
IT'S GRIM UP NORTH	Justified Ancients Of Mu Mu	1991
IT'S GROWING	Temptations	1965
IT'S HAPPENIN'	Plus One featuring Sirron	1990
IT'S HARD TO BE HUMBLE	Mac Davis	1980
IT'S IMPOSSIBLE	Perry Como	1970
IT'S IN HIS KISS	Linda Lewis	1975
IT'S IN HIS KISS (THE SHOOP SHOOP SONG)		
	Betty Everett	1968
IT'S IN OUR HANDS	Bjork	2002
IT'S IN YOUR EYES	Phil Collins	1996
IT'S INEVITABLE	Charlie	1983
IT'S JUST PORN MUM	Trucks	2002
(IT'S JUST) THE WAY YOU LOVE ME		
	Paula Abdul	1988
IT'S LATE	Shakin' Stevens	1983
(IT'S LIKE A) SAD OLD KINDA MOVIE		
	Pickettywitch	1970
IT'S LIKE THAT	Run DMC vs Jason Nevins	1998
IT'S LIKE THAT Y'ALL/I GOT DA FEELIN'		
	Sweet Tee	1988
IT'S LOVE	Ken Dodd	1966
IT'S LOVE (TRIPPIN')	Goldtrix presents Andrea Brown	2002
IT'S LOVE THAT REALLY COUNTS		
	Merseybeats	1963

SONG TITLE	ARTIST	DATE
IT'S LULU	Boo Radleys	1995
IT'S ME	Alice Cooper	1994
IT'S MY HOUSE	Storm	1979
IT'S MY HOUSE	Diana Ross	1979
IT'S MY LIFE	Animals	1965
IT'S MY LIFE	Dr. Alban	1992
IT'S MY LIFE	Bon Jovi	2000
IT'S MY LIFE	Talk Talk	1984
IT'S MY LIFE/BATHWATER	No Doubt	2004
IT'S MY PARTY	Lesley Gore	1963
IT'S MY PARTY	Dave Stewart & Barbara Gaskin	1981
IT'S MY TIME	Everly Brothers	1968
IT'S MY TURN	Angelic	2000
IT'S MY TURN	Diana Ross	1980
IT'S NO CRIME	Babyface	1989
IT'S NO GOOD	Depeche Mode	1997
IT'S NO SECRET	Kylie Minogue	1988
IT'S NOT ENOUGH	Starship	1989
IT'S NOT OVER ('TIL IT'S OVER)		
	Starship	1987
IT'S NOT RIGHT BUT IT'S OKAY		
	Whitney Houston	1999
IT'S NOT THE END OF THE WORLD?		
	Super Furry Animals	2002
IT'S NOT UNUSUAL	Tom Jones	1965
IT'S NOW OR NEVER	Elvis Presley	1960

SONG TITLE	ARTIST	DATE
IT'S NOW OR NEVER	John Schneider	1981
IT'S NOW WINTERS DAY	Tommy Roe	1966
IT'S O.K.	Beach Boys	1976
IT'S OH SO QUIET	Bjork	1995
IT'S OK	Delirious?	2000
IT'S OK!	Atomic Kitten	2002
IT'S ON YOU (SCAN ME)	Eurogroove	1995
IT'S ON/EGG RUSH	Flowered Up	1991
IT'S ONE OF THOSE NIGHTS (YES LOVE)		
	Partridge Family	1971
IT'S ONLY LOVE	Bryan Adams & Tina Turner	1985
IT'S ONLY LOVE	Simply Red	1989
IT'S ONLY LOVE	Tommy James & The Shondells	1966
IT'S ONLY LOVE/BEYOND THE REEF		
	Elvis Presley	1980
IT'S ONLY MAKE BELIEVE	Glen Campbell	1970
IT'S ONLY MAKE BELIEVE	Child	1978
IT'S ONLY MAKE BELIEVE	Billy Fury	1964
IT'S ONLY NATURAL	Crowded House	1992
IT'S ONLY ROCK 'N ROLL (BUT I LIKE IT)		
	Rolling Stones	1974
IT'S ONLY ROCK 'N' ROLL	Various	1999
IT'S OVER	Kurupt	2001
IT'S OVER	Clock	1997
IT'S OVER	Funk Masters	1983
IT'S OVER	Level 42	1987

SONG TITLE	ARTIST	DATE
IT'S OVER	Roy Orbison	1964
IT'S OVER	Jimmie Rodgers	1966
IT'S OVER	Boz Scaggs	1976
IT'S OVER (DISTORTION)	Pianoheadz	1998
IT'S OVER LOVE	Todd Terry presents Shannon	1997
IT'S OVER NOW	112	2001
IT'S PROBABLY ME	Sting With Eric Clapton	1992
IT'S RAINING	Darts	1978
IT'S RAINING	Shakin' Stevens	1981
IT'S RAINING AGAIN	Supertramp	1982
IT'S RAINING MEN	Weather Girls	1984
IT'S RAINING MEN	Geri Halliwell	2001
IT'S RAINING MEN... THE SEQUEL		
	Martha Wash featuring Rupaul	1998
IT'S SAD TO BELONG	England Dan & John Ford Coley	1977
IT'S SO EASY	Andy Williams	1970
IT'S SO EASY	Linda Ronstadt	1977
IT'S SO HARD TO SAY GOODBYE TO YESTERDAY		
	Boyz II Men	1991
IT'S STILL ROCK AND ROLL TO ME		
	Billy Joel	1980
IT'S THE END OF THE WORLD AS WE KNOW IT		
	R.E.M......................1991	
IT'S THE SAME OLD SONG	Four Tops	1965
IT'S THE SAME OLD SONG	Weathermen	1971
IT'S THE SAME OLD SONG	KC & The Sunshine Band	1978

SONG TITLE	ARTIST	DATE
IT'S THE WAY YOU MAKE ME FEEL/TOO BUSY THINKING 'BOUT MY BABY	Steps	2001
IT'S TIME FOR LOVE	Chi-Lites	1975
IT'S TOO LATE	Quartz Introducing Dina Carroll	1991
IT'S TOO LATE	Bobby Goldsboro	1966
IT'S TOO LATE NOW	Swinging Blue Jeans	1963
IT'S TOO LATE NOW	Long John Baldry	1969
IT'S TOO LATE/I FEEL THE EARTH MOVE	Carole King	1971
IT'S TRICKY	Run DMC	1987
IT'S TRICKY 2003	Run DMC featuring Jacknife Lee	2003
IT'S TRUE	Queen Pen	1998
IT'S UP TO YOU	Ricky Nelson	1963
IT'S UP TO YOU (SHINING THROUGH)	Layo & Bushwacka!	2003
IT'S WHAT WE'RE ALL ABOUT	Sum 41	2002
IT'S WHAT'S UPFRONT THAT COUNTS	Yosh presents Lovedeejay Akemi	1995
IT'S WONDERFUL	Jimmy Ruffin	1970
IT'S WONDERFUL	Young Rascals	1967
IT'S WRITTEN IN THE STARS	Paul Weller	2002
IT'S YER MONEY I'M AFTER BABY	Wonder Stuff	1988
IT'S YOU	EMF	1992

SONG TITLE	ARTIST	DATE
IT'S YOU	Freddie Starr	1974
IT'S YOU THAT I NEED	Enchantment	1978
IT'S YOUR DAY TODAY	P.J. Proby	1968
IT'S YOUR LIFE	Smokie	1977
IT'S YOUR LOVE	Tim McGraw With Faith Hill	1997
IT'S YOUR THING	Isley Brothers	1969
IT'S YOURS	Jon Cutler featuring E-Man	2002
ITCHYCOO PARK	Small Faces	1968
ITCHYCOO PARK	M People	1995
ITSY BITSY TEENY WEENY YELLOW POLKA DOT BIKINI	Bombalurina	1990
IZ U	Nelly	2003
IZZO (H.O.V.A.)	Jay-Z	2001
J.J. TRIBUTE	Asha	1995
JACK & DIANE	John Cougar Mellencamp	1982
JACK AND JILL	Raydio	1978
JACK IN THE BOX	Moments	1977
JACK IN THE BOX	Clodagh Rodgers	1971
JACK LE FREAK	Chic	1987
JACK MIX II	Mirage	1987
JACK MIX IV	Mirage	1987
THE JACK THAT HOUSE BUILT	Jack 'n' Chill	1988
JACK THE GROOVE	Raze	1987
JACK TO THE SOUND OF THE UNDERGROUND	Hithouse	1988

SONG TITLE	ARTIST	DATE
JACK YOUR BODY	Steve 'Silk' Hurley	1987
JACKIE	Scott Walker	1967
JACKIE BLUE	Ozark Mountain Daredevils	1975
JACKIE WILSON SAID	Dexy's Midnight Runners	1982
JACKSON	Nancy Sinatra & Lee Hazlewood	1967
JACKY	Marc Almond	1991
JACOB'S LADDER	Huey Lewis & The News	1987
JADED	Aerosmith	2001
JAILBIRD	Primal Scream	1994
JAILBREAK	Thin Lizzy	1976
JAILHOUSE ROCK	Elvis Presley	1983
JAM	Michael Jackson	1992
JAM J/SAY SOMETHING	James	1994
JAM SIDE DOWN	Status Quo	2002
JAM TONIGHT	Freddie Jackson	1987
JAM UP JELLY TIGHT	Tommy Roe	1969
JAM, JAM, JAM (ALL NIGHT LONG)		
	People's Choice	1978
JAMAICAN IN NEW YORK	Shinehead	1993
JAMBALAYA	Carpenters	1974
JAMBALAYA (ON THE BAYOU)		
	Blue Ridge Rangers	1972
JAMBOREE	Naughty By Nature featuring Zhane	1999
JAMES BOND THEME	Moby	1997

SONG TITLE	ARTIST	DATE
JAMES DEAN (I WANNA KNOW)		
	Daniel Bedingfield	2002
JAMIE	Ray Parker Jr.	1984
JAMMIN' ME	Tom Petty & The Heartbreakers	1987
JAMMING/PUNKY REGGAE PARTY		
	Bob Marley & The Wailers	1977
JANE	Jefferson Starship	1979
JANIE'S GOT A GUN	Aerosmith	1989
JANIE, DON'T TAKE YOUR LOVE TO TOWN		
	Jon Bon Jovi	1997
JANUARY	Pilot	1975
JANUARY FEBRUARY	Barbara Dickson	1980
JAPANESE BOY	Aneka	1981
JARROW SONG	Alan Price	1974
JAVA	Al Hirt	1964
JAWS	Lalo Schifrin	1976
JAZZ CARNIVAL	Azymuth	1980
JAZZ IT UP	Reel 2 Real	1996
JAZZMAN	Carole King	1974
JE NE SAIS PAS POURQUOI	Kylie Minogue	1988
JE SUIS MUSIC	Cerrone	1979
JE T'AIME (MOI NON PLUS)		
	Judge Dread	1975
JE T'AIME... MOI NON PLUS		
	Jane Birkin & Serge Gainsbourg	1969

SONG TITLE	ARTIST	DATE
JEALOUS GUY	Roxy Music	1981
JEALOUS KIND OF FELLA	Garland Green	1969
JEALOUS MIND	Alvin Stardust	1974
JEALOUSY	Pet Shop Boys	1991
JEALOUSY	Natalie Merchant	1996
JEAN	Oliver	1979
THE JEAN GENIE	David Bowie	1972
JEANS ON	David Dundas	1976
JEEPSTER	T. Rex	1971
JENNIFER ECCLES	Hollies	1968
JENNIFER JUNIPER	Donovan	1968
JENNIFER SHE SAID	Lloyd Cole	1988
JENNIFER TOMKINS	Street People	1970
JENNY FROM THE BLOCK	Jennifer Lopez	2002
JENNY TAKE A RIDE!	Mitch Ryder & The Detroit Wheels	1965
JEOPARDY	Greg Kihn Band	1983
JEREMY	Pearl Jam	1992
THE JERK	Larks	1964
JERK OUT	Time	1990
JERUSALEM	Fat Les 2000	2000
JESAMINE	Casuals	1968
JESSE	Roberta Flack	1973
JESSE	Carly Simon	1980
JESSE HOLD ON	B*Witched	1999
JESSIE	Joshua Kadison	1993

SONG TITLE	ARTIST	DATE
JESSIE'S GIRL	Rick Springfield	1981
JESUS	Cliff Richard	1972
JESUS CHRIST POSE	Soundgarden	1992
JESUS HE KNOWS ME	Genesis	1992
JESUS IS A SOUL MAN	Lawrence Reynolds	1969
JESUS IS JUST ALRIGHT	Doobie Brothers	1972
JESUS SAYS	Ash	1998
JESUS TO A CHILD	George Michael	1996
JESUS WALKS	Kanye West	2004
JET	Paul McCartney	1974
JET	Olivia Newton-John	1980
JET AIRLINER	Steve Miller Band	1977
JET CITY WOMAN	Queensryche	1991
JEWEL	Cranes	1993
JIG-A-JIG	East Of Eden	1971
JIGGA MY NIGGA	Jay-Z	1999
JILTED JOHN	Jilted John	1978
JIM DANDY	Black Oak Arkansas	1973
JIMMY JIMMY	Undertones	1979
JIMMY LEE	Aretha Franklin	1986
JIMMY LOVES MARY-ANNE	Looking Glass	1973
JIMMY MACK	Martha & The Vandellas	1967
JIMMY OLSEN'S BLUES	Spin Doctors	1993
JINGLE JANGLE	Archies	1969
JINGO	FKW	1994

SONG TITLE	ARTIST	DATE
JINGO	Jellybean	1987
JITTERBUGGIN'	Heatwave	1981
JIVE TALKIN'	Bee Gees	1975
JIVE TALKIN'	Boogie Box High	1987
JOAN OF ARC	Orchestral Manoeuvres In The Dark	1981
JOANNA	Mrs Wood	1997
JOANNA	Scott Walker	1968
JOANNA/TONIGHT	Kool & The Gang	1984
JOANNE	Michael Nesmith & The First National Band	1970
THE JOCK JAM	ESPN Presents	1997
JODY'S GOT YOUR GIRL AND GONE	Johnnie Taylor	1971
JOE	Inspiral Carpets	1995
JOE LE TAXI	Vanessa Paradis	1988
JOEY	Concrete Blonde	1990
JOGI/BEWARE OF THE BOYS	Panjabi MC featuring Jay-Z	2003
JOHN I'M ONLY DANCING (AGAIN)	David Bowie	1979
JOHN I'M ONLY DANCING/BIG GREEN CAR	Polecats	1981
JOHN KETTLEY (IS A WEATHERMAN)	Tribe Of Toffs	1988

SONG TITLE	ARTIST	DATE
JOHN WAYNE IS BIG LEGGY	Haysi Fantayzee	1982
JOHN, I'M ONLY DANCING	David Bowie	1972
JOHNNY B. GOODE	Jimi Hendrix	1972
JOHNNY COME HOME	Fine Young Cannibals	1985
JOHNNY FRIENDLY	Joboxers	1983
JOHNNY REGGAE	Piglets	1971
JOIN OUR CLUB/PEOPLE GET REAL	Saint Etienne	1992
JOIN THE PARTY	Honky	1977
JOIN TOGETHER	Who	1972
JOINING YOU	Alanis Morissette	1999
JOJO	Boz Scaggs	1980
THE JOKER	Steve Miller Band	1973
THE JOKER WENT WILD	Brian Hyland	1966
JOLENE	Dolly Parton	1976
THE JOLLY GREEN GIANT	Kingsmen	1965
JONATHAN DAVID	Belle & Sebastian	2001
JONES vs JONES/SUMMER MADNESS	Kool & The Gang	1981
JONESTOWN MIND	Almighty	1995
JORDAN: THE EP	Prefab Sprout	1991
JOSEPH MEGA-REMIX	Jason Donovan	1991
JOSEPHINE	Terrorvision	1998
JOSEY	Deep Blue Something	1996
JOSIE	Steely Dan	1978

SONG TITLE	ARTIST	DATE
JOURNEY	Duncan Browne	1972
THE JOURNEY	911	1997
JOURNEY TO THE CENTER OF THE MIND		
	Amboy Dukes	1968
JOURNEY TO THE PAST	Aaliyah	1998
JOY	Staxx	1993
JOY	Band AKA	1983
JOY	Mark Ryder	2001
JOY	Soul II Soul	1992
JOY	Apollo 100	1972
JOY!	Gay Dad	1999
JOY (PT 1)	Isaac Hayes	1973
JOY AND HEARTBREAK	Movement 98/Carroll Thompson	1990
JOY AND PAIN	Donna Allen	1989
JOY OF LIVING	Hank Marvin	1970
THE JOY OF LIVING	Cliff Richard	1970
JOY RIDE	Roxette	1991
JOY TO THE WORLD	Three Dog Night	1971
JOYBRINGER	Manfred Mann's Earth Band	1973
JOYRIDE	Roxette	1991
JU JU HAND	Sam The Sham & The Pharoahs	1965
JUDGE FUDGE	Happy Mondays	1991
JUDY IN DISGUISE (WITH GLASSES)		
	John Fred & His Playboy Band	1967
JUDY MAE	Boomer Castleman	1975
JUDY TEEN	Cockney Rebel	1974

SONG TITLE	ARTIST	DATE
JUICY	Wrecks-N-Effect	1990
JUICY	Notorious B.I.G.	1994
JUICY FRUIT	Mtume	1983
A JUICY RED APPLE	Skin Up	1992
JUKE BOX HERO	Foreigner	1982
JUKE BOX JIVE	Rubettes	1974
JULIA	Chris Rea	1993
JULIA SAYS	Wet Wet Wet	1995
JULIE ANNE	Kenny	1975
JULIE EP	Levellers	1994
JULIE, DO YA LOVE ME	White Plains	1970
JULIE, DO YA LOVE ME	Bobby Sherman	1970
JULIET	Four Pennies	1964
JULIET (KEEP THAT IN MIND)		
	Thea Gilmore	2003
JULY/I AM THE NEWS	Ocean Colour Scene	2000
JUMBO	Underworld	1999
JUMBO/THE SINGER SANG HIS SONG		
	Bee Gees	1968
JUMP	Bus Stop	1999
JUMP	Van Halen	1984
JUMP	Kris Kross	1992
JUMP	Girls Aloud	2003
JUMP (FOR MY LOVE)	Pointer Sisters	1984
JUMP AROUND/TOP O' THE MORNING TO YA		
	House Of Pain	1993

SONG TITLE	ARTIST	DATE
JUMP BACK (SET ME FREE)		
	Dhar Braxton	1986
JUMP DOWN	B*Witched	2000
JUMP INTO THE FIRE	Nilsson	1972
JUMP JIVE AN' WAIL	Brian Setzer Orchestra	1999
JUMP N' SHOUT	Basement Jaxx	1999
THE JUMP OFF	Lil' Kim featuring Mr. Cheeks	2003
JUMP ON DEMAND	Spunge	2002
JUMP START	Natalie Cole	1987
JUMP THEY SAY	David Bowie	1993
JUMP TO IT	Aretha Franklin	1982
JUMP TO MY BEAT	Wildchild	1996
JUMP TO MY LOVE/ALWAYS THERE		
	Incognito	1996
JUMP TO THE BEAT	Stacy Lattisaw	1980
JUMP TO THE BEAT	Dannii Minogue	1991
JUMPER	Third Eye Blind	1998
JUMPIN'	Liberty X	2003
JUMPIN' JACK FLASH	Aretha Franklin	1986
JUMPIN' JACK FLASH	Rolling Stones	1968
JUMPIN, JUMPIN	Destiny's Child	2000
JUNEAU	Funeral For A Friend	2003
JUNGLE BOOGIE	Kool & The Gang	1973
THE JUNGLE BOOK GROOVE		
	Jungle Book	1993
JUNGLE BROTHER	Jungle Brothers	1998

SONG TITLE	ARTIST	DATE
JUNGLE FEVER	Chakachas	1972
JUNGLE LOVE	Steve Miller Band	1977
JUNGLE LOVE	Time	1984
JUNGLE ROCK	Hank Mizell	1976
JUNGLE ROCK	Jungle Boys	2004
JUNIOR'S FARM/SALLY G	Paul McCartney	1974
JUNK FOOD JUNKIE	Larry Groce	1976
JUNKIES	Easyworld	2003
JUS I KISS	Basement Jaxx	2001
JUS' A RASCAL	Dizzee Rascal	2003
JUST	Radiohead	1995
JUST	Jamie Scott	2004
JUST A DAY (EP)	Feeder	2001
JUST A FEELING	Bad Manners	1981
JUST A FEW THINGS THAT I AIN'T		
	Beautiful South	2003
JUST A FRIEND	Mario	2003
JUST A FRIEND	Biz Markie	1990
JUST A GIGOLO/I AIN'T GOT NOBODY		
	David Lee Roth	1985
JUST A GIRL	No Doubt	1995
JUST A GROOVE	Nomad	1991
JUST A LITTLE	Liberty X	2002
JUST A LITTLE	Beau Brummels	1965
JUST A LITTLE BIT	Roy Head	1965
JUST A LITTLE BIT BETTER	Herman's Hermits	1965

SONG TITLE	ARTIST	DATE
JUST A LITTLE BIT OF YOU		
	Michael Jackson	1975
JUST A LITTLE BIT TOO LATE		
	Wayne Fontana & The	
	Mindbenders	1965
JUST A LITTLE GIRL	Amy Studt	2002
JUST A LITTLE MISUNDERSTANDING		
	Contours	1970
JUST A LITTLE MORE LOVE		
	David Guetta featuring	
	Chris Willis	2003
JUST A LITTLE WHILE	Janet	2004
JUST A MIRAGE	Jellybean featuring Adele Bertei	1988
JUST A SHADOW	Big Country	1985
JUST A SMILE	Pilot	1975
JUST A SONG BEFORE I GO		
	Crosby, Stills & Nash	1977
JUST A STEP FROM HEAVEN		
	Eternal	1994
JUST A TOUCH	Keith Sweat	1996
JUST A TOUCH OF LOVE (EVERYDAY)		
	C&C Music Factory	1991
JUST AN ILLUSION	Imagination	1982
JUST ANOTHER BROKEN HEART		
	Sheena Easton	1981
JUST ANOTHER DAY	Jonathan Wilkes	2001

SONG TITLE	ARTIST	DATE
JUST ANOTHER DAY	Jon Secada	1992
JUST ANOTHER DAY IN PARADISE		
	Phil Vassar	2000
JUST ANOTHER DREAM	Cathy Dennis	1990
JUST ANOTHER ILLUSION	Hurricane #1	1997
JUST ANOTHER NIGHT	Mick Jagger	1985
JUST AROUND THE HILL	Sash!	2000
JUST AS I AM	Air Supply	1985
JUST AS MUCH AS EVER	Bobby Vinton	1967
JUST BE A MAN ABOUT IT	Toni Braxton	2000
JUST BE DUB TO ME	Revelation	2003
JUST BE GOOD TO ME	S.O.S. Band	1984
JUST BE TRUE	Gene Chandler	1964
JUST BECAUSE	Jane's Addiction	2003
JUST BECAUSE	Anita Baker	1989
JUST BEFORE YOU LEAVE	Del Amitri	2002
JUST BETWEEN YOU AND ME		
	April Wine	1981
JUST BETWEEN YOU AND ME		
	DC Talk	1996
JUST BETWEEN YOU AND ME		
	Lou Gramm	1989
JUST CALL	Sherrick	1987
JUST CAN'T GET ENOUGH	Harry 'Choo Choo' Romero/	
	Inaya Day	1999
JUST CAN'T GET ENOUGH	Depeche Mode	1981

SONG TITLE	ARTIST	DATE
JUST CAN'T GET ENOUGH (NO NO NO NO)		
	Eye To Eye/Taka Boom	2001
JUST CAN'T GIVE YOU UP	Mystic Merlin	1980
JUST CAN'T WIN 'EM ALL	Stevie Woods	1982
JUST CRUISIN'	Will Smith	1997
JUST DON'T WANT TO BE LONELY		
	Freddie McGregor	1987
JUST DON'T WANT TO BE LONELY		
	Main Ingredient	1974
JUST DROPPED IN (TO SEE WHAT CONDITION MY		
CONDITION WAS IN)	First Edition	1968
JUST FOR KICKS	Mike Sarne	1963
JUST FOR MONEY	Paul Hardcastle	1985
JUST FOR TONIGHT	Vanessa Williams	1992
JUST FOR YOU	Glitter Band	1974
JUST FOR YOU	M People	1997
JUST FOR YOU	Lionel Richie	2004
JUST FRIENDS (SUNNY)	Musiq	2000
JUST GETS BETTER	TJR featuring Xavier	1997
JUST GOT LUCKY	Joboxers	1983
JUST GOT PAID	Johnny Kemp	1988
JUST HOLD ON	Toploader	2000
JUST IN CASE	Jaheim	2001
JUST IN LUST	Wildhearts	1995
JUST KEEP ROCKIN'	Double Trouble & Rebel M.C.	1989
JUST KICKIN' IT	Xscape	1993

SONG TITLE	ARTIST	DATE
JUST LET ME DO MY THING		
	Sine	1978
JUST LIKE A MAN	Del Amitri	1992
JUST LIKE A PILL	Pink	2002
JUST LIKE A WOMAN	Manfred Mann	1966
JUST LIKE A WOMAN	Bob Dylan	1966
JUST LIKE EDDIE	Heinz	1963
JUST LIKE FRED ASTAIRE	James	1999
JUST LIKE HEAVEN	Cure	1987
JUST LIKE JESSE JAMES	Cher	1989
JUST LIKE ME	Hollies	1963
JUST LIKE ME	Paul Revere & The Raiders	1965
JUST LIKE PARADISE	David Lee Roth	1988
JUST LIKE YOU	Robbie Nevil	1991
(JUST LIKE) ROMEO & JULIET		
	Reflections	1964
(JUST LIKE) STARTING OVER		
	John Lennon	1980
JUST LISTEN TO MY HEART		
	Spotnicks	1963
JUST LOOKIN'/BULLET COMES		
	Charlatans	1995
JUST LOOKING	Stereophonics	1999
JUST LOSE IT	Eminem	2004
JUST LOVING YOU	Anita Harris	1967

SONG TITLE	ARTIST	DATE
JUST MY IMAGINATION (RUNNING AWAY WITH ME)		
	Temptations	1971
JUST MY SOUL RESPONDING		
	Smokey Robinson	1974
JUST ONCE	Quincy Jones featuring	
	James Ingram	1981
JUST ONCE IN MY LIFE	Righteous Brothers	1965
JUST ONE LOOK	Faith, Hope And Charity	1976
JUST ONE LOOK	Hollies	1964
JUST ONE MORE NIGHT	Yellow Dog	1978
JUST ONE SMILE	Gene Pitney	1966
JUST OUT OF REACH (OF MY TWO EMPTY ARMS)		
	Ken Dodd	1972
JUST OUTSIDE OF HEAVEN	H2O	1983
JUST PLAYIN'	JT Playaz	1997
JUST REMEMBER I LOVE YOU		
	Firefall	1977
JUST RIGHT	Soul II Soul	1992
JUST SAY NO	Grange Hill Cast	1986
JUST SEVEN NUMBERS (CAN STRAIGHTEN OUT MY LIFE)		
	Four Tops	1971
JUST SO LONELY	Get Wet	1981
JUST TAH LET U KNOW	Eazy-E	1996
JUST TAKE MY HEART	Mr. Big	1992
JUST THE ONE	Levellers	1995
JUST THE TWO OF US	Will Smith	1998

SONG TITLE	ARTIST	DATE
JUST THE TWO OF US	Grover Washington Jr.	1981
JUST THE WAY	Alfonzo Hunter	1997
JUST THE WAY I'M FEELING		
	Feeder	2003
JUST THE WAY IT IS, BABY		
	Rembrandts	1991
JUST THE WAY YOU ARE	Billy Joel	1977
JUST THE WAY YOU ARE	Barry White	1978
JUST THE WAY YOU ARE	Milky	2002
JUST THE WAY YOU LIKE IT		
	S.O.S. Band	1984
JUST THIS SIDE OF LOVE	Malandra Burrows	1990
JUST TO BE CLOSE TO YOU		
	Commodores	1976
JUST TO SEE HER	Smokey Robinson	1987
JUST TOO MANY PEOPLE	Melissa Manchester	1975
JUST WALK IN MY SHOES	Gladys Knight & The Pips	1972
JUST WANNA KNOW/FE REAL		
	Maxi Priest	1992
JUST WANT TO HOLD YOU	Jasmine Guy	1991
JUST WAVE HELLO	Charlotte Church	1999
JUST WHAT I ALWAYS WANTED		
	Mari Wilson	1982
JUST WHAT I NEEDED	Cars	1978
JUST WHEN I NEEDED YOU MOST		
	Randy Vanwarmer	1979

SONG TITLE	ARTIST	DATE
JUST WHEN I NEEDED YOU MOST		
	Barbara Jones	1981
JUST WHEN YOU'RE THINKIN' THINGS OVER		
	Charlatans	1995
JUST WHO IS THE FIVE O'CLOCK HERO		
	Jam	1982
JUST YOU	Sonny & Cher	1965
JUST YOU 'N' ME	Chicago	1973
JUST YOU AND I	Melissa Manchester	1976
(JUST) YOU AND ME	New Vision	2000
JUSTIFIED AND ANCIENT	KLF/Tammy Wynette	1991
JUSTIFY MY LOVE	Madonna	1990
JUSTIFY THE RAIN	Cosmic Rough Riders	2003
JUXTAPOSED WITH U	Super Furry Animals	2001
K-JEE	Nite-Liters	1971
KA-CHING!	Shania Twain	2003
KANSAS CITY	Trini Lopez	1963
KANSAS CITY STAR	Roger Miller	1965
KARA, KARA	New World	1971
KARAOKE QUEEN	Catatonia	1999
KARMA CHAMELEON	Culture Club	1983
KARMA HOTEL	Spooks	2001
KARMA POLICE	Radiohead	1997
KARMACOMA	Massive Attack	1995
KARMADROME/EAT ME DRINK ME...		
	Pop Will Eat Itself	1992

SONG TITLE	ARTIST	DATE
KATE	Ben Folds Five	1997
KATE BUSH ON STAGE (EP)		
	Kate Bush	1979
KAYLEIGH	Marillion	1985
KEEM-O-SABE	Electric Indian	1969
KEEP COMING BACK	Richard Marx	1991
(KEEP FEELING) FASCINATION		
	Human League	1983
KEEP FISHIN'	Weezer	2002
KEEP GIVIN' ME YOUR LOVE		
	Ce Ce Peniston	1994
KEEP IT COMIN'	Keith Sweat	1991
KEEP IT COMIN' LOVE	KC & The Sunshine Band	1977
KEEP IT COMIN' (DANCE TILL YOU CAN'T DANCE NO		
MORE)	C&C Music Factory featuring	
	Q Unique & Deborah Cooper	1992
KEEP IT DARK	Genesis	1981
KEEP IT OUT OF SIGHT	Paul & Barry Ryan	1967
KEEP IT TOGETHER	Madonna	1990
KEEP IT UP	Sharada House Gang	1995
KEEP LOVE TOGETHER	Love To Infinity	1995
KEEP LOVE TOGETHER	Soda Club featuring	
	Andrea Anatola	2003
KEEP ME A SECRET	Ainslie Henderson	2003
KEEP ME CRYIN'	Al Green	1976
KEEP ME IN MIND	Boy George	1987

SONG TITLE	ARTIST	DATE
KEEP ON	Bruce Channel	1968
KEEP ON DANCIN'	Gary's Gang	1979
KEEP ON DANCIN' (LET'S GO)	Perpetual Motion	1998
KEEP ON DANCING	Bay City Rollers	1971
KEEP ON DANCING	Gentrys	1965
KEEP ON JUMPIN'	Lisa Marie Experience	1996
KEEP ON JUMPIN'	Todd Terry/Martha Wash & Jocelyn Brown	1996
KEEP ON KEEPIN' ON	MC Lyte featuring Xscape	1997
KEEP ON LOVIN' ME HONEY	Marvin Gaye & Tammi Terrell	1968
KEEP ON LOVING YOU	REO Speedwagon	1980
KEEP ON MOVIN'	Soul II Soul	1989
KEEP ON MOVIN'	5ive	1999
KEEP ON MOVING	Bob Marley & The Wailers	1995
KEEP ON PUSHING	Impressions	1964
KEEP ON PUSHING OUR LOVE	Nightcrawlers/John Reid/ Alysha Warren	1996
KEEP ON RUNNIN'	Spencer Davis Group	1965
KEEP ON SINGING	Helen Reddy	1974
KEEP ON SMILIN'	Wet Willie	1974
KEEP ON TRUCKIN'	Eddie Kendricks	1973
KEEP ON WALKIN'	Ce Ce Peniston	1992

SONG TITLE	ARTIST	DATE
(KEEP ON) SHINING/HOPE (NEVER GIVE UP)	Loveland featuring Rachel McFarlane	1994
KEEP ON, KEEPIN' ON	MC Lyte featuring Xscape	1996
KEEP SEARCHIN' (WE'LL FOLLOW THE SUN)	Del Shannon	1964
KEEP THE BALL ROLLIN'	Jay & The Techniques	1967
KEEP THE FAITH	Bon Jovi	1992
KEEP THE FIRE	Kenny Loggins	1980
KEEP THE FIRE BURNIN'	REO Speedwagon	1982
KEEP THE FIRES BURNING	Clock	1994
KEEP THE HOME FIRES BURNING	Bluetones	2000
KEEP THE MUSIC STRONG	Bizarre Inc.	1996
KEEP THEIR HEADS RINGIN'	Dr. Dre	1995
KEEP WARM	Jinny	1995
KEEP WHAT YA GOT	Ian Brown	2004
KEEP YA HEAD UP	2Pac	1993
KEEP YOUR EYE ON ME	Herb Alpert	1987
KEEP YOUR HANDS OFF MY BABY	Little Eva	1962
KEEP YOUR HANDS TO YOURSELF	Georgia Satellites	1986
KEEPER OF THE CASTLE	Four Tops	1972

SONG TITLE	ARTIST	DATE
KEEPING THE DREAM ALIVE		
	Freiheit	1988
KEEPING THE FAITH	Billy Joel	1985
KELLY WATCH THE STARS	Air	1998
KELLY'S HEROES	Black Grape	1995
KENNEDY	Wedding Present	1989
KENTUCKY RAIN	Elvis Presley	1970
KENTUCKY WOMAN	Deep Purple	1968
KENTUCKY WOMAN	Neil Diamond	1967
KERNKRAFT 400	Zombie Nation	2000
KEVIN CARTER	Manic Street Preachers	1996
THE KEY	Matt Goss	1995
KEY LARGO	Bertie Higgins	1981
THE KEY THE SECRET	Urban Cookie Collective	1993
KEY TO MY LIFE	Boyzone	1995
KEY WEST INTERMEZZO (I SAW YOU FIRST)		
	John Mellencamp	1996
KICK IT	Peaches featuring Iggy Pop	2004
KICK IT IN	Simple Minds	1989
KICKIN' HARD	Klubbheads	1998
KICKS	Paul Revere & The Raiders	1966
KICKSTART MY HEART	Motley Crue	1989
KID	Pretenders	1979
KID 2000	Hybrid featuring Chrissie Hynde	2000
THE KID'S AMERICAN	Matthew Wilder	1984
KIDS	Robbie Williams/Kylie Minogue	2000

SONG TITLE	ARTIST	DATE
THE KIDS ARE BACK	Twisted Sister	1983
THE KIDS AREN'T ALRIGHT		
	Offspring	1999
KIDS IN AMERICA	Kim Wilde	1982
KILL ALL HIPPIES	Primal Scream	2000
KILLER	Adamski	1990
KILLER	ATB	2000
KILLER (EP)	Seal	1991
KILLER ON THE LOOSE	Thin Lizzy	1980
KILLER QUEEN	Queen	1975
KILLERS LIVE (EP)	Thin Lizzy	1981
KILLIN' TIME	Tina Cousins	1999
KILLIN' TIME	Fred Knoblock & Susan Anton	1980
KILLING IN THE NAME	Rage Against The Machine	1993
KILLING ME SOFTLY	Fugees	1996
KILLING ME SOFTLY WITH HIS SONG		
	Roberta Flack	1973
THE KILLING MOON	Echo & The Bunnymen	1984
THE KILLING OF GEORGIE (PARTS I & II)		
	Rod Stewart	1977
KIND OF A DRAG	Buckinghams	1966
A KIND OF MAGIC	Queen	1986
KINDA LOVE	Darius	2004
KINETIC	Golden Girls	1998
THE KING AND QUEEN OF AMERICA		
	Eurythmics	1990

SONG TITLE	ARTIST	DATE
KING FOR A DAY	Jamiroquai	1999
KING FOR A DAY	Thompson Twins	1986
KING HEROIN	James Brown	1972
KING IN A CATHOLIC STYLE (WAKE UP)	China Crisis	1985
THE KING IS GONE	Ronnie McDowell	1977
THE KING IS HALF UNDRESSED	Jellyfish	1991
KING MIDAS IN REVERSE	Hollies	1967
KING OF EMOTION	Big Country	1988
THE KING OF KISSINGDOM	My Life Story	1997
KING OF MISERY	Honeycrack	1996
KING OF NEW YORK	Fun Lovin' Criminals	1997
KING OF PAIN	Police	1983
THE KING OF ROCK 'N' ROLL	Prefab Sprout	1988
KING OF SNAKE	Underworld	1999
KING OF THE CASTLE	Wamdue Project	1999
KING OF THE COPS	Billy Howard	1975
KING OF THE DANCEHALL	Beenie Man	2004
KING OF THE HILL	Rick Pinette and Oak	1980
KING OF THE KERB	Echobelly	1995
KING OF THE ROAD	Roger Miller	1965
KING OF THE ROAD	Proclaimers	1990

SONG TITLE	ARTIST	DATE
THE KING OF WISHFUL THINKING	Go West	1990
KING ROCKER	Generation X	1979
KING TUT	Steve Martin	1978
KING'S CALL	Philip Lynott	1980
KING/FOOD FOR THOUGHT	UB40	1980
KINGS OF THE PARTY	Brownsville Station	1974
KINGS OF THE WILD FRONTIER	Adam & The Ants	1980
KINGSTON TOWN	UB40	1990
KINKY AFRO	Happy Mondays	1990
KINKY BOOTS	Patrick Macnee & Honor Blackman	1990
KISS	Art Of Noise featuring Tom Jones	1988
KISS	Prince & The Revolution	1986
KISS (WHEN THE SUN DON'T SHINE)	Vengaboys	1999
KISS AN ANGEL GOOD MORNIN'	Charley Pride	1971
KISS AND SAY GOODBYE	Manhattans	1976
KISS AND TELL	Brownstone	1997
KISS AND TELL	Bryan Ferry	1988
KISS AWAY	Ronnie Dove	1965

SONG TITLE	ARTIST	DATE
KISS FROM A ROSE/I'M ALIVE		
	Seal	1995
KISS HIM GOODBYE	Nylons	1987
KISS IN THE DARK	Pink Lady	1979
KISS KISS	Holly Valance	2002
KISS ME	Stephen 'Tin Tin' Duffy	1985
KISS ME	Sixpence None The Richer	1999
KISS ME DEADLY	Lita Ford	1988
KISS ME GOODBYE	Petula Clark	1968
KISS ME IN THE RAIN	Barbra Streisand	1980
KISS ME QUICK	Elvis Presley	1964
KISS ME SAILOR	Diane Renay	1964
KISS OF LIFE	Supergrass	2004
KISS ON MY LIST	Daryl Hall & John Oates	1981
KISS ON THE LIPS	The Dualers	2004
KISS THE BRIDE	Elton John	1983
KISS THE GIRL	Peter Andre	1998
KISS THE RAIN	Billie Myers	1997
KISS THEM FOR ME	Siouxsie & The Banshees	1991
KISS THIS THING GOODBYE		
	Del Amitri	1990
KISS YOU ALL OVER	Exile	1978
KISS YOU ALL OVER	No Mercy	1997
KISS YOU BACK	Digital Underground	1991
KISSES ON THE WIND	Neneh Cherry	1989
KISSIN' COUSINS	Elvis Presley	1964

SONG TITLE	ARTIST	DATE
KISSIN' IN THE BACK ROW OF THE MOVIES		
	Drifters	1974
KISSIN' YOU	Total	1996
KISSING A FOOL	George Michael	1988
KISSING GATE	Sam Brown	1990
KISSING MY LOVE	Bill Withers	1973
KISSING WITH CONFIDENCE		
	Will Powers	1983
KISSING YOU	Keith Washington	1991
KITES	Simon Dupree & The Big Sound	1967
KITSCH	Barry Ryan	1970
KLUBBHOPPING	Klubbheads	1996
KNIGHT IN RUSTY ARMOUR		
	Peter & Gordon	1966
KNIVES OUT	Radiohead	2001
KNOCK KNOCK WHO'S THERE?		
	Mary Hopkin	1970
KNOCK ON WOOD	Otis Redding & Carla Thomas	1967
KNOCK ON WOOD	David Bowie	1974
KNOCK ON WOOD	Eddie Floyd	1966
KNOCK ON WOOD/LIGHT MY FIRE		
	Amii Stewart	1985
KNOCK OUT	Triple Eight	2003
KNOCK THREE TIMES	Dawn	1970
KNOCKED IT OFF	B.A. Robertson	1979
KNOCKED OUT	Paula Abdul	1990

SONG TITLE	ARTIST	DATE
KNOCKIN' BOOTS	Candyman	1990
KNOCKIN' DA BOOTS	H-Town	1993
KNOCKIN' ON HEAVEN'S DOOR	Eric Clapton	1975
KNOCKIN' ON HEAVEN'S DOOR	Bob Dylan	1973
KNOCKIN' ON HEAVEN'S DOOR	Guns N' Roses	1992
KNOCKIN' ON HEAVEN'S DOOR/THROW THESE GUNS AWAY	Dunblane	1996
KNOW BY NOW	Robert Palmer	1994
KNOW YOU WANNA	3rd Edge	2003
KNOWING ME KNOWING YOU	ABBA	1977
KNOWING ME, KNOWING YOU	ABBA	1977
KODACHROME	Paul Simon	1973
KOKOMO	Beach Boys	1988
KOMODO (SAVE A SOUL)	Mauro Picotto	2001
KOOCHY	Armand Van Helden	2000
KOOL IN THE KAFTAN	B.A. Robertson	1980
KOOTCHI	Neneh Cherry	1996
KOREAN BODEGA	Fun Lovin' Criminals	1999
KOWALSKI	Primal Scream	1997
KRUPA	Apollo 440	1996
KRYPTONITE	3 Doors Down	2000

SONG TITLE	ARTIST	DATE
KUMBAYA	Sandpipers	1969
KUNG FU	Curtis Mayfield	1974
KUNG FU FIGHTING	Carl Douglas	1974
KUNG FU FIGHTING	Bus Stop featuring Carl Douglas	1998
KUNG-FU	187 Lockdown	1998
KYRIE	Mr Mister	1986
KYRILA (EP)	Demis Roussos	1977
L'ESPERANZA	Airscape	1999
L'L'LUCY	Mud	1975
L-O-N-E-L-Y	Bobby Vinton	1965
L-O-V-E (LOVE)	Al Green	1975
L.A. CONNECTION	Rainbow	1978
THE L.A. RUN	Carvells	1977
L.O.D. (LOVE ON DELIVERY)	Billy Ocean	1976
L.S.F.	Kasabian	2004
L.S.I.	Shamen	1992
LA	Marc Et Claude	1998
LA BAMBA	Los Lobos	1987
LA BOOGA ROOGA	Surprise Sisters	1976
LA DERNIERE VALSE	Mireille Mathieu	1967
LA ISLA BONITA	Madonna	1987
LA LA (MEANS I LOVE YOU)	Swing Out Sister	1994
LA-LA MEANS I LOVE YOU	Delfonics	1968

SONG TITLE	ARTIST	DATE
LA LA LA (IF I HAD YOU)	Bobby Sherman	1969
LA LA LA HEY HEY	Outhere Brothers	1995
LA LA LAND	Green Velvet	2002
LA LA PEACE SONG	Al Wilson	1974
LA LUNA	Belinda Carlisle	1989
LA MUSICA	Ruff Driverz presents Arrola	1999
LA PRIMAVERA	Sash!	1998
LA SERENISSIMA	DNA	1990
LA TRISTESSE DURERA (SCREAM TO A SIGH)		
	Manic Street Preachers	1993
LABELLED WITH LOVE	Squeeze	1981
LABOUR OF LOVE	Hue And Cry	1987
LADIES NIGHT	Kool & The Gang	1979
LADIES NIGHT	Atomic Kitten featuring	
	Kool & The Gang	2003
LADY	D'Angelo	1996
LADY	Kenny Rogers	1980
LADY	Jack Jones	1967
LADY	Little River Band	1979
LADY	Styx	1974
LADY	Whispers	1980
LADY (HEAR ME TONIGHT)	Modjo	2000
LADY BARBARA	Herman's Hermits	1970
LADY BIRD	Nancy Sinatra & Lee Hazlewood	1967
LADY BLUE	Leon Russell	1975
LADY D'ARBANVILLE	Cat Stevens	1970

SONG TITLE	ARTIST	DATE
LADY ELEANOR	Lindisfarne	1972
LADY GODIVA	Peter & Gordon	1966
LADY IN RED	Chris De Burgh	1987
LADY JANE	David Garrick	1966
LADY JANE	Rolling Stones	1966
LADY LOVE	Lou Rawls	1978
LADY LOVE BUG	Clodagh Rodgers	1971
LADY LOVE ME (ONE MORE TIME)		
	George Benson	1983
LADY LYNDA	Beach Boys	1979
LADY MADONNA	Beatles	1968
LADY MARMALADE	Christina Aguilera, Lil' Kim,	
	Mya & Pink	2001
LADY MARMALADE (VOULEZ-VOUS COUCHER AVEC MOI		
CE SOIR?)	Labelle	1975
LADY ROSE	Mungo Jerry	1971
LADY WILLPOWER	Gary Puckett & The Union Gap	1968
LADY YOU BRING ME UP	Commodores	1981
THE LADYBOY IS MINE	Stuntmasterz	2001
LADYKILLERS	Lush	1996
LAID	James	1993
LAID SO LOW (TEARS ROLL DOWN)		
	Tears For Fears	1992
LAKINI'S JUICE	Live	1997
LALENA	Donovan	1968
LAMBADA	Kaoma	1989

SONG TITLE	ARTIST	DATE
LAMENT	Ultravox	1984
LAMPLIGHT	David Essex	1973
LANA	Roy Orbison	1966
LAND OF 1,000 DANCES	Wilson Pickett	1966
LAND OF 1000 DANCES	Cannibal And The Headhunters	1965
LAND OF CONFUSION	Genesis	1986
LAND OF MAKE BELIEVE	Bucks Fizz	1981
THE LAND OF MAKE BELIEVE		
	Allstars	2002
THE LAND OF MILK AND HONEY		
	Vogues	1966
LAND OF THE LIVING	Milk Inc.	2003
LANDSLIDE	Harmonix	1996
LANDSLIDE	Spin City	2000
LANDSLIDE	Olivia Newton-John	1982
LANDSLIDE OF LOVE	Transvision Vamp	1989
THE LANE	Ice-T	1996
THE LANGUAGE OF LOVE	Dan Fogelberg	1984
LAPDANCE	N E R D featuring Lee Harvey & Vita	2001
LARGER THAN LIFE	Backstreet Boys	1999
LAS PALABRAS DE AMOR	Queen	1982
LAS VEGAS	Tony Christie	1971
LAST CHANCE TO TURN AROUND		
	Gene Pitney	1965
LAST CHILD	Aerosmith	1976

SONG TITLE	ARTIST	DATE
LAST CHRISTMAS/BIG TIME		
	Whigfield	1995
LAST CHRISTMAS	Wham!	1984
LAST DANCE	Donna Summer	1978
LAST DROP	Kevin Lyttle	2004
THE LAST FAREWELL	Roger Whittaker	1975
LAST FILM	Kissing The Pink	1983
THE LAST GAME OF THE SEASON		
	David Geddes	1975
THE LAST GOODBYE/BE WITH YOU		
	Atomic Kitten	2002
LAST KISS	Pearl Jam	1999
LAST KISS	Wednesday	1973
LAST KISS	J. Frank Wilson & The Cavaliers	1964
THE LAST KISS	David Cassidy	1985
THE LAST MILE	Cinderella	1989
LAST NIGHT	Az Yet	1996
LAST NIGHT	Merseybeats	1964
LAST NIGHT A D.J. SAVED MY LIFE		
	Indeep	1983
LAST NIGHT A DJ BLEW MY MIND		
	Fab For featuring Robert Owens	2003
LAST NIGHT A DJ SAVED MY LIFE		
	Sylk 130	1998
LAST NIGHT I DREAMT THAT SOMEBODY LOVED ME		
	Smiths	1987

SONG TITLE	ARTIST	DATE
LAST NIGHT IN SOHO	Dave Dee, Dozy, Beaky, Mick & Tich	1968
LAST NIGHT ON EARTH	U2	1997
(LAST NIGHT) I DIDN'T GET TO SLEEP AT ALL	5th Dimension	1972
LAST NITE	Strokes	2001
LAST OF THE FAMOUS INTERNATIONAL PLAYBOYS	Morrissey	1989
LAST ONE STANDING	Girl Thing	2000
LAST RESORT	Papa Roach	2001
LAST SONG	Edward Bear	1972
THE LAST SONG	Elton John	1992
LAST STOP: THIS TOWN	Eels	1998
LAST SUMMER	Lostprophets	2004
LAST THING ON MY MIND	Steps	1998
LAST THING ON MY MIND	Ronan Keating & Leann Rimes	2004
THE LAST TIME	Rolling Stones	1965
THE LAST TIME I MADE LOVE	Joyce Kennedy & Jeffrey Osborne	1984
LAST TIME I SAW HIM	Diana Ross	1974
LAST TO KNOW	Pink	2004
LAST TRAIN HOME	Lostprophets	2004
LAST TRAIN TO CLARKSVILLE	Monkees	1966
LAST TRAIN TO LONDON	Electric Light Orchestra	1979

SONG TITLE	ARTIST	DATE
LAST TRAIN TO TRANCENTRAL	KLF	1991
THE LAST WALTZ	Engelbert Humperdinck	1967
THE LAST WORD IN LONESOME IS ME	Eddy Arnold	1966
THE LAST WORTHLESS EVEING	Don Henley	1989
LATE IN THE DAY	Supergrass	1997
LATE IN THE EVENING	Paul Simon	1980
LATELY	Skunk Anansie	1999
LATELY	Stevie Wonder	1981
LATELY	Samantha Mumba	2001
LATELY	Lisa Scott-Lee	2003
LATELY	Divine	1998
LATELY	Jodeci	1993
LAUGH AT ME	Sonny	1965
LAUGH, LAUGH	Beau Brummels	1965
LAUGHING	Guess Who	1969
THE LAUGHING GNOME	David Bowie	1973
LAUGHTER IN THE RAIN	Neil Sedaka	1974
THE LAUNCH	DJ Jean	1999
LAUNDROMAT/DON'T MESS WITH MY MAN	Nivea	2003
LAURA	Scissor Sisters	2004
LAUREL AND HARDY	Equals	1968

SONG TITLE	ARTIST	DATE
LAURIE (STRANGE THINGS HAPPEN)		
	Dickey Lee	1965
LAVA	Silver Sun	1997
LAVENDER	Marillion	1985
LAWYERS IN LOVE	Jackson Browne	1983
LAY A LITTLE LOVIN' ON ME		
	Robin McNamara	1970
LAY ALL YOUR LOVE ON ME		
	ABBA	1981
LAY BACK IN THE ARMS OF SOMEONE		
	Smokie	1977
LAY DOWN	Strawbs	1972
LAY DOWN (CANDLES IN THE RAIN)		
	Melanie/Edwin Hawkins Singers	1970
LAY DOWN SALLY	Eric Clapton	1978
LAY DOWN YOUR ARMS	Belinda Carlisle	1993
LAY IT DOWN	Ratt	1985
LAY LADY LAY	Bob Dylan	1969
LAY LOVE ON YOU	Luisa Fernandez	1978
LAY YOUR HANDS ON ME	Bon Jovi	1989
LAY YOUR HANDS ON ME	Thompson Twins	1985
(LAY YOUR HEAD ON MY) PILLOW		
	Tony Toni Tone	1994
LAY YOUR LOVE ON ME	Roachford	1994
LAY YOUR LOVE ON ME	Racey	1978
LAYLA	Derek & The Dominos	1972

SONG TITLE	ARTIST	DATE
LAYLA	Eric Clapton	1992
LAZY	Suede	1997
LAZY	X-Press 2 featuring David Byrne	2002
LAZY BONES	Jonathan King	1971
LAZY DAY	Spanky & Our Gang	1967
LAZY DAYS	Robbie Williams	1997
LAZY ELSIE MOLLY	Chubby Checker	1964
LAZY LOVER	Supernaturals	1996
LAZY SUNDAY	Small Faces	1968
LE DISC JOCKEY	En-Core	1998
LE FREAK	Chic	1978
LE VOIE LE SOLEIL	Subliminal Cuts	1996
LEAD ME ON	Maxine Nightingale	1979
LEADER OF THE BAND	Dan Fogelberg	1981
LEADER OF THE LAUNDROMAT		
	Detergents	1964
LEADER OF THE PACK	Shangri-Las	1964
LEAFY MYSTERIES	Paul Weller	2002
LEAN BACK	Terror Squad featuring Fat Joe & Remy	2004
LEAN ON ME	Club Nouveau	1987
LEAN ON ME	Michael Bolton	1994
LEAN ON ME	Mud	1976
LEAN ON ME	Bill Withers	1972
LEAN ON ME (AH-LI-AYO)	Red Box	1985

SONG TITLE	ARTIST	DATE
LEAN ON ME I WON'T FALL OVER		
	Carter The Unstoppable	
	Sex Machine	1993
LEAN ON YOU	Cliff Richard	1989
LEANING ON THE LAMP POST		
	Herman's Hermits	1966
LEAP UP AND DOWN (WAVE YOUR KNICKERS IN THE		
AIR)	St. Cecilia	1971
LEARN TO FLY	Foo Fighters	1999
LEARNING TO FLY	Tom Petty & The Heartbreakers	1991
LEATHER AND LACE	Stevie Nicks	1981
LEAVE (GET OUT)	Jojo	2004
LEAVE A LIGHT ON	Belinda Carlisle	1989
LEAVE A LITTLE LOVE	Lulu	1965
LEAVE A TENDER MOMENT/GOODNIGHT SAIGON		
	Billy Joel	1984
LEAVE HOME	Chemical Brothers	1995
LEAVE IN SILENCE	Depeche Mode	1982
LEAVE IT	Mike McGear	1974
LEAVE IT	Yes	1984
LEAVE IT ALONE	Living Colour	1993
LEAVE IT UP TO ME	Aaron Carter	2002
LEAVE ME ALONE	Michael Jackson	1989
LEAVE ME ALONE (RUBY RED DRESS)		
	Helen Reddy	1973
LEAVE RIGHT NOW	Will Young	2003
LEAVE THEM ALL BEHIND	Ride	1992
LEAVING ME	Independents	1973
LEAVING ME NOW	Level 42	1985
LEAVING NEW YORK	R.E.M.	2004
LEAVING ON A JET PLANE	Peter, Paul & Mary	1969
THE LEBANON	Human League	1984
LEEDS UNITED	Leeds United F.C.	1972
LEFT BEHIND	Slipknot	2001
LEFT OF CENTER	Suzanne Vega featuring	
	Joe Jackson	1986
LEFT OUTSIDE ALONE	Anastacia	2004
LEFT TO MY OWN DEVICES		
	Pet Shop Boys	1988
LEGACY (SHOW ME LOVE)	Space Brothers	1999
LEGACY (EP)	Mansun	1998
THE LEGACY	Push	2001
LEGAL MAN	Belle & Sebastian	2000
LEGEND OF A COWGIRL	Imani Coppola	1997
THE LEGEND OF WOOLEY SWAMP		
	Charlie Daniels Band	1980
THE LEGEND OF XANADU	Dave Dee, Dozy, Beaky, Mick	
	& Tich	1968
LEGENDS OF THE DARK BLACK (PT 2)		
	Wildchild	1995
LEGO SKANGA	Rupie Edwards	1975
LEGS	ZZ Top	1984

SONG TITLE	ARTIST	DATE
LEMON TREE	Fool's Garden	1996
LEMON TREE	Trini Lopez	1965
LENNY	Supergrass	1995
LENNY AND TERENCE	Carter The Unstoppable Sex Machine	1993
LES BICYCLETTES DE BELSIZE	Engelbert Humperdinck	1968
THE LESSON	Vikki Carr	1967
LESSON IN LEAVIN'	Jo Dee Messina	1999
LESSON LEARNED	Tracy Lawrence	2000
LESSONS IN LOVE	Level 42	1987
LESSONS LEARNED FROM ROCKY I TO ROCKY III	Cornershop	2002
LET 'EM IN	Billy Paul	1977
LET 'EM IN	Paul McCartney	1976
LET A BOY CRY	Gala	1997
LET A MAN COME IN AND DO THE POPCORN (PART 1)	James Brown	1969
LET A WOMAN BE A WOMAN – LET A MAN BE A MAN	Dyke & The Blazers	1969
LET FOREVER BE	Chemical Brothers	1999
LET GO	Sharon Bryant	1989
LET HER CRY	Hootie & The Blowfish	1995
LET HER DOWN EASY	Terence Trent D'Arby	1993
LET HER FEEL IT	Simplicious	1985
LET HER IN	John Travolta	1976

SONG TITLE	ARTIST	DATE
LET HIM GO	Animotion	1985
LET IT ALL BLOW	Dazz Band	1984
LET IT ALL HANG OUT	Jonathan King	1970
LET IT BE	Beatles	1970
LET IT BE	Ferry Aid	1987
LET IT BE ME	Justin	2000
LET IT BE ME	Jerry Butler & Betty Everett	1964
LET IT BE ME	Glen Campbell & Bobbie Gentry	1969
LET IT BE ME	Willie Nelson	1982
LET IT FLOW	Spiritualized Electric Mainline	1995
LET IT GO	Ray J	1997
LET IT LAST	Carleen Anderson	1995
LET IT OUT (LET IT ALL HANG OUT)	Hombres	1967
LET IT RAIN	East 17	1995
LET IT RIDE	Bachman-Turner Overdrive	1974
LET IT ROLL	Raze presents Doug Lazy	1989
LET IT SHINE/HE AIN'T HEAVY HE'S MY BROTHER	Olivia Newton-John	1975
LET IT SNOW	Boyz II Men	1993
LET IT WHIP	Dazz Band	1982
LET LOVE BE YOUR ENERGY	Robbie Williams	2001
LET LOVE COME BETWEEN US	James & Bobby Purify	1987
LET LOVE RULE	Lenny Kravitz	1990

SONG TITLE	ARTIST	DATE
LET LOVE SHINE	Amos	1995
LET ME	Paul Revere & The Raiders	1969
LET ME BE	Turtles	1965
LET ME BE THE BLOCK	Smokey Robinson	1980
LET ME BE THE ONE	Five Star	1985
LET ME BE THE ONE	Shadows	1975
LET ME BE THE ONE	Cliff Richard	2002
LET ME BE THE ONE	Blessid Union Of Souls	1995
LET ME BE THE ONE	Expose	1987
LET ME BE THERE	Olivia Newton-John	1973
LET ME BE YOUR ANGEL	Stacy Lattisaw	1980
LET ME BE YOUR FANTASY		
	Baby D	1994
LET ME BE YOUR UNDERWEAR		
	Club 69	1992
LET ME BLOW YA MIND	Eve featuring Gwen Stefani	2001
LET ME CLEAR MY THROAT		
	DJ Kool	1997
LET ME CRY ON YOUR SHOULDER		
	Ken Dodd	1967
LET ME ENTERTAIN YOU	Robbie Williams	1998
LET ME GO	Ray Parker Jr.	1982
LET ME GO TO HIM	Dionne Warwick	1970
LET ME GO, LOVE	Nicolette Larson	1980
LET ME GO, LOVER!	Kathy Kirby	1964

SONG TITLE	ARTIST	DATE
LET ME HEAR YOU SAY 'OLE OLE'		
	Outhere Brothers	1997
LET ME IN	Osmonds	1973
LET ME IN	OTT	1997
LET ME IN	Young Buck	2004
LET ME KISS YOU	Morrissey	2004
LET ME KNOW (I HAVE A RIGHT)		
	Gloria Gaynor	1979
LET ME LET GO	Faith Hill	1998
LET ME LIVE	Queen	1996
LET ME LOVE YOU TONIGHT		
	Pure Prairie League	1980
LET ME RIDE	Dr. Dre	1993
LET ME SERENADE YOU	Three Dog Night	1973
LET ME SHOW YOU	Camisra	1998
LET ME SHOW YOU	K-Klass	1993
LET ME TAKE YOU THERE	Betty Boo	1992
LET ME TALK	Earth, Wind & Fire	1980
LET ME TICKLE YOUR FANCY		
	Jermaine Jackson	1982
LET ME TRY AGAIN	Tammy Jones	1975
LET MY LOVE OPEN THE DOOR		
	Pete Townshend	1980
LET MY PEOPLE GO-GO	Rainmakers	1987
LET ROBESON SING	Manic Street Preachers	2001

SONG TITLE	ARTIST	DATE
LET THE BEAT CONTROL YOUR BODY		
	2 Unlimited	1994
LET THE BEAT HIT 'EM	Shena	1997
LET THE BEAT HIT 'EM	Lisa Lisa & Cult Jam	1991
LET THE GOOD TIMES ROLL & FEEL SO GOOD		
	Bunny Sigler	1967
LET THE HEALING BEGIN	Joe Cocker	1994
LET THE HEARTACHES BEGIN		
	Long John Baldry	1967
LET THE LOVE	Q-Tex	1996
LET THE MUSIC HEAL YOUR SOUL		
	Bravo All Stars	1998
LET THE MUSIC LIFT YOU UP		
	Loveland vs Darlene Lewis	1994
LET THE MUSIC PLAY	Shannon	1983
LET THE MUSIC PLAY	Barry White	1975
LET THE MUSIC PLAY	Mary Kiani	1996
LET THE SUNSHINE IN	Milk & Sugar/Lizzy Pattinson	2003
LET THE WATER RUN DOWN		
	P.J. Proby	1965
LET THERE BE LOVE	Simple Minds	1991
LET THERE BE PEACE ON EARTH		
	Michael Ward	1973
LET THIS BE A PRAYER	Rollo Goes Spiritual with	
	Pauline Taylor	1996
LET U GO	ATB	2001
LET YOUR BODY GO DOWNTOWN		
	Martyn Ford Orchestra	1977
LET YOUR HAIR DOWN	Temptations	1973
LET YOUR HEART DANCE	Secret Affair	1979
LET YOUR LOVE FLOW	Bellamy Brothers	1976
LET YOUR LOVE GO	Bread	1971
LET YOUR SOUL BE YOUR PILOT		
	Sting	1996
LET YOUR YEAH BE YEAH	Ali Campbell	1995
LET YOUR YEAH BE YEAH	Pioneers	1971
LET YOURSELF GO	Sybil	1987
LET'S ALL CHANT	Gusto	1996
LET'S ALL CHANT	Pat & Mick	1988
LET'S ALL CHANT	Michael Zager Band	1978
LET'S ALL GO TOGETHER	Marion	1995
LET'S BE US AGAIN	Lonestar	2004
LET'S CALL IT QUITS	Slade	1976
LET'S CLEAN UP THE GHETTO		
	Philadelphia International All-Stars	1977
LET'S DANCE	David Bowie	1983
LET'S DANCE	Chris Montez	1962
LET'S DANCE	Chris Rea	1987
LET'S DANCE	5ive	2001
LET'S DO IT AGAIN	Staple Singers	1975
LET'S DO ROCK STEADY	Bodysnatchers	1980

SONG TITLE	ARTIST	DATE
LET'S DO THE FREDDIE	Chubby Checker	1965
LET'S DO THE LATIN HUSTLE	Eddie Drennon & B.B.S. Unlimited	1976
LET'S DO THE LATIN HUSTLE	M. & O. Band	1976
LET'S FACE THE MUSIC AND DANCE	Nat 'King' Cole	1994
LET'S FALL IN LOVE	Peaches & Herb	1966
LET'S FLY AWAY	Voyage	1979
LET'S GET AWAY	T.I.	2004
LET'S GET BACK TO BED... BOY	Sarah Connor featuring TQ	2001
LET'S GET BRUTAL	Nitro Deluxe	1988
LET'S GET DOWN	Mark Morrison	1995
LET'S GET DOWN	Tony Toni Tone featuring DJ Quik	1997
LET'S GET DOWN	Spacedust	1999
LET'S GET ILL	P. Diddy featuring Kelis	2003
LET'S GET IT ON	Shabba Ranks	1995
LET'S GET IT ON	Marvin Gaye	1973
LET'S GET IT STARTED	Black Eyed Peas	2004
LET'S GET IT UP	AC/DC	1982
LET'S GET MARRIED	Proclaimers	1994
LET'S GET MARRIED	Al Green	1974
LET'S GET MARRIED	Jagged Edge	2000

SONG TITLE	ARTIST	DATE
LET'S GET READY TO RUMBLE	PJ And Duncan	1994
LET'S GET ROCKED	Def Leppard	1992
LET'S GET SERIOUS	Jermaine Jackson	1980
LET'S GET TATTOOS	Carter The Unstoppable Sex Machine	1994
LET'S GET THIS STRAIGHT	Dexy's Midnight Runners	1982
LET'S GET TOGETHER	Alexander O'Neal	1996
LET'S GET TOGETHER	We Five	1965
LET'S GET TOGETHER AGAIN	Glitter Band	1974
LET'S GO	Cars	1979
LET'S GO	Wang Chung	1987
LET'S GO	Trick Daddy featuring Lil Jon & Twista	2004
LET'S GO ALL THE WAY	Sly Fox	1985
LET'S GO ROUND AGAIN	Louise	1997
LET'S GO CRAZY	Prince & The Revolution	1985
LET'S GO DISCO	Real Thing	1978
LET'S GO GET STONED	Ray Charles	1966
LET'S GO ROUND AGAIN (PT 1)	Average White Band	1980
LET'S GO TO SAN FRANCISCO	Flowerpot Men	1967
LET'S GO TOGETHER	Change	1985
LET'S GROOVE	Earth, Wind & Fire	1981

SONG TITLE	ARTIST	DATE
LET'S HANG ON	Johnny Johnson & The Bandwagon	1969
LET'S HANG ON	Darts	1980
LET'S HANG ON	Barry Manilow	1982
LET'S HANG ON!	Four Seasons	1965
LET'S HAVE A QUIET NIGHT IN	David Soul	1977
LET'S HEAR IT FOR THE BOY	Deniece Williams	1984
LET'S JUMP THE BROOMSTICK	Coast To Coast	1981
LET'S LIVE FOR TODAY	Grass Roots	1967
LET'S LIVE IT UP (NITE PEOPLE)	David Joseph	1983
LET'S LIVE TOGETHER	Road Apples	1975
LET'S LOCK THE DOOR (AND THROW AWAY THE KEY)	Jay & The Americans	1964
LET'S MAKE A BABY	Billy Paul	1976
LET'S MAKE A NIGHT TO REMEMBER	Bryan Adams	1996
LET'S PARTY	Jive Bunny & The Mastermixers	1989
LET'S PRETEND	Lulu	1967
LET'S PRETEND	Raspberries	1973
LET'S PUSH IT	Innocence	1990
LET'S PUSH IT	Nightcrawlers featuring John Reid	1996

SONG TITLE	ARTIST	DATE
LET'S PUSH THINGS FORWARD	Streets	2002
LET'S PUT IT ALL TOGETHER	Stylistics	1974
LET'S RIDE	Montell Jordan	1998
LET'S SEE ACTION	Who	1971
LET'S SPEND THE NIGHT TOGETHER	Rolling Stones	1967
LET'S START ALL OVER AGAIN	Ronnie Dove	1966
LET'S STAY HOME TONIGHT	Joe	2002
LET'S STAY TOGETHER	Pasadenas	1992
LET'S STAY TOGETHER	Al Green	1971
LET'S STAY TOGETHER	Tina Turner	1984
LET'S STICK TOGETHER	Bryan Ferry	1976
LET'S STRAIGHTEN IT OUT	Latimore	1974
LET'S SWING AGAIN	Jive Bunny & The Mastermixers	1990
LET'S TALK ABOUT SEX	Salt 'N 'Pepa	1991
LET'S TRY AGAIN	New Kids On The Block	1990
LET'S TURKEY TROT	Little Eva	1963
LET'S TWIST AGAIN	John Asher	1975
LET'S TWIST AGAIN	Chubby Checker	1962
LET'S WAIT AWHILE	Janet Jackson	1987

SONG TITLE	ARTIST	DATE
LET'S WOMBLE TO THE PARTY TONIGHT		
	Wombles	1975
LET'S WORK	Mick Jagger	1987
LET'S WORK IT OUT	Raghav featuring Jahaziel	2004
LET'S WORK TOGETHER	Canned Heat	1970
LET'S WORK TOGETHER (PART 1)		
	Wilbert Harrison	1969
LETHAL INDUSTRY	DJ Tiesto	2002
LETITGO	Prince	1994
THE LETTER	Long And The Short	1964
THE LETTER	Joe Cocker	1970
THE LETTER	Box Tops	1967
THE LETTER	PJ Harvey	2004
THE LETTER	Arbors	1969
THE LETTER/PARADISE BIRD		
	Amii Stewart	1980
LETTER FROM AMERICA	Proclaimers	1987
A LETTER TO ELISE	Cure	1992
LETTER TO LUCILLE	Tom Jones	1973
LETTER 2 MY UNBORN	2Pac	2001
A LETTER TO MYSELF	Chi-Lites	1973
A LETTER TO YOU	Shakin' Stevens	1984
LETTERS FROM HOME	John Michael Montgomery	2004
LETTERS TO YOU	Finch	2003
LETTING GO	Paul McCartney	1975
LEVI STUBB'S TEARS	Billy Bragg	1986

SONG TITLE	ARTIST	DATE
LEVON	Elton John	1971
LFO	LFO	1990
LIAR	Profyle	2000
LIAR	Three Dog Night	1971
LIAR/DISCONNECT	Rollins Band	1994
LIAR, LIAR	Castaways	1965
LIBERATION	Liberation	1992
LIBERATION	Pet Shop Boys	1994
LIBERATION (TEMPTATION – FLY LIKE AN ANGEL)		
	Matt Darey/Mash Up	1999
LIBERIAN GIRL	Michael Jackson	1989
LIBIAMO/LA DONNA E MOBILE		
	Carreras/Domingo/Pavarotti/	
	Mehta	1994
LICENCE TO KILL	Gladys Knight	1989
LICENSE TO CHILL	Billy Ocean	1989
LICK A SHOT	Cypress Hill	1994
LICK IT UP	Kiss	1983
LICKING STICK-LICKING STICK		
	James Brown	1968
LIDO SHUFFLE	Boz Scaggs	1977
LIE TO ME	Bon Jovi	1995
LIES	EMF	1991
LIES	Jonathan Butler	1987
LIES	En Vogue	1990
LIES	Knickerbockers	1966

SONG TITLE	ARTIST	DATE
LIES	Thompson Twins	1983
LIES/DON'T DRIVE MY CAR		
	Status Quo	1980
THE LIES IN YOUR EYES	Sweet	1976
LIFE	Des'ree	1998
LIFE	Haddaway	1993
LIFE AIN'T EASY	Cleopatra	1998
LIFE AT A TOP PEOPLE'S HEALTH FARM		
	Style Council	1988
LIFE BECOMING A LANDSLIDE		
	Manic Street Preachers	1994
LIFE FOR RENT	Dido	2003
LIFE GOES ON	Leann Rimes	2002
LIFE GOES ON	Poison	1991
LIFE GOT COLD	Girls Aloud	2003
LIFE IN A NORTHERN TOWN		
	Dream Academy	1985
LIFE IN ONE DAY	Howard Jones	1985
LIFE IN THE FAST LANE	Eagles	1977
LIFE IN TOKYO	Japan	1982
LIFE IS A FLOWER	Ace Of Base	1998
LIFE IS A HIGHWAY	Tom Cochrane	1992
LIFE IS A LONG SONG/UP THE POOL		
	Jethro Tull	1971
LIFE IS A MINESTONE	10cc	1975

SONG TITLE	ARTIST	DATE
LIFE IS A ROCK (BUT THE RADIO ROLLED ME)		
	Reunion	1974
LIFE IS A ROLLERCOASTER	Ronan Keating	2000
LIFE IS JUST A BALLGAME	Womack & Womack	1988
LIFE IS SWEET	Chemical Brothers	1995
LIFE IS TOO SHORT GIRL	Sheer Elegance	1976
A LIFE LESS ORDINARY	Ash	1997
A LIFE OF ILLUSION	Joe Walsh	1981
THE LIFE OF RILEY	Lightning Seeds	1992
LIFE OF SURPRISES	Prefab Sprout	1993
LIFE ON MARS?	David Bowie	1973
LIFE ON YOUR OWN	Human League	1984
LIFE STORY	Angie Stone	2000
LIFE'S BEEN GOOD	Joe Walsh	1978
LIFE'S TOO SHORT	Hole In One	1997
LIFE'S TOO SHORT	Lightning Seeds	1999
LIFE'S WHAT YOU MAKE IT		
	Talk Talk	1986
LIFE, LOVE & HAPPINESS	Brian Kennedy	1996
LIFEFORMS	Future Sound Of London	1994
LIFELINE	Spandau Ballet	1982
LIFESTYLES OF THE RICH AND FAMOUS		
	Good Charlotte	2003
LIFETIME	Maxwell	2001
LIFETIME LOVE	Joyce Sims	1987

SONG TITLE	ARTIST	DATE
LIFT/OPEN YOUR MIND	808 State	1991
LIFT EVERY VOICE (TAKE ME AWAY)	Mass Order	1992
LIFT IT HIGH (ALL ABOUT BELIEF)	1999 Manchester United Squad	1999
LIFT ME UP	Red 5	1997
LIFT ME UP	Reel	2001
LIFT ME UP	Geri Halliwell	1999
LIFT ME UP	Howard Jones	1992
LIFTED	Lighthouse Family	1996
LIFTING ME HIGHER	Gems For Jem	1995
LIGHT A CANDLE	Daniel O'Donnell	2000
LIGHT A RAINBOW	Tukan	2001
LIGHT AND DAY	The Polyphonic Spree	2003
LIGHT MY FIRE	Doors	1967
LIGHT MY FIRE	Clubhouse featuring Carl	1994
LIGHT MY FIRE	Jose Feliciano	1968
LIGHT MY FIRE	Will Young	2002
LIGHT MY FIRE – 137 DISCO HEAVEN	Amii Stewart	1979
LIGHT MY FIRE/PLEASE RELEASE ME	Mike Flowers Pops	1996
LIGHT OF DAY	Barbusters (Joan Jett & The Blackhearts)	1987
(LIGHT OF EXPERIENCE) DOINA DE JALE	Georghe Zamfir	1976

SONG TITLE	ARTIST	DATE
LIGHT OF LOVE	T. Rex	1974
LIGHT OF MY LIFE	Louise	1995
LIGHT UP THE FIRE	Parchment	1972
LIGHTNIN' STRIKES	Lou Christie	1965
LIGHTNING	Zoe	1991
LIGHTNING CRASHES	Live	1996
THE LIGHTNING TREE	Settlers	1971
LIGHTNING'S GIRL	Nancy Sinatra	1967
LIGHTS OF CINCINNATI	Scott Walker	1969
LIGHTS OUT	Lisa Marie Presley	2003
LIGHTS OUT	Peter Wolf	1984
LIGHTS, CAMERA, ACTION!	Mr. Cheeks	2001
LIKE A BABY	Len Barry	1966
LIKE A BUTTERFLY	Mac & Katie Kissoon	1975
LIKE A CHILD	Julie Rogers	1964
LIKE A CHILD AGAIN	Mission	1992
LIKE A PRAYER	Madonna	1989
LIKE A PRAYER	Mad'house	2002
LIKE A ROCK	Bob Seger & The Silver Bullet Band	1986
LIKE A ROLLING STONE	Bob Dylan	1965
LIKE A ROLLING STONE	Rolling Stones	1995
LIKE A ROSE	Al	2000
LIKE A SAD SONG	John Denver	1976
LIKE A SATELLITE (EP)	Thunder	1993
LIKE A STONE	Audioslave	2003

SONG TITLE	ARTIST	DATE
LIKE A SUNDAY IN SALEM (THE AMOS & ANDY SHOW)		
	Gene Cotton	1978
LIKE A VIRGIN	Madonna	1984
LIKE A WOMAN	Tony Rich Project	1996
LIKE AN OLD TIME MOVIE	Scott McKenzie	1967
LIKE CLOCKWORK	Boomtown Rats	1978
LIKE DREAMERS DO	Applejacks	1964
LIKE DREAMERS DO	Mica Paris	1988
LIKE DREAMERS DO	Courtney Pine	1988
LIKE GLUE	Sean Paul	2003
LIKE I LOVE YOU	Justin Timberlake	2002
LIKE I'VE NEVER BEEN GONE		
	Billy Fury	1963
LIKE LOVERS DO	Lloyd Cole	1995
LIKE MARVIN GAYE SAID (WHAT'S GOING ON)		
	Speech	1996
LIKE NO OTHER NIGHT	38 Special	1986
LIKE SISTER AND BROTHER		
	Drifters	1973
LIKE THIS AND LIKE THAT	Monica	1996
LIKE THIS LIKE THAT	Mauro Picotto	2001
LIKE TO GET TO KNOW YOU		
	Spanky & Our Gang	1968
LIKE TO GET TO KNOW YOU WELL		
	Howard Jones	1984
LIKE WE USED TO BE	Georgie Fame	1965

SONG TITLE	ARTIST	DATE
LIKE WHAT	Tommi	2003
A LIL' AIN'T ENOUGH	David Lee Roth	1991
LIL' DEVIL	Cult	1987
LIL' RED RIDING HOOD	Sam The Sham & The Pharaohs	1966
LILAC WINE	Elkie Brooks	1978
LILY THE PINK	Scaffold	1968
LILY WAS HERE	David A. Stewart featuring Candy Dulfer	1990
LINE DANCE PARTY	Woolpackers	1997
LINE UP	Elastica	1994
LINES	Planets	1979
LINGER	Cranberries	1993
THE LION SLEEPS TONIGHT (WIMOWEH)		
	Dave Newman	1972
THE LION SLEEPS TONIGHT		
	Tight Fit	1982
THE LION SLEEPS TONIGHT		
	Robert John	1972
THE LION'S MOUTH	Kajagoogoo	1984
LIP SERVICE	Wet Wet Wet	1992
LIP UP FATTY	Bad Manners	1980
LIPS LIKE SUGAR	Echo & The Bunnymen	1987
LIPSMACKIN' ROCK 'N' ROLLIN'		
	Peter Blake	1977
LIPSTICK POWDER & PAINT		
	Shakin' Stevens	1985

SONG TITLE	ARTIST	DATE
LIQUID COOL	Apollo 440	1994
LIQUID DREAMS	O-Town	2001
LIQUIDATOR	Harry J. & The All Stars	1969
LISTEN (EP)	Stiff Little Fingers	1982
LISTEN PEOPLE	Herman's Hermits	1966
LISTEN TO ME	Hollies	1968
LISTEN TO THE MUSIC	Doobie Brothers	1972
LISTEN TO THE RADIO (ATMOSPHERICS)		
	Tom Robinson	1983
LISTEN TO WHAT THE MAN SAID		
	Paul McCartney	1975
LISTEN TO YOUR FATHER	Feargal Sharkey	1984
LISTEN TO YOUR HEART	Sonia	1989
LISTEN TO YOUR HEART/DANGEROUS		
	Roxette	1990
LITHIUM	Nirvana	1992
LITTLE ARROWS	Leapy Lee	1968
LITTLE BABY NOTHING	Manic Street Preachers	1992
LITTLE BAND OF GOLD	James Gilreath	1963
LITTLE BIRD/LOVE SONG FOR A VAMPIRE		
	Annie Lennox	1993
A LITTLE BIT	Rosie Ribbons	2003
A LITTLE BIT ME, A LITTLE BIT YOU		
	Monkees	1967
A LITTLE BIT MORE	Kym Sims	1992
A LITTLE BIT MORE	Dr. Hook	1976

SONG TITLE	ARTIST	DATE
A LITTLE BIT MORE	911	1999
LITTLE BIT O' SOUL	Music Explosion	1967
LITTLE BIT OF HEAVEN	Lisa Stansfield	1993
A LITTLE BIT OF HEAVEN	Ronnie Dove	1965
LITTLE BIT OF LOVE	Free	1972
A LITTLE BIT OF LOVE (IS ALL IT TAKES)		
	New Edition	1986
LITTLE BIT OF LOVIN'	Kele Le Roc	1998
A LITTLE BIT OF LUCK	DJ Luck & MC Neat	1999
A LITTLE BIT OF SOAP	Nigel Olsson	1979
A LITTLE BIT OF SOAP	Showaddywaddy	1978
LITTLE BITTY PRETTY ONE		
	Jackson Five	1972
LITTLE BLACK BOOK	Belinda Carlisle	1992
A LITTLE BOOGIE WOOGIE (IN THE BACK OF MY MIND)		
	Shakin' Stevens	1987
A LITTLE BOOGIE WOOGIE (IN THE BACK OF MY MIND)		
	Gary Glitter	1977
LITTLE BRITAIN	Dreadzone	1996
LITTLE BROTHER	Blue Pearl	1990
LITTLE BY LITTLE	Dusty Springfield	1966
LITTLE BY LITTLE	Robert Plant	1985
LITTLE BY LITTLE/SHE IS LOVE		
	Oasis	2002
LITTLE CHILDREN	Billy J. Kramer & The Dakotas	1964
LITTLE DARLING	Rubettes	1975

SONG TITLE	ARTIST	DATE
LITTLE DISCOURAGE	Idlewild	1999
LITTLE DOES SHE KNOW	Kursaal Flyers	1976
LITTLE DROPS OF SILVER	Gerry Monroe	1971
LITTLE DRUMMER BOY	Royal Scots Dragoon Guards	1972
LITTLE FLUFFY CLOUDS	Orb	1993
LITTLE GIRL	Troggs	1968
LITTLE GIRL	Banned	1977
LITTLE GIRL	Syndicate Of Sound	1966
THE LITTLE GIRL I ONCE KNEW		
	Beach Boys	1965
THE LITTLE GIRL	John Michael Montgomery	2000
LITTLE GREEN APPLES	Roger Miller	1968
LITTLE GREEN APPLES	O.C. Smith	1968
LITTLE GREEN BAG	George Baker Selection	1970
LITTLE HONDA	Hondells	1964
A LITTLE IN LOVE	Cliff Richard	1980
LITTLE JACKIE WANTS TO BE A STAR		
	Lisa Lisa & Cult Jam	1989
LITTLE JEANNIE	Elton John	1980
LITTLE L	Jamiroquai	2001
LITTLE LATIN LUPE LU	Mitch Ryder & The Detroit	
	Wheels	1966
A LITTLE LESS CONVERSATION		
	Elvis vs JXL	2002
LITTLE LIAR	Joan Jett & The Blackhearts	1988
LITTLE LIES	Fleetwood Mac	1987

SONG TITLE	ARTIST	DATE
A LITTLE LOVE	Corey Hart	1990
A LITTLE LOVE AND UNDERSTANDING		
	Gilbert Becaud	1975
A LITTLE LOVIN'	Neil Sedaka	1974
A LITTLE LOVING	Fourmost	1964
LITTLE MAN	Sonny & Cher	1966
LITTLE MAN	Alan Jackson	1999
LITTLE MIRACLES (HAPPEN EVERY DAY)		
	Luther Vandross	1993
LITTLE MISS CAN'T BE WRONG		
	Spin Doctors	1992
LITTLE MISS PERFECT	Summer Matthews	2004
LITTLE MOMENTS	Brad Paisley	2003
A LITTLE MORE LOVE	Olivia Newton-John	1978
THE LITTLE OLD LADY (FROM PASADENA)		
	Jan & Dean	1964
LITTLE OLE MAN (UPTIGHT – EVERYTHING'S ALRIGHT)		
	Bill Cosby	1967
LITTLE OLE WINE DRINKER ME		
	Dean Martin	1967
A LITTLE PEACE	Nicole	1982
A LITTLE PIECE OF LEATHER		
	Donnie Elbert	1972
LITTLE PINK STARS	Radish	1997
LITTLE RED CORVETTE	Prince & The Revolution	1983
LITTLE RED ROOSTER	Rolling Stones	1964

SONG TITLE	ARTIST	DATE	SONG TITLE	ARTIST	DATE
A LITTLE RESPECT	Erasure	1989	**LIVE IN TROUBLE**	Barron Knights	1977
A LITTLE RESPECT	Wheatus	2001	**LIVE IS LIFE**	Opus	1986
A LITTLE SOUL	Pulp	1998	**LIVE IT UP**	Mental As Anything	1987
LITTLE THINGS	Dave Berry	1965	**LIVE LIKE HORSES**	Elton John & Luciano Pavarotti	1996
LITTLE THINGS	Bobby Goldsboro	1965	**LIVE LIKE YOU WERE DYING**		
LITTLE THOUGHTS/TULIPS				Tim McGraw	2004
	Bloc Party	2004	**LIVE MY LIFE**	Boy George	1987
A LITTLE TIME	Beautiful South	1990	**LIVE THE DREAM**	Cast	1997
LITTLE TOO LATE	Pat Benatar	1983	**LIVE TO TELL**	Madonna	1986
LITTLE TOWN	Cliff Richard	1982	**LIVE TOGETHER**	Lisa Stansfield	1990
LITTLE TOWN FLIRT	Del Shannon	1962	**LIVE YOUR LIFE BE FREE**	Belinda Carlisle	1991
LITTLE WILLY	Sweet	1973	**LIVERPOOL LOU**	Scaffold	1974
LITTLE WOMAN	Bobby Sherman	1969	**LIVIN' FOR THE WEEKEND**		
LITTLE WONDER	David Bowie	1997		O'Jays	1976
A LITTLE YOU	Freddie & The Dreamers	1965	**LIVIN' FOR YOU**	Al Green	1973
LIVE AND LEARN	Joe Public	1992	**LIVIN' IN DESPERATE TIMES**		
LIVE AND LET DIE	Paul McCartney	1973		Olivia Newton-John	1984
LIVE AND LET DIE	Guns N' Roses	1991	**LIVIN' IN THE LIFE**	Isley Brothers	1977
THE LIVE EP	Gary Numan	1985	**LIVIN' IN THE LIGHT**	Caron Wheeler	1990
LIVE EVERY MOMENT	REO Speedwagon	1985	**LIVIN' IT UP**	Northern Uproar	1996
LIVE FOR LOVING YOU	Gloria Estefan	1991	**LIVIN' IT UP**	Ja Rule featuring Case	2001
LIVE FOREVER	Oasis	1994	**LIVIN' IT UP (FRIDAY NIGHT)**		
LIVE IN A HIDING PLACE	Idlewild	2002		Bell & James	1979
LIVE IN MANCHESTER (PTS 1 & 2)			**LIVIN' IT UP (LIVE)**	Ja Rule featuring Case	2002
	N-Joi	1992	**LIVIN' LA VIDA LOCA**	Ricky Martin	1999
LIVE IN THE SKY	Dave Clark Five	1968	**LIVIN' ON A PRAYER**	Bon Jovi	1986

SONG TITLE	ARTIST	DATE
LIVIN' ON THE EDGE	Aerosmith	1993
LIVIN' THING	Electric Light Orchestra	1976
LIVIN' THING	Beautiful South	2004
LIVING A LITTLE, LAUGHING A LITTLE		
	Spinners	1975
LIVING AFTER MIDNIGHT	Judas Priest	1980
LIVING AND LIVING WELL		
	George Strait	2002
LIVING BY NUMBERS	New Muzik	1980
THE LIVING DAYLIGHTS	A-Ha	1987
LIVING DOLL	Cliff Richard & The Young Ones	1986
LIVING FOR THE CITY	Stevie Wonder	1973
LIVING IN A BOX	Living In A Box	1987
LIVING IN A FANTASY	Leo Sayer	1981
LIVING IN A HOUSE DIVIDED		
	Cher	1972
LIVING IN AMERICA	James Brown	1985
LIVING IN DANGER	Ace Of Base	1994
LIVING IN HARMONY	Cliff Richard	1972
LIVING IN SIN	Bon Jovi	1989
LIVING IN THE PAST	Jethro Tull	1972
LIVING IN THE SUNSHINE	Clubhouse featuring Carl	1994
LIVING INSIDE MYSELF	Gino Vannelli	1981
LIVING NEXT DOOR TO ALICE		
	Smokie	1976
LIVING NEXT DOOR TO ALICE (WHO THE FK IS ALICE?)**	Smokie featuring	
	Roy Chubby Brown	1995
LIVING ON AN ISLAND	Status Quo	1979
LIVING ON MY OWN	Freddie Mercury	1993
LIVING ON THE CEILING	Blancmange	1982
LIVING ON THE FRONT LINE		
	Eddy Grant	1979
LIVING ON VIDEO	Trans-X	1985
LIVING TOGETHER, GROWING TOGETHER		
	5th Dimension	1973
THE LIVING YEARS	Mike & The Mechanics	1989
LIZARD (GONNA GET YOU)		
	Mauro Picotto	1999
LIZZIE & THE RAINMAN	Tanya Tucker	1975
LK (CAROLINA CAROL BELA)		
	DJ Marky & XRS featuring	
	Stamina MC	2002
LO MUCHO QUE TE QUIERO (THE MORE I LOVE YOU)		
	Rene & Rene	1968
LOADED	Primal Scream	1990
LOADED	Ricky Martin	2001
LOADSAMONEY (DOIN' UP THE HOUSE)		
	Harry Enfield	1988
LOCAL BOY IN THE PHOTOGRAPH		
	Stereophonics	1998

SONG TITLE	ARTIST	DATE
LOCK UP YA DAUGHTERS/MINISTRY OF MAYHEM		
	Noise Next Door	2004
LOCK UP YOUR DAUGHTERS		
	Slade	1981
LOCKED OUT	Crowded House	1994
LOCKED UP	Akon featuring Styles P.	2004
LOCO	Fun Lovin' Criminals	2001
LOCO IN ACAPULCO	Four Tops	1988
THE LOCO-MOTION	Little Eva	1962
THE LOCO-MOTION	Kylie Minogue	1988
THE LOCO-MOTION	Grand Funk	1974
LOCOMOTION	Orchestral Manoeuvres In	
	The Dark	1984
THE LODGERS	Style Council	1985
THE LOGICAL SONG	Supertramp	1979
THE LOGICAL SONG	Scooter	2002
LOLA	Kinks	1970
LOLA STARS AND STRIPES	The Stills	2004
LOLA'S THEME	Shapeshifters	2004
LOLLIPOP (CANDYMAN)	Aqua	1997
LONDINIUM	Catatonia	1999
LONDON BOYS	T. Rex	1976
LONDON CALLING	Clash	1979
LONDON NIGHTS	London Boys	1989
A LONDON THING	Scott Garcia featuring MC Styles	1997
LONDON TONIGHT	Collapsed Lung	1996

SONG TITLE	ARTIST	DATE
LONDON TOWN	Bucks Fizz	1983
LONDON TOWN	Paul McCartney	1978
THE LONE RANGER	Quantum Jump	1979
THE LONELIEST MAN IN THE WORLD		
	Tourists	1979
LONELINESS	Des O'Connor	1969
LONELINESS	Tomcraft	2003
(LONELINESS MADE ME REALIZE) IT'S YOU THAT I NEED		
	Temptations	1967
LONELY	Peter Andre	1997
LONELY BOY	Andrew Gold	1977
LONELY BOY LONELY GUITAR		
	Duane Eddy & The Rebelettes	1963
THE LONELY BULL (EL SOLO TORRO)		
	Herb Alpert	1963
LONELY, CRYIN' ONLY	Therapy?	1998
LONELY DAYS	Bee Gees	1970
LONELY DAYS, LONELY NIGHTS		
	Don Downing	1973
LONELY NIGHT (ANGEL FACE)		
	Captain & Tennille	1976
LONELY OL' NIGHT	John Cougar Mellencamp	1985
THE LONELY ONE	Alice Deejay	2000
LONELY PEOPLE	America	1974
LONELY SYMPHONY	Frances Ruffelle	1994
LONELY THIS CHRISTMAS	Mud	1974

SONG TITLE	ARTIST	DATE
LONELY TOGETHER	Barry Manilow	1980
LONESOME DAY	Bruce Springsteen	2002
LONESOME LOSER	Little River Band	1979
LONG AFTER TONIGHT IS ALL OVER		
	Jimmy Radcliffe	1965
LONG AGO AND FAR AWAY		
	James Taylor	1971
THE LONG AND WINDING ROAD		
	Ray Morgan	1970
THE LONG AND WINDING ROAD/FOR YOU BLUE		
	Beatles	1970
THE LONG AND WINDING ROAD/SUSPICIOUS MINDS		
	Will Young & Gareth Gates	2002
LONG AS I CAN SEE THE LIGHT		
	Creedence Clearwater Revival	1970
LONG COOL WOMAN (IN A BLACK DRESS)		
	Hollies	1972
LONG DARK ROAD	Hollies	1972
LONG DISTANCE	Turin Brakes	2002
THE LONG GOODBYE	Ronan Keating	2003
THE LONG GOODBYE	Brooks & Dunn	2001
LONG HAIRED LOVER FROM LIVERPOOL		
	Little Jimmy Osmond	1972
LONG HOT SUMMER	Style Council	1983
LONG LEGGED WOMAN DRESSED IN BLACK		
	Mungo Jerry	1974
LONG LIVE LOVE	Olivia Newton-John	1974
LONG LIVE LOVE	Sandie Shaw	1965
LONG LIVE OUR LOVE	Shangri-Las	1966
LONG LIVE ROCK'N'ROLL	Rainbow	1978
LONG LONELY NIGHTS	Bobby Vinton	1965
LONG LONESOME HIGHWAY		
	Michael Parks	1970
LONG LONG TIME	Linda Ronstadt	1970
LONG LONG WAY TO GO	Def Leppard	2003
LONG LOST LOVER	Three Degrees	1975
THE LONG RUN	Eagles	1979
LONG SHOT KICK DE BUCKET		
	Pioneers	1969
LONG TALL GLASSES (I CAN DANCE)		
	Leo Sayer	1975
LONG TIME	Arrow	1985
LONG TIME	Boston	1977
LONG TIME COMING	Delays	2004
LONG TIME GONE	Galliano	1994
LONG TIME GONE	Dixie Chicks	2002
LONG TRAIN RUNNIN'	Doobie Brothers	1993
LONG TRAIN RUNNING	Bananarama	1991
LONG, LONG WAY FROM HOME		
	Foreigner	1977
LONGER	Dan Fogelberg	1979
THE LONGEST TIME	Billy Joel	1984

SONG TITLE	ARTIST	DATE
LONGFELLOW SERENADE	Neil Diamond	1974
LONGVIEW	Green Day	1995
LOO-BE-LOO	Chucks	1963
THE LOOK	Roxette	1989
THE LOOK '95	Roxette	1995
LOOK AROUND (AND YOU'LL FIND ME THERE)		
	Vince Hill	1971
LOOK AT ME	Geri Halliwell	1999
LOOK AT ME (I'M IN LOVE)		
	Moments	1975
LOOK AT ME NOW	Jessy	2003
LOOK AT US	Northern Heightz	2004
LOOK AT YOURSELF	David McAlmont	1997
LOOK AWAY	Big Country	1986
LOOK AWAY	Chicago	1988
LOOK BUT DON'T TOUCH (EP)		
	Skin	1994
LOOK IN MY EYES PRETTY WOMAN		
	Tony Orlando & Dawn	1974
LOOK INTO MY EYES	Bone Thugs-N-Harmony	1997
LOOK MAMA	Howard Jones	1985
LOOK ME IN THE HEART	Tina Turner	1990
LOOK OF LOVE	Lesley Gore	1964
THE LOOK OF LOVE	Gladys Knight & The Pips	1973
THE LOOK OF LOVE	Madonna	1987
THE LOOK OF LOVE	ABC	1982

SONG TITLE	ARTIST	DATE
THE LOOK OF LOVE	Sergio Mendes & Brasil '66	1968
THE LOOK OF LOVE	Dusty Springfield	1967
LOOK OUT ANY WINDOW	Bruce Hornsby & The Range	1988
LOOK THROUGH ANY WINDOW		
	Hollies	1965
LOOK THROUGH ANY WINDOW		
	Mamas & The Papas	1966
LOOK WHAT THEY'VE DONE TO MY SONG MA		
	New Seekers featuring	
	Eve Graham	1970
LOOK WHAT YOU DONE FOR ME		
	Al Green	1972
LOOK WHAT YOU'VE DONE		
	Jet	2004
LOOK WHAT YOU'VE DONE		
	Pozo-Seco Singers	1966
LOOK WHAT YOU'VE DONE TO ME		
	Boz Scaggs	1980
LOOK WOT YOU DUN	Slade	1972
LOOKIN' AT ME	Mase featuring Puff Daddy	1998
LOOKIN' FOR A LOVE	Bobby Womack	1974
LOOKIN' FOR LOVE	Johnny Lee	1980
LOOKIN' OUT MY BACK DOOR		
	Creedence Clearwater Revival	1970
LOOKIN' THROUGH THE WINDOWS		
	Jackson 5	1972

SONG TITLE	ARTIST	DATE
LOOKIN' THRU THE EYES OF LOVE		
	Partridge Family	1973
LOOKING AFTER NUMBER ONE		
	Boomtown Rats	1977
LOOKING AT MIDNIGHT	Imagination	1983
LOOKING FOR A LOVE	Joyce Sims	1989
LOOKING FOR A LOVE	J. Geils Band	1971
LOOKING FOR A NEW LOVE		
	Jody Watley	1987
LOOKING FOR A PLACE	Mania	2004
LOOKING FOR A STRANGER		
	Pat Benatar	1983
LOOKING FOR CLUES	Robert Palmer	1980
LOOKING FOR LINDA	Hue & Cry	1989
LOOKING FOR LOVE	Karen Ramirez	1998
LOOKING FOR SPACE	John Denver	1976
LOOKING THROUGH PATIENT EYES		
	P.M. Dawn	1993
LOOKING THROUGH YOUR EYES/COMMITMENT		
	Leann Rimes	1998
LOOKING THRU THE EYES OF LOVE		
	Gene Pitney	1965
LOOKING THRU THE EYES OF LOVE		
	Partridge Family	1972
LOOKING UP	Michelle Gayle	1993
LOOKS LIKE WE MADE IT	Barry Manilow	1977

SONG TITLE	ARTIST	DATE
LOOKS, LOOKS, LOOKS	Sparks	1975
LOOP DE LOOP	Frankie Vaughan	1963
LOOP DI LOVE	Shag	1972
LOOPS OF FURY EP	Chemical Brothers	1996
LOOSE	Therapy?	1995
LOOSE CANNON	Killing Joke	2003
LOOSE FIT	Happy Mondays	1991
LOPEZ	808 State	1997
THE LORD'S PRAYER	Sister Janet Mead	1974
LORDS OF THE NEW CHURCH		
	Tasmin Archer	1993
LORELEI	Styx	1976
LORRAINE	Bad Manners	1981
LOSE CONTROL	James	1990
LOSE MY BREATH	Destiny's Child	2004
LOSE YOURSELF	Eminem	2002
LOSER	Beck	1994
LOSING GRIP	Avril Lavigne	2003
LOSING MY MIND	Liza Minnelli	1989
LOSING MY RELIGION	R.E.M.	1991
LOSING YOU	Brenda Lee	1963
LOSING YOU	Dusty Springfield	1964
THE LOST ART OF KEEPING A SECRET		
	Queens Of The Stone Age	2000
LOST FOR WORDS	Ronan Keating	2003
LOST HER IN THE SUN	John Stewart	1979

SONG TITLE	ARTIST	DATE
LOST IN AMERICA	Alice Cooper	1994
LOST IN EMOTION	Lisa Lisa & Cult Jam	1987
LOST IN FRANCE	Bonnie Tyler	1976
LOST IN LOVE	Up Yer Ronson featuring Mary Pearce	1995
LOST IN LOVE	Air Supply	1980
LOST IN LOVE	New Edition	1985
LOST IN MUSIC	Sister Sledge	1984
LOST IN SPACE	Apollo 440	1998
LOST IN SPACE	Lighthouse Family	1998
LOST IN YOU	Rod Stewart	1988
LOST IN YOU	Garth Brooks As Chris Gaines	1999
LOST IN YOUR EYES	Debbie Gibson	1989
LOST MYSELF	Longpigs	1996
LOST WEEKEND	Lloyd Cole & The Commotions	1985
LOST WITHOUT YOU	Delta Goodrem	2003
LOST WITHOUT YOUR LOVE	Bread	1976
LOST YOU SOMEWHERE	Chicane	1997
LOTTA LOVE	Nicolette Larson	1978
LOTUS	R.E.M.	1998
LOUIE LOUIE	Kingsmen	1963
LOUIE LOUIE	Three Amigos	1999
LOUIE, LOUIE	Sandpipers	1966
LOUISE	Human League	1984
LOUNGIN'	LL Cool J	1996

SONG TITLE	ARTIST	DATE
LOVE	Jimmy Nail	1995
LOVE	Musiq Soulchild	2001
LOVE & AFFECTION	Mr Pink presents The Program	2002
LOVE & KISSES	Dannii Minogue	1991
LOVE (CAN MAKE YOU HAPPY)	Mercy	1969
LOVE ACTION (I BELIEVE IN LOVE)	Human League	1981
LOVE AIN'T HERE ANYMORE	Take That	1994
LOVE ALL DAY	Nick Heyward	1984
LOVE AND AFFECTION	Joan Armatrading	1976
LOVE AND ANGER	Kate Bush	1990
LOVE AND EMOTION	Stevie B	1990
LOVE AND PRIDE	King	1985
LOVE AND REGRET	Deacon Blue	1989
LOVE AND TEARS	Naomi Campbell	1994
LOVE AND UNDERSTANDING	Cher	1991
LOVE AT 1ST SIGHT	Mary J. Blige featuring Method Man	2003
LOVE AT FIRST SIGHT	Kylie Minogue	2002
LOVE AT FIRST SIGHT	Styx	1991
LOVE AT FIRST SIGHT (JE T'AIME... MOI NON PLUS)	Sounds Nice	1969
LOVE ATTACK	Shakin' Stevens	1989

SONG TITLE	ARTIST	DATE
LOVE BALLAD	George Benson	1979
LOVE BALLAD	L.T.D.	1976
LOVE BITES	Def Leppard	1988
A LOVE BIZARRE	Sheila E	1985
LOVE BLONDE	Kim Wilde	1983
LOVE BUG – SWEETS FOR MY SWEET (MEDLEY)		
	Tina Charles	1977
LOVE BUG LEAVE MY HEART ALONE		
	Martha & The Vandellas	1967
LOVE BURNS	Black Rebel Motorcycle Club	2002
LOVE CAN BUILD A BRIDGE		
	Cher, Chrissie Hynde & Neneh	
	Cherry With Eric Clapton	1995
LOVE CAN MOVE MOUNTAINS		
	Celine Dion	1992
LOVE CAN'T TURN AROUND		
	Farley 'Jackmaster' Funk	1986
LOVE CAN'T TURN YOU AROUND		
	Farley 'Jackmaster' Funk	
	featuring Daryl Pandy	1996
THE LOVE CATS	Cure	1983
LOVE CHANGES (EVERYTHING)		
	Climie Fisher	1988
LOVE CHANGES EVERYTHING		
	Michael Ball	1989
LOVE CHILD	Diana Ross & The Supremes	1968

SONG TITLE	ARTIST	DATE
LOVE CHILD	Sweet Sensation	1990
LOVE CITY GROOVE	Love City Groove	1995
LOVE COME DOWN	Alison Limerick	1994
LOVE COME DOWN	Evelyn 'Champagne' King	1982
LOVE COMES AGAIN	Tiesto featuring BT	2004
LOVE COMES QUICKLY	Pet Shop Boys	1986
LOVE DOESN'T HAVE TO HURT		
	Atomic Kitten	2003
LOVE DON'T COST A THING		
	Jennifer Lopez	2001
LOVE DON'T LIVE HERE ANYMORE		
	Double Trouble	1990
LOVE DON'T LIVE HERE ANYMORE		
	Jimmy Nail	1985
LOVE DON'T LIVE HERE ANYMORE		
	Rose Royce	1978
LOVE DON'T LOVE NOBODY (PT I)		
	Spinners	1974
LOVE DON'T LOVE YOU	En Vogue	1993
LOVE ENUFF	Soul II Soul	1995
LOVE EVICTION	Quartz Lock featuring	
	Lonnie Gordon	1995
LOVE EYES	Nancy Sinatra	1967
LOVE FIRE	Jigsaw	1976
LOVE FOOLOSOPHY	Jamiroquai	2002
LOVE FOR LIFE	Lisa Moorish	1996

SONG TITLE	ARTIST	DATE
LOVE GAMES	Drifters	1975
LOVE GAMES	Belle & The Devotions	1984
LOVE GAMES	Level 42	1981
LOVE GETS ME EVERY TIME	Shania Twain	1997
LOVE GROWS (WHERE MY ROSEMARY GOES)	Edison Lighthouse	1970
LOVE GUARANTEED	Damage	1997
LOVE HANGOVER	Pauline Henry	1995
LOVE HANGOVER	Diana Ross	1976
LOVE HANGOVER/18 CARAT LOVE AFFAIR	Associates	1982
LOVE HAS PASSED AWAY	Supernaturals	1997
LOVE HER	Walker Brothers	1965
LOVE HER MADLY	Doors	1971
LOVE HERE I COME	Bad Boys Inc	1994
LOVE HIT ME	Maxine Nightingale	1977
LOVE HOUSE	Samantha Fox	1988
LOVE HOW YOU FEEL	Sharon Redd	1983
LOVE HURTS	Peter Polycarpou	1993
LOVE HURTS	Jim Capaldi	1975
LOVE HURTS	Nazareth	1975
THE LOVE I LOST (PT 1)	Harold Melvin & The Blue Notes	1973
THE LOVE I LOST	West End featuring Sybil	1993

SONG TITLE	ARTIST	DATE
THE LOVE I SAW IN YOU WAS JUST A MIRAGE	Smokey Robinson & The Miracles	1967
LOVE II LOVE	Damage	1996
LOVE IN 'C' MINOR (PT 1)	Cerrone	1977
LOVE IN A PEACEFUL WORLD	Level 42	1994
LOVE IN AN ELEVATOR	Aerosmith	1989
LOVE IN ITSELF	Depeche Mode	1983
LOVE IN STORE	Fleetwood Mac	1982
LOVE IN THE FIRST DEGREE	Alabama	1981
LOVE IN THE FIRST DEGREE/MR. SLEAZE	Bananarama	1987
LOVE IN THE KEY OF C	Belinda Carlisle	1996
LOVE IN THE NATURAL WAY	Kim Wilde	1989
LOVE IN THE SHADOWS	Neil Sedaka	1976
LOVE IN THE SUN	Glitter Band	1975
THE LOVE IN YOUR EYES	Vicky Leandros	1972
THE LOVE IN YOUR EYES	Eddie Money	1989
LOVE IS	Alannah Myles	1990
LOVE IS	Vanessa Williams & Brian McKnight	1993
LOVE IS A BATTLEFIELD	Pat Benatar	1983
LOVE IS A HURTIN' THING	Lou Rawls	1966

SONG TITLE	ARTIST	DATE
LOVE IS A STRANGER	Eurythmics	1983
LOVE IS A WONDERFUL COLOUR	Icicle Works	1983
LOVE IS A WONDERFUL THING	Michael Bolton	1991
LOVE IS ALIVE	Gary Wright	1976
LOVE IS ALL	Malcolm Roberts	1969
LOVE IS ALL	Rapture	2004
LOVE IS ALL AROUND	Troggs	1968
LOVE IS ALL AROUND	Wet Wet Wet	1994
LOVE IS ALL IS ALRIGHT	UB40	1982
LOVE IS ALL WE NEED	Mary J. Blige	1997
LOVE IS ALRIGHT TONITE	Rick Springfield	1981
LOVE IS BLIND	Eve featuring Faith Evans	2000
LOVE IS BLUE	Jeff Beck	1968
LOVE IS BLUE (L'AMOUR EST BLEU)	Paul Mauriat & His Orchestra	1968
LOVE IS CONTAGIOUS	Taja Sevelle	1988
LOVE IS EVERYWHERE	Cicero	1992
LOVE IS FOREVER	Billy Ocean	1986
LOVE IS HERE AND NOW YOU'RE GONE	Supremes	1967
LOVE IS HOLY	Kim Wilde	1992
LOVE IS IN CONTROL (FINGER ON THE TRIGGER)	Donna Summer	1982
LOVE IS IN THE AIR	John Paul Young	1978

SONG TITLE	ARTIST	DATE
LOVE IS IN THE AIR	Milk & Sugar vs John Paul Young	2002
LOVE IS JUST THE GREAT PRETENDER	Animal Nightlife	1985
LOVE IS LIFE	Hot Chocolate	1970
LOVE IS LIKE A ROCK	Donnie Iris	1981
(LOVE IS LIKE A) BASEBALL GAME	Intruders	1968
LOVE IS LIKE AN ITCHING IN MY HEART	Supremes	1966
LOVE IS LIKE OXYGEN	Sweet	1978
LOVE IS LOVE	Barry Ryan	1969
LOVE IS NOT A GAME	J. Majik featuring Kathy Brown	2001
LOVE IS ON THE WAY	Luther Vandross	1993
LOVE IS ON THE WAY	Saigon Kick	1992
LOVE IS ONLY A FEELING	Darkness	2004
LOVE IS STRANGE	Everly Brothers	1965
LOVE IS STRANGE	Peaches & Herb	1967
LOVE IS STRONG	Rolling Stones	1994
LOVE IS STRONGER THAN DEATH	The The	1993
LOVE IS THE ANSWER	England Dan & John Ford Coley	1979
LOVE IS THE DRUG	Roxy Music	1975
LOVE IS THE DRUG	Grace Jones	1986
LOVE IS THE KEY	Charlatans	2001
LOVE IS THE LAW	Seahorses	1997

SONG TITLE	ARTIST	DATE
LOVE IS THE SEVENTH WAVE		
	Sting	1985
LOVE IS THE SLUG	We've Got A Fuzzbox and	
	We're Gonna Use It	1986
(LOVE IS) THICKER THAN WATER		
	Andy Gibb	1977
LOVE JONES	Brighter Side Of Darkness	1972
LOVE KILLS	Freddie Mercury	1984
LOVE LADY	Damage	1997
LOVE LAND	Charles Wright & The Watts	
	103 Street Rhythm Band	1970
LOVE LETTERS	Alison Moyet	1987
LOVE LETTERS	Elvis Presley	1966
LOVE LETTERS IN THE SAND		
	Vince Hill	1967
LOVE LIES LOST	Helen Terry	1984
LOVE LIGHT IN FLIGHT	Stevie Wonder	1984
LOVE LIKE A FOUNTAIN	Ian Brown	1999
LOVE LIKE A MAN	Ten Years After	1970
LOVE LIKE A RIVER	Climie Fisher	1988
LOVE LIKE BLOOD	Killing Joke	1985
LOVE LIKE THIS	Faith Evans	1998
LOVE LIKE YOU AND ME	Gary Glitter	1975
A LOVE LIKE YOURS	Ike & Tina Turner	1966
LOVE LOVE LOVE	Bobby Hebb	1972

SONG TITLE	ARTIST	DATE
LOVE, LOVE, LOVE – HERE I COME		
	Rollo Goes Mystic	1995
LOVE LOVES TO LOVE LOVE		
	Lulu	1967
LOVE MACHINE	Miracles	1975
LOVE MACHINE	Girls Aloud	2004
LOVE MADE ME	Vixen	1989
LOVE MAKES A WOMAN	Barbara Acklin	1968
LOVE MAKES NO SENSE	Alexander O'Neal	1993
LOVE MAKES THE WORLD GO ROUND		
	Don-E	1992
LOVE MAKES THE WORLD GO ROUND		
	Jets	1982
LOVE MAKES THE WORLD GO ROUND		
	Deon Jackson	1966
LOVE MAKES THINGS HAPPEN		
	Pebbles	1990
LOVE ME	Yvonne Elliman	1976
LOVE ME	Diana Ross	1974
LOVE ME	112 featuring Mase	1998
LOVE ME ALL UP	Stacy Earl	1991
LOVE ME AND LEAVE ME	Seahorses	1997
LOVE ME BABY	Susan Cadogan	1975
LOVE ME DO	Beatles	1964
LOVE ME FOR A REASON	Boyzone	1994
LOVE ME FOR A REASON	Osmonds	1974

SONG TITLE	ARTIST	DATE
LOVE ME FOR LIFE	Stevie B	1990
LOVE ME LIKE A LOVER	Tina Charles	1976
LOVE ME LIKE I LOVE YOU		
	Bay City Rollers	1976
LOVE ME LOVE MY DOG	Peter Shelley	1975
LOVE ME RIGHT (OH SHEILA)		
	Angel City featuring	
	Lara McAllen	2003
LOVE ME TENDER	Roland Rat Superstar	1984
LOVE ME TENDER	Percy Sledge	1967
LOVE ME THE RIGHT WAY	Rapination/Kym Mazelle	1992
LOVE ME TOMORROW	Chicago	1982
LOVE ME TONIGHT	Tom Jones	1969
LOVE ME TONIGHT	Trevor Walters	1981
LOVE ME TWO TIMES	Doors	1967
LOVE ME WITH ALL OF YOUR HEART		
	Bachelors	1966
LOVE ME WITH ALL YOUR HEART		
	Karl Denver	1964
LOVE ME WITH ALL YOUR HEART		
	Ray Charles Singers	1964
LOVE MEANS (YOU NEVER HAVE TO SAY YOU'RE		
SORRY)	Sounds Of Sunshine	1971
LOVE MISSILE F1-11	Sigue Sigue Sputnik	1986
LOVE MOVES (IN MYSTERIOUS WAYS)		
	Julia Fordham	1992

SONG TITLE	ARTIST	DATE
LOVE NEEDS NO DISGUISE		
	Gary Numan & Dramatis	1981
LOVE OF A LIFETIME	Honeyz	1999
LOVE OF A LIFETIME	Firehouse	1991
LOVE OF A WOMAN	Travis Tritt	2001
LOVE OF MY LIFE	Dooleys	1977
LOVE OF MY LIFE (AN ODE TO HIP HOP)		
	Erykah Badu featuring Common	2002
THE LOVE OF RICHARD NIXON		
	Manic Street Preachers	2004
LOVE OF THE COMMON PEOPLE		
	Nicky Thomas	1970
LOVE OF THE COMMON PEOPLE		
	Paul Young	1983
LOVE OF THE LOVED	Cilla Black	1963
LOVE ON A MOUNTAIN TOP		
	Robert Knight	1973
LOVE ON A MOUNTAIN TOP		
	Sinitta	1989
LOVE ON A ROOFTOP	Desmond Child	1991
LOVE ON A TWO WAY STREET		
	Stacy Lattisaw	1981
LOVE ON A TWO-WAY STREET		
	Moments	1970
LOVE ON LOVE	Candi Staton	1999
LOVE ON THE LINE	Blazin' Squad	2002

SONG TITLE	ARTIST	DATE
LOVE ON THE NORTHERN LINE		
	Northern Line	2000
LOVE ON THE ROCKS	Neil Diamond	1980
LOVE ON THE RUN	Chicane featuring Peter Cunnah	2003
LOVE ON YOUR SIDE	Thompson Twins	1983
LOVE OR LEAVE	Spinners	1975
LOVE OR LET ME BE LONELY		
	Paul Davis	1982
LOVE OR LET ME BE LONELY		
	Friends Of Distinction	1970
LOVE OR SOMETHING LIKE THAT		
	Kenny Rogers	1978
LOVE OVERBOARD	Gladys Knight & The Pips	1988
LOVE PAINS	Yvonne Elliman	1979
LOVE PATROL	Dooleys	1980
LOVE PLUS ONE	Haircut 100	1982
LOVE POTION NUMBER NINE		
	Searchers	1964
LOVE POWER	Sandpebbles	1967
LOVE POWER	Dionne Warwick &	
	Jeffrey Osborne	1987
LOVE PROFUSION	Madonna	2003
LOVE REALLY HURTS WITHOUT YOU		
	Billy Ocean	1976
LOVE REARS ITS UGLY HEAD		
	Living Colour	1991

SONG TITLE	ARTIST	DATE
LOVE REMOVAL MACHINE	Cult	1987
LOVE RENDEZVOUS	M People	1995
LOVE RESURRECTION	Alison Moyet	1984
LOVE REVOLUTION	Phixx	2004
LOVE ROLLERCOASTER	Red Hot Chili Peppers	1997
LOVE ROLLERCOASTER	Ohio Players	1975
THE LOVE SCENE	Joe	1997
LOVE SCENES	Beverley Craven	1993
LOVE SEE NO COLOUR	Farm	1993
LOVE SENSATION	911	1996
LOVE SHACK	B-52's	1989
LOVE SHINE A LIGHT	Katrina & The Waves	1997
LOVE SHOULD BE A CRIME		
	O-Town	2002
LOVE SHOULDA BROUGHT YOU HOME		
	Toni Braxton	1992
LOVE SHY	Kristine Blond	1998
LOVE SLAVE	Wedding Present	1992
LOVE SNEAKIN' UP ON YOU		
	Bonnie Raitt	1994
A LOVE SO BEAUTIFUL	Michael Bolton	1995
LOVE SO RIGHT	Bee Gees	1976
LOVE SO STRONG	Secret Life	1995
LOVE SOMEBODY	Rick Springfield	1984
LOVE SONG	Utah Saints	2000
LOVE SONG	Damned	1979

SONG TITLE	ARTIST	DATE
LOVE SONG	Cure	1989
LOVE SONG	Anne Murray	1973
LOVE SONG	Tesla	1989
LOVE SONG	Simple Minds	1992
LOVE SONGS ARE BACK AGAIN (MEDLEY)	Band Of Gold	1984
THE LOVE SONGS EP	Daniel O'Donnell	1997
LOVE SPREADS	Stone Roses	1994
LOVE STIMULATION	Humate	1999
LOVE STINKS	J. Geils Band	1980
LOVE STORY	Jethro Tull	1969
LOVE STORY	Layo & Bushwacka	2002
LOVE STORY (VS FINALLY)	Layo & Bushwacka	2003
A LOVE SUPREME	Will Downing	1988
LOVE TAKE OVER	Five Star	1985
LOVE TAKES TIME	Mariah Carey	1990
LOVE TAKES TIME	Orleans	1979
LOVE THE LIFE	JTQ With Noel McKoy	1993
LOVE THE ONE YOU'RE WITH	Luther Vandross	1994
LOVE THE ONE YOU'RE WITH	Stephen Stills	1970
LOVE THE ONE YOU'RE WITH	Isley Brothers	1971
LOVE THE WORLD AWAY	Kenny Rogers	1980
LOVE THEM	Eamon featuring Ghostface	2004

SONG TITLE	ARTIST	DATE
LOVE THEME FROM 'EYES OF LAURA MARS' (PRISONER)	Barbra Streisand	1978
LOVE THEME FROM 'THE GODFATHER' (SPEAK SOFTLY LOVE)	Andy Williams	1972
LOVE THEME FROM 'THE THORN BIRDS'	Juan Martin	1984
LOVE THEME FROM ROMEO & JULIET	Henry Mancini & His Orchestra	1969
LOVE THEME FROM ST. ELMO'S FIRE	David Foster	1985
LOVE THING	Pasadenas	1990
LOVE THING	Tina Turner	1992
LOVE THING	Evolution	1993
LOVE... THY WILL BE DONE	Martika	1991
LOVE TO HATE YOU	Erasure	1991
LOVE TO LOVE YOU BABY	Donna Summer	1975
LOVE TO SEE YOU CRY	Enrique Iglesias	2002
LOVE TOUCH	Rod Stewart	1986
LOVE TOWN	Booker Newberry III	1983
LOVE TRAIN	Holly Johnson	1989
LOVE TRAIN	O'Jays	1973
LOVE TRUTH AND HONESTY	Bananarama	1988
LOVE U 4 LIFE	Jodeci	1995
LOVE U MORE	Sunscreem	1993

SONG TITLE	ARTIST	DATE
LOVE UNLIMITED	Fun Lovin' Criminals	1998
LOVE WALKED IN	Thunder	1991
LOVE WALKS IN	Van Halen	1986
LOVE WARS	Womack & Womack	1984
THE LOVE WE HAD (STAYS ON MY MIND)	Dells	1971
LOVE WHAT YOU DO	Divine Comedy	2001
LOVE WILL COME	Tomski featuring Jan Johnston	2000
LOVE WILL COME THROUGH	Travis	2004
LOVE WILL CONQUER ALL	Lionel Richie	1986
LOVE WILL FIND A WAY	David Grant	1983
LOVE WILL FIND A WAY	Jackie Deshannon	1969
LOVE WILL FIND A WAY	Pablo Cruise	1978
LOVE WILL FIND A WAY	Yes	1987
LOVE WILL KEEP US TOGETHER	Captain & Tennille	1975
LOVE WILL LEAD YOU BACK	Taylor Dayne	1990
LOVE WILL NEVER DO (WITHOUT YOU)	Janet Jackson	1990
LOVE WILL SAVE THE DAY	Whitney Houston	1988
LOVE WILL SET YOU FREE (JAMBE MYTH)	Starchaser	2002

SONG TITLE	ARTIST	DATE
LOVE WILL SHOW US HOW	Christine McVie	1984
LOVE WILL TEAR US APART	Joy Division	1980
LOVE WILL TURN YOU AROUND	Kenny Rogers	1982
LOVE WON'T LET ME WAIT	Major Harris	1975
LOVE WON'T WAIT	Gary Barlow	1997
A LOVE WORTH WAITING FOR	Shakin' Stevens	1984
LOVE X LOVE	George Benson	1980
LOVE YOU ANYWAY	De Nada	2001
LOVE YOU DOWN	Inoj	1998
LOVE YOU DOWN	Ready For The World	1986
LOVE YOU INSIDE OUT	Bee Gees	1979
LOVE YOU LIKE I NEVER LOVED BEFORE	John O'Banion	1981
LOVE YOU LIKE MAD	Vs	2004
LOVE YOU MORE	Buzzcocks	1978
LOVE YOU OUT LOUD	Rascal Flatts	2003
THE LOVE YOU SAVE	Jackson 5	1970
LOVE YOUR MONEY	Daisy Chainsaw	1992
LOVE ZONE	Billy Ocean	1986
LOVE'S A LOADED GUN	Alice Cooper	1991

SONG TITLE	ARTIST	DATE
LOVE'S ABOUT TO CHANGE MY HEART	Donna Summer	1989
LOVE'S BEEN A LITTLE BIT HARD ON ME	Juice Newton	1982
LOVE'S BEEN GOOD TO ME	Frank Sinatra	1969
LOVE'S COMIN' AT YA	Melba Moore	1982
LOVE'S GOT A HOLD ON MY HEART	Steps	1999
LOVE'S GOTTA HOLD ON ME	Dollar	1979
LOVE'S GREAT ADVENTURE	Ultravox	1984
LOVE'S GROWN DEEP	Kenny Nolan	1977
LOVE'S JUST A BROKEN HEART	Cilla Black	1966
LOVE'S LINES, ANGLES AND RHYMES	5th Dimension	1971
LOVE'S MADE A FOOL OF YOU	Buddy Holly	1964
LOVE'S MADE A FOOL OF YOU	Bobby Fuller Four	1966
LOVE'S SUCH A WONDERFUL THING	Real Thing	1977
LOVE'S SWEET EXILE/REPEAT	Manic Street Preachers	1991

SONG TITLE	ARTIST	DATE
LOVE'S THEME	Love Unlimited Orchestra	1973
LOVE'S UNKIND	Sophie Lawrence	1991
LOVE'S UNKIND	Donna Summer	1977
LOVEFOOL	Cardigans	1997
LOVELY	Bubba Sparxxx	2002
LOVELY DAY	Bill Withers	1977
LOVELY DAZE	D.J. Jazzy Jeff & The Fresh Prince	1998
LOVELY ONE	Jacksons	1980
LOVER	Joe Roberts	1994
LOVER	Rachelle McFarlane	1998
LOVER COME BACK TO ME	Dead Or Alive	1985
THE LOVER IN ME	Sheena Easton	1988
A LOVER SPURNED	Marc Almond	1990
THE LOVER THAT YOU ARE	Pulse featuring Antoinette Roberson	1996
A LOVER'S CONCERTO	Toys	1965
LOVER'S HOLIDAY	Peggy Scott & Jo Jo Benson	1968
LOVERBOY	Mariah featuring Cameo	2001
LOVERBOY	Billy Ocean	1984
LOVERGIRL	Teena Marie	1984
A LOVERS HOLIDAY/THE GLOW OF LOVE	Change	1980

SONG TITLE	ARTIST	DATE
LOVERS OF THE WORLD UNITE		
	David & Jonathan	1966
LOVES ME LIKE A ROCK	Paul Simon	1973
LOVESONG	Cure	1989
LOVESTRUCK	Madness	1999
LOVIN' EACH DAY	Ronan Keating	2001
LOVIN' EVERY MINUTE OF IT		
	Loverboy	1985
LOVIN' IS EASY	Hear'say	2002
LOVIN' THINGS	Marmalade	1968
LOVIN', TOUCHIN', SQUEEZIN'		
	Journey	1979
LOVIN' YOU	Minnie Riperton	1975
LOVIN' YOU	Bobby Darin	1967
LOVIN' YOU AIN'T EASY	Pagliaro	1972
LOVING AND FREE/AMOUREUSE		
	Kiki Dee	1973
LOVING EVERY MINUTE	Lighthouse Family	1996
LOVING HER WAS EASIER (THAN ANYTHING I'LL EVER		
DO AGAIN)	Kris Kristofferson	1971
LOVING JUST FOR FUN	Kelly Marie	1980
LOVING ON THE LOSING SIDE		
	Tommy Hunt	1976
LOVING THE ALIEN	David Bowie	1985
LOVING YOU	Massivo featuring Tracy	1990
LOVING YOU	Feargal Sharkey	1985

SONG TITLE	ARTIST	DATE
LOVING YOU '03	Marc Et Claude	2003
LOVING YOU (OLE OLE OLE)		
	Brian Harvey and The Refugee	
	Crew	2001
LOVING YOU HAS MADE ME BANANAS		
	Guy Marks	1978
LOVING YOU IS SWEETER THAN EVER		
	Four Tops	1966
LOVING YOU IS SWEETER THAN EVER		
	Nick Kamen	1987
LOVING YOU JUST CROSSSED MY MIND		
	Sam Neely	1972
LOVING YOU MORE	BT featuring Vincent Covello	1996
LOW	Foo Fighters	2003
LOW FIVE	Sneaker Pimps	1999
LOW LIFE IN HIGH PLACES		
	Thunder	1992
LOW RIDER	War	1975
LOW/THE TROUBLE WITH US		
	Kelly Clarkson	2003
LOWDOWN	Boz Scaggs	1976
LOWDOWN	Chicago	1971
LOWRIDER/TROUBLE	Cypress Hill	2001
LUCAS WITH THE LID OFF	Lucas	1994
LUCILLE	Kenny Rogers	1977

SONG TITLE	ARTIST	DATE
LUCKENBACH, TEXAS (BACK TO THE BASICS OF LOVE)		
	Waylon Jennings	1977
LUCKY	Britney Spears	2000
LUCKY	Greg Kihn	1985
LUCKY IN LOVE	Mick Jagger	1985
LUCKY LIPS	Cliff Richard	1963
LUCKY LOVE	Ace Of Base	1996
LUCKY MAN	Verve	1997
LUCKY NUMBER	Lene Lovich	1979
LUCKY ONE	Amy Grant	1994
THE LUCKY ONE	Laura Branigan	1984
LUCKY STAR	Madonna	1964
LUCKY STAR	Basement Jaxx featuring	
	Dizzee Rascal	2003
LUCKY STARS	Dean Friedman	1978
LUCKY YOU	Lightning Seeds	1995
LUCRETIA MAC EVIL	Blood, Sweat & Tears	1970
LUCRETIA MY REFLECTION		
	Sisters Of Mercy	1988
LUCY IN THE SKY WITH DIAMONDS		
	Elton John	1974
LUDI	Dream Warriors	1991
LUKA	Suzanne Vega	1987
LULLABY	Starsailor	2001
LULLABY	Cure	1989
LULLABY	Melanie B	2001

SONG TITLE	ARTIST	DATE
LULLABYE	Shawn Mullins	1998
LUMP	Presidents Of The United States	1996
THE LUNATICS HAVE TAKEN OVER THE ASYLUM		
	Fun Boy Three	1981
LUST FOR LIFE	Iggy Pop	1996
LUTON AIRPORT	Cats U.K.	1979
LUV 4 LUV	Robin S.	1993
LUV DA SUNSHINE	Intenso Project	2002
LUV ME LUV ME	Shaggy	2001
LUV U BETTER	LL Cool J	2002
LUVSTRUCK	Southside Spinners	2000
LYDIA	Dean Friedman	1978
LYIN' EYES	Eagles	1975
LYIN' TO MYSELF	David Cassidy	1990
LYRIC ON MY LIP	Tali	2004
M'LADY	Sly & The Family Stone	1968
MA BAKER	Boney M	1977
MA BAKER – SOMEBODY SCREAMED		
	Boney M vs Horny United	1999
MA BELLE AMIE	Tee Set	1970
MA! (HE'S MAKING EYES AT ME)		
	Lena Zavaroni	1974
MA, I DON'T LOVE HER	Clipse featuring Faith Evans	2003
MA-MA-MA-BELLE	Electric Light Orchestra	1974
MACARENA	Los Del Rio	1996
MACARTHUR PARK	Richard Harris	1968

SONG TITLE	ARTIST	DATE
MACARTHUR PARK	Donna Summer	1978
MACARTHUR PARK (PART II)	Four Tops	1971
MACH 5	Presidents Of The United States	1996
MACHINE	The Yeah Yeah Yeahs	2002
MACHINE GUN	Commodores	1974
MACHINERY	Sheena Easton	1982
MACHO MAN	Village People	1978
MACUSHLA	Bernie Nolan	2004
MAD ABOUT YOU	Bruce Ruffin	1972
MAD ABOUT YOU	Belinda Carlisle	1986
MAD EYED SCREAMER	Creatures	1981
MAD WORLD	Tears For Fears	1982
MAD WORLD	Michael Andrews featuring Gary Jules	2003
MADAME BUTTERFLY	Malcolm McLaren	1984
MADAME HELGA	Stereophonics	2003
MADCHESTER RAVE ON EP	Happy Mondays	1989
MADE FOR LOVIN' YOU	Anastacia	2001
MADE IN ENGLAND	Elton John	1995
MADE IT BACK	Beverley Knight featuring Redman	1998
MADE OF STONE	Stone Roses	1990
MADE YOU LOOK	Nas	2002
MADEMOISELLE	Styx	1976
MADLY IN LOVE	Bros	1990

SONG TITLE	ARTIST	DATE
MADNESS THING	Leilani	1999
MAGGIE	Foster And Allen	1983
MAGGIE MAY	Rod Stewart	1971
MAGIC	Sasha With Sam Mollison	1994
MAGIC	Pilot	1975
MAGIC	Nick Drake	2004
MAGIC	Cars	1984
MAGIC	Olivia Newton-John	1980
MAGIC BUS	Who	1968
MAGIC CARPET RIDE	Mighty Dub Katz	1997
MAGIC CARPET RIDE	Steppenwolf	1968
MAGIC FLY	Space	1977
MAGIC FLY	Minimalistix	2003
MAGIC FRIEND	2 Unlimited	1992
MAGIC HOUR	Cast	1999
THE MAGIC IS THERE	Daniel O'Donnell	1998
MAGIC MAN	Heart	1976
THE MAGIC NUMBER/BUDDY	De La Soul	1989
THE MAGIC PIPER (OF LOVE)	Edwyn Collins	1997
MAGIC SMILE	Rosie Vela	1987
MAGIC TOUCH	Loose Ends	1985
MAGIC TOWN	Vogues	1966
MAGICAL MYSTERY TOUR	Ambrosia	1977

SONG TITLE	ARTIST	DATE
MAGICAL MYSTERY TOUR (DOUBLE EP)		
	Beatles	1967
MAGNET AND STEEL	Walter Egan	1978
THE MAGNIFICENT SEVEN	Clash	1981
MAH-NA, MAH-NA	Piero Umiliani	1977
MAID OF ORLEANS (THE WALTZ JOAN OF ARC)		
	Orchestral Manoeuvres In The Dark	1982
THE MAIN EVENT/FIGHT	Barbra Streisand	1979
MAIN OFFENDER	The Hives	2002
MAIN THEME FROM 'THE THORN BIRDS'		
	Henry Mancini	1984
MAIN TITLE (THEME FROM 'JAWS')		
	John Williams	1975
MAINSTREET	Bob Seger & The Silver Bullet Band	1977
MAJOR TOM (COMING HOME)		
	Peter Schilling	1983
MAKE A DAFT NOISE FOR CHRISTMAS		
	Goodies	1975
MAKE A LITTLE MAGIC	Nitty Gritty Dirt Band	1980
MAKE A MOVE ON ME	Olivia Newton-John	1982
MAKE BELIEVE	Toto	1982
MAKE BELIEVE	Wind	1969
MAKE EM' SAY UHH!	Master P featuring Fiend, Silkk The Shocker, Mia X & M	1998

SONG TITLE	ARTIST	DATE
MAKE IT CLAP	Busta Rhymes featuring Spliff Star	2003
MAKE IT EASY ON YOURSELF		
	Walker Brothers	1965
MAKE IT EASY ON YOURSELF		
	Dionne Warwick	1970
MAKE IT FUNKY	James Brown	1971
MAKE IT GOOD	A1	2002
MAKE IT HAPPEN	Mariah Carey	1992
MAKE IT HOT	Vs	2004
MAKE IT HOT	Nicole featuring Miss 'Misdemeanor' Elliott & Mocha	1998
MAKE IT LAST	Embrace	2001
MAKE IT ON MY OWN	Alison Limerick	1992
MAKE IT REAL	Jets	1988
MAKE IT RIGHT	Christian Falk featuring Demetreus	2000
MAKE IT TONIGHT	Wet Wet Wet	1991
MAKE IT UP WITH LOVE	ATL	2004
MAKE IT WITH YOU	Universal	1997
MAKE IT WITH YOU	Bread	1970
MAKE IT WITH YOU	Pasadenas	1992
MAKE IT WITH YOU	Let Loose	1996
MAKE LOVE LIKE A MAN	Def Leppard	1992
MAKE LOVE STAY	Dan Fogelberg	1983

SONG TITLE	ARTIST	DATE
MAKE LUV	Room 5 featuring	
	Oliver Cheatham	2003
MAKE ME AN ISLAND	Joe Dolan	1969
MAKE ME BAD	Korn	2000
MAKE ME BELONG TO YOU		
	Barbara Lewis	1966
MAKE ME LAUGH	Anthrax	1988
MAKE ME LOSE CONTROL	Eric Carmen	1988
MAKE ME SMILE	Chicago	1970
MAKE ME SMILE (COME UP AND SEE ME)		
	Steve Harley & Cockney Rebel	1975
MAKE ME SMILE (COME UP AND SEE ME)		
	Erasure	2003
MAKE ME THE WOMAN THAT YOU GO HOME TO		
	Gladys Knight & The Pips	1971
MAKE ME WANNA SCREAM	Blu Cantrell	2003
MAKE ME YOUR BABY	Barbara Lewis	1965
MAKE ME YOURS	Bettye Swann	1967
MAKE THAT MOVE	Shalamar	1981
MAKE THE DEAL	Ocean Colour Scene	2003
MAKE THE WORLD GO AWAY		
	Eddy Arnold	1965
MAKE THE WORLD GO AWAY		
	Donny & Marie Osmond	1975
MAKE THE WORLD GO ROUND		
	Sandy B	1998

SONG TITLE	ARTIST	DATE
MAKE WAY FOR NODDY	Noddy	2003
MAKE WAY FOR THE INDIAN		
	Apache Indian With Tim Dog	1995
MAKE YOU SWEAT	Keith Sweat	1990
MAKE YOUR OWN KIND OF MUSIC		
	Mama Cass	1969
MAKE YOURS A HAPPY HOME		
	Gladys Knight & The Pips	1976
MAKES ME LOVE YOU	Eclipse	1999
MAKES ME WANNA DIE	Tricky	1997
MAKIN' GOOD LOVE	Avant	2002
MAKIN' HAPPY	Crystal Waters	1991
MAKIN' IT	David Naughton	1979
MAKIN' OUT	Mark Owen	2004
MAKING EVERY MINUTE COUNT		
	Spanky And Our Gang	1967
MAKING LOVE	Roberta Flack	1982
MAKING LOVE IN THE RAIN		
	Herb Alpert	1987
MAKING LOVE OUT OF NOTHING AT ALL		
	Air Supply	1983
MAKING MEMORIES	Frankie Laine	1967
MAKING OUR DREAMS COME TRUE		
	Cyndi Grecco	1976
MAKING PLANS FOR NIGEL		
	XTC	1979

SONG TITLE	ARTIST	DATE
MAKING UP AGAIN	Goldie	1978
MAKING YOUR MIND UP	Bucks Fizz	1981
MALE STRIPPER	Man 2 Man Meet Man Parrish	1987
MALIBU	Hole	1999
MALT AND BARLEY BLUES	McGuinness Flint	1971
MAMA	Kim Appleby	1991
MAMA	Dave Berry	1966
MAMA	Genesis	1983
MAMA	B.J. Thomas	1966
MAMA – WHO DA MAN?	Richard Blackwood	2000
MAMA CAN'T BUY YOU LOVE	Elton John	1979
MAMA NEVER TOLD ME	Sister Sledge	1975
MAMA SAID	Carleen Anderson	1994
MAMA SAID	Metallica	1996
MAMA SAID KNOCK YOU OUT	LL Cool J	1991
MAMA TOLD ME (NOT TO COME)	Three Dog Night	1970
MAMA TOLD ME NOT TO COME	Tom Jones & Stereophonics	2000
MAMA USED TO SAY	Junior	1982
MAMA WEER ALL CRAZEE NOW	Slade	1972
MAMA'S BOY	Suzi Quatro	1980
MAMA'S PEARL	Jackson 5	1971

SONG TITLE	ARTIST	DATE
MAMA, I'M COMING HOME	Ozzy Osbourne	1992
MAMA/WHO DO YOU THINK YOU ARE	Spice Girls	1997
MAMACITA	Public Announcement	2000
MAMBO ITALIANO	Shaft	2000
MAMBO NO. 5	Bob The Builder	2001
MAMBO NO. 5 (A LITTLE BIT OF...)	Lou Bega	1999
MAME	Herb Alpert & The Tijuana Brass	1966
MAMMA GAVE BIRTH TO THE SOUL CHILDREN	Queen Latifah & De La Soul	1990
MAMMA MIA	ABBA	1976
MAMMA MIA	A Teens	1999
MAMMY BLUE	Roger Whittaker	1971
MAMY BLUE	Los Pop Tops	1971
MAN BEHIND THE MUSIC	Queen Pen	1998
THE MAN DON'T GIVE A FUCK	Super Furry Animals	2004
MAN! I FEEL LIKE A WOMAN!	Shania Twain	1999
THE MAN I LOVE	Kate Bush And Larry Adler	1994
A MAN I'LL NEVER BE	Boston	1978
THE MAN IN BLACK	Cozy Powell	1974
MAN IN THE MIRROR	Michael Jackson	1988

SONG TITLE	ARTIST	DATE
A MAN NEEDS TO BE TOLD		
	Charlatans	2001
MAN OF STEEL	Meat Loaf	2003
MAN OF THE WORLD	Fleetwood Mac	1969
MAN ON THE CORNER	Genesis	1982
MAN ON THE EDGE	Iron Maiden	1995
MAN ON THE MOON	R.E.M.	1992
MAN ON YOUR MIND	Little River Band	1982
MAN SIZE LOVE	Klymaxx	1986
MAN TO MAN	Hot Chocolate	1976
MAN TO MAN	Gary Allan	2003
THE MAN WHO SOLD THE WORLD		
	Lulu	1974
THE MAN WHO TOLD EVERYTHING		
	Doves	2000
THE MAN WITH THE CHILD IN HIS EYES		
	Kate Bush	1978
A MAN WITHOUT LOVE	Kenneth McKellar	1966
A MAN WITHOUT LOVE	Engelbert Humperdinck	1968
MANCHILD	Neneh Cherry	1989
MANDINKA	Sinead O'Connor	1988
MANDOLIN RAIN	Bruce Hornsby & The Range	1987
MANDY	Barry Manilow	1974
MANDY	Westlife	2003
MANEATER	Daryl Hall & John Oates	1982
MANHATTAN SKYLINE	A-Ha	1987

SONG TITLE	ARTIST	DATE
MANIAC	Michael Sembello	1983
MANIC MONDAY	Bangles	1986
MANSIZE ROOSTER	Supergrass	1995
MANTRA FOR A STATE OF MIND		
	S'Express	1989
MANY RIVERS TO CROSS	UB40	1983
MAPS	Yeah Yeah Yeahs	2003
MARBLEHEAD JOHNSON	Bluetones	1996
MARCH OF THE MODS	Joe Loss & His Orchestra	1964
MARGARITAVILLE	Jimmy Buffett	1977
MARGUERITA TIME	Status Quo	1983
MARIA	Blondie	1999
MARIA	P.J. Proby	1965
MARIA (I LIKE IT LOUD)	Scooter vs Marc Acardipane & Dick Rules	2003
MARIA ELENA	Gene Pitney	1969
MARIA ELENA	Los Indios Tabajaras	1963
MARIA MARIA	Santana featuring The Product G&B	2000
MARIANA	Gibson Brothers	1980
MARIANNE	Cliff Richard	1968
MARIE	Bachelors	1965
MARIE MARIE	Shakin' Stevens	1980
MARLENE ON THE WALL	Suzanne Vega	1986
MAROC 7	Shadows	1967
MARQUEE MOON	Television	1977

SONG TITLE	ARTIST	DATE
MARRAKESH EXPRESS	Crosby, Stills And Nash	1969
MARRIED MAN	Bette Midler	1979
MARRIED MEN	Bonnie Tyler	1979
MARTA	Bachelors	1967
MARTA'S SONG	Deep Forest	1995
MARTHA'S HARBOUR	All About Eve	1988
MARTIKA'S KITCHEN	Martika	1991
MARVELLOUS	Lightning Seeds	1995
MARY	Supergrass	1999
MARY	Scissor Sisters	2004
MARY ANNE	Shadows	1965
MARY HAD A LITTLE BOY	Snap!	1990
MARY HAD A LITTLE LAMB/LITTLE WOMAN LOVE		
	Paul McCartney	1972
MARY IN THE MORNING	Al Martino	1967
MARY JANE	Del Shannon	1964
MARY JANE (ALL NIGHT LONG)		
	Mary J. Blige	1995
MARY JANE'S LAST DANCE	Tom Petty & The Heartbreakers	1993
MARY OF THE FOURTH FORM		
	Boomtown Rats	1977
MARY'S BOY CHILD/OH MY LORD		
	Boney M	1978
MARY'S PRAYER	Danny Wilson	1987
MAS QUE MANCADA	Ronaldo's Revenge	1998
MAS QUE NADA	Tamba Trio	1998

SONG TITLE	ARTIST	DATE
MAS QUE NADA	Echobeatz	1998
MASQUERADE	Skids	1979
MASS DESTRUCTION	Faithless	2004
MASSACHUSETTS (THE NIGHT THE LIGHTS WENT OUT IN)		
	Bee Gees	1967
THE MASSES AGAINST THE CLASSES		
	Manic Street Preachers	2000
MASSIVE ATTACK (EP)	Massive Attack	1992
MASTER AND SERVANT	Depeche Mode	1984
MASTER BLASTER (JAMMIN')		
	Stevie Wonder	1980
MASTER JACK	Four Jacks & A Jill	1968
MASTER OF EYES (THE DEEPNESS OF YOUR EYES)		
	Aretha Franklin	1973
MASTERBLASTER 2000	DJ Luck & MC Neat featuring JJ	2000
MASTERPIECE	Atlantic Starr	1992
MASTERPIECE	Temptations	1973
THE MASTERPLAN	Diana Brown & Barrie K. Sharpe	1990
THE MATADOR	Major Lance	1964
MATCHBOX	Beatles	1964
MATCHSTALK MEN AND MATCHSTALK CATS AND DOGS (LOWRY'S SONG)	Brian & Michael (Burke & Jerk)	1978
MATED	David Grant & Jaki Graham	1985
MATERIAL GIRL	Madonna	1985
MATINEE	Franz Ferdinand	2004

SONG TITLE	ARTIST	DATE
A MATTER OF FACT	Innocence	1990
A MATTER OF TRUST	Billy Joel	1986
MATTHEW AND SON	Cat Stevens	1967
MAXIMUM OVERDRIVE	2 Unlimited	1993
MAY EACH DAY	Andy Williams	1966
MAY I	Bill Deal & Rhondels	1969
MAY I HAVE THE NEXT DREAM WITH YOU		
	Malcolm Roberts	1968
MAY THE BIRD OF PARADISE FLY UP YOUR NOSE		
	Little Jimmy Dickens	1965
MAY THE SUNSHINE	Nazareth	1979
MAYBE	Thom Pace	1979
MAYBE	Enrique Iglesias	2002
MAYBE	Emma Bunton	2003
MAYBE	N E R D	2004
MAYBE	Three Degrees	1970
MAYBE (WE SHOULD CALL IT A DAY)		
	Hazell Dean	1988
MAYBE I DESERVE	Tank	2001
MAYBE I KNOW	Lesley Gore	1964
MAYBE I KNOW	Seashells	1972
MAYBE I'M A FOOL	Eddie Money	1979
MAYBE I'M AMAZED	Carleen Anderson	1998
MAYBE I'M AMAZED	Paul McCartney	1977
MAYBE THAT'S WHAT IT TAKES		
	Alex Parks	2003

SONG TITLE	ARTIST	DATE
MAYBE TOMORROW	Chords	1980
MAYBE TOMORROW	UB40	1987
MAYBE TOMORROW	Stereophonics	2003
MAYBE TOMORROW	Jackson 5	1971
MAYBELLINE	Johnny Rivers	1964
MAYBERRY	Rascal Flatts	2004
ME AGAINST THE MUSIC	Britney Spears featuring	
	Madonna	2003
ME & MRS. JONES	Freddie Jackson	1992
ME AND BABY BROTHER	War	1973
ME AND BOBBY MCGEE	Janis Joplin	1971
ME AND BOBBY MCGEE	Jerry Lee Lewis	1971
ME AND JULIO DOWN BY THE SCHOOLYARD		
	Paul Simon	1972
ME AND MR SANCHEZ	Blue Rondo A La Turk	1981
ME AND MRS JONES	Billy Paul	1973
ME AND MY ARROW	Nilsson	1971
ME AND MY GIRL (NIGHT-CLUBBING)		
	David Essex	1982
ME AND MY LIFE	Tremeloes	1970
ME AND THE FARMER	Housemartins	1987
ME AND YOU AND A DOG NAMED BOO		
	Lobo	1971
ME AND YOU VERSUS THE WORLD		
	Space	1996
ME. IN TIME	Charlatans	1991

SONG TITLE	ARTIST	DATE
ME JULIE	Ali G & Shaggy	2002
ME MYSELF AND I	De La Soul	1989
ME, MYSELF AND I	Beyonce	2004
ME MYSELF I	Joan Armatrading	1980
ME NO POP I	Kid Creole & The Coconuts	1981
ME SO HORNY	2 Live Crew	1989
ME, THE PEACEFUL HEART	Lulu	1968
ME (WITHOUT YOU)	Andy Gibb	1981
MEAN GIRL	Status Quo	1973
MEAN MAN	W.A.S.P.	1989
THE MEANING OF LOVE	Depeche Mode	1982
MEANT TO LIVE	Switchfoot	2004
MEANWHILE	George Strait	1999
MECCA	Cheetahs	1964
THE MEDAL SONG	Culture Club	1984
MEDICINE MAN (PART 1)	Buchanan Brothers	1969
MEDICINE SHOW	Big Audio Dynamite	1986
THE MEDICINE SONG	Stephanie Mills	1984
MEET EL PRESIDENTE	Duran Duran	1987
MEET HER AT THE LOVE PARADE	Da Hool	1998
MEET ME HALF WAY	Kenny Loggins	1987
MEET ME ON THE CORNER	Lindisfarne	1972
MEET VIRGINIA	Train	1999

SONG TITLE	ARTIST	DATE
(MEET) THE FLINTSTONES	BC-52s	1994
MEGABLAST/DON'T MAKE ME WAIT	Bomb The Bass	1988
MEGALOMANIAC	Incubus	2004
MEGAMIX	Crystal Waters	1992
MEGAMIX	Corona	1997
MEGAMIX	Technotronic	1990
MELLOW DOUBT	Teenage Fanclub	1995
MELLOW MELLOW RIGHT ON	Lowrell	1979
MELLOW YELLOW	Donovan	1966
MELODY OF LOVE (WANNA BE LOVED)	Donna Summer	1994
MELT/YEH YEH YEH	Melanie C	2003
MELTING POT	Blue Mink	1969
MEMO FROM TURNER	Mick Jagger	1970
MEMORIES	Elvis Presley	1969
MEMORIES ARE MADE OF THIS	Val Doonican	1967
MEMORY	Elaine Paige	1981
MEMORY	Barbra Streisand	1982
MEMORY	Barry Manilow	1982
THE MEMORY REMAINS	Metallica	1997
MEMPHIS	Johnny Rivers	1964
MEMPHIS SOUL STEW	King Curtis	1967

SONG TITLE	ARTIST	DATE
MEMPHIS TENNESSEE	Chuck Berry	1963
MEMPHIS TENNESSEE	Dave Berry	1963
MEN ARE GETTIN' SCARCE	Joe Tex	1968
MEN IN BLACK	Frank Black	1996
MEN IN BLACK	Will Smith	1997
THE MEN IN MY LITTLE GIRL'S LIFE		
	Mike Douglas	1969
MENDOCINO	Sir Douglas Quintet	1969
MENTAL	Manic MC's featuring	
	Sara Carlson	1989
MENTAL PICTURE	Jon Secada	1994
MENTIROSA	Mellow Man Ace	1990
MERCEDES BOY	Pebbles	1988
MERCI CHERI	Vince Hill	1966
MERCURY AND SOLACE	BT	1999
MERCY	Ohio Express	1969
MERCY MERCY	Don Covay	1964
MERCY MERCY ME (THE ECOLOGY)		
	Marvin Gaye	1971
MERCY MERCY ME/I WANT YOU		
	Robert Palmer	1991
MERCY, MERCY, MERCY	Cannonball Adderley	1967
MERCY, MERCY, MERCY	Buckinghams	1967
MERKINBALL	Pearl Jam	1995
MERMAIDS	Paul Weller	1997
MERRYE GENTLE POPS	Barron Knights	1965

SONG TITLE	ARTIST	DATE
MERRY CHRISTMAS DARLING/CLOSE TO YOU		
	Carpenters	1990
MERRY CHRISTMAS EVERYBODY '98 REMIX		
	Slade vs Flush	1998
MERRY CHRISTMAS EVERYONE		
	Shakin' Stevens	1985
A MERRY JINGLE	Greedies	1979
MERRY XMAS EVERYBODY	Slade	1973
MESMERIZE	Ja Rule featuring Ashanti	2003
A MESS OF THE BLUES	Status Quo	1983
THE MESSAGE	Grandmaster Flash, Melle Mel & The Furious Five	1982
MESSAGE IN A BOTTLE	Police	1979
MESSAGE IN THE BOX	World Party	1990
THE MESSAGE IS LOVE	Arthur Baker /Backbeat Disciples featuring Al Green	1989
MESSAGE OF LOVE	Lovehappy	1995
MESSAGE OF LOVE	Pretenders	1981
MESSAGE TO MARTHA (KENTUCKY BLUEBIRD)		
	Lou Johnson	1964
A MESSAGE TO MARTHA (KENTUCKY BLUEBIRD)		
	Adam Faith	1964
MESSAGE TO MICHAEL	Dionne Warwick	1966
A MESSAGE TO YOU RUDY/NITE KLUB		
	Specials featuring Rico	1979

SONG TITLE	ARTIST	DATE
A MESSAGE TO YOUR HEART		
	Samantha Janus	1991
MESSAGE UNDERSTOOD	Sandie Shaw	1965
MESSAGES	Orchestral Manoeuvres In The Dark	1980
MESSIN'	Ladies First	2001
METAL GURU	T. Rex	1972
METAL MICKEY	Suede	1992
METHOD OF MODERN LOVE		
	Daryl Hall & John Oates	1984
MEXICAN GIRL	Smokie	1978
MEXICO	Long John Baldry	1968
MFEO	Kavana	1997
MI CHICO LATINO	Geri Halliwell	1999
MI TIERRA	Gloria Estefan	1993
MIAMI	Will Smith	1998
MIAMI HIT MIX/CHRISTMAS THROUGH YOUR EYES		
	Gloria Estefan	1992
MIAMI VICE THEME	Jan Hammer	1985
MICHAEL	Franz Ferdinand	2004
MICHAEL (THE LOVER)	Geno Washington & The Ram Jam Band	1967
MICHAEL AND THE SLIPPER TREE		
	Equals	1969
MICHAEL CAINE	Madness	1984
MICHELLE	David & Jonathan	1966

SONG TITLE	ARTIST	DATE
MICHELLE	Overlanders	1966
MICKEY	Toni Basil	1982
MICKEY	Lolly	1999
MICRO KID	Level 42	1983
MIDAS TOUCH	Midnight Star	1986
THE MIDDLE	Jimmy Eat World	2002
MIDDLE OF THE ROAD	Pretenders	1983
MIDDLEMAN	Terrorvision	1994
MIDLIFE CRISIS	Faith No More	1992
MIDNIGHT	Un-Cut	2003
MIDNIGHT AT THE LOST AND FOUND		
	Meat Loaf	1983
MIDNIGHT AT THE OASIS	Brand New Heavies	1994
MIDNIGHT AT THE OASIS	Maria Muldaur	1974
MIDNIGHT BLUE	Lou Gramm	1987
MIDNIGHT BLUE	Melissa Manchester	1975
MIDNIGHT CONFESSIONS	Grass Roots	1968
MIDNIGHT COWBOY	Ferrante & Teicher	1969
MIDNIGHT IN CHELSEA	Jon Bon Jovi	1997
MIDNIGHT RIDER	Paul Davidson	1975
MIDNIGHT RIDER	Gregg Allman	1973
MIDNIGHT RIDER	Joe Cocker	1972
MIDNIGHT ROCKS	Al Stewart	1980
MIDNIGHT SPECIAL	Johnny Rivers	1965
MIDNIGHT SUMMER DREAM		
	Stranglers	1983

SONG TITLE	ARTIST	DATE
MIDNIGHT TRAIN TO GEORGIA		
	Gladys Knight & The Pips	1973
MIDNIGHT WIND	John Stewart	1979
MIDNITE DYNAMOS	Matchbox	1980
MIGHTY CLOUDS OF JOY	B.J. Thomas	1971
MIGHTY LOVE (PT 1)	Spinners	1974
MIGHTY MIGHTY	Earth, Wind & Fire	1974
THE MIGHTY POWER OF LOVE		
	Tavares	1977
MIGHTY QUINN	Manfred Mann	1968
MILES AWAY	Winger	1990
MILK	Garbage	1996
MILK AND ALCOHOL	Dr. Feelgood	1979
MILKMAN'S SON	Ugly Kid Joe	1995
MILKSHAKE	Kelis	2004
MILKY WAY	Sheer Elegance	1975
MILLENNIUM	Killing Joke	1994
MILLENNIUM	Robbie Williams	1998
THE MILLENNIUM PRAYER		
	Cliff Richard	1999
MILLER'S CAVE	Bobby Bare	1964
A MILLION LOVE SONGS (EP)		
	Take That	1992
MILLION MILES AWAY	Offspring	2001
A MILLION TO ONE	Donny Osmond	1973
MILLIONAIRE	Kelis featuring Andre 3000	2004

SONG TITLE	ARTIST	DATE
MILLY MOLLY MANDY	Glyn Poole	1973
MIND	Farm	1991
MIND BLOWIN'	Smooth	1995
MIND BLOWING DECISIONS		
	Heatwave	1978
MIND GAMES	John Lennon	1973
MIND OF A TOY	Visage	1981
A MIND OF ITS OWN	Victoria Beckham	2002
THE MIND OF THE MACHINE		
	N-Trance	1997
MIND OVER MONEY	Turin Brakes	2001
MIND PLAYING TRICKS ON ME		
	Geto Boys	1991
MIND UP TONIGHT	Melba Moore	1983
MIND, BODY AND SOUL	Flaming Ember	1969
MINDCIRCUS	Way Out West featuring Tricia Lee Kelshall	2002
MINE ALL MINE/PARTY FREAK		
	Ca$hflow	1986
MINERVA	Deftones	2003
MINISTRY OF LOVE	Hysteric Ego	1997
MINNIE THE MOOCHER	Reggae Philharmonic Orchestra	1988
MINORITY	Green Day	2000
THE MINOTAUR	Dick Hyman & His Electric Eclectics	1969
MINT CAR	Cure	1996

SONG TITLE	ARTIST	DATE
MINUETTO ALLEGRETTO	Wombles	1974
MINUTE BY MINUTE	Doobie Brothers	1979
A MINUTE OF YOUR TIME	Tom Jones	1968
THE MINUTE YOU'RE GONE		
	Cliff Richard	1965
MIRACLE	Jon Bon Jovi	1990
MIRACLE	Whitney Houston	1991
THE MIRACLE	Queen	1989
THE MIRACLE	Cliff Richard	1999
MIRACLE GOODNIGHT	David Bowie	1993
THE MIRACLE OF LOVE	Eurythmics	1986
MIRACLES	Pet Shop Boys	2003
MIRACLES	Jefferson Starship	1975
MIRACLES	Stacy Lattisaw	1983
MIRAGE	Tommy James & The Shondells	1967
MIRROR IN THE BATHROOM		
	Beat	1980
MIRROR MAN	Human League	1983
MIRROR MIRROR	Pinkerton's Assorted Colours	1966
MIRROR MIRROR	Diana Ross	1982
MIRROR MIRROR (MON AMOUR)		
	Dollar	1981
MIRRORS	Sally Oldfield	1978
MIS-SHAPES/SORTED FOR ES & WIZZ		
	Pulp	1995
MISDEMEANOR	Foster Sylvers	1973

SONG TITLE	ARTIST	DATE
MISERERE	Zucchero with Luciano Pavarotti	1992
MISERY	Soul Asylum	1995
MISFIT	Curiosity Killed The Cat	1987
MISFIT	Amy Studt	2003
MISHALE	Andru Donalds	1994
MISLED	Celine Dion	1994
MISLED	Kool & The Gang	1984
MISS AMERICA	Big Dish	1991
MISS CALIFORNIA	Dante Thomas featuring Pras	2001
MISS HIT AND RUN	Barry Blue	1974
MISS INDEPENDENT	Kelly Clarkson	2003
MISS LUCIFER	Primal Scream	2002
MISS ME BLIND	Culture Club	1984
MISS PARKER	Benz	1996
MISS PERFECT	ABS featuring Nodesha	2003
MISS SARAJEVO	Passengers	1995
MISS SUN	Boz Scaggs	1980
MISS THE GIRL	Creatures	1983
MISS YOU	Rolling Stones	1978
MISS YOU	Jimmy Young	1963
MISS YOU IN A HEARTBEAT		
	Def Leppard	1993
MISS YOU LIKE CRAZY	Natalie Cole	1989
MISS YOU MUCH	Janet Jackson	1989
MISS YOU NIGHTS	Cliff Richard	1976
MISSED OPPORTUNITY	Daryl Hall & John Oates	1988

SONG TITLE	ARTIST	DATE
MISSING	Everything But The Girl	1995
MISSING WORDS	Selecter	1980
MISSING YOU	Soul II Soul	1990
MISSING YOU	Chris De Burgh	1988
MISSING YOU	Mary J. Blige	1997
MISSING YOU	John Waite	1984
MISSING YOU	Tina Turner	1996
MISSING YOU	Lucy Carr	2003
MISSING YOU	Brandy, Tamia, Gladys Knight & Chaka Khan	1996
MISSING YOU	Case	2001
MISSING YOU	Dan Fogelberg	1982
MISSING YOU	Diana Ross	1984
MISSING YOU NOW	Michael Bolton featuring Kenny G	1992
MISSION OF LOVE	Jason Donovan	1992
MISSIONARY MAN	Eurythmics	1986
MISSISSIPPI	Pussycat	1976
MISSISSIPPI	John Phillips	1970
MISSISSIPPI QUEEN	Mountain	1970
MISTAKE NO. 3	Culture Club	1984
MISTER CAN'T YOU SEE	Buffy Sainte-Marie	1972
MISTER MENTAL	Eighties Matchbox B-Line Disaster	2004
MISTER SANDMAN	Emmylou Harris	1981
MISTI BLU	Amillionsons	2002

SONG TITLE	ARTIST	DATE
MISTLETOE AND WINE	Cliff Richard	1988
MISTY	Ray Stevens	1975
MISTY BLUE	Dorothy Moore	1976
MISUNDERSTANDING	Genesis	1980
MISUNDERSTOOD	Bon Jovi	2002
MISUNDERSTOOD MAN	Cliff Richard	1995
MIXED BIZNESS	Beck	2000
MIXED EMOTIONS	Rolling Stones	1989
MIXED-UP, SHOOK-UP, GIRL	Patty & The Emblems	1964
MIXED UP WORLD	Sophie Ellis-Bextor	2003
MMM MMM MMM MMM	Crash Test Dummies	1994
MMMBOP	Hanson	1997
MO MONEY MO PROBLEMS	Notorious B.I.G. featuring Puff Daddy & Mase	1997
MO' FIRE	Bad Company	2003
MOAN & GROAN	Mark Morrison	1997
MOBSCENE	Marilyn Manson	2003
MOCKINBIRD	Inez & Charlie Foxx	1969
MOCKINGBIRD	Carly Simon & James Taylor	1974
MOCKINGBIRD HILL	Migil Five	1964
THE MODEL/COMPUTER LOVE	Kraftwerk	1981
MODERN DAY DELILAH	Van Stephenson	1984
MODERN GIRL	Sheena Easton	1981

SONG TITLE	ARTIST	DATE
MODERN GIRL	Meat Loaf	1984
MODERN LOVE	David Bowie	1983
A MODERN WAY OF LETTING GO	Idlewild	2003
MODERN WOMAN	Billy Joel	1986
THE MODERN WORLD	Jam	1977
MOHAIR SAM	Charlie Rich	1965
MOI... LOLITA	Alizee	2002
MOIRA JANE'S CAFE	Definition Of Sound	1992
MOLLY'S CHAMBERS	Kings Of Leon	2003
A MOMENT LIKE THIS	Kelly Clarkson	2002
MOMENT OF MY LIFE	Bobby D'Ambrosio featuring Michelle Weeks	1997
MOMENTS IN SOUL	JT And The Big Family	1990
MOMENTS OF PLEASURE	Kate Bush	1993
MONA	Craig McLachlan & Check 1-2	1990
MONDAY MONDAY	Mamas & The Papas	1966
MONDAY MORNING	Candyskins	1997
MONDAY MORNING 5:19	Rialto	1997
MONEY	Bern Elliott & The Fenmen	1963
MONEY	Charli Baltimore	1998
MONEY	Flying Lizards	1979
MONEY	Jamelia featuring Beenie Man	2000
MONEY	Kingsmen	1964
MONEY	Pink Floyd	1973

SONG TITLE	ARTIST	DATE
(MONEY CAN'T) BUY ME LOVE	Blackstreet	1997
MONEY CHANGES EVERYTHING	Cyndi Lauper	1984
MONEY DON'T MATTER 2 NIGHT	Prince	1992
THE MONEY EP	Skin	1994
MONEY FOR NOTHING	Dire Straits	1985
MONEY GO ROUND (PT 1)	Style Council	1983
MONEY GREEDY/BROKEN HOMES	Tricky	1998
MONEY HONEY	Bay City Rollers	1976
MONEY IN MY POCKET	Dennis Brown	1979
MONEY LOVE	Neneh Cherry	1992
MONEY TO BURN	Richard Ashcroft	2000
MONEY'S TOO TIGHT (TO MENTION)	Simply Red	1986
MONEY, MONEY, MONEY	ABBA	1976
MONEY, POWER & RESPECT	Lox (featuring DMX & Lil' Kim)	1998
MONEYTALKS	AC/DC	1990
THE MONKEES (EP)	Monkees	1989
MONKEY	George Michael	1988
MONKEY BUSINESS	Skid Row	1991
MONKEY CHOP	Dan-I	1979
MONKEY SPANNER	Dave & Ansil Collins	1971

SONG TITLE	ARTIST	DATE
MONKEY WRENCH	Foo Fighters	1997
MONSIEUR DUPONT	Sandie Shaw	1969
MONSTER	L7	1992
MONSTER	Steppenwolf	1969
MONSTER MASH	Bobby 'Boris' Pickett & The Crypt Kickers	1962
MONSTERS AND ANGELS	Voice Of The Beehive	1991
MONTEGO BAY	Amazulu	1986
MONTEGO BAY	Bobby Bloom	1970
MONTEREY	Eric Burdon & The Animals	1967
MONTREAL	Wedding Present	1997
MONTREUX (EP)	Simply Red	1992
MONY MONY	Amazulu	1987
MONY MONY	Billy Idol	1987
MONY MONY	Tommy James & The Shondells	1968
MOODSWINGS/THE GENTLE ART OF CHOKING	My Vitriol	2002
MOODY BLUE/SHE THINKS I STILL CARE	Elvis Presley	1976
MOODY WOMAN	Jerry Butler	1969
MOON	Virus	1997
MOON RIVER	Greyhound	1972
MOON SHADOW	Cat Stevens	1971
MOONCHILD	Fields Of The Nephilim	1988
MOONFLIGHT	Vik Venus	1969
MOONLIGHT AND MUZAK	M	1979

SONG TITLE	ARTIST	DATE
MOONLIGHT & ROSES	Jim Reeves	
MOONLIGHT FEELS RIGHT	Starbuck	1976
MOONLIGHT SERENADE/LITTLE BROWN JUG	Glenn Miller	1976
MOONLIGHT SHADOW	Mike Oldfield	1983
MOONLIGHTING	Leo Sayer	1975
MOONLIGHTING (THEME)	Al Jarreau	1987
MOONSHINE SALLY	Mud	1975
MOR	Blur	1997
MORE	Sisters Of Mercy	1990
MORE & MORE	Spoiled & Zigo	2000
MORE AND MORE	Captain Hollywood Project	1993
MORE BEATS & PIECES	Coldcut	1997
MORE GOOD OLD ROCK'N'ROLL	Dave Clark Five	1970
THE MORE I GET, THE MORE I WANT	KWS featuring Teddy Pendergrass	1994
THE MORE I SEE YOU	Joy Marshall	1966
THE MORE I SEE YOU	Chris Montez	1966
MORE LIFE IN A TRAMP'S VEST	Stereophonics	1997
MORE LIKE THE MOVIES	Dr. Hook	1978
MORE LOVE	Next Of Kin	1999
MORE LOVE	Kim Carnes	1980

SONG TITLE	ARTIST	DATE
MORE LOVE	Smokey Robinson & The Miracles	1967
MORE MORE MORE	Rachel Stevens	2004
MORE, MORE, MORE	Bananarama	1993
MORE, MORE, MORE	Carmel	1984
MORE, MORE, MORE	Andrea True Connection	1976
MORE THAN A FEELING	Boston	1976
MORE THAN A LOVER	Bonnie Tyler	1977
MORE THAN A WOMAN	Tavares	1977
MORE THAN A WOMAN	911	1998
MORE THAN A WOMAN	Aaliyah	2002
MORE THAN EVER	Nelson	1991
MORE THAN I CAN SAY	Leo Sayer	1980
MORE THAN I NEEDED TO KNOW	Scooch	2000
MORE THAN IN LOVE	Kate Robbins	1981
MORE THAN JUST THE TWO OF US	Sneaker	1981
MORE THAN LIKELY	P.M. Dawn	1993
MORE THAN LOVE	Ken Dodd	1966
MORE THAN LOVE	Wet Wet Wet	1992
MORE THAN THAT	Backstreet Boys	2001
MORE THAN THIS	Emmie	1999
MORE THAN THIS	Roxy Music	1982
MORE THAN THIS	10,000 Maniacs	1997
MORE THAN US EP	Travis	1998

SONG TITLE	ARTIST	DATE
MORE THAN WORDS	Extreme	1991
MORE THAN WORDS CAN SAY	Alias	1990
MORE THAN YOU KNOW	Martika	1989
MORE TO LIFE	Cliff Richard	1991
MORE TO LOVE	Volcano	1994
MORE TO THIS WORLD	Bad Boys Inc	1994
MORE TODAY THAN YESTERDAY	Spiral Staircase	1969
THE MORE YOU IGNORE ME, THE CLOSER I GET	Morrissey	1994
THE MORE YOU LIVE, THE MORE YOU LOVE	Flock Of Seagulls	1984
MORNIN'	Al Jarreau	1983
MORNIN' BEAUTIFUL	Tony Orlando & Dawn	1975
MORNING	Val Doonican	1971
MORNING	Wet Wet Wet	1996
THE MORNING AFTER (FREE AT LAST)	Strike	1995
THE MORNING AFTER	Maureen McGovern	1973
MORNING AFTERGLOW	Electrasy	1998
MORNING DANCE	Spyro Gyra	1979
MORNING GIRL	Neon Philharmonic	1969
MORNING GLORY	James & Bobby Purify	1976
MORNING HAS BROKEN	Neil Diamond	1992
MORNING HAS BROKEN	Daniel O'Donnell	2000

SONG TITLE	ARTIST	DATE
MORNING HAS BROKEN	Cat Stevens	1972
THE MORNING OF OUR LIVES	Jonathan Richman & The Modern Lovers	1978
MORNING SIDE OF THE MOUNTAIN	Donny & Marie Osmond	1974
MORNING TRAIN (A.K.A. 9 TO 5)	Sheena Easton	1981
MORNINGTOWN RIDE	Seekers	1966
THE MOST BEAUTIFUL GIRL	Charlie Rich	1973
THE MOST BEAUTIFUL GIRL IN THE WORLD	TAFKAP	1994
MOST GIRLS	Pink	2000
MOST HIGH	Page & Plant	1998
MOST OF ALL	B.J. Thomas	1970
MOTHER	M Factor	2002
MOTHER & CHILD REUNION	Paul Simon	1972
MOTHER FREEDOM	Bread	1971
MOTHER OF MINE	Neil Reid	1972
MOTHER POPCORN (YOU GOT TO HAVE A MOTHER FOR ME)	James Brown	1969
MOTHER UNIVERSE	Soup Dragons	1990
MOTHER'S LITTLE HELPER	Rolling Stones	1966
MOTHERS TALK	Tears For Fears	1986
MOTIVATION	Sum 41	2002
THE MOTIVE (LIVING WITHOUT YOU)	Then Jericho	1987
MOTOR BIKIN'	Chris Spedding	1975
MOTORCYCLE EMPTINESS	Manic Street Preachers	1992
MOTORCYCLE MAMA	Sailcat	1972
MOTORHEAD LIVE	Motorhead	1981
MOTORMANIA	Roman Holliday	1983
MOTORTOWN	Kane Gang	1987
THE MOTOWN SONG	Rod Stewart	1991
MOTOWNPHILLY	Boyz II Men	1991
MOULDY OLD DOUGH	Lieutenant Pigeon	1972
MOUNTAIN OF LOVE	Johnny Rivers	1964
MOUNTAINS	Prince	1986
MOUTH	Merril Bainbridge	1996
MOVE	Moby	1993
MOVE ANY MOUNTAIN	Shamen	1991
MOVE AWAY	Culture Club	1986
MOVE AWAY JIMMY BLUE	Del Amitri	1990
MOVE BITCH	Ludacris featuring Mystikal & Infamous 2.0	2002
MOVE CLOSER	Phyllis Nelson	1985
MOVE IN A LITTLE CLOSER BABY	Harmony Grass	1969
MOVE IT BABY	Simon Scott & The Leroys	1964

SONG TITLE	ARTIST	DATE
MOVE IT LIKE THIS	Baha Men	2002
MOVE IT UP/BIG BEAT	Cappella	1994
MOVE MANIA	Sash! featuring Shannon	1998
MOVE ME NO MOUNTAIN	Soul II Soul	1992
MOVE MOVE MOVE (THE RED TRIBE)		
	Manchester United FA Cup Squad	1996
MOVE ON BABY	Cappella	1994
MOVE ON UP	Curtis Mayfield	1971
MOVE ON UP	Trickster	1998
MOVE OVER	Steppenwolf	1969
MOVE OVER DARLING	Doris Day	1964
MOVE OVER DARLING	Tracey Ullman	1983
MOVE THAT BODY	Technotronic featuring Reggie	1991
MOVE THIS	Technotronic featuring Ya Kid K	1992
MOVE YA BODY	Nina Sky	2004
THE MOVE YOUR ASS EP	Scooter	1995
MOVE YOUR BODY	Anticappella featuring MC Fixx It	1994
MOVE YOUR BODY	Eurogroove	1995
MOVE YOUR BODY	Gene Farrow & The G.F. Band	1978
MOVE YOUR BODY	Eiffel 65	2000
MOVE YOUR BODY (ELEVATION)		
	Xpansions	1991
MOVE YOUR FEET	Junior Senior	2003
MOVIE STAR	Harpo	1976
MOVIES	Alien Ant Farm	2002

SONG TITLE	ARTIST	DATE
MOVIESTAR	Stereophonics	2004
MOVIN'	Marathon	1992
MOVIN'	Brass Construction	1976
MOVIN' ON	Bananarama	1992
MOVIN' ON	Bad Company	1975
MOVIN' ON	Mya featuring Silkk The Shocker	1998
MOVIN' OUT (ANTHONY'S SONG)		
	Billy Joel	1978
MOVIN TOO FAST	Artful Dodger & Romina Johnson	2000
MOVING	Supergrass	1999
MOVING ON UP	M People	1994
MOZART 40	Sovereign Collection	1971
MOZART SYMPHONY NO. 40 IN G MINOR		
	Waldo De Los Rios	1971
MR BRIGHTSIDE	The Killers	2004
MR DEVIL	Big Time Charlie featuring Soozy Q	2000
MR DJ	Blackout	2001
MR FRIDAY NIGHT	Lisa Moorish	1996
MR RAFFLES (MAN, IT WAS MEAN)		
	Steve Harley & Cockney Rebel	1975
MR SECOND CLASS	Spencer Davis Group	1968
MR WRITER	Stereophonics	2001
MR. BASS MAN	Johnny Cymbal	1963
MR. BIG STUFF	Queen Latifah, Shades & Free	1997

SONG TITLE	ARTIST	DATE
MR. BIG STUFF	Jean Knight	1971
MR. BLOBBY	Mr. Blobby	1993
MR. BLUE SKY	Electric Light Orchestra	1978
MR. BOJANGLES	Nitty Gritty Dirt Band	1970
MR. BUSINESSMAN	Ray Stevens	1968
MR. DIEINGLY SAD	Critters	1966
MR. DJ	Concept	1985
MR. DREAM MERCHANT	Jerry Butler	1967
MR. E'S BEAUTIFUL BLUES	Eels	2000
MR. HANKEY THE CHRISTMAS POO		
	Mr. Hankey	1999
MR. JAWS	Dickie Goodman	1975
MR. LONELY	Bobby Vinton	1964
MR. LOVERMAN	Shabba Ranks	1992
MR. PRESIDENT	D.B.M. And T	1970
MR. ROBOTO	Styx	1983
MR. SOFT	Cockney Rebel	1974
MR. SOLITAIRE	Animal Nightlife	1984
MR. SPACEMAN	Byrds	1966
MR. SUN, MR. MOON	Paul Revere & The Raiders	1969
MR. TAMBOURINE MAN	Byrds	1965
MR. TELEPHONE MAN	New Edition	1984
MR. VAIN	Culture Beat	1993
MR. WENDAL/REVOLUTION	Arrested Development	1993
MRS ROBINSON	Booker T. & The M.G.'s	1969

SONG TITLE	ARTIST	DATE
MRS. BROWN YOU'VE GOT A LOVELY DAUGHTER		
	Herman's Hermits	1965
MRS. ROBINSON	Simon & Garfunkel	1968
MRS. ROBINSON/BEIN' AROUND		
	Lemonheads	1992
MS GRACE	Tymes	1974
MS. JACKSON	Outkast	2000
MUCH LOVE	Shola Ama	1998
(MUCHO MAMBO) SWAY	Shaft	1999
MUHAMMAD ALI	Faithless	2001
MULDER AND SCULLY	Catatonia	1998
MULE (CHANT NO. 2)	Beggar & Co	1981
MULE TRAIN	Frank Ifield	1963
MULL OF KINTYRE	Paul McCartney	1977
MULTIPLICATION	Showaddywaddy	1981
MULTIPLY	Xzibit	2002
MUM'S GONE TO ICELAND		
	Bennet	1997
THE MUMMER'S DANCE	Loreena McKennitt	1998
MUNDIAN TO BACH KE	Panjabi MC	2003
THE MUPPET SHOW MUSIC HALL EP		
	Muppets	1977
MURDER ON THE DANCEFLOOR		
	Sophie Ellis-Bextor	2001
MURDER SHE WROTE	Chaka Demus & Pliers	1994
MURPHY'S LAW	Cheri	1982

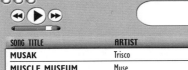

SONG TITLE	ARTIST	DATE
MUSAK	Trisco	2001
MUSCLE MUSEUM	Muse	2000
MUSCLEBOUND/GLOW	Spandau Ballet	1981
MUSCLES	Diana Ross	1982
MUSEUM	Herman's Hermits	1967
MUSIC	Fargetta And Anne-Marie Smith	1993
MUSIC	Erick Sermon featuring Marvin Gaye	2001
MUSIC	John Miles	1976
MUSIC	Madonna	2000
MUSIC & YOU	Room 5 featuring Oliver Cheatham	2003
MUSIC AND LIGHTS	Imagination	1982
MUSIC BOX DANCER	Frank Mills	1979
MUSIC FOR CHAMELEONS	Gary Numan	1982
MUSIC GETS THE BEST OF ME	Sophie Ellis-Bextor	2002
THE MUSIC I LIKE	Alexia	1998
MUSIC IN MY MIND	Adam F	1998
MUSIC IS MY RADAR	Blur	2000
MUSIC IS THE ANSWER (DANCIN & PRANCIN')	Danny Tenaglia & Celeda	1998
MUSIC MAKES YOU FEEL LIKE DANCING	Brass Construction	1980
MUSIC OF MY HEART	*NSYNC/Gloria Estefan	2000

SONG TITLE	ARTIST	DATE
THE MUSIC OF THE NIGHT/WISHING YOU WERE SOMEHOW HERE AGAIN	Michael Crawford/Sarah Brightman	1987
THE MUSIC OF TORVILL & DEAN EP	Richard Hartley/Michael Reed Orchestra	1984
MUSIC PART I	D Train	1983
MUSIC SOUNDS BETTER WITH YOU	Stardust	1998
MUSIC TIME	Styx	1984
MUSIC TO WATCH GIRLS BY	Andy Williams	1967
MUSIC TO WATCH GIRLS BY	Bob Crewe Generation	1966
THE MUSIC'S GOT ME	Bass Bumpers	1994
THE MUSIC'S NO GOOD WITHOUT YOU	Cher	2001
MUSICAL FREEDOM (MOVING ON UP)	Paul Simpson featuring Adeva	1989
MUSICAL MELODY/WEIGHT FOR THE BASS	Unique 3	1990
MUSKRAT LOVE	Captain & Tennille	1976
MUST BE LOVE	FYA featuring Smujji	2004
MUST BE THE MUSIC	Hysterix	1994
MUST BE THE MUSIC	Joey Negro featuring Taka Boom	2000

SONG TITLE	ARTIST	DATE
MUST OF GOT LOST	J. Geils Band	1974
A MUST TO AVOID	Herman's Hermits	1965
MUSTANG SALLY	Wilson Pickett	1966
MUTATIONS (EP)	Orbital	1992
MUTUALLY ASSURED DESTRUCTION		
	Gillan	1981
MY ALL	Mariah Carey	1998
MY ANGEL BABY	Toby Beau	1978
MY BABY	Lil' Romeo	2001
MY BABY	Temptations	1965
MY BABY DADDY	B-Rock & The Bizz	1997
MY BABY JUST CARES FOR ME		
	Nina Simone	1987
MY BABY LEFT ME	Dave Berry	1964
MY BABY LEFT ME BUT THAT'S ALRIGHT MAMA		
	Slade	1977
MY BABY LOVES LOVIN'	White Plains	1970
MY BABY LOVES ME	Martha & The Vandellas	1966
MY BABY MUST BE A MAGICIAN		
	Marvelettes	1966
MY BACK PAGES	Byrds	1967
MY BAND	D12	2004
MY BEAUTIFUL FRIEND	Charlatans	1999
MY BEST FRIEND	Tim McGraw	1999
MY BEST FRIEND'S GIRL	Cars	1978
MY BODY	LSG (Levert.Sweat.Gill)	1998

SONG TITLE	ARTIST	DATE
MY BONNIE	Beatles/Tony Sheridan	1964
MY BOO	Ghost Town DJ's	1996
MY BOO	Usher & Alicia Keys	2004
MY BOY	Elvis Presley	1975
MY BOY LOLLIPOP	Millie	1964
MY BRAVE FACE	Paul McCartney	1989
MY BROTHER JAKE	Free	1971
MY CAMERA NEVER LIES	Bucks Fizz	1982
MY CHERIE AMOUR	Stevie Wonder	1969
MY CHILD	Connie Francis	1965
MY COO-CA-CHOO	Alvin Stardust	1973
MY CULTURE	1 Giant Leap	2002
MY CUP RUNNETH OVER	Ed Ames	1967
MY DEFINITION OF A BOMBASTIC JAZZ STYLE		
	Dream Warriors	1990
MY DESIRE	Amira	2001
MY DESTINY	Lionel Richie	1992
MY DING-A-LING	Chuck Berry	1972
MY EVER CHANGING MOOD		
	Style Council	1984
MY EVERYTHING	98 Degrees	2000
MY EYES ADORED YOU	Frankie Valli	1974
MY FAIR SHARE	Seals & Crofts	1977
MY FATHER'S EYES	Eric Clapton	1998
MY FATHER'S SON	Conner Reeves	1997
MY FAVORITE GIRL	Dave Hollister	1999

SONG TITLE	ARTIST	DATE
MY FAVORITE MISTAKE	Sheryl Crow	1998
MY FAVOURITE GAME	Cardigans	1998
MY FAVOURITE WASTE OF TIME		
	Owen Paul	1986
MY FEELING	Junior Jack	2000
MY FEET KEEP DANCING	Chic	1979
MY FIRST LOVE	Avant featuring Ketara Wyatt	2000
MY FIRST NIGHT WITH YOU		
	Mya	1999
MY FORBIDDEN LOVER	Chic	1979
MY FRIEND	Groove Armada	2001
MY FRIEND	Roy Orbison	1969
MY FRIEND STAN	Slade	1973
MY FRIENDS	Red Hot Chili Peppers	1995
MY FRIENDS OVER YOU	New Found Glory	2002
MY FRONT PORCH LOOKING IN		
	Lonestar	2003
MY GENERATION	Who	1965
MY GENERATION	Limp Bizkit	2000
MY GIRL	Madness	1980
MY GIRL	Otis Redding	1965
MY GIRL	Temptations	1965
MY GIRL	Whispers	1980
MY GIRL	Rod Stewart	1980
MY GIRL	Donnie Iris	1982
MY GIRL	Suave	1988

SONG TITLE	ARTIST	DATE
MY GIRL (GONE, GONE, GONE)		
	Chilliwack	1981
MY GIRL BILL	Jim Stafford	1974
MY GIRL HAS GONE	Miracles	1965
MY GIRL JOSEPHINE	Super Cat featuring Jack Radics	1995
MY GIRL JOSEPHINE	Jerry Jaye	1967
MY GIRL LOLLIPOP (MY BOY LOLLIPOP)		
	Bad Manners	1982
MY GIRL MY GIRL	Warren Stacy	2002
MY GIRL SLOOPY	Vibrations	1964
MY GIRL/HEY GIRL (MEDLEY)		
	Bobby Vee	1968
MY GUY	Mary Wells	1964
MY GUY	Tracey Ullman	1984
MY GUY	Sister Sledge	1982
MY GUY – MY GIRL (MEDLEY)		
	Amii Stewart & Johnny Stewart	1980
MY HAND OVER MY HEART		
	Marc Almond	1992
MY HAPPY ENDING	Avril Lavigne	2004
MY HEAD'S IN MISSISSIPPI		
	ZZ Top	1991
MY HEART BELONGS TO ME		
	Barbra Streisand	1977
MY HEART BELONGS TO ONLY YOU		
	Bobby Vinton	1964

SONG TITLE	ARTIST	DATE
MY HEART BELONGS TO YOU	Russ Irwin	1991
MY HEART CAN'T TELL YOU NO	Rod Stewart	1989
MY HEART CRIES FOR YOU	Ray Charles	1964
MY HEART GOES BANG (GET ME TO THE DOCTOR)	Dead Or Alive	1985
MY HEART IS FAILING ME	Riff	1991
MY HEART SKIPS A BEAT	Cover Girls	1989
MY HEART WILL GO ON	Celine Dion	1998
MY HEART'S SYMPHONY	Gary Lewis & The Playboys	1966
MY HERO	Foo Fighters	1998
MY HOMETOWN	Bruce Springsteen	1985
MY HOUSE	Terrorvision	1994
MY IMMORTAL	Evanescence	2003
MY IRON LUNG (EP)	Radiohead	1994
MY KIND OF GIRL	Frank Sinatra	1964
MY KIND OF LADY	Supertramp	1983
MY KINDA GIRL	Babyface	1990
MY KINDA LIFE	Cliff Richard	1977
MY KINGDOM	Future Sound Of London	1996
MY LAST DATE (WITH YOU)	Joni James	1969
MY LAST NIGHT WITH YOU	Arrows	1975

SONG TITLE	ARTIST	DATE
MY LIFE	Billy Joel	1978
MY LIST	Toby Keith	2002
MY LITTLE BABY	Mike Berry	1963
MY LITTLE GIRL	Autumn	1971
MY LITTLE GIRL	Crickets	1963
MY LITTLE LADY	Tremeloes	1968
MY LITTLE ONE	Marmalade	1971
MY LITTLE SECRET	Xscape	1998
MY LITTLE TOWN	Simon & Garfunkel	1975
MY LOVE	Mary J. Blige	1994
MY LOVE	Petula Clark	1965
MY LOVE	Julio Iglesias (featuring Stevie Wonder)	1988
MY LOVE	Paul McCartney	1973
MY LOVE	Kele Le Roc	1999
MY LOVE	Westlife	2000
MY LOVE	Lionel Richie	1983
MY LOVE IS A FIRE	Donny Osmond	1990
MY LOVE IS ALWAYS	Saffron Hill featuring Ben Onono	2002
MY LOVE IS DEEP	Sara Parker	1997
MY LOVE IS FOR REAL	Paula Abdul	1995
MY LOVE IS FOR REAL	Strike	1996
MY LOVE IS LIKE... WO	Mya	2003
MY LOVE IS SO RAW	Alyson Williams featuring Nikki-D	1989

SONG TITLE	ARTIST	DATE
MY LOVE IS THE SHHH!	Somethin' For The People featuring Trina & Tamara	1997
MY LOVE IS WAITING	Marvin Gaye	1983
MY LOVE IS YOUR LOVE	Whitney Houston	1999
MY LOVE LIFE	Morrissey	1991
MY LOVE, FORGIVE ME (AMORE, SCUSAMI)	Robert Goulet	1964
MY LOVER'S PRAYER	Otis Redding	1966
MY LOVIN'	En Vogue	1992
MY LOVIN' (YOU'RE NEVER GONNA GET IT)	En Vogue	1992
MY MAGIC MAN	Rochelle	1986
MY MAMMY	Happenings	1967
MY MAN AND ME	Lynsey De Paul	1975
MY MARIA	B.W. Stevenson	1973
MY MARIE	Engelbert Humperdinck	1970
MY MATE PAUL	David Holmes	1998
MY MELODY OF LOVE	Bobby Vinton	1974
MY MIND'S EYE	Small Faces	1966
MY MISTAKE (WAS TO LOVE YOU)	Marvin Gaye & Diana Ross	1974
MY MOTHER'S EYES	Bette Midler	1980
MY MUM IS ONE IN A MILLION	Children Of Tansley School	1981
MY MUSIC	Loggins & Messina	1973
MY MY MY	Armand Van Helden	2004

SONG TITLE	ARTIST	DATE
MY, MY, MY	Johnny Gill	1990
MY NAME IS	Eminem	1999
MY NAME IS JACK	Manfred Mann	1968
MY NAME IS NOT SUSAN	Whitney Houston	1991
MY NAME IS PRINCE	Prince & The New Power Generation	1992
MY NECK MY BACK (LICK IT)	Khia	2004
MY NEXT THIRTY YEARS	Tim McGraw	2000
MY OH MY	Aqua	1998
MY OH MY	Sad Cafe	1980
MY OH MY	Slade	1984
MY OLD PIANO	Diana Ross	1980
MY ONE TEMPTATION	Mica Paris	1988
MY OWN SUMMER (SHOVE IT)	Deftones	1998
MY OWN WAY	Duran Duran	1981
MY OWN WORST ENEMY	Lit	1999
MY PERFECT COUSIN	Undertones	1980
MY PLACE/FLAP YOUR WINGS	Nelly	2004
MY PLEDGE OF LOVE	Joe Jeffrey Group	1969
MY PRAYER	Gerry Monroe	1970
MY PREROGATIVE	Bobby Brown	1988
MY PRETTY ONE	Cliff Richard	1987
MY RECOVERY INJECTION	Biffy Clyro	2004

SONG TITLE	ARTIST	DATE
MY RESISTANCE IS LOW	Robin Sarstedt	1976
MY RISING STAR	Northside	1990
MY SACRAMENT	Him	2003
MY SACRIFICE	Creed	2001
MY SENTIMENTAL FRIEND	Herman's Hermits	1969
MY SHARONA	Knack	1979
MY SHIP IS COMING IN	Walker Brothers	1965
MY SIDE OF THE BED	Susanna Hoffs	1991
MY SIMPLE HEART	Three Degrees	1979
MY SONG	Aretha Franklin	1968
MY SPECIAL ANGEL	Vogues	1968
MY SPECIAL DREAM	Shirley Bassey	1964
MY STAR	Ian Brown	1998
MY SWEET LADY	Cliff DeYoung	1974
MY SWEET LADY	John Denver	1977
MY SWEET LORD/ISN'T IT A PITY		
	George Harrison	1970
MY SWEET ROSALIE	Brotherhood Of Man	1976
MY THANG	James Brown	1974
MY TIME	Dutch featuring Crystal Waters	2003
MY TOOT TOOT	Denise La Salle	1985
MY TOWN	Glass Tiger featuring Rod Stewart	1991
MY TOWN	Montgomery Gentry	2002
MY TOWN	Michael Stanley Band	1983

SONG TITLE	ARTIST	DATE
MY TOWN, MY GUY AND ME		
	Lesley Gore	1965
MY VISION	Jakatta featuring Seal	2002
MY WAY	Shane Macgowan	1996
MY WAY	Eddie Cochran	1963
MY WAY	Dorothy Squires	1970
MY WAY	Elvis Presley	1977
MY WAY	Frank Sinatra	1969
MY WAY	Limp Bizkit	2001
MY WAY	Usher	1998
MY WAY OF THINKING/I THINK IT'S GOING TO RAIN		
	UB40	1980
MY WEAKNESS IS NONE OF YOUR BUSINESS		
	Embrace	1998
MY WHITE BICYCLE	Nazareth	1975
MY WHOLE WORLD ENDED (THE MOMENT YOU LEFT ME)	David Ruffin	1969
MY WORLD	Bee Gees	1972
MY WORLD	Secret Affair	1980
MY WORLD IS EMPTY WITHOUT YOU		
	Supremes	1966
MY WORLD OF BLUE	Karl Denver	1964
MYSTERIOUS GIRL	Peter Andre featuring Bubbler Ranx	1996
MYSTERIOUS TIMES	Sash! featuring Tina Cousins	1998
MYSTERIOUS WAYS	U2	1991

SONG TITLE	ARTIST	DATE
MYSTERY	Dio	1984
MYSTERY SONG	Status Quo	1976
MYSTIC EYES	Them	1965
MYSTICAL MACHINE GUN	Kula Shaker	1999
MYSTIFY	INXS	1989
N-N-NINETEEN NOT OUT	Commentators	1985
N-R-G	Adamski	1990
N.Y., YOU GOT ME DANCING		
	Andrea True Connection	1977
N.Y.C. (CAN YOU BELIEVE THIS CITY)		
	Charles & Eddie	1993
NA NA HEY HEY KISS HIM GOODBYE		
	Steam	1969
NA NA HEY HEY KISS HIM GOODBYE		
	Bananarama	1983
NA NA IS THE SADDEST WORD		
	Stylistics	1975
NA NA NA	Cozy Powell	1974
NADIA'S THEME (THE YOUNG & THE RESTLESS)		
	Barry Devorzon & Perry Botkin	1976
NADINE (IS IT YOU?)	Chuck Berry	1964
NAILS IN MY FEET	Crowded House	1993
NAKASAKAI EP (I NEED A LOVER TONIGHT)		
	Ken Doh	1996
NAKED	Reef	1995
NAKED	Louise	1996

SONG TITLE	ARTIST	DATE
NAKED AND SACRED	Maria Nayler	1998
NAKED EYE	Luscious Jackson	1996
NAKED IN THE RAIN	Blue Pearl	1990
NAKED LOVE (JUST SAY YOU WANT ME)		
	Quartz With Dina Carroll	1991
NAME	Goo Goo Dolls	1995
NAME AND NUMBER	Curiosity Killed The Cat	1989
THE NAME GAME	Shirley Ellis	1964
THE NAME OF THE GAME	ABBA	1977
THE NAMELESS ONE	Wendy James	1993
NANCY BOY	Placebo	1997
A NANNY IN MANHATTAN	Lilys	1998
NAPPY LOVE/WILD THING	Goodies	1975
NASHVILLE CATS	Lovin' Spoonful	1966
NASTRADAMUS	Nas	2000
NASTY	Janet Jackson	1986
NATHAN JONES	Bananarama	1988
NATHAN JONES	Supremes	1971
NATIONAL EXPRESS	Divine Comedy	1999
NATIVE NEW YORKER	Odyssey	1977
NATURAL	Peter Andre	1997
NATURAL	S Club 7	2000
NATURAL BLUES	Moby	2000
NATURAL BORN BUGIE	Humble Pie	1969
NATURAL HIGH	Bloodstone	1973
A NATURAL MAN	Lou Rawls	1971

SONG TITLE	ARTIST	DATE
NATURAL ONE	Folk Implosion	1995
NATURAL SINNER	Fair Weather	1970
NATURAL THING	Innocence	1990
A NATURAL WOMAN (YOU MAKE ME FEEL LIKE)		
	Aretha Franklin	1967
NATURALLY STONED	Avant-Garde	1968
NATURE BOY	George Benson	1977
NATURE BOY	Central Line	1983
NATURE BOY	Nick Cave & The Bad Seeds	2004
NATURE'S TIME FOR LOVE	Joe Brown	1963
NAUGHTY CHRISTMAS (GOBLIN IN THE OFFICE)		
	Fat Les	1998
NAUGHTY GIRL	Holly Valance	2002
NAUGHTY GIRL	Beyonce	2004
NAUGHTY GIRLS (NEED LOVE TOO)		
	Samantha Fox featuring	
	Full Force	1988
NAUGHTY NAUGHTY	John Parr	1984
NAUGHTY NAUGHTY NAUGHTY		
	Joy Sarney	1977
THE NAUGHTY NORTH & THE SEXY SOUTH		
	E-Motion	1996
NAVY BLUE	Diane Renay	1964
NAZIS	Roger Taylor	1994
NE-NE NA-NA NA-NA NU-NU		
	Bad Manners	1980

SONG TITLE	ARTIST	DATE
NEANDERTHAL MAN	Hotlegs	1970
NEAR WILD HEAVEN	R.E.M.	1991
NEAR YOU	Migil Five	1964
NEARER THAN HEAVEN	The Delays	2004
THE NEED TO BE	Jim Weatherly	1974
NEED YOU TONIGHT	INXS	1987
NEED YOUR LOVE SO BAD	Fleetwood Mac	1968
NEEDIN' U	David Morales presents	
	The Face	1998
NEEDIN' U II	David Morales presents The Face	
	featuring Juliet Robert	2001
NEEDLES AND PINS	Searchers	1964
NEEDLES AND PINS	Smokie	1977
NEEDLES AND PINS	Tom Petty & The Heartbreakers	
	with Stevie Nicks	1986
NEGATIVE	Mansun	1998
NEHEMIAH	Hope Of The States	2004
NEIGHBOR	Ugly Kid Joe	1992
NEIGHBOURHOOD	Zed Bias	2000
NEIGHBOURHOOD	Space	1996
NEITHER ONE OF US (WANTS TO BE THE FIRST TO SAY GOODBYE)	Gladys Knight & The Pips	1973
NELLIE THE ELEPHANT	Toy Dolls	1984
NELSON MANDELA	Special AKA	1984
NEON KNIGHTS	Black Sabbath	1980
NEON RAINBOW	Box Tops	1967

SONG TITLE	ARTIST	DATE
NERVOUS BREAKDOWN	Carleen Anderson	1994
NERVOUS SHAKEDOWN	AC/DC	1984
NERVOUS WRECK	Radio Stars	1978
NESSAJA	Scooter	2002
NESSUN DORMA	Luciano Pavarotti	1990
NEUROTICA	Cud	1994
NEUTRON DANCE	Pointer Sisters	1984
NEVER	Jomanda	1993
NEVER	Heart	1985
NEVER A TIME	Genesis	1992
NEVER AGAIN	Mission	1992
NEVER AGAIN	Nickelback	2002
NEVER AS GOOD AS THE FIRST TIME		
	Sade	1986
NEVER BE THE SAME	Christopher Cross	1980
NEVER BE THE SAME AGAIN		
	Melanie C/Lisa 'Left Eye' Lopes	2000
NEVER BEEN IN LOVE	Randy Meisner	1982
NEVER BEEN TO SPAIN	Three Dog Night	1971
NEVER BEFORE	Deep Purple	1972
NEVER CAN SAY GOODBYE	Communards	1987
NEVER CAN SAY GOODBYE	Gloria Gaynor	1974
NEVER CAN SAY GOODBYE	Jackson 5	1971
NEVER CAN SAY GOODBYE	Isaac Hayes	1971
NEVER ENDING SONG OF LOVE		
	New Seekers	1971

SONG TITLE	ARTIST	DATE
NEVER ENDING SONG OF LOVE		
	Delaney & Bonnie & Friends	1971
NEVER ENDING STORY	Limahl	1985
NEVER ENOUGH	Cure	1990
NEVER ENOUGH	Boris Dlugosch featuring	
	Roisin Murphy	2001
NEVER EVER	All Saints	1998
NEVER FELT LIKE THIS BEFORE		
	Shaznay Lewis	2004
NEVER FORGET	Take That	1995
NEVER FOUND A LOVE LIKE THIS BEFORE		
	Upside Down	1996
NEVER GIVE UP ON A GOOD THING		
	George Benson	1982
NEVER GIVE YOU UP	Sharon Redd	1982
NEVER GIVE YOU UP	Jerry Butler	1968
NEVER GOING NOWHERE	Bluetones	2003
NEVER GONNA FALL IN LOVE AGAIN		
	Dana	1976
NEVER GONNA FALL IN LOVE AGAIN		
	Eric Carmen	1976
NEVER GONNA GIVE YOU UP		
	Rick Astley	1987
NEVER GONNA GIVE YOU UP		
	Musical Youth	1983

SONG TITLE	ARTIST	DATE
NEVER GONNA LEAVE YOUR SIDE	Daniel Bedingfield	2003
NEVER GONNA LET YOU DOWN	Surface	1991
NEVER GONNA LET YOU GO	Tina Moore	1997
NEVER GONNA LET YOU GO	Faith Evans	1999
NEVER GONNA LET YOU GO	Sergio Mendes	1983
NEVER HAD A DREAM COME TRUE	Stevie Wonder	1970
NEVER HAD A DREAM COME TRUE	S Club 7	2001
NEVER HAD IT SO GOOD Take 5		1999
NEVER KEEPING SECRETS Babyface		1993
NEVER KNEW LOVE Oleta Adams		1995
NEVER KNEW LOVE LIKE THIS	Pauline Henry featuring Wayne Marshall	1996
NEVER KNEW LOVE LIKE THIS	Cherelle	1988
NEVER KNEW LOVE LIKE THIS	Alexander O'Neal	1988
NEVER KNEW LOVE LIKE THIS BEFORE	Stephanie Mills	1980

SONG TITLE	ARTIST	DATE
NEVER LEAVE YOU (OH OOOH, UH OOOH)	Lumidee	2003
NEVER LET GO	Cliff Richard	1993
NEVER LET HER GO	David Gates	1975
NEVER LET HER SLIP AWAY	Andrew Gold	1978
NEVER LET HER SLIP AWAY	Undercover	1992
NEVER LET ME DOWN	David Bowie	1987
NEVER LET ME DOWN AGAIN	Depeche Mode	1987
NEVER LET YOU DOWN	Honeyz	1999
NEVER LET YOU GO	Third Eye Blind	2000
NEVER LIE	Immature	1994
NEVER LOOK BACK	Dumonde	2001
NEVER MAKE A PROMISE	Dru Hill	1997
NEVER MIND THE PRESENTS	Barron Knights	1980
NEVER MY LOVE	Association	1967
NEVER MY LOVE	Blue Swede	1974
NEVER MY LOVE	5th Dimension	1971
NEVER NEVER	Warm Jets	1998
NEVER NEVER	Assembly	1983
NEVER NEVER LOVE	Simply Red	1996
NEVER, NEVER GONNA GIVE YA UP	Barry White	1973

SONG TITLE	ARTIST	DATE
NEVER, NEVER GONNA GIVE YOU UP		
	Lisa Stansfield	1997
NEVER, NEVER, NEVER (GRANDE, GRANDE, GRANDE)		
	Shirley Bassey	1973
NEVER SAW A MIRACLE	Curtis Stigers	1992
NEVER SAY DIE	Black Sabbath	1978
NEVER SAY DIE (GIVE A LITTLE BIT MORE)		
	Cliff Richard	1983
NEVER SAY GOODBYE	Bon Jovi	1987
NEVER SCARED	Bonecrusher featuring Killer Mike & T.I.	2003
NEVER SHOULD'VE LET YOU GO		
	Hi-Five	1993
NEVER STOP	Echo & The Bunnymen	1983
NEVER SURRENDER	Saxon	1981
NEVER SURRENDER	Corey Hart	1985
NEVER TAKE ME ALIVE	Spear Of Destiny	1987
NEVER TEAR US APART	Inxs	1988
NEVER TOO FAR/DON'T STOP (FUNKIN' 4 JAMAICA)		
	Mariah Carey	2001
NEVER TOO LATE	Kylie Minogue	1989
NEVER TOO MUCH	Luther Vandross	1981
NEVER TOO MUCH (89 REMIX)		
	Luther Vandross	1989
NEVER TRUST A STRANGER		
	Kim Wilde	1988

SONG TITLE	ARTIST	DATE
NEVER TURN YOUR BACK ON MOTHER EARTH		
	Sparks	1974
NEVERTHELESS	Frankie Vaughan	1968
NEVERTHELESS (I'M IN LOVE WITH YOU)		
	New Seekers	1973
NEW	No Doubt	1999
NEW AGE GIRL	Deadeye Dick	1994
NEW AMSTERDAM	Elvis Costello	1980
NEW ATTITUDE	Patti Labelle	1985
NEW BEGINNING (MAMBA SAYRA)		
	Bucks Fizz	1986
NEW BEGINNING/BRIGHT EYES		
	Stephen Gately	2000
NEW DAY	Wyclef Jean featuring Bono	1999
A NEW DAY HAS COME	Celine Dion	2002
NEW DIRECTION	S Club Juniors	2002
NEW EMOTION (EP)	Time Frequency	1993
A NEW ENGLAND	Kirsty MacColl	1985
A NEW FASHION	Bill Wyman	1982
A NEW FLAME	Simply Red	1989
NEW GENERATION	Suede	1995
THE NEW GIRL IN SCHOOL		
	Jan & Dean	1964
NEW KID IN TOWN	Eagles	1976
NEW KIND OF MEDICINE	Ultra Nate	1998
NEW LIFE	Depeche Mode	1981

SONG TITLE	ARTIST	DATE
NEW LIVE AND RARE (EP)	Deep Purple	1977
NEW MOON ON MONDAY	Duran Duran	1984
NEW ORLEANS	Bern Elliott & The Fenman	1964
NEW ORLEANS	Gillan	1981
NEW ORLEANS	Harley Quinne	1972
THE NEW POLLUTION	Beck	1997
NEW POWER GENERATION	Prince	1990
NEW ROMANCE (IT'S A MYSTERY)		
	Spider	1980
NEW SENSATION	INXS	1988
NEW SONG	Howard Jones	1984
A NEW SOUTH WALES/THE ROCK		
	Alarm	1989
NEW WORLD IN THE MORNING		
	Roger Whittaker	1970
NEW WORLD MAN	Rush	1982
NEW YEAR	Sugababes	2000
NEW YEAR'S DAY	U2	1983
NEW YEAR'S DUB	Musique vs U2	2001
NEW YORK CITY	T. Rex	1975
NEW YORK CITY BOY	Pet Shop Boys	1999
NEW YORK GROOVE	Hello	1975
NEW YORK GROOVE	Ace Frehley	1976
NEW YORK MINING DISASTER 1941		
	Bee Gees	1967

SONG TITLE	ARTIST	DATE
NEW YORK UNDERCOVER 4-TRACK EP		
	Various	1996
NEW YORK'S A LONELY TOWN		
	Trade Winds	1965
NEWBORN	Muse	2001
NEWS OF THE WORLD	Jam	1978
THE NEXT EPISODE	Dr. Dre featuring Snoop Dogg	2001
NEXT LIFETIME	Erykah Badu	1997
NEXT PLANE TO LONDON	Rose Garden	1967
THE NEXT TIME I FALL	Peter Cetera & Amy Grant	1986
NEXT TO YOU	ASWAD	1990
NI-TEN-ICHI-RYU	Photek	1997
NICE & SLOW	Usher	1998
NICE 'N' SLEAZY	Stranglers	1978
NICE 'N' TASTY	Salsoul Orchestra	1976
NICE AND SLOW	Jesse Green	1976
NICE GIRLS	Eye To Eye	1982
NICE GUY EDDIE	Sleeper	1996
NICE IN NICE	Stranglers	1986
NICE LEGS SHAME ABOUT HER FACE		
	Monks	1979
NICE ONE CYRIL	Cockerel Chorus	1973
NICE TO BE WITH YOU	Gallery	1972
NICE WEATHER FOR DUCKS		
	Lemon Jelly	2003
NICETY	Michel'le	1990

SONG TITLE	ARTIST	DATE
THE NICKEL SONG	Melanie	1972
NICOLE	Point Black	1981
THE NIGHT	Frankie Valli & The Four Seasons	1975
THE NIGHT	Soft Cell	2003
THE NIGHT	Scooter	2003
A NIGHT AT DADDY GEES	Showaddywaddy	1979
NIGHT BIRDS	Shakatak	1982
THE NIGHT CHICAGO DIED	Paper Lace	1974
NIGHT FEVER	Fatback Band	1976
NIGHT FEVER	Bee Gees	1978
NIGHT FEVER	Adam Garcia	1998
THE NIGHT FEVER MEGAMIX	UK Mixmasters	1991
NIGHT GAMES	Graham Bonnet	1981
THE NIGHT HAS A THOUSAND EYES	Bobby Vee	1962
NIGHT IN MOTION	Cubic 22	1991
NIGHT IN MY VEINS	Pretenders	1994
A NIGHT IN NEW YORK	Elbow Bones & The Racketeers	1984
THE NIGHT IS STILL YOUNG	Billy Joel	1985
NIGHT MOVES	Marilyn Martin	1986
NIGHT MOVES	Bob Seger & The Silver Bullet Band	1976

SONG TITLE	ARTIST	DATE
NIGHT NURSE	Sly And Robbie featuring Simply Red	1997
NIGHT OF FEAR	Move	1967
NIGHT OF THE LONG GRASS	Troggs	1967
NIGHT OWL	Gerry Rafferty	1979
THE NIGHT OWLS	Little River Band	1981
NIGHT PORTER	Japan	1982
THE NIGHT THE LIGHTS WENT OUT IN GEORGIA	Vicki Lawrence	1973
THE NIGHT THE WINE AND THE ROSES	Liquid Gold	1980
THE NIGHT THEY DROVE OLD DIXIE DOWN	Joan Baez	1971
NIGHT TIME	Strangeloves	1966
NIGHT TO REMEMBER	911	1996
A NIGHT TO REMEMBER	Shalamar	1982
A NIGHT TO REMEMBER	Joe Diffie	1999
NIGHT TRAIN	Visage	1982
NIGHT VISION	Hell Is For Heroes	2002
THE NIGHT YOU MURDERED LOVE	ABC	1987
NIGHTBIRD	Convert	1992
NIGHTBIRD	Stevie Nicks (with Sandy Stewart)	1983
NIGHTIME	Pretty Poison	1988

SONG TITLE	ARTIST	DATE
NIGHTINGALE	Carole King	1975
NIGHTLIFE	Kenickie	1997
NIGHTMARE	Brainbug	1997
NIGHTMARE	Gillan	1981
A NIGHTMARE ON MY STREET		
	D.J. Jazzy Jeff & The Fresh Prince	1988
NIGHTRAIN	Guns N' Roses	1989
NIGHTS ARE FOREVER WITHOUT YOU		
	England Dan & John Ford Coley	1976
NIGHTS IN WHITE SATIN	Dickies	1979
NIGHTS IN WHITE SATIN	Elkie Brooks	1982
NIGHTS IN WHITE SATIN	Moody Blues	1972
NIGHTS LIKE THIS	After 7	1991
NIGHTS ON BROADWAY	Candi Staton	1977
NIGHTS ON BROADWAY	Bee Gees	1975
NIGHTSHIFT	Commodores	1985
NIGHTSWIMMING	R.E.M.	1993
THE NIGHTTRAIN	Kadoc	1996
NIKI HOEKY	P.J. Proby	1967
NIKITA	Elton John	1986
9 A.M. (THE COMFORT ZONE)		
	Londonbeat	1988
911	Wyclef Jean featuring Mary J. Blige	2000
9 TO 5	Dolly Parton	1980

SONG TITLE	ARTIST	DATE
9 TO 5 (A.K.A. MORNING TRAIN)		
	Sheena Easton	1980
9PM (TILL I COME)	ATB	1999
19	Paul Hardcastle	1985
1980	Estelle	2004
1985	Bowling For Soup	2004
1900 YESTERDAY	Liz Damon's Orient Express	1970
1999	Prince & The Revolution	1985
1998	Binary Finary	1998
1979	Smashing Pumpkins	1996
19 SOMETHIN'	Mark Wills	2002
19/2000	Gorillaz	2001
1963	New Order	1995
19TH NERVOUS BREAKDOWN		
	Rolling Stones	1966
90S GIRL	Blackgirl	1994
98.6	Keith	1966
99	Toto	1979
99 LUFTBALLONS	Nena	1983
99 PROBLEMS/DIRT OFF YOUR SHOULDER		
	Jay-Z	2004
99 RED BALLOONS	Nena	1984
96 TEARS	Stranglers	1990
96 TEARS	Question Mark & The Mysterions	1966
92 DEGREES	Pop Will Eat Itself	1991
NITE AND DAY	Al B. Sure!	1988

SONG TITLE	ARTIST	DATE
NITE LIFE	Kim English	1994
THE NITTY GRITTY	Gladys Knight & The Pips	1969
NO ARMS CAN EVER HOLD YOU		
	Bachelors	1964
NO BETTER LOVE	Young Gunz featuring Rell	2004
NO CHANCE (NO CHANGE)	Billy Connolly	1976
NO CHARGE	J.J. Barrie	1976
NO CHARGE	Melba Montgomery	1974
NO CHEAP THRILL	Suzanne Vega	1997
NO CHRISTMAS	Wedding Present	1992
NO DIGGITY	Blackstreet featuring Dr. Dre	1996
NO DISTANCE LEFT TO RUN		
	Blur	1999
NO DOUBT ABOUT IT	Hot Chocolate	1980
NO DREAM IMPOSSIBLE	Lindsay	2001
NO EASY WAY OUT	Robert Tepper	1986
NO FACE, NO NAME, NO NUMBER		
	Traffic	1968
NO FLOW	Lisa Roxanne	2001
NO FRONTS – THE REMIXES		
	Dog Eat Dog	1996
NO GOOD	Da Fool	1999
NO GOOD (START THE DANCE)		
	Prodigy	1994
NO GOOD 4 ME	Oxide & Neutrino featuring	
	Megaman, Romeo & Lisa Maffi	2000

SONG TITLE	ARTIST	DATE
NO GOOD ADVICE	Girls Aloud	2003
NO HONESTLY	Lynsey De Paul	1974
NO LAUGHING IN HEAVEN	Gillan	1981
NO LETTING GO	Wayne Wonder	2003
NO LIMIT	2 Unlimited	1993
NO LOOKIN' BACK	Michael McDonald	1985
NO LOVE AT ALL	B.J. Thomas	1971
NO MATTER HOW I TRY	Gilbert O'Sullivan	1971
NO MATTER WHAT	Badfinger	1970
NO MATTER WHAT	Boyzone	1998
NO MATTER WHAT I DO	Will Mellor	1998
NO MATTER WHAT SHAPE (YOUR STOMACH'S IN)		
	T-Bones	1965
NO MATTER WHAT SIGN YOU ARE		
	Supremes	1969
NO MATTER WHAT THEY SAY		
	Lil' Kim	2000
NO MATTER WHAT YOU DO		
	Benny Benassi presents The Biz	2004
NO MEMORY	Scarlet Fantastic	1987
NO MERCY	Stranglers	1984
NO MILK TODAY	Herman's Hermits	1967
NO MISTAKES	Patty Smyth	1992
NO MORE	A1	2001
NO MORE	Ruff Endz	2000
NO MORE 'I LOVE YOUS'	Annie Lennox	1995

SONG TITLE	ARTIST	DATE
NO MORE (BABY I'MA DO RIGHT)		
	3LW	2001
NO MORE (I CAN'T STAND IT)		
	Maxx	1994
NO MORE ALCOHOL	Suggs featuring Louchie Lou &	
	Michie One	1996
NO MORE DRAMA	Mary J. Blige	2001
NO MORE HEROES	Stranglers	1977
NO MORE LIES	Sharpe & Numan	1988
NO MORE LIES	Michel'le	1989
NO MORE LONELY NIGHTS	Paul McCartney	1984
NO MORE MR. NICE GUY	Alice Cooper	1973
NO MORE MR. NICE GUY	Megadeth	1990
NO MORE RHYME	Debbie Gibson	1989
NO MORE TALK	Dubstar	1997
NO MORE TEARS	Ozzy Osbourne	1991
NO MORE TEARS (ENOUGH IS ENOUGH)		
	Donna Summer &	
	Barbra Streisand	1979
NO MORE TEARS (ENOUGH IS ENOUGH)		
	Kym Mazelle & Jocelyn Brown	1994
NO MORE THE FOOL	Elkie Brooks	1986
NO MORE WORDS	Berlin	1984
NO MULE'S FOOL	Family	1969
NO MYTH	Michael Penn	1990
NO NIGHT SO LONG	Dionne Warwick	1980

SONG TITLE	ARTIST	DATE
NO, NO, NO	Destiny's Child	1997
NO NO SONG/SNOOKEROO	Ringo Starr	1975
NO NOT MUCH	Vogues	1969
NO, NOT NOW	Hot Hot Heat	2003
NO ONE	Ray Charles	1963
NO ONE	2 Unlimited	1994
NO-ONE BUT YOU	Queen	1998
NO ONE CAN	Marillion	1992
NO ONE CAN BREAK A HEART LIKE YOU		
	Dave Clark Five	1968
NO ONE CAN STOP US NOW		
	Chelsea Football Club	1994
NO-ONE DRIVING (DOUBLE SINGLE)		
	John Foxx	1980
NO ONE ELSE	Total	1995
NO ONE IS INNOCENT (A PUNK PRAYER BY RONALD		
BIGGS)/MY WAY	Sex Pistols	1978
NO ONE IS TO BLAME	Howard Jones	1986
NO ONE KNOWS	Queens Of The Stone Age	2002
NO ONE SPEAKS	Geneva	1996
NO ONE TO CRY TO	Ray Charles	1964
NO ONE TO DEPEND ON	Santana	1972
NO ONE WILL EVER KNOW	Frank Ifield	1966
NO ONE'S DRIVING	Dave Clarke	1996
NO ORDINARY LOVE	Sade	1992

SONG TITLE	ARTIST	DATE
NO ORDINARY MORNING/HALYCON		
	Chicane	2000
NO PARTICULAR PLACE TO GO		
	Chuck Berry	1964
NO PIGEONS	Sporty Thievz	1999
NO PLACE THAT FAR	Sara Evans	1998
NO PLACE TO HIDE	Korn	1996
NO PROBLEM	Lil Scrappy	2004
NO RAIN	Blind Melon	1993
NO REGRETS	Shirley Bassey	1965
NO REGRETS	Midge Ure	1982
NO REGRETS	Walker Brothers	1976
NO REGRETS/ANTMUSIC	Robbie Williams	1998
NO REPLY AT ALL	Genesis	1981
NO REST	New Model Army	1985
NO SCRUBS	TLC	1999
NO SELF CONTROL	Peter Gabriel	1980
NO SHOES, NO SHIRT, NO PROBLEMS		
	Kenny Chesney	2003
NO SLEEP TILL BROOKLYN		
	Beastie Boys	1987
NO SON OF MINE	Genesis	1991
NO SUCH THING	John Mayer	2002
NO SURPRISES	Radiohead	1998
NO SURRENDER	Deuce	1996
NO SWEAT '98	North And South	1998

SONG TITLE	ARTIST	DATE
NO TELL LOVER	Chicago	1978
NO TENGO DINERO	Los Umbrellos	1998
NO TIME	Guess Who	1969
NO TIME	Lil' Kim featuring Puff Daddy	1996
NO TIME FOR TALK	Christopher Cross	1983
NO TIME TO BE 21	Adverts	1978
NO TIME TO PLAY	Guru featuring Dee C. Lee	1993
NO WAY	Freak Power	1998
NO WAY NO WAY	Vanilla	1997
NO WAY OUT	Jefferson Airplane	1984
NO WOMAN NO CRY	Bob Marley	1975
NO WOMAN NO CRY	Fugees	1996
NO. 1	Nelly	2001
NO. 9 DREAM	John Lennon	1975
THE NOBODIES	Marilyn Manson	2001
NOBODY	Tongue 'n' Cheek	1990
NOBODY	Keith Sweat featuring Athena Cage	1996
NOBODY	Sylvia	1982
NOBODY BETTER	Tina Moore	1998
NOBODY BUT ME	Human Beinz	1967
NOBODY BUT YOU	Gladys Knight & The Pips	1977
NOBODY BUT YOU BABE	Clarence Reid	1969
NOBODY DOES IT BETTER	Carly Simon	1977
NOBODY DOES IT BETTER	Nate Dogg featuring Warren G	1998
NOBODY ELSE	Tyrese	1998

SONG TITLE	ARTIST	DATE
NOBODY I KNOW	Peter & Gordon	1964
NOBODY KNOWS	Tony Rich Project	1995
NOBODY NEEDS YOUR LOVE		
	Gene Pitney	1966
NOBODY SAID IT WAS EASY (LOOKIN' FOR THE LIGHTS)		
	Le Roux	1982
NOBODY TOLD ME	John Lennon	1984
NOBODY WANTS TO BE LONELY		
	Ricky Martin & Christina Aguilera	2001
NOBODY WANTS YOU WHEN YOU'RE DOWN AND OUT		
	Bobby Womack	1973
NOBODY WINS	Elton John	1981
NOBODY'S BUSINESS	H2O featuring Billie	1996
NOBODY'S CHILD	Karen Young	1969
NOBODY'S DARLIN' BUT MINE		
	Frank Ifield	1963
NOBODY'S DIARY	Yazoo	1983
NOBODY'S FOOL	Haircut 100	1982
NOBODY'S FOOL	Jim Reeves	1970
NOBODY'S FOOL	Cinderella	1986
NOBODY'S FOOL	Kenny Loggins	1988
NOBODY'S HERO/TIN SOLDIERS		
	Stiff Little Fingers	1980
NOBODY'S SUPPOSED TO BE HERE		
	Deborah Cox	1998

SONG TITLE	ARTIST	DATE
NOCTURNE	T99	1991
NOLIA CLAP	Juvenile, Wacko & Skip	2004
NOMANSLAND (DAVID'S SONG)		
	DJ Sakin & Friends	1999
NON HO L'ETA PER AMARTI		
	Gigliola Cinquetti	1964
NONE OF YOUR BUSINESS	Salt 'N 'Pepa	1994
NORMAN BATES	Landscape	1981
NORTH COUNTRY BOY	Charlatans	1997
NORTH, SOUTH, EAST, WEST		
	Marvin And Tamara	1999
NORTHERN LIGHTS	Renaissance	1978
NORTHERN LITES	Super Furry Animals	1999
NORTHERN STAR	Melanie C	1999
NOT A DAY GOES BY	Lonestar	2002
NOT A DRY EYE IN THE HOUSE		
	Meat Loaf	1996
NOT A JOB	Elbow	2004
NOT A MINUTE TOO SOON	Vixen	1991
NOT ALONE	Bernard Butler	1998
NOT ANYONE	Black Box	1995
NOT ENOUGH LOVE IN THE WORLD		
	Cher	1996
NOT ENOUGH LOVE IN THE WORLD		
	Don Henley	1985
NOT ENOUGH TIME	INXS	1992

SONG TITLE	ARTIST	DATE
NOT EVEN GONNA TRIP	Honeyz	2000
NOT FADE AWAY	Rolling Stones	1964
NOT FOR YOU	Pearl Jam	1995
NOT GON' CRY	Mary J. Blige	1996
NOT GONNA GET US	t.A.T.u.	2003
NOT IF YOU WERE THE LAST JUNKIE ON EARTH		
	Dandy Warhols	1998
NOT IN LOVE	Enrique featuring Kelis	2004
NOT JUST ANOTHER GIRL	Ivan Neville	1988
NOT ME NOT I	Delta Goodrem	2003
NOT NOW JOHN	Pink Floyd	1983
NOT OVER YET	Grace	1995
NOT OVER YET 99	Planet Perfecto featuring Grace	1999
NOT OVER YOU YET	Diana Ross	1999
NOT SLEEPING AROUND	Ned's Atomic Dustbin	1992
NOT SO MANIC NOW	Dubstar	1996
NOT SUCH AN INNOCENT GIRL		
	Victoria Beckham	2001
NOT THAT KIND	Anastacia	2001
NOT THE GIRL YOU THINK YOU ARE		
	Crowded House	1996
NOT THE LOVIN' KIND	Dino, Desi & Billy	1965
NOT THE ONLY ONE	Bonnie Raitt	1992
(NOT THE) GREATEST RAPPER		
	1000 Clowns	1999
NOT TODAY	Mary J. Blige featuring Eve	2003

SONG TITLE	ARTIST	DATE
NOT TONIGHT	Lil' Kim	1997
NOT TOO LATE FOR LOVE	Beverley Knight	2004
NOT TOO LITTLE – NOT TOO MUCH		
	Chris Sandford	1963
NOT UNTIL THE NEXT TIME		
	Jim Reeves	1965
NOT WHERE IT'S AT	Del Amitri	1997
NOTHIN (THAT COMPARES 2 U)		
	Jacksons	1989
NOTHIN'	N.O.R.E.	2002
NOTHIN' AT ALL	Heart	1986
NOTHIN' BUT A GOOD TIME		
	Poison	1988
NOTHIN' BUT THE CAVI HIT		
	Mack 10 & Tha Dogg Pound	1996
NOTHIN' MY LOVE CAN'T FIX		
	Joey Lawrence	1993
(NOTHIN' SERIOUS) JUST BUGGIN'		
	Whistle	1986
NOTHIN' TO HIDE	Poco	1989
NOTHING	A	2002
NOTHING 'BOUT ME	Sting	1994
NOTHING AS IT SEEMS	Pearl Jam	2000
NOTHING BROKEN BUT MY HEART		
	Celine Dion	1992

SONG TITLE	ARTIST	DATE
NOTHING BUT A HEARTACHE		
	Flirtations	1969
NOTHING BUT HEARTACHES		
	Supremes	1965
NOTHING BUT LOVE	Optimystic	1994
NOTHING BUT YOU	Paul Van Dyk featuring	
	Hemstock	2003
NOTHING CAN DIVIDE US	Jason Donovan	1988
NOTHING CAN STOP ME	Gene Chandler	1965
NOTHING COMES EASY	Sandie Shaw	1966
NOTHING COMPARES 2 U	Sinead O'Connor	1990
NOTHING ELSE MATTERS	Metallica	1992
NOTHING EVER HAPPENS	Del Amitri	1990
NOTHING FROM NOTHING	Billy Preston	1974
NOTHING HAS BEEN PROVED		
	Dusty Springfield	1989
NOTHING HURTS LIKE LOVE		
	Daniel Bedingfield	2004
NOTHING IN THIS WORLD	Keke Wyatt featuring Avant	2002
NOTHING IS REAL BUT THE GIRL		
	Blondie	1999
NOTHING LASTS FOREVER	Echo & The Bunnymen	1997
NOTHING LEFT	Orbital	1999
NOTHING REALLY MATTERS		
	Madonna	1999
NOTHING RHYMED	Gilbert O'Sullivan	1970

SONG TITLE	ARTIST	DATE
NOTHING SACRED – A SONG FOR KIRSTY		
	Russell Watson	2002
NOTHING TO FEAR	Chris Rea	1992
NOTHING TO LOSE	S'Express	1990
NOTHING WITHOUT ME	Manchild	2001
NOTHING'S GONNA CHANGE MY LOVE FOR YOU		
	Glenn Medeiros	1987
NOTHING'S GONNA STOP ME NOW		
	Samantha Fox	1987
NOTHING'S GONNA STOP US NOW		
	Starship	1987
NOTHING'S TOO GOOD FOR MY BABY		
	Stevie Wonder	1966
NOTICE ME	Nikki	1990
NOTORIOUS	Duran Duran	1986
NOTORIOUS	Loverboy	1987
NOTORIOUS B.I.G.	Notorious B.I.G. featuring	
	Puff Daddy & Lil' Kim	2000
NOVEMBER RAIN	Guns N' Roses	1992
NOVEMBER SPAWNED A MONSTER		
	Morrissey	1990
NOVOCAINE FOR THE SOUL		
	Eels	1997
NOW	Def Leppard	2002
NOW AND FOREVER	Richard Marx	1994

SONG TITLE	ARTIST	DATE
NOW I KNOW WHAT MADE OTIS BLUE		
	Paul Young	1993
NOW I'M HERE	Queen	1975
NOW IS THE TIME	Jimmy James & The Vagabonds	1976
NOW IT'S ON	Grandaddy	2003
NOW THAT I'VE FOUND YOU		
	Sean Maguire	1995
NOW THAT THE MUSIC HAS GONE		
	Joe Cocker	1992
NOW THAT WE FOUND LOVE		
	Heavy D. & The Boyz	1991
NOW THAT WE'VE FOUND LOVE		
	Third World	1978
NOW THAT YOU'VE GONE	Mike & The Mechanics	1999
NOW THEY'LL SLEEP	Belly	1995
NOW THOSE DAYS ARE GONE		
	Bucks Fizz	1982
NOW WE ARE FREE	Gladiator featuring Izzy	2004
NOW WE'RE THRU	Poets	1964
NOW YOU'RE GONE	Whitesnake	1990
NOWHERE	Therapy?	1994
NOWHERE MAN	Beatles	1966
NOWHERE TO GO	Melissa Etheridge	1996
NOWHERE TO RUN	Martha & The Vandellas	1965
NU FLOW	Big Brovaz	2002
NU NU	Lidell Townsell	1992

SONG TITLE	ARTIST	DATE
NUCLEAR	Ryan Adams	2002
NUCLEAR DEVICE (THE WIZARD OF AUS)		
	Stranglers	1979
NUCLEAR HOLIDAY	3 Colours Red	1997
NUFF VIBES (EP)	Apache Indian	1993
NUMB	Linkin Park	2003
NUMBER 1	Tweenies	2000
THE NUMBER OF THE BEAST		
	Iron Maiden	1982
NUMBER ONE	EYC	1994
THE NUMBER ONE SONG IN HEAVEN		
	Sparks	1979
NUMBERS/BARRIERS	Soft Cell	1983
NUMERO UNO	Starlight	1989
NURSERY RHYMES	Iceburg Slimm	2000
NUT ROCKER	B. Bumble & The Stingers	1962
NUTBUSH CITY LIMITS	Ike & Tina Turner	1973
NUTHIN' BUT A 'G' THANG/LET ME RIDE		
	Dr. Dre	1994
NUTTIN' BUT LOVE	Heavy D. & The Boyz	1994
O BABY	Siouxsie & The Banshees	1995
O SUPERMAN	Laurie Anderson	1981
O' MY FATHER HAD A RABBIT		
	Ray Moore	1986
O-O-O CHILD	Five Stairsteps	1970
O.K.	Rock Follies	1977

SONG TITLE	ARTIST	DATE
O.K. FRED	Erroll Dunkley	1979
O.P.P.	Naughty By Nature	1991
OB-LA-DI, OB-LA-DA	Bedrocks	1968
OB-LA-DI, OB-LA-DA	Marmalade	1968
OBJECT OF MY DESIRE	Starpoint	1985
OBJECTION (TANGO)	Shakira	2002
OBJECTS IN THE REAR VIEW MIRROR MAY APPEAR		
CLOSER THAN THEY ARE	Meat Loaf	1994
OBLIVION	Terrorvision	1994
OBLIVIOUS	Aztec Camera	1983
OBSCENE PHONE CALLER	Rockwell	1984
OBSESSION	Animotion	1985
OBSESSIONS	Suede	2002
OBVIOUS	Westlife	2004
THE OBVIOUS CHILD	Paul Simon	1990
OBVIOUSLY	McFly	2004
OCEAN AVENUE	Yellowcard	2004
OCEAN DRIVE	Lighthouse Family	1996
OCEAN PIE	Shed Seven	1994
OCEAN SPRAY	Manic Street Preachers	2001
OCTOBER SWIMMER	JJ72	2000
ODE TO BILLIE JOE	Bobbie Gentry	1967
ODE TO BILLIE JOE	King Curtis	1967
ODE TO JOY (FROM BEETHOVEN'S SYMPHONY NO. 9)		
	BBC Concert Orchestra/	
	BBC Symphony Chorus	1996

SONG TITLE	ARTIST	DATE
ODE TO MY FAMILY	Cranberries	1994
OF COURSE I'M LYING	Yello	1989
OFF THE WALL	Wisdome	2000
OFF THE WALL	Michael Jackson	1980
OFFSHORE	Chicane	1996
OFFSHORE '97	Chicane With Power Circle	1997
OFFSHORE BANKING BUSINESS		
	Members	1979
OH BABE, WHAT WOULD YOU SAY		
	Hurricane Smith	1972
OH BABY	Rhianna	2002
OH BABY DON'T YOU WEEP (PART I)		
	James Brown	1964
OH BABY I...	Eternal	1994
OH BOY	Fabulous Baker Boys	1997
OH BOY	Mud	1975
OH BOY	Cam'ron featuring	
	Juelz Santana	2002
OH BOY (THE MOOD I'M IN)		
	Brotherhood Of Man	1977
OH CAROL	Smokie	1978
OH! CAROL (EP)	Neil Sedaka	1972
OH CAROLINA	Shaggy	1993
OH! DARLING	Robin Gibb	1978
OH DIANE	Fleetwood Mac	1982
OH FATHER	Madonna	1989

SONG TITLE	ARTIST	DATE
OH GIRL	Paul Young	1990
OH GIRL	Chi-Lites	1972
OH GIRL	Boy Meets Girl	1985
OH HAPPY DAY	Edwin Hawkins Singers	1969
OH HAPPY DAY	Glen Campbell	1970
OH HOW HAPPY	Shades Of Blue	1966
OH HOW I MISS YOU	Bachelors	1967
OH JULIE	Shakin' Stevens	1982
OH JULIE	Barry Manilow	1982
OH L'AMOUR	Dollar	1987
OH L'AMOUR	Erasure	2003
OH LA DE DA	Staple Singers	1973
OH LA LA LA	2 Eivissa	1997
OH, LORI	Alessi	1977
OH ME OH MY (I'M A FOOL FOR YOU BABY)		
	Lulu	1969
OH MY MY	Ringo Starr	1974
OH NO	Mos Def & Nate Dogg featuring Pharoahe Monch	2001
OH NO	Commodores	1981
OH NO NOT MY BABY	Cher	1992
OH NO NOT MY BABY	Maxine Brown	1964
OH NO, NOT MY BABY	Manfred Mann	1965
OH! NO NOT MY BABY	Rod Stewart	1973
OH PATTI (DON'T FEEL SORRY FOR LOVERBOY)		
	Scritti Politti	1988

SONG TITLE	ARTIST	DATE
(OH) PRETTY WOMAN	Van Halen	1982
OH, PEOPLE	Patti Labelle	1986
OH, PRETTY WOMAN	Roy Orbison	1964
OH SHEILA	Ready For The World	1985
OH, SHERRIE	Steve Perry	1984
OH VERY YOUNG	Cat Stevens	1974
OH WELL	Oh Well	1989
OH WELL	Fleetwood Mac	1969
OH WELL	Rockets	1979
OH WHAT A CIRCUS	David Essex	1978
OH WHAT A NIGHT	Clock	1996
OH WHAT A NIGHT FOR DANCING		
	Barry White	1978
OH WHAT A NITE	Dells	1969
OH WHAT A SHAME	Roy Wood	1975
OH! WHAT A WORLD	Sister Bliss With Colette	1995
OH YEAH	Caprice	1999
OH YEAH	Foxy Brown	2001
OH YEAH	Ash	1996
OH YEAH	Shadows Of Knight	1966
OH YEAH (ON THE RADIO)	Roxy Music	1980
OH YES! YOU'RE BEAUTIFUL		
	Gary Glitter	1974
OH YOU PRETTY THING	Peter Noone	1971
OHIO	Crosby, Stills, Nash & Young	1970

SONG TITLE	ARTIST	DATE
OI!	Platinum 45 featuring More Fire Crew	2002
OK	Big Brovaz	2003
OKAY!	Dave Dee, Dozy, Beaky, Mick & Tich	1967
OL' RAG BLUES	Status Quo	1983
OLD BEFORE I DIE	Robbie Williams	1997
OLD DAYS	Chicago	1975
OLD FASHIONED BOY (YOU'RE THE ONE)	Stallion	1977
AN OLD FASHIONED LOVE SONG	Three Dog Night	1971
THE OLD-FASHIONED WAY (LES PLAISIRS DEMODES)	Charles Aznavour	1973
OLD-FASHIONED LOVE	Commodores	1980
OLD MAN	Neil Young	1972
OLD MAN & ME (WHEN I GET TO HEAVEN)	Hootie & The Blowfish	1996
THE OLD MAN DOWN THE ROAD	John Fogerty	1984
OLD POP IN AN OAK	Rednex	1995
OLD RED EYES IS BACK	Beautiful South	1992
THE OLD RUGGED CROSS	Ethna Campbell	1975
OLD SIAM SIR	Paul McCartney	1979
THE OLD SONGS	Barry Manilow	1981
OLD TIME ROCK & ROLL	Bob Seger	1979

SONG TITLE	ARTIST	DATE
OLDER/I CAN'T MAKE YOU LOVE ME	George Michael	1997
OLDEST SWINGER IN TOWN	Fred Wedlock	1981
OLE OLA (MUHLER BRASILEIRA)	Rod Stewart	1978
THE OLIVE TREE	Judith Durham	1967
OLIVER'S ARMY	Elvis Costello	1979
OLYMPIAN	Gene	1995
AN OLYMPIC RECORD	Barron Knights	1968
THE OMD REMIXES	OMD	1998
OMEN III	Magic Affair	1994
ON	Aphex Twins	1993
ON & ON	Erykah Badu	1997
ON A CAROUSEL	Hollies	1967
ON A DAY LIKE TODAY	Bryan Adams	1998
ON A LITTLE STREET IN SINGAPORE	Manhattan Transfer	1978
ON A NIGHT LIKE THIS	Kylie Minogue	2000
ON A RAGGA TIP	SL2	1992
ON A ROPE	Rocket From The Crypt	1996
ON A SUNDAY AFTERNOON	Lighter Shade Of Brown	1991
ON AND ON	ASWAD	1989
ON AND ON	Longpigs	1996
ON AND ON	Stephen Bishop	1977

SONG TITLE	ARTIST	DATE
ON AND ON	Gladys Knight & The Pips	1974
ON BENDED KNEE	Boyz II Men	1994
ON BROADWAY	George Benson	1978
ON FIRE	T-Connection	1978
ON FIRE	Lloyd Bank$	2004
ON HER MAJESTY'S SECRET SERVICE		
	Propellerheads/David Arnold	1997
ON MOTHER KELLY'S DOORSTEP		
	Danny La Rue	1968
ON MY KNEES	411 featuring Ghostface Killah	2004
ON MY OWN	Patti Labelle &	
	Michael McDonald	1986
ON MY OWN	Peach Union	1997
ON MY RADIO	Selecter	1979
ON MY WAY	Mike Koglin featuring Beatrice	1999
ON MY WAY HOME	Enya	1996
ON MY WORD	Cliff Richard	1965
ON OUR OWN	Bobby Brown	1989
ON POINT	House Of Pain	1994
ON SILENT WINGS	Tina Turner	1996
ON STANDBY	Shed Seven	1996
ON THE BEACH	Cliff Richard	1964
ON THE BEACH	York	2000
ON THE BEACH SUMMER 88		
	Chris Rea	1988
ON THE BIBLE	Deuce	1995

SONG TITLE	ARTIST	DATE
ON THE DARK SIDE	John Cafferty & The Beaver	
	Brown Band	1984
ON THE HORIZON	Melanie C	2003
ON THE INSIDE (THEME FROM 'PRISONER CELL		
BLOCK H')	Lynne Hamilton	1989
ON THE LEVEL	Yomanda	2000
ON THE LOOSE	Saga	1982
ON THE MOVE	Barthezz	2001
ON THE RADIO	Donna Summer	1980
ON THE RADIO	Martine McCutcheon	2001
... ON THE RADIO (REMEMBER THE DAYS)		
	Nelly Furtado	2002
ON THE ROAD AGAIN	Canned Heat	1968
ON THE ROAD AGAIN	Willie Nelson	1980
ON THE ROPES (EP)	Wonder Stuff	1993
ON THE RUN	Big Time Charlie	1999
ON THE RUN	Tillman Uhrmacher	2002
ON THE SHELF	Donny & Marie Osmond	1978
ON THE STREET WHERE YOU LIVE		
	Andy Williams	1964
ON THE WAY DOWN	Ryan Cabrera	2004
ON THE WAY UP	Elisa Fiorillo	1990
ON THE WINGS OF LOVE	Jeffrey Osborne	1982
ON TOP OF THE WORLD	Diva Surprise featuring	
	Georgia Jones	1998
ON YA WAY	Helicopter	1994

SONG TITLE	ARTIST	DATE
ON YOUR OWN	Verve	1995
ON YOUR OWN	Blur	1997
ONCE AROUND THE BLOCK	Badly Drawn Boy	2000
ONCE AROUND THE SUN	Caprice	2001
ONCE BITTEN TWICE SHY	Ian Hunter	1975
ONCE BITTEN TWICE SHY	Vesta Williams	1986
ONCE BITTEN TWICE SHY	Great White	1989
ONCE IN A LIFETIME	Talking Heads	1981
ONCE MORE	Orb	2001
ONCE UPON A LONG AGO	Paul McCartney	1987
ONCE UPON A TIME	Marvin Gaye & Mary Wells	1964
ONCE UPON A TIME/NOT RESPONSIBLE		
	Tom Jones	1966
ONCE YOU GET STARTED	Rufus featuring Chaka Khan	1975
ONCE YOU UNDERSTAND	Think	1971
ONCE YOU'VE TASTED LOVE		
	Take That	1992
ONE	Mica Paris	1995
ONE	Busta Rhymes featuring Erykah Badu	1998
ONE	Metallica	1989
ONE	U2	1992
ONE	Bee Gees	1989
ONE	Three Dog Night	1969
ONE (EP)	Mansun	1996
THE ONE	Backstreet Boys	2000

SONG TITLE	ARTIST	DATE
THE ONE	Elton John	1992
THE ONE	Dee Dee	2003
ONE & ONE	Robert Miles featuring Maria Nayler	1996
ONE AND ONE IS ONE	Medicine Head	1973
ONE AND ONLY MAN	Steve Winwood	1990
THE ONE AND ONLY	Chesney Hawkes	1991
THE ONE AND ONLY	Gladys Knight & The Pips	1978
ONE BAD APPLE	Osmonds	1971
ONE BETTER DAY	Madness	1984
ONE BETTER WORLD	ABC	1989
ONE BIG FAMILY EP	Embrace	1997
ONE BROKEN HEART FOR SALE		
	Elvis Presley	1963
ONE BY ONE	Cher	1996
ONE CALL AWAY	Chingy featuring J. Weav	2004
ONE COOL REMOVE	Shawn Colvin with Mary Chapin Carpenter	1995
ONE DANCE WON'T DO	Audrey Hall	1986
ONE DAY AT A TIME	Lena Martell	1979
ONE DAY AT A TIME	Marilyn Sellars	1974
ONE DAY I'LL FLY AWAY	Randy Crawford	1980
ONE DAY IN YOUR LIFE	Michael Jackson	1981
ONE DAY IN YOUR LIFE	Anastacia	2002
ONE DRINK TOO MANY	Sailor	1977
ONE DYIN' AND A BURYIN'	Roger Miller	1965

SONG TITLE	ARTIST	DATE
ONE FINE DAY	Chiffons	1963
ONE FINE DAY	Jakatta	2003
ONE FINE DAY	Carole King	1980
ONE FINE MORNING	Lighthouse	1971
THE ONE FOR ME	Joe	1994
ONE FOR SORROW	Steps	1998
ONE FOR THE MOCKINGBIRD		
	Cutting Crew	1987
ONE FOR THE MONEY	Horace Brown	1996
ONE FOR YOU, ONE FOR ME		
	Jonathan King	1978
1432 FRANKLIN PIKE CIRCLE HERO		
	Bobby Russell	1968
I (FRIDAY NIGHT)	Dubstar	2000
ONE GOOD REASON	Paul Carrack	1988
ONE GOOD WOMAN	Peter Cetera	1988
ONE GOODBYE IN TEN	Shara Nelson	1993
ONE GREAT THING	Big Country	1986
ONE HAS MY NAME (THE OTHER HAS MY HEART)		
	Barry Young	1965
ONE HEART	Celine Dion	2003
ONE HEARTBEAT	Smokey Robinson	1987
ONE HELL OF A WOMAN	Mac Davis	1974
ONE HIT (TO THE BODY)	Rolling Stones	1986
ONE HORSE TOWN	Thrills	2003
100 MILES AND RUNNIN'	N.W.A.	1990

SONG TITLE	ARTIST	DATE
100%	Sonic Youth	1992
100%	Mary Kiani	1997
100% PURE LOVE	Crystal Waters	1994
138 TREK	DJ Zinc	2000
ONE HUNDRED WAYS	Quincy Jones featuring	
	James Ingram	1981
100 YEARS	Five For Fighting	2004
THE ONE I GAVE MY HEART TO/HOT LIKE FIRE		
	Aaliyah	1997
THE ONE I LOVE	R.E.M.	1987
ONE IN A MILLION	Romantics	1984
ONE IN A MILLION YOU	Larry Graham	1980
ONE IN TEN	808 State	1992
ONE IN TEN	UB40	1981
ONE INCH ROCK	T. Rex	1968
ONE KISS FOR OLD TIME'S SAKE		
	Ronnie Dove	1965
ONE KISS FROM HEAVEN	Louise	1996
ONE LAST BREATH	Creed	2002
ONE LAST CRY	Brian McKnight	1993
ONE LAST KISS	J. Geils Band	1978
ONE LAST LOVE SONG	Beautiful South	1994
ONE LESS BELL TO ANSWER		
	5th Dimension	1970
ONE LESS SET OF FOOTPRINTS		
	Jim Croce	1973

SONG TITLE	ARTIST	DATE
ONE LONELY NIGHT	REO Speedwagon	1985
ONE LOVE	Stone Roses	1990
ONE LOVE	Prodigy	1993
ONE LOVE	Blue	2002
ONE LOVE/PEOPLE GET READY		
	Bob Marley & The Wailers	1984
ONE LOVE IN A LIFETIME	Diana Ross	1976
ONE LOVE IN MY LIFETIME		
	Innocence	1992
ONE MAN	Chanelle	1989
ONE MAN BAND	Leo Sayer	1974
ONE MAN BAND	Three Dog Night	1970
ONE MAN BAND (PLAYS ALL ALONE)		
	Ronnie Dyson	1973
ONE MAN IN MY HEART	Human League	1995
ONE MAN WOMAN	Sheena Easton	1980
ONE MAN WOMAN/ONE WOMAN MAN		
	Paul Anka/Odia Coates	1974
ONE MINUTE MAN	Missy 'Misdemeanor' Elliott	
	featuring Ludacris	2001
ONE MOMENT IN TIME	Whitney Houston	1988
ONE MONKEY DON'T STOP NO SHOW (PT 1)		
	Honey Cone	1971
ONE MORE CHANCE	Maxi Priest	1993
ONE MORE CHANCE	EYC	1994
ONE MORE CHANCE	One	1997

SONG TITLE	ARTIST	DATE
ONE MORE CHANCE	Madonna	1996
ONE MORE CHANCE	Michael Jackson	2003
ONE MORE CHANCE/STAY WITH ME		
	Notorious B.I.G.	1995
ONE MORE DANCE	Esther & Abi Ofarim	1968
ONE MORE DAY	Diamond Rio	2001
ONE MORE HEARTACHE	Marvin Gaye	1966
ONE MORE NIGHT	Phil Collins	1985
ONE MORE TIME	Daft Punk	2000
ONE MORE TIME	Ray Charles Singers	1964
ONE MORE TIME	Real McCoy	1997
ONE MORE TRY	George Michael	1988
ONE MORE TRY	Divine	1999
ONE MORE TRY	Timmy T	1990
ONE NATION UNDER A GROOVE (PT 1)		
	Funkadelic	1978
ONE NIGHT	Mud	1975
ONE NIGHT IN BANGKOK	Murray Head	1985
ONE NIGHT IN HEAVEN	M People	1993
ONE NIGHT LOVE AFFAIR	Bryan Adams	1985
ONE NIGHT STAND	Aloof	1996
ONE NIGHT STAND	Let Loose	1995
ONE NIGHT STAND	Mis-Teeq	2001
ONE NIGHT STAND	J-Shin featuring Latocha Scott	1999
10538 OVERTURE	Electric Light Orchestra	1972

SONG TITLE	ARTIST	DATE
ONE OF A KIND (LOVE AFFAIR)		
	Spinners	1973
ONE OF THE LIVING	Tina Turner	1985
ONE OF THESE NIGHTS	Eagles	1975
ONE OF THOSE NIGHTS	Bucks Fizz	1981
ONE OF US	ABBA	1981
ONE OF US	Joan Osborne	1995
ONE ON ONE	Daryl Hall & John Oates	1983
ONE PERFECT SUNRISE	Orbital	2004
ONE PIECE AT A TIME	Johnny Cash	1976
ONE REASON WHY	Craig McLachlan	1992
ONE ROAD	Love Affair	1969
ONE RULE FOR YOU	After The Fire	1979
ONE SHINING MOMENT	Diana Ross	1992
ONE SMALL DAY	Ultravox	1984
ONE STEP AWAY	Tavares	1977
ONE STEP BEYOND...	Madness	1979
ONE STEP CLOSER	Linkin Park	2001
ONE STEP CLOSER	S Club Juniors	2002
ONE STEP CLOSER	Doobie Brothers	1980
ONE STEP CLOSER TO YOU		
	Gavin Christopher	1986
ONE STEP FURTHER	Bardo	1982
ONE STEP OUT OF TIME	Michael Ball	1992
ONE STEP TOO FAR	Faithless featuring Dido	2002
ONE STEP UP	Bruce Springsteen	1988

SONG TITLE	ARTIST	DATE
ONE SWEET DAY	Mariah Carey & Boyz II Men	1995
THE ONE THAT YOU LOVE	Air Supply	1981
ONE THING	Finger Eleven	2004
THE ONE THING	INXS	1983
ONE THING LEADS TO ANOTHER		
	Fixx	1983
ONE TIN SOLDIER	Coven	1971
ONE TIN SOLDIER	Original Caste	1969
ONE TO ANOTHER	Charlatans	1996
ONE TOKE OVER THE LINE		
	Brewer And Shipley	1971
ONE TRICK PONY	Paul Simon	1980
1-2-3	Gloria Estefan & The Miami Sound Machine	1988
1-2-3	Len Barry	1965
ONE, TWO, THREE	Dina Carroll	1998
ONE, TWO, THREE O'LEARY	Des O'Connor	1968
1,2,3, RED LIGHT	1910 Fruitgum Co.	1968
1-2-3-4 GET WITH THE WICKED		
	Richard Blackwood featuring Deetah	2000
1, 2, 3, 4 (SUMPIN' NEW)	Coolio	1996
ONE VISION	Queen	1985
ONE VOICE	Bill Tarmey	1993
ONE VOICE	Billy Gilman	2000
ONE WAY	Levellers	1999

SONG TITLE	ARTIST	DATE
ONE WAY LOVE	Cliff Bennett & The Rebel Rousers	1964
ONE WAY OR ANOTHER	Blondie	1979
ONE WAY TICKET	Eruption	1979
ONE WEEK	Barenaked Ladies	1998
ONE WILD NIGHT	Bon Jovi	2001
ONE WISH	Shystie	2004
ONE WOMAN	Jade	1993
THE ONE YOU LOVE	Glenn Frey	1982
ONION SONG	Marvin Gaye & Tammi Terrell	1969
ONLY	Anthrax	1993
ONLY A LONELY HEART SEES	Felix Cavaliere	1980
ONLY CRYING	Keith Marshall	1981
ONLY FOOLS (NEVER FALL IN LOVE)	Sonia	1991
ONLY FOR A WHILE	Toploader	2001
ONLY FOR LOVE	Limahl	1983
ONLY GOD KNOWS WHY	Kid Rock	2000
ONLY HAPPY WHEN IT RAINS	Garbage	1995
ONLY HUMAN	Dina Carroll	1996
ONLY IN AMERICA	Brooks & Dunn	2001
ONLY IN MY DREAMS	Debbie Gibson	1987

SONG TITLE	ARTIST	DATE
THE ONLY LIVING BOY IN NEW CROSS	Carter The Unstoppable Sex Machine	1992
ONLY LOVE	Nana Mouskouri	1986
ONLY LOVE CAN BREAK YOUR HEART	Neil Young	1970
ONLY LOVE CAN BREAK YOUR HEART/FILTHY	Saint Etienne	1991
ONLY LOVE IS REAL	Carole King	1976
ONLY LOVE REMAINS	Paul McCartney	1986
ONLY ME	Hyperlogic	1995
ONLY ONE	Peter Andre	1996
THE ONLY ONE I KNOW	Charlatans	1990
ONLY ONE ROAD	Celine Dion	1995
THE ONLY ONE	Gun	1995
THE ONLY ONE	Thunder	1998
THE ONLY ONE	Transvision Vamp	1989
ONLY ONE WOMAN	Marbles	1968
THE ONLY RHYME THAT BITES	MC Tunes vs 808 State	1990
ONLY SIXTEEN	Dr. Hook	1976
ONLY TENDER LOVE	Deacon Blue	1993
ONLY THE GOOD DIE YOUNG	Billy Joel	1978
ONLY THE HEARTACHES	Houston Wells & The Marksmen	1963
ONLY THE LONELY	T'Pau	1989

SONG TITLE	ARTIST	DATE
ONLY THE LONELY	Motels	1982
ONLY THE LOOT CAN MAKE ME HAPPY/WHEN A WOMAN'S FED UP/I CAN'T SLEEP	R. Kelly	2000
ONLY THE STRONG SURVIVE	Billy Paul	1977
ONLY THE STRONG SURVIVE	Jerry Butler	1969
ONLY THE STRONGEST WILL SURVIVE	Hurricane #1	1998
ONLY THE YOUNG	Journey	1985
THE ONLY THING THAT LOOKS GOOD ON ME IS YOU	Bryan Adams	1996
ONLY TIME	Enya	2001
ONLY TIME WILL TELL	Asia	1982
ONLY TIME WILL TELL	Nelson	1991
ONLY TO BE WITH YOU	Roachford	1994
ONLY WANNA BE WITH YOU	Hootie & The Blowfish	1995
THE ONLY WAY IS UP	Yazz & The Plastic Population	1988
THE ONLY WAY OUT	Cliff Richard	1982
ONLY WHEN I LOSE MYSELF	Depeche Mode	1998
ONLY WHEN YOU LEAVE	Spandau Ballet	1984
ONLY WOMEN	Alice Cooper	1975
ONLY WOMEN BLEED	Julie Covington	1977

SONG TITLE	ARTIST	DATE
ONLY YESTERDAY	Carpenters	1975
ONLY YOU	Portishead	1998
ONLY YOU	Yazoo	1982
ONLY YOU	Jeff Collins	1972
ONLY YOU	Flying Pickets	1983
ONLY YOU	Praise	1991
ONLY YOU	Ringo Starr	1974
ONLY YOU	112 featuring The Notorious B.I.G.	1996
ONLY YOU (AND YOU ALONE)	Mark Wynter	1964
ONLY YOU (AND YOU ALONE)	Child	1979
ONLY YOU CAN	Fox	1975
ONLY YOU KNOW & I KNOW	Delaney & Bonnie	1971
ONLY YOUR LOVE	Bananarama	1990
OO WEE BABY, I LOVE YOU	Fred Hughes	1965
007	Musical Youth	1983
007 (SHANTY TOWN)	Desmond Dekker & The Aces	1967
OOCHIE COOHIE	M.C. Brains	1992
OOCHIE WALLY	QB Finest featuring Nas & Bravehearts	2001
THE OOGUM BOOGUM SONG	Brenton Wood	1967

SONG TITLE	ARTIST	DATE
OOH AAH (G-SPOT)	Wayne Marshall	1994
OOH AAH... JUST A LITTLE BIT	Gina G	1996
OOH BABY	Gilbert O'Sullivan	1973
OOH BABY BABY	Miracles	1965
OOH BABY BABY	Linda Ronstadt	1978
OOH CHILD	Dino	1993
OOH I DO	Lynsey De Paul	1974
OOH LA LA	Coolio	1997
OOH LA LA	Rod Stewart	1998
OOH LA LA	Wiseguys	1999
OOH LA LA (I CAN'T GET OVER YOU)	Perfect Gentlemen	1990
OOH LA LA LA (LET'S GO DANCING)	Kool & The Gang	1982
OOH OOH SONG	Pat Benatar	1985
OOH STICK YOU!	Daphne & Celeste	2000
OOH TO BE AH	Kajagoogoo	1983
OOH WEE	Mark Ronson featuring Ghostface Killah & Nate Dogg	2003
OOH!	Mary J. Blige	2003
OOH! AAH! CANTONA	1300 Drums featuring Unjustified Ancients Of Mu	1996
OOH! WHAT A LIFE	Gibson Brothers	1979
OOH-AH-AA- (I FEEL IT)	EYC	1995

SONG TITLE	ARTIST	DATE
OOH-WAKKA-DOO-WAKKA-DAY	Gilbert O'Sullivan	1972
OOOH	De La Soul featuring Redman	2000
OOPS (OH MY)	Tweet	2002
OOPS UP	Snap!	1990
OOPS UPSIDE YOUR HEAD	Gap Band	1980
OOPS UPSIDE YOUR HEAD	DJ Casper featuring The Gap Band	2004
OOPS!... I DID IT AGAIN	Britney Spears	2000
OPAL MANTRA	Therapy?	1993
OPEN ARMS	Mariah Carey	1996
OPEN ARMS	Tina Turner	2004
OPEN ARMS	Journey	1982
AN OPEN LETTER TO MY TEENAGE SON	Victor Lundberg	1967
OPEN ROAD	Gary Barlow	1997
OPEN ROAD	Bryan Adams	2004
OPEN SESAME	Leila K	1993
OPEN THE DOOR TO YOUR HEART	Darrell Banks	1966
OPEN UP	Mungo Jerry	1972
OPEN UP	Leftfield Lydon	1993
OPEN YOUR HEART	Human League	1981
OPEN YOUR HEART	Madonna	1986
OPEN YOUR HEART	M People	1995
OPEN YOUR MIND	U.S.U.R.A.	1993

SONG TITLE	ARTIST	DATE
OPEN YOUR MIND 97	U.S.U.R.A.	1997
THE OPERA SONG (BRAVE NEW WORLD)	Jurgen Vries featuring CMC	2003
OPERATION BLADE (BASS IN THE PLACE)	Public Domain	2000
OPERATOR	Manhattan Transfer	1975
OPERATOR	Midnight Star	1984
OPERATOR (THAT'S NOT THE WAY IT FEELS)	Jim Croce	1972
OPPORTUNITIES (LET'S MAKE LOTS OF MONEY)	Pet Shop Boys	1986
OPPOSITES ATTRACT	Paula Abdul	1990
OPTIMISTIC	Sounds Of Blackness	1992
OPUS 17 (DON'T YOU WORRY 'BOUT ME)	Four Seasons	1966
OPUS 40	Mercury Rev	1999
ORANGE CRUSH	R.E.M.	1989
ORCHARD ROAD	Leo Sayer	1983
ORDINARY DAY	Curiosity Killed The Cat	1987
ORDINARY DAY	Vanessa Carlton	2002
ORDINARY LIFE	Chad Brock	1999
ORDINARY WORLD	Aurora featuring Naimee Coleman	2000
ORDINARY WORLD	Duran Duran	1993
ORIGINAL	Leftfield featuring Toni Halliday	1995
ORIGINAL BIRD DANCE	Electronicas	1981

SONG TITLE	ARTIST	DATE
ORIGINAL NUTTAH	UK Apachi With Shy FX	1994
ORIGINAL PRANKSTER	Offspring	2000
ORIGINAL SIN	Elton John	2002
ORINOCO FLOW (SAIL AWAY)	Enya	1989
ORPHEUS	Ash	2004
ORVILLE'S SONG	Keith Harris & Orville	1982
OSSIE'S DREAM (SPURS ARE ON THEIR WAY TO WEMBLEY)	Tottenham Hotspur F.A. Cup Final Squad	1981
THE OTHER GUY	Little River Band	1982
THE OTHER MAN'S GRASS IS ALWAYS GREENER	Petula Clark	1967
THE OTHER SIDE OF LOVE	Yazoo	1982
THE OTHER SIDE	David Gray	2002
THE OTHER SIDE	Aerosmith	1990
THE OTHER WOMAN	Ray Parker Jr.	1982
OTHERSIDE	Red Hot Chili Peppers	2000
'03 BONNIE & CLYDE	Jay-Z featuring Beyonce Knowles	2003
OUIJA BOARD, OUIJA BOARD	Morrissey	1989
OUR DAY WILL COME	Ruby & The Romantics	1963
OUR DAY WILL COME	Frankie Valli	1975
OUR FRANK	Morrissey	1991
OUR HOUSE	Madness	1983
OUR HOUSE	Crosby, Stills, Nash & Young	1970

SONG TITLE	ARTIST	DATE
OUR LAST SONG TOGETHER		
	Neil Sedaka	1973
OUR LIPS ARE SEALED	Fun Boy Three	1983
OUR LIPS ARE SEALED	Go-Go's	1981
OUR LIVES	Calling	2004
OUR LOVE	Natalie Cole	1978
(OUR LOVE) DON'T THROW IT ALL AWAY		
	Andy Gibb	1978
OUR RADIO ROCKS	PJ And Duncan	1995
OUR WORLD	Blue Mink	1970
OUT & ABOUT	Tommy Boyce & Bobby Hart	1967
OUT DEMONS OUT	Edgar Broughton Band	1970
OUT HERE ON MY OWN	Irene Cara	1980
OUT IN THE COUNTRY	Three Dog Night	1970
OUT IN THE FIELDS	Gary Moore & Phil Lynott	1985
OUT OF CONTROL	Chemical Brothers	1999
OUT OF CONTROL (BACK FOR MORE)		
	Darude	2001
OUT OF MY HEAD	Marradona	1994
OUT OF MY HEAD	Fastball	1999
OUT OF MY HEART	BBmak	2002
OUT OF MY MIND	Duran Duran	1997
OUT OF MY MIND	Johnny Tillotson	1963
OUT OF REACH	Gabrielle	2001
OUT OF REACH	Primitives	1988
OUT OF SIGHT	James Brown	1964

SONG TITLE	ARTIST	DATE
OUT OF SIGHT OUT OF MIND		
	Models	1986
OUT OF SPACE/RUFF IN THE JUNGLE		
	Prodigy	1992
OUT OF TEARS	Rolling Stones	1994
OUT OF THE BLUE	Debbie Gibson	1988
OUT OF THE BLUE	System F	1999
OUT OF THE QUESTION	Gilbert O'Sullivan	1973
OUT OF THE SILENT PLANET		
	Iron Maiden	2000
OUT OF THE SINKING	Paul Weller	1996
OUT OF TIME	Chris Farlowe	1966
OUT OF TIME	Blur	2003
OUT OF TOUCH	Daryl Hall & John Oates	1984
OUT OF WORK	Gary (US) Bonds	1982
OUT OF YOUR MIND	True Steppers & Dane Bowers	
	featuring Victoria Beckham	2000
OUT WITH HER	Blow Monkeys	1987
OUTA-SPACE	Billy Preston	1972
OUTERSPACE GIRL	Beloved	1993
OUTLAW	Olive	1997
OUTRAGEOUS	Stix 'n' Stoned	1996
OUTSIDE	Staind	2001
OUTSIDE	George Michael	1998
OUTSIDE WOMAN	Bloodstone	1974
OUTSTANDING	Kenny Thomas	1991

SONG TITLE	ARTIST	DATE
OUTTATHAWAY	Vines	2002
OVER	Portishead	1997
OVER & OVER	Plux featuring Georgia Jones	1996
OVER AND OVER	Puff Johnson	1997
OVER AND OVER	James Boys	1973
OVER AND OVER	Shalamar	1983
OVER AND OVER	Dave Clark Five	1965
OVER AND OVER	Nelly featuring Tim McGraw	2004
OVER MY HEAD	Lit	2000
OVER MY HEAD	Fleetwood Mac	1975
OVER MY SHOULDER	Mike & The Mechanics	1995
OVER RISING	Charlatans	1991
OVER THE EDGE	Almighty	1993
OVER THE HILLS AND FAR AWAY	Gary Moore	1986
OVER THE RAINBOW/YOU BELONG TO ME (MEDLEY)	Matchbox	1980
OVER THE RIVER	Bitty McLean	1995
OVER THERE (I DON'T CARE)	House Of Pain	1995
OVER TO YOU JOHN (HERE WE GO...)	Jive Bunny & The Mastermixers	1991
OVER UNDER SIDEWAYS DOWN	Yardbirds	1966
OVER YOU	Freddie & The Dreamers	1964
OVER YOU	Roxy Music	1980

SONG TITLE	ARTIST	DATE
OVER YOU	Justin	1999
OVER YOU	Gary Puckett & The Union Gap	1968
OVERCOME	Tricky	1995
OVERDRIVE	DJ Sandy vs Housetrap	2000
OVERJOYED	Stevie Wonder	1986
OVERKILL	Men At Work	1983
OVERKILL	Motorhead	1979
OVERLOAD	Sugababes	2000
OVERLOAD	Voodoo & Serano	2003
OVERNIGHT CELEBRITY	Twista	2004
OVERNIGHT SENSATION (HIT RECORD)	Raspberries	1974
OVERPROTECTED	Britney Spears	2002
OVERRATED	Siobhan Donaghy	2003
OVERTURE FROM TOMMY	Assembled Multitude	1970
OWNER OF A LONELY HEART	Yes	1983
OXBOW LAKES	Orb	1995
OXYGEN	JJ72	2000
OXYGENE 10	Jean Michel Jarre	1997
OXYGENE 8	Jean Michel Jarre	1997
OXYGENE PART IV	Jean Michel Jarre	1977
OYE	Gloria Estefan	1998
OYE COMO VA	Tito Puente Jr & The Latin Rhythm	1996
OYE COMO VA	Santana	1971

SONG TITLE	ARTIST	DATE
OYE MI CANTO	N.O.R.E. featuring Daddy Yankee, Nina Sky	2004
OYE MI CANTO (HEAR MY VOICE)	Gloria Estefan	1989
P.A.S.S.I.O.N.	Rythm Syndicate	1991
P.E. 2000	Puff Daddy featuring Hurricane G	1999
P.I.M.P.	50 Cent	2003
P.OWER OF A.MERICAN N.ATIVES	Dance 2 Trance	1993
P.S. I LOVE YOU	Beatles	1964
P.Y.T. (PRETTY YOUNG THING)	Michael Jackson	1983
PAC-MAN FEVER	Buckner & Garcia	1982
PACIFIC	808 State	1989
PACIFIC/CUBIK	808 State	1998
PACIFIC MELODY	Airscape	1997
PAGAN POETRY	Bjork	2001
PAID IN FULL	Eric B. & Rakim	1987
PAID MY DUES	Anastacia	2001
PAIN	Jimmy Eat World	2004
THE PAIN INSIDE	Cosmic Rough Riders	2001
PAIN KILLER	Turin Brakes	2003
PAINT IT BLACK	Rolling Stones	1966
PAINT ME DOWN	Spandau Ballet	1981
PAINTED LADIES	Ian Thomas	1973

SONG TITLE	ARTIST	DATE
PAINTER MAN	Creation	1966
PAINTER MAN	Boney M	1979
PAISLEY PARK	Prince & The Revolution	1985
PALE MOVIE	Saint Etienne	1994
PALE SHELTER	Tears For Fears	1983
PALOMA BLANCA	George Baker Selection	1975
PAMELA	Toto	1988
PAMELA, PAMELA	Wayne Fontana	1966
PANAMA	Van Halen	1984
THE PANDEMONIUM SINGLE	Killing Joke	1994
PANDORA'S BOX	Procol Harum	1975
PANDORA'S BOX	OMD	1991
PANDORA'S GOLDEN HEEBIE JEEBIES	Association	1966
PANDORA'S KISS	Louise	2003
PANIC	Smiths	1986
PANINARO '95	Pet Shop Boys	1995
PAPA DON'T PREACH	Madonna	1986
PAPA DON'T PREACH	Kelly Osbourne	2002
PAPA DON'T TAKE NO MESS (PART 1)	James Brown	1974
PAPA OOM MOW MOW	Gary Glitter	1975
PAPA OOM MOW MOW	Sharonettes	1975
PAPA WAS A ROLLIN' STONE	Temptations	1972

SONG TITLE	ARTIST	DATE
PAPA WAS A ROLLING STONE		
	Was (Not Was)	1990
PAPA'S GOT A BRAND NEW BAG		
	James Brown	1965
PAPA'S GOT A BRAND NEW BAG		
	Otis Redding	1968
PAPA'S GOT A BRAND NEW PIGBAG		
	Pigbag	1982
PAPER CUP	5th Dimension	1967
PAPER DOLL	P.M. Dawn	1992
PAPER IN FIRE	John Cougar Mellencamp	1987
PAPER PLANE	Status Quo	1973
PAPER ROSES	Marie Osmond	1973
PAPER SUN	Traffic	1967
PAPER TIGER	Sue Thompson	1965
PAPERBACK WRITER	Beatles	1966
PAPERCUT	Linkin Park	2001
PAPERLATE	Genesis	1982
PAPUA NEW GUINEA	Future Sound Of London	1992
PARADISE	Frank Ifield	1965
PARADISE	Black	1988
PARADISE	Kaci	2001
PARADISE	Sade	1988
PARADISE	LL Cool J featuring Amerie	2002
PARADISE BY THE DASHBOARD LIGHT		
	Meat Loaf	1978

SONG TITLE	ARTIST	DATE
PARADISE CITY	N-Trance	1998
PARADISE CITY	Guns N' Roses	1989
PARADISE LOST	Herd	1967
PARANOID	Black Sabbath	1970
PARANOID ANDROID	Radiohead	1997
PARANOIMIA	Art Of Noise	1986
PARENTS JUST DON'T UNDERSTAND		
	D.J. Jazzy Jeff & The Fresh Prince	1988
PARISIENNE WALKWAYS	Gary Moore	1979
PARKLIFE	Blur	1994
PART OF THE PLAN	Dan Fogelberg	1975
PART OF THE PROCESS	Morcheeba	1998
PART OF THE UNION	Strawbs	1973
PART TIME LOVE	Elton John	1978
PART TIME LOVE	Gladys Knight & The Pips	1975
PART TIME LOVER	Stevie Wonder	1985
THE PARTY	Kraze	1988
PARTY ALL NIGHT	Mytown	1999
PARTY ALL THE TIME	Eddie Murphy	1985
THE PARTY CONTINUES	JD featuring Da Brat	1998
PARTY FEARS TWO	Associates	1982
PARTY HARD	Pulp	1998
PARTY HARD	Andrew W.K.	2001
PARTY IN PARIS	UK Subs	1980
PARTY LIGHTS	Gap Band	1980

SONG TITLE	ARTIST	DATE
PARTY PEOPLE... FRIDAY NIGHT		
	911	1997
PARTY UP (UP IN HERE)	DMX	2000
PARTY UP THE WORLD	D:ream	1995
THE PARTY'S OVER (HOPELESSLY IN LOVE)		
	Journey	1981
PARTYMAN	Prince	1989
PASILDA	Afro Medusa	2000
PASS & MOVE (IT'S THE LIVERPOOL GROOVE)		
	Liverpool FC & The Boot	
	Room Boys	1996
PASS IT ON	Bitty McLean	1993
PASS IT ON	Coral	2003
PASS THAT DUTCH	Missy Elliott	2003
PASS THE COURVOISIER (PART II)		
	Busta Rhymes featuring	
	P. Diddy & Pharrell	2002
PASS THE DUTCHIE	Musical Youth	1982
PASS THE VIBES	Definition Of Sound	1995
THE PASSENGER	Iggy Pop	1998
PASSENGERS	Elton John	1984
PASSING STRANGERS	Joe Longthorne & Liz Dawn	1994
PASSING STRANGERS	Billy Eckstine & Sarah Vaughan	1969
PASSION	Gat Decor	1996
PASSION	Jon Of The Pleased Wimmin	1995
PASSION	Amen! UK	1997

SONG TITLE	ARTIST	DATE
PASSION	Rod Stewart	1980
PASSIONATE FRIEND	Teardrop Explodes	1981
PAST THE MISSION	Tori Amos	1994
PATA PATA	Miriam Makeba	1967
PATCHES	Clarence Carter	1970
PATHWAY TO THE MOON	MN8	1996
PATIENCE	Guns N' Roses	1989
PATIENCE OF ANGELS	Eddi Reader	1994
PAY TO THE PIPER	Chairmen Of The Board	1970
PAY YOU BACK WITH INTEREST		
	Hollies	1967
THE PAYBACK (PART I)	James Brown	1974
PAYING THE COST TO BE BOSS		
	B.B. King	1968
PAYING THE PRICE OF LOVE		
	Bee Gees	1993
PEACE	Sabrina Johnson	1991
PEACE IN OUR TIME	Big Country	1989
PEACE IN OUR TIME	Cliff Richard	1993
PEACE IN OUR TIME	Eddie Money	1989
PEACE OF MIND	Boston	1977
PEACE ON EARTH/LITTLE DRUMMER BOY		
	David Bowie & Bing Crosby	1982
PEACE PIPE	B.T. Express	1975
PEACE TRAIN	Cat Stevens	1971

SONG TITLE	ARTIST	DATE
PEACE WILL COME (ACCORDING TO PLAN)		
	Melanie	1970
PEACEFUL	Georgie Fame	1969
PEACEFUL	Helen Reddy	1973
PEACEFUL EASY FEELING	Eagles	1972
PEACH	Prince	1993
PEACHES	Presidents Of The United States	1996
PEACHES/GO BUDDY GO	Stranglers	1977
PEACHES & CREAM	112	2001
PEACHES 'N' CREAM	Ikettes	1965
PEACOCK SUIT	Paul Weller	1996
PEAKIN'	Bleachin'	2000
PEARL IN THE SHELL	Howard Jones	1984
PEARL RIVER	Three 'N One presents Johnny Shaker featuring Serial D	1999
PEARL'S A SINGER	Elkie Brooks	1977
PEARL'S GIRL	Underworld	1996
PEARLY-DEWDROPS DROPS		
	Cocteau Twins	1984
PEEK-A-BOO	New Vaudeville Band	1967
PEEK-A-BOO	Siouxsie & The Banshees	1988
PEEK-A-BOO	Stylistics	1973
PEG	Steely Dan	1977
PEGGY SUE	Buddy Holly	1957
PENETRATION	Pyramids	1964
PENNIES FROM HEAVEN	Inner City	1992

SONG TITLE	ARTIST	DATE
PENNY ARCADE	Roy Orbison	1969
A PENNY FOR YOUR THOUGHTS		
	Tavares	1982
PENNY LANE	Beatles	1967
PENNY LOVER	Lionel Richie	1984
PEOPLE	Tymes	1968
PEOPLE	Barbra Streisand	1964
PEOPLE ARE PEOPLE	Depeche Mode	1985
PEOPLE ARE STILL HAVING SEX		
	Latour	1991
PEOPLE ARE STRANGE	Echo & The Bunnymen	1988
PEOPLE ARE STRANGE	Doors	1967
PEOPLE EVERYDAY	Arrested Development	1992
PEOPLE GET READY	Impressions	1965
PEOPLE GOT TO BE FREE	Rascals	1968
PEOPLE GOTTA MOVE	Gino Vannelli	1974
PEOPLE HOLD ON	Coldcut featuring Lisa Stansfield	1989
PEOPLE HOLD ON (THE BOOTLEG MIXES)		
	Lisa Stansfield vs The Dirty Rotten Scoundrels	1997
PEOPLE IN LOVE	10cc	1977
PEOPLE LIKE YOU AND PEOPLE LIKE ME		
	Glitter Band	1976
PEOPLE MAKE THE WORLD GO ROUND		
	Stylistics	1972
PEOPLE OF LOVE	Amen! UK	1997

SONG TITLE	ARTIST	DATE
PEOPLE OF THE SOUTH WIND		
	Kansas	1979
PEOPLE OF THE SUN	Rage Against The Machine	1996
PEOPLE SAY	Dixie Cups	1964
PEPPER BOX	Peppers	1974
PER SEMPRE AMORE (FOREVER IN LOVE)		
	Lolly	2000
PER-SO-NAL-LY	Wigan's Ovation	1975
PERFECT	Smashing Pumpkins	1998
PERFECT	Fairground Attraction	1988
PERFECT	Lightning Seeds	1995
PERFECT	PJ And Duncan	1995
PERFECT	Simple Plan	2003
PERFECT 10	Beautiful South	1998
PERFECT BLISS	Bellefire	2001
PERFECT DAY	EMF	1995
PERFECT DAY	Duran Duran	1995
PERFECT DAY	Skin	1996
PERFECT DAY	Various	1997
THE PERFECT DAY	Saints	1977
A PERFECT DAY ELISE	PJ Harvey	1998
PERFECT GENTLEMAN	Wyclef Jean	2001
PERFECT MOMENT	Martine McCutcheon	1999
PERFECT MOTION	Sunscreem	1992
PERFECT PLACE	Voice Of The Beehive	1992
PERFECT SKIN	Lloyd Cole & The Commotions	1984

SONG TITLE	ARTIST	DATE
PERFECT WAY	Scritti Politti	1985
PERFECT WORLD	Huey Lewis & The News	1988
THE PERFECT YEAR	Dina Carroll	1993
PERPETUAL DAWN	Orb	1994
PERRY MASON	Ozzy Osbourne	1995
PERSEVERANCE	Terrorvision	1996
PERSONAL JESUS	Depeche Mode	1989
PERSONAL JESUS	Marilyn Manson	2004
PERSONAL TOUCH	Errol Brown	1987
PERSONALITY	Eugene Wilde	1985
PERSONALLY	Karla Bonoff	1982
A PESSIMIST IS NEVER DISAPPOINTED		
	Theaudience	1998
PETER GUNN	Art Of Noise featuring Duane Eddy	1986
THE PHANTOM OF THE OPERA		
	Sarah Brightman & Steve Harley	1986
PHASED (EP)	All About Eve	1992
PHATT BASS	Warp Brothers vs Aquagen	2000
PHENOMENON	LL Cool J	1997
PHILADELPHIA FREEDOM	Elton John	1975
THE PHOENIX LOVE THEME (SENZA FINE)		
	Brass Ring	1966
PHOREVER PEOPLE	Shamen	1992
PHOTOGRAPH	Ringo Starr	1973
PHOTOGRAPH	Def Leppard	1983

SONG TITLE	ARTIST	DATE
PHOTOGRAPH OF MARY	Trey Lorenz	1993
PHUTURE 2000	Carl Cox	1999
PHYSICAL	Olivia Newton-John	1981
PIANO IN THE DARK	Brenda Russell	1988
PIANO LOCO	DJ Luck & MC Neat	2001
PIANO MAN	Billy Joel	1974
PICCADILLY PALARE	Morrissey	1990
PICK A PART THAT'S NEWS		
	Stereophonics	1999
PICK UP THE PIECES	Average White Band	1974
PICK UP THE PIECES	Hudson-Ford	1973
PICKIN' WILD MOUNTAIN BERRIES		
	Peggy Scott & Jo Jo Benson	1968
PICTURE OF YOU	Boyzone	1997
PICTURE THIS	Blondie	1978
PICTURES OF LILY	Who	1967
PICTURES OF MATCHSTICK MEN		
	Status Quo	1968
PICTURES OF YOU	Cure	1990
PIE JESU	Sarah Brightman & Paul Miles-Kingston	1985
PIECE BY PIECE	Kenny Thomas	1993
PIECE OF MY HEART	Shaggy featuring Marsha	1997
PIECE OF MY HEART	Big Brother & The Holding Company	1968
PIECE OF MY HEART	Tara Kemp	1991

SONG TITLE	ARTIST	DATE
PIECE OF THE ACTION	Bucks Fizz	1981
PIECES OF A DREAM	Incognito	1994
PIECES OF APRIL	Three Dog Night	1972
PIECES OF ICE	Diana Ross	1983
PIECES OF ME	Ashlee Simpson	2004
PIED PIPER	Bob & Marcia	1971
PIED PIPER (THE BEEJE)	Steve Race	1963
THE PIED PIPER	Crispian St. Peters	1966
PILLOW TALK	Sylvia	1973
PILLS & SOAP	Imposter	1983
PILOT OF THE AIRWAVES	Charlie Dore	1980
PIN	The Yeah Yeah Yeahs	2003
PINBALL	Brian Protheroe	1974
PINBALL WIZARD	Elton John	1976
PINBALL WIZARD	Who	1969
PINBALL WIZARD/SEE ME, FEEL ME (MEDLEY)		
	New Seekers	1973
PINCH ME	Barenaked Ladies	2000
PINCUSHION	ZZ Top	1994
PINEAPPLE HEAD	Crowded House	1994
PINK	Aerosmith	1998
PINK CADILLAC	Natalie Cole	1988
PINK HOUSES	John Cougar Mellencamp	1983
THE PINK PANTHER (EP)	Graham Parker	1977
THE PINK PANTHER THEME		
	Henry Mancini	1964

SONG TITLE	ARTIST	DATE
PINK SUNSHINE	Fuzzbox	1989
PINKY BLUE	Altered Images	1982
PIPELINE	Chantays	1963
PIPELINE	Bruce Johnston	1977
PIPES OF PEACE	Paul McCartney	1983
PISSING IN THE WIND	Badly Drawn Boy	2001
PISTOL WHIP	Joshua Ryan	2001
PITCHIN' (IN EVERY DIRECTION)		
	Hi-Gate	2000
A PLACE IN THE SUN	Shadows	1966
A PLACE IN THE SUN	Stevie Wonder	1966
PLACE IN THIS WORLD	Michael W. Smith	1991
THE PLACE WHERE YOU BELONG		
	Shai	1994
PLACE YOUR HANDS	Reef	1996
PLACES THAT BELONG TO YOU		
	Barbra Streisand	1992
PLANET CARAVAN	Pantera	1994
PLANET EARTH	Duran Duran	1981
PLANET LOVE	DJ Quicksilver	1998
PLANET OF SOUND	Pixies	1991
PLANETARY SIT-IN	Julian Cope	1996
THE PLASTIC AGE	Buggles	1980
PLASTIC DREAMS	Jaydee	1997
PLASTIC MAN	Kinks	1969
THE PLASTIC MAN	Temptations	1973

SONG TITLE	ARTIST	DATE
PLAY	Jennifer Lopez	2001
PLAY (EP)	Ride	1990
PLAY DEAD	Bjork & David Arnold	1993
PLAY IT COOL	Super Furry Animals	1997
PLAY ME	Neil Diamond	1972
PLAY ME LIKE YOU PLAY YOUR GUITAR		
	Duane Eddy & The Rebelettes	1975
PLAY SOMETHING SWEET (BRICKYARD BLUES)		
	Three Dog Night	1974
PLAY THAT FUNKY MUSIC	Thunder	1998
PLAY THAT FUNKY MUSIC	Vanilla Ice	1990
PLAY THAT FUNKY MUSIC	Wild Cherry	1976
PLAY THE GAME	Queen	1980
PLAY THIS GAME TONIGHT		
	Kansas	1982
PLAYA HATA	Luniz	1996
PLAYAS GON' PLAY	3LW	2001
PLAYAZ CLUB	Rappin' 4-Tay	1994
PLAYBOY	Gene & Debbe	1968
PLAYED-A-LIVE (THE BONGO SONG)		
	Safri Duo	2001
PLAYER'S ANTHEM	Junior M.A.F.I.A.	1995
PLAYER'S BALL	Outkast	1994
PLAYGROUND	Another Bad Creation	1991
PLAYGROUND IN MY MIND		
	Clint Holmes	1973

SONG TITLE	ARTIST	DATE
PLAYGROUND LOVE	Air	2000
PLAYGROUND TWIST	Siouxsie & The Banshees	1979
PLAYING WITH KNIVES	Bizarre Inc.	1991
PLEASANT VALLEY SUNDAY		
	Monkees	1967
PLEASE	Elton John	1996
PLEASE	U2	1997
PLEASE	Robin Gibb	2003
PLEASE COME HOME FOR CHRISTMAS		
	Eagles	1978
PLEASE COME HOME FOR CHRISTMAS		
	Bon Jovi	1994
PLEASE COME TO BOSTON	Dave Loggins	1974
PLEASE DON'T BE SCARED	Barry Manilow	1989
PLEASE DON'T FALL IN LOVE		
	Cliff Richard	1983
PLEASE DON'T GO	KC & The Sunshine Band	1979
PLEASE DON'T GO	Donald Peers	1968
PLEASE DON'T GO	No Mercy	1997
PLEASE DON'T GO	Immature	1996
PLEASE DON'T GO/GAME BOY		
	KWS	1992
PLEASE DON'T GO GIRL	New Kids On The Block	1988
PLEASE DON'T LEAVE	Lauren Wood	1979
PLEASE DON'T MAKE ME CRY		
	UB40	1983

SONG TITLE	ARTIST	DATE
PLEASE DON'T TURN ME ON		
	Artful Dodger featuring Lifford	2000
PLEASE FORGIVE ME	Bryan Adams	1993
PLEASE FORGIVE ME	David Gray	2000
PLEASE LOVE ME FOREVER		
	Bobby Vinton	1967
PLEASE MR. PLEASE	Olivia Newton-John	1975
PLEASE MR. POSTMAN	Carpenters	1974
PLEASE PLEASE ME	Beatles	1964
PLEASE PLEASE ME	David Cassidy	1974
PLEASE REMEMBER ME	Tim McGraw	1999
PLEASE RETURN YOUR LOVE TO ME		
	Temptations	1968
PLEASE SAVE ME	Sunscreem vs Push	2001
PLEASE STAY	Cryin' Shames	1966
PLEASE STAY	Kylie Minogue	2000
PLEASE TELL HIM I SAID HELLO		
	Dana	1975
PLEASE TELL ME WHY	Dave Clark Five	1966
THE PLEASURE PRINCIPAL	Janet Jackson	1987
PLUG IN BABY	Muse	2001
PLUG IT IN	Basement Jaxx featuring	
	JC Chasez	2004
PLUSH	Stone Temple Pilots	1993
PO PIMP	Do Or Die featuring Twista	1996

SONG TITLE	ARTIST	DATE
PO' FOLKS	Nappy Roots featuring Anthony Hamilton	2002
THE POACHER	Ronnie Lane & Slim Chance	1974
POCKET CALCULATOR	Kraftwerk	1981
POEMS	Nearly God	1996
POETRY MAN	Phoebe Snow	1975
POGUETRY IN MOTION (EP)	Pogues	1986
POING	Rotterdam Termination Source	1992
POINT IT OUT	Smokey Robinson & The Miracles	1969
POINT OF KNOW RETURN	Kansas	1977
POINT OF NO RETURN	Expose	1987
POINT OF NO RETURN	Nu Shooz	1986
POINT OF VIEW	DB Boulevard	2002
POINT OF VIEW (SQUEEZE A LITTLE LOVIN)	Matumbi	1979
POISON	Bell Biv Devoe	1990
POISON	Alice Cooper	1989
POISON	Prodigy	1995
POISON ARROW	ABC	1983
POISON IVY	Paramounts	1964
POISON IVY	Lambrettas	1980
POLICE AND THIEVES	Junior Murvin	1980
POLICE OFFICER	Smiley Culture	1984
POLICEMAN SKANK ... (THE STORY OF MY LIFE)	Audioweb	1998

SONG TITLE	ARTIST	DATE
POLICY OF TRUTH	Depeche Mode	1990
THE POLITICS OF DANCING	Re-Flex	1983
POLK SALAD ANNIE	Elvis Presley	1973
POLK SALAD ANNIE	Tony Joe White	1969
PON DE RIVER, PON DE BANK	Elephant Man	2003
PONY	Ginuwine	1996
POOL HALL RICHARD/I WISH IT WOULD RAIN	Faces	1973
POOR LENO	Royksopp	2002
POOR MAN'S SON	Rockin' Berries	1965
POOR MAN'S SON	Survivor	1981
POOR MISGUIDED FOOL	Starsailor	2002
POOR POOR PITIFUL ME	Linda Ronstadt	1978
POOR SIDE OF TOWN	Johnny Rivers	1966
POP	*NSYNC	2001
POP GO THE WORKERS	Barron Knights	1965
POP GOES MY LOVE	Freeez	1983
POP GOES THE MOVIES (PART 1)	Meco	1982
POP GOES THE WEASEL	3rd Bass	1991
POP GOES THE WORLD	Men Without Hats	1987
POP LIFE	Prince & The Revolution	1985
POP MUZIK	M	1979
POP SINGER	John Cougar Mellencamp	1989

SONG TITLE	ARTIST	DATE
THE POP SINGER'S FEAR OF THE POLLEN COUNT		
	Divine Comedy	1999
POP THAT BOOTY	Marques Houston featuring	
	Jermaine 'JD' Dupri	2004
POP THAT THANG	Isley Brothers	1972
POP YA COLLAR	Usher	2001
POP!ULAR	Darren Hayes	2004
POPCORN	Hot Butter	1972
THE POPCORN	James Brown	1969
POPPA JOE	Sweet	1972
POPSCENE	Blur	1992
POPSICLE	Jan & Dean	1966
PORCELAIN	Moby	2000
PORTRAIT OF MY LOVE	Tokens	1967
PORTSMOUTH	Mike Oldfield	1976
POSITIVELY 4TH STREET	Bob Dylan	1965
POSITIVITY	Suede	2002
POSSE (I NEED YOU ON THE FLOOR)		
	Scooter	2002
POSSESSED	Vegas	1992
POSSESSION	Bad English	1990
POSSESSION OBSESSION	Daryl Hall & John Oates	1985
POSSIBLY MAYBE	Bjork	1996
POST MODERN SLEAZE	Sneaker Pimps	1997
POSTCARD FROM HEAVEN	Lighthouse Family	1999
POUNDING	Doves	2002

SONG TITLE	ARTIST	DATE
POUR SOME SUGAR ON ME		
	Def Leppard	1988
POWER	Nu Colours	1993
THE POWER	Snap!	1990
THE POWER (OF ALL THE LOVE IN THE WORLD)		
	D:ream	1995
THE POWER (OF BHANGRA)		
	Snap vs Motivo	2003
POWER AND THE GLORY	Saxon	1983
POWER OF A WOMAN	Eternal	1995
THE POWER OF GOLD	Dan Fogelberg/Tim Weisberg	1978
THE POWER OF GOODBYE/LITTLE STAR		
	Madonna	1998
POWER OF LOVE	Laura Branigan	1987
POWER OF LOVE	Joe Simon	1972
POWER OF LOVE/DEEE-LITE THEME		
	Deee-Lite	1990
THE POWER OF LOVE	Celine Dion	1993
POWER OF LOVE/LOVE POWER		
	Luther Vandross	1991
THE POWER OF LOVE	Frankie Goes To Hollywood	1984
THE POWER OF LOVE	Jennifer Rush	1985
THE POWER OF LOVE	Huey Lewis & The News	1986
POWER RANGERS	Mighty Morph'n Power Rangers	1994
POWER TO ALL OUR FRIENDS		
	Cliff Richard	1973

SONG TITLE	ARTIST	DATE
POWER TO THE PEOPLE	John Lennon & The Plastic Ono Band	1971
POWER WINDOWS	Billy Falcon	1991
THE POWER ZONE (EP)	Time Frequency	1993
POWERLESS (SAY WHAT YOU WANT)	Nelly Furtado	2003
POWERTRIP	Monster Magnet	1999
PRACTICE WHAT YOU PREACH/LOVE IS THE ICON	Barry White	1995
PRAISE YOU	Fatboy Slim	1999
PRAY	Tina Cousins	1998
PRAY	M.C. Hammer	1990
PRAY	Take That	1993
PRAY	Lasgo	2002
PRAY	Syntax	2003
PRAYER	Disturbed	2002
PRAYER FOR THE DYING	Seal	1994
PRAYIN' FOR DAYLIGHT	Rascal Flatts	2000
PRAYING FOR TIME	George Michael	1990
PREACHER MAN	Bananarama	1991
PRECIOUS	Annie Lennox	1992
PRECIOUS AND FEW	Climax	1972
PRECIOUS HEART	Tall Paul vs INXS	2001
PRECIOUS LOVE	Bob Welch	1979
PRECIOUS PRECIOUS	Jackie Moore	1970
PRECIOUS TIME	Van Morrison	1999

SONG TITLE	ARTIST	DATE
PRECIOUS TO ME	Phil Seymour	1981
PREDICTABLE	Good Charlotte	2004
PREGNANT FOR THE LAST TIME	Morrissey	1991
PRESS	Paul McCartney	1986
PRESSURE	Drizabone	1994
PRESSURE	Billy Joel	1982
PRESSURE POINT	Zutons	2004
PRESSURE US	Sunscreem	1993
PRETEND	Alvin Stardust	1981
PRETEND BEST FRIEND	Terrorvision	1994
PRETEND WE'RE DEAD	L7	1992
PRETENDERS TO THE THRONE	Beautiful South	1995
PRETTIEST EYES	Beautiful South	1994
PRETTY BALLERINA	Left Banke	1967
PRETTY BROWN EYES	Jim Reeves	1968
PRETTY FLAMINGO	Manfred Mann	1966
PRETTY FLY (FOR A WHITE GUY)	Offspring	1999
PRETTY GIRL	Jon B.	1995
PRETTY GIRLS	Melissa Manchester	1979
PRETTY GOOD YEAR	Tori Amos	1994
PRETTY GREEN EYES	Ultrabeat	2003
PRETTY IN PINK	Psychedelic Furs	1986

SONG TITLE	ARTIST	DATE
PRETTY LITTLE ANGEL EYES		
	Showaddywaddy	1978
PRETTY LITTLE BABY	Marvin Gaye	1965
PRETTY NOOSE	Soundgarden	1996
PRETTY PAPER	Roy Orbison	1963
PRETTY THING	Bo Diddley	1963
PRETTY VACANT	Sex Pistols	1977
PRICE OF LOVE	Bad English	1989
THE PRICE OF LOVE	Everly Brothers	1965
PRICE TO PLAY	Staind	2003
PRIDE (IN THE NAME OF LOVE)		
	Clivilles & Cole	1992
PRIDE (IN THE NAME OF LOVE)		
	U2	1984
PRIMAL SCREAM	Motley Crue	1991
PRIMARY	Cure	1983
PRIME MOVER	Zodiac Mindwarp	1987
PRIME TIME	Tubes	1979
PRIME TIME	Alan Parsons	1984
A PRINCE AMONGST ISLANDS (EP)		
	Capercaillie	1992
PRINCE CHARMING	Adam & The Ants	1981
PRINCE IGOR	Warren G featuring Sissel	1998
THE PRINCE	Madness	1979
PRINCES OF THE NIGHT	Blast featuring VDC	1994
PRINCESS IN RAGS	Gene Pitney	1965

SONG TITLE	ARTIST	DATE
PRINCIPAL'S OFFICE	Young M.C.	1989
THE PRISONER	Howard Jones	1989
A PRISONER OF THE PAST	Prefab Sprout	1997
PRISONER OF YOUR LOVE	Player	1978
PRIVATE DANCER	Tina Turner	1985
PRIVATE EMOTION	Ricky Martin featuring Meja	2000
PRIVATE EYES	Daryl Hall & John Oates	1981
PRIVATE INVESTIGATIONS	Dire Straits	1982
PRIVATE LIFE	Grace Jones	1980
PRIVATE NUMBER	Judy Clay & William Bell	1968
PRIVATE NUMBER	911	1999
PROBABLY A ROBBERY	Renegade Soundwave	1990
PROCESSED BEATS	Kasabian	2004
PROCESSION/EVERYTHING'S GONE GREEN		
	New Order	1981
PRODIGAL SON	Steel Pulse	1978
PRODUCT OF THE WORKING CLASS		
	Little Angels	1991
PROFESSIONAL WIDOW (IT'S GOT TO BE BIG)		
	Tori Amos	1997
PROFIT IN PEACE	Ocean Colour Scene	1999
PROMISE	Delirious?	1997
PROMISE	Jagged Edge	2000
THE PROMISE	Essence	1998
THE PROMISE	Arcadia	1986
THE PROMISE	When In Rome	1988

SONG TITLE	ARTIST	DATE
PROMISE ME	Beverley Craven	1991
PROMISE ME	Cover Girls	1988
THE PROMISE OF A NEW DAY	Paula Abdul	1991
THE PROMISE YOU MADE	Cock Robin	1986
PROMISED LAND	Style Council	1989
PROMISED LAND	Elvis Presley	1974
THE PROMISED LAND	Chuck Berry	1965
PROMISED YOU A MIRACLE	Simple Minds	1982
PROMISES	Take That	1991
PROMISES	Eric Clapton	1978
PROMISES	Buzzcocks	1978
PROMISES	Ken Dodd	1966
PROMISES	Cranberries	1999
PROMISES IN THE DARK	Pat Benatar	1981
PROMISES PROMISES	Cooper Temple Clause	2003
PROMISES PROMISES	Dionne Warwick	1968
PROMISES, PROMISES	Naked Eyes	1983
PROPER CRIMBO	Bo Selecta	2003
THE PROPHET	CJ Bolland	1997
PROTECT YOUR MIND (FOR THE LOVE OF A PRINCESS)	DJ Sakin & Friends	1999
PROTECTION	Massive Attack	1995
PROUD	Heather Small	2000
PROUD MARY	Checkmates Ltd.	1969

SONG TITLE	ARTIST	DATE
PROUD MARY	Creedence Clearwater Revival	1969
PROUD MARY	Ike & Tina Turner	1971
THE PROUD ONE	Osmonds	1975
PROVE IT	Television	1977
PROVE IT ALL NIGHT	Bruce Springsteen	1978
PROVE YOUR LOVE	Taylor Dayne	1988
PROVIDER/LAPDANCE	N E R D	2003
PSYCHEDELIC SHACK	Temptations	1970
PSYCHONAUT	Fields Of The Nephilim	1989
PSYCHOSIS SAFARI	Eighties Matchbox B-Line Disaster	2003
PSYCHOTIC REACTION	Count Five	1966
PUBLIC IMAGE	Public Image Ltd	1978
PUCKER UP BUTTERCUP	Jr. Walker & The All Stars	1967
PULL UP TO THE BUMPER/LA VIE EN ROSE	Grace Jones	1986
PULSAR 2002	Mauro Picotto	2002
PUMP IT UP	Elvis Costello	1978
PUMP IT UP	Joe Budden	2003
PUMP IT UP	Danzel	2004
PUMP UP THE BITTER	Star Turn On 45 Pints	1988
PUMP UP THE JAM	Technotronic featuring Felly	1989
PUMP UP THE JAM '96	Technotronic	1996
PUMP UP THE VOLUME	M/A/R/R/S	1987
PUMPIN	Novy vs Eniac	2000

SONG TITLE	ARTIST	DATE
PUMPING ON YOUR STEREO		
	Supergrass	1999
PUMPKIN	Tricky	1995
PUMPS AND A BUMP	Hammer	1994
PUNCH AND JUDY	Marillion	1984
PUNK	Ferry Corsten	2002
PUNK ROCK PRINCESS	Something Corporate	2003
PUNKA	Kenickie	1997
PUPPET MAN	5th Dimension	1970
PUPPET MAN	Tom Jones	1971
PUPPET ON A STRING	Sandie Shaw	1967
PUPPET ON A STRING	Elvis Presley	1965
PUPPY LOVE	Donny Osmond	1972
PUPPY LOVE	Barbara Lewis	1964
PUPPY LOVE/SLEIGH RIDE	S Club Juniors	2002
PURE	3 Colours Red	1997
PURE	Lightning Seeds	1990
PURE AND SIMPLE	Hear'say	2001
PURE MORNING	Placebo	1998
PURE PLEASURE	Digital Excitation	1992
PURE PLEASURE SEEKER	Moloko	2000
PURE SHORES	All Saints	2000
PURELY BY COINCIDENCE	Sweet Sensation	1975
PUREST OF PAIN (A PURO DOLOR)		
	Son By Four	2000
PURPLE HAZE	Jimi Hendrix Experience	1967

SONG TITLE	ARTIST	DATE
PURPLE HAZE	Groove Armada	2002
PURPLE HEATHER	Rod Stewart with The Scottish Euro '96 Squad	1996
PURPLE HILLS	D12	2001
PURPLE LOVE BALLOON	Cud	1992
PURPLE MEDLEY	Prince	1995
PURPLE RAIN	Prince & The Revolution	1984
PUSH	Moist	1995
PUSH	Matchbox Twenty	1998
PUSH	Ghostface featuring Missy Elliott	2004
PUSH IT	Garbage	1998
PUSH IT ALL ASIDE	Alisha's Attic	2001
PUSH IT/TRAMP	Salt 'N' Pepa	1988
PUSH THE FEELING ON	Nightcrawlers	1995
PUSH UP	Freestylers	2004
PUSH UPSTAIRS	Underworld	1999
THE PUSHBIKE SONG	Mixtures	1971
PUSHIN' ME OUT	D-Side	2004
PUSHIN' TOO HARD	Seeds	1966
PUSHIN' WEIGHT	Ice Cube featuring Mr. Short Khop	1998
PUSS/OH, THE GUILT	Jesus Lizard/Nirvana	1993
PUSS 'N BOOTS	Adam Ant	1983
PUT 'EM HIGH	Stonebridge featuring Therese	2004
PUT A LITTLE LOVE IN YOUR HEART		
	Dave Clark Five	1969

SONG TITLE	ARTIST	DATE
PUT A LITTLE LOVE IN YOUR HEART		
	Annie Lennox & Al Green	1988
PUT A LITTLE LOVE IN YOUR HEART		
	Jackie Deshannon	1969
PUT HIM OUT	Ms. Dynamite	2002
PUT IT IN A MAGAZINE	Sonny Charles	1982
PUT IT ON ME	Ja Rule featuring Lil' Mo & Vita	2000
PUT IT THERE	Paul McCartney	1990
PUT THE MESSAGE IN THE BOX		
	Brian Kennedy	1997
PUT THE NEEDLE ON IT	Dannii Minogue	2002
PUT YOUR ARMS AROUND ME		
	Texas	1997
PUT YOUR ARMS AROUND ME		
	Natural	2002
PUT YOUR HAND IN THE HAND		
	Ocean	1971
PUT YOUR HANDS TOGETHER		
	D. Mob featuring Nuff Juice	1990
PUT YOUR HANDS TOGETHER		
	O'Jays	1973
PUT YOUR HANDS WHERE MY EYES COULD SEE		
	Busta Rhymes	1997
PUT YOUR LOVE IN ME	Hot Chocolate	1977
PUT YOUR MOUTH ON ME	Eddie Murphy	1989

SONG TITLE	ARTIST	DATE
PUT YOURSELF IN MY PLACE		
	Elgins	1971
PUT YOURSELF IN MY PLACE		
	Isley Brothers	1969
PUT YOURSELF IN MY PLACE		
	Kylie Minogue	1994
PUTTIN' ON THE RITZ	Taco	1983
PYJAMARAMA	Roxy Music	1973
PYRAMID SONG	Radiohead	2001
QUADROPHONIA	Quadrophonia	1991
QUALITY TIME	Hi-Five	1992
QUANDO M'INNAMORORO (A MAN WITHOUT LOVE)		
	Sandpipers	1968
QUANDO QUANDO QUANDO		
	Engelbert Humperdinck	1999
QUE SERA MI VIDA (IF YOU SHOULD GO)		
	Gibson Brothers	1979
QUEEN FOR TONIGHT	Helen Shapiro	1963
QUEEN JANE	Kingmaker	1993
THE QUEEN OF 1964	Neil Sedaka	1975
QUEEN OF BROKEN HEARTS		
	Loverboy	1983
QUEEN OF CLUBS	KC & The Sunshine Band	1974
QUEEN OF HEARTS	Dave Edmunds	1979
QUEEN OF HEARTS	Juice Newton	1981
QUEEN OF MY HEART	Westlife	2001

SONG TITLE	ARTIST	DATE
QUEEN OF MY SOUL	Average White Band	1976
QUEEN OF NEW ORLEANS	Jon Bon Jovi	1997
THE QUEEN OF OUTER SPACE		
	Wedding Present	1992
QUEEN OF RAIN	Roxette	1992
QUEEN OF THE HOUSE	Jody Miller	1965
QUEEN OF THE NEW YEAR	Deacon Blue	1990
QUEEN OF THE NIGHT	Whitney Houston	1993
QUEEN OF THE RAPPING SCENE (NOTHING EVER GOES		
THE WAY YOU PLAN)	Modern Romance	1982
THE QUEEN'S BIRTHDAY SONG		
	St. John's College Choir & Band	
	Grenadier Guards	1986
QUEEN'S FIRST EP	Queen	1977
QUEER	Garbage	1995
QUENTIN'S THEME (FROM TV SERIES 'DARK SHADOWS')		
	Charles Randolph Green Sounde	1969
QUESTION	Moody Blues	1970
QUESTION OF FAITH	Lighthouse Family	1998
A QUESTION OF LUST	Depeche Mode	1986
A QUESTION OF TEMPERATURE		
	Balloon Farm	1968
A QUESTION OF TIME	Depeche Mode	1986
QUESTIONS & ANSWERS	Biffy Clyro	2003
QUESTIONS 67 AND 68	Chicago	1971
QUESTIONS AND ANSWERS	Sham 69	1979

SONG TITLE	ARTIST	DATE
QUESTIONS I CAN'T ANSWER		
	Heinz	1964
QUICK JOEY SMALL (RUN JOEY RUN)		
	Kasenentz-Katz Singing	
	Orchestral Circus	1968
QUIEREME MUCHO (YOURS)		
	Julio Iglesias	1982
QUIET LIFE	Japan	1981
THE QUIET THINGS THAT NO ONE EVER KNOWS		
	Brand New	2004
QUIT PLAYING GAMES (WITH MY HEART)		
	Backstreet Boys	1997
QUIT THIS TOWN	Eddie & The Hotrods	1978
R TO THE A	CJ Lewis	1995
R U READY	Salt 'N 'Pepa	1997
R U SLEEPING	Indo	1998
R.O.C.K. IN THE U.S.A. (A SALUTE TO 60'S ROCK)		
	John Cougar Mellencamp	1986
R.S.V.P.	Jason Donovan	1991
RABBIT	Chas & Dave	1980
RACE	Tiger	1996
RACE FOR THE PRIZE	Flaming Lips	1999
THE RACE IS ON	Dave Edmunds	1981
THE RACE IS ON	Stray Cats	1981
THE RACE IS ON	Jack Jones	1965
THE RACE	Yello	1988

SONG TITLE	ARTIST	DATE
RACE WITH THE DEVIL	Gun	1968
RADANCER	Marmalade	1972
RADAR LOVE	Golden Earring	1974
RADIATION VIBE	Fountains Of Wayne	1997
RADICAL YOUR LOVER	Little Angels	1990
RADICCIO (EP)	Orbital	1992
RADIO	Shaky featuring Roger Taylor	1992
RADIO	Teenage Fanclub	1993
RADIO	Corrs	1999
RADIO	Robbie Williams	2004
RADIO AFRICA	Latin Quarter	1986
RADIO GAGA	Queen	1984
RADIO HEART	Radio Heart featuring Gary Numan	1987
RADIO NO 1	Air	2001
RADIO ON	Ricky Ross	1996
RADIO RADIO	Elvis Costello	1978
RADIO ROMANCE	Tiffany	1989
RADIO SONG	R.E.M.	1991
RADIO WALL OF SOUND	Slade	1991
RADIOACTIVE	Firm	1985
RAG DOLL	Four Seasons	1964
RAG DOLL	Aerosmith	1988
RAG MAMA RAG	Band	1970
RAGAMUFFIN MAN	Manfred Mann	1969
RAGE HARD	Frankie Goes To Hollywood	1986

SONG TITLE	ARTIST	DATE
RAGE TO LOVE	Kim Wilde	1985
RAGGAMUFFIN GIRL	Apache Indian featuring Frankie Paul	1995
RAGS TO RICHES	Elvis Presley	1971
RAIN	Cult	1985
RAIN	Bruce Ruffin	1971
RAIN	Status Quo	1976
RAIN	Madonna	1993
RAIN	Beatles	1966
RAIN	SWV	1998
THE RAIN	Oran 'Juice' Jones	1986
THE RAIN (SUPA DUPA FLY)	Missy 'Misdemeanor' Elliott	1997
RAIN AND TEARS	Aphrodite's Child	1968
RAIN DANCE	Guess Who	1971
RAIN DOWN ON ME	Kane	2004
RAIN FOREST	Biddu Orchestra	1976
RAIN IN THE SUMMERTIME	Alarm	1987
RAIN ON ME	Ashanti	2003
RAIN ON THE ROOF	Lovin' Spoonful	1966
RAIN ON THE SCARECROW	John Cougar Mellencamp	1986
RAIN OR SHINE	Five Star	1986
THE RAIN, THE PARK & OTHER THINGS	Cowsills	1967
RAINBOW	Marmalade	1970

SONG TITLE	ARTIST	DATE
RAINBOW	Peters & Lee	1974
RAINBOW CHASER	Nirvana	1969
RAINBOW CONNECTION	Kermit (Jim Henson)	1979
RAINBOW COUNTRY	Bob Marley vs Funkstar De Luxe	2000
RAINBOW VALLEY	Love Affair	1968
RAINBOWS OF COLOUR	Grooverider	1998
RAINCLOUD	Lighthouse Family	1997
RAINDROPS KEEP FALLIN' ON MY HEAD	Sacha Distel	1970
RAINDROPS KEEP FALLIN' ON MY HEAD	Bobbie Gentry	1970
RAINDROPS KEEP FALLIN' ON MY HEAD	B.J. Thomas	1969
RAININ' THROUGH MY SUNSHINE	Real Thing	1978
RAINING IN MY HEART	Leo Sayer	1978
RAINING ON SUNDAY	Keith Urban	2003
RAINMAKER	Iron Maiden	2003
THE RAINS CAME	Sir Douglas Quintet	1966
RAINY DAY PEOPLE	Gordon Lightfoot	1975
RAINY DAY WOMEN #12 & 35	Bob Dylan	1966
RAINY DAYS AND MONDAYS	Carpenters	1971
RAINY DAYZ	Mary J. Blige featuring Ja Rule	2002

SONG TITLE	ARTIST	DATE
RAINY NIGHT IN GEORGIA	Randy Crawford	1981
RAINY NIGHT IN GEORGIA	Brook Benton	1970
RAISE	Hyper Go-Go	1994
RAISE THE ROOF	Luke featuring No Good But So Good	1998
RAISE UP	Petey Pablo	2001
RAISE YOUR HANDS	Big Room Girl featuring Daryl Pandy	1999
RAISE YOUR HANDS	Reel 2 Real featuring The Mad Stuntman	1994
RAISED ON ROCK	Elvis Presley	1973
RAMA LAMA DING DONG	Rocky Sharpe & The Replays	1978
RAMBLIN' GAMBLIN' MAN	Bob Seger System	1968
RAMBLIN' MAN	Allman Brothers Band	1973
RAMONA	Bachelors	1964
RANDY	Blue Mink	1973
RAOUL AND THE KINGS OF SPAIN	Tears For Fears	1995
RAP DIS/ONLY WANNA KNOW U COS URE FAMOUS	Oxide & Neutrino	2001
(RAP) SUPERSTAR/(ROCK) SUPERSTAR	Cypress Hill	2000
RAPP PAYBACK (WHERE IZ MOSES?)	James Brown	1981
THE RAPPER	Jaggerz	1970
RAPPER'S DELIGHT	Sugarhill Gang	1979

SONG TITLE	ARTIST	DATE
RAPTURE	Blondie	1981
RAPTURE	IIO	2001
RASPBERRY BERET	Prince & The Revolution	1985
RASPUTIN	Boney M	1978
RAT IN MI KITCHEN	UB40	1987
RAT RACE/RUDE BOYS OUTA JAIL		
	Specials	1980
RAT RAPPING	Roland Rat Superstar	1983
RAT TRAP	Boomtown Rats	1978
RATAMAHATTA	Sepultura	1996
THE RATTLER	Goodbye Mr Mackenzie	1989
RAVE ALERT	Praga Khan	1992
RAVE GENERATOR	Toxic Two	1992
RAVEL'S PAVANE POUR UNE INFANTE DEFUNTE		
	William Orbit	2000
RAVING I'M RAVING	Shut Up And Dance	1992
RAW POWER	Apollo 440	1997
A RAY OF HOPE	Rascals	1968
RAY OF LIGHT	Madonna	1998
RAYS OF THE RISING SUN	Mozaic	1996
RAZZAMATAZZ	Quincy Jones	1981
RE-OFFENDER	Travis	2003
RE-REWIND THE CROWD SAY BO SELECTA		
	Artful Dodger featuring	
	Craig David	1999
RE:EVOLUTION	Shamen/Terence McKenna	1993

SONG TITLE	ARTIST	DATE
REACH	Judy Cheeks	1994
REACH	Lil Mo' Yin Yang	1996
REACH	Gloria Estefan	1996
REACH	S Club 7	2000
REACH OUT AND TOUCH (SOMEBODY'S HAND)		
	Diana Ross	1970
REACH OUT FOR ME	Dionne Warwick	1964
REACH OUT I'LL BE THERE	Michael Bolton	1993
REACH OUT I'LL BE THERE	Four Tops	1966
REACH OUT I'LL BE THERE	Diana Ross	1971
REACH OUT, I'LL BE THERE		
	Gloria Gaynor	1975
REACH OUT OF THE DARKNESS		
	Friend And Lover	1968
REACH UP (PAPA'S GOT A BRAND NEW PIG BAG)		
	Perfecto Allstarz	1995
(REACH UP FOR THE) SUNRISE		
	Duran Duran	2004
REACHIN	House Of Virginism	1994
REACHING FOR THE BEST	Exciters	1975
REACT	Erick Sermon featuring Redman	2002
READ 'EM AND WEEP	Barry Manilow	1983
READ MY LIPS	Alex Party	1996
READ MY LIPS (ENOUGH IS ENOUGH)		
	Jimmy Somerville	1990
READ MY MIND	Conner Reeves	1998

SONG TITLE	ARTIST	DATE
READY	Cat Stevens	1974
READY FOR A NEW DAY	Todd Terry	1998
READY OR NOT	Course	1997
READY OR NOT	Lightning Seeds	1996
READY OR NOT	Fugees	1996
READY OR NOT	After 7	1990
READY OR NOT HERE I COME (CAN'T HIDE FROM LOVE)		
	Delfonics	1968
READY TO GO	Republica	1997
READY TO RUN	Dixie Chicks	1999
READY TO TAKE A CHANCE AGAIN		
	Barry Manilow	1978
REAL	Donna Allen	1995
REAL A LIE	Auf Der Maur	2004
REAL FASHION (REGGAE STYLE)		
	Carey Johnson	1987
REAL GONE KID	Deacon Blue	1988
REAL GOOD MAN	Tim McGraw	2003
REAL GOOD TIME	Alda	1998
REAL LIFE	Simple Minds	1991
REAL LIFE	Bon Jovi	1999
THE REAL LIFE	Raven Maize	2001
REAL LOVE	Jody Watley	1989
REAL LOVE	Mary J. Blige	1992
REAL LOVE	Driza Bone	1991
REAL LOVE	Beatles	1996

SONG TITLE	ARTIST	DATE
REAL LOVE	Doobie Brothers	1980
REAL LOVE '93	Time Frequency	1993
THE REAL LOVE	Bob Seger & The Silver Bullet Band	1991
THE REAL ME	W.A.S.P.	1989
REAL REAL REAL	Jesus Jones	1991
THE REAL SLIM SHADY	Eminem	2000
THE REAL THING	Tony Di Bart	1994
THE REAL THING	Jellybean featuring Steven Dante	1987
THE REAL THING	2 Unlimited	1994
THE REAL THING	Lisa Stansfield	1997
THE REAL THING	Simply Red	1987
REAL THINGS	Javine	2003
REAL TO ME	Brian McFadden	2004
REAL WILD CHILD (WILD ONE)		
	Iggy Pop	1986
THE REAL WILD HOUSE	Raul Orellana	1989
REAL WORLD	D-Side	2003
REAL WORLD	Matchbox Twenty	1998
REALITY USED TO BE A FRIEND OF MINE		
	P.M. Dawn	1992
REALLY FREE	John Otway & Wild Willy Barrett	1977
REALLY SAYING SOMETHING		
	Bananarama with Fun Boy Three	1982

SONG TITLE	ARTIST	DATE
REALLY WANNA KNOW YOU		
	Gary Wright	1981
REAP THE WILD WIND	Ultravox	1982
REASON	Ian Van Dahl	2002
THE REASON	Celine Dion	1997
THE REASON	Hoobastank	2004
REASON TO BELIEVE	Rod Stewart	1993
REASON TO LIVE	Kiss	1987
REASONS	Kleshay	1998
REASONS TO BE CHEERFUL (PT 3)		
	Ian Dury & The Blockheads	1979
REBEL REBEL	David Bowie	1974
REBEL RUN	Toyah	1983
REBEL WITHOUT A PAUSE	Public Enemy	1987
REBEL YELL	Scooter	1996
REBEL YELL	Billy Idol	1985
REBIRTH OF SLICK (COOL LIKE DAT)		
	Digable Planets	1993
RECIPE FOR LOVE/IT HAD TO BE YOU		
	Harry Connick Jr.	1991
RECKLESS	Afrika Bambaataa and Family	
	featuring UB40	1988
RECKLESS GIRL	Beginerz	2002
RECONSIDER ME	Johnny Adams	1969
RECOVER YOUR SOUL	Elton John	1998
RECOVERY	Fontella Bass	1966

SONG TITLE	ARTIST	DATE
RED	Elbow	2001
RED ALERT	Basement Jaxx	1999
THE RED BALLOON	Dave Clark Five	1968
RED BLOODED WOMAN	Kylie Minogue	2004
RED DIRT ROAD	Brooks & Dunn	2003
RED DRESS	Alvin Stardust	1974
RED GUITAR	David Sylvian	1984
RED HOT	Vanessa-Mae	1995
A RED LETTER DAY	Pet Shop Boys	1997
RED LIGHT – GREEN LIGHT (EP)		
	Wildhearts	1996
RED LIGHT SPECIAL	TLC	1995
RED LIGHT SPELLS DANGER		
	Billy Ocean	1977
RED RAG TOP	Tim McGraw	2002
RED RED WINE	Jimmy James & The Vagabonds	1968
RED RED WINE	UB40	1988
RED ROSES FOR A BLUE LADY		
	Vic Dana	1965
RED ROSES FOR A BLUE LADY		
	Bert Kaempfert	1965
RED ROSES FOR A BLUE LADY		
	Wayne Newton	1965
RED RUBBER BALL	Cyrkle	1966
RED SAILS IN THE SUNSET	Fats Domino	1963
THE RED SHOES	Kate Bush	1994

SONG TITLE	ARTIST	DATE
RED SKY	Status Quo	1986
THE RED STROKES/AIN'T GOING DOWN (TIL THE SUN COMES UP)	Garth Brooks	1994
RED SUN RISING	Lost Witness	1999
THE RED THE WHITE THE BLACK THE BLUE	Hope Of The States	2004
REDNECK WOMAN	Gretchen Wilson	2004
REDUNDANT	Green Day	1998
REELIN' & ROCKIN'	Chuck Berry	1972
REELIN' AND ROCKIN'	Dave Clark Five	1965
REELING IN THE YEARS	Steely Dan	1973
REET PETITE	Jackie Wilson	1986
REFLECTIONS	Diana Ross & The Supremes	1967
REFLECTIONS OF MY LIFE	Marmalade	1970
THE REFLEX	Duran Duran	1984
REFUGEE	Tom Petty & The Heartbreakers	1980
REGGAE FOR IT NOW	Bill Lovelady	1979
REGGAE LIKE IT USED TO BE	Paul Nicholas	1976
REGGAE MUSIC	UB40	1994
REGGAE TUNE	Andy Fairweather-Low	1974
REGRET	New Order	1993
REGULATE	Warren G & Nate Dogg	1994
REILLY	Olympic Orchestra	1983
RELAX	Crystal Waters	1995
RELAX	Deetah	1998

SONG TITLE	ARTIST	DATE
RELAX	Frankie Goes To Hollywood	1985
RELAY	Who	1973
THE RELAY	Who	1972
RELEASE ME	Wilson Phillips	1990
RELEASE ME (AND LET ME LOVE AGAIN)	Engelbert Humperdinck	1967
RELEASE THE PRESSURE	Leftfield	1996
RELIGHT MY FIRE	Take That featuring Lulu	1993
RELOAD	PPK	2002
REMEDY	Black Crowes	1992
REMEMBER	BT	1998
REMEMBER (SHA-LA-LA)	Bay City Rollers	1974
REMEMBER (WALKIN' IN THE SAND)	Shangri-Las	1964
REMEMBER ME	Blue Boy	1997
REMEMBER ME	Diana Ross	1970
REMEMBER ME	Cliff Richard	1987
REMEMBER ME	British Sea Power	2003
REMEMBER ME	Zutons	2004
REMEMBER ME	Rita Pavone	1964
REMEMBER ME THIS WAY	Gary Glitter	1974
REMEMBER ME WITH LOVE	Gloria Estefan	1991
(REMEMBER ME) I'M THE ONE WHO LOVES YOU	Dean Martin	1965

SONG TITLE	ARTIST	DATE
(REMEMBER THE DAYS OF THE) OLD SCHOOLYARD		
	Cat Stevens	1977
REMEMBER THE NIGHTS	Motels	1983
REMEMBER THE TIME	Michael Jackson	1992
REMEMBER THEN	Showaddywaddy	1979
REMEMBER WHAT I TOLD YOU TO FORGET/MY SHIP		
	Tavares	1975
REMEMBER WHEN	Alan Jackson	2003
REMEMBER YESTERDAY	John Miles	1976
REMEMBER YOU'RE A WOMBLE		
	Wombles	1974
REMEMBERING THE FIRST TIME		
	Simply Red	1995
REMIND ME/SO EASY	Royksopp	2002
REMINISCE	Mary J. Blige	1993
REMINISCE/WHERE THE STORY ENDS		
	Blazin' Squad	2003
REMINISCING	Little River Band	1978
REMOTE CONTROL/3 MCS & 1 DJ		
	Beastie Boys	1999
RENAISSANCE	M People	1994
RENDEZ-VOUS '98	Jean Michel Jarre & Apollo 440	1998
RENDEZ-VU	Basement Jaxx	1999
RENDEZVOUS	Tina Charles	1977
RENDEZVOUS	Craig David	2001
RENEE	Lost Boyz	1996

SONG TITLE	ARTIST	DATE
RENEGADE	Michael Murphey	1976
RENEGADE	Styx	1979
RENEGADE MASTER	Wildchild	1995
RENEGADES OF FUNK	Afrika Bambaataa & The Soul Sonic Force	1984
RENT	Pet Shop Boys	1987
RENTA SANTA	Chris Hill	1975
REPEATED LOVE	A.T.G.O.C.	1998
REPRESENT	Soul II Soul	1997
REPTILIA	Strokes	2004
REPUBLICAN PARTY REPTILE (EP)		
	Big Country	1991
REPUTATION	Dusty Springfield	1990
REQUEST & LINE	Black Eyed Peas featuring Macy Gray	2001
REQUEST LINE	Zhane	1997
REQUIEM	London Boys	1989
REQUIEM	Slik	1976
RESCUE ME	Fontella Bass	1965
RESCUE ME	Madonna	1991
RESCUE ME	Ultra	1999
RESPECT	Adeva	1989
RESPECT	Aretha Franklin	1967
RESPECT	Otis Redding	1965
RESPECT YOURSELF	Kane Gang	1984
RESPECT YOURSELF	Bruce Willis	1987

SONG TITLE	ARTIST	DATE
RESPECT YOURSELF	Staple Singers	1971
RESPECTABLE	Girls At Play	2001
RESPECTABLE	Mel & Kim	1987
RESPECTABLE	Rolling Stones	1978
RESPECTABLE	Outsiders	1966
REST & PLAY (EP)	Orbital	2002
REST IN PEACE	Extreme	1992
RESTLESS	Status Quo	1994
RESTLESS	Gillan	1982
RESTLESS	JX	2004
RESTLESS HEART	Peter Cetera	1992
RESURRECTION	PPK	2001
RESURRECTION	Brian May With Cozy Powell	1993
RESURRECTION SHUFFLE	Ashton Gardner & Dyke	1971
RESURRECTION SHUFFLE	Tom Jones	1971
RETREAT	Hell Is For Heroes	2003
THE RETURN OF DJ ANGO/DOLLAR IN THE TEETH		
	Upsetters	1969
THE RETURN OF PAN	Waterboys	1993
RETURN OF THE LOS PALMAS 7		
	Madness	1981
RETURN OF THE MACK	Mark Morrison	1997
RETURN OF THE RED BARON		
	Royal Guardsmen	1967
RETURN TO INNOCENCE	Enigma	1994
REUNITED	Peaches & Herb	1979

SONG TITLE	ARTIST	DATE
REVELATION	Electrique Boutique	2000
REVERENCE	Jesus & Mary Chain	1992
REVERENCE	Faithless	1997
REVEREND BLACK GRAPE	Black Grape	1995
REVIVAL	Eurythmics	1989
REVIVAL	Martine Girault	1993
REVOL	Manic Street Preachers	1994
REVOLUTION	Cult	1985
REVOLUTION	Beatles	1968
REVOLUTION (IN THE SUMMERTIME)		
	Cosmic Rough Riders	2001
REVOLUTION BABY	Transvision Vamp	1988
REVOLVING DOOR	Crazy Town	2001
REWARD	Teardrop Explodes	1981
REWIND	Celetia	1998
REWIND	Precious	2000
REWIND (FIND A WAY)	Beverley Knight	1998
RHAPSODY	Four Seasons	1977
RHAPSODY IN THE RAIN	Lou Christie	1966
RHIANNON (WILL YOU EVER WIN)		
	Fleetwood Mac	1976
RHINESTONE COWBOY	Glen Campbell	1975
RHINESTONE COWBOY (GIDDY UP GIDDY UP)		
	Rikki & Daz featuring	
	Glen Campbell	2002
RHYTHM	Major Lance	1964

SONG TITLE	ARTIST	DATE	SONG TITLE	ARTIST	DATE
THE RHYTHM	Clock	1994	RIDDLE	En Vogue	2000
RHYTHM & BLUES ALIBI	Gomez	1999	THE RIDDLE	Nik Kershaw	1984
RHYTHM AND GREENS	Shadows	1964	RIDDUM	US3 FEAT TUKKA YOOT	1993
RHYTHM BANDITS	Junior Senior	2003	RIDE	Ana Ann	2002
RHYTHM DIVINE	Enrique Iglesias	1999	RIDE	Vines	2004
RHYTHM IS A DANCER	Snap!	1992	RIDE 'EM COWBOY	Paul Davis	1974
RHYTHM IS A MYSTERY	K-Klass	1991	RIDE A ROCKET	Lithium And Sonya Madan	1997
RHYTHM IS GONNA GET YOU			RIDE A WHITE SWAN	T. Rex	1970
	Gloria Estefan	1988	RIDE A WILD HORSE	Dee Clark	1975
RHYTHM NATION	Janet Jackson	1989	RIDE AWAY	Roy Orbison	1965
RHYTHM OF LIFE	Oleta Adams	1995	RIDE CAPTAIN RIDE	Blues Image	1970
RHYTHM OF LOVE	Yes	1987	RIDE LIKE THE WIND	East Side Beat	1991
RHYTHM OF MY HEART	Runrig	1996	RIDE LIKE THE WIND	Christopher Cross	1980
RHYTHM OF MY HEART	Rod Stewart	1991	RIDE ON BABY	Chris Farlowe	1966
RHYTHM OF THE NIGHT	Powerhouse	1997	RIDE ON THE RHYTHM	Little Louie & Marc Anthony	1998
RHYTHM OF THE NIGHT	Debarge	1985	RIDE ON TIME	Black Box	1989
THE RHYTHM OF THE NIGHT			RIDE RIDE RIDE	Brenda Lee	1967
	Corona	1994	RIDE THE TIGER	Boo Radleys	1997
RHYTHM OF THE RAIN	Cascades	1963	RIDE THE WILD SURF	Jan & Dean	1964
RHYTHM OF THE RAIN	Jason Donovan	1990	RIDE THE WIND	Poison	1991
RICH AND STRANGE	Cud	1992	RIDE WID US	So Solid Crew	2002
RICH GIRL	Daryl Hall & John Oates	1977	RIDE WIT ME	Nelly featuring City Spud	2001
RICH KIDS	Rich Kids	1978	RIDE WIT U/MORE & MORE		
RICHARD III	Supergrass	1997		Joe featuring G-Unit	2004
RICO SUAVE	Gerardo	1991	RIDE YOUR PONY	Lee Dorsey	1965
RICOCHET	Faith No More	1995	RIDERS IN THE SKY	Shadows	1980

SONG TITLE	ARTIST	DATE
RIDERS ON THE STORM	Doors	1971
RIDERS ON THE STORM	Annabel Lamb	1983
RIDICULOUS THOUGHTS	Cranberries	1995
RIDING ON A TRAIN	Pasadenas	1988
RIDING WITH PRIVATE MALONE		
	David Ball	2001
RIGHT BACK WHERE WE STARTED FROM		
	Maxine Nightingale	1976
RIGHT BACK WHERE WE STARTED FROM		
	Sinitta	1989
RIGHT BEFORE MY EYES	N'n'G featuring Kallaghan	2000
RIGHT BESIDE YOU	Sophie B. Hawkins	1994
RIGHT BY YOUR SIDE	Eurythmics	1984
THE RIGHT DECISION	Jesus Jones	1993
RIGHT DOWN THE LINE	Gerry Rafferty	1978
RIGHT HERE	SWV	1993
RIGHT HERE	Ultimate Kaos	1995
RIGHT HERE RIGHT NOW	Disco Citizens	1995
RIGHT HERE RIGHT NOW	Fierce	1999
RIGHT HERE RIGHT NOW	Fatboy Slim	1999
RIGHT HERE WAITING	Richard Marx	1989
RIGHT HERE, RIGHT NOW	Jesus Jones	1991
RIGHT IN THE NIGHT (FALL IN LOVE WITH MUSIC)		
	Jam & Spoon featuring Plavka	1994
THE RIGHT KIND OF LOVE	Jeremy Jordan	1992
RIGHT NOW	Atomic Kitten	1999

SONG TITLE	ARTIST	DATE
RIGHT NOW	Creatures	1983
RIGHT ON THE TIP OF MY TONGUE		
	Brenda & The Tabulations	1971
RIGHT ON TRACK	Breakfast Club	1987
RIGHT OR WRONG	Ronnie Dove	1964
RIGHT PLACE WRONG TIME		
	Dr. John	1973
THE RIGHT STUFF	Bryan Ferry	1987
THE RIGHT THING	Simply Red	1987
THE RIGHT THING TO DO	Carly Simon	1973
RIGHT THURR	Chingy	2003
THE RIGHT TIME	Ultra	1998
RIGHT TIME OF THE NIGHT		
	Jennifer Warnes	1977
THE RIGHT WAY	Peter Andre	2004
RIKKI DON'T LOSE THAT NUMBER		
	Steely Dan	1974
RING DANG DOO	Sam The Sham & The Pharoahs	1965
RING MY BELL	Monie Love vs Adeva	1991
RING MY BELL	Anita Ward	1979
RING MY BELL	D.J. Jazzy Jeff & The Fresh Prince	1991
RING OF FIRE	Eric Burdon & The Animals	1969
RING OF ICE	Jennifer Rush	1985
RING OUR SOLSTICE BELLS (EP)		
	Jethro Tull	1976

SONG TITLE	ARTIST	DATE
RING RING	ABBA	1974
RING RING RING	Aaron Soul	2001
RING RING RING (HA HA HEY)		
	De La Soul	1991
RING THE BELLS	James	1992
RING THE LIVING BELL	Melanie	1972
RINGO	Lorne Greene	1964
RINGS	Cymarron	1971
RIO	Duran Duran	1983
RIO	Michael Nesmith	1977
RIOT RADIO	Dead 60s	2004
RIP	Gary Numan	2002
RIP IT UP	Orange Juice	1983
RIP VAN WINKLE	Devotions	1964
RIPGROOVE	Double 99	1997
RISE	Herb Alpert	1979
RISE	Eddie Amador	2000
RISE	Public Image Ltd	1986
RISE	Gabrielle	2000
RISE & FALL	Craig David featuring Sting	2003
THE RISE & FALL OF FLINGEL BUNT		
	Shadows	1964
RISE & SHINE	Cardigans	1996
RISE OF THE EAGLES	Eighties Matchbox B-Line Disaster	2004
RISE TO THE OCCASION	Climie Fisher	1987

SONG TITLE	ARTIST	DATE
RISING FREE (EP)	Tom Robinson Band	1978
RISING SUN	Medicine Head	1973
RISINGSON	Massive Attack	1997
RITUAL	Dan Reed Network	1988
THE RIVER	Bruce Springsteen	1981
THE RIVER	Breed 77	2004
THE RIVER (LE COLLINE SONO IN FIORE)		
	Ken Dodd	1965
RIVER DEEP MOUNTAIN HIGH		
	Ike & Tina Turner	1966
RIVER DEEP MOUNTAIN HIGH		
	Supremes & Four Tops	1970
THE RIVER IS WIDE	Grass Roots	1969
THE RIVER OF DREAMS	Billy Joel	1993
RIVER OF PAIN	Thunder	1995
RIVER'S RISIN'	Edgar Winter	1974
THE RIVERBOAT SONG	Ocean Colour Scene	1996
RIVERDANCE	Bill Whelan	1994
RIVERS OF BABYLON/BROWN GIRL IN THE RING		
	Boney M	1978
ROAD RAGE	Catatonia	1998
THE ROAD TO HELL (PT 2)		
	Chris Rea	1989
ROAD TO NOWHERE	Talking Heads	1985
ROAD TO YOUR SOUL	All About Eve	1989
ROAD TRIPPIN'	Red Hot Chili Peppers	2001

SONG TITLE	ARTIST	DATE
ROADBLOCK	Stock Aitken Waterman	1987
ROADHOUSE MEDLEY (ANNIVERSARY WALTZ PART 25)		
	Status Quo	1992
ROADRUNNER	Jonathan Richman & The Modern Lovers	1977
ROAM	B-52's	1989
ROBERT DE NIRO'S WAITING		
	Bananarama	1984
ROBIN'S RETURN	Neville Dickie	1969
ROBOT	Tornados	1963
THE ROBOTS	Kraftwerk	1991
ROCHDALE COWBOY	Mike Harding	1975
ROCK & ROLL PART 2	Gary Glitter	1972
ROCK 'N ROLL SOUL	Grand Funk Railroad	1972
ROCK 'N ROLL WINTER (LOONY'S TUNE)		
	Wizzard	1974
ROCK 'N' ROLL	Status Quo	1981
ROCK 'N' ROLL (I GAVE YOU THE BEST YEARS OF MY LIFE)	Kevin Johnson	1975
ROCK 'N' ROLL (I GAVE YOU THE BEST YEARS OF MY LIFE)	Mac Davis	1974
ROCK 'N' ROLL AIN'T NOISE POLLUTION		
	AC/DC	1980
ROCK 'N' ROLL CHILDREN	Dio	1985
ROCK 'N' ROLL DAMNATION		
	AC/DC	1978

SONG TITLE	ARTIST	DATE
ROCK 'N' ROLL FANTASY	Bad Company	1979
A ROCK 'N' ROLL FANTASY		
	Kinks	1978
ROCK 'N' ROLL IS KING	Electric Light Orchestra	1983
ROCK 'N' ROLL LADY	Showaddywaddy	1974
ROCK 'N' ROLL MERCENARIES		
	Meat Loaf featuring John Parr	1986
ROCK'N'ROLL SUICIDE	David Bowie	1974
ROCK 'TIL YOU DROP	Status Quo	1992
ROCK AND A HARD PLACE	Rolling Stones	1989
ROCK AND ROLL ALL NITE (LIVE VERSION)		
	Kiss	1975
ROCK AND ROLL DREAMS COME THROUGH		
	Meat Loaf	1994
ROCK AND ROLL DREAMS COME THROUGH		
	Jim Steinman	1981
ROCK AND ROLL GIRLS	John Fogerty	1985
ROCK AND ROLL HEAVEN	Righteous Brothers	1974
ROCK AND ROLL HOOCHIE KOO		
	Rick Derringer	1974
ROCK AND ROLL IS DEAD	Lenny Kravitz	1995
ROCK AND ROLL LULLABY	B.J. Thomas	1972
ROCK AND ROLL MUSIC	Beach Boys	1976
ROCK AROUND THE CLOCK		
	Bill Haley & His Comets	1955

SONG TITLE	ARTIST	DATE
ROCK AROUND THE CLOCK	Telex	1979
ROCK AROUND THE CLOCK	Ten Pole Tudor	1979
ROCK BOTTOM	Lynsey De Paul & Mike Moran	1977
ROCK DA FUNKY BEATS	Public Domain featuring Chuck D	2001
ROCK DA HOUSE	Tall Paul	1997
ROCK DJ	Robbie Williams	2000
ROCK IS DEAD	Marilyn Manson	1999
ROCK LOBSTER/PLANET CLAIRE	B-52's	1986
ROCK ME	Steppenwolf	1969
ROCK ME AMADEUS	Falco	1960
ROCK ME BABY	David Cassidy	1972
ROCK ME BABY	B.B. King	1964
ROCK ME GENTLY	Andy Kim	1974
ROCK ME GOOD	Universal	1997
ROCK ME TONIGHT (FOR OLD TIMES SAKE)	Freddie Jackson	1985
ROCK ME TONITE	Billy Squier	1984
ROCK MY HEART	Haddaway	1994
ROCK MY WORLD	Five Star	1988
ROCK OF AGES	Def Leppard	1983
ROCK OF LIFE	Rick Springfield	1988
ROCK ON	David Essex	1973

SONG TITLE	ARTIST	DATE
ROCK ON	Michael Damian	1989
ROCK ON BROTHER	Chequers	1975
THE ROCK SHOW	Blink-182	2001
ROCK STAR	N E R D	2002
ROCK STEADY	Whispers	1987
ROCK STEADY	Aretha Franklin	1971
ROCK THE BELLS	Kadoc	1997
ROCK THE BOAT	Forrest	1983
ROCK THE BOAT	Hues Corporation	1974
ROCK THE BOAT	Aaliyah	2001
ROCK THE CASBAH	Clash	1982
ROCK THE FUNKY BEAT	Natural Born Chillers	1997
ROCK THE HOUSE	Gorillaz	2001
ROCK THE NIGHT	Europe	1987
ROCK THIS TOWN	Stray Cats	1982
ROCK WIT U (AWWW BABY)	Ashanti	2003
ROCK WIT'CHA	Bobby Brown	1989
ROCK WITH YOU	D'Influence	1998
ROCK WITH YOU	Michael Jackson	1979
ROCK YOU LIKE A HURRICANE	Scorpions	1984
ROCK YOUR BABY	George McCrae	1974
ROCK YOUR BABY	KWS	1992
ROCK YOUR BODY	Clock	1998
ROCK YOUR BODY	Justin Timberlake	2003

SONG TITLE	ARTIST	DATE
ROCK YOUR BODY ROCK	Ferry Corsten	2004
ROCK'N ME	Steve Miller Band	1976
ROCK-A-DOODLE-DOO	Linda Lewis	1973
ROCKABILLY GUY	Polecats	1981
ROCKABILLY REBEL	Matchbox	1979
THE ROCKAFELLER SKANK	Fatboy Slim	1998
ROCKARIA	Electric Light Orchestra	1977
ROCKET	Def Leppard	1989
ROCKET	Mud	1974
ROCKET 2 U	Jets	1988
ROCKET MAN	Elton John	1972
ROCKET MAN (I THINK IT'S GOING TO BE A LONG LONG TIME)	Kate Bush	1991
ROCKET RIDE	Kiss	1978
THE ROCKFORD FILES	Mike Post	1975
ROCKIN' ALL OVER THE WORLD	Status Quo	1977
ROCKIN' ALL OVER THE WORLD	John Fogerty	1975
ROCKIN' AROUND THE CHRISTMAS TREE	Kim Wilde & Mel Smith	1987
ROCKIN' AT MIDNIGHT	Honeydrippers	1985
ROCKIN' CHAIR	Magnum	1990
ROCKIN' CHAIR	Gwen McCrae	1975
ROCKIN' FOR MYSELF	Motiv 8	1994
A ROCKIN' GOOD WAY	Shaky & Bonnie	1984

SONG TITLE	ARTIST	DATE
ROCKIN' MY BODY	49ers featuring Anne-Marie Smith	1995
ROCKIN' OVER THE BEAT	Technotronic featuring Ya Kid K	1990
ROCKIN' PNEUMONIA & THE BOOGIE WOOGIE FLU	Johnny Rivers	1972
ROCKIN' ROBIN	Michael Jackson	1972
ROCKIN' ROLL BABY	Stylistics	1973
ROCKIN' SOUL	Hues Corporation	1974
ROCKIN' TO THE MUSIC	Black Box	1993
ROCKING MUSIC	Martin Solveig	2004
ROCKIT	Herbie Hancock	1983
ROCKS/FUNKY JAM	Primal Scream	1994
ROCKY	Austin Roberts	1975
ROCKY MOUNTAIN HIGH	John Denver	1972
ROCKY MOUNTAIN WAY	Joe Walsh	1973
RODRIGO'S GUITAR CONCERTO DE ARANJUEZ	Manuel & The Music Of The Mountains	1976
ROK DA HOUSE	Beatmasters featuring The Cookie Crew	1988
ROLENE	Moon Martin	1979
ROLL AWAY THE STONE	Mott The Hoople	1973
ROLL ME AWAY	Bob Seger	1983
ROLL ON DOWN THE HIGHWAY	Bachman-Turner Overdrive	1975

SONG TITLE	ARTIST	DATE
ROLL ON/THIS IS HOW WE DO IT		
	Mis-Teeq	2002
ROLL OVER BEETHOVEN	Electric Light Orchestra	1973
ROLL OVER LAY DOWN	Status Quo	1975
ROLL TO ME	Del Amitri	1995
ROLL WITH IT	Oasis	1995
ROLL WITH IT	Steve Winwood	1988
ROLLER	April Wine	1979
ROLLERBLADE	Nick Heyward	1996
ROLLERCOASTER	B*Witched	1998
ROLLERCOASTER	Grid	1994
ROLLIN'	Limp Bizkit	2001
ROLLIN' IN MY 5.0	Vanilla Ice	1991
ROLLIN' STONE	David Essex	1975
ROLLING HOME	Status Quo	1986
A ROLLING SKATING JAM NAMED SATURDAYS		
	De La Soul	1991
ROLLOUT (MY BUSINESS)	Ludacris	2002
ROLLOVER DJ	Jet	2003
ROMANCING THE STONE	Eddy Grant	1984
ROMANTIC	Karyn White	1991
ROME WASN'T BUILT IN A DAY		
	Morcheeba	2000
ROMEO	Basement Jaxx	2001
ROMEO	Mr. Big	1977
ROMEO	Dino	1990

SONG TITLE	ARTIST	DATE
ROMEO & JULIET	Stacy Earl	1992
ROMEO AND JULIET	Dire Straits	1981
ROMEO AND JULIET	Sylk-E. Fyne featuring Chill	1998
ROMEO DUNN	Romeo	2002
ROMEO ME	Sleeper	1997
ROMEO'S TUNE	Steve Forbert	1979
RONDO	Kenny Ball	1963
RONI	Bobby Brown	1989
RONNIE	Four Seasons	1964
ROOBARB & CUSTARD	Shaft	1991
ROOM AT THE TOP	Adam Ant	1990
ROOM IN YOUR HEART	Living In A Box	1989
ROOM TO MOVE	Animotion	1989
ROOMS ON FIRE	Stevie Nicks	1989
ROOTS BLOODY ROOTS	Sepultura	1996
ROSALIE (COWGIRLS' SONG) (MEDLEY)		
	Thin Lizzy	1978
ROSANNA	Toto	1982
ROSEABILITY	Idlewild	2000
ROSE GARDEN	Lynn Anderson	1970
ROSE GARDEN	New World	1971
A ROSE HAS TO DIE	Dooleys	1978
A ROSE IS A ROSE	Aretha Franklin	1998
A ROSE IS STILL A ROSE	Aretha Franklin	1998
THE ROSE	Bette Midler	1980
ROSES	Haywoode	1986

SONG TITLE	ARTIST	DATE
ROSES	Outkast	2004
ROSES ARE RED	Bobby Vinton	1990
ROSES ARE RED	Mac Band featuring The McCampbell Brothers	1988
ROSES IN THE HOSPITAL	Manic Street Preachers	1993
ROSES OF PICARDY	Vince Hill	1967
ROSETTA	Fame And Price Together	1971
ROSIE	Don Partridge	1968
ROTATION	Herb Alpert & The Tijuana Brass	1979
ROTTERDAM	Beautiful South	1996
ROUGH BOY	ZZ Top	1986
ROUGH BOYS	Pete Townshend	1980
ROUGH JUSTICE	Bananarama	1984
ROUGH WITH THE SMOOTH	Shara Nelson	1995
ROUND & ROUND	New Order	1989
ROUND AND ROUND	Jaki Graham	1985
ROUND AND ROUND	Spandau Ballet	1984
ROUND AND ROUND	Tevin Campbell	1990
ROUND AND ROUND	Ratt	1984
ROUND EVERY CORNER	Petula Clark	1965
ROUND ROUND	Sugababes	2002
ROUNDABOUT	Yes	1972
THE ROUSSOS PHENOMENON (EP)	Demis Roussos	1976

SONG TITLE	ARTIST	DATE
ROUTE 101	Herb Alpert & The Tijuana Brass	1982
ROXANNE	Police	1979
RSVP/FAMILUS HORRIBILUS	Pop Will Eat Itself	1993
RUB A DUB DUB	Equals	1969
RUB IT IN	Billy 'Crash' Craddock	1974
RUB YOU THE RIGHT WAY	Johnny Gill	1990
RUBBER BAND MAN	T.I.	2004
RUBBER BISCUIT	Blues Brothers	1979
RUBBER BULLETS	10cc	1973
RUBBER DUCKIE	Ernie	1970
RUBBERBAND GIRL	Kate Bush	1993
THE RUBBERBAND MAN	Spinners	1976
RUBBERNECKIN'	Elvis Presley	2003
RUBBISH	Carter The Unstoppable Sex Machine	1992
RUBEN JAMES	Kenny Rogers & The First Edition	1969
RUBY ANN	Marty Robbins	1962
RUBY BABY	Billy 'Crash' Craddock	1974
RUBY TUESDAY	Melanie	1970
RUBY TUESDAY	Rod Stewart	1993
RUBY TUESDAY	Rolling Stones	1967

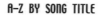
SONG TITLE	ARTIST	DATE
RUBY, DON'T TAKE YOUR LOVE TO TOWN		
	Kenny Rogers & The First Edition	1969
RUDE BOY ROCK	Lionrock	1998
RUDI'S IN LOVE	Locomotive	1968
RUFF MIX	Wonder Dog	1982
RUFFNECK	MC Lyte	1993
RUINED IN A DAY	New Order	1993
RUMBLE IN THE JUNGLE	Fugees	1997
RUMBLESEAT	John Cougar Mellencamp	1986
RUMORS	Timex Social Club	1986
RUMOUR HAS IT	Donna Summer	1978
RUMOURS	Damage	2000
RUMP SHAKER	Wreckx-N-Effect	1992
RUN	Sandie Shaw	1966
RUN	Lighthouse Family	2002
RUN	Snow Patrol	2004
RUN	George Strait	2001
RUN AWAY	(MC Sar &) The Real McCoy	1995
RUN AWAY CHILD, RUNNING WILD		
	Temptations	1969
RUN, BABY, RUN (BACK INTO MY ARMS)		
	Newbeats	1965
RUN, BABY, RUN	Sheryl Crow	1995
RUN BACK	Carl Douglas	1978
RUN FOR COVER	Sugababes	2001
RUN FOR HOME	Lindisfarne	1978
RUN FOR THE ROSES	Dan Fogelberg	1982
RUN FOR YOUR LIFE	Bucks Fizz	1983
RUN FOR YOUR LIFE	Northern Line	1999
RUN JOEY RUN	David Geddes	1975
RUN ON	Moby	1999
RUN RUDOLPH RUN	Chuck Berry	1963
RUN RUN RUN	Jo Jo Gunne	1972
RUN, RUN, LOOK AND SEE		
	Brian Hyland	1966
RUN, RUNAWAY	Slade	1984
RUN TO ME	Bee Gees	1972
RUN TO MY LOVIN' ARMS	Billy Fury	1965
RUN TO THE DOOR	Clinton Ford	1967
RUN TO THE HILLS	Iron Maiden	1982
RUN TO THE SUN	Erasure	1994
RUN TO YOU	Roxette	1994
RUN TO YOU	Bryan Adams	1984
RUN TO YOU	Rage	1992
RUN TO YOU	Whitney Houston	1993
RUN'S HOUSE	Run DMC	1988
RUNAGROUND	James	1998
RUN-AROUND	Blues Traveler	1995
RUNAROUND SUE	Racey	1980
RUNAROUND SUE	Leif Garrett	1977
THE RUNAWAY	Grass Roots	1972

SONG TITLE	ARTIST	DATE
RUNAWAY	E'voke	1995
RUNAWAY	Nuyorican Soul featuring India	1997
RUNAWAY	Corrs	1999
RUNAWAY	Janet Jackson	1995
RUNAWAY	Bon Jovi	1984
RUNAWAY	Jefferson Starship	1978
RUNAWAY BOYS	Stray Cats	1980
RUNAWAY HORSES	Belinda Carlisle	1990
RUNAWAY LOVE	En Vogue	1993
RUNAWAY TRAIN	Elton John & Eric Clapton	1992
RUNAWAY TRAIN	Soul Asylum	1993
RUNNER	Manfred Mann's Earth Band	1984
THE RUNNER	Three Degrees	1979
RUNNIN'	Pharcyde	1996
RUNNIN'	2Pac & Notorious B.I.G.	1998
RUNNIN'	Mark Picchiotti presents Basstoy featuring Dana	2002
RUNNIN' ALL OVER THE WORLD	Status Quo	1988
RUNNIN' AWAY	Sly & The Family Stone	1972
RUNNIN' DOWN A DREAM	Tom Petty	1989
RUNNIN' FOR THE RED LIGHT (I GOTTA LIFE)	Meat Loaf	1996
RUNNIN' ON EMPTY	Jackson Browne	1978
RUNNIN' (DYING TO LIVE)	Tupac featuring Notorious B.I.G.	2004

SONG TITLE	ARTIST	DATE
RUNNING AROUND TOWN	Billie Ray Martin	1995
RUNNING BACK TO YOU	Vanessa Williams	1991
RUNNING FREE	Iron Maiden	1980
RUNNING IN THE FAMILY	Level 42	1987
RUNNING OUT OF TIME	Digital Orgasm	1991
RUNNING UP THAT HILL	Kate Bush	1985
RUNNING WITH THE NIGHT	Lionel Richie	1983
RUPERT	Jackie Lee	1971
RUSH	Kleshay	1999
RUSH	Big Audio Dynamite II	1991
RUSH HOUR	Joyrider	1996
RUSH HOUR	Jane Wiedlin	1988
RUSH RUSH	Paula Abdul	1991
RUSHES	Darius	2002
RUSHING	Loni Clark	1993
RUSSIANS	Sting	1986
RUST	Echo & The Bunnymen	1999
RUSTY BELLS	Brenda Lee	1965
S CLUB PARTY	S Club 7	1999
S-S-S-SINGLE BED	Fox	1976
S.O.S.	ABC	1984
S.O.S.	ABBA	1975
S.Y.S.L.J.F.M. (THE LETTER SONG)	Joe Tex	1966
SABRE DANCE	Love Sculpture	1968

SONG TITLE	ARTIST	DATE
THE SACRAMENT	Him	2003
SACRAMENTO (A WONDERFUL TOWN)		
	Middle Of The Road	1972
SACRED EMOTION	Donny Osmond	1989
SACRED TRUST/AFTER YOU'RE GONE (I'LL STILL BE		
LOVING YOU)	One True Voice	2002
SACRIFICE	Elton John	1990
SAD BUT TRUE	Metallica	1993
SAD EYES	Robert John	1979
SAD, SAD GIRL	Barbara Mason	1965
SAD SONGS (SAY SO MUCH)		
	Elton John	1984
SAD SWEET DREAMER	Sweet Sensation	1975
SADDLE UP	David Christie	1982
SADNESS (PART 1)	Enigma	1991
SAFE FROM HARM	Massive Attack	1991
SAFE FROM HARM	Narcotic Thrust	2002
THE SAFETY DANCE	Men Without Hats	1983
SAID I LOVE YOU... BUT I LIED		
	Michael Bolton	1993
SAIL AWAY	David Gray	2001
SAIL AWAY	Urban Cookie Collective	1994
SAIL ON	Commodores	1979
SAILING	Rod Stewart	1975
SAILING	Christopher Cross	1980

SONG TITLE	ARTIST	DATE
SAILING ON THE SEVEN SEAS		
	OMD	1991
THE SAINT	Orbital	1997
SAINT OF ME	Rolling Stones	1998
SALE OF THE CENTURY	Sleeper	1996
SALLY	Gerry Monroe	1970
SALLY ANN	Joe Brown	1963
SALSOUL NUGGET (IF U WANNA)		
	M&S presents Girl Next Door	2001
THE SALT IN MY TEARS	Martin Briley	1983
SALTWATER	Chicane featuring Maire Brennan	
	Of Clannad	1999
SALTWATER	Julian Lennon	1991
SALVA MEA	Faithless	1996
SALVATION	Cranberries	1996
SAM	Keith West	1967
SAM	Olivia Newton-John	1977
SAMBA DE JANEIRO	Bellini	1997
SAMBA PA TI	Santana	1974
SAMBUCA	Wideboys featuring Dennis G	2001
SAME OLD BRAND NEW YOU		
	A1	2000
SAME OLD LANG SYNE	Dan Fogelberg	1980
THE SAME OLD SCENE	Roxy Music	1980
SAME OLD STORY	Ultravox	1986
SAMSON AND DELILAH	Middle Of The Road	1972

SONG TITLE	ARTIST	DATE
SAN BERNADINO	Christie	1970
SAN DAMIANO (HEART AND SOUL)		
	Sal Solo	1984
SAN FRANCISCO (BE SURE TO WEAR FLOWERS IN		
YOUR HAIR)	Scott McKenzie	1967
SANCTIFY YOURSELF	Simple Minds	1986
SANCTUARY	Iron Maiden	1980
SANCTUARY	New Musik	1980
SANCTUS (MISSA LUBA)	Troubadours Du Roi Baudouin	1969
SAND IN MY SHOES	Dido	2004
SANDMAN	Blue Boy	1997
SANDS OF TIME	Kaleef	1998
SANDSTORM	Cast	1996
SANDSTORM	Darude	2000
SANDWICHES	Detroit Grand Pu Bahs	2000
SANDY	John Travolta	1978
SANDY	Ronny & The Daytonas	1965
SANTA CLAUS IS COMIN' TO TOWN		
	Carpenters	1975
SANTA CLAUS IS COMIN' TO TOWN/MY HOMETOWN		
	Bruce Springsteen	1985
SANTA CLAUS IS ON THE DOLE/FIRST ATHEIST		
TABERNACLE CHOIR	Spitting Image	1986
SANTA CRUZ (YOU'RE NOT THAT FAR)		
	Thrills	2003
SANTA MARIA	Tatjana	1996

SONG TITLE	ARTIST	DATE
SANTA MARIA	DJ Milano featuring	
	Samantha Fox	1998
SANTA MONICA (WATCH THE WORLD DIE)		
	Everclear	1996
SANTA'S LIST	Cliff Richard	2003
SARA	Fleetwood Mac	1979
SARA	Starship	1985
SARA SMILE	Daryl Hall & John Oates	1976
SARAH	Thin Lizzy	1979
SAT IN YOUR LAP	Kate Bush	1981
SATAN	Orbital	1997
SATAN REJECTED MY SOUL		
	Morrissey	1998
SATELLITE	Beloved	1996
SATELLITE	Hooters	1987
SATELLITE	Oceanlab	2004
SATELLITE KID	Dogs D'Amour	1989
SATELLITE OF LOVE '04	Lou Reed	2004
SATIN PILLOWS	Bobby Vinton	1965
SATIN SHEETS	Jeanne Pruett	1973
SATIN SOUL	Love Unlimited Orchestra	1975
SATISFACTION	Wendy & Lisa	1989
SATISFACTION	Vanilla Ice	1991
SATISFACTION	Aretha Franklin	1968
SATISFACTION	Eve	2002
SATISFACTION	Benny Benassi presents The Biz	2003

SONG TITLE	ARTIST	DATE
SATISFACTION	Otis Redding	1966
SATISFACTION GUARANTEED (OR TAKE YOUR LOVE BACK)	Harold Melvin & The Bluenotes	1974
SATISFIED	Richard Marx	1989
A SATISFIED MIND	Bobby Hebb	1966
SATISFY MY SOUL	Bob Marley	1978
SATISFY YOU	Puff Daddy featuring R. Kelly	1999
SATURDAY	East 57th Street featuring Donna Allen	1997
SATURDAY (OOOH! OOOOH!)	Ludacris featuring Sleepy Brown	2002
SATURDAY IN THE PARK	Chicago	1972
SATURDAY LOVE	Cherelle With Alexander O'Neal	1986
SATURDAY MORNING CONFUSION	Bobby Russell	1971
SATURDAY NIGHT	Herman Brood	1979
SATURDAY NIGHT	Whigfield	1994
SATURDAY NIGHT	Suede	1997
SATURDAY NIGHT	UD Project	2004
SATURDAY NIGHT	Bay City Rollers	1975
SATURDAY NIGHT AT THE MOVIES	Drifters	1964
SATURDAY NIGHT PARTY (READ MY LIPS)	Alex Party	1994
SATURDAY NIGHT SPECIAL	Lynyrd Skynyrd	1975

SONG TITLE	ARTIST	DATE
SATURDAY NIGHT'S ALRIGHT FOR FIGHTING	Elton John	1973
SATURDAY NIGHT, SUNDAY MORNING	T-Empo	1994
SATURDAY NIGHT, SUNDAY MORNING	Thelma Houston	1979
SATURDAY NITE	Brand New Heavies	1999
SATURDAY NITE	Earth, Wind & Fire	1976
SATURDAY NITE AT THE DUCK-POND	Cougars	1963
SATURN 5	Inspiral Carpets	1994
SAVANNA DANCE	Deep Forest	1994
SAVANNAH NIGHTS	Tom Johnston	1979
SAVE A PRAYER	Duran Duran	1985
SAVE IT 'TIL THE MOURNING AFTER	Shut Up And Dance	1995
SAVE IT FOR A RAINY DAY	Stephen Bishop	1976
SAVE IT FOR ME	Four Seasons	1964
SAVE ME	Embrace	2000
SAVE ME	Dave Dee, Dozy, Beaky, Mick & Tich	1966
SAVE ME	Queen	1980
SAVE ME	Silver Convention	1975
SAVE ME	Fleetwood Mac	1990
SAVE OUR LOVE	Eternal	1994
SAVE SOME LOVE	Keedy	1991

SONG TITLE	ARTIST	DATE
SAVE THE BEST FOR LAST	Vanessa Williams	1992
SAVE THE COUNTRY	5th Dimension	1970
SAVE THE LAST DANCE FOR ME		
	DeFranco Family featuring Tony DeFranco	1974
SAVE TONIGHT	Eagle-Eye Cherry	1998
SAVE UP ALL YOUR TEARS	Cher	1991
SAVE YOUR HEART FOR ME		
	Gary Lewis & The Playboys	1965
SAVE YOUR KISSES FOR ME		
	Brotherhood Of Man	1976
SAVE YOUR LOVE	Renee And Renato	1982
SAVED	Mr Roy	1995
SAVED	Octopus	1996
SAVED BY THE BELL	Robin Gibb	1969
SAVED BY ZERO	Fixx	1983
SAVING ALL MY LOVE FOR YOU		
	Whitney Houston	1985
SAVING FOREVER FOR YOU		
	Shanice	1992
SAVIOUR'S DAY	Cliff Richard	1990
SAY A LITTLE PRAYER	Bomb The Bass	1988
SAY A PRAYER	Breathe	1990
SAY CHEESE (SMILE PLEASE)		
	Fast Food Rockers	2003

SONG TITLE	ARTIST	DATE
SAY GOODBYE/LOVE AIN'T GONNA WAIT FOR YOU		
	S Club	2003
SAY GOODBYE TO HOLLYWOOD		
	Billy Joel	1981
SAY HELLO WAVE GOODBYE		
	David Gray	2001
SAY HELLO WAVE GOODBYE		
	Soft Cell	1982
SAY HOW I FEEL	Rhian Benson	2004
SAY I AM (WHAT I AM)	Tommy James & The Shondells	1966
SAY I WON'T BE THERE	Springfields	1963
SAY I'M YOUR NO. 1	Princess	1985
SAY IT	Maria Rubia	2001
SAY IT	Voices Of Theory	1998
SAY IT AGAIN	Jermaine Stewart	1988
SAY IT AGAIN	Precious	1999
SAY IT ISN'T SO	Weezer	1995
SAY IT ISN'T SO	Bon Jovi	2000
SAY IT ISN'T SO	Gareth Gates	2003
SAY IT ISN'T SO	Daryl Hall & John Oates	1983
SAY IT LOUD – I'M BLACK AND I'M PROUD		
	James Brown	1968
SAY IT ONCE	Ultra	1998
SAY MY NAME	Zee	1997
SAY MY NAME	Destiny's Child	1999
SAY NO GO	De La Soul	1989

SONG TITLE	ARTIST	DATE
SAY NOTHIN'	Omar	1997
SAY SAY SAY	Paul McCartney & Michael Jackson	1983
SAY SOMETHING	Haven	2002
SAY SOMETHING ANYWAY	Bellefire	2004
SAY SOMETHING FUNNY	Patty Duke	1965
SAY THAT YOU'RE HERE	Fragma	2001
SAY WHAT	Jesse Winchester	1981
SAY WHAT!	X-Press 2	1993
SAY WHAT YOU WANT/INSANE	Texas featuring Wu-Tang Clan	1998
SAY WHEN	Lene Lovich	1979
SAY WONDERFUL THINGS	Ronnie Carroll	1963
SAY YEAH	Limit	1985
SAY YES	Floetry	2003
SAY YOU	Ronnie Dove	1964
SAY YOU DO	Ultra	1998
SAY YOU DON'T MIND	Colin Blunstone	1972
SAY YOU LOVE ME	Fleetwood Mac	1976
SAY YOU LOVE ME	Simply Red	1998
SAY YOU REALLY WANT ME	Kim Wilde	1987
SAY YOU, SAY ME	Lionel Richie	1985
SAY YOU WILL	Foreigner	1987
SAY YOU'LL BE MINE	QFX	1999
SAY YOU'LL BE MINE	Christopher Cross	1981

SONG TITLE	ARTIST	DATE
SAY YOU'LL BE MINE/BETTER THE DEVIL YOU KNOW	Steps	1999
SAY YOU'LL BE THERE	Spice Girls	1997
SAY YOU'LL STAY UNTIL TOMORROW	Tom Jones	1977
SAY YOU'RE WRONG	Julian Lennon	1985
(SAY) YOU'RE MY GIRL	Roy Orbison	1965
SAY, HAS ANYBODY SEEN MY SWEET GYPSY ROSE	Dawn featuring Tony Orlando	1973
SAY... IF YOU FEEL ALRIGHT	Crystal Waters	1997
SAYIN' SORRY (DOESN'T MAKE IT RIGHT)	Denise Lopez	1988
SCALES OF JUSTICE	Living In A Box	1987
SCANDAL	Queen	1989
SCANDALOUS	Mis-Teeq	2004
SCAR TISSUE	Red Hot Chili Peppers	1999
SCARBOROUGH FAIR	Sergio Mendes & Brasil '66	1968
SCARBOROUGH FAIR/CANTICLE	Simon & Garfunkel	1968
SCARED	Slacker	1997
SCARLET	All About Eve	1990
SCARLETT O'HARA	Jet Harris & Tony Meehan	1963
SCARY MONSTERS (AND SUPER CREEPS)	David Bowie	1981

SONG TITLE	ARTIST	DATE
SCATMAN (SKI-BA-BOP-BA-DOP-BOP)		
	Scatman John	1995
SCATMAN'S WORLD	Scatman John	1995
SCHOOL BOY CRUSH	Awb	1975
SCHOOL LOVE	Barry Blue	1974
SCHOOL'S OUT	Alice Cooper	1972
SCHOOL'S OUT	Daphne & Celeste	2000
SCIENCE OF SILENCE	Richard Ashcroft	2003
THE SCIENTIST	Coldplay	2002
SCOOBY SNACKS	Fun Lovin' Criminals	1996
SCORCHIO	Sasha/Emerson	2000
SCORPIO	Dennis Coffey & The Detroit Guitar Band	1971
SCORPIO RISING	Death In Vegas with Liam Gallagher	2002
SCOTCH ON THE ROCKS	Band Of The Black Watch	1975
THE SCRATCH	Surface Noise	1980
SCREAM/CHILDHOOD	Michael Jackson & Janet Jackson	1995
SCREAM IF YOU WANNA GO FASTER	Geri Halliwell	2001
SCREAM UNTIL YOU LIKE IT	W.A.S.P.	1987
THE SCREAMER	Yosh presents Lovedeejay Akemi	1996
SCULLERY	Clifford T. Ward	1974
SE A VIDA E (THAT'S THE WAY LIFE IS)	Pet Shop Boys	1996

SONG TITLE	ARTIST	DATE
SE LA	Lionel Richie	1987
SEA OF LOVE	Honeydrippers	1964
SEA OF LOVE	Del Shannon	1981
SEAGULL	Rainbow Cottage	1976
SEAL MY FATE	Belly	1995
SEAL OUR FATE	Gloria Estefan	1991
SEALED WITH A KISS	Jason Donovan	1989
SEALED WITH A KISS	Brian Hyland	1962
SEALED WITH A KISS	Gary Lewis & The Playboys	1968
SEALED WITH A KISS	Bobby Vinton	1972
SEARCH FOR THE HERO	M People	1995
THE SEARCH IS OVER	Survivor	1985
SEARCHIN'	Hazell Dean	1984
SEARCHIN'	Hollies	1963
SEARCHIN' MY SOUL	Vonda Shepard	1998
SEARCHING	Change	1980
SEARCHING	China Black	1994
SEARCHING FOR A SOUL	Conner Reeves	1998
SEARCHING FOR MY LOVE	Bobby Moore & The Rhythm Aces	1966
SEARCHING FOR THE GOLDEN EYE	Motiv 8 With Kym Mazelle	1995
SEASIDE	Ordinary Boys	2004
SEASIDE SHUFFLE	Terry Dactyl & The Dinosaurs	1972
SEASONS CHANGE	Expose	1987
SEASONS IN THE SUN	Terry Jacks	1974

SONG TITLE	ARTIST	DATE
SEASONS OF GOLD	Gidea Park	1981
SEATTLE	Perry Como	1969
SECOND AVENUE	Garfunkel	1974
SECOND CHANCE	38 Special	1989
SECOND HAND ROSE	Barbra Streisand	1965
SECOND NATURE	Electronic	1997
SECOND NATURE	Dan Hartman	1985
SECOND ROUND K.O.	Canibus	1998
THE SECOND SUMMER OF LOVE		
	Danny Wilson	1989
THE SECOND TIME	Kim Wilde	1984
THE SECOND TIME AROUND		
	Shalamar	1979
SECRET	Madonna	1994
SECRET	Orchestral Manoeuvres In The Dark	1985
SECRET AGENT MAN	Johnny Rivers	1966
SECRET GARDEN	T'Pau	1988
SECRET GARDEN	Bruce Springsteen	1997
SECRET GARDEN	Quincy Jones (featuring Al B. Sure, J. Ingram, E. DeBarge	1990
THE SECRET GARDEN	Quincy Jones	1990
SECRET KISS	Coral	2003
SECRET LOVE	Daniel O'Donnell & Mary Duff	1995
SECRET LOVE	Kelly Price	1999
SECRET LOVE	Bee Gees	1991

SONG TITLE	ARTIST	DATE
SECRET LOVE	Kathy Kirby	1963
SECRET LOVE	Freddy Fender	1975
SECRET LOVE	Billy Stewart	1966
SECRET LOVERS	Atlantic Starr	1985
SECRET RENDEZVOUS	Karyn White	1989
SECRET SEPARATION	Fixx	1986
SECRET SMILE	Semisonic	1999
THE SECRET VAMPIRE SOUNDTRACK (EP)		
	Bis	1996
SECRETLY	Skunk Anansie	1999
SECRETS	Sunscreem	1996
SECRETS	Eternal	1996
SECRETS	Sutherland Brothers And Quiver	1976
THE SECRETS THAT YOU KEEP		
	Mud	1975
SECURITY	Etta James	1968
THE SEDUCTION (LOVE THEME)		
	James Last Band	1980
SEE	Rascals	1969
SEE EMILY PLAY	Pink Floyd	1967
SEE IT IN A BOY'S EYES	Jamelia	2004
SEE ME, FEEL ME	Who	1970
SEE MY BABY JIVE	Wizzard	1973
SEE MY FRIEND	Kinks	1965
SEE SAW	Aretha Franklin	1968
SEE SEE RIDER	Eric Burdon & The Animals	1966

SONG TITLE	ARTIST	DATE
SEE THE DAY	Dee C. Lee	1985
SEE THE FUNNY LITTLE CLOWN		
	Bobby Goldsboro	1964
SEE THE LIGHTS	Simple Minds	1991
SEE THE STAR	Delirious?	1999
SEE THOSE EYES	Altered Images	1982
SEE YA	Atomic Kitten	2000
SEE YOU	Depeche Mode	1982
SEE YOU IN SEPTEMBER	Happenings	1966
THE SEED (2.0)	Roots featuring Cody Chesnutt	2003
THE SEEKER	Who	1970
SEEN THE LIGHT	Supergrass	2003
SELF CONTROL	Laura Branigan	1984
SELF ESTEEM	Offspring	1995
SELF!	Fuzzbox	1989
SELFISH ONE	Jackie Ross	1964
SELLING THE DRAMA	Live	1995
SEMI-CHARMED LIFE	Third Eye Blind	1997
SEMI-DETACHED SUBURBAN MR. JAMES		
	Manfred Mann	1966
SEND HER MY LOVE	Journey	1983
SEND HIS LOVE TO ME	PJ Harvey	1995
SEND IN THE CLOWNS	Judy Collins	1977
SEND ME AN ANGEL	Scorpions	1991
SEND ME AN ANGEL	Real Life	1983

SONG TITLE	ARTIST	DATE
SEND ME THE PILLOW THAT YOU DREAM ON		
	Dean Martin	1965
SEND ONE YOUR LOVE	Stevie Wonder	1979
SEND YOUR LOVE	Sting	2003
SENDING ALL MY LOVE	Linear	1990
SENDING MY LOVE	Zhane	1994
SENDING OUT AN S.O.S.	Retta Young	1975
SENORITA	Justin Timberlake	2003
SENSATIONAL	Michelle Gayle	1997
SENSE	Lightning Seeds	1992
SENSES WORKING OVERTIME		
	XTC	1982
SENSITIVITY	Ralph Tresvant	1990
SENSUAL SOPHIS-TI-CAT/THE PLAYER		
	Carl Cox	1996
THE SENSUAL WORLD	Kate Bush	1989
SENSUALITY	Lovestation	1998
SENTIMENTAL	Deborah Cox	1995
SENTIMENTAL	Kym Marsh	2003
SENTIMENTAL LADY	Bob Welch	1977
SENTIMENTAL STREET	Night Ranger	1985
SENTINEL	Mike Oldfield	1992
SENZA UNA DONNA (WITHOUT A WOMAN)		
	Zucchero/Paul Young	1991
SEPARATE LIVES	Phil Collins & Marilyn Martin	1985
SEPARATE TABLES	Chris De Burgh	1992

SONG TITLE	ARTIST	DATE
SEPARATE WAYS	Elvis Presley	1972
SEPARATE WAYS (WORLDS APART)		
	Journey	1983
SEPARATED	Avant	2000
SEPTEMBER	Earth, Wind & Fire	1978
SEPTEMBER 99	Earth, Wind & Fire	1999
SEPTEMBER MORN	Neil Diamond	1979
SEQUEL	Harry Chapin	1980
SERIOUS	Maxwell D	2001
SERIOUS	Donna Allen	1987
SERPENTINE FIRE	Earth, Wind & Fire	1977
SESAME'S TREET	Smart E's	1992
SET ADRIFT ON MEMORY BLISS		
	P.M. Dawn	1991
SET IT OFF	Peaches	2002
SET ME FREE	Jaki Graham	1986
SET ME FREE	Kinks	1965
SET ME FREE	Utopia	1980
SET THE NIGHT TO MUSIC	Roberta Flack With Maxi Priest	1991
SET THE RECORD STRAIGHT		
	Reef	2000
SET U FREE	Planet Soul	1995
THE SET UP (YOU DON'T KNOW)		
	Obie Trice featuring Nate Dogg	2004
SET YOU FREE	N-Trance featuring Kelly Llorenna	1994

SONG TITLE	ARTIST	DATE
SET YOUR LOVING FREE	Lisa Stansfield	1992
SETTING SUN	Chemical Brothers	1996
7	Prince & The New Power Generation	1992
SEVEN	David Bowie	2000
7 AND 7 IS	Love	1966
SEVEN BRIDGES ROAD	Eagles	1980
SEVEN CITIES	Solar Stone	1999
7 COLOURS	Lost Witness	2000
SEVEN DAFFODILS	Cherokees	1964
SEVEN DAFFODILS	Mojos	1964
7 DAYS	Craig David	2001
SEVEN DAYS	Mary J. Blige	1998
SEVEN DAYS	Sting	1993
SEVEN DAYS AND ONE WEEK		
	BBE	1996
SEVEN DAYS IN THE SUN	Feeder	2001
SEVEN DRUNKEN NIGHTS	Dubliners	1967
747 (STRANGERS IN THE NIGHT)		
	Saxon	1980
SEVEN LITTLE GIRLS SITTING IN THE BACK SEAT		
	Bombalurina	1990
7 NATION ARMY	White Stripes	2003
7 O'CLOCK	Quireboys	1989
SEVEN O'CLOCK NEWS/SILENT NIGHT		
	Simon And Garfunkel	1991

SONG TITLE	ARTIST	DATE
SEVEN ROOMS OF GLOOM	Four Tops	1967
SEVEN SEAS	Echo & The Bunnymen	1984
SEVEN SEAS OF RHYE	Queen	1974
7 SECONDS	Youssou N'Dour featuring Neneh Cherry	1994
SEVEN TEARS	Goombay Dance Band	1982
$7000 AND YOU	Stylistics	1977
7 WAYS TO LOVE	Cola Boy	1991
SEVEN WONDERS	Fleetwood Mac	1987
SEVEN YEAR ACHE	Rosanne Cash	1981
7-6-5-4-3-2-1 (BLOW YOUR WHISTLE)	Rimshots	1975
7:7 EXPANSION	System 7	1993
17	Rick James	1984
7 TEEN	Regents	1979
SEVENTEEN	Let Loose	1994
SEVENTEEN	Winger	1989
17 AGAIN	Eurythmics	2000
SEVENTH SON	Georgie Fame	1969
SEVENTH SON	Johnny Rivers	1965
'74-'75	Connells	1995
SEVERINA	Mission	1987
SEX AND CANDY	Marcy Playground	1998
SEX AS A WEAPON	Pat Benatar	1985
SEX BOMB	Tom Jones & Mousse T	2000
SEX ME	R. Kelly	1993
THE SEX OF IT	Kid Creole & The Coconuts	1990
SEX ON THE BEACH	T-Spoon	1998
SEX ON THE STREETS	Pizzaman	1995
SEX TALK (LIVE)	T'Pau	1988
SEXCRIME (NINETEEN EIGHTY FOUR)	Eurythmics	1984
SEXED UP	Robbie Williams	2003
SEXIEST MAN IN JAMAICA	Mint Royale	2002
SEXUAL	Amber	2000
SEXUAL GUARANTEE	Alcazar	2002
SEXUAL HEALING	Marvin Gaye	1982
SEXUALITY	Billy Bragg	1991
SEXX LAWS	Beck	1999
SEXY	MFSB	1975
SEXY BOY	Air	1998
SEXY CINDERELLA	Lynden David Hall	1998
SEXY EYES	Dr. Hook	1980
SEXY GIRL	Lillo Thomas	1987
SEXY GIRL	Glenn Frey	1984
SEXY MAMA	Moments	1974
SEXY MF/STROLLIN'	Prince	1992
SGT ROCK (IS GOING TO HELP ME)	XTC	1981
SHA LA LA	Manfred Mann	1964
SHA LA LA LA LEE	Plastic Bertrand	1978

SONG TITLE	ARTIST	DATE
SHA-LA-LA (MAKE ME HAPPY)		
	Al Green	1974
SHA-LA-LA-LA-LEE	Small Faces	1966
SHACKLES (PRAISE YOU)	Mary Mary	2000
SHADDAP YOU FACE	Joe Dolce	1981
SHADOW DANCING	Andy Gibb	1978
THE SHADOW OF LOVE	Damned	1985
SHADOWS IN THE MOONLIGHT		
	Anne Murray	1979
SHADOWS OF THE NIGHT	Pat Benatar	1982
SHADY LADY	Gene Pitney	1970
SHADY LANE	Pavement	1997
SHAGGY DOG	Mickey Lee Lane	1964
SHAKALAKA BABY	Preeya Kalidas	2002
SHAKE	Otis Redding	1967
SHAKE	Sam Cooke	1965
SHAKE A TAIL FEATHER	James & Bobby Purify	1967
SHAKE AND FINGERPOP	Jr. Walker & The All Stars	1965
SHAKE FOR THE SHEIK	Escape Club	1988
SHAKE IT	Ian Matthews	1978
SHAKE IT (MOVE A LITTLE CLOSER)		
	Lee-Cabrera featuring Alex Cartana	2003
SHAKE IT DOWN	Mud	1976
SHAKE IT UP	Cars	1981

SONG TITLE	ARTIST	DATE
SHAKE ME WAKE ME (WHEN IT'S OVER)		
	Four Tops	1966
(SHAKE, SHAKE, SHAKE) SHAKE YOUR BOOTY		
	KC & The Sunshine Band	1976
SHAKE THE DISEASE	Depeche Mode	1985
SHAKE UR BODY	Shy FX & T-Power featuring Di	2002
SHAKE YA ASS	Mystikal	2000
SHAKE YA BODY	N-Trance	2000
SHAKE YA SHIMMY	Porn Kings vs Flip & Fill featuring 740 Boys	2003
SHAKE YOU DOWN	Gregory Abbott	1986
SHAKE YOUR BODY (DOWN TO THE GROUND)		
	Full Intention	1997
SHAKE YOUR BODY (DOWN TO THE GROUND)		
	Jacksons	1979
SHAKE YOUR BON-BON	Ricky Martin	1999
SHAKE YOUR FOUNDATIONS	AC/DC	1986
SHAKE YOUR GROOVE THING		
	Peaches & Herb	1978
SHAKE YOUR HEAD	Was (Not Was)	1992
SHAKE YOUR LOVE	Debbie Gibson	1987
SHAKE YOUR RUMP TO THE FUNK		
	Bar-Kays	1976
SHAKE YOUR THANG (IT'S YOUR THANG)		
	Salt 'N 'Pepa	1988
SHAKE, RATTLE & ROLL	Arthur Conley	1967

SONG TITLE	ARTIST	DATE
SHAKEDOWN	Bob Seger & The Silver Bullet Band	1987
SHAKEDOWN CRUISE	Jay Ferguson	1979
SHAKERMAKER	Oasis	1994
SHAKESPEARE'S (WAY WITH) WORDS	One True Voice	2003
SHAKESPEARE'S SISTER	Smiths	1985
SHAKEY GROUND	Temptations	1975
SHAKIN' ALL OVER	Guess Who	1965
THE SHAKIN' STEVENS EP	Shakin' Stevens	1982
SHALALA LALA	Vengaboys	2000
SHAMBALA	Three Dog Night	1973
SHAME	Evelyn 'Champagne' King	1978
SHAME	Motels	1985
SHAME	Zhane	1994
SHAME AND SCANDAL IN THE FAMILY	Lance Percival	1965
SHAME ON THE MOON	Bob Seger & The Silver Bullet Band	1982
SHAME ON YOU	Gun	1990
SHAME SHAME	Magic Lanterns	1968
SHAME SHAME SHAME	Sinitta	1992
SHAME, SHAME, SHAME	Shirley And Company	1975
SHAMROCKS & SHENANIGANS/WHO'S THE MAN	House Of Pain	1993

SONG TITLE	ARTIST	DATE
SHANG-A-LANG	Bay City Rollers	1974
SHANGHAI BREEZES	John Denver	1982
SHANGRI-LA	Vic Dana	1964
SHANGRI-LA	Robert Maxwell, His Harp & His Orchestra	1964
SHANNON	Henry Gross	1976
SHAPE	Sugababes	2003
SHAPE OF MY HEART	Backstreet Boys	2000
SHAPE OF THINGS TO COME	Max Frost & The Troopers	1968
SHAPES OF THINGS	Yardbirds	1966
SHAPES THAT GO TOGETHER	A-Ha	1994
SHARE THE FALL	Reprazent/Roni Size	1997
SHARE THE LAND	Guess Who	1970
SHARE YOUR LOVE	Kenny Rogers	1981
SHARE YOUR LOVE WITH ME	Aretha Franklin	1969
SHARING THE NIGHT TOGETHER	Dr. Hook	1978
SHARP DRESSED MAN	ZZ Top	1984
SHATTERED	Rolling Stones	1978
SHATTERED DREAMS	Johnny Hates Jazz	1988
SHAVING CREAM	Benny Bell	1975
SHE	Charles Aznavour	1974
SHE	Elvis Costello	1999

SONG TITLE	ARTIST	DATE
SHE	Tommy James & The Shondells	1969
SHE AIN'T WORTH IT	Glenn Medeiros featuring Bobby Brown	1990
SHE BANGS	Ricky Martin	2000
SHE BANGS THE DRUMS	Stone Roses	1989
SHE BELIEVES (IN ME)	Ronan Keating	2004
SHE BELIEVES IN ME	Kenny Rogers	1979
SHE BELONGS TO ME	Ricky Nelson	1969
SHE BLINDED ME WITH SCIENCE	Thomas Dolby	1983
SHE BOP	Cyndi Lauper	1984
SHE CAME IN THROUGH THE BATHROOM WINDOW	Joe Cocker	1969
SHE COMES IN THE FALL	Inspiral Carpets	1990
SHE COULDN'T CHANGE ME	Montgomery Gentry	2001
SHE CRIES YOUR NAME	Beth Orton	1997
SHE DID IT	Eric Carmen	1977
SHE DON'T FOOL ME	Status Quo	1982
SHE DON'T LET NOBODY	Chaka Demus & Pliers	1993
SHE DRIVES ME CRAZY	Fine Young Cannibals	1989
SHE DROVE ME TO DAYTIME TELEVISION	Funeral For A Friend	2003
SHE GOT GAME	Tymes 4	2001
SHE HATES ME	Puddle Of Mudd	2002
SHE HITS ME	4 Of Us	1993

SONG TITLE	ARTIST	DATE
SHE IS STILL A MYSTERY	Lovin' Spoonful	1967
SHE IS SUFFERING	Manic Street Preachers	1994
SHE KISSED ME	Terence Trent D'Arby	1993
SHE KISSED ME (IT FELT LIKE A HIT)	Spiritualized	2003
SHE LEFT ME ON FRIDAY	Shed Seven	1998
SHE LOVES ME NOT	Papa Roach	2002
SHE LOVES YOU	Beatles	1964
SHE MAKES MY DAY	Robert Palmer	1988
SHE MAKES MY NOSE BLEED	Mansun	1997
SHE MEANS NOTHING TO ME	Phil Everly & Cliff Richard	1983
SHE NEEDS LOVE	Wayne Fontana & The Mindbenders	1965
SHE SAID	Longpigs	1996
SHE SELLS SANCTUARY	Cult	1985
SHE SOLD ME MAGIC	Lou Christie	1969
SHE TALKS TO ANGELS	Black Crowes	1991
SHE TAUGHT ME HOW TO YODEL	Frank Ifield/Backroom Boys	1991
SHE UNDERSTANDS ME	Johnny Tillotson	1964
SHE WANTS TO DANCE WITH ME	Rick Astley	1989
SHE WANTS TO MOVE	N E R D	2004
SHE WANTS YOU	Billie	1998

SONG TITLE	ARTIST	DATE
SHE WEARS MY RING	Solomon King	1968
SHE WILL BE LOVED	Maroon5	2004
SHE WILL HAVE HER WAY	Neil Finn	1998
SHE WON'T TALK TO ME	Luther Vandross	1989
SHE WORKS HARD FOR THE MONEY	Donna Summer	1983
SHE'D RATHER BE WITH ME	Turtles	1967
SHE'LL LEAVE YOU WITH A SMILE	George Strait	2002
SHE'S A BAD MAMA JAMA (SHE'S BUILT, SHE'S STACKED)	Carl Carlton	1981
SHE'S A BEAUTY	Tubes	1983
SHE'S A GOOD GIRL	Sleeper	1997
SHE'S A HEARTBREAKER	Gene Pitney	1968
SHE'S A LADY	Tom Jones	1971
SHE'S A LITTLE ANGEL	Little Angels	1990
SHE'S A MYSTERY TO ME	Roy Orbison	1989
SHE'S A RAINBOW	Rolling Stones	1967
SHE'S A RIVER	Simple Minds	1995
SHE'S A STAR	James	1997
SHE'S A WIND UP	Dr. Feelgood	1977
SHE'S A WOMAN	Scritti Politti featuring Shabba Ranks	1991
SHE'S A WOMAN	Beatles	1964

SONG TITLE	ARTIST	DATE
SHE'S ABOUT A MOVER	Sir Douglas Quintet	1965
SHE'S ALL I EVER HAD	Ricky Martin	1999
SHE'S ALL I GOT	Jimmy Cozier	2001
SHE'S ALL I GOT	Freddie North	1971
SHE'S ALL ON MY MIND	Wet Wet Wet	1995
SHE'S ALWAYS A WOMAN	Billy Joel	1978
SHE'S GONE	Matthew Marsden featuring Destiny's Child	1998
SHE'S GONE	Daryl Hall & John Oates	1976
SHE'S GONNA BREAK SOON	Less Than Jake	2003
SHE'S GOT A WAY	Billy Joel	1981
SHE'S GOT CLAWS	Gary Numan	1981
SHE'S GOT THAT VIBE	R. Kelly	1994
SHE'S IN FASHION	Suede	1999
SHE'S IN LOVE WITH YOU	Suzi Quatro	1979
SHE'S IN PARTIES	Bauhaus	1983
SHE'S JUST MY STYLE	Gary Lewis & The Playboys	1965
SHE'S LIKE THE WIND	Patrick Swayze featuring Wendy Fraser	1988
SHE'S LOOKIN' GOOD	Wilson Pickett	1968
SHE'S MINE	Cameo	1987
SHE'S MINE	Steve Perry	1984
SHE'S MORE	Andy Griggs	2000
SHE'S MY GIRL	Turtles	1967

SONG TITLE	ARTIST	DATE
SHE'S MY KIND OF RAIN	Tim McGraw	2003
SHE'S NOT JUST ANOTHER WOMAN		
	8th Day	1971
SHE'S NOT THERE	Neil MacArthur	1969
SHE'S NOT THERE	Santana	1977
SHE'S NOT THERE	Zombies	1964
SHE'S NOT THERE/KICKS (EP)		
	UK Subs	1979
SHE'S ON IT	Beastie Boys	1987
SHE'S OUT OF MY LIFE	Michael Jackson	1980
SHE'S PLAYING HARD TO GET		
	Hi-Five	1992
SHE'S SO BEAUTIFUL	Cliff Richard	1985
SHE'S SO COLD	Rolling Stones	1980
SHE'S SO FINE	Thunder	1990
SHE'S SO HIGH	Tal Bachman	1999
SHE'S SO HIGH	Kurt Nilsen	2004
SHE'S SO MODERN	Boomtown Rats	1978
SHE'S STRANGE	Cameo	1985
SHE'S THE ONE	Chartbusters	1964
SHE'S THE ONE/IT'S ONLY US		
	Robbie Williams	1999
(SHE'S) SEXY AND 17	Stray Cats	1983
SHED A TEAR	Wet Wet Wet	1993
SHEENA IS A PUNK ROCKER		
	Ramones	1977

SONG TITLE	ARTIST	DATE
SHEILA TAKE A BOW	Smiths	1987
SHELLSHOCK	New Order	1986
SHELTER	Brand New Heavies	1998
SHELTER ME	Cinderella	1990
SHERIFF FATMAN	Carter The Unstoppable	
	Sex Machine	1991
SHERRI DON'T FAIL ME NOW!		
	Status Quo	1994
SHERRY	Adrian Baker	1975
SHIFTER	Timo Maas featuring	
	MC Chickaboo	2002
SHILO	Neil Diamond	1970
SHINDIG	Shadows	1963
SHINE	Space Brothers	1997
SHINE	Aswad	1994
SHINE	Collective Soul	1994
SHINE 2000	Space Brothers	2000
SHINE A LITTLE LOVE	Electric Light Orchestra	1979
SHINE LIKE A STAR	Berri	1995
SHINE ON	Scott & Leon	2001
SHINE ON	Degrees Of Motion featuring	
	Biti	1994
SHINE ON	House Of Love	1990
SHINE ON	L.T.D.	1980
SHINE ON SILVER SUN	Strawbs	1973
SHINE SHINE	Barry Gibb	1984

SONG TITLE	ARTIST	DATE
SHINE SO HARD (EP)	Echo & The Bunnymen	1981
SHININ' ON	Grand Funk	1974
SHINING	Kristian Leontiou	2004
SHINING LIGHT	Ash	2001
SHINING STAR	Earth, Wind & Fire	1975
SHINING STAR	Manhattans	1980
SHINING STAR (EP)	INXS	1991
SHINY DISCO BALLS	Who Da Funk featuring Jessica Eve	2002
SHINY HAPPY PEOPLE	R.E.M.	1991
SHINY SHINY	Haysi Fantayzee	1983
SHIP OF FOOLS	Erasure	1988
SHIP OF FOOLS (SAVE ME FROM TOMORROW)	World Party	1987
SHIPBUILDING	Tasmin Archer	1994
SHIPBUILDING	Robert Wyatt	1983
SHIPS	Barry Manilow	1979
SHIPS (WHERE WERE YOU?)	Big Country	1993
SHIPS IN THE NIGHT	Be Bop Deluxe	1976
SHIRLEY	Shakin' Stevens	1982
SHIT ON YOU	D12	2001
SHIVER	Coldplay	2000
SHIVER	George Benson	1986
SHIVERING SAND	Mega City Four	1992
SHO' YOU RIGHT	Barry White	1987

SONG TITLE	ARTIST	DATE
SHOCK THE MONKEY	Peter Gabriel	1982
SHOCK TO THE SYSTEM	Billy Idol	1993
SHOCKED	Kylie Minogue	1991
SHOESHINE BOY	Eddie Kendricks	1975
SHOO DOO FU FU OOH!	Lenny Williams	1977
SHOO-BE-DOO-BE-DOO-DA-DAY	Stevie Wonder	1968
SHOOP	Salt 'N 'Pepa	1993
SHOOP SHOOP SONG (IT'S IN HIS KISS)	Betty Everett	1964
THE SHOOP SHOOP SONG (IT'S IN HIS KISS)	Cher	1990
SHOORAH! SHOORAH!	Betty Wright	1975
SHOOT ALL THE CLOWNS	Bruce Dickinson	1994
SHOOT ME WITH YOUR LOVE	D:ream	1995
SHOOT THE DOG	George Michael	2002
SHOOT YOUR GUN	22-20s	2004
SHOOT'EM UP BABY	Andy Kim	1968
SHOOTING STAR	Dollar	1978
SHOOTING STAR	Flip & Fill	2002
SHOP AROUND	Captain & Tennille	1976
SHOPLIFTERS OF THE WORLD UNITE	Smiths	1987
SHOPPING	Supersister	2001

SONG TITLE	ARTIST	DATE
SHORT DICK MAN	20 Fingers featuring Gillette	1994
SHORT PEOPLE	Randy Newman	1977
SHORT SHORT MAN	20 Fingers featuring Gillette	1995
SHORTSHARPSHOCK (EP)	Therapy?	1993
SHORTY (GOT HER EYES ON ME)	Donell Jones	2000
SHORTY (YOU KEEP PLAYIN' WITH MY MIND)	Imajin featuring Keith Murray	1998
SHOT IN THE DARK	Ozzy Osbourne	1986
SHOT SHOT	Gomez	2002
SHOTGUN	Jr. Walker & The All Stars	1965
SHOTGUN WEDDING	Rod Stewart	1993
SHOTGUN WEDDING	Roy 'C'	1966
SHOULD I DO IT	Pointer Sisters	1982
SHOULD I EVER (FALL IN LOVE)	Nightcrawlers featuring John Reid	1996
SHOULD I STAY	Gabrielle	2000
SHOULD I STAY OR SHOULD I GO? STRAIGHT TO HELL	Clash	1982
SHOULD'VE KNOWN BETTER	Richard Marx	1987
SHOULD'VE NEVER LET YOU GO	Neil Sedaka & Dara Sedaka	1980
SHOULDA WOULDA COULDA	Beverley Knight	2002

SONG TITLE	ARTIST	DATE
A SHOULDER TO CRY ON	Tommy Page	1989
SHOUT	Lulu	1964
SHOUT	Tears For Fears	1985
SHOUT	Louchie Lou & Michie One	1993
SHOUT	Ant & Dec	1997
SHOUT IT OUT LOUD	Kiss	1976
SHOUT SHOUT (KNOCK YOURSELF OUT)	Rocky Sharpe & The Replays	1982
SHOUT TO THE TOP	Fire Island featuring Loleatta Holloway	1998
SHOUT TO THE TOP	Style Council	1984
SHOUTING FOR THE GUNNERS	Arsenal FA Cup Squad '93	1993
THE SHOW	Doug E. Fresh & The Get Fresh Crew	1985
THE SHOW	Girls Aloud	2004
THE SHOW (THEME FROM 'CONNIE')	Rebecca Storm	1985
SHOW A LITTLE LOVE	Ultimate Kaos	1995
SHOW AND TELL	Al Wilson	1973
SHOW ME	Dana Dawson	1996
SHOW ME	Dexy's Midnight Runners	1981
SHOW ME	Pretenders	1984
SHOW ME	Joe Tex	1967
SHOW ME A SIGN	Kontakt	2003
SHOW ME GIRL	Herman's Hermits	1964

SONG TITLE	ARTIST	DATE
SHOW ME HEAVEN	Tina Arena	1995
SHOW ME HEAVEN	Maria McKee	1990
SHOW ME HEAVEN	Saint featuring Suzanna Dee	2003
SHOW ME LOVE	Robin S.	1993
SHOW ME LOVE	Robyn	1997
SHOW ME THE MEANING OF BEING LONELY		
	Backstreet Boys	2000
SHOW ME THE MONEY	Architechs	2001
SHOW ME THE WAY	Peter Frampton	1976
SHOW ME THE WAY	Styx	1990
SHOW ME YOUR SOUL	Lenny Kravitz/P.Diddy/Loon/	
	Pharrell Williams	2004
SHOW ME YOU'RE A WOMAN		
	Mud	1975
THE SHOW MUST GO ON	Leo Sayer	1973
THE SHOW MUST GO ON	Queen	1991
THE SHOW MUST GO ON	Three Dog Night	1974
SHOW SOME RESPECT	Tina Turner	1985
SHOW YOU THE WAY TO GO		
	Dannii Minogue	1992
SHOW YOU THE WAY TO GO		
	Jacksons	1977
SHOWDOWN	Electric Light Orchestra	1973
SHOWDOWN	Jody Lei	2003
SHOWER ME WITH YOUR LOVE		
	Surface	1989

SONG TITLE	ARTIST	DATE
SHOWER THE PEOPLE	James Taylor	1976
SHOWER YOUR LOVE	Kula Shaker	1999
SHOWING OUT	Mel & Kim	1986
SHOWROOM DUMMIES	Kraftwerk	1982
(SHU-DOO-PA-POO-POOP) LOVE BEING YOUR FOOL		
	Travis Wammack	1975
THE SHUFFLE	Van McCoy	1977
SHUT 'EM DOWN	Public Enemy	1992
SHUT UP	Madness	1981
SHUT UP	Kelly Osbourne	2003
SHUT UP	Black Eyed Peas	2003
SHUT UP AND DANCE	Aerosmith	1994
SHUT UP AND FORGET ABOUT IT		
	Dane	2001
SHUT UP AND KISS ME	Mary Chapin Carpenter	1995
SHUT YOUR MOUTH	Julian Cope	1986
SHUT YOUR MOUTH	Garbage	2002
SHY BOY	Bananarama	1982
SHY GIRL	Mark Wynter	1963
(SI SI) JE SUIS UN ROCK STAR		
	Bill Wyman	1981
SI TU DOIS PARTIR	Fairport Convention	1969
SIC TRANSIT GLORIA GLORY FADES		
	Brand New	2004
SICK & TIRED	Cardigans	1995
SICK AND TIRED	Anastacia	2004

SONG TITLE	ARTIST	DATE
SICK OF DRUGS	Wildhearts	1996
SICK OF IT	Primitives	1989
SIDE	Travis	2001
SIDE SHOW	Barry Biggs	1976
SIDESHOW	Blue Magic	1974
SIDEWALK SURFIN'	Jan & Dean	1964
SIDEWALK TALK	Jellybean	1985
SIDEWALKING	Jesus & Mary Chain	1988
THE SIDEWINDER SLEEPS TONITE	R.E.M.	1993
SIGHT FOR SORE EYES	M People	1994
THE SIGN	Ace Of Base	1994
SIGN 'O' THE TIMES	Prince	1987
THE SIGN OF FIRE	Fixx	1983
SIGN OF THE TIMES	Bryan Ferry	1978
SIGN OF THE TIMES	Belle Stars	1983
A SIGN OF THE TIMES	Petula Clark	1966
SIGN YOUR NAME	Terence Trent D'Arby	1988
SIGNED, SEALED, DELIVERED (I'M YOURS)	Peter Frampton	1977
SIGNED, SEALED, DELIVERED, I'M YOURS	Stevie Wonder	1970
SIGNED, SEALED, DELIVERED, I'M YOURS	Blue/Stevie Wonder/Angie Stone	2003
SIGNS	Five Man Electrical Band	1971
SIGNS	Tesla	1991

SONG TITLE	ARTIST	DATE
SILENCE	Delerium featuring Sarah McLachlan	2000
THE SILENCE	Mike Koglin	1998
SILENCE IS EASY	Starsailor	2003
SILENCE IS GOLDEN	Tremeloes	1967
SILENT ALL THESE YEARS	Tori Amos	1992
SILENT LUCIDITY	Queensryche	1991
SILENT PRAYER	Shanice	1992
SILENT RUNNING (ON DANGEROUS GROUND)	Mike & The Mechanics	1985
SILENT SCREAM	Richard Marx	1994
SILENT SIGH	Badly Drawn Boy	2002
SILENT TO THE DARK II	Electric Soft Parade	2002
SILENT VOICE	Innocence	1990
SILHOUETTE	Kenny G	1988
SILHOUETTES	Herman's Hermits	1965
SILHOUETTES	Cliff Richard	1990
SILLY GAMES	Janet Kay	1979
SILLY GAMES	Lindy Layton/Janet Kay	1990
SILLY LOVE	10cc	1974
SILLY LOVE SONGS	Paul McCartney	1976
SILLY THING/WHO KILLED BAMBI	Sex Pistols	1979
SILVER	Echo & The Bunnymen	1984
SILVER	Hundred Reasons	2002
SILVER BIRD	Mark Lindsay	1970

SONG TITLE	ARTIST	DATE
SILVER DREAM MACHINE (PT 1)		
	David Essex	1980
SILVER LADY	David Soul	1977
SILVER MACHINE	Hawkwind	1972
SILVER SCREEN SHOWER SCENE		
	Felix Da Housecat	2002
SILVER SHORTS	Wedding Present	1992
SILVER STAR	Four Seasons	1976
SILVERY RAIN	Cliff Richard	1971
SIMON SAYS	Pharoahe Monch	2000
SIMON SAYS	1910 Fruitgum Co.	1968
SIMON SMITH & HIS AMAZING DANCING BEAR		
	Alan Price Set	1967
SIMON TEMPLER/TWO PINTS OF LAGER AND A PACKET		
OF CRISPS PLEASE	Splodgenessabounds	1980
SIMPLE GAME	Four Tops	1971
SIMPLE KIND OF LIFE	No Doubt	2000
SIMPLE LIFE	Elton John	1993
THE SIMPLE THINGS	Joe Cocker	1994
THE SIMPLE TRUTH	Chris De Burgh	1991
SIMPLY IRRESISTIBLE	Robert Palmer	1988
SIN	Nine Inch Nails	1991
SINCE I DON'T HAVE YOU	Guns N' Roses	1994
SINCE I DON'T HAVE YOU	Art Garfunkel	1979
SINCE I DON'T HAVE YOU	Don McLean	1981
SINCE I LEFT YOU	Avalanches	2001

SONG TITLE	ARTIST	DATE
SINCE I LOST MY BABY	Temptations	1965
SINCE I MET YOU LADY/SPARKLE OF MY EYES		
	UB40 featuring LADY SAW	2001
SINCE I TOLD YOU IT'S OVER		
	Stereophonics	2003
SINCE YESTERDAY	Strawberry Switchblade	1984
SINCE YOU SHOWED ME HOW TO BE HAPPY		
	Jackie Wilson	1967
SINCE YOU'RE GONE	Cars	1982
SINCE YOU'VE BEEN GONE	Rainbow	1979
SINCE YOU'VE BEEN GONE	Outfield	1987
SINCERE	MJ Cole	1998
SINCERELY YOURS	Sweet Sensations with Romeo	
	J.D	1989
SINFUL	Pete Wylie	1986
SING	Travis	2001
SING	Carpenters	1973
SING A HAPPY SONG	O'Jays	1979
SING A HAPPY SONG	George McCrae	1975
SING A LITTLE SONG	Desmond Dekker & The Aces	1975
SING A SONG	Byron Stingily	1997
SING A SONG	Earth, Wind & Fire	1975
SING A SONG OF FREEDOM		
	Cliff Richard	1971
SING BABY SING	Stylistics	1975
SING DON'T SPEAK	Blackfoot Sue	1972

SONG TITLE	ARTIST	DATE
SING FOR ABSOLUTION	Muse	2004
SING FOR THE MOMENT	Eminem	2003
SING HALLELUJAH!	Dr. Alban	1993
SING IT (THE HALLELUJAH SONG)		
	Mozaic	1995
SING IT BACK	Moloko	1999
SING ME	Brothers	1977
SING ME AN OLD FASHIONED SONG		
	Billie Jo Spears	1976
SING OUR OWN SONG	UB40	1986
SING UP FOR THE CHAMPIONS		
	Reds United	1997
SING YOUR LIFE	Morrissey	1991
SING-A-LONG	Shanks & Bigfoot	2000
SINGALONG-A-SANTA	Santa Claus & The Christmas	
	Trees	1982
SINGALONG-A-SANTA AGAIN		
	Santa Claus & The Christmas	
	Trees	1983
SINGIN' IN THE RAIN (PT I)		
	Sheila B. Devotion	1978
SINGING IN MY SLEEP	Semisonic	2000
SINGING THE BLUES	Daniel O'Donnell	1994
SINGING THE BLUES	Dave Edmunds	1980
SINGLE	Everything But The Girl	1996
SINGLE	Pet Shop Boys	1996

SONG TITLE	ARTIST	DATE
SINGLE	Natasha Bedingfield	2004
SINGLE GIRL	Lush	1996
SINGLE GIRL	Sandy Posey	1966
SINGLE LIFE	Cameo	1985
SINGLE WHITE FEMALE	Chely Wright	1999
SINNER	Neil Finn	1998
SINS OF THE FAMILY	P.F. Sloan	1965
SIR DANCEALOT	Olympic Runners	1979
SIR DUKE	Stevie Wonder	1977
SISSYNECK	Beck	1997
SISTA SISTA	Beverley Knight	1999
SISTER	Bros	1989
SISTER	Sister 2 Sister	2000
SISTER CHRISTIAN	Night Ranger	1984
SISTER GOLDEN HAIR	America	1975
SISTER JANE	New World	1972
SISTER MARY ELEPHANT (SHUDD-UP!)		
	Cheech & Chong	1973
SISTER OF MERCY	Thompson Twins	1984
SISTER PAIN	Electrafixion	1996
SISTER SISTER	Sister Bliss	2000
SISTER SURPRISE	Gary Numan	1983
THE SISTERS (EP)	Pulp	1994
SISTERS ARE DOIN' IT FOR THEMSELVES		
	Eurythmics & Aretha Franklin	1985
SIT AND WAIT	Sydney Youngblood	1989

SONG TITLE	ARTIST	DATE
SIT DOWN	James	1991
SIT DOWN, I THINK I LOVE YOU	Mojo Men	1967
SIT YOURSELF DOWN	Stephen Stills	1971
SITTIN' IN THE LAP OF LUXURY	Louie Louie	1990
SITTIN' IN THE PARK	Georgie Fame	1966
SITTIN' ON A FENCE	Twice As Much	1966
SITTIN' ON TOP OF THE WORLD	Da Brat	1996
(SITTIN' ON) THE DOCK OF THE BAY	Otis Redding	1968
(SITTIN' ON) THE DOCK OF THE BAY	Michael Bolton	1988
SITTIN' UP IN MY ROOM	Brandy	1995
SITTING	Cat Stevens	1972
SITTING AT HOME	Honeycrack	1996
SITTING AT THE WHEEL	Moody Blues	1983
SITTING DOWN HERE	Lene Marlin	2000
SITTING IN THE PARK	Billy Stewart	1965
SITUATION	Yazoo	1990
SIX	Mansun	1999
SIX DAYS	DJ Shadow	2002
SIX FEET DEEP	Geto Boys	1993
643 (LOVE'S ON FIRE)	DJ Tiesto featuring Suzanne Palmer	2002

SONG TITLE	ARTIST	DATE
SIX O'CLOCK	Lovin' Spoonful	1967
SIX PACK	Police	1980
THE SIX TEENS	Sweet	1974
634-5789	Wilson Pickett	1966
6 UNDERGROUND	Sneaker Pimps	1996
SIXTEEN	Musical Youth	1984
SIXTEEN BARS	Stylistics	1976
68 GUNS	Alarm	1983
'65 LOVE AFFAIR	Paul Davis	1982
SIXTY MILE SMILE	3 Colours Red	1997
60 MILES AN HOUR	New Order	2001
SIXTY MINUTE MAN	Trammps	1975
THE SIZE OF A COW	Wonder Stuff	1991
SK8ER BOI	Avril Lavigne	2002
SKATEAWAY	Dire Straits	1981
SKELETONS	Stevie Wonder	1987
SKIING IN THE SNOW	Wigan's Ovation	1975
SKIN DEEP	Stranglers	1984
SKIN O' MY TEETH	Megadeth	1992
SKIN ON SKIN	Grace	1996
SKIN TIGHT	Ohio Players	1974
SKIN TRADE	Duran Duran	1987
SKINNY LEGS AND ALL	Joe Tex	1967
SKIP A ROPE	Henson Cargill	1967
SKIP TO MY LU	Lisa Lisa	1994
SKWEEZE ME PLEEZE ME	Slade	1973

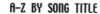

SONG TITLE	ARTIST	DATE
SKY	Sonique	2000
SKY HIGH	Jigsaw	1975
SKY PILOT	Eric Burdon & The Animals	1968
SKY'S THE LIMIT/GOING BACK TO CALI		
	Notorious B.I.G./112	1997
SKYDIVE (I FEEL WONDERFUL)		
	Freefall featuring Jan Johnston	2001
THE SKYE BOAT SONG	Roger Whittaker &	
	Des O'Connor	1986
SKYWRITER	Jackson 5	1973
SLAM	Onyx	1993
SLAM DUNK (DA FUNK)	5ive	1997
SLAM JAM	WWF Superstars	1992
SLANG	Def Leppard	1996
SLAP & TICKLE	Squeeze	1979
SLASH 'N' BURN	Manic Street Preachers	1992
SLASHDOTDASH	Fatboy Slim	2004
SLAUGHTER ON TENTH AVENUE		
	Ventures	1964
SLAVE TO LOVE	Bryan Ferry	1985
SLAVE TO THE RHYTHM	Grace Jones	1985
SLAVE TO THE VIBE	Aftershock	1993
SLAVE TO THE WAGE	Placebo	2000
SLEAZY BED TRACK	Bluetones	1998
SLEDGEHAMMER	Peter Gabriel	1986
SLEEP	Marion	1996

SONG TITLE	ARTIST	DATE
SLEEP	Little Willie John	1980
SLEEP ON THE LEFT SIDE	Cornershop	1998
SLEEP TALK	A.T.F.C. featuring Lisa Millett	2002
SLEEP TALK	Alyson Williams	1989
SLEEP WELL TONIGHT	Gene	1994
SLEEP WITH ME	Birdland	1990
SLEEPING BAG	ZZ Top	1985
SLEEPING IN	Menswear	1995
SLEEPING IN MY CAR	Roxette	1994
SLEEPING SATELLITE	Tasmin Archer	1993
SLEEPING WITH THE LIGHT ON		
	Busted	2003
SLEEPWALK	Ultravox	1980
SLEEPY JOE	Herman's Hermits	1968
SLEEPY SHORES	Johnny Pearson Orchestra	1971
SLICE OF DA PIE	Monie Love	2000
SLIDE	Goo Goo Dolls	1998
SLIDE	Slave	1977
SLIDE ALONG SIDE	Shifty	2004
SLIGHT RETURN	Bluetones	1996
THE SLIGHTEST TOUCH	Five Star	1987
SLIP AND SLIDE	Medicine Head	1974
SLIP AWAY	Clarence Carter	1968
SLIP SLIDIN' AWAY	Paul Simon	1977
SLIPPERY WHEN WET	Commodores	1975
SLIPPIN'	DMX	1999

SONG TITLE	ARTIST	DATE
SLIPPIN' INTO DARKNESS	War	1972
SLIPPING AWAY	Dave Edmunds	1983
SLITHER	Velvet Revolver	2004
SLOOP JOHN B	Beach Boys	1966
SLOW	Kylie Minogue	2003
SLOW AND SEXY	Shabba Ranks featuring Johnny Gill	1992
SLOW DANCIN' DON'T TURN ME ON	Addrisi Brothers	1977
SLOW DOWN	John Miles	1977
SLOW DOWN	Loose Ends	1986
SLOW DOWN	Beatles	1964
SLOW EMOTION REPLAY	The The	1993
SLOW FLOW	Braxtons	1997
SLOW HAND	Pointer Sisters	1981
SLOW HANDS	Interpol	2004
SLOW IT DOWN	East 17	1993
SLOW JAMZ	Twista	2004
SLOW MOTION	Ultravox	1981
SLOW MOTION	Color Me Badd	1992
SLOW RIDE	Foghat	1975
SLOWDOWN	John Miles	1977
SLY	Massive Attack	1994
THE SLY, SLICK, AND THE WICKED	Lost Generation	1970
SMACK MY BITCH UP	Prodigy	1997

SONG TITLE	ARTIST	DATE
SMALL BEGINNINGS	Flash	1972
SMALL BIT OF LOVE	Saw Doctors	1994
SMALL TOWN	John Cougar Mellencamp	1985
A SMALL VICTORY	Faith No More	1992
SMALL WORLD	Huey Lewis & The News	1988
SMALLTOWN BOY	Bronski Beat	1984
SMALLTOWN BOY (1991 REMIX)	Jimmy Somerville	1991
SMARTY PANTS	First Choice	1973
SMASH IT UP	Damned	1979
SMASH SUMTHIN'	Redman featuring Adam F	2001
SMELLS LIKE NIRVANA	'Weird Al' Yankovic	1992
SMELLS LIKE TEEN SPIRIT	Abigail	1994
SMELLS LIKE TEEN SPIRIT	Nirvana	1991
SMILE	Supernaturals	1997
SMILE	Audrey Hall	1986
SMILE	Pussycat	1976
SMILE	Lonestar	1999
SMILE	Scarface featuring 2Pac & Johnny P	1997
SMILE	Vitamin C featuring Lady Saw	1999
SMILE A LITTLE SMILE FOR ME	Flying Machine	1969

SONG TITLE	ARTIST	DATE
THE SMILE HAS LEFT YOUR EYES	Asia	1983
SMILING FACES SOMETIME	Undisputed Truth	1971
SMOKE	Natalie Imbruglia	1998
SMOKE FROM A DISTANT FIRE	Sanford/Townsend Band	1977
SMOKE GETS IN YOUR EYES	John Alford	1996
SMOKE GETS IN YOUR EYES	Blue Haze	1972
SMOKE GETS IN YOUR EYES	Bryan Ferry	1974
SMOKE ON THE WATER	Rock Aid Armenia	1989
SMOKE ON THE WATER	Deep Purple	1973
SMOKEY BLUES AWAY	New Generation	1968
SMOKIN' IN THE BOYS ROOM	Brownsville Station	1973
SMOKIN' IN THE BOYS ROOM	Motley Crue	1985
SMOKIN' ME OUT	Warren G featuring Ron Isley	1997
SMOKING GUN	Robert Cray Band	1987
SMOKY MOUNTAIN RAIN	Ronnie Milsap	1980
SMOOTH	Santana featuring Rob Thomas	1999
SMOOTH CRIMINAL	Alien Ant Farm	2001
SMOOTH CRIMINAL	Michael Jackson	1988
SMOOTH OPERATOR	Sade	1985

SONG TITLE	ARTIST	DATE
SMUGGLER'S BLUES	Glenn Frey	1985
THE SMURF SONG	Father Abraham & The Smurfs	1978
SNAKE	R. Kelly featuring Big Tigger	2003
THE SNAKE	Al Wilson	1968
SNAKE IN THE GRASS	Dave Dee, Dozy, Beaky, Mick & Tich	1969
SNAP MEGA MIX	Snap!	1991
SNAPPINESS	BBG featuring Dina Taylor	1990
SNATCHING IT BACK	Clarence Carter	1969
SNOOKER LOOPY	Matchroom Mob With Chas & Dave	1986
SNOOP DOGG	Snoop Dogg	2001
SNOOP'S UPSIDE YA HEAD	Snoop Doggy Dogg featuring Charlie Wilson	1996
SNOOPY VS THE RED BARON	Hotshots	1973
SNOOPY VS THE RED BARON	Royal Guardsmen	1966
SNOT RAP	Kenny Everett	1983
SNOW	JJ72	2001
SNOWBIRD	Anne Murray	1970
SO ALIVE	Ryan Adams	2004
SO ALIVE	Love And Rockets	1989
SO ALONE	Men At Large	1993
SO AMAZING	Luther Vandross	1987

SONG TITLE	ARTIST	DATE
SO ANXIOUS	Ginuwine	1999
SO BAD	Paul McCartney	1983
SO BEAUTIFUL	Chris De Burgh	1997
SO CALLED FRIEND	Texas	1993
SO CLOSE	Dina Carroll	1992
SO CLOSE	Daryl Hall & John Oates	1990
SO CLOSE	Diana Ross	1983
SO CLOSE TO LOVE	Wendy Moten	1994
SO COLD THE NIGHT	Communards	1986
SO CONFUSED	2Play featuring Raghav & Jucxi	2004
SO DAMN BEAUTIFUL	Poloroid	2003
SO DEEP IS THE NIGHT	Ken Dodd	1964
SO EMOTIONAL	Whitney Houston	1987
SO FAR AWAY	Dire Straits	1986
SO FAR AWAY	Staind	2003
SO FAR AWAY/SMACKWATER JACK		
	Carole King	1971
SO FINE	Fiestas	1969
SO FRESH, SO CLEAN	Outkast	2001
SO GOOD	Roy Orbison	1967
SO GOOD	Eternal	1994
SO GOOD	Boyzone	1995
SO GOOD TO BE BACK HOME AGAIN		
	Tourists	1980
SO GOOD TOGETHER	Andy Kim	1969
SO GOOD, SO RIGHT	Brenda Russell	1979

SONG TITLE	ARTIST	DATE
SO GOOD/FREE LOVE 98	Juliet Roberts	1998
SO HARD	Pet Shop Boys	1990
SO HELP ME GIRL	Gary Barlow	1997
SO HERE I AM	UB40	1982
SO I BEGIN	Galleon	2002
SO I CAN LOVE YOU	Emotions	1969
SO IN LOVE	Orchestral Manoeuvres In The Dark	1985
SO IN LOVE (THE REAL DEAL)		
	Judy Cheeks	1993
SO IN LOVE WITH TWO	Mikaila	2000
SO IN LOVE WITH YOU	Texas	1994
SO IN LOVE WITH YOU	Duke	1996
SO IN LOVE WITH YOU	Spear Of Destiny	1988
SO INTO YOU	Atlanta Rhythm Section	1977
SO INTO YOU	Wildhearts	2003
SO INTO YOU	Tamia	1998
(SO IT IS... SO IT WAS) SO IT WILL ALWAYS BE		
	Everly Brothers	1963
SO LET ME GO FAR	Dodgy	1995
SO LONELY	Police	1980
SO LONELY	Jakatta	2002
SO LONG	Fierce	1999
SO LOW	Ocean Colour Scene	1999
SO MACHO/CRUISING	Sinitta	1986
SO MANY WAYS	Braxtons	1997

SONG TITLE	ARTIST	DATE
SO MANY WAYS	Ellie Campbell	1999
SO MUCH IN LOVE	Tymes	1963
SO MUCH IN LOVE	All-4-One	1994
SO MUCH LOVE	Tony Blackburn	1968
SO NATURAL	Lisa Stansfield	1993
SO NEAR TO CHRISTMAS	Alvin Stardust	1984
SO PURE	Alanis Morissette	1999
SO PURE	Baby D	1996
SO REAL	Love Decade	1991
SO RIGHT	K-Klass	1992
SO SAD THE SONG	Gladys Knight & The Pips	1976
SO SEXY	Twista featuring R. Kelly	2004
SO TELL ME WHY	Poison	1991
SO THE STORY GOES	Living In A Box featuring Bobby Womack	1987
SO THIS IS ROMANCE	Linx	1981
SO TIRED	Frankie Vaughan	1967
SO TIRED	Ozzy Osbourne	1984
SO VERY HARD TO GO	Tower Of Power	1973
SO WHAT!	Ronny Jordan	1992
SO WHAT IF I	Damage	2001
SO WHY SO SAD	Manic Street Preachers	2001
SO WRONG	Patrick Simmons	1983
SO YESTERDAY	Hilary Duff	2003
SO YOU ARE A STAR	Hudson Brothers	1974

SONG TITLE	ARTIST	DATE
SO YOU WANT TO BE A ROCK 'N' ROLL STAR	Byrds	1967
SO YOU WIN AGAIN	Hot Chocolate	1977
SO YOUNG	Suede	1993
SO YOUNG	Corrs	1998
SOAK UP THE SUN	Sheryl Crow	2002
SOAPBOX	Little Angels	1993
SOCIETY'S CHILD (BABY I'VE BEEN THINKING)	Janis Ian	1967
SOCK IT TO ME BABY!	Mitch Ryder & The Detroit Wheels	1967
SOCKIT2ME	Missy 'Misdemeanor' Elliott featuring Da Brat	1997
SOFT LIKE ME	Saint Etienne	2003
SOFTLY WHISPERING I LOVE YOU	Paul Young	1990
SOFTLY WHISPERING I LOVE YOU	Congregation	1971
SOFTLY, AS I LEAVE YOU	Frank Sinatra	1964
SOLACE OF YOU	Living Colour	1991
SOLD	Boy George	1987
SOLD MY ROCK 'N' ROLL (GAVE IT FOR FUNKY SOUL)	Linda & The Funky Boys	1976
SOLDIER BLUE	Buffy Sainte-Marie	1971
SOLDIER BOY	Cheetahs	1965
SOLDIER GIRL	Polyphonic Spree	2003

SONG TITLE	ARTIST	DATE
SOLDIER OF LOVE	Donny Osmond	1989
SOLEY SOLEY	Middle Of The Road	1971
SOLID	Ashford & Simpson	1984
SOLID BOND IN YOUR HEART		
	Style Council	1983
SOLID GOLD EASY ACTION	T. Rex	1972
SOLITAIRE	Carpenters	1975
SOLITAIRE	Andy Williams	1973
SOLITAIRE	Laura Branigan	1983
SOLITARY MAN	Him	2004
SOLITARY MAN	Neil Diamond	1970
SOLOMON BITES THE WORM		
	Bluetones	1998
SOLSBURY HILL	Peter Gabriel	1977
SOLSBURY HILL	Erasure	2003
SOLVED	Unbelievable Truth	1998
SOME CANDY TALKING	Jesus & Mary Chain	1986
SOME DAY WE'RE GONNA LOVE AGAIN		
	Searchers	1964
SOME DAYS ARE DIAMONDS (SOME DAYS ARE STONE)		
	John Denver	1981
SOME ENCHANTED EVENING		
	Jay & The Americans	1965
SOME GIRLS	Racey	1979
SOME GIRLS	Ultimate Kaos	1994
SOME GIRLS	Rachel Stevens	2004

SONG TITLE	ARTIST	DATE
SOME GIRLS (DANCE WITH WOMEN)/BLOWIN' ME UP		
(WITH HER LOVE)	JC Chasez	2004
SOME GUYS HAVE ALL THE LUCK		
	Robert Palmer	1982
SOME GUYS HAVE ALL THE LUCK		
	Maxi Priest	1987
SOME GUYS HAVE ALL THE LUCK		
	Rod Stewart	1984
SOME GUYS HAVE ALL THE LUCK		
	Persuaders	1973
SOME JUSTICE	Urban Shakedown	1992
SOME KIND OF BLISS	Kylie Minogue	1997
SOME KIND OF FRIEND	Barry Manilow	1983
SOME KIND OF LOVER	Jody Watley	1988
SOME KIND OF WONDERFUL		
	Grand Funk	1974
SOME KINDA FUN	Chris Montez	1963
SOME LIKE IT HOT	Power Station	1985
SOME MIGHT SAY	Oasis	1995
SOME OF YOUR LOVIN'	Dusty Springfield	1965
SOME OTHER GUY	Big Three	1963
SOME PEOPLE	Belouis Some	1986
SOME PEOPLE	Cliff Richard	1987
SOME PEOPLE SAY	Terrorvision	1995
SOME THINGS ARE BETTER LEFT UNSAID		
	Daryl Hall & John Oates	1985

SONG TITLE	ARTIST	DATE
SOME THINGS YOU NEVER GET USED TO		
	Supremes	1968
SOME VELVET MORNING	Nancy Sinatra & Lee Hazlewood	1968
SOMEBODY	Shortie vs Black Legend	2001
SOMEBODY	Bryan Adams	1985
SOMEBODY	Reba McEntire	2004
SOMEBODY ELSE'S GIRL	Billy Fury	1963
SOMEBODY ELSE'S GUY	Jocelyn Brown	1984
SOMEBODY ELSE'S GUY	Ce Ce Peniston	1998
SOMEBODY HELP ME	Spencer Davis Group	1966
SOMEBODY LIKE YOU	Elate	1997
SOMEBODY LIKE YOU	Keith Urban	2002
SOMEBODY TO LOVE	Queen	1976
SOMEBODY TO LOVE	Boogie Pimps	2004
SOMEBODY TO LOVE	Jefferson Airplane	1967
SOMEBODY TO LOVE	George Michael And Queen	1993
SOMEBODY TO SHOVE	Soul Asylum	1993
SOMEBODY TOLD ME	Killers	2004
SOMEBODY'S BABY	Jackson Browne	1982
SOMEBODY'S BEEN SLEEPING		
	100 Proof Aged In Soul	1970
SOMEBODY'S GETTIN' IT	Johnnie Taylor	1976
SOMEBODY'S KNOCKIN'	Terri Gibbs	1981
SOMEBODY'S OUT THERE	Triumph	1986
SOMEBODY'S WATCHING ME		
	Rockwell	1984

SONG TITLE	ARTIST	DATE
SOMEBODY'S WATCHING YOU		
	Little Sister	1970
(SOMEBODY) HELP ME OUT		
	Beggar & Co	1981
SOMEDAY	Mariah Carey	1991
SOMEDAY	M People	1992
SOMEDAY	Eternal	1996
SOMEDAY	Gap Band	1984
SOMEDAY	Strokes	2002
SOMEDAY	Rezonance Q	2003
SOMEDAY	Nickelback	2003
SOMEDAY	All-4-One	1996
SOMEDAY	Glass Tiger	1986
SOMEDAY	Sugar Ray	1999
SOMEDAY (I'M COMING BACK)		
	Lisa Stansfield	1992
SOMEDAY I'LL BE SATURDAY NIGHT		
	Bon Jovi	1995
SOMEDAY I'LL FIND YOU/I'VE BEEN TO A MARVELLOUS PARTY	Shola Ama	1998
SOMEDAY NEVER COMES	Creedence Clearwater Revival	1972
SOMEDAY ONE DAY	Seekers	1966
SOMEDAY WE'LL BE TOGETHER		
	Diana Ross & The Supremes	1969
SOMEDAY WE'RE GONNA LOVE AGAIN		
	Searchers	1964

SONG TITLE	ARTIST	DATE
SOMEDAY, SOMEWAY	Marshall Crenshaw	1982
SOMEONE	SWV featuring Puff Daddy	1997
SOMEONE COULD LOSE A HEART TONIGHT	Eddie Rabbitt	1981
SOMEONE LIKE YOU	Dina Carroll	2001
SOMEONE LIKE YOU	Russell Watson & Faye Tozer	2002
SOMEONE LOVES YOU HONEY	Lutricia McNeal	1998
SOMEONE SAVED MY LIFE TONIGHT	Elton John	1975
SOMEONE, SOMEONE	Brian Poole & The Tremeloes	1964
SOMEONE SOMEWHERE	Wannadies	1996
SOMEONE SOMEWHERE (IN SUMMERTIME)	Simple Minds	1982
SOMEONE THAT I USED TO LOVE	Natalie Cole	1980
SOMEONE THERE FOR ME	Richard Blackwood	2000
SOMEONE TO CALL MY LOVER	Janet Jackson	2001
SOMEONE TO HOLD	Trey Lorenz	1992
SOMEONE TO LOVE	East 17	1996
SOMEONE TO LOVE	Sean Maguire	1994
SOMEONE TO LOVE	Jon B. featuring Babyface	1995
SOMEONE YOU USED TO KNOW	Collin Raye	1998

SONG TITLE	ARTIST	DATE
SOMEONE'S LOOKING AT YOU	Boomtown Rats	1980
SOMEONE'S TAKEN MARIA AWAY	Adam Faith	1965
SOMETHIN' 'BOUT 'CHA	Latimore	1977
SOMETHIN' 4 DA HONEYZ	Montell Jordan	1995
SOMETHIN' IS GOIN' ON	Cliff Richard	2004
SOMETHIN' STUPID	Ali & Kibibi Campbell	1995
SOMETHIN' STUPID	Nancy & Frank Sinatra	1967
SOMETHIN' STUPID	Robbie Williams & Nicole Kidman	2001
SOMETHING	Georgie Fame	1965
SOMETHING	Shirley Bassey	1970
SOMETHING	Lasgo	2002
SOMETHING	Beatles	1969
SOMETHING 'BOUT YOU BABY	Status Quo	1981
SOMETHING 'BOUT YOU BABY I LIKE	Tom Jones	1974
SOMETHING ABOUT THE WAY YOU LOOK TONIGHT	Elton John	1997
SOMETHING ABOUT YOU	Level 42	1986
SOMETHING ABOUT YOU	New Edition	1997
SOMETHING ABOUT YOU	Four Tops	1965
SOMETHING BEAUTIFUL	Robbie Williams	2003

SONG TITLE	ARTIST	DATE
SOMETHING BEAUTIFUL REMAINS	Tina Turner	1996
SOMETHING BETTER BEGINNING	Honeycombs	1965
SOMETHING BETTER CHANGE/STRAIGHTEN OUT	Stranglers	1977
SOMETHING BETTER TO DO	Olivia Newton-John	1975
SOMETHING CHANGED	Pulp	1996
SOMETHING DEEP INSIDE	Billie Piper	2000
SOMETHING DIFFERENT/THE TRAIN IS COMING	Shaggy	1996
SOMETHING ELSE/FRIGGIN' IN THE RIGGIN'	Sex Pistols	1979
SOMETHING FOR THE GIRL WITH EVERYTHING	Sparks	1975
SOMETHING FOR THE PAIN	Bon Jovi	1995
SOMETHING FOR THE WEEKEND	Fred & Roxy	2000
SOMETHING FOR THE WEEKEND	Divine Comedy	1996
SOMETHING 4 THE WEEKEND	Super Furry Animals	1996
SOMETHING GOIN' ON	Todd Terry	1997
SOMETHING GOOD	Utah Saints	1992

SONG TITLE	ARTIST	DATE
SOMETHING GOT ME STARTED	Simply Red	1991
SOMETHING HAPPENED ON THE WAY TO HEAVEN	Phil Collins	1990
SOMETHING HE CAN FEEL	Aretha Franklin	1976
SOMETHING HERE IN MY HEART (KEEPS A-TELLIN' ME NO)	Paper Dolls	1968
SOMETHING IN COMMON	Bobby Brown & Whitney Houston	1994
SOMETHING IN MY HEART	Michel'le	1991
SOMETHING IN MY HOUSE	Dead Or Alive	1987
SOMETHING IN THE AIR	Thunderclap Newman	1969
SOMETHING IN YOUR EYES	Ed Case	2000
SOMETHING IN YOUR EYES	Bell Biv Devoe	1993
(SOMETHING INSIDE) SO STRONG	Michael Ball	1996
(SOMETHING INSIDE) SO STRONG	Labi Siffre	1987
(SOMETHING INSIDE) SO STRONG	Rik Waller	2002
SOMETHING LIKE THAT	Tim McGraw	1999
SOMETHING OLD, SOMETHING NEW	Fantastics	1971

SONG TITLE	ARTIST	DATE
SOMETHING OUTA NOTHING		
	Letitia Dean & Paul Medford	1986
SOMETHING REAL (INSIDE ME/INSIDE YOU)		
	Mr. Mister	1987
SOMETHING SO STRONG	Crowded House	1987
SOMETHING TELLS ME (SOMETHING IS GONNA HAPPEN TONIGHT)	Cilla Black	1971
SOMETHING THAT I SAID	Ruts	1979
SOMETHING THAT YOU SAID		
	Bangles	2003
SOMETHING TO BELIEVE IN		
	Poison	1990
SOMETHING TO TALK ABOUT		
	Badly Drawn Boy	2002
SOMETHING TO TALK ABOUT		
	Bonnie Raitt	1991
SOMETHING WORTHWHILE	Gun	1995
SOMETHING YOU GOT	And Why Not?	1990
SOMETHING'S BEEN MAKING ME BLUE		
	Smokie	1976
SOMETHING'S BURNING	Kenny Rogers & The First Edition	1970
SOMETHING'S GOIN' ON	U.N.V.	1993
SOMETHING'S GOTTEN HOLD OF MY HEART		
	Marc Almond featuring Gene Pitney	1989
SOMETHING'S GOTTEN HOLD OF MY HEART		
	Gene Pitney	1967
SOMETHING'S HAPPENING		
	Herman's Hermits	1968
SOMETHING'S JUMPIN' IN YOUR SHIRT		
	Malcolm McLaren	1989
SOMETHING'S WRONG WITH ME		
	Austin Roberts	1972
SOMETIMES	Ash	2001
SOMETIMES	Erasure	1986
SOMETIMES	Brand New Heavies	1997
SOMETIMES	James	1993
SOMETIMES	Tin Tin Out featuring Shelley Nelson	1998
SOMETIMES	Britney Spears	1999
SOMETIMES	Facts Of Life	1977
SOMETIMES A FANTASY	Billy Joel	1980
SOMETIMES ALWAYS	Jesus & Mary Chain	1994
SOMETIMES IT'S A BITCH	Stevie Nicks	1991
SOMETIMES LOVE JUST AIN'T ENOUGH		
	Patty Smyth With Don Henley	1992
SOMETIMES SHE CRIES	Warrant	1990
SOMETIMES WHEN WE TOUCH		
	Newton	1997
SOMETIMES WHEN WE TOUCH		
	Dan Hill	1977

SONG TITLE	ARTIST	DATE
SOMEWHERE	P.J. Proby	1964
SOMEWHERE	Pet Shop Boys	1997
SOMEWHERE	Len Barry	1966
SOMEWHERE DOWN THE CRAZY RIVER		
	Robbie Robertson	1988
SOMEWHERE DOWN THE ROAD		
	Barry Manilow	1981
SOMEWHERE I BELONG	Linkin Park	2003
SOMEWHERE IN MY HEART	Aztec Camera	1988
SOMEWHERE IN THE COUNTRY		
	Gene Pitney	1968
SOMEWHERE IN THE NIGHT		
	Barry Manilow	1978
SOMEWHERE IN THE NIGHT		
	Helen Reddy	1975
SOMEWHERE IN YOUR HEART		
	Frank Sinatra	1964
SOMEWHERE MY LOVE	Michael Sammes Singers	1967
SOMEWHERE, MY LOVE	Ray Conniff & The Singers	1966
SOMEWHERE ONLY WE KNOW		
	Keane	2004
SOMEWHERE OUT THERE	Linda Ronstadt and	
	James Ingram	1987
SOMEWHERE OVER THE RAINBOW/WHAT A		
WONDERFUL WORLD	Cliff Richard	2001
SOMEWHERE SOMEBODY	Five Star	1987

SONG TITLE	ARTIST	DATE
SOMEWHERE SOMEHOW	Wet Wet Wet	1995
SOMEWHERE THERE'S A SOMEONE		
	Dean Martin	1966
SON OF A GUN	JX	1995
SON OF A GUN (I BETCHA THINK THIS SONG IS ABOUT		
YOU)	Janet With Carly Simon	
	featuring Missy Elliott	2001
THE SON OF HICKORY HOLLER'S TRAMP		
	O.C. Smith	1968
SON OF MY FATHER	Chicory Tip	1972
SON OF SAGITTARIUS	Eddie Kendricks	1974
SON-OF-A PREACHER MAN	Dusty Springfield	1968
SONG 2	Blur	1997
SONG FOR GUY	Elton John	1978
SONG FOR LOVE	Extreme	1992
A SONG FOR MAMA	Boyz II Men	1997
A SONG FOR THE LOVERS	Richard Ashcroft	2000
SONG FOR WHOEVER	Beautiful South	1989
SONG OF JOY	Miguel Rios	1970
SONG OF MEXICO	Tony Meehan	1964
THE SONG OF MY LIFE	Petula Clark	1971
SONG ON THE RADIO	Al Stewart	1979
SONG SUNG BLUE	Neil Diamond	1972
THE SONG THAT I SING (THEME FROM 'WE'LL MEET		
AGAIN')	Stutz Bearcats & The Denis	
	King Orchestra	1982

SONG TITLE	ARTIST	DATE
SONGBIRD	Kenny G	1987
SONGBIRD	Oasis	2003
SONGBIRD	Barbra Streisand	1978
SONGS FOR CHRISTMAS (EP)		
	Mini Pops	1987
SONIC BOOM BOY	Westworld	1987
SOOLAIMON (AFRICAN TRILOGY II)		
	Neil Diamond	1970
SOON AS I GET HOME	Faith Evans	1995
SOONER OR LATER	Grass Roots	1971
SOOTHE ME	Sam & Dave	1967
SOPHISTICATED CISSY	Meters	1969
SOPHISTICATED LADY (SHE'S A DIFFERENT LADY)		
	Natalie Cole	1976
SORRENTO MOON (I REMEMBER)		
	Tina Arena	1996
SORROW	David Bowie	1973
SORROW	Merseys	1966
SORRY (I DIDN'T KNOW)	Monsta Boy featuring Denzie	2000
SORRY DOESN'T ALWAYS MAKE IT RIGHT		
	Diana Ross	1975
SORRY I'M A LADY	Baccara	1978
SORRY SEEMS TO BE THE HARDEST WORD		
	Elton John	1976
SORRY SEEMS TO BE THE HARDEST WORD		
	Blue featuring Elton John	2002

SONG TITLE	ARTIST	DATE
SORRY SUZANNE	Hollies	1969
THE SOS EP	Shamen	1993
SOUL CHA CHA	Van McCoy	1977
SOUL CITY	Partland Brothers	1987
THE SOUL CITY WALK	Archie Bell & The Drells	1976
SOUL CLAP '69	Booker T. & The MG's	1969
SOUL DEEP	Council Collective	1984
SOUL DEEP	Box Tops	1969
SOUL DRACULA	Hot Blood	1976
SOUL FINGER	Bar-Kays	1967
SOUL HEAVEN	Goodfellas featuring Lisa Millett	2001
SOUL INSIDE	Soft Cell	1983
SOUL KISS	Olivia Newton-John	1985
SOUL LIMBO	Booker T. & The MG's	1968
SOUL MAKOSSA	Manu Dibango	1973
SOUL MAN	Sam & Dave	1967
SOUL MAN	Blues Brothers	1978
SOUL OF MY SOUL	Michael Bolton	1994
SOUL POWER (PT I)	James Brown	1971
SOUL PROVIDER	Michael Bolton	1989
SOUL SERENADE	Willie Mitchell	1968
SOUL SHAKE	Peggy Scott & Jo Jo Benson	1969
SOUL SISTER BROWN SUGAR		
	Sam & Dave	1969
SOUL SONG	Joe Stampley	1973
SOUL SOUND	Sugababes	2001

SONG TITLE	ARTIST	DATE
SOUL TO SQUEEZE	Red Hot Chili Peppers	1993
SOUL TRAIN	Swans Way	1984
SOULFUL STRUT	Young-Holt Unlimited	1968
SOULJACKER (PART 1)	Eels	2001
SOULS	Rick Springfield	1983
SOUND	James	1991
THE SOUND	X Press 2	1996
SOUND AND VISION	David Bowie	1977
THE SOUND OF BAMBOO	Flickman	2000
THE SOUND OF CRYING	Prefab Sprout	1992
SOUND OF DRUMS	Kula Shaker	1998
THE SOUND OF EDEN	Shades Of Rhythm	1991
SOUND OF LOVE	Five Americans	1967
THE SOUND OF SILENCE	Bachelors	1966
SOUND OF SPEED (EP)	Jesus & Mary Chain	1993
THE SOUND OF THE CROWD	Human League	1981
SOUND OF THE SUBURBS	Members	1979
SOUND OF THE UNDERGROUND	Girls Aloud	2002
THE SOUND OF YOUR VOICE	38 Special	1991
SOUND YOUR FUNKY HORN	KC & The Sunshine Band	1974
THE SOUNDS OF SILENCE	Simon & Garfunkel	1965
SOUNDS OF WICKEDNESS	Tzant	1998

SONG TITLE	ARTIST	DATE
SOUR TIMES	Portishead	1995
SOUTH AFRICAN MAN	Hamilton Bohannon	1975
SOUTH OF THE BORDER	Robbie Williams	1997
SOUTH SIDE	Moby featuring Gwen Stefani	2000
THE SOUTH'S GONNA DO IT	Charlie Daniels Band	1975
SOUTHAMPTON BOYS	Red 'n' White Machines	2003
SOUTHERN CROSS	Crosby, Stills & Nash	1982
SOUTHERN FREEEZ	Freeez	1981
SOUTHERN HOSPITALITY	Ludacris	2001
SOUTHERN NIGHTS	Glen Campbell	1977
SOUTHERN SUN/READY STEADY GO	Oakenfold	2002
SOUTHSIDE	Dave Clarke	1996
SOUTHSIDE	Lloyd featuring Ashanti	2004
SOUTHTOWN U.S.A.	Dixiebelles	1964
SOUVENIR	Orchestral Manoeuvres In The Dark	1981
SOWETO	Malcolm McLaren & The McLarenettes	1983
SOWING THE SEEDS OF LOVE	Tears For Fears	1989
SPACE	New Model Army	1991
SPACE AGE LOVE SONG	Flock Of Seagulls	1982
SPACE BASS	Slick	1979
THE SPACE BETWEEN	Dave Matthews Band	2001

SONG TITLE	ARTIST	DATE
SPACE COWBOY	Jamiroquai	1994
SPACE JAM	Quad City DJ's	1996
THE SPACE JUNGLE	Adamski	1990
SPACE ODDITY	David Bowie	1972
SPACE RACE	Billy Preston	1973
SPACE WALK	Lemon Jelly	2002
SPACED INVADER	Hatiras featuring Slarta John	2001
SPACEMAN	Babylon Zoo	1996
SPACEMAN	Nilsson	1972
A SPACEMAN CAME TRAVELLING/THE BALLROOM OF		
ROMANCE	Chris De Burgh	1986
SPACER	Sheila And B. Devotion	1979
SPANISH	Craig David	2003
SPANISH EDDIE	Laura Branigan	1985
SPANISH EYES	Al Martino	1965
SPANISH FLEA	Herb Alpert	1965
SPANISH HARLEM	Sounds Incorporated	1964
SPANISH HARLEM	Aretha Franklin	1971
SPANISH STROLL	Mink Deville	1977
SPANISH WINE	Chris White	1976
SPARE PARTS	Bruce Springsteen	1988
SPARK	Tori Amos	1998
SPARKLE	My Life Story	1996
SPARKY'S DREAM	Teenage Fanclub	1995
THE SPARROW	Ramblers	1979
THE SPARTANS	Sounds Incorporated	1964

SONG TITLE	ARTIST	DATE
SPEAK LIKE A CHILD	Style Council	1983
SPEAK TO ME SOMEONE	Gene	1997
SPEAK TO THE SKY	Rick Springfield	1972
SPEAKEASY	Shed Seven	1994
SPECIAL	Garbage	1998
SPECIAL AKA LIVE! (EP)	Specials	1980
SPECIAL BREW	Bad Manners	1980
SPECIAL CASES	Massive Attack	2003
SPECIAL DELIVERY	1910 Fruitgum Co.	1969
SPECIAL KIND OF LOVE	Dina Carroll	1992
SPECIAL KIND OF LOVER	Nu Colours	1996
SPECIAL KIND OF SOMETHING		
	Kavana	1998
SPECIAL LADY	Ray, Goodman & Brown	1980
SPECIAL NEEDS	Placebo	2003
SPECIAL OCCASION	Smokey Robinson &	
	The Miracles	1968
THE SPECIAL YEARS	Val Doonican	1965
SPECTACULAR	Graham Coxon	2004
SPEECHLESS	D-Side	2003
SPEED YOUR LOVE TO ME		
	Simple Minds	1984
SPELLBOUND	Siouxsie & The Banshees	1981
SPEND MY LIFE	Slaughter	1990
SPEND MY LIFE WITH YOU		
	Eric Benet featuring Tamia	1999

SONG TITLE	ARTIST	DATE
SPEND SOME TIME	Brand New Heavies	1994
SPEND THE NIGHT	Danny J Lewis	1998
SPEND THE NIGHT	Coolnotes	1985
SPENDING MY TIME	Roxette	1991
SPICE OF LIFE	Manhattan Transfer	1983
SPICE UP YOUR LIFE	Spice Girls	1997
SPIDERS & SNAKES	Jim Stafford	1973
SPIDERWEBS	No Doubt	1997
SPIES LIKE US	Paul McCartney	1985
SPILL THE WINE	Eric Burdon & War	1970
SPILLER FROM RIO (DO IT EASY)		
	Laguna	1997
SPIN SPIN SUGAR	Sneaker Pimps	1997
SPIN THAT WHEEL (TURTLES GET REAL)		
	Hi Tek 3 featuring Ya Kid K	1990
SPIN THE BLACK CIRCLE	Pearl Jam	1994
SPINNING AROUND	Kylie Minogue	2000
SPINNING ROCK BOOGIE	Hank C. Burnette	1976
SPINNING THE WHEEL	George Michael	1996
SPINNING WHEEL	Blood, Sweat & Tears	1969
SPINOUT	Elvis Presley	1966
SPIRAL SCRATCH (EP)	Buzzcocks	1979
SPIRIT	Sounds Of Blackness	1997
SPIRIT, BODY AND SOUL	Nolans	1979
SPIRIT IN THE DARK	Aretha Franklin	1970
SPIRIT IN THE NIGHT	Manfred Mann's Earth Band	1977

SONG TITLE	ARTIST	DATE
SPIRIT IN THE SKY	Doctor & The Medics	1986
SPIRIT IN THE SKY	Norman Greenbaum	1970
SPIRIT IN THE SKY	Gareth Gates featuring	
	The Kumars	2003
SPIRIT INSIDE	Spirits	1995
THE SPIRIT IS WILLING	Peter Straker & The Hands	
	Of Dr Teleny	1972
SPIRIT OF '76	Alarm	1986
SPIRIT OF THE BOOGIE	Kool & The Gang	1975
THE SPIRIT OF THE RADIO		
	Rush	1980
SPIRITS (HAVING FLOWN)	Bee Gees	1980
SPIRITS IN A MATERIAL WORLD		
	Pato Banton With Sting	1996
SPIRITS IN THE MATERIAL WORLD		
	Police	1982
SPIRITUAL LOVE	Urban Species	1994
SPIRITUALIZED	Finley Quaye	2000
SPIT IN THE RAIN	Del Amitri	1990
SPIT IT OUT	Slipknot	2000
SPITTING GAMES	Snow Patrol	2004
SPLACKAVELLIE	Pressha	1998
SPOOKY	New Order	1993
SPOOKY	Atlanta Rhythm Section	1979
SPOONMAN	Soundgarden	1994
SPOT THE PIGEON (EP)	Genesis	1977

SONG TITLE	ARTIST	DATE
SPREAD A LITTLE HAPPINESS		
	Sting	1982
SPREAD YOUR LOVE	Black Rebel Motorcycle Club	2002
SPREAD YOUR WINGS	Queen	1978
SPRING RAIN	Silvetti	1977
SPRINGTIME MAMA	Henry Gross	1976
SPY IN THE HOUSE OF LOVE		
	Was (Not Was)	1988
SPYBREAK!	Propellerheads	1997
SQUEEZE BOX	Who	1975
SSSST (LISTEN)	Jonah	2000
ST ANGER	Metallica	2003
ST. ELMO'S FIRE (MAN IN MOTION)		
	John Parr	1985
ST. TERESA	Joan Osborne	1996
ST. VALENTINE'S DAY MASSACRE (EP)		
	Headgirl	1981
STACY'S MOM	Fountains Of Wayne	2003
STAG-O-LEE	Wilson Pickett	1967
STAGE ONE	Space Manoeuvres	2000
STAGES	ZZ Top	1986
STAGGER LEE	Tommy Roe	1971
STAINSBY GIRLS	Chris Rea	1985
THE STAIRCASE (MYSTERY)		
	Siouxsie & The Banshees	1979
STAIRWAY TO HEAVEN	Far Corporation	1985

SONG TITLE	ARTIST	DATE
STAIRWAY TO HEAVEN	Rolf Harris	1993
STAKKER HUMANOID	Humanoid	1988
STALEMATE	Mac Band featuring The McCampbell Brothers	1988
STAMP!	Jeremy Healy & Amos	1996
STAN	Eminem	2000
STAN BOWLES	Others	2004
STAND	Poison	1993
STAND	R.E.M.	1989
STAND	Sly & The Family Stone	1969
STAND ABOVE ME	Orchestral Manoeuvres In The Dark	1993
STAND AND DELIVER	Adam & The Ants	1981
STAND BACK	Linus Loves featuring Sam Obernik	2003
STAND BACK	Stevie Nicks	1983
STAND BESIDE ME	Jo Dee Messina	1998
STAND BY LOVE	Simple Minds	1991
STAND BY ME	Kenny Lynch	1964
STAND BY ME	Ben E. King	1986
STAND BY ME	Oasis	1997
STAND BY ME	4 The Cause	1998
STAND BY ME	John Lennon	1976
STAND BY ME	Mickey Gilley	1980
STAND BY ME	Spyder Turner	1966
STAND BY YOUR MAN	Tammy Wynette	1968

SONG TITLE	ARTIST	DATE
STAND BY YOUR MAN	Candi Staton	1970
STAND INSIDE YOUR LOVE	Smashing Pumpkins	2000
STAND TALL	Burton Cummings	1976
STAND TOUGH	Point Break	2000
STAND UP	Thunder	1995
STAND UP	Love Tribe	1996
STAND UP	Ludacris	2003
STAND UP (KICK LOVE INTO MOTION)		
	Def Leppard	1992
STAND UP FOR YOUR LOVE RIGHTS		
	Yazz	1988
STAND UP TALL	Dizzee Rascal	2004
STANDING AT THE END OF THE LINE		
	Lobo	1974
STANDING IN THE NEED OF LOVE		
	River City People	1992
STANDING IN THE ROAD	Blackfoot Sue	1972
STANDING IN THE SHADOWS OF LOVE		
	Four Tops	1966
STANDING ON THE INSIDE	Neil Sedaka	1973
STANDING OUTSIDE THE FIRE		
	Garth Brooks	1994
STANDING STILL	Jewel	2001
STANLEY (HERE I AM)	Airheadz	2001
STAR	Bryan Adams	1996
STAR	Kiki Dee	1981

SONG TITLE	ARTIST	DATE
STAR	Earth, Wind & Fire	1979
STAR	Erasure	1990
STAR	Primal Scream	1997
STAR	Stealer's Wheel	1974
STAR 69	Fatboy Slim	2001
STAR BABY	Guess Who	1974
STAR GUITAR	Chemical Brothers	2002
STAR ON A TV SHOW	Stylistics	1975
STAR PEOPLE '97	George Michael	1997
THE STAR SPANGLED BANNER		
	Whitney Houston	2001
STAR TREKKIN'	Firm	1987
STAR WARS (MAIN TITLE)	John Williams	1977
STAR WARS THEME/CANTINA BAND		
	Meco	1977
STAR/I LIKE IT	D:ream	1993
STARBUCKS	A	2002
STARCROSSED	Ash	2004
STARDATE 1990/RAINBOW CHILD		
	Dan Reed Network	1990
STARDUST	David Essex	1974
STARDUST	Menswear	1995
STARING AT THE RUDE BOYS		
	Ruts	1980
STARING AT THE SUN	U2	1997
STARLIGHT	Supermen Lovers	2001

SONG TITLE	ARTIST	DATE
STARMAKER	Kids From 'Fame'	1982
STARMAN	David Bowie	1972
STARRY EYED SURPRISE	Oakenfold	2002
A STARRY NIGHT	Joy Strings	1964
STARS	Felix	1993
STARS	Dubstar	1996
STARS	Hear 'n' Aid	1986
STARS	China Black	1994
STARS	Simply Red	1991
STARS	Morjac featuring Raz Conway	2003
STARS ON 45	Starsound/Stars on 45	1981
STARS ON 45 (VOL 2)	Starsound/Stars on 45	1981
STARS ON 45 (VOL 3)	Starsound/Stars on 45	1981
STARS ON STEVIE	Starsound/Stars on 45	1982
STARS OVER 45	Chas & Dave	1981
START	Jam	1980
START CHOPPIN	Dinosaur Jr.	1993
START ME UP	Salt 'N 'Pepa	1992
START ME UP	Rolling Stones	1981
START TALKING LOVE	Magnum	1988
START THE COMMOTION	Wiseguys	2001
STARTING ALL OVER AGAIN		
	Mel & Tim	1972
STARTING OVER AGAIN	Dolly Parton	1980
STARTING TOGETHER	Su Pollard	1986
STARTOUCHERS	Digital Orgasm	1992

SONG TITLE	ARTIST	DATE
STARTRAX CLUB DISCO	Startrax	1981
STARVATION/TAM-TAM POUR L'ETHIOPE		
	Starvation	1985
STATE OF INDEPENDENCE	Donna Summer	1996
STATE OF MIND	Fish	1989
STATE OF MIND	Holly Valance	2003
STATE OF SHOCK	Jacksons	1984
STATE OF THE HEART	Rick Springfield	1985
STATE OF THE NATION	New Order	1986
STATUESQUE	Sleeper	1996
STAY	Kenny Thomas	1993
STAY	Mica Paris	1998
STAY	Jackson Browne	1978
STAY	Eternal	1994
STAY	Bernard Butler	1998
STAY	Hollies	1963
STAY	Shakespear's Sister	1992
STAY	Lisa Loeb & Nine Stories	1994
STAY	Sash! featuring La Trec	1997
STAY	Stephen Gately	2001
STAY	Barry Manilow	1982
STAY	Four Seasons	1964
STAY	Rufus And Chaka Khan	1978
STAY (FARAWAY, SO CLOSE!)/I'VE GOT YOU UNDER		
MY SKIN	U2	1993
STAY (TONIGHT)	Isha-D	1995

SONG TITLE	ARTIST	DATE
STAY/THE LOAD-OUT	Jackson Browne	1978
STAY ANOTHER DAY	East 17	1994
STAY AWHILE	Dusty Springfield	1964
STAY AWHILE	Bells	1971
STAY BEAUTIFUL	Manic Street Preachers	1991
STAY GONE	Jimmy Wayne	2003
STAY IN MY CORNER	Dells	1968
STAY ON THESE ROADS	A-Ha	1988
STAY OUT OF MY LIFE	Five Star	1987
STAY THE NIGHT	Chicago	1984
STAY THE NIGHT	IMX	1999
STAY THE NIGHT	Benjamin Orr	1986
STAY THE SAME	Gabrielle	2004
STAY THE SAME	Joey McIntyre	1999
STAY THIS WAY	Brand New Heavies	1992
STAY TOGETHER	Suede	1994
STAY WITH ME	Ultra High	1995
STAY WITH ME	Mission	1986
STAY WITH ME	Angelic	2001
STAY WITH ME	Blue Mink	1972
STAY WITH ME	Erasure	1995
STAY WITH ME	Faces	1972
STAY WITH ME (BABY)	Rebecca Wheatley	2000
STAY WITH ME BABY	Ruby Turner	1994
STAY WITH ME BABY	Walker Brothers	1967

SONG TITLE	ARTIST	DATE
STAY WITH ME HEARTACHE/I FEEL FINE		
	Wet Wet Wet	1990
STAY WITH ME TILL DAWN		
	Lucid	1999
STAY WITH ME TILL DAWN		
	Judie Tzuke	1979
STAY WITH ME TONIGHT	Human League	1996
STAY WITH ME TONIGHT	Jeffrey Osborne	1983
STAY YOUNG	Ultrasound	1998
STAYIN' ALIVE	Bee Gees	1977
STAYIN' ALIVE	N-Trance featuring Ricardo Da Force	1995
STAYING OUT FOR THE SUMMER		
	Dodgy	1994
STAYING TOGETHER	Debbie Gibson	1988
STAYING WITH IT	Firefall	1981
STEAL AWAY	Robbie Dupree	1980
STEAL AWAY	Jimmy Hughes	1964
STEAL AWAY	Johnnie Taylor	1970
STEAL MY SUNSHINE	Len	1999
STEAL THE NIGHT	Stevie Woods	1981
STEAL YOUR FIRE	Gun	1992
STEAL YOUR LOVE AWAY	Gemini	1996
STEAM	East 17	1994
STEAM	Peter Gabriel	1992

SONG TITLE	ARTIST	DATE
STEAMROLLER BLUES/FOOL		
	Elvis Presley	1973
STEAMY WINDOWS	Tina Turner	1989
STEEL BARS	Michael Bolton	1992
STEELO	702	1996
STEP BACK IN TIME	Kylie Minogue	1990
STEP BY STEP	New Kids On The Block	1990
STEP BY STEP	Joe Simon	1973
STEP BY STEP	Whitney Houston	1997
STEP BY STEP	Eddie Rabbitt	1981
STEP IN THE NAME OF LOVE/THOIA THOING		
	R. Kelly	2003
A STEP IN THE RIGHT DIRECTION		
	Truth	1983
STEP INSIDE LOVE	Cilla Black	1968
STEP INTO A DREAM	White Plains	1973
STEP INTO A WORLD	KRS One	1997
STEP INTO CHRISTMAS	Elton John	1973
STEP INTO MY OFFICE BABY		
	Belle & Sebastian	2003
STEP INTO MY WORLD	Hurricane #1	1997
STEP IT UP	Stereo MC's	1992
STEP OFF (PT 1)	Grandmaster Melle Mel &	
	The Furious Five	1984
STEP ON	Happy Mondays	1990

SONG TITLE	ARTIST	DATE
STEP ON MY OLD SIZE NINES		
	Stereophonics	2001
STEP OUT OF YOUR MIND	American Breed	1967
STEP RIGHT UP	Jaki Graham	1986
STEPPIN' IN A SLIDE ZONE		
	Moody Blues	1978
STEPPIN' OUT	Joe Jackson	1982
STEPPIN' OUT	Kool & The Gang	1981
STEPPIN' OUT	Neil Sedaka	1976
STEPPIN' OUT (GONNA BOOGIE TONIGHT)		
	Tony Orlando & Dawn	1974
STEPPING STONE	PJ And Duncan	1996
STEPTOE & SON AT BUCKINGHAM PALACE (PARTS 1 & 2)		
	Wilfred Brambell & Harry	
	H. Corbett	1963
STEREOTYPE/INTERNATIONAL JET SET		
	Specials	1980
STEREOTYPES	Blur	1996
STICK AROUND	Julian Lennon	1986
STICK IT OUT	Right Said Fred	1993
STICK-UP	Honey Cone	1971
STICKY	Wedding Present	1992
STILL	Ken Dodd	1963
STILL	Commodores	1979
STILL	Karl Denver	1963
STILL	Macy Gray	2000

SONG TITLE	ARTIST	DATE
STILL A G THING	Snoop Doggy Dogg	1998
STILL BE LOVIN' YOU	Damage	2001
STILL BELIEVE	Shola Ama	1999
STILL CRAZY AFTER ALL THESE YEARS		
	Paul Simon	1976
STILL D.R.E.	Dr. Dre featuring Snoop Dogg	2000
STILL FLY	Big Tymers	2002
STILL GOT THE BLUES (FOR YOU)		
	Gary Moore	1990
STILL IN SAIGON	Charlie Daniels Band	1982
STILL NOT A PLAYER	Big Punisher featuring Joe	1998
STILL OF THE NIGHT	Whitesnake	1987
STILL ON YOUR SIDE	BBmak	2001
STILL RIGHT HERE IN MY HEART		
	Pure Prairie League	1981
STILL THE ONE	Orleans	1976
STILL THE SAME	Bob Seger & The Silver	
	Bullet Band	1978
STILL THEY RIDE	Journey	1982
STILL WAITING	Sum 41	2002
STILL WATER (LOVE)	Four Tops	1970
STILL WATERS (RUN DEEP)		
	Bee Gees	1997
STILLNESS IN TIME	Jamiroquai	1995
THE STING	Ragtimers	1974

SONG TITLE	ARTIST	DATE
STING ME RED (YOU THINK YOU'RE SO CLEVER)		
	Who Da Funk featuring	
	Terra Deva	2003
STINGRAY	Shadows	1965
STINGY	Ginuwine	2002
STINKIN THINKIN	Happy Mondays	1992
STIR IT UP	Johnny Nash	1973
STOLE	Kelly Rowland	2002
STOLEN	Jay Sean	2004
STOLEN CAR	Beth Orton	1999
STOMP	Steps	2000
STOMP!	Brothers Johnson	1980
STOMP – THE REMIXES	Quincy Jones	1996
STONE BLUE	Foghat	1978
STONE BY STONE	Catatonia	2001
STONE COLD	Rainbow	1982
STONE COLD GENTLEMAN	Ralph Tresvant	1991
STONE LOVE	Kool & The Gang	1987
STONED LOVE	Supremes	1970
STONED OUT OF MY MIND	Chi-Lites	1973
STONED SOUL PICNIC	5th Dimension	1968
STONES	Neil Diamond	1971
STONEY END	Barbra Streisand	1970
STONEY GROUND	Guys And Dolls	1976
THE STONK	Hale & Pace	1991
STOOL PIGEON	Kid Creole & The Coconuts	1982

SONG TITLE	ARTIST	DATE
STOP	Mega City Four	1992
STOP	Sam Brown	1989
STOP	Spice Girls	1998
STOP	Black Rebel Motorcycle Club	2003
STOP AND GO	David Grant	1983
STOP AND SMELL THE ROSES	Mac Davis	1974
STOP AND THINK IT OVER	Dale & Grace	1964
STOP CRYING YOUR HEART OUT	Oasis	2002
STOP DRAGGIN' MY HEART AROUND	Stevie Nicks with Tom Petty & The Heartbreakers	1981
STOP FEELING SORRY FOR YOURSELF	Adam Faith	1965
STOP HER ON SIGHT (SOS)	Edwin Starr	1968
STOP IN THE NAME OF LOVE	Hollies	1983
STOP! IN THE NAME OF LOVE	Supremes	1965
STOP LIVING THE LIE	David Sneddon	2003
STOP LOOK AND LISTEN	Wayne Fontana & The Mindbenders	1964
STOP LOOK LISTEN (TO YOUR HEART)	Diana Ross & Marvin Gaye	1974

SONG TITLE	ARTIST	DATE
STOP, LOOK, LISTEN (TO YOUR HEART)	Stylistics	1971
STOP LOVING ME, STOP LOVING YOU	Daryl Hall	1994
STOP ME (IF YOU'VE HEARD IT ALL BEFORE)	Billy Ocean	1976
STOP MY HEAD	Evan Dando	2003
STOP PLAYING WITH MY MIND	Barbara Tucker featuring Darryl D'Bonneau	2000
STOP SIGN	ABS	2003
STOP STOP STOP	Hollies	1966
STOP THAT GIRL	Chris Andrews	1966
STOP THE CAVALRY	Jona Lewie	1980
STOP THE ROCK	Apollo 440	1999
STOP THE WAR NOW	Edwin Starr	1970
STOP THE WORLD	Extreme	1992
STOP THIS CRAZY THING	Coldcut	1988
STOP TO LOVE	Luther Vandross	1986
STOP YOUR CRYING	Spiritualized	2001
STOP YOUR SOBBING	Pretenders	1979
STORIES	Therapy?	1995
STORIES OF JOHNNY	Marc Almond	1985
STORM	Storm	1998
STORM ANIMAL	Storm	2000
STORM IN A TEACUP	Fortunes	1972

SONG TITLE	ARTIST	DATE
THE STORM IS OVER NOW	R. Kelly	2001
STORMY	Santana	1979
STORMY IN THE NORTH – KARMA IN THE SOUTH		
	Wildhearts	2003
THE STORY IN YOUR EYES	Moody Blues	1971
THE STORY OF LOVE	OTT	1998
STORY OF MY LIFE	Kristian Leontiou	2004
STORY OF THE BLUES	Gary Moore	1992
THE STORY OF THE BLUES	Wah!	1982
STRAIGHT AHEAD	Kool & The Gang	1983
STRAIGHT AHEAD	Tube & Berger featuring Chrissie Hynde	2004
STRAIGHT AT YER HEAD	Lionrock	1996
STRAIGHT FROM THE HEART		
	Doolally	1999
STRAIGHT FROM THE HEART		
	Bryan Adams	1983
STRAIGHT FROM THE HEART		
	Allman Brothers Band	1981
THE STRAIGHT LIFE	Bobby Goldsboro	1966
STRAIGHT ON	Heart	1978
STRAIGHT SHOOTIN' WOMAN		
	Steppenwolf	1974
STRAIGHT UP	Paula Abdul	1988
STRAIGHT UP	Chante Moore	2001
STRAIGHT UP NO BENDS	Brian Harvey	2001

SONG TITLE	ARTIST	DATE
STRANDED	Lutricia McNeal	1998
STRANDED	Heart	1990
STRANGE	Wet Wet Wet	1997
STRANGE AND BEAUTIFUL (I'LL PUT A SPELL ON YOU)		
	Aqualung	2002
STRANGE BAND	Family	1970
STRANGE BREW	Cream	1967
STRANGE BUT TRUE	Times Two	1988
STRANGE CURRENCIES	R.E.M.	1995
STRANGE GLUE	Catatonia	1998
STRANGE KIND OF WOMAN		
	Deep Purple	1971
STRANGE LITTLE GIRL	Stranglers	1982
STRANGE LITTLE GIRL	Sad Cafe	1980
STRANGE MAGIC	Electric Light Orchestra	1976
STRANGE RELATIONSHIP	Darren Hayes	2002
STRANGE TOWN	Jam	1979
STRANGE WAY	Firefall	1978
STRANGE WORLD	Push	2001
STRANGELOVE	Depeche Mode	1987
STRANGER IN A STRANGE LAND		
	Iron Maiden	1986
STRANGER IN MOSCOW	Michael Jackson	1996
STRANGER IN MY HOUSE	Ronnie Milsap	1983
STRANGER IN MY HOUSE	Tamia	2001
STRANGER IN TOWN	Del Shannon	1965

SONG TITLE	ARTIST	DATE
STRANGER IN TOWN	Toto	1984
STRANGERS IN THE NIGHT	Frank Sinatra	1966
STRANGERS WHEN WE MEET/THE MAN WHO SOLD THE WORLD (LIVE)	David Bowie	1995
THE STRANGEST PARTY (THESE ARE THE TIMES)	INXS	1994
STRANGLEHOLD	UK Subs	1979
STRAWBERRY FIELDS FOREVER	Candy Flip	1990
STRAWBERRY FIELDS FOREVER	Beatles	1967
STRAWBERRY LETTER 23	Brothers Johnson	1977
STRAWBERRY SHORTCAKE	Jay & The Techniques	1968
STRAY CAT STRUT	Stray Cats	1982
THE STREAK	Ray Stevens	1974
A STREET CALLED HOPE	Gene Pitney	1970
STREET CORNER SERENADE	Wet Willie	1977
STREET DANCE	Break Machine	1984
STREET DREAMS	Nas	1996
STREET FIGHTING MAN	Rolling Stones	1971
STREET LIFE	Crusaders	1979
STREET LIFE	Roxy Music	1973
STREET LIFE	Beenie Man	2003
STREET OF DREAMS	Nia Peeples	1991
STREET SINGER	Lady Flash	1976

SONG TITLE	ARTIST	DATE
STREET SPIRIT (FADE OUT)	Radiohead	1996
STREET TUFF	Rebel MC/Double Trouble	1989
STREETS OF LONDON	Ralph McTell	1974
STREETS OF PHILADELPHIA	Bruce Springsteen	1994
STREETWALKIN'	Shakatak	1982
STRENGTH	Alarm	1985
STRESSED OUT	A Tribe Called Quest	1996
STRICT MACHINE	Goldfrapp	2004
STRIKE IT UP	Black Box	1991
STRINGS FOR YASMIN	Tin Tin Out	1997
STRIPPED	Depeche Mode	1986
THE STROKE	Billy Squier	1981
STROKE YOU UP	Changing Faces	1994
STROLLIN' ON	Maxi Priest	1986
STRONG	Robbie Williams	1999
STRONG AS STEEL	Five Star	1987
STRONG ENOUGH	Sheryl Crow	1994
STRONG ENOUGH	Cher	1999
STRONG IN LOVE	Chicane	1998
STRONGER	Gary Barlow	1999
STRONGER	Britney Spears	2000
STRONGER THAN BEFORE	Carole Bayer Sager	1981
STRONGER THAN THAT	Cliff Richard	1990
STRONGER/ANGELS WITH DIRTY FACES	Sugababes	2002

SONG TITLE	ARTIST	DATE
STRUMPET	My Life Story	1997
STRUNG OUT	Steve Perry	1994
STRUT	Sheena Easton	1984
STRUT YOUR FUNKY STUFF		
	Frantique	1979
THE STRUTT	Bamboo	1998
STRUTTIN'	Billy Preston	1974
STUCK	Stacie Orrico	2003
STUCK IN A GROOVE	Puretone	2003
STUCK IN A MOMENT YOU CAN'T GET OUT OF		
	U2	2001
STUCK IN THE MIDDLE	Clea	2004
STUCK IN THE MIDDLE WITH YOU		
	Stealer's Wheel	1973
STUCK IN THE MIDDLE WITH YOU		
	Louise	2001
STUCK ON U	PJ And Duncan	1995
STUCK ON YOU	Lionel Richie	1984
STUCK ON YOU	Trevor Walters	1984
STUCK WITH ME	Green Day	1996
STUCK WITH YOU	Huey Lewis & The News	1986
STUFF LIKE THAT	Quincy Jones	1978
STUMBLE & FALL	Razorlight	2004
STUMBLIN' IN	Suzi Quatro & Chris Norman	1979
STUNT 101	G-Unit	2003
STUPID GIRL	Garbage	1996

SONG TITLE	ARTIST	DATE
STUPID QUESTION	New Model Army	1989
STUPIDISCO	Junior Jack	2004
STUTTER	Joe featuring Mystikal	2001
STUTTER RAP (NO SLEEP 'TIL BEDTIME)		
	Morris Minor & The Majors	1987
STYLE	Orbital	1999
STYLE	Mis-Teeq	2003
SUAVECITO	Malo	1972
SUBSTITUTE	Clout	1978
SUBSTITUTE	Liquid Gold	1980
SUBSTITUTE	Who	1966
SUBTERRANEAN HOMESICK BLUES		
	Bob Dylan	1965
SUBURBIA	Pet Shop Boys	1986
SUCCESS	Dannii Minogue	1991
SUCCESS	Sigue Sigue Sputnik	1988
SUCCESS HAS MADE A FAILURE OF OUR HOME		
	Sinead O'Connor	1992
SUCH A FEELING	Bizarre Inc.	1991
SUCH A GOOD FEELING	Brothers In Rhythm	1991
SUCH A NIGHT	Elvis Presley	1964
SUCH A PHANTASY (EP)	Time Frequency	1994
SUCH A WOMAN	Tycoon	1979
(SUCH AN) EASY QUESTION		
	Elvis Presley	1965
SUCKER DJ	Dimples D	1990

SONG TITLE	ARTIST	DATE
SUCKERPUNCH	Wildhearts	1994
SUDDENLY	Angry Anderson	1988
SUDDENLY	Olivia Newton-John & Cliff Richard	1980
SUDDENLY	Billy Ocean	1985
SUDDENLY	Sean Maguire	1995
SUDDENLY LAST SUMMER	Motels	1983
SUDDENLY YOU LOVE ME	Tremeloes	1968
SUDS IN THE BUCKET	Sara Evans	2004
SUE'S GOTTA BE MINE	Del Shannon	1963
SUEDEHEAD	Morrissey	1988
SUFFER NEVER	Finn	1995
SUFFOCATE	Feeder	1998
SUFFOCATE	King Adora	2001
SUGAH	Ruby Amanfu	2003
SUGAR AND SPICE	Searchers	1963
SUGAR BABY LOVE	Rubettes	1974
SUGAR BOX	Then Jericho	1989
SUGAR CANDY KISSES	Mac & Katie Kissoon	1975
SUGAR COATED ICEBERG	Lightning Seeds	1997
SUGAR DADDY	Jackson 5	1971
SUGAR DADDY	Thompson Twins	1989
SUGAR DON'T BITE	Sam Harris	1984
SUGAR DUMPLING	Sam Cooke	1965
SUGAR FOR THE SOUL	Steve Balsamo	2002
SUGAR FREE	Wa Wa Nee	1987
SUGAR HILL	AZ	1995
SUGAR HONEY ICE TEA	Goodfellas	1997
SUGAR IS SWEETER	CJ Bolland	1996
SUGAR KANE	Sonic Youth	1993
SUGAR LIPS	Al Hirt	1964
SUGAR ME	Lynsey De Paul	1972
SUGAR MICE	Marillion	1987
SUGAR ON SUNDAY	Clique	1969
SUGAR SUGAR	Duke Baysee	1994
SUGAR SUGAR	Archies	1969
SUGAR SUGAR	Sakkarin	1971
SUGAR SUGAR	Wilson Pickett	1970
SUGAR TOWN	Nancy Sinatra	1966
SUGAR WALLS	Sheena Easton	1984
SUICIDE BLONDE	INXS	1990
SUITE: JUDY BLUE EYES	Crosby, Stills, Nash & Young	1969
SUKIYAKI	Kenny Ball	1963
SUKIYAKI	Kyu Sakamoto	1963
SUKIYAKI	4 P.M.	1994
SUKIYAKI	Taste Of Honey	1981
SULKY GIRL	Elvis Costello	1994
SULTANA	Titanic	1971
SULTANS OF SWING	Dire Straits	1979
SUMERLAND (DREAMED)	Fields Of The Nephilim	1990
SUMMER	Charlotte Hatherley	2004
SUMMER	War	1976

SONG TITLE	ARTIST	DATE
SUMMER (THE FIRST TIME)	Bobby Goldsboro	1973
SUMMER BREEZE	Isley Brothers	1974
SUMMER BREEZE	Seals & Crofts	1972
SUMMER BUNNIES	R. Kelly	1994
SUMMER FUN	Barracudas	1980
SUMMER GIRLS	Lyte Funkie Ones	1999
SUMMER GIRLS	LFO	1999
SUMMER HOLIDAY	Cliff Richard	1963
SUMMER HOLIDAY MEDLEY	Darren Day	1996
SUMMER IN THE CITY	Lovin' Spoonful	1966
SUMMER IS OVER	Frank Ifield	1964
SUMMER JAM	UD Project vs Sunclub	2003
SUMMER MOVED ON	A-Ha	2000
SUMMER NIGHT CITY	ABBA	1978
SUMMER NIGHTS	Marianne Faithfull	1965
SUMMER NIGHTS	John Travolta & Olivia Newton-John	1978
SUMMER OF '42	Biddu Orchestra	1975
SUMMER OF '69	Bryan Adams	1985
SUMMER OF LOVE	Lonyo	2000
THE SUMMER OF MY LIFE	Simon May	1976
SUMMER RAIN	Belinda Carlisle	1990
SUMMER RAIN	Johnny Rivers	1967
SUMMER SAMBA (SO NICE)	Walter Wanderley	1966

SONG TITLE	ARTIST	DATE
SUMMER SAND	Dawn	1971
SUMMER SON	Texas	1999
A SUMMER SONG	Chad & Jeremy	1964
SUMMER SUNSHINE	Corrs	2004
SUMMER WIND	Frank Sinatra	1966
SUMMERLOVE SENSATION	Bay City Rollers	1974
SUMMERS MAGIC	Mark Summers	1991
SUMMERTIME	Billy Stewart	1966
SUMMERTIME	Another Level featuring TQ	1999
SUMMERTIME	D.J. Jazzy Jeff & The Fresh Prince	1991
SUMMERTIME	Fun Boy Three	1982
SUMMERTIME	Sundays	1997
SUMMERTIME BLUES	Eddie Cochran	1958
SUMMERTIME BLUES	Who	1970
SUMMERTIME BLUES	Blue Cheer	1968
SUMMERTIME CITY	Mike Batt	1975
SUMMERTIME HEALING	Eusebe	1995
SUMMERTIME OF OUR LIVES	Al	1999
SUMTHIN' SUMTHIN' THE MANTRA	Maxwell	1997
SUN	Slusnik Luna	2001
THE SUN AIN'T GONNA SHINE (ANYMORE)	Walker Brothers	1966

SONG TITLE	ARTIST	DATE
THE SUN AIN'T GONNA SHINE ANYMORE		
	Cher	1996
THE SUN ALWAYS SHINES ON TV		
	A-Ha	1985
THE SUN AND THE RAIN	Madness	1983
SUN ARISE	Rolf Harris	1962
SUN CITY	Artists United Against Apartheid	1985
THE SUN GOES DOWN (LIVING IT UP)		
	Level 42	1983
THE SUN HAS COME YOUR WAY		
	Sam & Mark	2004
SUN HITS THE SKY	Supergrass	1997
SUN IS SHINING	Bob Marley vs Funkstar De Luxe	1999
THE SUN IS SHINING (DOWN ON ME)		
	DT8 PROJECT	2004
SUN KING	Cult	1989
THE SUN RISING	Beloved	1989
SUN STREET	Katrina & The Waves	1986
SUNBURN	Michelle Collins	1999
SUNBURN	Muse	2000
SUNCHYME	Dario G	1997
SUNDANCE	Sundance	1997
SUNDAY AND ME	Jay & The Americans	1965
SUNDAY FOR TEA	Peter & Gordon	1967
SUNDAY GIRL	Blondie	1979

SONG TITLE	ARTIST	DATE
SUNDAY MORNIN'	Oliver	1969
SUNDAY MORNING	Spanky & Our Gang	1968
SUNDAY MORNING CALL	Oasis	2000
SUNDAY SHINING	Finley Quaye	1997
SUNDAY SUNDAY	Blur	1993
SUNDAY WILL NEVER BE THE SAME		
	Spanky & Our Gang	1967
SUNDOWN	Gordon Lightfoot	1974
SUNDOWN	S Club 8	2003
SUNFLOWER	Paul Weller	1993
SUNFLOWER	Glen Campbell	1977
SUNGLASSES	Tracey Ullman	1984
SUNGLASSES AT NIGHT	Tiga And Zyntherius	2002
SUNGLASSES AT NIGHT	Corey Hart	1984
SUNLIGHT	DJ Sammy	2003
SUNMACHINE	Dario G	1998
SUNNY	Cher	1966
SUNNY	Boney M	1977
SUNNY	Georgie Fame	1966
SUNNY	Bobby Hebb	1966
SUNNY	Boogie Pimps	2004
SUNNY AFTERNOON	Kinks	1966
SUNNY CAME HOME	Shawn Colvin	1997
SUNNY DAYS	Lighthouse	1972
SUNNY HONEY GIRL	Cliff Richard	1971
SUNRISE	Simply Red	2003

SONG TITLE	ARTIST	DATE
SUNRISE	Norah Jones	2004
SUNRISE	Eric Carmen	1976
SUNRISE/THE TREES	Pulp	2001
SUNSET & BABYLON	W.A.S.P.	1993
SUNSET (BIRD OF PREY)	Fatboy Slim	2000
SUNSET GRILL	Don Henley	1985
SUNSET NOW	Heaven 17	1984
SUNSHINE	Jay-Z featuring Babyface & Foxy Brown	1997
SUNSHINE	Umboza	1996
SUNSHINE	Gabrielle	1999
SUNSHINE	Yomanda	2000
SUNSHINE	Twista featuring Anthony Hamilton	2004
SUNSHINE	Lil' Flip	2004
SUNSHINE	Dino	1989
SUNSHINE	Jonathan Edwards	1971
SUNSHINE AFTER THE RAIN	Elkie Brooks	1977
THE SUNSHINE AFTER THE RAIN	New Atlantic	1994
THE SUNSHINE AFTER THE RAIN	Berri	1995
SUNSHINE DAY	Osibisa	1976
SUNSHINE GIRL	Herman's Hermits	1968
SUNSHINE GIRL	Parade	1967

SONG TITLE	ARTIST	DATE
SUNSHINE, LOLLIPOPS & ROSES	Lesley Gore	1965
SUNSHINE OF YOUR LOVE	Cream	1968
SUNSHINE OF YOUR SMILE	Mike Berry	1980
SUNSHINE ON A RAINY DAY	Zoe	1991
SUNSHINE ON MY SHOULDERS	John Denver	1974
SUNSHINE SUPERMAN	Donovan	1966
SUNSTORM	Hurley & Todd	2000
SUNSTROKE	Chicane	1997
SUNTAN	Stan	1993
SUPER BAD (PTS 1 & 2)	James Brown	1970
SUPER DUPER LOVE (ARE YOU DIGGIN ON ME?)	Joss Stone	2004
SUPER FLY MEETS SHAFT	John & Ernest	1973
SUPER FREAK (PT 1)	Rick James	1981
SUPER GIRL	Graham Bonney	1966
SUPER GRAN	Billy Connolly	1985
SUPER TROUPER	A Teens	1999
SUPER TROUPER	ABBA	1980
SUPER WOMBLE	Wombles	1975
SUPERFLY	Curtis Mayfield	1972
SUPERFLY GUY	S'Express	1988
SUPERMAN	Herbie Mann	1979
SUPERMAN (GIOCA JOUER)	Black Lace	1983

SONG TITLE	ARTIST	DATE
SUPERMAN (IT'S NOT EASY)		
	Five For Fighting	2001
SUPERMARIOLAND	Ambassadors Of Funk/MC Mario	1992
SUPERMODEL (YOU BETTER WORK)		
	Rupaul	1993
SUPERNATURAL THING (PART 1)		
	Ben E. King	1975
SUPERNATURE	Cerrone	1978
SUPERSHIP	George Benson	1975
SUPERSONIC	HWA featuring Sonic The Hedgehog	1992
SUPERSONIC	Oasis	1994
SUPERSONIC	Jamiroquai	1999
SUPERSONIC	J.J. Fad	1988
SUPERSONIC ROCKET SHIP		
	Kinks	1972
SUPERSTAR	Novy vs Eniac	1998
SUPERSTAR	Lydia Murdock	1983
SUPERSTAR	Jamelia	2003
SUPERSTAR	Paul Davis	1976
SUPERSTAR	Murray Head	1971
SUPERSTAR (REMEMBER HOW YOU GOT WHERE YOU ARE)	Temptations	1971
SUPERSTAR	Carpenters	1971
SUPERSTITION	Stevie Wonder	1972
SUPERSTITIOUS	Europe	1988

SONG TITLE	ARTIST	DATE
SUPERSTRING	Cygnus X	2001
SUPERSTYLIN'	Groove Armada	2001
SUPERTHUG	Noreaga	1998
SUPERWOMAN	Karyn White	1989
SUPERWOMAN (WHERE WERE YOU WHEN I NEEDED YOU)	Stevie Wonder	1972
SUPERWOMAN (PT II)	Lil' Mo featuring Fabolous	2001
SUPREME	Robbie Williams	2000
SURE	Take That	1994
SURE AS I'M SITTIN' HERE	Three Dog Night	1974
SURE GONNA MISS HER	Gary Lewis & The Playboys	1966
SURE SHOT	Beastie Boys	1994
SURF CITY	Jan And Dean	1963
SURFIN' U.S.A.	Beach Boys	1974
SURFIN' U.S.A.	Leif Garrett	1977
SURFIN' USA	Aaron Carter	1998
SURPRISE	Bizarre Inc.	1996
SURRENDER	Roger Taylor	1999
SURRENDER	Diana Ross	1971
SURRENDER	Swing Out Sister	1987
SURRENDER	Lasgo	2004
SURRENDER (YOUR LOVE)	Javine	2003
SURRENDER TO ME	Ann Wilson & Robin Zander	1989
SURRENDER YOUR LOVE	Nightcrawlers featuring John Reid	1995

SONG TITLE	ARTIST	DATE
SURROUND YOURSELF WITH SORROW		
	Cilla Black	1969
SURVIVE	David Bowie	2000
SURVIVOR	Destiny's Child	2001
SUSAN	Buckinghams	1967
SUSAN'S HOUSE	Eels	1997
SUSANNA	Art Company	1984
SUSANNAH'S STILL ALIVE	Dave Davies	1967
SUSIE DARLIN'	Tommy Roe	1962
SUSPICION	Terry Stafford	1964
SUSPICION	Elvis Presley	1976
SUSPICIONS	Eddie Rabbitt	1979
SUSPICIOUS MINDS	Fine Young Cannibals	1986
SUSPICIOUS MINDS	Elvis Presley	1969
SUSPICIOUS MINDS	Candi Staton	1982
SUSSUDIO	Phil Collins	1985
SUZANNE	Journey	1986
SUZANNE BEWARE OF THE DEVIL		
	Dandy Livingstone	1972
SUZIE Q. (PT. 1)	Creedence Clearwater Revival	1968
SVEN SVEN SVEN	Bell & Spurling	2001
SW LIVE EP	Peter Gabriel	1994
SWALLOW MY PRIDE	Ramones	1977
SWALLOWED	Bush	1997
SWAMP THING	Grid	1994
SWAMP WITCH	Jim Stafford	1973

SONG TITLE	ARTIST	DATE
SWASTIKA EYES	Primal Scream	1999
SWAYIN' TO THE MUSIC (SLOW DANCIN')		
	Johnny Rivers	1977
SWEAR IT AGAIN	Westlife	1999
SWEARIN' TO GOD	Frankie Valli	1975
SWEAT	Usura	1993
SWEAT (A LA LA LA LA LONG)		
	Inner Circle	1993
SWEATING BULLETS	Megadeth	1993
SWEEET SURRENDER	Rod Stewart	1983
SWEET AND INNOCENT	Donny Osmond	1971
SWEET BABY	Macy Gray featuring Erykah Badu	2001
SWEET BABY	Stanley Clarke & George Duke	1981
SWEET BLINDNESS	5th Dimension	1968
SWEET CAROLINE	Neil Diamond	1969
SWEET CHEATIN' RITA	Alvin Stardust	1975
SWEET CHERRY WINE	Tommy James & The Shondells	1969
SWEET CHILD O' MINE	Sheryl Crow	1999
SWEET CHILD O' MINE	Guns N' Roses	1988
SWEET CITY WOMAN	Stampeders	1971
SWEET CREAM LADIES, FORWARD MARCH		
	Box Tops	1968
SWEET DREAM	Jethro Tull	1969
SWEET DREAMS	DJ Scott featuring Lorna B	1995
SWEET DREAMS	Roy Buchanan	1973

SONG TITLE	ARTIST	DATE
SWEET DREAMS	Air Supply	1981
SWEET DREAMS	La Bouche	1996
SWEET DREAMS	Tommy McLain	1966
SWEET DREAMS (ARE MADE OF THIS)		
	Eurythmics	1983
SWEET DREAMS MY L.A. EX		
	Rachel Stevens	2003
SWEET EMOTION	Aerosmith	1975
SWEET FREEDOM	Positive Gang	1993
SWEET FREEDOM	Michael McDonald	1986
SWEET HARMONY	Beloved	1993
SWEET HARMONY/ONE LOVE FAMILY		
	Liquid	1995
SWEET HITCH-HIKER	Creedence Clearwater Revival	1971
SWEET HOME ALABAMA/DOUBLE TROUBLE		
	Lynyrd Skynyrd	1976
SWEET ILLUSION	Junior Campbell	1973
SWEET IMPOSSIBLE YOU	Brenda Lee	1963
SWEET INSPIRATION	Johnny Johnson & The	
	Bandwagon	1970
SWEET INSPIRATION	Sweet Inspirations	1968
SWEET INSPIRATION	Barbra Streisand	1972
SWEET LADY	Tyrese	1999
SWEET LIFE	Paul Davis	1978
SWEET LIKE CHOCOLATE	Shanks & Bigfoot	1999
SWEET LIPS	Monaco	1997

SONG TITLE	ARTIST	DATE
SWEET LITTLE MYSTERY	Wet Wet Wet	1987
SWEET LITTLE ROCK 'N' ROLLER		
	Showaddywaddy	1979
SWEET LOVE	Anita Baker	1986
SWEET LOVE	M-Beat featuring Nazlyn	1994
SWEET LOVE	Commodores	1977
SWEET LOVE 2K	Fierce	2000
SWEET LUI-LOUISE	Ironhorse	1979
SWEET LULLABY	Deep Forest	1994
SWEET MARY	Wadsworth Mansion	1970
SWEET MAXINE	Doobie Brothers	1975
SWEET MEMORY	Belle Stars	1983
SWEET MUSIC	Showaddywaddy	1975
SWEET PEA	Manfred Mann	1967
SWEET PEA	Tommy Roe	1966
SWEET POTATOE PIE	Domino	1994
SWEET SEASONS	Carole King	1972
SWEET SIXTEEN	Billy Idol	1987
SWEET SOMEBODY	Shannon	1984
SWEET SOUL MUSIC	Arthur Conley	1967
SWEET SOUTHERN COMFORT		
	Buddy Jewell	2004
SWEET STICKY THING	Ohio Players	1975
SWEET SURRENDER	Wet Wet Wet	1989
SWEET SURRENDER	Bread	1972
SWEET SURRENDER	John Denver	1974

SONG TITLE	ARTIST	DATE
SWEET SURRENDER	Sarah McLachlan	1998
(SWEET SWEET BABY) SINCE YOU'VE BEEN GONE		
	Aretha Franklin	1968
SWEET, SWEET SMILE	Carpenters	1978
SWEET TALKIN' GUY	Chiffons	1966
SWEET TALKIN' WOMAN	Electric Light Orchestra	1978
SWEET THING	Mick Jagger	1993
SWEET THING	Mary J. Blige	1993
SWEET THING	Rufus featuring Chaka Khan	1976
SWEET TIME	REO Speedwagon	1982
SWEET UNDERSTANDING LOVE		
	Four Tops	1973
SWEET WILLIAM	Millie Small	1964
A SWEET WOMAN LIKE YOU		
	Joe Tex	1965
THE SWEETEST DAYS	Vanessa Williams	1994
SWEETEST GIRL	Madness	1986
THE SWEETEST THING THIS SIDE OF HEAVEN		
	Chris Bartley	1967
SWEETEST SMILE	Black	1987
THE SWEETEST TABOO	Sade	1985
SWEETEST THING	U2	1998
THE SWEETEST THING (I'VE EVER KNOWN)		
	Juice Newton	1981
THE SWEETEST THING	Refugee Allstars/Lauryn Hill	1997
SWEETHEART	Engelbert Humperdinck	1970

SONG TITLE	ARTIST	DATE
SWEETHEART	Franke & The Knockouts	1981
SWEETNESS	Michelle Gayle	1994
SWEETNESS	Jimmy Eat World	2002
SWEETS FOR MY SWEET	Searchers	1963
SWEETS FOR MY SWEET	CJ Lewis	1994
SWEPT AWAY	Diana Ross	1984
SWIMMING HORSES	Siouxsie & The Banshees	1984
SWING LOW	UB40 featuring United Colours Of Sound	2003
SWING LOW '99	Russell Watson	1999
SWING LOW SWEET CHARIOT		
	Eric Clapton	1975
SWING LOW SWEET CHARIOT		
	Ladysmith Black Mambazo featuring China Black	1995
SWING MY WAY	KP & Envyi	1997
SWING, SWING	All-American Rejects	2003
SWING THAT HAMMER	Mike Cotton's Jazzmen	1963
SWING THE MOOD	Jive Bunny & The Mastermixers	1989
SWING YOUR DADDY	Jim Gilstrap	1975
SWINGING ON A STAR	Big Dee Irwin	1963
SWINGTOWN	Steve Miller Band	1977
SWITCH	Senser	1994
SWORDS OF A THOUSAND MEN		
	Ten Pole Tudor	1981
SYLVIA	Focus	1973

SONG TITLE	ARTIST	DATE
SYLVIA'S MOTHER	Dr. Hook	1972
SYLVIE	Saint Etienne	1998
SYMMETRY C	Brainchild	1999
SYMPATHY	Marillion	1992
SYMPATHY	Rare Bird	1970
SYMPATHY FOR THE DEVIL	Guns N' Roses	1995
SYMPATHY FOR THE DEVIL	Rolling Stones	2003
SYMPHONY OF DESTRUCTION		
	Megadeth	1992
SYMPTOMS OF TRUE LOVE	Tracie Spencer	1988
SYNAESTHESIA (FLY AWAY)		
	Thrillseekers featuring	
	Sheryl Deane	2001
SYNCHRONICITY II	Police	1983
SYNTH & STRINGS	Yomanda	1999
SYSTEM ADDICT	Five Star	1986
T-R-O-U-B-L-E	Elvis Presley	1975
T.L.C.	Linear	1992
TABOO	Glamma Kid featuring	
	Shola Ama	1999
TAHITI (FROM MUTINY ON THE BOUNTY)		
	David Essex	1983
TAINTED LOVE	Soft Cell	1982
TAINTED LOVE	Marilyn Manson	2002
TAKE 5	Northside	1991
TAKE A BOW	Madonna	1994

SONG TITLE	ARTIST	DATE
TAKE A CHANCE ON ME	ABBA	1978
TAKE A CHANCE WITH ME	Roxy Music	1982
TAKE A FREE FALL	Dance 2 Trance	1993
TAKE A HEART	Sorrows	1965
TAKE A LETTER MARIA	R.B. Greaves	1969
TAKE A LITTLE RHYTHM	Ali Thomson	1980
(TAKE A LITTLE) PIECE OF MY HEART		
	Erma Franklin	1992
TAKE A LOOK	Level 42	1988
TAKE A LOOK AROUND	Temptations	1972
TAKE A LOOK AROUND (THEME FROM M:I2)		
	Limp Bizkit	2000
TAKE A PICTURE	Filter	1999
TAKE CARE OF YOUR HOMEWORK		
	Johnnie Taylor	1969
TAKE CARE OF YOURSELF	Level 42	1989
TAKE CONTROL	Jaimeson featuring Angel Blu	
	and CK	2004
TAKE DOWN THE UNION JACK		
	Billy Bragg And The Blokes	2002
TAKE GOOD CARE OF MY BABY		
	Smokie	1980
TAKE GOOD CARE OF MY BABY		
	Bobby Vinton	1968
TAKE GOOD CARE OF YOURSELF		
	Three Degrees	1975

SONG TITLE	ARTIST	DATE
TAKE IT	Flowered Up	1991
TAKE IT AND RUN	The Bandits	2003
TAKE IT AWAY	Paul McCartney	1982
TAKE IT BACK	Pink Floyd	1994
TAKE IT EASY	Let Loose	1996
TAKE IT EASY	3SL	2002
TAKE IT EASY	Eagles	1972
TAKE IT EASY	Andy Taylor	1986
TAKE IT EASY ON ME	Little River Band	1981
TAKE IT LIKE A MAN	Bachman-Turner Overdrive	1976
TAKE IT OFF	Donnas	2003
TAKE IT ON THE RUN	REO Speedwagon	1981
TAKE IT OR LEAVE IT	Searchers	1966
TAKE IT TO THE LIMIT	Eagles	1975
TAKE IT TO THE STREETS	Rampage featuring Billy Lawrence	1997
TAKE IT TO THE TOP	Kool & The Gang	1981
TAKE ME	Dream Frequency	1992
TAKE ME AWAY	Cappella featuring Loleatta Holloway	1992
TAKE ME AWAY	D:ream	1994
TAKE ME AWAY (I'LL FOLLOW YOU)	Bad Boys Inc	1994
(TAKE ME AWAY) INTO THE NIGHT	4 Strings	2002

SONG TITLE	ARTIST	DATE
TAKE ME BACK	Little Anthony & The Imperials	1965
TAKE ME BAK 'OME	Slade	1972
TAKE ME BY THE HAND	Sub Merge featuring Jan Johnston	1997
TAKE ME DOWN	Alabama	1982
TAKE ME FOR A LITTLE WHILE	Coverdale Page	1993
TAKE ME FOR A LITTLE WHILE	Vanilla Fudge	1968
TAKE ME FOR WHAT I'M WORTH	Searchers	1965
TAKE ME GIRL I'M READY	Jr. Walker & The All-Stars	1973
TAKE ME HIGH	Cliff Richard	1973
TAKE ME HIGHER	Diana Ross	1995
TAKE ME HOME	Phil Collins	1986
TAKE ME HOME	Cher	1979
TAKE ME HOME (A GIRL LIKE ME)	Sophie Ellis-Bextor	2001
TAKE ME HOME TONIGHT	Eddie Money	1986
TAKE ME HOME, COUNTRY ROADS	Olivia Newton-John	1973
TAKE ME HOME, COUNTRY ROADS	John Denver	1971
TAKE ME I'M YOURS	Squeeze	1978
TAKE ME IN YOUR ARMS (ROCK ME A LITTLE WHILE)	Doobie Brothers	1975

SONG TITLE	ARTIST	DATE
TAKE ME OUT	Franz Ferdinand	2004
TAKE ME THERE	Blackstreet & Mya featuring Mase & Blinky Blink	1998
TAKE ME TO HEART	Quarterflash	1983
TAKE ME TO HEAVEN	Baby D	1996
TAKE ME TO THE CLOUDS ABOVE	LMC vs U2	2004
TAKE ME TO THE MARDI GRAS	Paul Simon	1973
TAKE ME TO THE RIVER	Skin	1995
TAKE ME TO THE RIVER	Talking Heads	1978
TAKE ME TO YOUR HEART	Rick Astley	1988
TAKE ME TO YOUR HEART AGAIN	Vince Hill	1966
TAKE ME TO YOUR HEAVEN	Charlotte Nilsson	1999
TAKE ME WITH U	Prince	1985
TAKE ME WITH YOU	Cosmos	2002
TAKE MY ADVICE	Kym Sims	1992
TAKE MY BREATH AWAY	Berlin	1986
TAKE MY BREATH AWAY	Emma Bunton	2001
TAKE MY BREATH AWAY	Soda Club featuring Hannah Alethea	2002
TAKE MY HAND	Jurgen Vries featuring Andrea Britton	2004

SONG TITLE	ARTIST	DATE
TAKE MY HEART (YOU CAN HAVE IT IF YOU WANT IT)	Kool & The Gang	1981
TAKE OFF	Bob & Doug McKenzie	1982
TAKE ON ME	A-Ha	1985
TAKE ON ME	Al	2000
TAKE ON THE WORLD	Judas Priest	1979
TAKE THAT LOOK OFF YOUR FACE	Marti Webb	1980
TAKE THAT SITUATION	Nick Heyward	1983
TAKE THAT TO THE BANK	Shalamar	1978
TAKE THE LONG ROAD AND WALK IT	Music	2002
TAKE THE LONG WAY HOME	Faithless	1998
TAKE THE LONG WAY HOME	Supertramp	1979
TAKE THE MONEY AND RUN	Steve Miller Band	1976
TAKE THESE CHAINS FROM MY HEART	Ray Charles	1963
TAKE THIS HEART	Richard Marx	1992
TAKE THIS TIME	Sean Maguire	1994
TAKE TIME	Chris Walker	1992
TAKE TIME TO KNOW HER	Percy Sledge	1968
TAKE TO THE MOUNTAINS	Richard Barnes	1970
TAKE YOU OUT	Luther Vandross	2001

SONG TITLE	ARTIST	DATE
TAKE YOUR MAMA	Scissor Sisters	2004
TAKE YOUR MAMA FOR A RIDE	Lulu	1975
TAKE YOUR SHOES OFF	Cheeky Girls	2003
TAKE YOUR TIME	Mantronix featuring Wondress	1990
TAKE YOUR TIME (DO IT RIGHT) (PT 1)	S.O.S. Band	1980
TAKEN FOR GRANTED	Sia	2000
TAKEN IN	Mike & The Mechanics	1986
TAKES A LITTLE TIME	Total Contrast	1985
TAKIN' CARE OF BUSINESS	Bachman-Turner Overdrive	1974
TAKIN' IT TO THE STREETS	Doobie Brothers	1976
TAKING EVERYTHING	Gerald Levert	1999
TALK ABOUT OUR LOVE	Brandy featuring Kanye West	2004
TALK DIRTY TO ME	Poison	1987
TALK IT OVER	Grayson Hugh	1989
TALK OF THE TOWN	Pretenders	1980
TALK TALK	Talk Talk	1982
TALK TALK	Music Machine	1966
TALK TALK TALK	Ordinary Boys	2004
TALK TO ME	60ft Dolls	1996
TALK TO ME	Chico DeBarge	1986
TALK TO ME	Stevie Nicks	1985
TALKING ABOUT MY BABY	Impressions	1964
TALKING IN YOUR SLEEP	Bucks Fizz	1984

SONG TITLE	ARTIST	DATE
TALKING IN YOUR SLEEP	Crystal Gayle	1978
TALKING IN YOUR SLEEP	Romantics	1983
TALKING IN YOUR SLEEP/LOVE ME	Martine McCutcheon	1999
TALKING LOUD AND CLEAR	Orchestral Manoeuvres In The Dark	1984
TALKING LOUD AND SAYING NOTHING (PART 1)	James Brown	1972
TALKING OFF	Cure	2004
TALKING WITH MYSELF	Electribe 101	1990
TALKING WITH MYSELF 98	Electribe 101	1998
TALL COOL ONE	Robert Plant	1988
TALL COOL ONE	Wailers	1964
TALLYMAN	Jeff Beck	1967
TALULA	Tori Amos	1996
TANGERINE	Salsoul Orchestra	1976
TANGLED UP IN BLUE	Bob Dylan	1975
TANTALISE (WO WO EE YEH YEH)	Jimmy The Hoover	1983
TAP THE BOTTLE	Young Black Teenagers	1994
TAP TURNS ON THE WATER	C.C.S.	1971
TAPIOCA TUNDRA	Monkees	1968
TAR AND CEMENT	Verdelle Smith	1966

SONG TITLE	ARTIST	DATE
TARA'S THEME	Spiro And Wix	1996
TARANTINO'S NEW STAR	North And South	1997
TARANTULA	Faithless	2001
TARZAN BOY	Baltimora	1993
TASTE IN MEN	Placebo	2000
TASTE IT	INXS	1992
A TASTE OF AGGRO	Barron Knights	1978
TASTE OF BITTER LOVE	Gladys Knight & The Pips	1980
A TASTE OF HONEY	Mr. Acker Bilk & The Leon Young String Chorale	1963
A TASTE OF HONEY	Herb Alpert	1965
THE TASTE OF YOUR TEARS	King	1985
TASTE THE PAIN	Red Hot Chili Peppers	1990
TATTOO	Mike Oldfield	1992
TATTOOED MILLIONAIRE	Bruce Dickinson	1990
TATTVA	Kula Shaker	1996
TAURUS	Dennis Coffey & The Detroit Guitar Band	1972
TAXI	Harry Chapin	1972
TAXLOSS	Mansun	1997
TCHAIKOVSKY ONE	Second City Sound	1966
TEACH YOUR CHILDREN	Crosby, Stills, Nash & Young	1970
THE TEACHER	Big Country	1986
TEACHER TEACHER	38 Special	1984
TEAR ME APART	Suzi Quatro	1977

SONG TITLE	ARTIST	DATE
TEAR THE ROOF OFF THE SUCKER (GIVE UP THE FUNK)	Parliament	1976
TEARDROP	Massive Attack	1998
TEARDROPS	Lovestation	1998
TEARDROPS	Shakin' Stevens	1984
TEARDROPS	Womack & Womack	1988
TEARIN' UP MY HEART	*NSYNC	1999
TEARS	Ken Dodd	1965
TEARS	John Waite	1984
TEARS AND ROSES	Al Martino	1964
TEARS ARE NOT ENOUGH	ABC	1981
TEARS DON'T LIE	Mark' Oh	1995
TEARS FROM HEAVEN	Heartbeat	1987
THE TEARS I CRIED	Glitter Band	1975
TEARS IN HEAVEN	Eric Clapton	1992
THE TEARS OF A CLOWN	Smokey Robinson & The Miracles	1970
TEARS OF A CLOWN/RANKING FULL STOP	Beat	1979
TEARS OF THE DRAGON	Bruce Dickinson	1994
TEARS ON MY PILLOW	Kylie Minogue	1990
TEARS ON MY PILLOW	Johnny Nash	1975
TEARS ON THE TELEPHONE	Claude Francois	1976
TEARS ON THE TELEPHONE	Hot Chocolate	1983

SONG TITLE	ARTIST	DATE
TEARS RUN RINGS	Marc Almond	1988
TEARS WON'T WASH AWAY THESE HEARTACHES		
	Ken Dodd	1969
TEASE ME	Chaka Demus & Pliers	1993
TECHNOCAT	Technocat featuring Tom Wilson	1995
TEDDY BEAR	Red Sovine	1976
TEDDY BEAR SONG	Barbara Fairchild	1973
TEENAGE	UK Subs	1980
TEENAGE ANGST	Placebo	1996
TEENAGE DEPRESSION	Eddie & The Hotrods	1976
TEENAGE DIRTBAG	Wheatus	2001
TEENAGE DREAM	Marc Bolan & T. Rex	1974
TEENAGE KICKS	Undertones	1978
TEENAGE LAMENT '74	Alice Cooper	1974
TEENAGE RAMPAGE	Sweet	1974
TEENAGE SENSATION	Credit To The Nation	1994
TEENAGE WARNING	Angelic Upstarts	1979
TEETHGRINDER	Therapy?	1992
TELEFONE (LONG DISTANCE LOVE AFFAIR)		
	Sheena Easton	1983
TELEFUNKIN'	N-Tyce	1998
TELEGRAM SAM	T. Rex	1972
THE TELEPHONE ALWAYS RINGS		
	Fun Boy Three	1982
TELEPHONE LINE	Electric Light Orchestra	1977
TELEPHONE MAN	Meri Wilson	1977

SONG TITLE	ARTIST	DATE
TELETUBBIES SAY EH-OH!	Teletubbies	1997
TELL HER	Lonestar	2000
TELL HER ABOUT IT	Billy Joel	1983
TELL HER NO	Juice Newton	1983
TELL HER NO	Zombies	1965
TELL HER THIS	Del Amitri	1995
TELL HIM	Quentin & Ash	1996
TELL HIM	Billie Davis	1963
TELL HIM	Hello	1974
TELL HIM	Barbra Streisand & Celine Dion	1997
TELL IT ALL BROTHER	Kenny Rogers & The First Edition	1970
TELL IT LIKE IT IS	Heart	1980
TELL IT LIKE IT IS	Aaron Neville	1966
TELL IT ON THE MOUNTAIN		
	Peter, Paul & Mary	1964
TELL IT TO MY HEART	Q-Club	1996
TELL IT TO MY HEART	Taylor Dayne	1987
TELL IT TO MY HEART	Kelly Llorenna	2002
TELL IT TO THE RAIN	Four Seasons	1966
TELL MAMA	Etta James	1967
TELL ME	Groove Theory	1995
TELL ME	Dru Hill	1996
TELL ME	Billie Myers	1998
TELL ME	Melanie B	2000
TELL ME	Nick Kamen	1988

SONG TITLE	ARTIST	DATE
TELL ME (WHAT'S GOIN' ON)		
	Smilez & Southstar	2003
TELL ME (YOU'RE COMING BACK)		
	Rolling Stones	1964
TELL ME A LIE	Sami Jo	1974
TELL ME DO U WANNA	Ginuwine	1997
TELL ME IS IT TRUE	UB40	1997
TELL ME IT'S REAL	K-CI & Jojo	1999
TELL ME MA	Sham Rock	1998
TELL ME SOMETHING	Indecent Obsession	1990
TELL ME SOMETHING GOOD		
	Rufus	1974
TELL ME THE WAY	Cappella	1995
TELL ME THERE'S A HEAVEN		
	Chris Rea	1990
TELL ME TO MY FACE	Keith	1967
TELL ME TOMORROW	Princess	1986
TELL ME TOMORROW (PART 1)		
	Smokey Robinson	1982
TELL ME WHAT YOU WANT		
	Jimmy Ruffin	1974
TELL ME WHAT YOU WANT ME TO DO		
	Tevin Campbell	1991
TELL ME WHEN	Applejacks	1964
TELL ME WHEN	Human League	1995

SONG TITLE	ARTIST	DATE
TELL ME WHEN THE FEVER ENDED		
	Electribe 101	1989
TELL ME WHY	Genesis	1993
TELL ME WHY	Elvis Presley	1966
TELL ME WHY	Alvin Stardust	1974
TELL ME WHY	Musical Youth	1983
TELL ME WHY	Declan featuring Young Voices Choir	2002
TELL ME WHY	Expose	1989
TELL ME WHY	Bobby Vinton	1964
TELL ME WHY (THE RIDDLE)		
	Paul Van Dyk featuring Saint Etienne	2000
TELLIN' STORIES	Charlatans	1997
TEMMA HARBOUR	Mary Hopkin	1970
TEMPERTEMPER	Goldie	1998
TEMPLE OF DREAMS	Messiah	1992
TEMPLE OF DREAMS	Future Breeze	2002
TEMPLE OF LOVE	Harriet	1991
TEMPLE OF LOVE (1992)	Sisters Of Mercy	1992
TEMPO FIESTA (PARTY TIME)		
	Itty Bitty Boozy Woozy	1995
TEMPTATION	Heaven 17	1983
TEMPTATION	Wet Wet Wet	1988
TEMPTATION	New Order	1982
TEMPTATION	Corina	1991

SONG TITLE	ARTIST	DATE
TEMPTATION EYES	Grass Roots	1970
10 IN 01	Members Of Mayday	2001
TEN MILES HIGH	Little Angels	1994
10-9-8	Face To Face	1984
TEN ROUNDS WITH JOSE CUERVO	Tracy Byrd	2002
TEN STOREY LOVE SONG	Stone Roses	1995
10 YEARS ASLEEP	Kingmaker	1993
TENDER	Blur	1999
TENDER HEART	Lionel Richie	2001
TENDER IS THE NIGHT	Jackson Browne	1983
TENDER LOVE	Kenny Thomas	1991
TENDER LOVE	Force M.D.'s	1986
TENDER LOVER	Babyface	1989
TENDER YEARS	John Cafferty & Beaver Brown Band	1984
TENDERNESS	General Public	1984
TENNESSEE	Arrested Development	1992
TENNESSEE BIRDWALK	Jack Blanchard & Misty Morgan	1970
TENNESSEE WALTZ	Sam Cooke	1964
TEQUILA	Terrorvision	1999
TEQUILA SUNRISE	Cypress Hill	1998
TERESA	Joe Dolan	1969
TERRY	Twinkle	1964
TESLA GIRLS	Orchestral Manoeuvres In The Dark	1984

SONG TITLE	ARTIST	DATE
TESTIFY	M People	1998
TESTIFY (I WONNA)	Johnnie Taylor	1969
TETRIS	Doctor Spin	1992
TEXAS COWBOYS	Grid	1994
THA CROSSROAD	Bone Thugs-N-Harmony	1996
THA DOGGFATHER	Snoop Doggy Dogg	1998
THA HORNS OF JERICHO	DJ Supreme	1998
THA WILD STYLE	DJ Supreme	1997
THANK ABBA FOR THE MUSIC	Various Artists	1999
THANK GOD I FOUND YOU	Mariah Carey featuring Joe & 98 Degrees	1999
THANK GOD I'M A COUNTRY BOY	John Denver	1975
THANK GOD IT'S CHRISTMAS	Queen	1984
THANK GOD IT'S FRIDAY	R. Kelly	1996
THANK GOD IT'S FRIDAY	Love And Kisses	1978
THANK THE LORD FOR THE NIGHT TIME	Neil Diamond	1967
THANK U	Alanis Morissette	1998
THANK U VERY MUCH	Scaffold	1967
THANK YOU	Boyz II Men	1995
THANK YOU	Dido	2001
THANK YOU (FALETTINME BE MICE ELF AGIN)/ EVERYBODY IS A STAR	Sly & The Family Stone	1970

SONG TITLE	ARTIST	DATE
THANK YOU BABY	Shania Twain	2003
THANK YOU FOR BEING A FRIEND		
	Andrew Gold	1978
THANK YOU FOR HEARING ME		
	Sinead O'Connor	1994
THANK YOU FOR LOVING ME		
	Bon Jovi	2000
THANK YOU FOR THE MUSIC		
	ABBA	1983
THANK YOU GIRL	Beatles	1964
THANK YOU MY LOVE	Imagination	1984
THANKS FOR MY CHILD	Cheryl 'Pepsii' Riley	1988
THANKS FOR SAVING MY LIFE		
	Billy Paul	1974
THANKS FOR THE MEMORY (WHAM BAM THANK		
YOU MAM)	Slade	1975
THAT AIN'T LOVE	REO Speedwagon	1987
THAT CERTAIN SMILE	Midge Ure	1985
THAT DAY	Natalie Imbruglia	2001
THAT DON'T IMPRESS ME MUCH		
	Shania Twain	1999
THAT GIRL	Maxi Priest	1996
THAT GIRL	Stevie Wonder	1982
THAT GIRL	McFly	2004
THAT GIRL BELONGS TO YESTERDAY		
	Gene Pitney	1964

SONG TITLE	ARTIST	DATE
THAT GIRL COULD SING	Jackson Browne	1980
THAT GREAT LOVE SOUND	The Raveonettes	2003
THAT LADY	Isley Brothers	1973
THAT LOOK	De'Lacy	1996
THAT LOOK IN YOUR EYE	Ali Campbell	1995
THAT MEANS A LOT	P.J. Proby	1965
THAT OLD SONG	Ray Parker Jr. & Raydio	1981
THAT OLE DEVIL CALLED LOVE		
	Alison Moyet	1985
THAT SAME OLD FEELING	Pickettywitch	1970
THAT SOUND	Michael Moog	1999
THAT SOUNDS GOOD TO ME		
	Jive Bunny & The Mastermixers	1990
THAT THING YOU DO!	Wonders	1997
THAT WAS THEN BUT THIS IS NOW		
	ABC	1983
THAT WAS THEN, THIS IS NOW		
	Monkees	1986
THAT WAS YESTERDAY	Foreigner	1985
THAT WOMAN'S GOT ME DRINKING		
	Shane Macgowan and The Popes	1994
THAT'D BE ALRIGHT	Alan Jackson	2003
THAT'LL BE THE DAY	Everly Brothers	1965
THAT'LL BE THE DAY	Linda Ronstadt	1976
THAT'S ALL RIGHT	Elvis Presley	2004
THAT'S ALL!	Genesis	1983

SONG TITLE	ARTIST	DATE
THAT'S HOW I'M LIVIN'	Ice-T	1993
THAT'S JUST THE WAY IT IS		
	Phil Collins	1990
THAT'S LIFE	Frank Sinatra	1966
THAT'S LIVING (ALRIGHT)	Joe Fagin	1984
THAT'S LOVE	Jim Capaldi	1983
THAT'S LOVE, THAT IT IS	Blancmange	1983
THAT'S NICE	Neil Christian	1966
THAT'S ROCK 'N' ROLL	Shaun Cassidy	1977
THAT'S THE WAY	Honeycombs	1965
THAT'S THE WAY	Katrina & The Waves	1989
THAT'S THE WAY	Jo Dee Messina	2000
THAT'S THE WAY (I LIKE IT)		
	Dead Or Alive	1984
THAT'S THE WAY (I LIKE IT)		
	Clock	1998
THAT'S THE WAY (I LIKE IT)		
	KC & The Sunshine Band	1975
THAT'S THE WAY BOYS ARE		
	Lesley Gore	1964
THAT'S THE WAY GOD PLANNED IT		
	Billy Preston	1969
THAT'S THE WAY I FEEL ABOUT CHA		
	Bobby Womack	1971
THAT'S THE WAY I WANNA ROCK 'N' ROLL		
	AC/DC	1988

SONG TITLE	ARTIST	DATE
THAT'S THE WAY I'VE ALWAYS HEARD IT SHOULD BE		
	Carly Simon	1971
THAT'S THE WAY IT IS	Celine Dion	1999
THAT'S THE WAY IT IS	Mel & Kim	1988
THAT'S THE WAY LOVE GOES		
	Charles Dickens	1965
THAT'S THE WAY LOVE GOES		
	Janet Jackson	1993
THAT'S THE WAY LOVE IS	Byron Stingily	2000
THAT'S THE WAY LOVE IS	Ten City	1989
THAT'S THE WAY LOVE IS	Marvin Gaye	1969
THAT'S THE WAY OF THE WORLD		
	Earth, Wind & Fire	1975
THAT'S THE WAY YOU DO IT		
	Purple Kings	1994
THAT'S WHAT FRIENDS ARE FOR		
	Dionne Warwick & Friends	1985
THAT'S WHAT FRIENDS ARE FOR		
	Deniece Williams	1977
THAT'S WHAT I LIKE	Jive Bunny & The Mastermixers	1989
THAT'S WHAT I THINK	Cyndi Lauper	1993
THAT'S WHAT LOVE CAN DO		
	Boy Krazy	1993
THAT'S WHAT LOVE IS ALL ABOUT		
	Michael Bolton	1987

SONG TITLE	ARTIST	DATE
THAT'S WHAT LOVE IS FOR	Amy Grant	1991
THAT'S WHAT LOVE IS MADE OF	Miracles	1964
THAT'S WHAT LOVE WILL DO	Joe Brown & The Bruvvers	1963
THAT'S WHEN I LOVE YOU	Phil Vassar	2002
THAT'S WHEN THE MUSIC TAKES ME	Neil Sedaka	1975
THAT'S WHERE I WENT WRONG	Poppy Family	1970
THAT'S WHERE THE HAPPY PEOPLE GO	Trammps	1976
THAT'S WHY I'M CRYING	Ivy League	1965
(THE BEST PART OF) BREAKIN' UP	Ronettes	1964
(THE LAMENT OF THE CHEROKEE) INDIAN RESERVATION	Don Fardon	1968
(THE SYSTEM OF) DOCTOR TARR AND PROFESSOR FETHER	Alan Parsons Project	1976
THEM BONES	Alice In Chains	1993
THEM GIRLS THEM GIRLS	Zig And Zag	1994
THEME FOR YOUNG LOVERS	Shadows	1964
THEME FROM 'A SUMMER PLACE'	Lettermen	1965

SONG TITLE	ARTIST	DATE
THEME FROM 'CLOSE ENCOUNTERS OF THE THIRD KIND'	John Williams	1977
THEME FROM 'E.T.'	John Williams	1982
THEME FROM 'GREATEST AMERICAN HERO' (BELIEVE IT OR NOT)	Joey Scarbury	1981
THEME FROM 'HILL STREET BLUES'	Mike Post featuring Larry Carlton	1982
THEME FROM 'HONG KONG BEAT'	Richard Denton & Martin Cook	1978
THEME FROM 'SHAFT'	Isaac Hayes	1971
THEME FROM 'SUMMER OF '42'	Peter Nero	1971
THEME FROM 'SUPERMAN' (MAIN TITLE)	London Symphony Orchestra	1979
THEME FROM 'THE LEGION'S LAST PATROL'	Ken Thorne & His Orchestra	1963
THEME FROM 'THE ONEDIN LINE'	Vienna Philharmonic Orchestra	1971
THEME FROM CLEOPATRA JONES	Joe Simon featuring The Main Streeters	1973
THEME FROM CLOSE ENCOUNTERS	Meco	1978
THEME FROM GUTBUSTER	Bentley Rhythm Ace	2000

SONG TITLE	ARTIST	DATE
THEME FROM HARRY'S GAME	Clannad	1982
THE THEME FROM HILL STREET BLUES	Mike Post featuring Larry Carlton	1981
THEME FROM LOVE STORY	Henry Mancini & His Orchestra	1971
THEME FROM M.A.S.H./EVERYTHING I DO	Manic Street Preachers/ Fatima Mansion	1992
THEME FROM MAGNUM P.I.	Mike Post	1982
THEME FROM MAHOGANY(DO YOU KNOW WHERE YOU'RE GOING TO)	Diana Ross	1975
THEME FROM MISSION:IMPOSSIBLE	Adam Clayton & Larry Mullen	1996
THEME FROM M*A*S*H*(SUICIDE IS PAINLESS)	Mash	1980
THEME FROM NEW YORK, NEW YORK	Frank Sinatra	1980
THEME FROM S'EXPRESS	S'Express	1988
THEME FROM S.W.A.T.	Rhythm Heritage	1974
THEME FROM SHAFT	Eddy & The Soul Band	1985
THEME FROM THE DEER HUNTER (CAVATINA)	Shadows	1979
THEME FROM THE DUKES OF HAZZARD (GOOD OL' BOYS)	Waylon Jennings	1980

SONG TITLE	ARTIST	DATE
THEME FROM THE MEN	Isaac Hayes	1972
THEME FROM THE PERSUADERS	John Barry Orchestra	1971
THEME FROM THE PROFESSIONALS	Laurie Johnson's London Big Band	1997
THEME FROM THE WIZARD OF OZ	Meco	1978
(THEME FROM) VALLEY OF THE DOLLS	Dionne Warwick	1968
THEME SONG FROM 'WHICH WAY IS UP'	Stargard	1978
THE THEME	Dreem Teem	1997
THE THEME	Jurgen Vries	2002
THEN	Charlatans	1990
THEN CAME YOU	Junior Giscombe	1992
THEN CAME YOU	Dionne Warwick & Spinners	1974
THEN HE KISSED ME	Crystals	1963
THEN I KISSED HER	Beach Boys	1967
THEN THE MORNING COMES	Smash Mouth	1999
THEN YOU CAN TELL ME GOODBYE	Casinos	1967
THERE AIN'T NOTHING LIKE SHAGGIN'	Tams	1987

SONG TITLE	ARTIST	DATE
THERE ARE MORE QUESTIONS THAN ANSWERS		
	Johnny Nash	1972
THERE BUT FOR FORTUNE		
	Joan Baez	1965
THERE BUT FOR THE GRACE OF GOD		
	Fire Island	1994
THERE BY THE GRACE OF GOD		
	Manic Street Preachers	2002
THERE GOES ANOTHER LOVE SONG		
	Outlaws	1975
THERE GOES MY BABY	Donna Summer	1984
THERE GOES MY EVERYTHING		
	Engelbert Humperdinck	1967
THERE GOES MY EVERYTHING		
	Elvis Presley	1971
THERE GOES MY FIRST LOVE		
	Drifters	1975
THERE GOES MY LIFE	Kenny Chesney	2003
THERE GOES THE FEAR	Doves	2002
THERE GOES THE NEIGHBORHOOD		
	Sheryl Crow	1998
THERE IS	Dells	1968
THERE IS A LIGHT THAT NEVER GOES OUT		
	Smiths	1992
THERE IS A MOUNTAIN	Donovan	1967

SONG TITLE	ARTIST	DATE
THERE IS ALWAYS SOMETHING THERE TO REMIND ME		
	Housemartins	1988
THERE IS NO ARIZONA	Jamie O'Neal	2000
THERE IT IS	Shalamar	1982
THERE IT IS	Tyrone Davis	1973
THERE MUST BE A WAY	Frankie Vaughan	1967
THERE MUST BE AN ANGEL (PLAYING WITH MY HEART)		
	Eurythmics	1985
THERE SHE GOES	La's	1990
THERE SHE GOES	Sixpence None The Richer	1999
THERE SHE GOES	Babyface	2001
THERE SHE GOES AGAIN/MISLED		
	Quireboys	1990
THERE THERE	Radiohead	2003
THERE THERE MY DEAR	Dexy's Midnight Runners	1980
THERE WAS A TIME	James Brown	1968
THERE WILL NEVER BE ANOTHER TONIGHT		
	Bryan Adams	1991
THERE WILL NEVER BE ANOTHER YOU		
	Chris Montez	1966
THERE WON'T BE ANYMORE		
	Charlie Rich	1974
THERE WON'T BE MANY COMING HOME		
	Roy Orbison	1966
THERE YOU GO	Pink	2000
THERE YOU'LL BE	Faith Hill	2001

SONG TITLE	ARTIST	DATE
THERE! I'VE SAID IT AGAIN		
	Bobby Vinton	1963
THERE'LL BE SAD SONGS (TO MAKE YOU CRY)		
	Billy Ocean	1986
THERE'LL NEVER BE	Switch	1978
THERE'S A GHOST IN MY HOUSE		
	Fall	1987
THERE'S A GHOST IN MY HOUSE		
	R. Dean Taylor	1974
THERE'S A GUY WORKS DOWN THE CHIPSHOP		
SWEARS HE'S ELVIS	Kirsty Maccoll	1981
THERE'S A HEARTACHE FOLLOWING ME		
	Jim Reeves	1964
THERE'S A KIND OF HUSH	Herman's Hermits	1967
THERE'S A KIND OF HUSH (ALL OVER THE WORLD)		
	Carpenters	1976
THERE'S A STAR	Ash	2002
THERE'S A WHOLE LOT OF LOVING		
	Guys & Dolls	1975
THERE'S ALWAYS SOMETHING THERE TO REMIND ME		
	Naked Eyes	1983
(THERE'S GONNA BE A) SHOWDOWN		
	Archie Bell & The Drells	1973
(THERE'S GOTTA BE) MORE TO LIFE		
	Stacie Orrico	2003
THERE'S MORE TO LOVE	Communards	1988

SONG TITLE	ARTIST	DATE
THERE'S NO ONE QUITE LIKE GRANDMA		
	St. Winifred's School	1980
THERE'S NO OTHER WAY	Blur	1991
THERE'S NOTHING I WON'T DO		
	JX	1996
THERE'S NOTHING LIKE THIS		
	Omar	1991
THERE'S SOMETHING WRONG IN PARADISE		
	Kid Creole & The Coconuts	1983
THERE'S THE GIRL	Heart	1987
THERE'S YOUR TROUBLE	Dixie Chicks	1998
(THERE'S) ALWAYS SOMETHING THERE TO REMIND ME		
	Sandie Shaw	1964
(THERE'S) NO GETTIN' OVER ME		
	Ronnie Milsap	1981
THESE ARE THE DAYS	O-Town	2003
THESE ARE THE DAYS/FRONTIN'		
	Jamie Cullum	2004
THESE ARE THE TIMES	Dru Hill	1998
THESE BOOTS ARE MADE FOR WALKIN'		
	Nancy Sinatra	1966
THESE DAYS	Bon Jovi	1996
THESE DAYS	Rascal Flatts	2002
THESE DREAMS	Heart	1986
THESE EYES	Guess Who	1969
THESE EYES	Jr. Walker & The All Stars	1969

SONG TITLE	ARTIST	DATE
THESE THINGS WILL KEEP ME LOVING YOU		
	Velvelettes	1971
THESE WOODEN IDEAS	Idlewild	2000
THESE WORDS	Natasha Bedingfield	2004
(THEY CALL HER) LA BAMBA		
	Crickets	1964
THEY DON'T CARE ABOUT US		
	Michael Jackson	1996
THEY DON'T KNOW	Jon B	1998
THEY DON'T KNOW	Tracey Ullman	1984
THEY DON'T KNOW	So Solid Crew	2001
THEY JUST CAN'T STOP IT (THE GAMES PEOPLE PLAY)		
	Spinners	1975
THEY LIKE IT SLOW	H-Town	1997
(THEY LONG TO BE) CLOSE TO YOU		
	Carpenters	1970
(THEY LONG TO BE) CLOSE TO YOU		
	Gwen Guthrie	1986
THEY SHOOT HORSES DON'T THEY?		
	Racing Cars	1977
THEY WANT EFX	Das EFX	1992
THEY'LL COME A TIME	Betty Everett	1969
THEY'RE COMING TO TAKE ME AWAY, HA-HAAA!		
	Napoleon XIV	1966
THEY'RE HERE	EMF	1992
THIEVES IN THE TEMPLE	Prince	1990

SONG TITLE	ARTIST	DATE
THIEVES LIKE US	New Order	1984
A THIN LINE BETWEEN LOVE & HATE		
	H-Town	1996
THIN LINE BETWEEN LOVE AND HATE		
	Persuaders	1971
THE THIN WALL	Ultravox	1981
A THING CALLED LOVE	Johnny Cash	1972
THE THING I LIKE	Aaliyah	1995
THINGS CAN ONLY GET BETTER		
	D:ream	1994
THINGS CAN ONLY GET BETTER		
	Howard Jones	1985
THINGS GET BETTER	Eddie Floyd	1967
THINGS I SHOULD HAVE SAID		
	Grass Roots	1967
THINGS I'D LIKE TO SAY	New Colony Six	1968
THINGS I'VE SEEN	Spooks	2001
THINGS THAT ARE	Runrig	1995
THINGS THAT GO BUMP IN THE NIGHT/IS THERE SOMETHING I SHOULD KNOW		
	Allstars	2001
THINGS THAT MAKE YOU GO HMMMM...		
	C&C Music Factory featuring Freedom Williams	1991
THINGS WE DO FOR LOVE	Horace Brown	1996
THINGS WE DO FOR LOVE	10cc	1977

SONG TITLE	ARTIST	DATE
THINGS WILL GO MY WAY	Calling	2004
THINGS'LLL NEVER CHANGE/RAPPER'S BALL		
	E-40 featuring Bo-Rock	1997
THE THINGS/TURNED AWAY		
	Audio Bullys	2003
THINK	Chris Farlowe	1966
THINK	Aretha Franklin	1968
THINK	Brenda Lee	1964
THINK	Information Society	1990
THINK ABOUT...	D.J.H. featuring Stefy	1991
THINK ABOUT ME	Artful Dodger featuring	
	Michelle Escoffery	2001
THINK ABOUT ME	Fleetwood Mac	1980
THINK ABOUT YOUR CHILDREN		
	Mary Hopkin	1970
THINK FOR A MINUTE	Housemartins	1986
THINK I'LL GO SOMEWHERE AND CRY MYSELF TO		
SLEEP	Al Martino	1966
THINK I'M GONNA FALL IN LOVE WITH YOU		
	Dooleys	1977
THINK I'M IN LOVE	Eddie Money	1982
THINK IT OVER	Cheryl Ladd	1978
THINK OF LAURA	Christopher Cross	1983
THINK OF ME (WHEREVER YOU ARE)		
	Ken Dodd	1975
THINK OF YOU	Whigfield	1995

SONG TITLE	ARTIST	DATE
THINK SOMETIMES ABOUT ME		
	Sandie Shaw	1966
THINK TWICE	Celine Dion	1994
THINKIN' ABOUT IT	Gerald Levert	1998
THINKIN' AIN'T FOR ME	Paul Jones	1967
THINKIN' BACK	Color Me Badd	1992
THINKIN' PROBLEM	David Ball	1994
THINKING ABOUT YOUR LOVE		
	Kenny Thomas	1991
THINKING ABOUT YOUR LOVE		
	Skipworth & Turner	1985
THINKING IT OVER	Liberty	2001
THINKING OF YOU	Hanson	1998
THINKING OF YOU	Colour Field	1985
THINKING OF YOU	Maureen	1990
THINKING OF YOU	Sister Sledge	1984
THINKING OF YOU	Loggins & Messina	1973
THINKING OF YOU	Sa-Fire	1989
THINKING OF YOU	Tony Toni Tone	1997
THINKING OF YOU ('93 REMIXES)		
	Sister Sledge	1993
THINKING OF YOU BABY	Dave Clark Five	1964
THINKING OVER	Dana Glover	2003
THIRD FINGER LEFT HAND	Pearls	1972
THIRD RAIL	Squeeze	1993
THIRD RATE ROMANCE	Amazing Rhythm Aces	1975

SONG TITLE	ARTIST	DATE
THIRD TIME LUCKY (FIRST TIME I WAS A FOOL)		
	Foghat	1979
THE 13TH	Cure	1996
THIRTY THREE	Smashing Pumpkins	1996
32 FLAVORS	Alana Davis	1997
THIS AIN'T A LOVE SONG	Bon Jovi	1995
THIS BEAT IS TECHNOTRONIC		
	Technotronic featuring MC Eric	1990
THIS BOY	Justin	1998
THIS CHARMING MAN	Smiths	1992
THIS CORROSION	Sisters Of Mercy	1987
THIS COULD BE THE NIGHT		
	Loverboy	1986
THIS COWBOY SONG	Sting	1995
THIS D.J.	Warren G	1994
THIS DIAMOND RING	Gary Lewis & The Playboys	1965
THIS DOOR SWINGS BOTH WAYS		
	Herman's Hermits	1966
THIS FEELING	Puressence	1998
THIS FLIGHT TONIGHT	Nazareth	1973
THIS GARDEN	Levellers	1993
THIS GENERATION	Roachford	1994
THIS GIRL IS A WOMAN NOW		
	Gary Puckett & The Union Gap	1969
THIS GIRL'S IN LOVE WITH YOU		
	Dionne Warwick	1969

SONG TITLE	ARTIST	DATE
THIS GOLDEN RING	Fortunes	1966
THIS GROOVE/LET YOUR HEAD GO		
	Victoria Beckham	2004
THIS GUY'S IN LOVE WITH YOU		
	Herb Alpert	1968
THIS HEART	Gene Redding	1974
THIS HOUSE	Alison Moyet	1991
THIS HOUSE	Tracie Spencer	1990
THIS HOUSE (IS WHERE YOUR LOVE STANDS)		
	Big Sound Authority	1985
THIS I PROMISE YOU	*NSYNC	2000
THIS IS A CALL	Foo Fighters	1995
THIS IS ENGLAND	Clash	1985
THIS IS FOR THE LOVER IN YOU		
	Babyface	1996
THIS IS HARDCORE	Pulp	1998
THIS IS HOW IT FEELS	Inspiral Carpets	1990
THIS IS HOW WE DO IT	Montell Jordan	1995
THIS IS HOW WE PARTY	S.O.A.P.	1998
THIS IS IT	State Of Mind	1998
THIS IS IT	Dan Hartman	1979
THIS IS IT	Melba Moore	1976
THIS IS IT	Dannii Minogue	1993
THIS IS IT	Kenny Loggins	1979
THIS IS LOVE	Gary Numan	1986
THIS IS LOVE	Paul Anka	1978

SONG TITLE	ARTIST	DATE
THIS IS ME	Climie Fisher	1988
THIS IS ME	Saw Doctors	2002
THIS IS ME	Dream	2001
THIS IS MINE	Heaven 17	1984
THIS IS MUSIC	Verve	1995
THIS IS MY COUNTRY	Impressions	1968
THIS IS MY NIGHT	Chaka Khan	1985
THIS IS MY SONG	Petula Clark	1967
THIS IS MY SONG	Harry Secombe	1967
THIS IS MY SOUND	DJ Shog	2002
THIS IS MY TIME	3 Colours Red	1999
THIS IS NOT A LOVE SONG	Public Image Ltd	1983
THIS IS NOT AMERICA	David Bowie & Pat Metheny Group	1985
THIS IS THE NEW SHIT	Marilyn Manson	2003
THIS IS THE RIGHT TIME	Lisa Stansfield	1990
THIS IS THE STORY OF MY LOVE (BABY)	Wizzard	1974
THIS IS THE TIME	Billy Joel	1986
THIS IS THE WAY	Dannii Minogue	1993
THIS IS THE WAY THAT I FEEL	Marie Osmond	1977
THIS IS THE WORLD CALLING	Bob Geldof	1986
THIS IS THE WORLD WE LIVE IN	Alcazar	2004

SONG TITLE	ARTIST	DATE
THIS IS TOMORROW	Bryan Ferry	1977
THIS IS WHERE I CAME IN	Bee Gees	2001
THIS IS YOUR LAND	Simple Minds	1989
THIS IS YOUR LIFE	Blow Monkeys	1988
THIS IS YOUR LIFE	Banderas	1991
THIS IS YOUR NIGHT	Heavy D. & The Boyz	1994
THIS IS YOUR NIGHT	Amber	1996
THIS KISS	Faith Hill	1998
THIS LIL' GAME WE PLAY	Subway featuring 702	1995
THIS LITTLE BIRD	Nashville Teens	1965
THIS LITTLE BIRD	Marianne Faithfull	1965
THIS LITTLE GIRL	Gary U.S. Bonds	1981
THIS LOVE	Maroon5	2004
THIS MAGIC MOMENT	Jay & The Americans	1968
THIS MAN IS MINE	Heart	1982
THIS MASQUERADE	George Benson	1976
THIS NEW YEAR	Cliff Richard	1992
THIS NIGHT WON'T LAST FOREVER	Michael Johnson	1979
THIS OLD HEART OF MINE	Isley Brothers	1966
THIS OLD HEART OF MINE	Rod Stewart	1975
THIS OLE HOUSE	Shakin' Stevens	1981
THIS ONE	Paul McCartney	1989
THIS ONE'S FOR THE CHILDREN	New Kids On The Block	1989

SONG TITLE	ARTIST	DATE
THIS ONE'S FOR THE GIRLS	Martina McBride	2003
THIS ONE'S FOR YOU	Barry Manilow	1976
THIS PICTURE	Placebo	2003
THIS SONG	George Harrison	1976
THIS STRANGE EFFECT	Dave Berry	1965
THIS SUMMER	Squeeze	1996
THIS TIME	Dina Carroll	1993
THIS TIME	Curtis Stigers	1995
THIS TIME	Bryan Adams	1983
THIS TIME	John Cougar	1980
THIS TIME/RESPECT	Judy Cheeks	1995
THIS TIME (WE'LL GET IT RIGHT)/ENGLAND, WE'LL FLY THE FLAG	England World Cup Squad	1982
THIS TIME AROUND	Phats & Small	2001
THIS TIME AROUND	Hanson	2000
THIS TIME I FOUND LOVE	Rozalla	1994
THIS TIME I KNOW IT'S FOR REAL	Donna Summer	1989
THIS TIME I KNOW IT'S FOR REAL	Kelly Llorenna	2004
THIS TIME I'M IN IT FOR LOVE	Player	1978
THIS TIME OF YEAR	Runrig	1995
THIS TOWN AIN'T BIG ENOUGH FOR BOTH OF US	Sparks	1974

SONG TITLE	ARTIST	DATE
THIS TOWN AIN'T BIG ENOUGH FOR BOTH OF US	Sparks vs Faith No More	1997
THIS TRAIN DON'T STOP THERE ANYMORE	Elton John	2002
THIS USED TO BE MY PLAYGROUND	Madonna	1992
THIS WAY	Dilated Peoples	2004
THIS WHEEL'S ON FIRE	Julie Driscoll, Brian Auger & The Trinity	1968
THIS WHEEL'S ON FIRE	Siouxsie & The Banshees	1987
THIS WILL BE	Natalie Cole	1975
THIS WOMAN	Kenny Rogers	1984
THIS WOMAN'S WORK	Kate Bush	1989
THIS WORLD	Staple Singers	1972
THIS WORLD IS NOT MY HOME	Jim Reeves	1965
THIS WRECKAGE	Gary Numan	1980
THIS YEAR'S LOVE	David Gray	2001
THONG SONG	Sisqo	2000
THORN IN MY SIDE	Eurythmics	1986
THOSE SIMPLE THINGS/DAYDREAM	Right Said Fred	1992
THOSE WERE THE DAYS	Mary Hopkin	1968
THOU SHALT NOT STEAL	Dick & Deedee	1964
THOUGHT I'D DIED AND GONE TO HEAVEN	Bryan Adams	1992

SONG TITLE	ARTIST	DATE
THE THOUGHT OF IT	Louie Louie	1992
THOUGHTLESS	Korn	2002
A THOUSAND MILES	Vanessa Carlton	2002
A THOUSAND TREES	Stereophonics	1997
THREE	Wedding Present	1992
THREE (EP)	Mansun	1996
3 A.M. ETERNAL	KLF	1991
THREE BELLS	Brian Poole & The Tremeloes	1965
3 IS FAMILY	Dana Dawson	1995
THREE LIONS (THE OFFICIAL SONG OF THE ENGLAND FOOTBALL TEAM)	Baddiel & Skinner & The Lightning Seeds	1996
THREE LITTLE BIRDS	Bob Marley & The Wailers	1980
THREE LITTLE PIGS	Green Jelly	1993
THREE LITTLE WORDS	Applejacks	1964
THREE MINUTE HERO	Selecter	1980
THREE O'CLOCK IN THE MORNING	Bert Kaempfert	1965
THREE RING CIRCUS	Barry Biggs	1977
THREE RING CIRCUS	Blue Magic	1974
3..6..9.. SECONDS OF LIGHT (EP)	Belle & Sebastian	1997
3 SONGS (EP)	Wedding Present	1990
THREE STEPS TO HEAVEN	Showaddywaddy	1975
THREE TIMES A LADY	Commodores	1978
THREE TIMES IN LOVE	Tommy James	1980
THREE WINDOW COUPE	Rip Chords	1964
THREE WOODEN CROSSES	Randy Travis	2003
3 X 3 (EP)	Genesis	1982
THE THRILL IS GONE	B.B. King	1969
THRILL ME	Simply Red	1992
THRILL ME	Junior Jack	2002
THRILLER	Michael Jackson	1984
THROUGH THE BARRICADES	Spandau Ballet	1986
THROUGH THE RAIN	Mariah Carey	2002
THROUGH THE STORM	Aretha Franklin & Elton John	1989
THROUGH THE YEARS	Kenny Rogers	1981
THROW AWAY THE KEY	Linx	1981
THROW DOWN A LINE	Cliff & Hank	1969
THROW YA GUNZ	Onyx	1993
THROW YOUR HANDS UP/GANGSTA'S PARADISE	LV	1995
THROW YOUR SET IN THE AIR	Cypress Hill	1995
THROWING IT ALL AWAY	Genesis	1986
THUG LOVIN'	Ja Rule featuring Bobby Brown	2002
THUGGISH RUGGISH BONE	Bone Thugs-N-Harmony	1994
THUGZ MANSION	2 Pac	2003
THUNDER	Prince & The New Power Generation	1992
THUNDER	East 17	1995

SONG TITLE	ARTIST	DATE
THUNDER AND LIGHTNING	Thin Lizzy	1983
THUNDER AND LIGHTNING	Chi Coltrane	1972
THUNDER IN MOUNTAINS	Toyah	1981
THUNDER IN MY HEART	Leo Sayer	1977
THUNDER ISLAND	Jay Ferguson	1977
THUNDERBALL	Tom Jones	1965
THUNDERBIRDS/3 A.M.	Busted	2004
THUNDERBIRDS ARE GO	Fab featuring MC Parker	1990
THUNDERDOME	Messiah	1993
THUNDERSTRUCK	AC/DC	1990
THURSDAY'S CHILD	David Bowie	1999
THUS SPAKE ZARATHUSTRA	Philharmonic Orchestra	1969
TI AMO	Gina G	1997
TIC-TAC-TOE	Kyper	1990
TICKET TO RIDE	Beatles	1965
TICKET TO THE MOON/HERE IS THE NEWS	Electric Light Orchestra	1982
THE TIDE IS HIGH	Blondie	1980
THE TIDE IS HIGH (GET THE FEELING)	Atomic Kitten	2002
TIE A YELLOW RIBBON ROUND THE OLD OAK TREE	Dawn featuring Tony Orlando	1973
TIE YOUR MOTHER DOWN	Queen	1977
TIED TO THE 90'S	Travis	1997
TIED UP	Olivia Newton-John	1983

SONG TITLE	ARTIST	DATE
TIGER FEET	Mud	1974
TIGHT ROPE	Leon Russell	1972
TIGHTEN UP	Archie Bell & The Drells	1968
TIGHTEN UP (I JUST CAN'T STOP DANCIN')	Wally Jump Jr & The Criminal Element	1987
TIGHTER, TIGHTER	Alive & Kicking	1970
TIJUANA TAXI	Herb Alpert & The Tijuana Brass	1965
'TIL MY BABY GETS HOME	Luther Vandross	1985
'TIL THE DAY	Easyworld	2004
TIL THE END	Haven	2002
'TIL YOU DO ME RIGHT	After 7	1995
TILL	Dorothy Squires	1970
TILL	Tom Jones	1971
TILL	Vogues	1968
TILL I HEAR IT FROM YOU	Gin Blossoms	1996
TILL I LOVED YOU	Placido Domingo & Jennifer Rush	1989
TILL I LOVED YOU	Barbra Streisand & Don Johnson	1988
TILL THE END OF THE DAY	Kinks	1965
TILL THE WORLD ENDS	Three Dog Night	1975
TIME	Marion	1996
TIME	Freddie Mercury	1986

SONG TITLE	ARTIST	DATE
TIME	Hootie & The Blowfish	1995
TIME	Alan Parsons Project	1981
TIME (CLOCK OF THE HEART)		
	Culture Club	1983
TIME AFTER TIME	Changing Faces	1998
TIME AFTER TIME	Cyndi Lauper	1984
TIME AFTER TIME	Distant Soundz	2002
TIME AFTER TIME	Novaspace	2003
TIME AFTER TIME	Inoj	1998
TIME AFTER TIME	Chris Montez	1966
TIME AFTER TIME	Timmy T	1990
TIME AND CHANCE	Color Me Badd	1993
TIME AND TIDE	Basia	1988
TIME DRAGS BY	Cliff Richard	1966
TIME FOR ACTION	Secret Affair	1979
TIME FOR HEROES	The Libertines	2003
TIME FOR LETTING GO	Jude Cole	1990
TIME FOR LIVIN'	Association	1968
TIME FOR LIVIN'	Sly & The Family Stone	1974
TIME HAS COME TODAY	Chambers Brothers	1968
TIME IN A BOTTLE	Jim Croce	1973
THE TIME IN BETWEEN	Cliff Richard	1965
THE TIME IS NOW	Moloko	2000
TIME IS ON MY SIDE	Rolling Stones	1964
TIME IS TIGHT	Booker T. & The MG's	1969
TIME IS TIME	Andy Gibb	1980

SONG TITLE	ARTIST	DATE
TIME OF MY LIFE	Toploader	2002
TIME OF OUR LIVES	Alison Limerick	1994
TIME OF OUR LIVES/CONNECTED		
	Paul Van Dyk featuring Vega 4	2003
TIME OF THE SEASON	Zombies	1969
TIME OF YOUR LIFE (GOOD RIDDANCE)		
	Green Day	1998
TIME OUT OF MIND	Steely Dan	1981
TIME PASSAGES	Al Stewart	1978
TIME SELLER	Spencer Davis Group	1967
TIME TO BURN	Storm	2000
TIME TO GET DOWN	O'Jays	1973
TIME TO MAKE THE FLOOR BURN		
	Megabass	1990
TIME TO MAKE YOU MINE		
	Lisa Stansfield	1992
TIME TO MOVE ON	Sparkle	1998
TIME TO SAY GOODBYE (CON TE PARTIRO)		
	Sarah Brightman & Andrea Bocelli	1997
THE TIME WARP (SAW REMIX)		
	Damian	1989
TIME WILL CRAWL	David Bowie	1987
TIME WILL REVEAL	DeBarge	1983
TIME WON'T LET ME	Outsiders	1966

SONG TITLE	ARTIST	DATE
TIME, LOVE AND TENDERNESS		
	Michael Bolton	1991
TIMELESS	Daniel O'Donnell	1996
TIMES LIKE THESE	Foo Fighters	2003
TIMES OF YOUR LIFE	Paul Anka	1975
TIMES THEY ARE A-CHANGIN'		
	Bob Dylan	1965
TIMOTHY	Buoys	1971
TIN MAN	America	1974
TIN SOLDIER	Small Faces	1967
THE TIP OF MY FINGERS	Des O'Connor	1970
TIP TOE THRU THE TULIPS WITH ME		
	Tiny Tim	1968
TIPSY	J-Kwon	2004
TIRED OF BEING ALONE	Al Green	1971
TIRED OF BEING ALONE	Texas	1992
TIRED OF TOEIN' THE LINE		
	Rocky Burnette	1980
TIRED OF WAITING FOR YOU		
	Kinks	1965
TISHBITE	Cocteau Twins	1996
TO ALL THE GIRLS I'VE LOVED BEFORE		
	Julio Iglesias & Willie Nelson	1984
TO BE A LOVER	Billy Idol	1986
TO BE IN LOVE	Maw presents India	1999
TO BE OR NOT TO BE	B.A. Robertson	1980

SONG TITLE	ARTIST	DATE
TO BE OR NOT TO BE (THE HITLER RAP)		
	Mel Brooks	1984
TO BE REBORN	Boy George	1987
TO BE WITH YOU	Mr. Big	1991
TO BE WITH YOU AGAIN	Level 42	1987
TO CUT A LONG STORY SHORT		
	Spandau Ballet	1980
TO EARTH WITH LOVE	Gay Dad	1999
TO GET DOWN	Timo Maas	2002
TO GIVE (THE REASONS I LIVE)		
	Frankie Valli	1967
TO HAVE AND TO HOLD	Catherine Stock	1986
TO HERE KNOWS WHEN	My Bloody Valentine	1991
TO KNOW YOU IS TO LOVE YOU		
	Peter & Gordon	1965
TO KNOW YOU IS TO LOVE YOU		
	B.B. King	1973
TO KNOW YOU IS TO LOVE YOU		
	Bobby Vinton	1969
TO LIVE & DIE IN L.A.	Makaveli	1997
TO LOVE A WOMAN	Lionel Richie featuring Enrique Iglesias	2003
TO LOVE SOMEBODY	Michael Bolton	1992
TO LOVE SOMEBODY	Nina Simone	1969
TO LOVE SOMEBODY	Jimmy Somerville	1990
TO LOVE SOMEBODY	Bee Gees	1967

SONG TITLE	ARTIST	DATE
TO MAKE A BIG MAN CRY P.J. Proby		1966
TO SIR WITH LOVE	Lulu	1967
TO SUSAN ON THE WEST COAST WAITING		
	Donovan	1969
TO THE BEAT OF THE DRUM (LA LUNA)		
	Ethics	1995
TO THE DOOR OF THE SUN (ALLE PORTE DEL SOLE)		
	Al Martino	1974
TO THE END	Blur	1994
TO THE MOON AND BACK	Savage Garden	1997
TO THE WORLD	O.R.G.A.N.	1998
TO WHOM IT CONCERNS	Chris Andrews	1965
TO WIN JUST ONCE	Saw Doctors	1996
TO YOU I BELONG	B*Witched	1998
TOAST AND MARMALADE FOR TEA		
	Tin Tin	1971
TOAST OF LOVE	Three Degrees	1976
TOAST/HOLD ON	Streetband	1978
TOBACCO ROAD	Nashville Teens	1964
TOCA ME	Fragma	1999
TOCA'S MIRACLE	Fragma	2000
TOCCATA	Sky	1980
TOCCATA & FUGUE	Vanessa-Mae	1995
TODAY	Sandie Shaw	1968
TODAY	Talk Talk	1982
TODAY	New Christy Minstrels	1964

SONG TITLE	ARTIST	DATE
TODAY FOREVER (EP)	Ride	1991
TODAY'S THE DAY	Sean Maguire	1997
TODAY'S THE DAY	America	1976
TOGETHER	O.C. Smith	1977
TOGETHER	P.J. Proby	1964
TOGETHER	Artificial Funk featuring	
	Nellie Ettison	2003
TOGETHER	Tierra	1980
TOGETHER AGAIN	Janet Jackson	1997
TOGETHER AGAIN	Ray Charles	1966
TOGETHER FOREVER	Rick Astley	1988
TOGETHER FOREVER	Lisette Melendez	1991
TOGETHER IN ELECTRIC DREAMS		
	Giorgio Moroder & Phil Oakey	1984
TOGETHER LET'S FIND LOVE		
	5th Dimension	1972
TOGETHER WE ARE BEAUTIFUL		
	Fern Kinney	1980
TOKOLOSHE MAN	John Kongos	1971
TOKYO JOE	Bryan Ferry	1977
TOKYO MELODY	Helmut Zacharias Orchestra	1964
TOM HARK	Piranhas	1980
TOM JONES INTERNATIONAL		
	Tom Jones	2002
TOM SAWYER	Rush	1981
TOM THE PEEPER	Act One	1974

SONG TITLE	ARTIST	DATE
TOM TRAUBERT'S BLUES (WALTZING MATILDA)		
	Rod Stewart	1992
TOM'S DINER	DNA featuring Suzanne Vega	1990
TOM'S PARTY	T-Spoon	1999
TOM-TOM TURNAROUND	New World	1971
TOMB OF MEMORIES	Paul Young	1985
TOMMY GUN	Clash	1978
TOMORROW	Communards	1987
TOMORROW	Sandie Shaw	1966
TOMORROW	Tongue 'n' Cheek	1990
TOMORROW	James	1997
TOMORROW	Strawberry Alarm Clock	1967
TOMORROW COMES TODAY		
	Gorillaz	2002
TOMORROW DOESN'T MATTER TONIGHT		
	Starship	1986
TOMORROW NEVER DIES	Sheryl Crow	1997
TOMORROW NIGHT	Atomic Rooster	1971
TOMORROW PEOPLE	Ziggy Marley & The Melody Makers	1988
TOMORROW'S (JUST ANOTHER DAY)/MADNESS (IS ALL IN THE MIND)	Madness	1983
TOMORROW'S GIRLS	UK Subs	1979
TOMORROW, TOMORROW	Bee Gees	1969
TONGUE	R.E.M.	1995
TONGUE TIED	Cat	1993

SONG TITLE	ARTIST	DATE
TONIGHT	Def Leppard	1993
TONIGHT	Move	1971
TONIGHT	New Kids On The Block	1990
TONIGHT	Rubettes	1974
TONIGHT	Kool & The Gang	1984
TONIGHT/MISS YOU NIGHTS		
	Westlife	2003
TONIGHT I CELEBRATE MY LOVE		
	Peabo Bryson & Roberta Flack	1983
TONIGHT I'M ALRIGHT	Narada Michael Walden	1980
TONIGHT I'M GONNA LET GO		
	Syleena Johnson	2002
TONIGHT I'M YOURS (DON'T HURT ME)		
	Rod Stewart	1982
TONIGHT IN TOKYO	Sandie Shaw	1967
TONIGHT SHE COMES	Cars	1985
TONIGHT, TONIGHT	Smashing Pumpkins	1996
TONIGHT TONIGHT TONIGHT		
	Genesis	1987
TONIGHT'S THE NIGHT	Solomon Burke	1965
TONIGHT'S THE NIGHT (GONNA BE ALRIGHT)		
	Rod Stewart	1976
TONITE	Supercar	1999
TONITE	Phats & Small	1999
TONITE'S THA NIGHT	Kris Kross	1995
TOO BAD	Nickelback	2002

SONG TITLE	ARTIST	DATE
TOO BEAUTIFUL TO LAST	Engelbert Humperdinck	1972
TOO BIG	Suzi Quatro	1974
TOO BLIND TO SEE IT	Kym Sims	1991
TOO BUSY THINKING ABOUT MY BABY		
	Marvin Gaye	1969
TOO BUSY THINKING ABOUT MY BABY		
	Mardi Gras	1972
TOO CLOSE	Next	1998
TOO CLOSE	Blue	2001
TOO DRUNK TO FUCK	Dead Kennedys	1981
TOO FAR GONE	Lisa Scott-Lee	2003
TOO FUNKY	George Michael	1992
TOO GONE, TOO LONG	En Vogue	1997
TOO GOOD TO BE FORGOTTEN		
	Amazulu	1986
TOO GOOD TO BE FORGOTTEN		
	Chi-Lites	1974
TOO GOOD TO BE TRUE	Tom Petty & The Heartbreakers	1992
TOO HOT	Coolio	1995
TOO HOT	Kool & The Gang	1980
TOO HOT TA TROT/ZOOM	Commodores	1978
TOO HOT TO HANDLE/SLIP YOUR DISC TO THIS		
	Heatwave	1977
TOO LATE	Junior	1982
TOO LATE FOR GOODBYES	Julian Lennon	1985

SONG TITLE	ARTIST	DATE
TOO LATE TO SAY GOODBYE		
	Richard Marx	1990
TOO LATE TO TURN BACK NOW		
	Cornelius Brothers &	
	Sister Rose	1972
2 LEGIT 2 QUIT	Hammer	1991
TOO LOST IN YOU	Sugababes	2003
TOO MANY BROKEN HEARTS		
	Jason Donovan	1989
TOO MANY DJ'S	Soulwax	2000
TOO MANY FISH	Frankie Knuckles featuring	
	Adeva	1995
TOO MANY FISH IN THE SEA		
	Marvelettes	1964
TOO MANY FISH IN THE SEA & THREE LITTLE FISHES		
	Mitch Ryder & The Detroit	
	Wheels	1967
TOO MANY GAMES	Maze featuring Frankie Beverly	1985
TOO MANY MC'S/LET ME CLEAR MY THROAT		
	Public Domain	2002
TOO MANY PEOPLE	Pauline Henry	1993
TOO MANY RIVERS	Brenda Lee	1965
TOO MANY RIVERS TO CROSS		
	Cher	1993
TOO MANY WALLS	Cathy Dennis	1991
TOO MUCH	Bros	1989

SONG TITLE	ARTIST	DATE
TOO MUCH	Spice Girls	1998
TOO MUCH FOR ONE HEART		
	Michael Barrymore	1995
TOO MUCH HEAVEN	Bee Gees	1978
TOO MUCH INFORMATION	Duran Duran	1993
TOO MUCH LOVE WILL KILL YOU		
	Brian May	1992
TOO MUCH LOVE WILL KILL YOU		
	Queen	1996
TOO MUCH OF NOTHING	Peter, Paul & Mary	1967
TOO MUCH PASSION	Smithereens	1992
TOO MUCH TALK	Paul Revere & The Raiders	1968
TOO MUCH TIME ON MY HANDS		
	Styx	1981
TOO MUCH, TOO LITTLE, TOO LATE		
	Johnny Mathis & Deniece Williams	1978
TOO MUCH, TOO LITTLE, TOO LATE		
	Silver Sun	1998
TOO MUCH TOO YOUNG	Little Angels	1992
TOO NICE TO TALK TO	Beat	1980
TOO SHY	Kajagoogoo	1983
TOO SOON TO KNOW	Roy Orbison	1966
TOO TIGHT	Con Funk Shun	1981
TOO WEAK TO FIGHT	Clarence Carter	1968
TOO YOUNG	Donny Osmond	1972

SONG TITLE	ARTIST	DATE
TOO YOUNG TO DIE	Jamiroquai	1993
TOOK MY LOVE	Bizarre Inc.	1993
TOOK THE LAST TRAIN	David Gates	1978
TOOTSIE ROLL	69 Boyz	1994
TOP OF THE POPS	Rezillos	1978
TOP OF THE STAIRS	Skee-Lo	1996
TOP OF THE WORLD	Carpenters	1973
TOP OF THE WORLD	Brandy featuring Mase	1998
TOP OF THE WORLD	Wildhearts	2003
TOP OF THE WORLD	Van Halen	1991
TOP OF THE WORLD (OLE, OLE, OLE)		
	Chumbawamba	1998
TORCH	Soft Cell	1982
TORN	Natalie Imbruglia	1997
TORN BETWEEN TWO LOVERS		
	Mary Macgregor	1976
TORNIQUET	Marilyn Manson	1997
TORTURE	Jacksons	1984
TORTURE	King	1986
TOSH	Fluke	1995
TOSS IT UP	Makaveli	1997
TOSSING AND TURNING	Ivy League	1965
TOSSING AND TURNING	Windjammer	1984
TOTAL ECLIPSE OF THE HEART		
	Bonnie Tyler	1983

SONG TITLE	ARTIST	DATE
TOTAL ECLIPSE OF THE HEART		
	Nicki French	1995
TOTAL ECLIPSE OF THE HEART		
	Jan Wayne	2003
THE TOTAL MIX	Black Box	1990
TOTALLY HOT	Olivia Newton-John	1979
TOTTENHAM TOTTENHAM	Tottenham Hotspur FA Cup Final Squad	1982
TOUCH A HAND MAKE A FRIEND		
	Staple Singers	1974
TOUCH AND GO	Cars	1980
TOUCH IT	Monifah	1998
TOUCH ME	Rui Da Silva featuring Cassandra	2001
TOUCH ME	49ers	1989
TOUCH ME	Angel City	2004
TOUCH ME	Doors	1968
TOUCH ME	Fancy	1974
TOUCH ME (ALL NIGHT LONG)		
	Cathy Dennis	1991
TOUCH ME (I WANT YOUR BODY)		
	Samantha Fox	1986
TOUCH ME IN THE MORNING		
	Diana Ross	1973
TOUCH ME TEASE ME	Case featuring Foxy Brown	1996
TOUCH ME TEASE ME	3SL	2002

SONG TITLE	ARTIST	DATE
TOUCH ME, TOUCH ME	Dave Dee, Dozy, Beaky, Mick & Tich	1967
TOUCH ME WHEN WE'RE DANCING		
	Carpenters	1981
TOUCH MYSELF	T-Boz	1996
TOUCH OF GREY	Grateful Dead	1987
A TOUCH OF LOVE	Cleopatra	1999
TOUCH TOO MUCH	AC/DC	1980
A TOUCH TOO MUCH	Arrows	1974
TOUCHED BY THE HAND OF CICCIOLINA		
	Pop Will Eat Itself	1990
TOUCHED BY THE HAND OF GOD		
	New Order	1987
TOUCHY!	A-Ha	1988
TOUGH ALL OVER	John Cafferty	1985
TOUGH LITTLE BOYS	Gary Allan	2003
TOUGHER THAN THE REST	Bruce Springsteen	1988
TOUR DE FRANCE	Kraftwerk	1983
TOURNIQUET	Headswim	1998
TOUS LES GARCONS ET LES FILLES		
	Francoise Hardy	1964
TOWER OF STRENGTH	Mission	1988
TOWER OF STRENGTH	Skin	1994
TOWERS OF LONDON	XTC	1980
TOWN CALLED MALICE/PRECIOUS		
	Jam	1982

SONG TITLE	ARTIST	DATE
TOWN CRIER	Craig Douglas	1963
TOWN WITHOUT PITY	Eddi Reader	1996
TOXIC	Britney Spears	2004
TOXICITY	System Of A Down	2002
TOXYGENE	Orb	1997
TOY	Casuals	1968
TOY BOY	Sinitta	1987
TOY SOLDIERS	Martika	1989
TRACES	Classics IV	1969
TRACEY IN MY ROOM	EBTG vs Soul Vision	2001
TRACIE	Level 42	1989
TRACKIN'	Billy Crawford	2003
TRACKS OF MY TEARS	Go West	1993
TRACKS OF MY TEARS	Linda Ronstadt	1975
THE TRACKS OF MY TEARS	Johnny Rivers	1967
TRACY	Cuff Links	1969
TRADE IT ALL	Fabolous featuring P. Diddy & Jagged Edge	2002
TRAFFIC	Stereophonics	1997
TRAGEDY	Argent	1972
TRAGEDY	Bee Gees	1979
TRAGEDY	John Hunter	1984
TRAGIC COMIC	Extreme	1993
THE TRAIL OF THE LONESOME PINE	Laurel & Hardy	1975
TRAIN	Goldfrapp	2003

SONG TITLE	ARTIST	DATE
TRAIN IN VAIN (STAND BY ME)	Clash	1980
THE TRAIN IS COMING	UB40	1999
TRAIN OF CONSEQUENCES	Megadeth	1995
TRAIN OF THOUGHT	Escrima	1995
TRAIN OF THOUGHT	A-Ha	1986
TRAIN OF THOUGHT	Cher	1974
TRAIN ON A TRACK	Kelly Rowland	2003
TRAIN TO SKAVILLE	Ethiopians	1967
TRAIN TOUR TO RAINBOW CITY	Pyramids	1967
TRAIN, TRAIN	Blackfoot	1979
TRAINS AND BOATS AND PLANES	Burt Bacharach	1965
TRAINS AND BOATS AND PLANES	Billy J. Kramer & The Dakotas	1965
TRAINS AND BOATS AND PLANES	Dionne Warwick	1966
TRAMP	Otis Redding & Carla Thomas	1967
TRAMPLED UNDER FOOT	Led Zeppelin	1975
TRAMPOLENE	Julian Cope	1987
TRANQUILLIZER	Geneva	1997
TRANSAMAZONIA	Shamen	1995
TRANSFER AFFECTION	Flock Of Seagulls	1983
TRANZY STATE OF MIND	Push	2002
TRAPPED	Colonel Abrams	1985

SONG TITLE	ARTIST	DATE
TRAPPED BY A THING CALLED LOVE		
	Denise La Salle	1971
TRASH	Suede	1996
TRASH	Roxy Music	1979
TRASHED	Skin	2003
TRAVELIN' BAND/WHO'LL STOP THE RAIN		
	Creedence Clearwater Revival	1970
TRAVELIN' SOLDIER	Dixie Chicks	2003
TRAVELLERS TUNE	Ocean Colour Scene	1997
TRAVELLING MAN	Studio 2	1998
TRAVLIN' MAN	Stevie Wonder	1967
TREASON (IT'S JUST A STORY)		
	Teardrop Explodes	1981
TREAT HER LIKE A LADY	Celine Dion	1999
TREAT HER LIKE A LADY	Temptations	1984
TREAT HER LIKE A LADY	Cornelius Brothers & Sister Rose	1971
TREAT HER RIGHT	Roy Head	1965
TREAT INFAMY	Rest Assured	1998
TREAT ME GOOD	Yazz	1990
TREAT ME LIKE A LADY	Zoe Birkett	2003
TREAT ME RIGHT	Pat Benatar	1981
TREMBLE	Marc Et Claude	2002
TREMOR CHRIST	Pearl Jam	1994
TRES DELINQUENTES	Delinquent Habits	1996
TRIBAL BASE	Rebel M.C./Tenor Fly/	
	Barrington Levy	1991

SONG TITLE	ARTIST	DATE
TRIBAL DANCE	2 Unlimited	1993
TRIBUTE (RIGHT ON)	Pasadenas	1988
A TRIBUTE TO A KING	William Bell	1968
A TRIBUTE TO JIM REEVES	Larry Cunningham & The	
	Mighty Avons	1964
TRICK ME	Kelis	2004
TRICK OF THE NIGHT	Bananarama	1987
TRICKY DISCO	Tricky Disco	1990
TRICKY KID	Tricky	1997
TRIGGER HIPPIE	Morcheeba	1996
TRIGGER INSIDE	Therapy?	1994
TRIP II THE MOON	Acen	1992
A TRIP TO TRUMPTON	Urban Hype	1992
TRIPLE TROUBLE	Beastie Boys	2004
TRIPPIN ON SUNSHINE	Pizzaman	1994
TRIPPIN'	Mark Morrison	1996
TRIPPIN'	Total featuring Missy Elliott	1998
TRIPPIN' ON SUNSHINE	Pizzaman	1996
TRIPPIN' ON YOUR LOVE	Kenny Thomas	1993
TROUBLE IS MY MIDDLE NAME		
	Four Pennies	1966
TROCADERO	Showaddywaddy	1976
TROGLODYTE (CAVE MAN)	Jimmy Castor Bunch	1972
THE TROOPER	Iron Maiden	1983
TROPIC ISLAND HUM	Paul McCartney	2004
TROPICALIA	Beck	1998

SONG TITLE	ARTIST	DATE
TROUBLE	Shampoo	1994
TROUBLE	Lindsey Buckingham	1981
TROUBLE	Coldplay	2000
TROUBLE	Gillan	1980
TROUBLE	Pink	2003
TROUBLE	Nia Peeples	1988
TROUBLE IN PARADISE	Al Jarreau	1983
TROUBLE IS MY MIDDLE NAME		
	Brook Brothers	1963
TROUBLE MAN	Marvin Gaye	1972
TRUCK ON	Simple Kid	2004
TRUCK ON (TYKE)	T. Rex	1973
TRUE	Spandau Ballet	1983
TRUE	Jaimeson featuring Angel Blu	2003
TRUE BLUE	Madonna	1986
TRUE BLUE LOVE	Lou Gramm	1990
TRUE COLORS	Phil Collins	1998
TRUE COLORS	Cyndi Lauper	1986
TRUE FAITH	New Order	1987
TRUE GRIT	Glen Campbell	1969
TRUE LOVE	Richard Chamberlain	1963
TRUE LOVE	Elton John & Kiki Dee	1993
TRUE LOVE	Shakin' Stevens	1988
TRUE LOVE	Glenn Frey	1988
TRUE LOVE FOR EVERMORE		
	Bachelors	1965

SONG TITLE	ARTIST	DATE
TRUE LOVE NEVER DIES	Flip & Fill featuring Kelly Llorenna	2002
TRUE LOVE WAYS	David Essex & Catherine Zeta-Jones	1994
TRUE LOVE WAYS	Peter & Gordon	1965
TRUE LOVE WAYS	Cliff Richard	1983
TRUE SPIRIT	Carleen Anderson	1994
TRUE STEP TONIGHT	True Steppers featuring Brian Harvey & Donell Jones	2000
TRUE TO US	Vanilla	1998
TRUGANINI	Midnight Oil	1993
TRULY	Steven Houghton	1998
TRULY	Hinda Hicks	1998
TRULY	Lionel Richie	1982
TRULY MADLY DEEPLY	Savage Garden	1997
TRUST	Ned's Atomic Dustbin	1991
TRUST ME	Guru featuring N'Dea Davenport	1993
THE TRUTH IS NO WORDS		
	Music	2003
THE TRUTH	Tami Show	1991
TRY	Bros	1991
TRY	Ian Van Dahl	2002
TRY	Nelly Furtado	2004
TRY A LITTLE KINDNESS	Glen Campbell	1969
TRY A LITTLE TENDERNESS		
	Otis Redding	1966

SONG TITLE	ARTIST	DATE
TRY A LITTLE TENDERNESS		
	Three Dog Night	1969
TRY AGAIN	Aaliyah	2000
TRY AGAIN	Champaign	1983
TRY AGAIN TODAY	Charlatans	2004
TRY IT BABY	Marvin Gaye	1964
TRY ME OUT	Corona	1995
TRY MY WORLD	Georgie Fame	1967
TRY TOO HARD	Dave Clark Five	1966
TRY TO UNDERSTAND	Lulu	1965
TRY TRY TRY	Julian Cope	1995
TRYIN' TO GET THE FEELING AGAIN		
	Barry Manilow	1976
TRYIN' TO LIVE MY LIFE WITHOUT YOU		
	Bob Seger & The Silver	
	Bullet Band	1981
TRYIN' TO LOVE TWO	William Bell	1977
TRYING TO FORGET	Jim Reeves	1967
TRYING TO HOLD ON TO MY WOMAN		
	Lamont Dozier	1973
TRYING TO MAKE A FOOL OF ME		
	Delfonics	1970
TSOP (THE SOUND OF PHILADELPHIA)		
	MFSB featuring The Three	
	Degrees	1974
TSUNAMI	Manic Street Preachers	1999

SONG TITLE	ARTIST	DATE
TU AMOR	Kaci	2001
TU M'AIMES ENCORE (TO LOVE ME AGAIN)		
	Celine Dion	1995
TUBTHUMPING	Chumbawamba	1997
TUBULAR BELLS	Mike Oldfield	1974
TUCKER'S TOWN	Hootie & The Blowfish	1996
TUESDAY AFTERNOON (FOREVER AFTERNOON)		
	Moody Blues	1968
TUESDAY MORNING	Pogues	1993
TUFF ACT TO FOLLOW	MN8	1996
TUFF ENUFF	Fabulous Thunderbirds	1986
TULANE	Steve Gibbons Band	1977
TULSA TIME	Eric Clapton	1980
TUM BIN JIYA	Bally Sagoo	1997
TUMBLING DICE	Rolling Stones	1972
TUMBLING DICE	Linda Ronstadt	1978
THE TUNE	Suggs	1995
TUNES SPLITS THE ATOM	MC Tunes Versus 808 State	1990
TUNNEL OF LOVE	Bruce Springsteen	1987
THE TUNNEL OF LOVE	Fun Boy Three	1983
TURN	Feeder	2001
TURN	Travis	1999
TURN AROUND	Phats & Small Present Mutant	
	Disco	1999
TURN AROUND LOOK AT ME		
	Vogues	1968

SONG TITLE	ARTIST	DATE
TURN BACK THE CLOCK	Johnny Hates Jazz	1987
TURN BACK THE HANDS OF TIME	Tyrone Davis	1970
TURN BACK TIME	Aqua	1998
TURN IT AROUND	Alena	1999
TURN IT INTO LOVE	Hazell Dean	1988
TURN IT ON AGAIN	Genesis	1980
TURN IT UP	Conway Brothers	1985
TURN IT UP (SAY YEAH)	DJ Duke	1994
TURN IT UP/FIRE IT UP	Busta Rhymes	1998
TURN ME LOOSE	Loverboy	1981
TURN ME ON	Kevin Lyttle	2003
TURN ME ON TURN ME OFF	Honey Bane	1981
TURN ME OUT (TURN TO SUGAR)	Praxis featuring Kathy Brown	1997
TURN OFF THE LIGHT	Nelly Furtado	2001
TURN ON, TUNE IN, COP OUT	Freak Power	1995
TURN THE BEAT AROUND	Gloria Estefan	1994
TURN THE BEAT AROUND	Vicki Sue Robinson	1976
TURN THE MUSIC UP!	Players Association	1979
TURN TO STONE	Electric Light Orchestra	1977
TURN TO YOU	Go-Go's	1984
TURN UP THE BASS	Tyree featuring Kool Rock Steady	1989

SONG TITLE	ARTIST	DATE
TURN UP THE NIGHT	Black Sabbath	1982
TURN UP THE POWER	N-Trance	1994
TURN UP THE RADIO	Autograph	1984
TURN YOUR LIGHTS DOWN LOW	Bob Marley featuring Lauryn Hill	1999
TURN YOUR LOVE AROUND	George Benson	1981
TURN YOUR RADIO ON	Ray Stevens	1972
TURN! TURN! TURN! (TO EVERYTHING THERE IS A SEASON)	Byrds	1965
TURN-DOWN DAY	Cyrkle	1966
TURNING AWAY	Shakin' Stevens	1986
TURNING JAPANESE	Vapors	1980
TURQUOISE	Donovan	1965
TURTLE POWER	Partners In Kryme	1990
TURTLE RHAPSODY	Orchestra On The Half Shell	1990
TUSH	ZZ Top	1975
TUSK	Fleetwood Mac	1979
TUXEDO JUNCTION	Manhattan Transfer	1976
TV CRIMES	Black Sabbath	1992
TVC 15	David Bowie	1976
TWANGLING THREE FINGERS IN A BOX	Mike	1994
TWEEDLE DEE, TWEEDLE DUM	Middle Of The Road	1971

SONG TITLE	ARTIST	DATE
TWEEDLEE DEE	Little Jimmy Osmond	1973
THE TWELFTH OF NEVER	Elvis Presley	1995
THE TWELFTH OF NEVER	Donny Osmond	1973
THE TWELFTH OF NEVER	Cliff Richard	1964
12 REASONS WHY I LOVE HER	My Life Story	1996
TWELVE STEPS TO LOVE	Brian Poole & The Tremeloes	1964
TWELVE THIRTY (YOUNG GIRLS ARE COMING TO THE CANYON)	Mamas & The Papas	1967
12:51	Strokes	2003
20TH CENTURY BOY	T. Rex	1973
21ST CENTURY	Weekend Players	2001
TWENTY FIRST CENTURY BOY	Sigue Sigue Sputnik	1986
21ST CENTURY GIRLS	21st Century Girls	1999
25 MILES	Edwin Starr	1969
25 MILES 2001	Three Amigos	2001
25 OR 6 TO 4	Chicago	1970
TWENTY FOREPLAY	Janet Jackson	1996
24 HOURS	Betty Boo	1990
TWENTY FOUR HOURS FROM TULSA	Gene Pitney	1963
24 HOURS FROM YOU	Next Of Kin	1999
24 SYCAMORE	Gene Pitney	1973
24-7-365	Charles & Eddie	1995
24/7	Kevon Edmunds	1999

SONG TITLE	ARTIST	DATE
24/7	3T	1996
29 PALMS	Robert Plant	1993
21 QUESTIONS	50 Cent featuring Nate Dogg	2003
21 SECONDS	So Solid Crew	2001
20 SECONDS TO COMPLY	Silver Bullet	1989
22 DAYS	22-20s	2004
TWENTY YEARS	Placebo	2004
20-75	Willie Mitchell	1964
20/20	George Benson	1985
TWENTYFOURSEVEN	Artful Dodger featuring Melanie Blatt	2001
TWILIGHT	Electric Light Orchestra	1978
TWILIGHT CAFE	Susan Fassbender	1981
TWILIGHT WORLD	Swing Out Sister	1987
TWILIGHT ZONE	2 Unlimited	1992
TWILIGHT ZONE	Golden Earring	1982
TWILIGHT ZONE/TWILIGHT TONE	Manhattan Transfer	1980
TWILIGHT ZONE/WRATH CHILD	Iron Maiden	1981
TWINE TIME	Alvin Cash & The Crawlers	1965
TWINKIE-LEE	Gary Walker	1966
TWINKLE TOES	Roy Orbison	1966
TWIST	Goldfrapp	2003
TWIST (ROUND 'N' ROUND)	Chill Fac-Torr	1983

SONG TITLE	ARTIST	DATE
THE TWIST (YO, TWIST)	Fat Boys & Chubby Checker	1988
TWIST & SHOUT	Deacon Blue	1991
TWIST AND SHOUT	Chaka Demus & Pliers/Jack Radics/Taxi Gang	1993
TWIST AND SHOUT	Brian Poole & The Tremeloes	1963
TWIST AND SHOUT	Salt 'N' Pepa	1988
TWIST AND SHOUT	Beatles	1986
TWIST 'EM OUT	Dillinja featuring Skibadee	2003
TWIST IN MY SOBRIETY	Tanita Tikaram	1988
TWIST OF FATE	Olivia Newton-John	1983
TWISTED	Keith Sweat	1996
TWISTED (EVERYDAY HURTS)	Skunk Anansie	1996
TWISTERELLA	Ride	1992
TWISTING BY THE POOL	Dire Straits	1983
2 + 2 = 5	Radiohead	2003
2 BECOME 1	Spice Girls	1997
TWO CAN PLAY THAT GAME	Bobby Brown	1994
TWO DIVIDED BY LOVE	Grass Roots	1971
TWO DOORS DOWN	Dolly Parton	1978
TWO EP	Mansun	1996
2 FACED	Louise	2000
TWO FATT GUITARS (REVISITED)	Direckt	1994
TWO FINE PEOPLE	Cat Stevens	1975

SONG TITLE	ARTIST	DATE
2-4-6-8 MOTORWAY	Tom Robinson Band	1977
TWO HEARTS	Phil Collins	1988
TWO HEARTS	Cliff Richard	1988
TWO HEARTS	Stephanie Mills With Teddy Pendergrass	1981
TWO HEARTS BEAT AS ONE	U2	1983
TWO IN A MILLION/YOU'RE MY NUMBER ONE	S Club 7	1999
TWO KINDS OF TEARDROPS	Del Shannon	1963
TWO LESS LONELY PEOPLE IN THE WORLD	Air Supply	1982
TWO LITTLE BOYS	Rolf Harris	1969
TWO LITTLE BOYS/HORSE	Splodgenessabounds	1980
TWO LITTLE KIDS	Peaches & Herb	1967
2 MINUTES TO MIDNIGHT	Iron Maiden	1984
TWO MONTHS OFF	Underworld	2002
TWO OCCASIONS	Deele	1988
TWO OF HEARTS	Stacey Q	1986
TWO OUT OF THREE AIN'T BAD	Meat Loaf	1978
TWO PAINTINGS AND A DRUM	Carl Cox	1996
2 PEOPLE	Jean Jacques Smoothie	2001
TWO PEOPLE	Tina Turner	1986

SONG TITLE	ARTIST	DATE
TWO PLACES AT THE SAME TIME		
	Ray Parker Jr. & Raydio	1980
TWO PRINCES	Spin Doctors	1993
TWO SIDES TO LOVE	Sammy Hagar	1984
TWO SILHOUETTES	Del Shannon	1963
2 STEP ROCK	Bandits	2003
TWO STEPS BEHIND	Def Leppard	1993
TWO STREETS	Val Doonican	1967
TWO TEARDROPS	Steve Wariner	1999
2000 MILES	Pretenders	1983
TWO TICKETS TO PARADISE		
	Eddie Money	1978
2 TIMES	Ann Lee	1999
TWO TO MAKE IT RIGHT	Seduction	1989
THE 2 TONE EP	Special AKA/Madness/Selecter/	
	Beat	1993
TWO TRIBES	Frankie Goes To Hollywood	1984
TWO WORLDS COLLIDE	Inspiral Carpets	1992
TWO WRONGS (DON'T MAKE A RIGHT)		
	Wyclef Jean/Claudette Ortiz	2002
2/231	Anticappella	1991
TWYFORD DOWN	Galliano	1994
TYPICAL MALE	Tina Turner	1986
U	Loni Clark	1994
U & ME	Cappella	1994
U BLOW MY MIND	Blackstreet	1995

SONG TITLE	ARTIST	DATE
U CAN'T TOUCH THIS	M.C. Hammer	1990
U DON'T HAVE TO CALL	Usher	2002
U DON'T HAVE TO SAY U LOVE ME		
	Mash!	1994
U GIRLS (LOOK SO SEXY)	Nush	1995
U GOT 2 KNOW	Cappella	1993
U GOT 2 LET THE MUSIC	Cappella	1993
U GOT IT BAD	Usher	2001
U GOT THE LOOK	Prince	1987
U KNOW WHAT'S UP	Donell Jones	2000
U KRAZY KATZ	PJ And Duncan	1995
U MAKE ME WANNA	Blue	2003
U R THE BEST THING	D:ream	1994
U REMIND ME	Usher	2001
U SEND ME SWINGIN'	Mint Condition	1994
U SEXY THING	Clock	1997
U SHINE ON	Matt Darey & Marcella Woods	2002
U SURE DO	Strike	1995
U WILL KNOW	BMU	1995
U-TURN	Usher	2002
U.N.I.T.Y.	Queen Latifah	1993
U.S. MALE	Elvis Presley	1968
U16 GIRLS	Travis	1997
UBIK	Timo Maas featuring	
	Martin Bettinghaus	2000
UGLY	Daphne & Celeste	2000

SONG TITLE	ARTIST	DATE
UGLY	Bubba Sparxxx	2001
THE UGLY DUCKLING	Mike Reid	1975
UH HUH	B2K	2002
UH HUH OH YEH	Paul Weller	1992
UH LA LA LA	Alexia	1998
UHH AHH	Boyz II Men	1991
UK BLAK	Caron Wheeler	1990
'ULLO JOHN GOT A NEW MOTOR?	Alexei Sayle	1984
ULTIMATE TRUNK FUNK (EP)	Brand New Heavies	1992
ULTRA FLAVA	Heller And Farley Project	1996
UM, UM, UM, UM, UM, UM	Major Lance	1964
UM, UM, UM, UM, UM, UM	Wayne Fontana & The Mindbenders	1964
UN BANC, UN ABRE, UNE RUE	Severine	1971
(UN, DOS, TRES) MARIA	Ricky Martin	1997
UN-BREAK MY HEART	Toni Braxton	1996
UN-CONNECTED	Stereo MC's	1992
UNA PALOMA BLANCA (WHITE DOVE)	Jonathan King	1975
UNBEARABLE	Wonder Stuff	1994
UNBELIEVABLE	EMF	1991

SONG TITLE	ARTIST	DATE
UNBELIEVABLE	Diamond Rio	1998
UNBREAKABLE	Westlife	2002
UNBROKEN	Tim McGraw	2002
UNCHAIN MY HEART	Joe Cocker	1992
UNCHAINED MELODY	Righteous Brothers	1990
UNCHAINED MELODY	Gareth Gates	2002
UNCHAINED MELODY/WHITE CLIFFS OF DOVER	Robson Green & Jerome Flynn	1995
UNCLE ALBERT/ADMIRAL HALSEY	Paul & Linda McCartney	1971
UNCLE JOHN FROM JAMAICA	Vengaboys	2000
UNCLE SAM	Madness	1985
UNCONDITIONAL LOVE	Donna Summer	1983
UNDER ATTACK	ABBA	1982
UNDER MY THUMB	Wayne Gibson	1974
UNDER NEW MANAGEMENT	Barron Knights	1966
UNDER ONE ROOF	Rubettes	1976
UNDER PRESSURE	Queen & David Bowie	1981
UNDER THE BOARDWALK	Tom Tom Club	1982
UNDER THE BOARDWALK	Bruce Willis	1987
UNDER THE BOARDWALK	Drifters	1964
UNDER THE BRIDGE	Red Hot Chili Peppers	1992
UNDER THE BRIDGE/LADY MARMALADE	All Saints	1998

SONG TITLE	ARTIST	DATE
UNDER THE GUN	Sisters Of Mercy	1993
UNDER THE MILKY WAY	Church	1988
UNDER THE MOON OF LOVE		
	Showaddywaddy	1976
UNDER THE THUMB	Amy Studt	2003
UNDER THE WATER	Brother Brown featuring	
	Frank'ee	1999
UNDER YOUR SPELL AGAIN		
	Johnny Rivers	1965
UNDER YOUR THUMB	Godley & Creme	1981
UNDERCOVER ANARCHIST	Silver Bullet	1991
UNDERCOVER ANGEL	Alan O'Day	1977
UNDERCOVER OF THE NIGHT		
	Rolling Stones	1983
UNDERDOG (SAVE ME)	Turin Brakes	2001
UNDERGROUND	Ben Folds Five	1996
UNDERGROUND	David Bowie	1986
UNDERNEATH IT ALL	No Doubt featuring Lady Saw	2002
UNDERNEATH THE BLANKET		
	Gilbert O'Sullivan	1971
UNDERNEATH YOUR CLOTHES		
	Shakira	2002
UNDERPASS	John Foxx	1980
UNDERSTAND YOUR MAN	Johnny Cash	1964
UNDERSTANDING	Bob Seger & The Silver	
	Bullet Band	1984

SONG TITLE	ARTIST	DATE
UNDERSTANDING	Xscape	1993
UNDERWATER	Delerium featuring Rani	2001
UNDERWATER LOVE	Smoke City	1997
UNDIVIDED LOVE	Louise	1996
UNDONE – THE SWEATER SONG		
	Weezer	1995
UNDUN	Guess Who	1969
UNEASY RIDER	Charlie Daniels Band	1973
UNEXPLAINED EP	EMF	1992
UNFINISHED SYMPATHY	Massive	1991
UNFORGETTABLE	Natalie Cole & Nat 'King' Cole	1991
THE UNFORGETTABLE FIRE		
	U2	1985
UNFORGIVABLE SINNER	Lene Marlin	2000
UNFORGIVEN	D:ream	1993
THE UNFORGIVEN	Metallica	1991
THE UNFORGIVEN II	Metallica	1998
UNGENA ZA ULIMWENGU (UNITE THE WORLD)		
	Temptations	1970
UNHOLY	Kiss	1992
THE UNICORN	Irish Rovers	1968
UNINTENDED	Muse	2000
UNION CITY BLUE	Blondie	1979
UNION MAN	Cate Brothers	1976
UNION OF THE SNAKE	Duran Duran	1983
UNITED	Judas Priest	1980

SONG TITLE	ARTIST	DATE
UNITED (WE LOVE YOU)	Manchester United & The Champions	1993
UNITED CALYPSO '98	Reds United	1998
UNITED STATES OF WHATEVER	Liam Lynch	2002
UNITED WE STAND	Brotherhood Of Man	1970
THE UNIVERSAL	Blur	1995
UNIVERSAL	Small Faces	1968
UNIVERSAL NATION	Push	1999
UNIVERSALLY SPEAKING	Red Hot Chili Peppers	2003
THE UNKNOWN SOLDIER	Doors	1968
UNLEASH THE DRAGON	Sisqo	2000
UNO MAS	Daniel O'Donnell	1999
UNPRETTY	TLC	1999
UNSKINNY BOP	Poison	1990
UNTIL IT SLEEPS	Metallica	1996
UNTIL IT'S TIME FOR YOU TO GO	Four Pennies	1965
UNTIL IT'S TIME FOR YOU TO GO	Elvis Presley	1972
UNTIL MY DYING DAY	UB40	1995
UNTIL THE END OF TIME	2Pac	2001
UNTIL THE TIME IS THROUGH	5ive	1998
UNTIL YOU COME BACK TO ME (THAT'S WHAT I'M GONNA DO)	Aretha Franklin	1973

SONG TITLE	ARTIST	DATE
UNTIL YOU LOVED ME	Moffatts	1999
UNTIL YOU SUFFER SOME (FIRE AND ICE)	Poison	1993
UNTIL YOUR LOVE COMES BACK AROUND	RTZ	1992
UNTITLED (HOW DOES IT FEEL)	D'Angelo	2000
UNTOUCHABLE	Rialto	1998
UP & DOWN	Scent	2004
UP AGAINST THE WALL	Tom Robinson Band	1978
UP ALL NIGHT	Slaughter	1990
UP AND DOWN	Vengaboys	1998
UP AROUND THE BEND/RUN THROUGH THE JUNGLE	Creedence Clearwater Revival	1970
UP AT THE LAKE	Charlatans	2004
UP IN A PUFF OF SMOKE	Polly Brown	1975
UP JUMPS DA BOOGIE	Magoo And Timbaland	1997
UP MIDDLE FINGER	Oxide & Neutrino	2001
UP ON CRIPPLE CREEK	Band	1969
UP ON THE CATWALK	Simple Minds	1984
UP ON THE DOWN SIDE	Ocean Colour Scene	2001
UP ON THE ROOF	Julie Grant	1963
UP ON THE ROOF	James Taylor	1979
UP ROCKING BEATS	Bomfunk MC's	2000
UP THE BRACKET	Libertines	2002
UP THE HILL BACKWARDS	David Bowie	1981

SONG TITLE	ARTIST	DATE
UP THE JUNCTION	Squeeze	1979
UP THE LADDER TO THE ROOF		
	Supremes	1970
UP TO NO GOOD	Porn Kings	1996
UP TO THE WILDSTYLE	Porn Kings vs DJ Supreme	1999
UP UP & AWAY	5th Dimension	1967
UP-UP AND AWAY	Johnny Mann Singers	1967
UP WHERE WE BELONG	Joe Cocker & Jennifer Warnes	1982
UPS AND DOWNS	Paul Revere & The Raiders	1967
UPSIDE DOWN	A Teens	2001
UPSIDE DOWN	Diana Ross	1980
UPTIGHT	Stevie Wonder	1966
UPTIGHT	Shara Nelson	1994
UPTIGHT (EVERYTHING'S ALRIGHT)		
	Stevie Wonder	1965
UPTOWN FESTIVAL	Shalamar	1978
UPTOWN GIRL	Billy Joel	1983
UPTOWN GIRL	Westlife	2001
UPTOWN TOP RANKING	Ali And Frazier	1993
UPTOWN TOP RANKING	Althia And Donna	1977
UPTOWN UPTEMPO WOMAN		
	Randy Edelman	1976
URBAN CITY GIRL	Benz	1996
URBAN GUERRILLA	Hawkwind	1973
URBAN TRAIN	DJ Tiesto featuring Kirsty Hawkshaw	2001

SONG TITLE	ARTIST	DATE
URGE	Wildhearts	1997
URGENT	Foreigner	1981
USE IT UP AND WEAR IT OUT		
	Pat & Mick	1990
USE IT UP AND WEAR IT OUT		
	Odyssey	1980
USE ME	Bill Withers	1972
USE TA BE MY GIRL	O'Jays	1978
USE YOUR HEAD	Mary Wells	1965
USE YOUR HEART	SWV	1996
USELESS	Depeche Mode	1997
V.I.P.	Jungle Brothers	1999
VACATION	Connie Francis	1992
VACATION	Go-Go's	1982
VADO VIA	Drupi	1973
VAGABONDS	New Model Army	1989
VALENTINE	T'Pau	1988
VALERIE	Steve Winwood	1987
VALLERI	Monkees	1968
VALLEY GIRL	Frank Zappa	1982
VALLEY OF THE DOLLS	Generation X	1979
THE VALLEY ROAD	Bruce Hornsby & The Range	1988
VALOTTE	Julian Lennon	1984
VANILLA RADIO	Wildhearts	2002
VAPORS	Snoop Doggy Dogg	1997

SONG TITLE	ARTIST	DATE
VAYA CON DIOS (MAY GOD BE WITH YOU)		
	Millican & Nesbitt	1973
VEGAS	Sleeper	1995
VEGAS TWO TIMES	Stereophonics	2002
VEHICLE	Ides Of March	1970
VELCRO FLY	ZZ Top	1986
VELOURIA	Pixies	1990
VENTURA HIGHWAY	America	1972
VENUS	Bananarama	1986
VENUS	Don Pablo's Animals	1990
VENUS	Shocking Blue	1969
VENUS AND MARS	Jo Breezer	2001
VENUS AND MARS ROCK SHOW		
	Paul McCartney	1975
VENUS AS A BOY	Bjork	1993
VERMILION	Slipknot	2004
VERONICA	Elvis Costello	1989
VERTIGO	U2	2004
VERY SPECIAL	Big Daddy Kane	1993
A VERY SPECIAL LOVE SONG		
	Charlie Rich	1974
THE VERY THOUGHT OF YOU		
	Tony Bennett	1965
THE VERY THOUGHT OF YOU		
	Ricky Nelson	1964
VIBEOLOGY	Paula Abdul	1992

SONG TITLE	ARTIST	DATE
VICE	Razorlight	2004
VICIOUS CIRCLES	Poltergeist	1996
VICTIM OF LOVE	Erasure	1987
VICTIM OF LOVE	Bryan Adams	1987
VICTIM OF LOVE	Elton John	1979
VICTIMS	Culture Club	1983
VICTIMS OF SUCCESS	Dogs D'Amour	1990
VICTORIA	Fall	1988
VICTORIA	Kinks	1970
VICTORY	Kool & The Gang	1986
VICTORY	Puff Daddy & Family featuring The Notorious B.I.G. & Busta Rhymes	1998
VIDEO	India.Arie	2001
VIDEO KILLED THE RADIO STAR		
	Buggles	1979
VIDEOTHEQUE	Dollar	1982
VIENNA	Ultravox	1981
VIENNA CALLING	Falco	1986
VIEW FROM A BRIDGE	Kim Wilde	1982
A VIEW TO A KILL	Duran Duran	1985
VINCENT	Don McLean	1972
VINDALOO	Fat Les	1998
VIOLENCE OF SUMMER (LOVE'S TAKING OVER)		
	Duran Duran	1990
VIOLENTLY (EP)	Hue & Cry	1989

SONG TITLE	ARTIST	DATE
VIOLENTLY HAPPY	Bjork	1994
VIOLET	Seal	1992
VIOLET	Hole	1995
VIRGINIA PLAIN	Roxy Music	1972
VIRTUAL INSANITY	Jamiroquai	1996
VIRTUALITY	Vbirds	2003
VIRUS	Iron Maiden	1996
VISAGE	Visage	1981
VISION INCISION	Lo Fidelity Allstars	1998
VISION OF LOVE	Mariah Carey	1990
THE VISION	Mario Piu presents DJ Arabesque	2001
VISIONS	Cliff Richard	1966
VISIONS IN BLUE	Ultravox	1983
VISIONS OF CHINA	Japan	1981
VISIONS OF YOU	Jah Wobble's Invaders Of The Heart	1992
VIVA BOBBIE JOE	Equals	1969
VIVA FOREVER	Spice Girls	1998
VIVA LA MEGABABES	Shampoo	1994
VIVA LA RADIO	Lolly	1999
VIVA LAS VEGAS	Elvis Presley	1964
VIVA LAS VEGAS	ZZ Top	1992
VIVA TIRADO – PART 1	El Chicano	1970
VIVID	Electronic	1999
VIVRANT THING	Q-Tip	1999

SONG TITLE	ARTIST	DATE
VOGUE	Madonna	1990
THE VOICE	Eimear Quinn	1996
THE VOICE	Ultravox	1981
THE VOICE	Moody Blues	1981
THE VOICE WITHIN	Christina Aguilera	2003
VOICES	Ann Lee	2000
VOICES	Dario G	2000
VOICES	Cheap Trick	1979
VOICES CARRY	Til Tuesday	1985
VOICES IN THE SKY	Moody Blues	1968
VOICES OF BABYLON	Outfield	1989
VOICES THAT CARE	Voices That Care	1991
VOLARE	Al Martino	1975
VOLUME 1 (WHAT YOU WANT WHAT YOU NEED)	Industry Standard	1998
VOODOO	Warrior	2001
VOODOO CHILE	Jimi Hendrix Experience	1970
VOODOO PEOPLE	Prodigy	1994
VOODOO RAY (EP)	A Guy Called Gerald	1989
VOODOO WOMAN	Bobby Goldsboro	1965
VOX HUMANA	Kenny Loggins	1985
VOYAGE VOYAGE	Desireless	1988
VOYEUR	Kim Carnes	1982
W.O.L.D.	Harry Chapin	1974
WACK ASS MF	Rhythmkillaz	2001
WACK WACK	Young-Holt Unlimited	1966

SONG TITLE	ARTIST	DATE
WADE IN THE WATER	Ramsey Lewis	1972
WADE IN THE WATER	Herb Alpert & The Tijuana Brass	1967
WAGES DAY	Deacon Blue	1989
WAIT	Robert Howard & Kym Mazelle	1989
WAIT	White Lion	1988
WAIT A MINUTE	Ray J featuring Lil' Kim	2001
WAIT AND BLEED	Slipknot	2000
WAIT FOR ME	Daryl Hall & John Oates	1979
WAIT FOR ME MARIANNE	Marmalade	1968
WAIT UNTIL TONIGHT (MY LOVE)	Galaxy featuring Phil Fearon	1983
WAITING	Green Day	2001
THE WAITING	Tom Petty & The Heartbreakers	1981
WAITING FOR A GIRL LIKE YOU	Foreigner	1981
WAITING FOR A STAR TO FALL	Boy Meets Girl	1988
WAITING FOR A TRAIN	Flash And The Pan	1983
WAITING FOR AN ALIBI	Thin Lizzy	1979
WAITING FOR LOVE	Alias	1991
WAITING FOR THAT DAY	George Michael	1991
WAITING FOR THE SUMMER	Delirious?	2001
WAITING FOR THE SUN	Ruff Driverz	1999
WAITING FOR TONIGHT	Jennifer Lopez	1999

SONG TITLE	ARTIST	DATE
(WAITING FOR) THE GHOST TRAIN	Madness	1986
WAITING IN VAIN	Annie Lennox	1995
WAITING IN VAIN	Bob Marley	1977
WAITING ON A FRIEND	Rolling Stones	1981
WAKE ME UP BEFORE YOU GO-GO	Wham!	1984
WAKE UP (MAKE A MOVE)	Lostprophets	2004
WAKE UP (NEXT TO YOU)	Graham Parker & The Shot	1985
WAKE UP BOO!	Boo Radleys	1995
WAKE UP EVERYBODY (PT 1)	Harold Melvin & The Blue Notes	1975
WAKE UP LITTLE SUSIE	Simon & Garfunkel	1982
WAKE UP SUSAN	Spinners	1977
WAKING UP	Elastica	1995
WALHALLA	Gouryella	1999
WALK	Pantera	1993
WALK A MILE IN MY SHOES	Joe South	1970
WALK AWAY	Matt Monro	1964
WALK AWAY	Joyce Sims	1988
WALK AWAY	Donna Summer	1980
WALK AWAY FROM LOVE	David Ruffin	1975
WALK AWAY RENEE	Four Tops	1968

SONG TITLE	ARTIST	DATE
WALK AWAY RENEE	Left Banke	1966
WALK HAND IN HAND	Gerry & The Pacemakers	1965
WALK IDIOT WALK	The Hives	2004
WALK IN LOVE	Manhattan Transfer	1978
A WALK IN THE BLACK FOREST	Horst Jankowski	1965
WALK IN THE NIGHT	Jr. Walker & The All-Stars	1972
A WALK IN THE PARK	Nick Straker Band	1980
WALK LIKE A CHAMPION	Kaliphz featuring Prince Naseem	1996
WALK LIKE A MAN	Divine	1985
WALK LIKE A MAN	Four Seasons	1963
WALK LIKE A MAN	Grand Funk	1973
WALK LIKE A PANTHER '98	All Seeing I featuring Tony Christie	1999
WALK LIKE AN EGYPTIAN	Bangles	1986
WALK OF LIFE	Billie Piper	2000
WALK OF LIFE	Dire Straits	1985
WALK ON	Roy Orbison	1968
WALK ON	U2	2001
WALK ON BY	Stranglers	1978
WALK ON BY	Sybil	1990
WALK ON BY	Dionne Warwick	1964
WALK ON BY	Gabrielle	1997
WALK ON BY	Isaac Hayes	1969

SONG TITLE	ARTIST	DATE
WALK ON THE OCEAN	Toad The Wet Sprocket	1992
WALK ON THE WILD SIDE	Jamie J. Morgan	1990
WALK ON THE WILD SIDE	Lou Reed	1973
WALK ON WATER	Milk Inc.	2002
WALK ON WATER	Neil Diamond	1972
WALK ON WATER	Eddie Money	1988
WALK RIGHT BACK	Perry Como	1973
WALK RIGHT IN	Rooftop Singers	1963
WALK RIGHT NOW	Jacksons	1981
WALK TALL	Val Doonican	1964
THE WALK	Cure	1983
THE WALK	Inmates	1979
WALK THE DINOSAUR	Was (Not Was)	1989
WALK THIS LAND	E-Z Rollers	1999
WALK THIS WAY	Run DMC	1986
WALK THIS WAY	Aerosmith	1976
WALK THROUGH FIRE	Bad Company	1991
WALK THROUGH THIS WORLD	Marc Cohn	1993
WALK WITH FAITH IN YOUR HEART	Bachelors	1966
WALK WITH ME	Seekers	1966
WALK WITH ME TALK WITH ME DARLING	Four Tops	1972

SONG TITLE	ARTIST	DATE
WALK DON'T RUN '64	Ventures	1964
WALKAWAY	Cast	1996
WALKED OUTTA HEAVEN	Jagged Edge	2004
WALKIN'	C.C.S.	1971
WALKIN' IN THE RAIN	Jay & The Americans	1969
WALKIN' IN THE RAIN WITH THE ONE I LOVE		
	Love Unlimited	1972
WALKIN' IN THE SUNSHINE		
	Bad Manners	1981
WALKIN' IN THE SUNSHINE		
	Roger Miller	1967
A WALKIN' MIRACLE	Limmie & The Family Cookin'	1974
WALKIN' MY CAT NAMED DOG		
	Norma Tanega	1966
WALKIN' ON THE SUN	Smash Mouth	1997
WALKIN' TALL	Adam Faith	1963
WALKING AFTER YOU/BEACON LIGHT		
	Foo Fighters/Ween	1998
WALKING ALONE	Richard Anthony	1963
WALKING AWAY	Craig David	2000
WALKING AWAY	Information Society	1989
WALKING DEAD	Puressence	2002
WALKING DOWN MADISON		
	Kirsty MacColl	1991
WALKING DOWN YOUR STREET		
	Bangles	1987

SONG TITLE	ARTIST	DATE
WALKING IN MEMPHIS	Marc Cohn	1991
WALKING IN MEMPHIS	Cher	1995
WALKING IN MY SHOES	Depeche Mode	1993
WALKING IN RHYTHM	Blackbyrds	1975
WALKING IN THE AIR	Peter Autry	1987
WALKING IN THE AIR	Aled Jones	1985
WALKING IN THE RAIN	Walker Brothers	1967
WALKING IN THE RAIN	Modern Romance	1983
WALKING IN THE RAIN	Partridge Family	1973
WALKING IN THE RAIN	Ronettes	1964
WALKING IN THE SUN	Travis	2004
WALKING ON A THIN LINE		
	Huey Lewis & The News	1984
WALKING ON AIR	Bad Boys Inc.	1993
WALKING ON BROKEN GLASS		
	Annie Lennox	1992
WALKING ON SUNSHINE	Katrina & The Waves	1985
WALKING ON SUNSHINE	Rocker's Revenge	1982
WALKING ON THE CHINESE WALL		
	Philip Bailey	1985
WALKING ON THE MILKY WAY		
	OMD	1996
WALKING ON THE MOON	Police	1979
WALKING ON THIN ICE	Yoko Ono	1981
WALKING ON WATER	Madasun	2000
WALKING THE DOG	Dennisons	1964

SONG TITLE	ARTIST	DATE
WALKING WOUNDED	Everything But The Girl	1996
WALKS LIKE A LADY	Journey	1980
THE WALL STREET SHUFFLE	10cc	1974
WALLS COME TUMBLING DOWN!	Style Council	1985
WALTZ AWAY DREAMING	Toby Bourke with George Michael	1997
WALTZ DARLING	Malcolm McLaren	1989
WALTZING ALONG	James	1997
WAM BAM	Handley Family	1973
WAND'RIN' STAR	Lee Marvin	1970
THE WANDERER	Dion	1961
THE WANDERER	Status Quo	1984
THE WANDERER	Donna Summer	1980
WANNA BE STARTIN' SOMETHING	Michael Jackson	1983
WANNA BE WITH YOU	Jinny	1995
WANNA GET TO KNOW YOU	G-Unit	2004
WANNA GET UP	2 Unlimited	1998
WANNABE	Spice Girls	1997
WANNABE GANGSTER/LEROY	Wheatus	2002
WANNAGIRL	Jeremy Jordan	1993
WANT ADS	Honey Cone	1971

SONG TITLE	ARTIST	DATE
WANT LOVE	Hysteric Ego	1996
WANT YOU BAD	Offspring	2001
WANTED	Dooleys	1979
WANTED	Style Council	1987
WANTED DEAD OR ALIVE	Bon Jovi	1987
WANTED DEAD OR ALIVE	2Pac And Snoop Doggy Dogg	1997
WAR	Bruce Springsteen	1986
WAR	Edwin Starr	1970
WAR BABY	Tom Robinson	1983
WAR CHILD	Blondie	1982
THE WAR LORD	Shadows	1965
WAR OF NERVES	All Saints	1998
THE WAR SONG	Culture Club	1984
WARHEAD	UK Subs	1980
WARM AND TENDER LOVE	Percy Sledge	1966
WARM IT UP	Kris Kross	1992
WARM RIDE	Rare Earth	1978
WARM WET CIRCLES	Marillion	1987
WARNING	Green Day	2000
WARNING	Adeva	1989
WARNING SIGN	Nick Heyward	1984
WARPED	Red Hot Chili Peppers	1995
WARRIOR	Warrior	2000
THE WARRIOR	Scandal featuring Patty Smyth	1984
WARRIORS	ASWAD	1994

SONG TITLE	ARTIST	DATE
WARRIORS	Gary Numan	1983
WARRIORS (OF THE WASTELAND)		
	Frankie Goes To Hollywood	1986
WAS IT NOTHING AT ALL	Michael Damian	1989
WAS IT WORTH IT	Pet Shop Boys	1991
WAS THAT ALL IT WAS	Kym Mazelle	1990
WASH IN THE RAIN	Bees	2004
WASH YOUR FACE IN MY SINK		
	Dream Warriors	1990
WASN'T THAT A PARTY	Rovers	1981
WASSUUP	Da Muttz	2000
WASTED DAYS AND WASTED NIGHTS		
	Freddy Fender	1975
WASTED IN AMERICA	Love/Hate	1992
WASTED ON THE WAY	Crosby, Stills & Nash	1982
WASTED TIME	Skid Row	1991
WASTED YEARS	Iron Maiden	1986
WASTELAND	Mission	1987
WASTING MY TIME	Default	2002
WATCH ME	Labi Siffre	1972
WATCH ME DO MY THING	Immature featuring Smooth	
	and Ed From Good Burger	1997
WATCH OUT FOR LUCY	Eric Clapton	1979
WATCH THE FLOWERS GROW		
	Four Seasons	1967
WATCH THE WIND BLOW BY		
	Tim McGraw	2003
WATCH WHAT YOU SAY	Guru featuring Chaka Khan	1995
WATCHDOGS	UB40	1987
A WATCHER'S POINT OF VIEW		
	P.M. Dawn	1991
WATCHIN' THE DETECTIVES		
	Elvis Costello	1977
WATCHING	Thompson Twins	1983
WATCHING SCOTTY GROW	Bobby Goldsboro	1970
WATCHING THE RIVER FLOW		
	Bob Dylan	1971
WATCHING THE WHEELS	John Lennon	1981
WATCHING THE WILDLIFE	Frankie Goes To Hollywood	1987
WATCHING THE WORLD GO BY		
	Maxi Priest	1996
WATCHING WINDOWS	Roni Size/Reprazent	1998
WATCHING XANADU	Mull Historical Society	2002
WATCHING YOU WATCHING ME		
	David Grant	1983
WATER	Geno Washington & Ram Jam Band	1966
THE WATER MARGIN	Godiego	1977
THE WATER MARGIN	Pete Mac Jr.	1977
WATER ON GLASS/BOYS	Kim Wilde	1981
WATER RUNS DRY	Boyz II Men	1995

SONG TITLE	ARTIST	DATE
WATERFALL	Stone Roses	1992
WATERFALL	Atlantic Ocean	1996
WATERFALLS	Paul McCartney	1980
WATERFALLS	TLC	1995
WATERFRONT	Simple Minds	1983
WATERLOO	ABBA	1974
WATERLOO SUNSET	Cathy Dennis	1997
WATERLOO SUNSET	Kinks	1967
THE WAVE OF THE FUTURE	Quadrophonia	1991
WAVE ON WAVE	Pat Green	2003
WAVES	Blancmange	1983
THE WAY	Fastball	1998
THE WAY (PUT YOUR HAND IN MY HAND)	Divine Inspiration	2003
WAY BACK HOME	Jr. Walker & The All-Stars	1973
WAY BEHIND ME	Primitives	1988
WAY DOWN	Elvis Presley	1977
THE WAY DREAMS ARE	Daniel O'Donnell	1999
THE WAY HE MAKES ME FEEL	Barbra Streisand	1983
THE WAY I AM	Eminem	2000
THE WAY I FEEL	Roachford	1997
THE WAY I FEEL ABOUT YOU	Karyn White	1991
THE WAY I FEEL TONIGHT	Bay City Rollers	1977

SONG TITLE	ARTIST	DATE
THE WAY I WANT TO TOUCH YOU	Captain & Tennille	1975
WAY IN MY BRAIN/DRUMBEATS	SL2	1992
THE WAY IT GOES	Status Quo	1999
THE WAY IT IS	Chameleon	1996
THE WAY IT IS	Bruce Hornsby & The Range	1986
THE WAY IT USED TO BE	Engelbert Humperdinck	1969
A WAY OF LIFE	Family Dogg	1969
THE WAY OF LOVE	Cher	1972
WAY OF THE WORLD	Tina Turner	1991
THE WAY SHE LOVES ME	Richard Marx	1994
THE WAY TO YOUR LOVE	Hear'say	2001
THE WAY WE WERE	Barbra Streisand	1973
THE WAY WE WERE/TRY TO REMEMBER (MEDLEY)	Gladys Knight & The Pips	1975
THE WAY YOU ARE	Tears For Fears	1983
THE WAY YOU DO THE THINGS YOU DO	Rita Coolidge	1978
THE WAY YOU DO THE THINGS YOU DO	Temptations	1964
THE WAY YOU DO THE THINGS YOU DO	UB40	1990
THE WAY YOU DO THE THINGS YOU DO/MY GIRL	Daryl Hall & John Oates	1985
THE WAY YOU LOVE ME	Faith Hill	2001

SONG TITLE	ARTIST	DATE
THE WAY YOU LOVE ME	Karyn White	1988
THE WAY YOU MAKE ME FEEL	Michael Jackson	1987
THE WAY YOU MAKE ME FEEL	Ronan Keating	2000
THE WAY YOU WORK IT	EYC	1994
WAYWARD WIND	Frank Ifield	1963
(WE AIN'T GOT) NOTHIN' YET	Blues Magoos	1966
WE ALL FOLLOW MAN. UNITED	Manchester United Football Club	1985
WE ALL SLEEP ALONE	Cher	1988
WE ALL STAND TOGETHER	Paul McCartney	1984
WE ARE	Ana Johnsson	2004
WE ARE ALIVE	Paul Van Dyk	2000
WE ARE ALL MADE OF STARS	Moby	2002
WE ARE DA CLICK	Da Click	1999
WE ARE DETECTIVE	Thompson Twins	1983
WE ARE EACH OTHER	Beautiful South	1992
WE ARE FAMILY	Sister Sledge	1979
WE ARE GLASS	Gary Numan	1980
WE ARE IN LOVE	Adam Faith	1963
WE ARE LOVE	DJ Eric	1999

SONG TITLE	ARTIST	DATE
WE ARE RAVING – THE ANTHEM	Slipstreem	1992
WE ARE THE CHAMPIONS	Queen	1977
WE ARE THE PIGS	Suede	1994
WE ARE THE WORLD	USA For Africa	1985
WE ARE THE YOUNG	Dan Hartman	1984
WE BELONG	Pat Benatar	1984
WE BUILT THIS CITY	Starship	1985
WE CALL IT ACIEED	D. Mob featuring Gary Haisman	1988
WE CAME TO DANCE	Ultravox	1983
WE CAN	Leann Rimes	2003
WE CAN DO IT	Liverpool F.C.	1977
WE CAN FLY	Cowsills	1968
WE CAN WORK IT OUT	Four Seasons	1976
WE CAN WORK IT OUT	Stevie Wonder	1971
WE CAN WORK IT OUT	Beatles	1965
WE CAN'T BE FRIENDS	Deborah Cox With R.L.	1999
WE CAN'T GO WRONG	Cover Girls	1989
WE CAN'T HIDE IT ANYMORE	Larry Santos	1976
WE CLOSE OUR EYES	Go West	1985
WE CLOSE OUR EYES '93	Go West	1993
WE COME I	Faithless	2001
WE COME TO PARTY	N-Tyce	1997
WE CONNECT	Stacey Q	1986
WE COULD BE KINGS	Gene	1997

SONG TITLE	ARTIST	DATE
WE COULD BE TOGETHER	Debbie Gibson	1989
WE DANCED	Brad Paisley	2000
WE DIDN'T START THE FIRE	Billy Joel	1989
WE DO IT	R & J Stone	1976
WE DON'T CARE	Audio Bullys	2003
WE DON'T HAVE TO TAKE OUT CLOTHES OFF	Jermaine Stewart	1986
WE DON'T NEED ANOTHER HERO (THUNDERDOME)	Tina Turner	1985
(WE DON'T NEED THIS) FASCIST GROOVE THANG	Heaven 17	1993
WE DON'T TALK ANYMORE	Cliff Richard	1979
WE FIT TOGETHER	O-Town	2001
WE GOT A LOVE THANG	Ce Ce Peniston	1992
WE GOT IT	Immature featuring Smooth	1996
WE GOT MORE SOUL	Dyke & The Blazers	1969
WE GOT THE BEAT	Go-Go's	1982
WE GOT THE FUNK	Positive Force	1979
WE GOT THE LOVE	Lindy Layton	1993
WE GOT THE WHOLE WORLD IN OUR HANDS	Nottingham Forest with Paper Lace	1978

SONG TITLE	ARTIST	DATE
WE GOTTA GET OUT OF THIS PLACE	Animals	1965
WE GOTTA GET YOU A WOMAN	Runt	1970
WE HATE IT WHEN OUR FRIENDS BECOME SUCCESSFUL	Morrissey	1992
WE HAVE A DREAM	Scotland World Cup Squad	1982
WE HAVE ALL THE TIME IN THE WORLD	Louis Armstrong	1994
WE HAVE EXPLOSIVE	Future Sound Of London	1997
WE HAVEN'T TURNED AROUND	Gomez	1999
WE JUST BE DREAMIN'	Blazin' Squad	2003
WE JUST DISAGREE	Dave Mason	1977
WE JUST WANNA PARTY WITH YOU	Snoop Doggy Dogg featuring JD	1997
WE KILL THE WORLD (DON'T KILL THE WORLD)	Boney M	1981
WE LIKE TO PARTY! (THE VENGABUS)	Vengaboys	1999
WE LIVE FOR LOVE	Pat Benatar	1980
WE LOVE EACH OTHER	Charlie Rich	1975
WE LOVE YOU	Menswear	1996
WE LOVE YOU/DANDELION	Rolling Stones	1967
WE LOVE YOU BEATLES	Carefrees	1964

SONG TITLE	ARTIST	DATE
WE MAY NEVER PASS THIS WAY (AGAIN)		
	Seals & Crofts	1973
WE NEED A RESOLUTION	Aaliyah featuring Timbaland	2001
WE SAIL ON THE STORMY WATERS		
	Gary Clark	1993
WE SHALL OVERCOME	Joan Baez	1965
WE SHOULD BE TOGETHER		
	Cliff Richard	1991
WE TAKE MYSTERY (TO BED)		
	Gary Numan	1982
WE THUGGIN'	Fat Joe featuring R. Kelly	2001
WE TRYING TO STAY ALIVE		
	Wyclef Jean And The Refugee	
	Allstars	1997
WE TWO	Little River Band	1983
WE USED TO BE FRIENDS	Dandy Warhols	2003
WE WANT THE FUNK	Gerardo	1991
WE WANT YOUR SOUL	Freeland	2003
(WE WANT) THE SAME THING		
	Belinda Carlisle	1990
WE WERE MEANT TO BE LOVERS		
	Photoglo	1980
WE WILL	Gilbert O'Sullivan	1971
WE WILL ROCK YOU	5ive & Queen	2000
WE WILL SURVIVE	Warp Brothers	2001
WE'LL BE TOGETHER	Sting	1987

SONG TITLE	ARTIST	DATE
WE'LL BE WITH YOU	Potters	1972
WE'LL BRING THE HOUSE DOWN		
	Slade	1981
WE'LL FIND OUR DAY	Stephanie De Sykes	1975
WE'LL NEVER HAVE TO SAY GOODBYE AGAIN		
	England Dan & John Ford	
	Coley	1978
WE'LL SING IN THE SUNSHINE		
	Gale Garnett	1964
WE'RE A WINNER	Impressions	1967
WE'RE ALL ALONE	Rita Coolidge	1977
WE'RE ALL IN THE SAME GANG		
	West Coast Rap All-Stars	1990
WE'RE AN AMERICAN BAND		
	Grand Funk	1973
WE'RE FREE	Beverly Bremmers	1972
WE'RE GETTING CARELESS WITH OUR LOVE		
	Johnnie Taylor	1974
WE'RE GOING TO IBIZA!	Vengaboys	1999
WE'RE GONNA DO IT AGAIN		
	Manchester United 1995	
	Football Squad featuring	
	Stryker	1995
WE'RE GONNA MAKE IT	Little Milton	1965
(WE'RE GONNA) ROCK AROUND THE CLOCK		
	Bill Haley	1974

SONG TITLE	ARTIST	DATE
WE'RE IN THIS LOVE TOGETHER	Al Jarreau	1981
WE'RE IN THIS TOGETHER	Nine Inch Nails	1999
WE'RE IN THIS TOGETHER	Simply Red	1996
WE'RE NOT GONNA SLEEP TONIGHT	Emma Bunton	2001
WE'RE NOT GONNA TAKE IT	Twisted Sister	1984
WE'RE NOT MAKING LOVE NO MORE	Dru Hill	1997
WE'RE ON THE BALL	Ant And Dec	2002
WE'RE READY	Boston	1986
WE'RE REALLY SAYING SOMETHING	Buffalo G	2000
WE'RE THROUGH	Hollies	1964
WE'VE GOT IT GOIN' ON	Backstreet Boys	1996
WE'VE GOT TO GET IT ON AGAIN	Addrisi Brothers	1972
WE'VE GOT TO LIVE TOGETHER	R.A.F.	1992
WE'VE GOT TONIGHT	Bob Seger & The Silver Bullet Band	1995
WE'VE GOT TONIGHT	Sheena Easton & Kenny Rogers	1983
WE'VE GOT TONIGHT	Ronan Keating featuring Lulu	2002
WE'VE GOT TONITE	Bob Seger & The Silver Bullet Band	1978

SONG TITLE	ARTIST	DATE
WE'VE ONLY JUST BEGUN	Bitty McLean	1995
WE'VE ONLY JUST BEGUN	Carpenters	1970
WEAK	SWV	1993
WEAK	Skunk Anansie	1996
WEAK BECOME HEROES	Streets	2002
WEAK IN THE PRESENCE OF BEAUTY	Alison Moyet	1987
WEAK SPOT	Evelyn Thomas	1976
WEAR YOU TO THE BALL	UB40	1990
WEAR YOUR LOVE LIKE HEAVEN	Definition Of Sound	1991
WEAR YOUR LOVE LIKE HEAVEN	Donovan	1967
WEATHER WITH YOU	Crowded House	1992
THE WEAVER (EP)	Paul Weller	1993
THE WEDDING	Cliff Richard featuring Helen Hobson	1996
THE WEDDING	Julie Rogers	1964
WEDDING BELL BLUES	5th Dimension	1969
WEDDING BELLS	Godley & Creme	1981
WEDDING SONG (THIS IS LOVE)	Paul Stookey	1971
WEDNESDAY WEEK	Undertones	1980
WEE RULE	Wee Papa Girl Rappers	1988
WEEK IN WEEK OUT	Ordinary Boys	2004
WEEKEND	Todd Terry Project	1995

SONG TITLE	ARTIST	DATE
WEEKEND	Mick Jackson	1979
WEEKEND	Wet Willie	1979
WEEKEND!	Scooter	2003
WEEKEND IN NEW ENGLAND		
	Barry Manilow	1976
WEEKENDER	Flowered Up	1992
THE WEIGHT	Band	1968
THE WEIGHT	Aretha Franklin	1969
WEIRD	Reef	1995
WEIRD	Hanson	1998
WEIRDO	Charlatans	1992
WELCOME	Gino Latino	1990
WELCOME BACK	John Sebastian	1976
WELCOME BACK	Mase	2004
WELCOME HOME	Peters & Lee	1973
WELCOME TO ATLANTA	Jermaine Dupri & Ludacris	2001
WELCOME TO HEARTLAND	Kenny Loggins	1983
WELCOME TO MY WORLD	Jim Reeves	1963
WELCOME TO PARADISE	Green Day	1994
WELCOME TO THE BOOMTOWN		
	David & David	1986
WELCOME TO THE CHEAP SEATS (EP)		
	Wonder Stuff	1992
WELCOME TO THE JUNGLE/NIGHTRAIN		
	Guns N' Roses	1988

SONG TITLE	ARTIST	DATE
WELCOME TO THE PLEASUREDOME		
	Frankie Goes To Hollywood	1993
WELCOME TO THE TERRORDOME		
	Public Enemy	1990
WELCOME TO TOMORROW		
	Snap! featuring Summer	1994
(WELCOME) TO THE DANCE		
	Des Mitchell	2000
A WELL RESPECTED MAN	Kinks	1965
WEREWOLVES OF LONDON		
	Warren Zevon	1978
WEST END GIRLS	East 17	1993
WEST END GIRLS	Pet Shop Boys	1986
WEST END PAD	Cathy Dennis	1996
WESTBOUND NO. 9	Flaming Ember	1970
WESTERN UNION	Five Americans	1967
WESTSIDE	TQ	1998
WET DREAM	Max Romeo	1969
WHADDA U WANT (FROM ME)		
	Frankie Knuckles featuring Adeva	1995
WHAM BAM	Candy Girls featuring Sweet Pussy Pauline	1996
WHAM BAM (SHANG-A-LANG)		
	Silver	1976
WHAM RAP	Wham!	1983

SONG TITLE	ARTIST	DATE
WHAT	Soft Cell	1982
WHAT A BEAUTIFUL DAY	Levellers	1997
WHAT A DIFFERENCE A DAY MADE	Esther Phillips	1975
WHAT A FOOL BELIEVES	Peter Cox	1998
WHAT A FOOL BELIEVES	Doobie Brothers	1979
WHAT A GIRL WANTS	Christina Aguilera	1999
WHAT A NIGHT	City Boy	1978
WHAT A WASTE!	Ian Dury & The Blockheads	1978
WHAT A WASTER	Libertines	2002
WHAT A WOMAN IN LOVE WON'T DO	Sandy Posey	1967
WHAT A WONDERFUL WORLD/CABARET	Louis Armstrong	1968
(WHAT A) WONDERFUL WORLD	Johnny Nash	1976
(WHAT A) WONDERFUL WORLD	Art Garfunkel, James Taylor & Paul Simon	1978
WHAT ABOUT LOVE	Heart	1988
WHAT ABOUT LOVE	'Til Tuesday	1986
WHAT ABOUT LOVE?	Heart	1985
WHAT ABOUT ME	Moving Pictures	1982
WHAT ABOUT ME?	Kenny Rogers With Kim Carnes & James Ingram	1984
WHAT ABOUT NOW	Lonestar	2000
WHAT ABOUT US	Point Break	2000
WHAT ABOUT US	Total	1997
WHAT ABOUT US?	Brandy	2002
WHAT ABOUT YOUR FRIENDS	TLC	1992
WHAT AM I CRYING FOR?	Classics IV	1972
WHAT AM I GONNA DO (I'M SO IN LOVE WITH YOU)	Rod Stewart	1983
WHAT AM I GONNA DO WITH YOU	Barry White	1975
WHAT AM I TO YOU	Kenny Lynch	1964
WHAT ARE WE DOIN' IN LOVE	Dottie West & Kenny Rogers	1981
WHAT ARE WE GONNA GET 'ER INDOORS	Dennis Waterman & George Cole	1983
WHAT ARE YOU DOING SUNDAY	Dawn	1971
WHAT BECAME OF THE LIKELY LADS	The Libertines	2004
WHAT BECOMES OF THE BROKEN HEARTED/SATURDAY NIGHT AT THE MOVIES	Robson Green & Jerome Flynn	1996
WHAT BECOMES OF THE BROKENHEARTED	Dave Stewart: Guest Vocals Colin Blunstone	1981

SONG TITLE	ARTIST	DATE
WHAT BECOMES OF THE BROKENHEARTED	Jimmy Ruffin	1966
WHAT BECOMES OF THE BROKENHEARTED	Paul Young	1992
WHAT CAN I DO?	Corrs	1998
WHAT CAN I SAY	Boz Scaggs	1977
WHAT CAN YOU DO FOR ME	Utah Saints	1991
WHAT CHA GONNA DO ABOUT IT	Small Faces	1965
WHAT CHA GONNA DO WITH MY LOVIN'	Stephanie Mills	1979
WHAT COLOR (IS A MAN)	Bobby Vinton	1965
WHAT COMES NATURALLY	Sheena Easton	1991
WHAT DID I DO TO YOU? (EP)	Lisa Stansfield	1990
WHAT DIFFERENCE DOES IT MAKE	Smiths	1984
WHAT DO I DO	Phil Fearon & Galaxy	1984
WHAT DO I DO NOW?	Sleeper	1995
WHAT DO I GET?	Buzzcocks	1978
WHAT DO I HAVE TO DO	Kylie Minogue	1991
WHAT DO YOU SAY	Chubby Checker	1963
WHAT DO YOU SAY	Reba McEntire	1999
WHAT DO YOU WANT FROM ME?	Monaco	1997

SONG TITLE	ARTIST	DATE
WHAT DO YOU WANT TO MAKE THOSE EYES AT ME FOR	Shakin' Stevens	1987
WHAT DOES IT TAKE	Then Jericho	1989
WHAT DOES IT TAKE (TO WIN YOUR LOVE)	Jr. Walker & The All Stars	1969
WHAT EVER HAPPENED TO OLD FASHIONED LOVE	Daniel O'Donnell	1993
WHAT GOD WANTS (PART I)	Roger Waters	1992
WHAT GOES AROUND	Bitty McLean	1994
WHAT GOOD AM I?	Cilla Black	1967
WHAT HAVE I DONE TO DESERVE THIS	Pet Shop Boys & Dusty Springfield	1987
WHAT HAVE THEY DONE TO MY SONG MA	Melanie	1971
WHAT HAVE THEY DONE TO THE RAIN	Searchers	1965
WHAT HAVE YOU DONE FOR ME LATELY	Janet Jackson	1986
WHAT I AM	Edie Brickell & The New Bohemians	1989
WHAT I AM	Tin Tin Out featuring Emma Bunton	1999
WHAT I GO TO SCHOOL FOR	Busted	2002

SONG TITLE	ARTIST	DATE
WHAT I GOT IS WHAT YOU NEED		
	Unique	1983
WHAT I LIKE ABOUT YOU	Michael Morales	1989
WHAT I REALLY MEANT TO SAY		
	Cyndi Thomson	2001
WHAT I SAW	Kings Of Leon	2003
WHAT I'VE GOT IN MIND	Billie Jo Spears	1976
WHAT IF	Kate Winslet	2001
WHAT IF SHE'S AN ANGEL	Tommy Shane Steiner	2002
WHAT IF...	Lightning Seeds	1996
WHAT IN THE WORLD'S COME OVER YOU		
	Rockin' Berries	1965
WHAT IN THE WORLD'S COME OVER YOU		
	Tam White	1975
WHAT IS A MAN	Four Tops	1969
WHAT IS LIFE	Olivia Newton-John	1972
WHAT IS LIFE	George Harrison	1971
WHAT IS LOVE	Haddaway	1993
WHAT IS LOVE?	Howard Jones	1984
WHAT IS THE PROBLEM?	Grafiti	2003
WHAT IS TRUTH?	Johnny Cash	1970
WHAT IT FEELS LIKE FOR A GIRL		
	Madonna	2001
WHAT IT TAKES	Aerosmith	1990
WHAT IT'S LIKE	Everlast	1998
WHAT KIND OF FOOL	All About Eve	1988

SONG TITLE	ARTIST	DATE
WHAT KIND OF FOOL	Kylie Minogue	1992
WHAT KIND OF FOOL	Barbra Streisand & Barry Gibb	1981
WHAT KIND OF FOOL AM I		
	Rick Springfield	1982
WHAT KIND OF FOOL DO YOU THINK I AM		
	Bill Deal & The Rhondels	1969
WHAT KIND OF MAN WOULD I BE		
	Mint Condition	1996
WHAT KIND OF MAN WOULD I BE?		
	Chicago	1989
WHAT KINDA BOY YOU LOOKING FOR (GIRL)		
	Hot Chocolate	1983
WHAT MAKES A MAN	Westlife	2000
WHAT MAKES YOU CRY	Proclaimers	1994
WHAT MY HEART WANTS TO SAY		
	Gareth Gates	2002
WHAT NOW	Adam Faith	1963
WHAT NOW	Gene Chandler	1964
WHAT NOW MY LOVE	Sonny & Cher	1966
WHAT NOW MY LOVE	Herb Alpert & The Tijuana Brass	1966
WHAT NOW MY LOVE	Mitch Ryder	1967
WHAT THE WORLD NEEDS NOW IS LOVE		
	Jackie Deshannon	1965
WHAT THE WORLD NEEDS NOW IS LOVE/ABRAHAM, MARTIN & JOHN	Tom Clay	1971
WHAT THEY DO	Roots	1997

SONG TITLE	ARTIST	DATE
WHAT TIME IS IT?	Dust Junkys	1998
WHAT TIME IS LOVE	KLF/Children of the Revolution	1990
WHAT TO DO	Buddy Holly	1963
WHAT TOOK YOU SO LONG?		
	Emma Bunton	2001
WHAT 'U' WAITIN' '4'	Jungle Brothers	1990
WHAT WAS I THINKIN'	Dierks Bentley	2003
WHAT WOULD I BE	Val Doonican	1966
WHAT WOULD YOU DO?	City High	2001
WHAT YA GOT 4 ME	Signum	2002
WHAT YA WANT	Eve & Nokio	1999
WHAT YOU DO TO ME (EP)		
	Teenage Fanclub	1992
WHAT YOU DON'T KNOW	Expose	1989
WHAT YOU GET	Hundred Reasons	2004
WHAT YOU GET IS WHAT YOU SEE		
	Tina Turner	1987
WHAT YOU GOT	Abs	2002
WHAT YOU NEED	Powerhouse featuring	
	Duane Harden	1999
WHAT YOU NEED	INXS	1986
WHAT YOU NEED IS...	Sinead Quinn	2003
WHAT YOU SEE IS WHAT YOU GET		
	Glen Goldsmith	1988
WHAT YOU SEE IS WHAT YOU GET		
	Tina Turner	1987

SONG TITLE	ARTIST	DATE
WHAT YOU SEE IS WHAT YOU GET		
	Brenda K. Starr	1988
WHAT YOU WAITIN' FOR	Stargard	1978
WHAT YOU WANT	Mase featuring Total	1998
WHAT YOU WON'T DO FOR LOVE		
	Go West	1993
WHAT YOU WON'T DO FOR LOVE		
	Bobby Caldwell	1978
WHAT YOU'RE MADE OF	Lucie Silvas	2004
WHAT YOU'RE MISSING	K-Klass	1994
WHAT YOU'RE PROPOSING		
	Status Quo	1980
WHAT'CHA GONNA DO	Eternal	1999
WHAT'CHA GONNA DO?	Shabba Ranks featuring	
	Queen Latifah	1993
WHAT'CHU LIKE	Da Brat featuring Tyrese	2000
WHAT'D I SAY	Elvis Presley	1964
WHAT'S ANOTHER YEAR	Johnny Logan	1980
WHAT'S FOREVER FOR	Michael Murphey	1982
WHAT'S GOING ON	Artists Against Aids Worldwide	2001
WHAT'S GOING ON	All Star Tribute	2001
WHAT'S GOING ON	Marvin Gaye	1971
WHAT'S GOING ON	Cyndi Lauper	1987
WHAT'S HAPPENIN'	Method Man featuring	
	Busta Rhymes	2004
WHAT'S IN A KISS	Gilbert O'Sullivan	1980

SONG TITLE	ARTIST	DATE
WHAT'S IN A WORD	Christians	1992
WHAT'S IN THE BOX? (SEE WHATCHA GOT)		
	Boo Radleys	1996
WHAT'S IT GONNA BE?	Busta Rhymes featuring Janet	1999
WHAT'S LOVE GOT TO DO WITH IT		
	Tina Turner	1984
WHAT'S LOVE GOT TO DO WITH IT		
	Warren G featuring Adina Howard	1996
WHAT'S LUV?	Fat Joe featuring Ashanti	2002
WHAT'S MY AGE AGAIN?	Blink-182	1999
WHAT'S MY NAME?	Snoop Doggy Dogg	1993
WHAT'S NEW PUSSYCAT?	Tom Jones	1965
WHAT'S ON TONIGHT	Montell Jordan	1997
WHAT'S ON YOUR MIND (PURE ENERGY)		
	Information Society	1988
WHAT'S SO DIFFERENT?	Ginuwine	1999
WHAT'S THAT TUNE? (DOO-DOO-DOO-DOO-DOO-DOO-DOO-DOO-DOO-DOO)	Dorothy	1995
WHAT'S THE COLOUR OF MONEY?		
	Hollywood Beyond	1986
WHAT'S THE FREQUENCY, KENNETH?		
	R.E.M.	1994
WHAT'S THE MATTER WITH YOU BABY		
	Marvin Gaye & Mary Wells	1964

SONG TITLE	ARTIST	DATE
WHAT'S THE USE OF BREAKING UP?		
	Jerry Butler	1969
WHAT'S UP	DJ Miko	1994
WHAT'S UP	4 Non Blondes	1993
WHAT'S UP DOC? (CAN WE ROCK)		
	Fu-Schnickens with Shaquille O'Neal	1993
(WHAT'S WRONG WITH) DREAMING?		
	River City People	1990
WHAT'S YOUR NAME, WHAT'S YOUR NUMBER		
	Andrea True Connection	1978
WHAT'S YOUR FANTASY	Ludacris	2001
WHAT'S YOUR FLAVA?	Craig David	2002
WHAT'S YOUR NAME	Chicory Tip	1972
WHAT'S YOUR NAME	Lynyrd Skynyrd	1977
WHAT'S YOUR NAME?	Angel Lee	2000
WHAT'S YOUR PROBLEM	Blancmange	1985
WHAT'S YOUR SIGN	Des'ree	1998
(WHAT) IN THE NAME OF LOVE		
	Naked Eyes	1984
WHATCHA GONE DO?	Link	1998
WHATCHA GONNA DO	Pablo Cruise	1977
WHATCHA GONNA DO ABOUT IT		
	Doris Troy	1964
WHATCHA GONNA DO NOW?		
	Chris Andrews	1966

SONG TITLE	ARTIST	DATE
WHATCHA GONNA DO WITH MY LOVIN'		
	Inner City	1989
WHATCHA SEE IS WHATCHA GET		
	Dramatics	1971
WHATCHULOOKINAT	Whitney Houston	2002
WHATEVER	Oasis	1994
WHATEVER	Ideal Us featuring Lil' Mo	2000
WHATEVER	En Vogue	1997
WHATEVER GETS YOU THRU THE NIGHT		
	John Lennon With The Plastic Ono Nuclear Band	1974
WHATEVER GETS YOU THRU' THE NIGHT		
	John Lennon	1974
WHATEVER HAPPENED TO COREY HAIM?		
	Thrills	2004
WHATEVER HAPPENED TO YOU ('LIKELY LADS' THEME)		
	Highly Likely	1973
WHATEVER I DO (WHEREVER I GO)		
	Hazell Dean	1984
WHATEVER U WANT	Christina Milian featuring Joe Budden	2004
WHATEVER YOU GOT, I WANT		
	Jackson 5	1974
WHATEVER YOU NEED	Tina	2000
WHATEVER YOU SAY	Martina McBride	1999
WHATEVER YOU WANT	Tina Turner	1996

SONG TITLE	ARTIST	DATE
WHATEVER YOU WANT	Status Quo	1979
WHATS HAPPNIN!	Ying Yang Twins featuring Trick Daddy	2004
WHATTA MAN	Salt 'N 'Pepa	1994
WHAZZUP	True Party	2000
WHEEL OF FORTUNE	Ace Of Base	1993
THE WHEEL OF HURT	Margaret Whiting	1966
WHEELS OF STEEL	Saxon	1980
THE WHEELS ON THE BUS		
	Mad Donna	2002
WHEN	Showaddywaddy	1977
WHEN	Shania Twain	1998
WHEN A CHILD IS BORN (SOLEADO)		
	Johnny Mathis	1976
WHEN A HEART BEATS	Nik Kershaw	1985
WHEN A MAN LOVES A WOMAN		
	Jody Watley	1994
WHEN A MAN LOVES A WOMAN		
	Michael Bolton	1991
WHEN A MAN LOVES A WOMAN		
	Percy Sledge	1966
WHEN A MAN LOVES A WOMAN		
	Bette Midler	1980
WHEN A WOMAN	Gabrielle	2000
WHEN A WOMAN'S FED UP		
	R. Kelly	1998

SONG TITLE	ARTIST	DATE
WHEN ALL IS SAID AND DONE		
	ABBA	1982
WHEN AM I GONNA MAKE A LIVING		
	Sade	1984
WHEN CAN I SEE YOU	Babyface	1994
WHEN CHILDREN RULE THE WORLD		
	Red Hill Children	1996
WHEN DO I GET TO SING 'MY WAY'		
	Sparks	1995
WHEN DOVES CRY	Prince & The Revolution	1984
WHEN DOVES CRY	Ginuwine	1997
WHEN FOREVER HAS GONE		
	Demis Roussos	1976
WHEN HE SHINES	Sheena Easton	1982
WHEN I ARGUE I SEE SHAPES		
	Idlewild	1999
WHEN I CALL YOUR NAME	Mary Kiani	1995
WHEN I CLOSE MY EYES	Shanice	1999
WHEN I COME AROUND	Green Day	1995
WHEN I COME HOME	Spencer Davis Group	1966
WHEN I DIE	Motherlode	1969
WHEN I FALL IN LOVE	Nat 'King' Cole	1957
WHEN I FALL IN LOVE	Donny Osmond	1973
WHEN I FALL IN LOVE	Ant & Dec	1996
WHEN I FALL IN LOVE	Celine Dion & Clive Griffin	1993

SONG TITLE	ARTIST	DATE
WHEN I FALL IN LOVE/MY ARMS KEEP MISSING YOU		
	Rick Astley	1987
WHEN I GET HOME	Searchers	1965
WHEN I GROW UP	Garbage	1999
WHEN I GROW UP (TO BE A MAN)		
	Beach Boys	1964
WHEN I LOOK INTO YOUR EYES		
	Firehouse	1992
WHEN I LOOKED AT HIM	Expose	1989
WHEN I LOST YOU	Sarah Whatmore	2002
WHEN I NEED YOU	Leo Sayer	1977
WHEN I NEED YOU	Will Mellor	1998
WHEN I SAID GOODBYE/SUMMER OF LOVE		
	Steps	2000
WHEN I SAID I DO	Clint Black	1999
WHEN I SEE YOU	Macy Gray	2003
WHEN I SEE YOU SMILE	Bad English	1989
WHEN I THINK ABOUT ANGELS		
	Jamie O'Neal	2001
WHEN I THINK OF YOU	Kenny Thomas	1995
WHEN I THINK OF YOU	Janet Jackson	1986
WHEN I WANTED YOU	Barry Manilow	1979
WHEN I WAS YOUNG	Eric Burdon & The Animals	1967
WHEN I'M BACK ON MY FEET AGAIN		
	Michael Bolton	1990

SONG TITLE	ARTIST	DATE
WHEN I'M CLEANING WINDOWS (TURNED OUT NICE AGAIN)	2 In A Tent	1994
WHEN I'M DEAD AND GONE	McGuinness Flint	1970
WHEN I'M GONE	Brenda Holloway	1965
WHEN I'M GOOD AND READY	Sybil	1993
WHEN I'M WITH YOU	Sheriff	1988
WHEN IT'S LOVE	Van Halen	1988
WHEN IT'S OVER	Sugar Ray	2001
WHEN IT'S OVER	Loverboy	1982
WHEN JULIE COMES AROUND	Cuff Links	1970
WHEN LIKING TURNS TO LOVING	Ronnie Dove	1966
WHEN LOVE & HATE COLLIDE	Def Leppard	1995
WHEN LOVE BREAKS DOWN	Prefab Sprout	1985
WHEN LOVE COMES AROUND	Ken Dodd	1971
WHEN LOVE COMES TO TOWN	U2 With B.B. King	1989
WHEN MY BABY	Scooch	1999
WHEN SHE CRIES	Restless Heart	1992

SONG TITLE	ARTIST	DATE
(WHEN SHE NEEDS GOOD LOVIN') SHE COMES TO ME	Chicago Loop	1966
WHEN SHE WAS MY GIRL	Four Tops	1981
WHEN SMOKEY SINGS	ABC	1987
WHEN THE CHILDREN CRY	White Lion	1988
WHEN THE FINGERS POINT	Christians	1987
WHEN THE GOING GETS TOUGH	Boyzone	1999
WHEN THE GOING GETS TOUGH, THE TOUGH GET GOING	Billy Ocean	1985
WHEN THE HEART RULES THE MIND	GTR	1986
WHEN THE HEARTACHE IS OVER	Tina	1999
WHEN THE LAST TIME	Clipse	2002
WHEN THE LIGHTS GO OUT	5ive	1998
WHEN THE LIGHTS GO OUT	Naked Eyes	1983
WHEN THE NIGHT COMES	Joe Cocker	1989
WHEN THE RIVER ROLLS OVER YOU	Stands	2003
WHEN THE SH.. GOES DOWN	Cypress Hill	1993

SONG TITLE	ARTIST	DATE
WHEN THE SUMMERTIME IS OVER	Jackie Trent	1965
WHEN THE SUN COMES SHINING THRU	Long John Baldry	1968
WHEN THE SUN GOES DOWN	Kenny Chesney & Uncle Kracker	2004
WHEN THE TIGERS BROKE FREE	Pink Floyd	1982
WHEN THE WORLD IS RUNNING DOWN	Different Gear vs The Police	2000
WHEN TOMORROW COMES	Eurythmics	1986
WHEN TWO WORLDS COLLIDE	Jim Reeves	1969
WHEN TWO WORLDS DRIFT APART	Cliff Richard	1977
WHEN WE ARE TOGETHER	Texas	1999
WHEN WE DANCE	Sting	1994
WHEN WE KISS	Bardeux	1988
WHEN WE WAS FAB	George Harrison	1988
WHEN WE WERE YOUNG	Solomon King	1968
WHEN WE WERE YOUNG	Bucks Fizz	1983
WHEN WILL I BE FAMOUS?	Bros	1987
WHEN WILL I BE LOVED	Linda Ronstadt	1975
WHEN WILL I SEE YOU AGAIN	Three Degrees	1974
WHEN WILL THE GOOD APPLES FALL	Seekers	1967
WHEN WILL YOU MAKE MY TELEPHONE RING	Deacon Blue	1988
WHEN WILL YOU SAY I LOVE YOU	Billy Fury	1963
WHEN YOU ARE A KING	White Plains	1971
WHEN YOU ASK ABOUT LOVE	Matchbox	1980
WHEN YOU BELIEVE	Mariah Carey & Whitney Houston	1998
WHEN YOU CLOSE YOUR EYES	Night Ranger	1984
WHEN YOU COME BACK TO ME	Jason Donovan	1989
WHEN YOU GET RIGHT DOWN TO IT	Ronnie Dyson	1971
WHEN YOU GONNA LEARN?	Jamiroquai	1993
WHEN YOU KISS ME/UP!	Shania Twain	2003
WHEN YOU LOOK AT ME	Christina Milian	2002
WHEN YOU LOVE A WOMAN	Journey	1996
WHEN YOU SAY LOVE	Sonny & Cher	1972
WHEN YOU SAY NOTHING AT ALL	Ronan Keating	1999

SONG TITLE	ARTIST	DATE
(WHEN YOU SAY YOU LOVE SOMEBODY) IN THE HEART	Kool & The Gang	1984
WHEN YOU TELL ME THAT YOU LOVE ME	Diana Ross	1991
WHEN YOU WALK IN THE ROOM	Status Quo	1995
WHEN YOU WALK IN THE ROOM	Child	1978
WHEN YOU WALK IN THE ROOM	Searchers	1964
WHEN YOU WALK IN THE ROOM	Agnetha Faltskog	2004
WHEN YOU WERE SWEET SIXTEEN	Fureys & Davie Arthur	1981
WHEN YOU WERE YOUNG	Del Amitri	1993
WHEN YOU'RE GONE	Bryan Adams featuring Melanie C	1998
WHEN YOU'RE HOT, YOU'RE HOT	Jerry Reed	1971
WHEN YOU'RE IN LOVE WITH A BEAUTIFUL WOMAN	Dr. Hook	1979
WHEN YOU'RE YOUNG	Jam	1979
WHEN YOU'RE YOUNG AND IN LOVE	Flying Pickets	1984
WHEN YOU'RE YOUNG AND IN LOVE	Marvelettes	1976

SONG TITLE	ARTIST	DATE
WHEN YOUR HEART IS WEAK	Cock Robin	1985
WHENEVER GOD SHINES HIS LIGHT	Van Morrison With Cliff Richard	1989
WHENEVER HE HOLDS YOU	Bobby Goldsboro	1964
WHENEVER I CALL YOU 'FRIEND'	Kenny Loggins	1978
WHENEVER I'M AWAY FROM YOU	John Travolta	1976
WHENEVER YOU NEED ME	T'Pau	1991
WHENEVER YOU NEED SOMEBODY	Rick Astley	1987
WHENEVER YOU NEED SOMEONE	Bad Boys Inc	1993
WHENEVER YOU WANT MY LOVE	Real Thing	1978
WHENEVER YOU'RE READY	Five Star	1987
WHENEVER, WHEREVER	Shakira	2001
WHERE ARE THEY NOW?	Gene	1997
WHERE ARE YOU	Kavana	1996
WHERE ARE YOU	Imaani	1998
WHERE ARE YOU BABY?	Betty Boo	1990
WHERE ARE YOU GOING	Dave Matthews Band	2002
WHERE ARE YOU GOING TO MY LOVE	Brotherhood Of Man	1970

SONG TITLE	ARTIST	DATE
WHERE ARE YOU NOW	Jimmy Harnen With Sync	1989
WHERE ARE YOU NOW (MY LOVE)	Jackie Trent	1965
WHERE CAN I FIND LOVE	Livin' Joy	1997
WHERE DID ALL THE GOOD TIMES GO	Donny Osmond	1974
WHERE DID I GO WRONG	UB40	1988
WHERE DID OUR LOVE GO	Donnie Elbert	1971
WHERE DID OUR LOVE GO	Supremes	1964
WHERE DID OUR LOVE GO/JE VOULAIS (TE DIRE QUE JE T'ATTENDS)	Manhattan Transfer	1978
WHERE DID THEY GO, LORD	Elvis Presley	1971
WHERE DO BROKEN HEARTS GO	Whitney Houston	1988
(WHERE DO I BEGIN) LOVE STORY	Andy Williams	1971
WHERE DO I STAND?	Montrose Avenue	1998
WHERE DO THE CHILDREN GO	Hooters	1986
WHERE DO YOU GO	No Mercy	1996
WHERE DO YOU GO	Cher	1965
WHERE DO YOU GO TO (MY LOVELY)	Peter Sarstedt	1969
WHERE DOES MY HEART BEAT NOW	Celine Dion	1990

SONG TITLE	ARTIST	DATE
WHERE HAS ALL THE LOVE GONE	Yazz	1989
WHERE HAVE ALL THE COWBOYS GONE?	Paula Cole	1997
WHERE HAVE ALL THE FLOWERS GONE	Johnny Rivers	1965
WHERE HAVE YOU BEEN TONIGHT?	Shed Seven	1995
WHERE I COME FROM	Alan Jackson	2001
WHERE I FIND MY HEAVEN	Gigolo Aunts	1995
WHERE I WANNA BE	Shade Sheist featuring Nate Dogg & Kurupt	2001
WHERE I WANNA BE	Donell Jones	2000
WHERE I'M HEADED	Lene Marlin	2001
WHERE IS MY MAN	Eartha Kitt	1983
WHERE IS THE FEELING?	Kylie Minogue	1995
WHERE IS THE LOVE	Roberta Flack & Donny Hathaway	1972
WHERE IS THE LOVE	Mica Paris & Will Downing	1989
WHERE IS THE LOVE	Betty Wright	1975
WHERE IS THE LOVE?	Black Eyed Peas	2003
WHERE IS THE LOVE (WE USED TO KNOW)	Delegation	1977
WHERE IS TOMORROW?	Cilla Black	1968
WHERE IT'S AT	Beck	1996

SONG TITLE	ARTIST	DATE
WHERE LOVE LIVES (COME ON IN)		
	Alison Limerick	1991
WHERE MY GIRLS AT?	702	1999
WHERE THE BLACKTOP ENDS		
	Keith Urban	2001
WHERE THE HEART IS	Soft Cell	1982
WHERE THE HOOD AT?	DMX	2003
WHERE THE PARTY AT?	Jagged Edge featuring Nelly	2001
WHERE THE POOR BOYS DANCE		
	Lulu	2000
WHERE THE ROSE IS SOWN		
	Big Country	1984
WHERE THE STARS AND STRIPES AND THE EAGLE FLY		
	Aaron Tippin	2001
WHERE THE STREETS HAVE NO NAME		
	U2	1987
WHERE THE STREETS HAVE NO NAME/CAN'T TAKE MY EYES OFF YOU	Pet Shop Boys	1991
WHERE THE WILD ROSES GROW		
	Nick Cave & Kylie Minogue	1995
WHERE WERE YOU (WHEN THE WORLD STOPPED TURNING)	Alan Jackson	2001
WHERE WERE YOU HIDING WHEN THE STORM BROKE?		
	Alarm	1984
WHERE WERE YOU WHEN I NEEDED YOU		
	Grass Roots	1966

SONG TITLE	ARTIST	DATE
WHERE WERE YOU WHEN I WAS FALLING IN LOVE?		
	Lobo	1979
WHERE WILL THE WORDS COME FROM		
	Gary Lewis & The Playboys	1966
WHERE WILL YOU BE	Sue Nicholls	1968
WHERE YOU GOIN' NOW	Damn Yankees	1992
WHERE YOU LEAD	Barbra Streisand	1971
WHERE'S MY..?	Adam F featuring Lil' Mo	2002
WHERE'S THE LOVE	Hanson	1997
WHERE'S THE PLAYGROUND SUSIE?		
	Glen Campbell	1969
WHERE'S YOUR HEAD AT?	Basement Jaxx	2001
WHEREVER I LAY MY HAT (THAT'S MY HOME)		
	Paul Young	1983
WHEREVER I MAY ROAM	Metallica	1992
WHEREVER YOU ARE	Neil Finn	2001
WHEREVER YOU GO	Voices Of Theory	1998
WHEREVER YOU WILL GO	Calling	2001
WHICH WAY SHOULD I JUMP?		
	Milltown Brothers	1991
WHICH WAY YOU GOIN' BILLY?		
	Poppy Family	1970
WHIGGLE IN LINE	Black Duck	1994
WHILE YOU SEE A CHANCE		
	Steve Winwood	1981
WHINE AND GRINE	Prince Buster	1998

SONG TITLE	ARTIST	DATE
WHIP APPEAL	Babyface	1990
WHIP IT	Devo	1980
WHIPPIN' PICCADILLY	Gomez	1998
WHIRLY GIRL	Oxo	1983
WHISKEY GIRL	Toby Keith	2004
WHISKEY IN THE JAR	Metallica	1999
WHISKY IN THE JAR	Thin Lizzy	1973
THE WHISPER	Selecter	1980
WHISPER TO A SCREAM (BIRDS FLY)		
	Icicle Works	1984
WHISPERING	Bachelors	1963
WHISPERING	Nino Tempo & April Stevens	1963
WHISPERING GRASS	Windsor Davies & Don Estelle	1975
WHISPERING YOUR NAME	Alison Moyet	1994
WHISPERING/CHERCHEZ LA FEMME/SE SI BON		
	Dr. Buzzard's Original 'Savannah' Band	1976
WHISPERS	Ian Brown	2002
WHISPERS (GETTIN' LOUDER)		
	Jackie Wilson	1966
WHISTLE DOWN THE WIND		
	Tina Arena	1998
WHISTLE DOWN THE WIND		
	Nick Heyward	1983
THE WHISTLE SONG (BLOW MY WHISTLE BITCH)		
	DJ Aligator Project	2002

SONG TITLE	ARTIST	DATE
THE WHISTLE SONG	Frankie Knuckles	1991
WHITE BOY WITH A FEATHER		
	Jason Downs featuring Milk	2001
WHITE BOYS AND HEROES	Gary Numan	1982
WHITE CHRISTMAS	Bing Crosby	1977
WHITE CHRISTMAS	Keith Harris & Orville	1985
THE WHITE CLIFFS OF DOVER		
	Righteous Brothers	1966
WHITE FLAG	Dido	2003
WHITE HORSE	Laid Back	1984
WHITE HORSES	Jacky	1968
THE WHITE KNIGHT	Cledus Maggard & The Citizen's Band	1975
WHITE LIES, BLUE EYES	Bullet	1971
WHITE LINES	Grandmaster Flash, Melle Mel & The Furious Five	1983
WHITE LINES (DON'T DO IT)		
	Duran Duran	1995
(WHITE MAN) AT HAMMERSMITH PALAIS		
	Clash	1978
WHITE ON WHITE	Danny Williams	1964
WHITE PUNKS ON DOPE	Tubes	1977
WHITE RABBIT	Jefferson Airplane	1967
WHITE RIOT	Clash	1977
WHITE ROOM	Cream	1968
WHITE SKIES	Sunscreem	1996

SONG TITLE	ARTIST	DATE
WHITE WEDDING	Billy Idol	1983
WHITE WEDDING	Murderdolls	2003
A WHITER SHADE OF PALE	Procol Harum	1967
A WHITER SHADE OF PALE	Annie Lennox	1995
WHO AM I	Beenie Man	1998
WHO AM I	Petula Clark	1966
WHO ARE YOU	Who	1978
WHO CAN I TURN TO	Tony Bennett	1964
WHO CAN IT BE NOW?	Men At Work	1982
WHO?	Ed Case & Sweetie Irie	2001
WHO CAN I RUN TO	Xscape	1995
WHO CAN MAKE ME FEEL GOOD?	Bassheads	1992
WHO COMES TO BOOGIE	Little Benny & The Masters	1985
WHO DAT	JT Money featuring Sole	1999
WHO DO U LOVE	Deborah Cox	1996
WHO DO YOU GIVE YOUR LOVE TO	Michael Morales	1989
WHO DO YOU LOVE	Juicy Lucy	1970
WHO DO YOU LOVE	Sapphires	1964
WHO DO YOU LOVE NOW? (STRINGER)	Riva featuring Dannii Minogue	2001
WHO DO YOU THINK YOU ARE	Bo Donaldson & The Heywoods	1974

SONG TITLE	ARTIST	DATE
WHO DO YOU THINK YOU ARE?	Candlewick Green	1974
WHO DO YOU THINK YOU'RE FOOLIN'	Donna Summer	1981
WHO FEELS LOVE?	Oasis	2000
WHO FOUND WHO	Jellybean featuring Elisa Fiorillo	1987
WHO GETS THE LOVE	Status Quo	1988
WHO I AM	Jessica Andrews	2001
WHO IS GONNA LOVE ME?	Dionne Warwick	1968
WHO IS IT	Michael Jackson	1993
WHO IS IT	Mantronix	1987
WHO IS IT	Bjork	2004
WHO LET IN THE RAIN	Cyndi Lauper	1994
WHO LET THE DOGS OUT	Baha Men	2000
WHO LOVES YOU	Four Seasons	1975
WHO MADE WHO	AC/DC	1986
WHO NEEDS ENEMIES?	Cooper Temple Clause	2002
WHO NEEDS LOVE (LIKE THAT)	Erasure	1992
WHO PAYS THE FERRYMAN?	Yannis Markopoulos	1977
WHO PAYS THE PIPER?	Gary Clail On-U Sound System featuring Bim Sherman	1992
WHO PUT THE BOMP (IN THE BOMP-A-BOMP-A-BOMP)	Showaddywaddy	1982

SONG TITLE	ARTIST	DATE
WHO PUT THE LIGHTS OUT	Dana	1971
WHO SAID (STUCK IN THE UK)	Planet Funk	2003
WHO THE HELL ARE YOU	Madison Avenue	2000
WHO TOLD YOU	Roni Size/Reprazent	2000
WHO WANTS THE WORLD	Stranglers	1980
WHO? WHERE? WHY?	Jesus Jones	1991
WHO WANTS TO BE THE DISCO KING	Wonder Stuff	1989
WHO WANTS TO LIVE FOREVER	Queen	1986
WHO WAS IT	Hurricane Smith	1972
WHO WE BE	DMX	2001
WHO WEARS THESE SHOES?	Elton John	1984
WHO WERE YOU WITH IN THE MOONLIGHT	Dollar	1979
WHO WILL ANSWER?	Ed Ames	1967
WHO WILL SAVE YOUR SOUL	Jewel	1996
WHO WILL YOU RUN TO	Heart	1987
WHO WOULDN'T WANT TO BE ME	Keith Urban	2003
WHO YOU ARE	Pearl Jam	1996
WHO'D SHE COO?	Ohio Players	1976

SONG TITLE	ARTIST	DATE
WHO'LL BE THE FOOL TONIGHT	Larsen-Feiten Band	1980
WHO'LL BE THE NEXT IN LINE	Kinks	1965
WHO'S CRYING NOW	Journey	1981
WHO'S DAVID	Busted	2004
WHO'S GONNA LOVE ME	Imperials	1977
WHO'S GONNA RIDE YOUR WILD HORSES	U2	1992
WHO'S GONNA ROCK YOU	Nolans	1980
WHO'S HOLDING DONNA NOW	DeBarge	1985
WHO'S IN THE HOUSE	Beatmasters featuring Merlin	1989
WHO'S IN THE STRAWBERRY PATCH WITH SALLY	Dawn featuring Tony Orlando	1974
WHO'S JOHNNY	El DeBarge	1986
WHO'S LEAVING WHO	Hazell Dean	1988
WHO'S LOVING MY BABY	Shola Ama	1997
WHO'S MAKING LOVE	Blues Brothers	1980
WHO'S MAKING LOVE	Johnnie Taylor	1968
WHO'S SORRY NOW	Marie Osmond	1975
WHO'S THAT GIRL	Eve	2001
WHO'S THAT GIRL	Madonna	1987
WHO'S THAT GIRL?	Eurythmics	1984
WHO'S THE DADDY	Lovebug	2003
WHO'S THE MACK!	Mark Morrison	1997

SONG TITLE	ARTIST	DATE
WHO'S YOUR BABY?	Archies	1970
WHO'S YOUR DADDY	Toby Keith	2002
WHO'S ZOOMIN' WHO	Aretha Franklin	1985
WHODUNIT	Tavares	1977
WHOLE AGAIN	Atomic Kitten	2001
WHOLE LOTTA LOVE	Led Zeppelin	1969
WHOLE LOTTA LOVE	C.C.S.	1970
WHOLE LOTTA LOVE	Goldbug	1996
WHOLE LOTTA ROSIE	AC/DC	1980
A WHOLE NEW WORLD (ALADDIN'S THEME)		
	Peabo Bryson & Regina Belle	1992
THE WHOLE OF THE MOON		
	Waterboys	1991
WHOLE WIDE WORLD	A'me Lorain	1990
THE WHOLE WORLD LOST ITS HEAD		
	Go-Go's	1995
THE WHOLE WORLD	Outkast featuring Killer Mike	2001
WHOOMP THERE IT IS	BM Dubs presents Mr Rumble featuring Brasstooth & Kee	2001
WHOOMP! (THERE IT IS)	Tag Team	1993
WHOOMPH! (THERE IT IS)	Clock	1995
WHOOPS NOW/WHAT'LL I DO		
	Janet Jackson	1995
WHOOT, THERE IT IS	95 South	1993
WHOSE LAW (IS IT ANYWAY?)		
	Guru Josh	1990

SONG TITLE	ARTIST	DATE
WHY	D. Mob featuring Cathy Dennis	1994
WHY	Carly Simon	1982
WHY	Annie Lennox	1992
WHY	3T featuring Michael Jackson	1996
WHY	Glamma Kid	1999
WHY	Mis-Teeq	2001
WHY?	Bronski Beat	1984
WHY?	Agent Sumo	2002
WHY/LONELY BOY	Donny Osmond	1972
WHY CAN'T I BE YOU	Cure	1987
WHY CAN'T I BE YOU?	Shed Seven	2003
WHY CAN'T I HAVE YOU	Cars	1985
WHY (MUST WE FALL IN LOVE)		
	Diana Ross & The Supremes & The Temptations	1970
WHY CAN'T I	Liz Phair	2003
WHY CAN'T I WAKE UP WITH YOU?		
	Take That	1993
WHY CAN'T THIS BE LOVE	Van Halen	1986
WHY CAN'T WE BE FRIENDS?		
	War	1975
WHY CAN'T WE BE LOVERS		
	Holland-Dozier featuring Lamont Dozier	1972
WHY CAN'T WE LIVE TOGETHER		
	Timmy Thomas	1972

SONG TITLE	ARTIST	DATE
WHY DID YOU DO IT	Stretch	1975
WHY CAN'T YOU FREE SOME TIME		
	Armand Van Helden	2001
WHY DIDN'T YOU CALL ME		
	Macy Gray	2000
WHY DO FOOLS FALL IN LOVE		
	Diana Ross	1981
WHY DO LOVERS BREAK EACH OTHER'S HEARTS?		
	Showaddywaddy	1980
WHY DOES IT ALWAYS RAIN ON ME?		
	Travis	1999
WHY DOES IT HURT SO BAD		
	Whitney Houston	1996
WHY DOES MY HEART FEEL SO BAD		
	Moby	1999
WHY DON'T WE FALL IN LOVE		
	Amerie featuring Ludacris	2002
WHY DON'T YOU GET A JOB?		
	Offspring	1999
WHY DON'T YOU TAKE ME?		
	One Dove	1994
WHY I LOVE YOU SO MUCH/AIN'T NOBODY		
	Monica	1996
WHY ME	Kris Kristofferson	1973
WHY ME	Styx	1979
WHY ME?	PJ And Duncan	1994

SONG TITLE	ARTIST	DATE
WHY ME?	Irene Cara	1983
WHY MUST WE WAIT UNTIL TONIGHT		
	Tina Turner	1993
WHY NOT ME	Fred Knoblock	1980
WHY NOT TONIGHT	Mojos	1964
WHY, OH WHY, OH WHY	Gilbert O'Sullivan	1973
WHY YOU TREAT ME SO BAD		
	Shaggy featuring Grand Puba	1996
WHY YOU TREAT ME SO BAD?		
	Club Nouveau	1987
WHY'D YOU LIE TO ME	Anastacia	2002
WICHITA LINEMAN	Glen Campbell	1968
WICKED GAME	Chris Isaak	1990
WICKED LOVE	Oceanic	1991
THE WICKER MAN	Iron Maiden	2000
WIDE BOY	Nik Kershaw	1985
WIDE EYED AND LEGLESS	Andy Fairweather-Low	1975
WIDE OPEN SPACE	Mansun	1996
WIFEY	Next	2000
WIG WAM BAM	Sweet	1972
WIGGLE IT	2 In A Room	1990
WIGGLY WORLD	Mr. Jack	1997
WIKKA WRAP	Evasions	1981
WILD AS ANGELS (EP)	Levellers	2003
WILD AS THE WIND	David Bowie	1981
WILD BOYS	Phixx	2004

SONG TITLE	ARTIST	DATE
THE WILD BOYS	Duran Duran	1984
WILD FLOWER	Cult	1987
WILD FRONTIER	Gary Moore	1987
WILD HEARTED SON	Cult	1991
WILD HEARTED WOMAN	All About Eve	1988
WILD HONEY	Beach Boys	1967
WILD HORSES	Rolling Stones	1971
WILD LOVE	Mungo Jerry	1973
WILD NIGHT	John Mellencamp featuring Me'shell Ndegeocello	1994
WILD NIGHT	Van Morrison	1971
WILD ONE	Martha & The Vandellas	1964
THE WILD ONE	Suzi Quatro	1974
THE WILD ONES	Suede	1994
WILD SIDE OF LIFE	Tommy Quickly & The Remo Four	1964
WILD SIDE OF LIFE	Status Quo	1976
WILD SURF	Ash	1998
WILD THING	Troggs	1966
WILD THING	Fancy	1974
WILD THING	Senator Bobby	1967
WILD THING/LOC'ED AFTER DARK...	Tone Loc	1989
WILD WEST HERO	Electric Light Orchestra	1978
WILD WILD LIFE	Talking Heads	1986
WILD WILD WEST	Will Smith featuring Dru Hill	1999

SONG TITLE	ARTIST	DATE
WILD WILD WEST	Escape Club	1988
WILD WOMEN DO	Natalie Cole	1990
WILD WOOD	Paul Weller	1993
WILD WORLD	Jimmy Cliff	1970
WILD WORLD	Maxi Priest	1988
WILD WORLD	Mr. Big	1993
WILD WORLD	Cat Stevens	1971
WILDERNESS	Jurgen Vries featuring Shena	2003
WILDEST DREAMS	Iron Maiden	2003
WILDFIRE	Michael Murphey	1975
WILDFLOWER	Skylark	1973
WILDSIDE	Marky Mark & The Funky Bunch	1991
WILDWOOD WEED	Jim Stafford	1974
WILL 2K	Will Smith	1999
WILL I	Ian Van Dahl	2001
WILL I EVER	Alice Deejay	2000
WILL IT GO ROUND IN CIRCLES	Billy Preston	1973
WILL WE BE LOVERS	Deacon Blue	1993
WILL YOU	Hazel O'Connor	1981
WILL YOU BE STAYING AFTER SUNDAY	Peppermint Rainbow	1969
WILL YOU BE THERE	Michael Jackson	1993
WILL YOU BE THERE (IN THE MORNING)	Heart	1993

SONG TITLE	ARTIST	DATE
WILL YOU LOVE ME TOMORROW		
	Bryan Ferry	1993
WILL YOU LOVE ME TOMORROW		
	Melanie	1974
WILL YOU LOVE ME TOMORROW		
	Four Seasons	1968
WILL YOU MARRY ME?	Paula Abdul	1992
WILL YOU STILL LOVE ME?	Chicago	1986
WILL YOU STILL LOVE ME TOMORROW		
	Dave Mason	1978
WILL YOU WAIT FOR ME	Kavana	1999
WILLIAM IT WAS REALLY NOTHING		
	Smiths	1984
WILLIE AND THE HAND JIVE		
	Eric Clapton	1974
WILLING TO FORGIVE	Aretha Franklin	1994
WILLOW WEEP FOR ME	Chad & Jeremy	1964
WILMOT	Sabres Of Paradise	1994
WIMMIN'	Ashley Hamilton	2003
WIN PLACE OR SHOW (SHE'S A WINNER)		
	Intruders	1974
WINCHESTER CATHEDRAL	New Vaudeville Band	1966
THE WIND	PJ Harvey	1999
WIND BENEATH MY WINGS		
	Bill Tarmey	1994

SONG TITLE	ARTIST	DATE
WIND BENEATH MY WINGS		
	Bette Midler	1989
WIND BENEATH MY WINGS		
	Steven Houghton	1997
THE WIND CRIES MARY	Jimi Hendrix Experience	1967
WIND IT UP (REWOUND)	Prodigy	1993
WIND ME UP (LET ME GO)		
	Cliff Richard	1965
WIND OF CHANGE	Scorpions	1991
A WINDMILL IN OLD AMSTERDAM		
	Ronnie Hilton	1965
THE WINDMILLS OF YOUR MIND		
	Noel Harrison	1969
THE WINDMILLS OF YOUR MIND		
	Dusty Springfield	1969
WINDOW SHOPPING	R. Dean Taylor	1974
WINDOWLICKER	Aphex Twins	1999
THE WINDOWS OF THE WORLD		
	Dionne Warwick	1967
WINDPOWER	Thomas Dolby	1982
WINDS OF CHANGE	Jefferson Airplane	1983
WINDY	Association	1967
SWING LOW (RUN WITH THE BALL)		
	Union featuring England Rugby World Cup Squad	1991
WINGS OF A DOVE	Madness	1983

SONG TITLE	ARTIST	DATE
THE WINKER'S SONG (MISPRINT)		
	Ivor Biggun	1978
THE WINKLE MAN	Judge Dread	1976
THE WINNER TAKES IT ALL		
	ABBA	1980
WINNERS AND LOSERS	Hamilton, Joe Frank & Reynolds	1975
WINNING	Santana	1981
WINTER	Tori Amos	1992
WINTER IN JULY	Bomb The Bass	1991
WINTER MELODY	Donna Summer	1976
WINTER SONG	Chris Rea	1991
WINTER WORLD OF LOVE	Engelbert Humperdinck	1969
A WINTER'S TALE	David Essex	1982
A WINTER'S TALE	Queen	1995
WIPE OUT	Animal	1994
WIPE OUT	Surfaris	1966
WIPEOUT	Fat Boys & The Beach Boys	1987
WIRED FOR SOUND	Cliff Richard	1981
WISER TIME	Black Crowes	1995
WISH	Soul II Soul	1993
WISH I COULD FLY	Roxette	1999
WISH I DIDN'T MISS YOU	Angie Stone	2002
WISH I WERE YOU	Alisha's Attic	1999
WISH SOMEONE WOULD CARE		
	Irma Thomas	1964

SONG TITLE	ARTIST	DATE
WISH YOU DIDN'T HAVE TO GO		
	James & Bobby Purify	1967
WISH YOU WERE HERE	Wyclef Jean	2001
WISH YOU WERE HERE	Incubus	2002
WISH YOU WERE HERE	Mark Wills	1999
WISHES OF HAPPINESS & PROSPERITY (YEHA-NOHA)		
	Sacred Spirit	1995
WISHFUL THINKING	China Crisis	1984
WISHIN' AND HOPIN'	Merseybeats	1964
WISHIN' AND HOPIN'	Dusty Springfield	1964
WISHING	Buddy Holly	1963
WISHING (IF I HAD A PHOTOGRAPH OF YOU)		
	Flock Of Seagulls	1982
WISHING I WAS LUCKY	Wet Wet Wet	1987
WISHING I WAS THERE	Natalie Imbruglia	1998
WISHING ON A STAR	Cover Girls	1992
WISHING ON A STAR	Fresh 4	1989
WISHING ON A STAR	Rose Royce	1978
WISHING ON A STAR	Jay-Z featuring Gwen Dickey	1998
WISHING ON A STAR	Paul Weller	2004
WISHING WELL	Terence Trent D'Arby	1988
WISHING WELL	Free	1973
THE WISHING WELL	G.O.S.H.	1987
WISHING YOU WERE HERE		
	Chicago	1974
WISHLIST	Pearl Jam	1998

SONG TITLE	ARTIST	DATE
THE WITCH	Rattles	1970
WITCH DOCTOR	Cartoons	1999
THE WITCH QUEEN OF NEW ORLEANS	Redbone	1971
THE WITCH'S PROMISE/TEACHER	Jethro Tull	1970
WITCHY WOMAN	Eagles	1972
WITH A GIRL LIKE YOU	Troggs	1966
WITH A LITTLE HELP FROM MY FRIENDS	Joe Brown	1967
WITH A LITTLE HELP FROM MY FRIENDS	Joe Cocker	1968
WITH A LITTLE HELP FROM MY FRIENDS	Young Idea	1967
WITH A LITTLE HELP FROM MY FRIENDS/MEASURE OF A MAN	Sam & Mark	2004
WITH A LITTLE HELP FROM MY FRIENDS/SHE'S LEAVING HOME	Wet Wet Wet/Billy Bragg with Cara Tivey	1988
WITH A LITTLE LUCK	Paul McCartney	1978
WITH ARMS WIDE OPEN	Creed	2001
WITH EVERY BEAT OF MY HEART	Taylor Dayne	1989
WITH ME	Destiny's Child	1998
WITH MY OWN EYES	Sash!	2000
WITH ONE LOOK	Barbra Streisand	1993

SONG TITLE	ARTIST	DATE
WITH OR WITHOUT YOU	U2	1987
WITH PEN IN HAND	Vikki Carr	1969
WITH THE EYES OF A CHILD	Cliff Richard	1969
WITH THESE HANDS	Tom Jones	1965
WITH THIS RING	Platters	1967
WITH YOU	Jessica Simpson	2004
WITH YOU	Tony Terry	1991
WITH YOU I'M BORN AGAIN	Billy Preston & Syreeta	1979
WITH YOUR LOVE	Jefferson Starship	1976
WITHOUT HER	Herb Alpert & The Tijuana Brass	1969
WITHOUT LOVE	Donna Lewis	1997
WITHOUT LOVE	Dina Carroll	1999
WITHOUT LOVE (THERE IS NOTHING)	Tom Jones	1969
WITHOUT ME	Eminem	2002
WITHOUT YOU	Motley Crue	1990
WITHOUT YOU	Matt Monro	1965
WITHOUT YOU	Nilsson	1971
WITHOUT YOU	Dixie Chicks	2000
WITHOUT YOU (NOT ANOTHER LONELY NIGHT)	Franke & The Knockouts	1982
WITHOUT YOU/NEVER FORGET YOU	Mariah Carey	1994

SONG TITLE	ARTIST	DATE
WITHOUT YOUR LOVE	Roger Daltrey	1980
WITHOUT YOUR LOVE	Toto	1986
THE WIZARD	Paul Hardcastle	1986
WIZARDS OF THE SONIC	Westbam	1995
WIZZY WOW	Blackstreet	2003
WOBBLE WOBBLE	504 Boyz	2000
WOE IS ME	Helen Shapiro	1963
WOLD	Harry Chapin	1974
WOLF CREEK PASS	C.W. McCall	1975
WOMAN	Peter & Gordon	1966
WOMAN	Neneh Cherry	1996
WOMAN	John Lennon	1981
WOMAN IN CHAINS	Tears For Fears	1989
WOMAN IN LOVE	Barbra Streisand	1980
WOMAN IN LOVE	Three Degrees	1979
THE WOMAN IN ME	Donna Summer	1982
THE WOMAN IN YOU	Bee Gees	1983
A WOMAN NEEDS LOVE (JUST LIKE YOU DO)		
	Ray Parker Jr. & Raydio	1981
WOMAN TO WOMAN	Beverley Craven	1991
WOMAN TO WOMAN	Shirley Brown	1974
WOMAN TROUBLE	Artful Dodger & Robbie Craig	
	featuring Craig David	2000
WOMAN'S GOT SOUL	Impressions	1965
WOMAN, WOMAN	Union Gap featuring	
	Gary Puckett	1967

SONG TITLE	ARTIST	DATE
A WOMAN'S WORTH	Alicia Keys	2001
WOMANKIND	Little Angels	1993
WOMBLING MERRY CHRISTMAS		
	Wombles	1974
THE WOMBLING SONG (UNDERGROUND OVERGROUND)		
	Wombles	1998
WOMBLING WHITE TIE AND TAILS (FOX TROT)		
	Wombles	1975
WOMEN IN UNIFORM	Iron Maiden	1980
WOMEN'S LOVE RIGHTS	Laura Lee	1971
WON'T GET FOOLED AGAIN		
	Who	1971
WON'T GIVE IN	Finn Brothers	2004
WON'T LET THIS FEELING GO		
	Sundance	2000
WON'T SOMEBODY DANCE WITH ME		
	Lynsey De Paul	1973
WON'T TAKE IT LYING DOWN		
	Honeyz	2000
WON'T TALK ABOUT IT	Beats International	1990
WON'T TALK ABOUT IT/BLAME IT ON THE BASS		
	Norman Cook featuring Billy Bragg/MC Wildski	1989
WON'T YOU HOLD MY HAND NOW		
	King	1985
WONDER	Embrace	2001

SONG TITLE	ARTIST	DATE
WONDER	Natalie Merchant	1995
THE WONDER OF YOU/MAMA LIKED THE ROSES		
	Elvis Presley	1970
WONDERBOY	Kinks	1968
WONDERBOY	Tenacious D	2002
WONDERFUL	Runrig	1993
WONDERFUL	Adam Ant	1995
WONDERFUL	Everclear	2000
WONDERFUL	Brian Wilson	2004
WONDERFUL	Ja Rule featuring R. Kelly & Ashanti	2004
WONDERFUL CHRISTMASTIME		
	Paul McCartney	1979
WONDERFUL DREAM	Ann-Marie David	1973
WONDERFUL LIFE	Black	1987
WONDERFUL TONIGHT	Damage	1997
WONDERFUL TONIGHT	Eric Clapton	1978
WONDERFUL WORLD	Sam Cooke	1960
WONDERFUL WORLD	Herman's Hermits	1965
WONDERFUL WORLD, BEAUTIFUL PEOPLE		
	Jimmy Cliff	1969
WONDERING WHERE THE LIONS ARE		
	Bruce Cockburn	1980
WONDERING WHY	MJ Cole	2003
WONDERLAND	Paul Young	1986
WONDERLAND	Commodores	1979

SONG TITLE	ARTIST	DATE
WONDERLAND	Psychedelic Waltons featuring Roisin Murphy	2002
WONDERLAND	Big Country	1984
WONDERLAND	911	1999
WONDEROUS STORIES	Yes	1977
WONDERWALL	Oasis	1996
WONDERWALL	Mike Flowers Pops	1995
WONDERWALL	Ryan Adams	2004
WOO HOO	5.6.7.8.'s	2004
WOO-HAH!! GOT YOU ALL IN CHECK		
	Busta Rhymes	1996
WOOD BEEZ (PRAY LIKE ARETHA FRANKLIN)		
	Scritti Politti	1984
WOODSTOCK	Matthews' Southern Comfort	1970
WOODSTOCK	Crosby, Stills, Nash & Young	1972
WOOF WOOF	69 Boyz	1998
WOOLY BULLY	Sam The Sham & The Pharaohs	1965
WOPBABALUBOP	Funkdoobiest	1993
THE WORD GIRL (featuring RANKING ANN)		
	Scritti Politti	1985
A WORD IN SPANISH	Elton John	1988
THE WORD IS LOVE (SAY THE WORD)		
	Voices Of Life	1998
WORD IS OUT	Kylie Minogue	1991
WORD OF MOUTH	Mike & The Mechanics	1991
WORD UP	Cameo	1986

SONG TITLE	ARTIST	DATE
WORD UP	Gun	1994
WORD UP	Melanie G	1999
WORDS	Rita Coolidge	1978
WORDS	Bee Gees	1968
WORDS	Christians	1989
WORDS	F.R. David	1983
WORDS	Boyzone	1996
WORDS	Monkees	1967
WORDS ARE NOT ENOUGH/I KNOW HIM SO WELL	Steps	2001
WORDS GET IN THE WAY	Miami Sound Machine	1986
WORDS OF LOVE	Mamas & The Papas	1966
WORDY RAPPINGHOOD	Tom Tom Club	1981
WORK	Technotronic featuring Reggie	1991
WORK ALL DAY	Barry Biggs	1976
WORK IN PROGRESS	Alan Jackson	2002
WORK IT	Missy Elliott	2002
WORK IT	Nelly featuring Justin Timberlake	2003
WORK IT OUT	Shiva	1995
WORK IT OUT	Def Leppard	1996
WORK IT OUT	Beyonce	2002
WORK REST & PLAY (EP)	Madness	1980
THE WORK SONG	Herb Alpert & The Tijuana Brass	1966
WORK THAT BODY	Diana Ross	1982
WORKAHOLIC	2 Unlimited	1992

SONG TITLE	ARTIST	DATE
WORKIN' AT THE CAR WASH BLUES	Jim Croce	1974
WORKIN' ON A GROOVY THING	5th Dimension	1969
WORKIN' OVERTIME	Diana Ross	1989
WORKING FOR THE WEEKEND	Loverboy	1981
WORKING FOR THE YANKEE DOLLAR	Skids	1979
WORKING IN A GOLDMINE	Aztec Camera	1988
WORKING IN THE COAL MINE	Lee Dorsey	1966
WORKING MAN	Rita McNeil	1990
WORKING MY WAY BACK TO YOU	Four Seasons	1966
WORKING MY WAY BACK TO YOU/FORGIVE ME, GIRL	Spinners	1980
WORKING ON A BUILDING OF LOVE	Chairmen Of The Board	1972
WORLD	Bee Gees	1967
WORLD (PART 1)	James Brown	1969
WORLD (THE PRICE OF LOVE)	New Order	1993
WORLD CUP '98 – PAVANE	Wimbledon Choral Society	1998

SONG TITLE	ARTIST	DATE
WORLD FILLED WITH LOVE		
	Craig David	2003
THE WORLD I KNOW	Collective Soul	1995
WORLD IN MOTION	Englandneworder	1990
WORLD IN MY EYES	Depeche Mode	1990
WORLD IN OUR HANDS	Culture Beat	1994
WORLD IN UNION	Shirley Bassey/Bryn Terfel	1999
WORLD IN UNION	Kiri Te Kanawa	1991
THE WORLD IS A GHETTO	War	1972
THE WORLD IS FLAT	Echobelly	1997
THE WORLD IS NOT ENOUGH		
	Garbage	1999
THE WORLD IS STONE	Cyndi Lauper	1992
THE WORLD OF BROKEN HEARTS		
	Amen Corner	1967
WORLD OF GOOD	Saw Doctors	1996
WORLD OF OUR OWN	Westlife	2002
A WORLD OF OUR OWN	Seekers	1965
THE WORLD OF WATER	New Musik	1980
THE WORLD SHE KNOWS	Dmac	2002
THE WORLD TONIGHT	Paul McCartney	1997
THE WORLD WE KNEW (OVER AND OVER)		
	Frank Sinatra	1967
A WORLD WITHOUT LOVE	Peter & Gordon	1964
WORLD WITHOUT YOU	Belinda Carlisle	1988
THE WORLD'S GREATEST	R. Kelly	2001

SONG TITLE	ARTIST	DATE
WORRIED GUY	Johnny Tillotson	1964
WORST COMES TO WORST	Dilated Peoples	2002
WORST THAT COULD HAPPEN		
	Brooklyn Bridge	1968
WORZEL'S SONG	Jon Pertwee	1980
WOT DO U CALL IT?	Wiley	2004
WOT!	Captain Sensible	1982
WOT'S IT TO YA	Robbie Nevil	1987
WOULD I LIE TO YOU	Whitesnake	1981
WOULD I LIE TO YOU?	Charles & Eddie	1992
WOULD I LIE TO YOU?	Eurythmics	1985
WOULD YOU BE HAPPIER?	Corrs	2001
WOULD YOU...?	Touch & Go	1998
WOULD?	Alice In Chains	1993
WOULDN'T CHANGE A THING		
	Kylie Minogue	1989
WOULDN'T IT BE GOOD	Nik Kershaw	1984
WOULDN'T IT BE NICE	Beach Boys	1966
WOW	Kate Bush	1979
WRACK MY BRAIN	Ringo Starr	1981
WRAP HER UP	Elton John	1985
WRAP ME UP	Alex Party	1995
WRAPPED AROUND	Brad Paisley	2001
WRAPPED AROUND YOUR FINGER		
	Police	1984
WRAPPING PAPER	Cream	1966

SONG TITLE	ARTIST	DATE
THE WRECK OF THE 'ANTOINETTE'		
	Dave Dee, Dozy, Beaky, Mick & Tich	1968
THE WRECK OF THE EDMUND FITZGERALD		
	Gordon Lightfoot	1976
THE WRECKONING	Boomkat	2003
WRECKX SHOP	Wreckx-N-Effect	1994
WRENCH	Almighty	1994
WRESTLEMANIA	WWF Superstars	1993
WRITE THIS DOWN	George Strait	1999
WRITING TO REACH YOU	Travis	1999
WRITTEN ALL OVER YOUR FACE		
	Rude Boys	1991
WRITTEN IN THE STARS	Elton John & Leann Rimes	1999
WRONG	Everything But The Girl	1996
WRONG AGAIN	Martina McBride	1998
WRONG FOR EACH OTHER	Andy Williams	1964
WRONG IMPRESSION	Natalie Imbruglia	2002
WUNDERBAR	Ten Pole Tudor	1981
WUTHERING HEIGHTS	Kate Bush	1978
X	Xzibit featuring Snoop Dogg	2001
THE X FILES	Mark Snow	1996
X GON' GIVE IT TO YA	DMX	2003
X, Y + ZEE	Pop Will Eat Itself	1991
X-FILES	DJ Dado	1996

SONG TITLE	ARTIST	DATE
XANADU	Olivia Newton-John & Electric Light Orchestra	1980
Y VIVA ESPANA	Sylvia	1974
Y VIVA SUSPENDERS	Judge Dread	1976
Y.M.C.A.	Village People	1978
YA DON'T SEE THE SIGNS	Mark B & Blade	2001
YA MAMA/SONG FOR SHELTER		
	Fatboy Slim	2001
YAAH/TECHNO TRANCE	D-Shake	1990
YABBA DABBA DOO	Darkman	1994
YAH MO B THERE	James Ingram & Michael McDonald	1983
YANKEE ROSE	David Lee Roth	1986
YEAH!	Usher featuring Lil' Jon & Ludacris	2004
YEAH! BUDDY	Royal House	1989
YEAH, YEAH, YEAH	Judson Spence	1988
YEAR 3000	Busted	2003
YEAR OF DECISION	Three Degrees	1974
YEAR OF THE CAT	Al Stewart	1976
YEAR OF THE RAT	Badly Drawn Boy	2004
YEARS	Wayne Newton	1980
YEARS MAY COME, YEARS MAY GO		
	Herman's Hermits	1970
YEH YEH	Matt Bianco	1985
YEH, YEH	Georgie Fame	1965

SONG TITLE	ARTIST	DATE
YEKE YEKE	Mory Kante	1988
YEKE YEKE – '96 REMIXES	Mory Kante	1996
YELLOW	Coldplay	2000
YELLOW BALLOON	Yellow Balloon	1967
YELLOW PEARL	Philip Lynott	1981
YELLOW RIVER	Christie	1970
YELLOW SUBMARINE	Beatles	1966
YEOVIL TRUE	Yeovil Town FC	2004
YER OLD	Reef	1997
YES	McAlmont & Butler	1995
YES!	Chad Brock	2000
YES I WILL	Hollies	1965
YES, I'M READY	Teri DeSario With K.C.	1979
YES, I'M READY	Barbara Mason	1965
YES SIR, I CAN BOOGIE	Baccara	1977
YES TONIGHT JOSEPHINE	Jets	1981
YES WE CAN CAN	Pointer Sisters	1973
YESTER LOVE	Smokey Robinson & The Miracles	1968
YESTER-ME, YESTER-YOU, YESTERDAY	Stevie Wonder	1969
YESTERDAY	Marianne Faithfull	1965
YESTERDAY	Beatles	1965
YESTERDAY	Matt Monro	1965
YESTERDAY	Wet Wet Wet	1997
YESTERDAY	Ray Charles	1967

SONG TITLE	ARTIST	DATE
YESTERDAY HAS GONE	Cupid's Inspiration	1968
YESTERDAY MAN	Chris Andrews	1965
YESTERDAY ONCE MORE	Carpenters	1973
YESTERDAY WENT TOO SOON	Feeder	1999
YESTERDAY'S DREAMS	Four Tops	1968
YESTERDAY'S GONE	Chad Stuart & Jeremy Clyde	1963
YESTERDAY'S MEN	Madness	1985
YESTERDAY'S SONGS	Neil Diamond	1981
YESTERDAY, WHEN I WAS MAD	Pet Shop Boys	1994
YESTERDAY, WHEN I WAS YOUNG	Roy Clark	1969
YESTERDAYS	Guns N' Roses	1992
YIM	Jez & Choopie	1998
YING TONG SONG	Goons	1973
YIPPIE-I-OH	Barndance Boys	2003
YO!!! SWEETNESS	M.C. Hammer	1991
YO-YO	Osmonds	1971
YOSHIMI BATTLES THE PINK ROBOTS (PT 1)	Flaming Lips	2003
YOU	Bonnie Raitt	1994
YOU	Johnny Johnson & The Bandwagon	1969
YOU	Ten Sharp	1992
YOU	Point Break	2000

SONG TITLE	ARTIST	DATE
YOU	George Harrison	1975
YOU	S Club 7	2002
YOU	Rita Coolidge	1978
YOU	Marvin Gaye	1968
YOU	Monifah	1996
YOU	Jesse Powell	1999
YOU & ME SONG	Wannadies	1996
YOU AIN'T LIVIN' TILL YOU'RE LOVIN'		
	Marvin Gaye & Tammi Terrell	1969
YOU AIN'T SEEN NOTHIN' YET		
	Bus Stop featuring	
	Randy Bachman	1998
YOU AIN'T SEEN NOTHIN' YET		
	Bachman-Turner Overdrive	1974
YOU ALL DAT	Baha Men	2001
YOU AND I	Rick James	1978
YOU AND I	Eddie Rabbitt with Crystal Gayle	1982
YOU AND I WILL NEVER SEE THINGS EYE TO EYE		
	Kingmaker	1995
YOU AND ME	Lisa B	1994
YOU AND ME	Alice Cooper	1977
YOU AND ME AGAINST THE WORLD		
	Helen Reddy	1974
YOU AND ME TONIGHT	Aurra	1986
YOU AND ME (TONIGHT)	Alistair Griffin	2004
YOU ARE	Lionel Richie	1983

SONG TITLE	ARTIST	DATE
YOU ARE ALIVE	Fragma	2001
YOU ARE EVERYTHING	Melanie Williams & Joe Roberts	1995
YOU ARE EVERYTHING	Diana Ross And Marvin Gaye	1974
YOU ARE EVERYTHING	Stylistics	1971
YOU ARE MY LADY	Freddie Jackson	1985
YOU ARE MY LOVE	Liverpool Express	1976
YOU ARE MY STARSHIP	Norman Connors	1976
YOU ARE MY WORLD	Communards	1985
YOU ARE NOT ALONE	Michael Jackson	1995
YOU ARE SO BEAUTIFUL	Joe Cocker	1975
YOU ARE THE GIRL	Cars	1987
YOU ARE THE ONE	A-Ha	1988
YOU ARE THE SUNSHINE OF MY LIFE		
	Stevie Wonder	1973
YOU ARE THE UNIVERSE	Brand New Heavies	1997
YOU ARE THE WOMAN	Firefall	1976
YOU BABY	Turtles	1966
YOU BE ILLIN'	Run DMC	1986
YOU BELONG IN ROCK N' ROLL		
	Tin Machine	1991
YOU BELONG TO ME	JX	1995
YOU BELONG TO ME	Gary Glitter	1976
YOU BELONG TO ME	Carly Simon	1978
YOU BELONG TO THE CITY		
	Glenn Frey	1985
YOU BET YOUR LOVE	Herbie Hancock	1979

SONG TITLE	ARTIST	DATE
YOU BETTER RUN	Young Rascals	1966
YOU BETTER SIT DOWN KIDS	Cher	1967
YOU BETTER WAIT	Steve Perry	1994
YOU BETTER YOU BET	Who	1981
YOU BLOW ME AWAY	Robert Palmer	1994
YOU BRING ME UP	K-Ci & Jojo	1997
YOU BRING ON THE SUN	Londonbeat	1992
YOU CAME	Kim Wilde	1988
YOU CAME, YOU SAW, YOU CONQUERED	Pearls	1972
YOU CAN CALL ME AL	Paul Simon	1986
YOU CAN DO IT	Al Hudson & The Soul Partners	1979
YOU CAN DO IT	Dobie Gray	1978
YOU CAN DO IT	Ice Cube featuring Mack 10 & Ms. Toi	1999
YOU CAN DO MAGIC	Limmie & The Family Cookin'	1973
YOU CAN DO MAGIC	America	1982
YOU CAN GET IT	Maxx	1994
YOU CAN GET IT IF YOU REALLY WANT	Desmond Dekker	1970
YOU CAN GO YOUR OWN WAY	Chris Rea	1994
YOU CAN HAVE HER	Sam Neely	1974
YOU CAN HAVE HIM	Dionne Warwick	1965
YOU CAN HAVE IT ALL	George McCrae	1974

SONG TITLE	ARTIST	DATE
YOU CAN MAKE ME DANCE SING OR ANYTHING	Rod Stewart & The Faces	1974
YOU CAN NEVER STOP ME LOVING YOU	Kenny Lynch	1963
YOU CAN TALK TO ME	Seahorses	1997
YOU CAN'T CHANGE ME	Roger Sanchez featuring Armand Van Helden	2001
YOU CAN'T CHANGE THAT	Raydio	1979
YOU CAN'T DENY IT	Lisa Stansfield	1990
YOU CAN'T GET WHAT YOU WANT (TILL YOU KNOW WHAT YOU WANT)	Joe Jackson	1984
YOU CAN'T GO HOME AGAIN	DJ Shadow	2002
YOU CAN'T HIDE (YOUR LOVE FROM ME)	David Joseph	1983
YOU CAN'T HIDE BEAUTIFUL	Aaron Lines	2002
YOU CAN'T HURRY LOVE	Phil Collins	1982
YOU CAN'T HURRY LOVE	Supremes	1966
YOU CAN'T PLAY WITH MY YO-YO	Yo-Yo featuring Ice Cube	1991
YOU CAN'T ROLLER SKATE IN A BUFFALO HERD	Roger Miller	1966
YOU CAN'T SIT DOWN	Phil Upchurch Combo	1966
YOU CAN'T STOP THE REIGN	Shaquille O'Neal	1997

SONG TITLE	ARTIST	DATE
YOU CAN'T TAKE THE HONKY TONK OUT OF THE GIRL		
	Brooks & Dunn	2003
YOU CAN'T TURN ME OFF (IN THE MIDDLE OF TURNING		
ME ON)	High Inergy	1977
YOU CAUGHT MY EYE	Judy Boucher	1987
YOU COULD BE MINE	Guns N' Roses	1991
YOU COULD HAVE BEEN A LADY		
	Hot Chocolate	1971
YOU COULD HAVE BEEN A LADY		
	April Wine	1972
YOU COULD HAVE BEEN WITH ME		
	Sheena Easton	1981
YOU COULD TAKE MY HEART AWAY		
	Silver Condor	1981
YOU DECORATED MY LIFE	Kenny Rogers	1979
YOU DIDN'T EXPECT THAT	Billy Crawford	2003
YOU DIDN'T HAVE TO BE SO NICE		
	Lovin' Spoonful	1965
YOU DO	McAlmont & Butler	1995
YOU DO SOMETHING TO ME		
	Dum Dums	2000
YOU DO SOMETHING TO ME		
	Paul Weller	1995
YOU DON'T BRING ME FLOWERS		
	Barbra & Neil	1978

SONG TITLE	ARTIST	DATE
YOU DON'T CARE ABOUT US		
	Placebo	1998
YOU DON'T FOOL ME	Queen	1996
YOU DON'T HAVE TO BE A BABY TO CRY		
	Caravelles	1963
YOU DON'T HAVE TO BE A STAR (TO BE IN MY SHOW)		
	Marilyn McCoo & Billy Davis Jr.	1977
YOU DON'T HAVE TO BE IN THE ARMY TO FIGHT IN		
THE WAR	Mungo Jerry	1971
YOU DON'T HAVE TO GO	Chi-Lites	1976
YOU DON'T HAVE TO GO HOME TONIGHT		
	Triplets	1991
YOU DON'T HAVE TO HURT NO MORE		
	Mint Condition	1997
YOU DON'T HAVE TO SAY YOU LOVE ME		
	Guys & Dolls	1976
YOU DON'T HAVE TO SAY YOU LOVE ME		
	Dusty Springfield	1966
YOU DON'T HAVE TO SAY YOU LOVE ME/CRY ME		
A RIVER	Denise Welch	1995
YOU DON'T HAVE TO SAY YOU LOVE ME/PATCH IT UP		
	Elvis Presley	1970
YOU DON'T HAVE TO WORRY		
	Mary J. Blige	1993
(YOU DON'T HAVE TO) PAINT ME A PICTURE		
	Gary Lewis & The Playboys	1966

SONG TITLE	ARTIST	DATE
YOU DON'T KNOW	Cyndi Lauper	1997
YOU DON'T KNOW	702	1999
YOU DON'T KNOW	Berlin	1987
YOU DON'T KNOW	Scarlett And Black	1988
YOU DON'T KNOW HOW IT FEELS		
	Tom Petty	1994
YOU DON'T KNOW ME	Armand Van Helden featuring	
	Duane Harden	1999
YOU DON'T KNOW MY NAME		
	Alicia Keys	2003
(YOU DON'T KNOW) HOW GLAD I AM		
	Kiki Dee	1975
(YOU DON'T KNOW) HOW GLAD I AM		
	Nancy Wilson	1964
YOU DON'T LOVE ME	Gary Walker	1966
YOU DON'T LOVE ME	Marilyn	1984
YOU DON'T LOVE ME (NO, NO, NO)		
	Dawn Penn	1994
YOU DON'T MESS AROUND WITH JIM		
	Jim Croce	1972
YOU DON'T WANT ME ANYMORE		
	Steel Breeze	1982
YOU DRIVE ME CRAZY	Shakin' Stevens	1981
(YOU DRIVE ME) CRAZY	Britney Spears	1999
YOU DROPPED A BOMB ON ME		
	Gap Band	1982

SONG TITLE	ARTIST	DATE
YOU DROVE ME TO IT	Hell Is For Heroes	2003
YOU GAVE ME A MOUNTAIN		
	Frankie Laine	1969
YOU GAVE ME LOVE	Crown Heights Affair	1980
YOU GAVE ME SOMEBODY TO LOVE		
	Manfred Mann	1966
YOU GET WHAT YOU GIVE	New Radicals	1998
YOU GETS NO LOVE	Faith Evans	2001
YOU GIVE GOOD LOVE	Whitney Houston	1985
YOU GIVE LOVE A BAD NAME		
	Bon Jovi	1986
YOU GIVE ME SOMETHING	Jamiroquai	2001
YOU GO TO MY HEAD	Bryan Ferry	1975
YOU GONNA MAKE ME LOVE SOMEBODY ELSE		
	Jones Girls	1979
YOU GOOD THING (IS ABOUT TO END)		
	Lou Rawls	1969
YOU GOT IT	Roy Orbison	1989
YOU GOT IT	Bonnie Raitt	1995
YOU GOT IT (THE RIGHT STUFF)		
	New Kids On The Block	1988
YOU GOT IT ALL	Jets	1986
YOU GOT LUCKY	Tom Petty & The Heartbreakers	1982
YOU GOT ME	Roots featuring Erykah Badu	1999
YOU GOT ME ROCKING	Rolling Stones	1994
YOU GOT ME RUNNIN'	Gene Cotton	1976

SONG TITLE	ARTIST	DATE
YOU GOT ME THINKING	Beloved	1993
(YOU GOT ME) BURNING UP		
	Cevin Fisher/Loleatta Holloway	1999
YOU GOT SOUL	Johnny Nash	1969
YOU GOT THE FLOOR	Arthur Adams	1981
YOU GOT THE LOVE	Source featuring Candi Staton	1997
YOU GOT THE LOVE	Rufus featuring Chaka Khan	1974
YOU GOT THE POWER	QFX	1996
YOU GOT THE STYLE	Athlete	2002
YOU GOT TO ME	Neil Diamond	1967
YOU GOT WHAT IT TAKES	Dave Clark Five	1967
YOU GOT WHAT IT TAKES	Showaddywaddy	1977
YOU GOT YOURS AND I'LL GET MINE		
	Delfonics	1969
YOU GOTTA BE	Des'ree	1994
YOU GOTTA BE A HUSTLER IF YOU WANNA GET ON		
	Sue Wilkinson	1980
YOU GOTTA HAVE LOVE IN YOUR HEART		
	Supremes & Four Tops	1971
YOU GOTTA LOVE SOMEBODY		
	Elton John	1990
YOU GOTTA STOP/THE LOVE MACHINE		
	Elvis Presley	1967
(YOU GOTTA) FIGHT FOR YOUR RIGHT (TO PARTY)		
	Beastie Boys	1986
YOU HAD ME	Joss Stone	2004

SONG TITLE	ARTIST	DATE
YOU HAD ME FROM HELLO		
	Kenny Chesney	1999
YOU HAVE BEEN LOVED/THE STRANGEST THING '97		
	George Michael	1997
YOU HAVE PLACED A CHILL IN MY HEART		
	Eurythmics	1988
YOU HAVEN'T DONE NOTHIN		
	Stevie Wonder	1974
YOU HELD THE WORLD IN YOUR ARMS		
	Idlewild	2002
YOU JUST MIGHT SEE ME CRY		
	Our Kid	1976
YOU KEEP IT ALL IN	Beautiful South	1989
YOU KEEP ME HANGIN' ON		
	Supremes	1966
YOU KEEP ME HANGIN' ON		
	Vanilla Fudge	1967
YOU KEEP ME HANGIN' ON		
	Kim Wilde	1987
YOU KEEP ME HANGIN' ON/STOP IN THE NAME OF LOVE	Roni Hill	1977
(YOU KEEP ME) HANGIN' ON		
	Cliff Richard	1974
(YOU KEEP ME) HANGIN' ON		
	Joe Simon	1968

SONG TITLE	ARTIST	DATE
YOU KEEP RUNNIN' AWAY	38 Special	1982
YOU KEEP RUNNING AWAY	Four Tops	1967
YOU KNOW HOW WE DO IT	Ice Cube	1994
YOU KNOW I LOVE YOU... DON'T YOU?	Howard Jones	1986
YOU KNOW THAT I LOVE YOU	Santana	1979
YOU KNOW WHAT I MEAN	Turtles	1967
YOU LAY SO EASY ON MY MIND	Andy Williams	1975
YOU LEARN/YOU OUGHTA KNOW	Alanis Morissette	1996
YOU LIED TO ME	Cathy Dennis	1992
YOU LIFE ME UP	Rebekah Ryan	1996
YOU LIGHT UP MY LIFE	Debby Boone	1977
YOU LITTLE THIEF	Feargal Sharkey	1986
YOU LITTLE TRUSTMAKER	Tymes	1974
YOU LOOK SO FINE	Garbage	1999
YOU LOVE US	Manic Street Preachers	1992
YOU MADE ME BELIEVE IN MAGIC	Bay City Rollers	1977
YOU MAKE IT MOVE	Dave Dee, Dozy, Beaky, Mick & Tich	1965

SONG TITLE	ARTIST	DATE
YOU MAKE LOVIN' FUN	Fleetwood Mac	1977
YOU MAKE ME FEEL (MIGHTY REAL)	Jimmy Somerville	1990
YOU MAKE ME FEEL (MIGHTY REAL)	Sylvester	1979
YOU MAKE ME FEEL (MIGHTY REAL)	Byron Stingily	1998
YOU MAKE ME FEEL BRAND NEW	Stylistics	1974
YOU MAKE ME FEEL BRAND NEW	Simply Red	2003
(YOU MAKE ME FEEL LIKE) A NATURAL WOMAN	Mary J. Blige	1995
YOU MAKE ME FEEL LIKE DANCING	Leo Sayer	1976
YOU MAKE ME FEEL LIKE DANCING	Groove Generation featuring Leo Sayer	1998
YOU MAKE ME GO OOOH	Kristine Blond	2002
YOU MAKE ME SICK	Pink	2001
YOU MAKE ME WANNA	Usher	1997
YOU MAKE MY DREAMS	Daryl Hall & John Oates	1981
YOU MAY BE RIGHT	Billy Joel	1980
YOU MEAN THE WORLD TO ME	Toni Braxton	1994
YOU MET YOUR MATCH	Stevie Wonder	1968

SONG TITLE	ARTIST	DATE
YOU MIGHT NEED SOMEBODY		
	Shola Ama	1997
YOU MIGHT NEED SOMEBODY		
	Randy Crawford	1981
YOU MIGHT THINK	Cars	1984
YOU MUST BELIEVE ME	Impressions	1964
YOU MUST HAVE BEEN A BEAUTIFUL BABY		
	Dave Clark Five	1967
YOU MUST LOVE ME	Madonna	1996
YOU NEED A WOMAN TONIGHT		
	Captain & Tennille	1978
YOU NEED LOVE LIKE I DO		
	Tom Jones & Heather Small	2000
YOU NEED LOVE LIKE I DO (DON'T YOU)		
	Gladys Knight & The Pips	1970
YOU NEED WHEELS	Merton Parkas	1979
YOU NEEDED ME	Boyzone	1999
YOU NEEDED ME	Anne Murray	1978
YOU NEVER CAN TELL	Chuck Berry	1964
YOU NEVER DONE IT LIKE THAT		
	Captain & Tennille	1978
YOU NEVER KNOW	Marly	2004
YOU NEVER KNOW WHAT YOU'VE GOT		
	Me And You featuring	
	We The People Band	1979

SONG TITLE	ARTIST	DATE
YOU NEVER LOVE THE SAME WAY TWICE		
	Rozalla	1994
YOU ON MY MIND	Swing Out Sister	1989
YOU ONLY LIVE TWICE/JACKSON		
	Nancy Sinatra	1967
YOU ONLY TELL ME YOU LOVE ME WHEN YOU'RE		
DRUNK	Pet Shop Boys	2000
YOU ONLY YOU	Rita Pavone	1967
YOU OUGHT TO BE WITH ME		
	Al Green	1972
YOU OUGHTA KNOW	Alanis Morissette	1995
YOU OWE IT ALL TO ME	Texas	1993
YOU PUT ME IN HEAVEN WITH YOUR TOUCH		
	Rhythm Of Life	2000
YOU RAISE ME UP	Daniel O'Donnell	2003
YOU REALLY GOT ME	Kinks	1964
YOU REALLY GOT ME	Van Halen	1978
YOU REALLY KNOW HOW TO HURT A GUY		
	Jan & Dean	1965
YOU REMIND ME	Mary J. Blige	1992
YOU REMIND ME OF SOMETHING		
	R. Kelly	1995
YOU ROCK MY WORLD	Michael Jackson	2001
YOU SAID NO	Busted	2003
YOU SANG TO ME	Marc Anthony	2000
YOU SAVED MY SOUL	Burton Cummings	1981

SONG TITLE	ARTIST	DATE
YOU SEE THE TROUBLE WITH ME		
	Black Legend	2000
YOU SEE THE TROUBLE WITH ME		
	Barry White	1976
YOU SEXY DANCER	Rockford Files	1995
YOU SEXY SUGAR PLUMB (BUT I LIKE IT)		
	Rodger Collins	1976
YOU SEXY THING	Hot Chocolate	1975
YOU SHOOK ME ALL NIGHT LONG		
	AC/DC	1980
YOU SHOULD BE DANCING		
	Bee Gees	1976
YOU SHOULD BE MINE (DON'T WASTE YOUR TIME)		
	Brian McKnight/Mase	1997
YOU SHOULD BE MINE (THE WOO WOO SONG)		
	Jeffrey Osborne	1986
YOU SHOULD BE...	Blockster	1999
YOU SHOULD HAVE SEEN THE WAY HE LOOKED AT ME		
	Dixie Cups	1964
YOU SHOULD HEAR HOW SHE TALKS ABOUT YOU		
	Melissa Manchester	1982
YOU SHOULD REALLY KNOW		
	Pirates featuring Enya, Shola Ama, naila Boss & Ishani	2004
YOU SHOULDN'T KISS ME LIKE THIS		
	Toby Keith	2000

SONG TITLE	ARTIST	DATE
YOU SHOWED ME	Salt 'N 'Pepa	1991
YOU SHOWED ME	Lightning Seeds	1997
YOU SHOWED ME	Turtles	1969
YOU SPIN ME ROUND	Dead Or Alive	2002
YOU SPIN ME ROUND (LIKE A RECORD)		
	Dead Or Alive	1985
YOU STILL TOUCH ME	Sting	1996
YOU STOLE THE SUN FROM MY HEART		
	Manic Street Preachers	1999
YOU SURROUND ME	Erasure	1989
YOU TAKE ME AWAY	Reel	2002
YOU TAKE ME UP	Thompson Twins	1984
YOU TAKE MY BREATH AWAY		
	Sureal	2000
YOU TAKE MY BREATH AWAY		
	Rex Smith	1979
YOU TAKE MY HEART AWAY		
	De Etta Little & Nelson Pigfoot	1977
YOU TALK TOO MUCH	Sultans Of Ping F.C.	1993
YOU TELL ME WHY	Beau Brummels	1965
YOU THINK YOU KNOW HER		
	Cause & Effect	1992
YOU THINK YOU OWN ME	Hinda Hicks	1998
YOU THINK YOU'RE A MAN		
	Divine	1984
YOU THRILL ME	Exile	1978

SONG TITLE	ARTIST	DATE
YOU TO ME ARE EVERYTHING	Real Thing	1976
YOU TO ME ARE EVERYTHING	Sonia	1991
YOU TO ME ARE EVERYTHING	Sean Maguire	1995
YOU TO ME ARE EVERYTHING (THE DECADE RE-MIX)	Real Thing	1986
YOU TOOK THE WORDS RIGHT OUT OF MY MOUTH	Meat Loaf	1978
YOU TURN ME ON	Ian Whitcomb	1965
YOU TURN ME ON, I'M A RADIO	Joni Mitchell	1972
YOU USED TO HOLD ME	Scott & Leon	2000
YOU USED TO LOVE ME	Faith	1995
YOU WANT IT, YOU GOT IT	Detroit Emeralds	1972
YOU WANT THIS/70'S LOVE GROOVE	Janet Jackson	1994
YOU WEAR IT WELL	Rod Stewart	1972
YOU WERE MADE FOR ME	Freddie & The Dreamers	1965
YOU WERE MEANT FOR ME	Jewel	1996
YOU WERE MINE	Dixie Chicks	1999
YOU WERE ON MY MIND	Crispian St. Peters	1967
YOU WERE ON MY MIND	We Five	1965

SONG TITLE	ARTIST	DATE
YOU WERE ONLY FOOLING	Vic Damone	1965
YOU WERE RIGHT	Badly Drawn Boy	2002
YOU WERE THE LAST HIGH	Dandy Warhols	2003
YOU WERE THERE	Heinz	1964
YOU WILL YOU WON'T	Zutons	2004
YOU WIN AGAIN	Bee Gees	1987
YOU WON'T BE LEAVIN'	Herman's Hermits	1966
YOU WON'T EVER BE LONELY	Andy Griggs	1999
YOU WON'T FIND ANOTHER FOOL LIKE ME	New Seekers	1973
YOU WON'T FORGET ABOUT ME	Dannii Minogue vs Flower Power	2004
YOU WON'T SEE ME	Anne Murray	1974
YOU WON'T SEE ME CRY	Wilson Phillips	1992
YOU YOU YOU	Alvin Stardust	1974
YOU'D BETTER COME HOME	Petula Clark	1965
YOU'LL ACCOMP'NY ME	Bob Seger & The Silver Bullet Band	1980
YOU'LL ALWAYS BE A FRIEND	Hot Chocolate	1972

SONG TITLE	ARTIST	DATE
YOU'LL ALWAYS FIND ME IN THE KITCHEN AT PARTIES		
	Jona Lewie	1980
YOU'LL BE IN MY HEART	Phil Collins	1999
YOU'LL BE MINE (PARTY TIME)		
	Gloria Estefan	1996
YOU'LL COME 'ROUND	Status Quo	2004
YOU'LL LOSE A GOOD THING		
	Freddy Fender	1976
YOU'LL NEVER BE ALONE	Anastacia	2002
YOU'LL NEVER FIND ANOTHER LOVE LIKE MINE		
	Lou Rawls	1976
YOU'LL NEVER GET TO HEAVEN (IF YOU BREAK MY HEART)	Dionne Warwick	1964
YOU'LL NEVER GET TO HEAVEN (IF YOU BREAK MY HEART)	Stylistics	1973
YOU'LL NEVER KNOW	Hi Gloss	1981
YOU'LL NEVER KNOW WHAT YOU'RE MISSSING		
	Real Thing	1977
YOU'LL NEVER STOP ME LOVING YOU		
	Sonia	1989
YOU'LL NEVER WALK ALONE		
	Carreras/Domingo/Pavarotti With Mehta	1998
YOU'LL NEVER WALK ALONE		
	Crowd	1985

SONG TITLE	ARTIST	DATE
YOU'LL NEVER WALK ALONE		
	Gerry & The Pacemakers	1963
YOU'LL NEVER WALK ALONE		
	Patti Labelle & Her Blue Belles	1964
YOU'LL SEE	Madonna	1995
YOU'LL THINK OF ME	Keith Urban	2004
YOU'RE A FRIEND OF MINE		
	Clarence Clemons & Jackson Browne	1985
YOU'RE A GOD	Vertical Horizon	2000
YOU'RE A LADY	Peter Skellern	1972
YOU'RE A PART OF ME	Gene Cotton With Kim Carnes	1978
YOU'RE A SPECIAL PART OF ME		
	Marvin Gaye & Diana Ross	1973
YOU'RE A SUPERSTAR	Love Inc.	2002
YOU'RE A WONDERFUL ONE		
	Marvin Gaye	1964
YOU'RE ALL I NEED TO GET BY		
	Marvin Gaye & Tammi Terrell	1968
YOU'RE ALL I NEED TO GET BY		
	Aretha Franklin	1971
YOU'RE ALL I NEED TO GET BY		
	Tony Orlando & Dawn	1975
YOU'RE ALL I NEED/WILD SIDE		
	Motley Crue	1988

SONG TITLE	ARTIST	DATE
YOU'RE ALL THAT MATTERS TO ME		
	Curtis Stigers	1992
YOU'RE AMAZING	Robert Palmer	1990
YOU'RE BEGINNING TO GET TO ME		
	Clay Walker	1998
YOU'RE BREAKIN' MY HEART		
	Keely Smith	1965
YOU'RE DRIVING ME OUT OF MY MIND		
	Little River Band	1983
YOU'RE EASY ON THE EYES		
	Terri Clark	1998
YOU'RE EVERYTHING TO ME		
	Boris Gardiner	1986
YOU'RE FREE	Yomanda	2003
YOU'RE GONE	Marillion	2004
YOU'RE GONNA GET NEXT TO ME		
	Bo Kirkland & Ruth Davis	1977
(YOU'RE GONNA) HURT YOURSELF		
	Frankie Valli	1966
YOU'RE GORGEOUS	Babybird	1996
YOU'RE HISTORY	Shakespear's Sister	1989
YOU'RE IN A BAD WAY	Saint Etienne	1993
YOU'RE IN LOVE	Wilson Phillips	1991
YOU'RE IN MY HEART (THE FINAL ACCLAIM)		
	Rod Stewart	1977
YOU'RE LYING	Linx	1980

SONG TITLE	ARTIST	DATE
YOU'RE MAKIN' ME HIGH/LET IT FLOW		
	Toni Braxton	1996
YOU'RE MORE THAN A NUMBER IN MY LITTLE		
RED BOOK	Drifters	1976
YOU'RE MOVING OUT TODAY		
	Carole Bayer Sager	1977
YOU'RE MY ANGEL	Mikey Graham	2000
YOU'RE MY BEST FRIEND	Queen	1976
YOU'RE MY BEST FRIEND	Don Williams	1976
YOU'RE MY EVERYTHING	Max Bygraves	1969
YOU'RE MY EVERYTHING	Temptations	1967
YOU'RE MY EVERYTHING	Lee Garrett	1976
YOU'RE MY GIRL	Rockin' Berries	1965
YOU'RE MY GIRL	Franke & The Knockouts	1981
YOU'RE MY LIFE	Barry Biggs	1977
YOU'RE MY MATE	Right Said Fred	2001
YOU'RE MY ONE AND ONLY (TRUE LOVE)		
	Seduction	1989
(YOU'RE MY) SOUL AND INSPIRATION		
	Donny & Marie Osmond	1977
(YOU'RE MY) SOUL AND INSPIRATION		
	Righteous Brothers	1966
YOU'RE MY WORLD	Cilla Black	1964
YOU'RE MY WORLD	Helen Reddy	1977
YOU'RE NO GOOD	Aswad	1995
YOU'RE NO GOOD	Swinging Blue Jeans	1964

SONG TITLE	ARTIST	DATE
YOU'RE NO GOOD	Linda Ronstadt	1974
YOU'RE NOBODY TILL SOMEBODY LOVES YOU		
	Dean Martin	1964
YOU'RE NOT ALONE	Embrace	2000
YOU'RE NOT ALONE	Olive	1997
YOU'RE NOT ALONE	Chicago	1989
YOU'RE ONLY HUMAN (SECOND WIND)		
	Billy Joel	1985
YOU'RE ONLY LONELY	J.D. Souther	1979
YOU'RE READY NOW	Frankie Valli	1970
YOU'RE SHINING	Styles & Breeze	2004
YOU'RE SIXTEEN	Ringo Starr	1973
YOU'RE SO VAIN	Carly Simon	1972
YOU'RE STILL A YOUNG MAN		
	Tower Of Power	1972
YOU'RE STILL THE ONE	Shania Twain	1998
YOU'RE SUCH A GOOD LOOKING WOMAN		
	Joe Dolan	1970
YOU'RE SUPPOSED TO KEEP YOUR LOVE FOR ME		
	Jermaine Jackson	1980
YOU'RE THE FIRST, THE LAST, MY EVERYTHING		
	Barry White	1974
YOU'RE THE INSPIRATION	Chicago	1984
YOU'RE THE LOVE	Seals & Crofts	1978
YOU'RE THE ONE	Petula Clark	1965
YOU'RE THE ONE	Kathy Kirby	1964

SONG TITLE	ARTIST	DATE
YOU'RE THE ONE	SWV	1996
YOU'RE THE ONE	Vogues	1965
YOU'RE THE ONE (PT 2)	Little Sister	1970
YOU'RE THE ONE FOR ME	D Train	1982
YOU'RE THE ONE FOR ME, FATTY		
	Morrissey	1992
YOU'RE THE ONE I LOVE	Shola Ama	1997
YOU'RE THE ONE THAT I WANT		
	Hylda Baker & Arthur Mullard	1978
YOU'RE THE ONE THAT I WANT		
	John Travolta &	
	Olivia Newton-John	1978
YOU'RE THE ONE THAT I WANT		
	Craig McLachlan &	
	Debbie Gibson	1993
YOU'RE THE ONLY ONE	Val Doonican	1968
YOU'RE THE ONLY WOMAN		
	Brat Pack	1990
YOU'RE THE ONLY WOMAN (YOU & I)		
	Ambrosia	1980
YOU'RE THE REASON	Wamdue Project	2000
YOU'RE THE REASON WHY	Rubettes	1976
YOU'RE THE STAR	Rod Stewart	1995
YOU'RE THE STORY OF MY LIFE/AS LONG AS YOU'RE		
GOOD TO ME	Judy Cheeks	1995
YOU'RE THE VOICE	John Farnham	1987

SONG TITLE	ARTIST	DATE
(YOU'RE THE) DEVIL IN DISGUISE		
	Elvis Presley	1963
(YOU'RE) FABULOUS BABE	Kenny Williams	1977
(YOU'RE) HAVING MY BABY		
	Paul Anka/Odia Coates	1974
YOU'VE BEEN CHEATIN'	Impressions	1965
YOU'VE BEEN ON LOVE TOO LONG		
	Martha & The Vandellas	1965
YOU'VE COME BACK	P.J. Proby	1966
YOU'VE GOT A FRIEND	Big Fun & Sonia	1990
YOU'VE GOT A FRIEND	Brand New Heavies	1997
YOU'VE GOT A FRIEND	James Taylor	1971
YOU'VE GOT A FRIEND	Roberta Flack	1971
YOU'VE GOT A FRIEND	Donny Hathaway	1971
YOU'VE GOT A LOT TO ANSWER FOR		
	Catatonia	1996
YOU'VE GOT IT BAD	Ocean Colour Scene	1996
YOU'VE GOT LOVE	Buddy Holly & The Crickets	1964
(YOU'VE GOT ME) DANGLING ON A STRING		
	Chairmen Of The Board	1970
YOU'VE GOT MY NUMBER (WHY DON'T YOU USE IT!)		
	Undertones	1979
YOU'VE GOT TO CRAWL (BEFORE YOU WALK)		
	Eighth Day	1971
YOU'VE GOT TO HIDE YOUR LOVE AWAY		
	Silkie	1965

SONG TITLE	ARTIST	DATE
YOU'VE GOT YOUR TROUBLES		
	Fortunes	1965
(YOU'VE GOT) PERSONALITY		
	Lena Zavaroni	1974
YOU'VE LOST THAT LOVIN' FEELIN'		
	Cilla Black	1965
YOU'VE LOST THAT LOVIN' FEELIN'		
	Righteous Brothers	1964
YOU'VE LOST THAT LOVIN' FEELING		
	Daryl Hall & John Oates	1980
YOU'VE LOST THAT LOVIN' FEELING		
	Dionne Warwick	1969
YOU'VE MADE ME SO VERY HAPPY		
	Blood, Sweat & Tears	1969
YOU'VE MADE ME SO VERY HAPPY		
	Brenda Holloway	1967
YOU'VE NEVER BEEN THIS FAR BEFORE		
	Conway Twitty	1973
YOU'VE NOT CHANGED	Sandie Shaw	1967
(YOU'VE) NEVER BEEN IN LOVE LIKE THIS BEFORE		
	Unit Four Plus Two	1965
YOU, I	Rugbys	1969
YOUNG	Kenny Chesney	2002
YOUNG AMERICANS	David Bowie	1975
THE YOUNG AND THE HOPELESS/HOLD ON		
	Good Charlotte	2003

SONG TITLE	ARTIST	DATE
YOUNG AT HEART	Bluebells	1993
YOUNG BLOOD	UFO	1980
YOUNG BLOOD	Bad Company	1976
YOUNG BOY	Paul McCartney	1997
YOUNG FRESH N' NEW	Kelis	2001
YOUNG GIRL	Gary Puckett & The Union Gap	1968
YOUNG GODS	Little Angels	1991
YOUNG GUNS (GO FOR IT)	Wham!	1982
YOUNG HEARTS RUN FREE	Candi Staton	1976
YOUNG HEARTS RUN FREE	Kym Mazelle	1997
YOUNG LOVE	Donny Osmond	1973
YOUNG LOVE	Air Supply	1982
YOUNG LOVERS	Paul & Paula	1963
THE YOUNG NEW MEXICAN PUPPETEER	Tom Jones	1972
THE YOUNG OFFENDER'S MUM	Carter The Unstoppable Sex Machine	1995
YOUNG PARISIANS	Adam & The Ants	1980
YOUNG TURKS	Rod Stewart	1981
YOUNG'N (HOLLA BACK)	Fabolous	2001
YOUNG, FREE AND SINGLE	Sunfire	1983
YOUNG, GIFTED AND BLACK	Bob & Marcia	1970
YOUNGER GIRL	Critters	1966

SONG TITLE	ARTIST	DATE
YOUR BABY AIN'T YOUR BABY ANYMORE	Paul Da Vinci	1974
YOUR BABY NEVER LOOKED GOOD IN BLUE	Expose	1990
YOUR BODY IS A WONDERLAND	John Mayer	2002
YOUR BODY'S CALLIN'	R. Kelly	1994
YOUR BULLDOG DRINKS CHAMPAGNE	Jim Stafford	1974
YOUR CARESS (ALL I NEED)	DJ Flavours	1997
YOUR CHRISTMAS WISH	Smurfs	1996
YOUR EYES	Simply Red	2000
YOUR FACE	Slacker	1997
YOUR FAVOURITE THING	Sugar	1994
YOUR GAME	Will Young	2004
YOUR GENERATION	Generation X	1977
YOUR HONOUR	Pluto Shervington	1982
YOUR HURTIN' KINDA LOVE	Dusty Springfield	1965
YOUR IMAGINATION	Daryl Hall & John Oates	1982
YOUR KISS IS SWEET	Syreeta	1975
YOUR KISSES ARE CHARITY	Culture Club	1999
YOUR LATEST TRICK	Dire Straits	1986
YOUR LOVE	Inner City	1996

SONG TITLE	ARTIST	DATE
YOUR LOVE	Diana Ross	1993
YOUR LOVE	Larry Graham	1975
YOUR LOVE	Marilyn McCoo & Billy Davis Jr	1977
YOUR LOVE	Outfield	1986
YOUR LOVE GETS SWEETER		
	Finley Quaye	1998
(YOUR LOVE HAS LIFTED ME) HIGHER AND HIGHER		
	Rita Coolidge	1977
YOUR LOVE IS A 187	Whitehead Bros.	1995
YOUR LOVE IS DRIVING ME CRAZY		
	Sammy Hagar	1982
YOUR LOVE IS KING	Sade	1984
YOUR LOVE TAKES ME HIGHER		
	Beloved	1990
YOUR LOVING ARMS	Billie Ray Martin	1995
YOUR LUCKY DAY IN HELL		
	Eels	1997
YOUR MAGIC PUT A SPELL ON ME		
	LJ Johnson	1976
YOUR MAMA DON'T DANCE		
	Poison	1989
YOUR MAMA DON'T DANCE		
	Loggins & Messina	1972
YOUR MAMMA WON'T LIKE ME		
	Suzi Quatro	1975
YOUR MIRROR	Simply Red	1992

SONG TITLE	ARTIST	DATE
YOUR MOTHER'S GOT A PENIS		
	Goldie Lookin Chain	2004
YOUR MOVE	Yes	1971
YOUR MUSIC	Intenso Project featuring	
	Laura Jaye	2003
YOUR NEW CUCKOO	Cardigans	1997
YOUR PERSONAL TOUCH	Evelyn 'Champagne' King	1985
YOUR PRECIOUS LOVE	Marvin Gaye & Tammi Terrell	1967
YOUR SECRET LOVE	Luther Vandross	1996
YOUR SMILING FACE	James Taylor	1977
YOUR SONG	Elton John	1970
YOUR SONG	Billy Paul	1977
YOUR SWAYING ARMS	Deacon Blue	1991
YOUR TIME HASN'T COME YET BABY		
	Elvis Presley	1968
YOUR TOWN	Deacon Blue	1992
YOUR TURN TO CRY	Joe Simon	1970
YOUR UNCHANGING LOVE	Marvin Gaye	1967
YOUR WILDEST DREAMS	Moody Blues	1986
YOUR WOMAN	White Town	1997
YOURS FATALLY	Big Brovaz	2004
YOURS UNTIL TOMORROW	Gene Pitney	1968
YOUTH GONE WILD/DELIVERING THE GOODS		
	Skid Row	1992
YOUTH OF THE NATION	P.O.D.	2002
YOUTH OF TODAY	Musical Youth	1982

SONG TITLE	ARTIST	DATE
YUM, YUM (GIMME SOME)	Fatback Band	1975
YUMMY YUMMY YUMMY	Ohio Express	1969
ZABADAK!	Dave Dee, Dozy, Beaky, Mick & Tich	1967
ZAMBEZI	Piranhas	1982
THE ZEPHYR SONG	Red Hot Chili Peppers	2002
ZEROES AND ONES	Jesus Jones	1993
ZIGGY STARDUST	Bauhaus	1982
ZING WENT THE STRINGS OF MY HEART	Trammps	1974
ZIP CODE	Five Americans	1967
ZOMBIE	Adam featuring Amy	1995
ZOMBIE	Cranberries	1994
ZOOM	Dr. Dre & LL Cool J	1998
ZOOM	Fat Larry's Band	1982
ZORBA THE GREEK	Herb Alpert & Tijuana Brass	1965
ZORBA'S DANCE	LCD	1998
ZORBA'S DANCE	Marcello Minerbi	1965

SONG TITLE	ARTIST	DATE